CURRENT
BIOGRAPHY
YEARBOOK
1960

CURRENT BIOGRAPHY YEARBOOK

1960

EDITED BY

CHARLES MORITZ

THE H. W. WILSON COMPANY
NEW YORK, N. Y.

Preface

With the appearance of this twenty-first annual volume of CURRENT BIOGRAPHY, the publication enters its third decade. Like its predecessors, the volume covers some forty subject fields, ranging from the Madison Avenue world of advertising to the Broadway world of the theater. Winners of the 1960 Nobel Prizes and Pulitzer Prizes are again the subjects of biographical sketches.

An important difference between the 1960 CURRENT BIOGRAPHY YEARBOOK and the volumes preceding it is the increased number of revised biographical sketches. As time goes on, more and more persons who appeared in the CURRENT BIOGRAPHY yearbooks of the early 1940's need new articles bringing their careers up to date. The number of revised articles in the twenty-first volume more than triples the number included in the twentieth yearbook. There are updated biographical sketches on such figures of international interest as: Dr. Franz Alexander, Charles de Gaulle, Harold C. Urey, Marcel Breuer, Lillian Hellman, James Thurber, Frank Sinatra, Van Wyck Brooks, Marc Chagall, and many others. The new articles supersede the earlier ones, now outdated.

Sketches have been made as accurate and objective as possible through careful researching by CURRENT BIOGRAPHY writers in newspapers, magazines, authoritative reference books, and the news releases of government agencies. Immediately after their publication in monthly issues, the articles are submitted to the biographees to give them an opportunity to suggest corrections in time for CURRENT BIOGRAPHY YEARBOOK. Sketches have also been revised before inclusion in the yearbook to take account of major changes in the careers of biographees. With the exception of occasional interviews, the questionnaire remains the main source of direct information.

In the back of the volume under *Organizations* can be found the heads of veterans, industrial, fraternal, and professional organizations. Persons who are not authors by profession but who have written books are listed under *Nonfiction* or *Literature* in addition to their primary vocational fields.

The pages following contain: *Explanation; Key to Reference Abbreviations; Key to Pronunciation;* and *Key to Abbreviations.* The indexes at the end of the volume are: *Biographical References (consulted by Current Biography research staff); Periodicals and Newspapers Consulted; Necrology* (of persons whose biographies have appeared in previous volumes) ; *Classification by Profession; Cumulated Index, 1951-1960.* The 1940-1950 Index can be found in the 1950 Yearbook.

CHARLES MORITZ

Explanations

Authorities for biographees' full names, with some exceptions, are the bibliographical publications of The Wilson Company. When a biographee prefers a certain name form, that is indicated in the heading of the article: for example, Armstrong-Jones, Antony (Charles Robert) means that he is usually referred to as Antony Armstrong-Jones. When a professional name is used in the heading, as for example, Anne Bancroft, the real name (in this case Annemarie Italiano) appears in the article itself.

The heading of each article includes the pronunciation of the name if it is unusual, date of birth (if obtainable), and occupation. The article is supplemented by a list of references to sources of biographical information, in two alphabets: (1) newspapers and periodicals and (2) books. See the section *Biographical References.*

KEY TO REFERENCE ABBREVIATIONS

References to newspapers and periodicals are listed in abbreviated form; for example, "Sat Eve Post 217:14-15 S 30 '44 por" means *Saturday Evening Post,* volume 217, pages 14-15, September 30, 1944, with portrait. (For full names, see the section *Periodicals and Newspapers Consulted,* found in the rear of this volume.)

January—Ja	July—Jl	Journal—J
February—F	August—Ag	Magazine—Mag
March—Mr	September—S	Monthly—Mo
April—Ap	October—O	Weekly—W
May—My	November—N	Portrait—por
June—Je	December—D	Review—R

KEY TO PRONUNCIATION
(Based on Webster's Guide to Pronunciation*)

ā	āle	N	Not pronounced, but indicates the nasal tone of the preceding vowel, as in the French *bon* (bōN).	û	ûrn; French eu, as in *jeu* (zhû); German ö, oe, as in *schön* (shûn), *Goethe* (gû'tĕ)
à	câre				
ă	ădd			ŭ	tŭb
ȧ	ȧccount			ŭ	circŭs
ä	ärm			ü	Pronounced approximately as ē, with rounded lips: French u, as in *menu* (mē-nü'); German ü, as in *grün*
à	àsk	ō	ōld		
a	sofȧ	ô	ôrb		
		ŏ	ŏdd		
ē	ēve	oi	oil		
ĕ	ĕnd	oo	ooze		
ẽ	makẽr	oo	foot		
		ou	out		
g	go			zh	azure
		th	then		
I	Ice	th	thin	′ =	main accent
ĭ	Ill			″ =	secondary accent
ᴋ	German ch as in *ich* (ĭᴋ).	û	cūbe		

(*Exceptions : *th* in then; main and secondary accents.)

KEY TO ABBREVIATIONS

AAAA	Amateur Athletic Association of America	FPC	Federal Power Commission	OBE	Officer of (the Order of) the British Empire
A.A.U.	Amateur Athletic Union	FSA	Federal Security Agency	OCD	Office of Civilian Defense
ABC	American Broadcasting Company	FTC	Federal Trade Commission	OEEC	Organization for European Economic Cooperation
A.C.L.U.	American Civil Liberties Union	G.B.E.	Knight or Dame, Grand Cross Order of the British Empire	OPA	Office of Price Administration
ADA	Americans for Democratic Action			OPM	Office of Production Management
AEC	Atomic Energy Commission	G.C.B.	Knight Grand Cross of the Bath	OWI	Office of War Information
AEF	American Expeditionary Force	G.O.P.	Grand Old Party		
AFL	American Federation of Labor	H.M.	His Majesty; Her Majesty	P.E.N.	Poets, Playwrights, Editors, Essayists and Novelists (International Association)
AFL-CIO	American Federation of Labor and Congress of Industrial Organizations	ICA	International Cooperation Administration	Ph.B.	Bachelor of Philosophy
A.L.A.	American Library Association	ICBM	Intercontinental Ballistic Missile	Ph.D.	Doctor of Philosophy
A.M.A.	American Medical Association	ICC	Interstate Commerce Commission	PWA	Public Works Administration
A.P.	Associated Press	I.C.F.T.U.	International Confederation of Free Trade Unions		
ASCAP	American Society of Composers, Authors and Publishers	IGY	International Geophysical Year	Q.C.	Queen's Counsel
ASNE	American Society of Newspaper Editors	I.L.A.	International Longshoremen's Association	RAF	Royal Air Force
				RCA	Radio Corporation of America
B.A.	Bachelor of Arts	I.L.G.W.U.	International Ladies' Garment Workers' Union	REA	Rural Electrification Administration
BBC	British Broadcasting Corporation	I.L.O.	International Labor Organization	RFC	Reconstruction Finance Corporation
B.D.	Bachelor of Divinity	IRO	International Refugee Organization	RKO	Radio-Keith-Orpheum
B.L.S.	Bachelor of Library Science			ROTC	Reserve Officers' Training Corps
B.S.	Bachelor of Science	J.D.	Doctor of Jurisprudence		
CAA	Civil Aeronautics Administration	K.B.E.	Knight of (the Order of) the British Empire	SAC	Strategic Air Command
CAB	Civil Aeronautics Board			SCAP	Supreme Command for the Allied Powers
C.B.	Companion of the Bath	K.C.	King's Counsel	SEATO	Southeast Asia Treaty Organization
C.B.E.	Commander of (the Order of) the British Empire	K.C.B.	Knight Commander of the Bath	SEC	Securities and Exchange Commission
CBS	Columbia Broadcasting System	L.H.D.	Doctor of Humanities	SHAEF	Supreme Headquarters, Allied Expeditionary Force
C.E.	Civil Engineer	Litt.D.	Doctor of Letters		
CEA	Council of Economic Advisers	LL.B.	Bachelor of Laws	SHAPE	Supreme Headquarters, Allied Powers Europe
C.E.D.	Committee for Economic Development	LL.D.	Doctor of Laws	S.J.D.	Doctor of Juridical Science
CIO	Congress of Industrial Organizations	M.A.	Master of Arts	S.T.B.	Bachelor of Sacred Theology
C.M.G.	Companion of (the Order of) St. Michael and St. George	M.B.A.	Master of Business Administration	S.T.D.	Doctor of Sacred Theology
Com.	Commodore	MBS	Mutual Broadcasting System		
		M.C.E.	Master of Civil Engineering	TVA	Tennessee Valley Authority
D.A.R.	Daughters of the American Revolution	M.D.	Doctor of Medicine	T.W.U.A.	Textile Workers Union of America
D.C.L.	Doctor of Civil Law	M.E.	Master of Engineering		
D.D.	Doctor of Divinity	METO	Middle East Treaty Organization	U.A.W.	United Automobile, Aircraft, and Agricultural Implement Workers of America
D.Eng.	Doctor of Engineering	MGM	Metro-Goldwyn-Mayer		
DEW	Distant Early Warning Line	M.Lit.	Master of Literature	UAR	United Arab Republic
D.F.C.	Distinguished Flying Cross	M.P.	Member of Parliament	UMT	Universal Military Training
D.J.	Doctor of Jurisprudence	M.P.P.D.A.	Motion Picture Producers and Distributors of America	U.M.W.A.	United Mine Workers of America
D.Lit.	Doctor of Literature	MRP	Mouvement Républicain Populaire	U.N.	United Nations
D.Mus.	Doctor of Music	MSA	Mutual Security Agency	UNESCO	United Nations Educational, Scientific, and Cultural Organization
DP	Displaced Person	M.Sc.	Master of Science		
D.Pol.Sc	Doctor of Political Science	Msgr.	Monsignor, Monseigneur	UNRRA	United Nations Relief and Rehabilitation Administration
D.Sc.	Doctor of Science	NAACP	National Association for the Advancement of Colored People	U.P.I.	United Press and International News Service
D.S.C.	Distinguished Service Cross	NAB	National Association of Broadcasters	USO	United Service Organizations
D.S.M.	Distinguished Service Medal	NAM	National Association of Manufacturers	U.S.S.R.	Union of Soviet Socialist Republics
D.S.O.	Distinguished Service Order	NASA	National Aeronautics and Space Administration	U.S.W.A.	United Steel Workers of America
		NATO	North Atlantic Treaty Organization		
ECA	Economic Cooperation Administration	NBC	National Broadcasting Company	VA	Veterans Administration
ECOSOC	Economic and Social Council	N.E.A.	National Education Association	V.F.W.	Veterans of Foreign Wars
EDC	European Defense Community	NLRB	National Labor Relations Board		
ERP	European Recovery Program	N.M.U.	National Maritime Union	W.E.U.	Western European Union
ESA	Economic Stabilization Administration	NRA	National Recovery Administration	W.F.T.U.	World Federation of Trade Unions
		NRPB	National Resources Planning Board	WHO	World Health Organization
FAO	Food and Agriculture Organization	NYA	National Youth Administration	WMC	War Manpower Commission
FBI	Federal Bureau of Investigation			WPA	Work Projects Administration
FCA	Farm Credit Administration	O.A.S.	Organization of American States	WPB	War Production Board
FCC	Federal Communications Commission				
FEPC	Fair Employment Practice Committee				
FHA	Federal Housing Administration				
FOA	Foreign Operations Administration				

CURRENT BIOGRAPHY
YEARBOOK
1960

ADAMS, FRANKLIN P(IERCE) Nov. 15, 1881-Mar. 23, 1960 Author; often called F.P.A.; conducted "The Conning Tower" column for the New York *Tribune* (1914-21) and other newspapers; wrote several volumes of light verse; panelist on the *Information Please* radio program for a number of years beginning in 1938. See *Current Biography* (July) 1941.

Obituary

N Y Times p1+ Mr 24 '60

AGA KHAN IV, THE (KARIM AL HUSSAINI SHAH) Dec. 13, 1937- Religious leader
Address: h. 76 Eaton Square, London, S.W. 1, England

The youthful Aga Khan IV, the spiritual leader of millions of Moslems of the Ismaili sect in some parts of Asia and Africa, has in his few years as the forty-ninth Imam demonstrated that he does not intend to ignore the economic and social welfare of his followers. Reared and educated in the West, he has brought a sober dedication to the position left vacant in July 1957 by the death of his grandfather, Aga Khan III, who passed over his two worldly sons, Aly and Sadruddin, to choose the Harvard undergraduate student of Oriental history as his successor.

Prince Karim Khan was born in Geneva, Switzerland, on December 13, 1937. Since Moslems consider an infant one year old at birth, his age is generally reported as older than he is by Western reckoning. He is the son of Prince Aly Khan and the former Joan Barbara Yarde-Buller, eldest daughter of England's Baron Churston. A second son, Amyn, was born in 1938. The parents were divorced in 1949 after thirteen years of marriage; Aly Khan was given custody of both sons, although Prince Karim subsequently spent much of his free time at his mother's home in Eaton Square in London.

Although he is predominantly European in ancestry, Prince Karim through his father is a direct descendant of the Prophet Mohammed; Ismaili Moslems consider him to be the forty-ninth Imam in direct descent from Fatima, the daughter of the Prophet. His great-great-grandfather was the first Aga Khan who, after a dispute with the Shah of Persia, went to India and was there rewarded for his services to the British crown.

Wide World

THE AGA KHAN IV

By tradition, the Khans have been staunch supporters of Great Britain. Aga Khan II continued the ties during his regime, which lasted from 1881 to 1885, as did Aga Khan III from 1885 until his death in 1957. Toward the end of his long and much publicized life, the third Aga Khan lived in a lakeside villa in Switzerland, where he was a king without a country. He was the acknowledged leader of the Shiah Moslems, regarded as a god by the rich Khoja sub-sect, and as the hereditary Unrevealed Imam by the Ismaili sect. A statesman and religious leader as well as a playboy whose riches were legendary, he embarked in the later years of his life on an ambitious program to elevate the living standards of his estimated 20,000,000 followers.

It was to be expected that the grandson of the Aga Khan, Prince Karim, would be trained in his Moslem heritage, although he was a British subject, reared in Europe, who did not learn Arabic until he came to the United States. He was graduated from Le Rosey preparatory school, located between Geneva and Lausanne in Switzerland. With his brother, he then toured Ismaili communities in East Africa before enrolling at Harvard.

(Continued next page)

AGA KHAN IV, THE—*Continued*

As an undergraduate in residence at Harvard's Leverett House in Cambridge, Massachusetts, Prince Karim earned the respect of his fellow students. Entering into the American university routine, he joined the Islamic Association, played on the freshman soccer team, and competed in intramural hockey games. He was elected to the Signet, Delphic, and Hasty Pudding clubs. His standard of living was modest.

One of his roommates was John Fell Stevenson, the youngest son of Adlai Stevenson. He recalled in *This Week* magazine (November 10, 1957): " 'K,' as we soon came to call Karim, was dressed casually in a plain brown leather jacket, open white shirt, creaseless baggy trousers, and shoes which I believe had never been shined. . . . Karim impressed me when we first met as freshmen because he had a purpose —he wanted to help people."

Realizing that he had to devote his future to the Ismailis, Prince Karim began to study civil engineering, in response to a need of his people. When he was defeated by the required chemistry courses, he changed his major subject to Oriental history. A student whose name often appeared on the "dean's list," he once seriously considered making Oriental studies his life work. He planned to attend the Sorbonne in Paris after he completed his courses at Harvard.

In 1957 Prince Karim was forced to withdraw from Harvard to be with his grandfather during the Aga Khan's last illness. Unknown to his people, the dying Imam had passed over his two sons to choose Prince Karim as his successor. "In view of the fundamentally altered conditions of the world," he wrote in his will, "I should be succeeded by a young man who has been brought up and developed in midst of the new age." He died on July 11, 1957, and two days later Prince Karim proclaimed the start of his reign as Aga Khan IV.

In the course of an extensive tour of Ismaili communities in Africa and Asia, he was officially invested in a ceremony at Dar Es Salaam, Tanganyika, on October 19, 1957. The ceremony was repeated in Kenya, Uganda, India, Pakistan, and other countries. In the meantime his grandfather's widow, the Begum Aga Khan, emerged as his most influential advisor.

In September 1958 the new Aga Khan returned to Harvard to complete his studies. He carried an unusually heavy load of courses in order to graduate in June, and in addition devoted much time to his religious duties. With him in Cambridge were a secretary, Gaetane Beguel, a blonde Frenchwoman who had formerly served his grandfather in the same capacity, and a personal aide, Michael Curtis, formerly an editor of the London *News Chronicle*. In spite of his double workload, he found time to play left wing on the varsity soccer team.

On June 11, 1959 the Aga Khan received his Bachelor of Arts degree (with honors) in history. Two days earlier, he had given $50,000 to Harvard to establish a ten-year scholarship fund for Moslem students from the Middle East, an amount which the university planned to duplicate out of its own funds. He then resumed his travels through the Moslem world with a visit to Syria in August.

After the ceremony in Syria, the Aga Khan announced that a central bank for Ismailis was being formed at Damascus, and that he was bringing two engineers to Salamiyeh to search for underground water. He also appointed an eleven-member Ismaili council to handle community affairs, organized a group of forty youthful Ismailis to recommend projects to the central bank, and created a small educational committee. By means of these and similar projects he hoped to alleviate the abysmal poverty of his disciples in Syria. When a reporter asked Karim about his functions, he answered: "The primary function is the Imamate itself. That is the link which holds together our people, who live in many different kinds of cultures and speak so many different languages" (New York *Herald Tribune,* August 16, 1959).

Multiplied many times over, the problems that the Aga Khan is facing in Syria are the same as those he is confronting in other parts of the Ismaili Moslem world. Every week he receives reports from every Ismaili center; with them pour in the riches that make his projects possible. Although he did not share in his grandfather's enormous estate, all Ismaili Moslems contribute from 2 to 10 per cent of their incomes to his treasury. Most of the money returns to them in the form of social welfare projects.

In addition to his religious and economic duties, the Aga Khan is inevitably concerned with the cold war as it impinges on the Arab world. During a visit to Washington, D.C. in November 1959 he declared that each Ismaili must approach Communism according to his own conscience. "I can only answer for myself," he said, "and I personally am not sure that monotheism can live side by side with Communism." He hopes to visit the Ismailis who live in the southern part of the Soviet Union.

Unmarried, the Aga Khan maintains his residence at his mother's home in London. In 1957 Queen Elizabeth II conferred upon him the title, "His Highness," and also awarded him the Brilliant Star of Zanzibar. He speaks several European languages as well as Arabic and Urdu. Slender and darkly handsome, he is six feet tall, and has brown hair and hazel eyes. As a devout Moslem, he neither drinks nor smokes.

The Aga Khan sees no paradox in being the Western-oriented leader of 20,000,000 Moslems. "Often," he has said, "one can better understand their problems living away from them and visiting them occasionally." Since his visits have been more than occasional, he is perhaps the ideal man to lead his followers into the twentieth century.

References

N Y Herald Tribune p1 Jl 13 '57 por
N Y Post p3 Jl 14 '57 por
N Y Times p1 Jl 13 '57 por
N Y World-Telegram p1+ Jl 12 '57 por
This Week p8+ N 10 '57 por
Time 70:24+ Jl 22 '57 por
Who's Who, 1959

AHERNE, BRIAN (DE LACY) (ä-hûrn')
May 2, 1902- Actor
Address: b. 121 S. Beverly Dr., Beverly Hills, Calif.; h. 1038 Ocean Front, Santa Monica, Calif.

It was fitting that when *Dear Liar* began its second year on tour throughout the United States in 1960, it was on its way to a fame comparable to that achieved on the road by *The Barretts of Wimpole Street* in 1933-34. Its stars—Katharine Cornell and Brian Aherne—were the same. After establishing his reputation in the British theater, Aherne came to the United States in 1930 to star with Miss Cornell in *The Barretts of Wimpole Street*. Ever since, to the pleasure of audiences on two continents, Aherne and Miss Cornell have often linked their careers. Although Aherne has also played leading roles in more than twenty-five motion pictures, he has always achieved his most notable successes opposite Miss Cornell on the stage.

The male half of this theatrical team was born Brian de Lacy Aherne in King's Norton, Worcestershire, England, on May 2, 1902, the son of William de Lacy and Louise (Thomas) Aherne. His parents were both of Irish stock. The elder Aherne was an architect, his wife an amateur actress; of these family careers Brian chose the maternal one. He went to London when he was ten to study drama with Italia Conti; among his fellow students were Noel Coward and Gertrude Lawrence. A year later, in 1913, he made his debut in *Where the Rainbow Ends* at London's Garrick Theatre.

Aherne was educated at Malvern College (Worcestershire) and at Edgbaston in Birmingham, where he began to study architecture. Experience in Birmingham and the Liverpool Green Room Club rekindled his acting ambitions, however, and he decided to become a professional. He forsook his architectural studies to play a small part in *Paddy, the Next Best Thing* in 1923.

In the next seven years, Aherne quickly moved up to starring roles and became one of England's leading actors. His outstanding youthful performance was that as Langford in *White Cargo*, a part which he played for two years. His engagement was interrupted in 1926 by a tour of Australia with Dion Boucicault where he played in *Quality Street*, *What Every Woman Knows*, *The Admirable Crichton*, *Mary Rose*, and *Aren't We All?*

In 1930 Aherne came to the United States to play opposite Katharine Cornell in *The Barretts of Wimpole Street*. He made his Broadway debut on February 9, 1931. "Brian Aherne's Robert Browning is all strength, kindliness, and sincerity," wrote a New York *Times* reviewer (February 22, 1931). The play was a notable success in New York, and throughout the United States in a tour which lasted through 1933 and into 1934.

Aherne left Miss Cornell's tour in 1933 to make his American film debut opposite Marlene Dietrich in *The Song of Songs*. Disappointed with the results, he returned to London to star in *The Constant Nymph*. Again,

BRIAN AHERNE

in 1934 Miss Cornell brought him back to Broadway to play Mercutio in her production of *Romeo and Juliet,* and for the next decade he alternated between Broadway and Hollywood.

His most durable co-star was Miss Cornell, with whom he appeared in *Lucrece* and *St. Joan;* he also played Iago opposite Walter Huston's Othello. His film credits include *What Every Woman Knows* (1934), *I Live My Life* (1935), *Beloved Enemy* (1936), *The Great Garrick* (1937), *Merrily We Live* (1938), *Juarez* (1939), *Captain Fury* (1939), *My Son, My Son* (1940), *The Lady in Question* (1940), *Hired Wife* (1940), *The Man Who Lost Himself* (1941), *Skylark* (1941), *Smilin' Through* (1941), and *My Sister Eileen* (1942).

In 1943 Aherne announced that he was leaving film work to become a flight instructor for the Royal Air Force at Falcon Field, Arizona. When he realized that he could make a greater contribution to the war effort in his own profession, he toured American military camps in the winter of 1943-44 as an entertainer. In August 1944 he went overseas for the American Theater Wing, to recreate his role as Robert Browning in Miss Cornell's production of *The Barretts of Wimpole Street*. The cast gave 140 performances in Italy, France, and the Netherlands, and returning to New York six months later, staged the play on Broadway.

"Mr. Aherne acted Browning with a wealth of humorous and romantic effect, and a sensibility that matched that of Miss Cornell," observed a *Christian Science Monitor* reviewer (March 27, 1945). One critic felt that his performance was overdone—"an overemphasis no doubt caused by a worthy desire that the last GI in a huge theater get an impression of Browning's character" (New York *Times,* April 1, 1945).

After a short-lived production of *The French Touch* on Broadway in December

AHERNE, BRIAN—*Continued*

1945, Aherne returned to Hollywood to make *The Locket* for RKO in 1947. He was again on the New York stage in December 1949, when he acted Young Marlow in a City Center production of *She Stoops to Conquer*. In December 1951 he joined Miss Cornell in a successful revival of the Somerset Maugham comedy, *The Constant Wife*. Recalling how Aherne had made his American debut opposite Miss Cornell twenty years before, a *Theatre Arts* reviewer noted (February 1952): "He remains today one of our few romantic leading men, and an actor of distinction."

In quick succession, Aherne then made three films in Hollywood. He was the prosecutor in *I Confess* (1953), the ship's captain in *Titanic* (1953), and King Arthur in *Prince Valiant* (1954). Before the latter film was released, Aherne returned to the New York stage in an "accomplished, delightful performance" in a British comedy, *Escapade*.

The play collapsed after thirteen performances and Aherne recrossed the United States to play the father to Jean Simmons in *A Bullet is Waiting* (1954). His next film was *The Swan*, virtually his swan song in Hollywood, in which he portrayed the sympathetic monk-prince who abetted a royal romance. The film was released by Metro-Goldwyn-Mayer in 1956.

In 1958 Aherne emerged from semiretirement to play Professor Higgins in the touring company of *My Fair Lady*. The following year he appeared on the screen as the lecherous head of a publishing house in *The Best of Everything*, released by Twentieth Century-Fox in October 1959. He also appeared on television in June 1959 in *A Story Without a Moral* on the *Alcoa-Goodyear Theater*.

Drawn back to the world of one-night stand, Aherne again plunged into the hardships of a road tour at the request of Katharine Cornell. The play was *Dear Liar*, adapted by Jerome Kilty from the romantic correspondence between George Bernard Shaw and Mrs. Patrick Campbell. *Dear Liar* opened in Phoenix, Arizona in March 1959 and ended its "warm-up" tour six weeks later in Atlantic City, New Jersey. Aherne received his share of the critical plaudits along the way.

"Aherne's Shaw is a tour de force," wrote a *Variety* critic (March 25, 1959). A reviewer in the Toronto *Globe and Mail* (October 19, 1959) commented: "Mr. Aherne is the nimble, witty, blarneying Shaw, being deliberately preposterous, mischievously outrageous with much skill. He does characterize Shaw for us, and quite easily we substitute the remembered image of the crotchety dramatist for the urbane figure of Mr. Aherne." The play was presented on Broadway for a month beginning in March 1960.

Aherne has been married twice. His first marriage, to actress Joan Fontaine, ended in divorce in 1944; he was married to Mrs. Eleanor de Liagre Labrot January 27, 1946. He has a grape ranch in Thermal, California, which he manages when he is not appearing before the camera or the footlights. In recent years he has toured the summer theater circuit in *Dear Brutus* and in his own production of *The Beaux' Stratagem*.

"Few players could stand the road pace gaily set by [Miss Cornell and Aherne] and few would seem to have less incentive," remarked a *Time* reviewer (April 27, 1959). "Aherne has a profitable California grape farm, and hates the road. . . . But he feels bound to support (Miss) Cornell. . . . Shrugs Aherne: 'She's wedded to the road, and I'm wedded to her.'"

References

N Y Times IX p22 Jl 23 '33
Time 73:53 Ap 27 '59 por
Who's Who in America, 1950-51
Who's Who in the Theatre (1957)

ALEXANDER, FRANZ (GABRIEL) Jan. 22, 1891- Psychiatrist; psychoanalyst

Address: b. Mount Sinai Hospital, Levine Park, 8720 Beverly Blvd., Los Angeles 48, Calif; h. 1011 Ciello Dr., Palm Springs, Calif.

NOTE: This biography supersedes the article which appeared in *Current Biography* in 1942.

"Like all science, psychoanalysis is continually expanding and being modified. In our young field, new knowledge is paramount," Dr. Franz Alexander once said. In his native Hungary and in the United States, where he became a naturalized citizen in 1938, Dr. Alexander has become known for his contributions to psychoanalysis. He has become equally noted for his research on personality development, psychoneuroses and psychoses, psychosomatic medicine, psychoanalytic technique, criminology, and social psychology, and has written many books and articles on his findings. After almost twenty-five years as director of the Chicago Institute for Psychoanalysis, he became in 1956 the head of the psychiatric department and the Psychiatric and Psychosomatic Research Institute at Mount Sinai Hospital in Los Angeles.

Franz Gabriel Alexander was born in Budapest, Austria-Hungary (later Hungary), on January 22, 1891, the son of Bernard and Regina (Brössler) Alexander. He had four sisters and one brother. His father was an eminent professor of philosophy at the University of Budapest from 1880 until his death in 1927 and an author of works on the history of aesthetics and on Shakespeare. After his graduation from the Humanistic Gymnasium in Budapest with a B.A. degree in 1908, he entered the medical school of the University of Budapest. During the next several years he also studied medicine at the University of Göttingen and at the Physiological Institute in Cambridge, England. "Looking back upon my intellectual development," Alexander has said, "the struggle to synthesize my two major interests, that in science and that in philosophy and the humanities, remained for long years a main problem in finding my own identity. . . . This synthesis I found eventually in psychiatry and, in particular, in psychoanalysis."

From 1910 to 1913 Alexander was a research associate in physiology at the Institute for Experimental Pathology at the University of Budapest under Franz Tangl; during this period he published three experimental studies on the metabolism of the brain. He received his M.D. degree in 1913 from the university and for the next year he was a research associate in bacteriology at the university's Institute for Hygiene under the physiological chemist, Leo Lieberman.

During World War I Alexander served at the front as a commander of a Red Cross medical unit. In 1918 he became the head of a field laboratory, whose purpose was to organize malaria prophylaxis on the Italian front, and he later published an article on the epidemiology of malaria as a result of this experience. Discharged with the rank of first lieutenant, he received the Merit Cross with the crown and the Red Cross, second class.

After the war Alexander was invited to continue his research in brain physiology as an assistant at the Neuropsychiatric Clinic of the University of Budapest. Although he was primarily interested in blood chemistry, he soon began to consider the patients' psychological problems, and, eventually, the problems of the psychological understanding of the insane. He read the works of Sigmund Freud, and, convinced of the tremendous importance of Freud's approach to medicine, decided to study psychoanalysis.

At the invitation of Dr. Max Eitingon, who had just opened the Psychoanalytic Institute in Berlin, Alexander went there as its first training candidate in 1919. From 1920 to 1921 he did postgraduate work in the Psychiatric Hospital (Charite) of the University of Berlin, studied psychoanalysis, and underwent a training analysis with Dr. Hanns Sachs. In 1921 he became an assistant at the Psychoanalytic Institute and in this year he won the Freud Prize of the International Psychoanalytic Association for his research on the castration complex and the formation of character (his article on this topic was later published in English in the *International Journal of Psychoanalysis*, volume 4, 1923).

Dr. Alexander became a lecturer in psychoanalysis at the institute in 1924; some of his lectures were published under the title of *Psychoanalyse der Gesamtpersönlichkeit; neun Vorlesungen über die Anwendung von Freuds Ichtheorie auf die Neurosenlehre* (Internationaler Psychoanalytischer Verlag, 1927). This was published in English in 1930 in the Nervous and Mental Disease Monograph Series, number 52, under the title: *Psychoanalysis of the Total Personality; The Application of Freud's Theory of the Ego to Neuroses.*

Pursuing his interest in the problems of criminal personalities, Dr. Alexander worked on the application of psychoanalysis to criminology. With his co-worker Hugo Staub, a lawyer, he wrote *Der Verbrecher und seine Richter* (1929), which was published in English in 1931 by the Macmillan Company under the title, *The Criminal, the Judge, and the Public; A Psychological Analysis.* It was republished in

Black Star—Nolan Patterson

DR. FRANZ ALEXANDER

English in 1956 by the Free Press. In 1929 the two men started a seminar on criminology for judges and lawyers at the Psychoanalytic Institute.

In 1930 Dr. Alexander came to the United States as a visiting professor of psychoanalysis in various departments and schools of the University of Chicago, occupying the first university chair for psychoanalysis ever created. In the following year he undertook a research project in criminal psychology in collaboration with Dr. William Healy at the Judge Baker Foundation in Boston. The result of this study was published under the title of *Roots of Crime; Psychoanalytic Studies* (Knopf, 1935). In 1932 Dr. Alexander became the first director of the Chicago Institute for Psychoanalysis, an organization financed by private contributions and the Rockefeller Foundation, and devoted to the training of psychiatrists and to research in psychoanalysis and psychosomatic medicine. He helped to prepare the way for the final integration of psychoanalysis in the medical schools and teaching hospitals.

Dr. Alexander remained at the institute until 1956. In 1938 he was made an associate professor of psychiatry at the University of Illinois College of Medicine in Chicago and attending physician of the Cook County (Illinois) Psychopathic Hospital. In 1943 he was appointed clinical professor of psychiatry at the University of Illinois College of Medicine, where he taught a seminar in psychosomatic medicine. In 1949 his Institute for Psychoanalysis and other psychiatric faculties organized the Associated Psychiatric Faculties of Chicago to avoid duplication of effort in the training of psychiatrists.

During his almost twenty-five years at the Institute for Psychoanalysis, Dr. Alexander continued his researches in two major fields: psychosomatic medicine and improvement in the

ALEXANDER, FRANZ—*Continued*

techniques of psychoanalysis. His work in the former has been devoted to studies of the influence of emotional factors on gastrointestinal, endocrinological, and cardiovascular disturbances.

His publications in this field include: *The Medical Value of Psychoanalysis* (Norton, 1932), which he revised and enlarged in 1936; with Dr. Thomas French and others, *Psychogenic Factors in Bronchial Asthma* (Psychosomatic Medicine Monographs, 1941); *Studies in Psychosomatic Medicine; An Approach to the Cause and Treatment of Vegetative Disturbances* (Ronald, 1948); and *Psychosomatic Medicine; Its Principles and Applications* (Norton, 1950), an outgrowth of his *The Medical Value of Psychoanalysis*. In 1939 he helped to organize a new medical journal, *Psychosomatic Medicine*, and served as one of its editors from 1939 to 1949.

After 1939 Dr. Alexander and his associates at the institute had been concerned with re-examining the principles of psychoanalytic treatment and with developing a more flexible approach in adapting therapy to individual needs. The results of this study by the staff were published in *Psychoanalytic Therapy; Principles and Applications* (Ronald Press, 1946). Staff members have also worked toward developing principles of "brief psychoanalysis."

Dr. Alexander wrote *Fundamentals of Psychoanalysis* (Norton, 1948) and edited with Helen Ross *Dynamic Psychiatry* (University of Chicago Press, 1952), which deals with the influence of psychoanalysis upon psychiatric knowledge. Dr. Alexander and Helen Ross also edited *20 Years of Psychoanalysis; A Symposium in Celebration of the Twentieth Anniversary of the Chicago Institute for Psychoanalysis* (Norton, 1953).

He has also written books of broader philosophical import. In 1942 the J. B. Lippincott Company published *Our Age of Unreason; A Study of the Irrational Forces in Social Life,* which deals with political thought through the ages and applies the principles of modern dynamic psychology to the nature of totalitarian and democratic systems. An enlarged and revised edition was published by Lippincott in 1951. More recently, he has written the semiautobiographical *The Western Mind in Transition; An Eyewitness Story* (Random House, 1960), in which he analyzes the changing foundations of the modern world, using his own life as an "inner-directed" man as a case history in miniature.

While he was spending a year, 1955-56, at the Ford Foundation's Center for Advanced Study in the Behavioral Sciences in Palo Alto, California, Alexander completed his *Psychoanalysis and Psychotherapy; Developments in Theory, Technique and Training* (Norton, 1956). He returned to Chicago, but left it later in 1956 to become the head of a new psychiatric department of Mount Sinai Hospital in Los Angeles and the director of the Psychiatric and Psychosomatic Research Institute at the hospital. There the Ford Foundation supported his research project in which both the patient and the therapist are observed during psychotherapy and psychoanalysis by trained observers. Out of the project may emerge the principles by which the right kind of analyst can be selected for an emotionally unstable person.

In 1957 Alexander was awarded the Semmelweis Medal of the American-Hungarian Medical Association and in 1958, the Samuel Rubin Foundation Award. He belongs to many scientific societies and has held offices in some.

Franz Alexander was married to Anita Venier, an artist, in Berlin in 1921. They have two daughters: Sylvia and Francesca. He has brown eyes and gray hair. His religious affiliation is with the Roman Catholic Church. For recreation he enjoys reading, skiing, swimming, playing golf and tennis, and photography.

References

Newsweek 43:98+ Ap 26 '54; 51:91 My 12 '58

Alexander, Franz The Western Mind in Transition (1960)

National Cyclopaedia of American Biography current vol H (1952)

Who's Who in America, 1960-61

World Biography (1954)

ALLPORT, GORDON W(ILLARD) Nov. 11, 1897- Psychologist

Address: b. Emerson Hall, Harvard University, Cambridge 38, Mass.; h. 6 Arlington St., Cambridge 40, Mass.

The human personality and the complexities of social interaction have been the special concerns throughout his career of Dr. Gordon W. Allport, a professor of psychology at Harvard University, who has won international recognition for his research. His books, articles, and lectures on religion, rumor, prejudice, and public opinion have been praised for their lucidity and erudition, and his *Personality: A Psychological Interpretation* (Holt, 1937) has become a standard book in its field. Dr. Allport, who helped to found the department of social relations at Harvard University, has served as chairman of its department of psychology.

Gordon Willard Allport was born to Dr. John Edwards and Nellie Edith (Wise) Allport in Montezuma, Indiana on November 11, 1897. His father, a physician, whose ancestors came to the United States from England at the time of the Revolutionary War. Allport had three brothers, Harold E., Floyd H., and Fay W. (who died in 1957).

When Gordon Allport was six years old, he moved with his family to Cleveland, Ohio, where he received his primary and secondary school education. When he was fifteen years old, he ran his own multigraph business, and he edited the school newspaper at Glenville High School. After he was graduated in 1915, Allport enrolled at Harvard College. There he held various scholarships and majored in philosophy and economics. He was a dedicated student, who allowed himself little time for extracurricular activities; he was later to characterize himself as "a bit of a grind" as an undergraduate, who "didn't belong to many things." He received his B.A. degree in 1919, with Phi Beta Kappa honors.

Before returning to Harvard for his advanced degrees, he taught English and sociology at Robert College in Constantinople for a year. Allport returned to his alma mater in 1920, and earned his M.A. degree in 1921 and his Ph.D. degree in 1922. Under the influence of his brother Floyd (now a noted psychologist) and the famous experimental psychologist Hugo Münsterberg, he had chosen psychology as his major field of interest. His doctoral thesis, dealing with the experimental study of personality traits, was perhaps the first university thesis done on the topic in the United States.

After studying for two years (1922-24) in Berlin, Hamburg, and Cambridge, England, under a Sheldon Traveling Fellowship, Dr. Allport obtained a post at Harvard as instructor in social ethics (1924-26). From 1926 to 1930 he was an assistant professor of psychology at Dartmouth College, after which he returned to Harvard for the rest of his academic career. He was made associate professor of psychology in 1937 and full professor of psychology in 1942. When Harvard established the department of social relations in 1946 (partly under Dr. Allport's inspiration), he became chairman of its committee on higher degrees.

As a student of human psychology, Dr. Allport has explored the problems confronting man as a social being with a conscience. He has been outspoken on the question of racial and religious prejudice, and his book *The Nature of Prejudice* (Beacon, 1954) has been called a "notable contribution" which "will become a standard work" in the field. He takes a generally optimistic stand on the problem of prejudice. "There has been a very rapid drop in prejudice among students and educated people," Dr. Allport has said. "There is much more awareness of the stupidity and danger of bigotry."

At the University of Natal in Durban, South Africa, where he was visiting overseas consultant of the Institute for Social Research in 1956, Allport examined the racial issue at close range. He concluded that the problems of prejudice in South Africa "are very similar to the problems in our own South," and that in both areas "white supremacy cannot be maintained."

In *The Individual and His Religion* (Macmillan, 1950), Dr. Allport viewed religious belief through the eyes of a psychologist. Some reviewers praised the book as the most significant contribution of its kind since William James's *The Varieties of Religious Experience,* published almost half a century earlier. In spite of his sympathy with religion in general, Dr. Allport has on occasion roundly criticized some aspects of organized religion. During the tenth annual Race Relations Institute held at Fisk University in July 1953, he warned that "institutionalized" churchgoing engenders bigotry when the conscience is not strengthened by "interior revelation." "The institutionalized churchgoer," he asserted, "is like a super-patriot or a

GORDON W. ALLPORT

super-fraternal member. He attends church to find a safety island from which he can define the 'outgroup' and buttress his prejudices in a world of personal frustrations."

Another social problem that has attracted Dr. Allport's attention is the spread of rumor. As a member of the emergency committee of the National Research Council in psychology during World War II, he specialized in problems of morale and rumor among civilians. He also served as consultant to the Boston *Sunday Herald* rumor clinic, which dealt with dangerous rumors spread through Boston during the war. His study of rumor resulted in *The Psychology of Rumor* (Oxford, 1947), written with the help of Leo J. Postman, which Tomatsu Shibutani found "probably the most comprehensive and best single work on rumor now available" (*Journal of Sociology,* January 1948).

Dr. Allport has held high positions in many American professional organizations concerned with psychology. He has represented the American Psychological Association, of which he was president in 1937, on the National and Social Science Research Councils. He served as president of the Eastern Psychological Association in 1943 and as president of the Society for the Psychological Study of Social Issues in 1944. He was a director of the National Opinion Research Center.

Foreign governments have also honored Dr. Allport. He is an honorary Fellow of the British Psychological Society and an honorary member of the Deutsche Gesellschaft für Psychologie and Österreichische Ärztegesellschaft für Psychotherapie. He has been elected *membre associé (à titre étranger)* of the Société Française de Psychologie. Active in international scholarship, he is a former member of the national commission for UNESCO.

(Continued next page)

ALLPORT, GORDON W.—*Continued*

A frequent contributor to scholarly journals, Dr. Allport was editor of the *Journal of Abnormal and Social Psychology* from 1937 to 1949. His other published works include: *Studies in Expressive Movement* (with Philip E. Vernon, Macmillan, 1933); *The Psychology of Radio* (with Hadley Cantril, 1935); *The Use of Personal Documents in Psychological Science* (Social Science Research Council, 1942); *The Nature of Personality* (Addison-Wesley, 1950); *Becoming: Basic Considerations for a Psychology of Personality* (Yale University, 1955); and *Personality and Social Encounter* (Beacon, 1960).

A member of the Society of Colonial Wars, Dr. Allport belongs also to the Harvard Club of New York, the American Psychological Association, and the Eastern Psychological Association. In 1958 he received an honorary L.H.D. degree from Boston University. He has been president of the Ella Lyman Cabot Foundation and is a member of Sigma Xi honorary society. He is an Episcopalian and a Democrat.

Gordon Willard Allport was married to the former Ada Lufkin Gould of Lincolnville, Maine on June 30, 1925. They have one son, Robert Bradlee Allport, a pediatrician. Although he spends much of his time in his office in Harvard's Emerson Hall (he calls himself "the Methuselah of Emerson Hall"), he manages to indulge in his favorite recreations: music (he plays the piano "a little") and gardening. When he wearies of city living, he departs for one of his two country homes—"a simple farmhouse in Lincolnville and a small cottage at Rockport."

Rollo May has written of Gordon W. Allport: "He shares with William James and John Dewey the resolute capacity to see man as human regardless of whatever particular scientific trends may hold sway at any given moment. Allport helps fulfill his own prediction, that 'soon . . . psychology will offer an image of man more in accord with the democratic ideals by which psychologists as individuals live'" (*Saturday Review*, September 17, 1955).

References

Boston Sunday Herald III p2 F 28 '60
Who's Who in America, 1960-61

ALY (SULEIMAN) KHAN, PRINCE

June 13, 1911- Pakistani Representative to the United Nations; sportsman
Address: b. Pakistan House, 8 E. 65th St., New York 21; h. Carlton House, 680 Madison Ave., New York 21

Bulletin: Prince Aly Khan died on May 12, 1960.

The leader of the Asian-African bloc at the United Nations is Prince Aly Khan, the Permanent Representative of Pakistan to the United Nations. The son of the late Aga Khan III, father of the Aga Khan IV, and former husband of Rita Hayworth, the Prince has undergone a considerable transformation since he first presented his credentials to U.N. Secretary General Dag Hammarskjöld in 1958.

Even while he had been noted as a playboy, sportsman, and horse breeder, Aly Khan had displayed a sense of social responsibility. As a young man, he attended a conference in 1931 that considered constitutional reform for India, and he acquired a distinguished military record during World War II. For the past twenty-five years he has made annual visits to the Middle and Far East in order to meet with members of the Moslem Ismaili sect.

Prince Aly Suleiman Khan was born in Turin, Italy on June 13, 1911, the second son of Aga Sultan Sir Mahomed Shah Aga Khan (see *C.B.*, May 1946) and the former Italian ballerina Teresa Magliano. The death of his brother later that year made Prince Aly Khan the probable heir to his father's Imamah.

Although born and reared in Europe, Prince Aly traces his ancestry to Fatima, daughter of the Prophet Mohammed. His great-grandfather was the first Aga Khan, who settled in India after a dispute with the Shah of Persia and was rewarded for services to the British crown. Aga Khan II maintained close ties with England during his reign, 1881-1885, as did the Aga Khan III from 1885 until his death in 1957. The Aga Khans are in a sense kings without a country, as the hereditary Unrevealed Imams (or popes) to the Ismaili sect of Moslems, numbering about 20,000,000 persons in Asia and Africa.

A delicate child, Prince Aly spent his early summers in a villa at Deauville on the northern coast of France and his winters on the French Riviera. He was educated by a succession of Swiss tutors until he was fourteen, when he was sent to England to be tutored by C. W. Waddington, former principal of Mayo College in India.

While Aly was living and studying at his tutor's home outside Cambridge, his mother died and his father remarried. About this time he discovered the magic of horses and racing, and he soon became a hard-riding member of the Southdown Hunt in Sussex, where friends described him as "absolutely fearless, bright and gay and filled with energy."

Although he continued his studies (he was accepted at Cambridge University but settled for tutelage in law at Lincoln's Inn in London), Aly soon became one of Europe's most publicized sportsmen and playboys. He first rode as a gentleman jockey in 1930, and a year later he won the Southdown Welter Handicap and registered his own racing colors in England. He also drove in major European auto races, hunted in African safaris, and in 1932 flew a plane on a hazardous 10,000-mile round trip between Bombay and Singapore. After Loel Guinness named him as correspondent in a divorce suit in 1936, he was married to Mrs. Joan Barbara Yarde-Buller Guinness, daughter of the 3d Baron Churston.

Aly Khan's first playboy period had ended a few years earlier. Already he had displayed a serious turn of mind by serving as a secretary to the British-Indian delegation at the second Round Table Conference in 1931 which discussed constitutional reforms for India. At the outbreak of World War II, he joined the Sixth Regiment of the French Foreign Legion as a second lieutenant.

After basic training, Aly served one year at the Legion's desert headquarters in Sidi-bel-Abbès, then was attached to General Maxime Weygand's headquarters in Syria. He deserted when the French army came under the command of Marshal Henri Philippe Pétain after the German occupation. Joining the Royal Wiltshire Yeomanry in 1940, Aly was subaltern in British intelligence in Jerusalem, making propaganda broadcasts and organizing a network of Ismaili spies throughout the Middle East. Later he was a liaison officer assigned to the Free French Army and then to the United States Sixth Army during the invasion of southern France. It is reported that one of his last acts in uniform was to free at gun point some of the valuable horses taken from his father's stables by the Nazis.

Discharged with the rank of lieutenant colonel in 1945, the Prince became a full partner in his father's racing interests in the following year. As chief administrator of one of the world's finest stables, he managed 3,000 acres of land in France and Ireland and bloodstock valued at some $8,000,000. Until 1953, when the Aga Khan sold many of his horses in order to reinvest his money, Aly Khan increased the number of his father's English Derby winners to a record five.

Aly remained on the gossip pages of the world's newspapers, as well, by virtue of his fast cars and his whirlwind romances. Perhaps his most-publicized exploit was his marriage to movie actress Rita Hayworth in 1949. The lavish wedding did not improve his standing with his father, nor with the Ismailian Moslems who were already manifesting disapproval of the adventures of their prospective Imam. Aly Khan curtailed his social activities somewhat when the declining health of the Aga obliged his son to perform missions in the Middle and Far East. When the Aga died in 1957, however, the Imamah passed to Aly's elder son, Prince Karim Khan, who became the Aga Khan IV (see *C.B., March 1960*).

In February 1958 Prince Aly Khan received an appointment as Pakistan's Representative to the United Nations, with the rank of Ambassador. After spending a week at the Pakistani Foreign Office being briefed on the nation's policies, the Prince flew to New York and assumed his new duties on March 4. During the General Assembly's thirteenth session he served as chairman of the Pakistani delegation and vice-president of the General Assembly. He was elected vice-president of the U.N. Peace Observation Commission in 1959.

While in New York, Aly lives at the Carlton House and works at the Pakistan House on East 65th Street. He walks to his office. A writer for the Toronto *Globe and Mail* (April 25, 1958) commented: "He has largely withdrawn from the glitter of the international set, spends long hours at his job, and has learned to be smoothly noncommittal with all the bland good humor of a man who has spent his life in diplomacy."

Blackstone Studios

PRINCE ALY KHAN

Yet the name of Aly Khan continues to appear on the sports and society pages of newspapers and magazines. Some of his 280 horses still win races, and his former marriage to Rita Hayworth still attracts headlines when questions concerning the custody and education of their daughter, Princess Yasmin, arise. The Prince and Miss Hayworth were married in 1949; four years later, their marriage was dissolved. His first marriage, to Joan Yarde-Buller Guinness, was dissolved in 1949 after the birth of two sons, Karim and Amyn.

In addition to his New York apartment, Aly has homes in Ireland, France, Switzerland, and Venezuela. He is a lavish entertainer, a far-ranging traveler, and a man of exuberant energy during his average nineteen-hour day. He speaks fluent French and English as well as some Arabic. In recognition of his World War II service he became an officer in the French Legion of Honor and received the French Croix de Guerre with palms and the American Bronze Star Medal. He is the colonel commandant of the Pakistani Fourth Cavalry. Prince Aly Khan is an attractive, stockily built man, standing just under five feet six inches tall and weighing 165 pounds, who has thinning black hair and black eyes. His club is the Athenæum in London.

"I've never been conscious of being a playboy," the Prince told Walter Ames (Los Angeles *Times*, March 17, 1959). "Some columnist gives you a tag and you have to live with it for the rest of your life. However, I've always believed in playing hard when one is playing. I also believe in working hard when one is working. The latter is what I have been doing for years—but not many people seem to know about it."

Although he has not yet achieved the diplomatic prestige of his father, who was five times India's delegate to the League of Nations and

ALY KHAN, PRINCE—*Continued*

once chairman of the League Assembly, there is no doubt that Prince Aly Khan has found a new mission in his U.N. work. Speaking of the United Nations, he said in April 1958: "It is the only future. There is no future outside it."

References

N Y Times p4 F 7 '58 por; p31 My 9 '58 por
Sports Illus 10:60+ Mr 23; 61+ Mr 30 '59 pors
Toronto Globe and Mail p24 F 7 '58
Who's Who, 1959

ANDREWS, ROY CHAPMAN Jan. 26, 1884-Mar. 11, 1960 Explorer; naturalist; author; conducted famed expeditions to Central Asia in the 1920's; was associated with the American Museum of Natural History in New York for more than fifty years. See *Current Biography* (July) 1953.

Obituary

N Y Times p1+ Mr 12 '60

ARANHA, OSWALDO Feb. 15, 1894-Jan. 27, 1960 Brazilian diplomat and advocate of Pan-American solidarity; Minister of Justice and Internal Affairs (1930-31); Minister of Finance (1931-34 and 1953-55); Ambassador to the United States (1934-38); Foreign Minister (1938-44); President of the General Assembly of the United Nations (1947). See *Current Biography* (March) 1942.

Obituary

N Y Times p31 Ja 28 '60

ARMSTRONG-JONES, ANTONY (CHARLES ROBERT) Mar. 7, 1930- Husband of Princess Margaret of Great Britain

Address: Kensington Palace, London, England

London gossip columnists in February 1960 were astonished when they heard the news that had been building up under their noses for two years: Princess Margaret was going to marry court photographer Antony Armstrong-Jones, a commoner and a leader of London's sophisticated Bohemia. His friends wondered how Armstrong-Jones, who had always flouted convention and reveled in informality, would meet the rigorous demands of his new life. Nevertheless, as the months went by, Armstrong-Jones seemed to have readily adapted himself to his role as a member of the royal family. A professional photographer before his marriage to Princess Margaret on May 6, 1960, Armstrong-Jones is noted for the unorthodox quality of his portraits of society people, his fashion photography, and his genre glimpses of life in the parks and streets of London.

Although zealous genealogists have traced his lineage to the thirteenth-century King Edward I, Antony Charles Robert Armstrong-Jones was born a commoner, i.e., not royal nor a British peer, on March 7, 1930 in London. The only son of Sir Ronald Owen Lloyd Armstrong-Jones, Q. C., and the former Anne Messel, he is descended from landed gentry; his father's family occupies a seat at Plâs Dinas, Caernarvon, North Wales. His grandfather, Sir Robert Armstrong-Jones, a distinguished physician, added "Armstrong" to his surname by deed poll in 1913. Antony had dropped the hyphen when he became a photographer, but reassumed it after his engagement to the Princess.

Antony's parents were divorced in 1934, and his mother the following year married Sir Laurence Michael Harvey Parsons, the Sixth Earl of Rosse. Armstrong-Jones has one sister, Susan, now the Viscountess de Vesci, and two half brothers (the children of his mother and the Earl of Rosse), Lord Oxmanton and the Honorable Desmond Parsons. His father, a prominent barrister, is now married to the former Jenifer Unite, his third wife.

Tony—as he was invariably called until his betrothal—entered Sandroyd School in Wiltshire when he was eight and went on to Mr. J. D. Upcott's house at Eton in 1943. At Eton he displayed a talent for radio engineering, boxing, and coxing, but for little else. Typical of his end-of-term reports was one in which the master is reported to have commented, "Maybe he is interested in some subject, but it isn't a subject we teach here." Tony has recalled of the reports that "They were so awful I used to give them to my parents and then disappear for the rest of the day."

When he was still at Eton he suffered an attack of poliomyelitis which he fought with such determined exercise that he today displays no vestige of it except a barely noticeable limp when he is nervous or tired. While he was recovering from polio, his mother, to keep him amused, gave him the camera that started his interest in photography.

In 1948 he entered Jesus College of Cambridge University, where, at the prompting of his mother, he studied architecture, but with less enthusiasm and energy than he expended on photography and rowing. He received his rowing Blue as coxswain of Jesus College's first boat and he directed the university's eight in its 1950 victory over Oxford. After two years at Cambridge he failed his second examination and was sent down.

Following his expulsion from Cambridge in 1951 Armstrong-Jones worked with Baron Bahum, a court photographer better known simply as Baron. After serving a six-month apprenticeship with Baron, he went into partnership with David Sim in a basement studio on Shaftesbury Avenue for a few months before opening his own studio in a former ironmonger's shop at 20 Pimlico Road. He renovated and decorated the studio and his living quarters above it, building a wood and copper spiral staircase to connect the two areas. Here his friends from Chelsea, Fleet Street, and the theater and fashion worlds could enjoy clever conversation, blaring jazz, and informal meals cooked by Antony himself.

He became a familiar figure in the neighborhood. He carried his wash to the self-service laundry, and washed down meat pies with ale in nearby pubs and restaurants. He gave and attended many parties, where he liked to indulge in mimicry or clowning, enjoying himself most when he tricked his friends with his outlandish disguises. At one party he posed undetected as an old flower lady at the gate; at another, a "baby party," he came in a baby carriage, sucking a pacifier.

Armstrong-Jones began his career as a society photographer. His persistence and his imaginative approach gradually won him popularity in fashionable circles. His pictures of society dowagers for the *Tatler* were lighthearted examples of their kind. In 1956 he staged a successful exhibit at Kodak House in Kingsway, London. The same year he was asked to take the Duke of Kent's twenty-first birthday portrait; after that, he did not lack commissions.

Appointed an official court photographer in 1958, Armstrong-Jones took pictures of the royal family that were handed out to the press on birthdays and other festive occasions. He gratified the royal family with frequent departures from conventional portraiture. One photograph of Prince Charles and Princess Anne showed the children sitting and reading on the floor of a large hall in Buckingham Palace. On the other hand, a photograph of Princess Margaret taken in 1959, showing a pensive princess posed between two hobby horses she had played with as a child, was criticized by many Englishmen who felt that the royal family should be presented only in traditional poses.

For magazines like *Vogue*, Armstrong-Jones engaged in fashion and advertising photography. He also became interested in theater design (spurred on perhaps by his uncle, Oliver Messel, the stage designer) and in 1957 he made the first photographic sets ever used on the English stage —blown-up photographs of London for the musical, *Keep Your Hair On*. In 1959 Armstrong-Jones visited New York to take photographs of the Broadway play, *Rashomon*. His portraits of theater personalities include those of Sir Alec Guinness, Dame Edith Evans, and Marlene Dietrich; he has also photographed the poet-playwright, T. S. Eliot.

"Many [of his photographs] show a perceptive eye and wit and the patient energy needed to catch telling moments in the lives of all sorts of people," a *Life* (March 14, 1960) reporter wrote. For a while Armstrong-Jones roamed around London—to Hyde Park, Victoria, Chelsea, Kew Gardens—trying to catch "the local feeling." The photos he took on these rambles were displayed in *London* (Weidenfeld, 1958 and Dutton, 1959), a book which drew high praise from British critics. The photographs in Sacheverell Sitwell's *Malta* (Batsford, 1958) are also by Armstrong-Jones.

At the peak of his career, Armstrong-Jones was earning about $12,000 a year; he received over $200 for each portrait that he took and autographed. Having now given up commercial

Wide World

ANTONY ARMSTRONG-JONES

photography in deference to a Buckingham Palace tradition that no one should make money out of the prestige of royalty, Armstrong-Jones may seek a new career in stage design, according to the London *Evening Standard* (June 29, 1960).

Princess Margaret and Antony Armstrong-Jones first met formally at a London evening party early in 1958. They continued to see each other at informal gatherings given by the Princess at Clarence House; at Mayfair and Belgravia affairs; and, after a while, at Balmoral, the royal family's residence in Scotland, and Sandringham, the royal country house in the east of England. They also met—more rarely—in Antony's Pimlico studio and in his rooms overlooking the Thames River near Paradise Street in the East End. So successfully did they keep the courtship a secret that the closest linking of their names in the press was a mention in a London newspaper of their being two in a party of six at *West Side Story* in May 1959.

Armstrong-Jones and Princess Margaret agreed to be married in January 1960. Margaret told the Most Rev. Dr. Geoffrey Francis Fisher, Archbishop of Canterbury, of the proposal. The Archbishop, who had disapproved of her engagement to Peter Townsend five years before because of Townsend's previous divorce, was quoted as being "very pleased." The Queen and Prince Philip were "delighted" at the "obviously happy match."

The engagement was announced by Queen Elizabeth, the Queen Mother, in a court circular on February 26, 1960. After the announcement Armstrong-Jones abandoned his Pimlico studio, his photographic career, his easygoing life, his "drainpipe" blue jeans and loud shirts, and, putting on a suit tailored in Saville Row, moved into Buckingham Palace. He resided there until the marriage.

(Continued next page)

ARMSTRONG-JONES, ANTONY—Cont.

The wedding of Princess Margaret Rose of Great Britain and Antony Charles Robert Armstrong-Jones took place before 2,000 spectators (and an estimated 300,000,000 more on live and taped television) in Westminster Abbey on the morning of May 6, 1960. The Most Rev. Dr. Geoffrey Fisher, Archbishop of Canterbury, officiated. The couple then boarded the royal yacht, H.M.S. *Britannia,* for a forty-three-day honeymoon in the Caribbean.

Antony Armstrong-Jones is about five feet five inches tall—"tall enough to look over the top of Princess Margaret's most bouffant hairdo" *(Ladies' Home Journal,* June 1960). He is fair-haired, slight of build, and blue-eyed. His eyesight is not as good as he pretends; he often uses glasses but snatches them off when a stranger appears. He has a poor public speaking voice and a tendency to stammer slightly when tense or excited. Armstrong-Jones likes to read books on furnishing, architecture, and other subjects which appeal to his practical artistic sense. His associates speak of his great vitality and singlemindedness.

References

Christian Sci Mon p9 Ap 27 '60 por
Illus London N 226:797+ My 14 '60 pors
Ladies Home J 77:46+ Je '60 por
Life 48:91+ Mr 14 '60 pors
London Observer p9 Ap 24 '60 por
London Sunday Times p31 F 28 '60
N Y Times p6 F 27 '60 por
Time 75:18 Mr 7 '60 por
Glenton, R. and King, S. Antony Armstrong-Jones (1960)

BAKER, MELVIN H(OUSTON) Aug. 11, 1885- Corporation executive

Address: b. 325 Delaware Ave., Buffalo 2, N.Y.; h. 751 West Ferry St., Buffalo, N.Y.

In its thirty-five year history the National Gypsum Company has grown from a small-scale venture into a multimillion dollar enterprise. Melvin H. Baker, its chairman of the board, has guided the development from the start of National Gypsum Company both as founder of the firm and as its president for twenty-five years. The company is now the nation's second largest purveyor of building materials; it has assets of $247 million, including forty-three plants east of the Rockies in twenty-eight states and Canada. Its headquarters are in Buffalo, New York.

The National Gypsum Company began with one product and one plant in 1925. Today it markets some 300 products in eleven major lines (gypsum, lime, metal lathe, asbestos, acoustical materials, insulation, insulation board, paper, paint, ceramic tile, and cement). It ranks as the 247th industrial concern in size in the United States and in its field is not far behind the giant U.S. Gypsum Company, which has $300 million in assets. In 1959 Baker announced a five-year plan to expand his company by spending some $125 million for new

plants, acquisitions, and increased production. "Growth," Baker has said "has always been a guiding and motivating factor in my life."

Melvin Houston Baker was born on August 11, 1885 in Sevierville, Tennessee, the son of Joseph and Amanda (Fox) Baker. His family background includes several generations of American ancestors of Scotch-Irish origin. His father was a tenant farmer. The boy received his elementary education in a one-room schoolhouse, after which he worked his way through high school. After his high school graduation, he walked more than twenty miles to register at Carson-Newman College in Jefferson City, Tennessee. To support himself and at the same time assist his parents, he worked after school hours firing furnaces and doing other odd jobs. Because the college curriculum was designed to prepare students for the Baptist ministry, Baker was unable to study engineering as he wished. At twenty-five years of age, Baker left Carson-Newman College and took a job as assistant to an auctioneer in a warehouse containing slow-moving hardware. He then became a distributor for a window screen manufacturer in a new territory that had been set up in four southeastern states. In 1912 he joined the Beaver Products Company as a southern sales representative.

Once, when calling on a dealer in a mining area, Baker was told that the local market had small use for Beaverboard. He ignored the advice, took his samples to a mining company, and showed how his product could be used to build houses for mine superintendents. As a result, he returned to the dealer with an order for a carload of Beaverboard. In three years he was promoted to general sales manager of the company. When Beaver Products Company failed in 1921, Baker joined the American Manufacturers' Foreign Credit Underwriters in New York City. He served as a vice-president from 1922 to 1924.

In 1925 Baker and two associates from the Beaver Products Company, Joseph Haggerty and Clarence Williams, founded the National Gypsum Company. Baker became vice-president that year, president in 1928, and chairman of the board in 1952.

During his career as chief executive of National Gypsum, Baker has achieved a long and successful record of moving counter to storm warnings in the economy and the industry. When the firm began, investment houses refused to finance it because they insisted that the wallboard field was overcrowded. Baker and his associates, who had accumulated $150,000 in capital, estimated that they needed $2 million. Instead of selling wallboard, their salesmen went from door to door, selling shares of stock in the new enterprise. In four months the necessary funds had been raised and production began at Clarence Center, New York.

In the 1930's when other companies were liquidated, Baker added new products, expanded plant capacity and opened new markets. During the depression he amazed the business world by selling more materials in 1930 than in 1929. Seeking new funds to build a $2 million gypsum plant in 1938, he invited ten prominent financiers to a dinner in New York. He explained his proposed project and by morning his project had been oversubscribed.

After World War II, when many businessmen feared an economic collapse, Baker again expanded the output of gypsum board and other products to meet the postwar housing boom. He spent $50 million for expansion, added seven new plants, bought three companies and three ships, and completely mechanized production lines. Since 1930, the National Gypsum Company has never failed to make a profit.

In July 1959 Baker announced his intention to spend about $125 million on the expansion of National Gypsum Company during the first half of the 1960's. A projected new plant to be erected in California at the cost of $10 million will put the company west of the Rockies for the first time. According to Baker, National Gypsum wants to expand its markets to include the entire North American continent.

Noting his excellent sales ability, *Forbes* magazine (December 1, 1954) quoted Baker as saying: "Maybe, I can't do anything else. But I sure can whip up enthusiasm in people." The magazine continued: "To such a man retirement does not come easy. Though he talks freely enough about 'spending more time in my Florida home' and has stepped out of the presidency, Baker is still undeniably the boss at National Gypsum, quite noticeably talks of retirement in a rather ambiguous fashion. In one breath he speaks of dropping out of harness. In the next, and with far more bounce, he vows that 'I will be with this company in one capacity or another as long as I am physically competent. The National Gypsum Company is my baby.' "

Through the years, Baker has worked hard in many business, religious, and community organizations. He has been a director of the United States Chamber of Commerce, the National Industrial Conference Board, past director of the National Association of Manufacturers, and chairman of the board of the Buffalo Redevelopment Foundation. He is a trustee of the National Safety Council and a former president of the Buffalo Chamber of Commerce. He is a trustee of the General Assembly of the Presbyterian Church in the United States of America, and was president of the board of trustees of Westminster Church in Buffalo. For three years he served as general chairman of the American Cancer Crusade for the state of New York and in 1956 he was chairman of National Bible Week.

The Alumni Association of the University of Buffalo named Baker as The Outstanding Businessman of the Niagara Frontier in 1950. Later in 1950 he was selected as one of fifty industrialists to receive the Boston Jubilee Award, and he was named one of the outstanding citizens of Buffalo by the Buffalo *Evening News.* Baker has been cited for "industrial pioneering" by the University of Buffalo and "for his efforts in promotion of the Free Enterprise System" by the University of Maryland "M" Club. In 1953 Baker was granted honorary degrees by Carson-Newman College and the University of Maryland. In

MELVIN H. BAKER

1956 he received honorary degrees from Canisius College in Buffalo and Alfred University in Alfred, New York.

On April 19, 1920 Melvin Baker was married to Frances Yeager. They have two children, Melvin H. Baker, Jr., and Jevene Hope. Baker stands five feet five inches in height, weighs 150 pounds, and has brown eyes and gray hair. He is a Republican. Baker, who occupies one of the few penthouse apartments in Buffalo, has been called by *House and Home* (September 1959) "a meticulous dresser, two-packs-a-day cigarette smoker who relaxes with golf, fishing, hunting (mostly duck and pheasant), and an occasional good book." His optimism is based not upon a self-hypnotizing Pollyanna attitude, but upon a solid knowledge of facts and figures and the conviction that industrialists may think themselves into a depression psychology.

Reference

Who's Who in America, 1958-59

BANCROFT, ANNE Sept. 17, 1931-
Actress

Address: b. Actors' Equity Association, 226 W. 47th St., New York 36

A newcomer to Broadway, actress Anne Bancroft, of Italian-American background, has scored two hits in succession—first as a Jewish girl in *Two for the Seesaw* in 1958 and as an American educator in *The Miracle Worker* in 1959. Her portrayal of Annie Sullivan, the teacher of Helen Keller, won her an ANTA award for the best performance of the 1959-60 season. Miss Bancroft has been called "a female Marlon Brando" and "a young Magnani." Before she made her Broadway debut in *Two for the Seesaw* she had appeared in some fifteen second-rate movies and about ninety television shows.

(Continued next page)

ANNE BANCROFT

Anne Bancroft, whose real name is Annemarie (some sources give Anna Maria) Italiano, was born on September 17, 1931 in the Bronx, New York, to Michael and Mildred (DiNapoli) Italiano. Her father was a dress pattern maker and her mother, a telephone operator at Macy's department store. She has two sisters, Jo Anne and Phyllis. It was Mrs. Italiano who decided that of her three daughters Anne would be the actress. Anne admits that she was born a show-off. When she was three or four years old she sang for WPA workers on the streets of the East Bronx. "I was the personality kid," she told a *Time* interviewer (December 21, 1959). "When I wasn't sick, I was singing."

After Public School Number 35, Anne entered Christopher Columbus High School in the Bronx, where she was active in the drama club and a member of Arista. In her senior year, in 1947, she decided to become a laboratory technician instead of an actress, but her mother scraped up the tuition to send her to the American Academy of Dramatic Arts.

Her first professional performance was on television in the *Studio One* production of Ivan Turgenev's *The Torrents of Spring*. Using the name of Anne Marno, she had a role in the TV series *The Goldbergs* and appeared occasionally on such programs as *Danger, Suspense,* and *Studio One,* on which Fred Coe first saw her act. In this period she also worked in drugstores and taught English to Peruvian singer Yma Sumac.

After a screen test, Anne immediately won a Twentieth Century-Fox Film Corporation contract. Choosing the name of Anne Bancroft from a list submitted to her by Darryl F. Zanuck, then head of production at Fox, she appeared in a featured role in *Don't Bother To Knock* (1952). She portrayed the wife of S. Hurok in *Tonight We Sing* (1953), a film

biography of the impresario; a Roman lady in *Demetrius and the Gladiators* (1954), a spectacle about early Christianity; the gangster's unhappy daughter who has everything but respectability in *New York Confidential* (1955), a drama about syndicated crime; and the blonde wife of the colonel in *The Last Frontier* (1956), a western.

After two years under contract to Twentieth Century-Fox and five years of free-lancing, Miss Bancroft took inventory of herself. "Not only hadn't I arrived," she told interviewer Stanley Richards (*Theatre,* December 1959), "but there was a great deal of work and study ahead. . . . I learned a great deal in Hollywood, even though I'm not particularly proud of the fifteen or so films I made."

After reading the script of *Two for the Seesaw* she yearned for the part of Gittel Mosca, a ballet dancer who has exchanged the Bronx for Bohemia. When she met Fred Coe, the play's producer, she decided to impress him not so much by acting the role of Gittel as by making herself over as Gittel. "I made sure he found me with one shoe off, scratching my foot," she told an interviewer from *Time.* She succeeded. Coe, Arthur Penn, the director, and William Gibson, the playwright, agreed that she was a perfect choice for the Bohemian girl in the two-character play about an affair between an Omaha lawyer on the brink of divorce and a generous Greenwich Village stray.

At rehearsals Anne Bancroft demonstrated that she could learn to take direction admirably. "At first," Arthur Penn informed a *Time* reporter, "she could hardly find the stage. She'd play with her back to the audience. She was too broad and too vulgar. Even the lawyers and agents connected with the show said, 'She's no good; dump her.' I even had to tell her where the jokes were, but once was enough."

Playing opposite the veteran actor Henry Fonda, Miss Bancroft won immediate recognition as an accomplished actress when the play opened on Broadway on January 16, 1958. As the black-stockinged beatnik in search of self-respect, "Miss Bancroft . . . turns out to be a deliriously captivating comic, a rich discovery, a youngster who should do much for the West 40's," wrote Frank Aston in the New York *World-Telegram and Sun* (January 17, 1958). She won the Antoinette Perry, Theatre World, and Variety awards for her performance.

When Gibson, Penn, and Coe turned to their second enterprise, *The Miracle Worker,* they never questioned that the fourth member of their team, Anne Bancroft, would play the role of Annie Sullivan. In the play the governess at first takes on the job of merely taming the spoiled and savage child, Helen Keller. Soon she dedicates herself to opening up the entire universe by means of language to Helen, who is triply handicapped by blindness, muteness, and deafness.

To groom herself for her demanding role, Anne Bancroft observed blind and disturbed children at the Institute of Physical Medicine and Rehabilitation in New York City. "I became so completely absorbed that I stayed three weeks to work with them," Miss Bancroft told

Stanley Richards. In order to know what it was like to be blind, she attached adhesive strips to her eyelids and wore dark glasses for two days. Then she visited the Vacation Camp for the Blind to practise the manual alphabet she had learned. Soon Miss Bancroft and Patty Duke, who had been assigned the role of the young Helen Keller, were carrying on private conversations and cracking jokes in the manual alphabet.

The play opened on October 19, 1959 at the Playhouse Theatre, and both Miss Bancroft and Patty Duke received unanimous critical praise. Anne's picture appeared on the covers of numerous magazines. "Miss Bancroft has an amazing talent for onstage concentration and a willingness to work disciplinedly and hard," noted Henry Hewes (*Saturday Review,* November 7, 1959). "She has an extraordinary spontaneity which makes it all seem 'natural.'"

Despite shoulder, knee, and shin pads, both actresses have been injured in the nightly pummeling they give each other during a scene based on an actual "battle royal" described in one of Annie Sullivan's letters. "Since Miss Bancroft and Patty are inventive," reported Nan Robertson (New York *Times,* December 20, 1959), "the scene is never played exactly the same way twice. . . . It is invariably followed by amazed applause. Depending on the audience, the scene may be played for laughs, tears, or tension . . . on occasion, it has been hilarious. Annie is a natural clown."

Anne Bancroft is happiest and most satisfied when she is working. She has no objection to television or film assignments, but for her a live audience is the most exciting. Twice a week she studies at the Actors Studio, where she is concentrating on Shakespearean and Restoration roles. She is also taking voice lessons because she wants to appear in a Broadway musical.

Standing five feet six inches in height and weighing about 120 pounds, Anne Bancroft has a round face, a mobile mouth, brown eyes, and brown hair. Among her favorite clothes are black cotton stockings, flat shoes, and shapeless sweaters. She makes her home in an apartment in a remodeled Greenwich Village brownstone, where she likes to read biography and paint in water colors. She is currently undergoing psychoanalysis. Her marriage to Martin A. May on July 4, 1954 ended in divorce on February 13, 1958. Of the $150,000 she earns a year she reserves $50 a week for spending money, investing a large part of the rest of her funds in Manhattan real estate, a California bank, and a Texas oil well.

She still works with blind children. When one little boy learned how to load his spoon with food, she wept at "one of the most wonderful sights she had ever seen." She told Richard Harrity (*Cosmopolitan,* February 1960) that in getting to know the blind children and their teachers, she has a compulsion to help. When Harrity asked her about her future plans, she said: "I want to do everything, and while that may sound greedy it really isn't. I feel that if you limit your hopes, you limit your horizons."

Her hunger for experience transcends the limits of her daily life. She told Gilbert Millstein of the New York *Times Magazine* (February 9, 1958): "I like to be alone when I want to be alone; I like to be with people when I like to be with people; walk when I want to walk, take baths when I want to take baths, sleep when I'm sleepy. I would like the right to die. My philosophy is that life is here only to be lived so that we can, through life, earn the right to death, which to me is paradise, really. . . . Paradise to me is knowledge, the answers to all the questions you think of and all the questions you never think of in life."

References

Cue 28:18 O 17 '59 por
N Y Herald Tribune IV p1 N 8 '59
N Y Times Mag p22+ F 9 '58 pors
International Motion Picture Almanac, 1960
Who's Who of American Women, 1958-59

BANNOW, RUDOLPH F(REDERICK)

April 15, 1897- Organization official; manufacturer

Address: b. 500 Lindley St., Bridgeport, Conn.; h. 26 Flat Rock Dr., Easton, Conn.

The sixty-five-year-old National Association of Manufacturers, with its more than 20,000 member companies who together are responsible for about 75 per cent of the manufacturing output of the United States, has been widely regarded as a spokesman for big business. Rudolph F. Bannow, its president for 1960, rejects this idea. The president of the nonunion Bridgeport Machines, Inc., a concern which employs only about 400 workers, Bannow has called himself "one of the little guys that make up 83 per cent of the NAM" (New York *Times,* December 4, 1959).

Among the measures that Bannow advocates as indispensable to a thriving economy are lowering of individual and corporation taxes; prevention of spiraling inflation by curbing wage and price rises; and revision of "outdated" union work laws. In his own twenty-one-year-old company, Bannow has eschewed mandatory retirement regulations and has instituted a profit-sharing plan.

"Up until the 1650's, half my ancestors were Norwegian. After that we were Swedish," says Rudolph Frederick Bannow, who was born on April 15, 1897 in Göteborg, Sweden. After having attended elementary and manual training schools in that city, Rudolph migrated at the age of thirteen to Holyoke, Massachusetts, where his mother supported her daughter and two sons by running a boarding house.

At fourteen, after an additional year of schooling in Holyoke, Bannow became an apprentice patternmaker with the Deane Steam Pulp Company and was, he says, "grossly underpaid" at six and a half cents an hour. Five years later he moved to Bridgeport, Connecticut, where he worked as a patternmaker for various concerns until 1919. He then sailed as a stoker aboard a

RUDOLPH F. BANNOW

freighter which made a one-year trip around the world.

In 1920 he became a foreman at the Bridgeport Pattern and Model Works, which he purchased in 1927 with $80 of his own and a loan of some $3,000 from his mother. Rudolph Bannow and Magnus Wahlstrom, also a native of Sweden, formed a partnership in 1929. After introducing the Bridgeport high-speed milling attachment, the firm began making its own all-angle, self-powered milling head, which was then attached to a complete turret milling machine now known as the "Bridgeport miller." In 1939 the company was incorporated under the name of Bridgeport Machines, which today manufactures machines used to make other machines and tools. The company today is worth $6,500,000 and can produce a machine every twenty minutes on its assembly line.

For ten years Bannow carried a patternmaker's union card and is said to have been at one time the only union member in an open shop. Bridgeport Machines, Inc., has never been unionized, however. It has also never had a strike. "I guess I'm a better union representative than a real union representative is," Bannow has said (New York *Sunday News,* December 20, 1959). Bannow pays an hourly wage higher than the Bridgeport average. Each worker, regardless of his length of service or pay grade, also receives a yearly gift of about $400. Employees with five years of service are eligible for a profit-sharing plan financed by sums drawn from the concern's annual net operating income. There is no mandatory retirement age, and employees may go on working as long as health and inclination permit.

If Bannow has a special aversion, it is inflation. Though wages, taxes, and costs of raw materials have increased for Bridgeport Machines as they have for everyone, the company raised its prices only once in twenty years. This

was a 12 per cent increase in the cost of the miller, raised in 1951 to $1,575. Bannow ascribes his ability to stand firm against inflation to increased mechanization within his plant. He also resisted the pressures of a slump in the machine tools industry during 1957 and 1958. Although other plants were forced to lay off workers, Bannow's concern geared down to a thirty-two-hour work week and stockpiled its products. In subsequent periods of good business, the stockpile was sold out and today Bridgeport Machines, Inc., is able to give its workers employment for forty-five hours a week (including overtime).

Bannow headed the Bridgeport Manufacturers Association from 1951 through 1955, and joined the board of directors of the National Association of Manufacturers in 1956. In 1958 he became chairman of its patents committee. He also worked on the industrial problems committee and executive committee and on the interassociation, educational, general economic problems, and public relations advisory groups. He took a particular interest, too, in NAM's efforts to solve the employment problems of the handicapped. (He employs a number of handicapped workers at Bridgeport Machines, Inc.)

Bannow was elected vice-president of the National Association of Manufacturers at the sixty-third congress of American industry which met in December 1958 in New York City. The office is regarded as the equivalent of "president elect." On December 3, 1959 Bannow became NAM president for 1960, succeeding Stanley C. Hope. The following day Bannow declared that "a lower tax rate, say a 47 per cent ceiling for both individuals and corporations would spur expansion of the U.S. economy, boosting the tax revenues of Uncle Sam" (New York *World-Telegram and Sun,* December 5, 1959). Later the same month Bannow called for a tax reform that would enable persons in all income brackets to save more of their incomes.

Although once a union man himself, Bannow disagrees with labor leaders on many current issues. He feels that the labor movement has not developed in the directions envisaged by one of its early organizers, Samuel Gompers. "I believe with Gompers that membership in any organization should be voluntary to be effective," Bannow has stated (*Christian Science Monitor,* March 5, 1959). "A basic principle we all have to believe is that of the independence of the individual. The NAM does not believe in compulsory membership for itself as an organization. Anyone joins because he wants to."

In December 1959 Bannow criticized, as detrimental to industrial operation, "antiquated" work rules that have been enforced by the labor unions for the past twenty years. In the early part of 1960 he crusaded for the right of management to retain full authority in organizing men, money, and materials to achieve the best economic results. "Management must have authority to improve efficiency in every possible way. . . . Any roadblocks which impede the exercise of the management function need to be re-examined carefully and reduced or eliminated wherever possible" (New York *World-Telegram and Sun,* March 14, 1960).

President Eisenhower conferred separately with Bannow and with George Meany, president of the AFL-CIO, during April 1960 in connection with an administration proposal for a top-level meeting of labor and industrial leaders. A planning group of six delegates (three executives of the AFL-CIO and three working leaders of major companies having contracts with unions) was chosen for preliminary meetings. When Bannow said that he planned to attend these meetings, the unions protested that he was ineligible (since Bridgeport Machines, Inc., is a nonunion concern). Bannow agreed to confine his participation to one initial planning session.

Early in 1959 Bannow represented the National Association of Manufacturers in a tour of French industries as a guest of the French Chamber of Commerce. He is a director of the Bridgeport City Trust Company, the Bridgeport Hospital, the Crippled Children's Bureau, and the United Fund of Bridgeport, and a trustee of the University of Bridgeport. Another of his community interests is the Bridgeport Young Men's Christian Association, of which he is a trustee and past president (1947-49).

A New York *Times* writer (December 4, 1959) described Bannow as a "nice, friendly, bluff, self-made businessman" who looks like Spencer Tracy. He has a "ruddy, rugged face, blue eyes and white silky hair, and he is solidly built." Bannow kept his athletic physique by playing soccer and softball with the Swedish Athletic Club from 1916 to 1936. He has now, he says, "degenerated into golf." At his modest home in Bridgeport he has a workshop where he still turns out new patterns in wood and metal. He has sung first bass in the North Star Singers, a male chorus, for twenty-six years.

Rudolph Frederick Bannow and Swedish-born Elsa Erickson, a former dressmaker, were married in 1920. They have two married daughters, Lillian and Dorothy, and several grandchildren. For promoting Swedish-American friendship, Bannow received the Royal Order of Vasa (first class) from the Swedish government on December 4, 1959 and the Swedish-American of the Year award at the Swedish-American Day celebration in Stockholm on August 7, 1960.

References

Bridgeport (Conn.) Sunday Post My 17 '59
N Y Sunday News p68+ D 20 '59 pors
N Y Times p20 D 4 '59 por
Who's Who in America, 1960-61

BARDOT, BRIGITTE Sept. 28(?) 1934-
Actress
Address: b. Columbia Pictures, 711 Fifth Ave., New York 22

Like sports cars and vintage wines, the films of Brigitte Bardot rank high among the money-making exports of France to the United States. In her own country Miss Bardot has become the high priestess of a cult of adulation known as *Bardolatrie*; internationally, the initials "B.B." have become symbols of an appeal that combines the allure of the ingénue and the vamp, the child and the woman, the innocent and the sensual. In the American "art" movie houses her films have grossed more receipts at the box office than those of any other foreign film star.

Originally fabricated by the elaborate machinery of publicity, the Bardot legend has exercised its spell on the young rebels of the Parisian Left Bank and even upon such older intellectuals as Simone de Beauvoir, who has written a learned essay on the subject. Critics of Miss Bardot have insisted that the actress, believing in the legend herself, has lived up to it away from the movie set. In 1959 she decided to refashion her public image by making the film *Babette Goes to War*. In it she appears as a dedicated and respectable member of the French Resistance. The metamorphosis startled her fans, whose admiration had made her the most highly publicized movie actress in the world.

The center of this furor was born Brigitte Bardot in the fashionable Passy district of Paris in 1934, probably on September 28, the daughter of Louis and Anne-Marie Bardot. The family was wealthy: M. Bardot was an industrial engineer who owned a liquified-air factory; his wife managed a chic dress shop. Brigitte has a younger sister, Mijanou, who is now beginning a motion-picture career.

Brigitte's childhood has been characterized as "the easy, thoughtless life of a sheltered little French girl," and much has been written about the bourgeois atmosphere in which she grew to adolescence. She studied at Hattemer's, an exclusive private school. From the age of seven she learned ballet from dance teacher Mme. Bourgat, who regarded her as an outstanding pupil; Brigitte won an excellency award from the Paris Conservatory when she was thirteen. Her vacations from school were spent at the family villa at St. Tropez on the French Riviera.

But young Brigitte was not satisfied with this sedate environment. "When I was fifteen," she has said, "I was seeking something. Not just excitement—I don't know what it was. Perhaps a fulfillment of myself." The direction of her fulfillment was determined when a family friend asked her to pose for the cover of *Elle*, the leading women's magazine in France. The photograph appeared on May 8, 1950.

Although at fifteen Brigitte's face contained small trace of the sulky charms that have since made her famous, the *Elle* cover attracted the attention of movie director Marc Allégret, who in 1934 had "discovered" Simone Simon. Allégret was searching for a new star for a film version of *Les Lauriers Sont Coupés (The Laurels Are Cut)*, which was never produced. He directed his assistant, Roger Vadim Plemiannikov, to get in touch with the prim-looking adolescent wearing the striped shirtwaist on the cover of *Elle*.

Vadim, as he prefers to be called, did not succeed in his first attempt to make an actress of Miss Bardot, either because her parents objected or because the screen test was not promising. She quit her studies, however, and put herself under Vadim's direction as protégée and fiancée. After small parts in two minor films, *Le Trou Norman* and *Manina, la Fille sans Voile,* she married Vadim in 1952.

As an aspiring script writer and film director, Vadim had become well-schooled in the arts of publicity. More than anyone else, he was responsible for creating the Bardot legend and for tutoring the actress in the mannerisms that were to make her famous on and off the movie set. Through his connections with the popular French pictorial weekly, *Paris-Match,* he arranged for a two-page spread of photographs on the Vadim-Bardot wedding. His publicity campaign won Miss Bardot bit parts in ten movies.

The first of Miss Bardot's films to be shown in the United States was *An Act of Love* (released by United Artists in December 1953), in which she had a brief walk-on part. She was not mentioned in the reviews; nor was she noticed as the slave girl in *Helen of Troy* (Warner Brothers, January 1956). After a small part in Marc Allégret's *Future Stars,* she was signed for the female lead in the British film, *Doctor at Sea.*

"The most eye-catching member of the cast," wrote Alton Cook prophetically in the New York *World-Telegram and Sun* (March 1, 1956), "is Brigitte Bardot, a tiny, piquant French crooner, whose measurements are likely to become an object of international attention as soon as her press agents get around to them." Cook also singled her out for attention in René Clair's *The Grand Maneuver* (October 1956).

After starring in *This Crazy Kid, The Light Across the Street,* and *Please! Mr. Balzac,* all for French distribution, Miss Bardot was cast in *And God Created Woman,* written and directed by Vadim and produced by Raoul Levy. The movie was filmed at St. Tropez, France in June 1956; it marked the end of her marriage to Roger Vadim and the beginning of her career as the leading erotic hoyden of the cinema.

And God Created Woman opened in Paris in November 1956. Although it was successful, it did not recoup its $400,000 production costs until it was released in the United States a year later. Not all the critics were impressed. "If sex is the object," commented a *Time* reviewer (November 11, 1957), "there is just about as much to be seen in almost any Hollywood film, and in promulgating Brigitte as a full-blown enchantress, the French have clearly sent a girl to do a woman's job." Nevertheless, the film broke all records for foreign-made movies exhibited in the United States, and eventually grossed $8,500,000 throughout the world.

American distributors immediately rushed a series of Bardot movies to the theaters. *Mam'zelle Pigalle* was already in distribution, and *Please! Mr. Balzac* was also released in the United States in November 1957. In 1958 distributors dusted off *Nero's Weekends* (filmed in 1955) and *The Girl in the Bikini (Manina, la Fille sans Voile,* 1952) for American release; in the latter, Miss Bardot appeared as a seventeen-year-old brunette.

Meanwhile Miss Bardot was adding new films to her credit. In 1956 she appeared in *The Bride Is Much Too Beautiful* and *La Parisienne;* in 1957 she made *The Night Heaven Fell*

United Artists Corp.

BRIGITTE BARDOT

and *In Case of Emergency* (released in the United States as *Love Is My Profession*), which was completed the following year; and in 1958 she made *The Woman and the Puppet,* her twenty-third motion picture. Each exploited the physical splendors that had made her famous.

The film *La Parisienne* did more for Miss Bardot than that; it established her as a comedienne rather than as a pouting and seductive adolescent. "Brigitte Bardot shows marked improvement," wrote a New York *Times* correspondent (February 9, 1958), while a *New Yorker* critic assessed her as "an accomplished comedienne, whose style and dash enable her . . . to turn this preposterous romp into an hour of reasonable entertainment."

By 1959 Miss Bardot was the highest-paid actress in France and able to impose her own conditions upon producers. Like many a popular star before her, she wanted the chance to become an actress. "Some people say I am not a very good actress," she told one reporter (Washington *Post and Times Herald,* January 11, 1959). "Maybe so. But I have not had very much chance to act. Mostly I have had to undress. That is not acting, and I know it. I would like to be a good actress." The first film tailored to Miss Bardot's specifications was *Babette Goes to War,* which had its première at the Moscow film festival in September 1959. In it she portrays a girl of the French Resistance who, clad in helmet and uniform, undertakes a dangerous mission in enemy territory. The movie was cordially received by its Russian viewers.

Whatever her future as an actress may be, there appears to be little doubt in most informed quarters that Miss Bardot will continue her reign as a box-office star. Her nonconformity has made her a pet with French intellectuals, who have adopted her as a symbol of rebellion against the *bourgeoisie,* while the average movie-goer is attracted by the fascination exerted by an actress who in her twenties retains both the bloom of a teen-ager and a sensuous presence.

Although her name has been linked with those of many admirers, Miss Bardot has only been married twice. She was married to Roger Vadim Plemiannikov on December 20, 1952 and was divorced from him on December 6, 1957. She was married to Jacques Charrier, her co-star in *Babette Goes to War,* in a publicized ceremony on June 18, 1959. They have a son, Nicolas Jacques Charrier. For recreation, Miss Bardot likes to speed around the French countryside in sports cars; she reads Simenon, Gide, and Faulkner and collects rock 'n' roll, mambo, and cha-cha-cha records. She likes to surround herself with live and stuffed animals, especially Teddy bears.

Brigitte Bardot is five feet six inches tall and weighs 121 pounds. She has blond hair (originally brunette) and brown eyes. Her childlike face is oval, with a small, upturned nose; her protuberant teeth are usually hidden by the pout of her lower lip. An accomplished dancer, she appeared in a ballet on French television on December 31, 1958, causing an observer from *Dance Magazine* to write: "Her performance was excellent."

Miss Bardot would like to hear movie critics say the same thing about her acting. "I am now spending my life trying to erase the Bardot legend," she has said (*Newsweek,* February 16, 1959). ". . . I am going to be a girl without anything unhealthy or equivocal about her, and I am going to be good if it kills me. I want to be cute and tender and warm, in the hope that people will forget the idea that I am a brainless, bosomy girl. I can be more than *that.*"

References

Am Weekly O 26 '58 pors
Esquire 52:32+ Ag '59 pors
Life 44:51+ Je 30 '58 pors
N Y Times VI p34+ S 14 '58 por

BARRETTE, (JOSEPH MARIE) ANTONIO May 26, 1899- Former Prime Minister of the Province of Quebec

Address: b. Barrette et Lépine, Joliette, Quebec, Canada; h. 804 Boulevard Manseau, Joliette, Quebec, Canada

The eighteenth Prime Minister of the Canadian province of Quebec and the third leader of the Union Nationale (or National Union) party, Antonio Barrette succeeded Paul Sauvé in office on January 8, 1960. Sauvé, who died 114 days after he became Prime Minister, had followed Maurice Duplessis in office. (Duplessis founded the Union Nationale, a provincial Conservative party, in 1936.) After his party lost its majority in the provincial election of June 22, 1960, Barrette yielded the Prime Ministership to Liberal Jean Lesage in July, and resigned both his legislative seat and his leadership of the Union Nationale party in September.

An insurance broker and former railway machinist, Barrette was the first Prime Minister of the Canadian province to have begun his career as a workingman. As the Minister of Labour from 1944 to 1960, he was known for his successful efforts in behalf of industrial and agricultural workers. Under his leadership, the Union Nationale party tried to co-operate with the national government and with other provinces, in the belief that Quebec stands to benefit by modifying its tradition of strict autonomy.

Joseph Marie Antonio Barrette was born on May 26, 1899 in Joliette, a town in the province of Quebec, about forty miles northeast of Montreal. His brother, Donatien, and his three sisters, Gabrielle, Marguerite, and Cécile, live in Canada. Overriding the objections of his well-educated parents, Ernest and Robéa (Côté) Barrette, Antonio left the local Académie St. Viateur at the age of fourteen to become a night messenger for the Canadian National Railways at a wage of 5 cents an hour.

"I was something of a bronco," Barrette has explained. "I had no use for schooling . . . but soon the urge to learn overpowered me and I became as stubborn about education as about getting the nickel-an-hour job." He taught himself correct French and English and began to read history, philosophy, economics, and science. The "veritable passion for reading" to which he then succumbed has continued throughout his life.

By 1915, the sixteen-year-old Barrette had become an apprentice machinist. During World War I, he took his first political step at the age of eighteen when he rallied to the support of the Conservative party and advocated conscription—a highly explosive issue at that time. He then worked as a railway machinist in Quebec and Ontario until 1930. He is still a member of the International Association of Machinists, and once served as its secretary. After five years (1930 to 1935) as a mechanical engineer with the Acme Glove Company in his native town, Barrette became a senior partner in a Joliette insurance brokerage firm, Barrette and Lépine. He maintains the partnership today.

In the 1935 election, Barrette ran as the Conservative candidate for the Joliette County seat in the Quebec provincial legislature, but was defeated. In 1936, however, the newly formed and liberalized Conservative party, the Union Nationale, led by Maurice Duplessis, won a resounding victory over the Liberal government which, after thirty-nine years of ascendancy, had become entrenched in power. Barrette was elected deputy for Joliette County on the Union Nationale ticket at that time. He was re-elected in this constituency in 1939, 1944, 1948, 1952, and 1956, with steadily increasing majorities. In 1956, he received 11,500 votes to his Liberal opponent's 6,225 votes.

From the outset of his career as deputy of a largely rural county, Barrette tried to improve conditions for the agricultural population. He encouraged the building and improvement of roads, bridge construction, land drain-

ANTONIO BARRETTE

ing, electrification, and the erection of new schools and hospitals. He promoted the revival of tobacco growing in the district of Joliette. He worked for the adoption of progressive labor legislation and served as the secretary of the Seignorial Rent Abolition Commission. After the Union Nationale lost its majority in 1939, Barrette, as a member of the Opposition, led many debates on the social laws introduced by the Liberals.

On August 30, 1944, after Duplessis had once again become Prime Minister of Quebec, Barrette was appointed Minister of Labour. He represented the province at the International Conference of Labor at Paris in 1945 and at the International Labor Office conferences at Montreal in 1946 and Geneva in 1951. Until December 1946 he served as chairman of the Regional War Labor Board.

As Quebec's Minister of Labour, Barrette has encouraged harmonious industrial relations and established new labor benefits. His efforts resulted in the adoption of vacations-with-pay stamps; the setting up of apprenticeship centers (the apprenticeship system is known as the "Barrette formula"); the founding of rehabilitation clinics and employment services for ex-tubercular and crippled workers; and the creation of a department of industrial hygiene within Quebec's Workman's Compensation Commission.

His mediation of industrial disputes brought about the successful resolution of several serious strikes, notably a textile industry strike in 1947 and a strike of aluminum workers in 1957. Before 1944, 300 strikes had occurred in Quebec during one two-year period; during 1958-59 only eight work stoppages took place throughout the entire province. As time went by, Barrette found himself increasingly at odds with the isolationist and antilabor Du-

plessis regime. During the last twenty-one months of Duplessis' rule, Barrette ran his department from Joliette and virtually boycotted cabinet meetings.

Barrette was for many years an intimate friend of Paul Sauvé, who became Prime Minister of Quebec after the death of Duplessis in September 1959. He also won the high esteem of national political leaders like John Diefenbaker, Progressive Conservative party Prime Minister of Canada. After Barrette's party colleagues in the Legislative Assembly and Legislative Council had voted unanimously to appoint him as their Prime Minister, Barrette promised that he would continue Sauvé's programs, particularly his policy of co-operation with the English Canadian provinces and the federal government.

As a first step in this program, Barrette concluded an agreement with the national government whereby Quebec would accept some $25,000,000 in federal grants to education that it had previously refused, in order to improve conditions in its universities and colleges. Provincial leaders had long maintained that federal education grants infringed upon provincial autonomy. Barrette also endorsed for eventual adoption Sauvé's proposal that Quebec institute a hospitalization scheme similar to that of other provinces. Barrette was the first Premier of Quebec to have spoken before the Ontario Parliament since 1867, and his visit to the English-speaking province in April 1960 was regarded as having inaugurated "a new era of understanding" between Quebec and Ontario.

In December 1949 Barrette represented the province of Quebec at the Holy Year inauguration in the Vatican. He returned to Rome in the same capacity in 1951 for the sixtieth anniversary of the encyclical, *Rerum Novarum,* and in 1956 for the seventeenth anniversary of the accession of Pope Pius XII. He is a Grand Officer of the Roman Catholic Order of St. Gregory, an honorary lieutenant colonel of the Joliette regiment, and a member of the Société des Oliviers and of the Club Renaissance. Barrette was awarded honorary D.S.Sc. degrees by Laval University in Quebec in June 1945 and by Montreal University in 1948. Bishop's University at Lennoxville, Quebec granted him an honorary LL.D. degree in 1954.

Joseph Marie Antonio Barrette and Estelle Guilbault of Joliette were married on July 2, 1924. They have two sons, Alain and Serge, two daughters, Lise (Mrs. Gérard Notebaert) and Nicole (Mrs. Guy Barrette), and several grandchildren. In 1959 Barrette left his ten-room house at Joliette with its library of some 5,000 volumes in French and English for a pleasure trip around the world. A New York *Times* biographical sketch (January 9, 1960) described Barrette as a forceful and personable man with slightly gray hair, who seems taller than his five feet ten inches. Barrette believes that "the most important problem for the [Union Nationale] party is to keep social, cultural, and educational progress abreast of economic and industrial developments that have characterized the postwar years in Quebec."

References

Canadian Labour 1:31+ S '56 por
N Y Times p10 Ja 9 '60 por
Time 75:34+ Ja 18 '60 por
Toronto Globe and Mail p1+ Ja 8 '60 por
Biographies Françaises d'Amérique (1950)
Canadian Parliamentary Guide, 1959
Canadian Who's Who, 1955-57

BEACH, EDWARD (LATIMER) Apr. 20, 1918- United States Navy officer; author
Address: b. USS *Triton,* FPO, New York; h 848 Lee Pl., Falls Church, Virginia

The best known officer of the United States Navy's "silent service" is Captain Edward Latimer Beach, who commanded the world's largest nuclear-powered submarine, the USS *Triton,* on her historic eighty-four-day circumnavigation of the globe that ended on May 10, 1960. A veteran of twenty-one years of military service, the much-decorated naval officer is no stranger to unusual achievement. In two fields, he has equalled or surpassed his father, the late Captain Edward L. Beach, who commanded the battleship *New York* in 1918-19. Like his father, Captain Beach commands a ship and four-stripe rank, and he too is a writer. His books, *Submarine!* and *Run Silent, Run Deep,* are for adults; his father wrote stories of navy life for children. From 1953 to 1957 Captain Beach served as President Dwight D. Eisenhower's first naval aide.

Edward Latimer Beach was born in New York City on April 20, 1918 to Captain Edward Latimer Beach, USN, and Mrs. Alice (Fouché) Beach. Soon after his graduation from high school in Palo Alto, California in 1935, he was appointed to the United States Naval Academy in Annapolis, Maryland by Senator Hiram Johnson. Active in athletics, he was regimental commander in his first class year, was named the midshipman who had done most to promote naval spirit and loyalty in his regiment, and was awarded the Sword of the Class of 1897. He was graduated second in his class and was commissioned an ensign on June 1, 1939.

Assigned first to the USS *Chester,* Beach served on that cruiser from June until September 1939. He then joined the USS *Lea,* a destroyer engaged in neutrality patrol, and took part in the initial occupation of Iceland. Before his detachment in September 1941, the USS *Lea* was assigned to convoy duty in the North Atlantic.

Captain Beach's Navy career began in earnest when he was a student for three months at the submarine school in New London, Connecticut, where he graduated with the highest standing in his class in December 1941. When World War II started, he was assigned to the USS *Trigger,* then being built at the Navy Yard at Mare

U. S. Navy

CAPT. EDWARD BEACH

Island, California. From her commissioning on January 30, 1942 until May 1944, he served aboard in various capacities—as diving officer, executive officer, and co-approach officer. During these two and a half years the USS *Trigger* participated in the Battle of Midway and in nine war patrols, and sank or damaged thirty-six enemy ships during that period.

The USS *Trigger* received the Presidential Unit Citation and the Navy Unit Commendation. Captain Beach was awarded the Silver Star Medal, a gold star in lieu of the second Silver Star Medal, the Bronze Star Medal with combat distinguishing device "V", and two Letters of Commendation with ribbon star, and "V" from the Commander in Chief of the Pacific Fleet.

In July 1944 Beach reported to the USS *Tirante* and undertook one war patrol, the submarine's maiden cruise, during which she sank nine enemy vessels. The USS *Tirante* received the Presidential Unit Citation, and Beach was awarded the Navy Cross. The citation stated in part: "For extraordinary heroism as Navigator and Assistant Approach Officer . . . [for] expertly navigating his ship through extremely shallow and dangerous enemy waters and skillfully handling attack problems . . . in penetrating the Japanese inner defenses and in launching destructive attacks."

Detached from the USS *Tirante* in April 1945, Beach received his first command, that of the USS *Piper,* in June 1945, and served as her commanding officer until after the Japanese surrender. The USS *Piper,* on her third war patrol, entered the Sea of Japan through the Straits of Tsushina mine field with a group of submarines, but the war ended before severe damage could be inflicted upon the enemy. The USS *Piper* had the honor of being the last submarine to return from patrol after the war

BEACH, EDWARD L.—*Continued*

ended. Beach was awarded a Gold Star in lieu of the second Bronze Star Medal, with a combat "V" for his meritorious service on the vessel.

Returning to the United States in December 1945, Beach reported to the Navy Department in Washington D.C., where he served first as personal aide to the Chief of Navy Personnel, and from March 1947 until May 1948 in the Office of the Chief of Naval Operations. During this period Captain Beach began to write of his war experiences. His efforts resulted in his first book, *Submarine!* (Holt, 1952), a first-person account of the service of USS *Trigger* and other submarines during World War II, which Beach dedicated "as a memorial" to his lost ship and shipmates.

In May 1948 Beach went back to sea for fifteen months as commanding officer of the submarine USS *Amberjack*. He was then assigned to shore duty, from August 1949 to March 1951, as naval aide to General Omar Bradley, who was then the chairman of the Joint Chiefs of Staff.

Captain Beach scored a service "first" when he became commander of the new USS *Trigger* (SS-564), the first "guppy snorkel" type of submarine, which was commissioned on March 31, 1952. He then was appointed as naval aide to President Eisenhower and served in this capacity from 1953 to 1957. He was advanced to the rank of captain on October 1, 1956.

Run Silent, Run Deep (Holt, 1955), Beach's second best-seller, was published during his assignment at the White House. A *Time* magazine reviewer called this semifictionalized war story "he-man's seaman's reading with only a dash of home-base romance." The book was made into a movie starring Clark Gable and Burt Lancaster that was released by United Artists in 1958.

Eager to go back to sea duty, Captain Beach was given command of the deep-draft tanker *Salamonie* for nine months in the Mediterranean before his shore duty in preparation for the command of the USS *Triton,* then being built at the General Dynamics Corporation, Groton, Connecticut. In January 1958 he became special assistant in submarine matters to the chief of the naval reactors branch, division of reactor development, Atomic Energy Commission, where he was instructed in technical aspects of submarine nuclear propulsion.

Within naval circles, the assignment of Captain Beach as commander of the world's largest submarine, and the first equipped with twin nuclear reactors, occasioned some surprise, for underwater vessels are usually skippered by commanders. Observers were of the opinion that unusual achievements were to be expected of the USS *Triton.* They were not disappointed. On February 16, 1960 the submarine, with its crew of 183 officers and men, began its unprecedented submerged circumnavigation of the world, following much the same course taken by Ferdinand Magellan's crew on their voyage from 1519 to 1522. The voyage of the USS *Triton,* lasting eighty-four days, covered 41,500 miles.

What the officers and men learned on the voyage of the USS *Triton,* Captain Beach reported in his log, "can be extremely important to the Polaris program." According to the New York *Times* (May 11, 1960) "the Triton's log, a literary product in its own right, rivals in spots the suspense and drama of an adventure from the pages of Captain Hornblower."

At forty-two, Captain Beach is a stern-faced man of serious disposition. A writer of a biographical sketch for the New York *Times* (August 20, 1958) reported: "His 'strictly business' attitudes earn him respect, but not open friendship. He is not the sort of man one would slap on the back. . . . Even at Annapolis he was of a serious nature. Classmates recall that as the five-stripe Commander of the regiment of midshipmen, young Beach turned out the men after the Orson Welles broadcast of 1938, and reported to the commandant that they were ready to stand by to repel Martians."

In addition to the awards and medals mentioned above, Captain Beach also has the American Defense Service Medal, with the Atlantic Fleet Clasp; the Asiatic-Pacific Campaign Medal with three engagement stars; the American Campaign Medal; the World War II Victory Medal; and the National Defense Service Medal.

On June 4, 1944 Captain Edward Latimer Beach was married to the former Ingrid Bergstrom Schenck of Palo Alto, California, a daughter of a professor of paleontology at the Leland Stanford University. They have two sons, Edward L., Jr., and Hubert, and a daughter, Ingrid Alice. A believer in do-it-yourself, Beach has made extensive repairs on his homes at Falls Church, Virginia and at Mystic, Connecticut.

References

Christian Sci Mon p6 My 24 '60 por
N Y Herald Tribune p10 Ag 19 '58 por
N Y Times p3 Ag 20 '58 por
Who's Who in America, 1960-61

BELAÚNDE (Y DIEZ CANSECO), VÍCTOR ANDRÉS (bä"lä-ōōn'dä) Dec. 15, 1883- Peruvian Representative to the United Nations; educator; writer; lawyer

Address: b. Peruvian Mission to the United Nations, 350 5th Ave., New York 1; h. Av. San Isidro 196, Lima, Peru

At every session of the United Nations General Assembly for more than a decade, Peru has been represented by Víctor Andrés Belaúnde, who also attended the founding conference of the U.N. in 1945. He is a well-known exponent of Pan-Americanism, a colorful figure who is internationally respected as a diplomat, educator, writer, and lawyer. During 1959 he served as president of the fourteenth session of the General Assembly, and in September 1960 he presided over the General Assembly's emergency session, which reviewed the crisis of the new Republic of Congo. In speaking for Peru, he has upheld the rights of all small nations and has been an articulate advocate of membership of all nations in the U.N. and of freedom and social justice.

Víctor Andrés Belaúnde y Diez Canseco was born to Mariano A. and Mercedes (Diez Canseco) Belaúnde in Arequipa, Peru on December 15, 1883. Another son in the family, Rafael Belaúnde, also became prominent as a diplomat. The education that helped make Víctor Belaúnde a noted humanist began in Arequipa's schools of San Vicente and San José and the University of Arequipa. He later enrolled at the University of San Marcos in Lima, which awarded him the LL.D. degree in 1908, the doctorate in political science in 1910, and the Litt.D. degree in 1911.

Considerable practical experience, meanwhile, had enriched Belaúnde's years of study at the university. In 1903 he became secretary of boundary archives in the Peruvian Ministry of Foreign Affairs and from 1907 to 1911 he served as director of the boundary archives division. Before attaining this promotion he had been a member of the Spanish-Argentine mission involving a dispute with Bolivia in 1905-06, his first diplomatic appointment.

From 1911 to 1919 Belaúnde maintained his association with the University of San Marcos as professor of international law and constitutional law. During part of this period he also carried out diplomatic assignments for the Peruvian government, as chargé d'affaires in Germany (1914) and in Bolivia (1915) and as minister plenipotentiary to Uruguay (1919).

Belaúnde presented many of his observations on issues in international relations, as well as on philosophy and politics, in a number of early books beginning with *La Filosofiá del derecho y el método positivo* (1904) and including *La Cuestión de límites peruano-boliviana* (1908) and *Idealismo político* (1918). He founded in 1918 the review *Mercurio Peruano,* of which he was director until 1932 and for a period after 1938.

A champion of civil rights, Belaúnde left Peru in 1921 in opposition to the dictatorial government of Augusto Leguía, who had returned to the presidency of Peru in 1919. During his nine years as a political exile, mainly in the United States, Belaúnde taught Hispanic-American culture at Columbia University, Rice Institute (Houston, Texas), the University of Virginia, and the University of Miami. He was a member of the founding faculty of the last-named university in 1926 and a member of its board of trustees from 1926 to 1932. Besides lecturing at other American universities, he spent some time in France. Books of Belaúnde published during his years of exile include *The Treaty of Ancón* (Washington, 1922), *Hispanic-American Culture* (Houston, 1925), and *La Realidad nacional* (Paris, 1930).

With the end of Leguía's rule in 1930, Belaúnde returned to Peru. After taking part in the constituent assembly in Lima in 1930, he was elected to serve in the Chamber of Deputies from 1931 to 1933. Also resuming his work in education, he accepted an appointment in 1931 as dean of the faculty of political and economic science at the Catholic University of Peru in Lima and in 1940 became pro-rector of that

United Nations
VÍCTOR ANDRÉS BELAÚNDE

university. In 1939 he established at the University of San Marcos a summer school of which he was also the director.

Again in Peru's diplomatic service, Belaúnde was a delegate to the League of Nations in Geneva in 1936; during that year he also attended the International Labor Conference and represented Latin America in the league's committee of international co-operation. He has taken part in several diplomatic meetings to settle Peru's border disputes and was a delegate to the eighth Pan-American Conference, in Lima in 1938. On another diplomatic mission, he acted as Special Ambassador during the visit in 1942 of Peru's President Manuel Prado Ugarteche to the United States.

In April 1945 Dr. Belaúnde represented Peru at the United Nations Conference on International Organization in San Francisco, which drew up the U.N. charter. He has been chairman of the Peruvian delegation to every session of the General Assembly since 1949. In a recent brief intermission he served from January to April 1958 as Minister of Foreign Affairs in President Prado's cabinet.

At the U.N., Belaúnde became identified with the representatives of small nations who, comparatively free of big-power competition, are developing the tradition of striving to reconcile the differences between East and West. He contributed to the work of many committees and commissions and filled the rotating office of president of the Security Council a number of times.

Perhaps his most important accomplishment in strengthening the U.N. concerned the seven-year old controversy over admission of new members, in which the application of twenty-one nations had been blocked because of rivalry between the Soviet Union and some Western nations. In the fall of 1953 Belaúnde presented a resolution calling for the creation of a three-

BELAÚNDE, VÍCTOR ANDRÉS—*Cont.*

member committee of good offices to explore, in consultation with the Security Council, various means of reaching agreement.

Subsequently appointed chairman of the committee he had sponsored, Belaúnde pursued his universality-of-membership principle and during the next two years assisted in working out a formula for admitting sixteen new nations. When the U.N. General Assembly finally decided to accept the committee's compromise resolution in December 1955, much of the credit for breaking the long deadlock was given to Belaúnde. The following year President Giovanni Gronchi of Italy conferred on Belaúnde the Order of Knight of the Great Cross of Merit for his part in securing the agreement which had brought Italy into the U.N.

On September 15, 1959 Belaúnde was named on eighty-one of eighty-two ballots (one being invalid) as president of the fourteenth session of the U.N. General Assembly; his nomination was supported by the nine members of the Soviet bloc. In his talk to the delegates after the election he warned, "Our forefathers were faced by but one alternative to the advantages of peace: the dangers and inconveniences of war. Our world, in the atomic age, faces a different alternative: either peace, which will safeguard life and progress for all peoples, or war, which will bring death and universal destruction."

Belaúnde's "reputation of being one man at the U.N. with no enemies," as Gertrude Samuels reported in a New York *Times Magazine* article (December 8, 1957), does not mean that he declines to take a stand for or against an issue. During the Hungarian revolt of late 1956, for instance, he charged in the U.N. that the Soviet Union's intervention had been an extreme form of Stalinist policy.

A full General Assembly debate in December 1959 on the continuing troubled situation in Hungary was a high point of the fourteenth session. Other outstanding developments during Belaúnde's term as president included a resolution expressing concern over the denial of human rights in Tibet, a resolution calling on France to refrain from exploding its first atomic weapon, and a debate on the question of Algerian independence.

Among the books that Belaúnde wrote during the years that he centered most of his attention on the U.N. are *La Conferencia de San Francisco* (Lima, Talleres gráficos de la Editorial Lumen, 1945); *La Sintesis viviente* (Madrid, Ediciones Cultura Hispánica, 1950); *Inquietud, serenidad, plenitud* (Lima, Imprenta Santa Maria, 1951), and *Palabras de fé* (Lima, 1952).

In both the United States and Spain, as well as in South America, Belaúnde belongs to many professional organizations, including Institutio Histórico del Perú, Sociedad Peruana de Filosofiá (founder and president), Sociedad Chilena de Historia y Geografiá, Academia Histórica de Madrid, and the American Academy of Arts and Sciences. His decorations are the Grand Cross of Alfonso XII (Spain), Order of Boyacá (Colombia), and Grand Cross of El Sol (Peru), among others. One of his recent honorary awards is the LL.D. degree conferred by St. John's University in Jamaica, New York in November 1959.

Although Belaúnde also speaks French, English, and Latin (and understands Portuguese and Italian), he prefers to address U.N. delegates in Spanish. He usually talks without a manuscript, believing that eloquence depends upon emotion of the moment. Because of his gestures while speaking, he has been described as an "oratorical windmill." He is a slightly built man, with brown eyes and gray hair and a gray mustache. As a *Newsweek* (September 28, 1959) writer pictured him, he "has a bristle to his mustache, a twinkle to his eye, and his words crack with wit and wisdom." His religion is Roman Catholic, and he attends Mass every morning before work.

Belaúnde has been married twice. His two daughters by his first wife, Sofiá (Irigoyen) Belaúnde (deceased), are Sofiá and Mercedes. He is now married to Teresa (Moreyra) Belaúnde, and their children are Andrés, Antonio, José, Pedro, Teresa, and Martín. He has eighteen, or more, grandchildren. Walking, reading, listening to music, talking with people, and dancing are his hobbies.

References

N Y Times p2 S 16 '59 por
N Y Times Mag p88 D 8 '57 por
U S News 47:20 S 28 '59
Who's Who in Latin America pt 4 (1947)
Who's Who in the United Nations (1951)
World Biography (1948)

BENNETT, HUGH H(AMMOND) Apr. 15, 1881-July 7, 1960 Conservationist; soil scientist; first chief of the soil conservation service, United States Department of Agriculture (1935-52). See *Current Biography* (December) 1946.

Obituary

N Y Times p21 Jl 8 '60

BERDING, ANDREW H(ENRY) Feb. 8, 1902- United States government official

Address: b. Department of State, Washington 25, D.C.; h. 3111 Foxhall Rd., Washington, D.C.

In an age when weapons of propaganda are important in the battle for the minds of men, Andrew H. Berding is playing a central role. As Assistant Secretary of State for Public Affairs, he serves as a point of contact between the public and the shapers of American foreign policy. The chief spokesman for the Department of State, he accompanies Secretary of State Christian Herter on diplomatic missions and to press conferences. He conducts a careful watch over the public image of United States foreign policy and plays an important part in combating Soviet propaganda. Not a State Department career man, Berding worked as a newspaperman for nineteen years before he went into government service in 1948 as an information officer and expert on public relations.

Of Swedish descent, Andrew Henry Berding was born in Cincinnati, Ohio on February 8, 1902 to Andrew and Catherine (Weber) Berding. Educated in Cincinnati, he received his B.A. degree from Xavier University in 1926, working his way through by writing for the Cincinnati *Commercial Tribune* and the *Times Star*. After having failed in his two attempts to be selected as a Rhodes Scholar, he went to Oxford on his own, supporting himself by rewriting mail features for the Associated Press. He received a B.A. degree and an M.A. degree in English literature from Oxford University in 1928.

Staying in Europe after his Oxford graduation, Berding became a correspondent for the Associated Press. In 1933 he was appointed chief of the Associated Press bureau in Rome, a position that he held until 1937. He returned to the United States in 1937 to become chief Associated Press correspondent covering the Department of State in Washington. In 1940 he joined the Buffalo *Evening News* as an editorial writer and radio commentator.

After World War II broke out, Berding volunteered for duty and was called by the Army Air Force. After several assignments in the United States, he was assigned to the Office of Strategic Services. He became chief of counterintelligence in Italy and, later, in Germany. He was awarded the Legion of Merit and the Bronze Star Medal and attained the rank of lieutenant colonel before his discharge in January 1946.

At the State Department before the war, Berding made the acquaintance of Cordell Hull, who was then the Secretary of State. After the war, from 1946 to 1948, he collaborated with Hull in writing the two-volume *Memoirs of Cordell Hull* (Macmillan, 1948).

Entering government service in July 1948, Berding returned to Italy where he served until 1950 as chief of the information division of the Marshall Plan mission to that country. He then served, in succession, as director of information for the Office of Defense Mobilization (1950-51), the Mutual Security Administration (1951-52), and the Department of Defense (1952-53).

When the United States Information Agency was detached from the Department of State to become an independent organization in 1953, Berding left the Department of Defense to become its deputy director. He supervised plans and policy for the United States Information Agency and embarked on his travels to international conferences throughout the world.

In March 1957 Berding was named Assistant Secretary of State for Public Affairs, the principal adviser on public relations to the Secretary of State at home and abroad. Before taking this post, he had handled foreign press relations for Secretary of State John Foster Dulles, whom he accompanied in 1955 to the Southeast Asia Treaty Conference in Bangkok and the Summit Conference in Geneva. He served as United

Wide World

ANDREW H. BERDING

States spokesman for the press at conferences in Paris, Bonn, Copenhagen, Karachi, Canberra, Manilla, Ankara, London, Bermuda, and Santiago. All in all, he flew more than 200,000 miles with Dulles.

Berding's most demanding diplomatic assignment to date was his job as briefing officer at the Foreign Ministers Conference in Geneva from May to July 1959. He accompanied President Dwight D. Eisenhower when he flew to Bonn, London, and Paris in August 1959, and was present at Camp David, Maryland in September 1959, when the Eisenhower-Khrushchev conversations took place.

But attending foreign conferences is only one of Berding's responsibilities. He also has to direct the bureau of public affairs, which is made up of six divisions. The news division, serving the press, maintains around-the-clock service. The public services division, serving the public, maintains liaison with national organizations, handles speaking engagements, distributes publications on foreign affairs, and answers about 100,000 letters a year from the public.

The other four divisions are engaged in work that aids policy formulation. The historical division conducts research into the history of American foreign policy and publishes the results. The public studies division analyzes American public opinion on foreign policy. The policy guidance staff furnishes guidance on foreign policy to the United States Information Agency and plans future undertakings in the information field. The mutual security information staff provides information on the mutual security program.

Roscoe Drummond, the nationally syndicated Washington columnist, once wrote of the bureau of public affairs that "the work of this office is far more than a convenient service to

BERDING, ANDREW H.—*Continued*

the press. It is vital to the effective functioning of the whole department because a Secretary of State today can accomplish little without public understanding and support" (New York *Herald Tribune,* February 25, 1957). Drummond credited Berding with some of the most important qualifications for the job, including the confidence and support of the Secretary of State and independence of character to stand up on his own.

As an official spokesman for government policy in the past six years, Berding has figured in controversies on everything from abstract art shown in American exhibits overseas to the recognition of Red China. He has often delivered major policy speeches for the State Department. The most crucial of his responsibilities, however, has been the countering of Soviet propaganda.

Berding claims that he plays no part in actual policy formulation, beyond advising the Secretary of State on the probable effect of any proposed policy. After the policy has been formulated, he tells the world what the Department of State is doing and why. Because of this, a New York *Times* writer has called him "a virtuoso on the musical saw." But, continued the *Times* writer, "reporters like him and know what to expect of him. They know that, unlike some briefing officers, he will never be irritated by any question, no matter how ill-informed or indiscreet. He will never be sarcastic. His tongue has no barb" (October 17, 1959).

Although Berding has been offered public relations jobs with private industry at a much higher salary than the $20,000 he receives from the government, he stays because he likes "the big sweep of things" in his work. He belongs to the Overseas Writers Club and the National Press Club, and spends his spare time puttering around in his ninety-year-old frame house on top of a hill in the Foxhall Road area of Washington.

Andrew H. Berding was married to the former Alice Godley Jones of Dallas, Texas on December 30, 1930. They have two children: a daughter, Mrs. Anne Broaddus, the wife of a Naval surgeon, and a son, Drew, a student at Rensselaer Polytechnic Institute. Berding is a tall and lanky man, with a low voice and a long and deeply creased face that somehow manages to be serious and friendly at the same time. He takes his notes in shorthand at the meetings he attends, and, according to observers, he has a tenacious memory and a knack for penetrating to the core of complicated diplomatic proceedings. Eddy Gilmore of the Washington *Post and Times-Herald* summed up his impressions of Berding with the adjectives "informative, scholarly, kind, and friendly" (May 18, 1959).

References

Ed & Pub 90:14 Mr 9 '57 por
N Y Times p2 O 17 '59 por
U S News 42:22 Mr 15 '57
Who's Who in America, 1958-59

BERG, GERTRUDE Oct. 3, 1899- Actress; author; producer

Address: b. and h. 829 Park Ave., New York 21

> NOTE: This biography supersedes the article which appeared in *Current Biography* in 1941.

During the last three decades Gertrude Berg has won the hearts of radio, television, screen, and stage audiences with her portrayal of Molly Goldberg, a chatty and maternal Jewish housewife. Since *The Rise of the Goldbergs*—the oldest of soap operas—first appeared on the radio in 1929, she has written, acted in, and produced over 5,000 scripts dealing with the fictitious Bronx family. Mrs. Berg played the same disarming role on television, beginning in 1949, and she brought the Goldbergs to the screen in *Molly* (Paramount, 1951), which she wrote together with N. Richard Nash. She made her Broadway debut as an actress in her own play, *Me and Molly,* in 1948, and eleven years later played a plump Jewish widow in *A Majority of One.*

Gertrude Berg was born Gertrude Edelstein in New York City on October 3, 1899, the only child of Jacob and Diana Netta (Goldstein) Edelstein. Her father was in the hotel business. She was educated in the public schools of her native city, graduating from Wadleigh High School. While taking extension courses in playwriting at Columbia University, she met Lewis Berg, an engineering student. They were married on December 1, 1918.

She spent the early years of her marriage on a sugar plantation near Reserve, Louisiana, where her husband worked as a mechanical engineer for sugar refineries. When they returned to New York, Mrs. Berg began to write for radio. Her first script, *Effie and Laura,* which was supposed to have been a series, was cancelled after the first program.

Two years later Mrs. Berg fared much more successfully when she created the Goldberg family consisting of Mr. and Mrs. Goldberg, intent on bettering their lot; teen-aged Rosalie and Sammy, their offspring; and comical Uncle David. When she submitted her script to the National Broadcasting Company, she read it aloud to bring the characters to life equipped with accurate Yiddish vocal inflections. NBC executives not only accepted the script, but also decided that Mrs. Berg was the ideal choice to play the role of Molly Goldberg.

The Rise of the Goldbergs was first heard on the air on November 20, 1929 on the NBC radio network. For the weekly series Mrs. Berg received $75, out of which she had to meet the payroll for the cast. Four weeks later, when Mrs. Berg contracted a sore throat and a substitute played Molly, some 11,000 listeners protested to the radio station. By 1931 the program had a soap company for a sponsor and was broadcast five times a week. For her services as actress and author of the series, Mrs. Berg then received $2,000 a week.

Gradually winning millions of listeners, *The Rise of the Goldbergs* became a radio classic, second only to *Amos and Andy* in popularity and staying power. The program usually opened with Molly Goldberg shouting her "Yoo-hoo! Mrs. Bloo-oom!" up the air shaft of her Bronx apartment to her neighbor. "As Molly, Mrs. Berg 'shmoosed' with the neighbors, henpecked her irascible, financially erratic husband, Jake, plotted marriages, prepared kreplach, battled against overweight, and tossed off celebrated Goldbergisms like: 'Enter, whoever!' and 'If it's nobody, I'll call back'" (New York *Times,* February 15, 1959).

Forced to be prolific, Mrs. Berg prepared her fifteen-minute scripts three weeks in advance and often worked nine hours a day in longhand. Each day's episode pointed to a climax at the end of the five-day week, calculated to leave the listener eager to tune in again the following Monday. "It's hard to say where I get my ideas for my sketches," she once observed (*Commentary,* April 1956). "My sense of Jewishness comes not from my father and mother so much as from my grandparents. We scarcely spoke Yiddish at home; my mother came from England. You'll notice there's no dialect [on the program], just intonation and word order."

Out of Mrs. Berg's observation of people and situations emerged over 200 different characters for the program. As its producer, she occasionally used amateur actors in their real-life roles—elevator operators, grocery clerks, and delivery boys, for instance. She of course also employed professionals; among the "graduates" of the Goldberg program were John Garfield, Allan Jones, Martin Wolfson, Joseph Cotten, Anne Bancroft, Van Heflin, Jan Peerce, Allyn Joslyn, and George Tobias.

When *The Goldbergs* went off the air temporarily in 1934, the cast made a personal appearance tour on the vaudeville circuit. In 1935 Mrs. Berg wrote and produced *The House of Glass,* a series based on her memories of summer vacations at a Catskill mountain resort hotel owned by her father. The program was moderately successful, but never attained the popularity of *The Goldbergs.* She also wrote scripts for *Kate Hopkins,* a serial about a visiting nurse.

The Goldbergs returned to the radio in 1936 for a six-month run on Columbia Broadcasting System stations. The following year Mrs. Berg worked on her first motion picture, *Make a Wish* (RKO), and also piloted a short four-month run of *The Goldbergs* on NBC. The series then played on twenty-three CBS stations from January 1938 to March 1945. In 1941 it was also broadcast on thirty NBC stations for four months and was heard on the Mutual Broadcasting System station WOR.

Before *The Goldbergs* resumed radio broadcasts from September 1949 to June 1950, Mrs. Berg took advantage of the hiatus to write her first Broadway play. *Me and Molly* opened at the Belasco Theatre in New York on February 26, 1948, starring Gertrude Berg as Molly. "No wonder the Goldbergs have been popular on radio," commented Brooks Atkinson (New

Friedman—Abeles

GERTRUDE BERG

York *Times,* February 27, 1948). "Mrs. Berg is a real human being who believes in the people she writes about and is not ashamed of their simplicity. . . . The result is a leisurely, intimate, cheerful portrait of interesting people and the humor is kind-hearted. It is something for a playwright to preserve that much integrity amid the gag traps of Broadway."

In 1949 a television version of *The Goldbergs* was launched on the CBS network and soon attracted some 13,000,000 viewers. The series ran until June 1951 and then played on NBC television in 1952 and the summer of 1953. In 1954 the program appeared on WABD (Channel 5). Mrs. Berg also wrote with N. Richard Nash the 1951 movie version of *The Goldbergs,* a Paramount picture entitled *Molly,* in which she played the title role.

During 1956 and 1957 Mrs. Berg acted in summer stock on the "straw-hat circuit," in *The Solid Gold Cadillac* (in the role created by Josephine Hull) and *The Matchmaker* (in the role first played by Ruth Gordon). She also played a benign Jewish landlady in the star-studded but indifferently received *Main Street to Broadway* (MGM, 1953). In *A Majority of One,* which opened on Broadway in February 1959, Mrs. Berg played Mrs. Jacoby, a Jewish widow from Brooklyn, who lost a son in World War II and who on a visit to Japan becomes romantically involved with Mr. Asano, a rich Japanese widower (played by Sir Cedric Hardwicke), who lost a daughter at Hiroshima.

Her performance in this play by Leonard Spigelgass was unanimously praised by the New York critics. The play was presented 570 times. "Mrs. Berg's bustling, warm-hearted, knowing mother from Brooklyn is the salt of the earth," wrote Brooks Atkinson (New York *Times,* February 22, 1959). "As an actress, Mrs. Berg knows how to project a character

BERG, GERTRUDE—*Continued*

on the stage. But the qualities that make it endearing are, one feels, extensions of herself —her simplicity of manner, her nobility of soul."

Mrs. Berg has written *The Rise of the Goldbergs* (Barse & Company, 1931) and *The Molly Goldberg Cookbook* (Doubleday, 1955). She received the Antoinette Perry (Tony) Award as the best actress of 1959. In 1950 the Girls Clubs of America, Inc., cited her as the Radio and TV Mother of the Year. Mrs. Berg has appeared on several television shows as a guest star and as an actress in television dramas. She is generous with her time, talent, and money and has made numerous appearances for charity drives.

The Rise of the Goldbergs, which attracts listeners from many cultural and religious groups, has often been commended for promoting intercultural and interfaith understanding. Among the awards it has received are: the citation of distinguished merit, National Conference of Christians and Jews (1950); interfaith award, Cinema Lodge, B'nai Brith (1949); commendation award, Veterans of Foreign Wars (1950); citation, American Heritage Foundation; award, Federation of Jewish Philanthropies of New York (1949); and awards from the Community Chests and Councils of America, the United Cerebral Palsy Association, Inc., the American Cancer Society, and Hadassah.

Mr. and Mrs. Lewis W. Berg have a daughter, Harriet, a son, Cherney Robert (who is now a television producer and writer), and several grandchildren. They live in a duplex Park Avenue apartment filled with the art objects and antiques that Mrs. Berg has collected. They also own a country home at Bedford Hills, New York, where Mrs. Berg likes to cook cherry dumplings and almond pastry in her old-fashioned kitchen. Gertrude Berg is five feet three and one-half inches tall and admits that she is overweight. Her eyes and hair are brown. In politics she is an independent, and she attends Temple Emanu-El in New York City.

Gertrude Berg's philosophy is that poverty is bearable where there is love and family solidarity. "Some people want their children to have everything that money can buy," she said once (*American Magazine*, October 1952), "but I want them to have everything money can't buy. I've found out that it's perfectly possible to have both and I don't see why one shouldn't be well off as well as happy. It isn't money—or the lack of it either—that makes people miserable. It's something inside them."

References

Am Mag 154:108+ O '52 pors
Christian Sci Mon p2 Jl 10 '59 por
Commentary 21:359+ Ap '56
N Y Times II p1 F 15 '59
Who's Who in America, 1960-61
Who's Who in World Jewry (1955)
Who's Who of American Women, 1958-59

BERGMAN, (ERNST) INGMAR (băr' y'-màn) July 14, 1918- Film writer and director

Address: b. c/o Janus Films, Inc., 100 W. 55th St., New York 19; Royal Dramatic Theater, Stockholm, Sweden

In October 1959 five motion pictures in which a world-famous Swedish director asked some disturbing questions about man's relation to woman and to God were on view at the same time in the art theaters of New York City. The work of Ingmar Bergman, they were noteworthy for their pictorial beauty in black and white, their technical brilliance, and their bewildering obscurity. Tracking down the symbols in Bergman movies had become a parlor game among American intellectuals who had wearied of the cryptograms in Eliot and Joyce.

In his native Sweden, however, Bergman continued to be a film prophet unhonored by mass audiences. Even his acknowledged masterpieces, like *The Seventh Seal* and *The Magician*, failed to make money at the box office, though his earlier films were beginning to make up their losses. His motion pictures have attracted the most attention in France (where they won four times at the Cannes International Film Festival) and in England, South America, and the United States.

Ernst Ingmar Bergman was born on July 14, 1918 in the Swedish university town and archbishopric of Uppsala. His father was a Lutheran clergyman, who seems to have governed his children's lives with stern restraint, but who did not succeed in curbing Ingmar Bergman's early attraction to the world of make-believe. "When you are born and brought up in a vicarage, you are bound, at an early age, to peep behind the scenes of life and death," Bergman has said. "Father has a funeral, father has a wedding, father has a christening, father is writing his sermon. The devil was an early acquaintance, and I felt a child's need to give him concrete form. This is where the magic lantern came in, a little metal box with a paraffin lamp." In the mind of the imaginative child, the wolf in "Little Red Ridinghood" embodied evil on the flowered wallpaper of his nursery. He improvised dramas on the stage of his cardboard toy theater, including the plays of Strindberg and the adventures of Punch.

After his father had become the chaplain to the Royal Court in Stockholm, Ingmar Bergman saw his first motion picture in 1924 when he accompanied his brother to the screening of a film at a secondary school. His habit of going to the cinema at least once a week redoubled his search for expression. He later left the University of Stockholm (one source says Stockholm High School), which he had entered in 1937 to study the history of literature and art, in order to follow a career in the theater.

Although Bergman is mainly known outside Sweden for his work in films, he began his career with legitimate theaters and with the Stockholm Royal Opera where, as an assistant director, he learned a great deal about music, production, and lighting. In the early 1940's he broke into the Swedish cinema when he obtained a position with the script department of Svensk Filmindustri. The head of the department remembers him as having been "shabby, rude, and a bit of a scamp," and a "natural buffoon." It was the heyday of Bergman's Bohemianism, when, dressed in an old sweater, he sometimes slept on a mat in the theater in which he happened to be working, established a reputation as an amorist, drove an ancient automobile, and lived in a modest apartment that housed his private film library.

Since the early 1940's, Bergman has alternated between motion pictures and the legitimate theater. "The theater is like a faithful wife," he says. "The film is the great adventure, the costly, exacting mistress. One adores them both, but in different ways." Although the films bring him more money, the theater imposes more discipline and gives him the opportunity to direct the work of other artists.

In 1944 Bergman began his cinematic career when *Hets* (known as *Torment* in the United States and as *Frenzy* in England), for which he had written the script, was shown for the first time. Directed by Alf Sjöberg and featuring Stig Jarrel, Alf Kjellin, and Mai Zetterling, the film dealt with the emotional development of a confused and persecuted schoolboy. *Torment* had won eight "Charlies" (the Swedish equivalent of the American Oscar) and the Grand Prix du Cinéma at Cannes in 1946 before it made its debut in the United States on April 21, 1947 to much enthusiasm from the critics.

Although he continued to write film scripts from 1944 to 1952, Bergman also added the directing of films to his list of professional skills. During this period he wrote *Woman Without a Face (Kvinna utan ansikte)* and *Eva*, and both wrote and directed *For Joy (Till glädje);* he also directed *Crisis (Kris), Seaport (Hamnstad), Three Strange Loves (Törst),* and *Summer with Monica (Sommaren med Monika).*

He had by no means abandoned the legitimate theater, but continued his double career. In 1944 he was made head of the municipal theater of Hälsingborg, a city in southern Sweden. In 1946 he changed the scene of his activities to Göteborg, where he became a producer at the municipal theater. Four years later he left Göteborg to act as a guest producer in various Swedish theaters until 1952. With the film *Waiting Women (Kvinnors vantan)* in 1952, Bergman (who by now usually both wrote and directed his films) exhibited his flair for comedy for the first time. The leading players in this episodic film about the marital lives of four sisters-in-law were Eva Dahlbeck and Gunnar Björnstrand; for them Bergman concocted a comedy in the following year called *A Lesson in Love,* concerning the problem of marital fidelity.

The Naked Night (Gycklarnas afton), made in 1953, was released in the United States on April 9, 1956. A brutally realistic representation of circus life, the film elicited praise for its acting and direction. But

INGMAR BERGMAN

William K. Zinsser of the New York *Herald Tribune* (April 10, 1956) posted a warning in his column that "as entertainment, it's not exactly sprightly."

The next film by Bergman to be screened in the United States was *Smiles of a Summer Night (Sommarnattens leende),* which was made in 1955 but did not have its first New York showing until December 23, 1957. In reviewing it for the New York *Times* on December 24, 1957, Bosley Crowther wrote: "Mr. Bergman skips us gaily through a mix-up of youthful and adult love affairs, which, while timed around the turn of the century, are as spicy as any such today." Ulla Jacobsson, Eva Dahlbeck, Harriet Andersson, Margit Carlquist, and Gunnar Björnstrand were featured in the romantic romp, which won the prize for comedy at Cannes in 1956.

In 1956 Ingmar Bergman wrote and directed *The Seventh Seal (Det sjunde inseglet),* one of his most widely acclaimed productions. As stark as a medieval ballad, the allegorical tale was set in the plague-ridden Middle Ages and dealt with the search of a returned Crusader for God and the ultimate meaning of life and death. When it had its New York première on October 13, 1958, Bosley Crowther warned that the film presented serious problems of interpretation to the viewer.

Of *The Seventh Seal* Ingmar Bergman wrote: "My intention has been to paint in the same way as the medieval church painter, with the same objective interest, with the same tenderness and joy." In spite of its baffling allegory and its pestilential atmosphere, the picture won a special award at Cannes in 1957 and proved to be a popular success when it was exhibited in the United States.

(Continued next page)

BERGMAN, INGMAR—Continued

Wild Strawberries (Smultronstället), produced in 1957, is Bergman's symbol-laden treatment of one day in the life of an honored but lonely old man (played by Victor Sjöström) as he muses upon his past. The film opened in New York on June 22, 1959 to much praise for its visual beauty and much speculation about its meaning. *Wild Strawberries* won the first prize at the International Berlin Film Festival.

Filmed in 1957, *Brink of Life (Nära livet),* which Bergman directed from a script by Ulla Isaksson, was released in New York on November 7, 1959. Critical favor carried little weight with American filmgoers, who stayed away in droves from this depiction of the effect of childbirth on three women, played by Ingrid Thulin, Bibi Andersson, and Eva Dahlbeck. *Brink of Life* received a prize for direction at Cannes in 1958.

Featuring Max von Sydow, Ingrid Thulin, and Gunnar Björnstrand, Bergman's 1958 production called *Ansiktet*, or *The Face*, came to New York on August 27, 1959 as *The Magician*. It concerns a Swedish theatrical charlatan who comes to Stockholm in the 1840's. American reviewers again tempered their acclaim with warnings of the film's opacity of meaning, although the central theme seemed to be the warfare between faith as represented by the conjuror and reason as represented by a rationalist doctor.

In the summer of 1959 Bergman completed *The Virgin Spring (Jungfrukällan)*, again with a script by Ulla Isaksson. The Stockholm audience which first viewed it on February 8, 1960 was stunned by its bold treatment of rape and medieval brutality; some reviewers, however, called it a masterpiece. During 1960 Bergman completed work on a comedy, *The Devil's Eye*, which he wrote himself and which has for its leading character Don Juan in one of his many disguises.

While fulfilling his crowded film schedule, Bergman found time to serve with the municipal theater at Malmö, Sweden from 1952 to 1959. He then received an appointment to the Royal Dramatic Theater in Stockholm, where he is the youngest director in the long history of that institution. To Bergman the stage is more important than the cinema in expressing his talents. "Theater is my love and the basis of my existence," he told Frederic Fleisher (*Christian Science Monitor,* June 7, 1960). "Through theater I can create films, but I could never do the reverse. If I ever had to choose, I am convinced that I could live without films." He is also directing productions on radio and television.

Ingmar Bergman is married to Käbi Laretei, a concert pianist, with whom he shares a villa in a wooded suburb of Stockholm. He was married three times previously and is the father of six children by his former wives. His dark complexion and dark eyes place Bergman at a far remove from the stereotyped Swede. Alan Cole in the New York *Herald Tribune* (October 25, 1959) compared his appearance to that of a Puritan preacher, reasonably enough in view of his family background and the moral obsession of his films. One of his actors has said of Bergman's preoccupation with the powers of darkness: "It is like wandering in the mountains. He shows you the most entrancing views, but you always feel that the prerequisite for the view is an abyss." Bergman has no intention of making films in Hollywood, and rarely travels outside of Sweden. The superior technical resources of a Hollywood studio are less important to him than the freedom to continue to produce his enigmatic motion pictures in black and white and without a wide sweep of screen.

References

N Y Herald Tribune IV p1+ O 25 '59 por; IV p1+ N 1 '59; IV p1+ N 8 '59 por
N Y Times Mag p20+ D 20 '59 por
Newsweek 54:116+ N 23 '59 por
Time 75:60 Mr 14 '60 pors
Vem är Det, 1959

BERIOSOVA, SVETLANA (bĕr'yo-zo"vȧ svĕt'lȧ-nȧ) Sept. 24, 1932- British ballerina

Address: b. c/o Royal Opera House, Covent Garden, London, W.C. 2, England; Hurok Attractions, 730 5th Ave., New York 19

Dedicated to continuing a family tradition in ballet, Lithuanian-born Svetlana Beriosova is considered "one of the most radiant, poetic, and technically elegant" of the Royal Ballet (formerly Sadler's Wells Ballet) ballerinas. She is regarded as a possible successor to Margot Fonteyn. Miss Beriosova made her professional debut in 1947 and danced leading parts while still a teen-ager.

Before she became associated with the famous London company in 1952, she had performed with the Grand Ballet de Monte Carlo, London Metropolitan Ballet, and Sadler's Wells Theatre Ballet. Miss Beriosova, whose highly individual style distinguishes her from the rest of her company, was a featured ballerina during the Royal Ballet's four-week New York engagement in the fall of 1960 and on the American tour that followed.

On September 24, 1932 in Kaunas, Lithuania, Svetlana Beriosova was born into the world of dance. Her father, Nicholas Beriosoff, at the time of her birth was a member of the Lithuanian State Ballet and later became the leading character dancer in René Blum and Col. de Basil Ballets Russes de Monte Carlo (later the Ballet Russe de Monte Carlo). Two of her aunts and an uncle were also professional dancers.

She spent much of her early childhood in her father's dressing room and in the wings. She traveled throughout Europe with her parents and observed ballerinas performing all the classic roles. During these early, nomadic years she learned to develop her serenity and self-possession. At the age of eight she began to take ballet lessons, and made her first stage appearances about a year later with the Ballet Russe de Monte Carlo. She took the roles of a little girl skipping rope in *Le Beau Danube,* a dwarf in *Labyrinth,* and Clara in *The Nutcracker.* Recalling the first time she danced the part of Clara, Miss Beriosova told Pigeon Crowle: "I had to walk around the stage, wearing a long blue nightgown and holding the hand of Alexandra Danilova who, as the Sugar Plum Fairy, looked absolutely wonderful in pink—I was so proud!" (*Enter the Ballerina,* 1955).

Svetlana picked up a smattering of general education from her parents, and, while traveling with her father's troupe, she learned several languages. When the family moved to New York City, she enrolled in the Professional Children's School. She studied dance at the Vilzak-Shollar School and later at George Balanchine's School of American Ballet, with Olga Preobrajenska in Paris, and with Vera Volkova in London. When her father was not on tour, he observed his daughter in dance class and gave her corrections and lessons afterwards. Her mother died when Svetlana was ten years old, and her father married Lylene, a maker of tutus for ballerinas, with whom Svetlana became fast friends.

At the age of fourteen Svetlana Beriosova made her professional debut in March 1947 with the Ottawa Ballet Company in Canada, performing in *Les Sylphides* and *The Nutcracker.* Later that year she joined the *corps de ballet* of the Grand Ballet de Monte Carlo, whose ballet master, William Dollar, chose her as one of the leads in his ballet *Constantia.* When her father joined the newly organized Metropolitan Ballet in England as ballet master, Miss Beriosova became a soloist with the company, and her piquant beauty and fastidious technique soon attracted the notice of London audiences.

During 1948 she danced in the classical roles of the Blue Bird and Odette in *Le Lac des Cygnes* at the Scala Theatre in London. In that season she created a leading part in John Taras' *Designs with Strings,* dancing with haunting melancholy in an abstract role. She also interpreted the young girl who succumbs to the Seven Deadly Sins in the première of Frank Staff's *Fanciulla delle Rose.* In the ballet each Sin takes a rose from her wreath leaving her with a circlet of thorns. After a successful tour of the Continent with the Metropolitan Ballet, Miss Beriosova and her father performed together in *Le Beau Danube,* as the First Hand and the Strong Man, respectively.

At this time Miss Beriosova performed for the first time on television in *Stars of the Ballet* with Danilova and Léonide Massine. Later, viewers saw her with Alicia Markova in *Les Sylphides.* When the Metropolitan Ballet came to an untimely end in the 1949-50 season, the dancer received two offers: one from the Sadler's Wells second company and the other from the New York City Ballet. She decided to accept the invitation from Sadler's Wells. After she joined this company, Gladys Davidson wrote prophetically of the quality of Svetlana Beriosova's work in the book *Ballet Biographies* (1952): "This very young and most

SVETLANA BERIOSOVA

attractive dancer shows definite promise of becoming a future really fine ballerina in the grand Russian manner. She already has the true classical line and style, coupled with real artistry, and the assured easy carriage of the Russian School."

After touring in the United States and Canada with the Sadler's Wells Theatre Ballet, Miss Beriosova became a member of the senior company in 1952 and has since appeared in many full-length classic roles. In 1953 she danced a memorable Sylvia in the ballet of the same name with Philip Chatfield at New York City's Metropolitan Opera House. The New York engagement was followed by a five-month American and Canadian tour during which she replaced Violetta Elvin in *Homage to the Queen.* Miss Beriosova's impeccable technique, unusual musicality, and command of the stage drew praises when she created roles in John Cranko's *Pastorale* and *The Shadow.*

On June 1, 1954 she danced Princess Aurora in *The Sleeping Beauty.* Commenting on this milestone in her career, the young ballerina told Pigeon Crowle: "From the moment I knew I was to dance the Beauty, it was rarely out of my thoughts. All day I lived with it, and I dreamt about it at night, for it is a great honor, but a great responsibility, too. The more one studies the role, the more one becomes aware of its splendours and its difficulties. . . . The most nerve-racking moments, though, were those last few minutes in the wings, waiting for my cue. But once 'on', I forgot all this—there was the stage, the wonderful Tchaikovsky music sweeping me along, everything falling into its ordained pattern. I felt light and free and imagined I was Aurora."

Ranked as a ballerina by Sadler's Wells in 1955, she danced the role of Odette-Odile in *Le Lac des Cygnes (Swan Lake)* at Covent

BERIOSOVA, SVETLANA—*Continued*

Garden; she thus became part of an illustrious tradition of immortal Swans. In that year she also danced the first role created especially for her by Frederick Ashton, Armida in *Rinaldo and Armida,* opposite Michael Somes.

Other parts which Miss Beriosova has interpreted with the Sadler's Wells Ballet have been in *The Lady and the Fool, Checkmate, Firebird,* and *Coppélia.* She has participated in the Edinburgh International Festival and other festivals. In 1957 she danced the part of Belle Rose in John Cranko's *The Prince of the Pagodas,* which had its American première with Miss Beriosova at the Metropolitan Opera House on September 18, 1957. It was about this time that the Sadler's Wells became the Royal Ballet.

Dance critics have described Svetlana Beriosova as "blonde, exquisitely formed"; "tall," (five feet six and one-half inches); "serenely beautiful as a Botticelli madonna, with long almond eyes in a pale face"; "heart-shaped face and wide blue eyes." She has a gentle voice and a merry wit. Miss Beriosova was married to Dr. Mohammed Masud Khan, a Pakistani psychologist practising in London, on January 23, 1959. They maintain homes in London and in southern France. She collects paintings of Georges Braque and other artists, and numbers among her close friends painters, writers, and intellectuals, to whom she is known as Lana. She likes to swim, bicycle, sun-bathe, read books on religion and philosophy, listen to music, and attend the cinema and the theater. She is now a British subject.

Svetlana Beriosova prefers to dance roles in classic ballets. Her aim, she has said, is "to better each performance, to improve interpretation and technique, and to hope that in years to come one may even *begin* to give a performance that is satisfying to oneself." Interviewed by Margaret Lloyd (*Christian Science Monitor,* October 3, 1955), Miss Beriosova was asked to comment on modern dance movements. She replied: "Ballet is inclusive. It has everything. You don't have to go outside ballet to do any kind of step or movement or gesture."

In developing her artistry, Svetlana Beriosova has been inspired by the great ballerinas and *premiers danseurs* of the past. She told Pigeon Crowle: "They are rather like ancestors who have given us—the dancers of to-day —a wonderful heritage, for they strove very hard to make our art great, and all we enjoy now, they made possible. To them the laurel leaves—we must carry on the tradition as best we may."

References

N Y World-Telegram Mag p9 S 14 '57 por
This Week p24 O 25 '53 por
Chujoy, Anatole ed. The Dance Encyclopedia (1949)
Franks, Arthur H. Svetlana Beriosova (1958)
Swinson, Cyril Svetlana Beriosova (1956)
Who's Who, 1960

BERNAYS, EDWARD L. Nov. 22, 1891-
Public relations counselor

Address: b. 26 E. 64th St., New York 21; h. 480 Park Ave., New York 22

> NOTE: This biography supersedes the article which appeared in *Current Biography* in 1942.

A little more than forty years ago, Edward L. Bernays, public relations counselor, hung out his shingle in New York City. As he saw it, his vocation resembled medicine and law in that it could produce desired changes in individuals or groups through deliberate action based on precise, scientific principles. Often called the foremost publicist in the United States, Bernays has engineered public consent on behalf of many business and industrial enterprises, professional, civic, and welfare bodies, and governments at home and abroad. He is the founder and president of the Edward L. Bernays Foundation.

Edward L. Bernays was born in Vienna, Austria on November 22, 1891, one of five children of Ely and Anna (Freud) Bernays. His mother was a sister of Sigmund Freud, the founder of psychoanalysis. When Edward was one year old, the family moved to New York City, where his father became a successful grain merchant. Edward attended public school in upper Manhattan and was graduated from the De Witt Clinton High School at the age of sixteen.

To please his father, Bernays enrolled in the College of Agriculture at Cornell University, but by 1912, when he received his B.S. degree, he had decided that scientific farming was not his métier. Later the same year, he became the editor, copyreader, make-up man, and promotion manager of the *Dietetic and Hygienic Gazette* and the *Medical Review of Reviews.* His editorials at that time touched on such avant-garde subjects as the case against corset stays and the need for taking shower baths and for teaching children the facts of life.

Bernays made what was probably his first experiment in public relations in support of actor Richard Bennett, who wanted to produce a play about venereal disease, a taboo subject at the time. Creating a "sociological fund," Bernays invited leaders of politics, industry, and society to contribute endorsements and money to support the cause of sex education in exchange for first-night tickets to the play. The show was a tremendous success, and, what is more important, the venture turned Bernays towards public relations as a career.

From 1913 to 1917 Bernays worked as a publicist for such theatrical producers as Klaw & Erlanger and Henry Miller. He advertised the Diaghilev Russian ballet tour for the Metropolitan Opera Company and, as a partner in the Metropolitan Music Bureau, publicized its leading singers, including Enrico Caruso. In 1917 he contributed to *The Broadway Anthology* (Duffield). The following year he joined the staff of the United States committee on public information, headed by George Creel. Working for the committee during World War I at the foreign press bureau in New

York City and later at the Paris peace conference, Bernays wrote material that dramatized American war aims and ideals.

When Bernays returned to New York in 1919, he and his future wife, Doris Fleischman, opened an office where they dispensed what Bernays at first called "publicity direction" and later termed "counsel on public relations." The first agency to seek his services as an independent professional was the United States War Department, which hired him to conduct a nation-wide campaign to encourage the re-employment of ex-servicemen. At this time Lithuanian leaders also engaged his services to encourage recognition of Lithuania by the United States.

Bernays is generally regarded as the man who created the concept of the professional public relations counselor: one who studies the social sciences to understand, motivate, and direct the responses of large groups of people. Ivy Lee is said to have defined the public relations man as one who reports his clients' actions to the public; Bernays added that the publicist must educate his clients to take the kind of actions which are newsworthy enough to be reported. Bernays also believes that since the counselor manipulates mass opinion, he must never serve a cause out of keeping with his own view of the public interest.

Some examples of Bernays' methods are the promotion campaigns he directed in the 1920's to advertise Venida hair nets, Ivory soap, and electric lighting. For Venida, Bernays asked social leaders to declare their preference for long hair rather than the bobbed styles then popular; from labor and public health experts he elicited statements about the dangers of wearing long hair unconfined in factories and restaurants. As a result, some states passed laws requiring waitresses and women factory workers to wear hair nets.

To encourage the use of Proctor and Gamble's Ivory soap, Bernays created a national small sculptural committee which sponsored annual contests for the best sculptures created from Ivory soap. Over the years millions of school children carved away at millions of cakes of Ivory soap. It was his promotion of Light's Golden Jubilee held in 1929 at Dearborn, Michigan, however, that brought Bernays national recognition. Thomas Alva Edison himself attended the fiftieth anniversary of his invention of electric light, as the guest of honor of such dignitaries as Henry Ford, President Herbert Hoover, and John D. Rockefeller, Jr. Edison's birthplace was made a national shrine, twenty-five cities joined in the festivities, and a special United States postage stamp commemorated the Mazda lamp.

Since 1929 Bernays has worked—usually on a yearly retainer basis—for leading firms in the auto manufacturing, banking, construction, food, entertainment, oil, tobacco, real estate, public utilities, and transportation fields. His clients have included publishing firms like Condé Nast Publications and *McCalls Magazine,* radio and television corporations, and private educational and civic organizations like Columbia University and the National Associ-

EDWARD L. BERNAYS

ation for the Advancement of Colored People. Bernays served as assistant commissioner at the Paris Exhibition for the United States Department of Commerce in 1925 and was named public relations director of the New York World's Fair in 1939.

Bernays has also held many state and federal government positions in the United States. From 1930 to 1931 he was a member of President Hoover's emergency committee for employment and he served on the New York state committee on discrimination in employment in 1942. During World War II, the Army, Navy, Commerce, and Treasury departments asked for his advice. He was co-chairman of the Victory Book Campaign in 1943 and also headed the United States Department of the Treasury's national publicity advisory committee for the third war loan. In the spring of 1953 he recommended the establishment in the State Department of a psychological warfare office. The following year he was a consultant to the United States Air Force and since then has served as chairman of the national committee for an adequate overseas United States information program. Bernays has also done public relations work for the governments of India and Vienna, Austria.

Over the years Bernays has continued to make a sharp distinction between the public relations counselor and the press agent. "Bernays has taken the sideshow barker and given him a philosophy and a new language," wrote Stanley Walker in *City Editor* (1934). In his book *Crystallizing Public Opinion* (Boni and Liveright, 1923) Bernays defined for the first time the scope and function of the profession and set forth its ethical rules and practices. In 1923 he became the first instructor on public relations in the United States when he lectured at New York University.

(Continued next page)

BERNAYS, EDWARD L.—*Continued*

Bernays returned to New York University as an adjunct professor of public relations in 1949, and in 1950 was a visiting professor at the University of Hawaii. In 1958 he became an adjunct professor at Yeshiva University's Graduate School of Education. He has lectured on public relations before the Harvard Graduate School of Business Administration, Princeton University's School of Public and International Affairs, the Yale University Economics Club, the American Statistical Association, and the American Marketing Association.

Acting on his own oft-stated principle that a public relations counselor must advance the public good, Bernays wrote a booklet, *Take Your Place at the Peace Table* (Duell, Sloan, and Pearce, 1945), in which he told Americans how to express their support of the Dumbarton Oaks Conference in public. A *New York Times* (June 10, 1945) reviewer said of Bernays that "instead of pounding or insinuating ideas into our minds, he is trying to show us how to express our own ideas most effectively." In his earlier *Speak Up for Democracy* (Viking, 1940), Bernays had outlined the means by which each citizen could promote the democratic idea in his own community. Bernays was the editor of and a contributor to *Outline of Careers* (Doubleday, Doran and Co., 1927) and the author of *Propaganda* (Liveright, 1928). Other books in which he describes his vocation are *Public Relations* (Bellman, 1945), and *Public Relations* (1952) and *The Engineering of Consent* (1955), both published by the University of Oklahoma Press.

The first to admit that he has prospered through the years, Bernays has contributed generously to educational, artistic, and social causes. He established fellowships in journalism and public relations at Columbia and Western Reserve universities in 1943, and in 1944 sponsored lectures on civil liberties at Cornell University. The Edward L. Bernays Foundation, which he founded in 1946 and of which he is president, financed an industrial relations fund at Cornell University in 1947; contributed to the Barnard College fund for social science teaching in 1950; sponsored a psychologists' conference on juvenile delinquency in 1957; and helped the Educational Broadcasters' Association set up the WNYC Education Institute of the Air in 1954. In the summer of 1959 the foundation donated $10,000 to support free performances of Shakespeare in New York City's Central Park.

Bernays is counsel on public relations to the New York City department of commerce and public events. He is a director of the National Multiple Sclerosis Society; a trustee of the Hospital for Joint Diseases in New York City; a member of the board of governors of the New York state chapter of the Arthritis and Rheumatism Foundation; and, since 1942, a member of the national public relations committee, American Red Cross. Bernays is also a member of the advisory committee of Columbia University's School of General Studies and a trustee of the Metropolitan Educational Television Association.

In 1954 Bernays received a certificate of commendation from the University of Florida's School of Journalism and the bronze medallion award of the Southwest Journalism Forum and Southern Methodist University. In 1955 he received an award of appreciation from the Veterans of Foreign Wars. He has held the French rank of Officer of Public Instruction since 1926 and received the Danish King Christian Medal in 1946. Bernays is a member of the American Sociological Society, the Society for Applied Anthropology, and the Society for Psychological Study of Social Issues. He belongs to the Cornell Club of New York, the Harmonie Club, and the Overseas Press Club.

Edward L. Bernays and Doris E. Fleischman were married on September 16, 1922. They have two daughters, Doris (Mrs. Richard Held) and Anne (Mrs. Justin Kaplan), and several grandchildren. The Bernays enjoy listening to music and attend many concerts. A *Printers' Ink* (December 4, 1959) writer describes Bernays as "a small, rotund, scholarly-looking man with a cherubic face. . . . He has gray hair, a scraggly gray mustache, and wears old-fashioned suits, an oldish-looking black coat and hat. All told, he looks and carries himself like a learned scholar or great specialist, an appearance which is in keeping with the goals he has pursued throughout his life."

References

Med R of Rs 81:155 Mr '30
Ptr Ink 269:62 D 4 '59 pors
Author's & Writer's Who's Who (1948-49)
Who's Who in America, 1960-61
Who's Who in New York, 1952

BERNSTEIN, LEONARD Aug. 25, 1918-
Conductor; composer; musician

Address: b. c/o The Philharmonic-Symphony Society of New York, 113 W. 57th St., New York 19

NOTE: This biography supersedes the article which appeared in *Current Biography* in 1944.

When, at the age of forty, the versatile Leonard Bernstein began a three-year term as music director of the New York Philharmonic Symphony Orchestra, succeeding Dimitri Mitropoulos, he was the first musician born in the United States to hold such a position with a major American orchestra. But this achievement was only one among many in conducting, composing, playing the piano, and lecturing on music, in which Bernstein has achieved celebrity.

Leonard Bernstein was born on August 25, 1918, in Lawrence, Massachusetts, the son of Samuel Joseph and Jennie (Resnick) Bernstein, both Russian immigrants. The child's talent for music was not discovered until his tenth year, when an old upright piano was sent by a relative to be kept by the Bernsteins. Leonard found the instrument irresistible and soon decided upon a musical career for himself, a decision which his father opposed up to the time of his son's first professional successes.

His choice of a musical career did not interfere with Leonard Bernstein's normal boyhood activities: at the Boston Latin School, he enjoyed, and excelled in, athletics. He later attended Harvard University, where, with the intention of becoming a pianist, he studied piano with Heinrich Gebhard and composition with Walter Piston and Edward Burlinghame Hill.

After graduating from Harvard in 1939, Bernstein attended the Curtis Institute of Music in Philadelphia. His principal interest was now conducting, which he studied with Fritz Reiner, although he continued his piano work under Madame Isabella Vengerova. He also studied orchestration with Randall Thompson. During the summers he worked under Serge Koussevitzky, conductor of the Boston Symphony Orchestra, at the Berkshire Music Center in Tanglewood, Massachusetts.

Upon leaving the Curtis Institute, Bernstein spent the season of 1941-42 in teaching, composing his Clarinet Sonata, his first published composition, and producing operas for the Boston Institute of Modern Art. In September 1942 he was appointed assistant to Koussevitzky at the Berkshire Music Center.

Bernstein's first New York appearances as pianist and conductor took place in the 1942-43 season, when he received enthusiastic reviews for playing at a Town Hall music forum and for directing one of the "serenade" concerts at the Museum of Modern Art. He received his major conducting assignment late in the summer of 1943, when he accepted the offer of Artur Rodzinski, conductor of the New York Philharmonic, to become an assistant conductor of that orchestra.

On two consecutive days in 1943 Leonard Bernstein took two major steps forward in his musical career. On November 12, the mezzo-soprano Jennie Tourel performed his cycle *Five Kid Songs: I Hate Music* at a recital in Town Hall. On November 13, the young conductor was called upon at the last minute to take the place of Bruno Walter, who was indisposed, at a concert of the New York Philharmonic.

Bernstein's success at the concert brought his name into the glare of public notice. His conducting won him the acclaim of audience and critics, praise from Rodzinski and Koussevitzky, and a front-page story in the New York *Times*. After his New York triumph, Bernstein appeared as a conductor in Pittsburgh and Boston, where his symphony called *Jeremiah* was part of the program. On February 18, 1944, the work was performed for the first time in New York City. Despite a tepid reception on the part of certain critics, the work won the award of the New York City Music Critics' Circle as the most distinguished new orchestral work of American composition performed in the city during the season of 1943-44.

On April 18, 1944, the world première of the ballet *Fancy Free* was given by Ballet Theatre at the Metropolitan Opera House. Bernstein, who had composed the score, also conducted. The success of this production prompted Bernstein, Jerome Robbins, its choreographer, Adolph Green, and Betty Comden to expand the ballet into a full-length Broadway musical, *On*

LEONARD BERNSTEIN

the Town, which opened in New York City on December 28, 1944. Although not all the reviewers paid homage to Bernstein's musical score, most of them were well disposed toward the show, which prospered at the box office.

Since 1945 each of Bernstein's several musical careers has flourished. As a conductor, he led the New York City Symphony from 1945 until 1948. He has also conducted many major American and European orchestras, including the London Philharmonic (1946), the Orchestre National de Paris (1950), and the orchestra of the La Scala opera house in Milan (1953).

Leonard Bernstein has also kept in close touch with the Israel Philharmonic Symphony. After acting as its music adviser from 1945 to 1948, he shared with Koussevitzky the conducting of the orchestra's 1951 American tour; in 1957 he conducted the orchestra when it gave its first concert in the new Fredric H. Mann Auditorium in Tel-Aviv.

As a teacher, Bernstein has been a member of the faculty of the Berkshire Music Center in 1948. He succeeded Koussevitzky as head of its conducting department in the summer of 1951. He also taught music at Brandeis University in Waltham, Massachusetts from 1951 to 1956. Beginning with his first appearance on the *Omnibus* program during the 1954-55 season, he has often lectured on music over television.

Bernstein has written the scores for two highly successful musicals. One was *Wonderful Town,* which opened on Broadway on February 25, 1953, and the other was *West Side Story,* which had its New York première on September 26, 1957. A third Broadway venture, a musical version of Voltaire's *Candide* that opened on December 1, 1956, was less well received and closed after seventy-three performances.

(Continued next page)

BERNSTEIN, LEONARD—*Continued*

Among Bernstein's other compositions are a second symphony for piano and orchestra, *The Age of Anxiety* (1949); a song cycle called *La Bonne Cuisine* (1949); the incidental music for a Broadway production of *Peter Pan* (1950); a short opera, *Trouble in Tahiti* (both music and libretto, 1952); incidental music for the film *On the Waterfront* (1954), for which he received an Academy Award nomination; and a *Serenade for Violin and String Orchestra with Percussion* (1954).

Bernstein was appointed co-conductor (with Dimitri Mitropoulos) of the New York Philharmonic for its 1957-58 season, and was also made music director of the orchestra's young people's concerts, four of which were nationally televised. One year later, Bernstein took over the reins of the Philharmonic completely, bringing with him several departures from established tradition, including interrelated programs emphasizing the work of one composer or one type of music, and Thursday evening "preview" concerts, during which the conductor is free to speak to the audience about the music to be performed.

His reputation as conductor of the New York Philharmonic has not been confined to the United States. After the 1957-58 season, Bernstein led the orchestra through a tour of Latin America; after the 1958-59 season, the itinerary included twenty-nine cities in seventeen countries of Europe and Asia. The popular reaction to both tours was wildly enthusiastic, nowhere more so than in the Soviet Union and other Communist countries. In the Soviet Union, Bernstein performed works by contemporary American composers, including himself, and of the Russian-born Igor Stravinsky. Several of these compositions were heard for the first time in Soviet Russia.

When he returned from the Russian tour, Bernstein received many honors for his services to music and to international good will, including keys to the cities of New York and Washington. He also received the John H. Finley Medal for service to New York City from the City College of the City of New York on November 4, 1959. In the following year the Albert Einstein College of Medicine of Yeshiva University honored him with the Albert Einstein Commemorative Award in the Arts, and the Academy of Television Arts and Sciences gave him an "Emmy" award for his TV series of four programs entitled *New York Philharmonic Young People's Concerts*.

Although Leonard Bernstein's separate musical careers seem irreconcilable, he has, to some extent, brought them together on several occasions. For example, he frequently performs the solo part in piano concertos while conducting from the keyboard. He has conducted the overture to his musical *Candide* on a New York Philharmonic program. His television appearances for the Lincoln Division of the Ford Motor Company, inaugurated on November 30, 1959, are based on the words-plus-music technique of the New York Philharmonic previews.

On September 9, 1951, Leonard Bernstein was married to Chilean-born actress Felicia Montealegre Cohn. They have two children, a daughter, Jamie, born in 1952, and a son, Alexander Serge, born in 1955. The Bernsteins live in a nine-room duplex apartment near Carnegie Hall, the home of the New York Philharmonic. Bernstein has supported Democratic nominees for the Presidency. Although he has called writing only a "hobby," his avocation led to the publication of his book, *The Joy of Music*, by Simon and Schuster in 1959.

Leonard Bernstein is five feet, eight and one-half inches tall. His black hair is now quite generously threaded with gray. *Time* (February 4, 1957) has remarked that "he exudes sex appeal like a leaky electric eel"; there is no question that his boyish appearance and craggy good looks have helped to endear him to his public. But it is more than his appearance, more than his dynamic, extroverted manner of conducting and lecturing, more even than his innate musical gifts, that have made him the success story of American music. For, as the same *Time* article noted, he has a fifth career in addition to conducting, composing, playing the piano, and teaching—that of being a celebrity. This talent for making himself remembered is as impressive as any of his musical accomplishments.

References

Look 22:73+ N 11 '59 por
New Yorker 33:37+ Ja 11 '58; 33:35+ Ja 18 '58
Time 69:68+ F 4 '57 por
Ewen, D. Living Musicians (First Supplement, 1957); Leonard Bernstein (1960)
Goss, M. Modern Music Makers (1952)
International Who's Who (1959)
Who's Who in America, 1958-59
World Biography (1954)

BETANCOURT, RÓMULO (běh-tähn-cōr')

Feb. 22, 1908- President of Venezuela
Address: Palacio del Gobierno, Caracas, Venezuela

"The fundamental problem of Latin America," Rómulo Betancourt said shortly before he became President of Venezuela, "is the low standard of living, the hunger and misery, the underdevelopment, and in some countries, the presence of dictators." All of his life Betancourt has fought for political democracy in his country, and in 1959, when he took office as the second Venezuelan chief executive elected by direct universal suffrage, he set to work to end the extremes of wealth and poverty in Venezuela.

Because of his opposition to Venezuelan dictators, he spent eighteen of the fifty-two years of his life in exile. He served as provisional President of Venezuela from 1945 to 1948, organized and was secretary-general of the Acción Democrática (A.D.), a leftist political party, and has written a number of books on economics and politics. During his five-year term as President, he proposes to provide his nation with a stable and democratic government and to carry out various economic and social reforms, including the diversification of the economy. Venezuela, the world's second largest producer of oil, almost wholly depends on it for its income.

Rómulo Betancourt was born in Guatire, Miranda, not far from Caracas in Venezuela, on February 22, 1908, the son of Luis and Virginia Betancourt. His father was an accountant for a wholesale grocer and an amateur poet. Young Rómulo attended the local primary schools and the Liceo Caracas, where he studied under the novelist Rómulo Gallegos. He then worked as a bill collector for a wholesale tobacco firm and entered the law school of the Central University of Venezuela in Caracas in 1927.

Because he helped to organize a liberal student movement called the Boys of '28 and took part in student demonstrations against the Venezuelan dictator Juan Vicente Gómez in February 1928, Betancourt was put in prison for several weeks. After his release, he led an abortive rebellion in April 1928. He then escaped to Colombia, where he recounted his prison experience in *Dos meses en las cárceles de Gómez* (1928) and discussed Venezuelan politics in *En las huellas de la pezuña* (1929). He took part in various efforts to overthrow Gómez from Santo Domingo, Curaçao, and Trinidad and moved to Costa Rica, where he joined the Communist party in 1930. He now calls this "a youthful attack of small pox that left me immune to the disease" (*United States News & World Report,* December 19, 1958).

By the time that Betancourt returned to Venezuela in 1936, after the death of Gómez, he had left the Communist party and had associated himself with the anti-Communist left. He founded and edited the newspaper *Orve* and led a revolutionary underground political party. Ordered to leave Venezuela in 1937 by dictator Eleázar López Contreras, he managed to remain in hiding until 1939. Captured and sent into exile, he went to Chile and Argentina, where he continued to expound his democratic faith through his lectures and his writings. In his *Problemas venezolanos,* published in 1940, he examined the economics of petroleum in his country.

López allowed him to return in 1941, on the eve of national elections. Betancourt organized the Acción Democrática, a leftist, non-Communist political party. Its first Presidential candidate was the novelist Rómulo Gallegos, who lost to General Isaías Medina Angarita. (At that time, because of the lack of direct universal suffrage, Parliament determined elections.) In 1943 Betancourt founded another newspaper, *El Pais.* In 1945 he joined forces with some army officers, one of whose leaders was Major Marcos Pérez Jiménez, to overthrow successfully President Medina Angarita on October 18.

As head of the seven-man revolutionary junta, Betancourt served as provisional President from 1945 to 1948. He soon nettled conservatives by enforcing such reforms as an excess-profits tax, reduced rents and electricity rates, orders to businesses to distribute at least 10 per cent of their annual profits to employees, and the radical fifty-fifty oil formula, by which the Venezuelan government received half of the profits of

Wide World

RÓMULO BETANCOURT

petroleum companies. Betancourt promised free elections, and in December 1947 the A.D.'s candidate, Rómulo Gallegos, won the Presidential election in the first national contest decided by direct universal suffrage. In the following year Betancourt headed the Venezuelan delegation to the Ninth Pan American Conference, in Bogotá, Colombia.

Moved to action by reports that the A.D. was trying to minimize its co-operation with the military and to replace the army of professionals with a militia of peasants, the military groups turned against the A.D. and staged a bloodless coup on November 24, 1948. Marcos Pérez Jiménez became dictator of the country. Betancourt again went into exile, this time to Washington, D.C., New York City, Cuba, Costa Rica, and Puerto Rico, and the government ordered the press not to publish his name. During the nine years of banishment from his native land, he had time to ponder the mistakes of his regime and to talk with democratic leaders in the Western Hemisphere. He directed the underground activities of his party in Venezuela and wrote: *Trayectoria democrática de una revolución* (1948), *El Caso de Venezuela y el destino de la democracia en América* (1949), and *Venezuela: política y petróleo* (1956).

In January 1958 the armed forces turned against Pérez Jiménez and overthrew his regime. Rear Admiral Wolfgang Larrazábal Ugueto headed the new temporary junta, which arranged for free elections and guided the country toward constitutionalism and democracy. Betancourt returned to Venezuela and reorganized his party, the Acción Democrática. He became his party's candidate for President in the December 1958 elections.

In a pre-election agreement the three major political parties, the A.D., the Unión Republicana Democrática, and Social Christian, promised to support the candidate elected by the

BETANCOURT, ROMULO—Continued

people and to participate in a coalition cabinet. Betancourt defeated his two major rivals, Larrazábal and Rafael Caldera. Sworn into office on February 13, 1959, he formed a cabinet composed of members of the A.D., the Unión Republicana Democrática, and the Social Christian party and several independents.

In his inaugural address, Betancourt promised a government of austerity and integrity; a program for improving health, sanitation, communications, and roads; friendly relations with the United States; and support for the United Nations. He said that he would recommend that the Organization of American States exclude dictatorships from its membership, and that he would work toward closer union among the Latin American countries, perhaps through a common market.

Much of Betancourt's first year as President was spent in planning, and he invited a mission of the International Bank for Reconstruction and Development to assist in outlining the most essential economic and social reforms. Under the terms of the Land Reform Act, passed in March 1960, some 700,000 farmers will acquire lands of their own through legal procedures and with compensation to former owners. The act also provides for the building of schools, hospitals, roads, and aqueducts in rural areas.

Many schools have already been built in Venezuela under the new government in an attempt to end the illiteracy of one half of a population of over 6,000,000. In March 1960 Parliament enacted a law establishing a National Institute of Culture and Fine Arts to develop the cultural interests of Venezuelans. Some of the reforms innovated by Betancourt's administration may help to siphon off students and workers from the Communist party, which is not represented in the cabinet, but which still enjoys a legal status.

The government has agreed to honor the debts of the Pérez Jiménez regime, in order to show good faith to private investors in Venezuela. (The American investment is about $3.5 billion.) Betancourt has said that he will not grant new oil concessions to foreign firms and plans to start a government oil company. His government will not expropriate the oil companies, but it appears to have accepted the decision of the Larrazábal junta to raise the government's share in oil profits from 50 per cent to 63 per cent. Threats to the government occurred in 1960 when a minor revolt took place in April and when an unsuccessful attempt on President Betancourt's life was made in June.

Betancourt was married to Carmen Valverde, a schoolteacher whom he met while in exile in Costa Rica during the 1930's. They have one daughter, Virginia, and several grandchildren. The short and stocky political leader wears dark horn-rimmed glasses and often smokes a pipe. He is an energetic worker and an astonishingly fast reader. Among the many honors he has received are decorations from Venezuela, Colombia, Peru, Ecuador, Cuba, Guatemala, Mexico, Panama, Chile, and Sweden.

References

N Y Herald Tribune p14 F 13 '59
N Y Times p2 D 11 '59
Time 72:30+ D 22 '58; 75:34+ F 8 '60
U N World 1:37+ My '47
International Who's Who, 1959
Who's Who in Latin America Pt 3 (1951)

BEVAN, ANEURIN

Nov. 15, 1897-July 6, 1960 Deputy leader of the British Labour party; Member of Parliament since 1929; cabinet member (1945-51); head of left-wing faction of party. See *Current Biography* (May) 1943.

Obituary

N Y Times p1+ Jl 7 '60

BIKEL, THEODORE

May 2, 1924- Actor; folk singer
Address: b. Elektra Records, 116 W. 14th St., New York 11

So unobtrusive is the performing of the multilingual Theodore Bikel, the character actor and folk singer, that he can play the male lead opposite Mary Martin in the new Rodgers and Hammerstein musical *The Sound of Music* and be seldom discussed at length in the reviews. Bikel has contributed supporting roles of power and depth to motion pictures, including the much honored 1958 film *The Defiant Ones,* in which he appeared as the humane Southern sheriff. For this performance he was nominated for an award from the Academy of Motion Picture Arts and Sciences.

For Elektra Records Bikel has made bestselling folk song albums that put to use his ability to sing in seventeen languages from Zulu to Greek. When he has appeared in oneman concerts in New York's Town Hall, accompanying himself on the guitar, overflow audiences have spilled on to the stage. Yet for all his success as international actor, folk singer, FM radio broadcaster, and restaurateur, Bikel has somehow dispensed with the trappings of celebrity. He remains a man known to many people but recognized by few.

Theodore Bikel was born in Vienna, Austria, on May 2, 1924, the son of Joseph and Maria Bikel. His Jewish family gave young "Theo" a head start as a linguist: he learned Yiddish and Hebrew at home and German in the Vienna schools. When he was fourteen, the family was forced to flee from Vienna when Austria succumbed to Nazi Germany in the *Putsch* of 1938.

The Bikels migrated to what was then Palestine, where they became British subjects in 1939. Joseph Bikel is now a director of the public health service in Israel. Theo continued his studies with the intention of teaching comparative linguistics; meanwhile he worked as a laborer on a *kibbutz* (communal farm settlement). When he displayed more flair for reciting Shakespeare than for farming, the elders of the *kibbutz* reassigned him to the library and allowed him to stage and direct local pageants.

In 1943, after four years in the *kibbutz,* Bikel joined the Habimah Theater in Tel Aviv, where the classics are performed in Hebrew, as an apprentice actor. He resigned after eighteen months, during which time he had been given only one microscopic role, to found the Tel Aviv Chamber Theater in 1944 with four other young actors. After playing diversified roles for two years, Bikel left the new troupe to study acting at the Royal Academy of Dramatic Arts in London, a venture that was financed by his parents.

After his graduation, Bikel won a series of roles in little theater productions off-Mayfair in London. His performance in *You Can't Take It With You* led to his being cast by Sir Laurence Olivier as Mitch in the first European production of *A Streetcar Named Desire,* starring Vivien Leigh. The play opened in Manchester on September 27, 1949, and moved to the Aldwych Theatre in London on October 12.

After a successful run in the Tennessee Williams play, Bikel was cast as a German sailor in John Huston's film, *The African Queen* (1951). Before it was released, he was back on the London stage as the Russian officer in Peter Ustinov's *The Love of Four Colonels,* which ran for two years. When it finally closed, Bikel devoted himself to supporting roles in British films and to American productions filmed in Europe. Among them were: *Moulin Rouge* (1952), *Never Let Me Go* (1953), *Melba* (1953), *A Day to Remember* (1954), *Love Lottery* (1954), *The Little Kidnappers* (1954), and *The Divided Heart* (1955).

Although Bikel was seldom mentioned in the American reviews of his films, Bosley Crowther noticed that he played "a lean and anguished romance touchingly" in *The Little Kidnappers* (New York *Times,* September 2, 1954). He did attract professional attention, however, and Herman Shumlin, the producer, persuaded him to come to the United States in 1954 to appear with Louis Jourdan in *Tonight in Samarkand* on Broadway.

The short-lived drama opened at the Morosco Theater on February 16, 1955. "As a forbearing police inspector," wrote a New York *Times* reviewer (February 17, 1955), "Theodore Bikel is responsible for two of the best scenes. In the midst of the circus ebullience, he plays with a relaxed deliberation that changes the pace and introduces order into disorder."

The subtle impact of Bikel's personality was also felt in *The Lark* when it opened at the Longacre Theatre in New York on November 17, 1955. When the next day's copies of the New York *Times* reached the newsstands, readers learned that Brooks Atkinson considered Theodore Bikel "artless and human enough to bring a cerebral play down to earth

THEODORE BIKEL

whenever he appears." Starring Julie Harris, the play ran on Broadway until June 2, 1956.

When *The Lark* closed after 229 performances, Bikel was signed for a supporting role in the film, *The Vintage* (1957). He then made his television debut on the *United States Steel Hour* (December 5, 1956), and followed this appearance with a part in *There Shall Be No Night* on the *Hallmark Hall of Fame* (March 7, 1957). He next appeared on the movie screen as a French general in *The Pride and the Passion* (1957), as a Dutch captain in *The Colditz Story* (1957), and as a German submarine officer in *The Enemy Below* (1957).

Bikel returned to Broadway in the supporting role of Dr. Jacobson, the tenement physician, in Morton Wishengrad's *The Rope Dancers,* which opened at the Cort Theatre on November 20, 1957. "Theodore Bikel's lumbering, tired, modest, knowing physician is superb," the New York *Times* reviewer reported the next morning. The play, co-starring Siobhan McKenna and Art Carney, closed on May 3, 1958.

For the next two years Bikel dedicated himself to films and video plays. In 1958 he portrayed a Russian colonel in *Fräulein,* a sheriff in *The Defiant Ones,* and a psychiatrist in *I Want to Live.* The following year he was seen in *The Angry Hills, Woman Obsessed,* and *The Blue Angel.* Television claimed a larger share of his time after an "exceptionally good" portrayal of Captain Alvarado in *The Bridge of San Luis Rey* over the *DuPont Show of the Month* on January 21, 1958. He has since appeared on most of the leading TV drama series as well as on his own "specials," notably a Passover program entitled *Look Up and Live* (April 12, 1959), which he wrote and in which he starred.

In addition to his acting, Bikel was also creating a reputation as a folk singer. The success of his Elektra records had assured

BIKEL, THEODORE—*Continued*

him of a large audience when he gave his first solo concert at New York's Town Hall on October 5, 1958. People outside the hall who had not been fortunate enough to obtain tickets offered high prices for any seat in the auditorium. The concert was recorded by Elektra under the title of *Bravo Bikel.*

His other Elektra record albums include *Folk Songs of Israel, A Young Man and a Maid, Jewish Folk Songs, More Jewish Folk Songs, Songs of a Russian Gypsy, An Actor's Holiday,* and *Folk Songs From Just About Everywhere.* Bikel has given concerts throughout the United States and Canada and conducts a weekly FM radio program, *At Home With Theodore Bikel,* which is broadcast in New York City, Los Angeles, and San Francisco. His interest in folk songs led him to write *Folksongs and Footnotes; An International Songbook* (Meridian Books, 1960), containing eighty-four selections with commentaries.

In August 1959 Bikel was finally given the chance to put all his talents to work when he was assigned the role of Georg Von Trapp, the male lead opposite Mary Martin, in *The Sound of Music.* Inspired by the story of the Trapp family singers, the Rodgers and Hammerstein musical opened on October 5, 1959 in New Haven, Connecticut, and after a Boston tryout moved to the Lunt-Fontanne Theatre in New York on November 16, where it settled down for a long run. It had accumulated the unprecedented amount of $2,500,000 in advance sales before the curtain went up on its New York opening. As usual, Bikel went almost unnoticed in the reviews.

Indeed, Bikel seems to defy definition. In an article entitled "The Star Nobody Knows" (*Coronet,* January 1960), writer Arnold Hano commented: "For one thing, no Bikel role ever seems to resemble another Bikel role. . . . Bikel has been as old as 83 in one film and as young as 25 in another; his real age is 35. Even his weight (he's six feet, one-and-a-half inches tall) varies from 190 to 220. He speaks languages—English, French, German, Hebrew, Yiddish, Spanish, and Russian—in a voice that oddly blends soft-middle European with the clipped hardness of the British." Once wedded to an Israeli girl whom he met in Paris, married in New York. and divorced in Mexico, Bikel shuns leisure and follows an unorthodox working schedule. He owns two espresso coffee houses in Los Angeles, and his 1959 income from his various activities exceeded $100,000.

"It isn't true that a man can do only one thing well," Bikel has said of his career. "This is a fallacy in our thinking; specialization has many disadvantages. Take, for instance, doctors; no one trusts a man who isn't a specialist. Yet a general practitioner sees the whole, not the part. But today the GP is maligned, no matter how competent. I'm a GP."

References

Coronet 47:157+ Ja '60 por
N Y Herald Tribune p20 My 24 '60 por
N Y Times II p7 Mr 1 '59 por
Newsweek 51:63 F 24 '58

BJOERLING, JUSSI

Feb. 2, 1911-Sept. 9, 1960 Swedish tenor; sang roles from the Italian repertory with the Metropolitan Opera Company, beginning in 1938; made many recordings. See *Current Biography* (September) 1947.

Obituary

N Y Times p21 S 10 '60

BLACKWELL, (SAMUEL) EARL, (JR.)

May 3, 1913- Business executive; publisher
Address: b. 140 W. 57th St., New York 19; h. 171 W. 57th St., New York 19

Celebrity Service, Inc., is a unique organization that provides its clients with information about noted persons in all fields of endeavor. As its co-founder and president, Earl Blackwell has not only achieved success in business but has also satisfied his lifelong desire to hobnob with celebrities. Blackwell and a friend started the service in 1939 with a file of some 300 names. It can now provide its subscribers with facts on 100,000 famous people.

The files of Celebrity Service, Inc., contain dossiers on the renowned in the arts, business, education, literature, politics, religion, science, society, and sport. The majority of the requests that Blackwell receives, however, ask for data on celebrities in the world of entertainment. People in show business often entrust Blackwell with details that they have concealed from their own agents and friends, perhaps because he does not abuse these confidences and because he is, for them, an amiable and dedicated escort and friend. "Earl lives in a world of make-believe . . . where the heroes and heroines can do no wrong," Gloria Swanson has said of him. "He loves everybody and the feeling seems to be mutual."

Samuel Earl Blackwell, Jr., was born at the home of his maternal grandfather in Atlanta, Georgia on May 3, 1913, the son of Samuel Earl and Carrie (Lagomarsino) Blackwell. He and his sister, who is now Mrs. Mary Alexander of Redwood City, California, were reared in Atlanta, where his father was a cotton broker. "My childhood in Atlanta was surely the happiest anyone ever experienced," Blackwell says. "It was also, to me, one of the most glamorous."

From an early age, Earl had been attracted to famous people. An impassioned movie-goer, he also came into contact with real-life celebrities in Atlanta: he caddied for champion golfer Bobby Jones and, at the age of thirteen, ran errands for soprano Rosa Ponselle during the Atlanta stopover of a Metropolitan Opera tour.

Earl attended the Ella W. Smiley Grammar School, and, as a second-grader, achieved local celebrity by portraying the Cheshire Cat in a school production of *Alice in Wonderland.* He subsequently studied at Boys' High School in Atlanta and the Culver Military Academy in Indiana. Throughout the summer of 1927 Earl parked cars at the Atlanta baseball stadium in order to finance his first trip to New York. His declared destination was the home of relatives in Montclair, New Jersey, but, he says, "it wasn't the relatives or Montclair that intrigued me; it was New York." Before he returned to Atlanta, he had seen most of the shows then running on Broadway.

At the age of fifteen-and-a-half, Blackwell entered Oglethorpe University in Atlanta. There he majored in journalism and took part in many activities. He became president of the student body, president of the Pi Kappa Phi fraternity, a member of two social organizations, Lords Club and Boar's Head, and campus correspondent for the Atlanta *Georgian*. Active in the drama society, he staged an annual musical revue entitled *Petrel Follies*, and he once wrote a one-act play. He was graduated with a B.A. degree in 1932 and received the president's medallion for outstanding contributions to the school.

That summer Blackwell drove to Hollywood, armed with the determination to become an actor and with a letter of introduction to the publishing magnate William Randolph Hearst. Although he won a screen test and some bit parts at MGM (1936), Blackwell saw little hope of attaining success as an actor. He returned to New York to try his hand at playwriting, which he studied at Columbia University. His play, *Aries is Rising,* opened on Broadway in November 1939 with a cast headed by Constance Collier, but it suffered a chilly reception and closed after a brief run.

After his play failed, Blackwell decided to accept the advice of a friend, and, in partnership with another writer, Ted Strong, founded a service providing information about celebrities and their past and current activities. The first subscriber to this service was the Columbia Broadcasting System, which now takes ten annual subscriptions.

Blackwell's fledgling firm expanded considerably in size and prestige when he and Strong were appointed directors of the celebrity department of the New York World's Fair of 1939-40. Since that time, Celebrity Service has continued to grow, and, when Strong sold his interest in the organization several years ago, Blackwell assumed full responsibility for its direction. He now employs a couple of dozen assistants and earns about $500,000 a year.

Blackwell's clients include the major newspapers, radio and television stations, manufacturers, hotels, stores, charitable and civic organizations, government agencies, and, of course, celebrities. Five times a week in New York and three times a week in Paris, London, Hollywood, and Rome they receive the *Celebrity Bulletin,* which details the comings and goings of famous persons, along with information on their current activities and ways to get in touch with them.

Celebrity Service circulates several other publications. The weekly *Theatrical Calendar* presents details of current and future activities of the New York legitimate stage. The annual *Contact Book* contains listings of businesses serving the needs of persons in the entertainment world.

Fabian Bachrach

EARL BLACKWELL

Another recent publication of Earl Blackwell's Celebrity Service has stirred up considerable interest, especially in New York City. Entitled *Celebrity Register,* the volume contains information about 2,240 celebrities. Although it is priced at $26 and can be bought only at such chic New York establishments as Tiffany's, Twenty One, and the Stork Club and a select number of bookstores, it has sold tens of thousands of copies. Its editor in chief, Cleveland Amory, makes clear in the introduction that "No one has paid to get in or, for that matter, to get out."

Subscribers may telephone the service at any time for further information; Blackwell's concern receives some 5,000 calls a week. Most of these request the telephone numbers or addresses of celebrities, but clients may also ask for the name of a star willing to endorse a cigarette or introduce a new tennis racket. Celebrities willing to appear at a trade fair, fashion show, or charity benefit, or at the opening of a new hotel or supermarket are also much in demand. A writer for movie magazines was given a list of stars interested in cats, and an organization seeking a lecturer on mathematics was supplied with a list of the ten leading mathematicians in the United States.

Although it takes pride in its ability to supply information, Celebrity Service, Inc., found itself unprepared on one occasion. A newspaper client wanted to know the name of Tommy Manville's seventh wife. Unable to find it in the files, the researcher called Manville himself. When Manville was unable to remember, the service got the information by calling the third Mrs. Manville.

From the earliest days of Celebrity Service, Blackwell has been vigilant in protecting the famous persons in his files. In order to spare them possible embarrassment, Blackwell will not

BLACKWELL, EARL—*Continued*

offer data to law firms, collection agencies, or other organizations which might use the information to harass the celebrities.

Blackwell is a director of the Mayor's Committee on Scholastic Achievement and of the Embassy Foundation, which annually sponsors a ball to benefit worthy organizations like the Childrens Asthma Research Institute. He is a Republican and a Roman Catholic. Described by Dean Jennings in the *Saturday Evening Post* (April 2, 1955) as "an unhurried, drawling man with big brown eyes and Southern-plantation manners," he is five feet eleven inches tall, weighs 165 pounds and has brown hair. He belongs to the New York Town Tennis Club and says that his hobbies are "traveling, the sea, and sun."

Blackwell spends almost six months of each year abroad—in Italy, where the press calls him "Mr. Celebrità"; in Paris, where he is known as "Monsieur Célèbre"; and in London. A bachelor, he is frequently seen in newspaper photographs, escorting such stars as Zsa Zsa Gabor, Tallulah Bankhead, and Ginger Rogers. He lives in a New York City penthouse, within walking distance of the main office of Celebrity Service. Jennings has suggested that, with his custom-tailored clothing, gold accessories (many of them the gifts of his celebrity friends), and dapper air, he might be taken for "an influential foreign emissary, living incognito in New York," or "an international banker," or "a mysterious manipulator of political strings."

Blackwell is glad that he abandoned his acting aspirations. "If I'd stayed in Hollywood I might have clicked in a small way . . . I might still be out there struggling for some small part. I was luckier. In fact, I must be the luckiest man who ever lived. I've always been interested in people in the limelight . . . and now . . . almost every moment of every day, I'm in personal contact with the most exciting people in the world. The most amazing thing of all is that I make a living by doing it!"

References

Atlanta Constitution p13 Ja 9 '60 por
Sat Eve Post 227:22 Ap 2 '55 pors

BOHLEN, CHARLES E(USTIS) Aug. 30, 1904- United States government official

Address: b. Department of State, Washington, 25, D.C.; h. 2811 Dumbarton Ave., N.W., Washington, D.C.

NOTE: This biography supersedes the article which appeared in *Current Biography* in 1948.

Appointed Acting Assistant Secretary of State for International Organization Affairs in September 1960, Charles E. Bohlen directed tactics and strategy at the U.N. General Assembly session which convened at that time. About a year before, in November, Bohlen, the dean of the Russian experts in the State Department, had left the Philippines, where he served as Ambassador, and returned to Washington to take up responsibilities as special

assistant for Soviet affairs to Secretary of State .Christian A. Herter. By his own estimate, Bohlen has engaged in some 4,000 hours of talk with Russian officials in the thirty-one years of his Foreign Service career. Since the end of World War II he has been a Russian interpreter and adviser on Soviet affairs to five Secretaries of State and has been present at all major meetings of United States and Soviet officials held during the past three decades. Senator Mike Mansfield of Montana has called Bohlen "one of the very few men qualified by training, experience, and linguistics to cope with the Russians." In June 1960 he was honored with the rank of career ambassador, the highest professional rating in the Foreign Service.

Charles Eustis Bohlen, one of three children of Charles and Celestine (Eustis) Bohlen, was born in Clayton, New York on August 30, 1904. He spent his early childhood in the winter health and pleasure resort of Aiken, South Carolina, where his father was a banker and well-known sportsman. When the boy was twelve, the family moved to Ipswich, Massachusetts. Bohlen was graduated from St. Paul's School in Concord, New Hampshire in 1923. He enrolled at Harvard, where he played on the scrub football team and became a member of the socially exclusive Porcellian Club. Although he majored in modern European history as an undergraduate (and elected a course in Russian history), he had no intention of becoming a diplomat. Soon after he obtained a B.A. degree from Harvard in 1927, he embarked on a tramp steamer for a trip around the world.

In 1929 Bohlen came back to Washington. He was one of a small group of candidates who passed the Foreign Service examination that year, and was assigned to a vice-consulship in Prague, where he remained from 1929 to 1931. The State Department, which had opened a division of Russian studies in anticipation of the resuming of relations between the United States and Russia, selected Bohlen as one of six men assigned to study Russian language, literature, history, and political theory. Another Foreign Service officer thus honored was George F. Kennan.

Bohlen went to Paris in 1931 as vice-consul and language officer. He studied at the Institute of Oriental Languages under the noted French teacher of Russian, Paul Boyer, and devoted his spare time to perfecting his working knowledge of the language by attending Russian church services and chatting with White Russian refugees in the Parisian cafés. One summer he dispensed with English altogether when he lived in Estonia with a Russian family. By the time of the Potsdam Conference in 1945, Bohlen was so fluent in the language that he could explain the technicalities of American baseball to Joseph Stalin. He now speaks Russian like a Muscovite and can exchange banter with Khrushchev in the Communist party chief's own racy vernacular.

The United States resumed diplomatic relations with Russia in 1933. William C. Bullitt, the United States Ambassador to the Soviet Union, selected Bohlen in 1934 to serve in the

United States Embassy in Moscow as a member of the first diplomatic mission. Bohlen started as vice-consul, but was soon promoted to third secretary. Since relations between the United States and the Soviet Union were at that time relaxed and friendly, Bohlen was free to travel in the Soviet Union and to meet its citizens.

In 1935 Bohlen returned to the Department of State in Washington where he joined the Division of Eastern European Affairs. In 1937 he returned to Moscow, stopping off en route at two international conferences at both of which he served as secretary for the American delegations. They were the International Sugar Conference in London and a conference in Brussels which unsuccessfully tried to reach a settlement in the Far East between Japan and China.

When Bohlen returned to Moscow in 1937 as second secretary and consul, he found that the atmosphere had changed. The political purges had engendered strain, imposed restrictions, and generated hostility and suspicion towards aliens. He remained in Moscow until 1940, when he was summoned to Tokyo to serve as second secretary of the American Embassy. He served in Japan until the Japanese attacked Pearl Harbor on December 7, 1941. Along with the rest of the American Embassy staff, he was placed in internment for six months. After he was released, he returned to Washington to serve as acting chief of the Division of Eastern European Affairs in the State Department.

Having accompanied Secretary of State Cordell Hull to the Moscow Conference in 1943, Bohlen remained at the American Embassy to serve as first secretary. At the end of the year President Franklin D. Roosevelt assigned him as his interpreter at the Big Three Conference in Teheran. After that meeting, Bohlen returned to Moscow to stay until the middle of 1944, when he was asked to come to Washington to advise the United States delegation at the Dumbarton Oaks conversations on international organization. In December 1944 he was designated assistant to the Secretary of State for White House liaison by Secretary of State Edward R. Stettinius.

International conferences occupied most of Bohlen's time in 1945. He accompanied President Roosevelt to the Big Three Conference at Yalta, where he served primarily as interpreter; he was political and liaison officer for the United States delegation at the United Nations Conference on International Organization at San Francisco; and he journeyed to Moscow as an adviser and interpreter for Harry Hopkins, who was trying to reach an understanding with Joseph Stalin on world problems and to work on a Russian-language version of the United Nations Charter. In the same year Bohlen served as a political adviser at the Berlin Conference, assisted the American delegates to the meeting of the Council of Foreign Ministers in London, and acted as President Truman's Russian interpreter at the Potsdam Conference.

Dept. of State—Whit Keith, Jr.

CHARLES E. BOHLEN

Between conferences Bohlen worked at his assignment as liaison officer between the State Department and the White House, a job to which he once referred in private as "the sewer-pipe between the White House and the State Department." In this capacity, he was one of the first to observe the growing and as yet unpublicized rift between the Soviet Union and the United States.

In 1946 and 1947 Secretary of State James F. Byrnes and his successor, Secretary of State George C. Marshall, enlisted the special services of Bohlen at international conferences. Although Bohlen had at first served only as a language interpreter, he was being increasingly called upon for advice in policy planning. In recognition of Bohlen's changing role, Secretary of State Marshall appointed him his personal adviser on Soviet affairs in 1947. In July of the same year Bohlen became the counselor of the Department of State, a post carrying equal rank with that of an Assistant Secretary of State.

In theory, the duties of a counselor of the Department of State consist of advising and assisting the Secretary of State in working out solutions to major problems in foreign relations. Actually, Bohlen had many additional tasks to perform. He was responsible for liaison between the State Department and Congress, he served as principal interpreter at major conferences, and he was the chief spokesman of the State Department to the press and radio corps. He was also a policy aide to Secretary of State George C. Marshall at the United Nations, and served as general adviser to Under Secretary of State Robert A. Lovett on questions of high policy. In June 1948 he was one of five diplomats whom President Harry S. Truman nominated for promotion to the rank of minister.

(Continued next page)

BOHLEN, CHARLES E.—*Continued*

In July 1948 the Russians imposed a blockade on Berlin after a dispute in which they had insisted that only Soviet Zone currency was valid in Berlin. In that month Bohlen went to Berlin to confer with General Lucius D. Clay, United States Military Governor in Germany, Lewis W. Douglas, Ambassador to Great Britain, and Lieutenant General Walter Bedell Smith, Ambassador to Russia. In London he explored the possibilities for finding a way out of the predicament with British and French officials. In September 1948 he accompanied Secretary of State Marshall to the meeting of the United Nations Assembly in Paris.

In 1949, soon after he was promoted to the rank of career minister, Bohlen transferred his activities to Paris as counselor of the American Embassy. In that capacity, he attended the 1949 conference of the Council of Foreign Ministers. In 1951 he returned to Washington to resume his responsibilities as counselor of the State Department. Now the third-ranking official in the State Department, he was the aide to Secretary of State John Foster Dulles at the Japanese Peace Conference in San Francisco and helped to draft replies to Soviet requests for a Big Four meeting.

The name of Charles E. Bohlen reached the headlines in 1953 when President Dwight D. Eisenhower nominated him as Ambassador to the Soviet Union. The nomination was bitterly contested by a group of ultraconservative Republican Senators headed by Joseph R. McCarthy who linked him with the Yalta Conference and with what they called the "Truman-Acheson policies of appeasement" of the Russians. Bohlen refused to see the Yalta agreements as a "great mistake"; the cold war, in his opinion, grew out of the violation of the agreements. During the hearings McCarthy called Bohlen "part and parcel of the Acheson-Hiss-Truman group in the State Department—the group we promised we'd repudiate when in power." But nobody leveled the charge of pro-Communism at him or turned up any evidence that impugned his loyalty. In spite of the controversy, the nomination of Bohlen was confirmed by a vote of 74 to 13.

In Moscow Bohlen witnessed the purge of Lavrenti P. Beria and the demotion of Georgi M. Malenkov in favor of Nikolai A. Bulganin. He read widely in Soviet periodicals and is reported to have drafted more dispatches than any other American Ambassador in recent history. His stay in Moscow ended in April 1957 when he was transferred to the Philippines by John Foster Dulles. Dulles was criticized for banishing the Soviet expert from a crucial post, and it was no secret that Dulles was unhappy with the Ambassador whose views on Soviet affairs differed so markedly from his own. The regret that Bohlen did not conceal when he left Moscow was not remedied when Premier Bulganin told him: "We do not understand why they are taking you from us." His friends entertained him with skits reviewing his career, and hundreds of members of the Western community in Moscow saw him off at the airport.

As Ambassador to the Philippines, Bohlen negotiated a military base agreement that represented a compromise between the pride of the Filipinos and the security requirements of the United States. He also worked on unsettled Philippine war claims against the United States, and dealt with other problems growing out of the island's drifting away from its former dependence on the United States. When Bohlen was about to leave Manila, President Carlos Garcia praised Bohlen for his statesmanship and his furtherance of Philippine-American friendship.

In Manila Bohlen kept up with Soviet affairs by reading Russian books and periodicals. After two and a half years in the Philippines he was restored to his primary interest by Secretary of State Christian A. Herter, who appointed him his special assistant for Soviet affairs. In order to accept the post, Bohlen waived the retirement that he had contemplated and accepted a reduction in salary from that which he had earned as Ambassador to the Philippines. In January 1960 he led the fruitless negotiations with the Russians that tried to settle the Soviet Union's lend-lease debt to the United States.

Charles Eustis Bohlen is married to Avis Howard Thayer, whom he met when she was visiting her brother, Charles Thayer, at the American Embassy in Moscow in 1943. They have two children, Avis and Charles. Bohlen stands six feet one inch in height and weighs about 180 pounds. Impatient with embassy formalities, he has been known to put his feet up on the desks of the State Department and to greet his colleagues with "hello, professor." In Moscow he sat in on the poker sessions of the Sunday Evening Society, but had to give up golf, a recreation unknown to the Russians. "The Soviet Union," Bohlen has said, "is not a mystery. It's just a secret."

References

N Y Times Mag p14+ O 18 '59
Sat Eve Post 224:34+ S 15 '51
U S News 47:58+ Jl 27 '59

International Who's Who, 1958
Who's Who in America, 1960-61
World Biography (1954)

BOLLING, RICHARD (WALKER) May 17, 1916- United States Representative from Missouri

Address: b. House Office Bldg., Washington 25, D.C.; 643 U.S. Courts Bldg., 811 Grand Ave., Kansas City, Mo.; h. 3409 Lowell St., Washington 16, D.C.; 648 W. 59th Ter., Kansas City, Mo.

The Representative in Congress of the Fifth Missouri District for the past eleven years is Richard Bolling, a Democrat, who has for most of that period been a member of the House Rules Committee and of the Joint Economic Committee. As a member of the House Rules

Committee, Bolling was instrumental in 1956 in bringing both the school construction aid bill and the civil rights bill out of the committee and on to the floor of the House. On the Joint Economic Committee he has served as chairman of several subcommittees investigating economic conditions. Before becoming a politician, Bolling was a teacher, university administrator, and organization director.

Born in New York City on May 17, 1916, Richard Walker Bolling was named after his surgeon father, Dr. Richard Walker Bolling; his mother's maiden name was Florence Losey Easton. One of two boys (his brother, John Minge Bolling, is deceased), Richard Bolling was brought up in New York City and Huntsville, Alabama. After completing grade school, he entered Phillips Exeter Academy at Exeter, New Hampshire. When he was fifteen his father died, and he returned to Huntsville. At the University of the South, Sewanee, Tennessee, he majored in French. He was elected to the Phi Delta Theta social fraternity and to several honorary societies, and headed the student body as president of the Order of Gownsmen. At Phillips Exeter he had belonged to the soccer and swimming teams; at the University of the South he won letters in football and track.

Awarded his B.A. degree in 1937, Bolling was engaged for one year as a teacher and coach at the Sewanee Military Academy before he re-entered the University of the South for postgraduate work in English literature. After he received his M.A. degree there in 1939, he did additional postgraduate work at Vanderbilt University, Nashville, Tennessee. Overseas for four years during World War II with the United States Army, Bolling saw service in Australia, New Guinea, the Philippines, and Japan, and advanced in rank from private to lieutenant colonel between April 1941 when he enlisted and July 1946 when he was released to the reserve. He was decorated with the Legion of Merit in 1945 and with the Bronze Star in 1946.

For one year after his discharge, Bolling served as director of student activities and veterans affairs at the University of Kansas City in Missouri. Having decided that his interests lay in politics rather than in education, Bolling accepted a position as Midwestern director of Americans for Democratic Action in 1947. When he became vice-chairman of the American Veterans Committee later that year, George Eckel (New York *Times*, June 23, 1947) said that Bolling made possible a "decisive disposal of the issue of Communist influence" in the organization's leadership and policy.

Entering the 1948 Congressional race as a Democrat in Missouri's Fifth District (a residential, business, and industrial area in northwest Kansas City), Bolling made his principal campaign issue repeal of the Taft-Hartley Act. In November he defeated the incumbent, Albert L. Reeves, Jr., a Republican, by 59,961 to 47,371 votes. Re-elected to each succeeding Congress, Bolling won the approval of his constituents in November 1958 by 53,622 votes to only 22,953 for his Republican opponent.

During his freshman term Bolling favored the administration's six-year housing program (July

Miller of Washington
RICHARD BOLLING

1949) and the voluntary Fair Employment Practice Commission bill (February 1950). He cast negative votes on the coalition, as opposed to the administration bill, for repealing the Taft-Hartley Act (May 1949) and the Lodge-Gossett constitutional amendment (July 1950).

In connection with his committee work, Bolling was one of four Democrats on the Joint Committee on the Economic Report who urged in April 1951 that Congress increase taxes by $10 billion in order to curb inflation. On the House Banking and Currency Committee he sought unsuccessfully in 1952 to add to the defense production bill an amendment authorizing the President to seize the strike-bound steel mills.

A revolt led by Bolling against Rules Committee chairman Howard W. Smith of Virginia in 1956 resulted in clearing for House action both the school construction aid bill and the Eisenhower administration's civil rights bill. Smith was able to delay consideration of the bills by the committee until June, when Bolling succeeded in effecting an 8 to 3 vote in favor of reporting the bills. Later, the House rejected the school aid bill. The civil rights bill, which won approval in the lower chamber, was not reported out of the Senate Judiciary Committee.

When the civil rights measure was again deliberated by the Rules Committee, in April 1957, Bolling charged that a "deal was on" between Republicans and Southern Democrats to prevent the bill from reaching the floor of the House. The measure, reported to the lower chamber on May 21 by a vote of 8 to 4, was passed by both House and Senate and signed into law in September.

The Joint Committee on the Economic Report, now known as the Joint Economic Committee, has on several occasions named Bolling chairman of subcommittees. As head of the economic statistics subcommittee, Bolling, with other members of the group, recommended in De-

BOLLING, RICHARD—Continued

cember 1955 that government statistics be improved by employing more trained statisticians and economic analysts.

In January 1956 Bolling's foreign economic policy subcommittee, after studying the relationship between American trade policy and domestic prosperity, proposed reducing tariffs and expanding technical aid to foreign nations. On another subcommittee, organized in March 1959, Bolling directed a comparative study of American and Soviet economic growth. After the unit began its hearings in November, Bolling said that the greatest need of the American economy is the removal of "special interest tax erosions," which would have the effect of adding to the tax base "fantastic sums—tens of billions of dollars" (New York *Herald Tribune,* November 16, 1959).

Bolling also presided over a special Rules subcommittee which in June 1956 urged that a standing committee on administrative practices and procedures be established. Dedicated to maintaining the traditional separation of powers in government, the proposed committee would study complaints concerning the abuses of administrative agencies, the need for legislative standards to limit their authority, and the effect of such laws once they are enacted.

On key labor issues over the years Congressman Bolling voted "yea" on increasing unemployment compensation benefits (July 1954), raising the minimum wage to $1 an hour (July 1955), and the labor-management reporting and disclosure bill (August 1958). He voted "nay" on using the Taft-Hartley Act to halt the steel strike (June 1952) and substituting the Landrum-Griffin bill for the labor-management reporting and disclosure measure (August 1959).

As for other domestic measures, Bolling favored maintaining 90 per cent farm price supports (June 1952), retaining the nonpartisan nature of the Tariff Commission (June 1953), raising the personal income tax exemption (March 1954), the Social Security amendments (July 1955), the Colorado River project (March 1956), the school construction bill (July 1956), the civil rights bills (July 1956 and June 1957), Alaskan statehood (May 1958), and Hawaiian statehood (March 1959).

Bolling cast negative votes on a measure to end consumer price controls (June 1952), revision of the Atomic Energy Act (July 1954), natural gas act exemptions (July 1955), the Powell amendment to the school aid bill (July 1956), and a motion to recommit the civil rights act with instructions to insert a provision for jury trials (June 1957).

Believing that the United States should assume an active role in international affairs, Bolling was against reducing economic aid to Europe by $615,000,000 (May 1952); he supported the authorization of the Eisenhower Middle East Doctrine (January 1957) and the mutual security bill (June 1959). He has also favored reciprocal trade, voting for the three-year extension of the Trade Agreements Act in February 1955 and the five-year extension in June 1958.

From time to time Representative Bolling has expressed his views on important issues in articles he has contributed to national magazines. In the *New Republic* (July 16, 1956) he attributed the defeat of the school construction bill of 1956 to the adoption of the Powell amendment. In September 1951 he wrote an article, "Politics in Dispersal," for the *Bulletin of the Atomic Scientists,* in which he underscored the importance of decentralizing vital industries and government services in the nuclear age.

Richard Bolling was married to the former Barbara Stratton, a chemistry teacher, on June 7, 1945. Their family includes a daughter, Andrea Walker, and Mrs. Bolling's three children by a previous marriage, Angus Roy 3d, Brenda Ann, and Deborah. The hazel-eyed, brown-haired Congressman is six feet one inch in height and weighs some 205 pounds. He is an Episcopalian. He is a past vice-president of the Missouri Association for Social Welfare and a member of the Jefferson's Island Club in Kansas City. For relaxation he goes fishing and gardens. A fan of folk music and jazz, Bolling encourages his wife's life-long interest in jazz, and in March 1959 they sponsored the Washington Jazz Jubilee in aid of charity.

References

Kansas City (Mo.) Star O 19 '50; Mr 31 '55
New Leader 37:3 N 29 '54
Parents Mag 25:32+ Mr '50 pors
St. Louis (Mo.) Post-Dispatch D 12 '58
Congressional Directory (1959)
Who's Who in America, 1958-59

BONOMI, MARIA (ANNA OLGA LUIZA) (bō-nô'mē) July 8, 1935- Artist

Address: b. c/o Lívio Abramo, Estúdio Gravura, Caixa Postal 340, São Paulo S.P., Brazil; h. Avenida Paulista 854, São Paulo, Brazil

A gifted twenty-five-year-old Brazilian artist, Maria Bonomi, who came to Brazil from her native Italy as a child, has received much acclaim in international art circles for the impressionist quality and inventive techniques of her woodcuts. She has had one-man shows at the Museum of Modern Art in São Paulo in 1956, the Roland de Aenlle Gallery in New York City in 1958, and the Pan American Union in Washington, D.C. in 1959. "Though amazingly intricate," wrote a critic in *Brazil* (number 4, 1958), "her work in black and white prints has interesting depth and attractiveness that is moving and arresting for the general public as well as for patrons and connoisseurs."

Maria Anna Olga Luiza Bonomi was born on July 8, 1935 in Meina, Italy on Lake Maggiore to Georgina (Martinelli) and Ambrogio Bonomi, an engineer. Her maternal grandfather, José Martinelli, migrated from Italy to Brazil and built the first South American skyscraper, the Prédio Martinelli, in São Paulo. Maria has one brother, Angelo.

Since childhood Maria has lived in São Paulo. She became fond of drawing when very young, and by the age of nine had attracted the attention of her teachers. When she was thirteen, the Brazilian artist Lasar Segall saw her drawings and encouraged her to study drawing and watercolor at the studio of Yolanda Mohalyi. Later she worked in oils under the supervision of Karl Plattner. She received her academic instruction at the Colégio das Cônegas de Sto. Agostinho in São Paulo, and the Gymnasio from which she was graduated in 1952 and the Lyceum Classic from which she was graduated in 1955.

During 1951 and 1952 Maria Bonomi took several trips through Brazil and Europe. In Brazil she was much inspired by the baroque church architecture that she saw around her. In Italy she studied graphic arts with Enrico Prampolini and Emilio Vedova. At this time she began to show her work in São Paulo art exhibitions: the group shows at the Gallery of Contemporary Art of the São Paulo Museum of Art in 1952 and 1954; the First Salon of August exhibition in 1953, where she won honorable mention for a painting; and the Third Biennial in 1955. Her work received much praise, and interest in it soon developed outside of São Paulo and Brazil. In 1955 she was the youngest artist shown in the Brazilian exhibition in Neuchâtel, Switzerland.

Concentrating more and more on engraving after 1954, she studied with Lívio Abramo in São Paulo. Within two years her prints were displayed at the Fourth Salon of Modern Art in São Paulo and the Fifth Salon of Modern Art in Rio de Janeiro.

The first solo exhibition of Miss Bonomi's art was held at the Museum of Modern Art in São Paulo in 1956. Especially noteworthy were her bold and skillful drawings of lepers, which she had made on a trip to Pernambuco in northeastern Brazil. As a result of this show she won the second prize for contemporary art in São Paulo and the Ingram-Merrill scholarship, under which she studied graphic art with Seong Moy at Pratt Institute in New York City in 1957 and 1958. She also studied with Hans Müller and Meyer Schapiro at Columbia University. When she returned to São Paulo, Miss Bonomi resumed working with Lívio Abramo in a private workshop called Estúdio Gravura. She is now an assistant professor at the Brazilian Graphic Art School in São Paulo.

Her first one-man show in New York City was held at the Roland de Aenlle Gallery in November and December 1958. The theme of most of the woodcuts, in which Miss Bonomi was at times guided by the wood grain and knotholes, is the destruction of New York. Many viewers felt that *Stillness in Motion* was one of the most outstanding of the forty-three prints displayed. Other striking prints were *City in Bloom,* which conveys the suggestion of tulips, *Soaring Aloft* (selected by Seong Moy as the best in his graphic arts course at Pratt), and *Restrained Hope,* a print with lines as delicate as gossamer threads.

Reviewing the de Aenlle show, Dore Ashton wrote in the New York *Times* (November 21, 1958): "It is rare to find a young artist today using woodcut as a primary means of

American Brazilian
Assn. Inc.

MARIA BONOMI

expression. . . . Miss Bonomi can twist her knife, scrape and incise with agility, and knows the value of variation. . . . Miss Bonomi uses assorted tools to create streaking white lines, or rounded white masses that often suggest the structures and artificial lighting of New York. . . . It is good to see a tradition, begun with Ballotton and continued with Munch and Kirchner, carried into contemporary terms."

In January and February 1959 an exhibit devoted exclusively to Miss Bonomi's creations was held at the Pan American Union in Washington, D.C. Among the woodcuts were *Foreboding, Thoughts, Drum Beat,* and *Oblivion.* In the following year two of her prints were exhibited with the work of other Brazilian graphic artists at the Smithsonian Institution in Washington, D.C.

Her work has been displayed at Belo Horizonte and Porto Alegre, Brazil under the auspices of the United States Cultural Association. In New York she has been represented at the National Arts Club, International Festival of Art of the Jewish Federation, Museum of Modern Art, and New York Public Library. The Print Club of Philadelphia has also exhibited her woodcuts and prints.

Miss Bonomi's art has found a place in some distinguished private collections in Brazil, Italy, and the United States, including that of Governor Nelson A. Rockefeller. The first of her illustrations to appear in book form were those accompanying the poems of the Brazilian poet, Geraldo Azevedo, entitled *Vesperal de Silêncio.*

Maria Bonomi is a member of the Museum of Modern Art in Rio de Janeiro, the Museum of Modern Art in São Paulo, and Print Club of Philadelphia. She has brown hair and brown

BONOMI, MARIA—*Continued*

eyes and is about five feet six inches in height and about 145 pounds in weight. Her favorite outdoor sports are fishing, horseback riding, and swimming. She is a Roman Catholic and a naturalized citizen of Brazil.

References

Brazil 32 no4:7 '58 por
Habitat 10:40 Jl '59 por

BORBOLLA, DANIEL F. RUBÍN DE LA
See Rubín de la Borbolla, Daniel F.

BOYD, LOUISE A(RNER) Sept. 16, 1887- Explorer; geographer

Address: b. c/o American Geographical Society, Broadway at 156th St., New York 32; 210 Post St., San Francisco 8, Calif.; h. "Maple Lawn," 1312 Mission Ave., San Rafael, Calif.

In an age of global problems, when the arctic regions have become more important in transportation and military strategy, the polar expeditions of Louise A. Boyd, begun some thirty-five years ago, have grown in value. She has broken trails both in increasing man's knowledge of the north and in opening exploration as a career for women. She has organized, financed, and led several scientific expeditions to the arctic, including a flight in 1955 which made her the first woman to reach the North Pole. The United States government and a number of foreign governments have honored her, and in February 1960 she became the first woman councilor of the American Geographical Society.

The daughter of a wealthy mining operator, Louise Arner Boyd was born to John Franklin and Louise Cook (Arner) Boyd in San Rafael, California on September 16, 1887. She was educated at Miss Stewart's School in San Rafael and at Miss Murison's School in San Francisco; shooting and horseback riding were among her girlhood accomplishments. In 1920, after the death of her father, she became president of the Boyd Investment Company, a private estate.

Reading about arctic exploration had made her interested in the polar regions, and in the summer of 1924 Louise Boyd went on a cruise to Iceland, Greenland, and Lapland. She returned to Greenland from California in 1926 to organize the first of her own expeditions. Chartering the motorship *Hobby*, she led a team of six researchers on an exploration that included microscopic study of arctic flora and fauna. On her early trips to the north she was also an enthusiastic hunter and reportedly shot twenty-nine polar bears. Her expeditions, however, were scientific in purpose. She handled all the photographic work, did much of the surveying, and planned each project so carefully in advance that she later had few tales to relate of hair-raising escape from disaster.

While in Norway in 1928, preparing for another venture into the arctic, she heard that the polar explorer Roald Amundsen had disappeared on a rescue flight in the north. She immediately joined in the search, putting her services, her ship *Hobby*, and other resources of her expedition under the direction of the Norwegian and French governments, which were undertaking the long, far-reaching hunt. The search was fruitless, but for her contributions Miss Boyd was awarded the decoration of the Order of St. Olaf, first class, of Norway and was named a Chevalier of the French Legion of Honor.

Other Boyd expeditions left Norway, aboard the S.S. *Veslekari*, in 1931, 1933, 1937, and 1938 to take hydrographical soundings and make cartographical, geological, botanical, and meteorological studies. Her explorations included regions in and around Franz Josef Land, Spitsbergen, Greenland, Jan Mayen Island, and eastern arctic Canada.

According to historical records, Louise Boyd's ship was the first to sail to the inner ends of Ice Fjord, Greenland. In recognition of her exploration in this area in 1931, the Danish government gave the name of Louise A. Boyd Land to the territory in the vicinity of the de Geer glacier. Unusually favorable weather in 1938 enabled her research team to travel further north along the Greenland coast than any other Americans had ever gone by sea.

Most of the several expeditions that Miss Boyd organized and financed between 1926 and 1938 were carried out under the auspices of the American Geographical Society, to which she reported her scientific findings. The society published her books on the arctic, *The Fiord Region of East Greenland* (1935) and *Coast of Northeast Greenland* (1949); and several of her articles appeared in its quarterly *Geographical Review*, including "Further Explorations of East Greenland" (July 1934). Another, nonarctic, book of Louise Boyd that the American Geographical Society published was *Polish Countrysides* (1937).

In June 1941, before the United States entered World War II (but was carefully studying its defense areas), Miss Boyd was chosen to head an investigation of magnetic and radio phenomena in the Greenland and other arctic waters. She worked in co-operation with the National Bureau of Standards, which installed its scientific equipment on the schooner *Effie M. Morrissey*. The veteran skipper of the northern seas, Robert Bartlett, served as captain for Miss Boyd.

Soon after completing her mission in early December 1941, Louise Boyd became a technical expert in the War Department. For some fifteen months during 1942 and 1943 she helped make available to government agencies thousands of maps, photographs, and scientific reports on strategic areas of the arctic and also offered her own firsthand information about the fjords of Greenland and Spitsbergen. The need for military secrecy left the value of her work unpublicized until March 1949 when the Department of the Army awarded her its Certificate of Appreciation for "outstanding patriotic service to the Army as a contributor of geographic knowledge and consultant during the critical period prior to and after the start of World War II."

At the time of receiving the award Louise Boyd was more or less in retirement from her arctic explorations. She was about to make a trip to Portugal to read a paper to the International Geographic Congress. Years earlier, in 1934, she had represented the American Geographical Society, the National Academy of Science, and the Department of State at an international geographical conference in Warsaw and had represented the Department of State at an international photogrammetrical conference in Paris. In 1939 she was a member of the advisory committee at the sixth Pacific Science Congress.

Since childhood Louise Boyd had dreamed of some day going to the North Pole; to fulfill this goal, she organized her eighth arctic expedition. On June 16, 1955, having chartered an airplane in Norway, she made a successful flight over and around the North Pole with a small group whose task was to photograph the area. She had made her other expeditions by ship and dog sled.

As a culmination of her long association with the American Geographical Society, Miss Boyd was elected on February 7, 1960 to the society's council, its chief policy-making body. She became the first woman to hold the position of councilor in the 108-year history of the organization, whose membership of 4,200 is made up mainly of professional geographers, explorers, and educators. Her contributions to the work of the society had included the establishment in 1956 of the Louise A. Boyd Publishing Fund.

Many American and foreign organizations have paid tribute to Miss Boyd for achievement in exploration. In 1939 the University of California and Mills College awarded her honorary LL.D. degrees. In June 1959 the American Polar Society named her to its short list of illustrious honorary members (as the first woman so honored) and credited her with having contributed more to the knowledge of Greenland, the Greenland Sea, Spitsbergen, and Franz Josef Land than any other explorer. She is also a member of the board of governors of the American Polar Society.

Other professional associations to which she belongs include the Royal Geological Society in London (Fellow), the American Society for Photogrammetry, and the National Institute of Social Sciences. Also interested in civic affairs, she held the position of park commissioner of the city of San Rafael for many years beginning in 1920. She serves on the executive committee and board of governors of the San Francisco Symphony Orchestra. She is a member of the Colonial Dames of America and is a Republican and an Episcopalian.

In appearance and manner Louise A. Boyd belies the popular conception of an arctic explorer. She is feminine, graceful, and gentle—with blue eyes and gray hair. One of her hobbies is gardening, and she belongs to several clubs and other organizations concerned with horticulture. Describing her feelings when she flew over the North Pole, in a brief article for *Parade* (February 2, 1958), Miss Boyd wrote, "Aside from the contribution which every scientist makes to our nation's welfare, great per-

Bakalar-Cosmo

LOUISE A. BOYD

sonal rewards, often intangible, also await him. The thrill of adventure as he probes an uncharted field—the sense of pride and gratification as he reaches an aimed-for goal—such things can be his meat and drink."

References

Christian Sci Mon p15 Je 19 '59
N Y Herald Tribune p4+ Mr 19 '49 por; p1+ F 8 '60 por
National Cyclopaedia of American Biography current vol G (1943-46)
Who's Who in America, 1960-61
Who's Who of American Women, 1958-59
World Biography (1954)

BREUER, MARCEL (LAJOS) (broi'ĕr)
May 21, 1902- Architect
Address: b. Marcel Breuer & Associates, Architects, 201 E. 57th St., New York 22; h. 75 West Rd., New Canaan, Conn.

> NOTE: This biography supersedes the article which appeared in *Current Biography* in 1941.

Born in Hungary and trained at Germany's Bauhaus, Marcel Breuer is regarded as a frontiersman of contemporary American architecture because of his early and successful introduction of European modernism into private homes and academic buildings in the United States and his adaptation of European design to American technology. Since moving to the United States in 1937, where he taught at Harvard University during his first nine years, he has greatly enhanced the reputation he had won in Europe as an influential "form-giver" of the twentieth century, especially in domestic architecture, including interior design.

(Continued next page)

Hans Namuth

MARCEL BREUER

Breuer's most important work to date, according to some of his admirers, is his contribution to the recently completed (1958) headquarters buildings of the United Nations Educational, Social and Cultural Organization in Paris. On this international integration of architecture, technology, and fine arts he collaborated with Italy's Pier Luigi Nervi and France's Bernard H. Zehrfuss.

It has been pointed out that Marcel Lajos Breuer and the twentieth century grew up together in a relationship of close interchange. He was born in the Danube valley city of Pécs, Hungary on May 21, 1902 to Jacques Breuer, a doctor, and Franciska (Kan) Breuer. He had a sister, Hermina, and a brother, Alexander (deceased). In his youth, while a student at the Magyar Királyi Föreáliskola in Pécs, he often spent his free time skiing and playing tennis. His chief interests were painting and sculpture, and after his graduation from the Gymnasium in 1920, he left Pécs for Vienna, Austria to study at the Art Academy.

Immediately dissatisfied with the teaching at the Vienna academy, Breuer went to work for a furniture designer, with the intention of learning a trade. He soon afterward heard about a new school, the Bauhaus, in Weimar, Germany, which was directed by architect Walter Gropius (see C.B., March 1952) and combined the teaching of the pure arts with training in functional craftsmanship and the technology of modern industrial problems. Enrolling in the Bauhaus, Breuer specialized in interior architecture, and finding himself in tune with the experimental emphasis of the school, he advanced rapidly. He was awarded his master's degree in 1924 and in that year also became head of the carpentry shop and interior department.

When the Bauhaus was moved to Dessau, Germany in 1925, Breuer moved with it, in the same capacity. He designed all the furniture and interiors for Gropius' new Bauhaus buildings. In Dessau, he bought his first bicycle. Fascinated by the handle bars, he conceived the idea in 1925 of the Bauhaus' best-known artifact, the tubular steel chair, which was commercially produced in 1928. Peter Blake regards Breuer's use of continuously bent tubular steel framing in furniture making as "the single most influential furniture-invention of this century to date" (Marcel Breuer, *Sun and Shadow;* Dodd, Mead, 1955). In later pioneer work in furniture design, Breuer experimented successfully with aluminum (1933) and plywood (1935).

Partly because of the limited opportunities to work in architecture at the Bauhaus, Breuer moved to Berlin in 1926 to set up a private architectural practice, emphasizing prefabricated housing and the use of concrete in building. Discouraged in 1931 by deteriorating economic and political conditions in Germany, he began a series of extensive tours in other European countries, traveling and studying vernacular architecture for the next four years in Spain, Morocco, Switzerland, Hungary, and Greece. He had returned to Germany in 1932 to build the Harnischmacher House in Wiesbaden, which because of its inventiveness and originality in solving aesthetic and functional problems came to be regarded as one of the outstanding houses in modern architecture.

Breuer's travels took him to England in 1935, and he remained there for two years, working in partnership with architect F. R. S. Yorke. An English furniture manufacturer produced some of his latest designs in aluminum and plywood. His stay in England was memorable also for his model of a civic center in Bristol, in which he used natural materials and textures and expressed architectural ideas that he later developed more fully.

Walter Gropius, who was also a voluntary exile from Hitler's Germany, had moved to the United States; and in 1937 as head of Harvard University's Graduate School of Design, he urged Breuer to join him at Harvard in the position of associate professor in the school's department of architecture. For the next nine years at Harvard, Breuer taught over-all aesthetic and structural problems of architecture. In 1937 he also began a four-year partnership with Gropius for the private practice of architecture, mainly building homes. One product of this association was a project for the 1938 Wheaton College Art Center Competition, in which they won second prize. Also notable was the New Kensington, Pennsylvania defense housing project for aluminum workers, built in 1941.

In order to give more time to his work as an architect, Breuer left Harvard in 1946 and opened an office in New York City. He has since worked with many associates and assistants and with collaborators from other arts. His house designs made a far-reaching impression on domestic architecture, particularly his development of the "bi-nuclear," or two-center house, planned to meet the living problems of twentieth century families. One of many important examples is the Robinson House in Williamstown, Massachusetts (1946), which has nighttime and daytime areas, or zones, on different floor levels adjusted to the landscape. He is credited with having done much to convince the American public of the advantages of split-leveling by his "butterfly" exhibition house for the garden of the Museum of Modern Art, which more than 70,000 people visited in 1949.

Outside the field of domestic architecture, Breuer has become known for educational buildings. His work includes several schools in Connecticut, a classroom building and library for Hunter College, a dormitory for Vassar College, an arts center for Sarah Lawrence College, and buildings for the Convent of the Annunciation (Dickens, North Dakota). In 1953 he submitted his designs for the multimillion-dollar rebuilding of St. John's Abbey in Collegeville, Minnesota for a community of Benedictine monks. He was chosen from a number of leading architects because, Abbot Baldwin Dworschak explained, "he struck us as being not only an outstanding architect, but as a simple, straightforward, sincere and rather humble person" (Time, April 26, 1954). Also in 1954 Breuer received the important commission of designing houses for members of the Institute for Advanced Study in Princeton, New Jersey.

As early as the summer of 1952 Breuer had been chosen as the American architect to help design the new headquarters in Paris for UNESCO, in association with Nervi and Zehrfuss. The three UNESCO structures at Place de Fontenoy, finished in 1958 at a cost of about $9,000,000, consist of a Y-shaped secretariat building, a wedge-shaped conference building, and a five-story-high delegation building. Use of gracefully sculptured concrete stilts, similar to those that support the secretariat building, had been made in early Breuer designs, and the structure's Y shape was the result of some twenty years of study of efficiency in office building planning, having been foreshadowed in his 1936 civic center of the future in Bristol, England.

Three other European commissions, all in the Netherlands, also occupied Breuer during the 1950's: a United States Embassy building in The Hague, a much-discussed ("Beehive") De Bijenkorf department store in Rotterdam, and a suburban office building in Amstelveen, near Amsterdam. Like the UNESCO headquarters, the office building has sun shields made of dark-gray solar glass panels supported by metal framework, standing away from the building for heat radiation.

Breuer takes pains to let his building materials, like stone and wood, express themselves in color and texture, and he is known for his original application of materials. He wants to express structure wherever possible, by using such devices as tension cables bracing canopies. He prefers to introduce color into a house by bringing in the actual flowers rather than by painting them on a wall. He does not like buildings to imitate natural forms, believing that buildings and nature belong together, but that their relationship is a "composition of contrasts." As he wrote in Sun and Shadow, "I feel it is a great mistake either to adapt building forms to organic forms, or to adapt natural forms to the crystallic, geometric forms of architecture, as it was done in the Rococo period." Skeptical about slogans and shortcuts in architecture, he also treats cautiously terms like "international style," "regional architecture," and "function follows form." In handling dualism in building—the needs of living and working as against aesthetic values—he strives for unity rather than compromise.

Among the awards that Breuer has won is the first international La Rinascente prize, given for outstanding work in the field of industrial design (1957). He is a Fellow of the American Institute of Architects (1958) and an honorary member of the architects' associations of Argentina and Colombia. He belongs also to the Architectural League, the Connecticut Society of Architects, and International Congress of Modern Architects, among other professional organizations, and to the Harvard Club.

Marcel Breuer has been married twice. His first marriage, to Martha Erps on August 14, 1926, was terminated by divorce in 1934. He was married to Constance Crocker Leighton March 30, 1940; their children are Thomas and Francesca. Breuer has blue eyes and close-clipped gray-brown hair and retains his athletic figure. He weighs 175 pounds and stands five feet nine and a half inches tall. He is a Protestant. Not unexpectedly, his hobbies are painting, drawing, and photography. His ideal concept of an architect is a designer of creative judgment who "organizes inventiveness, structure, material and function and imagination into one cohesive unit, who also relates this unit to our senses—to the eye, to the touch, to pleasure, and to the satisfaction caused by achievement."

References

Arch Rev 121:348 My '57 por

Time 68:90+ O 22 '56 por

Breuer, Marcel Sun and Shadow (1955)
International Who's Who, 1959
Who's Who in America, 1960-61

BRINKLEY, DAVID (MCCLURE) July 10, 1920- News commentator

Address: b. 4001 Nebraska Ave., Washington, 16, D.C.; h. 5 Admirals Way, Potomac, Md.

When the Academy of Television Arts and Sciences distributed its "Emmy" awards for 1958 and 1959, *Huntley-Brinkley Report* won in the reporting division. The junior half of the popular team on this program, David Brinkley, first attracted national attention with his coverage of the 1956 Presidential conventions. Ever since, Brinkley has won an increasing following by his shrewd comments on the news.

David McClure Brinkley was born in Wilmington, North Carolina, on July 10, 1920, the son of William Graham and Mary MacDonald (West) Brinkley. He has four brothers and sisters, William, Jesse, Mary, and Margaret.

DAVID BRINKLEY

His father was a railroader who quietly continued his wine-making hobby through the prohibition era, although David's mother was a staunch prohibitionist. Brinkley remarks that he has inherited none of his father's "rare skill."

Even before his graduation from Wilmington's New Hanover High School in 1938, Brinkley had entered the newspaper profession. Discussing factors that influenced him in becoming a newsman, he recalled, "Early exposure to newspaper business through a relative who owned a weekly newspaper in Wilmington and asked me at the age of 17 to write a column about high school activities. It was full of such racy items as who was buying ten cent sodas for whom, each separated by three dots." His other interests in high school had included baseball, rifle shooting, and the literary society. After leaving school he worked as a reporter for the Wilmington *Star-News* from 1938 to 1940. He also attended classes at the University of North Carolina in Chapel Hill, majoring in English.

In 1940 Brinkley joined the United States Army as an infantryman, and spent his brief military career as a supply sergeant in an infantry rifle company at Fort Jackson, South Carolina. He was discharged the following year with the rank of sergeant. In 1942 he was hired by the United Press news agency as a reporter assigned to the Atlanta, Georgia bureau. Subsequently he was entrusted with one-man bureaus in Montgomery, Alabama; Nashville, Tennessee; and Charlotte, North Carolina. He continued his education by studying English at Vanderbilt University while he was working in Nashville.

Brinkley left the United Press in 1943 to go to Washington, D.C. There he applied for a job with the National Broadcasting Company, which hired him as a news writer to prepare scripts for staff announcers. Before the year was out, he was delivering his own newscasts on television. "I had a chance to learn while nobody was watching," he has said: there were then only a few hundred television sets in the capital.

As television grew in importance, so did Brinkley's role in the new medium. At first, in addition to making his television newscasts, he worked on NBC radio, and from 1945 was the moderator for the network's *America United* program. He became a TV news commentator in 1950 and the following year took on the job of Washington correspondent for NBC's *News Caravan*.

During those years, in the opinion of some critics, video newscasts suffered from an overemphasis on the pictorial, with straight news subdued at the expense of the photogenic. In 1954 NBC returned to a radio-style format for its *Comment* series. Applauding the experiment, critic John Crosby singled out Brinkley and New York *Times* Washington commentator Arthur Krock for special mention.

"Of the two," Crosby wrote in the New York *Herald Tribune* (June 27, 1954), "Krock is infinitely more experienced and wise in the ways of Washington. Yet for this sort of work, I would unhesitatingly pick Brinkley, who has a pungent and economical style of prose, an engaging face and a dry, sardonic tone of voice which carries great authority."

Brinkley held a key position in NBC's coverage of the 1954 Congressional elections and was assigned to the same task in 1956. The political conventions that year increased his national prominence as a video newscaster. They also brought him together for the first time with Chet Huntley, with whom he was later to team in one of the most popular news-comment series on television.

"Mr. Brinkley quite possibly could be the forerunner of a new school of television commentator," Jack Gould observed in the New York *Times* (August 17, 1956). "He is not an earnest Voice of Authority. . . . He contributes his observations with assurance but not insistence. But during the many long hours in Chicago, where at times it has seemed there has only been a national convention of commentators, Mr. Brinkley's extraordinary accomplishment has been not to talk too much. He has the knack for the succinct phrase that sums up the situation."

Realizing the audience appeal of their new team, NBC officials put them on *NBC News* (later named *Huntley-Brinkley Report*), beginning on October 29, 1956. Brinkley was based in Washington, while Huntley reported from New York City. By November the program had full sponsorship, and in its fourth time on the air it outdrew competing programs for a 36.9 per cent share of the viewing audience (Trendex).

With his partner, Brinkley was NBC's anchor man in the November elections. He also covered President Eisenhower's inauguration the following March; the Brussels World's Fair and the Congressional elections in 1958; Queen Elizabeth's tour of Canada; the NATO summit meeting in Paris; and Premier Nikita S. Khrushchev's American visit in 1959. The network assigned him to several special-events analyses.

Among them were a critical study of school integration (*Outlook,* August 31, 1958), the Berlin crisis and the proposed summit meeting (April 2, 1959), a study of American education (*Back to School,* August 25, 1959), and a survey of the Presidential hopefuls (*Politics—1960,* November 15, 1959).

In 1959 NBC also sent Brinkley on a Mediterranean tour, films of which were telecast in May as *Our Man in the Mediterranean.* The program caused critic Harriet Van Horne to comment (New York *World-Telegram and Sun,* May 18, 1959): "It was a shock—and a delightful one—to tune in a travelogue on NBC yesterday and find the commentary so literate it far outshone the picture."

Brinkley's dry wit is perhaps the most frequently noted feature of his newscasts. Recalling that in Premier Khrushchev's statement, "Your children will live under socialism," the word "children" had been altered to "grandchildren," he commented: "We've saved one whole generation." Of a new missiles chief, Brinkley said: "He's a new man brought in to do in a hurry what the government should have done long ago."

Also notable is the fact that Brinkley and Huntley dare to moralize in their newscasts. "What distinguishes 'Chet' and 'David,'" wrote Robert Lewis Shayon in the *Saturday Review* (December 28, 1957), ". . . is their propensity to introduce, every now and then, a revelatory footnote to the mere facts. Try as they may to present the mask of neutrality (Huntley has been accused of having an over-solemn pokerface and Brinkley of undisguised boredom) the tones of their voices, ironies on their lips, and subtleties in their eyes betray their values—not to speak of the selectivity in their news items."

Together with Huntley, Brinkley won "Emmy" awards in 1959 and 1960 for the "best news reporting series." Earlier, David Brinkley had received an Alfred I. du Pont Commentator's Award which noted that he displayed "an inquiring mind sensitive to both the elusive fact and the background that illuminates its meaning." He also won a Peabody award in 1959, a Sylvania award in 1958, and the School Bell Award for Educational Broadcasts in 1957 and 1958.

Brinkley was married to Ann Fischer, also a reporter, on October 11, 1946; they have three sons, Alan, Joel, and John. At his Maryland home, Brinkley enjoys his hobby of woodworking. Travel and conservation are among his other interests. He belongs to the National Press Club and Sigma Delta Chi. He is a Presbyterian; for professional reasons he does not state his political affiliation. A slender man, he is six feet two inches tall, weighs 175 pounds, and has blue eyes and brown hair.

"Some of the most successful 'news' on the air is not news at all," Brinkley says of his craft. ". . . Instead, it is often no more than a report on a mood, a feeling, a texture, a shape or a movement. Possibly that is art and not journalism, but I think the two have a great deal in common and could stand some inbreeding."

References

N Y Times II p11 Je 7 '59
Newsweek 55:40 Ja 4 '60 por
Sat R 40:24 D 28 '57 por
Time 74:92 O 19 '59 por
Who's Who in America, 1958-59

BROOKS, VAN WYCK (văn wĭk) Feb. 16, 1886- Writer; critic
Address: b. c/o E. P. Dutton & Co., 300 Park Ave. S., New York 10; h. Bridgewater, Conn.

NOTE: This biography supersedes the article which appeared in *Current Biography* in 1941.

Over a period of more than fifty years Van Wyck Brooks, the scholar, biographer, sociologist, and critic, has written some twenty-seven books that have earned him a pre-eminent place among historians of literature in the United States. He is perhaps best known for the five-volume study of American writers that he began in 1936 with *The Flowering of New England.* Writing in his graceful, civilized, and pellucid style, he has done more than any other contemporary critic to discover and regain a "usable past" for Americans by recapturing the cultural life of the nineteenth and early twentieth centuries.

New England has been the home of Van Wyck Brooks for most of his life and the subject of much of his writing. As he has noted, however, he is by heredity only partly a New Englander; his two grandfathers were Vermonters, and his grandmothers were New Yorkers. He was born in Plainfield, New Jersey on February 16, 1886, one of two sons of Charles Edward Brooks, a stockbroker, and Sarah Bailey (Ames) Brooks. His brother, Charles Ames Brooks, died in 1932. Van Wyck received his early education in the public schools of Plainfield.

When he was twelve years old he went to Europe with his parents, spending a year in Germany, France, Italy, and England. One of several lasting influences of the trip was an interest in France which led to his later translations of French books. In 1904 he entered Harvard University, where he became one of the editors of the *Harvard Advocate* and was elected to Phi Beta Kappa. Although a member of the class of 1908, he took his A.B. degree a year earlier and soon afterward sailed for England.

During the next year and a half Brooks lived precariously in London, where he was employed mainly as a journalist. He contributed articles to several London and Manchester periodicals, was associated for part of that time with the literary agents Curtis Brown & Company, and made a number of visits to Paris. Also while in England he completed his first book, *The Wine of the*

Carola Gregor

VAN WYCK BROOKS

Puritans (Kennerley, 1909), in which he began to explore the idea that art must have roots in a fertile and receptive native soil.

Upon his return to the United States in 1909, Brooks worked on the *Standard Dictionary* and *Collier's Encyclopaedia* and, under Walter H. Page, on the *World's Work*. Moving to California in 1911, he taught English for the next two years at Leland Stanford University and while at Palo Alto wrote the biography *John Addington Symonds* (Kennerley, 1914). In 1913 he revisited England, where he taught a class for the Workers' Educational Association at South Norwood and also worked on several books, including *America's Coming of Age* (Huebsch, 1915) and *The World of H. G. Wells* (Kennerley, 1915).

A few months after the outbreak of World War I, Brooks went back to New York, entered the Century Company, and began to translate French literature. Among the thirty-one French books which he helped translate were the novels of Romain Rolland and the *Journal Intime* of Henri Frédéric Amiel. He was associate editor of *The Seven Arts* during the year of its existence, 1917-18, and in 1920 he became literary editor of *The Freeman* for a four-year period. Some of the essays that he wrote for that magazine's weekly page, "A Reviewer's Notebook," were reprinted in *Emerson and Others* (1927) and *Sketches in Criticism* (1932). They were among the first of his books to appear under the imprint of E. P. Dutton & Company, which published all his succeeding books.

Also in 1920 Brooks settled in Westport, Connecticut, the chief setting of his autobiographical volume *Days of the Phoenix; The Nineteen-Twenties I Remember* (1957), a continuation of his *Scenes and Portraits: Memories of Childhood and Youth* (1954). During the 1920's he became recognized as

an influential critic, the leader of a group of critics and writers whose outlook was then regarded as radical and rebellious. A Socialist, he deplored the cultural and economic shortcomings in American life that in his opinion tended to thwart creative genius. His *Ordeal of Mark Twain* (1920) and *The Pilgrimage of Henry James* (1925) are somewhat pessimistic in their presentation of the sense of unfulfillment that he sees in the work of both men.

In *Days of the Phoenix* Brooks relates how in the mid-1920's he became consumed with a feeling of his own frustration and failure and from 1926 to 1931 suffered a period of mental illness which he has called his "season in hell." During these years he was unable to do much work, but in 1932 he published his *Life of Emerson,* a critical study of the transcendentalist writer with whom he felt an affinity of spirit.

With *The Flowering of New England, 1815-1865* (1936), which won the Pulitzer Prize for history in 1937 and other awards, Van Wyck Brooks began his long-projected history of literature in America. The first of the five-volume chronicle deals with the "golden age" of New England culture and is first only in point of composition; in order of sequence it is second. Other volumes in the series are *The World of Washington Irving* (1944); *The Times of Melville and Whitman* (1947); *New England: Indian Summer, 1865-1915* (1940); and *The Confident Years, 1885-1915* (1951). The entire series is entitled "Maker and Finders: A History of the Writer i. America, 1800-1915." (In 1956 Otto L. Bettmann prepared an abridgment of the series, illustrated by more than 500 pictures, called *Our Literary Heritage: A Pictorial History of the Writer in America.*)

When he finished his literary history, Brooks began to write an introductory chapter explaining why he had undertaken the study. The chapter grew into a book, *The Writer in America,* in which he discusses his philosophy of life and literature. Malcolm Cowley summed up the views of many critics in his comment that "judged as a whole 'Makers and Finders' is the most impressive work undertaken and carried through by any single American scholar of our time" (New York *Herald Tribune Book Review,* January 6, 1952). Other reviewers remarked on Brooks's capacity for assimilation and synthesis of an enormous amount of material, for recreating the past as if painting an impressionistic picture, and for giving his readers a sense of shared experience.

Among Brooks's more recent books are biographies of Helen Keller (1955) and the painter John Sloan (1955), both of whom he knew personally. His *Dream of Arcadia; American Writers and Artists in Italy, 1760-1915* (1958) has been compared with the *The Flowering of New England* in its picturesque combination of history and artistic criticism. In *From a Writer's Notebook* (1958), in which he brings up to date his observations on life and letters, he shows himself out of tune with many tendencies of contemporary American society. Astringent without becoming ill-tempered, he deplores the negativeness and the tiresome concentration on the "mean" that he finds in much current literature.

The point of view that Brooks defended in *From a Writer's Notebook* was reflected in his sympathetic biography, *Howells: His Life and World* (1959). His concern for cultivating the "tender emotion" was attacked in K. S. Lynn's review: "The sweet charm of Brooks's narrative has been purchased, as is generally true of his books starting with 'The Flowering of New England,' at the sacrifice of everything sour" (*Christian Science Monitor,* October 8, 1959). Kenneth Millar also charged Brooks with having a "rose-colored" vision of the American past (San Francisco *Chronicle,* November 8, 1959).

The tone of affirmation and hope in regard to the American tradition that Brooks generally expressed in his books after the 1920's is perhaps in part responsible for the change in his position from a controversial critic to an author of best-selling books. He has been criticized for certain limitations in his biographical approach to the study of literature and for his condemnation of untraditional writers like James Joyce. His immense pioneering contribution to the development of mature and scholarly literary criticism in the United States remains, however, largely undisputed.

In addition to the Pulitzer Prize, Brooks's writings have won him the Dial Prize for distinguished critical work (1923), the Gold Medal of the National Institute of Arts and Letters (1946), the Theodore Roosevelt Medal (1954), and several honorary degrees, including the Litt.D. degree from Harvard, Columbia, Boston, and Northeastern universities. He is a member of the American Academy of Arts and Letters, the American Philosophical Society, the Century Club of New York, and the Royal Society of Literature in London (Fellow), among other associations.

Brooks was married to Eleanor Kenyon Stimson on June 1, 1911, and by that marriage he is the father of two sons, Charles Van Wyck and Oliver Kenyon. His first wife died in August 1946, and on June 2, 1947 he was married to Gladys (Rice) Billings, the author of *Gramercy Park; Memories of a New York Girlhood* (Dutton, 1958) and other books. Brooks has blue eyes and gray-brown hair, weighs 165 pounds, and stands five feet six and a half inches tall. He is an Episcopalian and, now, a Democrat.

Brooks's more recent autobiographical books and philosophical essays make him seem less mysterious and reticent than early biographical sketches pictured him, although even in his personal reminiscences some readers are struck by a note of detachment. He is reported to be gentle, genial, informal, and free of self-importance. His literary style reveals a man of wit, briskness, and suavity whose books, for all their tranquility of surface, probe to the depths beneath.

References
> Newsweek 51:70 Ja 6 '58 por
> Brooks, Van Wyck Scenes and Portraits (1954); Days of the Phoenix (1957)
> International Who's Who, 1959
> National Cyclopaedia of American Biography current vol D (1934)
> Twentieth Century Authors (1942; First Supplement, 1955)
> Who's Who in America, 1960-61
> World Biography (1954)

BROWN, CHARLES H(ARVEY) Dec. 28, 1875-Jan. 19, 1960 Librarian of Iowa State College (1922-46); president of the American Library Association (1941-42). See *Current Biography* (August) 1941.

Obituary

N Y Times p31 Ja 21 '60

BROWN, EDMUND G(ERALD) Apr. 21, 1905- Governor of California

Address: b. The Capitol, Sacramento, Calif.; h. Executive Mansion, Sacramento, Calif.

For only the second time in the twentieth century California voters elected a Democratic Governor when they gave Edmund G. Brown a victory over Senator William F. Knowland in November 1958. Brown succeeded Republican Goodwin Knight, in whose administration he had served the last four of his eight years as attorney general. The bipartisan support that Brown has received as Governor and the precedent-shattering co-operation with which the state legislature enacted most of his program during 1959 have greatly enhanced Brown's political prestige, both locally and nationally.

Since California, the third largest state in area (following Alaska and Texas), is the nation's second most populous state (following New York), its delegation to the Democratic National Convention controls a sizable bloc of votes. Brown first announced his intention to lead the California delegation as a favorite-son candidate for the Presidential nomination at the National Convention. However, just before the convention convened in July 1960, Brown endorsed Senator John F. Kennedy of Massachusetts, who won the race as the Democratic standard-bearer.

A native San Franciscan of Irish-German descent, Edmund Gerald Brown was born on April 21, 1905 to Edmund Joseph and Ida (Schuckman) Brown. There were three other children in the family, a girl and two boys. His father, who had moved to California during the Gold Rush, operated a cigar store, photo arcades, nickelodeons, and shooting galleries. During his boyhood, religious differ-

Wide World

EDMUND G. BROWN

ences between his Catholic father and his Protestant mother led to some question as to what church and school he should attend.

Although Brown did go to a Catholic parochial school for a while, he acquired most of his early education at Lowell High School in San Francisco. Politically ambitious in school and interested in a variety of activities, including sports and music, he held eleven student offices. He reportedly owes his nickname of Pat to his impressive oratorical manner in quoting Patrick Henry's "Give me liberty or give me death" during a speech for a Liberty Bond drive.

Lacking the money to enter college, Brown went to work in his father's cigar store-poker room establishment. His mother had a strong faith in the value of education, and with her encouragement he studied law at night. In 1927 he completed his University of California extension courses at the San Francisco Law School and received his LL.B. degree. Later in the same year, as soon as he was admitted to the California bar, he began a private law practice in San Francisco that he maintained until 1943.

Pat Brown began his career in politics as a Republican, running unsuccessfully in 1928 for the state Assembly. Eleven years later (1939) he became a candidate on the Democratic ticket for district attorney of San Francisco and was again defeated. He gradually gained public attention and political strength, however, as a member of the California Code Commission (beginning in 1939) and of the Golden Gate Bridge and Highway District (beginning in 1942) and as chairman of the speakers' bureau for President Roosevelt's campaigns (1940 and 1944) and delegate from California to the Democratic National Convention (1940 and subsequent Presidential election years).

Victorious in the 1943 election, Brown began the first of his two terms as district attorney for the city and county of San Francisco (1943-47 and 1947-50). He had to run twice also before he won the office of attorney general of California in 1950, having lost in 1946. When he campaigned for re-election in 1954 he won both the Democratic and Republican nomination in the primary, under the crossfiling system then in effect in California, which allowed a candidate to compete in the primary of all parties.

As attorney general, Brown was the only Democrat in a state-wide elective post. His office, with a staff of more than a hundred lawyers, annually handled thousands of civil and criminal cases and proceedings before boards and commissions. His progressive activities included an investigation of the scandal-ridden State Liquor Administration and special studies of problems of narcotics, interracial friction, and juvenile delinquency.

The June 1958 primary election, in which Pat Brown won the Democratic nomination for Governor of California, gave him the largest combined vote on both party tickets ever gained by a Democrat in the state. Also cross-filing in the primary was Senator William F. Knowland, who became the Republican nominee and Brown's opponent in the November election. In his campaign for Governor, Brown stressed what he called the "bread-and-butter" issues—jobs from new industries not dependent upon defense spending, education, mental health, and a solution to California's water problem. He called for reform of labor unions, but opposed the right-to-work legislation that Knowland advocated.

At the polls on November 4, 1958 Brown received 3,015,734 votes to Knowland's 2,007,247 votes. (The only other Democrat elected Governor of California in the twentieth century so far, Culbert L. Olson, had served from 1939 to 1943.) Because they also won a majority in the state Legislature, the Democrats controlled both houses for the first time since 1889.

Inaugurated the thirty-second Governor of California on January 5, 1959, Brown outlined in his address a program that he described as "liberal and responsible" and as "reasonable, rational, and realistic." It was also generally bipartisan. When the Legislature ended its 1959 session six months later, Brown was able to claim that 90 per cent of his program had been enacted, including a fair employment practice bill, a measure ending the cross-filing primary system, increased jobless benefits, and pensions for the blind and aged. His labor reform bill was one of his five proposals that were defeated.

Although Brown failed to get from the Legislature all that he had asked for in additional taxes to meet his budget of $2.1 billion, he did obtain some $220,000,000 in new tax revenues. One of his most important achievements was to put in motion a measure for water-resources development, subject to voters' ratification of a $1.2 billion bond proposal in the November 1960 election.

In Brown's leadership during his first year as Governor a number of political news writers saw a much greater decisiveness than had characterized his service as attorney general. He showed a readiness to study issues thoroughly and an ability to use skillfully the information that his aides and advisers provided. Drawing upon experts from both parties, he appointed advisory groups on old age, atomic, urban, economic, and other problems.

Brown has belonged to many professional organizations, including the District Attorneys' Association of California (past president), American Bar Association, and American College of Trial Lawyers (Fellow). He is an Elk, and his clubs are the Native Sons of the Golden West, the Commonwealth, and the Olympic (San Francisco). He is also a member of the St. Thomas More Society.

When Pat Brown was still in high school he met Bernice Layne, the daughter of a San Francisco police captain, and they were married some years later, on October 30, 1930. Their daughters are Mrs. Charles Casey, Jr., Mrs. Joseph Kelly, and teen-age Kathleen Brown. A son, Edmund G. Brown, Jr., is a former student at the Novitiate of the Sacred Heart in Los Gatos, California.

Unpretentious in appearance and behavior, Brown is black-haired, stands five feet ten and a half inches tall, weighs 195 pounds, and has a brisk, cheerful, and sincere manner. He is known as a voracious reader of newspapers and magazines. His principal hobby is an occasional game of golf, in which his wife usually beats him. Brown once told Gladwin Hill, of the New York *Times* Los Angeles bureau, "The success I've had as a lawyer and in public life I think has come mainly from the ability to bring divergent views together. I've always loved diplomacy and politics." To illustrate Brown's wry wit, Hill also quoted his remark, "The facts in this case are so simple as to defy explanation by political experts."

References

N Y Post Mag p2 Je 15 '58 por
N Y Times p24 O 31 '57 por
N Y Times Mag p15+ S 28 '58; p38+ D 6 '59 por
Reporter 21:12+ D 24 '59 por
American Catholic Who's Who, 1960 and 1961
Who's Who in America, 1958-59
Who's Who in United States Politics (1952)

BROWN, PAT *See* Brown, Edmund G.

BRYSON, LYMAN (LLOYD) July 12, 1888-Nov. 24, 1959 Educator; author; professor at Teachers College, Columbia University, since 1935; originator and moderator of radio and television adult education programs, including the CBS radio program *Invitation to Learning*. See *Current Biography* (September) 1951.

Obituary

N Y Times p37 N 26 '59

BUCHHOLZ, HORST (WERNER) Dec. 4, 1933- Actor
Address: 336 Central Park W., New York 25

The brooding face of Horst Buchholz, the young German film idol who has been called "the Teutonic James Dean," has become known in the United States in recent years through his foreign films and his 1959 Broadway debut in the title role of the play *Chéri*. It is certain to become familiar to a wider public when his scheduled Hollywood films are released for distribution outside the art movie houses.

The honor that Horst (or "Hotte" as he is known to his fans) Buchholz has already found in his own country was demonstrated when in 1957 and 1958 he was chosen the most popular German actor in a poll conducted by the fan magazine, *Film-Revue*. In 1959 he placed third in the same poll, the winner of which receives the so-called Bambi Prize. In 1957 Buchholz won a prize given by the city of Berlin to outstanding members of the younger generation.

The grandson and son of shoemakers, Horst Werner Buchholz was born on December 4, 1933 in Weissensee, a working-class quarter of what is now East Berlin. He has a sister, Heidi, who was born at Christmas time in 1941. His father and his mother, Maria, had to practise stringent economy in order to keep the family going. "I come from modest circumstances," Buchholz says. "The first thing I learned was how to count money. We saved every penny."

World War II brought many hardships to Horst Buchholz and his family. His father was conscripted into the German army, and the family became separated. Horst was placed under the care of the "KVL," an organization that looked after homeless children, and was evacuated from Berlin to Czechoslovakia. In

Friedman—Abeles
HORST BUCHHOLZ

BUCHHOLZ, HORST—*Continued*

spite of these precautions, he narrowly missed being killed in a bombing raid during the final phase of the war.

The Buchholz family resumed its normal routines soon after the war, when Horst returned to Berlin from Czechoslovakia and his father came back from a prison camp in France. Horst did everything he could to help support his family; he worked as a packager and as a delivery boy; at one time he even trafficked in cigarettes on the black market.

Although Horst hoped to study either medicine or speech after graduating from high school, he revised his ambitions when, in 1947, he took on a job as an extra at the Metropol Theatre in Berlin. He was fourteen years of age when he took his first solo part of the boy Mittenzwei in a stage production of Erich Kästner's *Emil und die Detektive* (*Emil and the Detectives*). In spite of objections from his family, he continued his theatrical career by contributing his voice to the dubbing of foreign movies into German and by acting in radio plays. In 1950 he left high school in order to devote himself full-time to his budding career.

Continuing his stage engagements in Berlin, Buchholz appeared in such works as Georg Kaiser's *Floss der Medusa* (*Raft of Medusa*), Jean-Paul Sartre's *Tote ohne Begräbnis* (*Death Without Burial*) and Shakespeare's *Richard III*. Buchholz often gives credit to his director in the Sartre play, Ernst Schröder, for having taught him much about the art of acting, and to Marlise Ludwig, with whom he studied during this period.

In 1955 Horst Buchholz made his film debut under the French director Julien Duvivier in *Marianne—meine Jugendliebe* (*Marianne, My Youthful Love*), opposite Marianne Hold. This film, in which Buchholz played a young man discovering romantic love, apparently enjoyed little commercial success. In the same year, he played Mischa, a young Russian gunner, in a film version of Helmut Käutner's *Himmel ohne Sterne* (known to English-speaking audiences as *No Star in the Sky* or *Heaven Without Stars*). His sensitive performance in this role, requiring very little dialogue, established his reputation in German films and won for him the 1956 *Bundesfilmpreis* (National Film Prize).

After portraying a revolutionary blast furnace worker in *Regine*, Buchholz went on to play a delinquent in *Die Halbstarken* (*The Half-Strong*), a low-budget film which proved highly successful, although its writer and director were virtually unknown. This film was shown in a version with English titles in the United States in 1959 under the title *Teen-Age Wolf Pack*.

In *Herrscher ohne Krone* (titled variously in English as *Ruler Without a Crown* or *The King in Shadow*) Buchholz appeared with one of the leading stars of the German screen, Otto Wilhelm Fischer. The younger actor was acclaimed for his performance in the taxing role of a mentally disturbed King of Denmark; among those who added their voices to the

chorus of praise was Herr Fischer who said on a television interview that "Buchholz is one of the young people who will reach the highest peaks."

By 1957, Buchholz' first five films had raised him to the heights of popularity in Germany. He went on to make *Robinson soll nicht sterben* (*Robinson Must Not Die*), the story of the later years of Daniel Defoe, the author of *Robinson Crusoe*, in which Buchholz played the novelist's scapegrace son. The popular German actress Romy Schneider also appeared in this film.

Horst Buchholz next starred in the title role of the film version of Thomas Mann's last novel *Bekenntnis des Hochstaplers Felix Krull*, seen in the United States as *The Confessions of Felix Krull*. He was reportedly recommended for the part by Mann's daughter, Erika. *Felix Krull* was favorably received in the United States and in Europe. Liselotte Pulver, Susi Nicoletti, and Paul Dahlke were also in the cast.

Buchholz co-starred once more with Romy Schneider in a romantic film, *Monpti*, which, when exported to the United States, provoked admiration from critics and audiences. He also appeared as a factory worker in *Endstation Liebe* (*Destination Love*). Another Buchholz film of this period, *Nasser Asphalt* (*Wet Asphalt*), aroused small enthusiasm in Germany. Rolf Hansen's screen version of Tolstoy's novel *Resurrection* provided Buchholz with his next screen vehicle.

A British mystery thriller, *Tiger Bay*, marked the debut of Horst Buchholz in English-language motion pictures. The film, also featuring John Mills and his daughter, Hayley, opened in New York on December 14, 1959, and Buchholz' performance as a Polish seaman who, after murdering his faithless lover, is shielded by a waif of the slums, was commended by most of the city's film critics.

After completing one more German film, *Das Totenschiff* (*The Death Ship*), Buchholz came to the United States to appear with Kim Stanley in *Chéri*, Anita Loos's unhappy adaptation of two novels by Colette. The drama, which opened on Broadway on October 12, 1959, disappointed most of the reviewers and had only a brief engagement, although the acting was eulogized in some quarters.

Brooks Atkinson in the New York *Times* (October 13, 1959) described Buchholz as "a slender, wiry young man who plays a nervous, panther-like boy—mocking and supercilious in the beginning; worn, disillusioned, hollow in eye and spirit at the end," and termed his performance "gorgeous." Less friendly reviewers, such as Frank Aston of the *World-Telegram and Sun* of the same date, attributed any shortcomings in Buchholz' playing to Anita Loos's writing and Robert Lewis' direction.

Horst Buchholz is now under contract for five films to the Hollywood producer and director Billy Wilder, who first became interested in Buchholz' work in *The Confessions of Felix Krull*. He has also been engaged by Joshua Logan for a motion-picture version (nonmusical) of Marcel Pagnol's *Fanny*. Charles Boyer and Maurice Chevalier have also been signed for the production.

On December 7, 1958 Horst Buchholz was married to French actress Miriam Bru, whom he had courted during the filming of *Resurrection*. To his proficiency in English, he is now adding a speaking knowledge of Russian, Italian, and French. Among his hobbies is driving his red Mercedes 300 S1 sports car, which he has christened "the tramp." The letters on the German license plate, reading "B—HW 300," stand for "Buchholz—Horst Werner."

A slim, lithe, and Slavic-looking young man, Horst Buchholz moves with the grace of a cat. His troubled, yet defiant face with its fine bone structure has prompted many comparisons with the late James Dean. But Buchholz told Seymour Peck of the New York *Times* (October 11, 1959) that he disclaims the resemblance. "My name is Horst Buchholz," he insisted, "and under that name and no one else's is my personality. I feel I am myself." He added: "I want to develop my possibilities in acting as much as I want to develop in life as a private person. I want to see where my limits are and I want to find out everything about me—and then one day I can tell you who I am."

References

N Y Times II p5 O 11 '59
Wer ist Wer, 1958

BUCHWALD, ART(HUR) Oct. 20, 1925-
Journalist; author
Address: b. 21 Rue de Berri, Paris, France; h. 50 Rue Monceau, Paris, France

One of the funniest and most popular of the American innocents abroad is the newspaper humorist Art Buchwald, who has been called the most comic American observer of the European scene since Mark Twain. His columns for the Herald Tribune syndicate appear in some eighty newspapers from Enid, Oklahoma to Israel. Ever since January 1949, when he began turning out his columns for the European (Paris) edition of the New York *Herald Tribune*, Buchwald has been entertaining readers with his spirited and sometimes irreverent comments on the celebrities and tourists who come and go on the European scene.

Arthur Buchwald was born in Mount Vernon, New York on October 20, 1925 to Joseph and Helen (Kleinberger) Buchwald. His father was a curtain manufacturer. His three sisters, Alice, Edith, and Doris, still live in the New York metropolitan area. Buchwald grew up in Hollis, New York, a residential community in the Queens borough of New York City, where he attended elementary school at Public School Number 35. He attended Jamaica High School and Forest Hills High School, both in the borough of Queens, but did not graduate. When he reached his seventeenth birthday in October 1942, he ran away to join the United States Marines.

ART BUCHWALD

From October 1942 to October 1945 Buchwald served with the United States Marine Corps as an enlisted man; he entered the service as a private and was discharged as a sergeant. Attached to the Fourth Marine Air Wing, he spent three and a half years in the Pacific. Most of that time he was stationed on Eniwetok, where he edited his outfit's newspaper. Shortly before he was discharged, he did public relations work for the Special Services department.

When he again became a civilian, Buchwald enrolled at the University of Southern California at Los Angeles to take liberal arts courses under the provisions of the G.I. Bill of Rights. At the university he was managing editor of the *Wampus*, the campus humor magazine, conducted a column for the college newspaper, the *Daily Trojan*, and wrote a variety show called *No Love Atoll*.

Impelled by an urge to sample the expatriate life in Paris, Buchwald left the University of Southern California in 1948 without taking a degree. With the $250 check he had received as a war bonus, he bought a one-way ticket to France. When his financial resources dwindled, Buchwald got the job of correspondent for *Variety* magazine in Paris. In January 1949 he took a trial column on which he had been working to the editorial offices of the European edition of the New York *Herald Tribune*. Titled "Paris After Dark," it was filled with scraps of offbeat information about Parisian night life. Buchwald was hired for the editorial staff. "Paris After Dark" caught on quickly, and Buchwald followed it in 1951 with another column, "Mostly About People," featuring interviews with celebrities in Paris.

Early in 1952 the editors of the New York *Herald Tribune* decided to bring Art Buchwald's columns to readers in the United States. The two columns, "Paris After Dark" and "Mostly About People," were fused into one

BUCHWALD, ART—*Continued*

with the title of "Europe's Lighter Side." They are now usually published with the title, "Art Buchwald in Paris."

Art Buchwald's columns about "the lighter things that take place in Europe" soon began to recruit readers on both sides of the Atlantic. By August 24, 1959 *Time* magazine, in reviewing the history of the European edition, was able to report that Buchwald's column had achieved "an institutional quality." The column in which Buchwald explained Thanksgiving Day to the French populace in 1953 is reprinted late in every November with ceremonial regularity.

Although Paris is usually his beat, Buchwald will go almost anywhere—and do almost anything—to gather the raw material for his columns. He has marched in a May Day parade in East Berlin, chased goats up and down the mountains of Yugoslavia, and climbed trees to get a better view of the races at Longchamps. He once traveled all the way to Turkey to get a firsthand impression of a Turkish bath.

On one occasion, Buchwald made a three-week trip behind the Iron Curtain in a limousine driven by a uniformed chauffeur. In his columns Buchwald explained that he had made the trip in the "interests of science" and to show the Communists what a "bloated, plutocratic capitalist really looked like." In the late summer of 1957 Buchwald inserted the following advertisement in the classified column of *The Times* (London): "Would like to hear from people who dislike Americans and their reasons why. Please write Box R.543." The ad drew 209 replies, ranging from the tersest of answers to lengthy tributes to Americans. They furnished Buchwald with the material for two columns.

In December 1957 Buchwald himself became the subject of newspaper headlines when White House Press Secretary James C. Hagerty attacked one of his columns as "unadulterated rot." President Dwight D. Eisenhower was attending a North Atlantic Treaty Organization conference in Paris at the time, and, while attending the press briefings conducted by Hagerty, Buchwald was struck by the detailed coverage that newspapermen gave to the President's routine activities. In the column that created the furor Buchwald had satirized the briefings by asking such questions as: "What time did the President start eating his grapefruit, Jim?" and "Jim, did the President speak to anyone before retiring?"

At a later news conference, Hagerty retorted that "at no time did the reports in the New York *Herald Tribune* even remotely resemble what I ever said at a public briefing." But it was reported that President Eisenhower did not share Hagerty's indignation over the column. It was said that he "laughed like mad" when he read it, then advised Hagerty to "simmer down, Jim, simmer down" (New York *Herald Tribune,* December 18, 1957).

As might have been predicted, Buchwald had the last word in the Hagerty affair. The day after the celebrated column appeared, Buchwald wrote another, taking note of Hagerty's objections. In this column Buchwald admitted that he "has been known to write adulterated rot, but never . . . unadulterated rot."

By the end of 1959, Buchwald had to his credit seven published books. Six are collections of his columns and of his miscellaneous writings; one—*A Gift from the Boys* (Harper, 1958)—is a novel. The collections are: *Paris After Dark* (Haef, 1950); *Art Buchwald's Paris* (Little, 1954); *The Brave Coward* (Harper, 1957); *I Choose Caviar* (Doubleday, Toronto, 1957); *More Caviar* (Harper, 1959); and *Don't Forget to Write* (World Publishing, 1960).

Although reviewers have usually looked upon Buchwald's books with favor, they have entered some reservations. William Hogan, in reviewing *The Brave Coward* for the San Francisco *Chronicle* (March 14, 1957), wrote: "By no means on a par with the greats in the humor-writing field (Perelman), Buchwald is nonetheless witty, disarming and more informed on the Mayfair-Cannes-Beverly Hills set than he should be." In judging the same book for the *Christian Science Monitor* (April 4, 1957), E. W. Foell warned: "Taken one column at a time, as they appear in the newspapers, Mr. Buchwald's pieces are nearly always hilarious; but assembled in book form they can surfeit the reader, who is not a careful sampler, with an overdose of upstartishness."

In his first venture into novel writing, *A Gift from the Boys,* Buchwald told the story of a racket czar who is deported from the United States to his native Sicily, where he settles down in his native fishing village after a series of wild mishaps. Although the *New Yorker* (September 6, 1958) dismissed it as "a souffle, which never quite rises," Al Morgan was more charitably inclined in the New York *Herald Tribune Book Review* (September 7, 1958). After calling Buchwald "an amusing, zany, literate commentator on the passing scene," Morgan observed: "If Mr. Buchwald seems to run out of invention and interest two-thirds of the way through, it is not completely fatal to his first excursion into novel-writing. Most of the way, 'A Gift from the Boys' is entertaining, amusing, and fun."

Arthur Buchwald was married to Ann McGarry, a former fashion co-ordinator for Neiman-Marcus, on October 12, 1952. They live with their three adopted children—Joel, Conchita Mathilda, and Marie Jennifer—in an apartment not too far from the office of the *Herald Tribune* and the Hotel George V. Buchwald is a member of the Overseas Press Club and the Anglo-American Press Club. He is five feet nine inches tall and weighs 180 pounds. James Thurber is reported to have said that Buchwald "bears a striking resemblance to the late Rudolph Valentino"; the writer Robert Ginna sees him as "a freshly-shaven owl in a Tattersall vest." For recreation, Buchwald prefers "anything that doesn't require physical exercise." "I think exercise is dangerous," he has declared. "People should stay in the horizontal position as much as possible." He enjoys his work more than his hobbies: playing chess, collecting chess sets, photography, and going to the race track. "I love my work," he says. "I wouldn't do anything else."

Reference

Who's Who in America, 1958-59

BUETOW, HERBERT P(AUL) Jan. 25, 1898- Business executive

Address: b. Minnesota Mining and Manufacturing Company, 900 Bush Ave., St. Paul, 6, Minn.; h. 1550 Edgecomb Rd., St. Paul, 16, Minn.

As president of the Minnesota Mining and Manufacturing Company, Herbert P. Buetow heads an organization dedicated to the proposition that the legal monopoly provided by patents constitutes the lifeblood of a corporation. Having started out in 1926 as a $150 a month bookkeeper with the research-minded firm, Buetow rose steadily through the ranks at a time when the vertical set-up of the St. Paul corporation made rapid promotion from the bottom easier than it is today, when the organization is divided into divisions.

Now the acknowledged leading producer of adhesive tapes, the Minnesota Mining and Manufacturing Company started out in 1902 to mine corundum ore, the source of an abrasive mineral almost as hard as a diamond. When this proved unsuccessful, the firm switched to the manufacture of flexible and waterproof sandpaper. With the production, beginning in 1931, of pressure-sensitive cellophane Scotch tape, the firm moved into the class of multimillion dollar business. Currently producing about forty different lines of products and about 25,000 separate items, the Minnesota Mining and Manufacturing Company corners about 80 per cent of the cellophane tape business and a huge share of the trade in coated abrasives. It conducts its operations in twenty-five plants in America and in fourteen factories located in nine foreign countries.

A native of St. Paul, Minnesota, Herbert Paul Buetow was born on January 25, 1898 to Charles A. and Henriette (Ramlow) Buetow. His father was a construction superintendent. Like his four brothers and sisters, Herbert P. Buetow attended local schools; he studied at the Mechanic Arts High School, the St. Paul Institute, and the Nichols Expert Business School. In 1921 he received a B.A. degree from the school of business administration at the University of Minnesota, and has, from time to time, taken extension courses in business at the university.

Buetow began his business career as a part-time office boy for the Waldorf Paper Company in St. Paul from 1913 to 1916. In 1918 he accepted a position as staff accountant for Bishop-Brissman and Company; in 1920 he became first senior accountant for the city of St. Paul. A young woman, Luella Witt, who was secretary of an advertising agency (and who shortly became his wife), told him that the Minnesota Mining and Manufacturing Company, one of her agency's clients, was looking for "a bright young auditor." Although Buetow was not too interested, he allowed himself to be persuaded to join the Minnesota Mining and Manufacturing Company as an auditor, a position that he held for nine years.

The policy of the Minnesota Mining and Manufacturing Company is to look within the ranks of its own employees for men to fill vacated positions. In accordance with this

HERBERT P. BUETOW

policy, Herbert P. Buetow was made controller in 1935, treasurer in 1939, director in 1940, executive vice-president in 1949, and president in 1953.

The business to which Buetow has devoted most of his career attributes its success to the application of a three-part formula. As outlined by *Business Week* (October 4, 1958), it includes: 1. Finding an "uninhabited" market where an unfilled need exists; 2. Developing a product to fit that market and getting strong patents on it; 3. Protecting a monopoly position fully—by licensing if advisable, by litigation if necessary. To maintain the patent on cellophane tape alone, for example, it cost the company about $1,000,000 in legal and related expenses.

Scotch tape represents a lion's share of the business of the Minnesota Mining and Manufacturing Company. Few of its purchasers are aware that the corporation also manufactures approximately 300 other pressure-sensitive tapes. Coated abrasives, insulating materials, magnetic recording tapes, and lithographing plates are only a few types of 3-M products developed in the research department and protected by a legal monopoly of patents.

Executives at the Minnesota Mining and Manufacturing Company have described their business as "pulling rabbits out of a bottomless hat." To Buetow and his associates the bottomless hat is the research department, and they have backed up their conviction by pouring more than $60,000,000 into research since Scotch tape was first developed, and by setting aside 4½ per cent of all sales for research. "If you can afford to do fundamental research at home or elsewhere," Buetow says, "you cannot afford not to." He interprets research as applying to the improving of existing products as well as the developing of new ones.

In keeping with a company policy adopted in 1951, Buetow has been expanding and strengthening the foreign operations of the Minnesota

BUETOW, HERBERT—*Continued*

Mining and Manufacturing Company. Late in 1959 its products were being manufactured in some fourteen plants in nine countries, including Germany, Brazil, Mexico, Australia, Canada, Argentina, and the Union of South Africa. Tapes and coated abrasives are produced in the main plant in St. Paul. The corporation further diversified its activities when it bought the Mutual Broadcasting Company, a national radio network, in April 1960.

Buetow hopes that by 1966 the Minnesota Mining and Manufacturing Company will reach $876,000,000 in sales. He believes that the corporation will achieve this goal if it continues to give its products close patent protection, improves its products through continuous research, and engages in effective sales promotion. In the years between 1952 and 1958 the company spent $58,000,000 on modernization, expansion, and research. Any year when profit margins are not up to 10 per cent after taxes Buetow calls a "lean year," and he hopes to double sales every five years.

Never one to spare himself, Buetow stays close to his desk throughout the working day. He even dislikes to take time to go downtown to lunch, preferring to eat in the company dining room where he can discuss business with his employees. He arrives in his office at 8:30 in the morning and lingers beyond closing time, when he often leaves with a loaded brief case.

As a leader in his field, Buetow is often called upon to write articles for professional publications. Among those he has written are: "The President Looks at the Controllership Function" (*The Controller*, March 1956); "Management Planning and Control at Minnesota Mining and Manufacturing Company"; and "Are You Growing Your Own Crop of Management-Able Men?" (*Sales Management*, February 7, 1958).

In St. Paul Buetow has been a director of the First Trust Company. From 1948 to 1955 he was chairman of the board and director of the First Merchants State Bank. Since 1955 he has been a director of the First National Bank. He has taken an active role in the Controllers Institute of America and in the Controller Foundation, and has held offices in these associations. His sense of civic obligation has led him to serve as a member of the Governor's advisory council on unemployment since 1945. Since 1955 he has also been a member of the advisory council of the National Business Aircraft Association, Inc.

On June 24, 1924 Herbert Paul Buetow was married to Luella R. Witt. They have one child, Janet. Erect in bearing, Buetow is six feet tall, weighs 200 pounds, and has brown eyes and graying hair. His preoccupation with the affairs of the Minnesota Mining and Manufacturing Company sometimes carries over into his recreation; he has been known to take his business associates along on hunting trips. Before he became an executive, he used to indulge in gardening at home, but this hobby, along with others, has had to recede into the background. In St. Paul he belongs to the Town and Country

Club, Minnesota Club, and the Athletic Club; in Chicago he belongs to the Union League Club. He is a Republican and a Lutheran.

Confident that the Minnesota Mining and Manufacturing Company will continue to grow in an expanding American economy, Buetow says: "All we need to do is to continue to improve existing products, introduce one or two new products annually, protect them with patents, produce them on a quality basis, and sell, sell, sell."

References

Bsns W p114+ O 4 '58 por
Forbes 81:51 Mr 15 '58 por
Who's Who in America, 1958-59

BUNDESEN, HERMAN NIELS Apr. 27, 1882-Aug. 25, 1960 Public health official; physician; president, Board of Health of Chicago since 1931; writer of books and syndicated columnist. See *Current Biography* (October) 1948.

Obituary

N Y Times p25 Ag 26 '60

BURDICK, USHER L(LOYD) Feb. 21, 1879-Aug. 19, 1960 Former United States Representative from North Dakota (1935-45, 1949-59); Lieutenant Governor (1911-13); Independent Republican who won support from the Nonpartisan League of North Dakota; lawyer; author of books on Western history. See *Current Biography* (April) 1952.

Obituary

N Y Times p19 Ag 20 '60

BURGESS, ROBERT W(ILBUR) July 25, 1887- United States government official; statistician

Address: b. Bureau of the Census, General Federal Office Bldgs., Nos. 3 and 4, Suitland, Md.; h. 1200 16th St., Washington 6, D.C.; 440 Pelham Manor Rd., Pelham 65, N.Y.

"The most important use of the census," Robert W. Burgess, the director of the Bureau of the Census, has said, "is the fact that the population in any given area is what determines its representation in the House of Representatives." A former mathematics teacher, Burgess took office as head of the Bureau of the Census on February 5, 1953, after a long career as senior statistician and chief actuary at the Western Electric Company. The 1960 census, which in April tallied approximately 180,000,000 persons at the cost of about $118,000,000, was the eighteenth full-scale decennial count in the history of the United States and the first that was directed by Burgess.

Born at Newport, Rhode Island on July 25, 1887, Robert Wilbur Burgess is one of the sons of Isaac Bronson (whose father came from England in 1830) and Ellen (Wilbur) Burgess. His younger brother is W. Randolph Burgess, the statistician, banker, and former Under Secretary of the Treasury, who is now Ambassador to the North Atlantic Treaty Organization. Their father, the author of several textbooks, was a teacher of Latin at preparatory schools in New England and Illinois, and their mother had been a teacher of German.

Like his younger brother, Burgess is a graduate of Morgan Park Military Academy in Chicago and of Brown University in Providence, Rhode Island. After having been graduated from Morgan Park in 1905, Burgess took first place in his entrance examinations for Brown in mathematics and Latin and tied for second place in Greek. At Brown University, where he was graduated with a B.A. degree in 1908 after only three years of study, he was elected to membership in Phi Beta Kappa and awarded a Rhodes Scholarship to Oxford University. A resident of Lincoln College at Oxford, Burgess received a B.A. degree in 1910, with a third class in mathematics, and remained at Oxford to take a third class in physics in the following year. He was a member of the Oxford team in chess matches with Cambridge from 1909 to 1911.

From 1911 to 1912 Burgess was an instructor in mathematics at Purdue University. He then taught at Cornell University as an assistant in mathematics while studying for his Ph.D. in applied mathematics, which he received in 1914. His doctoral dissertation, *The Uniform Motion of a Sphere Through a Viscous Liquid,* was published in the *American Journal of Mathematics* in 1916. Burgess remained at Cornell as a mathematics instructor until 1916, when he returned to his alma mater, Brown University, this time as a mathematics instructor. In October 1917 he was drafted for World War I service as a first lieutenant in the Officers' Reserve Corps and in May 1918, when his commission was confirmed in the National Army "for the duration," he was assigned to the statistical branch of the General Staff of the United States Army in Washington, D.C. By the time he was released from active duty in September 1919, he had attained the rank of major, which he held in the Officers' Reserve Corps until 1929.

While serving as an assistant professor at Brown University from 1919 to 1925, Burgess wrote a textbook, *Introduction to the Mathematics of Statistics,* which was published in the United States by Houghton Mifflin Company in 1927 and in England by Harrap in 1929. As an outgrowth of his military experience, Burgess had acquired an interest in statistics which prompted him to leave academic life for private industry. In 1924, while still teaching at Brown, he joined the staff of the Western Electric Company, and in 1925 he began to work for the corporation full-time, as senior statistician and chief actuary. His duties included actuarial studies of company pension plans and machinery depreciation rates and appraisals of business prospects.

In July 1952, when he turned sixty-five years of age, Burgess was automatically retired from the Western Electric Company after twenty-eight years of service. In August he was ap-

ROBERT W. BURGESS

pointed a consultant in business and economic statistics for the operations research office of Johns Hopkins University in Chevy Chase, Maryland. He also served as statistical consultant for the New York law firm of Root, Ballantine, Harlan, Bushby & Palmer just before he was nominated by President Dwight D. Eisenhower on January 16, 1953 for the post of director of the Bureau of the Census. In this appointment, which was confirmed by the Senate on February 4, he succeeded Roy Victor Peel.

On February 5, 1953 Burgess was installed in office. He superintended a special manufacturing census in 1955 and a national housing inventory in 1956. The Bureau of the Census, which uses electronic computers for processing information, was the first government agency to use automation. For this reason, Burgess was called in October 1955 before the Joint Senate-House Committee on the Economic Report that was investigating the effects of automation on the national economy. Citing benefits that mechanization had conferred on the economy in the past, Burgess endorsed automation as a method for improving employment standards and opportunities.

The counting of the American population, required by Article One of the United States Constitution as the basis for apportionment of representatives and for direct state taxation, began in 1790. Although the first decennial count was taken primarily for these purposes, a census of manufactures was added in 1810. By 1840 the census also covered agriculture, mineral industries, trade, and professional activities. The Bureau of the Census, established in 1902 and since 1913 a part of the Department of Commerce, is directed by law to conduct special censuses every five years.

The Bureau of the Census also makes monthly, quarterly, and annual sample surveys in order to obtain data on employment, housing,

BURGESS, ROBERT W.—Continued

migration, and population characteristics and will undertake special city censuses on request. Planning for the 1960 census, which had been preceded by a census of agriculture in 1959, began in 1957. Special advisory committees, consisting of leaders in business, government, labor, and education, helped to formulate the census questions. Eventually some 160,000 enumerators and 10,000 crew leaders were hired to gather the census data. Since the American Civil Liberties Union and certain religious bodies had raised objections to the query about religious preference, it was decided in December 1957 to drop the question. In the census of 1950 a United States population of 150,697,361 was reported; the census of 1960 was expected to reveal a population of approximately 180,-000,000 persons.

A productive writer through the years, Burgess contributed a chapter on "Research for General Administration" to the Taylor Society's volume, *Scientific Management in American Industry* (Harper, 1929), and subsequently contributed to *The American Individual Enterprise System* (McGraw, 1947). He also wrote articles for such periodicals as the *American Journal of Mathematics,* the *Physical Review, Social Forces,* the *American Oxonian,* and the *Journal of the American Statistical Association* and contributed to the *Encyclopaedia Britannica.*

Burgess served as the vice-president of the American Statistical Association in 1939 and is presently a Fellow of the organization. He is a member and former president of the Brown Engineering Association and also belongs to the American Economic Association, the Econometric Society, the Conference of Business Economists, the Institute of Mathematical Statistics, and the Population Association of America. In 1944 he was named to the economic principles commission of the National Association of Manufacturers; in 1948 he became a member of the business research advisory committee of the Bureau of Labor Statistics of the United States Department of Labor, later serving as its chairman. His social clubs include the Brown University Club in New York and the Cosmos Club in Washington. His fraternities are Delta Upsilon, Sigma Xi, and Phi Beta Kappa.

Robert Wilbur Burgess and Dorothy Cross of Barrington and Providence, Rhode Island were married on January 1, 1925. They have three daughters: Mary Ellen, Margaret Cross, and Dorothy Cleveland (Mrs. H. M. B. Voorhis). Newspapermen have commented upon Burgess' erect bearing and on his bushy eyebrows and thick gray hair. For recreation, he likes to play chess, read books about the American Civil War, and swim at the Huguenot Yacht Club in New Rochelle, New York. He is a Baptist and a Republican.

References

N Y Herald Tribune p10 Mr 24 '58 por
U S News 48:22 F 8 '60
New York Times Men in the News—1958
Who's Who in America, 1960-61

BURNS, EVELINE M(ABEL) March 16, 1900- Economist; university professor

Address: b. 2 E. 91st St., New York 28; h. 276 Riverside Dr., New York 25

Social economist and champion of social security, Dr. Eveline M. Burns has extended her career beyond the classrooms of the New York School of Social Work at Columbia University. As teacher, author, lecturer, and consultant to federal and state agencies, Mrs. Burns has applied her wide-ranging knowledge of social insurance. Her incisive thinking and concern for human welfare were assets during her service with the National Resources Planning Board, the National Planning Association, and the Social Security Board. Since 1948 she has been a consultant to the Social Security Administration. Her counsel has been sought by the United States Treasury, the Federal Reserve Board, the New York State Department of Labor, and the United Nations Division of Social Affairs.

Professor Burns has written pamphlets, contributed to encyclopedias and yearbooks, and has had over one hundred articles published in professional journals. She is the author of six books about economics, wage regulations, and social security. Dr. Burns and her husband came to the United States from England in 1926, joined the faculty of Columbia University two years later, and became American citizens in 1937. She received the 1960 Florina Lasker Social Work Award for her efforts in behalf of social security legislation.

Eveline Mabel Richardson was born in London, England on March 16, 1900, the daughter of Frederick Haig and Eveline Maud (Falkner) Richardson. She attended Seatham Secondary School. In 1920 she received a B.S. degree in economics with first class honors at the London School of Economics, University of London. She received her Ph.D. degree in 1926, after having written a thesis on the problems of state wage regulation. This was published the same year under the title of *Wages and The State,* the eighty-sixth in a series of studies in economic and political science issued by the London School of Economics.

Miss Richardson served as an administrative assistant in the British Ministry of Labour from 1917 to 1921. That year she joined the teaching staff at the London School of Economics as assistant lecturer, and two years later became assistant editor of *Economica,* a professional journal. She held both posts until 1926.

Mrs. Burns and her husband, to whom she was married in 1922, received the Laura Spelman Rockefeller fellowship for 1926-28. They spent these years traveling in the United States. In 1928 they both joined the faculty of the graduate department of economics at Columbia University. Except for a period of wartime service with federal agencies, Mr. Burns has maintained his professorship at Columbia.

Mrs. Burns left Columbia in 1942 for active work with the National Resources Planning Board. She was the Anna Howard Shaw lecturer at Bryn Mawr College in 1944; two years later she became professor of social work at the New York School of Social Work, Columbia University, a position she still holds. During the 1950-51 school year she was a visiting professor at Princeton University.

Her term as an administrative assistant in the British Ministry of Labour initiated Eveline Burns's career of service with government and social welfare agencies. Economic research and her own personal convictions were factors influencing her special interest in social security. She became chief of the economic security and health section of the National Resources Planning Board in 1939 and held this post until Congress dissolved the board in 1943 by cutting off its funds. As director of research she was responsible for one of the two illuminating reports issued by the board in 1943, outlining the problems and prospects to be faced in the postwar economy. The report, *Security, Work, and Relief,* received considerable attention from the press and public, but encountered a frigid reception in Congress, which regarded both documents as "New Dealish."

From 1943 to 1945 Dr. Burns was a consultant on social security to the National Planning Association, for which she prepared the *Discussion and Outline on Social Security.* She was one of the group of social security consultants to the Secretary of Health, Education, and Welfare whose recommendations led to the Old Age Survivors' Insurance (OASI) coverage extensions in 1954. Her cogent articles and statements during these years helped clarify many questions about the new system. In 1957 she chided the American Medical Association for its opposition to social security medical benefits to the aged. She told a session of the American Public Welfare Association that the medical profession in the United States "takes a narrow and self-interested view of the social responsibilities of the profession" (New York *Times,* December 6, 1957).

Professor Burns has deplored the relatively small proportion of national income spent on health, education, and welfare services. Recently she questioned whether "our very success in rising to new heights of economic productivity has not so entranced us that we may well be in danger of making economic progress an end in itself" (*Christian Science Monitor,* March 29, 1960).

She has attended White House conferences on children and youth. She is now chairman of the benefit financing and legislative committees of the Federal Advisory Council on Employment Security and a member of the welfare policy committee of the American Public Welfare Association.

Wages and the State (P. S. King, 1926) was Eveline Burns's first book. It was followed by *The Economic World* (Oxford, 1927), written with Arthur R. Burns. J. Fennelly, in a review for *Historical Outlook* (October 1928), called it "a new and interesting attempt by two prominent British economists to solve the apparently insoluble problem of writing a thoroughly satisfactory text for elementary students of economics. The outstanding merit of this book is its readability and clarity." In 1933 Dr. Burns returned to England on a grant from Columbia

EVELINE M. BURNS

University to observe the operation of unemployment programs during the depression. She went again in 1937, under the auspices of the Social Science Research Council, to examine a new comprehensive assistance plan. *British Unemployment Systems* (S.S.R.C., 1942) is the result of her investigations.

The first of her three books on social insurance was published as *Toward Social Security* (Whittlesey, 1936). Its objective was to explain the new Social Security Act to the average person. A New York *Times* (March 22, 1936) writer noted that "Mrs. Burns has a very definite gift for simplifying and clarifying complicated problems. Her vigorous and vitalizing exposition of the Social Security Act and her illuminating discussion of the reasons for its limitations and failings . . . will enlarge and enrich any reader's understanding of this new departure in America's quest for social justice. A vivid personality shines behind the book as a whole and in all its parts and helps to make it, even if it is an economic discussion, eminently readable."

The American Social Security System Houghton Mifflin, 1949) was written with teachers and students in mind, and is organized for their use. A writer for the *Annals of the American Academy for Political and Social Science* (May 1950) reported that "Mrs. Burns, in her marshaling of the facts of social insurance and public assistance, has once more demonstrated her ability to take a difficult and complex matter and assemble it for intelligent use."

Her latest book, *Social Security and Public Policy* (McGraw-Hill, 1956), employs the "problem" approach to analyze the factors involved in policy decisions in this field. Writing for students as well as laymen, Dr. Burns focuses on the American social security system but includes comparative data on other countries. She has contributed to the *Encyclopedia*

BURNS, EVELINE M.—*Continued*

of the Social Sciences, yearbooks, and anthologies, and has had many articles published in *Survey, American Economic Review,* and other professional journals.

Dr. Burns has held office in a number of professional associations. She was vice-president of the American Economic Association in 1953 and 1954, and a member of its executive committee from 1945 to 1948. She has served as secretary (1950-51) and vice-president (1955-56) of the National Conference on Social Welfare. While president (1957-58) of this organization, she asserted that there is no absence of great social issues, only a lack of leaders for them, and urged social workers to avoid the "cocoon" approach to their jobs. She is vice-president and a past president of the Consumers League of New York, and for some years was a member of the national social studies committee of the American Association of University Women. From 1935 to 1943 she was a vice-president of the American Association for Social Security. She has served on the social welfare committee of the National Board of the Y.W.C.A. and on the executive board of her club, Women's City (New York).

Eveline Burns was awarded the Adam Smith medal for outstanding economic research in 1926, the Laura Spelman Rockefeller Fellowship in 1926-28, and a Guggenheim Fellowship in 1954-55 for travel in Europe. She also held the Simon Visiting Professorship of Research at Manchester University, England during the summer term of 1955. In 1958-59 she was American delegate to the International Conference on Social Work in Tokyo, and traveled extensively in the Orient and Middle East under State Department auspices.

Eveline Mabel Richardson was married to Arthur Robert Burns, an economist, on April 8, 1922. She has been described as a keen, energetic, small brunette; her friends claim she has an excellent sense of humor. Both she and her husband are popular with their students. Her leisure activities include cooking and renovating old houses. The Burnses have a summer home at North Sanbornton, New Hampshire.

The 1960 Florina Lasker Social Work Award was given to Dr. Burns at the National Conference on Social Welfare in June 1960. Dr Clara A. Kaiser, chairman of the award committee, cited her as "an outstanding authority on social security systems throughout the world." This tribute is especially fitting since it comes in the year that marks the twenty-fifth anniversary of the Social Security Act, which was signed into law by President Franklin Delano Roosevelt on August 14, 1935. The original legislation has been amended several times and further changes are forecast for the coming year. "One essential aspect for all social legislation," Eveline Burns has said (*Survey,* October 1950), "is the fact that it is dynamic, not static. Times change, and resources and needs change with them. Laws designed to make human lives safer and happier must change, too, at whatever cost of legislative and administrative time and effort."

References

Newsweek 21:31 Mr 22 '43
American Men of Science vol 3 (1956)
Who's Who in America, 1960-61
Who's Who of American Women, 1958-59

BURNS, JOHN L(AWRENCE) Nov. 16, 1908- Corporation executive

Address: b. Radio Corporation of America, 30 Rockefeller Plaza, New York 20

A former teacher, engineer, and management consultant, John L. Burns is the fifth president to serve the Radio Corporation of America, the leading electronics corporation in the world, since its founding in 1919. He was chosen to succeed Frank M. Folsom in early 1957. Burns directs a corporation with annual sales of over $1 billion and with interests in the radio and television entertainment industry, the manufacture of electronic consumer goods, and the development of electronic space equipment. During the decade before he became the president of RCA, Burns was concerned with its organizational and policy matters as a partner in the management consultant firm of Booz, Allen & Hamilton.

John Lawrence Burns was born in Watertown, Massachusetts on November 16, 1908, the son of Michael P. and Ellen B. (Holihan) Burns. After attending elementary schools in Watertown, he was graduated from Watertown High School, where he had been a member of the football, baseball, and boxing teams. At Northeastern University in Boston he took part in the co-operative work-study program and gained engineering experience at Western Electric Company and the Dewey & Almy Chemical Company in Boston, Massachusetts. He received the B.S. degree in electrical engineering in 1930.

From Northeastern University, Burns went on to do postgraduate work at Harvard University, earning a M.Sc. degree in metallurgy in 1931 and a D.Sc. degree in metallurgy in 1934. From 1931 to 1933 Burns was the assistant to the noted metallurgist, Professor Albert Sauveur, at Harvard. In the following year he joined the faculty of Lehigh University in Bethlehem, Pennsylvania as an assistant professor of metallurgy.

Late in 1934 Burns decided to leave the academic field to acquire firsthand knowledge of the operation of industries; he became a laborer in the Republic Steel Corporation's mill in south Chicago. "I decided I knew enough of the theory and wanted to take a crack at actually doing the work," he explained (*New York Times,* May 17, 1959). Paid 59 cents an hour, Burns was required to do such jobs as wrestling with 450-pound coils of white-hot metal with a pair of tongs. His fellow mill hands never suspected that Burns was a doctor of science.

During the next seven years Burns rose through the ranks of Republic Steel. He held such positions as director of metallurgical laboratories, director of quality control, director of process engineering, superintendent of large ingot manufacture, manager of grand crossing works, and superintendent of the wire division.

At the age of thirty-three he was offered a job with the New York management consulting firm of Booz, Allen & Hamilton. He "bagged a partnership within a year (still a company record)" (*Time,* September 7, 1959), and became vice-chairman of the executive committee. In the next few years Burns and his associates helped to determine policy and drafted organizational programs for approximately one-third of the 100 biggest manufacturing and mercantile corporations in the United States, for nearly every department of the executive branch of the federal government, and for several foreign governments. Burns believes that "consulting is a science because it is a study of principles, an art because people are involved."

Among the corporations that used the advisory services of Booz, Allen & Hamilton was the Radio Corporation of America. Frank M. Folsom called on the help of the late Edwin G. Booz to find out how well RCA's many manufacturing plants were organized. When Burns took over as adviser to RCA in 1947, his chief concern was to develop modern management. To attain this goal, he prepared 100 lengthy reports that suggested changes in RCA. One report contained a formula for television programing for the National Broadcasting Company, a subsidiary of RCA. Burns recommended that NBC spend money lavishly on a few outstanding shows and fill in the other hours with low-cost programs. The formula proved so successful that other networks soon adopted it.

From 1947 to 1957 Burns worked on the management policies and problems of RCA. When RCA needed a new president in 1957, it therefore could find no one who knew more about the company than Burns. He was "hand-picked" by David Sarnoff, RCA chairman and chief executive officer. Granted full authority to run the company, Burns assumed the duties of president on March 1, 1957 succeeding Folsom. Burns and RCA reportedly signed a contract providing for a $150,000 annual salary, with increases to $200,000 over the next five years (*Time,* January 28, 1957). He was also elected as a director of the National Broadcasting Company, Inc., and of RCA Communications, Inc.

As president of RCA, Burns gave special emphasis to diversifying the company's activities. In the first two years after he took over, its nonentertainment business jumped 30 per cent. Many new products emerged from its laboratories, and it continued to extend its operations into such areas as missiles, satellites, automation including electronic-data processing, and atomic energy.

Karsh, Ottawa

JOHN L. BURNS

Burns's administration of RCA has been characterized by a tightly knit team operation. He maintains that only by an efficient team can a large corporation deal with its complex problems. Burns has also introduced advanced management systems and methods, and a cost-reduction and profit-improvement program, resulting in increased earnings. For the first nine months of 1959 profits rose to $27,300,000, a gain of 38 per cent over the first three quarters of 1958.

In addition to his responsibilities at RCA and its subsidiaries, Burns is a director of the Great Atlantic & Pacific Tea Company and the National Bank & Trust Company of Fairfield County, Connecticut. He is active in the Boys' Clubs of America, American Heritage Foundation, Committee for Economic Development, Defense Orientation Conference Association, and belongs to many social clubs. A member of the Northeastern University Corporation, he was awarded the honorary Doctor of Business Administration degree by Northeastern in 1957.

John Lawrence Burns was married to Beryl Spinney on August 29, 1937. The couple have two children, John Spinney and Lara Lacey Burns, and make their home in a stone house of twelve rooms in Greenwich, Connecticut. Golfing is Burns's favorite sport.

Usually Burns makes the trip from Greenwich to his office on the fifty-third floor of Manhattan's RCA building in a chauffeured limousine, accompanied by one or more RCA executives he picks up en route. By the time he has arrived at his office, he has already conducted his first business meeting of the day; he has also made notes on matchbook covers, which he drops on his secretary's desk for processing. His associates see nothing unusual in this, for Burns is a man who works

BURNS, JOHN L.—*Continued*

at top speed. He believes that American businesses are in need of men not only with high I.Q.'s, but also with high A.Q.'s ("accomplishment quotients").

References

Forbes 85:19+ F 15 '60 pors
N Y Times p41 Ja 16 '57 por
Who's Who in America, 1958-59

BURTON, RICHARD Nov. 10, 1925- Actor

Address: b. c/o Warner Brothers Pictures, Inc., 666 5th Ave., New York 19; h. 6 Lyndhurst Rd., Hampstead, N.W.3, London, England

Equally responsive to the challenges of classic and modern drama, the Welsh actor Richard Burton has divided his activities between films and the stage in both England and the United States. Known in England for his portrayals of Shakespearean characters with the Old Vic Company, he is also highly esteemed by Broadway theatergoers for his acting in Christopher Fry's *The Lady's Not for Burning* and Jean Anouilh's *Time Remembered*. On both sides of the Atlantic, movie-goers have seen him in such roles as the romantic hero in *My Cousin Rachel,* the Roman officer in *The Robe,* and the disgruntled young man in *Look Back in Anger.* In each part Burton tries to reach perfection. Film director Henry Koster once said: "Burton can thrill an audience. He is one of the few talents that can vibrate and glow."

Richard Burton was born Richard Jenkins on November 10, 1925 in Pontrhydfen, South Wales, the youngest of the thirteen children of Thomas and Edith Jenkins. His father, a coal miner, was determined that at least one of his sons would "live in sunshine" both literally and figuratively, and Richard was allowed to swim,

RICHARD BURTON

chase swans, and attend Port Talbot Secondary School. He learned to play Rugby and to box and won a prize fight when he was fifteen.

As a boy soprano, he earned the annual Eisteddfodau (singing festivals) certificate. He made his nonprofessional stage debut portraying fifty-year-old Magnus in Bernard Shaw's *The Apple Cart* in the New Theatre in Pontrhydfen. His high school teacher and dramatic coach and mentor, Philip Burton, whose name he adopted when he became a professional actor, taught him to speak English without a Welsh accent.

While waiting around for his eighteenth birthday so that he might enter Exeter College, Oxford University, where he had won a scholarship, he learned from a newspaper advertisement that Emlyn Williams wanted an actor who could speak Welsh and looked twenty-two. Richard auditioned for the part, and he was hired to play Glan in *The Druid's Rest,* which opened in Liverpool in November 1943 and later ran in London.

When he finally entered Exeter College, Burton studied English and Italian literature and found time to act with the Oxford University Dramatic Society. At the end of his first year at Oxford, in 1944, Burton entered the Royal Air Force and went to Winnipeg, Canada to receive training as a navigator. He was demobilized with the rank of sergeant in 1947.

When he returned to London, Burton called on Hugh Beaumont, managing director of a successful producer's company. He accepted Beaumont's offer of a one-year contract at the equivalent of $30 a week and performed in several plays during 1948. Cast as Richard the clerk, Burton acted with John Gielgud and Pamela Brown in Christopher Fry's poetical fantasy *The Lady's Not for Burning,* beginning in May 1949 at London's Globe Theatre. When the successful production was transplanted to New York in November 1950, Burton appeared for the first time on a Broadway stage. Between the London and Broadway productions of *The Lady's Not for Burning* he portrayed Cuthman in Fry's *The Boy with a Cart* in the Hammersmith borough of London and Tegeus in Fry's *A Phoenix Too Frequent* in Brighton, England.

For two weeks during the 1951-52 Broadway season he co-starred with Dorothy McGuire in the ill-fated *Legend of Lovers.* In this adaptation of Jean Anouilh's *Eurydice,* Orpheus is an impoverished street musician and Eurydice, an actress. After one day of love, the pair have to choose between continuing on an ecstatic plane in death and facing the disappointments of life. As Orpheus, Burton chose death. Again in London, Burton interpreted the part of Captain Montserrat in Lillian Hellman's *Montserrat,* which began its run in April 1952.

Appearing in Jean Anouilh's romantic comedy *Time Remembered,* which opened in New York on November 12, 1957, Burton acted the part of Prince Albert Troubiscoe. His aunt, played by Helen Hayes, hires a young milliner, portrayed by Susan Strasberg, to shock Albert out of his melancholia over a dead enchantress. Burton was credited by Walter Kerr (New York *Herald Tribune,* November 24, 1957) with having an "intuitive feeling for the author's arrogant and winning determination to build a house out of playing cards."

A brilliant Shakespearean actor, Burton took the title role of *Hamlet* with the Old Vic Company at the Edinburgh Festival in 1953. He remained with the Old Vic during 1953-54 when he again appeared as Hamlet and as John's half-brother, Philip, in *King John,* Sir Toby Belch in *Twelfth Night,* Caius Martius in *Coriolanus,* and Caliban in *The Tempest.* Two years later he was in *Henry V* and in *Othello,* alternating as Othello and Iago.

Burton made his motion-picture debut in the Welsh film *The Last Days of Dolwyn* shortly after his discharge from the RAF and several years later was in *Now Barrabas* and *Waterfront.* In 1952 he went to Hollywood for the first time, to star opposite Olivia de Havilland in *My Cousin Rachel* (Fox, 1952), adapted from Daphne Du Maurier's novel. As Philip Ashley, he was the young Englishman madly in love with the widow of his guardian, even though he suspects she was responsible for her husband's death. "Burton, lean and handsome, is the perfect hero of Miss Du Maurier's tale," wrote Bosley Crowther (New York *Times,* December 26, 1952). "His outbursts of ecstasy and torment are in the grand romantic style." For this role Burton was nominated for an Academy of Motion Picture Arts and Sciences Award.

In Twentieth Century-Fox's first CinemaScope production, *The Robe* (1953), Burton appeared as Marcellus, the Roman officer. Based on the novel by Lloyd C. Douglas, the story tells of the homespun robe worn by Jesus Christ that became a symbol for the conversion of the arrogant Roman tribune. Critics praised Burton's dynamic vigor and his forceful acting, and he was again nominated for an Oscar.

In the British film *Look Back in Anger* (Warner, 1959), Burton captured some of the frustration felt by Jimmy Porter, a university graduate educated beyond his background by the welfare state and married to a girl from a higher class. Although Richard L. Coe (Washington *Post and Times Herald,* September 17, 1959) wrote that "Burton's performance as Jimmy Porter is sensational," a *Time* critic (September 28, 1959) commented that he turnd the character into a "seething, snarling Elizabethan villain." Playing the opportunist, Zeb Kennedy, in *The Ice Palace* (1960), Burton aged from mid-twenty to mid-sixty in the Warner Brothers version of Edna Ferber's outsize novel about Alaska.

Some of Burton's other films are *The Desert Rats* (Fox, 1953), *The Prince of Players* (Fox, 1955), *The Rains of Ranchipur* (Fox, 1955), *Alexander the Great* (United Artists, 1956), *The Sea Wife* (Fox, 1957), *Bitter Victory* (Columbia, 1958), and *The Bramble Bush* (Warner, 1960).

Burton has appeared on television in both England and the United States. On the British Broadcasting Corporation he recited poetry three times a week and took part in several readings with James and Pamela Mason. In 1960 he signed a contract to become the leading narrator of the American Broadcasting Company's series on Sir Winston Churchill.

A lusty baritone who can sing some 2,000 Welsh ditties, Burton satisfied his long-entertained ambition to perform in a musical when he took the male lead in *Camelot.* This Lerner-Loewe show began its Broadway run in 1960.

Richard Burton's wife is the former Sybil Williams, who was a Welsh dramatics student when he met her while he was making *The Last Days of Dolwyn.* Mrs. Burton recalls in an article for *Photoplay* magazine (March 1954) that on their wedding day, February 5, 1949, Wales lost the Rugby championship to Scotland, and Burton was too busy "moaning with grief" to take her on a honeymoon. The Burtons have two children. Besides Rugby, Burton enjoys swimming and boxing. His more sedentary pastimes are chess, piano playing, and attending parties. His pet extravagances are fast automobiles and books.

The actor, who has curly light-brown hair and green eyes, is five feet eleven inches tall and weighs 165 pounds. In religion, he is a Protestant, and in politics, he is an admirer of the late fiery Welsh leftist, Aneurin Bevan. Sidney Skolsky (New York *Post,* October 4, 1959) said that Burton, although charming and humorous, cannot tolerate stupidity and actors who are unpunctual and do not know their lines. Mrs. Burton wrote in *Photoplay* that "he never goes to see his own pictures or reads reviews. In his work Rich is a complete perfectionist."

Burton's style of acting has been much discussed. Richard G. Hubler in the *Saturday Evening Post* (October 3, 1953) wrote: "The passion and energy which he crams into his roles make Burton a throwback to the grand old ideal of acting—in the tradition of John Barrymore, Sir Henry Irving, and Edmund Kean. Not that Burton's style is theirs—he is more intimate, less flamboyant—but his concept of the profession is the same. He has absorbing intensity in his work. He is not afraid to emotionalize offstage as well as on." "By heaven," Burton has said, "I'm going to be the greatest actor, or what's the point of acting?"

References

International Motion Picture Almanac, 1960
Who's Who in the Theatre (1957)
Who's Who, 1960

BYRD, ROBERT C(ARLYLE) Jan. 15, 1918- United States Senator from West Virginia

Address: b. Senate Office Bldg., Washington 25, D.C.; h. Sophia, W.Va.

Calling himself a middle-of-the-road Democrat, Senator Robert C. Byrd of West Virginia says that he can most accurately be characterized as a "liberal on some issues and a conservative on others." As the United States Representative from the Sixth District of his state from 1953 to 1959, he opposed reciprocal trade and liberal foreign aid programs and expressed dissatisfaction with the federal debt.

ROBERT C. BYRD

victorious in the state Senate race. At that time the West Virginia Legislature met only in odd-numbered years, and in 1950-51 and 1951-52 Byrd broadened his educational background by taking courses first at Morris Harvey College in Charleston, West Virginia and afterwards at Marshall College in Huntington, West Virginia. He later studied law at George Washington University and the American University in the nation's capital.

Elected as a Democrat on November 4, 1952 to the first of three successive terms in the United States House of Representatives, Byrd represented the Sixth West Virginia District which encompasses four counties (Boone, Kanawha, Logan, and Raleigh) and includes the city of Charleston.

In January 1953, after being sworn into the Eighty-third Congress, Byrd was assigned to the House Administration Committee. A labor-backed spokesman for a coal mining area, he not only recommended the repeal of the Taft-Hartley Law, but also urged re-enactment of the Wagner Act. Returned to Congress in November 1954, Byrd increased his percentage of the popular vote from 57.4 to 62.7.

During the latter part of his tenure in the House, he served on the Foreign Affairs Committee, as well as on the Administration Committee. In October 1955 he denounced as "dishonorable and unrealistic" the canceling of plans by the International Cooperation Administration to purchase 10,000,000 tons of coal for shipment overseas. In early 1956 he asserted that the West should not yield Chinese Nationalist-held islands to the Chinese Communists.

Requesting in June 1957 that Congress pay close attention to Federal Power Commission hearings on the purchase of natural gas from Canada, Byrd warned that the "importation of foreign natural gas would create a serious impact upon the economy of the coal regions of West Virginia and neighboring states" (Toronto Globe and Mail, June 24, 1957). By November 1959, however, the commission had granted permission to an American company to buy gas from Trans-Canada Pipe Lines Ltd.

While a member of the House of Representatives Byrd voted for the following labor measures: a proposal to increase unemployment compensation benefits (July 1954); the 8.3 per cent as opposed to the 7.6 per cent pay raise for postal workers (April 1955); raising the minimum wage to $1 an hour (July 1955); and the temporary unemployment compensation bill (May 1958). He opposed passage of the labor-management reporting and disclosure bill (August 1958).

On domestic matters he voted against raising Congressional salaries to $25,000 (February 1955); the Eisenhower highway construction bill (July 1955); exemption of natural gas producers from federal regulation (July 1955); and the Powell amendment to the school aid bill (July 1956). He favored increasing personal income tax exemptions to $700 (March 1954), restoration of rigid farm price supports (May 1955), and a revised highway construction bill (April 1956).

More liberal on domestic matters, he supported public housing, civil rights measures, federal aid for school construction, and grants to economically depressed areas. Byrd was elected to the Senate in November 1958, when he defeated the incumbent Republican, Chapman Revercomb, for the term ending in January 1965.

Born to Titus Dalton Byrd, a coal miner, and Vlurma (Sale) Byrd at North Wilkesboro, North Carolina on January 15, 1918, Robert Carlyle Byrd was orphaned at an early age and brought up on a dirt farm in southern West Virginia by foster parents. (Who's Who in America, 1958-59 records him as the son of Cornelius Sale Byrd and Ada Kirby Byrd.) Graduated from Mark Twain High School at Stotesbury, West Virginia in 1934, Robert went to junior college at Beckley, West Virginia and later to Concord College at Athens, West Virginia. For a time he worked as a store clerk and butcher.

At the age of twenty-eight, Byrd was elected to the West Virginia House of Delegates. He has "acknowledged a brief membership in the Ku Klux Klan at the age of 24" (Joseph A. Loftus, New York Times, November 6, 1958), and before becoming a state legislator wrote the Grand Wizard "as a former member," suggesting that the state was "ripe for some organizational work" (Wayne Phillips, New York Times, October 18, 1958). Byrd later called this letter "a mistake of youth," and while he was a United States Representative in Washington he placed Negroes and Catholics on his staff.

Robert Byrd has been characterized as a "tireless worker" who has "followed an announced political timetable with clocklike precision" (New York Times, November 6, 1958). Thus, after serving one term in the West Virginia House of Delegates, he sought and won re-election in 1948, then in November 1950 was

In the area of foreign policy Byrd voted "yea" on the authorization of the Eisenhower Middle East Doctrine (January 1957). He was recorded as voting "nay" on extension of the Trade Agreements Act (June 1954), postponement of British debt payments (April 1957), and authorization of the Mutual Security Act of 1958 (May).

Both West Virginia seats in the United States Senate were at stake in 1958. Chapman Revercomb, Republican, who had been elected in 1956 to fill out the term of the late Harley M. Kilgore, Democrat, ending in 1959, was a candidate for election to a full six-year term. The Republican John D. Hoblitzell, Jr., who was occupying the seat of the late Matthew M. Neely, Democrat, by appointment, was a candidate to fill out the remaining two years of Neely's term. At the primary on August 5, 1958 former Representative Jennings Randolph won the Democratic nomination for the Neely-Hoblitzell seat, and Representative Byrd led Dr. Fleming N. Anderson in the contest to oppose Revercomb by a vote of 167,000 to 24,000.

During the election campaign Byrd criticized the Eisenhower administration for its "lack of strong leadership" in foreign relations, its failure to keep abreast of the U.S.S.R. in the race for scientific achievements, and its incapacity to deal with the high cost of living. Most observers agreed that the biggest issue in the campaign, however, was the recession. Wayne Phillips (New York *Times,* October 18, 1958) pointed out that the number of persons receiving unemployment benefits in West Virginia had more than quintupled in the two preceding years. On November 4, 1958 Byrd unseated Revercomb by 381,745 to 263,172 votes, and Randolph won over Hoblitzell. The Democrats also kept control of both houses of the state Legislature and won all but one of the six Congressional contests.

After being sworn into the Senate, Byrd was named to the committees on Appropriations and on Banking and Currency. The Senator's voting record for 1959 indicates that he supported the amended housing bill authorizing $2.7 billion in loans and grants for a six-year period (February); the $389,500,000 bill for redevelopment of depressed areas (March); statehood for Hawaii (March); and the bill to give the Rural Electrification Administrator final authority over loans (April). He voted against confirmation of Mrs. Clare Boothe Luce as Ambassador to Brazil (April) and Lewis L. Strauss as Secretary of Commerce (June) and opposed extending foreign aid to Soviet satellites in Europe (September).

On the labor-management reporting and disclosure bill, passed in the 1959 session, Byrd voted in April for passage of the bill and favored an amendment providing a Bill of Rights, with criminal penalties, to protect union members from unfair actions by their unions; an amendment to permit state agencies or state courts to undertake the settling of labor disputes which the National Labor Relations Board declines to handle; and an amendment extending the secondary boycott provisions of the Taft-Hartley Act.

An astute campaigner, of whom it has been said that "everything he does is politically calculated," Byrd has "made the most of the poverty of his youth." The Senator "delights county audiences with his foot-stomping fiddling of 'Ida Red' ₁and₁ 'Old Joe Clark'. . . . It's said that he knows some 50,000 verses and ditties." His speeches abound in Biblical quotations, and he is a popular speaker in Protestant churches.

Senator Robert C. Byrd is five feet nine inches in height, about 160 pounds in weight, and has blue eyes and black hair. His church is the Baptist. He is a Mason, Odd Fellow, Moose, Elk, and Knight of Pythias, and a member of the Lions International. Married since May 29, 1936 to the former Erma Ora James, he has two daughters, Mona Carol and Marjorie Ellen.

References

N Y Herald Tribune p1 Ap 21 '60 por
N Y Times p24, 42 N 6 '58 por
U S News 45:55 N 14 '58 por

Congressional Directory (1959)
Congressional Quarterly Almanac, 1958
International Who's Who, 1959
Who's Who in America, 1958-59
Who's Who in the East (1959)

BYRNES, JOHN W(ILLIAM) June 12, 1913- United States Representative from Wisconsin

Address: b. House Office Bldg., Washington 25, D.C.; h. 1215 25th St. S., Arlington 2, Va.; 201 Main St., Green Bay, Wis.

One of a group of young Republican leaders who stand firmly in the conservative tradition of their party, John W. Byrnes is widely regarded as one of the ablest Congressmen in the House of Representatives. He has been chairman of the House Republican Policy Committee since January 1959, succeeding veteran politician Joseph W. Martin, Jr., in that post. Considered the Republicans' top expert on revenue and tax matters, Byrnes is also a key member of the powerful Ways and Means Committee, on which he has served since 1947. He has represented the Eighth Wisconsin District for sixteen years.

John William Byrnes was born June 12, 1913 at Green Bay, Wisconsin, where his father, Charles W. Byrnes, was formerly a teacher and the superintendent of buildings for the Board of Education. His mother was Harriet Schumacher before her marriage. He has a brother, William, and a sister, Betty. John was stricken with polio at the age of three and has ever since worn a brace on his left leg. He attended Green Bay parochial and public schools, and at East High School, from which he was graduated in 1932, he was active in dramatics, debating, and forensics and was a member of the band.

Byrnes received his B.A. degree from the University of Wisconsin at Madison in 1936 and an LL.B. degree from the university's Law School in 1938. The same year he was appointed special deputy commissioner of banking for the State of Wisconsin, a post he held until January

JOHN W. BYRNES

1941. Admitted to the Wisconsin bar in 1939, Byrnes opened an attorney's office in Green Bay, but had little time to practise there in subsequent years.

Only twenty-seven years old when elected to the Wisconsin state Senate for a four-year term (1940-44), John W. Byrnes was the first Republican in many years to represent Brown County in the upper chamber at Madison. In 1943 he was named majority floor leader. He also served as chairman of the Judiciary Committee, and he wrote the act that created the Veterans' Recognition Board and the Wisconsin Soldiers' Voting Law.

In November 1944 Byrnes became a candidate for election as United States Representative from the Eighth Wisconsin District embracing nine counties in the northeast section of the state, and defeated the incumbent Democrat by about seven thousand votes. He has been returned by his constituents to the House of Representatives in every biennial election since then, receiving a substantially increased number of votes.

Sworn into the primarily Democratic Seventy-ninth Congress in January 1945, Byrnes was assigned to the House Civil Service Claims and the War Claims committees. In the Republican-dominated Eightieth Congress, he was named to the tax-writing Ways and Means Committee, on which he has served continuously ever since. Although Byrnes is now the second-ranking G.O.P. member of this committee following Noah Mason of Illinois, "Mason . . . is a traditional 'loner,' and the Administration and House Republicans . . . will undoubtedly take their cues from . . . Byrnes" (*Wall Street Journal*, January 25, 1960). In July 1960 Byrnes expressed his hope that the Eighty-seventh Congress would enact legislation to lower income tax rates for individuals, small businesses, and corporations.

On Ways and Means subcommittees, he served with the foreign trade policy unit in 1957-58 and with the administration of foreign trade laws and policy unit in 1959-60. He is a member of the Joint Committee on Internal Revenue Taxation.

During the legislative session 1951-52, Byrnes served on the Republican Committee on Committees. In the Eighty-fourth Congress (1955-56), the Congressman was selected to represent Iowa, Minnesota, Missouri, and Wisconsin on the House Republican Policy Committee. Byrnes served as chairman of the Wisconsin Republican delegation in the House of Representatives during 1957-58.

In January 1959 Charles A. Halleck of Indiana replaced Massachusetts Representative Joseph W. Martin, Jr. as Republican floor leader. Byrnes was chosen to take over Martin's position as the chairman of the Republican Policy Committee, one of whose functions is to coordinate party action in Congress with the programs of the White House. Under Byrnes' leadership the committee became far more active than it had been under Martin. Byrnes felt that instead of merely implementing Administration recommendations, the committee should participate in formulating policies and should advise and counsel the President on the opinions of House Republicans as a group.

Byrnes has called himself an economy-minded conservative. According to a *Congressional Quarterly* (January 8, 1960) writer, he voted in 1959 for "76 per cent of the measures which offered a clear-cut opportunity to limit Federal spending," as compared with an average Republican "economy score" of 60 per cent. He has consistently opposed such "financially unsound" legislation as a 1949 bill which would have paid $90-a-month pensions to veterans over sixty-five.

In 1950 he cast the only negative vote on a social security bill proposing coverage of some 10,000,000 additional persons. He explained that, had a proper tax increase been made to cover the costs, he might have supported this bill. In 1960 he opposed the Forand Bill for medical aid to the aged, on the grounds that "priority should be given to the needs of persons who have no social security protection." Byrnes has also indicated his feeling that President Eisenhower "did not use his red pencil enough" on budgets since 1956, and that such Administration programs as the school aid and housing bills "go too far" in spending.

The Wisconsin legislator introduced in 1949 a bill to allow stockholders a 20 per cent income tax credit on dividends subject to corporation tax. Three years later he voted to end consumer price and rent controls. On a motion by Byrnes in 1954, the House voted working parents an income tax deduction of up to $600 for the expenses incurred in obtaining child care services. His proposal to reduce a contemplated raise in the national debt ceiling from $5 billion to about $3 billion was, however, rejected in January 1958, as was a Byrnes amendment to limit payments to previously insured workers under the billion-dollar unemployment relief program of 1958. In 1960 Byrnes opposed an across-the-board pay increase of 7½ per cent for federal workers.

As the representative of a semi-agricultural, semi-industrial district, Byrnes voted in 1954 to authorize the St. Lawrence Seaway construction. The following year he proposed a Great Lakes Basin compact involving eight states and possibly the Canadian provinces of Ontario and Quebec. Byrnes opposed a bill to grant the Rural Electrification Administration authority over loans (1959). He also disapproved of allowing the Tennessee Valley Authority to issue more bonds in order to finance new power facilities (1959). He has favored flexible farm price supports.

Although he supported President Eisenhower on the Civil Rights Bill in 1957, Byrnes did not approve the inclusion of a jury trial amendment. During the Eightieth Congress he favored giving individual states the possession of tideland oil deposits. In 1958 and 1959 he supported various bills which would limit the power of the federal government to encroach on state rights.

Byrnes voted in 1945 for the establishment of a permanent House Committee on Un-American Activities and in 1948 he supported the Mundt-Nixon Subversive Activities Control Bill. Six years later, however, he opposed making membership in the Communist Party a crime. Byrnes favored the Taft-Hartley Labor Law in 1947 and urged the use of its provisions to halt the strike of 1952. He also supported the Landrum-Griffin Labor Bill of 1959.

In foreign policy, Byrnes has consistently supported aid to needy nations, but he has often differed with the administration on the size of appropriations. In 1947 he favored a $200,000,-000 limit on foreign relief and two years later voted to cut European arms aid by 50 per cent. He voted for a $350,000,000 cut for economic aid to Europe in 1951. Byrnes has supported President Eisenhower's Mideast doctrine (1957). He has made at least two official trips abroad, once in 1955 to Finland as a delegate to the Interparliamentary Union and again in 1956 as a member of a Congressional group that visited Formosa.

Byrnes was keynote speaker at both the national convention of the Young Republican Federation in 1947 and the Wisconsin State Republican Convention of 1948, and he was one of a small group of Republicans, including Richard M. Nixon, which in 1949 organized the influential Chowder and Marching Club, a semisocial, semipolitical society. The Republican National Committee considered him for the post of the keynote speaker at the party's 1960 National Convention, but finally selected Representative Walter H. Judd of Minnesota.

John William Byrnes and Barbara Preston, a physical education instructor, were married on February 15, 1947. They have six children: John Robert, Michael Preston, Bonnie Jean, Charles Kirby, Barbara Harriet, and Elizabeth Alice. Byrnes has been described by a *Wall Street Journal* (January 25, 1960) writer as a "baby-faced, usually hatless, frequently grinning or laughing" man who looks younger than his age. "His marked limp . . . doesn't keep him from setting a brisk walking pace." Byrnes stands five feet seven inches tall, weighs 140 pounds,

and has brown eyes and black hair. He is an Elk and a member of the Wisconsin Bar Association. His church is the Roman Catholic. His favorite pastimes are golf, swimming, and photography.

Commenting on the Wisconsin Republican party's announcement in May 1960 of its intention to name Byrnes for the Vice-Presidential nomination, John Wyngaard of the Green Bay *Press-Gazette* (May 30, 1960) called the move an indication of the "respectful standing of this comparatively young man in the political life of his state." After describing Byrnes' rapid rise in politics, Wyngaard concluded: "Perhaps his real importance in the public life in his era is that he has shown that a conservative can be respected, and popular, and cumulatively more successful at the ballot box, if he combines a conservative inclination with intelligence and courage."

References

> Cong Q p55 Ja 8 '60
> Wall Street J (N.Y.) Ja 25 '60
> Washington (D.C.) Evening Star Ja 8 '59 por
>
> Congressional Directory (1960)
> Who's Who in America, 1960-61
> Who's Who in the Midwest (1956)
> Who's Who in U.S. Politics (1952)

CANDELA (OUTERIÑO), FÉLIX (căn' dĕ-lă) Jan. 27, 1910- Architect

Address: b. Insurgentes Sur 123-204, Mexico 4, D.F.; Cubiertas Ala, S.A., Ramón Guzmán 123-204, Mexico 4, D.F.; h. Calle Juárez 14, Tlacopac, Mexico 20, D.F.

"One of the best of the new magicians of concrete" is the Spanish-born Mexican architect Félix Candela, whose soaring, undulating, double-curving creations—from churches to bandstands to warehouses—display shells of concrete so thin that they seem to derive less from skill in engineering than from nature itself. Candela is a builder, engineer, and architect who believes that creative architecture can arise only when it achieves an intimate relationship with structure. He has been called a "master builder" in the old sense of the term, because he has helped to narrow the gap between architect and engineer.

At the end of the Spanish Civil War in 1939, Candela migrated to Mexico by way of an internment camp. He first received international recognition when he and Jorge González Reyna designed a concrete shell for Mexico's University City Cosmic Ray Pavilion. This roof is so precisely engineered that its minimum thickness is a mere five-eighths of an inch.

Félix Candela Outeriño was born in Madrid, Spain, on January 27, 1910 to Félix Candela Magro, a shoe dealer, and his wife, the former Julia Outeriño Echeverría. He has a sister, Julia, and a brother, Antonio, who is now his business partner and manager of Candela's firm, Cubiertas Ala, S.A., which specializes in the design and construction of laminar structures and thin concrete shells. Félix attended the

Concrete Quarterly,
London

FÉLIX CANDELA

Instituto del Cardenal Cisneros in Madrid, from which he was graduated in 1926. He had become proficient in skiing and Rugby while he was in high school, and in 1932 he won the ski jumping championship of Spain. In 1933 he played halfback on the national Spanish Rugby team.

Since Candela came from a home where money was not too plentiful, he helped to pay for his training as an architect in the Escuela Superior de Arquitectura in Madrid by coaching his fellow students in statics (that branch of mechanics which deals with the equilibrium of forces). Even during his student days Candela was much interested in structure, especially in shell design, although he has said that he chose his career "by chance." He studied French and German in order to read papers by leading foreign architects in the original languages. He was graduated from the school in 1935 and in 1936 was awarded an important architectural scholarship, the Beca del Conde de Cartagena, from the Academia de Bellas Artes de San Fernando.

His career was interrupted by the Spanish Civil War (1936-39), in which he served as a captain with a Loyalist corps of engineers. (His brother served with Franco's forces.) The defeat of the Loyalists led to his retreat to France, his imprisonment in an internment camp, and his escape to Mexico in 1939. On his arrival there he found work as an architect in charge of a newly established Spanish colony, La Colonia Santa Clara, in Chihuahua.

In 1940 Candela left the colony to work as a draftsman in an architects' office in Mexico City, and in 1941 he became a contractor in Acapulco. In 1942 he began work as an assistant architect in Jesús Martí's architectural office in Mexico City. He observed that reinforced concrete is a standard building material in Mex-

ico because of its economy, its responsiveness to handicraft methods, and because of the scarcity of steel. Furthermore, since the climate is temperate throughout the year, "open planning" is possible. Candela recalled that the Chaldeans and Sumerians had used the dome and vault in their mud-brick architecture, and he also realized that curved concrete "shells" were easy to build with unskilled labor—no more difficult than the traditional vaulting work he had seen being done in Spain with hollow bricks.

Often working in collaboration with other architects, Candela experimented with concrete reinforced with steel mesh and began to design curved concrete roofs for warehouses, factories, restaurants, bandstands, and churches. In 1945 he formed a partnership as architect and contractor with his brother, Antonio, who arrived from Spain at this time. Four years later he built his first structure in thin-shell concrete, and within six years had won recognition as the world's leading authority in this field.

In 1951 Candela established Cubiertas Ala, S.A., a firm that designs and constructs concrete shells. He acts as a building, engineering, and architectural consultant for many architectural firms in Mexico and abroad. He is in much demand because of his talent for thin-shell design; his ability to employ relatively simple building techniques; and because, above all, of the economy of his finished structures. They sometimes are constructed for as little as 50 cents per square foot.

Candela works as an architect, engineer, builder, and even, at times, as a foreman on the structures he creates. He feels that a designer must also be a builder and that education and practice will develop "integrated" architect-engineers. "It is in the separation of design and construction that we have sacrificed an intimate relationship between structure and expression," he has said. "The professions of architect and engineer were one and the same long ago and then the title of Master Builder had real significance." Candela is also a brilliant mathematician and is now a professor at the Escuela Nacional de Arquitectura in Mexico.

Describing Candela's Iglesia de la Virgen Milagrosa in *Arts and Architecture* (May 1957), Esther McCoy wrote: "The Iglesia de la Virgen Milagrosa was the first structure in which Candela had an opportunity to fuse his talents as architect and engineer. An authentic architecture, it blooms out of its own internal order, revealing a mysterious connection between the laws of physics and our aesthetic sensibility. Structurally, it is a series of hyperbolic paraboloidical shells of two heights. Visually it is sculpture of a rich complexity. It has the fancifulness of a flock of Japanese paper birds, but the poetry of its form was conceived as structure not as sculpture."

His Cosmic Ray Pavilion, designed for Mexico's University City in 1950, has the thinnest concrete roof ever constructed. In order to permit the passage of cosmic rays, the roof is five-eighths of an inch at its thinnest point and two inches at its thickest. Other notable concrete structures which Candela has built and designed are the Stock Exchange Building, the Church of San Antonio de las Huertas, Lederle Laboratories, and warehouses for the Rio Company, Cabero, and the Celestino's in Mexico City, a restaurant in Xochimilco and a housing estate's bandstand in Santa Fé.

Photographs of many of Candela's structures, in various stages of construction, are displayed in *Concrete Quarterly* (July-September 1959). The Chapel of St. Vincent at Coyoacán is formed of three one-and-a-half-inch hyperbolic paraboloid shells arranged on a triangular plan, and his Church of San Antonio de las Huertas, Mexico City, has a groined vault roof. The Plaza de los Abanicos, which he has called "somewhat surrealistic" will form the centerpiece in the residential area outside Cuernavaca. The entrance canopy to the Lederle Laboratories, Mexico is a thin V-shaped shell flattening to the tip. A major exhibition of Candela's architectural work was held in May 1957 at the University of Southern California under the sponsorship of the university's fine arts department, its school of architecture, and the southern California chapter of the American Institute of Architects.

Candela has expounded his theories and described his experiences with concrete shell structures in such publications as the *Journal of the American Concrete Institute, Progressive Architecture, Architectural Forum, Architectural Record, L'Architecture d'aujourd'hui, Architetiura,* and *Cement.* The architect has discussed the technical aspects of concrete-shell construction in his paper, "Structural Application of Hyperbolic Paraboloidal Shells" at the American Concrete Institute's convention in Denver, Colorado in February 1954.

Félix Candela and Eladio Martín Galán, a former fashion designer, were married on May 3, 1940. They have four children: Antonia, Manuela, and Pilar and Teresa (twins). Candela is five feet nine inches tall, weighs 160 pounds, and has brown eyes and dark-brown hair. He enjoys playing squash rackets. His professional memberships include the American Concrete Institute, Sociedad de Arquitectos Mexicanos (Mexico), International Association for Bridge and Structural Engineering (Zurich), and the Institut Technique du Bâtiment des Travaux Publiques (Paris). He is an honorary member of the Sociedad de Arquitectos Colombianos in Bogotá.

After Candela had lectured on architecture in a tour of five British cities in May 1959, Betty Campbell wrote in the *Concrete Quarterly* (July-September 1959) that he is "a remarkable man in every way . . . one of the leading structural designers in the world today. . . . He is a great imaginative engineer, because he is fundamentally a thinker."

References

Concrete Q 42:2+ Jl-S '59 por
Progressive Arch 36:106+ Jl '55
Time 72:80 S 8 '58

CANHAM, ERWIN D(AIN) (kăn'ăm)
Feb. 13, 1904- Editor; organization official
Address: b. 1 Norway St., Boston, Mass.; h. 6 Acorn St., Boston 8, Mass.

> NOTE: This biography supersedes the article which appeared in *Current Biography* in 1945.

The thirty-second president of the United States Chamber of Commerce was Erwin D. Canham, the well-known newspaper editor, writer, and public speaker. Since 1945 Canham has been editor of the *Christian Science Monitor,* a daily newspaper with an international circulation and an enviable reputation for accuracy, wealth of information, and uncompromising ethical standards. Described by columnist Roscoe Drummond as "a conservative who does not look upon a new idea as dangerous," Canham felt that his chief mission as president of the United States Chamber of Commerce was to publicize the "responsible, progressive, and liberal" nature of American capitalism today.

Erwin Dain Canham was born in Auburn, Maine on February 13, 1904, to Vincent Walter and Elizabeth May (Gowell) Canham. The Canhams were Christian Scientists, and the editor has said of his mother that her "understanding and love of Christian Science set the path of my life." His father was a part-time farmer and agricultural reporter for the Lewiston *Sun,* a small daily newspaper. The family moved to Lisbon, Maine in 1906, and Erwin grew up in this rural New England area.

Before he was eight years old the boy began to help his father collect local news for the *Sun,* and he started folding and selling papers at eleven, when his father became editor and publisher of a weekly in Sanford, Maine. He then learned to set type by hand. Because of a manpower shortage during World War I, Erwin was hired as a regular reporter by a local daily when he was only fourteen. He continued to work for various newspapers in the summers during his high school days.

Having been a poor student in high school, Erwin had a hard time getting into college, but he finally was enrolled in Bates College in Lewiston in 1921. There, his academic record improved so much that he graduated in 1925 as a Phi Beta Kappa number. In college, as a writer for a small local paper and correspondent for eight metropolitan dailies, he made more money than he later earned as a full-time reporter.

In debating contests at Bates College, Canham began the public speaking that was to become his secondary career. He took part in the first collegiate debate with Oxford University ever held in the United States, and as captain of the debating team in his senior year, he led a trip to England to debate with students of seven British universities. While he was abroad, Canham received a cable from the *Christian Science Monitor* offering him a job as a reporter.

Immediately after receiving his B.A. degree, Canham moved to Boston to join the *Monitor* reporter, Roscoe Drummond, who is now Washington columnist of the New York *Herald Tribune.* Drummond, still Canham's closest friend,

Harris & Ewing

ERWIN D. CANHAM

Monitor, as presented in an editorial in the first anniversary edition (and since reprinted many times) is, in part, that "whatever is of public importance or affects the public welfare, even though it be news of what is ordinarily reckoned as crime or disaster, is printed in the *Monitor* in completeness sufficient for information but without unnecessary embellishment or sensational display. The emphasis, however, is reserved for the helpful, the constructive, the encouraging, not for their opposites."

Because editor Erwin Canham and his staff have carried on in this idealistic tradition, the *Monitor* has for years been one of the most respected and influential newspapers in the United States. Although its circulation (about 160,000 in 1959) is not very large, it is international in its influence, and many of its subscribers are not Christian Scientists. Although the paper has been called stuffy and "too soft-spoken," it is known for its typographical excellence, its leisurely style, and its accurate and responsible reporting of national and international news.

In addition to his editorial activities, Erwin Canham has long been an energetic member of various commissions, boards, and societies. He was vice-chairman of the American delegation to the United Nations Geneva conference on freedom of information in 1948 and alternate American delegate to the General Assembly in 1949; he has also been chairman of the United States advisory commission on information for the United States Information Agency, president of the American Society of Newspaper Editors, chairman of the National Manpower Council, a radio commentator, and moderator of a weekly television program in Boston.

Before he was elected president of the United States Chamber of Commerce, Canham was a member of its board of directors. He served as chairman of its foreign policy committee, first chairman of its committee on commercial uses of atomic energy, and as chairman of a special committee on the Communist economic offensive. He was a delegate to the International Chamber of Congress in Tokyo in 1955. When he was named as president of the United States Chamber of Commerce in 1959, Canham became the first practising newspaperman to hold the office of "spokesman for the world's largest business organization" (*Nation's Business,* May 1959).

"My chief goal as president of the Chamber," Canham once said, "is to let people know about the tremendous change that has taken place in the American system of free enterprise. . . . Too many people—both in this country and abroad—do not realize the degree to which American business has accepted social accountability to its customers, its employees, its stockholders, and the entire community" (*Nation's Business,* May 1959).

In the time not taken up by his other activities, Canham has written four books: *Awakening; The World at Mid-Century* (written with members of the *Monitor* staff) (Longmans, 1951); *New Frontiers for Freedom* (Longmans, 1954), and *Commitment to Freedom; The Story of the Christian Science Monitor* (Houghton, 1958). In 1959 he edited *Man's Great Future*

gave him the nickname "Spike," which he still bears. "Erwin was such a scholarly type," says Drummond (*Nation's Business,* May 1959), "that I thought he needed a nickname. So I gave him the most incongruous one I could think of."

The following year the young reporter was awarded a Rhodes scholarship for graduate study. The *Christian Science Monitor* granted him a leave of absence, and Canham spent the next three years studying modern history at Oxford. During the long vacations he was assistant *Christian Science Monitor* correspondent at the sessions of the League of Nations assembly in Geneva. He earned B.A. and M.A. degrees from Oxford (finally awarded in 1936) and in 1929 returned to Boston, where he became a reporter for the city desk.

In 1930 Canham returned to Europe as chief *Christian Science Monitor* correspondent for the London Naval Conference; for the following two years he served as Geneva correspondent. Called back to the United States in 1932, he became chief of the *Monitor*'s Washington bureau, where he remained for the next seven years. On special assignment, he left Washington in 1933 to cover the London Economic Conference, in 1935 to report on the inauguration of the Philippine Commonwealth, and on several occasions to make nationwide political surveys and to report on Presidential candidates. During this period he also wrote a number of articles on the Far East. After his return to Boston in 1939, Canham became general news editor of the *Christian Science Monitor.* He rose to managing editor in two years and was named editor of the newspaper in January 1945.

Mary Baker Eddy, who founded the Christian Science Church, had established the *Monitor* in 1908 because she felt that the newspapers of the day, with their emphasis on death and crime, injured public morals. The news policy of the

(Longmans). Canham holds honorary degrees from thirteen colleges and universities, is a director of the John Hancock Mutual Life Insurance Company and of the Federal Reserve Bank of Boston, and a trustee of Bates College and of the Boston Museum of Fine Arts. He is an honorary Fellow of Sigma Delti Chi, the professional journalists' fraternity, and a member of Delta Sigma Rho and the Association of American Rhodes Scholars.

Erwin Dain Canham and Thelma Whitman Hart of Truro, Massachusetts were married on May 10, 1930. They have two daughters, Carolyn (Mrs. R. Shale Paul of Pittsburgh) and Elizabeth. The Canhams live in an ante-bellum brick house on Acorn Street in Boston. As a Christian Scientist, Canham neither drinks nor smokes (and smoking is not permitted in the *Monitor* building, by the wish of Mary Baker Eddy). Described by a *Time* writer as "square-faced, silver-haired . . . gentle, scholarly," Canham enjoys reading, playing folk songs on the piano, and vacationing on Cape Cod.

Generally considered one of the busiest men in the United States, Canham comments: "If I sat around playing bridge every night, no one would think anything of it. . . . It just happens that I get more real refreshment out of meeting with a committee of interesting people to talk about a stimulating problem than out of playing cards. I honestly relax and enjoy practically all of these activities that are credited to me as 'work.' "

References

Nat Bsns 47:38+ My '59 pors
Time 73:83 Mr 23 '59 por

Finkelstein, Louis ed. Thirteen Americans (1953)
International Who's Who (1958)
Stewart, Kenneth N. and Tebbel, John Makers of Modern Journalism (1952)
Who's Who in America, 1958-59
Who's Who in New England (1949)
World Biography (1954)

CANNON, HOWARD W(ALTER) Jan. 26, 1912- United States Senator from Nevada; lawyer

Address: b. Senate Office Bldg., Washington 25, D.C.; h. 10012 E. Bexhill Dr., Kensington, Md.; 1702 E. Charleston Blvd., Las Vegas, Nev.

Elected in November 1958 for the term ending in January 1965, the junior United States Senator from Nevada is Howard W. Cannon, a Democrat, who won over the incumbent, George W. Malone, a Republican. A much decorated veteran of World War II, Cannon practised law in Las Vegas and served for ten years as the attorney for that city.

Since taking his seat in the Senate, Cannon has promoted the improvement of the administration of economic aid to foreign countries and other reforms that would regain lost American prestige abroad. On domestic issues he favors helping economically depressed areas, decreasing farm price supports, balancing the budget, and carrying out the integration decisions of the Supreme Court "not through force, but through the use of slower and more natural processes."

Born on January 26, 1912 at St. George, Utah, Howard Walter Cannon is the only son of Walter Cannon, who was born in Utah and became a teacher, farmer, and banker, and Leah (Sullivan) Cannon. He has two sisters, Ramona (Mrs. Don Schmutz of Santa Monica, California) and Evelyn (Mrs. George M. Jay of Ogden, Utah). As a boy Howard learned to be an expert cowhand on his father's ranch.

Graduated from St. George's Dixie High School in 1929 and Dixie Junior College in 1931, he prepared for the teaching profession at Arizona State Teachers College, Flagstaff, Arizona and won election to the Kappa Delta Phi honorary education fraternity. After receiving his B.E. degree in 1933, he turned to the study of law at the University of Arizona, Tucson, Arizona, where he was awarded the LL.B. degree in 1937.

As an undergraduate, Cannon won letters in track, baseball, basketball, and football and attained an outstanding record in wrestling. At the University of Arizona he managed the concert band for three years, organized his own dance band, and became a life member of the Tucson musicians' union.

Admitted to the Arizona bar in 1937 and to the Utah bar in 1938, he began practice as an attorney in St. George. Becoming active in local politics, he was made secretary of the Washington county Democratic central committee. In 1939 he was named legal consultant to the Utah Senate; in the following year he was elected county attorney of Washington county, of which St. George is the administrative seat.

Joining the United States Army in March 1941, Cannon was commissioned a first lieutenant in the Air Forces and had advanced to the rank of lieutenant colonel when separated from the service in July 1946. During World War II he spent more than twenty months overseas, was shot down behind enemy lines in Holland, and evaded capture for forty-two days before rejoining Allied troops. He rode aboard the lead airplane during the invasion of France and later joined the French underground. For his bravery Cannon was decorated with the Distinguished Flying Cross, the Air Medal with two oak leaf clusters, the Purple Heart, the European Theatre Ribbon with seven battle stars, and the French Croix de Guerre with silver star. He has also received a Presidential Citation.

When he returned to civilian life, Cannon was admitted to the Nevada bar in 1946 and became a partner in a Las Vegas law firm. It handled corporation, real property, and federal tax matters and maintained a general civil and trial practice in state and federal courts. Continuing his interest in politics, Cannon was elected city attorney of Las Vegas in June 1949 and was returned to this post for three consecutive terms.

In the years after World War II Cannon was also active in professional law associations. He served with the American Bar Association

Wide World

HOWARD W. CANNON

as Nevada state chairman of the junior bar section and was his state's chairman in the National Institute of Municipal Law Officers. A member of the State Bar of Nevada, he was on its corporation committee, committee on unauthorized practice, and committee on judicial council, selection, and salaries. From 1950 to 1955 he was also a member of the state Board of Bar Examiners.

Entering the national political arena in 1956, Cannon sought the Democratic nomination for Nevada's only seat in the House of Representatives, then occupied by Clifton Young, a Republican. He was defeated, however, in the September primary by Walter S. Baring, who won in the regular election. Two years later Cannon filed against Dr. Fred Anderson of Reno for the Democratic nomination to oppose the re-election of Senator George W. Malone, who was running for a third term. Nevada's other Senate seat has been held by a Democrat, Alan Bible, since 1954.

Supporters of Dr. Anderson prevented labor from endorsing Cannon throughout the state, but Cannon won the allegiance of the Southern Nevada Central Labor Council and defeated Anderson in the primary. In a hard-hitting campaign using television, radio, and the newspapers, Cannon attacked Senator Malone's isolationism in foreign policy and conservatism on domestic matters.

It was more than widespread support from labor, however, that contributed to Cannon's victory over Malone in November 1958 by 48,732 votes to 35,760. His praiseworthy war record and a national Democratic trend also contributed their share. It was the first time in the history of Nevada that Clark County in which Las Vegas is located gave a majority of votes to a Democratic candidate.

Seated in the Eighty-sixth Congress on January 7, 1959, the new junior Senator from Nevada was assigned to the Senate's committees on Aeronautical and Space Sciences, on Armed Services, and on Rules and Administration. In March he was named to a new government operations for space activities subcommittee, headed by Senator Stuart Symington, Democrat of Missouri, which was empowered to investigate wasteful rivalry and duplication in space programs. In April he was named to a Rules and Administration subcommittee to consider a resolution by Senator Wayne Morse, Democrat of Oregon, to restore the publication of salaries of senatorial staff members.

On the floor of the Senate, on June 12, Senator Cannon urged that the "rampant" lobbying for approval of Lewis L. Strauss as Secretary of Commerce be investigated. He voted against confirmation. Among the legislative proposals Cannon submitted was a measure to repeal the "tombstone" act permitting promotion without salary increases upon retirement for Navy, Marine Corps, and Coast Guard officers who had been decorated in combat. Cannon also blocked a move to extend the expiration date of the act beyond November 1. With Senator Clair Engle of California, in April 1959 Cannon introduced another bill, sponsored by many Western Senators, to spend $10,000,000 over ten years for saving and increasing the water supply in the Colorado River basin.

The 1959 voting record indicates that on domestic matters Cannon favored authorizing $389,500,000 in federal loans for redevelopment of economically depressed areas (March), statehood for Hawaii (March), granting to the Rural Electrification Administration authority over REA loans (April), the labor-management reporting and disclosure bill (April), and the revised housing bill of 1959 (August). In the sphere of foreign policy he voted for increasing the United States subscription to the International Bank for Reconstruction and Development (March) and for the $3.2 billion mutual security appropriation bill (September). He opposed granting the President the right to approve aid to Communist countries (September).

Howard W. Cannon is a member of the permanent legal committee of the International Astronautical Foundation and space law and sociology committee of the American Rocket Society. In addition, the Senator is a former district governor and currently an international counsellor of Lions International; a past president (1955) of the Clark County Chamber of Commerce; a charter member of the Southern Nevada Industrial Foundation, a nonprofit organization to promote industry in the state; he is also a member of the Benevolent and Protective Order of Elks. His religious affiliation is with the Church of Jesus Christ of Latter-day Saints.

Mrs. Cannon, a secretary before her marriage, is the former Dorothy Pace. Married on December 21, 1945, the couple has two children, Nancy Lee and Alan Howard. Senator Cannon is five feet eight inches in height, 180 pounds in weight, and has blue eyes and black hair. Today a full colonel in the Air Force Reserve, he has flown over twenty different types of aircraft, including the F-100 supersonic jet. Flying remains a favorite recreation, along with horseback riding, hunting, and fishing.

References

Christian Sci Mon p5 N 10 '58
N Y Times p24 N 6 '58 por
U S News 45:87 D 26 '58 por
Congressional Directory (1959)
International Who's Who, 1959
Who's Who in the West (1954)

CARROLL, JOHN Aug. 14, 1892-Nov. 7, 1959 Artist; painted delicate portraits and landscapes which are represented in leading American museums; instructed at the Art Students League of New York (1926-27; 1944-55). See *Current Biography* (July) 1955.

Obituary

N Y Times p88 N 8 '59

CARTER, ELLIOTT (COOK) Dec. 11, 1908- Composer
Address: b. School of Music, Yale University, New Haven, Conn.

For a number of years, the composer Elliott Carter had been respected by an inner circle of musicians and critics, and he had often been honored with commissions from musical groups and foundations. But it was not until May 1960, when Carter was awarded the Pulitzer Prize in Music for his Second String Quartet, that he made the front pages of American newspapers. An editorial in the New York *Times* called attention to the fact that the award signalized the recognition of "a mature composer's talent."

Because of their frequent changes of speed and their dissonance, the austere chamber compositions of Elliott Carter demand a great deal from both performer and listener. Using polyrhythm or "metrical modulation" and allowing each instrumentalist relative independence, they explore new musical territory, the terrain of which becomes more meaningful with repeated hearings.

Elliott Cook Carter, Jr., the son of Elliott C. Carter, a lace importer, and Florence (Chambers) Carter, was born in New York City on December 11, 1908. He was reared in New York, where he attended Horace Mann High School. Although his early interest in music received little encouragement at home, Elliott Carter became aware of trends in contemporary musical composition through friends at Horace Mann. The noted American composer Charles Ives urged him to pursue a musical career.

After graduating from high school in 1926, Elliott Carter enrolled at Harvard, where he majored in English literature, since he was still uncertain about choosing music as a career. At the same time, he studied piano with Newton Swift and solfeggio with Hans Ebell at the Longy School in Cambridge, Massachusetts. His extracurricular activities reflected his musi-

Helen Merrill

ELLIOTT CARTER

cal bent: he belonged to the Harvard Glee Club, played in chamber music ensembles around the Cambridge-Boston area, and frequently attended concerts of the Boston Symphony Orchestra.

Carter took his B.A. degree from Harvard in 1930 and then decided to stay on for graduate work in music. His teachers included Walter Piston for harmony and counterpoint, A. T. Davison for choral composition, Edward Burlinghame Hill for the history of music, and the British composer Gustav Holst, then a visiting professor, for composition. He was awarded an M.A. degree in 1932.

In 1932 Elliott Carter journeyed to Paris to study with Nadia Boulanger, both as a private student in composition and as a member of her course in counterpoint at the École Normale de Musique. He emerged from the École Normale with a Licence de Contrepoint. He also sang in a madrigal group directed by Henri Expert and conducted a chorus of his own before he returned to the United States in 1935.

While in France, Elliott Carter was asked to compose the incidental music for a production of Sophocles' *Philoctetes* that was planned by the Harvard Classical Club. The production, which took place in Cambridge in the winter of 1933, represented the first public performance of an Elliott Carter score.

Settling in Cambridge upon his return from Paris, Carter found that the Depression had made a composer's financial situation even more precarious than usual. In the fall of 1936 he moved to New York and began contributing articles to the journal *Modern Music*. From 1937 to 1939 he was music director of the Ballet Caravan.

Compositions by Carter dating from this early period include a 1937 *Tarantella*, incidental music for a Mercury Theatre production of *The Merchant of Venice* (1938), and the ballet *Pocahontas* (1939), which was commis-

CARTER, ELLIOTT—*Continued*

sioned by the Ballet Caravan. In 1938 he won a prize from the music division of the Works Projects Administration for his choral work *To Music*. His suite from *Pocahontas* won the Juilliard Publication Award in 1941.

From 1939 to 1941 Carter served on the faculty of St. John's College, Annapolis, Maryland, where, in addition to supervising various musical activities around the college, he taught Greek and mathematics. In co-operation with the dean of St. John's, the philosopher Scott Buchanan, Carter devised a unique course, required of all students, in which music was studied for its mathematical as well as emotional qualities. Carter described this course in an article in *Modern Music* (October 1944).

In 1943 Elliott Carter became music consultant to the Office of War Information, a post he retained until 1945. From 1946 to 1948 he taught music theory and composition at the Peabody Conservatory in Baltimore. Later academic appointments include posts at Columbia University (1948 to 1950), the Salzburg Seminars in Austria (1958), and Yale University, where Carter is currently Professor of Musical Composition.

His many activities in several areas of American musical life have not dislodged composing from its central place in Elliott Carter's affections. During the 1940's he composed the choral work *The Defense of Corinth* (1941); the First Symphony (1942-43); *The Harmony of Morning* (1944) for women's chorus and small orchestra; a Quartet for Four Saxophones (1943), which received the American Composers Alliance prize; and a Piano Sonata (1945).

Carter wrote his ballet *The Minotaur* (1946-47) on a commission from the Ballet Society. During the late 1940's he composed a Woodwind Quintet (1947); a Sonata for Cello and Piano (1948); *Emblems* (1948) for men's chorus and piano; and *Eight Études and a Fantasy for Woodwind Quartet* (1949). His *Holiday Overture* won the 1954 prize of the Independent Music Publishers and his First String Quartet (1950-51) took first prize over scores submitted from twenty countries at the Concours International de Quatuors à Cordes in Liége, Belgium. In 1952 he received a commission from the League of Composers to write a symphony.

More recently, Carter has composed a Sonata for Flute, Oboe, Cello and Harpsichord (1952), which won the Walter W. Naumburg Musical Foundation Award; Variations for Orchestra (1955), which was commissioned by the Louisville Orchestra; and a Double Concerto (1956), which was commissioned by the Fromm Foundation. His output also includes several smaller works for voice with piano accompaniment.

Although Elliott Carter's compositions have always evoked approbation from the critics, his chamber music has been especially praised. Paul Henry Lang has called the First String Quartet "an authentic masterpiece by an American composer" and "one of the handful of truly significant works that open the second half of the twentieth century" (New York *Herald Tribune*, October 24, 1958).

Lang went on to describe the piece as "a difficult, intense, and aristocratic work, the product of a clear, cultivated, subtle, and enterprising mind. Its contrapuntal, metric, and rhythmic intricacies are extraordinary, yet Carter's narrative architecture is so skillful that one can 'listen' to much of his music without being aware of them." Lang discerned in the quartet the influence of earlier twentieth-century masters, Bartók, Schoenberg, Berg, and Ives.

Carter's second venture into quartet composition received equally ecstatic notices before it captured the 1959 Pulitzer Prize in Music. After its première by the Juillard String Quartet at the Juilliard School of Music on March 25, 1960, Howard Taubman wrote: "With his Second String Quartet Elliott Carter rivets his right to be regarded as one of the most distinguished of living composers" (New York *Times*, March 27, 1960).

Explaining his love of the quartet genre to Eric Salzman (New York *Times*, March 20, 1960), Carter said: "I find the human world of the quartet fascinating. You have four people who have cast their lot together in life. There's the problem of how they can stand each other for so long. There's the fascinating thing of how a communal ensemble group can become almost a solo, virtuoso instrument."

Carter has found time to be active in the League of Composers (having served on the board of directors from 1939 to 1952), the International Society of Contemporary Music (board of directors, 1946-1952; president of the United States section in 1952), and the American Composers Alliance (board of directors, 1939-1952; treasurer, 1949-50). In 1956 he was elected a member of the National Institute of Arts and Letters. He professes no political or religious affiliations.

In 1939 Elliott Carter was married to Helen H. Frost Jones, a sculptor and art critic. They have one son, David Chambers Carter. Youthful in appearance, Carter is five feet eight and one half inches tall, weighs about 150 pounds, and has gray eyes and graying hair. Travel has been his favorite recreation ever since he was introduced to Europe at the age of twelve. (His father's business maintained offices in Switzerland.) Carter has visited most of the interesting cities of Europe and has made many trips through remote sections of Greece and Italy. He is interested in architecture and painting and reads widely in literature and philosophy. He has said of his composing: "I just can't bring myself to do something that someone else has done before. Each piece is a kind of crisis in my life; it has to be something new, with an idea that is challenging."

CASTLE, LEWIS G(OULD) Aug. 12, 1889-June 4, 1960 United States government official; administrator, St. Lawrence Seaway Development Corporation since 1954; president, Northern Minnesota National Bank (1947-54). See *Current Biography* (July) 1958.

Obituary

N Y Times p85 Je 5 '60

CHAGALL, MARC (shä-gäl') July 7, 1887-
Artist

Address: Vence, France

> NOTE: This biography supersedes the article which appeared in *Current Biography* in 1943.

The man on the flying trapeze would find his element in a painting by Marc Chagall. Floating with him over the roof tops of a topsy-turvy village would be green cows, blissful lovers, decapitated peasants, old violinists, and grave rabbis. Chagall found the ever-recurrent images of his art in a youth spent in the Jewish section of a Russian town, and in a happy marriage. Often called a creator of fantasies and a dreamer, he protests that he has always shown a real and important part of human experience. "I want to introduce into my pictures a psychic shock . . . a fourth dimension," he says. "Therefore, let people cease talking about fairy tales, of the fantastic, of Chagall the flying painter, when they speak of me."

Marc Chagall, one of ten children of Zakhar and Ida (Tchernine) Chagall, was born on July 7, 1887 in Vitebsk, a town on the Russo-Polish border. His parents were Hasidim, members of a devout and mystical Jewish sect. Chagall's paternal grandfather was a teacher of religion; his mother's father, a master butcher. It was his maternal grandfather who, during a family holiday gathering, quietly climbed up on the roof, where he sat munching raw carrots. A figure astride a roof top often appears in Chagall's pictures. So does the violinist who recalls the artist's Uncle Neuch, who played that instrument "like a cobbler."

Marc's father worked as a laborer in a herring plant. His mother, sovereign within the household, dealt with all practical matters. It was she who set up a small grocery shop, furnishing it with wares obtained on credit. The fascination which his birthplace held for Chagall has endured throughout his life. Appearing in almost every one of the artist's paintings, the cottages of Vitebsk testify to his memory of his native town.

From an old man, a teacher and cantor who lived nearby, Marc first received elementary schooling. This did not interfere with his swimming in the Dvina River and watching fires from a first-row seat on the roof. It was only after he was confronted with the first of three rabbis with whom he continued his elementary education that river bathing gave way to Bible instruction on Saturdays. Marc next enrolled in the town school, which he reluctantly attended for some three years; at this time he began to stammer and refused to recite lessons which he knew perfectly. He excelled only in geometry.

From his earliest youth, a career as a singer, violinist, dancer, or poet attracted Marc more than life as a laborer or merchant. His parents apprenticed him to a photographer, but he did not like retouching the wrinkles and crow's feet which made faces interesting. The remark of a schoolmate who praised one of his drawings

Maywald, Paris

MARC CHAGALL

first prompted Chagall to consider painting as a vocation. Persuading his parents to give him the tuition, he enrolled in the Penne School of Painting and Design.

Influenced by a fellow student, Chagall decided to pursue art studies in St. Petersburg. Since the Tzarist régime required every Jew in that city to justify his presence there by presenting proof of a legitimate occupation, he arranged to go as the official representative of the merchants in his town in 1907.

Immediately on his arrival, Chagall took examinations for Baron Stieglitz's School of Arts and Crafts, but he failed to pass. In order not to forfeit his right to remain in the city, he became a third-year student at a school of lesser reputation, the Society for the Protection of the Arts. Although he attended the course for two years, Chagall was not satisfied with such academic and provincial training.

Hoping to find a mentor who would understand his creative goals, he studied for a few months with Leon Bakst. Here too Chagall found the instruction alien. "The truth is, I'm incapable of learning," he has explained. "Or rather it's impossible to teach me. . . . I get nothing except by instinct. . . . And academic theory has no hold on me."

Disappointed with his artistic progress, Chagall also found it difficult to obtain money and authorization to remain in St. Petersburg. For several months he received a small subsidy from an art patron; toward the end of his stay he lived as a servant in the house of a Jewish lawyer. He also apprenticed himself to a sign painter in order to learn a craft which would afford him an unchallenged residence permit. For the most part, however, he lived in penury, often sleeping in a corner of a room occupied by laborers. Arrested on one occasion for lack-

CHAGALL, MARC—*Continued*

ing residence papers, he spent a short term in prison. There he ate and slept better than he ever had since coming to St. Petersburg.

Chagall's early paintings record with compassion and humor his youthful impressions of the people of Vitebsk. Painting primarily in a low chromatic scale, he tried to attain emotional verity rather than exact description of external attributes. He returned to St. Petersburg after a short visit to Vitebsk, convinced that he must seek artistic fulfillment in Paris. A lawyer and political leader, Vinaver, bought two of his pictures and promised him a monthly subsidy which would enable Chagall to live in the French capital.

In the Paris of 1910 Chagall's art bloomed. He took pleasure in studying original paintings by old masters and those by his experimenting contemporaries. After living for a while in the impasse du Maine, he moved into La Ruche (The Beehive), a network of studios in rue Dantzig that housed indigent artists of many nationalities. Here Chagall made friends with poets Guillaume Apollinaire and Blaise Cendrars, who dedicated poems to him and encouraged him in his painting.

Always productive, Chagall now executed hundreds of paintings in which the colors became lighter and the figures lost their material weight and began to float. Although he experimented with the cubist style, he rejected all the new art theories as he had the old. "My art . . . is perhaps a wild art, a blazing quicksilver, a blue soul flashing on my canvases," he said.

Although he exhibited every year in the Salon des Indépendants, Chagall sold no pictures. Three paintings which he sent to the Salon of the Independents at Amsterdam were bought for 900 francs, but he never received the money because the gallery cashier absconded with it. In the spring of 1914 art dealer Charles Malpel contracted to pay Chagall 250 francs for seven pictures which Chagall was to supply each month. At the suggestion of Apollinaire, Herwarth Walden, founder of a German expressionist movement and editor of *Der Sturm,* arranged Chagall's first one-man show at the *Sturm* offices in Berlin in 1914. The artist sent the whole of his existing work—some 200 paintings—to the exhibition.

The letters that Chagall received from Bella, his childhood sweetheart and fiancée whom he had left in Russia, began to contain references to another suitor. Eager to see her, he returned to his birthplace, stopping off in Berlin to see his exhibition. In 1915 he and Bella were married. For nearly thirty years, until her death in 1944, Chagall found happiness in this union. Bella was also the most discerning critic of his art.

Two outstanding paintings of this period are *The Birthday* (1915-23) and *Self-Portrait with a Wineglass* (1917). Executed with striking clarity, the canvases communicate a bursting joy. The young man of *The Birthday* has caught his beloved by flying over her head and kissing her; his kiss draws her up with him in happy flight. In the *Self-Portrait,* Chagall sits on Bella's shoulders, tipsily flour-

ishing a wineglass. Dressed in a white wedding frock, Bella strides out confidently, sharing his satisfaction.

From 1915 to 1917 Chagall fulfilled his World War I military service by checking muster-rolls in a St. Petersburg office. Named by the Russian revolutionary régime as Minister of Arts for the province of Vitebsk, he stopped painting and devoted himself to building a school of art in his native town. For the first anniversary of the October revolution Chagall set his students to copying his designs for decorations. "On October 25," he writes, "my multicolored animals swung back and forth, swollen with revolution . . . [the] workers understood. Their Communist leaders appeared to be less satisfied. Why is the cow green and why is the horse flying in the sky? Why?

For two years Chagall struggled to establish a people's art in his school. He wore himself out seeking money, food, and art supplies for faculty and students. Frustrated at every turn, Chagall was finally ousted by them and given twenty-four hours to leave town. He went to Moscow, where he lived until 1922.

During this period he decorated the auditorium of Granovsky's Jewish State Theater with murals depicting the forerunners of contemporary actors: a popular musician, a wedding jester, a dancing woman, a copyist of the Torah, and a young couple twirling over the stage. The sets that he designed for the first production included properties which he himself sketched in, because he could not bear naturalism in the theater.

Unable to collect payment for his execution of the State Theater murals, Chagall lived for several months in Malachowka, a village near Moscow, where he gave art lessons to orphans in a state children's colony. He had had his fill of Russia, however. In 1922 a letter from a friend in Berlin advised Chagall that he had become famous in western Europe. He decided to return to Paris, stopping first at Berlin.

After spending several months in the German capital trying unsuccessfully to retrieve the paintings that he had left at the *Sturm* galleries eight years before, Chagall accepted the invitation of the French art dealer Ambroise Vollard to do a series of etchings for Gogol's *Dead Souls.* He worked on them in Paris for the next five years; in 1927 he began engravings commissioned by Vollard for the *Fables* of La Fontaine. One hundred preliminary gouaches for this work were exhibited in Paris in 1930. His drawings for *Dead Souls* were first published in 1948, those for the *Fables* in 1952 by Tériade.

Between 1931 and 1937 Chagall traveled to Egypt, Syria, Palestine, Holland, Spain, Poland, and Italy, searching for ideas for illustrations of the Old Testament which he began in 1931 at Vollard's request. The first forty etchings were shown in Paris in 1934. In 1956 Harcourt, Brace and Company brought out the American edition of 105 *Illustrations for the Bible,* and four years later the firm published additional engravings under the title, *Drawings for the Bible.* Chagall has also illustrated numerous books written by contemporaries with drawings that are simply done and freely interpret the spirit rather than the letter of the text.

Chagall's first retrospective exhibition was held at the Galerie Barbazange-Hodebert in Paris in 1924. Two years later his first one-man show in New York was held at the Reinhardt Galleries. His pictures have been on view almost every year since then in major cities throughout Europe, the United States, and Israel. In 1948, 1950, and 1952 Chagall exhibited at the Venice Biennale. He received the International Prize for Engraving at the Biennale of 1948.

The contentment of the 1920's and early 1930's when Chagall's pictures blossomed with flowers, the happiness of lovers, and acrobats and angels, gave way to anxiety and the horror of war. The familiar images persist in paintings like *White Crucifixion* (1938), *Cello Player* (1939), and *Martyrdom* (1940), but they communicate a feeling of wild disorder and fear. In 1939 Chagall moved to Gordes in southern France. Two years later, at the invitation of the director of the Museum of Modern Art, he, his wife, and his daughter, moved to New York. In 1942 he went to Mexico to design décor and costumes for Massine's ballet, *Aleko*. He did a curtain and sets for the Ballet Theater production of *The Firebird* in 1945.

Chagall returned to Paris in 1947 and moved two years later to his present home in Vence. He has done restoration work on stained glass windows in Europe, replacing those shattered in the war. He designed stained glass windows representing the Twelve Tribes of Israel for a synagogue built in the Hadassah Hebrew University Medical Center outside of Jerusalem. At Vence, a town which thrives on the pottery trade, Chagall has turned to ceramics and sculpture as new modes of artistic expression.

Marc Chagall was married to Bella Rosenfeld on July 25, 1915. She died on September 2, 1944. Chagall has one daughter, Ida (Mrs. Franz Meyer), who lives in Switzerland. He is a short, blue-eyed man with a wispy cloud of white hair. He was married to his second wife, Valentine, after he returned to France in 1947. He is the winner of a Carnegie Prize (1939) and holds the French title of Commandeur des Artes et des Lettres and honorary LL.D. degrees from Brandeis University and the University of Glasgow.

References

Chagall, Marc My Life (1960)
Erben, Walter Marc Chagall (1957)
Sweeney, J. J. Marc Chagall (1946)

CHAMBERLAIN, OWEN July 10, 1920-
Physicist; university professor
Address: b. Radiation Laboratory, University of California, Berkeley, Calif.,; h. 954 San Benito Rd., Berkeley, Calif.

The co-recipient of the Nobel Prize in Physics for 1959 is Dr. Owen Chamberlain, professor of physics at the University of California at Berkeley and a member of its Radiation Laboratory. He shared the award with his Berkeley colleague, Dr. Emilio Segrè, for the joint discovery in 1955 of the antiproton, the mirror image of the proton which composes the nucleus of ordinary atoms. The Chamberlain-Segrè discovery was made after nuclear researchers had tried in vain for more than twenty-five years to confirm the existence of the negatively charged proton which can annihilate the positive proton of matter found on earth. Discovery of the antiproton, which cannot exist permanently on earth, has increased man's knowledge of symmetry in nature and marked an immense advance in the study of anti-matter, reaching from atomic nuclei to the universe.

Owen Chamberlain was born on July 10, 1920 in San Francisco, California, where his father was a radiologist on the staff of Stanford University Hospital. The family moved to Philadelphia when Owen was ten years old, and he received his education in the public schools there. He attended Dartmouth College and took his A.B. degree with the last pre-World War II graduating class in June 1941. Chamberlain matriculated at the University of California at Berkeley in the fall to do graduate work in physics.

Within the year the United States entered the war and the government embarked upon a crash research program. Chamberlain abandoned his own studies in 1942 to join a group of scientists investigating uranium isotopes for the Manhattan District under the direction of Dr. Ernest O. Lawrence, inventor of the cyclotron and winner of the 1939 Nobel Prize. In mid-1943 Owen Chamberlain was transferred to Los Alamos, where he continued his atomic research and participated in the firing of the first atomic bomb test in 1945.

At the end of World War II Chamberlain continued to work in atomic physics, concentrating on slow-neutron diffraction in liquids at the Argonne National Laboratory in Chicago. He also studied at the University of Chicago with Professor Enrico Fermi and received the Ph.D. degree in physics in 1948. Chamberlain was invited to return to the Berkeley campus as an instructor in physics in 1948. He was appointed an assistant professor in 1950 and promoted to an associate professorship four years later.

When Chamberlain returned to the University of California he began a series of scientific investigations that laid the foundation for the work which later brought him fame. Using the giant cyclotron, Chamberlain concentrated on a study of the scattering of high-energy protons and neutrons. He was especially successful with proton polarization experiments, including the first triple-scattering experiments with polarized protons. These studies permitted the determination of components of the scattering matrix that were not made accessible in the simpler double-scattering experiments.

Dr. Chamberlain's work with protons, which have a positive charge, was superseded by a study of its opposite members, the antiprotons, which are negatively charged particles of the same mass as protons. These antiprotons had been the object of scientific investigation since their existence was first suggested by the Eng-

OWEN CHAMBERLAIN

lish physicist P.A.M. Dirac in 1928. Antiprotons, though stable in a vacuum, could not exist, however, with ordinary matter and were extremely elusive. Scientists could not establish their existence in atomic nuclei despite involved experiments with cosmic rays.

During the early 1950's Chamberlain established a fruitful scientific collaboration with Dr. Emilio Segrè, Italian-born scientist and fellow member of the Berkeley faculty, who was conducting research of a similar nature. Assisted by Clyde Wiegand and Tom Ypsilantis, the team discovered that antiprotons arose only outside the nucleus in high-energy nuclear collisions such as those occurring in cosmic radiation or in bombardments achieved with the Berkeley bevatron, the most powerful atom smasher in the world. Until the bevatron was built, high-energy nuclear bombardments sufficient to create antiprotons could not be performed. "It is the only energy source high enough to produce the anti-protons," says Dr. Chamberlain. "Even the stars are a million times too cool, while the hydrogen bomb, which is basically a star, is not in the same league" (*Christian Science Monitor,* January 20, 1956).

Using the bevatron to fire protons of 6.2 Bev (billion electron volts) at a copper target, the Chamberlain-Segrè team created antiprotons artificially and kept them alive long enough to identify them. From the target emerged a secondary beam of subatomic debris (protons, neutrons, mesons) that were presumed to contain antiprotons. This was shot into an experimental "maze" (selected apparatus consisting of magnetic fields and/or speed instruments) through which only particles with antiproton characteristics could and would pass.

Announcement of the California experiment was made in October 1955. Conclusions were not reached dramatically and, according to Dr. Chamberlain, "there was no moment of discov-

ery. It was more like a month. And most of that time was spent trying to prove that we hadn't made any discovery at all" (*Christian Science Monitor,* January 20, 1956). After another month, in December 1955, scientists from California and Rome reported that they had observed "the explosive disintegration of an atomic nucleus—a 'star'—by an anti-proton." Chamberlain and his associates had bombarded photoemulsion plates with antiprotons to obtain visible records of these strange, elusive particles when they met atoms of the emulsion. The star was actually the cosmic debris created when the proton and antiproton collided in the nucleus of the silver or bromine in the photographic emulsion.

The discovery of the antiproton lies completely within the realm of theory. Chamberlain has emphasized that the antiproton cannot be used to "produce a super bomb more powerful than the atomic or hydrogen bombs." Although the collision of a proton and antiproton causes an explosion of extreme power, it does not release a new source of energy since they both destroy each other. It requires as much energy to create an antiproton as is produced when it destroys itself colliding with a positive proton. The California team has not ventured to predict the ultimate significance of their experiment. "Perhaps physicists are never to understand a basic 'why,'" says Professor Chamberlain, "and thus they are settling for a lesser goal, trying to find as few man-made rules as possible to 'explain' the known facts."

A Guggenheim Fellowship awarded to Dr. Chamberlain in 1957 permitted him to further his investigations of the antiprotons and its interactions and to work with Dr. Edoardo Amaldi, an Italian physicist, who had joined the California scientists to confirm the existence of the antiproton. When he returned to his California post in 1958, Dr. Chamberlain was appointed a full professor of physics. During the 1959 fall semester Chamberlain was Loeb lecturer in physics at Harvard University.

In recognition of his outstanding work in discovering the antiproton, Dr. Chamberlain shared the 1959 Nobel Prize in Physics with his co-worker, Dr. Emilio Segrè. When he was told the news, Chamberlain remarked, "I'm stunned." He and Dr. Segrè, who will share $42,606, are the sixteenth recipients of the Nobel physics prize to be awarded to American teams or individuals—more than to any other nation.

Tall, angular, and bespectacled Owen Chamberlain was married to Babette Cooper in June 1943. Their children are daughters Karen, Lynn, and Pia, and son Darol. A prolific author, Dr. Chamberlain has published the results of his scientific investigations in foreign as well as American journals. He is a Fellow of the American Physical Society and a member of Phi Beta Kappa and Sigma Xi.

Dr. Ernest O. Lawrence has compared the discovery of the antiproton with the discovery of the positive electron which initiated "the remarkable developments in nuclear physics that followed. One cannot help but wonder whether the discovery of the anti-proton . . . likewise is a milestone on the road to a whole new realm of discoveries in high energy physics that are coming in the days and years ahead."

References

N Y Times p26 O 26 '59 por

American Men of Science vol I (1955)

CHAMBERLAIN, WILT(ON NORMAN)
Aug. 21, 1936- Basketball player

Address: h. 6205 Cobbs Creek Parkway, Philadelphia, Pa.

Perhaps no player has ever before made such a sensational impression on the sport of basketball as Wilt Chamberlain, the agile, seven-foot Negro athlete, former star of the University of Kansas varsity team and the professional Philadelphia Warriors. In one season (1959-60) with the Warriors, his first in the National Basketball Association, he set an all-time NBA single-season scoring record —one of eight league marks that he established. He was also named both the league's top rookie and the most valuable player by the New York basketball writers. During the summer of 1960 he rejoined a team on which he had played in 1958-59, the Harlem Globetrotters, for a tour of Europe, North Africa, and the Middle East.

Since his days at Overbrook High School in Philadelphia, where he led his team to lopsided wins over smaller boys of his age, Chamberlain has been an object of awe and a center of controversy. During his season in the NBA he frequently charged that referees and opposing players had "ganged up" on him —the players by their incessant fouls, and the referees by not noticing the fouls. At the end of the season, March 1960, he announced that he would no longer play in NBA games. By August 1960, however, Chamberlain had changed his mind and had signed a three-year contract with the Warriors to play in NBA contests.

Wilton Norman Chamberlain was born on August 21, 1936 in Philadelphia, Pennsylvania and was raised in a pleasant eight-room house in West Philadelphia. He was one of nine children (six sons and three daughters) born to William and Olivia Chamberlain. His father works as a porter for the Curtis Publishing Company, and his mother used to do outside housework a few days a week in addition to raising her family. Both parents are about five feet nine inches tall. Wilt Chamberlain's growth was normal until he reached the age of fourteen when he began to grow quickly, gaining four inches during one summer.

At Shoemaker Junior High School he first began to play basketball seriously. He also played at the Haddington Recreation Center and by the time he entered Overbrook High School in 1952, he was devoted to the sport. At that time he stood six feet eleven inches. In three years of basketball at Overbrook he scored 2,252 points.

Wide World

WILT CHAMBERLAIN

When Chamberlain was in his senior year at Overbrook, Eddie Gottlieb, owner of the Warriors, obtained a special ruling from the NBA on the territorial rights to high school players. That enabled him to claim Chamberlain as his first draft choice in 1959. (Under NBA rules, a player cannot compete in the league until after graduation of the college class of which he normally would be a member. This rule encourages an athlete to complete his education before becoming a professional. Chamberlain was not scheduled to graduate from college until June 1959.)

Gottlieb was fortunate in having no competition in his efforts to obtain Chamberlain. In order to lure Chamberlain to the University of Kansas in Lawrence, on the other hand, officials had to outbid seventy-seven major colleges and 125 smaller schools. When he finally chose Kansas in May 1955, he remarked that regardless of where he decided to go, there would be adverse comments. A number of sports writers did speculate about the lavishness of the offer Chamberlain had accepted and hinted at possible investigations by the National Collegiate Athletic Association.

In high school Chamberlain's best subject had been mathematics, and in college he intended to specialize in accounting. He changed his major subject, however, to language arts (communication), and in connection with this study he tape-recorded a show once a week on station KLWN in Lawrence, playing records and talking about sports.

During his three years at the University of Kansas Chamberlain played one year of freshman basketball and two years of varsity basketball. In his first varsity game as a sophomore, Chamberlain scored 52 points against Northwestern University. That set the tempo of his college career. In his initial varsity

CHAMBERLAIN, WILT—*Continued*

season Chamberlain led his team to the finals of the NCAA basketball tournament, but Kansas bowed to the University of North Carolina 54 to 53 in two overtime periods.

The University of Kansas won 42 of 50 games played during Chamberlain's two years of varsity basketball, and he averaged 30 points per contest. He was named All-American both years. But he was dissatisfied: he complained that he was being guarded by two, three, and sometimes four opposing players and felt that this type of game was retarding his continuing development as a basketball player.

After leaving college at the end of his junior year, Chamberlain joined the Harlem Globetrotters, a Negro professional basketball team which travels throughout the world. He was paid $65,000 while waiting to become eligible for NBA competition. As Abe Saperstein, owner of the Globetrotters, said at the time: "They all want to see Wilt." Chamberlain spent the year with the Globetrotters polishing his play for the tough competition of the NBA. He joined the Warriors for the start of the 1959-60 season and proceeded to dwarf the accomplishments of many excellent basketball players who had dominated the NBA in past years.

A sports writer for *Time* reported in the February 22, 1960 issue: "Last week Chamberlain was well on his way to smashing every record on the books. Even with 14 games still to play, he had scored more points and snared more rebounds than any other player ever had in a full season. . . . To stop Chamberlain, the pros have tried every trick in the book. They may double-team him (one man in front, one behind) with the hope of blocking off passes. When Chamberlain does get the ball, the defense swirls about him like a pack of hounds circling a bear at bay. Under the hoop, they beat a tattoo on him with elbow and hip."

It was this kind of treatment which caused Chamberlain to lash out at his opponents and league referees in an article written for the March 1, 1960 issue of *Look* entitled "Pro Basketball Has Ganged Up On Me." He charged that the NBA had two different standards of officiating: one for the league as a whole and another for him.

As the 1959-60 regular season drew to an end, the New York basketball writers named Chamberlain for both the Hy Turkin Award (leading rookie of the year) and the Sam Davis Award (most valuable player). Later, in March, he was credited with eight of the eleven marks set during the season in NBA records. They included his 37.6 point average for 75 games; 2,707 points for the season; the most field goals scored (1,065); and the most rebounds (1,941). He was also chosen for the Eastern Division All-Star team.

In spite of the generous recognition he had received, on March 24, 1960, just after the Boston Celtics had defeated the Warriors for the Eastern championship, Chamberlain announced that he was leaving the Warriors

and withdrawing from NBA play. He explained that if he continued to be subjected to the same conditions of the league, he would get into fights which would reflect upon himself and indirectly upon his race. The following month he agreed to join the Harlem Globetrotters on their forthcoming summer basketball tour. Later in 1960 he returned to the Warriors under a three-year contract.

Chamberlain's height is given in some publications as seven feet two inches. He places his height at seven feet one-sixteenth of an inch. He weighs 250 pounds. He is not the first seven-footer to play basketball, but he is by far the most successful, principally because he is a co-ordinated, all-around athlete. He is fast enough to run a quarter-mile in 47 seconds, strong enough to throw the sixteen-pound shot-put 55 feet, and agile enough to high jump 6 feet 10 inches. When he is playing basketball, at the height of a leap straight into the air, the top of his hand is thirteen feet three inches from the floor. Since his college days there has been talk of raising the baskets from the present height of ten feet to twelve feet.

Cars have been Wilt Chamberlain's hobby from the time he was a high school student. He also enjoys jazz music. Outwardly he is casual and relaxed. He has one announced personal peeve—the nickname of "Wilt the Stilt"; he prefers to be called "Dippy" or "The Big Dipper."

References

Look 22:91+ Je 10 '58 por; 24:51+
  Mr 1 '60 por
N Y Times p16 Mr 26 '60 por
Newsweek 48:96 D 17 '56
Sat Eve Post 229:33+ D 1 '56 por

CHANDY, ANNA May 4, 1905- Judge of the High Court of Kerala

Address: b. High Court of Kerala, Ernakulam-1, India

After many years as a practising lawyer and as a judge in India, Mrs. Anna Chandy was appointed in February 1959 to the High Court of the state of Kerala in India, the highest judiciary of this state, one of the fourteen in India. She is the first and only woman High Court judge in India and may be the first and only woman to have reached this rank in the judicial system of any country. She became the first woman lawyer in Kerala in 1928, and, after almost a decade of private practice and a term in the Travancore Legislative Assembly, she became the first woman judge in India in 1937. Noted for her integrity and courage, she is considered one of the outstanding women of her country.

Her rise in the judicial system was attained partly during the period of British rule in India and partly after India had become an independent member in the Commonwealth of Nations in 1947. India is now divided into fourteen states (much like the states in America) and six territories. All of the courts in the country form a single hierarchy with the Supreme Court at the head. Below the Supreme Court there are High Courts for each state, and below the High Court in each state there are subordinate courts.

Anna Jacob, the oldest daughter of M. J. Jacob and his wife, the former Sarah Daniel, was born in Alleppy, Kerala, India, on May 4, 1905. Her family belonged to the Syrian Christian Community in India. Her father, a doctor, died when she was five years old; her mother became a schoolteacher and brought up the two sisters in Trivandrum, Kerala, in southwestern India. "Mother wanted us both to study as high as we wanted," Anna Chandy remembers. "Younger sister, a good-looking girl, did not want to go any higher than high school, but she got her man before I did mine. She is now a house-frau, married to a government official."

After her graduation in 1920 from the Holy Angels' Convent in Trivandrum, Anna entered the Women's College in Trivandrum. There she completed the two-year intermediate course, a prerequisite for those who want to study for a degree. She was awarded a scholarship to take an advanced course in the Malayalam language, but decided not to accept it. Instead, she enrolled in the three-year course in history at Maharajas College in Trivandrum. There she received the Master of Arts degree in 1926.

Quite probably, like a number of other educated Indian women, she would have become a teacher. Her marriage to P. C. Chandy in 1926, however, introduced her to a different career. Chandy, a lawyer who was at that time a prosecuting inspector (public prosecutor) in the Travancore police service, persuaded her—"veritably compelled me," she has said—to study law.

Mrs. Chandy entered the Law College in Trivandrum as the first woman student of law in Kerala. She was awarded the Bachelor of Law degree in 1928 and began practising law before the district and sessions court of Kottayam, as the first practising woman lawyer in the country. She pleaded cases in several district courts and the High Court of Kerala. Becoming noted as a criminal lawyer, she often had more cases than she could handle.

While a practising lawyer, Mrs. Chandy also took part in some of the social and political activities in her state. She became an excellent speaker and worked with several women's organizations. She founded and edited a women's journal in the Malayalam language, called *Sreemathy*. In the 1931 election she ran for the Travancore Legislative Assembly from the constituency of Trivandrum, but lost to Pattom Thanu Pillai, who subsequently became a minister in the state government.

By government appointment, however, she gained a seat in the Travancore Legislative Assembly, which she held from 1932 to 1934 as the second woman member in its history. There she sought legislation which would better the position of women and reform the

The Royal Studio, Ernakulam

JUDGE ANNA CHANDY

conditions in jails, particularly in relation to women prisoners. After her term in the legislature, she returned to her thriving legal practice.

In 1937, according to the *Christian Science Monitor* (June 15, 1959), "the government persuaded her to join the judicial service of the state 'to bring it prestige' as the first woman in the Empire to preside over a judicial court." She was appointed a district *munsiff*, the lowest position in the civil judiciary. Six years later, in 1943, she was promoted to the office of additional district judge in Travancore state.

After seven years in this position she was appointed district and sessions judge in Travancore state, in 1950. The district and sessions judges in India, in addition to their duties as criminal judges, have responsibility for the management of all the inferior civil courts within their districts. Throughout her terms in the judiciary Mrs. Chandy became noted for her fairness and ability to mete out justice. Her judgments were rarely reversed by higher courts, and her work has been commended by both the public and her superior judicial officers.

When a position as judge of the High Court of Kerala became available, Mrs. Chandy was appointed on February 2, 1959, by the President of India. He had previously conferred about the appointment with the Chief Justice of the Supreme Court of India, the Governor of Kerala, and the Chief Justice of the High Court of Kerala. To be qualified for the position, a person must be a citizen of India and must have held judicial office or practised as an advocate for ten years in one of the states. Judges on the High Courts serve until they become sixty years of age, when they must retire.

(Continued next page)

CHANDY, ANNA—Continued

Mrs. Chandy thus became the first and only woman High Court judge in India, and perhaps the first and only woman in the world to have reached this rank in the judicial system of any country. The High Court in each of the fourteen states of India is the head of the judicial administration in each state, and has superintendence over all the lower courts and tribunals in each state. The Supreme Court of India is the highest court in the country. It has original jurisdiction in certain types of cases, and appellate jurisdiction in all cases from every High Court involving interpretation of the Indian Constitution. It also has appellate jurisdiction in certain civil and criminal cases originally tried in the state courts.

C. G. Kesavan wrote in the *Christian Science Monitor* (June 15, 1959): "Gentle and completely self-possessed, Mrs. Anna Chandy sits unruffled in the midst of conflicting issues and verbal play between lawyers. Her penetrating eyes discern and assess every manoeuvre, apparently without effort. . . . Eminent lawyers and judges of the Supreme Court of India have praised her as judge." She expresses herself easily and effectively and has a pleasant sense of humor.

The Judge and her husband, who has now retired after having risen to the post of deputy inspector general of the state, have one son, a lawyer. Anna Chandy has black eyes and black hair. For recreation, she enjoys walking. She has remained a member of the Syrian Christian Community of Kerala, in which she was raised. According to tradition, this community was converted to Christianity by the Apostle Thomas; thus it is one of the oldest Christian communities in the world.

References

Christian Sci Mon p10 Je 15 '59

Times of India Directory and Year Book, 1959-60

CHASINS, ABRAM (chā'sĭnz) Aug. 17, 1903- Composer; pianist; radio musical director

Address: b. c/o WQXR, The New York Times, 229 W. 43d St., New York 36; h. 19 E. 88th St., New York 28

The dedication to music that has made Abram Chasins a concert pianist acclaimed in the United States and abroad and a composer whose works have been played by leading pianists and orchestras has also brought him fulfillment of his desire to be known as an "educator in music." Since 1943 he has been the musical director of WQXR, the radio station of the New York *Times*. In October 1959 the WQXR-*Times* project, *Musical Talent in Our Schools,* which he initiated and directs, opened its tenth season of auditions for public, parochial, and private school pupils who have displayed exceptional talent in instrumental performance.

Abram Chasins was born in New York City on August 17, 1903, soon after his parents had moved to the United States from Russia. His father was Saul L. Chasins; his mother, Elizabeth (Hochstein) Chasins. It was early apparent to them that their son had a talent for music and was strongly attracted to the piano. When he was seven years old they took him to Bertha (Feiring) Tapper, who has been credited with having discovered Leo Ornstein. For three years preceding her death Chasins benefited by the careful training and "angelic patience" which helped build the foundations of his career as pianist.

In 1914 Chasins became a student at the Ethical Culture School of New York. Here he acquired the equivalent of a high school education; played on the chess, basketball, and ice hockey teams; and graduated in 1918. He later took an extension course in literature at Columbia University and continued his musical training through scholarships at the Juilliard School of Music in New York and the Curtis Institute of Music in Philadelphia.

At Juilliard, Chasins found a master piano teacher in Ernest Hutcheson, the famous concert pianist. Chasins pays tribute to "the erudition and lucidity of Hutcheson's mellow mind." At Juilliard too was Rubin Goldmark, composer, who became his master in musical analysis and composition. Two other men made important contributions: Richard Epstein, who gave him what Chasins calls "precise technical training," and Percy Goetschius, under whom he studied harmony, counterpoint, and form.

Chasins' first important composition, *Three Chinese Pieces,* was published in 1925. The work, which consisted of "Flirtation in a Chinese Garden," "Rush Hour in Hongkong," and "A Shanghai Tragedy," won him immediate recognition and was played internationally by many of the leading pianists of the time. In 1928 he published Twenty-four Preludes for Piano, an opus that some critics compared to Chopin. This was followed in 1930 by *Parade,* the first composition by an American to be performed by Arturo Toscanini, who directed it with the New York Philharmonic-Symphony Orchestra on April 18, 1931. On the same program Toscanini also directed an orchestral arrangement of "Flirtation in a Chinese Garden."

Within a year after the Chinese pieces were published, Chasins met the wife of pianist Josef Hofmann. She invited him to play the Chinese pieces for her husband, who was so pleased when he heard them that he made Chasins his protégé. Out of this grew an association of thirty years with a man whom Chasins considers his greatest teacher and inspiration. During 1926 he worked with Hofmann for four months, in London, Berlin, and Paris.

Upon his return to America, Chasins became a member of the faculty of the Curtis Institute of Music, a post he held until 1935. From 1934 to 1935 he was also musical consultant to the University of Pennsylvania. He collaborated on a precision study of piano touch and tone with Professors Harry C. Hart, Melville Fuller, and Walter Lusby of the Moore School of Electrical Engineering. Sir James Jeans later incorporated their findings in a book on the nature of sound.

After three years of study with Josef Hofmann, Chasins made his formal debut as a concert pianist in 1929, playing his own First Piano Concerto in F Minor with the Philadelphia Orchestra under Ossip Gabrilowitsch. In 1933 he played his Second Piano Concerto in F-Sharp Minor with the Philadelphia Orchestra under Leopold Stokowski. In 1938 he played this composition, completely revised, with the New York Philharmonic, John Barbirolli conducting. A second revision of this work, retitled *Symphonic Variations* for piano and orchestra in one movement, was played by the composer at the Berkshire Music Festival in Massachusetts, Serge Koussevitzky conducting, in the summer of 1945.

For a number of years, Chasins made most of his concert appearances as a performer of his own compositions. "It was as a composer," he has said (New York *Sun,* November 9, 1940) "that I first came before the public, although composition had been secondary to my piano studies. Many of my earlier works were taken up by well-known performers and I suppose it was natural that I should find myself identified by the general public only as a composer. . . . Musicians can be 'typed' just as actors are and I think it's just as bad for their artistic development." It was not until 1940 that he made his first New York appearance as soloist in a classic concerto, not his own. He played the Beethoven C Minor Concerto with the National Orchestral Association in Carnegie Hall.

In the twenty years from 1927 to his retirement from the concert platform in 1947, Chasins' musical life was one of complex activity. In addition to teaching, he toured the United States each year, appearing in recitals and with orchestras and covering as many as 15,000 miles by air in a single season. In 1931 and 1932 he toured Europe as soloist with leading orchestras. He published more than 100 compositions, many of which have become standard works in concert, radio, and teaching repertory. Among them were two-piano transcriptions of Bach, Gluck, Bizet, Johann Strauss, Richard Strauss, and Rimski-Korsakov. He also composed chamber music, preludes for violin and piano, and songs for soprano with orchestra.

Chasins' career in radio began in 1932. For six years over CBS and NBC, he broadcast his *Master Class of the Air,* originally called *Piano Pointers,* in which he played and talked about music. In 1943 he became musical director of WQXR, the position he now holds. Under his direction, WQXR programs came to be considered influential in building standards of musical taste for American listeners. Three evenings each week Chasins gives his educational comments on the music heard on WQXR's *Symphony Hall,* which is broadcast every evening except Saturday.

WQXR's *Musical Talent in Our Schools* offers qualified music students an audition before Chasins and a panel of five judges, which in 1959 included Artur Rubinstein and Leonard Bernstein. During the years from 1950 to 1959 the program gave 146 young instrumentalists the opportunity of radio broadcasts.

ABRAM CHASINS

Twenty-six of them appeared with either the New York Philharmonic Young People's Concerts or New York's Little Orchestra Society.

Chasins has been chairman of several prize or award juries for musical composition and performance, among them those for the Rachmaninoff Award, the Leventritt Prize, the Naumburg Award, the National Federation of Music Clubs Awards, and the New York Philharmonic Young People's Awards. He has lectured at leading universities and has contributed many articles on musical subjects to national magazines and to the New York *Times Magazine* and *Times Book Review.* He is the author of two books; *Speaking of Pianists* (Knopf, 1957) and *The Van Cliburn Legend* (Doubleday, 1959). In the former, Chasins relates his experiences with various well-known musicians and discusses musical subjects like hi-fi and concert management. Jan Holcman described it in the *Saturday Review* (November 16, 1957) as "a courageous, knowledgeable, and stimulating book."

Although he has been called a modern composer, Chasins has declined to ride on the modernist merry-go-round. "Only through evolution and not revolution," he says, "will the artist free himself and his art." John Tasker Howard noted, "In his music Chasins has a modern concept of tone relationships, but pays homage to his musical idols, Bach, Brahms, Wagner, Chopin and Rimsky-Korsakoff. He dislikes all that seems affected in modern music, has little patience with badly made music where technic is missing" (*Our American Music,* Crowell, 1954).

In 1944 the National Association for American Composers and Conductors awarded Chasins its Award of Merit for outstanding service to American music. He was cited four times by the United States government for meritorious service in radio in connection with World

CHASINS, ABRAM—*Continued*

War II bond drives. He is a member of ASCAP, Bohemians, Radio Pioneers of America, and other organizations.

Chasins was married to concert pianist Constance Keene in 1949. His first marriage, to Julia Haberman in 1935, was terminated by divorce in 1946. A slightly built brown-haired, brown-eyed man, he is five feet seven inches tall and weighs 138 pounds. His favorite recreations include swimming and ice hockey. He is devoted to chess, which he studied with the famous chess expert, José Capablanca, and to bridge. David Ewen quotes him as saying, "I am interested in almost anything in the world, and if I had to devote all my time and interest only to music I would consider my life misspent."

> *References*
>
> ASCAP Biographical Dictionary of Composers, Authors, and Publishers (1952)
> Ewen, D. ed. American Composers Today (1949)
> Thompson, O. ed. International Cyclopedia of Music and Musicians, 1956
> Who's Who in America, 1958-59

CLARK, BOBBY June 16, 1888-Feb. 12, 1960 Comedian; began career as circus clown and became a star in musical comedies; partner with Paul McCullough for thirty-six years in the Clark-McCullough comedy team. See *Current Biography* (May) 1949.

Obituary

N Y Times p19 F 13 '60

CLAXTON, BROOKE Aug. 23, 1898-June 13, 1960 Former Canadian Minister of National Defence (1946-54); Minister of National Health and Welfare (1944-46); chairman, Canadian Council (since 1957); insurance company executive. See *Current Biography* (December) 1947.

Obituary

N Y Times p34 Je 14 '60

COBB, LEE J. Dec. 9, 1911- Actor
Address: h. 1037 South Ogden St., Los Angeles 19, Calif.

Although he rarely takes star billing, Lee J. Cobb has been called "one of the world's great actors." In seventy-five motion pictures, a dozen stage plays, and several video dramas, he has portrayed a range of characters remarkable for both diversity and intensity, from that of a mobster in *On the Waterfront* to Willy Loman in *Death of a Salesman*.

Lee J. Cobb was born in New York City on December 9, 1911, the son of Benjamin Jacob and Kate (Neilecht) Cobb. His father worked as a compositor for a foreign-language newspaper in Manhattan. As a child, Lee studied

to become a concert violinist, but a broken wrist ended his lessons and his hopes of a musical career. He was educated at public elementary and secondary schools in New York City.

After his graduation from high school, Cobb went to Hollywood in 1929 with the intention of becoming a movie actor. He was unable to find work in the motion-picture capital, and soon returned to New York, where he sold radio tubes on commission during the day and studied accounting at City College of the City of New York at night. Two years later he again headed for California.

This time, he was accepted at the Pasadena Playhouse, where he was an actor and director from 1931 to 1933. He then worked as a free lance on tour and in New York City for two years. In 1935 he became a permanent member of the Group Theatre, a troupe of dedicated young actors in New York, with whom Cobb played character roles in *Johnny Johnson* (1936), *Waiting for Lefty* (1935), *Till the Day I Die* (1935), and *Thunder Rock* (1939).

Golden Boy (1937) was the Group's major success; Cobb played father Bonaparte at its première, and other roles in its cast during its run. He went to London for a British staging of the play in 1938, and was also cast in the movie version. Previously he had played minor roles in two Hopalong Cassidy westerns. *Golden Boy* proved to be his breakthrough in motion pictures, and until 1943 he alternated between Hollywood and Broadway.

Joining the Theatre Guild in 1940, Cobb appeared in its production of Hemingway's *The Fifth Column* (1940) and created the role of Jerry in *Clash By Night* (1941). He then made a trio of movies, *This Thing Called Love* (1941), *Men of Boys Town* (1941), and *Paris Calling* (1941), before returning to the stage in the title role of *Jason* (1942). A number of movies followed, including *The Moon is Down* (1943), *Tonight We Raid Calais* (1943), and *The Song of Bernadette* (1943).

In 1943 Cobb entered the United States Army Air Corps as a private, and was assigned to a California radio production unit. He was in the cast of the Moss Hart play, *Winged Victory,* produced by the Air Corps; the play opened in Los Angeles in November 1943 and was seen by 900,000 persons before it closed in New York six months later. Corporal Cobb was also seen in the film version, released in 1944.

After his discharge, Cobb returned to professional acting in Hollywood. He played the prime minister in *Anna and the King of Siam* (1946), a badgered police chief in Elia Kazan's *Boomerang!* (1947), a Spaniard in *Captain from Castile* (1947), the editor in *Call Northside 777* (1948), a scientist in *The Dark Past* (1949), and a crooked wholesaler in *Thieves' Highway* (1949)—all supporting roles of distinction.

Archer Winsten's praise in a review of *Captain from Castile* (New York *Post,* December 26, 1947) was echoed by other film critics and might have been written of any of Cobb's films. "They have discovered nothing that has not long been recognized in Lee J. Cobb's ability to handle a character part of power and color. His Juan Garcia sticks in the mind." Yet Cobb was restless, and he seized the chance to return to the legitimate stage in 1949.

The play was Arthur Miller's *Death of a Salesman*. "When I read the script, I knew there was no living unless I played Willy Loman's part," he has said. He took a leave of absence from Twentieth Century-Fox which was to last for two years. "It is hard to imagine anyone more splendid than Lee J. Cobb," wrote William Hawkins New York *World-Telegram* (February 11, 1949). Brooks Atkinson in the New York *Times* the same day termed Cobb's role "a heroic performance," and Howard Barnes in the New York *Herald. Tribune* called it "a mammoth and magnificent portrayal." He won the annual Donaldson Award for his part in the much-honored play.

Cobb's movies began to reach the screen again in 1951. He was featured in *The Man Who Cheated Himself* (1951), *Sirocco* (1951), *The Family Secret* (1951), *The Fighter* (1952), *The Tall Texan* (1953), *Yankee Pasha* (1954), and *Gorilla at Large* (1954). Between films, he recreated his youthful success in an ANTA revival of *Golden Boy* in March 1952, and starred in a short-lived production of *The Emperor's Clothes* the following February.

Cobb's next outstanding role was that of the gangster in *On the Waterfront* in 1954; he was one of five members of the cast who were nominated for Oscars for their performances in the movie. Cobb then appeared as a race-driver in *The Racers* (1955), a policeman in *Miami Exposé* (1956), a Chinese war lord in *The Left Hand of God* (1955), and the country judge in *The Man in the Gray Flannel Suit* (1956).

Before the last film was released, Cobb was stricken by a heart attack which nearly ended his career. But by 1957 he had returned to the screen as the star of *The Garment Jungle*, then as a juror in *Twelve Angry Men*. In 1958 he played a supporting role in *The Brothers Karamazov* which prompted critic William Peper to write (in the New York *World-Telegram & Sun*, February 21, 1958): "Much of the excitement comes from the powerful acting of a fine cast that is dominated, not by the stars, . . . but by Lee J. Cobb as the father. . . . Mr. Cobb roars and loves in grand style and when he is murdered, he is sorely missed."

After portraying an outlaw leader in *Man of the West*, and a mobster in *Party Girl*, Cobb finished 1958 with parts in *Green Mansions* and *The Trap*. In the Clark Gable comedy, *But Not For Me* (1959), Cobb portrayed a playwright; it was his seventy-fifth screen appearance.

In recent years, Cobb has also played occasional roles on television. He co-starred in *The Panic Button* over *Playhouse 90* in November 1957, and a few weeks later was seen on *Studio One* as a pathologist in *No Deadly Medicine*. In 1958 he played two sheriff roles

Columbia Pictures

LEE J. COBB

on the *Desilu Playhouse* and *Zane Grey Theater,* and in June 1959 returned to *Playhouse 90* as the scientist in *Project Immortality*.

Cobb's most notable video appearance was in *I, Don Quixote,* an ambitious adaptation of Cervantes' life and writings which most reviewers pronounced only a partial success. "Mr. Cobb, when he had the lines to share with (Colleen) Dewhurst, was superb," Jack Gould remarked in the New York *Times* (November 10, 1959). "But at the other extreme there were many long scenes in which his approach was far too broad and emphatic." A reviewer for *Time* (November 23, 1959), taking issue with this estimate, wrote that "Actor Cobb . . . put on a performance that was both poignant and terrifying but never out of control. His deeply felt *Don Quixote* seemed to overcome the world."

Lee J. Cobb has been twice married. His first marriage, to actress Helen Beverly on February 6, 1940, ended in divorce after twelve years; by that marriage he had two children. He was married to Mrs. Mary Hirsch, a Los Angeles schoolteacher, in Hollywood in July 1957. The couple has a son, who was born in 1960. In appearance, according to Cecil Smith in the Los Angeles *Times* (September 28, 1958), Cobb "seems a massive man . . . the face is big, each feature oversize—the large, soft, intelligent eyes; the big nose, jutting chin, wide cheekbones." Yet Cobb is not large: he is six feet tall, and weighs 190 pounds. He has blue eyes and brown hair. A private pilot, Cobb was a member of the Civil Air Patrol in the first part of World War II. He is an articulate critic of Hollywood films and dreams of the day when he can confine his film activities to directing.

"The character actor is gratified very few times," Lee J. Cobb said (*Newsweek*, January 26, 1959). "So far in Hollywood I have

COBB, LEE J.—*Continued*

come close to that feeling only twice, in *The Brothers Karamazov* and *On the Waterfront*. But nothing in Hollywood has come close to the reward I felt in roles I've done on the stage. . . . To act on stage and direct in films would be the best of everything."

References

Los Angeles Times V p1+ S 28 '58 por
Newsweek 53:98+ Ja 26 '59 por
New Yorker 25:21 Mr 26 '49
Who's Who in America, 1958-59

COCHRANE, EDWARD L(ULL) Mar. 18, 1892-Nov. 14, 1959 Former United States Navy officer; attained rank of vice-admiral (1942); served as chairman of Federal Maritime Board and head of Maritime Administration (1950-52); was vice-president of Massachusetts Institute of Technology (1954-57). See *Current Biography* (March) 1951.

Obituary

N Y Times p31 N 16 '59

COHEN, ARTHUR A(LLEN) June 25, 1928- Publisher; author
Address: b. 12 E. 22d St., New York 10; h. 103 E. 86th St., New York 28

For some six years Arthur A. Cohen was the president and executive editor of Meridian Books, Inc., a publishing house specializing in high-quality reprints and original titles in paper-back format. A Jewish scholar of the first rank, Cohen has contributed essays on theology, philosophy, contemporary literature, and Judaism to such periodicals as *Partisan Review, Jewish Frontier, Commonweal, Christian Century,* and *Harper's Magazine.* His book on the Jewish religious philosopher Martin Buber drew much critical acclaim. On April 7, 1960 Ben D. Zevin, the president of the World Publishing Company, announced that although his house had just acquired Meridian Books, Inc., the publishing program of Meridian would continue under the direction of its founder, Arthur A. Cohen.

Born on June 25, 1928 in New York City, Arthur Allen Cohen is the son of Isidore Meyer Cohen, a clothing manufacturer, and Bess Marion (Junger) Cohen, who were second-generation Americans. He has one sister, Doris Cohen Schaper. Arthur attended Cherry Lawn School in Darien, Connecticut and Friends Seminary in New York City. During his high school years, he took a lively interest in politics and, he says, "wrote one or two frightfully bad plays about the Spanish Civil War and a brief history of the War from its outbreak in 1936 to the collapse of the Loyalists." He was also editor of the school newspaper and president of the student body during his senior year.

At the age of sixteen Cohen enrolled in the University of Chicago, where he studied philosophy and comparative religion. Two years

later, in 1946, he received his B.A. degree and, in 1949, took an M.A. degree. His master's thesis was entitled "The Concept of Paradox in Kierkegaard and Nietzsche." In college he co-edited an ephemeral "little magazine," *The Critic* ("primarily, I think, to get a very mannered short story published"). He was active in campus politics and belonged for a time to the Labor Rights Society. He explains that this was "a Trotskyist organization of no influence or significance, but it gave me the distinction of being among the last of my generation to have any close contact with the political passion that characterized the thirties and early forties."

In 1950 Cohen received a fellowship to study medieval Jewish philosophy at the Jewish Theological Seminary of America in New York City. He studied there for three years and took courses at Columbia University, the New School for Social Research, and Union Theological Seminary. Cohen embarked on his publishing career purely by chance. The Jewish seminary instructors, he says, saw in him a future rabbi, but he did not agree with this estimate. Their pressure, paired with the desire of his friend, Cecil Hemley, to publish a volume of verse, turned Cohen away from the seminary and into publishing.

Hemley and Cohen founded the Noonday Press on a shoestring in 1951. They suffered "considerable financial agonies", but nevertheless continued to grow. Cohen was a director of Noonday until 1956 and then, having started Meridian Books, Inc., he sold his Noonday assets to Hemley. The Noonday Press has continued to publish general fiction and nonfiction works under Hemley's direction.

In 1954 Cohen organized Meridian Books, Inc., a publishing house which specializes in paper-cover books. The concern has released titles in both hard-cover and paper-back editions, primarily in fiction, literary criticism, art, history, religion, and philosophy. It has published the Meridian Documents of American History series; the *Noble Savage,* a semi-annual review of literature; *History* magazine; Living Age Books, a scholarly Protestant series; and Meridian Fiction, reprints of distinguished novels that have not previously found their way into mass market distribution.

In April 1960 the World Publishing Company acquired all the outstanding stock of Meridian Books, Inc. The acquisition left unchanged Cohen's direction of the publishing program and the editorial autonomy of Meridian Books, Inc. It did, however, effect the merging of production and other service operations of the two firms.

As a publisher, Cohen has made a significant contribution to secular intellectual life in the United States. As a writer and scholar, he has urged American Jews to re-examine and re-evaluate the ancient precepts of Judaism and to identify with and seek meaning in Judaism as a religion. "In the United States today it is at last possible to choose *not* to remain a Jew," Cohen wrote in his article, "Why I Choose to Be a Jew" (*Harper's Magazine,* April 1959). "The fear of anti-Semitism has waned and the hope for the restoration of Israel has been fulfilled; neither is now an effective reason for holding on to Jewish identity. Now as never before it will be possible for the Jewish people and the state of Israel to survive but for the Jewish *religion* to perish."

In the same article, Cohen explains his own "conversion" to Judaism. He came from an unobservant Jewish home, where the "flesh was nourished but the spirit left unattended." At the University of Chicago, he studied the fountainheads of Western culture, including the classics of Christian theology, and he soon came to recognize that "Western culture is a Christian culture; Western values are rooted in the Greek and Christian traditions." His contact with Christian literature, his own unreligious background, and a growing concern with religious problems directed his first religious steps towards Christianity.

In this crisis his parents rushed him not to a psychoanalyst, but to a rabbi—the late Milton Steinberg, a gifted and profound thinker. "Leading me gently," Cohen has written, "he retraced the path backwards through Christianity to Judaism, revealing Jewish thought and experience. It was extremely important to me to return to Judaism through the medium of Christianity. . . . I could only conclude that Judaism was not an unavoidable fate, but a destiny to be chosen freely." Through study and reflection Cohen returned to Judaism. Traditionally, Judaism has frowned upon theology, but Cohen has favored the revival of theological speculation and has tried to make "what is now only a minor chord in Jewish tradition sound a more commanding note."

Arthur A. Cohen edited *The Anatomy of Faith: The Theological Essays of Milton Steinberg* (Harcourt, Brace, 1960). His first book, *Martin Buber* (Hillary House, 1958), was commended by a *Saturday Review* critic, who said that Cohen had "proved himself more than equal to a prodigious task by producing a brilliant and penetrating study of Buber's pursuit of the holy."

In many articles Cohen has deplored the attrition of contemporary Jewish piety. Reviewing Howard Sachar's *Course of Modern Jewish History* for the *Saturday Review* (August 2, 1958), Cohen called the book a history of the Jews but not of Judaism. In an article, "The Problem of Pluralism," that he wrote for the volume, *Religion and the Free Society* (Fund for the Republic, 1958), Cohen lamented the secularization of religion in American life.

To the *Handbook of Christian Theology* (Meridian, 1958) Cohen contributed the chapters on atheism and Judaism. He contributed a chapter on "The Natural and the Supernatural Jew" to *American Catholics: A Protestant-Jewish View* (Sheed & Ward, 1959), and he took part in a discussion of religious tensions at the annual meeting of the Associated Church Press in April 1959.

From 1957 to 1960 Cohen was a consultant to Religion and the Free Society, a project of the Fund for the Republic. He serves on the advisory council of the Philip W. Lown Insti-

ARTHUR A. COHEN

tute of Advanced Judaic Studies at Brandeis University and is a co-chairman of the Franz Rosenzweig Society.

Arthur Allen Cohen was married to Elaine Firstenberg Lustig on October 14, 1956. Mrs. Cohen is a designer of interiors, much interested in the graphic arts, who has worked with Cohen at Meridian Books. They have one daughter, Tamar Judith. Cohen has brown hair, gray-green eyes, stands five feet eleven inches tall and weighs 185 pounds. He describes himself as a "passionless Democrat after two Stevenson defeats."

The Cohens collect primitive art. Their distinguished collection contains African, Polynesian, and pre-Columbian art objects; recently, they have been adding ancient Cycladic, Iberian, and Etruscan pieces. Paintings and some modern sculpture round out their collection. Cohen's favorite sport is horseback riding, primarily dressage. Discussing his basic attitude, he says: "As a believer, I can communicate my beliefs, but as a thinker, I cannot guarantee that they are certain or will never change."

References

Harper 218:61+ Ap '59

Who's Who in America (sup Mr-My '59)

COHEN, BENJAMIN A(LBERTO) Mar.
18, 1896-Mar. 12, 1960 Chilean diplomat; held important positions in the United Nations, including Assistant Secretary General for public information and Under Secretary for the department of trusteeship and information for non-self-governing territories. See *Current Biography* (May) 1948.

Obituary

N Y Times p86 Mr 13 '60

COMBS, BERT(RAM) T(HOMAS) Aug. 13, 1911- Governor of Kentucky; lawyer
Address: b. Governor's Office, Frankfort, Ky.; h. Governor's Mansion, Frankfort, Ky.

Since his inauguration as Governor of Kentucky in December 1959, Democrat Bert T. Combs has been fulfilling his promise to elevate "the moral and political tone of government." His plans include state constitutional revisions, a merit system for state employees to eliminate political patronage, home rule for cities, uniform election laws, better schools and highways, a veterans' bonus, and loans to bolster Kentucky's lagging economy.

BERT T. COMBS

Kentucky's first Governor from its eastern mountains in over thirty years, Combs defeated Republican John M. Robsion, Jr., in the November 1959 election with an all-time record majority of 180,093 votes. A lawyer by profession, he served as a judge on the state Court of Appeals from 1951 until he resigned in 1955 to enter the Democratic primary for Governor. In that election, running against A. B. (Happy) Chandler in a bitter factional campaign, Combs lost by a slim margin. As chief executive of his state, he is serving a four-year term that expires in December 1963.

Bertram Thomas Combs was born in Manchester, Kentucky on August 13, 1911, one of six children of Stephen Gibson Combs, a farmer, and Martha (Jones) Combs, a schoolteacher. In Kentucky kinship and genealogy are all-important, and members of the Combs family proudly trace their origins to English settlers who arrived in Virginia in 1619.

As a youth, Bert Combs showed unusual scholastic ability. He graduated first in his class at Clay County High School in Manchester in 1926, when only fifteen. He attended Cumberland College, Williamsburg,

Kentucky from 1929 to 1931, earning his expenses by firing furnaces and sweeping out buildings. For the next three years he worked as a clerk in the state highway department in order to continue his education. After entering the University of Kentucky Law School in 1934, Combs became managing editor of the *Kentucky Law Journal.* He was graduated with the LL.B. degree in 1937, ranking second in his class and winning the medal of the Order of the Coif, the highest honor for a law student.

Combs practised law in Manchester for a year before moving to the Kentucky mountain valley town of Prestonsburg, Floyd County; this remains his home town. In 1942 he enlisted as a private in the Army. He rose to the rank of captain and was sent to the South Pacific to serve on General Douglas MacArthur's staff. As chief of the investigating section of the War Crimes Department in the Philippine Islands, Combs assisted in the trial and prosecution of Japanese war criminals. He was awarded the Bronze Star and the Medal of Merit (Philippine Islands) upon his discharge in 1946.

Resuming the practice of law in Prestonsburg, he was a partner in Howard & Combs from 1946 to 1951. Meanwhile, in 1950 he served as city attorney for Prestonsburg and in 1951 became commonwealth attorney of the 31st judicial district. On the recommendation of several prominent judges he was appointed in April 1951 to fill a vacant chair on Kentucky's highest tribunal, the Court of Appeals. He later won his seat for an eight-year term in the elections of that year. In 1954 he served as chairman of the Judiciary Council of Kentucky.

When a group of Democrats, headed by United States Senator Earle C. Clements and Governor Lawrence Wetherby, drafted Combs to run for the gubernatorial nomination, he resigned his judgeship to campaign for the primary in the early months of 1955. Opposing him was A. B. (Happy) Chandler, onetime Governor, United States Senator, and baseball commissioner. Chandler had been warming up since 1952 in an effort to wrest party control from Clements, a political rival since 1935. His campaign was spectacular and noisy, with sound trucks blaring "Happy days are here again."

Chandler's goal, according to political observers, was the 1956 Democratic National Convention, where he hoped to be nominated as a Presidential candidate. To do this he had to remove Clements and the strong party organization backing Combs. He referred to the latter as a "captive candidate," using a proposed sales tax as an issue to discredit him.

Although Combs, a novice in politics, comparatively, got a late start, he waged a serious and impressive campaign. He stuck mainly to local issues and promises of reforms in the state government. He had the influential backing of Senator Alben W. Barkley, former Vice-President and the "Mr. Democrat" of Kentucky politics, as well as the support of Clements, the incumbent administration, and the Louisville *Courier-Journal*. Chandler defeated him in the August 6 primary and was elected Governor in November 1955; Combs returned to practise law in Prestonsburg.

Again in early 1959 the opposing factions, led by Clements and Chandler, drew up their slates for the Democratic primary race. This time, Combs's opponent was Chandler's Lieutenant Governor, Harry Lee Waterfield. A third contender for the governorship, Wilson Watkins Wyatt, Adlai E. Stevenson's campaign manager in 1952, was persuaded to run with Combs for Lieutenant Governor.

The primary campaign was another bitter race, with both Clements and Chandler looking ahead to gaining control of Kentucky's delegation at the 1960 Democratic National Convention. Combs, pledging to reform the state government and improve state economy, defeated both Waterfield in the May 26 primary and the Republican candidate, John M. Robsion, Jr., in the November election. He used the latter's support of Secretary Ezra Taft Benson's agricultural policies to influence rural voters and won in a landslide victory with a 180,093-vote margin. Kentucky eighteen-year-olds voted for the first time. Most political commentators and observers saw this election as a significant prelude to 1960.

One of Combs's first acts after becoming Governor was to cut the state payroll by 15 per cent. He and Wyatt then sent the General Assembly a sixteen-point reform program. The legislators approved, among other measures, a merit system for state employees, a fair-election bill which required state-wide use of voting machines, a cleanup of voting rolls, an average $1,100 increase in teachers' salaries, and the establishment of a $4,000,000 corporation to encourage business development. In February 1960 Combs signed into law a controversial veterans' bonus bill to compensate state veterans with a bonus of from $300 to $500.

To help finance his program and meet his billion-dollar budget, Governor Combs added a 3 per cent sales tax, while trimming the state income tax by 40 per cent. By April 1960 every major proposal in his sixteen-point platform had been enacted into law by the legislature or had been put into effect by executive order.

Governor Combs is chairman of the board of regents of the Eastern Kentucky Historical Society, a trustee of Campbellsville College, a member of the Junior Bar Association of Kentucky (president, 1946-47), and the Kentucky and American bar associations. He also belongs to the Order of the Coif and Phi Delta Phi, legal honorary societies, as well as to the American Legion, Forty and Eight, Veterans of Foreign Wars, and the Kiwanis and Lions clubs. He is a Mason and a Baptist.

On June 15, 1937 Bert Combs was married to Mabel Hall of Hindman, Knott County, Kentucky. They have two children, Lois and Thomas George. Governor Combs is five feet ten inches tall and has graying hair. Although mild-mannered and often reserved, he can express his own opinion with clarity and force. At his first cabinet meeting he reportedly overruled a proposal by Highway Commissioner Clements with a firm: "Nope, that ain't the way we're going to do it" (*Time*, March 28, 1960). In 1955 Louisville reporter Richard Harwood wrote in the *Nation*, "It seems no longer to be a compliment to call a man 'sincere' but that is Combs's biggest asset."

References

American Bar, 1959
Directory of American Judges (1955)
Martindale-Hubbell Law Directory, 1960
Who's Who in America, 1960-61

CONERLY, CHARLES Sept. 19, 1922-
Professional football player

Address: b. New York Football Giants, Inc., 10 Columbus Circle, New York 19; h. Alligator, Miss.

A battle-scarred veteran of twelve years in the National Football League, and the league's oldest player, Charles (Chuck) Conerly is one of the mainstays of the New York Football Giants. Conerly, a quarterback, has helped the New York Giants to win three Eastern Division titles in the last four years and one world's championship. Perhaps the most memorable year for Conerly was 1959, when for the first time in his professional career he won the passing championship of the National Football League and the fifth annual Jim Thorpe trophy as the league's Most Valuable Player. He was also named first-string quarterback on the All-Star team of the Eastern Division selected by writers of *Sporting News*.

Success came to Chuck Conerly just six years after fans of the New York Giants went to football games carrying placards reading "Conerly Must Go!" Near the end of the 1959 season, after the fans of New York and of Conerly's home state, Mississippi, had showered him and his wife with $25,000 worth of gifts, Conerly said in his acceptance speech, "I thank you all for sticking with me."

Charles Conerly, who was born on September 19, 1922 in Clarksdale, Mississippi, played his first competitive football for the local high school. Shortly after World War II broke out, he enlisted in the United States Marines and took part in the bloody landing on the Pacific island of Guam in the summer of 1944. Of that experience, he says with his usual simplicity: "Things were kinda hot for awhile." After his discharge from the Marines, Conerly enrolled at the University of Mississippi near Oxford. There he became one of the finest backs in the history of collegiate football in the South.

As a senior, Conerly was named an All-American and in 1947 he won the National Collegiate Athletic Association passing title with 133 completed throws in 233 attempts for 1,367 yards and 18 touchdowns. The University of Mississippi used the single-wing formation and Conerly passed out of the halfback position. A writer for *Look* magazine summed up his play during his senior year in this manner: "Writers generally underestimated Ole Miss in the pre-

CHARLES CONERLY

season roundups by not appreciating what experience in a key position can do for a team. As a left halfback, Charley did the passing, running, punting and was a defensive bulwark. His passing against Florida, South Carolina and Arkansas with a wet ball was phenomenal" (December 23, 1947).

After his graduation from college in June 1948, Conerly was signed by the New York Giants. His first year in the National Football League was a rousing success, and he was named the league's Rookie of the Year in a poll of football writers taken by the United Press. His record of 162 pass completions in 299 attempts for 1,175 yards and 22 scores overshadowed the first-year efforts of such great passers as Sammy Baugh of the Washington Redskins, Sid Luckman of the Chicago Bears, and Bob Waterfield of the Cleveland (later Los Angeles) Rams. "There's no doubt about it," predicted Steve Owen, who was the New York Giants coach at the time, "Conerly is going to become the greatest." During his first year Conerly also set an individual National Football League record that still stands—36 pass completions in one game—against the Pittsburgh Steelers on December 5, 1948.

In spite of this auspicious start, Conerly did not live up to the bright future predicted for him until his last four years. The New York Giants team began to come apart at the seams during his early years as a quarterback. The players managed to tie the Cleveland Browns for the divisional title in 1950, but lost a subsequent playoff and with it their only chance for a championship until 1956, when they swept everything before them. In the meantime, Conerly, as quarterback, was forced to bear the brunt of the wrath of football fans for the miserable showings of the team.

The billingsgate reached its peak in 1953 when the New York Giants finished the season with a record of three victories and nine defeats.

Fans went to the game with signs reading "Goodbye Charley" and "Get A New Quarterback!" The signs were augmented by raucous jeers and catcalls. "Some years it was so bad that my wife and I just wouldn't go out evenings," Conerly told W. C. Heinz (*Life*, December 1, 1958). "I'd be recognized, and it doesn't matter to me so much what they say, but I didn't want my wife to be embarrassed."

With some urging from the New York Giants coach, Jim Lee Howell, Conerly weathered the abuse, and as the team grew in ability Conerly grew with it. In 1956 the New York Giants captured the Eastern Division championship and went on to crush the Chicago Bears, winners of the Western Division title, in the championship playoff game at Yankee Stadium. In the following year the New York Giants fell to second place, behind Cleveland, but came back in 1958 to win again the Eastern crown, defeating the Browns 10-0 in a divisional playoff. But the New York Giants lost the championship game 23-17 to the Baltimore Colts in sudden death overtime in one of the most exciting games in the history of the National Football League.

The New York Giants were again the Eastern champions in 1959, although Baltimore again won the playoff, this time by a margin of 31-16. In the 1959 season Conerly truly came into his own. He completed 113 of 194 passes for 1,706 yards (an average of 8.79 yards per throw) and 14 touchdowns. Conerly's calling of plays all season was impeccable. His true value became obvious when he was forced to miss three games because of an ankle injury. In those three games the New York Giants failed to register a touchdown. They managed to score only by means of three-point field goals and were able to win two of the games principally because of a rock-ribbed defense.

"The guy has been our meal ticket for years," admits Coach Howell. "It takes guts to stand there and not panic. Charley has that courage, and has a lot of other things the public doesn't appreciate." As quarterback, Conerly is subjected again and again to brutal physical punishment. "He's taken more beatings than anybody I've ever seen," says Dr. Francis J. Sweeny, the Giants' physician since 1930. "Charley's a battered man." In more than ten years with the New York Giants, Conerly has contributed 158 touchdown passes to the Giants' cause, second only to Sammy Baugh's lifetime total of 187. He has completed 1,308 passes in 2,593 attempts, and his throws have amounted to 17,900 yards.

Charles Conerly and his wife, Perian, live on a 225-acre cotton farm four miles from Alligator, Mississippi. Mrs. Conerly writes a sports column for a local Mississippi newspaper during the football season and has written sports stories for the North American Newspaper Alliance. Conerly, who stands six feet tall and weighs 185 pounds, has been described by his teammate Kyle Rote as one who "commands respect with quiet confidence, [who is] never loud, never vociferous, but always capable." His seasonal salary with the New York Giants has been estimated at $20,000. Although a New York newspaper once ran the headline "Age

Catches Up With Conerly" when the New York Giants lost to the Baltimore Colts in the championship game, most football observers have detected no sign of it.

References

Life 45:57+ D 1 '58 por
Look 11:75 D 23 '47
N Y Herald Tribune p36 D 17 '48
N Y Times p50 D 6 '48
N Y World-Telegram p27 D 14 '59
Sports Illus 11:18+ D 7 '59 por; 11:21 D 21 '59

COOKE, MORRIS LLEWELLYN May 11, 1872-Mar. 5, 1960 Consulting engineer; specialist in the development of natural resources; first administrator of the Rural Electrification Administration (1935-37). See *Current Biography* (May) 1950.

Obituary

N Y Times p86 Mr 6 '60

COONS, ALBERT H(EWETT) June 28, 1912- Physician

Address: b. Harvard Medical School, Boston, Mass.; h. 132 High St., Brookline, Mass.

By developing a technique that differentiates antibodies from the surrounding body cells, Dr. Albert H. Coons has made possible the rapid and accurate diagnosis of certain diseases. An immunologist and bacteriologist, Dr. Coons has prepared antibodies with a fluorescent dye and has then placed them in contact with the microorganisms they are specifically intended to destroy. When the slide specimens are examined under an ultraviolet microscope, the existence of the germs is revealed by the telltale green-yellow glow of the attached test antibodies. If the specific suspect disease organism is not present, the fluorescent testing matter does not latch on to anything else in the specimen. Associated with Harvard University for two decades, Dr. Coons now works as a lifetime career investigator for the American Heart Association.

The son of Albert Selmser and Marion (Hewett) Coons, Albert Hewett Coons was born in Gloversville, New York on June 28, 1912. He received the B.A. degree from Williams College in Williamstown, Massachusetts in 1933 and the M.D. degree from Harvard University Medical School four years later. After completing his internship in 1939, Dr. Coons accepted a research fellowship in medicine at Harvard and a post as assistant resident in medicine at the Thorndike Memorial Laboratory of the Boston City Hospital.

At Thorndike Memorial Laboratory Dr. Coons became interested in the behavior of antibodies, the agents produced by body tissues to fight infection and disease. He especially wanted to test the hypothesis that heart damage in rheumatic fever was caused by some mistaken action in the protective nature of antibodies. The director of the laboratory,

Dr. George R. Minot, a Nobel laureate, provided Coons with a $50 grant to purchase chemicals to make the antibodies of rheumatic fever visible. His first researches in preparing colored antibodies proved unsuccessful. "I found," explains Dr. Coons, "that the color produced by a dye was too feeble to let me see an antibody the way I wanted to see it . . . in the tissues."

Having won a National Research Council Fellowship in 1940, Dr. Coons remained at Harvard to work under J. Howard Mueller and John F. Enders (who in 1954 received the Nobel Prize for his work on a poliomyelitis vaccine). Continuing his studies of antibodies, Dr. Coons initiated a series of experiments to differentiate antibodies from the surrounding body cells by using a fluorescent material. Again his investigations proved disappointing, but Coons soon learned of a group of organic chemists at Harvard who had succeeded in making proteins fluorescent. Since antibodies are also composed of protein matter, Dr. Coons reasoned that he could obtain similar results with them.

Working in collaboration with Hugh J. Creech and R. Norman Jones, Dr. Coons attached a fluorescent dye to the antibodies in the form of a glowing tail light to make the tiny particles visible under an ultraviolet microscope. For the antibodies Dr. Coons selected the bright apple-green dye of the chemical fluorescein, to distinguish the antibodies from the red and blue fluorescence taken on by normal tissues. The scientists also established that fluorescent labeling caused no damage whatsoever to the antibody under examination.

The first paper that Dr. Coons and his colleagues wrote describing the methods they used in the chemical manipulations of antibodies was published in the *Proceedings of the Society for Experimental Biology and Medicine* in 1941. A second treatise, which appeared in the *Journal of Immunology* (number 45, 1942), presented a more comprehensive picture of the fluorescent antibody technique. Dr. Coons's entrance into the United States Army Medical Corps, with the rank of captain, in 1942, abruptly suspended his research on antibodies.

After serving in the South Pacific for three years, Dr. Coons was discharged from the service in 1945 as a major. He returned to Harvard Medical School as a resident Fellow, and two years later he became an instructor in bacteriology and immunology. In 1948 Coons was promoted to an associateship, and in 1950 he was appointed the Silas Arnold Houghton assistant professor of bacteriology and immunology. Since 1953 he has been a lifetime career investigator for the American Heart Association, one of a small group of outstanding scientists who receive grants that enable them to work on research problems of their own choice. Dr. Coons is currently continuing his association with Harvard as a visiting professor.

Assisted by Dr. Melvin Kaplan and a staff of bacteriologists, virologists, and public health specialists, Dr. Coons spent the early postwar years in perfecting and extending the fluores-

Fabian Bachrach

DR. ALBERT H. COONS

serum for every important disease-causing organism will be manufactured.

A nationwide move to introduce the fluorescent antibody method for immediate diagnosis of streptococcal infections was made by the Department of Health, Education, and Welfare in the latter part of 1959. A plan was established to give federal assistance to the states for research programs on increased uses of the test and to expand laboratory facilities.

For significant contributions to public health procedures Dr. Coons received in 1958 the Kimble Methodology Award of the State and Provincial Public Health Laboratory Directors. In the following year the American Public Health Association honored him with a Lasker Award. He serves as editor of the *Journal of Immunology* and of the *Proceedings of the Society for Experimental Biology and Medicine.* Since 1956 he has been a consultant to the United States Public Health Service.

The professional organizations to which Dr. Coons belongs are the Society of Experimental Biology and Medicine, Society of American Bacteriologists, New York Academy of Sciences, and American Rheumatism Society. He has served as counselor of the Histochemical Society (1952-56) and the American Association of Immunologists (since 1956). Dr. Coons has been elected a Fellow of the American Association for the Advancement of Science and American Academy of Arts and Sciences. He is a member of the Harvard Club, Sigma Xi honorary society, and Phi Delta Theta fraternity.

A sparely built man, Dr. Coons has a prominent forehead and sleek black hair. He has been married to the former Phyllis Watts, a member of the society staff of the Boston *Globe,* since December 27, 1947. They are the parents of four daughters, Elizabeth Schuyler, Susan Wakefield, Hillary, and Wendy, and a son, Albert Hewett. Dr. Coons enjoys playing the piano and tinkering with mechanical gadgets.

References

Sat R 42:54+ O 3 '59 por

American Men of Science (1960)

Who's Who in America, 1960-61

cent-tagging technique. One reporter called Coons's research activities "a laborious struggle," since he and his colleagues were responsible for making the chemicals and instruments which they needed in their work. (Not until 1958 did commercial manufacturers provide the materials needed to label and identify antibodies.)

Considered one of the major original discoveries in medical science, Dr. Coons's method depends on the "exquisite specificity" of antibodies. It is known that antibodies will react only to a specific invader (antigen), so that an antibody for an influenza virus will attack only that particular virus strain. By labeling antibodies with the apple-green fluorescent dye and studying them under the ultraviolet microscope in contact with specific disease organisms in a patient's blood samples, Dr. Coons can identify and locate a virus-infected cell, and even parts of cells.

Dr. Coons's method has been adopted in research laboratories throughout the world and has provided an important new scientific tool that promises to revolutionize the diagnosis of disease. He has said that "it will probably take some years to work out details for each infectious agent to which the technique might be applied, particularly since there are about 400 of them. But fluorescein-labeled antibodies have been used to detect the antigens that cause mumps, influenza, chicken pox, pneumonia, measles, parrot fever, poliomyelitis, and rabies, among others." Although Coons still regards the process as "too complicated, tricky and expensive," several research hospitals, including the Public Health Service Communicable Disease Center in Atlanta, Georgia, are working at refining the technique so that diseases can be diagnosed within a few hours after the drawing of a blood sample. For the future, technicians believe it possible that a fluorescent

COOPER, R(ICHARD) CONRAD June 15, 1903- Steel executive

Address: b. United States Steel Corporation, 525 William Penn Place, Pittsburgh, Pa.; h. 2 Woodland Rd., Sewickley, Pa.

Throughout the prolonged strike of 500,000 steelworkers which began in the summer of 1959, R. Conrad Cooper held the key position of chairman of industry's four-man team which negotiated with labor representatives headed by David J. McDonald, president of the United Steelworkers of America. Trained as an engineer, Cooper had risen gradually from field work in his profession to the office of executive vice-president in charge of personnel services for the United States Steel Corporation. He was appointed to the position in February 1958,

A specialist in industrial relations, he has built his reputation on achievements in the spheres of job classification and wage incentives in the steel industry.

Richard Conrad Cooper, the fifth of eight children of Edwin Peter and Stella (Taylor) Cooper, was born in Beaver Dam, Kentucky on June 15, 1903. During Richard Conrad's boyhood, his father gave up his work as a coal miner and small-shaft operator in Beaver Dam, moved his family to South Dakota, and became a homesteader on a farm near Pierre. Here Cooper grew up and received most of his early education.

With engineering as his major subject, Cooper then studied at the University of Minnesota in Minneapolis, where he also played center for the football team and won the heavyweight boxing championship. He was graduated with the B.S. degree in 1926. Remaining in Minneapolis, he took a position as field engineer in the service department of the Universal Portland Cement Company.

Three years later, in 1929, Cooper moved to New York City to become a field engineer in consulting industrial engineering work. The firm with which he was employed during the next eight years is now called American Associated Consultants. At that time it specialized in installing for various companies the Bedaux system, which *Fortune* (March 1959) described as "an efficiency-engineering program that was long denounced by U.S. labor as 'the speedup system.'"

The Wheeling (West Virginia) Steel Corporation hired Cooper in 1937 as assistant to its vice-president in charge of operations and promoted him in 1940 to assistant vice-president in charge of operations. In 1944 the United States War Labor Board directed the steel industry to set up a system of standard job classifications and wages. Cooper accepted an assignment from the United States Steel Corporation of Delaware to head its negotiating committee in working out an agreement with the United Steelworkers; from 1945 to 1947, as the corporation's assistant vice-president for industrial relations, he negotiated with the union to reach a settlement on classifications.

Turning next to the problem of establishing a new wage-incentive program, Cooper tried to persuade the steelworkers' union to agree to a plan based on his estimates of a "fair day's work." During several years of drawn-out negotiations, union spokesmen charged Cooper with advocating the speedup, according to *Fortune* (March 1959). A settlement in 1952 resulted in a compromise which allowed the union to retain the right to challenge incentive rates set by management.

In the meantime, Cooper had been appointed in 1948 vice-president in charge of industrial engineering for the Delaware corporation and through successive company mergers retained that title—with the United States Steel Company from 1951 to 1953 and with the United States Steel Corporation from 1953 to 1955. He was appointed the corporation's vice-president for administrative planning in October 1955 and assumed his present title of executive vice-president for personnel services in February 1958.

R. CONRAD COOPER

The United States Steel Corporation has for some years provided leadership for management in settling disputes with the steelworkers' union. Cooper, therefore, was recognized early in 1959 as the man who would be the principal industry negotiator with labor representatives in the collective bargaining due to begin before the contract expired at the end of June. When formal talks between the two groups began in New York in May, Cooper headed a four-man team representing twelve steel companies, all major producers, accounting for about 87 per cent of the nation's steel.

When negotiations opened, Cooper urged in a statement that they be carried on in an atmosphere of "calm, dispassionate presentation and discussion . . . courtesy, consideration, and thoughtful contemplation" of divergent views. From the beginning he denounced the steelworkers' wage demands as inflationary, contending that an increase in the price of steel would be needed to offset the wage raise. He argued that such a price increase would make it more difficult for United States steel producers to withstand the encroachment of foreign steel producers, and that American steel would price itself out of world markets. (Labor, on the other hand, attributed industry's predicament to its own high profits.)

Another important issue in the dispute concerned local work rules. Industry insisted upon gaining greater authority over working practices at the plant level in order to eliminate what Cooper called "loafing, featherbedding and unjustifiable idle time." Industry negotiators stipulated that union agreement to work-rule changes would have to be a precondition to any specific offer of wage increase.

Eight weeks of negotiations failed to break the deadlock between labor and management. A strike set for June 30 was postponed through a two-week truce arranged by President Eisen-

COOPER, R. CONRAD—*Continued*

however, but on July 15 the steelworkers called a nationwide walkout. During the following months Cooper's group met frequently with McDonald's team, and both conferred occasionally with government representatives, such as the President's fact-finding panel headed by George W. Taylor. In October this panel investigated the issues in connection with the government's seeking an eighty-day strike-stopping injunction under the Taft-Hartley law.

A. H. Raskin, who covered the strike for the New York *Times,* remarked on November 3, 1959: "The settlement efforts have moved through so many hotel suites, Government offices and courtrooms in so many cities that one weary negotiator suggested last week that the bargaining table be mounted in a Greyhound bus." Raskin ascribed the delay in settlement largely to the unyielding conviction of each side that it was acting for the common good. Cooper's group, where the work-rule issue was concerned, in a sense represented "all management in an effort to restore the boss' right to be boss."

During the course of negotiations, in late October 1959, the Kaiser Steel Corporation, one of twelve companies that Cooper's team had represented, signed a separate pact with the union. Other major producers refused to follow Kaiser's lead on the grounds that for them a similar agreement would mean a rise in steel prices. Labor leaders tried to force "a S-Kaiser-high" settlement, Cooper punned in early November. He added, "Clearly they are interested only in perpetuating inflation in America and wasteful practices in the steel industry" (New York *Times,* November 3, 1959).

On November 7, 1959 the United States Supreme Court upheld a Taft-Hartley law injunction directing the steelworkers to return to work for eighty days. By this time the strike had reached its 116th day, having run more than twice as long as any previous work stoppage in the history of the steel industry; and many thousands of workers in the automotive, construction, and other industries had been thrown out of work because of the steel shortage.

The United States Steel Corporation announced in October that during the strike-ridden third quarter of 1959 it had suffered a loss of more than $31,000,000. It nevertheless was able to maintain its quarterly dividend of 75 cents because of heavy profits in the first half of the year—profits partly due to consumers' having built up inventories in expectation of a strike.

The steel dispute ended on Jannary 4, 1960 when an agreement was reached between the United Steelworkers of America and eleven major companies. Under the new contract the union won raises and other benefits amounting to about 40 cents an hour, and local committees were created to study work rules.

R. Conrad Cooper was married to Irene V. Johnson, his college sweetheart, on August 19, 1929. Athletic in appearance, he is about six feet one inch tall and weighs 192 pounds. He smokes cigars, plays golf, and is impatient with long-windedness. He attends the Episcopal Church and votes Republican. His clubs are the Duquesne (Pittsburgh), Edgeworth (Sewickley, Pennsylvania), and Allegheny (Sewickley Heights); and he belongs to the American Iron & Steel Institute, the American Institute of Industrial Engineers, the Engineers Society of Western Pennsylvania, and the Pennsylvania Society for the Advancement of Management.

Straightforward and taciturn in manner, Cooper is said to be "as tough as the product that his company produces—steel," as reported in a New York *Times* biographical sketch (May 6, 1959). "Yet he speaks so softly that sometimes his hearers have to lean forward to catch his words. . . . He is the kind of man whose mind is so ordered that when he is interrupted in a presentation he will go back to his take-off point."

References

Fortune 59:192 Mr '59 por
N Y Times p31 My 6 '59 por
Who's Who in Commerce and Industry (1957)
Who's Who in America, 1958-59

CORNELIUS, JOHN C(HURCH) Aug. 21, 1900- Foundation executive
Address: b. American Heritage Foundation, 11 W. 42d St., New York 36; Northwestern Bank Bldg., Minneapolis, Minn.; h. 2323 E. Lake of the Isles Blvd., Minneapolis, Minn.

To his nonpaying position as president of the American Heritage Foundation, John C. Cornelius has brought a background of over a quarter of a century in the advertising business, the greater part of it with Batten, Barton, Durstine & Osborn, from which he retired as executive vice-president in 1955. In Cornelius' view, the transition from selling ham (his first account at BBDO was Hormel) to "selling" Americans on the value of their political heritage is a natural one: "Advertising is the great mover," he once explained in an *Advertising Age* interview. "Just as it moves merchandise, it can also move citizens from passive to participating citizenship."

The son of John Church and Amy Salina (Davis) Cornelius, John Church Cornelius was born in Milford, Pennsylvania on August 21, 1900 and was raised on a cattle ranch in Texas. He worked as a movie extra, window decorator, bill collector, ticket taker, and dance park manager before getting his first taste of advertising when a student at the University of Wisconsin in Madison. It was there, in 1921, that he devised "The Varsity Blotter," the first of the advertising blotters now seen on practically every college campus. So successful was Cornelius' blotter that upon leaving the university in 1924 he was able to sell the business for $4,000.

After graduating with the B.A. degree, Cornelius joined the advertising department of the Chicago *Tribune,* where he stayed for one year. Then, with the Florida land boom underway, he went into the Chicago office of a Florida real estate company, remaining there until the boom collapsed in 1927. After an interlude in the newspaper business as a member of a group which unsuccessfully tried to establish a rival in Des Moines to the dominant *Register,* he returned to the advertising business in 1929 when he joined the Winter Advertising Agency. Two years later he moved on to the newly opened Minneapolis branch office of Batten, Barton, Durstine & Osborn, where, exactly two years after he had joined the firm, he was named vice-president in charge of the Minneapolis office.

In 1938 Cornelius, then only thirty-eight, was offered the presidency of BBDO. To the surprise of practically everyone (including Bruce Barton, who had offered him the job), Cornelius turned it down and, when Barton renewed the offer a year later, again declined. He subsequently became known as "the man who didn't want to be president," as four other advertising agencies, two large food companies and a soap concern each offered him their top management post—only to have him refuse. He remained, instead, with BBDO, which named him vice-president in charge of Western offices (including Chicago, San Francisco, and Los Angeles, as well as Minneapolis) in 1939 and executive vice-president in 1943. He has been a director of the agency since 1940.

In a tribute to Cornelius written upon his retirement, Paul H. Beuter, advertising manager of San Francisco's M. J. B. Coffee, a BBDO client, credited his success to a "willingness to understand the overall problems of somebody else's business" and "an extraordinary and uncanny ability to recruit and build people." He continued, "It is nice to have known someone in a cutthroat competitive field . . . who never took advantage of anyone, who kept his integrity, with friendliness and no false front, and was always willing to stretch out a friendly hand" (*Advertising Age,* January 3, 1955).

When Cornelius retired in 1955 it was with the intention of devoting a larger share of his time to his two absorbing pastimes—hunting and fishing. He was soon persuaded, however, to accept the voluntary post of president of the American Heritage Foundation, and as a result has been busier during his "retirement" than he was during his "active" career.

A nonpartisan, nonprofit, educational organization, the American Heritage Foundation "is an expression of faith in the democratic process and of determination to make that process work ever better." Its board of trustees, which represents every segment of American political and economic life, includes such diverse figures as Charles E. Wilson and Walter P. Reuther, Eleanor Roosevelt and Henry R. Luce.

The American Heritage Foundation was established in 1947. Its first project was sponsorship of the Freedom Train's 1947-1949 nationwide tour, which carried the originals of the country's most important historical documents (from the Mayflower Compact to the USS *Missouri*'s log for the day in 1945 that Japan surrendered) to over 3,000,000 Americans. The foundation supports Radio Free Europe and, with the American Bar Association, sponsors the annual Law Day Program. In 1952, 1956, and 1958 it organized national "Register, In-

JOHN C. CORNELIUS

form Yourself and Vote" campaigns, bringing out a record-breaking vote in all three elections.

In the 1956 election the foundation's activities were extended further. To meet constantly increasing campaign costs (Lincoln's entire 1860 election fund was reportedly $100,000; no more than the cost of *one* television program today) and to broaden the financial base of party support (only 2 per cent of Americans contribute to political parties, according to David Sarnoff, the foundation's chairman), the American Heritage Foundation, with the cooperation of the Advertising Council, organized its drive around the theme: "Don't Pass the Buck. . . . Give a Buck to the Party of Your Choice." The drive received the enthusiastic support of President Eisenhower and Adlai E. Stevenson and was endorsed by other leaders of both political parties: "It is the one thing we can agree on," said Meade Alcorn, chairman of the Republican National Committee.

When all the dollar bills were collected for the 1958 campaign (twenty-nine of them by former President Harry S. Truman, who rang doorbells and solicited contributions on San Francisco's "Dollars for Democrats" Day), Cornelius estimated that the foundation's drive had netted $5,000,000. Although this represented only a small part of the $200,000,000 which he believed the 1956 campaign to have cost, he was encouraged by the results: "We're bullish about the collections," he said; "after all, this is the first time in history it's been tried—and we think they've had a tremendous effect on voters."

Along with spending much of his time on country-wide speaking tours and other activities on behalf of the American Heritage Foundation, Cornelius still serves as a consultant to BBDO. He is vice-president of Muzart Company and a director of North Star Woolen Mill Company; Red Owl Stores, Inc.; Background

CORNELIUS, JOHN C.—*Continued*

Music, Inc.; Rexall Drug, Inc.; and General Securities. Cornelius has also held positions of leadership in organizations within the advertising field, serving the American Association of Advertising Agencies as a director (1944-45), vice-chairman (1946), chairman (1947), and as chairman of the advertising committee (1948). He is also a director of the Advertising Council.

Public service is not something Cornelius started when he retired, but something he has done all his life. He played a leading role in many war bond drives, particularly as state chairman of a United States defense bond drive and as a member of the national advisory committee of the Treasury Department's savings bond division. He headed the Minneapolis Community Fund drive in 1942 and served as general chairman of its century celebration. He is a director of the Minneapolis Chamber of Commerce, the Minneapolis Council of Social Agencies, the National Municipal League, and the Civic and Community Association.

The Minnesota Association for Crippled Children and Disabled Adults (of which he is president), St. Barnabas Hospital, the Orchestral Association, the Institute of Fine Arts, the Pop Warner Foundation, and the Acquatenial Association are among other organizations in which he is especially interested. He is also a director of Boys' Clubs of America. For some time Cornelius published *The American Boy* magazine—a financial failure, but an enterprise he is proud to have undertaken.

In addition, he finds some time for hunting and fishing and has contributed more than fifty articles to various sporting publications. Some of his recent pieces, all appearing in *Field and Stream,* include: "My Favorite Spot" (May 1954), "Brook Trout Heaven" (March 1955), "Listen, Bergen," a description of a pheasant hunting expedition with Charlie McCarthy's creator (March 1956), and "Ice Fishing Is Hot" (January 1957). All of Cornelius' sports articles are signed "Jack," the name his friends call him.

On May 29, 1924 Cornelius was married to Miriam A. Swartz. They have one son, John Church. Cornelius is an Episcopalian and a Republican. He belongs to the Minneapolis and the Minikahda clubs and the Newcomen Society. He has received the Gold Good Citizenship Medal of the Sons of the American Revolution, the National Municipal League's Citizenship Award, and the Young Men of Minnesota's Award.

References

N Y Herald Tribune II p10 Ja 2 '55 por
Who's Who in America, 1960-61

COUSINS, FRANK Sept. 8, 1904- British labor leader

Address: b. Transport House, Smith Sq., London S.W. 1, England; h. "Sherbrook," 29 Beech Grove, Epsom Downs, Surrey, England

The Transport and General Workers' Union, with a membership of over 1,250,000, is the largest labor union in Great Britain. It is also one of the largest voting blocs in the 8,300,000-member Trades Union Congress, which in turn exerts a major influence on the official policy of the Parliamentary Labour party. Since May 1956 Frank Cousins has headed the T. & G.W.U. as its fourth general secretary, having succeeded Arthur Tiffin. At the time of Cousins' election, *The Times* (London) described him as "definitely and consciously on the left" in the labor movement. He is a strong proponent of controlled economy and nationalized industry. Despite the relative failure of a costly London bus drivers' strike called by Cousins in 1958, he continues to be regarded as the most powerful British trade union leader.

The son of a miner, Frank Cousins was born at Bulwell, Nottinghamshire, England on September 8, 1904. He attended the King Edward School at Doncaster on the fringe of the Yorkshire coal fields before going to work in the pits at the age of fourteen and joining the miners' union. A job as a lorry driver delivering concessionary coal to the miners gave him the opportunity to leave the pits.

In the middle 1920's Cousins became a long-distance truck driver and joined the Transport and General Workers' Union. He was made a probationary officer within two years. Having caught the eye of the union's organizer and general secretary, Ernest Bevin, he was appointed in 1938 a full-time organizer for the road transport section. Cousins was still a full-time organizer when in 1940 Bevin was named Minister of Labour and National Service in the World War II coalition cabinet; his second-in-command, Arthur Deakin, became acting general secretary of the union. In 1944, or shortly before the war ended in Europe, Cousins was brought into union headquarters in London to become national officer for the road transport section.

The promotion led to widening activity for Cousins, including experience in various negotiating groups, during the next eleven years. According to the *New Statesman and Nation* (September 15, 1956), it was this experience as a national officer of his union's road haulage group which made Cousins "a 'militant' always ready to call a strike to better the condition of what he considered one of the most harshly exploited sections of workers."

Both Ernest Bevin, who became Foreign Secretary in Clement Attlee's Labour government in July 1945, and Arthur Deakin, who succeeded him as the union's general secretary in March 1956, were regarded as belonging to the moderate wing of the trade union movement. Between Deakin and Cousins a conflict developed which reached its height in January 1947 when 15,000 London truck drivers went on an eleven-day wildcat strike. "Cousins," the *New Statesman and Nation* reported, "did not trouble to hide his sympathy with their demands for better conditions, and, as a result of his efforts, the union executive finally agreed to meet a conference of unofficial strikers—an unprecedented step in Deakin's union. Deakin never forgave, and the lorry drivers never forgot."

In the following year, 1948, Cousins was made national secretary of the T. & G.W.U.'s road transport section. He was in touch with the government officials who planned the legislation bringing the road transport industry under public control. After the Conservative victory in the 1951 election, he was disappointed when the government restored the industry to private ownership.

Deakin died in the spring of 1955 and was succeeded as general secretary by Arthur Tiffin. In August 1955 Cousins was appointed assistant secretary. Then, as acting general secretary in place of Tiffin, who was ill, he represented his union at the Labour party conference in the autumn. In a forthright speech in private session he urged Aneurin Bevan and other Labour leaders to forget old discords and work together.

The death of Tiffin in December 1955 again left vacant the general secretaryship of the T. & G.W.U. Cousins announced his candidacy for the office in February 1956. Later in the month he was elected to membership in the general council of the Trades Union Congress, and on May 11, 1956 he was elected general secretary of the T. & G.W.U. by a record vote.

Cousins had been named to membership in the British Transport Joint Consultative Council in the previous year; in 1956 he was in addition named to the Ministry of Labour's National Joint Advisory Council and the executive council of the International Transport Workers Federation. He also served the latter as vice-president for two years before being elected to a term as president in 1958.

"I want to get as much for labor as can be obtained out of industry," Cousins has said in explaining his basic position. He rejected an offer made by Harold Macmillan, then Chancellor of the Exchequer, to address the Trades Union Congress in September 1956 on wage demands in relation to inflation. Cousins himself sponsored a decisively adopted resolution calling for return to "a planned economy based upon effective economic controls." A year later he again urged T.U.C. delegates to reject the Conservative government's anti-inflationary policy, arguing that prices and profits would remain uncontrolled while wages would be restrained.

A seven-week strike by some 50,000 London bus drivers and conductors in May and June 1958 ended in a settlement that Cousins felt allowed "no question of either surrenders or victories." He had threatened to call sympathy strikes by workers employed in distributing gasoline and in the power stations, but reportedly was frustrated in his attempt by the T.U.C. general council. Late in June the strikers voted to accept a wage increase of a little over one dollar, which an industrial court had awarded to 36,000 bus drivers and conductors before the strike. They also accepted a promise by the London Transport Executive both to review the wage position of the other 14,000 employees and to cancel projected cuts in services and payroll. The strike was estimated to have cost the union about half the total cost of $11,200,000.

Wide World

FRANK COUSINS

At the Labour party conference in October 1957, Frank Cousins spoke in support of a motion calling for unilateral nuclear disarmament by Great Britain. Both the party leader, Hugh Gaitskell, and Aneurin Bevan opposed the motion, however, and it was overwhelmingly rejected; a similar resolution in 1958 was defeated by another huge majority. In June 1959, with a general election in prospect, the party executive and the T.U.C. agreed on a policy that endorsed Great Britain's commitments to the North Atlantic Treaty Organization (NATO), but called for the formation of a "non-nuclear club," through which Great Britain would try to reach nuclear disarmament agreements with countries that do not yet have the hydrogen bomb.

An impassioned appeal from Cousins, however, at the T. & G.W.U.'s biennial conference in July 1959, persuaded all but about fifty of the 760 delegates to vote for a union policy statement which amounted to endorsement of unilateral nuclear disarmament. At the Labour party conference in early September the non-nuclear club plan was nevertheless approved by a two-to-one vote.

Commenting in his union's journal on Labour's loss in the general election of October 1959, Cousins declared that "the campaign for the next election must start now" and warned against one suggestion for remaking the party. "It is," he wrote, "to drop our demands for social justice and make sure that we do not offend the floating voter. I believe, however, that it would be wrong to trim our sails to any prevailing electoral wind—and unsuccessful, too."

"Frank Cousins believes in Frank Cousins. No one who talks to this pleasantly approachable man is left in any doubt of that," noted a writer for the *New Statesman and Nation.* He added that the labor leader is "no abstract

COUSINS, FRANK—*Continued*

thinker" and "makes all his deductions from his own experience." Over six feet tall, Cousins has an athletic build, and in earlier years he was active in outdoor sports and fond of dancing. As favorite recreations nowadays he prefers reading and gardening at his home in a southwestern suburb of London. Mrs. Cousins is the former Annie Elizabeth Judd. The couple were married in 1930 and have two sons and two daughters.

References

Fortune 54:236 N '56 por
Manchester Guardian p7 Ag 29 '57 por
N Y Herald Tribune p6 S 30 '57
New Statesman 52:304+ S 15 '56
Time 70:26 S 2 '57 por
U S News 41:24 S 14 '56
International Who's Who, 1959
Who's Who, 1959

CRUM, BARTLEY C(AVANAUGH) Nov. 28, 1900-Dec. 9, 1959 Lawyer, author; publisher of the New York *Star* in 1948; noted for handling cases involving civil rights. See *Current Biography* (May) 1947.

Obituary

N Y Times p33 D 11 '59

CULLEN, BILL Feb. 18, 1920- Radio and television entertainer

Address: b. National Broadcasting Co., Inc., 30 Rockefeller Plaza, New York 20

If entertainers were paid by the word, Bill Cullen, the amiable host of *The Price is Right*, might well be the highest-paid personality on radio and television. In addition to his quiz program, which draws as many as three million postcards a week from television viewers, he is a veteran of *I've Got a Secret* and the host of a daily radio program. His programs add up to a total of twenty-five hours of broadcast time each week.

William Lawrence Cullen was born on February 18, 1920 in Pittsburgh, Pennsylvania, the son of a local garage owner. He was stricken by infantile paralysis when he was eighteen months old; the disease left him with a decided limp and a restricted choice of career goals. "Polio moved me out of physical effort and forced me into a mental manner of living," he later remarked. Cullen believed he had discovered his life's work when he was hospitalized for the second time by an automobile accident. Nine months in bed made him decide to become a doctor.

After graduating from South High School, Cullen enrolled at the University of Pittsburgh as a premedical student. A shortage of funds soon forced him to withdraw from school, however, and he went to work in his father's garage as a mechanic and tow-truck driver. There he entertained his co-workers with imitations of local radio announcers. This pastime led to an audition for a radio job.

In 1939 Cullen was taken on as an unpaid announcer for radio station WWSW in Pittsburgh, working six hours a night every night of the week. Within two months he was a salaried announcer for the little 250-watt station. He later moved over to KDKA, and in 1943 became master of ceremonies for a variety program on that station. He was earning $250 a week before his twenty-fourth birthday.

Meanwhile, Cullen was exhibiting the remarkable energy that later made him one of the busiest personalities on television. He had resumed his studies at the University of Pittsburgh, where he earned a Bachelor of Arts degree in fine arts. His childhood illness made him ineligible for military duty during World War II, but he flew for the Civilian Air Defense as a patrol pilot and civilian instructor in Allegheny County, Pennsylvania.

Although he was now a successful announcer by local standards, Cullen felt he had gone as far as he could go in Pittsburgh. "I looked at other no-longer-young guys in a deep rut on stations like mine," he has remarked, "and said, 'No, I'm not gonna be like this—even if I starve.'" In 1944 he went to New York City. Far from starving, Cullen discovered that network radio was suffering from a wartime shortage of staff.

Within a week, Cullen was hired as a staff announcer by the Columbia Broadcasting System. He worked in that capacity until 1946, when the master of ceremonies for *Winner Take All* resigned because of an illness. Cullen, who had been announcing the quiz program, was made a temporary master of ceremonies and did so well that he was hired for the job at an eventual salary of $600 a week.

Cullen was now at the peak of his radio career. In quick succession he was heard by audiences of *The Arthur Godfrey Show, Skyline Roof, Sing Along, Waitin' for Clayton, Crime Photographer, Give and Take,* and *This is Nora Drake.* In 1949 television began to make an impact on the profession, but Cullen remained aloof from video for three years because of his physical disability.

In 1952, however, Cullen made his television debut on *I've Got a Secret,* a "panel-of-experts" program in which the panelists remained seated. He has served on the show ever since. He discovered that his collegiate face made him a favorite of video audiences and that the television cameramen could stay sufficiently far ahead of him to conceal his limp. He severed his ties with CBS and became a free lance. Although circumstance had made him a radio announcer, Cullen has carefully cultivated himself as a master of ceremonies. "I never considered myself a top-flight announcer," he has said. "I'm not an actor. . . . But this I can do."

Cullen moved quickly to the top of his new profession. "His patter is sometimes irrelevant but it is always fast," observed one writer (*Time,* August 16, 1954); "his smile gleams as brightly as the lens of his eyeglasses; and, whatever else may happen, he is never speechless." By 1954 Cullen was appearing on three coast-to-coast television programs and two network radio shows.

Since his first appearance on *I've Got a Secret,* Cullen has been master of ceremonies for such audience-participation shows as *Place the Face, Quick as a Flash, Hit the Jackpot, Give and Take,* and *Down You Go.* Cullen "hit the jackpot" himself in November 1956, when he was chosen as master of ceremonies for NBC-TV's *The Price is Right,* a new daytime program in which panelists selected from the studio audience try to price various articles of merchandise: the panelist who bids the highest for the article without over-valuing it wins it.

The Price is Right became one of the most durable quiz programs on television. In October 1957 a weekly evening version was added to Cullen's schedule; within a month it was attracting more than one million postcards each week from the home audience. The program's unusual format enabled it to survive the charges of corruption which ended many of the "give-away" shows in 1958.

With each change in his program schedule, Cullen was spending more and more time before the microphone. By 1958 he was on the air for twenty-five hours and thirty minutes each week (more time than even Arthur Godfrey undertook at the peak of his active career). Cullen maintained this exhausting pace through 1959. His working day began at 6 A.M. with *The Bill Cullen Show* (formerly called *Pulse*) over radio station WRCA (now WNBC) in New York. Cullen talked, played records, and read commercials for four hours every weekday morning.

At 10 A.M. Cullen went by taxi to the NBC-TV studio for a briefing in preparation for *The Price is Right,* telecast each weekday at 11 A.M. Although this program was also unrehearsed, the master of ceremonies had to know exactly where he was to be at every moment. "It's a complicated show mechanically," Cullen has said. "... You could break your neck if you didn't know where to stand."

The same problem faced Cullen every Wednesday night, when he appeared on the evening version of *The Price is Right* at 8:30 P.M. over NBC-TV. On the same evening he appeared as a panelist on *I've Got a Secret* at 9:30 P.M. over CBS-TV, a program which fortunately required no rehearsal for him. In addition to his weekday programs, Cullen was also on the air over WRCA for two hours every Saturday.

Both of Cullen's television programs are packaged by Goodson-Todman Productions, whose Mark Goodson has explained that Cullen combines two indispensable talents. "He has an adept sense of format; he remembers names, scores, and such details," Goodman has said. "He also has a remarkable sense of freewheeling association that lets him talk his way out of any situation that arises."

Cullen has been described as "the slim, alert man with the big horn-rimmed glasses, the large eyes, and the elfin grin which splits his face wide and lights it like a ball park at night" (New York *Times,* June 27, 1954). He is five feet nine inches tall and has brown hair and hazel-brown eyes. He has been married three times; his present wife is the former model, Anne Macomber. Cullen hopes some day to live in California and to make his living as a writer; he once wrote gags for Arthur Godfrey and

BILL CULLEN

Danny Kaye. He pilots his own plane, is an enthusiastic amateur photographer, and collects modern art.

"One thing I like very much about my jobs is that they want me to be myself," Cullen has said (New York *Times,* July 20, 1958). "When I used to be an announcer a friend once complained that I spoke so precisely on the air, that it was unlike my regular speech. Well, that's what I was paid for. Now some people say that I drop my g's on the air. Well, that's what I'm gettin' paid for now."

References

Look 22:28+ Jl 8 '58 por
N Y Post Mag p4+ My 11 '58 por
N Y Times II p13 Je 27 '54; p9 Jl 20 '58 por
N Y World-Telegram Mag p3 Mr 7 '59 por
Time 64:65 Ag 16 '54

DAHANAYAKE, W(IJAYANANDA) (dá-hăn-ī'ă-kĕ) Oct. 22, 1902- Former Prime Minister of Ceylon; teacher
Address: Richmond Hill, Galle, Ceylon

In Ceylon, the "Pearl of the Orient," W. Dahanayake was chosen Prime Minister on September 26, 1959, after S.W.R.D. Bandaranaike was assassinated. Once a Marxist, Dahanayake now favors the development of private enterprise and the outlawing of strikes in essential industries in order to solve some of Ceylon's economic problems. A schoolteacher before he entered politics, Dahanayake later served as Minister of Education in Bandaranaike's cabinet.

Ceylon is a former British crown colony which gained the status of a Dominion within the British Commonwealth on February 4, 1948. In recent years it has been plagued with re-

W. DAHANAYAKE

ligious strife and with labor problems. Increasing opposition to his efforts to deal with these problems and scandals over the investigation into the assassination of Bandaranaike compelled Dahanayake to form a caretaker government in December 1959 and to schedule a general election for March 1960.

In the election Dahanayake lost his Parliamentary seat to W. D. S. Abeygunewardene and he went back to his old teaching job. The Dahanayake administration was followed by a short-lived cabinet headed by Dudley Senanayake. He was succeeded on July 21 by the Sri Lanka Freedom party's Mrs. Sirimavo Bandaranaike, the widow of the late Prime Minister.

Wijayananda Dahanayake is the first Prime Minister of Ceylon to come from the middle class rather than from the wealthy upper class. One of five sons of Caroline (Gunasekera) and Dionysius Sepala P. Dahanayake, he was born on October 22, 1902 in Galle in southern Ceylon. His father, who was given the honorary title of Muhandiram, was an Oriental scholar of some repute and instructed several servants in Singhalese.

With his twin brother, Kalyanapriya, now a teacher, Wijayananda attended Richmond College in Galle and St. Thomas College in Dehiwala-Mount Lavinia. At Richmond he became known as a compelling orator who often spoke at meetings of the literary society. One of his teachers at St. Thomas College described him as the most mischievous pupil in the school. Nevertheless, he not only passed the London Matriculation examination, but also came through the Cambridge Junior examination with honors.

Unable to attend a university because of insufficient funds, Dahanayake studied at the Government Training College in Colombo-Maharagama, where he shocked other students by eating curried rice with his fingers. When

he was reported to the authorities, Dahanayake was penalized, but this did not discourage him from continuing to eat with his fingers. After completing his course at the Government Training College, he became a staff member of St. Aloysius College, a Roman Catholic institution in Galle. There he was put in charge of slow learners and distinguished himself when all of them earned the English School Leaving Certificate. While teaching, Dahanayake often digressed from the assigned lessons to tell his students tales about his beloved town of Galle.

In Galle, Dahanayake began to take part in local politics. At St. Aloysius College he led a student demonstration that protested the visit of the Prince of Wales to Ceylon. Finally, his interest in politics took precedence over his love of teaching. In 1935 he was elected to the Galle Municipal Council, and retained his seat in successive elections. Within four years he became the mayor of the town and was re-elected in 1940 and 1941. As the mayor of Galle, he introduced reforms and amended the bylaws of the council to permit its members to speak in Singhalese at council sessions. In those years, Dahanayake, who was without political affiliation, used to declare that his allegiance belonged to Galle.

As a zealous champion of independence for Ceylon, Dahanayake denounced in public British imperialism and Ceylon's participation in World War II. When he was jailed by the British in 1942 as a security risk, he spent his six months in prison studying political science. Two years after his release he was elected to the State Council, then Ceylon's central legislature, as a member from Bibile. In the State Council he attracted attention by his criticism of the British government, his eccentricities, and his oratory. He came to be known as the Voice from Bibile and His Majesty's Unpaid Opposition and well earned both nicknames.

In his often amusing speeches he recited limericks that parodied his opponents. During the budget debate in 1944 he spoke for thirteen hours in what was undoubtedly the longest speech in the legislative history of Ceylon. To demonstrate the poor quality of food distributed to the people, he exhibited a bag of rice that was ridden with weevils. To show the low grade of matches sold in the market, he lit a match and burned his fingers. During this period he belonged to various Marxist parties.

In 1947, just before Ceylon became a self-governing Dominion, Dahanayake was elected to the House of Representatives, the lower chamber of the new Parliament, where he became an outspoken critic of the first native government, headed by D. S. Senanayake. In the 1952 general election he was returned to the House of Representatives.

Having become an anti-Communist liberal by 1956, Dahanayake joined S.W.R.D. Bandaranaike's (see C.B., September 1956) Sri Lanka Freedom party. In the general elections of that year he campaigned as a candidate of the Mahajana Eskath Peremuna (People's United Front), a coalition of parties organized by Bandaranaike. The coalition won a landslide victory, and Dahanayake was again re-elected to the House.

In April 1956 Bandaranaike appointed Dahanayake as Minister of Education in his cabinet. Dahanayake arranged for free milk and buns to be served to school children and expressed his gratitude to the United States for assisting him in the project. In 1959 he led a movement against Left-wing cabinet members and, as a result, several Trotskyite and Sri Lanka Freedom ministers resigned.

When Prime Minister Bandaranaike died on September 26, 1959 from the bullet wounds he had received the preceding day, Dahanayake was chosen to succeed him. The immediate cause of the assassination was a medical controversy between Buddhists who prescribed herb brews and practised a massage called Ayur-Veda and those who followed modern Western techniques. Bandaranaike, who had tried to encourage the use of Western medical science, was assassinated by a Buddhist monk who practised Ayur-Veda. Another conflict, arising out of the dissension between Singhalese-speaking Buddhists and the Tamil-speaking Hindus, has been aggravated by Hindu aspirations to establish an independent republic.

When he was sworn into office, Dahanayake pledged himself to carrying out Bandaranaike's socialist-neutralist policies in an attempt to make Ceylon the "Switzerland of Asia." He also promised to remove restrictions from essential foodstuffs to lower the cost of living and to eliminate profiteering. He assured his people that minority groups would be protected. Departing from Bandaranaike's policy of promoting state ownership of certain industries, he promised to permit private traders to compete with state-owned ships in importing food. He said that he favored outlawing strikes in industries and occupations essential to the public welfare. Ceylon has been disturbed by over 900 strikes since April 1956, when Bandaranaike took office.

From the very beginning Dahanayake's government has been beset with discord and mounting opposition. His administration was charged with interfering with the investigation of Bandaranaike's assassination; one cabinet member was arrested and others were accused of complicity in the murder plot. In his attempts to achieve some kind of unity and order, Dahanayake imposed a state of emergency and a brief censorship of the press for which he was severely criticized. Attempts to remove the Prime Minister were instigated in the form of an October 30 and a November 27 no-confidence motion, both of which the government barely survived. Concerned for his personal safety, the Prime Minister ordered a protective wall built around his residence.

In December 1959 Dahanayake resigned from the Sri Lanka Freedom party when it refused to name him its leader. The party, in turn, declined his resignation, choosing rather to expel him. On December 8 the Prime Minister dissolved Parliament, dismissed five ministers, and formed a caretaker government to rule until elections were held.

W. Dahanayake, a gray-haired man with a tall, slightly stooped frame, wears his nation's traditional banian and sarong. He is a bachelor with an affection for children and has been called a "baby kisser par excellence." He has clung to his youthful belief in astrology and superstitions; he loves to walk barefoot and enjoys the society he finds at roadside kiosks and foodstalls. A Buddhist, he has said: "Religion is the most important thing in a man's life. The higher one goes the nearer one must get to God. If one fails God, one cannot but fail mankind." As a hobby Dahanayake writes verses which have frequently enlivened Parliamentary debates. One of his best remembered is a couplet he wrote about Bandaraike in 1952: "We do not love thee, Banda dear, because you change from year to year."

References

N Y Times p3 S 27 '59 por
Newsday p26 S 29 '59 por
Times of Ceylon S 23 '59
U S News 47:27 O 12 '59

D'ARCY, MARTIN (CYRIL), VERY REV. June 15, 1888- Roman Catholic priest of the Jesuit Order; writer; lecturer

Address: 114 Mount St., London W.1, England

Although St. Ignatius of Loyola might have been amazed at the intellectual sweep and power of Father Martin D'Arcy, S.J., the founder of the Roman Catholic Society of Jesus would certainly not have been disappointed in the devotion of "his latest disciple." Lionized by sophisticates, Father D'Arcy is first of all a Jesuit priest with the faith of a peasant—a fact which he never forgets, according to his friends. His numerous philosophical and religious works, including *The Mind and the Heart of Love*, praised by both secular and religious critics, have been turned out during a life filled with the duties of a preacher, lecturer, headmaster of the Jesuit college at Oxford, and provincial of the English Jesuits.

Martin Cyril D'Arcy was born in Bath, England, on June 15, 1888, the fourth of four sons of Martin Valentine D'Arcy, barrister-at-law, and Madoline (Keegan) D'Arcy. The family lineage was Norman-Irish. His paternal grandfather was Nicholas D'Arcy of Ballyforan and Gorteen, Ireland. There is, reportedly, evidence that the family descends from the kings of Ireland.

At the age of ten he entered Stonyhurst College, Lancashire. Seven years later, in 1905, he was graduated from the college but remained at Stonyhurst to put on cassock and cotta and begin his studies in philosophy at the Jesuit seminary attached to the school. In 1912 he entered the Literae Humaniores course at Oxford, where he passed his final exam for M.A. with first class honors. While at Oxford he won the Charles Oldham Prize, the John Locke Scholarship, and the Green Moral Philosophy Prize.

The young Jesuit scholastic returned to Stonyhurst to teach in 1916. "He would sit [on the rostrum] crooning lines from Virgil," Michael de la Bedoyere recalls (*Catholic Pro-*

VERY REV. MARTIN D'ARCY

files, Series I). Students misled by his delightful manner and appearance into thinking he would not bother to keep order found themselves "picked up bodily by a wiry pack of taut muscles and deposited under the rostrum."

He begun studying theology at St. Benno's College, North Wales in 1919, was ordained a priest of the Society of Jesus in 1921, and received his doctorate in theology at the Gregorian University in Rome in 1926. (He has since been given honorary doctorates by many universities, including Fordham, Georgetown, Marquette, and the National University of Ireland.)

Father D'Arcy became a lecturer in the Faculty of Philosophy at Oxford University in 1927 (a post he retained until 1945). In 1932 he became headmaster of Campion Hall, the first Roman Catholic college to be established at Oxford since the Reformation. (In becoming headmaster of Campion he also automatically became a member of the governing body of the university.) He rebuilt Campion Hall during his tenure and turned its three-story building into what was virtually a museum of valuable paintings and rare books. But the spiritual effect of his own personality was still greater. Campion Hall under Father D'Arcy became the center of a large and lively circle of young artists and writers, including Evelyn Waugh and Lord Cherwell. "His urbane charm and cultivated mind," commented *Time* (March 17, 1947), "have influenced a quarter century's crop of Oxonians and helped bring many a British highbrow into his broadbrowed church." While at Campion, Father D'Arcy became the Roman Catholic representative on the BBC's religious committee (1936-45). He delivered several talks over the BBC, some of which have been collected in his *Christian Morals* (Longmans, 1937).

Elected to head the English Province of the Society of Jesus in 1945, Father D'Arcy left Campion Hall and Oxford in the summer of that year and on August 2, in London, assumed leadership of all English Jesuits. He remained in the post until 1950.

His work as a lecturer has frequently taken Father D'Arcy away from England. He has represented his homeland in speaking trips abroad, including Spain, Malta, and Japan. In 1954 he was the English representative to the International Cultural Congress at Florence, Italy.

Father D'Arcy came to the United States in 1936 to deliver the Lenten sermons at Our Lady of Lourdes Church, New York City, and has returned several times since. He was acting dean of philosophy in the Graduate School of Fordham University during the school year 1939-40, and a member of the Institute of Advanced Study, Princeton, New Jersey, 1941-42. He visited the United States briefly in 1947. In 1954 he participated in the Columbia University bicentennial broadcasts. He was a visiting professor at Notre Dame University during the school year 1955-56 and at Georgetown University during 1957-58 and 1958-59. The Georgetown Graduate School catalogue for 1959-60 lists him as still being on the faculty there.

The first book to appear under the name of Martin D'Arcy was *The Problem of Evil* (1922). Soon after its appearance the author began submitting philosophical essays to the *Hibbert Journal,* the *Dublin Review,* and other periodicals. He is the author of the article on the Roman Catholic Church in *Chambers's Encyclopaedia,* the contributor of the essay on Gerard Manley Hopkins (on whom he has been called "the prime authority") to C. C. Williamson's *Great Catholics* (Macmillan, 1939), and a contributor to James L. May's *God and the Universe* (Dial, 1931), a Free Church-Anglican-Catholic symposium. He has contributed to such periodicals as T. S. Eliot's *Criterion,* the *Month,* and *Thought.*

His second book, *Mass and Redemption* (Burns, Oates, 1926), was followed two years later by *Catholicism; Christ as Priest and Redeemer* (Doubleday, 1928). His next book to appear was *The Spirit of Charity* (Burns, Oates, 1929). His *Thomas Aquinas* (E. Benn, 1930) was praised both in the United States and in England for its objectivity and freedom from bias. *The Nature of Belief* (Sheed, 1934) tried to identify belief with knowledge. *Mirage and Truth* (Macmillan, 1935) and *The Pain of This World and the Providence of God* (Longmans, 1935) wrestled with the problems of shaken faith and with the presence of evil and suffering in the world.

The book which Father D'Arcy is reported to consider his masterpiece is *The Mind and the Heart of Love* (Holt, 1947), an attempt to resolve the conflict between passionate love (Eros) and selfless charity (agape) emphasized by Nygren, de Rougemont, and others. D'Arcy concludes that Christian love must be both, that it cannot leave out Eros. "We are bound," he says, "to accept self-love as legitimate, to admit some place for Greek and other kinds of true thinking."

Father D'Arcy's uncommon capacity for recognizing and humbly accepting truth from whatever camp it emerges has not gone unnoticed by critics. "His book has virtues one too seldom finds in religious writings on Marxism," wrote William Clancy of *Communism and Christianity* (Devin-Adair, 1957) in the *Saturday Review* (March 8, 1958). "There is no stridency here; D'Arcy recognizes and brilliantly analyzes." In *The Meeting of Love and Knowledge* (Harper, 1957) Father D'Arcy discusses the shared awareness as well as the profound differences between the mysticisms of Buddhism and Christianity with what the London *Times Literary Supplement* (May 23, 1958) called "sympathy and understanding." In 1959 Father D'Arcy's *The Meaning and Matter of History* (Farrar, Straus, 1959) appeared, teaching its readers the lesson of humility as they confront the facts of history. The response T. S. Gregory once made in the *Spectator* (London), on May 10, 1935, to the writings of Father D'Arcy sums up that of many readers and still holds true: "When . . . he lifts up the Son of God crucified as 'the one sure way which leads to life,' it is as one who knows the tempting alternatives."

The head of Father D'Arcy, with its ascetic face, burning eyes, and cascades of gray hair, is the delight of graphic artists. It is the subject of a mosaic by Elsa Schmidt in the Museum of Modern Art, New York, of a bronze by Shrady in the Metropolitan Museum of Art, and of a painting by Augustus John in Campion Hall, Oxford. "He looks lean and ascetic," commented Alfred Eisenstaedt after photographing the priest in his cluttered room at London's Farm Street Church, "yet there is kindness written all over his unworldly face."

"The epitome of his society [the Jesuits] . . . an El Greco saint turned *homme d'affaires*" —in these words *Vogue* sums up the personality of Father Martin D'Arcy. Michael de la Bedoyere, a friend of long duration, does it a little differently. "Those wiry, taut muscles have their counterpart in a beautifully ordered brain—a brain deliberately directed toward the Greater Glory of God. . . . Don't be deceived by the preliminary flourishes! The end justifies the means! The entertainment, the paradoxes, the impish[ness] . . . as he leads the lively conversation among his guests . . ," the dilettantism in art, the unconventional political views—they all have their final end; and their effect is all the more deadly in that Father Martin D'Arcy also loves them all—all for their own sake."

References

Life 32:95 Ja 14 '52 por
N Y Times p6 O 16 '39; p1 S 19 '40 por
Sat Eve Post 231:36 Mr 7 '59
Time 59:52+ Mr 17 '47

Authors & Writers Who's Who (1948-49)
Catholic Who's Who, 1952
Hoehn, M. A. ed. Catholic Authors, 1930-47
International Who's Who, 1959
Who's Who, 1959
World Biography (1948)

DAVIDSON, JOHN F(REDERICK) May 3, 1908- United States Navy officer
Address: b. Office of the Superintendent, United States Naval Academy, Annapolis, Md.; h. 1 Buchanan Rd., United States Naval Academy, Annapolis, Md.

In June 1960 Rear Admiral John F. Davidson took office as the new superintendent of the United States Naval Academy in Annapolis, Maryland. His appointment came as the latest in a long series of top-level assignments that included administrative positions in Washington as well as important commands at sea. For the latter he has been honored with many decorations, including the Legion of Merit and the Silver Star Medal. He has been cited for his "inspiring devotion to duty" in battle and "conspicuous gallantry and intrepidity" as commander of the submarine USS *Blackfish* in the Pacific during World War II.

An alumnus of the Naval Academy, Rear Admiral Davidson served as head of its department of English, history, and government for three years. He was given the rank of rear admiral in 1956, and has recently served as chief of the Navy Group, joint United States military mission for aid to Turkey.

John Frederick Davidson was born on May 3, 1908 in Olean, New York, to Perry Allen Davidson, a department store owner, and Annie Marie (Smith) Davidson. Raised in Warren, Pennsylvania, he attended Warren High School from which he was graduated in 1925. One of six children, he has two sisters, Mrs. William M. Hill of Warren and Mrs. C. L. Brunke of Jamestown, New York, and three brothers, Captain R. A. Davidson, United States Navy, Perry A. Davidson, Jr., of Warren, and R. S. Davidson of Corry, Pennsylvania.

Davidson entered the United States Naval Academy on June 17, 1925, as a midshipman from Pennsylvania. After his graduation from the academy on June 6, 1929, when he was awarded a B.S. degree and commissioned ensign, he served as a junior officer in the engineering department of the USS *Utah*. In September 1930 he was transferred to the USS *Arizona*, where he was given communication and gunnery details.

A student at the submarine school at New London, Connecticut, from July to December 1933, Davidson was assigned to the USS *Cachalot* as communications officer in January 1934. Two years later he was transferred to the Bureau of Navigation (now the Bureau of Naval Personnel) in the Navy Department at Washington, D.C. In this office he performed duties in the detail section of the officer personnel division.

(Continued next page)

REAR ADM. JOHN F. DAVIDSON

Davidson received his first submarine command as executive officer and navigator of the USS S-45, an Atlantic fleet ship, in September 1938. Eight months later he was transferred to the command of the USS S-44, which also operated in the Atlantic. In October 1940 he was given command of the USS *Mackerel,* where he remained until June 1942.

Davidson's major wartime command was aboard the submarine USS *Blackfish,* on which he served until March 1944. First off the North African coast and finally in the Pacific Theater, the *Blackfish* distinguished itself for valuable reconnaissance activities and effective torpedo attacks on enemy shipping. While acting "as a navigational beacon for orientation of United States amphibious forces involved in the landing operations" in North Africa, the *Blackfish* under Davidson's command torpedoed a 5,000-ton enemy blockade runner. For his capable leadership in this and subsequent patrols, Davidson was later awarded the Legion of Merit with Combat "V". He was cited for having, with the *Blackfish,* helped to maintain a blockade of enemy shipping lanes, sunk an antisubmarine vessel, and evaded severe depth-charge attacks. He was also credited with having substantially aided successful landings in North Africa.

With the *Blackfish* in the Pacific, Davidson and his crew inflicted great damage on Japanese shipping. For his leadership in this phase of the war, he was awarded the Silver Star Medal for heroic service. At that time he was cited for "conspicuous gallantry and intrepidity," when "undeterred by extremely severe hostile countermeasures and the presence of numerous antisubmarine vessels, [he] maintained constant contact with the enemy ships for extended periods of time and, skillfully maneuvering his craft into advantageous striking position at every opportunity, pressed home a series of vigorous torpedo attacks which resulted in the sinking or damaging of an important amount of Japanese shipping."

From April to December 1944 Davidson was training officer on the staff of Commander, Submarine Training Command at Pearl Harbor. Thereafter, until May 1947, he again served in the officer detail of the Bureau of Naval Personnel. During this period he was advanced to the rank of captain (March 30, 1945). He was next assigned to command submarine division 62, the USS *Orion,* submarine tender, and submarine squadron two.

Once again a student, Davidson spent twelve months in the Canadian National Defense College at Kingston, Ontario, where he completed a course of study in August 1951. The following month he became the chairman of the department of English, history, and government at the United States Naval Academy in Annapolis. His next sea command was on the USS *Albany,* which he joined in May 1954 for a sixteen-month tour of duty.

Made assistant director of the politico-military policy division of the Office of the Chief of Naval Operations in September 1955, Davidson was appointed director of the division on January 4, 1957. After an assignment as commander of cruiser division five from December 1957 until October 1958, he was made chief of the Navy Group in the joint United States military mission for aid to Turkey, which operated from Ankara.

On March 29, 1960 Davidson was named to replace Rear Admiral Charles L. Melson as superintendent of the United States Naval Academy. Davidson's assignment as head of the Academy began in June 1960. At the same time he was appointed commandant of the Severn River Naval Command in Annapolis.

The Naval Academy, founded in 1845, is directed by the superintendent under the Chief of Naval Personnel. Appointments for admission are made by United States Senators and Representatives, each entitled to designate five midshipmen a year, while the President of the United States appoints seventy-five. There are also admissions from Canada and other countries, and from the regular Navy and Marine Corps and Reserves. Exacting scholastic and physical tests are required of entrants to the Academy, who must be between seventeen and twenty-two years old. Undergraduates are provided with a comprehensive college course in engineering and naval science that leads to the B.S. degree and usually an ensign's commission.

In addition to the Legion of Merit and Silver Star, other medals won by Rear Admiral Davidson are the American Defense Service Medal with Bronze "A"; the American Campaign Medal; European-African-Middle Eastern Campaign Medal with two stars; World War II Victory Medal; and the National Defense Service Medal.

Admiral Davidson was married to the former Ann Dorsey Rogers of Howard County, Maryland on May 10, 1947. Mrs. Davidson was the widow of Lieutenant Commander Charles F. Brindupke, the commanding officer of the World War II submarine *Tullibee.* Davidson has a daughter, Diane Raguet Davidson, and a step-daughter, Mrs. William S. Cole, Jr. Although his official residence is at 14 Hertzel Street, Warren, Pennsylvania, Davidson now lives in Annapolis on the grounds of the Naval Academy. He is a 170 pound six-footer, with brown hair and brown eyes. In Washington, D.C. he belongs to the Army-Navy Club and the Army and Navy Country Club, where he plays golf.

Reference

NY Times p6 Mr 30 '60 por

DEFAUW, DÉSIRÉ Sept. 5, 1885-July 25, 1960 Belgian violinist and conductor; musical director and conductor of Chicago Symphony Orchestra (1943-47); guest conductor of NBC Symphony Orchestra in 1939 and 1940; founder of National Orchestra of Belgium (1937). See *Current Biography* (January-February) 1940.

Obituary

N Y Times p30 Jl 26 '60

DE GAULLE, CHARLES *See* Gaulle, Charles de

DEMIKHOV, VLADIMIR P(ETRO-VICH) (dĕ-mē′kôv) 1916- Soviet surgeon
Address: b. Organ Transplantation Laboratory, First Medical Institute, Moscow, U.S.S.R.

A renowned Soviet surgeon, Vladimir P. Demikhov attracted world-wide attention in 1954 when he successfully grafted the head of one dog onto the neck of another. Since then he has repeated this feat on several occasions for foreign visitors. Earlier, he successfully replaced the heart of a dog with a mechanical instrument, and he also inserted an extra heart into a dog. These experiments are part of a long-range Soviet program to discover how mechanical substitutes can perform the function of organs and how healthy organs can replace damaged or diseased organs. Eventually, when medical knowledge expands and surgical techniques attain perfection, Soviet scientists hope to perform these operations on human beings.

Vladimir Petrovich Demikhov was born in 1916. The Soviet press has never carried biographical information about him. Foreigners who have visited him report that he was born in Moscow and was educated at the First Medical Institute, a hospital and medical school in his native city. Soviet publications in their earliest reports about him described Demikhov as a physiologist. More recently he is described as a surgeon. Foreigners who have talked with him say he is strictly a research scientist and has neither been trained as a physician nor has practised as one.

After World War II he began his experimental work at the Vishnevsky Surgical Institute of the Academy of Medical Sciences of the U.S.S.R. The institute was then headed by

Wide World

VLADIMIR P. DEMIKHOV

Aleksandr Vasilyevich Vishnevsky, who died in 1948. Vishnevsky had transplanted nerves from corpses to the bodies of living persons during the war.

Moscow News, an English-language newspaper published in the Soviet capital, in May 1947 described a series of experiments Demikhov had made, replacing the hearts and lungs of dogs with hearts and lungs from other dogs. The extra hearts continued their own rhythms, beating independently of the original heart. All of the dogs survived the operation, but none lived more than eight days. Just a year later, in May 1948, *Literaturnaya gazeta* reported an operation Demikhov had performed on September 26, 1947, in which he had given a dog an artificial mechanical heart with which it had lived for three months.

Komsomolskaya pravda on February 14, 1951 reported that Demikhov had received the Academician Burdenko Prize for his work in giving dogs a second or auxiliary heart. The article referred to Demikhov as the head of the experimental laboratory for transplanting organs at the Vishnevsky Institute, and quoted his speculation about future experiments: "Perhaps in time it will be possible to transplant organs in human beings also."

Soon after this article appeared, Soviet scientists working at the Institute for Experimental Surgical Instruments perfected a surgical-stapling machine which made it possible to stitch together severed blood vessels with more speed than before. The device was precisely what Demikhov needed in his experiments, and he has made extensive use of it ever since.

Some ten years ago Demikhov and his assistant, Vladimir Mikhailovich Goryainov, began experimenting with the transplanting of the head and forelegs of one dog to the body of

DEMIKHOV, VLADIMIR P.—*Continued*

another. In 1954, at a meeting of the Moscow Surgical Society, they exhibited a two-headed dog that had survived such an operation.

During the operation Demikhov had attached the head and forward appendages of a smaller dog to the neck of a larger dog. By using the surgical stapling machine, he connected the blood vessels of the smaller dog's head with the corresponding veins and arteries of the host dog, enabling the latter's heart to pump blood into both heads. After the completion of the operation, both heads could see, hear, smell, bark, and swallow.

Similar operations had been performed in 1908 by a United States scientist, Dr. Charles C. Guthrie. Some Soviet scientists knew of the work of Dr. Guthrie, but whether Demikhov did is not known. American scientists working in this field had all but forgotten his work until Soviet scientists pointed it out to them.

In May 1958 an American surgeon, Dr. Edgar F. Berman of Mount Sinai Hospital in Baltimore, Maryland, went to the Soviet Union to observe Demikhov's work. In 1957 Dr. Berman had been the first in this country to transplant a dog's heart successfully. But none of his dogs had lived more than six hours, while one of the dogs on which Demikhov has operated lived for two and a half months. At the time of Berman's visit Demikhov was no longer at the Vishnevsky Institute, but had his own laboratory at the First Medical Institute. In December 1958 Demikhov demonstrated the same operation at Leipzig University in East Germany. In the following month he appeared at a news conference in East Berlin where he declared that the transplanting of human hearts had become possible.

In April 1959 it was reported that Demikhov had succeeded in keeping one of his two-headed dogs alive for twenty-nine days. The previous record had been six days. Demikhov demonstrated the head grafting operation for Dr. Blair O. Rogers, of the Institute of Reconstructive Plastic Surgery at the New York University-Bellevue Medical Center, who was in Moscow under a scientific exchange agreement.

Life magazine in its July 20, 1959 issue carried an exclusive story by its correspondent Edmund Stevens, with pictures by its photographer Howard Sochurek, of another such operation. Demikhov told them it was the twenty-fourth time he performed it. He also told them he was planning to move his laboratory to the Sklifosovsky Institute, which is Moscow's largest emergency hospital.

"This is because we are swiftly outgrowing the experimental stage and must now go on to apply our knowledge to saving human lives," Demikhov told Stevens and Sochurek. "We will begin by establishing a tissue bank. It will eventually include every conceivable part of the human anatomy: corneas, eyeballs, livers, kidneys, hearts, even limbs. Everything will

be kept under refrigeration. When we are fully prepared, an accident victim will be brought in with a normally fatal injury to some essential organ. Since a man who is going to die anyway has absolutely nothing to lose, we will try to provide him with the necessary organ from our bank. If the transplanting is successful, he lives. If not—better luck next time."

The Soviet surgeon also told Stevens about a woman who had lost her leg under a street car. "For the past five years she has been nagging me to provide her with a leg, not a wooden or artificial leg but a real one," he said. "It may sound incredible to you, but I have just about decided to attempt it. The worst that could happen is that we will have to re-amputate the leg that we try to graft on."

The equipment and techniques developed by Demikhov have already been used on a human patient. The patient, whose hand was almost completely severed, now has a range of function in his reattached hand believed to be superior to that of an artificial hand.

In October 1959 Demikhov had an interview with Tom Lambert, the New York *Herald Tribune*'s Moscow correspondent. He told Lambert he was preparing to try linking an auxiliary heart to the body of a man with heart trouble. He added: "I hope to live until the time when it will be possible to replace hearts."

Vladimir P. Demikhov, who lives in a Moscow apartment, is married to an engineer and has two children. He looks younger than his age and has dark hair and a receding hairline. Visitors have described him as an enthusiastic, indefatigable, and determined worker and a "vigorously decisive man with a frank, open manner." Demikhov said in October 1959 that he is willing to share the results of his investigations with scientists of all nations. "They are not secret," he emphasized. "There is nothing political about this."

Among his colleagues Demikhov has the reputation of a man with whom it is difficult to work. His shift from the Vishnevsky Institute to the First Medical Institute is said to have been involuntary. Medical men, in particular, have indicated a distaste for the sensational publicity he has received. Although he is widely known, it is clear that he is neither one of the most honored nor best rewarded of Soviet scientists. Both Dr. Berman and Dr. Rogers praised the techniques which Demikhov had developed as his major contribution to medical science and commented on the limited staff and facilities which the Soviet Government had made available to him.

References

Cur Digest of the Soviet Press 10:22
    Jl 9 '58
Life 47:79 Jl 20 '59 por
N Y Herald Tribune p1+ O 26 '59 por
Time 65:62 Ja 17 '55

DENNISON, ROBERT LEE Apr. 13, 1901- United States Navy officer

Address: b. Headquarters, Commander in Chief, United States Atlantic Fleet, Norfolk 11, Va.; h. Warren, Pa.

As Supreme Allied Commander, Atlantic (SACLANT), Admiral Robert Lee Dennison is the counterpart for the NATO naval force to Lauris Norstad, Supreme Allied Commander, Europe and a general in the United States Air Force. On February 29, 1960 at the United States Naval Base in Norfolk, Virginia, Dennison took up the dual assignment that Admiral Jerauld Wright formerly held—Commander in Chief, United States Atlantic Fleet, as well as commander of NATO's fleet and naval air units. In the Navy for over thirty-five years, Dennison, an ex-submariner, served for five years as naval aide to President Truman, has had considerable experience in staff and strategic planning, and has commanded forces in the Pacific, the eastern Atlantic, and the Mediterranean.

Born to Ludovici Waters and Laura Florence (Lee) Dennison on April 13, 1901, Robert Lee Dennison is a native of Warren, the small city in northwestern Pennsylvania which is still his official home address. He studied at Kiskiminetas School in Saltsburg, Pennsylvania, before his appointment to the United States Naval Academy, Annapolis, Maryland. In 1923 he was graduated from the academy with the B.S. degree, commissioned an ensign, and assigned to duty on the battleship *Arkansas*.

Qualifying as a submariner after submarine training at New London, Connecticut in 1925, he joined the crew of the submarine *S-8*. He subsequently returned to Annapolis, where he completed the postgraduate course in diesel engineering at the Naval Postgraduate School in 1929. A year later he received the M.Sc. degree from Pennsylvania State College. From 1930 until 1933, when he began two years of further shore assignment at the Engineering Experiment Station in Annapolis, Dennison had duty afloat on the cruiser *Chester*. He received his Eng.D. degree from Johns Hopkins University in Baltimore in 1935.

Dennison commanded the rescue vessel USS *Ortolan* from 1935 to 1937, when he became commanding officer of the submarine *Cuttlefish*. From 1938 through 1939 he was again on shore assignment, this time as assistant Naval inspector of machinery at the Electric Boat Company, New London Ship and Engine Works, Groton, Connecticut. (The New London Naval Base, actually across the Thames River from New London, is the Navy's principal site for planning, building, and launching submarines.)

When he returned to sea in 1940, Dennison assumed command of the destroyer USS *John D. Ford*. By the time the Japanese attacked Pearl Harbor, however, he had already been assigned to the staff of the Commander in Chief, Asiatic Fleet, and in this assignment participated both in the defense of the Philippines in December 1941 and in the early

U. S. Navy

ADM. ROBERT LEE DENNISON

fighting with the Japanese in the East Indies. For his service in the Philippines, he was decorated with the Army Distinguished Unit Emblem.

Early in 1942 Dennison was appointed chief of staff to commander, Allied Naval Forces, East Australia, with similar duty on the staff of commander, Submarines, East Australia. Detached in August 1942 he became chief of staff to commander, Amphibious Force, Pacific Fleet (later Ninth Amphibious Force). As such, he took part in the recapture and occupation in the summer of 1943 of the Aleutian Islands of Attu and Kiska, taken by the Japanese in June 1942. In the recovery of Attu, he supervised the execution of a plan which enabled the United States forces to attack without loss of any Navy ships or personnel. For his conduct in Australia and later in the Aleutians area, he was awarded the Legion of Merit. Having served aboard the USS *Pennsylvania* in the Aleutians campaign, he wears that battleship's Navy Unit Commendation Ribbon.

During the latter part of the war Dennison served in the rank of captain on the joint war plans committee for the Joint Chiefs of Staff. He was also special adviser to the Under Secretary of the Navy. From 1945 until early 1947 he served as Assistant Chief of Naval Operations for politico-military affairs. In this office he was concerned with co-ordination of Navy and State Department policy.

Appointed commander of the USS *Missouri* early in February 1947, Captain Dennison took over his new duties at the beginning of March. He was in command of that battleship when it was selected to transport President Harry S. Truman and his party back to the United States from Brazil after the ceremony of signature of the Treaty of Rio de Janeiro on September 2, 1947. Among the

DENNISON, ROBERT LEE—*Continued*

honors conferred by the Brazilian government at that time was the Grand Officer, Order of Naval Merit, bestowed on Dennison.

His personality and capabilities impressed President Truman, and in January 1948 Captain Dennison was selected to succeed Rear Admiral James H. Foskett, who was returning to sea duty, as the President's naval aide. His function was to keep the President informed on naval matters, and after the outbreak of war in Korea, his briefings became particularly important. "When he talks, the Chief listens," was a comment at that time.

President Truman appointed his naval aide in June 1950 to serve with Howard A. Rusk and Arthur S. Abramson on a three-member committee directed to review veterans' hospitalization programs and the needs of disabled veterans, giving special attention to the problems of paraplegics and amputees. In its report in October the committee found that the administrative organization of the Veterans Administration was "cumbersome and unwieldy," but that the program for the care and rehabilitation of paraplegics surpassed the services available for civilian paraplegics. Dennison continued as Truman's naval aide until the change in administration in January 1953. By that time he held the rank of rear admiral (permanent), his promotion having been confirmed by the Senate in April 1952.

For one year beginning February 1953, Rear Admiral Dennison was back on sea duty as commander, Cruiser Division Four, operating in the Atlantic. In January 1954 he was detached to serve once again in Washington, this time as director of the strategic plans division in the Navy Department's Office of the Chief of Naval Operations. In November 1955 Dennison took on additional responsibility as Assistant Chief of Naval Operations (plans and policy).

With his promotion to the rank of vice-admiral, for which President Eisenhower nominated him in March 1956, Dennison also received appointment as chief of staff and aide to Admiral Jerauld Wright, Commander in Chief of the United States Atlantic Fleet and Supreme Allied Commander, Atlantic (SACLANT). From June 18, 1956 to July 21, 1958 he was in command of the First Fleet, United States Pacific Fleet, and at the same time was a member of the joint strategic plans committee of the Joint Chiefs of Staff. For eight months beginning July 23, 1958 he served as Deputy Chief of Naval Operations (plans and policy) in Washington.

After the Senate had approved Dennison's promotion to the rank of full admiral on March 10, 1959, he went to London, England to assume a new command, succeeding Admiral James L. Holloway, Jr., as Commander in Chief, Naval Forces, Eastern Atlantic and Mediterranean. Dennison's appointment to replace Admiral Wright as Supreme Allied Commander, Atlantic, and Commander in Chief of the United States Atlantic Fleet was announced from NATO headquarters in Paris, France on December 28, and the transfer of command became effective on February 29, 1960. Fleet and naval air units of eight NATO countries serve under Dennison. The responsibility of SACLANT, Admiral Wright once asserted, is to "make the Atlantic Ocean from the North Pole to the Tropic of Cancer and between Europe and North America a NATO lake, a protected body of water on which shipping can move with safety" (New York *Herald Tribune,* April 19, 1954).

Dennison was married to Mildred Fenton Mooney Neely of Washington, D.C. on May 10, 1937; they have a daughter, Lee, and a son, Robert Lee, Jr. Five feet eleven inches in height and about 180 pounds in weight, Dennison has been described as husky. He enjoys golf when he has time to play, and he belongs to Sigma Xi, the New York Yacht Club, and the Army-Navy Club of Washington.

References

N Y Times p47 Ja 25 '48 por; p1 D 17 '59 por; p16 Mr 1 '60 por
People Today 1:2+ S 12 '50 pors
U S News 48:14 Ja 4 '60
Navy Register, 1959
Who's Who in America, 1958-59

DENNY, GEORGE V(ERNON), JR. Aug. 29, 1899-Nov. 11, 1959 Radio broadcaster; founder and moderator (1935-52) of *America's Town Meeting of the Air* radio program; president of Town Hall, Inc. (1937-51). See *Current Biography* (September) 1950.

Obituary

N Y Times p35 N 12 '59

DILLMAN, BRADFORD Apr. 14, 1930-
Actor

Address: c/o Twentieth Century-Fox Film Corp., Beverly Hills, Calif.

Before Bradford Dillman's motion-picture career was more than one year old, he was named co-winner of the "best actor" award at the 1959 Cannes International Film Festival for his performance in *Compulsion*. Yet success was not sudden or easy for Dillman, who had served a difficult five-year apprenticeship on the stage and who had rejected a carefree way of life as a wealthy man's son to become a professional actor. One of his notable roles on the stage was Edmund Tyrone (Eugene O'Neill as a young man) in *Long Day's Journey Into Night*.

Bradford Dillman was born in San Francisco, California, on April 14, 1930, the son of socially prominent Dean and Josephine (Moore) Dillman. He is among the few actors who have not improved upon the names on their birth certificates: "Bradford Dillman sounded like a distinguished phony theatrical name," he has said, "so I liked it and kept it." He has one brother and two sisters. His parents are now divorced, and his father is a stockbroker and a partner in E. F. Hutton & Company in San Francisco. Bradford Dillman attended private schools, beginning with the Town School for Boys in San

Francisco. After one year at St. Ignatius High School in the same city, he transferred to the Hotchkiss School in Lakeville, Connecticut.

Dillman's first acting experience came in a Christmas pageant at the Town School when he was six years old. During his San Francisco boyhood he frequently attended the local movie houses, often sitting through three double features in a single day. He was a serious amateur actor at Hotchkiss, playing the title role in *Hamlet,* Malcolm in *Macbeth,* and parts in *The Hasty Heart, The Jest,* and *Home of the Brave.* He also played on the Hotchkiss soccer, basketball, and golf teams.

At Yale University, Dillman studied English literature in the classroom and drama on the stage. He performed in eight productions of the Yale Dramatic Association, including *Mannerhouse,* in which he had the role of young Thomas Wolfe. Among his classmates and admirers was writer John Knowles, who later recalled (*Holiday,* February 1957): "In the false dawn which University life can be, we were both coming up like thunder." Dillman was elected to the Yale Senior Society, the Fence Club, and the Torch Honor Society.

During his summer vacations Dillman returned to Santa Barbara, California, where his parents were then living and where he acted with the Youththeatre group and the Alcehama Theatre group. Among his plays were *Dark of the Moon, The Glass Menagerie,* and *John Loves Mary.* When he received his B.A. degree in English literature from Yale in 1951, he faced the possibility of military service in the Korean war.

Joining the United States Marine Corps in 1952, Dillman went through boot training at Parris Island, North Carolina. He was selected for Officers Candidate School in Quantico, Virginia and was commissioned a second lieutenant. During the war he served at an instructors' school, teaching combat veterans how to convey their military experience to new recruits. He was discharged as a first lieutenant in 1953.

Dillman was now determined to become a professional actor. He applied for a scholarship at the Royal Academy of Dramatic Arts in London and was selected, but changed his plans in favor of an off-Broadway role in *The Scarecrow.* He acted in three more plays with the same group, the Theatre De Lys in Greenwich Village, and also earned small roles in television plays and in a series of Signal Corps training movies.

Acting required an unleashing of personality quite foreign to his Ivy League training, Dillman was discovering, and acting jobs were few and irregular. Between engagements, he passed the time with crossword puzzles, old movies, and baseball. He shared an apartment with his former classmate John Knowles: four rooms overlooking a junk-yard in the Hell's Kitchen district of New York City.

Early in 1955 Dillman won a walk-on part in *Inherit the Wind.* Later in the year he was admitted to the famous Actors Studio of dramatic arts, one of nine students to be selected from some 1,000 applicants; among his classmates was Marilyn Monroe. He was then cast as the young soldier in *Third Person.* The play

BRADFORD DILLMAN

proved to be his breakthrough as an actor. "Bradford Dillman's lost soldier . . . is taut, reserved, carefully-carved portraiture," wrote Walter Kerr in the New York *Herald Tribune* (December 30, 1955). Brooks Atkinson, in the New York *Times* the same day, remarked that Dillman had the most sympathetic role to play, adding: "Of course, one must not confuse the part with the performance. But let's forget the rules and remark that Mr. Dillman gives the best performance in the drama."

Now Dillman was at the decisive point in his career, halfway between obscurity and fame. He crossed the line in July 1956, when he was chosen by José Quintero and approved by Mrs. Carlotta O'Neill to play the youthful playwright in Eugene O'Neill's *Long Day's Journey Into Night;* 500 actors had applied for the role. The play opened at the Helen Hayes Theatre in New York on November 7, 1956.

"It was such an opening night as the dreams of young actors are made on," wrote John Knowles in *Holiday* (February 1957). "There were twelve curtain calls, halted only by turning on the house lights. Immediately after, Dillman was engulfed in his dressing room by excited friends, and led along a route strewn with congratulations to Sardi's. A little later he and other members of the cast appeared at a glittering party which quickly became exuberant as the newspapers arrived."

Dillman's portrayal of the tortured young playwright was described as one of "swift, sensitive skill" in the New York *Herald Tribune* (November 8, 1956); as "winning, honest, and both callow and perceptive" in the New York *Times* of the same date; and as "an artful blend of strength and gentleness" in *Variety* (November 14, 1956). The Pulitzer Prize-winning play was sent to Europe by the State Department in June 1957.

(Continued next page)

DILLMAN, BRADFORD—*Continued*

Leaving the cast before the play went on tour in 1958, Dillman was signed to a motion-picture contract by Twentieth Century-Fox Film Corporation. He played the young law student in *A Certain Smile,* released in August 1958, and a Marine in *In Love and War,* released in October. "Both pictures embarrassed me," Dillman admitted (*Newsweek,* April 13, 1959). Then he was cast as the psychotic killer, Artie Straus, in *Compulsion,* based on the celebrated Loeb-Leopold "thrill killing" of 1924.

Compulsion was released in April 1959 and won a three-way "best actor" award for Orson Welles, Dean Stockwell, and Dillman at the Cannes International Film Festival in May. Press reviewers tended to choose one or another of the three principals for special notice; a *Newsweek* critic wrote (April 13, 1959) that Dillman played his role "with something touching on brilliance." Dillman's next picture was *Crack in the Mirror,* a Darryl F. Zanuck production filmed in Paris in the fall of 1959 and released in the spring of 1960.

Although he is a member of the Actors Studio, Dillman is unwilling to conform to the usual stereotype of "The Method" actor. "Much of the 'beatnik' nonsense that we see on television and in movies, and that passes for Actors Studio technique, is nothing of the sort," he has said (New York *Times,* April 19, 1959). "It's gross caricature and affectation. [Lee] Strasberg encourages honest individuality, not the weird, off-beat St. Vitus dancing that passes for 'The Method.'"

Dillman was married to Frieda Harding on June 16, 1956 at Hotchkiss School, Lakeville, Connecticut; they had met as co-workers at the Sharon Playhouse in Pennsylvania a year earlier. With their two children, they live in a rented home in Pacific Palisades, California, shunning Hollywood night life. In appearance, Dillman is a "spare, wiry, flashing-eyed young man" who is five feet eleven inches tall, weighs 165 pounds, and has brown hair and brown eyes. He likes to write and is working on a military analysis of the German Army in World War II. He holds the 1957 Blum Award as the outstanding new personality in the theater that year.

"Dillman is an individualist and a breaker of rules," wrote Lawrence J. Quirk in the New York *Times* (April 19, 1959). "He dares to dress neatly. He dares to be a gentleman.... He doesn't hate himself. He isn't lonely.... His ambition, pure and simple, is to be the best actor his endowments (natural) and training (disciplined) will permit."

References

Holiday 21:91+ F '57 por
N Y Post Mag p3 D 7 '58 por
N Y Sunday News II p6 Ap 26 '59 por
N Y Times II p2 Ap 19 '59 por
Newsweek 53:116 Ap 13 '59 por

DIMECHKIE, NADIM (dē-mǐsh-kē"à nà-dēm') Dec. 5, 1919- Lebanese Ambassador to the United States; Member of Lebanese Delegation to the United Nations

Address: b. Sheraton Park Hotel, Washington, D.C.; h. 2841 McGill Terrace, Washington, D.C.

Tiny though Lebanon may be, it plays an important role in international affairs because of the pivotal position it occupies in the power struggle between the East and West. Half-Christian, half-Moslem, it is strategically located on the fringes of Asia, Africa, and Europe. Its Ambassador to the United States is Nadim Dimechkie, a career diplomat trained in economics, who worked for a short time as a teacher and as a government economist before he joined Lebanon's foreign service. Since then he has held important posts in England, Canada, Egypt, and Switzerland, and has been a delegate to various international bodies, including the United Nations General Assembly.

Nadim Dimechkie was born on December 5, 1919 in Beirut, Lebanon to Badr and Julia (To'meh) Dimechkie, and was raised in the Moslem faith of his parents. He was educated in local elementary and secondary schools and received his B.A. and M.A. degrees in economics from the American University of Beirut, a former missionary school now sponsored by the Near East College Association in the United States.

Dimechkie began his career at the age of twenty-one as a teacher. He left his native country and traveled inland to Iraq where he taught in a public high school from 1940 to 1941. In 1942 he traveled to Syria where he became managing director of the Societé des Conserves et d'Industries Agricoles in Damascus, the first large corporation in Syria. It represented an association of food producers scattered through the country.

In 1943 Dimechkie started his career in government work when he was appointed to the Lebanese Ministry of Supply. His office was charged with the responsibility of procuring and distributing food and supplies during World War II. While with the ministry, he served as the Lebanese representative to the Joint Supply Board for Syria and Lebanon, and he served as the Lebanese delegate to the Office des Céréales Panifiables, the bureau for grain processing.

Before Dimechkie joined the diplomatic corps of his country's government, he served briefly in 1944 as the Lebanese Director of Economic Affairs, a post similar to that of an Under Secretary in the United States. In 1944 he joined the Ministry of Foreign Affairs. His first position was at the Lebanese Legation to the Court of St. James in London where he served as commercial counselor, advising on economic and commercial affairs. From 1947 to 1949 he was counselor of the legation.

During this period Dimechkie began his career with the United Nations and other international bodies. In 1945 he served as a member of the Lebanese delegation to the preparatory commission of UNESCO in London and the preparatory commission of the United Nations in London. In 1946 he was an alternate delegate to the first session of the United Nations General Assembly in London. In 1947 he was a delegate to the Palestine Conference in London and the International Wheat Conference in Paris.

His next diplomatic post was in Canada, where he was Lebanese Consul General in Ottawa from 1949 to 1951. He served as a delegate to the International Aviation Conference in Montreal and to the United Nations General Assembly in New York, both in 1950. In 1951 he returned to his native country in an official capacity for the last time. He served briefly as director of the Economic and Social Department of the Ministry of Foreign Affairs before devoting the next three and a half years to Arab problems.

In 1952 Dimechkie became counselor of the legation in Cairo, Egypt; and in 1953 he became Minister and Chargé d'Affaires at the Embassy of Lebanon in Cairo. From 1953 to 1955 he was the Lebanese delegate to the Arab League. He served as the president of the twenty-second session of the Arab League Council in 1954. Dimechkie was then transferred to Switzerland as Minister of Lebanon, a post he held from 1955 to 1957. During that time he also served as a member of the Lebanese delegation to the international Wheat Conference in Geneva in 1955, and in London in 1956. Before transferring to his next post in Washington, he went to New York City as a member of the Lebanese delegation to the twelfth session of the United Nations General Assembly in 1957. He served in the same capacity for the thirteenth session in 1958 and the fourteenth session in 1959.

Dimechkie came to Washington as Ambassador of Lebanon in 1958. On February 10, he was officially received by President Dwight D. Eisenhower, who upon accepting his credentials, said: "The devotion which the Lebanese people and their leaders have demonstrated for the principles of independence and human dignity has contributed significantly to the preservation of these principles in the world today."

One of the most cosmopolitan countries in the Middle East, the republic of Lebanon is a small country on the eastern end of the Mediterranean, bounded on the north and east by Syria and on the south by Israel. The country is about 120 miles long and from thirty to thirty-five miles wide, with a population of about 1,525,000 crowded into its 3,927 square miles.

Before September 1, 1920, the territory that is now the republic of Lebanon formed a part of the Turkish Empire. From 1920 to 1941 it was administered by France under a mandate of the League of Nations. Although Lebanon became free on January 1, 1944, foreign troops were not withdrawn until 1946. Lebanon is administered by a democratic parliamentary form of government, with a Chamber of Deputies of sixty-six members who are elected every four years. They select a President for a term of six years.

Steve Zweig

NADIM DIMECHKIE

Unlike any of the other Arab countries, Lebanon has a majority of Christians, who represent about 54 per cent of the population; Moslems represent about 44 per cent. Before 1958, the government tended to favor the West, but in 1958 pro-Nasser elements instigated an internal insurrection. In July 1958 the government appealed to the United Nations for help and United States Marines landed on the shores of Lebanon. Since then, although the internal struggle has quieted down and Lebanon has apparently recovered, the country has moved closer to a neutral position between East and West and has allied itself more closely with the United Arab Republic.

When Nadim Dimechkie took over as the Lebanese Ambassador to the United States, he called for continued co-operation between the two countries in "insuring the peace of our area through economic and cultural development" (New York *Herald Tribune*, February 11, 1958). Although he sees no conflict between his country's liaison with Nasser's United Arab Republic and the interests of the United States, he does feel that Eisenhower's good will mission to the Middle East in 1959 helped to cement relations between the United States and Lebanon, and will continue to do so.

Nadim Dimechkie has received several decorations during the course of his diplomatic career. He was named Commander of the Order of the Cedars by his own country. From Syria he received the Order of Merit, and from Egypt the award of Grand Officer of the Order of Ismail, and the Grand Cordon of Merit. His own family represents a kind of Lebanon in miniature—half-Moslem and half-Christian. He was married to Margaret Sherlock of Great Britain on February 14, 1946 while he was attached to the Court of St.

DIMECHKIE, NADIM—*Continued*

James in London. His wife is a member of the Church of England; he is a Moslem. They have two young sons, Riad and Ramez.

The Ambassador from Lebanon to the United States leads a busy life, dividing his time between the embassy in Washington and the delegation from Lebanon to the United Nations in New York City. He relaxes by playing tennis or going swimming. He and his family have traveled across the United States several times, and he and his wife are familiar figures on the Washington social scene. At a reception on November 23, 1959 to celebrate Lebanon's Independence Day, they entertained more than 400 guests, including prominent United States government officials and leading diplomats of many countries.

References

International Year Book and Statesmen's Who's Who, 1959
Middle East (1958)

DODGE, JOHN V. Sept. 25, 1909- Editor
Address: b. Encyclopaedia Britannica, 425 N. Michigan Ave., Chicago 11, Ill.; h. 1043 Briarwood Lane, Northwood, Ill.

One of the most exacting tasks in the field of American publishing is performed by John V. Dodge, who in 1960 was appointed to the newly created position of executive editor of all Britannica publications. Since 1950 he had been managing editor of the *Encyclopaedia Britannica,* and in the postwar period he had supervised the publication of *Ten Eventful Years,* a four-volume history of World War II, and the *Britannica World Language Dictionary,* which gives word equivalents in English, French, German, Italian, Spanish, Swedish, and Yiddish.

Before joining the Encyclopaedia Britannica, Inc., in 1938 as assistant editor of the *Encyclopaedia Britannica* and associate editor of the *Britannica Book of the Year,* Dodge had been editor of official publications at Northwestern University. As executive editor, Dodge supervises the continously revised *Encyclopaedia Britannica*'s attempt to capture in 40,000,000 words the essence of human activity, past and present. A staff of 250 staff members in the United States, 150 editorial consultants and advisers throughout the world, and approximately 6,000 contributing specialists aid him in achieving this annual objective.

John V. Dodge was born in Chicago on September 25, 1909 to George Dannel Dodge, a sales agent, and Helen (Porter) Dodge, a former teacher of piano and voice. On his father's side he can trace his ancestry back ten generations to Richard Dodge, who emigrated from East Coker in England "without royal permission" in 1638 and showed up in Salem, Massachusetts, "desiring accommodations." Later becoming a prosperous farmer, he contributed generously to Harvard College during its infancy. His descendants were farmers in Vermont until Luther Dodge moved from Vermont to Illinois in 1857. Dodge has two sisters, Mrs. Tran Mawicke and Mrs. Henry J. Dostal, both of Bronxville, New York, and one brother, William P. Dodge, of Whittier, California.

After graduating from Evanston Township High School in Evanston, Illinois in 1926, Dodge entered Northwestern University in Evanston, where he chose as his major subjects English and journalism. Interested in a publishing career, he worked on school publications, took a job as reporter on the Evanston *News Index,* and reviewed books for the literary supplement of the Chicago *Evening Post* under Llewellyn Jones. He won full scholarships that subsidized his freshman and sophomore years, took a prize in English in his freshman year, and received a Sigma Delta Chi scholarship award in his senior year. In 1930 he was graduated from Northwestern University with the degree of Bachelor of Science.

After his graduation from Northwestern, Dodge entered the University of Bordeaux at Bordeaux, France on a fellowship from the Institute of International Education. There he specialized in studying contemporary French journalism. In 1931 the University of Bordeaux granted him the Diplôme d'Études. Returning to the United States, he went to work in an expansion shield factory in the fall of 1931, from which, he says, he was "fired after two months."

Late in 1931 Dodge began his editorial career when he became assistant editor of the Northwestern University *Alumni News.* By 1934 he had been promoted to chief editor. From 1934 to 1938 he served as editor of the official publications of Northwestern University. He began his association with Encyclopaedia Britannica, Inc., in 1938 when he was appointed assistant editor of the *Encyclopaedia Britannica* and associate editor of the *Britannica Book of the Year.*

In 1943 Dodge entered the United States Army as a private, first with the antiaircraft artillery and later with military intelligence. He saw brief overseas service during World War II in France, Italy, Greece, Egypt, and Palestine. In 1945-46 he was attached to the General Staff at Washington, D.C. He was awarded the War Department Staff Citation and was discharged in 1946 with the rank of first lieutenant.

When John V. Dodge returned to Chicago as a civilian, his former job with Encyclopaedia Britannica, Inc., was waiting for him. From 1946 to 1950 he again served as assistant editor of the *Encyclopaedia Britannica* and associate editor of the *Britannica Book of the Year.* In 1950 he was promoted to managing editor of the *Encyclopaedia Britannica* and from then he has continued to provide the executive direction for carrying out the late Walter Yust's program of continuous revision. In February 1960 the announcement that Dodge had been appointed executive editor followed the announcement that Walter Yust had retired after twenty-two years of service as editor in chief. At the same time Dodge became a member of the board of editors.

Instituted in 1934, the program of continuous revision for the *Encyclopaedia Britannica* requiring that editorial changes proceed every working day of the year was a radical departure from the policy that had preceded it for 166 years. Beginning with the first edition of 1768, a single numbered edition was printed and distributed until it became too out-of-date to sell. Then the distribution force was abandoned, an editorial department was created, and years were spent in creating a new edition.

Under the program of continuous revision, Dodge supervises the preparation of new and revised material for the *Encyclopaedia Britannica* every year. This establishes a "web of scholarship" that includes committees of advisers or departmental editors who, as specialists in their own fields, assist the Chicago and London editorial offices. Each adviser makes a continuous study of the articles assigned to him and of the scholarly material bearing on each subject. From time to time he informs editors about articles that need major changes as a result of new developments. He also suggests the best authorities in each field to be considered as possible contributors, supervises the new articles when they are received, suggests changes, and follows the changes through with contributor and editor up to the point of publication.

Theoretically at least, it is the responsibility of Dodge to be acquainted with everything in the twenty-four volumes of the *Encyclopaedia Britannica,* to know the strengths and weaknesses of every article in the set, to know when an article is ripe for changes, and to know where to find the person best qualified in the world to make the changes. (He also has to practise the arts of persuasion so that the contributor will be willing to make the changes.) In a single year as much as one-quarter of the set may have to be changed, often adding up in total number of words to more editorial content than that found in other encyclopaedias.

Early in 1960 the *Encyclopaedia Britannica* became a center of controversy when Dr. Harvey Einbinder, a consulting physicist, charged that it contained obsolete articles and serious inaccuracies. Dr. Einbinder stated his case in the winter, 1960 issue of the Columbia University *Forum;* the spring, 1960 issue contained a reply from Dr. Robert Hutchins, the chairman of the board of editors, who cited the encyclopaedia's extensive-revision policy and its modern outlook. Calling Dr. Einbinder's examination of the reference set "superficial," Dr. Hutchins said: "One thing can be said with certainty and that is that the *Britannica* reflects modern scholarship. In the 1960 edition there are articles by forty winners of the Nobel Prize."

Dodge was married to Jean Elizabeth Plate on August 17, 1935. They have four children: Kathleen, Ann, John, and Gerald. Dodge stands just under five feet eight inches tall and weighs about 146 pounds. His eyes are brown, his hair a graying black. He is a Roman Catholic in religion and an independent in politics. Associates of Dodge mention his orderliness, "easygoing nature," and lack of pretension. They

JOHN V. DODGE

say that he insists on accuracy ("a kind of sane but dogged perfectionism") and that "he expects the best from everyone because he invariably delivers it himself." An associate calls him "a good raconteur," who knows that "when the party's over, it's totally over, when the job's put aside, it's totally put aside." Dodge is the president of the Northbrook, Illinois public library board and a member of the Quadrangle Club of Chicago.

A champion of clarity in expression, Dodge has written: "It is always baffling that a man can go through high school and a university, reach the top of his profession, and still be shaky in his spelling. If I had the power to choose the preference order of (1) more science subjects and (2) stiffer English courses in our secondary schools, I'd put (2) before (1). The mark of an educated person has never changed: he writes or talks so clearly that even the most uneducated can understand him. I applaud the recent inclination of many of our high schools to return to that simple fact."

Reference

Who's Who in America, 1960-61

DOI, PETER TATSUO, CARDINAL (doy) Dec. 22, 1892- Roman Catholic prelate *Address:* Archbishop's House, 19 Sekiguchi-Daimachi, Bunkyo-ku, Tokyo, Japan

Elevated to the College of Cardinals by Pope John XXIII in March 1960, Peter Tatsuo Cardinal Doi is the first native of Japan to become a prince in the hierarchy of the Roman Catholic Church. Pope John said that the elevation of Doi and the appointments of Archbishop Laurian Rugambwa as the first African cardinal and Archbishop Rufino J. Santos as the first Filipino cardinal "proclaims that Christ is the brother of all people, and that His Kingdom is

PETER TATSUO CARDINAL DOI

without boundaries or limits of any kind." Cardinal Doi has been Archbishop of Tokyo since December 1937.

Peter Tatsuo Doi was born on December 22, 1892 at Sendai, a large city in Japan's prefecture of Miyagi, about 200 miles north of Tokyo. His family traced itself to the samurai, who were hereditary lesser nobility of Japan's feudal system. When Peter was in his second year the entire family became Roman Catholic. The baptism took place at Sendai on Easter Sunday, 1894.

Peter received his early education at local Sendai institutions. When he completed his secondary studies at Sendai College, he entered the Roman Catholic seminary in Sendai, where his abilities impressed his superiors. He then went to Rome to study for six years at the Universitá de Propaganda Fide, earning degrees in philosophy and theology.

Ordained in Sendai on May 1, 1921, he was appointed a parish priest in Wakamatsu, less than 100 miles southwest of Sendai. He served at Wakamatsu until the mid-1930's, when he moved to Tokyo as private secretary to the Apostolic Delegate to Japan, Archbishop Paul Marella. After Doi served in this post for several years, Pope Pius XI named him to succeed the Most Reverend Alexis Chambon as Archbishop of Tokyo on December 2, 1937. When he was consecrated on February 13, 1938, with Archbishop Chambon officiating, he reached a level in the hierarchy of the Roman Catholic Church never before attained by a native of Japan.

In 1940 Japan signed a military treaty with Germany and Italy, and many foreign-born ordinaries, fearing the advent of war, resigned their sees in Japan. The administration of the Roman Catholic Church in Japan passed into native hands, with Archbishop Doi as ranking prelate. Doi remained in Tokyo throughout World War II, carrying on in the face of the troubles inflicted by Japanese militarists and American bombs. By the end of the war, eleven of Tokyo's parish churches had been destroyed.

The Archdiocese of Tokyo is the only Roman Catholic archiepiscopal see in Japan. Within its boundaries are 37,000 Roman Catholics, a small number in proportion to the total population figure of 11,000,000. (There are only 270,000 Roman Catholics in all of Japan.) The 37,000 represents, however, a four-fold increase since the end of World War II, and the Roman Catholics are reported to be influential in the life of the community.

Under the guidance of Archbishop Doi the number of parishes has grown to forty, and the archdiocese now has approximately forty native priests, 260 foreign missionaries, over 600 professed native sisters, and over 550 novices, postulants, and aspirants. The institutions of the Archdiocese include twelve elementary schools, eleven middle schools, and nine high schools. In the city of Tokyo there are two Roman Catholic universities: Sophia University, operated by the Jesuits, and the International University of the Sacred Heart, conducted by the Sisters of the Society of the Sacred Heart of Jesus. In promoting education, Archbishop Doi has especially emphasized preparation for the priesthood, and he has sponsored a large proportion of the seminarians trained at the Inter-Diocesan Seminary in Tokyo.

To meet the needs of Japan's laboring classes, Doi has encouraged the activities of the Young Christian Workers, a group recently established in Japan with headquarters in the capital city. Cells have been organized in most major industries. Doi has taken a strong anti-Communist stand. In recognition of Doi's many years of service to the Roman Catholic Church in Japan, Pope Pius XII conferred upon him the title of Assistant at the Pontifical Throne in November 1956.

Pope John XXIII named Archbishop Doi to the College of Cardinals, the Pope's Senate, on March 3, 1960. The only precedent nominations of Asiatics to the sacred college were those of Thomas Cardinal Tien, a Chinese, created cardinal in 1946, and Valerian Cardinal Gracias, an Indian, created cardinal in 1953. Among the six others named by Pope John the same day as Doi were another Oriental, Rufino Cardinal Santos of Manila, and the first native African Cardinal, Laurian Cardinal Rugambwa of Rutabo, Tanganyika.

The Japanese primate accepted his nomination as an honor bestowed upon the Japanese people and the Roman Catholic Church in Japan. "On this happy occasion," he said, "I wish to express . . . profound gratitude and appreciation to the Vicar of Christ who . . . has shown his special regard for this nation." He also thanked "the Government of Japan for the liberty and protection it accords to Catholicism." A writer for Time (March 14, 1960) attributed Doi's appointment to a loss of ground by the Roman Catholic Church in Japan "for lack of Japanese priests and trained personnel," and saw in the appointment a Vatican hope "that a Japanese cardinal will stimulate the faith in Japan as well as rally Catholics elsewhere in Asia."

The College of Cardinals convened in a secret consistory on March 28, 1960 for the formality of approving the nominations of Pope John. The thirty-seven cardinals present showed their approval of the nominations in the traditional manner—by silently raising their caps. At the secret consistory the Pope spoke at length on his reasons for naming a Negro and two Asiatics, pointing out the equality of all people before God and expressing the belief that the forthcoming Second Vatican Council would be helped by the presence of men of many diverse nations endowed with highest authority. The council is to be held in St. Peter's Basilica, Rome, "not before January 1962."

On March 31, 1960, at the public consistory held with great pageantry in St. Peter's Basilica in Rome, Pope John XXIII, aided by two assistants, held over the head of Cardinal Doi the big red felt *galero* with fifteen tassels hanging down either side of its broad brim. As he did so, he recited: "For the praise of Almighty God and the honor of the Apostolic See, receive the red hat, the special badge of the Cardinalitial rank. By this you are to understand that you must show yourself fearless, even to the shedding of blood, in making our Holy Faith respected, in securing peace for Christian people and in promoting the welfare of the Roman Church." A cardinal never wears his large *galero*. The smaller square scarlet biretta is used instead. The *galero* is again used publicly only after the Cardinal's death, when it is hung in his cathedral until it disintegrates.

Peter Cardinal Tatsuo Doi is a short, frail man, black-haired and gray-eyed. His manner is gentle. He enjoys following Japanese baseball. In addition to his archiepiscopal duties, he is chief of the board of directors of the National Catholic Committee of Japan and in this capacity faces many problems of the Roman Catholic Church in Japan as a whole.

References

N Y Herald Tribune p11 Mr 4 '60
N Y Times p3 Mr 4 '60 por
Time 75:48 Mr 14 '60 por
Japan Biographical Encyclopedia & Who's
    Who (1958)
Japan Who's Who, 1950-51

DONGEN, CORNÉLIUS THÉODORUS MARIE VAN See Dongen, Kees van

DONGEN, KEES VAN Jan. 26, 1877-
Artist
Address: h. 75 rue de Courcelles, Paris 8°, France; 7 ave. Hector Otto, Monte Carlo, Monaco

The exuberant pre-World War I era of the Fauves or "wild beasts" of Paris is still fresh in the mind of the artist Kees van Dongen. Now a successful portrait painter living in Paris and on the Riviera, van Dongen gleefully recalls the period when he and other rebellious young artists rejected the conventions of life and art and shocked turn-of-the-century connoisseurs with their riotous use of brilliant color.

Born in the Netherlands, he has worked in Paris since the age of twenty, first with the Fauves and, after World War I, as a portraitist of society figures, political leaders, and renowned artists. At his 1953 exhibition in the galleries of Wildenstein & Company, Inc., in New York, he displayed many vividly colored landscapes, which he has painted in recent years and which he calls the memoirs of his youth.

Cornélius Théodorus Marie van Dongen was born on January 26, 1877 in Delfshaven, a Dutch town near Rotterdam, to Jan van Dongen and the former Helena Geurts van Gestel. He and his brother and two sisters were raised in this area. His parents, noticing his talent for drawing, hoped their son would become an industrial designer, but young Cornélius preferred to frequent the quays, sketching the boats, the sailors, and the river scenery. When he was twelve he sold his first picture, a likeness of a cow, to a butcher.

As he worked with his father in a Rotterdam suburb making malt for breweries, Cornélius dreamed of going to the big city—in this case, Paris. One day in 1897 he boarded a Paris-bound excursion train, intending to return that evening. Instead, he related in an article for *Life* (February 8, 1960), "I had such fun that I stayed."

At first van Dongen lived on the outskirts of Paris, where, he remembers, he met "all kinds of people, bums who lived there and slept on the grass," and soon he "did what they did" (*Life*, February 8, 1960). Later he moved to the Montmartre section. This was a very difficult period for van Dongen, who turned his hand to several trades, such as selling newspapers and sketching portraits in the park, in order to earn a few sous. At this time he knew few painters. He saw artists like Pierre Auguste Renoir and Henri Toulouse-Lautrec pass in the streets but was afraid to speak to them because he was "simply a bum."

By 1901 van Dongen had made a name for himself as a contributor of cartoons and caricatures to newspapers and satirical journals like *L'Assiette au beurre*. He then began trying to find buyers for his paintings. At a show of his pictures which he arranged at the Salon des Indépendants, where many unknown painters exhibited, van Dongen met artists who were working in the style later known as Fauve.

Following Henri Matisse, painters like Maurice de Vlaminck and Raoul Dufy were vigorously rejecting the delicacy of impressionist palettes in favor of pure colors, often squeezed directly from the tube and laid thickly on the canvas. Their landscapes blazed with red trees and yellow skies, portraits sported green noses and blue hair, and still lifes jumped with vibrant patterns. Van Dongen, who had also been working with these raw, bright colors, was drawn to this group. "In Holland my paintings were darker and much heavier," he

KEES VAN DONGEN

has explained, "but in Paris everything seemed light and we all wanted to get that lightness into our painting."

In 1905 van Dongen began exhibiting his work at Berthe Weill's picture shop with other painters of this group. He also participated in the third Salon d'Automne, held that year in the Grand Palais des Champs-Élysées. It was at this show that Louis Vauxhall, expressing the public and critical hostility to the new art style, dubbed the creators of these intense canvases "Fauves" or "wild beasts." Van Dongen and the other Fauvists again displayed their pictures at the Salon d'Automne in the following year. Besides participating in Fauve shows, van Dongen exhibited with vanguard groups in Germany: Die Brücke (The Bridge) group in Dresden and the New Society of Artists in Munich.

Shortly before the 1905 Salon d'Automne, van Dongen had moved into a studio in a wooden shack which stood in a little tree-lined square, the Place Ravignan (now the Square Émile Goudeau), in Montmartre. Christened Bateau-lavoir by Max Jacob because it leaked, shook, and groaned during a rainstorm, the old house nevertheless served as the residence or meeting place of some of the most illustrious figures in twentieth-century art and literature. In the studio above van Dongen's lived Pablo Picasso. The steep steps and dark winding halls of the old shack were regularly traversed by many who later became famous: Edgar Degas, Henri Matisse, Georges Braque, Gertrude Stein, Jean Cocteau, among others.

Van Dongen recalls that Picasso, with whom he became friendly, "did not have the kind of flexibility I had, [for] making little stupidities for the newspapers. He was strictly a painter. So he would stay hungry or try to sell his paintings to the secondhand dealers for five francs, a fortune at that time." The two paint-

ers often had nothing to eat and sometimes helped themselves to milk and *croissants* which had been delivered to the doorsteps of the more affluent. After the 1906 Salon d'Automne, an increasing number of Fauve paintings were sold. "But most of us still had more fervor than money in our pockets," van Dongen recalls. "Still, we were young; we laughed and sang; thanks to color we had our little rebellion. Best of all, we had a good time being 'wild.' "

During the years before World War I, van Dongen revealed an unbridled enthusiasm for color contrast in his landscape paintings of Holland, Paris and its environs, and the Normandy coast. He also adapted the Fauve technique to his representations of the female figure. A. Salmon noted (*Jeune Peinture Française*, 1914) that van Dongen freely combined colors of the make-up box with those of the palette. Fritz Vanderpyl, writing of this phase in van Dongen's development (*Peintres de mon époque*, 1931), said: "The painted woman, like a countryside between Amstel and Alkmaar, but flowering with an exotic essence, became for him—born landscape painter that he is—the preferred landscape."

In the early 1920's the acrobats, gypsy girls, and black-stockinged nudes which had predominated as subjects of van Dongen's paintings gradually gave way to celebrities. His gift for figure painting soon made him a sought after portraitist, patronized by society people, statesmen, literary figures, and renowned actresses and dancers. Among the best known of his portraits are those of the Aga Khan III, the Countess Anna de Noailles, Anatole France, Maurice Chevalier, King Leopold II of Belgium, Sacha Guitry, and Brigitte Bardot. Maurice Raynal wrote in *Modern French Painters* (1928) that van Dongen never employed his talents as a portrait painter to make academic effigies or flattering likenesses.

In time, the great and the near-great whom van Dongen painted began calling him "Kiki," and he started to use the name "Kees." He participated in the Exposition of Masters of Independent Art in 1937 and exhibited at the Galerie de France in Paris in 1942. A retrospective show of his work was arranged at the Galerie Charpentier in 1949. In March 1952 at the Galerie Petridès in Paris he presented a new collection of landscapes which recalled his Fauve period.

Praising this show, a reporter for *Time* (March 17, 1952) wrote: "There, instead of society's faces and figures, were dazzling beaches, race tracks and fields, painted in brilliant yellows, blues and reds that seemed as bright as sunlight itself." An *Art Digest* (December 15, 1953) critic, however, wrote of the same show held at the Wildenstein galleries in New York that van Dongen's landscapes were "either diluted echoes of van Gogh's slashing strokes and vibrant yellows, or else banal, slap-dash performances." In general, critics have felt that although van Dongen's art possesses few qualities that might make it enduring—a matter of complete indifference to van Dongen—it is a brilliant reflection of his times.

Van Dongen has illustrated various books since 1918. That year he worked on a French translation by J. Mardrus, *Les contes des mille et une nuits,* and two years later he illustrated a French translation of some Rudyard Kipling stories *Les plus beaux contes.* Among his other contributions in this field are accompanying illustrations for Voltaire's *La princesse de Babylone,* Anatole France's *La révolte des anges,* and Henry de Montherlant's *Les lépreuses,* as well as drawings for some of Proust's works.

Kees van Dongen has traveled in Morocco, Spain, Italy, and Egypt in search of new subjects for his oil paintings, water colors, pastels, drawings, and lithographs. In 1901 he was married for the first time, to a girl whom he had met at art school in the Netherlands. He was married to Marie Claire Huguen, his second wife, in 1939. They have one son, Jean-Marie. The artist is tall and slender and has white hair, a Shavian beard, and blue eyes. He is an officer of the French Legion of Honor, the Belgian Legion of Honor, and the Tunisian Nicham-Iftikhar. In 1929 he was naturalized a French citizen.

The paintings of van Dongen may be seen in the Musée National d'Art Moderne in Paris and in museums of Belgium, the Netherlands, Canada, Japan, Australia, and the United States, as well as in private collections. His portraits today command as much as $25,000. Some critics attribute the current interest in van Dongen's work to period sentiment and to his reputation as a chronicler of the carefree and the rich during the years between the wars. The artist himself jocularly ascribes his success to the fact that he paints "the women slimmer than they are and their jewels fatter" (*Time,* March 17, 1952).

References

France Illus 5 :43 Ja 8 '49
Réalités no115 :64 Je '60
Bénézit, E. ed. Dictionnaire des Peintres, Sculpteurs, Dessinateurs et Graveurs (1948-55)
Dictionnaire Biographique des Artistes Contemporains, 1934
Dictionnaire Biographique Français Contemporain (1954)
Duthuit, Georges Les Fauves (1949)
Georges-Michel, Michel From Renoir to Picasso (1957)
Who's Who in France, 1959-60

DUCHAMP, MARCEL (dü'shäN) July 28, 1887- Artist; author

Address: b. c/o Grove Press, 64 University Pl., New York 3

In the years since 1913, when Marcel Duchamp's stroboscopic painting, *Nude Descending a Staircase,* caused a sensation at the New York Armory Show, the French-born artist, a legend in his lifetime, has continued to influence modern art and art collecting. After having been a leading practitioner of cubism, Dadaism, futurism, and surrealism, Duchamp abandoned creative activity at the height of his career in 1923, before he reached the age of forty. Now making his home in the United States, he gives over most of his time to his "ready-mades," occasional sculptures, and to chess.

An experimentalist and innovator, Duchamp has viewed the world with coolness and detachment, producing from time to time the witty creations that puncture the dogmas of art and affront the academicians. In 1957 the Solomon R. Guggenheim Museum of New York honored Marcel Duchamp, together with his brothers, Jacques Villon, the painter, and Raymond Duchamp-Villon, the sculptor, with a retrospective exhibition. In February 1960 Duchamp became a member of the National Institute of Arts and Letters.

Marcel Duchamp, the youngest of three sons of Eugène and Lucie (Nicolle) Duchamp, was born on July 28, 1887 in Blainville (Seine-Inférieure) near Rouen. Although Eugène Duchamp, a prosperous provincial notary, had little interest in art, he gave to the world through his offspring a concentration of talent unknown since the great families of Renaissance artists. Marcel's eldest brother, Gaston, who took the name of Jacques Villon (see *C.B.,* January 1956), became a world-famous painter; his brother, Raymond, known as Raymond Duchamp-Villon, was one of the first cubist sculptors before he died in World War I. Their sister Suzanne, who is married to French artist Jean Crotti, is a painter.

Marcel attended the *lycée* at Rouen and at seventeen went to Paris to live with his brother Jacques. For one year he studied at the Académie Julian, where he found the atmosphere among the artists "infectious." He later volunteered for military service and, after being invalided out, worked for a time as a librarian at the Bibliothèque Sainte-Geneviève in Paris.

Beginning his art career, Duchamp created accomplished Cézannesque paintings. One of these, *The Artist's Father* (1910), was exhibited in the 1910 Salon d'Automne in Paris. He worked in all the *avant-garde* idioms that characterized French painting from 1908 to 1912, including cubism. With his brothers he participated in the cubist Section d'Or (Golden Section) exhibition of 1912. The "golden section" refers to the ideal proportion between the side and diagonal of a square, a proportion existing in many natural and man-made forms. Among Duchamp's experimental paintings were *Sad Young Man on a Train,* in which he deals with dynamics, and *Yvonne and Magdeleine,* in which he conveys the passage of time.

When Duchamp's *Nude Descending a Staircase* was exhibited in the Salon des Indépendants show of 1911, it caused such an uproar that he was asked to remove it. The canvas contained a series of five schematized human forms, overlapping one another and descending a winding staircase with "marvelous rhythm and precision."

Regarding his *Nude Descending a Staircase,* Duchamp has written: "It is an organization of kinetic elements, an expression of time and space through the abstract presentation of mo-

Wide World

MARCEL DUCHAMP

Moving to New York in 1915, Duchamp became a leader of the American Dadaists. He found a sympathetic patron in Walter Arensberg and an impresario in Alfred Stieglitz, who opened a gallery at 291 Fifth Avenue. Turning to writing in order to promote his ideas, Duchamp contributed to the review *391,* helped to edit the publication *VVV,* and founded another magazine, *The Blind.*

In an effort to free painting from the limitations of the flat canvas, Duchamp worked sporadically from 1915 to 1923 on *The Bride Stripped Bare by her Bachelors, Even,* an oil painting on transparent glass with fragments of lead wire He did not want *The Bride* to hang passively on a wall, but wanted people to walk around it and to look through it. The title of the work is misleading. Instead of representing a woman, it expresses the machine state of machine men and the power of steel through the joy of steel.

Just when Duchamp seemed to have reached the height of his powers as a painter, he abandoned painting and turned to the design of "ready-mades," assuming what he called the "role of artistic clown." Ready-mades are objects transformed into works of art through the "accidental" choice of the artist. Labeled with metaphysical, punning titles, they are composed of such articles as gunny sacks, coat hangers, bottle racks, and weather vanes. Perhaps his most famous ready-made is *Why Not Sneeze?* (1921), a bird cage containing small squares of marble, a thermometer, a canceled postage stamp, and some parrot food.

In this period, Duchamp again shocked the art public when he submitted a reproduction of *Mona Lisa* with added eyebrows, moustache, and beard to a Paris show. In 1917 he was a founder of the Society of Independent Artists, and three years later joined with Katherine S. Dreier in establishing the Société Anonyme in New York, the world's first museum devoted exclusively to modern art. At the Société Anonyme he arranged the first one-man show of Louis Michel Eilshemius. Within three decades the contribution of the Dadaists and their influence upon other artists received recognition; in 1941 Yale University acquired the Société's collection.

Since 1923 Duchamp has devoted much of his time to chess. "Ah, but not to paint doesn't mean I've given up art," he told A. L. Chanin (New York *Times Magazine,* January 22, 1956). "All good painters have only about five masterpieces to their name. . . . If I've done five good things, it's enough. . . . And why isn't my playing chess an art activity? A chess game is very plastic. You construct it. It's mechanical sculpture, and with chess one creates beautiful problems. Besides, it's purer, socially, than painting, for you can't make money out of chess, eh?" When he became so proficient at chess that he could enter championship games, Duchamp turned away from playing in public and took to private games of a Dada chess in which only illegal moves were permitted.

The work of Duchamp has been exhibited in New York City at the Rose Fried Gallery (1952), the Sidney Janis Gallery (1956), and the Solomon R. Guggenheim Museum (1957).

tion. A painting is, of necessity, a juxtaposition of two or more colors on a surface. I purposely restricted the *Nude* to wood coloring so that the question of painting *per se* might not be raised. There are, I admit, many patterns by which this idea could be expressed. Art would be a poor muse if there were not. But remember, when we consider the motion of form through space in a given time, we enter the realm of geometry and mathematics, just as we do when we build a machine for that purpose. Now if I show the ascent of an airplane, I try to show what it does. I do not make a still-life picture of it. When the vision of the *Nude* flashed upon me, I knew that it would break for ever the enslaving chains of Naturalism."

When a second version of this work was shown at the International Exhibition of Modern Art at the New York Sixty-ninth Regiment Armory in February-March 1913, it produced an effect "like an explosion in a shingle factory." There were greater and more striking paintings on display, but the *Nude Descending the Staircase* became the symbol of the iconoclasm of the exhibition. Sold at the time for $300, it is now valued at over $50,000.

Believing that the cubists had become tame, Duchamp turned down a commission to paint other cubist pictures with the remark "No, thanks, I prefer my liberty." He went on to create *The King and Queen Surrounded by Swift Nudes* and *Chocolate Grinder,* which, though completed before the founding of Dadaism, were wholly in that mold. Dadaism, a name derived from a French nursery word for hobbyhorse, was launched in 1916 as an expression of disillusion with World War I. Its adherents regarded traditional aesthetic values as dead and believed that art had been replaced by industry.

It is included in the permanent collections of the Museum of Modern Art in New York and, as the gift of Louise and Walter Arensberg, in the Philadelphia Museum of Art.

"Everything important that I have done can be put into a small suitcase," Duchamp once said. He has made miniature reproductions of some of his work that fit into small valises, each selling for $300. Another aspect of Duchamp's art has been his contribution to abstract films directed by Hans Richter.

In 1938 Duchamp found time to arrange the displays for the International Surrealist Exhibition, held in Paris, for which he decorated the ceiling with coal sacks. More recently, he was an organizer of the International Surrealist Exhibition in Paris in 1960.

Marcel Duchamp was described by Winthrop Sargeant in *Life* (April 28, 1952) as "a wiry, genial, gray-eyed Frenchman who gesticulates rapidly with long lean hands as he talks. . . . He lives four flights up in a little garretlike studio on 14th Street. . . . His rent is $40 a month, fitting into an extremely economical budget." He has no telephone. Chess, pipe smoking, and philosophical discussions occupy his time. Duchamp became a United States citizen in 1955.

In 1959 Grove Press published Robert Lebel's *Marcel Duchamp,* a full-length biography of the artist. It contains 129 monochrome plates and reproductions of six major works in color. Reviewing the book, a critic for the *Times Literary Supplement* (December 11, 1959) wrote: "Now for forty years Duchamp's role has been that of an iconoclast who intends to provoke us; sets out to depreciate our inherited scale of aesthetic and artistic values . . . and invents pictorial mechanisms in order to express 'his rejection of the scientific spirit because it imposes mechanization in the field of affective relations.' "

References

Art Digest 26:11+ Ja 15 '52 por
New Yorker 33:99+ Mr 2 '57
Time 59:82 Mr 10 '52 por

Bénézit, E. ed. Dictionnaire des Peintres, Sculpteurs, Dessinateurs et Graveurs (1948-55)
Blesh, Rudi Modern Art USA (1956)
Brown, Milton W. American Painting from the Armory Show to the Depression (1955)
Dictionary of Modern Painting (1955)
Encyclopedia of Painting (1955)
International Who's Who, 1959
Pach, Walter Queer Thing, Painting (1938)

EISELEY, LOREN (COREY) (īz'lē)
Sept. 3, 1907- Anthropologist; university professor
Address: b. Box 14, Bennett Hall, University of Pennsylvania, Philadelphia, Pa.; h. Wyndon Apts., B-302, Wynnewood, Pa.

Throughout his distinguished academic and literary career, Dr. Loren Eiseley, chairman of the department of anthropology and provost of the University of Pennsylvania, has demonstrated an abiding interest in nature and man's past together with a desire to understand and interpret their significance for the modern world. Professor Eiseley, who serves as curator of early man in the university museum, is one of America's leading interpreters of the works and theories of Darwin and others who developed the theory of evolution. He has received much acclaim for the grace and lyricism of his many technical and popular scientific articles.

The only child of Clyde Edwin and Daisy (Corey) Eiseley, Loren Corey Eiseley was born on September 3, 1907 in Lincoln, Nebraska into a family which homesteaded in that region when it was still a territory. He grew up in Lincoln, where his father was a hardware salesman, and there he developed two major interests that have continued throughout his life: a love for books and a fascination with the natural world. Loren's first contact with nature came from the salt flats and ponds around Lincoln and from the mammoth bones housed in an old red brick building on the University of Nebraska campus. He collected pond life for a homemade aquarium, snared snakes and turtles, and set up his own museum of baked clay bones and skulls.

Eiseley attended Lincoln High School and was graduated from the University of Nebraska Teachers College High School in 1925. He majored in anthropology at the University of Nebraska, from which he received a B.A. degree in 1933. When his college literary fraternity, Sigma Upsilon, founded the *Prairie Schooner,* a "little magazine" devoted to young Western writers, Eiseley became one of the editors. He published poems, stories, and reviews in the *Schooner* and edited a poetry page that reprinted pieces from several other "little magazines" flourishing at that time. An issue of the *Schooner* (spring, 1930) called him "one of America's most promising young poets," while another (summer, 1934) noted that he, together with Witter Bynner and John Gould Fletcher, had been asked to read poems at a Santa Fe memorial ceremony for Mary Austin, the novelist and playwright.

Most of his writing, then as now, reflected his feeling for nature. Eiseley continued to have his work published in the *Prairie Schooner* after he left the University of Nebraska; one of his two accounts of hoboing experiences, *The Mop to K.C.,* was included on the honor roll of Edward O'Brien's *Best Short Stories of 1936,* and one of his sonnets appeared in Thomas Moult's collection, *Best Poems of 1942.* Eiseley also contributed to other "little magazines," such as *Midland, Books, Voices,* and *Poetry,* and some of his poems were reprinted in *American Mercury* and *Literary Digest.*

Eiseley studied at the University of Pennsylvania from 1933 to 1935, on a Harrison Scholarship, and received an M.A. degree in 1935. He was employed for a year as assistant sociologist at the University of Nebraska and then, as the recipient of a Harrison Fellowship,

Phillips Studio

LOREN EISELEY

returned to the University of Pennsylvania to get his Ph.D. degree in anthropology in 1937. His special fields of interest include human evolution, paleo-archaeology, early man in America, and floral and faunal problems relating to human dating and the rise of man.

For a number of years Eiseley was active in the search for early postglacial man in the western United States and worked extensively in the high plains, mountains, and deserts bordering the Rocky Mountains from Canada to Mexico. From 1931 to 1933 he was a member of the Morrill paleontological expeditions from the University of Nebraska. He joined the University of Pennsylvania and Carnegie Institute expedition to the Southwest in 1934 and worked with the Smithsonian Institute expedition to northern Colorado in 1935. Several of his literary reminiscences which date back to these expeditions are published in *Harper's Magazine* (October 1947, November 1948, and May 1951, for example).

In 1937 Eiseley returned to the West for his first major academic position, as assistant professor of anthropology and sociology at the University of Kansas in Lawrence. He became associate professor in 1942 and, two years later, moved to Oberlin College in Ohio, where he served as chairman of the department of sociology and anthropology from 1944 to 1947. He assumed his present position as professor of anthropology and chairman of the department of anthropology at the University of Pennsylvania in 1947 and became curator of early man in the University of Pennsylvania Museum in 1948. He was appointed provost of the university in 1959. Eiseley has been a visiting lecturer during the summer at a number of universities, including Columbia (1946, 1950), University of California at Berkeley (1949), and Harvard University (1952).

A postdoctoral fellowship from the Social Science Research Council had enabled Eiseley to take a leave of absence from his academic responsibilities to do research work at Columbia University and the American Museum of Natural History, New York City, in 1940-1941. Another research grant from the Wenner-Gren Foundation for Anthropology (1952-53) gave him leisure from his professional duties, during which he wrote a good deal.

Eiseley served as a member of the National Research Council's committee on interrelationships of Pleistocene research (1947-50) and as vice-chairman of its division of anthropology and psychology (1950-52). In 1953 he became a research associate of the American Philosophical Society, which later commissioned him to compile a bibliography and materials on evolution to shed light on the Darwin-Lyell correspondence which the society had just then acquired. He also edited a volume of papers for the society's Darwin centennial (1958-59) which commemorated the publication of Darwin's *Origin of Species* in 1859. Eiseley was co-editor of *An Appraisal of Anthropology Today* (University of Chicago, 1953) and editor of a book of monographs, *Early Man in the Eden Valley*, by John H. Moss and others (University of Pennsylvania Museum, 1951).

"When I am not teaching classes, preparing for classes or attending meetings of university committees, I am usually trying to get on with a book or article which must be written," Eiseley once explained. The persistence and success with which he has plied the pen (he writes slowly and by hand) are evidenced by the ubiquity of his published articles on evolution theory and history and on more general aspects of nature. He has written technical analyses for professional journals such as *American Antiquity, American Anthropologist,* and the *American Journal of Physical Anthropology,* and is equally at ease when he writes for lay periodicals like *Harper's Magazine, Reader's Digest, Scientific American,* the New York *Times Magazine,* and the *Saturday Evening Post.*

With his article "An Evolutionist Looks at Modern Man," in 1958 Eiseley began an "Adventures of the Mind" series in the *Saturday Evening Post.* The series provided a forum for communication with the public to "authorities of unquestioned competence and attainment" in the sciences, fine and applied arts, medicine, and the humanities; it included articles by J. Robert Oppenheimer and Walter Gropius. The same year, Doubleday published Eiseley's book *Darwin's Century,* a serious detailed study of the rise and growth of the evolution theory, which won the newly established 1959 Phi Beta Kappa Science Prize of $1,000. In the following year he contributed the article, "The Ethic of the Group," to *Social Control in a Free Society* (University of Pennsylvania Press), edited by Robert E. Spiller; and he wrote The *Firmament of Time* (Longmans).

The Immense Journey, a collection of essays published by Random House in 1957, evoked wide praise from literary critics for the "eloquence and imagination" with which Eiseley told the story of living organisms since they first appeared on earth. Eiseley's eloquence and scholarship, his love for and acute observation of nature, and his urge to draw from the past a significance for himself and others—all come together in *The Immense Journey.* "I set down certain experiences," he wrote, "in the hope that they will come to the eye of those who have retained a true taste for the marvelous and who are capable of discerning in the flow of ordinary events the point at which the mundane world gives way to quite another dimension."

For Eiseley, man is only "one of the many appearances of the thing called life, not its perfect image, for life is multitudinous and emergent in the stream of time." Yet man is also unique: he has "escaped out of the eternal present of the animal world into a knowledge of past and future" and "for the first time in four billion years, a living creature contemplated himself." "The most enormous extension of vision of which life is capable," Eiseley wrote, "is the projection of itself into other lives. This is the lonely, magnificent power of humanity."

Eiseley is a Fellow of the American Anthropological Association (vice-president, 1948-49) and of the American Association for the Advancement of Science. He belongs to the Institute of Human Paleontology (president 1949-52), the Philadelphia Anthropological Society (vice-president 1947; president 1948), the American Association of Physical Anthropologists, and the Society for American Archaeology. His club is the Franklin Inn Club in Philadelphia, and he is a member of the Society of Magazine Writers in New York, the American Association of University Professors, and the scientific fraternity, Sigma Xi.

On August 29, 1938 Eiseley was married to Mabel Langdon, former curator of American art collections at the University of Nebraska. Eiseley has brown eyes and dark-brown hair; he stands five feet eleven inches tall and weighs 190 pounds. In religion, he is a Protestant, and he is an independent politically. Since childhood his hobby has been book collecting.

In his essay "The Enchanted Glass" (*American Scholar,* autumn, 1957), Eiseley spoke of the need for the contemplative naturalist, a man who in a less-frenzied century had time to observe, to speculate, and to dream. He is a vital part of our society, Eiseley wrote, for "when the human mind exists in the light of reason and no more than reason, we may say with absolute certainly that man and all that made him will be in that instant gone."

References

Sci Amer 194:26 F '56
Sci Mo 62:517 Je '46
American Men of Science, vol III (1956)
Leaders in American Science, 1955-56
Who Knows—and What (1954)
Who's Who in America, 1960-61

ELDER, ALBERT L(AWRENCE) June 19, 1901- Chemist

Address: b. c/o Corn Products Co., P.O. Box 345, Argo, Ill.; h. 612 S. Stone, La Grange, Ill.

A chemist who has made a contribution in the fields of education, government, and industry, Dr. Albert L. Elder won election as the American Chemical Society's president for 1960. His predecessor in this post is Dr. John C. Bailar, Jr. Since 1944 Dr. Elder has headed the research facilities of the Corn Products Company at the George M. Moffett Research Laboratories in Argo, Illinois. There he has supervised research and development projects involving medicinal chemicals, proteins, starches, oils, sanitary and colloid chemistry, biochemical oxygen demand, and catalysis.

One of four children in a family of three boys and a girl, Albert Lawrence Elder was born on June 19, 1901 in Lexington, Illinois to George Clinton Elder and the former Ann Jane Rowlands. His father was a farmer. The boy attended school in Lexington, graduating from the town high school in 1918.

At the University of Illinois in Urbana, he majored in chemistry, won election to the honor societies Sigma Xi, Phi Lambda Upsilon, and Alpha Chi Sigma, and joined the social fraternity Sigma Pi. He received the B.A. degree in 1923, the M.Sc. degree in 1925, and the Ph.D. degree in 1928. An abstract of his doctoral dissertation, *Studies on the Fate of Sulfur Compounds in the Degradation of Organic Matter,* was published in 1928. While still a graduate student he served as an assistant with the Illinois State Water Survey from 1924 to 1928.

After having completed his formal education, Elder was appointed Charles M. Hall research instructor at Oberlin College in Ohio and taught there from 1928 to 1930. He remained in the field of education for the next eleven years, first as assistant professor, then as research professor at Syracuse University in New York. During this period he wrote three chemistry textbooks: *Laboratory Manual of General Chemistry* (Edwards Brothers, 1933), *Demonstrations and Experiments in General Chemistry* (Harper, 1937), and *Textbook of Chemistry* (Harper, 1941).

Dedicating his scientific knowledge to the war effort, Dr. Elder went to Washington, D.C. in 1941 as head chemical adviser to the War Production Board. He also served the government by dealing with labor problems in the chemical industry; represented the Patent Office on the War Production Board; and, by co-ordinating the board's penicillin program, helped twenty American and Canadian plants to begin mass production of the new drug.

Dr. Elder also played a significant role in the government's synthetic-rubber program, which became vitally important after the Japanese had occupied the major rubber-producing areas in the Dutch East Indies. At a 1942 meeting of the American Chemical Society, Elder said: "The Japs have completely underestimated our technical ability if they thought that by taking natural rubber away from us

ALBERT L. ELDER

with its membership of about 88,000, is now the largest professional scientific association in the world. Its objectives are to advance chemistry in all its branches, promote research in pure and applied chemistry, improve the ethical and educational standards of chemists, and foster scientific interest and inquiry through meetings, discussions, and publications.

Besides serving as president of ACS, Elder is associate chairman of the organization's building fund. (The society plans to erect a new headquarters building in Washington, D.C.) Dr. Elder also belongs to the American Institute of Chemists, Institute of Food Technologists, Society of the Chemical Industry, Industrial Research Institute, Chemists' Club of New York, Chicago Chemists' Club, and La Grange (Illinois) Country Club. He serves as a member of the board of directors of the University of Illinois Alumni Association.

For "service, loyalty, and devotion to duty" with the Army's Quartermaster Food and Container Institute from 1944 to 1947, Dr. Elder was honored with an Award of Appreciation. For two years beginning in 1951 he was president of the Research and Development Associates of the Army's Quartermaster Food and Container Institute. He now serves on the advisory board of the National Research Council.

Gray-haired and blue-eyed, Dr. Albert L. Elder is six feet tall and weighs 195 pounds. He is a Republican and a Presbyterian. His favorite recreations are golf and bridge. Married to the former Ruth Ludden Dixon since August 31, 1925, Elder is the father of a daughter, Louise Ann (Mrs. Marshall Gillispie) and a son, John Dixon. Mrs. Elder, also a graduate of the University of Illinois, is on the national executive committee of the United Presbyterian Women and on the national board of directors of Camp Fire Girls, Inc.

References

Chem & Eng N 38:100 Ja 4 '60 por
American Men of Science (1960)
Chemical Who's Who, 1956
Who's Who in America, 1960-61

we were licked. We will bounce right back with synthetic rubber." He predicted that by 1943 this substitute would pour out of American industrial plants at the rate of 1,000,000 tons a year. "I am not pessimistic regarding the synthetic rubber problem," he added. "In fact, I am not a pessimist and I don't see how anyone fortunate enough to live in the greatest country on earth can be one."

Leaving government service in 1944, Dr. Elder became director of research of the Corn Products Refining Company (which became the Corn Products Company in 1958 when it merged with Best Foods, Inc.). The world's largest corn refiner, the concern makes many industrial and consumer products. Since World War II Dr. Elder has supervised a $50,000,000 research program largely aimed at expanding the company's activities into areas other than corn products. As a result, it now manufactures such items as inosital, a drug for relieving hardening of the arteries, and glucuronolactone, a medicine for treating arthritic ailments, in addition to its traditional starches, syrups, sugars, and other corn derivatives.

While he was a student at the University of Illinois, Elder joined the American Chemical Society in 1925. He has held many posts on local and national levels. He was chairman of the Syracuse section; councilor, alternate councilor, and chairman of the board of the Chicago section; councilor and chairman of the board of the ACS division on agricultural and food chemistry; and chairman of the ACS council committee on professional and economic status.

In December 1958 Dr. Elder was chosen president-elect of the American Chemical Society, and in December 1959 he became president, succeeding Dr. John C. Bailar, Jr. (see *C.B.*, July 1959). The president for 1961 will be Dr. Arthur C. Cope, chairman of the chemistry department at the Massachusetts Institute of Technology. Founded in 1876, the ACS,

ELLINGTON, (E.) BUFORD June 27, 1907- Governor of Tennessee
Address: b. State Capitol, Nashville, Tenn.; h. Curtiswood Lane, Nashville, Tenn.

As the forty-second Governor of Tennessee, Buford Ellington heads a state that is undergoing two major revolutions: industrialization and integration. Only recently, Tennessee was an agricultural state steeped in Southern traditions. Today, it is more industrial than agricultural and in some localities is seeking solutions to the integration of Negro and white students in public schools. Although Governor Ellington has supported the industrial development of his state, he has opposed integration.

For most of his life, Buford Ellington has been a farmer. He served for one term in the Tennessee legislature, was state agriculture commissioner, and became Governor for a four-year term in 1959, succeeding Frank G. Clement. As the leader of the state's delegation to the Democratic National Convention in 1960, Ellington, who has represented the conservative strain in Southern politics, exerted a considerable influence on the sixty-six representatives from Tennessee.

E. Buford Ellington was born in Holmes County, Mississippi on June 27, 1907 to Abner Earl and Cora (Grantham) Ellington. His father was a farmer, and he spent his boyhood on the family farm. He attended the Agricultural High School in Goodman and Millsaps College in Jackson, Mississippi. During the Depression, he had to leave college to look for work. For a time he sold farm equipment, and later he bought a small store at Verona, Tennessee. Then, like his father, he turned to farming in 1944 and bought the small farm in Marshall County, Tennessee that he still operates.

His political career began in 1948, when he was elected to the state General Assembly from Marshall County. During the one term that he served, he helped to establish a farm and health insurance program for farmers. As a result, he was asked to organize and supervise the sales force of the Tennessee Farm Bureau Insurance Service.

Impressed by Ellington's work with farmers, Governor Clement appointed Ellington state agriculture commissioner in 1953. He remained agriculture commissioner until 1958 when he resigned to seek the governorship. In his campaign, Ellington ran as "an old-fashioned segregationist and States' righter" (*United States News & World Report*, August 22, 1958). He promised to close any public school involved in a serious controversy over court-ordered integration and said that if necessary he would strengthen the laws of his state aimed at circumventing the 1954 Supreme Court ruling on integration. In the Democratic primaries on August 7, 1958, Ellington won over four other candidates, two of whom took moderate positions on public school integration. He was subsequently elected in a three-way contest in November.

After he assumed office in January 1959, one of Ellington's first steps was to enact a program of austerity. He opposed a legislative proposal to raise his salary from $12,000 to $18,600. As part of his program, the General Assembly passed the Reorganization Act of 1959. This measure reduced the number of officials reporting directly to the governor from more than seventy to eighteen. The act also authorized the governor to revamp by executive order several departments for greater efficiency and economy.

With the help of the state administration, the 1959 General Assembly withstood efforts by segregationists to enact extreme measures against integration. It refused to excuse children from integrated schools, to give them a tuition allowance to enter private schools, or to establish a powerful state rights commission against desegregation. In 1959 Nashville reached the end of its second year of "stairstep" desegregation, integrating one new grade

BUFORD ELLINGTON

in the schools each year. In April 1960 the *Southern School News* survey reported that of a total of 146,700 Negro students in Tennessee public schools, 169 were in mixed classes.

During the Negro sit-down strikes against segregated lunch-counter service in Nashville and other Southern cities in 1960, Ellington charged that a CBS-television news team was purposely instigating the strikes. "If anything can be done by legislative action to curb such outside interference and agitation," he said, "I'm going to do whatever is necessary" (*New York Herald Tribune*, March 27, 1960). Dr. Frank Stanton, president of CBS, called the charges "unsupported" and asked for a retraction and apology.

During his first year in office, Governor Ellington laid great stress on a balanced budget and on industrial development. Although the budget was the largest in the history of the state, it was balanced and did not require increased taxes. To attract new industries to Tennessee, Ellington visited New York, New Jersey, and Connecticut to confer with businessmen. He was finally able to announce that more than $240,000,000 were to be invested in new industrial plants or expansions of existing plants, spread over 103 cities and towns and providing about 17,000 new jobs for Tennesseans. During 1959 the state reached the lowest level of unemployment in many years.

Although Tennessee was long an agricultural region, it is now predominantly industrial, producing chemicals, food, textiles, virgin aluminum, shoes, and lumber. Industrial growth has been largely due to the Tennessee Valley Authority which operates twenty-nine dams to facilitate flood control, navigation, and electrical power along the Tennessee and Cumberland rivers.

As leader of the Democratic party in Tennessee, Governor Ellington was designated to head the state's sixty-six-member delegation to

ELLINGTON, BUFORD—*Continued*

the Democratic National Convention in July 1960. He has failed to support Estes Kefauver in his campaign for re-election to the Senate. On the other hand, he has refused to support a third party made up of Southern champions of state rights. Instead, he voiced his strong loyalty to the Democratic party, and in a speech to the state convention in April 1960, he said: "The keynote of this convention today is unity and harmony. . . . Our loyalty to the party is as strong today as it was in the days of Andrew Jackson." When he accepted the vice-chairmanship of the Citizens-for-Johnson National Committee in June 1960, Ellington indicated his choice of his close friend Senator Lyndon B. Johnson of Texas for the Democratic Presidential candidacy.

Ellington was married to Catherine Ann Cheek, a schoolteacher, on January 24, 1929. They have two children, John Earl, who is a heavy-equipment salesman, and Ann. The Governor is six feet two inches in height and has thinning black hair. He has served on the board of stewards of the Verona Methodist Church and Nashville's Glendale Methodist Church and has taught men's Bible classes. He is a Scottish Rite Mason. He enjoys watching football and baseball and likes to fish, hunt, and play golf.

References

U S News 45:49 Ag 22 '58 por
Who's Who in America, 1960-61

ELLIOTT, HERBERT (JAMES) Feb. 25, 1938- Australian athlete
Address: b. Australian Shell Chemical Company Ltd., Melbourne, Victoria, Australia

The world's record for the one-mile run is held by Herb Elliott, a long and lean Australian, who set the mark of 3:54.5 minutes on August 6, 1958 in a race at Santry Stadium in Dublin, Ireland. The race has become known as the "miracle mile," in tribute not only to Elliott but also to the four runners who finished behind him, since they too were clocked in under four minutes.

By June 6, 1960, Elliott had run the mile in less than four minutes thirteen times. The once insurmountable four-minute mark is placed in jeopardy whenever Elliott steps onto a running track. For the 1,500-meter event he set the world record of 3:36 minutes on August 28, 1958 at Göteborg, Sweden. At the 1960 Summer Olympics he took a gold medal when he broke his own score for the 1,500-meter race to finish in 3:35.6 minutes.

Only by winning a victory at the Olympics did Elliott surpass the success that he achieved in 1958, when he was only twenty years old. In that year he broke through the four-minute barrier for the mile ten times, including his record-shattering performance in Dublin, and was named the Male Athlete of the Year in the annual Associated Press year-end poll, the second foreign athlete to win the award in its history.

Herbert James Elliott was born on February 25, 1938 in Perth, a city in western Australia. His father, Herbert Charles Elliott, is a furniture dealer who operates two stores in Perth, and a cyclist from whom the runner probably inherited his stamina. Although Herb Elliott first showed signs of his athletic distinction while in high school, when he raced the mile in 4:22 minutes, it was not until he came under the tutelage of the track coach Percy Cerutty that he began to develop his full potential. Cerutty had Elliott develop his chest muscles by lifting weights and his leg muscles by running along sandy beaches and up and down sandhills eighty feet in height. He placed his protégé under a Spartan-like diet, emphasizing such fare as oats, nuts, dried fruits, and diced bananas.

Something of a legend in track and field circles, Cerutty has trained several other Australian champions, including John Landy, whose mile mark of 3:58 minutes was broken by Elliott. His athletes are trained at a camp in Portsea, sixty miles from Melbourne, where they undergo a regimen of sand and sunshine in the daytime and poetry and philosophy and Bach and Beethoven in the evening. Instead of jogging along training tracks, they run up and down steep dunes until they give in to exhaustion. "We try to produce more than runners at the camp," Cerutty says. "We try to produce men—men who can appreciate beauty in music, literature, art, and nature."

Certainly Cerutty has molded Elliott into the finest miler the world has known. On March 9, 1957, less than two weeks after his nineteenth birthday, Elliott ran the mile in 4:00.4 minutes at Olympic Park in Melbourne. On January 25, 1958 he broke the mythical four-minute barrier when he covered the mile distance in 3:59.9 minutes. He thus became the eighteenth man in the history of track and field to run the mile in less than four minutes. Roger Bannister was the first, with a 3:59.4 clocking at Oxford, England, May 6, 1954. John Landy ran it in less than four minutes six times before he retired.

In May 1958 Elliott came to the United States and ran the mile in 3:57.8 minutes at the Los Angeles Coliseum. The mark was submitted to track officials for consideration as a new world record. But Elliott's achievement at Dublin made his previous performances seem academic. As 20,000 spectators watched in the new Santry Stadium, Elliott toed the starting line with two other Australians, Merv Lincoln and Albert Thomas, Ireland's Ron Delany, and Murray Halberg of New Zealand. With Thomas setting the pace for the first two laps, Lincoln took the lead on the third lap with Elliott a close second and Delany in challenging position. At the start of the final quarter-mile Elliott pulled away steadily from his competition and finished first in 3:54.5 minutes. Lincoln was second with 3:55.9 minutes, Delany was third with 3:57.5 minutes, Halberg was fourth with 3:57.5 minutes, and Thomas was fifth with 3:58.6 minutes. Elliott said later: "On the first half-mile I felt I was running

Australian News & Inf.
Bureau

HERBERT ELLIOTT

faster than I have ever run in my life. The race was run at a terrific pace. It was definitely my night."

A month later, the American sports promoter Leo Leavitt offered Elliott $238,000 to become the star attraction in a troupe of professional athletes. Because, as an amateur, Elliott had been paying his expenses out of his own pocket, he was sorely tempted by the offer. After five weeks of mulling it over, however, he rejected it in favor of a proposal made by his employer, the Australian Shell Chemical Company Ltd. that he attend college while working on its payroll. In March 1959 Elliott commented: "I am satisfied that my future is secure."

Elliott confined himself to only a few races in 1959, since he preferred to take an extended leave from training for the better part of the year. He did, however, manage to run a mile in 3:58.9 minutes at Brisbane, Australia on March 14, and he apologized for not producing a faster clocking. It was his only mile under four minutes in the entire year. On March 23 he ran the final leg of an all-Australian four-mile relay which established an international record of 16:25.6 minutes.

Early in 1960 Elliott embarked on a routine of training that was intended to bring him to his competitive peak for the Olympic Games in Rome. With four companions and his beloved Alsatian dog Sandy, he took to the Australian Alps near Mansfield, Victoria, over 100 miles from Melbourne. "I get bloody sick of training," Elliott confided to a reporter from *Sports Illustrated* (January 18, 1960). "I don't think a trip like this should be a pleasure." Following a route originally laid out by John Landy, Elliott and his companions waded through water up to their knees, ascended 60-degree slopes, and descended the face of bluffs.

By the time the excursion ended, they had hiked fifty hard miles.

On February 6, 1960 Elliott ran his twelfth race in less than four minutes. Competing on grass at Melbourne, he returned a clocking of 3:59.8 minutes. "I am really happy now," he said. Two weeks later he ran the mile in four minutes even, again at Melbourne. Ahead of him lay the grind of building himself up for the Summer Olympics. Elliott has said that 3:45 minutes is the probable ultimate in human speed for the mile run. "No man must set a limit on his capabilities. Nobody must be limited by what's around him."

Herb Elliott was married to Anne Dudley, a former hairdresser of Perth, on May 2, 1959. They have one child, a son. Elliott attended Melbourne University while he worked for Australian Shell Chemical Company Ltd., studying commercial courses. He planned to enter Cambridge University in October 1960. He stands under six feet in height and weighs between 148 and 154 pounds. An expert in the art of taking it easy, Elliott sleeps like a contented child before an important race and enjoys himself afterwards. Then he sleeps again. The superbly conditioned runner is so modest and so given to understatement that when he was asked how he felt about his record-breaking Dublin race on August 6 he replied: "I thought it was a rather good time." He runs, he says, not to set world records or to make money or to achieve fame, but to win. John Landy, the brilliant Australian miler, whose performance impelled Elliott to begin a career that will surpass his own once said of Elliott: "Herb is the greatest natural runner I've ever seen."

References

Sports Illus 12:30+ Ja 18 '60 por
Time 72:58 S 15 '58
Toronto Globe and Mail Globe Mag p12 Ap 11 '59 por

ESHELMAN, W(ALTER) W(ITMER)

Aug. 7, 1908- Educator; organization official
Address: b. Upper Dublin Township Schools, Fort Washington, Pa.; h. 15 N. Bethlehem Pike, Ambler, Pa.

The three basic R's of education—reading, writing, and arithmetic—remain as important as they ever were to the classroom, but they are not enough, in the opinion of Dr. W. W. Eshelman, the 1959-60 president of the National Education Association; he believes that responsibility, respect, and reverence should be added to the original three. For thirty years, in teaching, administration, and organizational work, he has been close to the problems of his profession, and he thinks that the most crucial need in education is improvement in quality. He succeeded Ruth A. Stout as president of the world's largest educational organization in July 1959. Since 1945 he has been supervising principal of Upper Dublin Township Schools in Pennsylvania.

A farmer's son, Walter Witmer Eshelman, was born near Elizabethtown, Pennsylvania on August 7, 1908 to John W. and Amanda F.

W. W. ESHELMAN

(Witmer) Eshelman. He was raised in Elizabethtown with several other children in the family. In 1926 he graduated from the local high school and entered Elizabethtown College to major in social studies. Before receiving his B.A. degree in 1930, he became class president, president of the Y.M.C.A. student organization, and a member of the debating team.

Education is the favored professional field of several members of Eshelman's family, including a brother who is a supervisory principal. At one time Walter Eshelman inclined toward a career in law. While still in college, he enrolled in a correspondence course offered by the Blackstone Institute of Chicago, Illinois, which awarded him the LL.B. degree in 1931. He has said, however, that he has never regretted having continued in teaching through the years instead of becoming a lawyer.

Eshelman's first appointment in education was as teacher-principal in Shohola, Pennsylvania, where from 1930 to 1936 his duties included teaching ninth and tenth grades as well as administrative work. By taking weekend and summer courses in social science and political science, he earned his M.A. degree at Columbia University in 1933. He moved to Stowe, Pennsylvania in 1936 as supervising principal of the West Pottsgrove schools.

Continuing his graduate work, this time in school administration, Eshelman was granted the Ed.D. degree in 1941 by New York University. In 1945 he accepted his present position of supervising principal of Upper Dublin schools in Fort Washington, near Philadelphia. His school system includes a high school with about 800 pupils and five grade schools which have some 1,400 pupils.

For Eshelman, service in educational organizations is an important way of strengthening the teaching profession throughout the country. He has been president of both the local and district branches of the Pennsylvania State Education Association and chairman of the resolutions committee of the National Education Association. The NEA, which has more than 665,000 members, represents over 47 per cent of the country's 1,396,000 teachers and education staff members. The association is dedicated to improving American education at all levels and in all states and to raising the standing of the teaching profession. Overall policy for the association is made by an elected representative assembly of about 600 delegates from state, territorial, and affiliated teacher organizations.

At the 101st convention of the NEA in 1958, Ruth A. Stout was elected the ninety-seventh president. The delegates, meeting in Cleveland, Ohio, selected Dr. Eshelman as vice-president. On July 3, 1959 at the next convention, in St. Louis, Missouri, Eshelman was elected president; Clarice Kline of Waukesha, Wisconsin was named president-elect. During his year as president, Eshelman traveled to various parts of the United States, visiting schools and local educational groups; he also spent some time at NEA headquarters at 1201 16th Street, N.W., Washington, D.C.

Some 5,000 delegates at the 1959 convention overwhelmingly reaffirmed the organization's previous stand on public school integration. They adopted a resolution calling upon all citizens to approach integration "with the spirit of fair play, good will and respect for law." The resolution also stated that "all problems of integration in our schools are capable of solutions at the state and local levels by citizens of intelligence, saneness and reasonableness working together in the interests of national unity for the common good of all." The debate on the resolution and on proposals for a stronger stand on integration severely tested the unity of the NEA, since in many Southern states the white and Negro members of affiliating associations belong to separate organizations.

As the 1960 session of Congress began, the NEA called for legislative action to provide substantial and continuing federal aid to education. The organization urged support for a bill that would provide $1.1 billion a year for four years to be used for classroom construction and teachers' pay increases. The funds would be used to alleviate a nationwide shortage of a large number of teachers and classrooms. State and local taxes, traditionally the mainstays of school support, no longer can provide the funds needed to insure quality education, according to an association study. Congress, however, failed in 1960 to enact legislation providing aid for school construction or for raising teachers' salaries.

Dr. Eshelman recently declared that the public school system is the strongest bulwark of democracy in America. "The miracle of modern times—and it was made possible by the public schools," he said, "is the assimilation here of people of different nationalities, cultures, and backgrounds, and their development into citizens who can think, and are willing to think." Instilling in pupils the ability and will to think independently is one of four major responsibilities that Eshelman believes a teacher has. Other responsibilities are "to create a democratic and challenging atmosphere in the classroom, to help develop children into dynamic participating citizens, to give students a broad cultural background."

In 1957 Eshelman worked on the commission that prepared *The Superintendent as Instructional Leader,* the yearbook of the American Association of School Administrators. Elizabethtown College awarded him an honorary Pd.D. degree in 1959. He is a Mason, a member of Phi Delta Kappa, and a member of the board of directors of the Kiwanis Club. He participates in Sunday school administrative work in a Protestant church. In politics he votes for Republicans.

W. W. Eshelman was married to Mary M. Minnich, a teacher, on December 26, 1931. Their ten-year-old daughter, Donna Faye, calls her father a "Doctor of Schools." The family lives in a large stone house of colonial design a few miles from the Philadelphia city limits. Eshelman has brown hair and brown eyes, is five feet ten inches tall, and weighs 180 pounds. He devotes much of his spare time to work in his house, having remodeled the kitchen a year or so ago, and in his garden.

References

Mich Educ J 37:5 S 1 '59 por
N Y Times p16 Jl 4 '59 por

EVERGOOD, PHILIP (HOWARD FRANCIS DIXON) Oct. 26, 1901- Artist

Address: A.C.A. Gallery, 63 E. 57th St., New York 22; h. Oxford, R.F.D. 2, Southbury, Conn.

NOTE: This biography supersedes the article which appeared in *Current Biography* in 1944.

Emerging in his sixtieth year as one of America's most imaginative "social" and "figurative" painters, Philip Evergood was honored by the Whitney Museum of American Art in April 1960 with a retrospective exhibition of paintings and drawings covering a span of forty years. Six other museums in various parts of the United States later showed the exhibition.

During the economic depression of the 1930's Evergood proved himself an incisive satirist and painter of social themes. Widening his scope in the 1940's, he demonstrated through successive exhibitions at the A.C.A. Gallery in New York City his "fertile gift of imagery, often fantastic, which springs from passionate convictions and emotions, and a strain of wild humor and an innate sense of irony." He is represented in the permanent collections of the Metropolitan Museum of Art, Museum of Modern Art, Whitney Museum of American Art, in New York; the Boston Museum of the Fine Arts; Carnegie Institute, Pittsburgh; and in many private collections.

Philip Howard Francis Dixon Evergood was born on October 26, 1901 in the studio of his father, Meyer Evergood Blashki, in New York City. His mother, Flora Jane Perry, came from a wealthy Gentile British family. His grandfather, Meyer Blashki, was a prosperous jeweler who had wandered from Poland to England and then to Australia. His father, who early broke away from his orthodox Jewish background, was an artist who painted in the South Seas and for a time did illustrations for San Francisco newspapers. Evergood has said of his father: "He was proud of his race, but he was never interested in religion."

As a child, Philip showed precocious musical ability and in 1908 appeared in a small auditorium in Carnegie Hall in a piano recital with his teacher, Madame Rabagliatti. His formal education had begun in 1907 at the Ethical Culture School in New York City, but when he was eight his mother took him to England to be educated. In 1914, after attending a succession of boarding schools, he was graduated from Stubbington House, which prepared boys for the Royal Naval Training College at Osborne.

An appendectomy and an attack of peritonitis prevented him, however, from becoming a naval officer. Moreover, the name of Blashki did not favorably impress the committee of Admirals. Philip's father wrote to Winston Churchill, then First Lord of the Admiralty, asking: "Is it because my son's name is Blashki that this doubt takes place in the minds of the Admirals?" Churchill advised him to change his name to Evergood. Philip's father had it legally changed, and from then on father and son were Miles and Philip Evergood. Admitted to Eton in 1915, Philip was blessed with "an understanding tutor with an uncommon veneration for the arts." He was encouraged to express his thoughts in biblical, allegorical, and historical drawings in crayon.

After graduation in 1919 he studied French, Latin, and mathematics in Belgium with a Catholic priest, l'Abbé de Moore. In his spare time he visited art museums. Entering Trinity Hall College at Cambridge University in 1919 and embarking upon a tripos in English, he had vague thoughts of taking up law or civil engineering. In the fall of 1921, after frequent trips to the Fitzwilliam Museum, he decided to become an artist. He was supported in his decision by Henry Bond, the head of Trinity Hall. His family permitted him to leave Cambridge and to study at the Slade School in London, with Henry Tonks, the principal, and with Havard Thomas, the sculptor.

After two years of rigorous training in drawing and sculpture, Evergood returned to the United States, convinced that America rather than England was his native country. He studied with George Luks, who tried to persuade him to concentrate on painting rather than drawing, and with William von Schlegell at the Art Students' League. In 1924 he went to Paris and, enrolling at the Académie Julian, started to paint seriously. He next studied briefly with André Lhote, but soon found that he could work better independently. He became acquainted with artists Maurice Utrillo, Jules Pascin, Tsugouharu Foujita, and Man Ray, and with the dramatist Eugene O'Neill.

His work was first exhibited in London and in Paris in 1925 and two years later in a one-

Deana Harris Hoffman
St. Paul, Minn.

PHILIP EVERGOOD

man show at the Dudensing Gallery in New York. The latter show received generally favorable reviews from the art critics. Succeeding exhibitions at the Montross Gallery in New York in 1929, 1933, and 1935 revealed his preoccupation with Biblical subjects. He emerged as a painter of the world about him in the Museum of Modern Art's "Murals by American Painters" in which Evergood exhibited three murals. Critics noted a brave new surge of color, and his increasing interest in realistic subject matter and in autobiographical painting. In 1935 he won the Kohnstamm Prize at the Art Institute of Chicago with his painting, *Evening Reading*. The painting depicted a Bohemian interior with a young man and his wife reading Tolstoi and radical leaflets. Under the influence of the Depression and his close association with John Sloan, his work soon widened to take in all of the city's pullulating humanity.

After a six-month stay in Spain, where he studied the work of El Greco, Goya, and Velasquez, he married Julia Cross, an artist and dancer, in New York in 1931. They both worked in the American Gallery of Indian Art, owned by his mother-in-law, Amelia White, Julia as a bookkeeper, Philip as a part-time handyman who carpentered shelves and mounted displays.

In 1934 he exhibited in the Whitney Museum's second biennial show and in all its subsequent annual exhibitions. He also worked for the Public Works of Art Project and for its successor, the Federal Art Project of the Work Projects Administration (WPA) from 1934 to 1937. During these years he became a militant propagandist in his painting and, impelled by his idealism and his sensitized social conscience, became deeply enmeshed in liberal and even radical causes. Among these were the rights of Negroes, the cause of the Spanish loyalists, and the promotion of Russian War Relief. He

joined the Artists Committee of Action, became a president of the Artists' Union which succeeded it and took an active part in the American Artists' Congress. He participated in the "219 sit-in strike" in 1936 to protest the layoffs of 219 artists by the Federal Art Project.

Recognition for his mural painting slowly came to Evergood during the 1930's. Some of his murals, like *The Story of Richmond Hill*, which was executed in 1937 for the Richmond Hill branch of the Queens Public Library in Long Island, stirred up controversy. Although the painting was defended by artists and critics, Evergood had to make alterations and omit "vulgar corporal references" before it was accepted.

When the National Gallery in Melbourne, Australia showed his painting, *Art on the Beach*, in 1937, a storm of resentment greeted it. Admirers like Sir John Longstaff, the noted Australian artist, however, raised funds to purchase it for the gallery. Other Evergood murals include *Cotton From Field to Mill* for the United States Post Office at Jackson, Georgia, and *The Bridge of Life* (on a Carnegie Foundation grant) at Kalamazoo College, Kalamazoo, Michigan, where Evergood was an artist in residence from 1940 to 1942.

Influenced by his friendship for artist John Sloan, Evergood continued to paint in the same genre: warm and humorous scenes of New York's teeming life, such as *Dance Marathon, Treadmill, Street Corner, Nude by the El,* and *The Siding*. Critics referred to Breughel and Daumier more and more in reviewing Evergood's work. He also acknowledges his debt to El Greco, Goya, Bosch, cave painting, child art, and early Charlie Chaplin movies. "Perhaps its most striking characteristic," wrote John I. H. Baur, "was the deliberate awkwardness of the drawing, sometimes veering toward satire. . ."

Among Evergood's easel paintings of this period were the notable *My Forebears Were Pioneers*, hung at the New York World's Fair (1939) and now in the Whitney Museum of American Art collection; *An American Tragedy,* a much disputed painting of steel strikers clashing with the police; and *Lily and the Sparrows* (shown at the Whitney Annual of 1940). In 1954 Evergood surpassed himself with his delightful painting, *American Shrimp Girl,* which one critic called a New World extension of Hogarth's eighteenth-century *Shrimp Girl.* The doll-like face personifies summertime on American shores.

Commenting on the retrospective exhibition of his work at the Whitney Museum, in April 1960, Robert M. Coates wrote in the *New Yorker* (April 16, 1960): "Such emotional ebullience, coupled with a readiness to tackle anything, has its penalties, and especially in the field of fantasy, Evergood fails about as often as he succeeds . . . he still has an oddly innocent earnestness, an unabashed willingness to go all out in the effort to convey his ideas that give his best work considerable impact and power." Emily Genauer observed in the New York *Herald Tribune* (April 6, 1960): "His pictures remain exuberant, astonishingly alive." On the other hand, John Canaday (New York *Times,*

May 1, 1960) expressed his opinion that he did not understand Evergood, "despite special effort."

Philip Evergood and Julia Vincent Cross (a ballet dancer with the Monte Carlo Ballet Russe and other groups) were married on August 15, 1931. Evergood, who somewhat resembles the British actor Charles Laughton in appearance, has a booming voice and a gentle manner. He is a successful lecturer and often writes for art periodicals.

Awards given to Evergood include the Carol H. Beck Gold Medal, Pennsylvania Academy (1949) ; Carnegie Institute of Art (1949-Second Prize) ; W. A. Clark Silver Medal ; Corcoran Gallery of Art (1951) ; First Prize, Baltimore Museum (1955) ; and a grant from the National Institute of Arts and Letters (1956). He won the $2,000 second prize in 1944 in the Pepsi-Cola Artists for Victory contest. In 1952 he won a first prize of $5,000 from the Terry Art Institute in Miami for the painting of his wife entitled *Happy Entrance*.

He has been represented in the United States group shows at the Venice, London, Brussels, and Paris international art exhibitions. He is a member of Artists' Equity Association and Kappa Pi (honorary) fraternity. He has illustrated a book of short stories by Gogol (1951).

References

Art N 50:30+ Ja '52 pors
Baur, John I. H. New Art in America (1957)
Baur, John I. H. Philip Evergood (1960)
Eliot, Alexander Three Hundred Years of American Painting (1957)

Twenty Years of Evergood-ACA Gallery (1946)
Who's Who in America, 1960-61
Who's Who in American Art (1959)

FASCELL, DANTE B(RUNO) (fä-sĕl') Mar. 9, 1917- United States Representative from Florida; lawyer

Address: b. House Office Bldg., Washington 25, D.C.; 157 Miracle Mile, Coral Gables, Fla.; h. 6300 S.W. 99th Terrace, Miami, Fla.; 900 Banks Place, Alexandria, Va.

Representing the largest Congressional District in the nation—the Fourth District of Florida, which covers Dade and Monroe counties—Dante B. Fascell serves more than 1,200,000 constituents in the United States House of Representatives. Fascell, a Miami lawyer and former state legislator, was elected to Congress on the Democratic ticket in November 1954, to the seat vacated by William C. Lantaff, and was re-elected in 1956 and 1958. As a member of the House Government Operations Committee he has promoted legislation to curb waste and inflation, and on the Foreign Affairs Committee he has been especially concerned with relations with Latin America.

Dante Bruno Fascell was born in Bridgehampton, Long Island, New York, on March 9, 1917 to Charles Angelo and Mary (Gullotti)

DANTE B. FASCELL

Fascell. He has a sister, Vera, and a brother, Rudy. His father was a dairyman. The family moved to Miami, Florida in 1925, in time to experience the "bust" of Florida real estate in 1926. Fascell attended Ponce de Leon High School in Coral Gables, where he was a member of the band and orchestra; he also belonged to the Greater Miami Drum and Bugle Corps.

A music scholarship enabled Fascell to study at the University of Miami after his high school graduation in 1933. He played in the university's symphonic band and orchestra and also found time for intramural wrestling and handball. His high scholastic record qualified him for membership in the Iron Arrow Society, an honorary fraternity. Deciding to follow a legal career, he enrolled in the university's law school and earned his LL.B. degree in 1938. In that same year he was admitted to the Florida bar and began the practice of law.

When the United States entered World War II, Fascell was a private in the Florida National Guard, which he had joined in January 1941. Commissioned a second lieutenant in the Army in May 1942, he fought in the African, Sicilian, and Italian campaigns. In January 1946 he received his honorable discharge with the rank of captain.

Becoming a member of the law firm of Turner, Hendrick & Fascell in 1946, he resumed his legal work and in 1947 was legal attaché at the state legislative delegation representing Dade County. He continued in this capacity until 1950 when he was elected a member of the Florida state Legislature for a two-year term. During his first year in the Legislature the state press named him one of the ten outstanding legislators, and he received this honor again in 1953. He was re-elected without opposition in 1952 and served until 1954 when he ran for election to the United States Congress

FASCELL, DANTE B.—*Continued*

as a Representative from the Fourth District of Florida. His slogan was "Ring the bell for Dante Fascell."

During the Eighty-fourth Congress, which opened in January 1955, Fascell worked on the Government Operations and Post Office and Civil Service committees. One of his earliest bills to pass the House proposed the repeal of the 10 per cent tax on travel to the Caribbean area and Canada. As a freshman Congressman, Representative Fascell was the first to preside over the House in the Eighty-fourth Congress. When a bill authorizing the Foreign Affairs Committee to investigate foreign policy came before the House, Speaker Sam Rayburn stepped down and asked the young legislator to preside. The bill was passed by voice vote.

In a House speech in April 1956 Fascell successfully urged an extension of the GI home loan program. He pointed out that more than 11,000,000 World War II veterans had not used their home loan rights because they had not reached the stage of financial stability which would permit them to purchase a home. He recommended that the termination of loans be gradual. In 1957 he won another extension of the program.

Although Fascell has supported federal aid for schools "given the need," he has opposed "any more than the bare necessities of a federal control over schools" (Miami *News*, February 23, 1956). He believes that such aid should be offered on a matching-money basis and that it should not involve any interference with the state government. In July 1956 he voted against the Adam Clayton Powell amendment to the school construction bill which would have withheld federal funds from states not complying with the decision of the United States Supreme Court regarding segregation.

On the matter of civil rights, Fascell was the only Florida Congressman who refused to sign the so-called Southern Segregation Manifesto in 1956. He pointed out that he disagreed with the Supreme Court ruling in the Brown segregation case because he believes that the school system is one for state and local control. "But once the Supreme Court establishes law," he declared, "it is my duty as an American citizen and public official, sworn to uphold the laws, to abide by the law."

Fascell's voting record in the Eighty-fourth Congress includes support for extension of Social Security (July 1955), the $2.5 billion foreign aid grant (July 1955), and the $3.6 billion appropriation for mutual security (June 1956). He opposed Eisenhower's highway program (July 1955) and the farm bills providing for high price supports and the soil bank program (April and May 1956).

Winning assignment in 1956 to the House Foreign Affairs Committee, Fascell gave up his membership on the Post Office and Civil Service Committee, and after his re-election to Congress he remained on both the Foreign Affairs and Government Operations committees. On his record in the Eighty-fifth Congress he scored high in bipartisan support. He approved the President's Mideast Doctrine (January 1957), postponement of interest payments on

the British loan (April 1957), the Alaska statehood bill (May 1958), increases in postal rates and salaries of postal workers (May 1958), and extension of reciprocal trade agreements (June 1958).

An interest in conservation had prompted Fascell in 1956 to co-sponsor a bill which reorganized the Fish and Wildlife Service of the Department of Interior. In April 1957 he introduced a measure to fix boundary lines of the Everglades National Park, and he has also won Congressional authorization to establish a refuge for the Florida Key deer.

Another proposal that he submitted, in February 1959, was an amendment to the National Housing Act to meet the needs of persons of sixty years and over by providing for lenient FHA terms in insuring mortgages for low-cost housing and medical centers to accommodate all age groups, in areas where at least half of the homes are owned by elderly people. In August 1959 he co-sponsored a bill that by controlling imports of shrimp would relieve the United States shrimp industry's suffering from the competition of foreign imports.

Diligent in exposing waste in government operations and spending, Fascell cited many examples of extravagance in the United States foreign aid program after his return from a tour of the Far East in the fall of 1959. As he had done in earlier years, however, he voted for mutual security funds in June 1959. In regard to other 1959 measures, he favored United States participation in the Inter-American Development Bank (July) and also voted "yea" on the controversial Landrum-Griffin labor bill (August); he opposed an amendment extending the life of the Civil Rights Commission (September).

Among the several key subcommittees on which Fascell serves is the inter-American affairs subcommittee of the House Foreign Affairs Committee. He has expressed concern over the government's relations with Panama and Cuba, "problems not subject to solution overnight." Speaking in the House on January 13, 1960 Fascell urged patience in dealing with Cuba and suggested that the United States "hold back funds paid for our sugar purchases. . . . These moneys could be held in trust for the reimbursement of all American properties taken in Cuba at a fair value to be fixed by impartial appraisers."

Dante B. Fascell and Jeanne-Marie Pelot were married on September 19, 1941. They have two daughters, Sandra Jeanne and Toni, and one son, Dante Jon. "I like living in Florida," Fascell has said. "It is the best place for my family. They practically live outdoors and we all enjoy the state's wonders and pleasures." His hobbies are fishing and photography. He belongs to the Coral Gables Country Club and the Annapolis (Maryland) Yacht Club.

Fascell's favorite foods are Italian. He is five feet five and a half inches tall, weighs 164 pounds, and has brown eyes and black hair. His religion is Protestant. He has many awards and decorations, one of which, Ordine della Stella della Solidarietà Italiana, he received from the Italian government in 1953 for fostering friendship between the United States and Italy. He has been cited by President José Maria Lemus of El Salvador for his work in bringing about better relations between Latin America and the United States.

References

Congressional Directory (1959)
Who's Who in America, 1958-59

FELLOWS, HAROLD E(VERETT) Mar. 22, 1899-Mar. 8, 1960 Broadcasting executive in New England (1932-51); president of the National Association of Radio and Television Broadcasters (1951-54) and chairman (from 1954). See *Current Biography* (February) 1952.

Obituary

N Y Times p33 Mr 9 '60

FERBER, HERBERT Apr. 30, 1906-
Sculptor
Address: 454 Riverside Dr., New York 27

Referred to by art critic S. Lane Faison, Jr., as "one of our most distinguished living sculptors," Herbert Ferber is a leading exponent of abstract expressionist art in the United States. His sculpure, which has been shown in art galleries and museums throughout the world since his first one-man show in 1937, has brought him international recognition. In 1953 he was a prize winner at the International Sculpture Competition held at the Institute of Contemporary Art in London; his 1952 construction, *And the Bush Was Not Consumed,* which decorates the façade of a New Jersey synagogue, is regarded as one of the finest pieces of architectural sculpture in the United States.

Herbert Ferber was born to Louis and Hattie (Lebowitz) Silvers on April 30, 1906 in New York City. His father, a compositor in the printing trade, later taught printing in a boys' trade school in New York's Lower East Side. Ferber attended Morris High School in New York, and after his graduation in 1923, continued his education at the City College of the City of New York. He later studied dentistry and oral surgery at Columbia University, where he received a B.S. degree in 1929. Enrolling as a student at the Beaux Arts Institute of Design in 1927, he decided upon a career as a "free and unattached sculptor."

During the 1930's Ferber exhibited his work at various galleries in the United States and in Paris, including the National Academy of Design in 1930, while he was in his final year at the Beaux Arts Institute; the Corcoran Gallery of Art in Washington, where his paintings were shown in 1933; and the Musée du Jeu de Paume, Paris, in 1938. He held his first one-man sculpture show in 1937, at New York's Midtown Gallery. He executed his early sculpture in wood, and according to S. Lane Faison,

HERBERT FERBER

Jr., it already showed "the wiry contours and expressive movement of his art today." His early works were also exhibited at the Golden Gate International Exposition in San Francisco in 1939, and at the New York World's Fair in 1940. In 1943 he won the Purchase Prize at the "Artists for Victory" show at the Metropolitan Museum of Art in New York.

Before the 1940's ended, Ferber discovered that he had "pushed wood-sculpture to the farthest limit it could go in the direction of the kind of freedom he sought," according to E. C. Goossen. Under the influence of Gonzales and his own contemporaries, Ferber began to work in metal, and he has ever since executed his major sculptural works in soldered metal. His *Apocalyptic Rider* and *Hazardous Encounter* were singled out for special praise when they were exhibited at the Betty Parsons Gallery in New York in 1947. Other works of Ferber that have received much acclaim are *The Flame* (lead and brass, 1949), *Sun Wheel* (brass, 1956), and *Heraldic* (brass, 1957).

Not until 1952 did Ferber's work begin to receive wide public recognition. At that time, his *And the Bush Was Not Consumed,* a metal construction commissioned for the façade of the B'nai Israel Synagogue in Millburn, New Jersey, was exhibited by the Museum of Modern Art in its "Fifteen Americans" show. Andrew Ritchie has called the work "one of the most successful applications of the abstract expressionists' manipulation of space for the presentation of a specific religious symbol." S. Lane Faison, Jr., has said of the work: "I could recall no more monumental and yet poignant work of recent sculpture."

In addition to the burning bush sculpture on the Millburn synagogue, several other Ferber pieces adorn Jewish houses of worship in the United States. In 1955 he completed a candelabrum and altar decoration for the chapel of

FERBER, HERBERT—*Continued*

Brandeis University in Waltham, Massachusetts. He has also done façade sculpture for Temple Anshe Chesed in Cleveland (1956) and Temple Aaron in St. Paul, Minnesota (1957).

Ferber's work was selected to be shown at the American National Exhibition in Moscow, in 1959. His sculpture has also been exhibited in Cassel, Germany, and at the Musée Rodin in Paris. Collections of his work may be found in such institutions as the Metropolitan Museum of Art, the Museum of Modern Art, and the Whitney Museum of American Art in New York, Williams College Art Gallery in Massachusetts, Grand Rapids Art Gallery in Michigan, and the Detroit Institute of Arts.

Although he has referred to himself as a "baroque sculptor," Ferber is usually considered an abstract expressionist by art historians and critics. Faison has pointed out that, while Ferber's sculpture "frequently has the interlaced movement of the baroque," it nevertheless does not "comprise a movement of masses in space, as the baroque has been aptly defined, but a movement of axes across space. His forms do not displace space, rather, they are penetrated by it." His work is "elegant and taut; it sheds all semblance of density and abundance; it defies the laws of gravity."

Ferber practises what is known as "space sculpture," and has been called by E. C. Goossen "one of the best who, within this modal ambience, has been able to prove its worth and richness." According to Carlyle Burrows, his "vigorously twisted, fluently curving and sometimes harshly spiked pieces" often suggest "still-life structures, or figures in seeming flight, or objects swept along as by the wind in tumbleweed fashion."

In the articles that he has contributed to art journals, including *Tiger's Eye, Art Students' League Quarterly,* and *Art in America,* Ferber expounds his theory of the use of space in modern sculpture. "The new sculpture," he wrote in *Art in America* (December 1954), "might be tested by its ability to withstand a hurricane because it offers so little surface. . . . Space is not displaced, the mark of traditional sculpture; rather it is pierced and held in tension." Traditionally sculpture had been solid and closed. It is now an art of forms that, suspended in space, are open, airy, and discontinuous.

In a lecture entitled, "Sculpture as Environment," delivered in May 1960 at Princeton University, Ferber discussed another development of the break with tradition in contemporary sculpture. It is the concept of "a sculpture and a space each of which would be meaningless if one were to be removed," as opposed to the traditional view in which "the space has a character and an existence apart from the existence of the sculpture." In terms of this new theory, according to Ferber, "the environment . . . is defined by the forms and the space in which the spectator finds himself." As a result of this advance in modern art theory, "the wedding of architecture and art . . . can become a reality."

Herbert Ferber lives with his wife, Ilse Falk, an art historian whom he married on September 19, 1944, in a studio penthouse at 454 Riverside Drive, New York City. (A previous marriage to Sonia Stirt in 1932 ended in divorce eleven years later.) Their apartment is decorated with paintings by such American abstract expressionists as Pollock, De Kooning, Rothko, Tomlin, Gottlieb, and Motherwell. His own sculpture adorns the terrace. During his trips to Europe in 1938 and 1948, Ferber studied Romanesque, Gothic, and Baroque art. He has also traveled in Mexico. His interest in pre-Columbian art and African and South Sea sculpture is reflected by his fine collection of primitive African and Tarascan sculpture.

Ferber works in his New York studio most of the year and at his farm in northern Vermont during the summer, where he likes to go bird watching and mushroom picking. E. C. Goossen has hailed him for "the extraordinary range" of his "imagination and ability" and has called him a sculptor whose work "is one of the real additions to the art of our time."

Reference

Goossen, E. C. Three American Sculptors (1959)

FISCHER, JOHN H(ENRY) July 16, 1910- Educator

Address: b. Teachers College, Columbia University, 525 W. 120th St., New York 27; h. 106 Morningside Dr., New York 27

Since taking office as dean of Teachers College of Columbia University in September 1959, John H. Fischer has administered the instructional and research program of a teacher-training center that has influenced educational ideas and practices throughout the United States and in other parts of the world. At the time of his appointment, in the spring of 1959, to succeed Stephen M. Corey, he was well known in professional circles for his contributions to the work of educational associations and for his achievements as superintendent of the Baltimore, Maryland school system, of which he had been a member for about thirty years.

Baltimore is also the native city and boyhood home of John Henry Fischer. He was born there on July 16, 1910 to Henry Fischer and Minnie (Muth) Fischer, who were also the parents of a daughter, now Mrs. Elizabeth F. Sheppard. His father was a stationary engineer. For his secondary school education John H. Fischer attended Baltimore City College, was graduated in 1927, and the following year entered Maryland State Teachers College in Towson.

Two years later, in 1930, having received a teacher's diploma from the college, Fischer began his career in education as an elementary school teacher in the Baltimore public schools. From 1933 to 1935 he taught in junior high school and then, in his first administrative appointment, became an assistant junior high school principal. In 1938 he was made special assistant in charge of Benjamin Franklin Junior High School in Baltimore.

At the same time that Fischer was acquiring practical experience, he was also gaining formal academic training. Johns Hopkins University in Baltimore granted him the B.S. degree in 1940. Later, at Teachers College, Columbia University, where he held a Shankland Memorial Scholarship, he studied for the M.A. degree, awarded in 1949, and the Ed.D. degree, awarded in 1951. His doctoral dissertation was entitled *A Plan for Reviewing and Revising the Program for the Preparation of School Executives at Teachers College, Columbia University.* In 1950-51 he was associate co-ordinator of the co-operative program in educational administration at Teachers College.

During his years of undergraduate and postgraduate study, meanwhile, Fischer had advanced in the Baltimore school system to director of attendance and child guidance in 1942 and to assistant superintendent for general administration in 1945. He became deputy superintendent of schools in 1952 and superintendent of public instruction in 1953.

One of the most challenging problems with which Dr. Fischer had to deal as superintendent of Baltimore's schools was that of racial integration, especially after the ruling of the United States Supreme Court in May 1954 outlawing segregation of white and Negro pupils in public schools. During a convention of the American Association of School Administrators in 1957 he noted that, in theory, schools have long professed to believe in equality. He suggested that schoolmen in some states at the present time are encountering difficulties "precisely because they are trying to adjust practices in public administration to historic American statements on equality and freedom of all men."

When Fischer was named dean of Columbia University's Teachers College in April 1959, the president of the college, Hollis L. Caswell, commented upon the outstanding reputation that Fischer had acquired through his achievements in Baltimore. "He is widely considered one of the ablest superintendents of schools in the United States," Caswell said, "and has given exceptional leadership in the development of an improved educational program in Baltimore." Caswell also called attention to Fischer's long interest in the education of teachers and his contributions to the in-service education program in his city.

The preparation of teachers for effective professional careers is the central purpose of Teachers College, whose students may receive either preservice training or the opportunity to increase their competence while they are in service. A large number of the 13,000 or more men and women who enroll yearly in the college (many from foreign countries) are already experienced teachers studying for advanced degrees or seeking special training that will qualify them for academic promotion.

Teachers College, founded in 1888, offers programs in all phases of instruction for all subjects and in guidance and educational administration. Its emphasis upon research has made it a pioneer in the investigation of learning, and the influence of some of its brilliant professors, such as the late Edward L. Thorndike and the late John Dewey, has conditioned classroom practices in the United States and

Fabian Bachrach

JOHN H. FISCHER

other countries. It is estimated that in the thirty-four largest American cities, with some 6,000,000 students, half of the school systems are headed by graduates of Teachers College.

Dr. Fischer assumed office as dean on September 1, 1959. In his first news conference the following November he defended the need for teacher training on the grounds that there are not enough "natural-born educators"; he denied that Teachers College stresses teaching technique to the neglect of knowledge of subject matter. On the issue of federal aid to education, he said that such assistance was necessary to assure quality education and that academic freedom would not suffer as a result of aid.

Quality education, priorities in education, and the need for teacher training have been among the subjects that Fischer has often canvassed in talks before professional groups and in educational periodicals. Taking into consideration the complexities and conflicts brought about by historical precedent and the demands of an accelerating rate of change, he is generally forthright in his statements on educational values and needs. He believes that "a principal measure of the effectiveness of our schools as instruments of universal education is their success in teaching the use of English" and that "to assure high quality teaching and learning, it is only sensible to make the greatest possible use of accumulated experience in teaching techniques and to apply to teaching all that can be drawn from the sciences which explore human development and learning." In his opinion, the increasing number of children from "disadvantaged homes" who were neglected until recently are the ones who need learning most of all.

In 1958 Fischer was chairman of the yearbook commission of the American Association of School Administrators which prepared *The*

FISCHER, JOHN H.—*Continued*

High School in a Changing World. Other professional organizations in which he has been active are the Maryland State Teachers Association (president in 1945) and the National Education Association (member of the educational policies commission). He has contributed articles to the journal of the latter organization and to a large number of other periodicals, including *School Executive, Teachers College Record, Nation's Schools,* and *Baltimore Bulletin of Education.* He is a member of the national advisory council of *Scholastic Magazine.*

Prominent as well in various civic groups in Maryland, Fischer has served as president of the Baltimore Council of Social Agencies and, in 1952, of the Maryland Prisoners Aid Association. He holds honorary LL.D. degrees from Morgan State College (1955) and Goucher College (1959). He belongs to the Johns Hopkins Club and to Phi Delta Kappa and Kappa Delta Pi.

John H. Fischer and his wife, Norma (Frederick) Fischer, who were married on November 28, 1934, have two sons, David Hackett and Miles Pennington. Fischer is five feet nine inches tall and weighs 175 pounds; his eyes are gray and his hair is brown-gray. One of his special interests is in the Boy Scouts of America, and he recently wrote "Scouting a Most Valuable Program" for *School Activities* (March 1959). For his services to the Boy Scouts, which include his membership on the national council and his vice-presidency of the Baltimore area council, he was awarded the Silver Beaver.

References

Sr Schol 74:2T+ Ap 17 '59 por
Leaders in Education (1948)
Who's Who in America, 1960-61

FLAGG, JAMES MONTGOMERY June 18, 1877-May 27, 1960 Illustrator; created patriotic posters during World War I and World War II; contributed drawings to magazines; collected some of his work in book form. See *Current Biography* (November) 1940.

Obituary

N Y Times p21 My 28 '60

FLEMMING, ARTHUR S(HERWOOD) June 12, 1905- United States Secretary of Health, Education and Welfare

Address: b. Health, Education and Welfare Bldg., 330 Independence Ave., S.W., Washington 25, D.C.; h. 7108 Lenhart Dr., Chevy Chase 15, Md.

NOTE: This biography supersedes the article which appeared in *Current Biography* in 1951.

"Dr. Flemming is one of our younger national leaders. He is not a politician in any sense. He is an educator and an administrator. He has . . . earned a splendid reputation for getting a good

job done and getting it done on time." This editorial appraisal appeared in the New York *Times* on May 9, 1958, two days after the appointment of Arthur S. Flemming to succeed Marion B. Folsom as Secretary of Health, Education and Welfare in the Eisenhower cabinet. Flemming came to his post after almost ten years as president of Ohio Wesleyan University. During that time he had been on leave of absence for four years (1953-57) as director of the Office of Defense Mobilization (and for an earlier, briefer period as assistant to the director). In other government assignments he has served on the Civil Service Commission, the War Manpower Commission, and commissions for the organization of the government.

Born in Kingston, New York on June 12, 1905, Arthur Sherwood Flemming is the only son of Harry Hardwicke Flemming, a lawyer who subsequently became judge of a surrogate court, and Harriet (Sherwood) Flemming. He has one sister, Mrs. Donald Sherbondy of Pittsburgh, Pennsylvania. At Kingston High School he excelled in public speaking. For a year after his graduation in 1922 he worked as a newspaper reporter before entering Ohio Wesleyan University, Delaware, Ohio. One of his many extracurricular interests in college was the Republican Club, of which he was president. He received the B.A. degree in 1927.

During the next three years Flemming was employed as an instructor in government and debate coach at American University, Washington, D.C., where he took his M.A. degree in political science in 1928. He was a member of the editorial staff of the *United States Daily* (which became the *United States News & World Report*) from 1930 to 1934, and in 1932 he began a three-year editorship of *Uncle Sam's Diary,* a current events weekly for high school students. Having also taken courses in law at George Washington University in Washington, he was awarded the LL.B. degree in 1933. He became director of American University's School of Public Affairs in 1934 and remained in that post until his appointment as executive officer of the university in October 1938.

Within a year, however, Flemming left American University to accept an appointment from President Roosevelt as the Republican member of the three-man United States Civil Service Commission. He served from July 1939 to August 1948 and during this period established a program to honor young employees making a career of government service. (This program was later taken over by the Junior Chamber of Commerce, which set up the annual Arthur S. Flemming Award in connection with it.)

Much of Flemming's work on the Civil Service Commission concerned recruiting of employees for the war effort. In related World War II assignments he was chief of labor supply with the Office of Production Management (1941-42) and a member of the War Manpower Commission (1942-45), of which he headed the management-labor policy committee. He received the Navy's Distinguished Civilian Service Award for his work on the Navy's manpower survey board in 1943-44, and from

October 1944 to March 1947 served on the advisory council of the Labor Department's retraining and re-employment administration. On July 17, 1947 he was one of four members named by President Truman to the twelve-member Commission on Organization of the Executive Branch of the Government, commonly known as the Hoover Commission.

The trustees of Ohio Wesleyan University elected Flemming president in June 1948. He had himself been a trustee for six years and had established the Institute of Practical Politics at Ohio Wesleyan. Resigning from the Civil Service Commission, he took office on August 31, 1948 as the ninth president of that Methodist-affiliated university and as the first alumnus and layman to be named its head since its founding in 1841.

The government continued to consult Flemming, who became chairman of the personnel advisory board of the Atomic Energy Commission in September 1948. On a leave of absence from the university, he began a new assignment in February 1951 as assistant to Director of Defense Mobilization, Charles E. Wilson, and as chairman of the manpower policy committee of the Office of Defense Mobilization. Since 1953 he has served on the three-man President's Advisory Committee on Government Organization, of which Milton S. Eisenhower is also a member.

With the change in administration from Democratic to Republican in January 1953, Flemming was made acting head of the Office of Defense Mobilization. Although he was eager to return to Ohio Wesleyan, pressure from the White House induced him to stay on as director of a reorganized and permanent ODM; he was sworn into the new office in June 1953. Through the abolition of the National Defense Administration, his responsibilities had been expanded to include the National Security Resources Board, the stockpiling functions of the Munitions Board, and supervision of the dissolution of the Office of Price Stabilization and the Wage Stabilization Board. A member of the National Security Council, he sat in on cabinet meetings.

By the end of 1954 Flemming had made considerable headway, with a staff of slightly over 200, on a comprehensive program for industrial mobilization, wage and price controls, rationing, and training of executive personnel for defense production—all designed to have the country prepared in the event of an atomic attack. He described the general nature of this program at some length in an interview in the *United States News & World Report* for March 1, 1957. The article appeared about three weeks after he had resigned as ODM director in order to return to Ohio Wesleyan University.

On May 7, 1958 President Eisenhower nominated Flemming to succeed Marion B. Folsom, who retired, as United States Secretary of Health, Education and Welfare. The appointment was confirmed by the Senate in July, and Flemming, having resigned as president of Ohio Wesleyan, took his oath of office on August 1. His department had been created in 1953 to unite a number of scattered agencies, including

Wide World

ARTHUR S. FLEMMING

the Public Health Service, the Social Security Administration, the Office of Vocational Rehabilitation, the Food and Drug Administration, and the Office of Education.

As soon as he entered the department Flemming plunged into the school integration crises. On September 10 he warned that aid to areas in which there were federal installations might be withdrawn if schools were closed to forestall integration. On December 1 he issued a statement describing the closing of schools in Arkansas and Virginia as "indefensible from the standpoint of what is being done to the children." Early the following year he said that he favored the administration's civil rights bill over Senator Lyndon B. Johnson's proposed "conciliation" measure.

Endeavoring to get school construction "out of the realm of argument and into the realm of action," Flemming announced in February 1959 an administration proposal whereby the federal government would help finance $5 billion worth of construction of educational facilities during the next five years, at a cost to the government of $100,000,000 a year for twenty-five years. Although he has strongly favored the 1958 National Defense Education Act, he has recommended repeal of the loyalty oath requirement from the loan program.

In the field of public health Secretary Flemming has called for sustained and vigorous attack on water pollution and has instituted a study of the effects of car fumes on human beings. In May 1959 he sent to Congress a proposal for a new method of regulation by the Food and Drug Administration of the use of color additives in foods, drugs, and cosmetics. Designated chairman of a new Federal Radiation Council in August 1959, Flemming promised in the following January "the most comprehensive water pollution clean-up ever instituted in this country" and the sampling,

FLEMMING, ARTHUR S.—*Continued*

beginning in July, of all milksheds for the presence of the radioactive material strontium 90.

Secretary Flemming was severely criticized by cranberry growers and some political figures because of the nationwide scare that followed his warning in November 1959 that certain cranberries grown in the Pacific Northwest had been found contaminated by a cancer-inducing weed-killer. "My position all along," he later said, "has been that when we in the Government develop information of this nature, we have an obligation to make it available to the public. We have no right to sit on it."

From 1946 to 1948 Flemming was the lay leader of the Washington Federation of Churches. He became the lay leader of the Ohio Conference of the Methodist Church in 1949 and vice-president of the National Council of Churches of Christ in America in 1951. He is a trustee of Temple University as well as of Ohio Wesleyan and has received honorary degrees from at least eleven colleges and universities.

Arthur S. Flemming and Bernice Virginia Moler were married on December 14, 1934 and have five children: Elizabeth Anne (Mrs. George Speese), Susan Harriet, Harry Sherwood, and the twins Arthur Henry and Thomas Madison. Tall and slender, Flemming is six feet one-half inch in height; he has brown eyes and graying brown hair. "He is pleasant and accessible." according to the *United States News & World Report* (December 7, 1959). "Amiability, however, stops short of joviality. . . ; He does not use tobacco, liquors, coffee or tea."

References

Harper 218 :91+ F '59
N Y Times Mag p9 O 5 '58 por
Newsweek 41 :23 F 9 '53
Reporter 12 :26 Ja 27 '55 por
Time 71 :16 My 19 '58
International Who's Who, 1959
New York Times   Men in the News—1958 (1959)
Who's Who in America, 1958-59
Who's Who in Methodism (1952)
World Biography (1954)

FLETCHER, SIR ANGUS (SOMERVILLE) May 13, 1883-Aug. 6, 1960 Former British government official; director, British Library of Information in New York (1928-41); chairman, headquarters commission of the United Nations (1946). See *Current Biography* (September) 1946.

Obituary

N Y Times p21 Ag 8 '60

FLOYD, CARLISLE (SESSIONS, JR.) June 11, 1926- Composer; teacher

Address: b. Florida State University, Tallahassee, Fla.; h. 1605 Redwood Dr., Tallahassee, Fla.

The composer and music educator Carlisle Floyd first attracted attention on a national scale in 1956 when his first opera, *Susannah*, became an instant success at its New York première. Floyd's next opera, *Wuthering Heights*, brought him further acclaim and led the critics to nominate him as one of the most promising composers for the lyric stage in America. The United States Junior Chamber of Commerce named Carlisle Floyd one of the ten outstanding young men of 1959, citing his "memorable contributions through one of the most rigorous of all art forms to the future of American music." Since 1947 Floyd has been on the faculty of the School of Music at Florida State University in Tallahassee, where he is now an associate professor.

Born in Latta, South Carolina, on June 11, 1926, Carlisle Floyd is the son of a Methodist minister whose French Huguenot ancestors came to Charleston in the late seventeenth century. His mother, the former Ida Fenegan, is a pianist who descends from a Scotch-Irish family that settled in the Carolinas before the American Revolution. He has one younger sister, Ermine Floyd Matheny. Because his father moved from parish to parish in South Carolina, Floyd grew up in several small towns throughout the state. He attended North High School, North, South Carolina, where he played on the basketball team, edited the school paper, and served as vice-president of the student body.

When he was ten, Floyd started to play the piano on his own initiative. (He did not receive any formal musical instruction until later.) Soon he discovered that he was also talented in the graphic arts and in literature. "In high school and college," he says, "it was a question of determining which would receive special concentration, and music won out." He now feels that in composing operas he is putting to work his talents in all of the arts.

At sixteen, Floyd won a scholarship to Converse College in Spartanburg, South Carolina, which he attended for two years, studying under Ernest Bacon, the composer. While at Converse he won a prize for a one-act play he had written. When Bacon took a post on the faculty at Syracuse University, Floyd transferred to Syracuse so that he could continue his studies under the composer. He received the degree of Bachelor of Music from Syracuse in 1946. At both Converse and Syracuse, Floyd majored in applied piano.

Although Carlisle Floyd had begun to teach at Florida State University in 1947, he returned to Syracuse University in 1949 on a leave of absence to study for his Master of Music degree, which he received in the same year. Up to this time he had been chiefly interested in becoming a performing pianist, having prepared for this career with both Sidney Foster and Rudolf Firkusny, and it was as an instructor in piano that he joined the faculty of the School of Music of Florida State University.

During his second sojourn at Syracuse University, Floyd began to settle down to serious composition. He wrote his first opera, the one-act *Slow Dusk*, which, produced at Syracuse in 1949, has since been performed at other universities and in opera workshops. For *Slow Dusk* Floyd wrote both the libretto and the music, an achievement he was to repeat in all his succeeding operas. His second opera, *Fugitives,* given only one mounting, at Florida State University in 1951, has since been withdrawn by the composer.

Susannah, Carlisle Floyd's third opera, was first produced at Florida State University in February 1955, with Mack Harrell and Phyllis Curtin in the leading roles. Both of the principals had become interested in *Susannah* when Floyd showed them the manuscript score at the Aspen Festival of Music and Art in Colorado. With Miss Curtin again singing the title role, the New York City Opera Company gave *Susannah* its New York première in September 1956. *Susannah* has been described by one enthusiast as "a hit show in the American operatic repertory if there ever was one." It has met with acclaim from both audience and critics and won the New York Music Critics Circle Award for the best new opera in 1956. One of the most durable operas in the New York City Opera's repertoire, *Susannah* was given its European première during the company's appearance at the Brussels World Fair of 1958. The Cedar Rapids (Iowa) Symphony performed an orchestral suite from the opera, arranged by Walter Hendl, in the same year.

A musical drama in two acts, each with five scenes, *Susannah* is based on the story of Susanna and the elders from the Apocrypha. Floyd wrote the libretto in only ten days, but he took his time in composing the music. He wrote the score during the years 1953 and 1954. *Susannah* takes place in a Tennessee country town during one week in July, and deals with the seduction of the flirtatious Susannah by a traveling evangelist and his subsequent murder by the girl's outraged brother. The townspeople try to force Susannah to leave town, but, driving them off with a gun, she stands alone in bitter triumph.

Analyzing *Susannah* in *Tempo* (Winter, 1956-57), Ronald Eyer found it "vitally, emotionally alive . . . a straightforward, unadorned story of malice, hypocrisy and tragedy of almost scriptural simplicity of language and characterization." He singled out as a key factor in the opera's impact the composer's approximation of natural speech inflections by using a continuous musical background "over which a mixture of speaking, speaking on pitch and in rhythm, and full singing voice are used without jarring transitions. This is a difficult thing to do convincingly, but Floyd has managed it extraordinarily well." The critic also noted the use of hymn tunes, modality, and folk music in the score.

The next opera composed by Carlisle Floyd was *Wuthering Heights,* based on the novel by Emily Brontë. Commissioned by the Santa Fe, New Mexico Opera Association, the world première of the opera took place in Santa Fe on July 16, 1958. Running about two and a half hours, *Wuthering Heights* has a prologue and three acts. Heathcliff is first seen as the

Evon Streetman

CARLISLE FLOYD

master of Wuthering Heights, and then, fifteen years earlier, as an orphaned youth living with the Earnshaws. He falls in love with Cathy Earnshaw, runs away when she becomes engaged to Edgar, a neighbor, then returns after a lapse of years to marry Edgar's sister and take over Wuthering Heights from Cathy's impoverished brother. At last, as Cathy lies dying, Heathcliff and Cathy are reconciled.

Critical reaction to the Santa Fe première was mixed. *Time* (July 28, 1958) noted that while the libretto was "cliché-ridden," the score pulsed "with moments of moving lyricism." In *Musical America* (September 1958), Marvin David Levy wrote that Floyd was trying to forge a new form of lyric theater by combining powerful drama with "music that the traditions associate with opera." Although he did not consider the end result wholly successful, he admired many things in the work, especially the end of Act II, Scene 1, when Cathy, while bathing Heathcliff's wounds, begins to weep quietly.

After the Santa Fe performances of *Wuthering Heights,* Floyd rewrote the third act, and the opera was given its New York première in this revised form by the New York City Opera Company on April 9, 1959. In the New York *Herald Tribune* the next day, Paul Henry Lang declared that the composer had ratified the promise he had shown in *Susannah* and now revealed "a maturity that promises still further. . . . Mr. Floyd appears made for the operatic stage. . . . From first to last the familiar story is handled in a manner that compels attention and strong sympathy." Robert Sabin of *Musical America* (May 1959) observed that *Wuthering Heights* is "a wholly successful and deeply moving opera—one of the best from an American composer," and

FLOYD, CARLISLE—*Continued*

said that the opera hypnotized its audience. The musical idiom reminded him of that used by Richard Strauss.

Other works by Carlisle Floyd include *Pilgrimage* (1956), a song cycle for baritone and orchestra dedicated to Mack Harrell, and a *Sonata for Piano* which was introduced in recital by Rudolf Firkusny.

In 1958 at Florida State University, Carlisle Floyd gave the first accredited course ever taught anywhere on the problems of co-ordinating music and text in opera to a class consisting of composers and librettists. Floyd works first on the libretto, making sure that every plot line is clear, every character revealed through dramatic situations and consistent behavior, and every line and action motivated. Until he has completed and polished the book, he does not think in terms of the specific music. He feels that operatic subjects should be limited to stories that rely on externalized thought and emotion, that are rich in dramatic situations, and responsive to concise treatment. If a composer is to avoid musical sterility, he must keep in contact with the public, Floyd believes. Because it furnishes precisely this kind of contact, music for the theater, films, and ballet interests Floyd as much as does opera. Floyd says, "As long as there is an outlet for my operas and other compositions, I think I'll just go on writing them."

In 1956 Floyd received a Guggenheim Fellowship, and in 1957 he won a citation of merit for outstanding service to American music from the National Association for American Composers and Conductors. He is a member of the American Society of Composers, Authors, and Publishers and of the National Association for American Composers and Conductors.

In November 28, 1957 Carlisle Floyd was married to Margery Kay Reeder, a former graduate student in English literature at Florida State University. Floyd is five feet eleven inches in height and has hazel eyes and brown hair. He plays tennis daily, is a fan of football and basketball, and enjoys reading history and politics. He is an Episcopalian and a Democrat.

FONG, HIRAM L(EONG) Oct. 1, 1907-
United States Senator from Hawaii; lawyer; businessman
Address: b. Senate Office Bldg., Washington 25, D.C.

In Hawaii's last election as a territory, on July 28, 1959, Hiram L. Fong, a self-made millionaire lawyer and businessman, was chosen as one of two Senators of the United States Congress who would represent Hawaii after it had been proclaimed the fiftieth state on August 21. Fong, whose term will end in January 1965, is Hawaii's senior Senator and a Republican. As the first person of Chinese descent to serve in the United States Congress, Fong feels that he has a unique opportunity to

increase understanding between the United States and the nations of Asia. Soon after Congress adjourned in 1959 he undertook an extended tour of Asia at his own expense.

Hiram Leong Fong was born on October 1, 1907 in Honolulu. His original given name was Yau, but in college he changed it to Hiram out of admiration for Hiram Bingham, a Congregationalist missionary who had gone to Hawaii in 1819. (He was the grandfather of the explorer and Republican Senator from Connecticut also named Hiram Bingham.) Hiram Fong's father, Lum Fong, and his mother Lum Fong Shee, had moved to Oahu from the Kwangtung province of China in 1872 to work as indentured laborers on a sugar plantation. His father earned $12 a month; his mother, nothing. Hiram, the seventh of eleven children, learned early to help support the family by shining shoes, selling newspapers and caddying. He grew up in the tough Kalihi slum section of Honolulu and attended Kalihi Waena Grammar School. Later he went to St. Louis College, a private school in Honolulu, and McKinley High School, one of Honolulu's largest public high schools.

Since he had no funds, Fong could not go to college immediately. He worked for three years as a clerk at the Pearl Harbor Naval Shipyard and saved enough to enter the University of Hawaii. He graduated from the university in only three years and with honors. During this time he held a wide variety of side jobs, including bill collecting and guiding tourists. He also found time to be editor of the school paper, associate editor of the school annual, adjutant of the ROTC, and a member of the debating, volley ball, and rifle teams.

In 1930 Fong went back to work full-time, this time with the Suburban Water System. After two years he saved $2,000. He borrowed $3,000 more and entered Harvard Law School. He returned home in 1935 with his law degree and "ten cents in [his] pocket." First he worked as a municipal clerk and later as deputy city attorney.

The law firm of Fong, Miho, Choy & Robinson, which Fong founded, was the first law office in Honolulu to make itself deliberately multiracial (Chinese, Japanese, Korean, and Caucasian). The firm was so successful that Fong began investing in real estate, insurance, shopping centers, finance, and a banana plantation. He is the president of Finance Factors, Grand Pacific Life Insurance Company, Finance Realty, Finance Investment Company, and Market City, Ltd. His annual earnings are now more than $50,000 and his personal assets are worth several million dollars.

During World War II Fong served as judge advocate of the 7th Fighter Command of the Seventh Air Force with the rank of major. For nineteen years he was an officer of the United States Army Reserve.

Politics has long been an important concern of Hiram L. Fong. He served fourteen years in the territorial House of Representatives, including three terms as speaker and two as vice-speaker. In 1954, when the Democrats gained control of the Legislature for the first time, Fong was one of the Republicans who was unseated. In the election of six representatives from the fifth district of Honolulu County, candidate number six received 16,066 votes; Fong received 16,035. He was a delegate to the Republican National Conventions of 1952 and 1956 and vice-president of the Territorial Constitutional Convention in 1950.

When Hawaiians went to the polls on June 27, 1959 to accept statehood in a plebiscite, they also voted in a primary election in which Fong was unopposed as a Republican candidate for the United States Senate. During his subsequent campaign against Democrat Frank F. Fasi, Fong's supporters labeled him the Man of the Pacific and stressed his hard climb from very humble beginnings. He received the unsolicited support of Harry Bridges' International Longshoremen's and Warehousemen's Union—the only Republican the union supported. The effect of this backing on his election is uncertain. Many observers believe, however, that ILWU endorsement hindered rather than helped John A. Burns, the defeated Democratic candidate for Governor.

On July 28, 1959, 93.8 per cent of Hawaii's 183,000 registered voters elected state officials for the first time. Republicans took the governorship, lieutenant governorship, one United States Senate seat, and a 14 to 11 margin in the state Senate. The Democrats won one seat in the Senate, one in the House, and a 33 to 18 majority in the state House of Representatives. Fong won over his opponent Fasi by 87,175 to 77,692 votes.

Hawaii was officially proclaimed the fiftieth state of the union on August 21, 1959. Three days later Fong and his colleagues, Oren E. Long in the Senate and Daniel K. Inouye in the House of Representatives, were sworn in as members of Congress. It was Fong's lucky day. By a flip of a coin and a draw he won both the title of senior Senator from Hawaii and the longer term—five and one-half years. Long's term will end in January 1963.

In the Eighty-sixth Congress, Fong was assigned to the Senate's Interior and Insular Affairs Committee and the Public Works Committee. During the last weeks of the 1959 session he voted on a number of legislative proposals, supporting appropriations for the Mutual Security Program and opposing the housing bill of 1959 and a measure to give the President authority to approve economic aid for Communist-dominated countries (other than Russia or those in the Far East) when it is important for national security.

In October 1959 Senator and Mrs. Fong embarked on a forty-five-day tour of fourteen Asian countries. His purpose was two-fold: to increase his understanding of Asia and its problems and to provide a living example of Hawaii's interracial equality. In Tokyo he told a reporter, "They say that a picture tells more than 10,000 words, I hope that my appearance in the flesh will do the same."

During his brief stay in the Philippines, Singapore, and elsewhere, Fong received a

HIRAM L. FONG

warm welcome from both government officials and the local Chinese populations. He expressed his conviction that both the Far East nations and their resident Chinese populations would benefit if the Chinese were integrated into the nations in which they live instead of remaining loyal to China.

The University of Hawaii in 1953 awarded Fong an honorary LL.D. degree and made him a foundation member of Phi Beta Kappa. He is a member of the Chinese American Club, Warriors of the Pacific, Commercial Associates, University of Hawaii Alumni Association, Harvard Club of Hawaii, Chinese Civic Club, Chamber of Commerce of Honolulu, and the Chinese Chamber of Commerce.

Hiram Fong was married to Ellyn Lo, also of Chinese ancestry, in Honolulu on June 25, 1938, soon after her graduation from the University of Hawaii. They have four children: Hiram, Jr., now at Lafayette College in Easton, Pennsylvania; Rodney, who is a student at Western Military Academy in Alton, Illinois; and twins, Merie-Ellen and Marvin-Allan. Besides their banana plantation, the Fongs have two homes in Hawaii—one on the heights in Honolulu and another on the beach. Fong is five feet ten inches tall and has graying black hair and dark-brown eyes. He is a member of the Congregational First Chinese Church of Christ.

References

N Y Herald Tribune p6 Jl 30 '59
N Y Times p14 Jl 30 '59
Newsweek 54:23 Ag 10 '59
Time 74:13 Ag 10 '59 por
Washington (D.C.) Post pF1 Ag 30 '59 por
Men and Women of Hawaii (1955)

FORAND, AIME J(OSEPH) (fôr'ănd)
May 23, 1895- United States Representative
from Rhode Island

Address: b. House Office Bldg., Washington
25, D.C.; h. Stony Brook Farm, Old Mendon
Rd., Route 2, Valley Falls, R.I.; 4108 Dresden
St., Kensington, Md.

During the Eighty-fifth and Eighty-sixth
Congresses Aime J. Forand, Democratic Representative of the First Rhode Island District
for twenty-two years, has been a center of
national attention as the sponsor of a much-
disputed bill to provide medical care for the
aged under the Social Security system. His
proposal, first introduced in 1957, has been
attacked by the American Medical Association
as a step toward socialized medicine and by
the National Association of Manufacturers as
an inflationary measure; organized labor vigorously supports the bill. The second Democrat
in rank on the House Ways and Means Committee, Forand is also a member of the Joint
Committee on Internal Revenue Taxation and
the Joint Committee on Reduction of Nones-
sential Federal Expenditures. In 1960 he announced that he would retire at the end of
the year.

Of French descent, Aime Joseph Forand was
born to François Xavier and Meli-Luce
(Ruest) Forand in Fall River, Massachusetts
on May 23, 1895. During his childhood the
family moved to the northern Rhode Island
township of Cumberland, which includes Valley
Falls, still Forand's home. He attended public
and Roman Catholic parish schools for several
years, but when he was twelve years old his
father became blind from cataracts over both
eyes, and Aime Forand had to go to work to
help support his seven brothers and sisters.

Although Forand's formal schooling ended
with the seventh grade, his education continued.

Wide World

AIME J. FORAND

Through evening study he learned bookkeeping
from a course sold by Sears, Roebuck &
Company. He later studied shorthand at the
Magnus Commercial School in Providence,
Rhode Island and then took a home extension
course offered by Columbia University. Meanwhile, he held dozens of jobs—in a cotton
mill, a grocery store, a roofing company and
as a salesman for lubricating oil, a private
chauffeur, a dump-truck driver, a radio re-
pairman.

In about 1914 Forand began working for a
wholesale baking company, in charge of twenty-
five delivery routes. He left the company in
1918 to join the Army for World War I
service and was assigned to the Motor Transport Corps. After a year in France with the
American Expeditionary Force, he was demobilized with the rank of sergeant and returned to his job in the baking company,
where he remained for four more years.

Becoming interested in politics after the war,
Forand was made a member in 1922 of the
city commission for Central Falls, Rhode
Island, a few miles south of Valley Falls.
A charter member of the Rhode Island Young
Men's Democratic League formed in 1923,
he served as president of the Central Falls
branch for the next three years. In 1923 he
also began the first of two terms as Democratic
member of the House of Representatives of
the Rhode Island General Assembly.

For six years, from 1924 to 1930, Forand
was employed by the Providence *News* and the
Providence *News-Tribune* as a reporter and
branch office manager at Pawtucket and Woon-
socket, Rhode Island. In addition, in 1929
he became the secretary to United States
Representative Jeremiah E. O'Connell from the
First District of Rhode Island. O'Connell
resigned from Congress in May 1930 to accept
appointment as an associate justice of the
Rhode Island Supreme Court, and Forand then
served as secretary to his successor, Representative Francis B. Condon, until January
1935, when Condon in turn resigned to become
an associate justice of the state's Supreme
Court.

A Republican, Charles F. Risk, was appointed to fill out Condon's unexpired Congressional term. During 1935-36, when Forand
was therefore away from Washington, he
served as chief of the Rhode Island Division
of Soldiers Relief and commandant of the
Rhode Island Soldiers Home. It was in part
his close experience here with the medical
needs of elderly people that led him to write
the Forand bill some twenty years later.
"The needy will never again be just statistics
to anyone who has to deal with their personal
problems," he has said (New York *Times,*
March 21, 1960).

Nominated in 1936 as the Democratic candidate to oppose Risk (described in the New
York *Times* as an "anti-New Deal champion"),
Forand won the November election by about
10,000 votes. He took his seat in the Seventy-
fifth Congress in January 1937 as Representative of Rhode Island's First District, which
covers the southeastern counties of Bristol

and Newport and part of Providence County. During his freshman term he was on the Post Office and Post Roads Committee and voted consistently as a New Deal Democrat.

Forand was defeated for re-election in 1938 by former Representative Risk, but won back his seat from the same opponent in 1940. He became a member of the Democratic National Congressional Committee in 1941 and a speaker for the committee in 1943. Assigned for the first time to the House Ways and Means Committee in 1943, he co-sponsored in April of that year the Forand-Robertson pay-as-you-go taxation bill, which proposed, as an alternative to the Ruml plan, to "forgive" that part of the 1942 income tax liability to which normal and first surtax rates would apply. (The measure passed the House, but not the Senate.)

In January 1944 Forand proposed creation of a fifteen-member commission for simplification of the tax laws, and during 1945-46 he headed an unofficial sixty-three member Congressional committee to protect the consumer, of which sixty members signed in March 1946 a manifesto urging continuation of the OPA and price controls. He became chairman of the House Democratic caucus in 1947.

Several bills that Forand sponsored during the 1950's also concerned taxation. In May 1950 he made the proposal, first adopted and afterward rejected by the Ways and Means Committee, that the Collector of Internal Revenue be instructed to accept voluntary disclosures of underpayments of taxes and not refer the taxpayer to the Department of Justice. As chairman of a subcommittee studying excise tax technical and administrative problems, he suggested in January 1956 that parochial schools be exempted from federal taxes on the purchase of buses and gasoline. The Treasury opposed both this recommendation and his proposal in July 1957 that the federal sales tax on night club cabaret checks be reduced from 20 to 10 per cent. (The bill was finally passed in the House in September 1959, but opposed in the Senate.)

In the area of welfare legislation, Forand headed a subcommittee in 1950 holding hearings on a bill to provide jobless benefits for federal, state, and municipal employees. In 1953 and 1954 he proposed measures to extend Social Security benefits to an additional million of the aged and to compel states to double their annual unemployment compensation payments.

Just before the close of Congress in 1957 Representative Forand introduced a bill to provide federal health insurance for old people as well as a 10 per cent increase in existing Social Security benefits. The Forand bill, which would have provided sixty days of hospital, surgical, and nursing home insurance for all Social Security beneficiaries, was assailed in May 1958 by Dr. David B. Allman, then president of the American Medical Association, as "another means of bringing in socialized medicine by the side door." Allman declared that a "voluntary" program was being worked out to provide care for persons over sixty-five.

Labor, however, strongly supported Forand's bill, which was reintroduced, to the Eighty-sixth Congress, in early 1959. About a year later, February 1960, President Eisenhower told a news conference that the administration was considering an alternative proposal to increase the Social Security payroll tax by one-fourth of 1 per cent for both employer and employee to finance better care for the aged. In March 1960 the National Association of Manufacturers came out in opposition to the Forand bill, calling it "inflationary" and recommending voluntary health insurance as a more realistic substitute. In 1960 Congress rejected measures for medical benefits under the Social Security system. Instead it passed a bill in August granting federal funds to state programs for elderly persons in need.

Key voting in the Eighty-fifth and Eighty-sixth Congresses found Forand opposed to both the Smith motion to strike out the enacting clause of the school construction assistance bill (July 1957) and the later Smith motion (July 1958) to bar courts from ruling that federal law nullifies state law in the same field. He voted against substituting the Landrum-Griffin amendment to the Taft-Hartley Law for the Elliott amendment (August 1959), but did approve the labor-management reporting and disclosure bill of 1959, which incorporated much of the Landrum-Griffin measure (September).

Among his other "yea" votes were those for extension of the Reciprocal Trade Act (June 1958), the TVA self-financing bill (May 1959), and the extension of the Civil Rights Commission (September 1959). He helped pass the public works bill over the President's veto (September 1959) and the water-pollution bill over the President's veto (February 1960). In the field of foreign affairs he favored the President's Mideast Doctrine (January 1957), postponement of British debt interest payments (April 1957), mutual security appropriation bills (July 1957, May 1958, September 1959), and increasing the United States subscription to the International Monetary Fund (March 1959).

Providence College awarded Forand an honorary LL.D. degree in June 1951. A Roman Catholic, he is a member of L'Union St. Jean Baptiste d'Amérique and the Knights of Columbus. His clubs are the Elks, Eagles, Lions, Marquette, and Le Foyer Franco-Américain; his service organizations are the American Legion and Veterans of Foreign Wars. Aime J. Forand and Gertrude Bedard of Central Falls were married on November 16, 1931. According to the New York *Times* (March 21, 1960), "Forand, a slightly bald, round, cigar-smoking man of medium size and somewhat lackluster manner, is an authentic example of

FORAND, AIME, J.—*Continued*

a traditional type of American—the self-made success."

References

American Catholic Who's Who, 1960 and 1961
Biographical Directory of the American Congress, 1774-1949 (1950)
Congressional Directory (1960)
Who's Who in America, 1960-61
Who's Who in New England (1949)
Who's Who in United States Politics (1952)

FORD, FREDERICK W(AYNE) Sept. 17, 1909- United States government official; lawyer

Address: b. New Post Office Bldg., Washington, D.C.; h. 316 Duke St., Alexandria, Va.

Since the recent disclosure of scandals in the broadcasting industry, the Federal Communications Commission has attracted much public attention. When its chairman, John C. Doerfer, resigned under fire for accepting "unusual hospitality" from a broadcaster, the spotlight inevitably fell on his successor, Frederick W. Ford, who was appointed by President Dwight D. Eisenhower on March 10, 1960. Doerfer had maintained that the commission could not regulate broadcasting practices effectively and appeared to abide by an essentially "hands-off" policy. Ford, on the other hand, has indicated that he intends to take a more vigorous position on the role of the FCC with regard to its relations with the broadcasting industry.

Ford has been in government service for over twenty years, and has served the FCC in various capacities between 1947 and 1953. As a commissioner on the FCC since 1957, he has

FREDERICK W. FORD
Harris & Ewing

added to his considerable experience in the working of federal agencies his knowledge of the FCC in particular.

Frederick Wayne Ford was born on September 17, 1909 in Bluefield, West Virginia, the only son of George M. and Annie Laurie (Linn) Ford. His father was State Superintendent of Free Schools of West Virginia, and his mother was a schoolteacher. Ford attended public schools in Charleston and in Dunbar, West Virginia, and in 1931 received his B.A. degree from West Virginia University. Three years later he earned his LL.B. degree from the law school of the university. While studying law, he had served on the editorial staff of the *West Virginia Law Quarterly*.

In 1934 Ford began the general practice of law before state and federal courts as a junior partner in the firm of Stathers and Cantrall of Clarksburg, West Virginia. After five years of private practice, he entered government service in the office of the general counsel of the Federal Security Agency, which at that time was responsible for the administration of Social Security benefits.

In 1942, shortly after he had left the FSA for the Office of Price Administration, Ford entered the United States Air Force as a second lieutenant. He was released in 1946, with the rank of major. He then returned to the OPA as a hearing commissioner. In 1947 he transferred to the FCC, where he worked in the hearing and review sections. He served the FCC in the special legal and technical group (now the office of opinions and reviews) and in the general counsel's office. In 1950 he was named an FCC trial attorney. He became the first chief of the hearing division of the broadcast bureau when the commission was reorganized in 1951. He left the commission in 1953 to join the United States Department of Justice.

In the Department of Justice Ford served as first assistant in the office of the legal counsel, then as acting assistant attorney general in charge of the office. In January 1957 he became assistant deputy attorney general under Deputy Attorney General William P. Rogers, who later became Attorney General of the United States.

On August 29, 1957 President Eisenhower appointed Ford as a member of the FCC to fill the vacancy left by the retiring chairman, George C. McConnaughey. As a commissioner, he acted as FCC liaison with the Office of Civil and Defense Mobilization in long-range frequency allocation planning. He also served as an alternate commission member of the interagency telecommunications advisory board, which advises the Director of Defense Mobilization in the area of national telecommunications plans; acted as an FCC alternate defense commissioner; and belonged to the commission's telephone and telegraph committees.

The FCC is the government agency established under the Federal Communications Act of 1934 to regulate interstate and foreign communications by cable, wire, and air "in the public interest." It is composed of seven commissioners appointed by the President subject to confirmation by the Senate, and employs around

1,200 persons, most of whom are Civil Service employees. The commission is responsible for the licensing of commercial and private radio and television operators, the allocation of radio and television frequencies for broadcasting, and the regulation of broadcasters in accordance with the Federal Communications Act.

In his new position Ford faces problems he considers "more serious than at any time in history" for the commission. His announcement, however, that a new complaints and compliance division has been established for the monitoring of programming has shown his determination to meet those problems by adopting a firm policy towards television and radio licensees.

John C. Doerfer, the former chairman of the FCC, had been of the opinion, according to the New York *Times* (March 11, 1960), that the broadcasting industry had the right to "clean its own house" and that the commission lacked jurisdiction and power to provide further regulation. In reviewing the question in his official report to President Eisenhower at the end of 1959, Attorney General William P. Rogers said, however: "The principal conclusion of this report . . . is that the Federal Communications Commission and the Federal Trade Commission appear to have authority adequate under existing law to eradicate most, if not all, of the deceptive and corrupt practices in broadcasting which have been disclosed—particularly if the agencies are accorded the full co-operation of the broadcasting industry."

Changes in legislation have been proposed. They include the use of temporary license suspension; stricter definition of the types of contacts permitted between commissioners and broadcasters; further delineation of the limitations on sponsors' favors to stations and their personnel; and the licensing of networks.

Ford seems to be providing the FCC with a new and challenging leadership. He has said that he thinks it possible "to rebuild the reputation of the commission under its present setup." But he also feels that when action is indicated on the part of the commission for which further legislation is required, "it becomes the commission's obligation to inform the Congress of that fact and propose the necessary legislation." Ford hopes to revitalize the FCC and make it an effective means to the ends for which it was originally intended.

While a student in law school, Frederick W. Ford was married to Virginia Lee Carter on August 12, 1933. She died on February 19, 1958. Ford was married on October 11, 1959 to Mary Margaret Mahoney of Blackstone, Massachusetts. He has one daughter, Mary Carter Ford, by his former marriage. The Fords are renovating and restoring an eighteenth-century house in Alexandria, Virginia, the second such project that Ford has undertaken. His interest in the American past is shared with his wife, who managed an antique shop before their marriage. For three years Ford served as president of the Alexandria Association, a group responsible for saving and restoring Ramsey House, the oldest home in Alexandria.

Although he no longer acts in plays, Ford is still interested in the little theater movement. He devotes most of his spare time to gardening and his restoration work, since his earlier interest in golf has slackened. A Republican, he was elected to the Harrison County (West Virginia) Republican executive committee in 1936, when he still engaged in private law practice. In 1938 he became president of the Young Republican Club of Harrison County.

Ford belongs to the American Law Institute, Scabbard and Blade (the ROTC honor society), Phi Delta Phi (a legal fraternity), and Sigma Chi (a social fraternity). An Episcopalian, he has served as a vestryman of Christ Church, Episcopal, in Alexandria.

References

N Y Times p8 Mr 11 '60 por
N Y World-Telegram p9 Mr 11 '60 por
Who's Who in America, 1960-61

FOWLER, GENE Mar. 8, 1890-July 2, 1960 Author; scenarist; newspaperman; wrote *Good Night, Sweet Prince* (1944), among other books. See *Current Biography* (March) 1944.

Obituary

N Y Times p1+ Jl 3 '60

FOX, JACOB NELSON *See* Fox, Nellie

FOX, NELLIE Dec. 25, 1927- Baseball player
Address: h. Lincoln Highway, St. Thomas, Pa.; b. c/o The Chicago White Sox, Comiskey Park, Chicago, 16, Ill.

When, in November 1959, the Baseball Writers Association named Nellie Fox, the diminutive second baseman of the Chicago White Sox, the Most Valuable Player of the American League for 1959, he became the first member of the Chicago team to be thus honored. Fox drew fourteen first-place votes and a total of 295 points, while his runner-up for the honor, Luis Aparicio, the White Sox shortstop, drew 255 points. When the awards were distributed, both players were given credit for helping the Chicago White Sox to earn their first pennant in forty years. Although the two men are gifted fielders, Fox's more consistent hitting was probably the decisive factor in the voting.

Over the 1959 season, Fox batted .306. His 191 hits included thirty-four doubles, six triples, and two home runs. Furthermore, he stretched his playing record in consecutive games to 669, a major league mark for second basemen. In the field, Fox made only ten errors, for a .988 average. He now ranks second in lifetime hits among active American League players with 1,902; only Ted Williams of the Boston Red Sox can claim more.

Jacob Nelson (Nellie) Fox was born on Christmas Day, 1927 in St. Thomas, Pennsylvania, an unincorporated community of some

NELLIE FOX

550 inhabitants 140 miles west of Philadelphia. The youngest of three sons born to Jacob and Mae Fox, he is of German-Irish descent. His oldest brother, Frank, died at the age of three months, long before Nellie was born; another brother, Wayne, is seven years older than Nellie. The elder Fox, a carpenter, was second baseman on the St. Thomas baseball team from 1917 until the early 1940's, when he decided to retire from active baseball competition.

The Chicago White Sox second baseman played his first competitive game of baseball at the age of nine, when he was sent into a local game as a pinch hitter, and, according to his father, "got a single over second." In the eighth grade he was playing on the St. Thomas Vocational High School nine, and slightly more than a year later, he was playing regularly on both the St. Thomas team and in the Chambersburg (Pennsylvania) Twilight League.

By the time he had reached his middle 'teens, Nellie Fox had made up his mind that he wanted to become a professional baseball player and that graduation from high school was not a prerequisite to the achievement of his ambition. In 1944 the Philadelphia (now Kansas City) Athletics were in spring training in Frederick, Maryland, only fifty miles from St. Thomas. The sixteen-year-old Fox pleaded with his parents to go to Frederick for a tryout. They finally relented, but for a strategic reason. "My idea was to keep him in high school," Nellie's father recalls. "I figured once he had a tryout and saw how good those big leaguers were, that maybe he'd be willing to wait awhile. I figured they'd just tell him at camp to go back to school."

Instead, the legendary Connie Mack, then managing the Athletics, decided that Fox deserved a chance in the minor leagues. When the elder Fox gave his consent, Nellie reported back to the Athletics, and remained with them for the greater part of spring training. He was then farmed out to Lancaster, Pennsylvania, in the now defunct Class B Interstate League.

Fox played twenty-four games at first base for Lancaster and was hitting .325 when he injured his left ankle. He was then sent to Jamestown, New York, in the Class D Pony League, finishing the season there with a .304 average. In 1945 he was moved to second base and led the league in hits, runs, and triples. Fox was assigned to Toronto in the International League in the following year, but in the middle of April he was drafted and sent to Korea for occupation duty.

Returning to Lancaster in May, 1947, Fox hit .281 in fifty-five games before being called by the Philadelphia Athletics, with whom he played in seven games. In 1948 he played with Lincoln, Nebraska, in the Class A Western League. When his impressive performance there earned him another trial with the Philadelphia Athletics, Fox was in the major leagues to stay.

Fox remained with the Philadelphia Athletics for only the 1949 season, hitting .255. In October 1949 he was traded to the Chicago White Sox for catcher Joe Tipton, who has long since faded from the major league scene. Fox became the Chicago White Sox full-time second baseman in the middle of the 1950 season and has held the position ever since. In his first year with the White Sox he batted only .247, but his hitting underwent a marked improvement during the following season, when he finished at .313.

Roger ("Doc") Cramer, who was the coach for the Chicago White Sox when Fox joined the team, is now given a great deal of the credit for Fox's emergence as a steady .300 hitter. Writing for the Chicago Daily News Service, Howard Roberts noted: "Cramer taught him how to bunt, broke him of the bad habit of hitting off his front foot, and persuaded him to use a heavier bat with a larger barrel" (Washington Post and Times Herald, August 22, 1959).

During his period with the Chicago White Sox, Fox has played under four managers. The latest is Al Lopez, who says of his eager second baseman: "Fox is what you call a 'manager's ball player.' He does his job expertly and he does it every day. He's the type of player you can count on. He's an 'old pro.' A great many times, he is hurting pretty badly from the dumpings he has taken on the field, but he's always ready to play. Fox is a self-made ball player. He has hustled his way to stardom."

Even rival managers have nothing but praise for Fox. Casey Stengel, the field general of the New York Yankees, has said: "That little feller, he ain't so big, but he's all fire. He's caused me more grief than any other player on the White Sox. He's in my hair all the time. He can beat you with his glove or with his bat." Fox is one of the few ball players ever to silence the ebullient Stengel. Once, during a game between the New York Yankees and the Chicago White Sox, a close play at second base brought Stengel running from the dugout.

As he arrived to give the umpire a piece of his mind, Fox snapped: "What're you doing out here? Gonna tell us a couple of your funny jokes?" (New York *Herald Tribune,* June 16, 1959).

Christmas is a significant day in the life of Nellie Fox, not just because it is his birthday. Christmas in 1943 marked his first date with Joanne Statler, a girl from St. Thomas. Engaged on Christmas Day in 1946, they were married in June 1948. Their daughter, Bonnie, was born on Christmas Day in 1949. They also have a son, Tracy.

By the standards of baseball, Nellie Fox is a short man, standing five feet, nine inches in height, and weighing 160 pounds. An inveterate chewer of tobacco, he can easily be singled out from the other players on the field by the chaw that distorts his cheeks. He dislikes fish and most vegetables but partakes of ice cream and pastries in great quantities. Away from the baseball field, Fox's hobbies consist of ping-pong, bowling, and hunting. He hopes in the future to play even better baseball than he has in the past. "They say," grins Fox, "a player's best years are between the ages of thirty-two and thirty-five."

References

N Y Herald Tribune III p1 Je 16 '59
N Y Times p35 N 13 '59
Sat Eve Post 227:30+ My 14 '55 por
Sports Illus 12:30 Ja 4 '60 por
Washington (D.C.) Post p12-A Ag 22 '59

FRENCH, PAUL COMLY Mar. 19, 1903- June 2, 1960 Former executive director of CARE (1946-55); executive director of the National Service Board for Religious Objectors (1940-46). See *Current Biography* (May) 1951.

Obituary

N Y Times p23 Je 4 '60

FRINGS, KETTI (HARTLEY) Writer
Address: 230 Ladera Dr., Beverly Hills, Calif.

Although she was generally unknown to audiences before *Look Homeward, Angel* opened on Broadway in 1957, Ketti Frings is an established screenwriter, who estimates that she regularly spends ten to twelve hours a day at her typewriter. For her dramatization of Thomas Wolfe's autobiographical novel Mrs. Frings won both the 1958 Pulitzer Prize in Drama and the New York Drama Critics Circle Award. The author of two novels and an earlier Broadway play, she has a secure reputation in Hollywood, where she is best known for notable screen adaptations of the stage plays, *Come Back, Little Sheba* and *The Shrike.*

It is not by accident that the theater has figured prominently in Mrs. Frings's success; she once wanted to become an actress and all her life she has "desperately wanted to write for the

KETTI FRINGS

stage." Her love of acting started her on her playwriting career. "When I was in school," she recalls. "I wrote plays so that I could write myself the best parts."

Katharine Hartley Frings ("Ketti" was her husband's nickname for her, which she now uses) was born in Columbus, Ohio, of Scottish and English descent, like Thomas Wolfe. Her father, Guy Herbert Hartley, was a Quaker who traveled all over the country as a paper box salesman, taking his wife, Pauline (Sparks) Hartley, and daughters with him. Before she had entered her teens Mrs. Frings had lived in thirteen cities, ranging from Brooklyn, New York, to Portland, Oregon. After her mother's death she and her two sisters went to live with an aunt in Milwaukee, where she attended the Lake School for Girls. After graduation she studied at Principia College in St. Louis, but she left after one year.

Mrs. Frings's dual love of acting and writing manifested itself early. At twelve she won her first literary prize—for an essay on "The Real Meaning of Santa Claus," published in a Dayton, Ohio newspaper the following year she earned a silver medal in a scholastic competition for her recitation, with gestures, of "Lochinvar."

Starting her professional writing career as an advertising copy writer for L. Bamberger & Company, a Newark, New Jersey, department store, Mrs. Frings went on to work as publicist, columnist, radio script writer, and movie magazine ghost writer. Having decided to write a novel, she spent a year in the South of France. Although she never got around to writing the novel, she met Kurt Frings, a former lightweight boxer in France and Belgium, to whom she was married on March 18, 1938.

Since the German-born Mr. Frings was not an American citizen, the couple waited for two years in Mexico until he could migrate to the United States. On the basis of this experience Mrs. Frings wrote both her first screen story,

FRINGS, KETTI—*Continued*

which was made into Paramount's *Hold Back the Dawn* (1941), starring Charles Boyer and Olivia de Havilland, and her first novel, also entitled *Hold Back the Dawn* (Duell, 1940). A reviewer for the *New Republic* called the novel "a moving and disturbing book, written in clipped, vivid sentences."

In 1942 Mrs. Frings's first Broadway play, *Mr. Sycamore,* was produced. Based on a story by Robert Ayre, this fantasy about a disgruntled postman who changed himself into a tree ran for only nineteen performances. Brooks Atkinson (New York *Times,* November 14, 1942) found it "mildly imaginative." Howard Barnes (New York *Herald Tribune,* November 14, 1942) reported that "it has its funny moments and certain glib philosophical underlinings . . . but [it] never rises to the true dimension of dramatic fantasy." Of this maiden effort, Mrs. Frings says: "I was not too bruised by its lack of success. . . . You can only learn from your mistakes."

Two years later Mrs. Frings wrote her second novel, *God's Front Porch* (Morrow, 1944). The story of a corporal, killed in action in North Africa, who makes his way to Heaven and finds it very much like earth, it was written, according to its author, "to try to dispel some of the world's gloom, to make those who are frightened a little less frightened." For that reason, perhaps, most critics thought their readers would like it better than they did. Ben Ray Redman (*Saturday Review of Literature,* February 26, 1944) thought it would "certainly delight many readers," but admitted that he was not one of them. Lewis Gannett (New York *Herald Tribune,* February 24, 1944) was sure it would have "a vast appeal in war time," but found it "a little too cute."

During the next few years Mrs. Frings worked in Hollywood, turning out a steady stream of screen plays. These included United Artists' *Guest in the House* (1944), Paramount Pictures' *The Accused* (1949), Paramount's *File on Thelma Jordan* (1949), and RKO's *The Company She Keeps* (1951). The last was inspired by a visit Mrs. Frings had made to Tehachapi Women's Prison.

In 1952 Paramount Pictures released two films with screen plays by Ketti Frings. The first of these, *Because of You,* was described by Otis L. Guernsey, Jr. (New York *Herald Tribune,* December 4, 1952) as "the kind of film which might be called a 'woman's picture' by those who tend to underestimate the fair sex." The second, however, was her screen adaptation of William Inge's *Come Back, Little Sheba,* which scored a critical and popular success and earned an Oscar for its star, Shirley Booth.

Mrs. Frings scored another success in 1955 with her scenario for *The Shrike,* a Universal-International release based on the Pulitzer Prize-winning play by Joseph Kramm. While her script was being shot, Mrs. Frings served as "a second pair of eyes" for José Ferrer, who not only directed but also starred in the film; she viewed from the camera position those scenes in which Ferrer played. This unusual arrangement was possible because, according to Ferrer, "Ketti knows exactly how I feel about every word in the script."

While working on these screen adaptations, Mrs. Frings was also planning the stage adaptation of Thomas Wolfe's *Look Homeward, Angel.* (Ironically, Wolfe himself had always wanted to be a dramatist, but did not succeed in having either of the two plays he completed produced during his lifetime.) In 1955 she asked Edward C. Aswell, Wolfe's last editor and literary executor, for dramatic rights to the novel and began work on her adaptation when Aswell gave his consent.

Her efforts were rewarded on November 28, 1957 when *Look Homeward, Angel,* starring Anthony Perkins and Jo Van Fleet, opened on Broadway to critical and popular acclaim. It ran for 564 performances and earned for its author the two highest accolades in the American theater, a New York Drama Critics Circle award and a Pulitzer Prize in Drama.

"What Thomas Wolfe could never do, Ketti Frings has done admirably," wrote Brooks Atkinson (New York *Times,* November 29, 1957). "She has mined a solid drama out of the craggy abundance of *Look Homeward, Angel.*" In adapting Wolfe's autobiographical novel of boardinghouse life in Asheville, North Carolina to the stage, Mrs. Frings compressed 626 pages of torrential prose into two hours of playing time, reduced its army of characters to nineteen, telescoped the time span of the novel to three weeks, and altered Wolfe's chronology. Nevertheless, in the view of Richard Watts, Jr. (New York *Post,* November 29, 1957), she had "captured the letter and spirit of the Wolfe novel in completely dramatic terms and given it truth, richness, abounding vitality, laughter and compassion, and enormous emotional impact."

In his introduction to the published text of the play (Scribner, 1955) Edward C. Aswell said: "Now, more than 19 years after his [Wolfe's] death, *Look Homeward, Angel* has come to Broadway, thanks to the extraordinary insight and dramatic skill of Ketti Frings. How Tom would have rejoiced in this event! It would have been for him the final consummation."

Mrs. Frings's other works include *Let the Devil Catch You* (Shakespere, 1947); short stories in *Collier's, Good Housekeeping, Woman's Home Companion,* and the *Saturday Evening Post;* she wrote the screen plays for Paramount Pictures' *About Mrs. Leslie* (1954) and Universal-International's *Foxfire* (1955). She was selected a Woman of the Year for 1958 by the Los Angeles *Times* and received the distinguished achievement award of Theta Sigma Phi, the honorary journalism sorority, in 1959.

Ketti Frings, who has two teen-aged children, Peter and Kathie, still resembles the actress she once wanted to be. She is tall (five feet seven inches) and slim (126 pounds) and deeply tanned, with brown eyes and graying hair. Her husband, Kurt Frings, is a well-known actors' agent who has numbered among his clients Elizabeth Taylor, Audrey Hepburn, and Maria Schell.

Mr. and Mrs. Frings live in Beverly Hills, in an ultramodern house, complete with swimming pool and Japanese garden, which Cleveland Amory has called "one of Hollywood's most showy showplaces." In the house, which gives the impression of being all glass, there is one room which has no windows, only a skylight. It is Mrs. Frings's favorite room, of which she says: "You can't look out. You have to look in. It's a darn good thing, too, not only for writing but for everything else."

About the craft of playwriting Ketti Frings has said: "The greatest mistake anyone can make is to undertake a play as a casual excursion in creative work, to treat it as an alternate occupation. It's quite the other way. It demands the most complete dedication. And even with that kind of dedication you can't be sure of the result, but you have to possess it anyway."

References

    Los Angeles Times IV p1 F 22 '59 por
    Sat Eve Post 216:4 N 20 '43 por
    Sat Rev 41:6+ S 6 '58

Wide World

R. BUCKMINSTER FULLER

FULLER, R(ICHARD) BUCKMINSTER, (JR.) July 12, 1895- Inventor; engineer

Address: b. Geodesics, Inc., and Synergetics, Inc., Raleigh, N.C.; h. 6 Burns St., Forest Hills 75, N.Y.

A mathematical genius, an engineer of rare and extraordinary foresight, and a philosopher "whose mind bestrides the most colossal problems of life and living," R. Buckminster Fuller has been a pioneer of revolutionary technical inventions since he constructed the Dymaxion house in 1927. The three-wheeled Dymaxion car served as a vehicle of unusual utility and speed, and his Dymaxion map, which has eliminated all distortions, was the first of its kind to receive a patent.

Although he denies that he is an architect, some authorities have hailed his space frames and enclosures as being the greatest advance in building since the invention of the arch. His geodesic dome, based on an advanced mathematical system he devised called "energetic synergetic geometry," has been employed with great success. When it sheltered the American exhibit in Moscow during the summer of 1959, it evoked favorable comment from the Russians, including Premier Nikita S. Khrushchev, who invited Fuller to lecture to Soviet engineers. Fuller is interested in using the dome to enclose entire communities, permitting total climatic control.

A descendant of a distinguished New England family, Richard Buckminster Fuller, Jr., was born on July 12, 1895 in Milton, Massachusetts to Richard Buckminster and Caroline Wolcott (Andrews) Fuller. His father was a successful Boston merchant dealing in tea and leather goods. A paternal great-aunt, Margaret Fuller, was the famous transcendentalist and associate of Ralph Waldo Emerson.

Fuller attended Milton Academy in his native city from 1904 to 1913 and then matriculated at Harvard University. He was expelled at the end of his sophomore year (1915), as he explains, "officially for cutting classes but actually for general irresponsibility" (*Business Week*, May 10, 1958). For a short time Fuller worked as a fitter's apprentice with an importer of cotton mill machinery and then as an apprentice with Armour & Company, but these jobs hardly provided the proper scope for his imagination.

When the United States entered World War I in 1917, Fuller was commissioned an ensign in the Navy. Here he was "involved in the new era of flying," and received some of the technical education he so sorely lacked. After his discharge as a lieutenant (j.g.) he returned to Armour and later for a few months in 1922 was a sales manager for a trucking firm. For the next five years Fuller was in the construction business with his father-in-law, the noted architect James Monroe Hewlett. But in 1927 he moved his family "to a poor section of Chicago" and began to develop and synthesize his radical theories of "comprehensive design."

According to a student of Fuller's work, Robert W. Marks, comprehensive design "is more a philosophy than a form of engineering," and Fuller has defined his ultimate goal as "finding ways of doing more with less to the end that all people—everywhere—can have more and more of everything" (New York *Times*, August 23, 1959). With the invention of the Dymaxion house in 1927, Fuller's dedication to the philosophy of "adequate preplanning and design" advanced from theory to reality. This luxury dwelling, which was uniquely suspended from a central mast and could be bought for the retail price of a 1927 Ford sedan, was a drastic departure from the typical architecture of the 1920's. The Dymaxion house, coined from "dynamic" and "maximum" to signify the "maximum gain of advantage from minimum

FULLER, R. BUCKMINSTER—*Continued*

energy output," represented Fuller's desire to build more efficiently along modern industrial lines with lighter, stronger materials.

The Dymaxion Corporation was founded by R. Buckminster Fuller in 1932 to produce and market his revolutionary inventions. As director and chief engineer, he was responsible for introducing a die-stamped bathroom unit which could be assembled in minutes. From 1932 to 1935 he manufactured the Dymaxion car, a three-wheeled auto that could attain a speed of 120 miles per hour, travel forty miles on a gallon of gasoline, cross open country like a jeep, and turn in its own length. He designed the Dymaxion steel igloo in 1940, and received a patent for the Dymaxion world map showing "all the continents without any visible distortion." The Wichita house, which Fuller built in 1946 entirely with airplane construction techniques, was a circular aluminum seven-room dwelling providing "spaciousness, portability and luxury living" for $6,400.

Despite public enthusiasm for Fuller's designs, commercial sponsors were indifferent, and in 1935 the Dymaxion Company was dissolved. Fuller was assistant to the director of research and development at the Phelps Dodge Corporation from 1936 to 1938. He re-established Dymaxion in 1941 but was forced to suspend production when the United States entered World War II. From 1942 to 1944 he served with the Board of Economic Warfare and as special assistant to the director of the Foreign Economic Administration. The Dymaxion Dwelling Machines Company was reorganized in 1944 and ten years later, Geodesics, Inc., and Synergetics, Inc., were founded.

Though the geodesic dome has become popular only recently, Fuller has claimed that it has been in constant evolution since 1917. In that year Fuller invented his system of "energetic synergetic geometry," an ingenious mathematical formula that closely resembles spherical trigonometry; it describes "the lines of force that occur in atoms, molecules, and crystals." He recognized that the tensile strength (resistance to pull) of building materials had changed markedly with the introduction of modern metal alloys while the compressive strength (resistance to being squeezed together) of materials had remained the same. Fuller "designed structures in which tension struts of high-strength alloy pulled against compression members—the way taut guy wires pull against the mast of a sailboat. . . . The result was enormous strength with minimum quantities of materials." He began to copy nature's own forms, especially the diamond, and his domes "consisted of a lattice arrangement of points in the shape of a tetrahedron (a pyramid with three sides plus its base). . . . A pressure applied to any part of a dome's surface was dissipated among the compression and tension struts of adjacent tetrahedrons, and the tetrahedrons adjacent to those" (New York *Times*, August 23, 1959).

Fuller's commercial acceptance was assured when he completed a geodesic dome for the Ford plant in Dearborn in 1953. Plastic and fiber-glass radomes dot the arctic Distant Early Warning Line; light enough to be flown in by airplane, they can be assembled in a few hours and can withstand winds of 125 miles per hour. His domes have been used by the United States Marine Corps, which cited Fuller in 1954 for providing "the first basic improvement in mobile military shelter in 2,600 years." The Union Tank Car Company dome is the largest clear-span building ever constructed, with a diameter of 384 feet and no inside posts. Fuller's domes have been used for restaurants, theaters, and community centers, and by the United States government for trade fairs and exhibitions.

Fuller calls his new designs "tensegrity sphere—for 'tensional integrity'—a system that makes them proof against internal and external pressure" (*Newsweek*, July 13, 1959). By utilizing tensile power, reported a New York *Times* writer (September 27, 1959), the sphere "has unprecedented strength; its rigidity increases, rather than weakens, as it grows larger . . . reversing the history of architecture, which has been a struggle against the strength limitations of buildings of increasing size." Fuller plans to change the architectural horizon with these structures, using them for space islands as launching platforms for missiles or underwater as bases for submarines, drilling equipment, or oceanographic surveys.

An enormously successful teacher and lecturer, Fuller has been associated with the architectural departments of leading American universities, including Cornell, Yale, Princeton, and Massachusetts Institute of Technology. In 1959 he was appointed to a professorship with life tenure at Southern Illinois University. Fuller is the author of *Nine Chains to the Moon* (J.B. Lippincott, 1938), and he served as technical editor of *Fortune* from 1938 to 1940. He is a Fellow of the American Association for the Advancement of Science, a member of the Harvard Engineering Society, and an honorary member of Alpha Chi Rho and the American Institute of Architects, whose New York chapter honored him in 1952. The Gran Premo Triennale of Milano was awarded to Fuller in 1954, and his works have been shown at the Metropolitan Museum of Art and the Museum of Modern Art (New York).

"Bucky" Fuller was described by Robert W. Marks as "an intense stocky man with crew-cut white hair and serious eyes that gaze fixedly from behind heavy tortoise-shell glasses" (New York *Times*, August 23, 1959). He was married to Anne Hewlett on July 12, 1917 and had two daughters, Alexandra, who died in childhood, and Allegra. Until the 1950's, when he was accepted by the engineering and architectural worlds, the couple lived precariously, with "scarcely enough money in the house for a bowl of soup." All fees and his own and his wife's inheritances were used to further his experiments. His habits, which have been pared down to the basic necessities, do not include smoking or drinking. He is generally oblivious to his surroundings, and his home, which consists of a three-room apartment, is simply a point of departure for a lecture tour or trip abroad. He prefers to be the independent "American maverick, keeping himself unlabeled and free from commitments that are exclusively money-making" (New York *Times,* August 23, 1959).

References

Bsns W p112+ My 10 '58
N Y Times Mag p14 Ag 23 '59 por
Newsweek 54:84 Jl 13 '59 por
Marks, Robert W. The Dymaxion World of Buckminster Fuller (1960)
Who's Who in America, 1958-59

FUNK, WALTHER (IMMANUEL) Aug. 18, 1890-May 31, 1960 Former German Minister of Economics (1938-45); was president of the Reichsbank (1939-45); convicted as a war criminal by the International Military Tribunal in Nuremberg, Germany (1946); author. See *Current Biography* (October) 1940.

Obituary

N Y Times p23 Je 4 '60

GALVIN, ROBERT W(ILLIAM) Oct. 9, 1922- Manufacturing executive

Address: b. Motorola, Inc., 4545 W. Augusta Blvd., Chicago 51, Ill.; h. 9519 Monticello Ave., Skokie, Ill.

One of Chicago's energetic and optimistic young business leaders, Robert W. Galvin, has been president of Motorola, Inc., since 1956. Now known as "the world's largest exclusive electronics manufacturer," Motorola grew out of a small firm established in 1928. Robert Galvin's father, Paul V. Galvin, a co-founder of the company, was its chief executive officer as chairman of the board at the time of his death in 1959. From 1940 Robert Galvin had worked closely with his father to help guide the wartime and postwar expansion of Motorola, which currently has annual sales of more than $200,000,-000 in radio and television sets, phonographs, two-way communications equipment, military electronics, and other products.

The only child of Paul Vincent and Lillian (Guinan) Galvin, Robert William Galvin was born October 9, 1922 in Marshfield, Wisconsin. He received most of his grammar school education in Chicago, Illinois, where in 1928 his father and his uncle Joseph Galvin established the small battery eliminator manufacturing business which developed into Motorola, Inc. "I grew up about like other kids in the neighborhood," Robert Galvin told an interviewer in 1955. "I never had a newspaper route, or worked outside for pay, but I wasn't given any special concessions at home."

His father's success in developing his company gave Robert what he has called a "definite gravitation toward responsibility." The family moved from Chicago to suburban Evanston, Illinois when he was in the seventh grade. At a new school in Evanston he worked hard at public speaking, was elected president of his class, and took part in debating and dramatics. (Years later, in the early 1950's he handled the

Shelburne Studios

ROBERT W. GALVIN

commercial announcements so skillfully for a television program sponsored by Motorola that some viewers believed him to be a professional actor.) After high school he attended the University of Chicago and the University of Notre Dame.

Early in 1929 the Galvin Manufacturing Company had gone into the making of radio chassis as well as battery eliminators. Looking for a new market during the depression, Paul Galvin turned his attention to developing an automobile radio which would sell for about $100. He named the radio Motorola. Although it continues to be the largest manufacturer of automobile radios, since 1937 the company has also been producing conventional radios.

A few years before World War II the Galvin company extended its production to mobile communications. For some time it manufactured special receiving sets for police departments and gradually developed a revolutionary mobile radio transmitter. At the Wisconsin National Guard maneuvers in 1939 this transmitter attracted the notice of the Army Signal Corps. As a result, the company made a portable unit called the Handie-Talkie for the Army and later, with Daniel E. Noble in charge of research, evolved the SCR300 FM Walkie-Talkie, which it supplied in mass quantities for use in World War II. Also for the armed services during the war the company produced radar equipment. According to *Fortune* (August 1954), "At the peak—in 1944—Motorola was producing more than $80 million of military equipment a year; its biggest total volume prewar had been less than $17 million."

Robert W. Galvin went to work for the family enterprise in 1940, starting as an apprentice in the stock room, and, except for a period of wartime service in the Army Signal Corps, he has been with Motorola ever since. During the first several years he held a variety

GALVIN, ROBERT W.—*Continued*

of jobs in almost every department of the factory, before gaining experience in engineering, sales, and administrative operations.

The Galvin company was self-financed and almost entirely family-owned until 1943. Then, because of the need to pay a large inheritance tax, after the death of Mrs. Paul Galvin in 1942, some 40,000 shares were sold to the public. Joseph Galvin, who had charge of production, credit, and labor relations, died in 1944; and Paul Galvin began to move his son rapidly into positions of increasing responsibility.

Having been made a director of the company in 1945, Robert Galvin had a voice in its decisions in 1946 when, as a result of the ending of the company's military business, its sales dropped sharply to $23,000,000. Price restrictions hampered immediate rebuilding of the market for car and home radios, and Paul Galvin therefore decided to concentrate on television. He also reorganized the company, which since 1946 has had the name Motorola, Inc. As the manufacturer of the first workable television set costing less than $200, in 1947 Motorola increased its sales to $47,000,000; and in 1948, after acquiring car-radio contracts, it could report sales of $62,000,000. The following year Motorola invaded the luxury television field.

In 1949 Robert Galvin was advanced to executive vice-president of Motorola. After the Korean war broke out in 1950, the company's government business boomed again, and sales that year shot up to $177,000,000. Early in 1952 Motorola established a separate national defense division headquarters in Chicago. It manufactured more mobile radio equipment than Radio Corporation of America, General Electric, Westinghouse, and International Telephone & Telegraph combined, and also led in the production of microwave-relay communications systems.

When he was elected president of Motorola, Inc., on November 15, 1956, Robert Galvin took over day-by-day direction of the corporation's enterprises from his father, who moved up to chairman of the board and continued as chief executive officer until his death in November 1959. The Galvins, father and son, controlled about 25 per cent of the stock of Motorola, whose sales reached $227,562,000 in 1956. Robert Galvin suggested in 1959 that sales for that year could possibly rise to $250,000,000.

In discussing the growth of Motorola, Galvin has stressed the importance of diversity. The company prepared its Phoenix, Arizona plant for volume production of transistors in 1955 and a few years later announced that it expected to market in 1960 the first "truly portable" television set at a moderate price. Motorola has also entered the field of guided missile design and of stereophonic equipment. In August 1959 it acquired control of the Dahlberg Company of Minneapolis, makers of hearing aids and special communications systems for hospitals.

Since the growth of a company requires delegation of authority and the development of a team structure, Galvin also attaches much im-portance to industrial human relations. Motorola has had a profit-sharing plan since 1947, and Galvin belongs to the Council of Profit-Sharing Industries, at whose annual conference in Chicago in 1959 he delivered the keynote address.

One of Galvin's close friends is Chicago industrialist Charles H. Percy, president of Bell & Howell Company, with whom he shares an interest in Republican politics and civic activities. Galvin is a trustee of the Illinois Institute of Technology, a member of the executive committee of the Armour Research Foundation, a vice-president of Junior Achievement of Chicago, and a director of the Harris Bank and Trust Company.

Tall and vigorous Galvin, whose hair is graying prematurely, enjoys what he calls "strenuous athletics" and has been an enthusiastic badminton, squash tennis, and golf player as well as a water skier. He has also played second baseman for the Kamikazees, a neighborhood baseball team that he helped to organize in Evanston in 1952. More recently he has learned to fly his own helicopter. Galvin and Mary Barnes were married in 1944. They have four children—Gale, Dawn, Chris, and Michael—and have bought a farm so that they and their children can acquire an interest in nature and outdoor activities like hunting and fishing.

References

Flying 64:33+ F '59 por
Forbes 76:31+ O 1 '55 por
Fortune 50:102+ Ag '54 por
N Y Herald Tribune II p6 D 15 '55 por
Elliott, Osborn Men at the Top (1959)
Poor's Register of Directors and Executives, 1959
Who's Who in America, 1958-59
Who's Who in Commerce and Industry (1959)

GAULLE, CHARLES (ANDRÉ JOSEPH MARIE) DE (gōl dĕ) Nov. 22, 1890-

President of the French Republic and French Community

Address: Palais de L'Élysée, Paris 8e, France; "La Boisserie," Colombey-les-deux-Églises, Haute-Marne, France

NOTE: This biography supersedes the articles which appeared in *Current Biography* in 1940 and 1949.

The restoration of French grandeur is the aim of General Charles de Gaulle, who in 1959 became President of the Fifth Republic and of the French Community. A year earlier he had been summoned to lead his country as Premier during a period of crisis. After almost two years, the authority and vision of de Gaulle have enhanced the prestige of his country abroad and restored economic equilibrium at home. The Free French leader of World War II withstood a serious threat to his regime when he quelled a revolt of Algerian colonists in January 1960. On February 13, 1960 he saw his country join the nuclear club to which the United States, Great Britain, and the Soviet Union already belonged, when the French exploded a nuclear bomb in the Sahara Desert.

Charles André Joseph Marie de Gaulle was born in Lille, France on November 22, 1890, the second of the five children of Henri and Jeanne (Maillot-Delannoy) de Gaulle. He had three brothers and a sister. He spent much of his youth in Paris, where his father had become a professor of philosophy and literature in a Jesuit school. After attending a secondary school in Paris and after completing his required military service, de Gaulle entered Saint-Cyr, the French military school, where he became an honor student.

In 1911 de Gaulle was graduated from Saint-Cyr and received a commission as a second lieutenant. He served in the Thirty-third Infantry Regiment, commanded by Colonel Henri Pétain. During World War I he was wounded at Dinant (1914), at Champagne (1915), and at Douaumont (1916); in the latter battle he was wounded so severely that he became a prisoner of the Germans. After his repatriation, he became a commandant, served with the French Army in Poland, and taught military history at Saint-Cyr for a year.

Upon his return to Paris, he attended the École Supérieure de Guerre (War College). During annual maneuvers he ran counter to current principles of French military science by using mobile tactics and, as a result, was demoted. When Pétain, who was then commander in chief and a marshal of the French Army, heard of the episode, he reinstated de Gaulle at the War College as an instructor and also appointed him to his own staff.

Later, in 1927, de Gaulle was assigned to the general staff of the Army of the Rhine and was made commander of the Nineteenth Battalion of the Chasseurs à Pied. During the years between 1929 and 1932 he headed French military missions in Egypt, Syria, Iraq, and Persia. When he returned to France, he became Secretary-General of the High Council of National Defense and was promoted to the rank of lieutenant colonel.

De Gaulle's book, *Vers l'armée de métier,* appeared in 1934. (It was published in the United States by Lippincott in 1941, under the title, *The Army of the Future.*) In it he attacked the French strategy based on the impregnability of the Maginot Line, forecast the blitzkrieg method of warfare, and proposed a plan for using armored columns. Although his ideas were not accepted by the French General Staff, de Gaulle and Paul Reynaud worked together for the next five years to develop an adequate mechanized force (particularly tanks)—for France. By the time of the German invasion, however, France had only three light mechanized and four heavily armored divisions. The validity of de Gaulle's thesis was established when German mechanized troops overran France in May and June of 1940.

French Embassy Press & Inf. Div.

CHARLES DE GAULLE

Promoted to brigadier general and placed in command of the remaining mechanized forces, de Gaulle held the Germans at Laon and Abbeville. In June 1940 he was named Under Secretary of National Defense and War by Premier Reynaud and went to London for conferences with Prime Minister Winston Churchill. He returned to France on June 15, 1940, but refused to accept the truce which the new Premier, Henri Pétain, had signed with the Germans.

Back in London, de Gaulle announced the formation of a French National Committee which would function as France's *de jure* government. He was made President. *In absentia,* he was tried by a French court-martial and condemned to death for treason. The British government, however, recognized de Gaulle as commander of the Free French Army, which was subject only to the British High Command.

De Gaulle led an abortive naval landing at the African port of Dakar in September 1941. He was named president of the Free French National Council, which received the co-operation of the Resistance groups in France. After the reconciliation between de Gaulle and General Henri Honoré Giraud at the Casablanca Conference in 1943, the two worked together to establish the French Committee of National Liberation in Algiers. Friction between the co-presidents led de Gaulle to become the sole president of Free French operations. A month after the Provisional Government of the French Republic was established in May 1944, its President, Charles de Gaulle, returned to London and awaited the Normandy invasion.

On August 24, 1944 he made a triumphal entry into Paris. During the travail of the early postwar years, from September to Janu-

GAULLE, CHARLES DE—*Continued*

ary 1946, de Gaulle headed the Provisional Government of France. In the debates over a new constitution for France, he proposed a strong presidency to balance the powers of the legislature, as distinct from the traditional system of an all-powerful legislature. Facing increased hostility to his views about the constitution, de Gaulle resigned on January 6, 1946. The French people on October 13, 1946 adopted a constitution for the Fourth Republic which maintained the traditional system.

In the following year de Gaulle called for a rally of French citizens to work toward reforming the state within the legal framework of the French constitution. The Rassemblement du Peuple Français (RPF), formed at Strasbourg in April 1947, named de Gaulle as its leader. The RPF did not regard itself as a political party, but as a rally open to all citizens, who were not required to forsake their party affiliations. In the 1947 municipal elections the RPF emerged as France's most popular party, with 40 per cent of the vote, and a number of its candidates were elected to office. De Gaulle remained the president of RPF until 1953, when the party suffered a 15 per cent loss of votes as compared to the 1947 results.

The Fourth Republic lasted for over a decade. The weaknesses of its constitution, which de Gaulle had foreseen, had led to many cabinet crises and had brought the nation close to bankruptcy and civil war. In May 1958, after eleven years of relative retirement, de Gaulle was asked by President René Coty to form a government. As Premier from June 1958 to January 1959, de Gaulle promulgated a new constitution, subordinating the legislature to a strong president, which was adopted by 78 per cent of the French voters on September 28, 1958. Elected to serve a seven-year term as president of the Fifth Republic on December 21, 1958, de Gaulle took office the following January.

As perhaps the first French leader since World War II with enough power and security of tenure to carry a program through to its conclusion, de Gaulle has been able to deal forcefully with problems both at home and abroad. He has re-established the economic stability of France, which now has a sound currency and a favorable balance of trade; he has awakened confidence on the part of businessmen. His financial reforms have included a devaluation of the franc, an almost balanced budget, reduction of certain social services, and elimination of certain subsidies to industry and agriculture.

In foreign affairs de Gaulle has sought to increase the prestige and power of France. Toward this end France exploded its first atomic device on February 13, 1959 as part of its plan to become an atomic power. Over issues concerning NATO, France's relations with her allies have become strained. De Gaulle has refused to allow intercontinental ballistic missiles to be placed in France and has withdrawn the French contingent from

NATO's Mediterranean fleet. His posture has caused difficulties with Great Britain and the United States over a common policy for negotiations with the Soviet Union; he was successful in delaying a summit conference until the spring of 1960. (When the conference was finally held in May, it collapsed within two days.)

De Gaulle's solution to some of France's colonial problems was the French Community, formed in 1958 when twelve French African territories approved the new constitution and voted to become autonomous republics of the Community. One territory, Guinea, rejected the constitution and automatically gained complete independence. Although the states of the Community have internal autonomy, their foreign affairs, defense, finance, and certain other matters are determined by their executive council. While some of these republics want fuller autonomy, with membership in the United Nations and responsibility for their own foreign policies, they also want to remain in the Community in order to continue receiving economic aid from France. De Gaulle is apparently beginning to feel that this may be possible.

Algeria remains an unsettled problem. De Gaulle has implemented the Constantine Plan to raise the natives' living standard and the Challe Plan to deal with the five-year-old Moslem rebellion. On September 16, 1959 he promised to give Algeria the right to self-determination after a cease-fire. Increased fear about Algerian independence caused the colons (French settlers) to rebel in January 1960 and some French troops serving in Algeria supported them.

On January 29 de Gaulle said that he would not renounce his decision about Algerian self-determination, and he ordered the Army to restore order in Algeria. Army discipline was immediately effected, and the insurgents surrendered. De Gaulle's position was strengthened when, on February 3, the National Assembly and the Senate granted the government special powers to rule by decree for one year.

His critics at home and abroad fear de Gaulle's tremendous reduction in the power of the legislature, his inability so far to encourage the development of middle-of-the-road political parties between the extreme right and the extreme left, and the problem of succession in the Fifth Republic, whose constitution was written so obviously for the man who became the President.

Among de Gaulle's other books are *La discorde chez l'ennemi* (1924); *Le fil de l'épée* (Berger-Levrault, 1932); and *La France et son armée* (Plon, 1938). Collections of his speeches and his three volumes of memoirs are available in both French and English. He has been awarded military decorations by his own country and has been honored by other nations.

De Gaulle was married to Yvonne Charlotte Anne-Marie Vendroux in April 1921 in Calais, France. They had three children: Philippe (a naval officer), Elisabeth (Madame Alain de Boissieu), and Anne (deceased). The French

President, who is six feet four inches tall, has blue eyes and brown hair. He is known for his austerity and aloofness and for his slow and deliberate speech. For recreation he enjoys walking and reading biography and history.

References

Holiday 27:62+ F; 80+ Mr '60 pors
Brogan, D. W. French Personalities and Problems (1947)
Dictionnaire Biographique Français Contemporain (1954)
Funk, A. L. Charles de Gaulle: The Crucial Years, 1943-1944 (1959)
Garas, F. Charles de Gaulle seul contre les pouvoirs (1957)
Who's Who in France, 1959-60

GAUSS, CLARENCE E(DWARD) Jan. 12, 1887-Apr. 8, 1960 Career diplomat; United States Ambassador to China (1941-44); director of Export-Import Bank of Washington. See *Current Biography* (January) 1941.

Obituary

N Y Times p33 Ap 9 '60

GEIS, BERNARD (J.) Aug. 30, 1909- Publisher; editor
Address: b. 130 E. 56th St., New York 22; h. 2 Sutton Pl. S., New York 22

Less than five months after the new publishing house of Bernard Geis Associates published its 'first book in August 1959, Bernard Geis, its editor and director, announced that the firm had ended its first season with a substantial profit, and that all of its titles had appeared at various times on lists of best sellers. Geis attributes this spectacular success to a sales promotion that makes full use of the mass media—a departure from the conservative advertising policies traditional in book publishing. Much of the promotion was provided informally by partners of the firm, the majority of whom are prominent in television and magazine publishing. Before he organized Bernard Geis Associates, Geis worked as an editor at Prentice-Hall, Inc. He arrived there by way of Grosset & Dunlap, Inc., where he had been editor in chief and vice-president.

Bernard J. Geis was born in Chicago, Illinois on August 30, 1909, the youngest of three sons of Harry M. and Bessie (Gesas) Geis. His father was a cigar manufacturer. One brother, Edward, is a clothing merchant; the other, Lester, is an architect. Bernard lived in Lima, Ohio, until he was halfway through high school, then moved with his family to Evanston, Illinois. At Evanston Township High School he played on the lightweight basketball team and the third team of the football squad. He was also associate editor of the school newspaper. In 1927 he was graduated from Evanston Township High School and was admitted to Northwestern University.

Walter Daran

BERNARD GEIS

As an undergraduate student at Northwestern, Geis was night editor of the *Daily Northwestern* and editor of the *"N" Book*. On weekends he worked as the North Shore correspondent of the Chicago *Herald-Examiner*. He received scholastic scholarships in his junior and senior years and was elected to several student boards. He was graduated from Northwestern with a B.A. degree in 1931, having majored in English.

After graduation, Geis worked for a year with an advertising agency. "This," he says, "inspired me to seek another career." He wrote for a time for newspapers and magazines on a free-lance basis, then joined the staff of a men's clothing trade magazine, *Apparel Arts,* in January 1933. Late that year he became its editor. In 1935 he became an assistant editor of *Esquire,* and in 1939 he became editor in chief of *Coronet,* retaining his editorial position with *Esquire.*

During the fall of 1943 and the spring of 1944 Geis was stationed in London as a war correspondent for both magazines. Back in New York, he continued to edit *Coronet* and *Esquire* until January 1945, when he left to become editor in chief at the publishing house of Grosset & Dunlap, Inc. Geis was also a vice-president of this company from 1949 to 1953. For the next three years Geis worked as editorial director of MTB, the publisher of Magic Talking Books, which he had invented. These were illustrated children's books, accompanied by records related to the text. From 1956 to 1958 Geis was an editor at Prentice-Hall, Inc., specializing in sports books.

One March evening in 1957 when Geis returned home from Prentice-Hall, his wife told him that she had just watched Art Linkletter talking to youngsters on television. She was convinced that Linkletter could write a good book about the things that children told

GEIS, BERNARD—*Continued*

him. Geis passed the suggestion on to Link-letter, who said that he had been thinking the same thing. That October Linkletter's *Kids Say the Darndest Things!* was published by Prentice-Hall, Inc.

Linkletter casually mentioned his book from time to time on his two television shows. The hard-cover edition sold 150,000 copies the first year and 250,000 the second, and the paperback edition has sold more than 2,000,000 copies. According to Everett C. Martin of the *Wall Street Journal* (July 16, 1959), "this is big business in the publishing industry where it is estimated that less than 5 per cent of the fiction and nonfiction published during a year sells more than 5,000 copies of each book." Geis resigned from Prentice-Hall in 1958 to become director of a publishing firm that would use this kind of promotion to sell books.

Bernard Geis Associates, which publishes under the imprint of Star Press Books, was organized in October 1958. The owners, who, except for Geis, are newcomers to book publishing are: Groucho Marx, Art Linkletter, Jack Bailey, and Ralph Edwards, television personalities; Mark Goodson, William Todman, and John Guedel, television producers; Esquire, Inc., publishers of *Esquire* and *Coronet* magazines, and Cowles Magazines, Inc., publishers of *Look;* Ralph E. Schneider, chairman, and Alfred Bloomingdale, president, of the Diners' Club; a lawyer, Jacques Leslie; and Bernard Geis. Random House handles the distribution of the firm's books.

Bernard Geis Associates has tried to develop a new concept of book publishing and merchandising: to select, edit, and promote books through all mass media so that maximum sales are achieved with a minimum number of titles. The firm's success has been attributed to the practice of some of its co-owners of "plugging" books on television, i.e., giving titles free publicity on their programs. A writer for *Barron's* (January 25, 1960) observed: "One highly successful publishing enterprise, Bernard Geis Associates, was formed by a group of TV performers, including Art Linkletter and Groucho Marx, who push each other's literary works on their programs." Indeed, when the Columbia Broadcasting System announced in December 1959 that no television program on its network was to carry "plugs" for any products except those being paid for by the shows' sponsors, a *Publishers' Weekly* (December 14, 1959) writer said: "One's first thought in this connection is of Bernard Geis Associates."

Geis has said that his associates reach more than 50,000,000 people every week, but he insists that the TV promotion is only a part of what his firm does to sell books. "Most publishing firms have been a bit stodgy about promotion," he has explained (Cleveland *Plain Dealer*, January 24, 1960). "We try to give a book widespread national promotion." Geis also notes that since his firm publishes only a few books a year, a more intensive creative and promotional job can be done on each individual book.

The first title published by Bernard Geis Associates was a novel by Max Shulman called *I Was a Teen-Age Dwarf*. It was issued in August 1959. Next came *Groucho and Me* by Groucho Marx; *The Secret World of Kids* by Art Linkletter; *Dear Teen-Ager* by Abigail Van Buren; and *My Eyes Are in My Heart* by Ted Husing with Cy Rice. One reason why nonfiction outnumbers fiction on the first Geis list may be that hard-cover fiction tends to lose money for the publisher, and Bernard Geis Associates does not intend to enter the field of paperbacks. Geis has explained that "nonfiction is easier to edit, too; we can direct an author to write what we want. That's something we can't do with fiction."

The list of publications for spring 1960 of Bernard Geis Associates consists of five nonfiction titles: Harry S. Truman's *Mr. Citizen,* in which he discusses his life since leaving the White House; Steve Allen's *The Question Man,* a book of pictures with captions; H. Allen Smith's *Let the Crab-Grass Grow,* a satirical look at life in the suburbs; Dr. George Gallup and Evan Hill's *The Secrets of Long Life,* in which American nonagenarians communicate their formulas for longevity; and *Burn This!,* a cartoon book based on the greeting cards of Bill Box.

On March 28, 1940 Bernard J. Geis was married to Darlene Stern, a writer of books for children and young people. They have two sons, Peter and Stephen. Geis is five feet ten inches tall and has black hair and blue eyes. He is Jewish in religion and maintains political ties with the Liberal party. He is a member of the New York Grand Jury Association. In his opinion, "Anything that can be done, short of using a knout, to drive more people into bookshops renders this nation a service and gives aid and comfort to booksellers, authors, and publishers."

References

N Y Times p81 Mr 22 '59
Who's Who in the East (1957)

GOULD, GLENN (HERBERT) Sept. 25, 1932- Pianist; composer
Address: h. 32 Southwood Dr., Toronto 8, Ont., Canada

Although much of the publicity about Glenn Gould has centered upon his idiosyncratic, extra-musical characteristics, critics and audiences have been quick to praise the genuine gifts of the young Canadian pianist and composer. So many feature articles have pointed out that Gould wears gloves, scarves, and overcoats in the summer for fear of catching cold, and that he soaks his hands in hot water for twenty minutes before beginning a piano recital or recording session that they have diverted attention from the undisputed fact that Glenn Gould, with his musicianship and dedicated approach, belongs in the front rank of concert pianists today. After having conducted a performance of Beethoven's Second Piano Concerto, in which

Glenn Gould was the featured pianist, Leonard Bernstein remarked: "He gives me a whole new interest in music."

Born in Toronto, Ontario, on September 25, 1932, Glenn Herbert Gould is the son of the Toronto furrier, Russell Herbert Gould, and Florence (Greig) Gould, an amateur pianist, who taught him to read music at the age of three. He was educated in Toronto, first at the Williamson Road Public School and later at the Malvern Collegiate Institute, where his senior matriculation took place in 1952.

From 1943 to 1952, Glenn Gould was also enrolled at Toronto's Royal Conservatory of Music, where he studied piano under the Chilean-born Alberto Guerrero, organ under Frederick Silvester, and composition under Leo Smith. By the time Glenn was twelve, when he received the degree of Associate at the conservatory, he was widely regarded as one of the most promising pianistic prodigies on the North American continent. Since leaving the conservatory, he has been largely self-taught, in a continuing attempt to evolve and to perfect his own styles of performing and composition.

While still in school, Glenn Gould made his professional debut as a pianist with the Toronto Symphony Orchestra under Sir Ernest MacMillan on January 14, 1957, playing Beethoven's Fourth Piano Concerto. On January 1, 1955, he played his first recital in the United States in Washington, D. C., and on January 12 of the same year made his New York debut at Town Hall. Both events were highly acclaimed.

A favorite in his own country, Glenn Gould has also made concert tours of the United States since 1956. In the spring of 1957 he enjoyed his first contact with European audiences. He concertized in Moscow and Leningrad as the first North American pianist to be invited by the government of the Soviet Union to perform in that country, and appeared, on his return trip to Canada, with the Berlin Philharmonic under Herbert von Karajan and at the Vienna International Music Festival.

Glenn Gould's eccentric behavior on the concert platform provides a bizarre contrast to his purely musical approach. Slouching in a specially constructed low chair, he sometimes provides a vocal and gestural counterpoint to the emotions of the pieces in question, at the same time performing the music with notable clarity and restraint. Disturbed by the spectacle of Gould's uninhibited responses, some listeners find him most satisfactory in recordings. They will not then be disturbed by the sight of the piano propped up on blocks and the lowered chair; the muffler, sweater, and heavy jacket in which Gould is usually swaddled against the ominous draughts of the concert hall; nor will they be distracted by the sound of his humming or his occasional outcries of ecstasy. Nevertheless, these oddities, along with the ever-present Oriental rug under his feet, the portable electric heater nearby, and the bottle of Poland Water, have become trademarks of which press agents have not failed to take advantage.

Several recordings by Glenn Gould have been released by Columbia Records. The first, a performance of Bach's long and intricate *Goldberg*

Columbia Records

GLENN GOULD

Variations, recorded in June 1955 and released in January of the following year, enjoyed a popular success unusual for music of such a cerebral character and challenged the late Wanda Landowska's long-standing authority in her recording of the same work for RCA Victor. Glenn Gould has gone on to record for Columbia Records works by Beethoven, Bach, Haydn, Mozart, Berg, Schönberg, and Křenek. Although he has generally received excellent notices for his recordings, Gould aroused the ire of some music critics with his interpretations of Beethoven's Sonatas of Opus 109, Opus 110, and Opus 111, works sometimes regarded as the private preserve of the late Artur Schnabel.

Broadcasting is another medium in which Glenn Gould has achieved fame. A frequent attraction on radio programs of the Canadian Broadcasting Corporation, he became the first concert pianist to appear on the CBS television outlet, and was recently featured in two half-hour CBS television episodes describing his career. His debut on American television took place on January 31, 1960, on the CBS show *Leonard Bernstein and the New York Philharmonic.*

Despite his success as a pianist, Glenn Gould insists that his first love is composing, to which he hopes to devote himself entirely some day. A shoulder injury sustained in December 1959 eventually forced him to cancel his remaining engagements for the 1959-60 season, and led him to consider a permanent retreat from live performing: "I have been announcing my retirement every year since I was 15," the Toronto *Globe and Mail* quoted him as saying. "This time I might just carry it off" (April 21, 1960).

The first published composition by Glenn Gould, a string quartet, was commissioned by CBS and was first performed on that network. On July 9, 1956 the work was played at the Second Annual Music Festival at Stratford,

GOULD, GLENN—*Continued*

Ontario; on the same program Glenn Gould performed works of Berg and Křenek on the piano and conducted Schönberg's Ode to Napoleon. Gould's quartet was later given its United States première by four members of the Cleveland Orchestra, who have also recorded the piece for release by Columbia Records in the fall of 1960.

As a composer, Glenn Gould is more influenced by the lush post-Romantic music of the later nineteenth century than by the leaner, more intellectual styles he usually selects for his piano recitals. Joseph Roddy in the *New Yorker* (May 14, 1960) quotes Gould as saying "It seems that I perform in the eighteenth and twentieth centuries and compose in the nineteenth. That must be just jammed with psychoanalytic significance, but I have never paid to find out what it means."

Gould's scholarly interest in the literature and history of music has led him to write extensive program notes for many of his own recordings. His analyses of Beethoven's last piano sonatas, for example, end with the following sentences written in his typically effusive rococo prose style: "These sonatas are a brief but an idyllic stopover in the itinerary of an intrepid voyageur. Perhaps they do not yield the apocalyptic disclosures that have been so graphically ascribed to them. Music is a malleable art, acquiescent and philosophically flexible, and it is no great task to mold it to one's want—but when, as in the works before us now, it transports us to a realm of such beatific felicity, it is the happier diversion not to try."

Although he was once interested in the art of orchestral conducting, Gould has given up the podium because of the physical strain involved in managing a symphonic group. He has to his credit, however, conducting engagements with orchestras in Toronto and Vancouver, as well as the Stratford appearance mentioned above.

A bachelor, Glenn Gould lives in Toronto but spends much of his time ninety miles to the north in his summer cottage retreat at Lake Simcoe, where he can devote himself entirely to his music and where he can go boating on his motorboat that he has named after Arnold Schönberg, one of his idolatries. In the district he has become something of a local celebrity—so much so that his favorite Chinese restaurant now stocks Poland Water for his convenience. Gould has a deep interest in world literature. He favors the nineteenth- and twentieth-century masters of central and eastern Europe, and once planned an opera based upon Kafka's short story "Metamorphosis."

Described by Jay Harrison in the *Reporter* (July 11, 1957) as "a slim, blond-haired young man with sensitive but not weak features," Gould attributes his hypochondriacal dependence upon pills, heavy clothing, and electric heaters, not to a desire to be thought eccentric but rather to a fear of illness. "I have a horror of catching colds," Gould told Harrison in the New York *Herald Tribune* (February 8, 1959), "an absolute horror." He then went on to say: "That's why I don't go to concerts. The halls are always filled with moving air, with drafts.

Besides, concerts unnerve me. I don't like to listen to music with thousands of people around. I'm narcissistic about hearing music—I like to do it alone, on a phonograph, so I can think."

References

New Yorker 36:51+ My 14 '60
Sat Eve Post 231:38 Ap 3 '59 por

Canadian Who's Who, 1955-57
Twentieth Century Musicians, First Supplement (1957) por
Who's Who in America, 1960-61

GRACE, EUGENE GIFFORD Aug. 27, 1876-July 25, 1960 President (1916-57) and chairman of the board (1945-57) of Bethlehem Steel Corporation. See *Current Biography* (April) 1941.

Obituary

NY Times p29 Jl 26 '60

GRACE, J(OSEPH) PETER, (JR.) May 25, 1913- Business executive
Address: b. W. R. Grace & Co., 7 Hanover Sq., New York 4; h. 41 Shelter Rock Rd., Manhasset, N.Y.

Representing the third generation of his family to hold the presidency of W. R. Grace & Co., J. Peter Grace assumed command in 1945 of the century-old shipping and trading company which his grandfather had established as a ship chandlery in Peru. Under J. Peter Grace's direction, the company, long known as "the old lady of Hanover Square," has been transformed into a diversified industrial complex which includes more than forty chemical plants in the United States and abroad. The company's numerous subsidiaries and affiliates are chiefly concerned also with air and ocean transportation, trading, banking, insurance, and advertising, as well as with many agricultural and manufacturing enterprises in Latin America.

Joseph Peter Grace, Jr., was born on May 25, 1913 in Manhasset, Long Island, New York, the son of Janet (Macdonald) and Joseph Peter Grace. He has two brothers, Michael and Charles, and one sister, Maureen. His paternal grandfather, William Russell Grace, founded W. R. Grace & Co., in Peru after voyaging from Ireland in 1846 to escape the potato famine.

"My grandfather learned to love Peru," J. Peter Grace related in an address before the Newcomen Society in 1953. "He made the Spanish tongue his own. His energy and application brought him forward speedily and by 1854 he was a full partner in [Bryce & Co., a ship supplier], which later became Bryce, Grace & Co." In 1865 he moved to New York City and gradually built up a triangular trade and shipping business between South America, Europe, and the United States.

When W. R. Grace died in 1904, his son, Joseph Peter Grace, became president of Grace & Co. He followed many of the practices and the techniques of expansion, diversification, and integration in which his father had pioneered. He continued to enter new businesses in South America, frequently in partnership with local investors, and also developed the famed *Santa* fleet of the Grace Line.

The company's "heir apparent," J. Peter Grace, meanwhile studied from 1927 to 1932 at St. Paul's School in Concord, New Hampshire and then attended Yale University, from which he received the B.A. degree in 1936. The year of his graduation he began his long career in W.R. Grace & Co., interrupted only by a period of service as a lieutenant (j.g.) in the United States Navy in 1942.

During his apprenticeship he circulated "through a series of less important jobs to get a broad understanding of the company he would head. He was insatiably curious. He devoured old letters and memos from the files and made a nuisance of himself asking questions" (*Catholic Digest,* May 1958). He was trained intensively in both the North American and South American enterprises of the company. In 1940 he became assistant secretary; in 1942, manager and then secretary; in 1943, director; and in May 1945, vice-president. In September 1945 he was named president, replacing David Stewart Iglehart, who had succeeded Grace's father.

J. Peter Grace soon won a reputation for running the company with "frenetic energy" and for promoting "diversification within diversification" (*Business Week,* January 25, 1958). Continual travel, on the average of about 150 days a year, enables him to keep in direct touch with the activities of the subsidiaries of the Grace industrial empire. Its principal companies include the thirty-three-vessel Grace Line, Inc., Panagra (Pan American-Grace Airways, Inc), Grace National Bank of New York, and Foster and Kleiser Division (an outdoor-advertising firm). The company's Libyan oil venture, in which it is associated with Texas Gulf Producing Company and Standard Oil Company of New Jersey, resulted in the discovery of oil in two wells in 1959.

As a result of studies made under Grace's direct supervision, W.R. Grace & Co. is now an important producer of petrochemicals, petroleum cracking catalysts, silica gel, fertilizers, container sealing compounds, Cryovac plastic bags, high-density polyethylene, and other basic and processed chemicals, manufactured through Grace Chemical, Polymer Chemicals and Research, Davison Chemical Corporation, and Dewey and Almy Company, the latter two now merged with W.R. Grace & Co. Its chemical business, in which it has invested some $180,000,000, represents more than half of Grace's assets, whereas in 1950 it accounted for only 3 per cent.

In Latin America, the Grace company's chief activities are in the production of paper, sugar and other foods, chemicals, textiles, paint, and metallurgical products. It also carries on extensive trading operations there. Besides increasing the interests of his own company in Latin America, Grace has done much to en-

J. PETER GRACE

courage other United States businessmen to invest in the industrialization of Latin America.

During recent years he has discussed United States-Latin American relations before such groups as the Alumni Society of the University of Pennsylvania's Wharton School of Finance and Commerce and the Commonwealth Club of California in San Francisco. In one of his series of articles for the *Christian Science Monitor* (November 24-29, 1958), he argued that building up the Latin American economy served the best interests of the United States: "A strong Latin America is vital to the future well-being and security of the United States and the western world."

A closely held family corporation, Grace & Co. had its stock listed on the New York Stock Exchange for the first time in 1953. It has more than 28,000 common stockholders and about 40,000 employees. During the first six months of 1959 the company earned a net income after taxes of over $7,000,000 from its operations in thirty countries.

Grace holds directorships in numerous business firms, including Kennecott Copper Corporation, Ingersoll-Rand Company, and Northern Insurance Company of New York. Throughout his career he has been called upon to serve on the boards of many educational and public service groups, and he is a director of the Downtown-Lower Manhattan Association and a member of the Mayor's Business and Finance Committee of the City of New York.

An active Roman Catholic layman, Grace is president of the Catholic Youth Organization in New York City and an officer of several Catholic educational, medical, and charitable associations. He has honorary LL.D. degrees from Mount St. Mary's College, Manhattan College, and Fordham University. He has been decorated by the governments of Chile,

GRACE, J. PETER—*Continued*

Ecuador, and Colombia, and in 1953 the American Legion conferred on him its Humanitarianism Award.

J. Peter Grace and Margaret Fennelly were married on May 24, 1941. His wife had been a secretarial student at the Grace Institute, founded in 1897 by his grandfather. The Graces have eight children: Joseph Peter 3d, William Russell, Michael Stephen, Margaret Mary, Mary Janet, Nora Mary, Patrick Peyton, and Teresa Mary. Grace is five feet nine inches tall, weighs 180 pounds, and has blue eyes and brown hair.

Believing that sports teach an individual to stand on his own ability, Grace encourages his children to play baseball and hockey and sometimes joins them in a game. He enjoys sailing and fishing with them during the summer in Maine and horseback riding on a 5,000-acre farm in South Carolina. Grace's clubs include the Meadow Brook, Links, Links Golf, Madison Square Garden, and Racquet & Tennis. In *Men at the Top* (Harper, 1959), however, Osborn Elliott wrote that "few men in American business work as hard as Peter Grace" and that Grace, "a onetime six-goal polo player, lists his hobbies, somewhat somberly, as 'economics and anti-Communism.'"

References

> Am Mercury 78:42+ Mr '54
> Bsns W p105+ Ja 25 '58 pors
> American Catholic Who's Who, 1960 and 1961
> Who's Who in America, 1958-59
> Who's Who in Commerce and Industry (1959)
> World Biography (1954)

GREEN, HOWARD (CHARLES) Nov. 5, 1895- Canadian Secretary of State for External Affairs
Address: b. Parliament Bldgs., Ottawa, Ontario, Canada; h. 4160 W. 8th Ave., Vancouver, British Columbia, Canada

Canada's foreign minister, Secretary of State for External Affairs Howard Green, was named to his present post in the Progressive Conservative government of John Diefenbaker on June 4, 1959 to succeed the late Sidney Smith. A Vancouver lawyer, he has represented British Columbia districts in Parliament in Ottawa continuously since 1935. After the victory of the Progressive Conservatives in June 1957, Green had become his party's floor leader in the House of Commons and had been appointed Minister of Public Works, a position that he held until August 1959. According to Blair Fraser (*Maclean's Magazine*, August 1, 1959), because of Green's "deep emotional attachment" to the British Commonwealth, Canada may become a more reliable supporter of British policy, while being "wary—not hostile to, just wary—of any closer entanglement with the United States."

Howard Charles Green was born in Kaslo in southeastern British Columbia on November 5, 1895, about two years after that small mining town was founded on the shore of Kootenay Lake. His father, Samuel Howard Green, had moved to Kaslo from Ontario as a baker with a railroad construction crew and had remained to establish, with his brother Robert, the first in a chain of general stores operating in the southern interior of Canada's Pacific province. His mother, Flora Isabel (Goodwin) Green, belonged to an old New Brunswick family staunchly loyalist at the time of the American Revolution. Largely because of the prominence of his uncle, Robert Green, in the provincial government, Howard Green grew up in an atmosphere of vigorous political activity and early decided to make politics his career.

A graduate of public elementary and high schools in the Kaslo area, Howard Green went east in 1912 to University College at the University of Toronto. When World War I broke out he joined the Officers Training Corps at the university, and in May 1915, after receiving his B.A. degree, he was commissioned a second lieutenant in the 54th (Kootenay) Battalion of the Canadian Expeditionary Force.

The "Kootenays" went to France in August 1916 and fought in the trenches for about a year. Green also served as an instructor at the Canadian Corps Infantry School in France and as a staff officer with the 6th Infantry Brigade. After the armistice he was assigned to headquarters duty with the occupation forces in Germany. He was discharged from the army in the rank of captain in July 1919.

Immediately resuming his studies, Green entered Osgoode Hall Law School in Toronto and ranked second in his class at graduation in 1920. In 1922, following two years of further reading of the law with firms in Toronto and Vancouver, he was admitted to the British Columbia bar.

In 1926 Green formed with F. K. Collins his own law partnership in Vancouver. Politically he was active in the South Vancouver Conservative Association. When, in 1930, the Conservatives lost the South Vancouver seat in the House of Commons at Ottawa to the candidate of the socialistic Cooperative Commonwealth Federation, he headed "a ginger group of young Conservatives determined to reorganize the riding from the bottom up and recapture it" (Harvey Hickey in the Toronto *Gobe Magazine*, July 4, 1959). At the general election of 1935, he was elected member for Vancouver South by a narrow 279 majority in a year which witnessed a decline in his party's strength across the nation. When Green went to the Commons at Ottawa he was one of only thirty-nine Conservatives in a legislature with a membership of 245.

Early interested in welfare legislation, in his maiden speech in the Commons Green urged pensions for the blind. He increased his majority to 5,919 at the general election of 1940, and in 1942 he sought, unsuccessfully, election as his party's leader. During World War II, as head of the Conservative caucus on the armed forces, Green criticized the Liberal government's "home defense complex," and in February 1942 he asserted that "Canadians on the

[Pacific] coast know that the Canadian armed forces are hopelessly inadequate to deal with an attempted invasion."

Through the Redistribution Act of 1947 much of Vancouver South was incorporated in the new riding, Vancouver-Quadra, which Green has represented since 1949. From the Opposition benches during the next eight years he continued to harass the Liberal government. He was interested in postwar reconstruction, veteran's affairs, conservation and development of resources, and also advocated the building up of Canada's maritime strength.

At the general election of June 10, 1957 Green raised his majority to 16,296, the widest margin yet attained in his six Parliamentary candidacies. (In the Conservative landslide election of April 1958 it was to swell to 19,069.) Nationally, in the 1957 election the Progressive Conservatives ran slightly behind the Liberals in total votes, but with some support from minor parties John Diefenbaker was able on June 21 to announce the formation of Canada's first Conservative federal government in twenty-two years.

Howard Green was sworn into the Privy Council and entered Diefenbaker's cabinet as Minister of Public Works and Acting Minister of Defence Production. (He held the latter post until May 1958.) In ensuing sessions of Parliament he served as head of the Conservative caucus, majority leader in the Commons, and as Acting Prime Minister during Diefenbaker's absences on state business.

A "querulous, persistent and obstinate" critic in opposition, Green as a majority leader became a "bland, mellow peacemaker . . . capable of joking in the House," Harvey Hickey wrote in the Toronto *Globe Magazine* (July 4, 1959). As Public Works Minister, Green not only fought the patronage system but, in preparation for the opening of the St. Lawrence Seaway, launched a $100,000,000 program for the improvement of Canada's Great Lakes harbors. Under Green's auspices 164,632 new housing units were started in 1958.

In view of the fact that Howard Green had not visited Europe since the days of World War I and had never been in Washington, some political observers were considerably surprised when Prime Minister Diefenbaker announced his appointment as Secretary of State for External Affairs on June 4, 1959. He succeeds the late Sidney Smith, former president of the universities of Manitoba and Toronto, who died March 17. In the interim the Prime Minister himself had taken over the External Affairs portfolio. "The position," commented *Time* (June 15, 1959), "crowns the career of a loyal retainer with no designs on the party leadership. Diefenbaker will set overall foreign policy, while Green will handle day-to-day problems and parliamentary rough-and-tumble."

Addressing the House of Commons on July 9, Green "defined Canada's long-term aims in foreign policy as working toward the lessening of world tensions within the framework of the Western alliance" and voiced his belief in "the fullest cooperation with the United States . . .

Capital Press Service

HOWARD GREEN

as long as no loss of sovereignty was involved" (New York *Times,* July 10, 1959). Commenting on recent disarmament proposals in an address to the United Nations General Assembly in New York on September 24, he observed that there is "an inseparable relationship between disarming and control and . . . the two must be negotiated in parallel and must be put into effect together." He told U.N. delegates that as a contribution to World Refugee Year his country would waive normal immigration requirements in order to admit "a substantial number of tubercular refugees and their families."

"There is a laconic 'Yankee' quality to his manner and wit," Maxwell Cohen wrote of Howard Green in *Saturday Night* (August 15, 1959), adding that he is "in many ways one of the best liked and most respected Conservative front benchers." He is tall and spare and does not drink or smoke. By his marriage to Marion Jean Mounce on August 7, 1923, he has two sons, Lewis Howard and John Willison. His first wife died in 1953. On March 29, 1956 he was married to Donna Enid Kerr, a bacteriologist and former professor at the University of British Columbia. His clubs are the Terminal City and the Lions, and he belongs to the United Church of Canada.

References

Christian Sci Mon p4 Je 5 '59 por
External Affairs 11:114 Je '59
Monetary Times 126:25+ Je '58 por
N Y Herald Tribune p4 Je 5 '59
N Y Times p2 Je 5 '59 por
Toronto Globe and Mail p7 Jl 20 '57 por; p7 S 12 '59 por
Canadian Parliamentary Guide, 1959
Canadian Who's Who, 1955-57
International Who's Who, 1958
Who's Who in Canada, 1958-59

GREENBIE, SYDNEY June 28, 1889-June 8, 1960 Author; lecturer; wrote books and collaborated on books and plays with his wife, Marjorie Barstow Greenbie; president of Floating University (1928-29) and president of Traversity (1929-32), both of which offered academic studies to traveling college students. See *Current Biography* (September) 1941.

Obituary

N Y Times p31 Je 10 '60

GRIFFIN, JOHN HOWARD June 16, 1920-
Writer; musicologist
Address: b. c/o Houghton Mifflin Co., 2 Park St., Boston, Mass.; h. Mansfield, Tex.

Firsthand experience and spiritual travail endow the writings of John Howard Griffin with authenticity and immediacy — with "the power of life itself." His books reflect tensions between body and soul, symbolism and realism. In the spring of 1960 he published in the Negro magazine *Sepia* a series of articles about the humiliations he endured when he traveled in the Deep South disguised as a Negro.

JOHN HOWARD GRIFFIN

Many people who saw his articles discussed in magazines and on television programs in the United States and abroad already knew Griffin as the Roman Catholic author of two novels, the best-selling *The Devil Rides Outside* (1952) and *Nuni* (1956). Both books deal with man's long struggle for salvation. A Texan, Griffin is a musicologist, historian, and lecturer who wrote the novels that brought him fame during a ten-year period of blindness caused by injuries he suffered during World War II.

John Howard Griffin, the son of Jack Walter and Lena Mae (Young) Griffin, was born in Dallas, Texas on June 16, 1920. He has one brother, E. W. Griffin, whose home is now in Maracaibo, Venezuela, and two sisters, Mrs. W. J. Culbertson and Mrs. G. M. Hamilton, both residents of Texas. Griffin's mother is a concert pianist, and from his schoolboy days music has been a dominant influence in his life.

Scientific studies were also among Griffin's chief interests when he was a student at E. M. Daggett Junior High School and Paschal High School in Fort Worth, Texas. He went to France in 1936, before finishing his secondary school course, entered the Lycée Descartes in Tours, and was graduated in 1938. Intending to become a psychiatrist, he then began to study medicine with private tutors, and as an assistant to the doctor in charge of the insane asylum in Tours, he carried on research in psychiatric techniques.

Experiments with musical therapy in the treatment of the insane led to Griffin's career in musicology. He learned theory and composition, studied under Robert Casadesus and Nadia Boulanger, and began historical research on Gregorian chant. Working with the organist of the Cathedral of Tours, he helped write an interpretation of ornaments of music for keyboard instruments of the seventeenth and eighteenth centuries.

Still in France when World War II broke out in 1939, Griffin joined the French Défense Passive. While serving as liaison agent for the evacuation of German and Austrian refugees from Tours to the coast, he barely escaped capture by the Gestapo. In 1942 he joined the United States Army as a private and for the next thirty-nine months fought in the South Pacific and Far East with the 13th Air Force. Shortly after the Japanese surrender he taught Georgian chant at a Benedictine convent in the Philippines. He was discharged from the Army in 1945 with the rank of technical sergeant, and for his war services he received awards from both the French and United States governments.

Twice injured during the war, Griffin returned to France with badly impaired eyesight, which doctors attributed at that time to a blockage of circulation in arteries carrying blood to the eyes. Since blindness made a career in medicine impossible, he resumed his musical studies, undertaking further research in Gregorian chant at the Monastery of Solesmes in Sarthe. In 1946 he was granted the Certificat d'Études of the Abbaye de Solesmes. While studying in France, he became totally blind and he has said that he regards it as his "good fortune" that at the time of this tragedy he was in a monastery "surrounded by dedicated men" (New York *Herald Tribune Book Review*, November 9, 1952).

In 1947 Griffin went home to Texas, studied Braille, and attended a school for the blind in New Orleans. He then moved to his parents' forty-acre ranch in Mansfield, some twenty miles south of Fort Worth, where he raised pure-bred cattle. Under the direction of the Discalced Carmelite Monks and the Basilian Fathers of Canada, he continued the studies of philosophy and theology that he had begun in France.

One day drama critic John Mason Brown visited Griffin on his farm and, after talking to the blind veteran, encouraged him to write. Within a few days Griffin started a memoir of his experiences in French monasteries. He then converted his record into a novel, *The Devil Rides Outside.* Published in 1952, it was the first book to appear under the imprint of Smiths, Inc., of Fort Worth. It was reprinted by Pocket Books (1952) and has also been published in England, France, the Netherlands, and South America.

Griffin's first novel, which takes its title from the French proverb, "The devil rides outside monastery walls," deals with the everlasting conflict between the forces of good and evil for possession of man's soul. Frank in its treatment of sex, "the work is brutal in its intensity, visceral in its images of flesh," Eugene McNamara noted in *America* (August 17, 1957). "But," he added, "it is triumphant in the contrasting spiritual side."

The Devil Rides Outside is less autobiographical, according to Griffin, than some readers believe; some of its characters are fictitious. As a record of spiritual development, however, it is self-revealing. "In the course of it I wrote my way into the Church," Griffin has said, "—I held out tooth and nail [like the hero of "The Devil Rides Outside"]—but when I had finished, my conscience wouldn't let me do anything else" (New York *Herald Tribune Book Review,* November 9, 1952).

Nuni (Houghton, 1956), Griffin's second novel, is written in the first person and in the present tense and is also a story of spiritual struggle. Its hero is a college professor, the only survivor of a plane crash, who lands on a Pacific island inhabited by a savage tribe and who has to free himself of all trappings of civilization and earthly values in order to find peace of mind. Griffin's picture of a primitive society has an anthropological interest and was probably based on his studies during the war of peoples in the Pacific.

In *Land of the High Sky,* published in 1959 by the First National Bank, Midland, Texas, Griffin turned from fiction to write a history of the Midland area of west Texas, including a detailed description of Indian culture. Among Griffin's books scheduled for eventual publication by Houghton Mifflin are *Street of the Seven Angels, Black Like Me,* and his autobiography, *Scattered Shadows.*

Suddenly one day in January 1957 Griffin regained his eyesight. For the first time in ten years he was able to see. *Time* magazine (January 21, 1957) reported that he belittled the possibility that his blindness had been due mainly to the emotional shock of bombing raids. Recovery of his vision enabled Griffin a few years later to undertake an extraordinary assignment for *Sepia,* a Negro monthly magazine published in Fort Worth. After darkening his skin by the use of drugs and vegetable dye, he posed for four weeks as a Negro, traveling through several Southern states.

Griffin's account of the hostility and discrimination that he suffered while in this disguise appeared in *Sepia* in five installments, begin-

ning in April 1960, under the title of "Journey into Shame." The articles attracted international attention and were featured in *Paris Match* and *France-Soir.* Griffin was interviewed on several television programs, including those of Mike Wallace and Paul Coates and Dave Garroway's *Today.* At home, in Mansfield, Griffin was hanged in effigy, but he expressed doubt that the townspeople as a whole had become unfriendly toward him.

As a novelist, Griffin has been compared with another Roman Catholic author, Graham Greene, in style and purpose. Maxwell Geismar in *American Moderns* (1959) ranks him high among new writers for talent and craftsmanship. A number of critics agree with B. R. Redman *(Saturday Review,* November 1, 1952), who found that *The Devil Rides Outside,* despite its faults, "has the power of life itself."

One of Griffin's greatest rewards upon recovering his sight was that after three and a half years of marriage he was able to see his wife, Elisabeth Ann (Holland) Griffin, whom he had married on June 7, 1953. They have three children, Susan-Michele, John Howard, Jr., and Gregory. Griffin, who covered his hazel eyes with dark glasses and polled his brown hair when masquerading as a Negro, is a huskily built man, standing six feet one and a half inches tall and weighing 196 pounds. He is a director of the Fort Worth Foundation for Visually Handicapped Children and a member of the Texas Institute of Letters. French cooking and French literature (Gide and Camus are favorites), as well as swimming and working with livestock, are among his recreations; and even in his leisure time he is preoccupied wth music, philosophical studies, and exploration of primitive cultures.

References

Lib J 77:1802 O 15 '52
N Y Herald Tribune Bk R p2 N 9 '52
  por
N Y Times Bk R p8 O 26 '52
Time 69:60 Ja 21 '57 por; 75:90 Mr 28
  '60 pors
Who's Who in America, 1951-52

GRIFFIN, ROBERT P. Nov. 6, 1923- United States Representative from Michigan; lawyer

Address: b. House Office Bldg., Washington 25, D.C.; h. Traverse City, Mich.; 5921 Gloster Rd., Washington 16, D.C.

When only in his second Congressional term, Representative Robert P. Griffin, Republican of Michigan, became in July of 1959 a focus of national attention through co-authorship with Representative Phil M. Landrum, Democrat of Georgia, of the Landrum-Griffin bill to effect reforms in the labor field. The bill, opposed by labor but endorsed by President Eisenhower, sought to curb racketeering by requiring unions to report on welfare fund expenditures and by imposing severe limitations on secondary boycotting and picketing. Most of its provisions

Wide World

ROBERT P. GRIFFIN

were approved by Congress. Griffin, a lawyer of Traverse City, has represented his state's Ninth District since January 1957.

The son of J.A. and Beulah M. Griffin, Robert P. Griffin was born in the greater Detroit area, Michigan on November 6, 1923. His father was a factory worker, and at one time Griffin himself worked on the automobile assembly lines. He attended public schools in Dearborn and Garden City and studied to be a teacher at the Central Michigan College of Education in Mount Pleasant, where he received both the B.A. and B.S. degrees in 1947. His attendance there, however, was interrupted by enlistment in the United States Army during World War II, in which he served for fourteen months overseas with the 71st Infantry Division.

By the time he had completed his courses in education, Griffin had decided to make the law rather than teaching his profession; he accordingly entered the Law School of the University of Michigan at Ann Arbor. During the first four months of 1949 he contributed to the *Michigan Law Review* his comment on certain cases involving the rights of alien enemies threatened with deportation and the effect of excusing procedure on the composition of a jury panel. Later in 1949, while still a student, Griffin was made an assistant editor of the *Michigan Law Review*, and in May 1950 he contributed ten pages of discussion on the question of whether corporations as well as individuals are protected by the Fourteenth Amendment.

Griffin was awarded his J.D. degree by the University of Michigan in 1951. A year before, however, having been admitted to the Michigan bar, he had begun practice as a member of the firm of Williams, Griffin, Thompson & Coulter. During six years of practice as an attorney, from 1950 to 1956, he handled many cases in the labor field and earned a reputation as a student of labor legislation.

At the primary in August 1956, running for the Republican nomination for United States Representative for the Ninth Michigan District, Griffin outpolled the state's first Congresswoman, the conservative Ruth Thompson. He went on in November to defeat the Democratic nominee, William E. Baker, by 68,166 votes to 53,609 in a half-agricultural, half-industrial area covering eleven counties in western Michigan.

Seated in the Eighty-fifth Congress in January 1957, Griffin quickly showed himself much less reactionary in his thinking on both foreign and domestic issues than was his predecessor. He favored military and economic implementation of the Eisenhower Mideast Doctrine (March 1957), permission to Britain to postpone seven debt interest payments (April 1957), and the mutual security appropriations of both 1957 (August) and 1958 (July). He did not support Eisenhower's objection to a bill raising the pay of postal workers (July 1957), but he sided with the President in opposing what the latter regarded as an extravagant authorization for rivers, harbors, and flood control (March 1958). He gave down-the-line support to the Eisenhower-Benson agricultural policies.

In keeping with his training as a teacher and his experience in labor problems, Griffin had been assigned at his own request to the House Education and Labor Committee at the convening of the Eighty-fifth Congress. The committee, headed by Democratic Representative Graham Barden of North Carolina, voted in May 1958 by 15 to 14 to set up a special subcommittee to study a welfare-fund control bill and other proposals that would require public disclosure of operations of pension and welfare funds of unions and employers. Griffin was the sole Republican to join Democrats in voting "yes."

Representative Griffin was also the ranking minority member of the regular labor-management relations subcommittee headed by Representative Phil Landrum, which at the same time (May 1958) was directed to hold hearings on broader legislative measures to reform abuses in labor unions. The subcommittee heard ninety-eight witnesses in forty days of hearings, but no substantial labor legislation was presented during the Eighty-fifth Congress.

After his re-election in November 1958, Griffin renewed his efforts to have Congress pass a strong labor bill, and he discussed labor problems at some length with Democratic Senator John L. McClellan of Arkansas, the chairman of the Senate's Select Committee to Investigate Improper Activities in Labor-Management Relations. The bill that the House Labor and Education Committee was preparing to report out during the Eighty-sixth Congress seemed to Griffin to be weak and inadequate. He began to work over some of the provisions of the bill, to make revisions and substitutions, at the same time keeping as much as possible of the original bill in order to win support for his revisions. Since his views coincided with those of Landrum, they decided to collaborate on the bill in the interests of bipartisanship.

On July 23, 1959 the House Education and Labor Committee approved by a vote of 16 to 14 a measure carrying the name of Representative

Carl Elliott of Alabama. It was a modification of the labor-management reporting and disclosure bill sponsored by Senators John F. Kennedy of Massachusetts and Samuel J. Ervin, Jr., of North Carolina which had been passed by the Senate in April by 90 votes to 1. The Elliott bill did impose certain restrictions on blackmail picketing and secondary boycotts and was not so mild as the labor bill sponsored by California Democrat John F. Shelley.

The bill that Griffin and Landrum introduced on July 24, 1959 was the third choice before the House. Their measure was more restrictive than the other two: it included provisions that put severe limitations on secondary boycotts and picketing and that forced union officials to respect a bill of rights for union members. Griffin said that the bill had been discussed with White House and Labor Department staff members and that he expected that the administration would support it.

In a radio and television appeal on August 6, 1959 President Eisenhower urged adoption of the Landrum-Griffin measure. The bill was offered a week later as an amendment to the Taft-Hartley Law of 1947 in place of the Elliott bill. Supported by conservative Democrats as well as by Republicans, the Landrum-Griffin amendment was adopted by the House by a vote of 229 to 201. Early in September, after twelve days of conference and compromise, an amended version was passed in both the Senate and the House and signed by President Eisenhower.

During the Eighty-sixth Congress, Griffin had the additional responsibilities of membership in the House Committee on Government Operations, headed by William L. Dawson of Illinois, and its subcommittee on foreign operations and monetary affairs. Griffin, who had voted in 1958 (May) for admission of Alaska as a state, favored statehood for Hawaii in 1959 (March). Also in 1959 he voted for a $3.5 billion mutual security authorization (June) and for United States participation in the Inter-American Development Bank. He opposed a Democrat-sponsored measure to give the Rural Electrification Administrator final authority over REA loans (April) and the self-financing bill for the Tennessee Valley Authority (May).

As his colleague Representative Landrum pictures him, Griffin is "a clean, courageous, clear-thinking young lawyer who can associate labor corruption with the legislative remedies needed to right these wrongs" (New York Herald Tribune, August 14, 1959). He is a member of the Michigan state and American bar associations and belongs to the Kiwanis and Elks clubs and to the American Legion, the Jaycees, and Phi Alpha Delta. His religious affiliation is with the Congregational Christian Church. Mrs. Griffin, a schoolteacher before her marriage, is the former Marjorie J. Anderson of Ludington, Michigan. The Griffins have three children.

References

N Y Herald Tribune p1 Ag 14 '59 por
N Y World-Telegram p3 Ag 22 '59 por
Congressional Directory (1960)
Martindale-Hubbell Law Directory, 1952
Who's Who in America, 1958-59

GRIFFITH, ANDY June 1, 1926- Actor
Address: b. c/o Richard Linke, Park Sheraton Hotel, 7th Ave. and 55th St., New York 19; h. Roanoke Island, Manteo, N.C.

Although Variety magazine on June 17, 1959 honored Andy Griffith for his performance in Destry Rides Again as the best by a male lead in a musical, Griffith is better known for his interpretation of the hillbilly draftee, Private Will Stockdale, in both the stage and screen versions of the comedy No Time for Sergeants. He rose to stardom in the theater, television, and motion pictures only six years after he was graduated from the University of North Carolina. After having demonstrated the scope of his talents in such films as A Face in the Crowd and Onionhead, the warm and ingratiating Griffith won further acclaim as the pacifistic deputy sheriff Tom Destry in the musical version of Max Brand's Destry Rides Again.

ANDY GRIFFITH

Born in the mountain town of Mt. Airy, North Carolina, Andrew Samuel Griffith is the only son of Carl Lee Griffith, who was a foreman in a chair factory, and Geneva (Nunn) Griffith. His birthdate is June 1, 1926. The boy attended the local Rockford Street Grammar School and Mt. Airy High School. Brought up on hillbilly music, he wanted to learn how to play the trombone, bass horn, guitar, and ukulele. In order to pay for his music lessons and instruments, he swept out the high school after classes every day. At first he wanted to become an opera singer, but later he changed his mind: he wanted to become a Moravian preacher instead. With that goal in view, he enrolled in the University of North Carolina in Chapel Hill in 1944 as a pre-divinity student.

At Chapel Hill, Andy soon became especially interested in acting, having found a sympathetic

GRIFFITH, ANDY—*Continued*

guide in a member of the university faculty, Foster Fitzsimmons, author of *Bright Leaf.* He joined the university drama group, the Carolina Players, not only attracted by the opportunities it offered for stage appearances, but also because one of its leading actresses was a girl he was to marry. One of his earliest stage appearances was as Ko Ko, the lord high executioner, in *The Mikado.* He also joined the cast of the outdoor pageant *The Lost Colony* by Paul Green, staged annually on Roanoke Island near Manteo, North Carolina, to commemorate the exploration of the territory under Sir Walter Raleigh. His association with the pageant outlasted his stay at Chapel Hill. For the last three of his seven-year association with the pageant he played Sir Walter. He had graduated from the University of North Carolina in 1949 as a music major. In 1949 he was also married to his fellow player Barbara Edwards, who had come to Chapel Hill after her graduation from Converse College in Spartanburg, South Carolina.

For the next three years Griffith and his wife dedicated themselves to teaching. While he directed high school choral groups, she supervised the music for a local church. In their spare time the couple worked up an act that featured singing, dancing, guitar playing, and monologues by Andy. They toured the Carolinas in a station wagon, staging their routines for clubs, conventions, and clambakes. One of the monologues was called *What It Was, Was Football,* a Carolina clergyman's drawled impressions of his first gridiron game. Griffith performed this specialty at a convention of the Jefferson Standard Life Insurance Company, in 1953. It was recorded, played on radio stations, and heard by a Capitol Records representative, who released it under commercial auspices. *What It Was, Was Football* is reported to have sold more than 800,000 albums. Griffith admirers rate it as his funniest number, with his recording of a hillbilly version of *Romeo and Juliet* running at a close second.

When the Griffiths tried to break into the New York entertainment business with their act, they made little progress. They were turned down by Fred Waring and the Paper Mill Playhouse, among other prospective employers. Discouraged, they went back to North Carolina and borrowed $1,000, with which sum they organized their own troupe and gave performances for clubs and conventions for a season. It was Ed Sullivan who gave Griffith his first big opportunity when he hired him to appear as a monologist on the *Ed Sullivan Show.*

A friend lent Griffith a copy of Mac Hyman's best-selling novel about the private war between a country bumpkin and the top brass in the United States Air Force called *No Time for Sergeants.* When Griffith heard that the Theatre Guild was planning a television version of the book for the *United States Steel Hour,* he saw in Will Stockdale a role that was custom-made for his talents. He went to the offices of the Theatre Guild for an audition and, although he found little encouragement in his first interview, he waited patiently outside the

office, hoping for another chance. While marooned in the waiting room, he performed his monologues before an audience of his fellow auditioners. Later, he was called inside and told that he had been hired.

When Ira Levin's dramatization of the novel was produced at the Alvin Theatre on October 20, 1955, Griffith made his debut before a Broadway audience as the mountain yokel reluctantly drafted into the United States Air Force. The play was greeted as a comedy sensation, and Griffith was applauded by both the audience and his fellow actors. The newspaper reviews made him a star overnight. He still remembers the Broadway opening of *No Time for Sergeants* as the most important night of his life. John McClain of the New York *Journal-American* might have been speaking for his critical colleagues when he wrote: "Andy Griffith is certainly one of the important discoveries of the new year on Broadway, an engaging and brilliant natural" (October 24, 1955).

If there had been any question of Andy Griffith's range of acting ability, he made a resounding answer with his performance as Lonesome Rhodes in *A Face in the Crowd,* Budd Schulberg's motion-picture adaptation of his short story "Your Arkansas Traveler," directed by Elia Kazan. Griffith played a complex and folksy vagrant whom a girl reporter discovers playing a guitar in an Arkansas jail. He develops a homespun charm that he wields over a television following of millions, acquires some megalomaniacal political ambitions, and is ultimately dethroned. The role was a radical departure from that of Will Stockdale, and Griffith later told Gilbert Millstein of the New York *Times* (June 2, 1957): "I *became* 'Lonesome Rhodes.' It was something bigger than I was and it might have got to control me. It started here in New York and continued on up to the last month of the picture. . . . The thing was I actually felt the power of 'Lonesome Rhodes.' I'll tell you the truth. You play an egomaniac and paranoid all day and it's hard to turn it off by bedtime." After the film had been completed, Schulberg told Griffith: "I think you can play any part in anything."

Of Griffith as Lonesome Rhodes, Alton Cook wrote in the New York *World-Telegram* (May 29, 1957): "Andy Griffith roars through this role at gale force. It is a remarkable demonstration of seemingly undisciplined vigor subtly guided through the picture's comedy and its underlying idea." William Zinsser observed in the New York *Herald Tribune* (May 29, 1957): "Griffith carries the movie almost single handed. His bountiful personality can't be described in mere words—it overflows the screen with vitality and laughter." Archer Winsten of the New York *Post* called Griffith's work a "prodigious performance" and *Cue* magazine's movie critic hailed it as "probably the best actor's performance of this year."

Griffith seemed the inevitable choice to play Will Stockdale for the film version of *No Time for Sergeants.* Directed by Mervyn Leroy, the film was first exhibited in New York on May 30, 1958. Among the local reviewers who paid tribute to Griffith's performance was Paul V. Beckley, who wrote in the New York *Herald Tribune* (June 1, 1958): "Every line and every situation seems intended by fate for Griffith." The next film vehicle for Griffith was *Onionhead*, adapted from Weldon Hill's novel about a cook on a Coast Guard buoy tender during World War II and directed by Norman Taurog. The film was released in October 1958, to a mixed reception from the critics.

Returning to the stage, Griffith appeared in his first musical comedy, *Destry Rides Again*, which opened at the Imperial Theatre in New York City on April 23, 1959, with a book by Leon Gershe and music and lyrics by Harold Rome. Griffith inherited a role played in films by Tom Mix in 1932, by James Stewart in 1939, Joel McCrea in 1950, and by Audie Murphy in 1954. The Griffith charm again carried the day. A typical response was that of George Oppenheimer in *Newsday* (April 30, 1959) who noted: "There isn't a more likeable personality around than Andy Griffith. That virginal innocence which exudes from his strapping, overgrown body and that simple face with the 'Oh, what a good boy am I' grin just has to put everybody on his side. As usual, he's wonderfully funny." After *Destry Rides Again* completed its Broadway run on July 18, 1960, Griffith starred in the television series *The Andy Griffith Show*, beginning on October 3, 1960.

Reminiscing about the interdenominational aspects of his marriage to Barbara Edwards in 1949, Griffith has said that he was "married in a copy of an Anglican chapel in Manteo, North Carolina, by a Methodist minister, to a Baptist maiden, while a Roman Catholic vibraphonist played the pump organ." The Griffiths have adopted a son, Sam, and it was reported in March 1960 that they are planning to adopt another child. Andy Griffith is over six feet tall and weighs about 175 pounds. He has reddish brown hair, regular features, and blue eyes. In religion Griffith is a Methodist, and in politics he is a Democrat. Between his commitments the Griffiths retreat to their fifty-three-acre farm on historic Roanoke Island in North Carolina, where they have only one acre under cultivation but 100,000 feet of timber.

Concerning his famous Southern drawl, Griffith comments: "I have found that there is a very thin line between the real and the phoney when you use Southern accents. . . . What most people don't realize is that there is a pleasure, a musical-like satisfaction, in using a definite Southern manner of speech. Southerners enjoy words, accenting them a certain way. In England the language is enjoyed much the same way." Concerning his professional plans, he has said: "I want to know my limitations. I don't think I should do anything but comedy."

References

N Y Times II p1 N 6 '55
N Y Times Mag p17 Je 2 '57 por

GROSVENOR, MELVILLE BELL

(grŏv'nēr) Nov. 26, 1901- Editor; association official

Address: b. National Geographic Society, 1146 16th St., N.W., Washington 6, D.C.; h. 5510 Grosvenor Lane, Bethesda 14, Md.

In 1902 a baby held in his great-grandfather's arms helped to lay the cornerstone of the first wing of the National Geographic Society building in Washington, D.C. Now the president of the society and editor of its world-famous *National Geographic Magazine,* Melville Bell Grosvenor thus took part in the group's first major expansion, and since 1924 when he joined its staff, he has helped to increase its international membership to 2,500,000. Organized in 1888 as a nonprofit association of professional geographers and interested laymen, the society is dedicated to "increasing and diffusing geographic knowledge and promoting research and exploration."

Melville Bell Grosvenor, a descendant of two victims of the Salem witchcraft trials of 1692, was born on November 26, 1901 to Gilbert Hovey and Elsie May (Bell) Grosvenor. He is a member of the fourth generation of his family to head the National Geographic Society: his great-grandfather, Gardiner Greene Hubbard, was founder and first president; his grandfather, Alexander Graham Bell, the famous inventor, was the second president.

Dr. Bell persuaded Gilbert Grosvenor to come to Washington in 1899 to edit the *National Geographic Magazine,* then a highly technical publication of limited circulation. During the next fifty-five years Grosvenor built the magazine into a publication combining popular appeal and scholarship, with "a roll call of contributors, lecturers and explorers that scans like a picket fence of U.S. history."

Melville Bell Grosvenor grew up with the magazine. Under his grandfather's auspices, he founded the rival *Wild Acres Weekly* for his own amusement; Melville was editor, writer, and staff photographer. "When I was a youngster," he has said, "[my father] never told me that he wanted me to join the Geographic staff. But he whetted my interest in geography by taking me all over the world."

For a while, however, his interest in sailing took precedence over geography. Young Grosvenor had learned the craft as helmsman of the family yawl in Nova Scotia, and he later attended the United States Naval Academy. Awarded the B.S. degree and commissioned an ensign in 1923, he was successively assigned to the battleships U.S.S. *Delaware* and *West Virginia.*

After a year's tour of duty, Grosvenor resigned his commission in 1924 to join the staff of the *National Geographic Magazine.* Under the tutelage of his father and of Dr. John Oliver La Gorce, then associate editor, Grosvenor served an apprenticeship in the magazine's editorial departments. His primary job, however, was as assistant chief of its illustrations division.

Grosvenor worked in this capacity from 1924 to 1935. His first by-line article in the *National Geographic Magazine* came from an assignment

MELVILLE BELL GROSVENOR

by La Gorce to take his camera aloft in a blimp to photograph New York City and Washington in color. The first natural-color aerial photographs ever published, they ran in the September 1930 issue of the magazine.

Named an assistant editor in 1935, Grosvenor began to devote more time to photographing and writing his own stories. He prepared articles about such diverse locales as Poland, Styria, England, Switzerland, Cuba, and Florida's Corkscrew Swamp and used his naval experience in writing two articles about American aircraft carriers during World War II.

Grosvenor was elected senior assistant editor in 1951, and three years later was named associate editor and vice-president of the society. At the same time, his father resigned as editor and president, and was succeeded by Dr. La Gorce. On January 8, 1957 Melville Bell Grosvenor in turn succeeded Dr. La Gorce as the society's president and editor. A New York *Herald Tribune* (January 9, 1957) reporter commented: "The retirement of Dr. La Gorce, following that of Dr. Gilbert Grosvenor in 1954, marked the transfer of direct supervision of the huge scientific and educational organization from its two architects and builders. Working as a team, the elder Dr. Grosvenor and Dr. La Gorce increased the society's membership from a few thousand in 1905 to 2,160,000 today."

Melville Bell Grosvenor has also helped to enhance the prestige of the society and to increase its membership to about 2,500,000. Inaugurating a map-atlas program, he sent cartographers to chart the entire world, region by region. The society has distributed some 17,000,-000 maps each year as free supplements to the magazine; when the project is completed, society members will own one of the most comprehensive of world atlases.

Grosvenor also installed the first production model of Linofilm, a new electronic composing device to speed production of the magazine. At the same time, he added natural-color photographs to its traditional black-yellow-white cover and expanded the society's book service, which provides books at nominal costs to members.

Larger grants have also been made available by Grosvenor for exploration and research. Among the society's geographical ventures since his election as president and editor have been excavations in Yucatán to explore the ruins of an ancient Mayan city; an underwater survey of the earthquake-drowned city of Port Royal, Jamaica; and the first precise scientific study of the abandoned Pueblo cliff dwellings in the Mesa Verde National Park of Colorado.

"To stay abreast of the missile era," wrote a *Time* commentator (June 15, 1959), "the magazine has added to its list of contributors many a starlit name from the ranks of space engineers. . . . But it remains solidly indentured to the principles laid down by Gilbert Grosvenor years ago, still segregates advertising and editorial copy, runs no liquor, tobacco or real-estate ads, hustles no lagging subscriber, still refuses to say anything controversial or unkind of any individual, race, country, or hemisphere.

"This rule gives an unrealistic hue to the *Geographic's* rose-colored world; the *Geographic* [had] not carried an article on Soviet Russia for 15 years. 'How can we do it,' said Editor Melville Bell Grosvenor, 'without making it sound friendly?'" Since that time the magazine has published Thomas Taylor Hammond's "Firsthand Look at the Soviet Union" in September 1959 and United States Vice-President Richard M. Nixon's "Russia as I Saw It" in December 1959.

Despite his policy-making chores, Grosvenor finds time to travel. He made a round-the-globe trip in the spring of 1959 to visit correspondents in the field, and a report on his journey was published in the December 1959 edition. His photographs and articles still appear in the pages of the magazine.

Melville Bell Grosvenor was married to Helen Rowland on January 4, 1924 and had three children by this first marriage: Helen Rowland (Mrs. Robert C. Watson, Jr.); Alexander Graham Bell Grosvenor, a Navy pilot; and Gilbert M. Grosvenor, an editorial staff member of the *National Geographic Magazine*. On August 12, 1950 Grosvenor was married to Anne Elizabeth Revis, and they have two children, Edwin S. and Sara A. Grosvenor. The editor lives at the family home in Bethesda, Maryland. In 1954 Grosvenor was awarded a D.Sc. degree by the University of Miami, and in 1959 he received an LL.D. degree from George Washington University.

In addition to being the editor and president of the National Geographic Society, Grosvenor is a member of its board of trustees and heads several of its committees. He is also a trustee of Robert College in Istanbul, Turkey; an associate of the Woods Hole Oceanographic Institution; a Fellow of the Royal Geographical Society of London; and a member of the American Museum of Natural History, the American Geographical Society, and the Explorers, Cosmos, National Press, and Overseas Writers clubs. He is a director of the Chesapeake & Potomac Telephone Company, a member of the advisory board of Riggs National Bank, and a trustee of the National Presbyterian Church of Washington.

A lifelong sailing enthusiast and former racing skipper, Grosvenor now confines his sailing to the cruising sloop *Lady Anne* during vacations on Bras d'Or Lake in Nova Scotia. And, of course, he participates in the same sort of armchair ocean voyages beloved by every faithful member of the National Geographic Society.

References

N Y Herald Tribune Ja 9 '57 por
Nat Geog Mag 111:419+ Mr '57 por
Who's Who in America, 1958-59

MOSES HADAS

HADAS, MOSES (hăd'ăs) June 25, 1900-
Classicist; author; translator; university professor
Address: b. Columbia University, 116th St. & Broadway, New York 27; h. 460 Riverside Dr., New York 27

The prolific and enthusiastic translating, editing, and writing done over the past quarter century by Moses Hadas, professor of Greek and Latin at Columbia University, have distinguished him as a classicist who is "scholarly without being pedantic." His numerous translations from Greek and Latin include *Three Greek Romances* and Caesar's *Gallic War, and Other Writings,* both of which he also edited. He has demonstrated the range of his competence and interest in the work he has done beyond the Greek and Latin classics. From German he has translated such books as Jakob Christoph Burckhardt's *Age of Constantine the Great* and from Hebrew he has translated Joseph ben Meir Zabara's *The Book of Delight.* He himself has written six books on classical literature, history, and culture. His recent *Hellenistic Culture: Fusion and Diffusion* (1959) displays a learning which fellow classicist C. A. Robinson, Jr., found "both deep and delightful" (New York *Herald Tribune Book Review,* November 1, 1959).

Moses Hadas was born to David and Gertrude (Draizen) Hadas in Atlanta, Georgia, on June 25, 1900. He earned his B.A. degree at Emory University in Atlanta in 1922. From 1922 to 1926 he was a student at the Jewish Theological Seminary, New York City. At the same time he pursued graduate work at Columbia University, receiving his M.A. degree in 1925 and becoming an instructor in Greek and Latin at the university that same year. From 1928 to 1930 he taught classics at the University of Cincinnati.

While Hadas was teaching at Cincinnati, Columbia University Press published his and Jacob Hammer's translation of Alfred Körte's *Hellenistic Poetry* (1929). The following year Hadas received his Ph.D. degree from Columbia University. The thesis he wrote for the degree became his first original published work: *Sextus Pompey* (Columbia University Press, 1930), a study of the manner in which the younger son of Pompey the Great carried on the traditions of his father after the latter lost his power struggle with Julius Caesar. J. J. Van Nostrand of the University of California, reviewing the book in the *American Historical Review* (April 1930), expressed dislike for what he called its "use of inferential treatment," but nevertheless praised it as a "useful study" with "excellent documentation."

In the fall of 1930 Hadas accepted an appointment to teach evening Bible classes in the preparatory department of the Hebrew Union College School for Teachers. At the same time he resumed his teaching of Greek and Latin at Columbia. He has been on the faculty of Columbia ever since, except for leaves of absence for travel and wartime service (1943-46) as a civilian with the Office of Strategic Services in North Africa and in Greece, where he was liaison officer to the Greek government forces. Columbia advanced him to the position of associate professor in 1946 and to that of full professor in 1953. In 1956 he was named sixth Jay Professor of Greek. The Jay Professorship, the university's oldest chair, was created in 1839 to honor John Jay, first Chief Justice of the Supreme Court and Columbia College graduate in 1764.

In 1932 Columbia University Press published Hadas' translation of Joseph ben Meir Zabara's twelfth century book of tales, discussions, and proverbs, *The Book of Delight,* the plays of Euripides were translated by Hadas and John Harvey McLean for the Dial Press and published in 1936. The translations Professor Hadas has published since that date include Herman Vogelstein's *Rome,* for the Jewish Communities series of the Jewish Publication Society of America (1941); Elias Bickerman's *The Maccabees; An Account of Their History*

HADAS, MOSES—*Continued*

from the Beginnings to the Fall of the House of Hasmoneans, for the Schocken Library (**1947**) ; also for the Schocken Library, Ferdinand Adolf Gregorovius' *The Ghetto and the Jews of Rome,* in the same volume with *Lament of the Children of Israel in Rome,* translated by Randall Jarrell (1948) ; Jakob Christoph Burckhardt's *Age of Constantine the Great,* published by Pantheon Books in 1949 and reissued as a Doubleday Anchor paperback in 1956; Karl Viëtor's *Goethe, the Poet* (Harvard University Press, 1949) ; and Walter Friedrich Otto's *The Homeric Gods* (Pantheon Books, 1954). The Liberal Arts Press published his translations of Seneca's *Medea* (1956) and *Thyestes* (1957), and the University of Michigan Press published his translation of Heliodorus of Emesa's *Ethiopian Romance* (1957).

As an editor, Professor Hadas has been responsible for the Modern Library editions of *The Complete Works of Tacitus* (1942), *The Basic Works of Cicero* (1951), and *The Greek Poets* (1953). He has edited and written an epilogue to Maimon Salomon's *Autobiography,* based on the translation of J. Clark Murray (Schocken, 1947). He has also edited a revision of the Jowett translation of Plato's *Euthyphro, Apology, Crito, and Symposium* (Regnery Gateway, 1953).

Professor Hadas both edited and translated *Aristeas to Philocrates; Letter of Aristeas* (1951) and *The Third and Fourth Books of the Maccabees* (1953), both published by Harper for the Dropsie College for Hebrew and Cognate Learning. For Doubleday Anchor Books he edited and translated *Three Greek Romances* (*Daphnis and Chloe* by Longus, *An Ephesian Tale* by Xenophon, and *The Hunters of Euboea* by Dio Chrysostom), published in 1953; *A History of Rome; From its Origins to 529 A.D. as Told by the Roman Historians,* published in 1956; and *The Stoic Philosophy of Seneca; Essays and Letters,* published in 1958. For the Modern Library he edited and translated Caesar's *Gallic War, and Other Writings,* published in 1957. Hugo Bieber's biographical anthology, *Heinrich Heine,* with some of the translation made by Hadas and the rest of it selected by him, was published by the Jewish Publication Society of America in 1956.

Hadas' own survey of writers from Homer to Lucian, *A History of Greek Literature,* was published by Columbia University Press in 1950. Robert Halsband, reviewing the book in the *Saturday Review of Literature* (September 2, 1950), described the "copiousness and familiarity" with which Hadas sketched the long history of literary works and ideas as "astonishing." A companion volume, *A History of Latin Literature,* appeared two years later (Columbia University Press, 1952). Its subject matter ranged from the origins of Latin literature to the sixth century A.D. "In this sweep of some seven centuries every writer, and almost every work, is discussed, described, and, in the best sense of the word, appreciated," said the Oxonian classicist Basil Davenport (New York *Times Book Review,* March 30, 1952). Davenport's

only negative criticism was that Professor Hadas "might have related his writers a little more clearly to the events of their time."

The same criticism could scarcely be leveled against Professor Hadas' next book, *Ancilla to Classical Reading* (Columbia University Press, 1954), written at the suggestion of Jacques Barzun as one of the scholarly works signalizing the Columbia bicentennial celebration. In the book, Hadas treats those matters that had been only peripheral in his histories : the daily lives of the writers themselves, their tools, and their relationships to the people around them. In *Hellenistic Culture: Fusion and Diffusion* (Columbia University Press, 1959) Hadas studied the adoption of Greek culture by large numbers of non-Greeks in the three centuries between the death of Alexander the Great and the beginning of the Christian era. In 1960 Harper & Brothers published Hadas' *Humanism; The Greek Ideal and its Survival.*

Moses Hadas and Elizabeth M. Chamberlayne were married in 1945. They have two children, Elizabeth and Rachel. By a previous marriage (1926), to Ethel J. Elkus, which terminated in divorce, he also has two children, Jane and David. Professor Hadas is a member of Phi Beta Kappa and the American Philological Association. Emory University awarded him an honorary doctorate (D. Lit.) in 1956.

References

Directory of American Scholars (1957)
Who's Who in America, 1958-59
Who's Who in World Jewry (1955)

HALIFAX, EDWARD FREDERICK LINDLEY WOOD, IST EARL OF Apr. 16, 1881-Dec. 23, 1959 British statesman; scholar; writer; Viceroy of India (1926-31) ; Secretary of State for Foreign Affairs (1938-40), during appeasement of Hitler at Munich; Ambassador to the United States (1941-46). See *Current Biography* (September) 1940.

Obituary

N Y Times p1+ D 24 '59

HALSMAN, PHILIPPE May 2, 1906-
Photographer; author
Address: 33 W. 67th St., New York 23

"Of the thousands of people, celebrated and unknown, who have sat before my camera," Philippe Halsman has said, "I am often asked who was the most difficult subject, or the easiest, or which picture is my favorite. This last question is like asking a mother which child she likes the most" (*American Magazine,* June 1953). Since he came to the United States in 1940 after ten years as a successful portraitist in Paris, the Latvian-born photographer has become famous for a distinctive style and technical skill that have kept him in demand for magazine and advertising work. Although he is not a staff member of *Life,* he has placed nearly ninety covers on that magazine, more than any other photographer. In an international poll that *Popular Photography* conducted in the spring of 1958, he was named as one of the world's ten greatest photographers.

Philippe Halsman was born in Riga, Latvia, on May 2, 1906 to Dr. Max Halsman, a dentist, and Ita (Grintouch) Halsman, a school principal. He has a sister, Liouba, who is now his secretary, retoucher, and photographic assistant. Philippe attended Riga's Vidus Skola and in 1924, after receiving his bachelor's degree, entered the Dresdner Technische Hochschule in Dresden, Germany, as an engineering candidate.

To Halsman, however, engineering proved unsatisfying, and he decided to turn to photography for a career. Opening a studio in Paris in 1930, he soon became a fashionable portrait photographer. Between 1930 and 1940 much of his work appeared in *Voilà,* a hat-fashion magazine, and in the Paris *Vogue.* In 1940 he moved to the United States. By 1944 he was so well established that he was chosen first president of the American Society of Magazine Photographers. (He held this office again in 1954.)

Experience has taught Halsman that men do not attach too much importance to details in a portrait so long as the picture reveals their intelligence, energy, or sensitivity, as the case may be. But a woman's appearance, he has concluded, plays "an enormous part in her life and in her thinking, and therefore she will go over every feature in her portrait, and usually will demand a number of improvements." He finally decided to accept orders only from magazine editors. "I still do my best to capture each woman's particular beauty and character," he wrote in "The People I've Shot" (*American Magazine,* June 1953), "but they, themselves, are no longer the ones to decide whether or not I have succeeded. This has helped to make my life more peaceful."

Traveling in many parts of the world, Halsman has taken more than 100,000 photographs, including portraits of most of the leading statesmen, scientists, entertainers, and other outstanding figures of the time. He has posed people and furniture floating in mid-air, and models rising out of the ground like plants. He once made a picture of the artist Salvador Dali as an unborn baby inside an egg. But he considers such "stunts" easy compared with the making of a "simple-looking, straightforward portrait of an individual."

It is only natural, he thinks, for people to feel self-conscious when a camera is pointed at them. This universal fear he calls "photo-phobia." He tries to overcome a sitter's fear by provoking him to talk, or by lulling him with silence, or by amusing him with jokes, or by asking impertinent questions.

Without hesitation Halsman has admitted that Sir Winston Churchill was the most difficult subject to photograph. Among the famous sitters whom he found unusually co-operative he has named Mrs. Eleanor Roosevelt; Wendell L. Willkie (Halsman's picture was used on the cover of *One World*); Katharine Cornell, Lynn Fontanne, and Helen Hayes (whom he photographed together as they exchanged recipes); and Albert Einstein (who, relaxed and smiling, wrote a series of equations on a pad while Halsman prepared his camera lights).

Yvonne Halsman

PHILIPPE HALSMAN

In January 1951 *Photography Workshop* devoted twenty-six pages to a study of Halsman's work and techniques. In the December 1958 issue of *Popular Photography* Halsman discussed technical and psychological measures involved in characterizing a person in a portrait. One of his most striking portraits is that of Dr. J. Robert Oppenheimer which he made for the "Mental Giants" series in the *Saturday Evening Post.* To emphasize Oppenheimer's intellectual power, he used a high camera position, thereby putting symbolic stress on the brain.

In discussing the psychology of the sitting, Halsman has also recalled the day that Gloria Swanson posed for him. She was tired and despondent until he asked her to put on her long, black gloves. Her mood changed, she became flirtatious, and he took a picture of her which revealed her usual gay personality. As Halsman explained in his *Popular Photography* article, putting the subject in the right frame of mind is only one achievement in a long creative process that depends upon the interrelation of technique and emotion. Since he believes that each technical step adds an important contribution to the characterization of the subject, he even makes most of his prints himself.

During 1955 Halsman spent three months in Europe. Using a portable speed-light studio, he photographed some of the foremost figures of the political, social, and entertainment world for *Picture Post.* This was the first time a British magazine had invited an American photographer to "shoot" British subjects.

The author of three humorous books, Halsman wrote and illustrated *The Frenchman; A Photographic Interview,* published by Simon and Schuster in 1949. It contains twenty-four photographs of the French comedian Fernandel, taken while he answered in pantomime (and with a

HALSMAN, PHILIPPE—Continued

wide range of facial expressions) Halsman's questions about art, international affairs, and other subjects typical of a shipboard interview.

Halsman's *Dali's Mustache* (1954) is also a Simon and Schuster publication, as is his *Jump Book* (1959). In the latter he expounds the "science" of "jumpology." He believes that the subject of a photograph best reveals his true character when he is suspended at the peak of a jump, since he cannot control his muscles. Halsman documents his theory with pictures of famous people jumping. In his pursuit of "jumpology," he admits that he met with some refusals, but 178 personages agreed to be photographed while jumping, thus—Halsman claims —exposing their real selves. His subjects include Judge Learned Hand, the Reverend Dr. Paul J. Tillich, Father Martin D'Arcy, Vice-President Richard M. Nixon, Brigitte Bardot, and the Duke and Duchess of Windsor.

Philippe Halsman and Yvonne Moser were married on April 1, 1937. They have two daughters, Irène Aline and Jane Ellen, for whom he wrote *Piccoli,* stories about a tiny creature small enough to fit in a walnut shell, published in 1953 by Simon and Schuster. Halsman has brown eyes and black hair and stands five feet nine inches tall and weighs 152 pounds. He is a student of modern art and enjoys reading Plato and Sartre. He speaks seven languages. His chief satisfaction as a photographer is to feel that in his characterization he is creating what may become the historic image of a great person.

References

Am Mag 155:40+ Je '53
Life 31:11+ O 15 '51
N Y Herald Tribune p21 My 5 '55
Pop Phot 42:65 My '58; 43:117+ D '58
por

HAMMERSTEIN, OSCAR, 2D July 12, 1895-Aug. 23, 1960 Librettist; lyricist; scenarist; producer; wrote book and songs for musical shows like *Oklahoma* (1943) and *South Pacific* (1949). See *Current Biography* (February) 1944.

Obituary

N Y Times p1+ Ag 23 '60

HANDLEY, HAROLD W(ILLIS) Nov. 27, 1908(?)- Governor of Indiana

Address: b. 206 State House, Indianapolis 4, Ind.; h. 4343 N. Meridian St., Indianapolis, Ind.

Indiana, the tenth largest state in population and one of the nation's greatest industrial centers and richest agricultural producers, has often been called a Midwestern citadel of conservative Republicanism. Its Governor, Harold W. Handley, stands squarely in the tradition of conservative Republican politics in his state, despite the fact that union growth and a more liberal Republicanism have sapped the strength of the old guard. Handley, a businessman, has

served in state politics as a state senator and Lieutenant Governor. His term as Governor expires in January 1961.

One of three sons of Harold Lowell and Lottie Margaret (Brackbill) Handley, Harold Willis Handley was born in La Porte, Indiana cn November 27, 1908 (some sources quote 1909). His brothers are Kenneth E. and S. Dwight Handley. His father was engaged in furniture manufacturing in La Porte, and Harold attended local public elementary and high schools.

In 1928, he went to Indiana University in Bloomington, where he studied economics. After receiving a B.A. degree in 1932, he entered business; he still prefers to call himself a businessman rather than a politician. For a time Handley followed in his father's footsteps as a sales representative for the Unagusta Furniture Corporation of Hazelwood, North Carolina. He is a former sales representative of Kling Film Productions in Chicago and Hollywood. From 1949 to 1953 he served as a vice-president of Darling Motion Picture Sales Company, and in 1952 he was Midwest sales representative for the John Sutherland Productions of Hollywood.

Handley was elected to his first public office in 1940, when he won a bid for a seat in the Indiana state Senate. He resigned this position in 1941, however, to enter the United States Army. During World War II he served with the 85th Infantry Division, rising from second lieutenant to lieutenant colonel before his discharge in 1945.

After the war Handley returned to business. He did not return to politics until 1948, when he was re-elected to the state Senate. He served in the Senate until 1953, when he became Lieutenant Governor of the state. In that capacity he presided over the state Senate, was state commissioner of agriculture, state commissioner of commerce and industry, and a member of various commissions and committees.

He has long been a conservative Republican. Godfrey Sperling, Jr., of the *Christian Science Monitor* called Handley a protégé of Indiana's arch-conservative former Senator William E. Jenner (December 31, 1957). In 1956 Handley was Jenner's choice for the Republican nomination for Governor. In a Republican party convention scarred by bitter battles with incumbent Governor George N. Craig, he won the nomination, and in the November elections he defeated his Democratic opponent at the polls.

Shortly after he took office in January 1957, a story of scandalous activity in the previous administration of Governor Craig came to light. The state highway commissioner and others in the state government, including two of Craig's principal advisers, were charged with bribery and embezzlement in connection with contracts for highway supplies and equipment, involving huge profits in the purchase and sale of land secretly earmarked for highway right-of-ways. The charges led to convictions and sentences for a number of men closely connected with Indiana politics.

Although both Craig and Handley are Republicans, Handley escaped suspicion since he had been continually at odds with the Craig administration. Instead, he claimed credit for having helped unearth the conspiracy after he became Governor. Godfrey Sperling wrote in the *Christian Science Monitor* (September 11, 1958) that even Handley's critics were forced to concede that Governor Handley and his aides moved fast to clean up a corruption that had its heyday in a previous administration.

But Governor Handley's administration had its own troubles. In addition to raising tax rates in his first year in office, Handley refused to veto a right-to-work bill passed by the state Legislature in March 1957 that banned the union shop in Indiana. The bill caused a riot at the state capitol, and nearly 10,000 union members marched into the State House in protest, but the Governor would not veto the measure.

When Senator Jenner announced that he would not seek renomination in 1958, he picked Handley to succeed him in the United States Senate (New York *Times,* March 23, 1958). Since a Governor is not allowed to succeed himself in Indiana, Handley accepted the nomination for the Senate, with the intention of resigning his Governorship if he should happen to win.

Handley's Democratic opponent for the vacant Senate seat was Vance Hartke, the mayor of Evansville. During his campaign Handley accused Hartke of corrupt administration in Evansville and of being a tool of Walter Reuther, chief of the United Auto Workers union. In the November elections, however, Hartke swept to a commanding victory as a result of a growing anti-Republican temper among Indiana voters. He thus became the state's first Democratic United States Senator in two decades. Many observers attributed the Republican defeat to Handley's conservatism and the scandals that had tainted the previous state administration.

Recently, Republicanism in Indiana has been divided into two camps. Godfrey Sperling, Jr., of the *Christian Science Monitor* called them "the anti-Eisenhower forces (represented by Senator Jenner and Governor Handley) against the Eisenhower forces (represented by Senator Capehart, Representative Halleck, and other Congressmen)" (December 31, 1957). Defining his own concept of Republicanism, Handley wrote for *United States News & World Report*: "I regard myself as a 'modern Republican' in the Hoosier sense of the word. Here in Indiana we jealously guard the constitutional sovereignty of the individual states and ardently champion the principle of home rule. We are opposed to overconcentration of power in the federal government, and we oppose the continued strangulation of state and local governments by Washington's pre-emption and domination of revenue sources" (May 3, 1957).

Handley has opposed federal aid in many forms, from rural electrification to education. "I am opposed to federal aid for the primary reason that we can take care of ourselves," he has said (*Time,* May 13, 1957). He has campaigned strenuously against obscene literature, and, through a group called the Youth Council, he has fought to remove "trash literature" from Indiana newsstands.

Mollett

HAROLD W. HANDLEY

The Governor is not opposed to taking the situation into his own hands when he wants to get things done. In 1959 he asked his state department of financial institutions to raise to 3 per cent the interest rate that banks could pay to customers. When the department turned down his request, Handley replaced four of the department's six board members.

Nevertheless, the Governor does not act in a dictatorial manner. A New York *Times* reporter said of him that his "oratory in cold print looks much like that of Senator Jenner," but he "eschews the Senator's slam-bang type of delivery. While Mr. Jenner frequently sheds his coat for shouting, arm-waving speeches, the Governor usually talks in conversational tones with cultivated diction" (October 31, 1958).

Handley backed Vice-President Richard M. Nixon for the 1960 Presidential nomination. At a 1959 meeting of the Council of State Government's board of governors, he was one of the most outspoken supporters of Nixon. He reported that the political sentiment in his state was "all Nixon. [Nelson] Rockefeller is a great governor and a fine fellow, and we all think very highly of him, but we're not for him," Handley said.

Several Indiana educational institutions have awarded Governor Handley honorary LL.D. degrees: Valparaiso University (1957), Indiana University (1957), Tri-State College (1958), Franklin College, and Vincennes University. He is a member of the Ancient Arabic Order of Nobles of the Mystic Shrine; the Ancient and Accepted Scottish Rite (Masons); the Masonic Lodge; Knights Templar; the American Legion; Eagles; Loyal Order of Moose; the Elks; and the International Association of Lions Clubs. His fraternity is Delta Tau Delta. He is a Presbyterian. For recreation Handley enjoys golfing and, when not in Indiana, deep-sea fishing.

(Continued next page)

HANDLEY, HAROLD W.—*Continued*

While he was in military service during World War II, Harold Willis Handley met Barbara Jean Winterble, a volunteer worker for the American Red Cross. On February 17, 1944 she became his wife. The Handleys have two children: Kenneth David and Martha Jean. Governor Handley is six feet tall and weighs 185 pounds. He has blue eyes and gray hair. A New York *Times* biographical sketch characterized him as a "trim, immaculately dressed man with a gray fringe framing a largely bald head. He favors a bow tie with white polka dots" (October 31, 1958).

References

Nations Bsns 47:34 My '59 por
International Who's Who, 1959
Who's Who in America, 1960-61

HANSEN, H(ANS) C(HRISTIAN SVANE) Nov. 8, 1906-Feb. 19, 1960 Premier of Denmark (since 1955) and political leader who supported NATO; former Finance Minister (1945-50); Minister of Trade (1950); Minister of Foreign Affairs (1953-58). See *Current Biography* (March) 1956.

Obituary

N Y Times p23 F 20 '60

HARKNESS, GEORGIA (ELMA), REV. DR. April 21, 1891- Teacher; theologian; author
Address: b. Pacific School of Religion, Berkeley, Calif.; h. 10 Kerr Ave., Berkeley 7, Calif.

As professor of applied theology at the Pacific School of Religion and as the author of many books and articles on religion, Georgia Harkness has proved that careers in theology are open to American women. Since 1926 she has been an ordained Methodist minister, and she has served on many church commissions, including the Board of World Peace and the Board of Social and Economic Relations. Her interest in the ecumenical movement has led her to take part in international religious conferences since 1937. She wrote the hymn, "Hope of the World," which was selected by the Hymn Society of America to honor the Evanston Assembly of the World Council of Churches in 1954.

In addition to fullfilling her professorial and conference responsibilities, Dr. Harkness has written twenty-two books and numerous articles on theological subjects. *Prayer and the Common Life* (Abingdon, 1947) was co-winner of the $7,500 Abingdon-Cokesbury Award for a book which would accomplish "the greatest good for the Christian faith and Christian living among all people." Her books, which present theological truths with clarity and force, have a particular appeal for the lay reader.

Georgia Elma Harkness was born in Harkness, New York on April 21, 1891, the youngest of four children of Joseph Warren and Lillie (Merrill) Harkness. Descendants of a Quaker family that had settled in the region in the eighteenth century, Georgia, her sister Hattie (now deceased), and her brothers Charles Merrill and Edward Everett grew up on the family farm in the small Adirondack town named for their grandfather. Family activities in the little country church and early reading habits (she pored over Methodist conference minutes) exerted a lasting spiritual influence on her life and helped determine her choice of a career.

After concluding postgraduate studies at Keeseville (New York) High School in 1908, Georgia won a scholarship to Cornell University, where she studied history and political science and took part in the YWCA and student volunteer movements. Her plans to enter foreign missionary work were curtailed by responsibilities at home. She was graduated from Cornell in 1912 with a B.A. degree and was elected to the Phi Beta Kappa society.

After teaching Latin and French in high schools at Schuylerville (1912-14) and Scotia (1915-18) in New York State, Dr. Harkness enrolled at Boston University's School of Religion, from which she received M.A. and M.R.E. degrees in 1920. At this time she also conducted courses in the English Bible. Although it was then unusual for a woman to pursue a career in theology, she obtained a Ph.D. degree in 1923 with an excellent scholastic record in that subject. Her thesis was entitled "The Relations Between the Philosophy of Religion and Ethics in the Thought of Thomas Hill Green."

For the next fifteen years Professor Harkness taught religion and philosophy at Elmira College for Women at Elmira, New York. During these years she spent her leisure time writing and continuing her divinity studies at Harvard University; at Yale Divinity School, from which she had received a Sterling Fellowship for 1928-29; and at Union Theological Seminary. In 1937 she became an associate professor of the history and literature of religion at Mount Holyoke College. Three years later she accepted an invitation to join the faculty of Garrett Biblical Institute, the Methodist graduate seminary in Evanston, Illinois, as professor of applied theology. "For one who believes as I do in the church and in the importance of theology for all our living, the opportunity to help prepare young people for religious leadership was most welcome," she says.

Dr. Harkness went to California in 1949 to deliver the Earl lectures at the Pacific School of Religion. The school offered her a teaching position which would allow six months a year for her study, travel, lecturing, and, of course, writing. This plan, coupled with Berkeley's scenic charms and beneficent climate, induced Miss Harkness to accept the professorship of applied theology. She was the first woman to be so honored. Miss Harkness spent her sabbatical year of 1956-57 teaching at the International Christian University in Japan, and at the Union Theological Seminary in Manila.

Theologians have described Georgia Harkness as a scholar to be respected. In the opinion of her colleagues, her theology is sound, although some feel that she is "not overawingly profound" (*Christian Century,* September 24, 1952). "She has too great a concern for humanity ever to be satisfied with theology for theology's sake alone," explains one former associate. "She always sees it in relation to life. Her approach is conditioned by her own convictions, her own spiritual reaction. She well represents the evangelical approach to theological questions." Her lectures have been described as "logical, clearcut, beautifully organized to move surely and neatly to a conclusion"; this appraisal also applies to her classroom techniques, sermons, and writings. Always well attended, her sermons and lecture series demonstrate a rare ability to create an atmosphere of fellowship and personal contact.

A prolific author, Dr. Harkness began her writing career while she was still a student. Her articles and poems have appeared in *Christian Century, Christian Advocate, Journal of Religion,* and other religious periodicals. Her first two major books, *Conflicts in Religious Thought* (Harper, 1929; 1949) and *John Calvin; The Man and his Ethics* (Holt, 1931), were favorably received by reviewers.

Despite a heavy teaching load and conference activities, Miss Harkness found time to publish eight more books before 1947. That year she won the Abingdon-Cokesbury award for *Prayer and the Common Life,* a guide to the use of prayer. K. B. Cully, reviewing it for *Christian Century* (August 18, 1948), said: "She can stand on her feet alongside any male theologian in the country. Her special genius, however, seems to be in making these great theological ideas simple enough for the average layman to comprehend."

This statement can be applied with equal pertinence to Dr. Harkness' later books; at least two have been effective study guides for lay religious groups. In *The Modern Rival of Christian Faith* (Abingdon, 1952) she cogently defined secularism as the "organization of life as if God did not exist," and found this secularism exemplified "in large areas of modern life by a superficial optimism and inner despair." L. H. DeWolf wrote in the *Christian Century* (May 28, 1952) that "It is a delight to read a book of such clarity, devout spirit, and prevailing fairness."

Her latest book, *Providence of God* (Abingdon, 1960) asks the question: Does God care? Her answers are based on sound theological reasoning and are presented in language that has a twentieth-century appeal. "Not much new is said here," Virginia Kirkus observed (June 1, 1960). "But everything that is said is offered with a conscious knowledge of atom bombs, power politics, the deterioration of personality, and the loss of a sense of corporateness without which the Church loses its very life."

Dr. Harkness served as a consultant at the 1937 Conference on Life and Work at Oxford, England. At the 1948 Amsterdam and 1954 Evanston (Illinois) assemblies of the World Council of Churches she helped draft official statements on social and economic issues. She was a delegate to the International Missionary

REV. DR. GEORGIA HARKNESS

Council in Madras, India in 1938 and to the third Conference on Faith and Order at Lund, Sweden in 1952. Her "felicitous gift of phrasing," as one of her colleagues called it, has been a valuable asset in her extensive work on committees.

A pacifist since 1924, Georgia Harkness has done a great deal to reconcile different points of view and join in statements on basic principles involving world peace. While a member of the Dun Commission of the Federal Council of Churches in 1950, she and Robert Calhoun signed a minority statement taking exception to the majority's approval of the use of atomic weapons in retaliation for their use against this nation or its allies. However, in the debate that followed, she did all she could to stress the points on which the committee agreed, and to encourage reconciliation of differences.

Although she was ordained in 1926 as a Methodist "local elder" who could administer the sacraments or preach, the Reverend Georgia Harkness, like others of her sex, did not become a full member of a Methodist conference until 1956. She had advocated equal clerical status on many occasions but took no part in the final verbal battle at Minneapolis in May 1956, when women were finally admitted to full pastoral status. "The Bible says that there is a time to speak and a time to be silent. This was the time for me to be silent," she declared with a smile after the decision had been approved (*Christian Science Monitor,* May 5, 1956).

Georgia Harkness has received wide recognition for her services to Methodism and to the ecumenical movement. In 1941 the General Federation of Women's Clubs awarded her a scroll for pioneer work in religion, and she was listed as one of the ten "most influential living Methodists" in a poll taken in 1947 by the *Christian Advocate. Christian Century* chose her as one of six subjects for a series on lead-

HARKNESS, GEORGIA, REV. DR.—
Continued

ing churchwomen in 1952; she was named Churchwoman of the Year by the Religious Heritage of America at the 1958 Washington Pilgrimage.

Dr. Harkness has been awarded the Litt.D. degree by Boston University (1938) and Mac-Murray College (1943); the D.D. degree by Wilson College (1943); and the LL.D. degree by Mills College (1958). She belongs to organizations like the American Association of University Professors, the American Association of University Women, the American Philosophical Society, and the National Association of Biblical Instructors. She has retained her membership at the little country Methodist church in Harkness, New York, which she attended in her youth. Politically, she is an independent.

Miss Harkness is a tall (five feet eight inches) woman, with brown eyes, gray hair, and a friendly smile that dispels any first impression of reserve. Cooking and gardening are her principal relaxations, and she spends many summers at her cottage near Lake Champlain, often visiting her brothers' families and her childhood friends. Although it was at first difficult to take up a career in theology, she has found many opportunities for service. "I have never been a militant feminist in the church," she says. "I have simply gone ahead doing what I saw to do, concentrating on the job at hand, and not trying to do anything unusual or world-shaking. Of course, I've been happy when recognition has come."

References

North Country Life 14:43 spring '60
Who's Who in America, 1952-53; 1960-61
Who's Who of American Women, 1958-59

HART, MOSS Oct. 24, 1904- Playwright; director; author

Address: b. 1501 Broadway, New York 18; h. 1185 Park Ave., New York 28

> NOTE: This biography supersedes the article which appeared in *Current Biography* in 1940.

For one sportive decade the playwriting team of Moss Hart and George S. Kaufman delighted Broadway audiences with their satirical foolery in such comedy hits as *Once in a Lifetime* (1930), *You Can't Take it With You* (1936), and *The Man Who Came to Dinner* (1939). When they parted company after 1940, Hart wrote his own comedies; he also ventured into a more serious medium with dramas like *Christopher Blake* (1946) and *Climate of Eden* (1952). For his direction of *My Fair Lady* in 1956 he received an Antoinette F. Perry (Tony) award. Acclaimed also as a writer of screen scenarios, Hart demonstrated his talent in yet another form when he wrote the best-selling autobiography about his early years, *Act One* (1959).

The elder son of English-born Barnett Hart and the former Lillian Solomon, Moss Hart was born on October 24, 1904 in New York City, where he grew up in the Bronx in "an atmosphere of unrelieved poverty." His father, a cigar maker who saw his livelihood vanish with the advent of the rolling machine, was too frail to undertake a new occupation, and the family eked out a living by renting rooms to boarders. "Poverty was always a living and evil thing to me," Hart has written in *Act One*.

The goad was poverty and the goal was the theater, Hart explains, describing the two main concerns of his youth. With his Aunt Kate, who instilled in him a passion for the theater, Moss saw shows at the Alhambra Theater and the Bronx Opera House on Thursday and Saturday afternoons. Meanwhile he attended Bronx public schools, where he was "an alien and lonely figure." Fond of reading and not skilled at sports, he stood apart from most of his schoolmates.

Having worked after school as a clerk in a neighbor's music store, Moss obtained his first summer job at the age of thirteen. Soon afterwards he left school to become a full-time employee. After working for two-and-a-half years in the storage vault of A. L. Neuberger Furs, Inc., he decided to find another job. When he scanned want ads for clerks and stock boys, one seemed "more miserable than the other." To console himself he paid a visit to his "only link with the theatre," an office boy who worked for the theatrical producer Augustus Pitou, Jr. Finding his friend gone and the job open, seventeen-year-old Moss eagerly became a part of what seemed to him to be the glamorous world of the theater.

Known as the "King of the One-Night Stands," Augustus Pitou, Jr., sent out six road troupes every winter to tour towns throughout the United States. For every company a new play was written each season by Pitou's principal dramatist, Anne Nichols. When Miss Nichols' play, *Abie's Irish Rose*, became a Broadway hit in 1922, Pitou was forced to rely on other, less satisfactory, writers. One day while reading through new scripts, Hart suddenly decided to write his own play. Fearful that this daring might cost him his job, he submitted it to Pitou under the pseudonym of Robert Arnold Conrad.

In Hart's own words, *The Hold-up Man* or *The Beloved Bandit* was "a composite of all the plays Anne Nichols had written for [the actor] Fiske O'Hara." Despite the fact that Pitou and Broadway backer Mrs. Henry B. Harris had envisioned a triumphant New York opening, audiences in Rochester and Chicago, where the play was previewed, recognized it as "a fake . . . a dishonest facsimile." Pitou lost some $45,000 on the production, and Hart's worst fears were justified: he was fired.

During the next six years Hart spent his winter evenings as a director of little theater groups in New York and New Jersey and his summers as a social director at adult resort camps in the Catskills. Hart undertook his first directing assignment at the prompting of Edward Chodorov. During his first season with the Labor Temple theater group, he staged three successful one-act plays and an abortive production of Ibsen's *Ghosts.* The following summer, after holding temporary jobs as a floorwalker at Macy's and as an advertisement classifier with the New York *Times,* Hart served his apprenticeship as a social director at Camp Utopia, which was owned by the sponsor of the Labor Temple project.

In *Act One* Hart describes the anguish he experienced during these summers. Constant inventiveness and sheer physical endurance were required to provide demanding vacationers with uninterrupted entertainment. By 1929 he had won an undisputed reputation as "King of the Borscht Circuit." Three years before, in November 1926, Hart had made his first and last appearance as a professional actor when he played Smithers in Eugene O'Neill's *The Emperor Jones* at the Mayfair Theater in New York.

Each fall, after returning to New York, Hart wrote a full-length serious play. Although he completed six manuscripts, he did not succeed in selling a single one. Undiscouraged, in September 1929 Hart began a new play—his first comedy. The script of *Once in a Lifetime,* a satire of Hollywood's reaction to the coming of talking pictures, won the approval of Sam H. Harris. He agreed to produce it on Broadway if Hart would rewrite it in collaboration with George S. Kaufman. After try-outs in Atlantic City and Brighton Beach and many revisions of the script, the comedy came to the Music Box in New York City in September 1930. *Once in a Lifetime* ran for two years and won the Roi Cooper McGrue prize. "I would like the audience to know," Kaufman said in a rare appearance in front of the curtain, "that eighty per cent of this play is Moss Hart." In 1932 Universal Studios produced a film version of *Once in a Lifetime.*

While *Once in a Lifetime* was still running on Broadway, Hart wrote the book for Irving Berlin's musical, *Face the Music,* which opened at the New Amsterdam Theater in February 1932. He also collaborated with Berlin on the successful musical revue, *As Thousands Cheer* (1933). The most serious of the Kaufman-Hart plays, *Merrily We Roll Along* (1934), dealt with the pitfalls of sudden success. Hart's operetta, *The Great Waltz* (1934), was set to the music of Johann Strauss, Senior, and Johann Strauss, Junior.

Written on a cruise around the world that Hart and composer Cole Porter made together in 1934, *Jubilee* (1935) tells of a royal family escaped incognito from the palace and indulging in a few days' spree in town. The following year Kaufman and Hart's *You Can't Take it With You,* which described the antic behavior of a pleasantly eccentric family, began its run of 837 performances. The play won a Pulitzer Prize in 1937.

I'd Rather Be Right (1937), their next comedy, satirized New Deal politicking and starred George M. Cohan as President Franklin D. Roosevelt. The theater itself was the protagonist of *The Fabulous Invalid* (1938). Burns

MOSS HART

Mantle characterized the first half of the patriotic spectacle *The American Way* (1939) as "one of America's superior folk plays," and the second half as a "ruthlessly revealing arraignment of the American way of meeting or dodging, ignoring or grappling with current social, racial, economic and political problems."

The Man Who Came to Dinner (1939), an acerbic comedy inspired by the crotchets of Alexander Woollcott, was Kaufman and Hart's last successful collaboration. With Monty Woolley in the title role, the play ran for 739 performances in New York. The less successful *George Washington Slept Here* (1940) was the last play that Hart and Kaufman wrote together.

"About this time," Mona Gardner noted in the *Saturday Evening Post* (November 25, 1944), "Hart found himself beset with the fear that the most he could hope from the future was to be known as a prominent collaborator-about-town . . . [and] he . . . took himself to a psychiatrist." In 1941 he wrote about psychoanalysis in a successful musical play, *Lady in the Dark,* for which Kurt Weill wrote the music and Ira Gershwin the lyrics. Paramount released a film version of the play in 1944.

Beginning with *Lady in the Dark,* Hart staged his own plays. In 1943, as his contribution to the war effort, he wrote the Army Air Forces' drama, *Winged Victory.* A simple and romantic story geared to the mood of the day, the play was performed 212 times by 350 nonprofessional actors—men of the Air Forces and their wives. A film version was released by Twentieth Century-Fox in 1944. *Light Up the Sky* (1948), another Hart success, was a bustling farce about the vicissitudes of show business.

Turning to serious drama, Hart wrote *Christopher Blake* (1946), an exploration of the shattering effects on a small boy of his par-

HART, MOSS—Continued

ents' divorce. Not as successful as his comedies, the play nevertheless had the distinction of penetrating with some depth into the privacy of the boy's mind. Brooks Atkinson in the New York *Times* (December 8, 1946) observed that "Despite a tendency toward garish showmanship where imaginative drama would be more effective, 'Christopher Blake' is well-planned, well-written, and wholly engrossing in the last scenes."

The Climate of Eden (1952) concerns an unorthodox missionary family in British Guiana whose members do not allow piety to stand in the way of their uninhibited conduct. After it failed, Hart felt unable to begin work on a new play. Instead, he started to work on his autobiography, which was published in 1959 by Random House as *Act One*.

Hart has directed many plays by other dramatists. In 1941 he staged *Junior Miss* for producer Max Gordon and three years later staged *Dear Ruth*, produced by his younger brother, Bernard, and Joseph Hyman. The following year he directed Robert Turney's *The Secret Room*. He staged *Miss Liberty* (1949) and *Anniversary Waltz* (1954), and he rehearsed several companies of *My Fair Lady*, beginning with the original troupe in 1956. In 1960 Hart also directed *Camelot*, a musical by Alan Jay Lerner and Frederick Loewe.

Since 1932 Hart has written screen plays. Films for which he has provided the scenarios are *Flesh* (MGM, 1932); *The Masquerader* (United Artists, 1933); *Broadway Melody of 1936* (MGM, 1935); *Frankie and Johnnie* (RKO, 1935); *Hans Christian Andersen* (RKO, 1952); a new version of *A Star is Born* (Warner, 1954); and *Prince of Players* (Twentieth Century-Fox, 1955). He also wrote the script for *Gentleman's Agreement* (Twentieth Century-Fox, 1947), which won an award from the Academy of Motion Picture Arts and Sciences as the best film of the year.

Moss Hart and actress Kitty Carlisle were married at New Hope, Pennsylvania on August 10, 1946. They have one son, Christopher, and one daughter, Cathy Carlisle. "Hart's physical appearance is as conflicting as his personality," Mona Gardner wrote in the *Saturday Evening Post* (November 18, 1944). "Well over six feet tall, with a long narrow head and black hair, there is a faintly Biblical look about him which is immediately contradicted by an imposing set of satyr eyebrows." He belongs to the Dramatists' Guild (president 1947-54), Actors' Equity Association, the Screen Writers Guild, the Lambs Club, the Players, and the Independent Committee of Arts and Sciences in New York.

References

Sat Eve Post 217:9+ N 18 '44 pors; 217:20+ N 25 '44 pors
Hart, Moss Act One (1959)
National Cyclopaedia of American Biography, current vol G (1946)
Who's Who, 1960
Who's Who in America, 1960-61
World Biography (1954)

HARTKE, (RUPERT) VANCE May 31, 1919- United States Senator from Indiana; lawyer

Address: b. Senate Office Bldg., Washington 25, D.C.; h. 1010 Kearn's Court, Falls Church, Va.

Indiana's junior Senator, Vance Hartke, can claim one of the more striking election victories of the 1958 Democratic landslide. Winning the seat of Republican William E. Jenner in a race with Governor Harold W. Handley, he became the first Democratic Senator elected in his state in twenty years. Hartke, who is a lawyer and former mayor of Evansville, Indiana, includes among his legislative interests the problems of the unemployed, flood control, and civil rights. His major assignments in the Eighty-sixth Congress are to the Senate's Finance Committee and the Interstate and Foreign Commerce Committee.

Rupert Vance Hartke, the fourth child of Hugo and Ida (Egbert) Hartke, was born in the mining town of Stendal, Pike County, Indiana on May 31, 1919. His father was a schoolteacher and Stendal's postmaster. When he was in the first grade, his teacher was his sister, Ruth Hartke, who became a school supervisor. He graduated from the high school in Stendal in 1935 and went on to Evansville College in Evansville, Indiana, where he was captain of the basketball team, president of the student government, and a member of Lambda Chi Alpha. He received the B.A. degree in 1939.

The winner of two scholarships, Hartke then attended Indiana University Law School. He edited the *Indiana Law Journal* and joined Phi Delta Phi and Tau Kappa Alpha. When the United States entered World War II in 1941, he gave up his studies for the time being to serve in the Coast Guard and Navy. Hartke, who rose to the rank of lieutenant, spent part of his time in military service taking charge of purchasing for the Underwater Sound Laboratory in New London, Connecticut.

Immediately after his discharge he returned to law school, where he acquired the degree of Doctor of Jurisprudence in 1948. He then entered the Evansville firm of John H. Jennings, one of Indiana's leading damage lawyers. Two years later he opened his own law office in Evansville, also specialising in damage law. At the same time he received a one-year appointment as deputy prosecutor for Vanderburgh County, Indiana, and in that office helped send a murderer to life imprisonment.

Hartke had become associated with the Democratic party in law school through his activities in the Young Democrats. For a time he headed the Eighth Congressional District Young Democrats and, in January 1952, following a Democratic November election defeat, he became Vanderburgh County's Democratic chairman. His reorganization of the local party prompted one editor on the opposing side to describe him as a "genius at political organization."

In 1955 Hartke defeated Republican Curtis Huber in the Evansville mayoralty contest. Hartke's supporters cite among the accomplishments of his "reform administration" as mayor a slum clearance program, lower taxes, polio vaccine clinics, sewer expansion, and new recreation programs. He also initiated a fire-prevention program and a police civil service plan and installed "no-fix" traffic tickets.

When William E. Jenner decided to retire from the Senate, Hartke campaigned vigorously during 1958 to win the Democratic nomination and then, in November, the Senate seat. With the support of former Democratic National Chairman Frank E. McKinney of Indianapolis, he defeated four rivals for the nomination and united behind him a formerly faction-ridden party. The thirty-nine-year-old mayor campaigned almost every hour of the day and was known to solicit votes through the open window of his car when it was stopped for a red light.

In his victory on November 4, 1958 Hartke carried four counties that had never before left the Republican fold, defeating Republican Governor Harold W. Handley by a majority of 242,000 votes. He attributed the success of his campaign to "farmers' discontent, highway scandals, the lack of flood control projects, and a fighting Democratic organization." After taking his place in the Senate in January 1959, he was assigned to three committees: Finance (which handles tax matters and veterans affairs), Interstate and Foreign Commerce (which is concerned with transportation and communication as well as trade), and the District of Columbia (of which he is chairman of the judiciary subcommittee).

Generally regarded as a moderate, middle-of-the-road Democrat, Senator Hartke tends to take a liberal approach to such matters as housing, labor, and civil rights; he tends to be more conservative in his fiscal policies. In a 1959 intraparty quarrel over legislative strategy he sided with the moderates headed by Senator Lyndon B. Johnson of Texas who preferred a compromise program which a Republican President might accept rather than a more liberal one which would invite Presidential veto.

Included in the forty-nine proposals that Hartke introduced as a freshman Senator were measures and resolutions which would provide $100-a-month pensions to veterans of World War I, set up a commission of intergovernment relations for exchange of information among officials of state and local governments, provide funds to help local communities restore and enlarge their airports for the jet age, have the Census Bureau give priority in its hiring to the aged and jobless, and give Congress more control over government spending.

A veteran worker for flood control, he belongs to the National Rivers and Harbors Congress, which makes recommendations to Congress on flood control and water resources measures, and a charter member of the Wabash Valley Association and Ohio Valley Improvement Association. He has introduced a bill to give Congressional approval to the Wabash Valley agreement between Indiana and Illinois for industrial development and flood control.

Hartke's most widely publicized measure during 1959 was an amendment to the Federal Communications Act which would prevent

VANCE HARTKE

radio and television broadcasters from being forced to make equal time available for political broadcasts to obscure and fringe candidates for the office of President or Vice-President. The main elements of this amendment, which was hailed by the broadcasting industry, were incorporated in the final legislation passed by the Senate.

Interested in improved civil rights legislation, during 1959 Hartke introduced a constitutional amendment to remove the poll tax as a prerequisite for voting in any state, voted for a revision of the rules to curb filibusters (January), and supported an extension of the Civil Rights Commission (September). He showed his concern for the workingman in his affirmative votes on a bill to aid depressed areas (March), a proposed extension of the Temporary Unemployment Compensation Act (March), the labor-management reporting and disclosure bill (April), and a proposal to increase federal public assistance to states (June).

On other measures brought before the Senate during 1959 Hartke voted in favor of Hawaiian statehood (March), an extension of the Airport Construction Act (June), the housing bill of 1959 (June), and the mutual security bill of 1959 (July). He opposed repeal of all farm price supports (May) and the nomination of Lewis L. Strauss as Secretary of Commerce (June).

Hartke was one of ten Senators present at a meeting of the Atlantic Congress in London in June 1959, during which fifteen NATO (North Atlantic Treaty Organization) countries discussed defense organization. In October 1959 he was appointed a United States representative to the NATO Parliamentary Conference in Washington. He is also a member of a nine-man Senate committee to study the causes and effects of unemployment.

(Continued next page)

HARTKE, VANCE—*Continued*

In June 1943 Hartke was married to Martha Tiernan, at that time a schoolteacher. They have six children: Sandra, Jan, Wayne, Keith, Paul, and Anita Ruth—ranging in age from fifteen years to about one year. The Senator belongs to St. Paul's Lutheran Church and the Lutheran Laymen's League, is a member of the Junior Chamber of Commerce and the Exchange Club, and is director of Evansville's Future, Inc. He is also active in support of the Community Chest and United Fund. He still enjoys basketball, but usually spends his small amount of spare time in recreation with his family.

Reference

Congressional Directory (1959)

HAYNES, GEORGE EDMUND May 11, 1880-Jan. 8, 1960 Sociologist; educator; specialist in Negro-white race relations; co-founder of National Urban League and its first director (1910-18). See *Current Biography* (March) 1946.

Obituary

N Y Times p87 Ja 10 '60

HAYWORTH, RITA Oct. 17, 1918- Actress
Address: b. c/o Twentieth Century-Fox Film Corporation, Beverly Hills, Calif.

The cinema "love goddess" who longs to be known as a dramatic actress has by now become a stereotype, but the indications are that Rita Hayworth has made the transition. In show business since 1932, she typified the international glamour girl both on and off the screen for many years. Since 1958, however, her screen appearances have displayed dramatic talents she had never exhibited before, while her personal life has been devoid of material for the nation's gossip columnists.

Rita Hayworth was born Margarita Carmen Cansino in New York City on October 17, 1918, the daughter of Eduardo and Volga (Haworth) Cansino. Her father's family had long been famous as dancers in Spain; her mother was descended from a long line of English actors. In 1913 Eduardo Cansino had immigrated to the United States to become a vaudeville headliner with his sister. Volga Cansino, too, had been a show business professional as a "Ziegfeld's follies" girl.

In 1927, when vaudeville was giving place to motion pictures, the Cansino family settled in Los Angeles, California, where Margarita's father taught dancing and worked as a dance director for the film studios. While attending Carthay School and Hamilton High School in Los Angeles, the girl took dancing and acting lessons in order to carry on the family name. She made her stage debut in a school play when she was eleven years old. "I found I liked it," she later recalled. "Not so much the dancing as the pretty costume." A while later, in 1932,

she made her professional bow in a stage prologue to the motion picture *Back Street,* at the Carthay Circle Theater in Los Angeles.

Her father decided that in his daughter he had a new dancing partner who might revive the family tradition. Margarita broke off her education in the ninth grade, and father and daughter were booked at the Foreign Club in Tijuana, Mexico, for an eighteen-month run. After that they performed on a California gambling boat, then were hired for seven months in the resort of Agua Caliente, Mexico.

Among the spectators at Agua Caliente was Winfield R. Sheehan of the Fox Film Corporation, who hired the sixteen-year-old girl to play a supporting role in *Dante's Inferno* (1935). The film, starring Spencer Tracy, was later characterized as "one of the worst big-budget movies ever made," but Margarita came out of the fiasco with a one-year contract with Fox. Her early roles were as unimportant, however, as the films in which she appeared.

After she portrayed an Egyptian dancer in *Charlie Chan in Egypt* (1935), an Argentine dancer in *Under the Pampas Moon* (1935), an Irish dancer in *Paddy O'Day* (1935), and a Russian dancer in *Human Cargo* (1936), Miss Cansino's contract expired along with the interest of Fox executives in her as studio property. It was not renewed. She spent the next year portraying Mexican girls and Indian princesses in several movies at $100 per role and won a new contract, from Columbia Pictures Corporation.

Margarita made fourteen low-budget films for Columbia before Howard W. Hawks cast her in *Only Angels Have Wings* (1939), also produced by Columbia. Although the film lifted her out of the B-movie class, it did not immediately win her any new roles. During an eight-month period of unemployment, Margarita prepared for a major assault upon stardom. She cut and bleached her hair, raised her forehead by electrolysis, and studied under acting and singing coaches. The result was Rita Hayworth—her mother's maiden name with a "y" added for marquee appeal. Another studio was the first to recognize star material in Rita Hayworth: Warner Brothers Pictures, Inc., which borrowed her to replace Ann Sheridan in *The Strawberry Blonde* (1941). She then went to Fox to make *Blood and Sand* (1941).

At twenty-three, a veteran of thirty-two motion pictures, Miss Hayworth was cast opposite Fred Astaire in *You'll Never Get Rich* in 1941 by her own studio, Columbia. The film made her a celebrity. In a cover story about the new star, *Time* magazine wrote that "the high spots of the show come when its six Cole Porter melodies . . . tickle the dancing feet of Astaire & Hayworth. . . . Rita Hayworth really knows dancing." In quick succession, she then starred in *My Gal Sal* (1942), *Tales of Manhattan* (1942), and again as Astaire's dancing partner in *You Were Never Lovelier* (1942).

By now Columbia's leading actress, Miss Hayworth was earning $6,500 a week. The stipend was justified by her next three pictures, *Cover Girl* (1944), *Tonight and Every Night* (1945), and *Gilda* (1946), which together grossed $20,000,000 at the box office. A print of a fourth film, *Down to Earth* (1947) along with other examples of twentieth century life, was placed in a time capsule for posterity.

The film thus immortalized was excoriated by Winthrop Sargeant in *Life* (November 10, 1947) as "one of the shoddier, duller, and more heavy-handed examples of a type produced with relentless regularity by the Hollywood studios. . . . It is a ritual in which the great American love goddess re-enacts her perpetual legend." Sargeant continued: "It seems incredible that at the center of these heroic industrial operations should exist a rather likable, simple and completely unaffected human being." The human element, however, was one in which the movie-going public was not especially interested.

Miss Hayworth made her first break with this Venusberg legend in *The Lady From Shanghai* (1948), in which she cut her hair and became a sophisticated blonde to co-star with her husband, Orson Welles. She resumed her screen personality as a sultry siren in *The Loves of Carmen* (1948) before retiring temporarily from movie-making in order to become the bride of Prince Aly Khan.

Returning to Columbia studios, Miss Hayworth starred in *Affair in Trinidad* (1952), *Salome* (1953), and *Miss Sadie Thompson* (1953), a screen adaptation of W. Somerset Maugham's short story "Rain." All three documented Otis L. Guernsey's comment (New York *Herald Tribune,* December 24, 1953) that "a Hayworth movie is a kind of medicine show, attracting as much attention as possible to a single product."

Again Miss Hayworth married in the glare of publicity, this time to singer Dick Haymes and again she temporarily retired from Hollywood. Her next film vehicle was *Fire Down Below* (Columbia, 1957), with a screenplay by Irwin Shaw which attracted some favorable reviews. She followed it with *Pal Joey* (1957), a film version of the Rodgers and Hart musical success, in which she played a Nob Hill matron up from burlesque, who befriends a graceless night club crooner. It was her last film as a studio star.

As a free lance, she chose for her first vehicle the Hecht-Hill-Lancaster production of *Separate Tables* (United Artists release, 1958), Terence Rattigan's story of a British seaside hotel which shelters the lonely and desperate. As Ann Shankland, Rita Hayworth played a neurotic who preys on her former husband and brings about his downfall.

A greater departure from traditional roles was offered her by *They Came to Cordura* (1959), which had to do with American troops on their way home after fighting Pancho Villa's forces. Playing a dissolute and traitorous American, "Miss Hayworth, looking haggard, drawn, and defeated, gives the best performance of her career," reported *Variety* (Septem-

20th Century—Fox

RITA HAYWORTH

ber 23, 1959). "If she shows only half the beauty she usually does, she displays twice the acting." In 1960 Miss Hayworth appeared in *The Story on Page One* (December, 1959), a courtroom drama in which she played the housewife who with her lover is unjustly charged with murdering her husband.

The deglamourizing of Rita Hayworth seems also to extend to her personal life; her most recent marriage, to producer James Hill on February 2, 1958, was relatively free from publicity. She was married to Edward C. Judson, a Texas oil man, in 1936 and was divorced from him in 1942; to Orson Welles in 1943, divorced in 1948; to Prince Aly Khan in 1949, divorced in 1953; and to Dick Haymes in 1953, divorced in 1955. She has custody of her two daughters, Rebecca Welles and Princess Yasmin.

Rita Hayworth likes to wear slacks and casual clothes. Interested in art, she especially appreciates impressionism and Chinese *objets d'art* of the Wei and T'ang dynasties. She is very athletic, and her favorite sports are swimming, tennis, and golf.

"I'm in a new phase of my career," Miss Hayworth said in 1959. "I'm a free-lance actress. I could have stayed under a studio contract; by not staying, I gave up a lot of money. But I felt that at some point in my life I had to choose my own roles. I looked at all the parts I had done and realized that, no matter how they were sliced, it was still Salome."

References

Am Mag 134:42+ D '42 por

International Motion Picture Almanac, 1960

Who's Who in America, 1950-51

HELLMAN, LILLIAN June 20, 1905-
Playwright
Address: h. 63 E. 82d St., New York 28

NOTE: This biography supersedes the article which appeared in *Current Biography* in 1941.

Since the sensational Broadway première of her first drama, *The Children's Hour*, in 1934, Lillian Hellman has generally been considered America's leading woman playwright. Her latest play, *Toys in the Attic*, was welcomed by reviewers as a long-needed tonic to the pervasive mediocrity of the 1959-60 Broadway season, and promised to be a popular as well as critical success. Like most of Miss Hellman's other work, *Toys in the Attic* is concerned with the problem of evil (in this instance, the nature of destructive love) and has a theatrical power deriving in large measure from sharp, perceptive characterization and an uncompromising precision of language.

Bender, N.Y.

LILLIAN HELLMAN

The only child of Max Bernard Hellman, a businessman, and Julia (Newhouse) Hellman, Lillian Hellman was born on June 20, 1905, in New Orleans, Louisiana. She was reared for the most part in New York City, where the family moved when she was five. Returning to New Orleans for long visits, she attended public schools there, as well as in New York. From 1922 to 1924 she was a student at New York University and in 1924 also took a course in Dante at Columbia University.

Lillian Hellman's first job upon leaving college was as a manuscript reader with the book publishing firm of Horace Liveright, Inc. The following year, in 1925, she began reviewing books for the New York *Herald Tribune* and reading plays for Broadway pro-

ducers. In 1930 she went to Hollywood, where she read scenarios for Metro-Goldwyn-Mayer, but returned to New York in 1932 to read plays for Herman Shumlin, who was later to produce and direct several of Miss Hellman's own dramatic works.

Her commercial activities during these early years did not prevent Miss Hellman from cultivating her own creative talents. A piece called *Introspective Writing*, published in the Paris *Comet*, and the unproduced play "Dear Queen," written in collaboration with Louis Kronenberger, were products of this period. By 1934 she had completed *The Children's Hour*, which was to establish her as a leading Broadway playwright.

Herman Shumlin's production of *The Children's Hour* took New York by storm when it opened in November 1934. This tense dramatization of the effects of a child's slanderous suggestion of abnormal relations between two of her teachers ran for 691 performances in New York, toured the United States, and was adapted by Miss Hellman into a film, *These Three* (United Artists, 1936).

Among Miss Hellman's other early screenplays were those for *Dark Angel* (United Artists, 1935) and *Dead End* (United Artists, 1937). Her second play for the stage, *Days to Come*, a study of a labor strike, opened in New York in 1936. The least successful of her plays, it was greeted with critical disfavor and closed within a single week.

Later in 1936 Lillian Hellman began a tour of Europe which included visits to Russia, France, and Spain. The month she spent in revolution-torn Spain in 1937 was of great moment to her: she sympathized deeply with the Loyalist cause and made strong public denunciations of the Franco regime upon her return to the United States. The hatred for fascism awakened in her by her experiences in Spain were later to find expression in her wartime dramas.

Tallulah Bankhead was the star of Lillian Hellman's third Broadway effort, *The Little Foxes*, which had its première in February 1939. This bristling indictment of selfishness and hypocrisy in a turn-of-the-century Southern family ran for 410 performances in New York. Also enthusiastically received was the 1941 film version starring Bette Davis, which Miss Hellman herself adapted for RKO Radio.

During the 1940's Miss Hellman divided her time between Broadway and Hollywood. Perhaps her greatest success of this period was *Watch on the Rhine*, the story of an anti-Nazi German and his sacrifice of personal happiness to the cause of freedom. The play came to New York on April 1, 1941, and on April 23 won the New York Drama Critics Circle Award as the best drama of the 1940-41 Broadway season.

After adapting *Watch on the Rhine* (Warner Brothers, 1943) for the screen and completing the film *The North Star* (RKO, 1943), about the heroism of the Russian people during World War II, Miss Hellman wrote *The Searching Wind*, which was presented in New York beginning in April 1944. Ward Morehouse in the New York *Sun* (April 13) called it "an acrid and powerful drama of anti-appeasement" and "the theatrical event of the season of 1943-44 to date." Although other reviewers were less impressed by the drama, all agreed upon the seriousness of its intentions. In the cast were Dennis King, Cornelia Otis Skinner, and Montgomery Clift.

In 1945, before the end of the war in Europe, Lillian Hellman made her second trip to the Soviet Union, this time as an honored guest of that country, for the purpose of observing wartime conditions. Her desire to understand the Russian situation brought her within shooting range of the front lines. Her report on Russian life and gallantry was published in *Collier's* (March 31, 1945).

Having completed her film adaptation of *The Searching Wind* (Paramount, 1946), Lillian Hellman turned her energies to a new play, *Another Part of the Forest,* which reached Broadway on November 20, 1946. Concerned with an earlier stage of the Hubbard family anatomized in *The Little Foxes,* this drama prompted many reviewers to say that it could compare favorably with its notable predecessor. Among the players were Percy Waram and Mildred Dunnock. Miss Hellman herself directed.

Lillian Hellman also directed her own version of the French play *Montserrat* by Emmanuel Robles, first performed in New York on October 29, 1949. Although some critics admired the work, which starred Emlyn Williams and dealt with Bolivar's attempts to emancipate Venezuela from Spanish oppression, Brooks Atkinson in the New York *Times* complained that "the effects it achieves are mechanical."

In *The Autumn Garden,* which opened on Broadway on March 7, 1951 with Fredric March and Florence Eldridge as the stars, Lillian Hellman turned to the theme of middle age and the necessity of properly preparing for one's later years. Not all the reviewers admired the play. George Jean Nathan, for example, observed that "all we see is a room full of men and women suffering for nothing but the calendar." John Chapman, on the other hand, who described *The Autumn Garden* as a comedy in the Chekhovian sense, thought that it was Lillian Hellman's best play.

On December 18, 1952 Lillian Hellman staged a Broadway revival of *The Children's Hour* starring Patricia Neal and Kim Hunter. Although less successful than the original presentation, the production lasted for 189 performances in New York before going on tour, and some critics felt that after eighteen years the play retained much of its impact.

Lillian Hellman's excellent adaptation of Jean Anouilh's treatment of the Joan of Arc story, *The Lark,* reached Broadway on November 17, 1955, with a cast headed by Julie Harris. Miss Hellman's next adaptation was of Voltaire's *Candide.* This musical version of the famous satire on optimism was first presented in New York on December 1, 1956 and featured a score by Leonard Bernstein. The

reviews were mixed, and the show lived up to *Variety's* prediction that it would be a "commercial flop."

Toys in the Attic, Lillian Hellman's first original play since 1951, was given its Broadway première on February 25, 1960. Some reviewers did not think the play one of Miss Hellman's best; all agreed that her study of greed and moral laxity in a Louisiana family ranked far above the dreary level of the season and that Miss Hellman had not lost her ability to provide rewarding assignments for her actors, who in this play included Jason Robards, Jr., Maureen Stapleton, Anne Revere, and Irene Worth. "*Toys in the Attic* binds us to it," Walter Kerr wrote, "with a cold, serpentine grace that is born of a clear head, a level eye, and a fierce respect for the unchanging color of the precisely used word" (New York *Herald Tribune,* March 6, 1960). In April 1960 it won the New York Drama Critics Circle Award as the best play of the year.

Because of her interest in left-wing causes Miss Hellman was invited to testify before the House Un-American Activities Committee in 1952. Denying that she was a member of the Communist party at that time, she refused to answer questions concerning possible earlier membership. In a letter to committee chairman John S. Wood, she explained that her sense of ethics prevented her from testifying about the political activities of her associates. Miss Hellman was not prosecuted for her refusal to answer these questions.

Lillian Hellman now divides her time between her Manhattan town house and her home on Martha's Vineyard. She lives alone, her marriage on December 30, 1925 to playwright and short story writer Arthur Kober having terminated in divorce seven years later. For recreation she fishes, swims, and cooks. She also reads extensively, enjoying especially the poems of Donne and Blake. In 1955 she edited *Selected Letters* of Anton Chekhov for Farrar, Straus & Cudahy's Great Letters Series.

The creator of plays famous for their heated intensity and biting language is herself a restrained, soft-spoken woman, gentle and affable in manner. Miss Hellman is five feet four inches tall and weighs 125 pounds; her hair and eyes are brown. She is Jewish. Her organizations include the National Institute of Arts and Letters and the Dramatists Guild. She is no longer an active participant in politics. In 1950 she received an honorary M.A. degree from Tufts College.

References

N Y Post Mag p2 Mr 6 '60 por
International Who's Who, 1959
National Cyclopaedia of American Biography current vol G (1943-46)
Oxford Companion to the Theatre (1957)
Twentieth Century Authors (1942; First Supplement, 1955)
Who's Who in America, 1960-61
Who's Who in the Theatre (1957)
World Biography (1954)

HENNINGS, THOMAS C(AREY), JR.
June 25, 1903-Sept. 13, 1960 United States Senator from Missouri since 1951; chairman, Senate Rules and Administration Committee since 1957; United States Representative (1935-41); Democrat; lawyer. See *Current Biography* (October) 1954.

Obituary

N Y Times p1+ S 14 '60

HENNOCK, FRIEDA B(ARKIN) Sept.
27, 1904-June 20, 1960 Lawyer; member of the Federal Communications Commission (1948-55); private practitioner in Washington, D.C. since 1955. See *Current Biography* (November) 1948.

Obituary

N Y Times p33 Je 21 '60

HILL, DAVID G(ARRETT) June 6, 1902-
Business executive
Address: b. Pittsburgh Plate Glass Co., 1 Gateway Center, Pittsburgh 22, Pa.; h. 309 S. Linden Ave., Pittsburgh 8, Pa.

Convinced that the United States is "only at the beginning of the new age of glass," David G. Hill, president and chief executive officer of the Pittsburgh Plate Glass Company since 1955, shares his company's outlook that conceivably "some day glass will compare with steel in both strength and machinability." Hill, who joined the company in 1924 as an industrial engineer, has devised new uses for glass in private homes and public buildings and has directed the company's development of products like fiber glass and glass shields against atomic radiation in nuclear research.

The diversified, seventy-seven-year-old Pittsburgh Plate Glass Company not only is a leading producer of flat glass, but also has become an important manufacturer of paint, chemicals, and plastics and has interests in oil and uranium. In addition, it maintains a well-developed merchandising system. Since World War II it has invested more than $150,000,000 in plant expansion.

David Garrett Hill was born in Edgewood, near Pittsburgh, Pennsylvania on June 6, 1902 to William Fulton Hill and Eleanor Patton (Garrett) Hill. Both of his parents were native Pittsburghers. He attended Schenley High School in Pittsburgh and was graduated in 1920. He then enrolled at Cornell University, Ithaca, New York, where he studied mechanical engineering and received the M.E. degree in 1924.

In the same year he joined the Pittsburgh Plate Glass Company as an industrial engineer. At first he worked at the company's Ford City, Pennsylvania plate-glass manufacturing plant, later moving to the Crystal City, Missouri plant and to the Creighton, Pennsylvania plant, where plate glass was manufactured. In 1929 he was transferred to the glass manufacturing department at the company's headquarters in Pittsburgh.

Before the end of 1929 Hill was made assistant to the vice-president of Pittsburgh Plate Glass Company; he served in this capacity until 1940 when he was appointed general superintendent of all the company's plate-glass factories. In 1952 he became vice-president in charge of glass manufacturing. In 1954 he was made a director and in December 1955 was elected president, succeeding Harry B. Higgins, who moved up to chairman of the board.

Pittsburgh Plate Glass Company was established in Creighton, Pennsylvania in 1883 by John Pitcairn, a Scottish immigrant, and his associates. *Fortune* (May 1956) described it as a half-billion-dollar "family" company, which turns out 40 per cent of all the plate glass made in the United States. Until 1945 it was not listed on the New York Stock Exchange. Thirty-one per cent of the stock is owned by Pitcairn Company of Philadelphia, which John Pitcairn's children organized in 1917, a year after his death.

From the beginning, industrial diversification was the company's policy. As early as 1896 it began making paints and related products, as well as glass. Today, it operates forty-seven plants and has 403 merchandising branches, stores, and, sales offices in the United States and Canada. It employs more than 35,000 men and women and is owned by over 20,000 shareholders. The company also has interests in Mexico, South America, and Europe, including a subsidiary glass company at Courcelles, Belgium, of which Hill is president and a director.

Among the domestic affiliates of Pittsburgh Plate Glass Company are Koppers Pittsburgh Company, which manufactures a raw material for paint, and Southern Pipe Line Corporation, which produces and transports crude oil and gas. Hill is chairman and a director of the affiliate Pittsburgh Corning Corporation, producer of glass block and Foamglas insulation, and a director of the subsidiaries Southern Minerals Corporation and Columbia-Southern Chemical Corporation. Besides manufacturing caustic soda, chlorine, and alkali products, the latter subsidiary has pioneered in chemical processing of titanium and zirconium—important metals in the age of space exploration. Canadian subsidiaries of which he is also a director are Canadian Pittsburgh Industries, Ltd., and Standard Chemical, Ltd.

Originally, when the company's only product was flat plate glass, its manufacturing process was entirely manual, and each batch had to be moved from place to place for each operation. Pittsburgh Plate Glass Company has introduced many steps to make the process continuous. In its present-day plants glass moves without stopping for three-quarters of a mile, from melting tank to packing boxes.

The most notable of the many improvements that the company has developed in window glass production is the Pennivernon process, which draws a continuous sheet of glass straight upward from a furnace. It also worked out one of the first commercially successful processes for producing laminated safety automotive glass and in 1934 made the first curved laminated safety plate glass windshield.

Other glass products include Solex, a heat-absorbing glass for buildings and automobiles; Spandrelite, a colored glass for building exteriors; Nesa, a coated glass which conducts electricity on its surface; and Twindow insulating glass. In 1952 it began making fiber glass which can be both soft and strong. Fiber glass yarn (continuous glass filaments) is used in reinforced plastics, reinforced paper products, and insulation for electrical wires and cables.

In an article in *Ceramic Industry* (August 1959) describing how Pittsburgh Corning Corporation makes improved glass blocks, George L. Vincent wrote that the company "found its product identified with stereotyped uses, due to lack of major design changes and long life of the material. To overcome this, the company is introducing new colors and shapes of glass block to broaden the application in various kinds of buildings." Increased use of color in glass has stimulated the company's sales, and the trend toward larger windows in private homes has more than doubled the demand for glass in the past several years.

In 1957 Pittsburgh Plate Glass Company reported a new high in consolidated net sales of $620,803,000 and net earnings of $57,963,000, or $5.86 a share. During 1958, largely because of an extended strike, net earnings dropped to $3.24. In 1959 they were raised to an estimated $4.40 a share.

Other business affiliations of Hill include membership on the board of directors of the Bell Telephone Company of Pennsylvania, Mellon National Bank and Trust Company, and National Union Fire Insurance Company, all of Pittsburgh. He is also a director of Duplate Canada, Ltd., and Smith & Stone, Ltd., both of Canada.

In addition to directing far-flung production and merchandising activities, Hill is prominent in civic affairs. He is a director of the Pittsburgh Symphony Society and ACTION Housing, Inc.; a trustee of Presbyterian Hospital in Pittsburgh, the Automotive Safety Foundation in Washington, D.C., and the Committee for Economic Development; and a member of the National Industrial Conference Board, the executive committee of the Pennsylvania Economy League, and the Cornell University Council. He is also president and a director of the Pittsburgh Plate Glass Foundation, a charitable organization.

David G. Hill and Eleanor Campbell Musser were married on October 6, 1928. They have two sons, William Fulton Hill 2d, now a graduate of Cornell University's School of Engineering, and John Howard Hill, a student at Yale University. Hill is an enthusiastic golfer; he belongs to the Fox Chapel Golf Club and the Laurel Valley Golf Club in Pittsburgh, the Rolling Rock Club in Ligonier, Pennsylvania, and the Ross Moun-

DAVID G. HILL

tain Club in New Florence, Pennsylvania, among others. His fraternity is Sigma Alpha Epsilon. He is a Mason, a Presbyterian, and a Republican.

References

> Fortune 53:106+ My '56 por
> Who's Who in America, 1958-59
> Who's Who in Commerce and Industry (1957)

HINES, FRANK T(HOMAS) Apr. 11, 1879-Apr. 3, 1960 Former United States government official; director of Veterans Bureau (1923-30); administrator of Veterans Affairs (1930-44); career officer in Army (1901-20) who attained rank of brigadier general. See *Current Biography* (April) 1944.

Obituary

N Y Times p37 Ap 5 '60

HITCHCOCK, ALFRED (JOSEPH) Aug. 13, 1899- Motion-picture and television director

Address: b. Paramount Pictures Corp., Hollywood, Calif.; h. 10957 Bellagio Road, Bel Air, Los Angeles, Calif.

> NOTE: This biography supersedes the article which appeared in *Current Biography* in 1941.

During the past thirty-five years, motion-picture and television director Alfred Hitchcock has gained a reputation as the entertainment industry's "cherubic master of suspense" and "portly master of the involuntary scream." His more than forty films, his fleeting appearances as a performer in his own movies, and his weekly television series, *Hitchcock*

Paramount Pictures Corp.

ALFRED HITCHCOCK

Presents, for which he acts as host and narrator, have made millions of his admirers acquainted with "the Hitchcock touch." In spite of all of his triumphs on television, Hitchcock still considers himself primarily a movie man. He has been four times nominated for an award for direction from the Academy of Motion Picture Arts and Sciences, and one of his films, *Rebecca,* won an award from the same organization as the best picture of 1940.

Alfred Joseph Hitchcock was born in London on August 13, 1899, to William Hitchcock, a poultry dealer and fruit importer, and Emma (Whelan) Hitchcock. As a boy, Hitchcock seems to have been possessed by more than the normal share of wanderlust. By the time he was eight, he had ridden every bus line in London and had explored all its docks and shipping terminals. His hobby was keeping track of the British merchant fleet by buying a daily shipping bulletin and plotting the ship positions on a huge wall chart at home.

He was educated at St. Ignatius College, a Jesuit institution, and the University of London, where he took courses leading toward a career as an electrical engineer. He also studied art, navigation, economics, and political science. His first job after leaving the university was with a cable company, making technical calculations on electrical systems installed by the firm. But Hitchcock soon abandoned technology for art. He took a job as assistant layout man in the advertising office of a London department store at a salary of 15 shillings (about $3.50) a week.

In 1920 Hitchcock entered the motion-picture industry with the Famous Players-Lasky Company (now Paramount Pictures Corp.), as a title writer and title artist. His persistence won him the position. Having heard

that a New York executive of the firm was arriving in London to film *The Sorrows of Satan,* Hitchcock assembled a portfolio of subtitle frames for the picture. He somehow managed to see the executive, who, after having looked at the frames, informed Hitchcock that he was not in England to make *The Sorrows of Satan,* but another film; consequently, he had no interest in Hitchcock's title frames. The next day, when Hitchcock returned with another portfolio of art work, this time for *The Great Day,* he got the job.

As a title writer for Famous Players-Lasky Company, Hitchcock added symbolic drawings to the titles—an innovation in the motion-picture industry. In 1923 he joined Gainsborough Pictures in Islington, England, as a scenario writer; he later became art director, assistant director, and production manager. In 1923 he also earned his first film credit—as art director of *Woman to Woman.* In 1925 he became a full-fledged director with the movie, *The Pleasure Garden,* which was made in Munich, Germany.

After *The Pleasure Garden* Hitchcock went on to direct *Murder, The Ring, Juno and the Paycock, The Manxman, The Farmer's Wife, Rich and Strange, Number 17, Champagne, The Skin Game,* and *The Case of Lady Camber* for British International. He also directed the first successful English talking picture, *Blackmail,* for British International. In association with Michael Balcon and Victor Saville, he directed *The Lodger, Downhill,* and *Easy Virtue.* Other films that he directed in England or on the Continent were *The Blackguard, Waltzes from Vienna, The Woman Alone, Young and Innocent,* and *Jamaica Inn.*

These films had already won for Hitchcock the reputation of an expert in the manipulation of suspense. He did not get into his genuine stride, however, until he made a series of six motion pictures for Gaumont-British from 1935 to 1938. Called the "Hitchcock cycle," the series brought him to the attention of American film industry executives. The films were: *The Lady Vanishes; The Man Who Knew Too Much; Secret Agent; Sabotage; The Girl Was Young;* and *The 39 Steps.* The film critics of New York City named *The 39 Steps* the best-directed motion picture of 1938.

In 1938 Hitchcock made his first visit to the United States in order, he has said, "to size up the place." He apparently liked what he saw, since he signed a contract with Selznick-International for five pictures before he returned to England. In 1939 he came back to the United States, this time to establish his permanent residence. His first film in America was *Rebecca* which, based on the best-selling novel by Daphne Du Maurier, starred Laurence Olivier and Joan Fontaine. The film won an award from the Academy of Motion Picture Arts and Sciences as the best picture of 1940, and Hitchcock was nominated for an award for his direction.

Since 1940, hardly a year has gone by without one Hitchcock film (and sometimes more) being produced. His American film credits include: *Foreign Correspondent* (United Artists, 1940); *Mr. and Mrs. Smith* (RKO,

1941); *Suspicion* (RKO, 1941); *Saboteur* (Universal, 1942); *Shadow of a Doubt* (Universal, 1943); *Lifeboat* (Twentieth Century-Fox, 1944); *Spellbound* (United Artists, 1945); *Notorious* (RKO, 1946); *The Paradine Case* (Selznick, 1948); *Rope* (Warner, 1948); *Under Capricorn* (Warner, 1949); *Stage Fright* (Warner, 1950); *Strangers on a Train* (Warner, 1951); *I Confess* (Warner, 1953); *Dial M for Murder* (Warner, 1954); *Rear Window* (Paramount, 1954); *To Catch a Thief* (Paramount, 1955); *The Trouble With Harry* (Paramount, 1956); *The Man Who Knew Too Much* (Paramount, 1956), a second version of the film of the same name previously produced in England; *The Wrong Man* (Warner, 1957); *Vertigo* (Paramount, 1958); *North by Northwest* (MGM, 1959); and *Psycho* (Paramount, 1960). Hitchcock was again nominated for awards for direction from the Academy of Motion Picture Arts and Sciences for *Lifeboat, Spellbound,* and *Rear Window.*

In general, Hitchcock's films are noted for their suspense and humor and for an occasional chilling touch of the macabre. He once said: "The fun of life has the skeleton of life hovering somewhere near. Conversely, sadness enacts itself with court jesters in the cast. When employing suspense, you have to give the audience a chance to laugh. If you don't, they will anyway—because the human body cannot stand the strain—and the whole affair will become ludicrous."

After having marketed suspense so long, Hitchcock, not surprisingly, is articulate about his chief commodity. In explaining suspense to Herbert Brean of *Life* magazine (July 13, 1959), Hitchcock said: "Let us suppose that three men are sitting in a room in which a ticking bomb has been planted. It is going to go off in ten minutes. The audience does not know it is there, and the men do not know it is there either, so they go on talking inanely about the weather or yesterday's baseball game. After ten minutes of desultory conversation, the bomb goes off. What's the result? The unsuspecting audience gets a surprise. . . . That's all. Suppose the story were told differently. This time while the men still do not know the bomb is there, the audience does know. The men still talk inanities, but now the most banal thing they say is charged with excitement. When one finally says, 'Let's leave,' the entire audience is praying for them to do so. But another man says, 'No. Wait a minute. I want to finish my coffee.' The audience groans inwardly and yearns for them to leave. That is suspense."

Hitchcock puts his theory of suspense into practice in his weekly television series, *Hitchcock Presents,* which began on the CBS television network in 1955. He supervises the production of the series, selects most of the stories, oversees their adaptation, collaborates on the dialogue, and prepares the shooting scripts. He directs many, but not all, of the television shows. *Hitchcock Presents* moved to the NBC television network in the fall of 1960.

On December 2, 1926 Alfred Joseph Hitchcock was married to Alma Reville, who was his assistant director when he filmed *The Pleasure Garden* in Munich, and who still works with him on many projects as writer, adviser, and general assistant. They have one married daughter, Patricia (Mrs. Joseph O'Connell). The Hitchcocks live in a hillside home in Bel Air, California, and also own a mountain ranch near San Francisco. Hitchcock, who at five feet eight inches in height, once weighed a monumental 290 pounds, slimmed himself down to 190 pounds during the first half of 1944, and has hovered around that weight ever since. "I am not really a heavy eater," he says, "unless you mean that I am heavy, and I eat."

He dislikes exercise, likes to travel, and gloats over practical jokes. One of his favorite pranks is to enter an elevator with a friend and begin to tell an exciting anecdote in a loud voice. Just as the story is about to reach its climax, he walks out of the elevator, leaving the other passengers intrigued but frustrated. Since Hitchcock has probably frightened more people than any other director, Marie Torre, the television columnist for the New York *Herald Tribune,* asked him in May 1957 if he himself scares easily. He replied: "Very easily. Here's a list in order of adrenalin production: 1. Little children; 2. Policemen; 3. High places; 4. That my next picture won't be as good as the last one."

References

Sat Eve Post 230:36+ Jl 27 '57 por
Cosmop 147:22+ O '59
Who's Who, 1959
Who's Who in America, 1960-61

HOYLE, FRED June 24, 1915- Astronomer; university professor

Address: b. Cambridge University, Cambridge, England; h. 1 Clarkson Close, Cambridge, England

An internationally famous cosmologist, Fred Hoyle is professor of astronomy at Cambridge University and visiting professor of astrophysics at the California Institute of Technology. He is the chief exponent of the Steady-State Theory of the origin of the universe. (Other important theories that try to probe the mysteries of time, space, and matter are the Explosion Theory and the Expansion-Contraction Theory.) Dr. Hoyle views the universe as a "fully self-operating system," with a continuing pattern of development having no beginning and no end, where space and time are both infinite. His recent observations suggesting that the universe has a temperature of 100,000,000 degrees are significant in evaluating and verifying the concept that the universe has always existed and will always exist.

Professor Hoyle's computations on the ages of stars led scientists in 1958 to revise the age of the Milky Way from ten to fifteen billion years. His estimate has recently been challenged by calculations that indicate that the

FRED HOYLE

Milky Way is about twenty-four billion years old. Hoyle's opinion and its opposite may throw new light on the conflicting theories explaining the birth of the universe.

The son of Ben Hoyle, Fred Hoyle was born on June 24, 1915 in Bingley, in the West Riding district of Yorkshire, England. After graduating from the Bingley Grammar School he matriculated at Emmanuel College, Cambridge, where he took his Mathematical Tripos in 1936 and qualified as a Mayhew Prizeman. As a graduate student at Cambridge he won the Smith Prize and was selected as Senior Exhibitioner of the Royal Commission of the Exhibition of 1851. In 1939 Hoyle was elected a Fellow of St. John's College, Cambridge.

With the outbreak of World War II Hoyle abandoned his studies and astronomical observations to work on radar development for the British Admiralty. When he returned to Cambridge he began his studies on the internal composition of stars with Raymond Arthur Lyttleton. These studies with man-made stars confirmed the theory that ordinary stars, including the sun, consisted of pure hydrogen, building up into helium. Hoyle suggested that matter found in the universe was created as hydrogen and that heavier elements were products of subsequent evolution.

The trustees of Cambridge University appointed Hoyle to the post of University Lecturer in Mathematics in 1945, though his theories differed from those of the more conservative astronomers on the faculty. Hoyle became a leading light of "the Cambridge cosmographers," a group of scientists applying modern mathematics and physics to the problems of the universe. Hoyle's cosmological observations and the philosophical criteria that he used in order to distinguish between the different pictures presented by astronomical data, led him

in the late 1940's to propose the Steady-State Theory of the origin of the universe. Working in conjunction with Professors Hermann Bondi and Thomas Gold, Hoyle suggested that the creation of the universe was a process of continuous growth.

Other prominent theories advanced by astronomers are the Explosion Theory, which pictures the universe as an offshoot of a single cataclysmic event or explosion, and the Expansion-Contraction Theory, which provides for a cyclic universe, in which stars and galaxies are formed during expansion and disrupted and broken down by high temperatures during contraction. The Steady-State Theory, on the other hand, eliminates any explanation of the beginning or end of the universe. "Every cluster of galaxies, every star, every atom," according to Dr. Hoyle, "had a beginning, but the universe itself did not." In Hoyle's opinion, stars are created by condensation and their growth and development proceed by the capture of further interstellar material until they combine galaxies or clusters of galaxies. As new matter forms, the universe expands without end, Hoyle believes, since it is infinite in space and time and the galaxies tend to space themselves more widely apart. As they do so, new galaxies come into being, at such a rate that their average density in space remains unchanged with time. Although the individual clusters evolve, the universe does not.

Hoyle's reputation as a cosmologist was recognized in 1956 when he was appointed to the staff of the Mt. Wilson and Palomar Observatories in California. In the same year his Steady-State Theory was both challenged and defended by professional astronomers. The findings of radio astronomy made by Martin Ryle and Allan R. Sandage upheld "the rival evolutionary theory that the universe is expanding from its beginnings as a dense state of matter." The scientists also showed that galaxies were moving away from the earth "6,200 miles per second faster than Hoyle's prediction," which calculated their "speed in direct proportion to their distance from earth" (Time, September 3, 1956). On the other hand, laboratory experiments on the transmutation of helium into carbon conducted by Dr. Thomas Lauritsen strengthened Hoyle's view that matter is in a continuous state of formation in the interior of stars and that the creation and destruction of matter is an eternal process.

Since 1958 Dr. Hoyle has held the Plumian Professorship of Astronomy and Experimental Philosophy at Cambridge and a visiting professorship at the California Institute of Technology. While in the United States in 1958 he worked with the giant computers at the Massachusetts Institute of Technology, reviewing the tens of billions of years of a star's life. In Hoyle's opinion, knowledge of the fusion reactions of stars (in which the lighter elements are fused into heavier ones under the influence of tremendous temperatures and pressures, resulting either in an explosion or a cooling off into what is known as a "dwarf star") is essential if astronomers are to judge the age of galaxies. Evidence as to whether galaxies are of the same or different ages would provide further proof of the accuracy of conflicting theories explaining the origin of the universe.

An important outcome of these studies was Dr. Hoyle's estimate of the age of the Milky Way at fifteen billion years, based on observations of two stars, Delta Eridani and Mu Hercules, between twenty and thirty light years from the earth. In December 1959 Dr. Allan Sandage, rejecting this calculation, judged the Milky Way to be twenty-four billion years old. Verification or rejection of these estimates may determine the worth of the leading theories of the origin of the universe.

An exciting new hypothesis suggesting that the tenuous hydrogen gas in space between the galaxies of stars in the universe probably has a temperature of 100,000,000 degrees was advanced by Dr. Hoyle and Dr. Thomas Gold in June 1959. This upset the established concept that the space in which the galaxies move was empty and cold. The Hoyle-Gold explanation sheds new light on the formation of galaxies resulting from the condensation process of the hot hydrogen gas and on the existence of high-energy cosmic rays. It also supports the Steady-State Theory of the universe, which holds that new galaxies must be created to take the place of the galaxies that race away beyond the regions accessible to the observer. According to Professor Hoyle, without new galaxies "the Steady-State Theory becomes untenable."

Many articles by Dr. Hoyle have appeared in scientific and professional journals. A firm believer in the popularization of science, he has often addressed his writings to a lay audience. *Some Recent Researches in Solar Physics* (Cambridge University Press, 1949) was followed by *The Nature of the Universe* (Harper, 1951), which was well received by the critics and sold more than 70,000 copies in the first six months of publication. *Frontiers of Astronomy* (Harper, 1955), an attempt at "bold theorizing" of contradictory cosmological concepts, received mixed reviews. Hoyle has also written two sociological treatises, *A Decade of Decision* (William Heinemann, 1953) and *Man and Materialism* (Harper, 1956), and two books of science fiction.

With his black curly hair, cleft chin, and narrow-rimmed spectacles, Fred Hoyle presents a scholarly appearance. He has been married to the former Barbara Clark since 1939 and is the father of a son and a daughter. He enjoys listening to music, mountain climbing, and playing cricket. He was elected a Fellow of the Royal Society in 1957 and is a member of the British National Committee on Space Research.

References

International Who's Who, 1959
Who's Who, 1959

HUDSON, MANLEY O(TTMER) May 19, 1886-Apr. 13, 1960 Jurist; Bemis Professor (and Professor Emeritus) of International Law at Harvard University (1923-54); judge of the Permanent Court of International Justice (1936-45). See *Current Biography* (June) 1944.

Obituary

N Y Times p31 Ap 14 '60

HUNTER, DARD Nov. 29, 1883- Authority on paper and papermaking; author
Address: b. The Institute of Paper Chemistry, Appleton, Wisconsin; h. "Mountain House," Chillicothe, Ohio

Probably no living man knows more about paper, its early history, and the craft of making it by hand than Dard Hunter, who, by making people more conscious of its importance, has done much to raise the quality of paper made in our time. His interest in the history and methods of papermaking has taken him to remote corners of the world to study primitive techniques, and he has written many authoritative books and articles on the craft. Foreign countries have honored him for his pioneering research; people from many countries have sought him out for his expert counsel. A. Edward Newton recognized the importance of Dard Hunter as early as 1928 when he wrote in *This Book-Collecting Game*: "He is the most interesting bookmaker in this, perhaps in any country, and although he never will become rich, he has the unique distinction of writing his name on an absolutely white page in the history of bookmaking."

Dard Hunter was born on November 29, 1883 in Steubenville, Ohio to William Henry and Harriet Rosemond (Browne) Hunter. His father owned and edited the Steubenville *Daily Gazette*; his grandfather, Joseph Hunter, had owned and edited the Cadiz (Ohio) *Sentinel*; and his great-grandfather, James Hunter, had set up a printing-office in the wilds of Ohio in 1812. Dard Hunter had one brother, Philip Courtney Hunter, two years his senior, who died at the age of twenty-seven. During his boyhood Dard learned the rudiments of printing by setting type by hand for the Steubenville *Daily Gazette*.

He first became interested in the art of fine bookmaking when his father purchased a book that had been printed at William Morris' Kelmscott Press. Fascinated by what his father told him about the work of William Morris, Hunter was eager to make a pilgrimage to England, but he agreed to postpone it until he had finished his formal schooling. From 1900 to 1903 he attended the Ohio State University in Columbus, where he majored in mechanical engineering and in architecture and took advantage of the opportunity to examine books from the Kelmscott Press and the Doves Press. This only sharpened his desire to visit Europe. He also became interested in the work of Elbert Hubbard's Roycroft Shop and

Milwaukee Journal

DARD HUNTER

Roycroft Press in East Aurora, New York whose handicrafts were inspired by the ideas of William Morris.

When Dard Hunter wrote to Elbert Hubbard asking for a position with the Roycrofters when he finished his courses at the university, Hubbard told him that no additional help was required. Undiscouraged, Hunter decided to spend a part of his summer vacation in East Aurora. What he intended to be a short visit lengthened into an entire summer, and Hubbard finally asked Hunter to remain with the Roycrofters as art director. He occupied that position from 1903 to 1908.

For years Hunter had wanted to attend the K.K. Graphische Lehr- und Versuchsanstalt in Vienna, operated in conjunction with the Royal Printing House of the Austrian government, which experts considered one of the best schools of graphic arts in the world. Denied admission at first because he lacked a degree from a government graphic arts school, Hunter fabricated a diploma which passed muster with the Herr Direktor, who permitted him to enroll. At the school he studied under some of the leading artists and calligraphers in Europe. Hunter also studied at the Kunstgewerbe Schule in Vienna. After his graduation from the K.K. Graphische Lehr- und Versuchsanstalt in 1911, he went to London, where he was employed as a commercial artist by the Carlton Studio and the Norfolk Studio. His visits to London's museums during his free time intensified his interest in the arts of the book and influenced his choice of a career.

In Europe, Hunter had sustained his extravagant admiration of the British private presses, and he finally decided to establish one of his own in the United States. "It was my desire to have my own private press," Hunter wrote in his autobiography *My Life With Paper* (Knopf, 1958), "but I wanted my work to be individual and personal, without reliance upon outside help from the typefounder or papermaker. I would return to America and attempt to make books by hand completely by my own labor—paper, type, printing."

Back in the United States in 1913, Hunter looked for a suitable piece of property on which he could carry out his plans. He finally found a stone blockhouse on an old fruit farm at Marlborough-on-Hudson in Ulster County, New York. Supplementing his income with the sale of fresh berries, Hunter discovered that it was easier to make paper by hand than it was to bring up a family in an old stone blockhouse. (He had been married in Vienna in 1908.)

In 1917 the Hunters sold the old fruit farm and, moving back to Ohio, settled down in Chillicothe at Mountain House, a castle-like structure of "mongrel Gothic architecture" that had been built by a German political refugee in 1851. At the Mountain House Press in 1923 he published his *Old Papermaking* in an edition of 200 copies, the first of several books that he produced entirely by hand. To his astonishment he received more orders for the book than he could fill, although he priced the book at $25 a copy.

Hunter had long been interested in the primitive bark papers produced by the natives of the South Seas. In the spring of 1926 he set out for the South Pacific and visited Tahiti, New Zealand, Tonga, and the Cook and Society islands, observing papermaking and gathering samples of equipment and specimens of paper. *Primitive Papermaking,* completed during the last month of 1927, was the result of his travels. Containing many specimens of bark paper, the folio volume sold successfully at $75 a copy. Hunter was now convinced that he had been justified in his decision not to write about papermaking without first seeing it carried on in the locality of its origin and gathering the material for writing and illustrating a book about it.

From 1928 to 1931 Hunter tried to revive the craft of making paper by hand in the United States by setting up the company of Dard Hunter Associates in an abandoned mill in Lime Rock, Connecticut. He obtained both the equipment and the workers from Great Britain. The firm expired in receivership in 1931, at a cost to Dard Hunter of about $60,000, but not before it had produced paper equal in quality to the best imported from Europe. The equipment was salvaged and eventually went to the Dard Hunter Paper Museum, and the paper produced in the mill was used for the printing of several of Hunter's later books. The mill itself was totally destroyed in the flood of 1955.

During the 1930's Dard Hunter visited the paper mills and papermakers of Japan, Korea, China, Siam, Indochina, and India (where he had an audience with Mohandas Gandhi). Out of his travels came such books as *Old Papermaking in China and Japan* (1932); *A Papermaking Pilgrimage to Japan, Korea, and China* (1936); *Papermaking in Southern Siam* (1936);

Chinese Ceremonial Paper (1937); *Papermaking by Hand in India* (1939); and *Papermaking in Indo-China* (1947). Since most of these books containing original specimens of the papers that Hunter had collected on his travels were produced by hand in extremely limited editions, they commanded high prices on their first publication. Over the years the prices for these much sought after books have soared.

Dard Hunter has also written books that have been published in trade editions for a wider public. They include *Papermaking Through Eighteen Centuries* (Rudge, 1930); *Papermaking; The History and Technique of an Ancient Craft* (Knopf, 1943; 1947); and *Papermaking in Pioneer America* (University of Pennsylvania, 1952). He has written articles on paper and related subjects for the *Encyclopaedia Britannica* and other leading encyclopedias.

In the summer of 1939 the Massachusetts Institute of Technology opened its Dard Hunter Paper Museum to the public. The only museum of its kind, it contained papermaking equipment from all over the world and specimens of paper from the earliest times to the present. Although the collection attracted visitors from everywhere, it met with only a mild interest from the faculty and students at M.I.T. "What the scientific-minded M.I.T. professors and students failed to realize, however," Hunter wrote in his autobiography, "was that the origin and development of papermaking as shown in the museum was the basis of all civilization, and that had it not been for this craft the world would have been totally unable to exist. Without paper there would have been no scientists!" In October 1954 the museum, of which Hunter has been curator since its inception, was moved to its permanent quarters at the Institute of Paper Chemistry in Appleton, Wisconsin.

The honorary degree of Litt.D. was granted to Dard Hunter by Lawrence College in 1931 and by the Ohio State University in 1939. Wooster College gave him an L.H.D. degree in 1947 and Lehigh University conferred an honorary M.A. degree upon him in 1949. In 1949 he was the Rosenbach Fellow in Bibliography at the University of Pennsylvania. He has gold medals from the American Institute of Graphic Arts, awarded in 1936, and from the Gutenberg Museum in Mainz, awarded in 1954.

On March 24, 1908 Dard Hunter was married to Helen Edith Cornell, whom he had met when she was the piano accompanist at the Roycroft concerts. They had two sons: Dard Hunter, Jr., and Cornell Choate. Mrs. Hunter died in 1951. Dard Hunter, who stands six feet tall and weighs 175 pounds, has gray hair and blue eyes. Since 1925 he has been blind in the left eye as the result of an accident ten years earlier. He lists his political affiliation as "changeable," and says that, in religion, he "leans toward Christian Science." His favorite recreation is the curatorship of the Dard Hunter Paper Museum. He is an honorary member of the Club of Odd Volumes in Boston, the Rowfant Club in Cleveland, the American Antiquarian Society, the Forest Historical Foundation (Canada), and the Technical Association of the Pulp and Paper Industry. He has been an honorary curator of graphic arts at Massachusetts Institute of Technology since 1939 and at Harvard University since 1950.

References

    Sat Eve Post 226:27+ F 27 '54

    Hunter, Dard My Life With Paper (1958)

    Who's Who in America, 1960-61

HURSTON, ZORA NEALE Jan. 7, 1901-Jan. 28, 1960 Author; folklorist; anthropologist; wrote short stories, novels, and nonfiction, using Negro folklore as source material; studied voodoo rites in Haiti (1935-37). See *Current Biography* (May) 1942.

Obituary

N Y Times p27 F 5 '60

HYDE, H(ENRY) VAN ZILE Mar. 3, 1906- Physician; government official

Address: b. Office of the Surgeon General, Washington, D.C.; h. 5107 Battery Lane, Bethesda, Md.

An eminent physician and distinguished authority in the field of public health, Dr. H. van Zile Hyde is the assistant to the United States Surgeon General in charge of international health. He participated in negotiations for joint meetings of American and Soviet doctors and scientists to discuss research techniques, medical standards, and methods of treatment. The scientific conferences, covering such diseases as cancer, heart disease, and poliomyelitis are scheduled to take place in the United States and the Soviet Union in 1960 and 1961.

Hyde has been a career officer in the United States Public Health Service since 1941. He entered the field of international medicine during World War II when he served in the Middle East. He has worked on projects for the United Nations Relief and Rehabilitation Administration and the government of Colombia and has been active in the U.N. World Health Organization and the Pan American Sanitary Organization.

Born in Syracuse, New York on March 3, 1906, Henry van Zile Hyde is the second of four sons of Madeleine (van Zile) and Henry Neal Hyde, an Episcopal clergyman. He attended Nicholas Senn High School in Chicago and Deerfield Academy in Massachusetts. Following his graduation in 1925, Hyde matriculated at Yale University, where he was elected to Phi Beta Kappa. Hyde received the B.A. degree in 1929, and four years later he took his medical degree at Johns Hopkins University School of Medicine. With the completion of his internship in 1934 at the Johns Hopkins Hospital, Dr. Hyde accepted an appointment as instructor in medicine at the University of Rochester. He also served as assistant resident (1934-35) and resident

Dept. of Health, Education &
Welfare—S. Stanton Singer

DR. H. VAN ZILE HYDE

(1935-36) at the Strong Memorial and Rochester Municipal hospitals, where he did research in the fields of pulmonary physiology and metabolism.

Returning to his native city in 1936, Dr. Hyde entered the private practice of medicine. He was attending physician at Syracuse Memorial Hospital, University Hospital, and Syracuse Free Dispensary and part-time school medical officer with the Department of Education. After receiving a diploma in 1938 from the Trudeau School of Tuberculosis, Dr. Hyde specialized in the treatment of patients afflicted with this disease; from 1938 to 1941 he held a part-time appointment as examining physician with the tuberculosis clinic of the Syracuse Department of Health. During this period Dr. Hyde taught at the medical school of the University of Syracuse and the Albany Medical College of Union University.

Leaving his private practice in 1941, Dr. Hyde turned to the field of public health. From February to May 1941 he was director of the bureau of pneumonia control of the New York State Department of Health. There he conducted research on the use of sulfadiazine in the treatment of pneumonia. Later in 1941 he began his long association with the United States Public Health Service commissioned corps, advancing through its grades to the rank of medical director, which is equivalent to an Army colonel. During World War II he was assigned to the Office of Civilian Defense by the Public Health Service. From 1941 to 1943 he served as regional medical officer for New York, New Jersey, and Delaware, and in 1943-44 he was chief of the field casualty section of the medical division.

The desire to broaden his sphere of action brought Dr. Hyde into the international field in 1944 when he accepted the directorship of the medical division of the Middle East Supply Center in Cairo. For a few months in 1945 Dr. Hyde served as chief of the health division of the United Nations Relief and Rehabilitation Administration in the Balkans and as chief of the Middle East office of UNRRA. The United States Department of State called him back to Washington in the latter part of 1945 as assistant chief of the health services branch of the division of international labor, social, and health affairs.

His next assignment was with the staff of the Public Health Service as assistant chief of the division of international health in 1948-49. He became associated with the Institute of Inter-American Affairs, a unit of the State Department, in 1950 and for the next two years was director of its division of health and sanitation. In this post he helped to initiate a campaign to combat malarial infection in five states of Colombia by co-ordinating assistance from the Colombian government, the institute, the U.N. World Health Organization, and the U.N. International Children's Emergency Fund (UNICEF).

When he came back to the United States in 1952, Dr. Hyde reported that in the area of Colombia in which he worked there were 200,000 malaria cases annually out of a population of 2,000,000 people. He declared that a thoroughgoing insect-control program could cope with the malaria epidemics and their ravages of the health and productivity of the Colombians. As one village introduces mosquito control, waterworks, sewage, and sanitation projects and health programs, others follow the pattern. "Once people have seen what they can have," Dr. Hyde has said, "the idea spreads." In addition to Colombia, Dr. Hyde cited Brazil, Ecuador, Paraguay, and Venezuela as nations with advanced health programs.

Hyde joined the Technical Cooperation Administration in 1952 as director of the health and sanitation staff, but returned to the staff of the Public Health Service the following year to serve as chief of the division of international health. Since 1958 Dr. Hyde has been assistant to the United States Surgeon General for international health. He assumed the additional post of chief of the division of international health in November 1959.

Through its division of international health, the Public Health Service, under the direction of the Surgeon General, contributes to the advancement of world health. It participates in international health organizations, provides program and policy guidance to the Department of State on international health matters, administers educational and training services for the government and international agencies, and extends technical aid to the International Cooperation Administration.

In November 1959 Dr. Hyde conducted negotiations with Soviet officials for a series of joint scientific meetings to discuss research on cancer, heart diseases, and poliomyelitis. He also arranged for each nation to send medical delegations to the other to participate in scientific research.

A principal organizer of the World Health Organization, Dr. Hyde was a member of the United States delegation to the technical preparatory committee for WHO; the committee met in 1946 to formulate plans for an international health organization. Later, at the International Health Conference, he helped to draft a constitution for WHO. As a member of the WHO interim commission he drew up a report outlining the world's most urgent medical needs that has shaped WHO's undertakings.

He has been active in many World Health Assemblies and since 1948 has been a member of WHO's executive board. When Dr. Hyde became chairman of the executive board for the 1954-55 term, a New York *Times* (May 28, 1954) reporter commented: "Dr. Hyde's election was a tribute to his steady rise in influence in international health circles and his effective support of the World Health Organization since its foundation." Dr. Hyde also serves as a member of the joint health policy committee of WHO and UNICEF.

Influential in the affairs of the Pan American Sanitary Organization, Dr. Hyde was the United States delegate to its conference in 1950, alternate representative to the directing council (1948-51, 1953, 1955-56), and representative to the executive committee (1949, 1950, 1951). He participated in the United States public health mission to the U.S.S.R. in 1957. His articles on international health and civilian defense have appeared in professional journals.

Dr. Hyde is a Service Fellow of the American Medical Association and a Fellow of the American Public Health Association. Other organizations in which he is an active participant are the committee on preventive medicine and social science of the Social Science Research Council, the policy board of the National Citizens Committee for the World Health Organization, the international advisory committee of the American Social Hygiene Association, and the international committees of both the American Hospital Association and the Association of American Medical Colleges. He qualified for the Board of Internal Medicine in 1941 and the Board of Preventive Medicine and Public Health ten years later. Dr. Hyde has also been elected a member of the Alpha Omega Alpha honorary society.

H. van Zile Hyde was married to the former Ellen Sedgwick Tracy on June 24, 1933. Their children are Henry van Zile, Jr., Susan Sedgwick, and Thomas Prentice. Dr. Hyde is an Episcopalian. His hobbies are reading history, drawing cartoons, and art.

References

> Directory of American Specialists (1951)
> Who's Who in America, 1958-59
> Who's Who in the United Nations (1951)

IAKOVOS, ARCHBISHOP (yà'kă-vŭs)
July 29, 1911- Greek Orthodox prelate

Address: Greek Archdiocese, 10 E. 79th St., New York 21

Archbishop Iakovos, a Greek Orthodox prelate, has been playing an important role in the

ARCHBISHOP IAKOVOS

world-wide movement toward the unity of all Christian communions. As head of the Greek Orthodox Archdiocese of North and South America since April 1959, he is the spiritual leader of more than 1,300,000 communicants; as one of the six presidents of the World Council of Churches, he is in close contact with the 172 Christian denominations, besides his own, that make up this international body. In both these positions he succeeds Archbishop Michael, who died on July 13, 1958.

Archbishop Iakovos was born Demetrios A. Coucouzis on the Turkish island of Imroz on July 29, 1911, the son of Athanasios and Maria Coucouzis. His father kept a general store and, as a child Demetrios worked in the store after school, selling everything from sugar to icons. At the age of sixteen, he realized his ambition to enter the Halki Theological School, on the island of Halki in Turkey, having passed the necessary examinations and having saved enough money to travel to the school. He was graduated with high honors in 1934.

In the same year he was ordained a deacon and assigned as archdeacon to the Metropolitan of Derkon. (There are five orders of the clergy in the Holy Orthodox Catholic Apostolic Eastern Church: the minor orders of lector and subdeacon, and the major orders of deacon, priest, and bishop.) In 1939, after having served the Metropolitan of Derkon for five years, Father Demetrios came to the United States as archdeacon of the Greek Archdiocese of North and South America and professor of the Archdiocese Theological School, then located in Pomfret, Connecticut.

When he was ordained a priest in Boston on June 14, 1940, in accordance with Greek Orthodox custom, he took the name of Iakovos (James). He first served in the capacity of priest in Hartford, Connecticut during 1940 and 1941. In the latter year he moved to the Cathedral of the Holy Trinity in New York

IAKOVOS, ARCHBISHOP—*Continued*

City where he was a preacher. For a brief period in 1942 he was sent to St. Louis, Missouri.

Later in 1942 Iakovos returned to Boston, where he remained for twelve years, as dean of the Cathedral of the Annunciation. While there he earned the S.T.M. degree from Harvard Divinity School in 1945. For a brief period in 1954 he served as director and president of the Holy Cross Theological School in Brookline, Massachusetts.

Attaining the highest order of the Orthodox Eastern clergy, on December 17, 1954 Iakovos became Bishop of Melita (Malta) in the Archdiocese of Central and Western Europe. In March 1955 he was appointed representative of the Greek church's Ecumenical Patriarchate at World Council of Churches' headquarters in Geneva. He traveled extensively in this capacity and attended many ecclesiastical councils. He also visited the United States several times, lecturing at Harvard and Boston universities and at a number of religious conferences. On April 4, 1956 he was elected a Metropolitan (the bishop of a large city.)

The Holy Synod of the Ecumenical Patriarchate elected Iakovos Archbishop of North and South America on February 14, 1959, to succeed the late Archbishop Michael. Returning to the United States on March 31, 1959, Archbishop Iakovos was enthroned the following day at the Cathedral of the Holy Trinity in New York City. The Archdiocese, the largest of the Orthodox Eastern bodies in the Americas, has about 1,150,000 communicants in 375 churches in the United States. About 150,000 additional adherents live in Canada and South America. The combined Orthodox Eastern church in the United States has approximately 2,500,000 members included in some eighteen communions, among them the Russian, Syrian, Ukranian, Bulgarian, Albanian, Nestorian, Coptic, and Armenian churches.

The Greek Archdiocese of North and South America is under the jurisdiction of the Ecumenical Patriarchate of Constantinople, now headed by Patriarch Athenagoras I. The 268th primate to hold this position, Athenagoras preceeded Archbishop Michael as Archbishop of America from 1931 to 1949. Although the communions of the Holy Orthodox Catholic Apostolic Eastern Church are self-governing, they are in full communication with each other and regard themselves as branches of the same spiritual organism. They embrace similar forms of worship, the same faith, canon laws, pattern of organization, and accept the first seven Ecumenical Councils. The Patriarch of Constantinople wields no authority over the Patriarchs of the other Orthodox Eastern groups, but he is regarded as the first among equals.

The history of the Orthodox Eastern church as a distinctly separate body dates from 1054 when the Patriarch of Constantinople, Michael Cerularius, closed the Roman Churches in his city. For this act he was excommunicated by Pope Leo IX. Although the officially discussed points of dissension between East and West were of a minor nature and included the questions of fasting on Saturday, the celibacy of priests, and the separation of confirmation from baptism, basic differences lay in the more mystical interpretation which Eastern theologians gave to the body of the Church and their rejection of the supremacy of the Pope. The Orthodox Eastern church claims to be a universal church and the only true heir of the apostles. So complete has the separation between East and West been that when Archbishop Iakovos called upon Pope John XXIII in the spring of 1959, he was the first Greek Orthodox bishop to have visited a Pope in over 350 years.

Despite doctrinal differences with other churches, Eastern Orthodoxy now favors the movement for Christian unity. Archbishop Iakovos, who is serving as one of six presidents of the World Council of Churches for a term ending in 1961, is an exponent of this viewpoint and co-operates with leaders of other denominations in furthering the cause. The World Council of Churches is an instrument of fellowship and co-operation among 173 denominations. The four major groups which remain outside the fold are the Southern Baptist Convention and the Missouri Synod (Lutheran) in the United States, the Russian Orthodox Church in Russia, and the Roman Catholic Church.

Iakovos emphasized in October 1959 that the ecumenical movement is "not a movement between Protestant and Orthodox, or between Orthodox and Roman Catholics, but a move towards the unity of all Christians." He believes, however, that the "natural course" toward Christian reunion would be first between the Orthodox Eastern and the Roman Catholic churches, because they are much closer than either is to the Protestant churches. "But I cannot see that happy day coming soon," he said in April 1959, "because we have been separated for nine centuries."

His pessimism was reinforced when informal unity talks between Greek Orthodox and Roman Catholic theologians, scheduled to take place in 1960, were called off by the Vatican. "We know her attitude," he said in October 1959, speaking of the Roman Catholic Church, "always acting as a Mother Church that opens her arms and expects the return of 'separate' children without even asking them to come back."

Seeking Christian unity somewhat closer to home, Archbishop Iakovos called a conference of the leaders of the various Orthodox Eastern bodies in the United States in March 1960. It was the first such conclave since the separate churches were established on this continent, and Iakovos said it "far exceeded" his expectations. Steps were taken to establish a standing Conference of Orthodox Bishops in America, and the relation of Orthodoxy with other religious groups was discussed. The bishops also unanimously adopted a resolution "deploring the allegations of Communist infiltration in Protestant churches made in connection with the recently withdrawn Air Force manual" (New York *Times,* March 16, 1960).

In the spring of 1960 Archbishop Iakovos attended meetings of the Holy Synod of the Ecumenical Patriarchate in Istanbul. There he reported on the appearance of tears in the eyes of Madonnas in three lithographic icons formerly in the possession of residents of Long Island, New York. The Holy Synod pronounced these weeping Madonnas "divine signs."

Archbishop Iakovos is black-bearded and handsome. He is unmarried. (Members of the Greek Orthodox clergy are permitted to marry before becoming priests. Bishops are chosen from among the celibate priests.) He has written books and pamphlets in Greek, French, English, and German. For a South American tour, undertaken in February 1960, he "picked up" Spanish. Archbishop Iakovos is president of St. Basil's Academy in Garrison, New York and is a trustee of Anatolia College in Salonika, Greece. He became a United States citizen in 1950. While in Boston he acquired a lasting affection for the Boston Red Sox baseball team.

References

Newsweek 53:100 Ap 13 '59 por
Time 73:55+ Mr 2 '59 por
Who's Who in America, 1960-61

IBÁÑEZ (DEL CAMPO), CARLOS Nov. 3, 1877-Apr. 28, 1960 Former President of Chile (1927-31, 1952-58); career officer in the Army. See *Current Biography* (December) 1952.

Obituary

N Y Times p31 Ap 29 '60

IGLESIAS, ROBERTO (ē-glä'syäs) Oct. 27, 1927- Dancer; choreographer
Address: b. c/o S. Hurok, 730 5th Ave., New York 22

A leading exponent of the Spanish dance, Roberto Iglesias has starred in performances ranging from the pure lyric beauty of classical Spanish numbers and the wild rhythms of gypsy flamenco to his own creations rooted in Hispanic folklore. When the virtually unknown Iglesias and his newly formed Ballet Español company presented a program at Carnegie Hall in New York on May 18, 1957, they were greeted by cries from the audience of "Olé! Olé!" In 1958 and 1959, under the sponsorship of S. Hurok, the group appeared in New York and toured the United States, Canada, Mexico, and Cuba. Before organizing his own company, Iglesias was the partner of the Spanish dancer Rosario and was a member of the San Francisco Ballet company.

Born on October 27, 1927 in Guatemala, Roberto Iglesias is the son of Rigoberto Iglesias and the former Esther Sandoval. His father and some of his paternal ancestors were artists. Roberto spent his childhood in Mexico, where his parents had moved. He studied art and organized theatrical performances with his play-

ROBERTO IGLESIAS

mates, but he yearned most of all to become a bullfighter in the big rings of Mexico. When he was a teen-ager he tried to realize this ambition by fighting a bull, but he was badly gored. He recovered slowly, and, at the suggestion of a doctor, attended ballet classes to rebuild his body.

Opposed to dancing as a profession, the elder Iglesias sent Roberto to San Francisco to work in a relative's upholstery business and to enter high school. Roberto saved up his lunch money to take lessons at the San Francisco ballet school, and he soon became a member of the San Francisco ballet company. Eager to learn everything he could about the dance, he read books on design, choreography, and all phases of the theater. He took lessons in the modern dance, and studied pantomime with a Japanese teacher. He practised using the castanets for six months before he performed with them in public; soon he was marking his dance rhythms with their sharp, clicking sounds.

Joining a Spanish dance company, he toured Spain. "I went all over and saw what the people danced," he said. "Dancing is a part of their daily lives." He also sought out leading authorities on the dance wherever he traveled. As a result of his observations, he created several group dances which project a genuine folk atmosphere.

In Madrid Iglesias studied the flamenco, a style of Andalusian gypsy dancing, with Estampio and La Quica. Accompanied by a guitarist and singer, the flamenco dancer mesmerizes the audience with his staccato rhythms. "If he is an artist, he soon leads his musicians," Iglesias has said. Although flamenco dancing is stylized in form, it leaves ample room for improvisation.

Describing Iglesias' performance in this gypsy dance, Robert Coleman reported (New York *Mirror*, May 26, 1957): "Attired in . . . tight-fitting pants and vest-like jacket . . . bright red

IGLESIAS, ROBERTO—*Continued*

shoes and flat-topped hat . . . Iglesias threw back his shoulders, put his chin almost on his chest—like a torero facing the bull—and for 10 minutes reeled off incredibly sustained and perfect bursts of zapateados." The zapateado is a heel and toe tap.

Invited to become a member of the company of Rosario and Antonio in 1947, Roberto Iglesias soon attracted the attention of critics and dance lovers. When Rosario and Antonio broke up their partnership in 1952, he replaced Antonio as Rosario's partner. Iglesias regretted that "this good fortune came at the expense of the separation of two great artists" whom he loved. After dancing several years with Rosario, Iglesias decided to form his own company. He has explained: "I didn't want to be just another Spanish dancer in night clubs."

In 1956 in Barcelona, Spain, Roberto Iglesias organized the Ballet Español and for it created a repertoire of traditional Spanish dances, his own compositions in the idiom of Spanish folklore, and dance patterns ranging from the Canary Islands to Catalonia. The character of Spanish dances, which probably date back to 550 B.C., lies in the carriage of head, torso, and arms and in the emotional expression of the performer.

After the Ballet Español had successfully toured Europe and Latin America, Iglesias decided to borrow money and risk one appearance at New York's Carnegie Hall on May 18, 1957. At this performance, which was sold out in advance, American dance enthusiasts roared their approval and Spanish sailors, stationed in New York, threw their hats on the stage. Most of the critics were equally moved by the excitement of the group's rapid, flashing movements.

One of the reviewers, Louis Biancolli (New York *World-Telegram and Sun,* May 20, 1957), wrote: "Roberto . . . is a first-class artist—a master of pantomime and expressive dance and a wizard of the Spanish variety of tap . . . endowed with prodigious energy and precision." Another observer, the critic in *Dance Magazine* (July 1957), who praised the relaxed power in the quick movements of his feet and the melancholy intensity of his dramatic projections, reluctantly noted that Iglesias had not realized his full potential as a dancer.

Signed by impresario S. Hurok, the Ballet Español returned to New York for a week's engagement at the Broadway Theatre in October 1958. Iglesias again displayed his polished and subtle acting in a variety of moods, his virtuosic techniques, and his experimental choreographic patterns. He brilliantly alternated between very slow and very fast rhythms in the zapateado *Punta Y Tacón* and interpreted some of Federico García Lorca's gypsy songs in an impassioned dance called *Soledad Montoya.* After their New York appearance, Iglesias and his group toured the United States and Canada coast to coast in 1958-59.

During a two-week run at the Winter Garden Theatre, beginning on September 22, 1959, the dancers introduced nine new numbers, six of them composed by Iglesias. In appraising the artistry of Iglesias, Walter Terry (New York *Herald Tribune,* September 27, 1959) noted: "Talent, naturally, is manifest both in his sensitive, rhythmic, beautifully phrased dancing and in his imaginative choreography. Technique also is present in the magnificently mastered footbeats, the perfectly controlled turns and lunges, the carriage of the body, the varied dynamics of action."

But John Martin in the New York *Times* (October 11, 1959) felt that Iglesias is a choreographer who lacks craftsmanship and a dancer who is not only eccentric in his mannerisms but who breaks all the rules. Martin conceded that Iglesias transfers his intensity to the audience and that he exhibits genius in his originality and departure from tradition. "Clearly something must be done about Iglesias," Martin concluded. "Not once in a generation do we find so tremendous a dancer—or one so much in need of saving." In the season of 1959-60 Iglesias and his troupe toured Cuba, Mexico, Canada, and the United States.

Roberto Iglesias, who has been described as light and wiry, with a face expressing intensity, is five feet eight inches tall and weighs 150 pounds. He is now a citizen of the United States. Still an aficionado of bullfighting, Iglesias is the patron of a younger brother who is a matador. Another brother, Enrique, is a member of the Ballet Español. Married on July 3, 1949 to Aïda Ramirez, a dancer, Iglesias is the father of two daughters, Rosario and Maria Dolores. He was married for a second time, in 1960, to Rosario Galan.

References

Dance Mag 32:28+ O '58 pors
Vogue 132:121 O 1 '58 por

INOUYE, DANIEL K(EN) (ê-nō'wä) Sept. 7, 1924- United States Representative from Hawaii

Address: b. House Office Bldg., Washington 25, D.C.; h. 5410 Connecticut Ave., Washington 15, D.C.; 4987 Kolohala Ave., Honolulu, Hawaii

The first United States Representative from Hawaii, the fiftieth state in the Union, is Daniel K. Inouye, a hero of World War II, lawyer, and former member of the territorial legislature of Hawaii. The proclamation of statehood for Hawaii on August 21, 1959 and the election of Inouye, the first Congressman of Japanese ancestry, and of Hawaiian Senator Hiram L. Fong, the first Congressman of Chinese ancestry, won increased respect for the United States throughout the Orient.

Daniel Ken Inouye was born in Honolulu, Hawaii on September 7, 1924, the eldest child of Hyotaro Inouye and Kame (Imanaga) Inouye. Hyotaro Inouye, a naturalized American citizen, is now retired from his job as a department store clerk. Daniel has two brothers, John T. and Robert K., and a sister, Mrs. May M. Tomita. He attended the Lunalilo Elementary School and Washington Intermediate School in Honolulu, and then went on to

McKinley High School, where he was elected to the National Honor Society. He was graduated in 1942.

Soon after his high school graduation, Inouye enlisted as a private in the 442d Infantry Regimental Combat Team, the "go-for-broke" outfit composed entirely of nisei volunteers which General Mark W. Clark called "the most decorated Army unit in history." In 1944 Inouye was commissioned a second lieutenant on the battlefield. In 1945 he led his platoon in destroying three German machine gun nests in the Po Valley in Italy. Shot in the stomach and legs, his right arm shattered by an exploded grenade, he insisted on continuing to direct the assault before he allowed himself to be evacuated. By the time he was discharged in 1947 Inouye had attained the rank of captain. Now when asked if he would defend America, Inouye holds up his empty sleeve and replies, "The country can have the other one, too."

With his return to civilian life, Inouye entered the University of Hawaii in Honolulu to major in government and economics. "I had originally intended to study medicine," he has explained, "But the loss of my right arm... caused me to go into the field of law; I had always been interested in politics." He earned the B.A. degree in 1950 and later attended George Washington University Law School in Washington, D.C., where he became a member of the board of editors of the *George Washington Law Review* and received the J.D. degree in 1952.

Back in Honolulu, Inouye started his own general law practice in 1954. His prevailing interest, however, was politics, and his climb in political affairs was rapid. In 1953-54 he was appointed assistant public prosecutor of Honolulu. In 1954 and 1956 he was elected to the territorial House of Representatives, and served there as majority leader for four years. In the next territorial election, he won a seat to the Senate. During this period Inouye served in a succession of posts in the Democratic party: precinct president, county committeeman, county committee secretary, central committeeman, chairman of the territorial convention in 1958, and delegate to the Democratic National Convention in 1956.

The Hawaiian Islands were annexed by the United States in 1898 and organized as a territory in 1900. For fifty-six years the inhabitants of the territory tried to obtain statehood for Hawaii. Only one other territory, New Mexico, waited a longer time. Some Congressmen opposed the granting of statehood to Hawaii on the basis of its racial composition. Because of Hawaii's geographical position, it has one of the most polyglot populations in the Pacific, and it has earned a reputation for practising a minimum of racial discrimination and segregation. The United States Congress finally passed a bill granting statehood to Hawaii in March 1959.

Territorial Senator Inouye had at first intended to run for the United States Senate. He withdrew from the race and became instead the Democratic candidate for the House of Representatives because, he said, "it would give some

DANIEL K. INOUYE

elder statesmen in our party a clear field" (*Time,* June 8, 1959). This demonstration of party loyalty is not likely to be one that Inouye will regret when the slates are chosen for future elections.

On July 28, 1959 Hawaiians elected a Governor, two United States Senators, and a United States Representative for the first time. Running for Hawaii's seat in the House, Inouye won 111,733 votes, the largest number of votes ever cast for a candidate in Hawaii, and defeated Republican Charles H. Silva. When it had become obvious on election night that he was the winner, Inouye confessed: "I'm a little scared." After being sworn in on August 24, 1959 for a term ending in January 1961, he was assigned to the Banking and Currency Committee.

Shortly after he arrived in Washington, D.C., Inouye underwent a thorough baptism in political hot water. During a television interview on August 22, 1959 he told a panel of newsmen: "I personally am not convinced that Washington is ready for territorial status." He said that Washingtonians were not "stable enough" to govern themselves under the limited territorial status proposed in legislation at that time before Congress. He pointed out that since many of them are in the service of the federal government, they already have "many voices" through the House and Senate District of Columbia committees, and that Washingtonians hold influential posts in executive agencies. He was soon taken to task by an editorial that appeared in the Washington *Post and Times Herald* on August 25, 1959.

When the second session of the Eighty-sixth Congress was convened in January 1960, Inouye was one of 186 House members to sign a discharge petition to bring the civil rights bill out of the rules committee and on to the floor of the lower chamber. During the year he voted for a resolution expressing the view held by a ma-

INOUYE, DANIEL K.—*Continued*

jority of Congressmen that the "traditional interpretation" of treaties with Panama should not be modified except by treaty procedure (February), a resolution indicating Congressional indignation over acts of religious desecration in the United States and abroad (February), a measure authorizing the federal government to withhold city payroll taxes from salaries of federal employees in cities levying such taxes (February), a proposal to amend the 1948 Water Pollution Control Act by raising to $90,000,000 the annual federal contribution for sewage plant construction (February), and an amendment to appropriate $50,000,000 to liquidate obligations incurred for urban renewal and slum clearance (February).

Congressman Inouye has urged that economic assistance to the millions of Asiatics living at poverty levels be extended and increased. "From their efforts to make a better life for themselves," he has said, "will come self-confidence and dignity." He is trying to obtain federal aid for the establishing of a cultural and technical institute in Hawaii which would conduct an exchange program between Americans and Orientals.

Daniel K. Inouye has brown eyes and black hair, stands five feet six inches tall, and weighs 155 pounds. Well-poised and personable, he is popular with his colleagues in Congress. On June 12, 1949 he was married to Margaret Shinobu Awamura, who has an M.A. degree from Columbia University and once taught speech at the University of Hawaii. Mr. and Mrs. Inouye are high-fidelity fans and own a large record collection ranging from jazz to grand opera. In spite of the loss of his right arm, Inouye continues to play the piano, upon which he once practised as a form of therapy, and works in his garden. He is a Methodist in religion.

In Hawaii, Inouye is a director of the Central Pacific Bank in Honolulu. Active in organizations, he is a director of the Kapahulu-Moiliili den of Lions International, Nuuanu branch of Y.M.C.A., Honolulu Council of Churches, and University of Hawaii Alumni Association. He is a trustee of Hawaii Pacific Homes for the retired and John Howard Association for the rehabilitation of former convicts; an adviser of the Hawaiian Amateur Athletic Union; an executive committee member of the Hawaii chapter of World Brotherhood; a former vice-president of the 442d Veterans Club; and a former commander of Disabled American Veterans for Hawaii. He is a member of Phi Delta Phi and the American and Hawaii bar associations.

Among the many military decorations Inouye holds are the Distinguished Service Cross, Bronze Star Medal, Purple Heart with two oak leaf clusters, Distinguished Unit Citation Ribbon with four clusters, and Occupation Medal (Japan). The United States Junior Chamber of Commerce named Inouye one of the nation's outstanding young men for 1959.

After he was elected to Congress Inouye said: "Because of my ethnic background I know a little more will be expected of me. . . . Hawaii is much more interested in what we can con-

tribute to the general welfare of the nation than in what we expect the nation to contribute to us. I will do my best to see Hawaii receives fair treatment as a state."

References

Look 24:28+ Mr 1 '60 por
Los Angeles Times Ag 10 '59 por
N Y Times p14 Jl 30 '59; p9 D 7 '59 por
Time 74:13 Ag 10 '59
Congressional Directory (1959)
Congressional Quarterly Almanac, 1959

IVES, BURL (ICLE IVANHOE) June 14, 1909- Folk singer; anthologist; actor
Address: b. 580 West End Ave., New York 24

NOTE: This biography supersedes the article which appeared in *Current Biography* in 1946.

Long celebrated as a singer of folk ballads and as a performer in musical shows, Burl Ives, "the wayfaring stranger," has in recent years gone on to prove his abilities as a stage and screen actor and as an anthologist and editor of folk music. In 1959 his performance in *The Big Country* won him an Oscar from the Academy of Motion Picture Arts and Sciences.

Burl Icle Ivanhoe Ives was born on June 14, 1909, in Hunt Township, Jasper County in the "Bible Belt" of Illinois to Frank and Cordella (White) Ives, who were tenant farmers. He can trace his ancestry back through a long line of preachers and farmers to seventeenth century America. Singing was always a large part of the Ives family life, and at the age of four Burl was beginning to earn money by performing in public, either alone or with his brothers and sisters in a group the neighbors called "those singing Ives." He learned many of his folk songs from his pipe-smoking, tobacco-chewing grandmother, who had mastered hundreds of American ballads of Scottish, English, and Irish origin by heart.

Between the seasons of tenant farming, Frank Ives studied engineering and helped to build bridges in the neighborhood. When he purchased a construction business in Newton, Illinois, the Ives family moved there, and after years of privation and of moving from farmstead to farmstead, began to prosper. Burl attended Newton High School, where he was a fullback on the football team. Upon graduating in 1927, he entered the Eastern Illinois State Teachers College at Charleston with the intention of becoming a professional football coach (earlier, he had wanted to become a preacher.) There he exercised his athletic and musical abilities, but, in his own words, "never did take to studies."

In 1930, during his junior year, Burl Ives found himself unable to withstand his wanderlust. He left college to hitchhike and ride the rods on a vagabond trek across the length and breadth of the United States and through Canada and Mexico, supporting himself by singing and playing the banjo and performing odd jobs here and there. He stopped off at steel mills and lumber camps, and sang for a while with a traveling company of evangelists. Along the way he added to his folk song repertoire by listening to the songs of lumberjacks, cowboys, steelworkers, and fishermen.

He finally came to a halt in Terre Haute, Indiana, where he registered at Indiana State Teachers College, obtained a job singing on the radio, and worked in a drugstore. Acting on the advice of his Terre Haute singing teacher, Mrs. Clara Lyon, he went to New York City to continue his musical training. He settled at International House on Riverside Drive near Columbia University at a weekly rental rate of $5.00. Meanwhile, he besieged the offices of Broadway booking agents, only to be told that they "weren't interested in hillbilly acts."

Odd jobs and singing in church choirs supported Burl Ives during his early days in New York, while he was studying with the vocal coach Ekka Toëdt. In the academic year of 1937-38 he also enrolled for formal music courses at New York University. But in spite of all his training in classical music, Ives decided to devote himself to the folk ballads he had known during his childhood and his vagabond days.

During the summer of 1938 Ives appeared on the stage for the first time professionally at the Rockridge Theater in Carmel, New York, performing character parts in *Ah, Wilderness!, Pocahontas Preferred,* and *Flight*. In the same year, he made his debut on Broadway in a non-singing role especially written for him in George Abbott's musical comedy *The Boys from Syracuse*. During the engagement, Ives studied the techniques of acting with Benno Schneider. A four-month hit engagement at Max Gordon's Village Vanguard night club followed.

A touring company of Rodgers and Hart's *I Married an Angel* provided Burl Ives with his next professional engagement. Early in 1940 he appeared on Broadway in Albert Bein's fantasy *Heavenly Express*. In the same year Ives obtained several singing engagements on NBC radio, but soon moved to CBS; he performed ballads on the program *Back Where I Come From* and later was given his own show *The Wayfarin' Stranger*.

Drafted into the United States Army in April 1942, Burl Ives made his stage debut as a singer soon afterwards in the cast of Irving Berlin's military musical, *This Is the Army*. While the show was in New York, he also had a radio program, *G. I. Jive*, which was broadcast to military bases overseas. In October 1943, after touring with *This Is the Army*, Private Ives received a medical discharge and devoted his time to entertaining soldiers and making recordings for the Office of War Information. In 1945 he introduced "Rodger Young," Frank Loesser's popular musical tribute to the United States Infantry.

In 1944 Ives embarked upon a long engagement at the New York night club Cafe Society Uptown. At the end of that year he appeared on Broadway in *Sing Out, Sweet Land,* a "cavalcade of American folk music." Although the show encountered a generally cool reception,

BURL IVES

Ives was praised for his renditions of such folk songs as "Blue Tail Fly," now popularly associated with him. For his work in this show Ives received the Donaldson Award as best supporting actor of the 1944-45 Broadway season.

Ives went to Hollywood in 1945 to make his film debut in a version of Will James's novel *Smoky* (Twentieth Century-Fox) and to appear with Josh White, Winston O'Keefe, and others in a feature-length film about folk songs. On December 1, 1945 Ives made his concert bow at New York's Town Hall, and on December 15, 1946 gave another recital at the same hall. In 1945 Burl Ives appeared as the weekly star of the *Radio Readers Digest,* and he also made guest appearances on other radio programs. On October 18, 1946 he introduced a series of recorded song shows over the Mutual Broadcasting System.

McGraw-Hill published Ives's autobiography, *Wayfaring Stranger,* in 1948. Morroe Berger, reviewing the book in the *Saturday Review of Literature* (January 8, 1949), wrote: "It is unlikely that readers who are not Burl Ives fans will enjoy his autobiography, but his fans will love it. This book has just the proper mixture of rustic sincerity and corn for the life story of one of America's most popular singers of folk songs." Ives has also published several collections of folk ballads and tales, including the *Burl Ives Song Book* (Ballantine, 1953), *Tales of America* (World, 1954), and the *Burl Ives Book of Irish Songs* (Duell, 1958); and a verse for children, *Sailing On a Very Fine Day* (Rand McNally, 1955).

Films in which Burl Ives has been featured include: *Green Grass of Wyoming* (Twentieth Century-Fox, 1948); Disney's *So Dear to My Heart* (RKO Radio, 1948); *Station West* RKO Radio, 1948); *Sierra* (Universal, 1950); and *East of Eden* (Warner, 1955). In *The Power and the Prize* (Metro-Goldwyn-Mayer,

IVES, BURL—*Continued*

1956) Ives donned "citified" clothes for the first time in his film career. He won much praise from the critics for his performance as a business tycoon in the film, which starred Robert Taylor.

Meanwhile, Ives had not been absent from the Broadway stage. He appeared as Captain Andy in a revival of the Jerome Kern musical *Show Boat*, which opened on May 5, 1954 at the New York City Center, and as Big Daddy in Tennessee Williams' electrifying *Cat on a Hot Tin Roof*, which came to the Morosco Theatre on Broadway on March 24, 1955. Walter F. Kerr of the New York *Herald Tribune* predicted that Ives's "Rabelasian contribution" to *Cat on a Hot Tin Roof* would become the "talk of the town" (March 25, 1955). Laudatory reviews also greeted Ives's work in the film version of the play, starring Elizabeth Taylor and Paul Newman (Metro-Goldwyn-Mayer, 1958).

Returning to films of the outdoors, Ives appeared in *Wind Across the Everglades* (Warner, 1958) and *The Big Country* (United Artists, 1958). It was for his performance in the latter film that he won an award from the Academy of Motion Picture Arts and Sciences. Ives has also starred in such recent films as the movie adaptation of Eugene O'Neill's *Desire Under the Elms* (Paramount, 1958) and *Our Man in Havana* (Columbia, 1960).

Although his most publicized enterprises have been associated with Broadway and Hollywood, Burl Ives continues to give the folk song recitals that have made him popular throughout the world. He has appeared in many plays in summer stock, and has made over three hundred commercial records for Decca and Columbia and a series *Historical America in Song* for the *Encyclopædia Britannica*.

Burl Ives stands six feet tall and weighs about 270 pounds. He has blue eyes and reddish-brown hair and wears a large moustache and a goatee. His wide smile and humorous eyes reflect his easygoing philosophy of life. On December 6, 1945 Ives was married to the former Helen Payne Ehrlich, Ph.D., whom he met when she was directing one of his radio folk song programs. They have one son, Alexander. Whenever possible, they escape from the city to the country, where they can indulge in houseboating and allow their dogs to range freely.

Among the organizations to which Burl Ives belongs are the American Federation of Television and Radio Artists, the Writers Guild, the American Federation of Musicians, and the Screen Actors Guild. He is a Democrat. Ives holds an honorary Doctor of Laws degree from Fairleigh Dickinson College, Rutherford, New Jersey.

Along with his continuing devotion to folk ballads, Burl Ives thrives on the group feeling which arises from a successful dramatic enterprise. "I know of no other calling," he says of the theatrical profession, "which holds higher hopes for richer returns in both professional and personal fulfillment."

References

> Coronet 47:158+ Mr '60 por
> Holiday 19:14+ F '56 pors
> N Y Post Mag p3 Ja 9 '49 pors
> Theatre Arts 40:70+ My '56
> International Who's Who, 1959
> Who's Who in America, 1958-59

IVEY, JOHN E(LI), JR. Jan. 21, 1919-
Educator; sociologist

Address: b. Learning Resources Institute, 680 5th Ave., New York 22; h. 14 Washington Mews, New York 3

The question of how existing community resources and technological innovations can be used to improve the quality of education and to serve increasing numbers of students has interested John E. Ivey, Jr., president of the Learning Resources Institute, throughout his career as sociologist and educator. One of the founders and first president (since 1959) of both the Learning Resources Institute and the Midwest Program on Airborne Television Instruction, Ivey is a former executive vice-president of New York University and was for eight years director of the Board of Control for Southern Regional Education, an interstate co-ordinating agency for higher education in the South which he helped to form in 1948.

John Eli Ivey, Jr., was born on January 21, 1919 in Raleigh, North Carolina, the son of John Eli and Vera (House) Ivey. He studied community organization and Southern regional sociology at Alabama Polytechnic Institute in Auburn and received a B.S. degree in 1940. While teaching sociology as an instructor at the University of North Carolina from 1941 to 1943, Ivey worked on his doctorate under Howard Odum, the renowned regional sociologist. At this time Ivey wrote book reviews for *Social Forces* and prepared many articles expressing his conviction that the university must contribute to social and economic planning in its community and region, and in turn draw on the resources of society to renew and vitalize the educational process.

Having submitted his dissertation, "Experiment in American State Planning," Ivey received the Ph.D. degree in 1944. He then served as a specialist in the evaluation of education with the Tennessee Valley Authority. Rejoining the faculty of the University of North Carolina as an associate professor of sociology in 1946, Ivey was also chief of the division of research interpretation and a member of the board of the university's extension division. In 1948 he became the university's youngest professor when he was appointed professor of city and regional planning and research professor of the Institute for Research in Social Science.

For five years beginning in 1943, Ivey was executive secretary of the committee on Southern regional studies and education of the

American Council on Education and editor of the committee's newsletter, *Resource-Use Education*. He also served as secretary and executive committee member of the American Council on Education (1949-53).

A frequent consultant for surveys of state and city school systems, Ivey was director of reorganization, North Carolina State Planning Board (1944) and chairman, resources division, North Carolina Educational Survey (1947-48). He helped plan a new university at Boca Raton, Florida as consultant to the state Board of Control and served as consultant to the Florida Survey of Education.

For the states of Louisiana, Illinois, and Florida he participated in reviews of higher educational systems, and in Wyoming he examined adult education programs. Columbia University requested his help in an analysis of science and rural educational programs (1946) and in a survey of schools of Puerto Rico (1948-50). Ivey also advised the Atlanta Board of Education (1946-48) and guided the reorganization of its schools; directed research communications studies for the Office of Naval Research; and served as director of the Regional Council on Education (1948-49).

His interest in promoting co-operation among Southern academic and industrial facilities to build up the South's educational system led Ivey to help establish the Board of Control for Southern Regional Education in 1948 and to serve as its director for eight years. The board with four members from each of sixteen states co-ordinates professional, graduate, and research programs in the South by directing students seeking special training to the particular university which offers it.

Ivey's concern that Southern academic institutions should share fully in governmental support of scientific research was expressed in his article on the National Science Foundation Act (*School and Society*, August 5, 1950). "Ivey is one of the top young men in the nation," Governor LeRoy Collins of Florida said in 1957. "He has preached the sound doctrine that the South should use the manpower and brains of the South to improve the South."

In 1957 Ivey resigned from the Board of Control for Southern Regional Education to become executive vice-president of New York University. As second in line of authority, preceded only by the president, Ivey took general charge of the education program for two years. In 1959 he left N.Y.U. to help form and become first president of two nonprofit organizations, the Learning Resources Institute in New York City and the Midwest Program on Airborne Television Instruction, with headquarters at Purdue University. Explaining the goals of the two organizations, Ivey said: "We are striving for a breakthrough in education on a scale with those of recent years in medicine, agriculture, and industry. This means that education must find its shape from a deeper understanding of how people learn."

The Learning Resources Institute, which is expected to become the principal co-ordinator of television education in the country, now ad-

New York University

JOHN E. IVEY, JR.

ministers two TV courses in mathematics and chemistry and plans to develop a full two-year (eventually four-year) liberal arts undergraduate curriculum. It seeks to improve instructional uses for television, films, radio, and learning machines and prepares materials and syllabi for use in teaching with the new media.

The Midwest Program on Airborne Television Instruction plans to beam taped academic courses from an airplane television transmitter to TV sets in classrooms of participating schools and colleges. By applying technological advances to education, both organizations hope to keep academic curricula abreast of rapid social change and to provide more knowledge for more students. The two organizations receive funds from foundations and private industry.

The American Council on Education published Ivey's *Channeling Research into Education* (1944) and two books which he edited, *Education for the Use of Regional Resources* (1945) and *Scientists Look at Resources* (1947). In collaboration with Nicholas J. Demerath and Woodrow W. Breland, Ivey wrote *Building Atlanta's Future* (University of North Carolina Press, 1948) and *Community Resources* (Winston, 1951); with Rupert Bayless Vance and Marjorie N. Bond, he wrote *Exploring the South* (University of North Carolina Press, 1949). His many articles have appeared in educational journals and other magazines. He serves on the editorial board of *Social Forces* and in 1946 edited a special issue of the *High School Journal* called "Education Helps Build a Region."

Awarded an Eisenhower Exchange Fellowship in 1956, Ivey made a seven-month trip to Europe, the Near East, India, and Pakistan to observe educational systems abroad. Three years later, Ivey visited the U.S.S.R. with nine

IVEY, JOHN E., JR.—*Continued*

American state governors for three weeks, where they made a comparative study of state governments and regional cultures.

Ivey is a member of the Southern Association of Science and Industry and served on its board of directors (1942-47) and on its executive committee (1947). He was executive secretary of North Carolina's Resource-Use Education Commission (1946-48); regional vice-president of the American Education Fellowship (1947); chairman of the regional conference in resource-use education of the Southern States Work Conference (1946-48); and member of the board of advisers of Films, Inc. (1947-50). He is now vice-president of the Purdue Research Foundation.

The educator belongs to the National Education Association, Society of Public Administration, American Academy of Political and Social Science, American, Southern, and Rural sociological societies, Southern Economics Association, and American Anthropological Association. He is also a member of Alpha Kappa Delta, Omicron Delta Kappa, Delta Sigma Pi, and Phi Beta Kappa.

John E. Ivey, Jr., was married to Melville Corbett, a sociologist, on July 25, 1942. They have three children: Melville Elizabeth, Howard William, and Lela Davis. For relaxation Ivey enjoys listening to music, raising livestock, and traveling in the United States and the Caribbean area. He is the recipient of a Freedoms Foundation Honor Medal (1951) and an honorary LL.D. degree from the University of Chattanooga in 1954.

"The central problem in educational design," Ivey wrote in the *Saturday Review* (February 13, 1960), "is to help students learn the most the quickest with the greatest relevance to their future needs. . . . To my mind, the surest hope for meeting the threefold challenge of cost-quantity-quality in American education lies in the marriage of the learning process with the technology of modern communications."

References

N Y Times p56 Mr 25 '56 por
Time 69:88+ Ap 15 '57 por
Leaders in Education (1948)
Who's Who in America, 1960-61
Who's Who in American Education, 1959-60

JENSEN, BEN(TON) F(RANKLIN)

Dec. 16, 1892- United States Representative from Iowa; lumberman

Address: b. House Office Bldg., Washington 25, D.C.; h. Exira, Ia; 2120 16th St., Washington 9, D.C.

"In Congress I am called the Watchdog of the Treasury, and I am proud of that title," United States Representative Ben F. Jensen tells his constituents in the Seventh Iowa District. He has been a member of the House Appropriations Committee for the greater part of eleven consecutive terms in Congress and is now the second Republican in rank on that committee. The manager of a retail lumber concern in a rural section of Iowa when first elected in November 1938, Representative Jensen frankly calls himself a Conservative and is a champion of free enterprise. While supporting the Rural Electrification Administration, he has fought the public power policies and the favored status of the Tennessee Valley Authority. Among his legislative proposals was an amendment extending the educational coverage of the G.I. Bill of Rights.

Both parents of Representative Jensen were natives of Denmark. His father, Martin Jensen, was a stableman and his mother, nee Gertrude Anna Andersen, a milkmaid on the same farm when they met and married. They were the parents of four daughters by 1881 when Martin Jensen immigrated to Iowa to work as a tile ditch digger and establish a home.

The tenth of their thirteen children, Benton Franklin Jensen was born December 16, 1892 in Marion, Linn County, Iowa, not far from Cedar Rapids. At seven years of age he moved with the family to a 200-acre farm near Brayton in Audubon County, Iowa, where he attended public grade school. When Ben was thirteen his father became so crippled with rheumatism that the bulk of the farm work fell on the shoulders of Ben and his brother Oscar. The large farm was sold when Ben was fifteen, and the family moved to Exira in the same county, where the boys for a time attended high school.

"Both Oscar and I were obliged to quit school before finishing high school," Jensen wrote in an autobiographical sketch. "I went to work that summer digging tile ditch, and that winter I worked in a grocery store." He was employed successively as a farm hand, pearl-button cutter, and grocery clerk in a department store before he joined the Green Bay Lumber Company in his home town of Exira in March 1914. "I took," he recalls, "every advantage of my limited education, by reading good books and working hard on every job."

After two years as a yardman and as an assistant auditor for the retail lumber concern, Jensen was advanced to extra manager. In 1917 he joined the United States Army as a private in World War I, and at Camp Pike, Arkansas in 1918 was commissioned a second lieutenant. When he was discharged in December 1918, he returned to Exira as manager for the Green Bay Lumber Company; he continued to manage it until he was elected to Congress twenty years later. "Since early childhood," he notes, "I have been deeply interested in the sciences of good government, local, county and state." By the middle 1920's he was active in local politics as well as the American Legion, in which he became the seventh Iowa district commander for 1936-37.

Elected as a Republican to the Seventy-sixth Congress in November 1938 and regularly re-elected every two years thereafter, Ben Jensen represents the Seventh Iowa District, embracing fourteen rural counties in the southwestern part of the state. He early criticized most policies of the Roosevelt administration and all trends towards socialism, and has consistently championed states' rights.

In 1940 Jensen suffered a severe heart attack which may have delayed the prominence he began to attain after 1944, when he was appointed to the Interior subcommittee of the House Appropriations Committee. There he assumed a watchdog role in connection with the public power activities of the Tennessee Valley Authority. ("The Interior subcommittee," he explained in a speech in the House in May 1959, "had, until 1955, the duty of recommending to the Congress the amount of money to be appropriated to the Interior Department for transmission lines, substation and other facilities to market Federal hydropower.") Jensen gained additional prominence as sponsor of an amendment to the G.I. Bill of Rights (1945) which (in the words of his campaigning material) "made it possible for the poor man's veteran son and daughter to receive an education under that law, whether or not their education had been interrupted by their military service."

While serving as chairman of the government corporations subcommittee of the Appropriations Committee in the Republican-controlled Eightieth Congress (1947-48), Jensen insisted that a clause directing the TVA to repay to the Treasury a percentage of its power profits be included in the Government Corporations Appropriation Act of 1948. Jensen again served as chairman of the Interior Subcommittee in 1948, 1953, and 1954.

In an economy move in the spring of 1951 Jensen pushed through the House a rider to the Department of the Interior appropriations bill. The purpose was to reduce personnel by prohibiting the department to refill more than 25 per cent of jobs as they fell vacant. The rider was later added also to the Labor, Commerce, State, Justice, and Agriculture bills, but was stricken from some of these bills by the Senate. Certain agencies, however, received a ten per cent payroll cut.

During the Korean war, in December 1951, Jensen and two other United States legislators made a brief inspection tour of rear areas to see that American soldiers in Korea were getting satisfactory food and medical care. Jensen visited India and Pakistan in 1953, and in December 1954 went to Geneva, Switzerland to represent the United States at the eighth session of the Intergovernmental Committee for European Migration. Earlier in the latter year, in March, Jensen had been one of five legislators wounded when Puerto Rican extremists fired about twenty shots without warning in the House of Representatives.

As a foe of public power projects, in May 1955 Jensen attacked the proposed federal Hell's Canyon Dam as likely to produce "less power at greater cost" than three smaller utility company dams on the Snake River. Since he represented an agricultural area, he was concerned with government price supports to farmers, and in January 1956 he proposed government beef and hog buying programs sufficient to raise prices 25 per cent. In July

Chase

BEN F. JENSEN

he joined Senator Karl E. Mundt of South Dakota in promoting a bill to reduce the government's grain surplus by prohibiting the sale of gasoline or motor fuel unless containing alcohol manufactured from grain. He reintroduced the measure to the House of Representatives in February 1959.

In July 1956 Representative Jensen supported the Powell amendment to the school construction aid bill, but voted against the measure as a whole, as well as against the civil rights bill. In July 1957 he favored striking out the enacting clauses of the school bill; and in July 1958 he supported the Smith bill to bar courts from ruling that federal laws nullify state laws in the same field, except in certain defined circumstances.

On measures concerning finance and foreign affairs, Jensen disapproved during 1957 extension of military and economic aid under the Eisenhower Middle East Doctrine (March), postponement of British debt payments (April), and appropriations for mutual security (July). During 1958 he voted "yea" on an increase in funds for the missile-defense program (January) and on a postal policy rate increase bill which would also raise the salaries of postal workers (May). In February when acting on an appropriations bill for the Interior Department, the House rejected Jensen's amendment to reduce federal employment by 10 per cent.

Among the proposals that Jensen supported during the first session of the Eighty-sixth Congress (1959) were the provision to admit Hawaii to statehood (March), an increase in United States' subscription to the International Monetary Fund (March), an amendment to limit the size of price-support loans by the Commodity Credit Corporation (May), and the Landrum-Griffin labor bill (August). He also voted for granting the Rural Electrification Administrator final authority on electrifi-

JENSEN, BEN F.—*Continued*

cation loans (April). In a lengthy address on May 4 Jensen assailed the pending bill for self-financing of the Tennessee Valley Authority through the issuance of bonds, and the favored position of the authority in competition with private utilities.

Representative Jensen is a thirty-second degree Mason, an Elk, a Moose, and a member of the Order of the Eastern Star. His church is the Lutheran. Ben Jensen stands at six feet two inches, weighs 200 pounds, and has blue eyes and brown hair. On December 13, 1917 he was married to Charlotte E. Hadden of Clearfield, Iowa, who had come to his home town of Exira four years earlier to teach school. The couple have one daughter, Betty Loraine, now Mrs. Donald G. Fitzpatrick of Marblehead, Massachusetts, and several grandchildren. Jensen's favorite recreations, he says, are "hard work and fishing when time permits."

References

N Y Herald Tribune p11 Mr 2 '54
N Y Times p8 Mr 2 '54

Biographical Directory of the American Congress, 1774-1949 (1950)
Congressional Directory (1959)
Who's Who in America, 1958-59
Who's Who in United States Politics (1952)

JOHNSON, ARNOLD M(ILTON) Jan. 11, 1907-Mar. 10, 1960 Banker; industrialist; owner of the Kansas City Athletics baseball team (since 1954). See *Current Biography* (October) 1955.

Obituary

N Y Times p31 Mr 10 '60

JORDAN, SARA M(URRAY) Oct. 20, 1884-Nov. 21, 1959 Physician; co-founder (1922) of Lahey Clinic and director of its gastroenterology department (1922-58). See *Current Biography* (March) 1954.

Obituary

N Y Times p86 N 22 '59

KAGAWA, TOYOHIKO July 10, 1888-Apr. 23, 1960 Japanese Christian leader; active in pacifist movements; author of a large number of books on economics, politics, religion, and other subjects. See *Current Biography* (September) 1941.

Obituary

N Y Times p88 Ap 24 '60

KATZ, LABEL A. Sept. 22, 1919- Lawyer; businessman; organization official

Address: b. 608 Baronne St., New Orleans 12, La.; h. 2000 Octavia St., New Orleans, La.

The Supreme Lodge of B'nai B'rith, holding its triennial convention for the first time in Jerusalem, in May 1959 elected Label A. Katz, a prominent Louisiana businessman, as fourteenth president of the 400,000-member Jewish service organization—the largest of its kind in the world. Katz, who succeeded Philip M. Klutznick for a three-year term, is the youngest president since the founding of B'nai B'rith in 1843.

Label A. Katz was born in New Orleans, Louisiana on September 22, 1919 to Ralph and Matilda (Conterman) Katz. He was educated in local public elementary and high schools. At the same time he became acquainted with Jewish culture and learning at the Communal Hebrew School, where he studied under the poet and scholar Dr. Ephraim E. Lisitsky. He attended Tulane University in New Orleans, receiving the B.A. degree in 1938, and went on to its law school, where he acquired an LL.B. degree in 1941.

After his graduation Katz practised law for several years and then turned to real estate investment. Also interested in housing rehabilitation, he has been responsible for transforming many of New Orleans' old, run-down buildings into modern apartment houses. This achievement led to his appointment in 1953 to the Mayor's Citizens Committee on Housing Improvement. That same year he founded and became the president of the Label A. Katz Investment Company, Inc.

Katz's formal affiliation with the B'nai B'rith began in 1934 when he joined the Abe A. Fried chapter of its youth organization for boys, Aleph Zadik Aleph, better known as AZA. Specializing in debating, he represented his chapter in contests for several years and in 1938 participated in the national debate finals. AZA gave him his earliest leadership training and an appreciation of the Jewish heritage. "Through the social service activities," he has said, "we had instilled within us a keen sense of our responsibilities to our fellow Jews and our fellow Americans" (*Shofar*, June 1959).

Because of this sense of responsibility, he continued his association with the youth groups when he became an adult. In 1942 he was appointed a district director of AZA. In the spring of 1953 he was elected by his district as its representative on the B'nai B'rith youth commission, which co-ordinates the activities of its four agencies, and two years later became the commission chairman. In 1956 AZA honored him with its Sam Beber Distinguished Alumnus Award.

His concern with developing in Jewish youth "a positive commitment to a meaningful Jewish life and a democratic ideal" led to his work in behalf of the B'nai B'rith Hillel Foundation program. Hillel provides cultural, religious, social, community service, personal guidance, and interfaith activities for Jewish college students. Katz helped establish two foundation centers and has served as chairman of the Hillel board for Sophie Newcomb College of Tulane University.

Along with helping the youth groups, Katz has been active in virtually every phase of the parent organization's work. B'nai B'rith, which was founded in 1843 to develop understanding among various groups of Jews in America and to contribute to the intellectual and moral advancement of people of the Jewish faith, now has special programs for women and young adults and offers adult education, social services, and emergency aid in areas hit by floods, tornadoes, and the like. In behalf of Jews suffering discrimination abroad, the organization, which has branches in thirty-seven countries, has brought formal complaints against governments attacking Jews and has given material assistance to refugees from such attacks.

In the United States its civil rights activities are carried on by the B'nai B'rith Anti-Defamation League, which fights discrimination of all kinds. An advocate of improved race relations in the South, Katz has been strongly identified with the work of the league. He is a past chairman of a regional board of the league which functions in Mississippi, Arkansas, and Louisiana and has served as a member of its national community service committee. As such he has been intimately involved in problems arising from the desegregation ruling of the United States Supreme Court.

For their stand against segregation Katz and the league were attacked by the New Orlean's White Citizens' Council, which charged that the league was under "criticism as a possible Communist-front organization." Katz defended the league on television and in the press, replying that "to differ with the views of the Citizens' Council does not make one a subversive or Communist sympathizer" and that "true Americanism is to respect the law of the United States" (*Shofar*, June 1959).

On the local level of the B'nai B'rith organization Katz served also from 1950 to 1952 successively as third, second, and first vice-president of district grand lodge number seven. In 1953 he was elected its president.

Nationally, Katz was a member of the executive committee of the B'nai B'rith Committee for Israel and has been an active fund raiser of the organization. He has served as a vice-chairman of the Joint Defense Appeal, which is the joint fund-raising machinery for the Anti-Defamation League and the American Jewish Committee. He was the co-chairman of the Henry Monsky Foundation mortgage redemption committee, whose work made possible the burning in Israel of the mortgage of the new B'nai B'rith building at 17th Street and Rhode Island Avenue in Washington, D.C.

In May 1959 in Jerusalem, at the first international convention of B'nai B'rith held outside the United States, Katz was elected president of the organization. As president he plans to concentrate on the expansion of the youth and international programs. The convention set up an eighteen-member council to strengthen contacts among B'nai B'rith affiliates throughout the world.

One of Katz's major concerns has been recent anti-Semitic outbreaks in West Germany and other countries. He discussed this subject in a meeting with Pope John XXIII in January 1960. Later that month he attended a meeting in Amsterdam of the B'nai B'rith international council, which condemned the Arab League boycott of Israeli shipping.

LABEL A. KATZ

Among the other civic and religious groups in which Katz has been active are the New Orleans Israel Bond Committee (co-founder), the Jewish Community Center (board member), and the Communal Hebrew School (past president, 1945-48). He is on the executive committee of the National Council of Jewish Federations and Welfare Funds and in the national cabinet of United Jewish Appeal. As a vice-president of the Urban League of New Orleans, he has also worked for improved economic conditions for Negroes. He is a board member of the New Orleans Baseball Club, a Shriner, and a member of the Louisiana and New Orleans bar associations. He is a Democrat.

Katz was married to Alice Mayer in July 1940. They have three children, William, Robert, and Walda. Katz is a member of the Anshe Sfard Congregation and the Temple Sinai Congregation. An article in the *Shofar* (June 1959) attributes his success in part to his "abundance of personal charm . . . tactful and conciliatory approach to people . . . sensitive regard for duty . . . optimistic and affirmative outlook toward life."

Reference

Who's Who in World Jewry (1955)

KEITA, MODIBO June 4, 1915- French West African government and political party leader

Address: Bamako, Republic of Mali

A nationalist leader, Modibo Keita, the President of the Council of the Republic of Mali, led his West African state through various stages before it attained its present status as an independent nation on September 23, 1960. Until November 1958, when it became the Sudanese Republic, a self-governing state, it was a French territory, the French Sudan.

(Continued next page)

French Embassy Press
& Inf. Div.

MODIBO KEITA

From January 1959 to August 1960 it was part of the Mali Federation. Like some other native West African leaders, Keita has also been concerned with the political affairs of metropolitan France and has held ministerial posts in Paris.

Modibo Keita was born on June 4, 1915 in Bamako, the capital of French Sudan. Some sources state that his ancestry can be traced back to the Keita dynasty which founded the Mali Empire and ruled that part of Africa during the thirteenth and fourteenth centuries. After finishing primary school near his home he attended Senegal's William Ponthy School. He graduated in 1936 and became a teacher.

After World War II the African territories were permitted to elect representatives to the French Constituent Assembly in Paris for the purpose of drawing up a new constitution. This marked the beginning of organized political activity in French Sudan. Keita was one of the organizers of Sudan's "le Bloc," which soon affiliated itself with a Senegalese political group that was an integral part of the French Socialist party. The alliance was short-lived, however, and "le Bloc" joined with other local political organizations to form the Rassemblement Démocratique Africain (RDA) at Bamako in 1946, under the leadership of Félix Houphouet-Boigny of the Ivory Coast.

At that time the French authorities opposed the RDA, which advocated full equality with France, and soon after the Bamako interterritorial congress, Keita was sent to prison. Upon his release in 1947, he was elected secretary-general of the Union Soudanaise, his territory's section of the RDA. Under the French constitution of 1946 each of the eight territories of French West Africa had been given a territorial assembly with certain limited powers. In July 1948 Keita was elected to the first territorial assembly of the French Sudan.

During its early years the RDA was allied with the Communists in hostility toward French administration of West Africa. Accused of being "an unrepentant Communist," Keita was assigned in 1950 to teach in a school in the remote Sahara region of the French Sudan. Two years later, in March 1952, he was re-elected to the territorial assembly and afterward became vice-president of that body. A break between the RDA and the Communists, beginning in late 1950, enabled Keita to return to Bamako and to gain favor with the French. He was again re-elected to Sudan's assembly in 1957. He has also served as mayor of Bamako for several years.

Other provisions of the 1946 constitution established the French Union, comprising both the mother country and the former empire, and created the Assembly of the French Union, to which the territories of West Africa had the right to send members. Keita was elected a councilor in this assembly in October 1953, and as such until 1956 he served as secretary of its committee for planning, equipment, and communications.

In further evidence of his political strength, Keita won election as deputy for French Sudan to the French National Assembly on January 2, 1956. He became the National Assembly's first African vice-president in June 1956, but resigned at the end of one year to accept an appointment as Secretary of State for France Overseas in Maurice Bourgès-Maunoury's cabinet. About four months later Bourgès-Maunoury lost power, and in November Keita was named Secretary of State to the Presidency of the Council in the cabinet of Félix Gaillard, an office in which he remained until May 1958.

Charles de Gaulle took over as Premier of France on June 1, 1958. His policies and his new constitution formed a climate in which leaders of French West Africa could seek their nationalistic objectives without having to fight France. The *loi cadre* decrees of February 3, 1957 had already created in each African territory and in Madagascar an executive council elected by the territorial assembly, and although the French-appointed governor would remain as president, the elected vice-president would be premier and, in fact, the leader of the government in internal affairs.

The constitution of 1958 proposed the formation of a French Community, to replace the French Union, composed of autonomous states sharing only foreign policy, defense, and common economic and financial questions—these to be handled by the Community's executive which consisted of the heads of each of the states. In the constitutional referendum of September 28, 1958 Sudan's vote was 97 per cent "yes" for membership in the Community. Most of French Africa voted "yes" with similarly large majorities. Only Guinea, under the leadership of Sékou Touré, voted an overwhelming "no," thereby seceding immediately from the Community.

On November 24, two months after the referendum, French Sudan became a self-governing republic, known as the Sudanese Republic, and a member state of the French

Community. Modibo Keita, who contributed to the work of the constituent assembly of the new state, in March 1959 was elected a deputy to the first Sudanese Legislative Assembly. The following month he became President of the Council of the Sudanese Republic, the chief executive office. He is also in charge of matters relating to information and youth.

While helping to establish the government of the new republic, Keita was also taking a leading part in organizing the Mali Federation. The former West African territories that voted for membership in the French Community had to decide how much independence they wanted in their links with France and with each other. Keita and certain other leaders, particularly in Sudan and Senegal, wanted a federation of West African states fully independent of France, but confederally related to France. In late December 1958 representatives from several West African states met in Bamako, and on January 17, 1959 leaders of Senegal, Sudan, Upper Volta, and Dahomey proclaimed the Mali Federation. Upper Volta and Dahomey, however, soon withdrew.

Mali, whose motto is "one people, one aim, one faith," set up a federal government responsible for financial, economic, and social matters common to the Sudanese Republic and the Republic of Senegal. Keita served as president of its constituent assembly until March 31, 1959, when he was elected to the Federal Assembly, which met in Dakar, Senegal, the capital of Mali. On April 4, 1959 Keita was named President of the Mali Federation. Just before becoming President of Mali and President of the Council of the Sudanese Republic, Keita had given up the office of President of the Grand Council of French West Africa, to which he had been elected in January 1959. This forty-member federal council, established under the 1946 constitution as one form of local authority, was dissolved on April 1, 1959.

Closely related to these various governmental developments was Keita's political break with Houphouet-Boigny, head of the interterritorial RDA, who opposed federation for French West Africa. Keita took the Sudan section of the party out of the RDA and joined it with Senegal's chief party, the Union Populaire Senegalais, to form another organization—the Parti Fédéraliste Africain. On March 25, 1959 Keita began serving as leader of the new party, and when the PFA held its first congress, in Dakar in July 1959, his position was confirmed by his election as secretary-general.

Mali gave formal notice of its intention to become fully independent (but still maintaining close ties with France) to a meeting of the executive of the French Community in Paris in September 1959. Negotiations between French and Mali officials, including Keita, opened in Paris on January 18, 1960 with the expectation that during the spring or early summer of 1960 simultaneous agreements would be signed granting full independence to Mali and stating the future relationship of the newly independent federation to France. Permitting a state to become fully sovereign yet remain in

the French Community necessitates a change in the French constitution, and some observers believe that it may have a profound effect on the rest of French Africa.

An accord granting full independence to the Mali Federation was signed on April 4, 1960, and the French constitution was amended in May to permit former colonies to become sovereign states and yet remain in the French Community. The Mali Federation, with Keita as its President, proclaimed its independence on June 20. However, two months later, it was dissolved when Senegal withdrew. Then, on September 23 the Sudanese Republic changed its name to the Republic of Mali. The chief executive of the new nation, Keita is also the head of the Union Soudanaise, the country's only political party.

Modibo Keita is about six feet four inches tall. He is graceful in movement, gentle in manner, and impressive in bearing. He is a member of the Bambara tribe and a Moslem and is said to admire both Gandhi and Stalin.

References

West Africa p437 My 9 '59
International Who's Who, 1959
Who's Who in France, 1959-60

KENNEDY, THOMAS Nov. 2, 1887-
Labor official

Address: b. United Mine Workers of America, 900 15th St., N.W., Washington, D.C.; h. 134 S. Poplar St., Hazleton, Pa.

When eighty-year-old John L. Lewis resigned as president of the United Mine Workers of America in early 1960, his seventy-two-year-old colleague, Thomas Kennedy, was appointed to take his place. Like Lewis, Kennedy has spent his entire adult life, more than sixty years, in the coal miners' labor union. He started working in the mines in 1889, at the age of twelve, for four cents an hour, and has risen through the years to the $50,000-a-year position as leader of the coal miners in their fight for better pay and better conditions. As president of the independent union (not affiliated with AFL-CIO), he is the chief spokesman for more than 500,000 coal workers. Formerly very prominent in the Pennsylvania Democratic party, he served from 1935 to 1939 as Lieutenant Governor of his state.

Thomas Kennedy was born in the anthracite mining community of Lansford, Pennsylvania on November 2, 1887, the first of eight children of Peter and Mary (Boyle) Kennedy. He attended local public schools until the age of twelve, when the economic circumstances of his family forced him to go to work as a slate picker in the mines. At the age of sixteen, while he himself was working underground, his father was killed in a mining accident and he became the chief support of his family.

Ever since he was an adolescent, Kennedy has been a member of the United Mine Workers of America. He joined the local union in 1903 and became an officer, at the age of

Chase, Ltd.

THOMAS KENNEDY

eighteen, in 1905. In that year he began a long record as a delegate to union conventions. When he was twenty-two, in 1910, he became president of UMWA District 7, one of the three districts in the hard coal fields of eastern Pennsylvania. He held that position for fifteen years.

As district president, Kennedy had the important job of organizing some 20,000 miners under his jurisdiction; he has done much of his union's organizing since that time. He was his district's representative to the joint anthracite wage negotiations in 1912, and he has participated in every anthracite joint wage agreement since then.

In 1925 the international executive board of the UMWA unanimously elected Kennedy as international secretary-treasurer, succeeding William Green, who became president of the AFL. He was union secretary-treasurer until 1947, and during that time he was one of the union's chief wage negotiators. Often testifying before Congress, he formulated his union's policies for presentation to Congress on such matters as the St. Lawrence Seaway, unemployment compensation, foreign trade, and national fuels. He successfully led opposition to the AFL policy against federal Social Security, and he became an expert in both the domestic and Canadian coal industry in problems of production and distribution.

For most of his adult life Kennedy has been active in Democratic politics. In 1934, as the running mate of George Earle, candidate for Governor, he was elected to a four-year term as Lieutenant Governor of Pennsylvania. In that office, while maintaining his position with the union, he presided over the state Senate and was chairman of the state Board of Pardons. After his bid for the Democratic nomination for Governor was defeated in 1938, he left the government but remained in politics as a Demo-

cratic national delegate. He was a delegate-at-large to the Democratic National Convention in 1936 and 1940, serving in the latter year on the resolutions committee.

During World War II, Kennedy was appointed a member of the National Defense Mediation Board in 1941 and the National War Labor Board in 1942, but he shortly resigned from both of those bodies over conflicts with his union. He served as a member of the advisory committee to the Department of Interior's bituminous coal division and of the department's solid fuels administration for war. President Roosevelt made him a member of his Committee on Vocational Education during the war.

Upon the death of John O'Leary in 1947, Kennedy was elected his successor in the vice-presidency of the UMWA. As relations between workers and management became more amicable in the coal mining industry during the last decade, Kennedy acquired less argumentative duties. He visited many European cities as his union's representative at the Miners' International Confederation of Free Trade Unions. In the United States he has served on various committees at national conventions of the AFL and CIO. He has been a member of the Pennsylvania Post-War Planning Commission and the Governor's Tax Advisory Committee in Pennsylvania.

In accordance with the UMWA rules by which the vice-president automatically succeeds to the presidency, when John L. Lewis resigned as president on January 14, 1960, the union's international executive board named Kennedy president. Lewis had headed the union for forty years. "I doubt if anyone, including myself, can take his place," Kennedy told reporters when the news of his appointment was released in December 1959. In an open letter in the *United Mine Workers Journal*, Lewis wrote that Kennedy was "amply qualified by training, character, executive ability and a lifetime of devoted and loyal service to function with credit and distinction in this office of high responsibility." Kennedy, who was appointed to fill out Lewis' unexpired term, announced that he would run for election to a four-year term in the referendum in late 1960.

Until union financial reporting became compulsory under the 1959 Labor-Management Reporting and Disclosure Act, the fiscal structure of the UMWA had never been made public. In April 1960 it was disclosed that the UMWA is perhaps the country's wealthiest union: its net assets total $110,315,080; in addition, the balance of the welfare and retirement fund exceeds $100,000,000.

Besides being president of the union, Kennedy is on the board of directors of two organizations begun by the union to promote the use of coal. These are American Coal Shipping, Inc., formed in 1957 to encourage shipment of American coal to other countries, and National Coal Policy Conference, Inc., formed in 1959 to publicize the economic importance of coal in America.

A member of the Roman Catholic faith, Kennedy has long participated in religious activities, especially in the promotion of Catholic charities. He is on the board of directors of the Hazleton Catholic Charities and the Hazleton United Givers Fund, and he was a director of White Haven Sanitorium for crippled persons from 1936 to 1956. He is a member of the National Catholic Welfare Conference and St. Gabriel's Roman Catholic Church in Hazleton.

Three Catholic colleges have awarded Kennedy honorary LL.D. degrees, St. Vincent College, St. Francis College, and the University of Scranton. He is a member of the American Academy of Political and Social Science, and his clubs are the Eagles, the Good Evening Club of Hazleton, the Knights of Columbus, and the Friendly Sons of St. Patrick.

Kennedy makes a striking contrast to the former UMA president, in appearance, in personality, and in his methods of conducting strategy. Where Lewis was famous as a firebrand who tongue-lashed his foes and seldom made friends of the coal management, Kennedy is, according to the New York *Times* (December 16, 1959), "a slight, mild-mannered man whose forte is that of friendly persuasion. His infectious Irish humor has won him a reputation as a shrewd and effective negotiator of labor disputes. He is respected by coal miners and operators alike."

Thomas Kennedy was married on July 23, 1912 to Helen Melley of Coaldale, Pennsylvania. There are two children from this marriage, Thomas Kennedy, Jr., an attorney in Hazleton, and Mrs. Thomas B. Noonan, of Barnesville, Pennsylvania, and five grandchildren. Widowed in December 1953, Kennedy was married to Evelyn Summers, a Washington secretary, on November 12, 1959.

Partly because he is short and stocky in build compared to Lewis, Kennedy is known as "The Little Giant of Anthracite." He is five feet six inches tall and weighs about 175 pounds. He has thinning white hair and gray eyes. He enjoys telling humorous tales about an imaginary Irish character whom he calls Donovan. He is now in Washington most of the time, but he likes to spend weekends at his home in Hazleton or trout fishing in the Pocono Mountains.

References

Bsns W p114 Ja 23 '60
Newsday p48 D 16 '59 por
U S News 47:17 D 28 '59
Who's Who in America, 1960-61
Who's Who in Labor (1946)

KESSELRING, ALBERT Nov. 30, 1885-July 16, 1960 Supreme commander of German forces in Italy (1942-45); sentenced by British military court to be shot for Nazi war crimes (1947); sentence commuted to twenty years of imprisonment; released from West German prison for health reasons and by British order in 1952. See *Current Biography* (November) 1942.

Obituary

N Y Times p60 Jl 17 '60

KIDD, MICHAEL 1919- Director; choreographer; former dancer

Address: b. c/o William Morris Agency, Inc.; 151 El Camino, Beverly Hills, Calif.

Although Michael Kidd once studied to become an engineer, he has made his mark in the entertainment world as a dancer, choreographer, and director. His gift for humor and for depicting types of American character has made him especially successful in musical comedies. On Broadway he was responsible for the dances in *Finian's Rainbow, Can-Can,* and *Guys and Dolls* and for the choreography and direction of *Li'l Abner* and *Destry Rides Again.* In Hollywood he has devised the dance sequences for several films, including *Merry Andrew.*

Kidd began his career as a ballet dancer with the American Ballet, the Dance Players, and Ballet Theatre, for which he created and danced the ballet *On Stage!* in 1945. He is the first person to receive four Antoinette Perry awards since the prizes were originated in 1947.

Michael Kidd was born in 1919 in Brooklyn, New York, the son of an immigrant barber. He attended New Utrecht High School, where he joined the track team; he later majored in chemical engineering at the City College of the City of New York. To meet his living expenses, he worked nights as a copy boy for the New York *Daily News.*

Nothing in his early background helps explain why Michael Kidd became a dancer. One evening, while he was in high school, he attended a performance of the modern dance given by the New Dance League. Kidd, who was very impressed, was "careless enough to say so, and before he knew it he was a scholarship pupil in a modern dance class" (John Martin, New York *Times Magazine,* May 4, 1947). In the next few years he studied with such teachers as Blanche Evan, Anatole Vilzak, Ludmila Shollar, and Muriel Stuart. By the end of his third year at City College, he had decided that he was not interested in science. "I felt it was too impersonal," he said. "It didn't deal with human beings." Turning completely to the dance, he attended the School of American Ballet on a scholarship, and used his technical training to work with dance groups as an electrician and property man.

In 1937 he made his stage debut in the chorus of Max Reinhardt's production of *The Eternal Road.* In the same year he joined the American Ballet and Lincoln Kirstein's Ballet Caravan. Touring the United States with the latter troupe during the next three years, he danced many roles, including the lead in *Billy the Kid.* At the New York World's Fair, in 1939 and 1940, he danced in *Railroads on Parade* and *American Jubilee.* In 1941 he joined the Dance Players as assistant director and soloist, and appeared in such ballets as *The Man from Midian, City Portrait,* and *Harlequin for President.*

Kidd's work with the Dance Players favorably impressed Antal Dorati, musical director of the Ballet Theatre, who invited him to join the group in 1942. During his five years with

MICHAEL KIDD

the company, Kidd danced leading parts in *Helen of Troy, Bluebeard, Aurora's Wedding, Interplay,* and other ballets.

The Ballet Theatre gave Kidd the opportunity to direct his original ballet *On Stage!* Based on the story of a backstage handy man who befriends a shy young dancer, the ballet had its première on October 4, 1945, with Kidd and Janet Reed taking the leading roles. The dance was praised by many critics, including Edwin Denby (New York *Herald Tribune,* October 14, 1945) who predicted the ballet would take Kidd to Broadway before winter's end. "The gift it shows is congenial to Broadway, a gift for using dancing as agreeable efficient entertainment rather than for poetic expression," Denby wrote.

Kidd admits that he wants his ballets to appeal to popcorn-crunching young movie goers as well as to discriminating balletomanes. "Dancing," he has said, "should be completely understandable—every move, every turn should mean something, should be crystal-clear to the audience. And if you can make them laugh or cry, move them emotionally, make them respond to the dancer as a real person doing something believable within your theatrical framework—well—you've done a job."

Within a year and a half after the first performance of *On Stage!* Kidd accepted an assignment as choreographer of *Finian's Rainbow,* a musical fantasy about an outsized leprechaun who solves the race problem in Missitucky. When *Finian's Rainbow* opened on Broadway on January 10, 1947, Kidd's dance creations won the favor of the reviewers. Other New York productions for which Kidd did the choreography, were *Hold It!* (1948), *Love Life* (1948), *Arms and the Girl* (1950), and *Can-Can* (1953). In all of these shows, Kidd's dances were not just *divertissements,* but integral parts of the story.

Michael Kidd gave his "magic touch" to the dances of *Guys and Dolls,* the musical based on Damon Runyon's stories about Broadway characters, which began its New York run on November 24, 1950. His Havana sequence, dice game ballet, and two night club routines accompanying the hit songs, "Bushel and a Peck" and "Take Back Your Mink," were particularly commended. Kidd went to Hollywood to stage the dances and musical numbers for the motion-picture version of *Guys and Dolls* in 1955. He also choreographed and staged the dances for the movies *The Band Wagon* (1953), *Knock on Wood* (1954), and *Seven Brides for Seven Brothers* (1954).

Kidd acted and danced in the motion-picture musical *It's Always Fair Weather* (1955), which satirized the human interest shows on television. He was cast as Angie, the proprietor of a glorified hamburger stand called the Cordon Bleu, who is reunited with his World War II buddies on a TV program. Taking still another role in the production of movies, Kidd directed the Danny Kaye comedy *Merry Andrew* (1958), about an amateur archaeologist looking for a Roman statue buried in a meadow where a circus is encamped.

The Broadway stage has also provided Kidd with vehicles for his directorial talents. He choreographed, staged, and co-produced *Li'l Abner,* which began its long run on November 15, 1956. Based on the famous comic strip by Al Capp, the musical show was not regarded by critics as a three-dimensional version of the world of Dogpatch, Kentucky. Kidd's choreography in the Sadie Hawkins Day ballet, and the other frenzied acrobatics and harum-scarum antics that he devised came closest in quality to the satiric comic strip, according to most critics.

When *Destry Rides Again* galloped into the Imperial Theatre in New York City on April 23, 1959, critics commented that director Michael Kidd was "firmly in the saddle." In this musical version of the story of Sheriff Tom Destry, who preaches pacifism in a rough frontier town, Kidd presented "razzle-dazzle, gun smoke, cracking bullwhips and some of the wildest, funniest and most high-spirited dancing in town" (*Life,* May 25, 1959).

Walter Kerr of the New York *Herald Tribune* (May 3, 1959) took Kidd to task for his "electronic-brain musical, forever returning the right answer." Kidd "no longer dares pause for that odd, foolish, grinning little gesture that made a leprechaun neighborly in 'Finian's Rainbow.' Now that Mr. Kidd is in charge of the over-all direction, he seems ready to . . . keep the tractor roaring at whatever cost in incidental delight." *Destry Rides Again* continued on Broadway until July 18, 1960.

Black-haired, brown-eyed Michael Kidd stands five feet six inches and weighs 145 pounds. He enjoys photography, cabinetmaking, tinkering with sound-recording equipment and old car motors, and reading popular science magazines. Of his own work, he prefers the ballet "Green Up Time," a polka from *Love Life.* Since 1940 he has been married to Mary Heater, by whom he has two daughters, Kristine and Susan. When he was asked if he wanted them to become dancers, Kidd replied: "I'm certainly not going to push them, but it's wonderful for girls to study dancing. It gives them poise and grace."

Kidd departs from the popular conception of the director as a man who gives instructions from a chair. Jacques d'Amboise has said: "He's willing to do anything himself that he expects of his dancers. And he's a great dancer himself." When dancers do not pick up his direction on cue, he does not yell or throw a tantrum. Instead, he indicates his displeasure by giving a loud whistle.

Increasingly interested in the theater, he admits that he finds it more exciting than pure ballet. He even hopes to be given the opportunity to direct some dramas. He regards himself as a follower of Chaplin. "I have a strong attraction for pantomime," he has said. "And I use it all the time. I like the mixture of pathos and comedy, which nobody has ever done like Chaplin."

References

Cue 25:18+ Ja 21 '56 por
N Y Sunday Mirror Mag p7 O 21 '56 por
N Y Sunday News II p4 My 3 '59 por
Chujoy, A. ed. Dance Encyclopedia (1949)
Wilson, G.B.L. A Dictionary of Ballet (1957)

KILPATRICK, JOHN REED June 15, 1889-May 7, 1960 Former sports arena executive; was president (1933-55), board chairman (1955-59), and honorary chairman (since 1959) of Madison Square Garden in New York; attained rank of brigadier general in the United States Army. See *Current Biography* (July) 1948.

Obituary

N Y Times p1+ My 8 '60

KINTNER, EARL W(ILSON) Nov. 6, 1912- Chairman of the Federal Trade Commission; lawyer
Address: b. Federal Trade Commission, Washington 25, D.C.; h. 3037 Dent Pl., N.W., Washington 7, D.C.

Traditionally the chiefs of federal agencies do their work with a minimum of publicity, but the 1958 and 1959 Congressional inquiries into television shows have put Earl W. Kintner of the Federal Trade Commission, among others, in the press spotlight. Probably no other FTC chairman in recent years is better equipped to answer the challenge. The commission's new chairman is not a newcomer to the agency: he has been a career attorney with the FTC since 1948. Before that, he was a member of the United Nations War Crimes Commission and a lawyer in private and governmental practice. On February 19, 1960 President Dwight D. Eisenhower nominated

Wide World

EARL W. KINTNER

Kintner for reappointment to a seven-year term on the Federal Trade Commission, but the Senate failed to confirm the appointment.

Earl Wilson Kintner was born in Corydon, Indiana on November 6, 1912, the son of Jacob Leroy and Lillie Florence (Chanley) Kintner. He had one brother and three sisters: William, Kathern, Cleola (now deceased), and Alice. A farm family, the Kintners were reared in Princeton, Indiana, where Earl worked at home and at various jobs while attending public schools. At Princeton High School, from which he was graduated in 1932, Kintner was an excellent scholar and a member of the school's championship debating team. His record won him a full-tuition scholarship to De-Pauw University in Greencastle, Indiana, where he supplemented his scholarship by work as a newspaper reporter. He also edited the student newspaper, was a member of the cross-country team, and was elected to Delta Sigma Rho (debating), Pi Sigma Alpha (political science), and Sigma Delta Chi (journalism) societies. He received his B.A. degree in history and political science in 1936.

His debating experience persuaded Kintner to study law. He enrolled in the School of Law of Indiana University in Bloomington, where he was one of the winners of the school's first moot court competition and later was a moot court judge under a special scholarship. Before graduating, he campaigned on the Republican ticket for the office of prosecuting attorney of the Sixty-sixth Indiana Judicial Circuit.

The bid was unsuccessful, and after receiving the J.D. degree with high honors in 1938 he returned to Princeton, where he maintained a general practice of law until he entered the United States Navy in 1944. He also held the position of city attorney from 1939 to 1942

KINTNER, EARL W.—*Continued*

and was elected prosecuting attorney of the Sixty-sixth Indiana Judicial Circuit, serving in 1943-44.

In the Navy he was commissioned an ensign in the amphibious forces, handling legal matters until tuberculosis left him physically disabled. Twice promoted, he was transferred to the war crimes office in Washington, D.C., going to London in late 1945 in the rank of lieutenant to serve as United States deputy commissioner on the U.N. War Crimes Commission. After his medical discharge the following year, he completed this assignment as a temporary legal officer of the State Department.

In London, Kintner had been co-chairman of the committee which reviewed war crimes cases later tried by the Allied nations. He was also a member of the commission's legal committee, chairman of its publications committee, and editor in charge of law reports. He edited an official history of the commission, *Development of the Laws of War* (H.M. Stationery Office, 1948), and *The Hadamar Trial* (Hodge, 1949).

Returning to the United States in 1948, Kintner joined the Federal Trade Commission as a trial attorney in antimonopoly cases. He was advanced to legal adviser in 1951 and to general counsel two years later. In 1953 and 1954 he served as FTC delegate to the President's Conference on Administrative Procedure, meanwhile planning and editing the commission's *Manual for Attorneys*.

"His record in the Court of Appeals and the Supreme Court, as the commission's chief legal officer, has been outstanding," wrote a correspondent for *Printers' Ink* (July 3, 1959). "Thanks to his experience as a news gatherer, he eschews doubletalk and other forms of bureaucratic gobbledegook—a trait that has won him the esteem of Washington correspondents, especially the business press."

On June 9, 1959 Kintner was sworn in as a member of the Federal Trade Commission, filling the unexpired term of former chairman John W. Gwynne. Two days later he was designated by President Dwight D. Eisenhower as the FTC's chairman, the first career member of the commission to fill its top post. His appointment was unanimously approved by the Senate, and he formally assumed the chairmanship on June 12. The five-member FTC, organized as an independent administrative agency in 1915, is charged with preventing the free enterprise system from being restrained by monopoly and corrupted by unfair or deceptive trade practices.

When Kintner became FTC chairman the commission was primarily occupied with its traditional concerns: discovering violations of fair trade, especially the practice of setting artificially high "list" prices to give the consumer the illusion he was purchasing a bargain and the parallel practice of discriminatory price-fixing by wholesalers. Later, however, inquiries into "rigged" TV quiz shows by the legislative oversight subcommittee of the

House Interstate and Foreign Commerce Committee spelled out another area of study for the commission: video advertising frauds.

Although Kintner believes that the abuses of advertising can best be stopped by the advertisers themselves, he admits that self-policing will not work in all instances. He has therefore declared that it has become the policy of the commission to "turn off the spigot of chicanery at its source with the handiest wrench that will fit the task" (New York *Times,* November 2, 1959).

Doubling the size of his radio and television monitoring staff, the FTC chairman gave notice that "any advertising of doubtful integrity will be investigated on a priority basis." Almost immediately the FTC charged Libbey-Owens Ford Glass Company and General Motors Corporation with deceptive practices —including advertising films shot through an open window to illustrate distortion-free qualities in window glass.

Meanwhile, public disapproval of advertising frauds began to mount. "Doesn't it strike you," asked columnist Roscoe Drummond (New York *Herald Tribune,* December 4, 1959), "that the Federal Communications Commission . . . and the Federal Trade Commission . . . are bestirring themselves an awfully long time after the horse has been stolen?" It was obvious that a chagrined public, like children discovering that the department store Santa has a cotton beard, wanted the FTC and other agencies to move harder and faster to clean up the broadcasting frauds.

In December 1959 the commission filed complaints against nine record companies with "unfair and deceptive acts," including the use of money payments to disc jockeys who played their records on the air. Two months later, as a result of commission findings, the nation's cigarette manufacturers agreed to discontinue all low-tar and low-nicotine claims in their advertisements. The FTC also reached an agreement with the Department of Justice to use criminal prosecution against false TV advertisements concerning food, drugs, and cosmetics. One TV critic, Harriet Van Horne (New York *World-Telegram and Sun,* January 15, 1960), predicted: "If nothing else emerges from the TV scandals you can bet some new programs will—high-minded, high-budget programs aimed at the discriminating audience that began to snap off the set long before the TV scandals and subsequent mass revulsion."

Kintner also drew upon his newspaper experience to increase public awareness of deceptive advertising, by scheduling a conference on "trickery in the market place" in Washington, D.C., in late December 1959. At its end, he announced that the FTC, equipped with a larger budget, intended to increase its activities "all along the line" to protect the public from advertising and merchandising frauds.

Twice married, Kintner had three children by his first wife: Jonathan, Anna, and Rosemary (deceased). He was married to Valerie Patricia Wildy on May 28, 1948; their son is Christopher. Kintner is a Republican, belongs to many professional, fraternal, and veterans organizations, and is a member of St. Thomas Episcopal Church in Washington. Legal writing is his hobby, and he is an inveterate pipe smoker. Kintner, who stands five feet ten inches and weighs 165 pounds, has twinkling blue eyes and a full shock of brown hair. In 1958 he was an adjunct professor at New York University's School of Law.

"Every commissioner has primary responsibility for deciding the merits of each case," Kintner has said, "and justice should be tailored to meet the situation under adjudication. Justice is not an institutional matter" (*Printers' Ink,* July 3, 1959).

References

N Y World-Telegram p27 O 14 '59
Who's Who in America, 1958-59

KIRK, NORMAN T(HOMAS) Jan. 3, 1888-Aug. 13, 1960 Former Surgeon General of the United States Army (1943-47); career officer who attained rank of major general; orthopedist; author of medical books. See *Current Biography* (February) 1944.

Obituary

N Y Times p93 Ag 14 '60

KIRK, WILLIAM T(ALBOT) Mar. 24, 1908- Social worker

Address: b. 14 rue de Hollande, Geneva, Switzerland; 345 E. 46th St., New York 17; h. 27 Caterson Terrace, Hartsdale, N.Y.

In his closely related positions of international director of International Social Service and general director of the I.S.S. American branch, William T. Kirk helps to administer an organization whose responsibilities have increased a hundredfold with the growth of air travel during the past few years. The I.S.S. is the only international nonsectarian casework agency in the world; it helps anyone in need whose personal problem crosses international boundaries. Before being appointed international director in 1952, Kirk had acquired almost twenty years of experience in social work and during World War II had directed relief and repatriation operations for the Allied Military Government.

William Talbot Kirk was born in Columbus, Ohio on March 24, 1908 to Emmet Lyle Kirk, a business executive, and Katherine (Talbot) Kirk. His brother, J. T. Kirk, lives in Westlake, Ohio. Since his boyhood William Kirk has been interested in sports, and while attending high school in Lakewood, Ohio, he was captain of the football team, a member of the track team, and the state 440 yards champion.

Entering Ohio State University after his graduation from high school in 1927, Kirk chose business administration as his major subject and specialized in personnel administration. At the university he was president of the freshman council, president of the Liberal Club, assistant manager of the football

Arthur Avedon

WILLIAM T. KIRK

team, and assistant business manager of the campus humor magazine, *Sun Dial.* He was awarded his B.S. degree in 1932, the same year in which he joined the Sun Oil Company in Cleveland. Starting as a truck driver, he rose to salesman and then to dealer supervisor in the operation of service stations.

Volunteer work in a Cleveland settlement house, meanwhile, helped convince Kirk that his greatest interest lay in working in a program of direct service to people. In 1934 he left the Sun Oil Company and enrolled in the New York School of Social Work at Columbia University. He received a graduate certificate in 1936, and his thesis, *Lobbying for Social Legislation,* was published by the National Social Work Publicity Council the following year.

While still studying at Columbia, in 1935 Kirk had become a caseworker at the Joint Application Bureau in New York City. He left this position in 1937 to serve as area director for American Red Cross disaster relief in Louisville, Kentucky, but the same year returned to New York City, where he was employed as a social worker for the WPA during the next several months. From 1938 to 1941 he was executive secretary of Protestant Family Welfare, Inc., in Albany, New York, and from 1941 to 1943 he was executive director of Provident Family & Children's Service, Kansas City, Missouri.

Kirk's first experience in welfare work of an international character occurred during World War II. In 1943 he received a diploma for a course at the Harvard University School for Overseas Administration. Then with the rank of captain in the United States Army, which he had entered in May 1943, he was assigned to the European theater of operations and attached to the Allied Military Government. He directed relief work in Naples, Italy and later took charge of the repatriation

KIRK, WILLIAM T.—*Continued*

of Allied displaced persons and refugees in Europe. During his two and a half years in the Army he was awarded five Battle Stars, a Bronze Star Medal, and a special commendation. He was discharged in December 1945 with the rank of major.

For five years immediately after the war Kirk directed the special services program of the Community Service Society of New York. In May 1951, when he was also chairman of the New York City chapter of the American Association of Social Workers, he addressed the National Conference of Social Workers in Atlantic City, New Jersey, calling upon private agencies to handle their programs for the aged with more imagination and enterprise. Later in May he resigned from the Community Service Society to accept the general directorship of the American branch of International Social Service, which has headquarters in New York City.

As director of American I.S.S., Kirk administers an agency that annually helps about 12,000 Americans at home and abroad. A component part of the parent organization, the local branch is professionally staffed to help Americans whose personal problems require action and attention outside their country. Supported by individuals, philanthropic foundations, United Funds, Community Chests, and WAIF chapters, I.S.S. service is extended on an individual, no-cost basis. Although the nature of its demands has changed, the need for its service remains constant. With the expansion overseas of American government, business, and industry, more people are seeking agency assistance. At the present time about 65 per cent of the American casework involves children. Many of the cases arise from the efforts of American couples to adopt foreign-born children.

On September 30, 1952, the international council, the governing body of I.S.S., appointed Kirk international director. Working through I.S.S. headquarters in Geneva, he became responsible for the implementation and administration of the general international program, while still directing the work of the American office. World-wide in scope, I.S.S. maintains independent, but closely interrelated branches in seventeen countries and close affiliation with social agencies in seventy other countries. It has consultative status with the United Nations Economic and Social Council and collaborative arrangements with numerous governmental, intergovernmental, and voluntary organizations. It contributes to the field of international social planning through special studies based on its own experience.

After Kirk became director, I.S.S. was faced with larger demands for its services than at any time since its formation in 1924. At the biennial council meeting in Geneva in June 1959, Kirk said: "In just five years our case load has doubled from 29,000 in 1953 to 60,000 in

1958." With the world "on the move," as he explained, family problems with international complications have kept the I.S.S. intercontinental network busy. Family separation, desertion, and nonsupport cases are some of the most common, partly because of the number of servicemen who have left Japanese or German wives behind. Refugee families have also been broken by migration.

Since World War II intercountry adoptions have been among the major concerns of I.S.S. In an interview with *Cosmopolitan* magazine in February 1955, Kirk said that application for the adoption of a foreign-born child had to start with a local adoption agency, as does an application for the adoption of an American-born child. After processing and approving the application, the local agency contacts I.S.S.

In discussing the subject at a meeting of the Adoption Service of Westchester, New York in May 1955, Kirk suggested that couples interested in adopting a foreign-born child seek special counsel to understand the cultural, linguistic, and other possible problems involved. He stressed that it is I.S.S. policy to encourage adoption in the country of the child's birth first and to bring to the United States only those children who would not have the opportunity for desirable placement in their native lands. Because of I.S.S.'s wealth of experience in this field, its representatives have been called in to advise Congress in formulating legislation to regulate overseas adoption in accordance with approved social work policies.

Kirk is a member of the advisory committee on international activities of the Department of Health, Education and Welfare and, by White House appointment, a member of the board of directors of the United States Committee for Refugees. He serves on the executive committee of the National Conference of Social Work and is a former president of both the school board in Hartsdale, New York and the alumni association of the New York School of Social Work. His fraternity is Beta Theta Pi.

On September 15, 1934 William T. Kirk was married to Ruth Van Voorhis, also a social worker; they have one son, David. Kirk is five feet ten inches tall, weighs 190 pounds, and has brown eyes and graying light-brown hair. In his leisure time he enjoys baseball, football, golf, fishing, and reading. He is a Democrat and a Methodist. "Practical means must be found," Kirk believes, "to give the people of the world an opportunity to work together in worthwhile causes that increase the possibility of achieving lasting peace. It is increasingly important that people understand the real enemies of mankind are poverty, ignorance and disease."

References

N Y Times p37 My 27 '51 por; p35 O 1 '52 por
Who's Who in New York, 1952
World Biography (1954)

KISTIAKOWSKY, GEORGE B(OGDAN)

(kĭs-tyä-kŭv'skĭ) Nov. 18, 1900- United States government official; university professor; chemist

Address: b. Executive Office Bldg., The White House, Washington 25, D.C.

A distinguished research chemist, George B. Kistiakowsky was named in May 1959 by President Dwight D. Eisenhower as his Special Assistant for Science and Technology to succeed James R. Killian, Jr. Kistiakowsky, on leave from his post as chemistry professor at Harvard University, is responsible for advising the President on national science policy. The position was created in 1957 to try to restore American scientific and technological leadership after the Soviet success with Sputnik I. Kistiakowsky has had a prominent career in teaching, government, and research; his work in thermodynamics, chemical kinetics, and spectroscopy has contributed to the success of nuclear weapons, chemical explosives, and rocket propellants.

George Bogdan Kistiakowsky was born in Kiev, the Ukraine, Russia on November 18, 1900 into a Cossack family. His father was Bogdan Kistiakowsky, a professor of international law at the University of Kiev; his mother was Mary (Berenstam) Kistiakowskaya. George attended schools in Kiev and Moscow until the fall of 1918, when he began fighting in the infantry and in the tank corps of the White Army against the Bolsheviks in the Russian Revolution.

In spite of a bad case of typhus, he stayed with the army, under General Pëtr Nikolaevich Wrangel, until the evacuation from the Crimea in the autumn of 1920. After being interned in the Ottoman Empire, he made his way to Yugoslavia, where an uncle offered to help him secure a university education. He enrolled at the University of Berlin in 1921 and wrote his thesis under Max Bodenstein. He received his Ph.D. degree in chemistry in 1925 and remained at the university until January 1926 as Bodenstein's research assistant.

As an International Education Board Fellow in physical chemistry, he came to the United States in 1926 to study at Princeton University under Professor H. S. Taylor. After two years in this capacity, he continued at the university as a research associate from 1928 to 1930, when he was invited to Harvard University as an assistant professor of chemistry. There he did research on the origin of chemical reactions, in addition to teaching. Three years later he was advanced to the rank of associate professor and in 1938 was named Abbott and James Lawrence Professor of Chemistry.

With the spread of war throughout Europe and Asia, the United States embarked on a defense program and began to seek the expertise of the nation's scientists. In July 1940 Kistiakowsky became a consultant for section A-1 (explosives) of division B for the National Defense Research Committee, and later he was acting chairman of this section.

Wide World

GEORGE B. KISTIAKOWSKY

He assumed the chairmanship of section B-1 (explosives-physical) of division B in the fall of 1941.

A year later, after the United States had entered World War II, he became the head of division B (explosives) of the National Defense Research Committee. In this post he was responsible for the explosives work of the committee, including the supervision of two laboratories (at Bruceton, Pennsylvania and Woods Hole, Massachusetts) and the planning, placement, and supervision of contracts for the work done by private companies and colleges.

The type of work over which he presided included the preparing of new explosives, testing the performance and safety of these explosives, determining the effect of the explosives on their surroundings (shock waves in water and air fragmentation), manufacturing explosives for military use, and developing gun propellants and rocket propellants. He is credited with making the "Aunt Jemima" powder, an explosive that looked like flour and was safely baked into bread and cookies. It was sent to Chinese guerrillas to use against the Japanese occupiers.

On projects devoted to the perfecting of the atomic bomb Kistiakowsky participated informally in the work that preceded the Manhattan District in 1940-41. He belonged to the committee on atomic energy of the National Academy of Sciences in 1941. Taking a more active role, he became a consultant to the Los Alamos Project in 1943, a full-time member of the project in February 1944, and later head of the explosives division of the Los Alamos Laboratory of the Manhattan District. At the laboratory he prepared the conventional explosives used to detonate the atomic bomb.

(Continued next page)

KISTIAKOWSKY, GEORGE B.—*Cont.*

After the war had come to an end, he returned to Harvard in February 1946. Kistiakowsky served as chairman of the chemistry department from 1947 to 1950. He also became for several years a member of the admissions committee for Harvard College and of the faculty committee on athletics. He was also able to return to his own research activities. About 150 articles by Kistiakowsky have been published in scientific journals describing his researches in such areas of physical chemistry as chemical kinetics of gas phase reactions, shock and detonation waves, kinetics of enzyme-catalyzed reactions, thermochemistry of organic compounds, gas phase equilibria, and molecular spectroscopy. His book, *Photochemical Processes* (Chemical Catalog Company, 1928), appeared as number 43 in the monograph series of the American Chemical Society.

In the postwar period Kistiakowsky has continued to serve the United States government in several capacities. As a member of the ballistic missiles advisory committee of the Department of Defense from 1953 to 1958, he had a hand in the historic decision of 1954 to accelerate work on the development of an Intercontinental Ballistic Missile. He belonged to the United States delegation of experts to the Conference for Prevention of Surprise Attack, held in Geneva in 1958. Since 1959 he has belonged to the research advisory committee on chemical energy of the National Aeronautics and Space Administration.

Kistiakowsky succeeded Killian as Special Assistant to the President for Science and Technology in July 1959. In this position he advises President Eisenhower on all science problems facing the federal government, from co-ordination of research and development in the various government departments to science education in the United States. Kistiakowsky is also chairman of the President's Science Advisory Committee and of the Federal Council for Science and Technology.

Honorary D.Sc. degrees were conferred on Kistiakowsky by Harvard in 1955, Williams College in 1958, and Oxford University in 1959. He received the President's Medal for Merit (1946), Army Ordnance Award and Navy Ordnance Award (1946), Nichols Medal of the New York section of the American Chemical Society (1947), King's Medal (United Kingdom) for Services in the Cause of Freedom (1948), Exceptional Services Award of the United States Air Force (1957), Joseph Priestley Award of Dickinson College (1958), and the Willard Gibbs Medal of the Chicago section of the American Chemical Society (1960).

Organizations in which Kistiakowsky is a member include the National Academy of Sciences (former chairman of the chemistry section), American Academy of Arts and Sciences, American Chemical Society, American Philosophical Society, American Physical Society, and Society of Sigma Xi. He was made an honorary Fellow of the Chemical Society of London in 1958.

George B. Kistiakowsky was married to Hildegard Moebius in 1926. By this marriage, they have a daughter, Vera (Mrs. G. E. Fischer). In 1942 the couple were divorced. In 1945 Kistiakowsky was married to Irma E. Shuler. The scientist is six feet three inches in height, has brown eyes, and is known to his friends as "Kisty." He likes to smoke cigarettes and pipes. For recreation he goes skiing and watches Harvard football games. He has sometimes described himself as "just a poor Russian immigrant"; in 1933 he became a naturalized American citizen.

"The next step for the future of our nation," Kistiakowsky said in 1960, "depends on investing an even greater fraction of our national resources in education. I mean by that, high-brow education—improvement of the intellect, intellectual excellence and basic research." He believes that the present method of extending federal research grants for specific projects is creating an artificial distinction between teaching and research, and fostering an imbalance in the universities in favor of the natural sciences. Under an experiment begun in 1960, universities may use federal funds allocated by the National Science Foundation to build their science programs as they see fit.

References

Chem & Eng N 24:2881 N 10 '46 por; 25:770+ Mr 17 '47 pors; 36:94 Ap 14 '58 por
N Y Times p2 My 29 '59 por; p25 D 11 '59 por
N Y Times Mag p15+ Je 12 '60 por
Nature 183:1639 Je 13 '59
Science 129:1598+ Je 12 '59
American Men of Science vol 1 (1955)
Who's Who in America, 1960-61
World Biography (1954)

KLUCKHOHN, CLYDE (KAY MABEN)

Jan. 11, 1905-July 29, 1960 Professor of anthropology at Harvard University (1946-60); assistant and associate professor of anthropology at Harvard (1937-46); authority on the Navajo Indians; helped to organize and directed (1947-54) the university's Russian Research Center. See *Current Biography* (November) 1951.

Obituary

N Y Times p68 Jl 31 '60

KOWALSKI, FRANK, JR.

Oct. 18, 1907- United States Representative from Connecticut; former Army officer

Address: b. House Office Bldg., Washington, D.C.; h. 121 Lincoln St., Meriden, Conn.; 405 Regent Dr., Alexandria, Va.

Elected for a two-year term as United States Representative-at-Large from Connecticut in that state's Democratic landslide of November 1958, Frank Kowalski, Jr., was assigned in the Eighty-sixth Congress to the House Armed Services Committee. A freshman legislator and a former Army officer, he has crusaded against the misuse of military manpower, particularly the assignment of enlisted men as officers' servants. Kowalski held various military positions in Japan from 1948 to 1952 and later served for four years as the first commandant of the Army Command Management School in this country. In 1958, after thirty-three years in the Army, he retired from military service with the rank of colonel in order to engage in political activity.

Of Polish ancestry on his father's side, Frank Kowalski, Jr., was born to Frank and Mary (Miller) Kowalski at Meriden, Connecticut on October 18, 1907. He attended local public schools and Alliance College in Pennsylvania and enlisted as a private in the United States Army in 1925. After eighteen months of service, Kowalski won an appointment through competitive examinations to the United States Military Academy at West Point, New York where he received his B.S. degree and a commission as a second lieutenant in 1930. During the next few years, he held various company, battalion, and regimental assignments, first in the infantry and later in ordnance. He received an M.Sc. degree from the Massachusetts Institute of Technology in 1936.

A staff officer with General Eisenhower in the last two years of World War II, Kowalski was named chief of training for the G-3 section at the European Theater headquarters in London in 1944 and later that year became director of the Disarmament School in the British capital. In this capacity he directed the program for the dismantling of the German war machine.

In 1945 Kowalski became deputy chief of the information and education division at European headquarters. He also took courses in international relations at Columbia University later that year. Sent to Japan in 1948 to head the military government in the Kyoto and Osaka prefectures, Kowalski was appointed deputy chief of Japanese Civil Affairs in 1949.

During the Korean War, from 1950 to 1952, he served first as chief of staff and later as acting chief for the military advisory group which helped the Japanese government to plan organization of defense forces. Kowalski returned to the United States to organize the new Army Command Management School, of which he was named the first commandant in 1954. For his wartime and postwar services Kowalski was awarded the Legion of Merit with oak leaf cluster and the Bronze Star Medal.

Reapportionment after the 1940 census gave Connecticut six instead of five seats in Congress. The state, however, remained divided into five districts, with the additional seat being occupied by a Representative-at-Large. In 1958, while still directing the Army Command Management School, Kowalski decided to make a bid for the Democratic nomination to oppose the election for a sixth term of the incumbent Republican Representative-at-Large, Antoni N. Sadlak.

Kowalski went as a "political unknown" to the Democratic state convention at Hartford, where he was nominated on June 28 by 364 votes to 112 votes for Joseph P. Lyford of

Wide World

FRANK KOWALSKI, JR.

Westford. So that he might be free to campaign, Kowalski was placed on the Army's temporary disability retired list as of August 1, 1958.

The *Christian Science Monitor* writer Courtney Sheldon reported that Kowalski "came to Washington before the election . . . to ask the Democratic National Committee how to run for Congress" and that "they helped him out, but didn't think much of his chances" (November 7, 1958). The popularity of Democratic Governor Abraham A. Ribicoff, however, was strong enough to carry to victory his party's entire Congressional ticket, and Kowalski drew 542,315 votes to Sadlak's 425,452 votes.

Kowalski was assigned to the House Armed Services Committee in January 1959. He aroused public interest and protest from military quarters when he charged, in his first Congressional speech, that the armed services were wastefully employing thousands of trained enlisted men as officers' servants. As a member of the special manpower utilization subcommittee which began a series of public hearings in May 1960 to investigate these charges, Kowalski cited a Defense Department report to a House Appropriations military subcommittee which disclosed that more than 20,000 enlisted men were serving as stewards, chauffeurs, orderlies, and messboys for officers.

"I can now conservatively raise that estimate to 50,000 enlisted men and noncoms in all three services," Kowalski wrote in an article for *True, the Man's Magazine* in November 1959. "Tens of thousands of servicemen—including many highly trained and high-ranking noncoms —are regularly assigned as bartenders, waiters, chefs, bedmakers, valets, chauffeurs, babysitters, yardmen, and so called 'orderlies' for officers." He added that the practice of using enlisted men as personal servants is illegal according to the United States military code and that the

KOWALSKI, FRANK, JR.—*Continued*

men thus employed might better be placed in combat divisions. "A reappraisal of our manpower situation," Kowalski concluded, "could accomplish two vital objectives: the preservation of the dignity of the GI and a trim fighting service ready to protect our safety in any emergency."

Shortly after *Reader's Digest* had published a condensation of his article in January 1960, Kowalski introduced in Congress a bill designed to penalize "improper utilization of services of enlisted men." Although Assistant Secretary of Defense Charles C. Finucane had defended these practices as traditional and denied that they were degrading, Kowalski's crusade brought about several changes in armed services procedures.

The Army reduced the number of enlisted men in officers' clubs throughout the country, and the Air Force abolished kitchen police duties for airmen. Two Air Force manuals— one which maintained that the "pastors of some of our churches are card-carrying Communists' and another which instructed officers' aides in performance of household and social chores such as polishing shoes and making Martinis— were withdrawn after arousing widespread criticism and after Kowalski had suggested that the House Armed Services Committee investigate all military manuals. The Air Force also rescinded a money collection drive among airmen for erection of a stadium at the Air Force Academy when Kowalski termed the campaign "high-pressure and coercive."

In January 1960 Kowalski submitted to the second session of the Eighty-sixth Congress legislation which proposed the amalgamation of the Army, Navy, Air Force, Marines, and Coast Guard into a single "flexible, streamlined defense force . . . to meet the realities of the missile age." The plan, which would give full command to a civilian Secretary of Defense topped only by the President as commander in chief, would, in Kowalski's opinion, save $3 billion annually and provide a better and stronger defense force.

A steady supporter of strong centralized government, Kowalski introduced in 1959 several bills designed to extend federal aid for improvement of unemployment and disability insurance programs at state level. He also favored passage over President Eisenhower's veto of a 1960 bill which would increase federal grants to communities for sewageplant construction. In 1959, Representative Howard W. Smith introduced a state rights measure, which was designed to prevent federal courts from construing acts of Congress as being intended to pre-empt the field to the exclusion of state laws on the same subjects, unless Congress had so specified or there was a direct conflict between the federal and state laws. Kowalski voted against the bill, which the *Congressional Quarterly Almanac, 1959,* called one of a series of "court bills" proposed by critics of recent Supreme Court decisions involving civil rights:

His prolabor position prompted Kowalski to oppose passage of the Landrum-Griffin labor

reform bill; in June 1959 he sponsored legislation which would provide federal medical insurance for the aged. Kowalski has contributed a number of articles to military journals and holds no fewer than six patents for military and engineering inventions. Noteworthy among these is a new type of hollow small-arms bullet, patented in his name in July 1942.

Frank Kowalski, Jr., and the former Helene Amelia Bober of New Britain, Connecticut were married on October 20, 1931. They have a son, Barry Frank, and a daughter, Carol Helene. Kowalski's church affiliation is Roman Catholic. He is a member of the Society for Advancement of Management, and his service organizations are the American Legion, Veterans of Foreign Wars, American Veterans of World War II and Korea, the Polish Legion, and the Retired Officers' Association.

References

Congressional Directory (1960)
Who's Who in America, 1960-61
Who's Who in the East (1959)

KRAUS, HANS P(ETER) Oct. 12, 1907-
Rare book dealer
Address: b. 16 E. 46th St., New York 17; h. 85 Overlook Circle, New Rochelle, N.Y.

Perhaps no dealer in rare books since the late Dr. A. S. W. Rosenbach has received so much publicity as Hans P. Kraus, who has brought home to his shop in New York City some of Europe's leading treasures in rare books and illuminated manuscripts. A familiar figure at international auctions, Kraus has made newspaper headlines with such spectacular bids as the $182,000 he paid for the thirteenth-century St. Albans manuscript of the Apocalypse at Sotheby & Company in London on December 1, 1959. He has several times outdistanced the record prices paid by J. P. Morgan and Dr. Rosenbach. All the publicity has somewhat obscured to public view the real purpose of Kraus's enterprise, which is, he says, "to bring the right books to the right collectors."

Hans Peter Kraus was born on October 12, 1907 in Vienna, Austria, the only child of Dr. Emil Kraus, a member of the medical faculty of the University of Vienna, and Hilda (Rix) Kraus. Dr. Kraus, an enthusiastic philatelist, had a huge collection of Austrian stamps of which he wanted Hans to become the curator. He did not succeed; Hans found fussing over stamps a tedious business compared to the hunting of books.

He was sixteen years of age and exploring attics for old stamps — not books — with his father, when he came upon a mouse-eaten atlas in a sixteenth-century chest in the attic of an old house in the mountains. The owner presented him with the atlas, and Hans discovered that he had stumbled on treasure: one of the maps was the celebrated 1578 Mercator map of the world. He sold it and on the proceeds enjoyed a two-week Easter vacation in Italy. His father, only slightly impressed, still wanted his son to collect stamps.

With money his grandmother had given him and money he had realized from selling his schoolbooks, Hans P. Kraus began to buy books when he was thirteen years old. Within a year, he was collecting the works of the classical German authors. Selling his textbooks the day after school opened had its disadvantages; he sometimes had to borrow his classmate's books in order to do his lessons.

"As a boy I collected everything from butterflies to cigar rings," he recalls. "In Vienna, where there are hundreds of bookstores, I found that a book I bought from some obscure shop in the suburbs might be worth double the price in a larger store in the city. I paid my way through school with such transactions. . . . Later, I bought rare books in one country, where they weren't appreciated at the time, such as Poland, and sold them in another."

Kraus attended the Gymnasium at Baden bei Wien about fifteen miles from Vienna. After secondary school, he attended the Academy of Commerce in Vienna, but left it at the age of seventeen to become apprenticed to R. Lechner Universitäts Buchhandlung in Vienna. He swept the floor, washed windows, ran errands, tied up packages, and fetched sausages for the staff. He did everything, in fact, for his first two years, except sell books. Before he could become a journeyman in his chosen profession, he had to pass an extensive written examination, because the guild system of bookselling was in force in Vienna. To prepare for it, Kraus received formal training at the booksellers' school in addition to his on-the-job training.

Kraus then joined the Vienna branch of the old and respected Berlin firm of Ernst Wasmuth, publisher, retailer, wholesaler, and specialist in books on art and architecture. It was his first position as a full-fledged member of the bookselling profession. He was soon transferred to the home office and traveled for Wasmuth in Poland, Romania, Bulgaria, Yugoslavia, Greece, and — later — in Scandinavian countries. In 1931 he joined the Leipzig firm of Karl W. Hiersemann, a dealer in both new and antiquarian books, an affiliation that afforded him his first professional contact in depth with antiquarian bookselling.

In 1932, when Kraus set up his own book business in Vienna, the trade was highly competitive and overcrowded. Included in his first stock was part of Count Thun-Hohenstein's library. Luckily, he was able to rent the Bellegarde Palais, the former residence of Baron Bellegarde, who had been *Hofstallmeister,* or equerry to Franz Joseph, Emperor of Austria. Because of a city ordinance, Kraus was not allowed to carry on the business from the street floor; he conducted it one flight up, without benefit of a sign. The new firm offered for sale old and rare books and manuscripts, with an emphasis on the classics; they remain the specialties of H. P. Kraus today.

When Hitler invaded Austria on March 11, 1938, Kraus decided to go to the United States while escape was still possible. Managing to salvage some of his book stock—and even more

HANS P. KRAUS

important—some of his reference collection, he arrived in New York City in 1939 on the *Kungsholm* of the Swedish-American Line.

The firm of H. P. Kraus settled in rather confined quarters on the fifth floor of a converted brownstone at 21 East 57th Street. Until an American bookseller informed him otherwise, Kraus at first believed that, as in Europe, he would have to pass an examination and apply for a license in order to practise in the United States. He obtained what he had been denied in Vienna: a plate on the door which read "H. P. Kraus—Rare Books."

The first quarters proved too small and the business was moved to a converted brownstone at 64 East 55th Street, where it occupied the second, third, and fourth floors. When even this became too cramped, the business moved again in 1945—this time to the old Lehman brownstone at 16 East 46th Street, where the firm now takes up five full floors. Each floor is self-contained and connected with other floors by means of an interior fire escape. The oak panelling that gives the Kraus establishment its Brahmin look originally covered the walls of the library of the Union League Club. Microscopes, ultraviolet lights, and other apparatus aid the staff in their bibliographical detective work. The reference collection of over 10,000 volumes is the largest of any book shop in the world.

Kraus Periodicals, Inc., another enterprise, is housed more prosaically in a converted rubber boot factory in Mamaroneck, New York. In charge of Mrs. Kraus, the company sells scholarly, scientific, and technical publications in many languages to corporation, school, and government libraries throughout the world. The building also shelters two more Kraus activities: the Back Issues Corporation, which handles single numbers of back issues of tech-

KRAUS, HANS P.—*Continued*

nical publications, and Kraus Reprints Corporation, which reissues out-of-print books and old periodicals.

In 1952 the firm of H. P. Kraus reached the front pages when it sold to Lessing J. Rosenwald the huge *Mainzer Riesenbibel* (Giant Bible of Mainz), a manuscript measuring nearly 23″ x 16″. The Library of Congress exhibited it to the public on April 4, 1952. In 1953 Kraus obtained the printed Constance Missal, believed to predate the Gutenberg Bible, from a Capuchin monastery in Romont, Switzerland. It is a scuffed and dusty copy on which the monastery cat once slept, but it is one of only three known existing copies printed in Mainz about 1450. It now reposes in the Pierpont Morgan Library in New York City, where it is valued at around $100,000, and may well be the first book to be printed from movable type. On July 9, 1955 a feature story in the New York *Times* announced that Kraus had discovered in Brussels the rare campaign maps that Marshal de Rochambeau used during the American Revolution when he helped Washington to defeat the British.

At Part I of the Dyson Perrins sale at Sotheby & Company in London on December 9, 1958, Kraus purchased for $109,200 the Helmarshausen Latin gospels and the Euselbian Canons. At the same sale he bought the thirteenth-century bestiary of Hugues de Fouilloy for $102,200. A few months later, on February 23, 1959, Kraus paid $42,560 at Sotheby's for a fifteenth-century manuscript of Chaucer's *Canterbury Tales*: the so-called Brudenell Chaucer Codex owned continuously by the Brudenell family since at least the late sixteenth century—possibly earlier. The manuscript consists of 308 leaves of vellum, written about 1450 by professional scribes.

At Part II of the Dyson Perrins sale at Sotheby's on December 1, 1959 H. P. Kraus set a world record for the price paid at a public auction for a bound vellum manuscript when for $182,000 he purchased an illuminated manuscript copy of the Apocalypse, produced at the Benedictine Abbey of St. Albans in England around 1250. Like other treasures that have come into the hands of Kraus, the manuscript with its eighty-two miniature paintings once belonged to the library of the leading British manufacturer of Worcestershire sauce. At the same sale Kraus bought a thirteenth-century Psalter of Wenceslas, King of Hungary and Bohemia, for $72,800.

On August 28, 1940 Hans Peter Kraus was married to Hanni Zucker-Hale, formerly of Austria. They live in New Rochelle, New York with their five children, who range in age from eighteen to two years: Mary Ann, Barbara, Evelyn, Susan, and the youngest child, Hans Peter, Jr. "It's a nice thing that we have this boy," Kraus once remarked. "I would like him to become interested in beautiful old books, like his father." Kraus has long been a generous contributor to the Bibliothèque Nationale, the national library of France, and on July 30, 1951 his benefactions were recognized when he was made a chevalier of the French Legion of Honor. He is a member of the Grolier Club in New York City and of the Boulderbrook Club of Scarsdale, New York.

In a postscript to his Catalogue 80, Kraus explained why he distributes some of the most sumptuous catalogues in the antiquarian book trade, and voiced some sentiments about his calling: "The rare book trade is certainly a strange profession. The genuine antiquarian bookseller is at heart a collector and booklover. . . . For only such a person could pour the best of himself into a lifelong chase for something he could never keep. . . . Let me confess that it is never easy to say goodbye to . . . great books for which I longed, for which I worked and struggled. To solve this emotional problem at least in part . . . I decided . . . to put these most cherished objects of my affection, my books, into catalogues, profusely illustrated, minutely described. In this way they are assembled around me and remain with me even though they may be living in other worthier homes than mine."

References

New Yorker 30:20 Ap 3 '54
Pub W 177:58+ Ja 4 '60 por
Who's Who in the East (1959)

KREISKY, BRUNO (krīs'kē) Jan. 22, 1911-
Austrian Minister of Foreign Affairs
Address: b. Ballhausplatz 2, Vienna I, Austria; h. Grinzinger Allee 17, Vienna XIX, Austria

The Big Four signatories of the 1955 State Treaty which restored independence to Austria and prefaced the withdrawal of Allied occupation forces from its territory had stipulated as a condition for Austria's renewed sovereignty her pledge to remain perpetually neutral. Bruno Kreisky, the Austrian Minister of Foreign Affairs, who was a member of the Austrian delegation at the 1954 and 1955 treaty negotiations, has spared no effort to keep the country out of alliances that might commit her to partisan action in wartime.

Kreisky, who spent the years of World War II in Sweden, succeeded Dr. Leopold Figl as Foreign Minister on July 16, 1959. He is the first Socialist to fill this key cabinet post in a coalition government equally divided between members of the People's party and of the Socialist party. He had previously served for six years as the State Secretary for Foreign Affairs in the federal chancellery.

Born on January 22, 1911 in Vienna into a well-to-do family, Bruno Kreisky is the son of Max and Irene (Felix) Kreisky. His father was managing director of the Austrian Textile Industry Ltd., and a board member of the Austrian National Bank. Bruno attended elementary and secondary schools in Vienna. At the age of fifteen, he joined the socialist youth movement and soon assumed various responsible positions within the Social Democratic party. Although the prewar authoritarian regime outlawed the party in February 1934, Kreisky continued to work for it illegally. As a result of his underground activities he was arrested in January 1935 and imprisoned for some eighteen months. Released from prison, Kreisky entered the University of Vienna and subsequently received a doctorate of law.

After Nazi Germany annexed Austria, Bruno Kreisky was once again arrested for political reasons and exiled to Sweden in 1938. Within a year he found employment as a staff member in the secretariat for scientific studies of the Svenska Kooperativa Förbundet, a large consumer sales co-operative. He retained this position until 1946. In 1943 he was also a correspondent for the English-language *Tribune* and for Swedish newspapers. In his capacity as an adviser on Austrian affairs for the Swedish government, Kreisky won the right of political asylum in Sweden for Austrians who had deserted the German *Wehrmacht*. He was a chairman of the Swedish-Austrian Society in 1945 and the founder of the Swedish-Austrian Relief Society the following year.

At the end of the war Kreisky returned to Austria and joined the foreign service. He immediately received an appointment as first secretary at the Austrian Legation in Stockholm (1946-50). Back in Vienna in 1951, Kreisky was assigned for a short time to the foreign affairs section of the federal chancellery, after which he was transferred to the office of the Austrian President as its acting deputy director.

On April 2, 1953 Kreisky became State Secretary for Foreign Affairs in the federal chancellery. During the next two years he took part in the parleys held in Berlin in 1954 and in Moscow in 1955 concerning the terms for restoration of Austrian independence. Representatives of Austria and the Allied powers agreed that Austria would maintain a neutrality similar to Switzerland's: it would not join any military alliance or permit the establishment of foreign bases on its land. Although this resolution was not embodied in the State Treaty signed in Vienna on May 15, 1955, it was adopted into law shortly thereafter by the Austrian Parliament and it has since been regarded as a guiding principle of the country's foreign policy.

Soon after it regained its sovereignty, Austria became a member of the United Nations on December 14, 1955. Kreisky made his first visit to the United States in the fall of 1957 as a delegate to the United Nations General Assembly and later was a representative at the twelfth (1957) and thirteenth (1958) sessions of the U.N. Economic Commission for Europe in Geneva.

Since World War II Austria has been governed by coalition cabinets. In an effort to compose a new government acceptable to Socialists and conservatives alike, Austrian Chancellor Julius Raab in June 1959 invited the Socialists to appoint a member of their party to fill the important cabinet post of Finance Minister. He withdrew this offer under pressure from his own People's party; instead he offered the portfolio of Foreign Minister.

Atelier Fayer, Vienna, Austria

BRUNO KREISKY

Kreisky was first chosen unanimously by the Socialists to assume the Finance Minister's duties, then selected by his party to fill the Foreign Minister's post. He was named to this position on July 14, 1959 and sworn in two days later.

Since 1956, Kreisky has been a member of Parliament. He serves on the executive committee of the Socialist party, and was elected its vice-chairman in November 1959. The party represents the majority of workers and part of the lower middle class and favors economic planning, extensive social services, and nationalization of key industries. Kreisky has been described as the minister who is most acceptable to the conservative faction in the coalition government. "Conservatives and Socialists alike praise Dr. Kreisky's balanced judgment and hardheaded approach to domestic and foreign affairs," a New York *Times* writer noted (July 21, 1959).

Soon after Kreisky became Minister of Foreign Affairs, Austrian leaders faced a critical choice as to which of two rival Western European economic unions their country should join. Since Austria carries on 80 per cent of its foreign trade with West Germany, France, Italy, and the Benelux nations, conservative leaders favored affiliation with these countries of the European Economic Community (common market). Kreisky and other Socialists asserted, however, that the overwhelming economic advantages of joining the common market must be subordinated to political and diplomatic considerations. He said that Austria's obligations to remain neutral precluded economic union with West Germany. In November 1959, despite persistent criticism from the conservative ranks, Kreisky joined representatives of Great Britain, Sweden, Norway, Portugal, Denmark, and Switzerland in agreement on

KREISKY, BRUNO—*Continued*

the establishment of a European Free Trade Association.

On his first official mission abroad as Foreign Minister, Kreisky went to Sweden for negotiations on the seven-power free trade union. His subsequent discussions with Soviet leaders in October 1959 and with West German representatives in March 1960 also touched on that topic. Early that year Kreisky pressed for a solution to the Italian-Austrian dispute over South Tirol, an Italian region with a minority of German-speaking inhabitants. He said that the area should be granted autonomy to safeguard minority rights in the legal, economic, and cultural spheres. (The South Tirol question was included in the agenda of the fifteenth session of the U.N. General Assembly.) Kreisky's discussions with officials of Yugoslavia during the same period, on the other hand, centered on that country's claims for the preservation of Slovene minority rights in Carinthia, an Austrian province bordering on Yugoslavia.

Kreisky has written numerous articles on economic problems and foreign affairs for Austrian and American and other foreign publications. He is the founder and vice-president of the Theodor Körner Fund for the Promotion of Arts and Sciences in his country. Austria awarded him the Silver Grand Cross of Honor for services rendered to the republic. He has also received the Swedish Grand Cross of the Order of the North Star and the French Grand Officer's Cross of the Legion of Honor, as well as decorations from Germany, Cambodia, Ethiopia, Greece, Luxembourg, the Netherlands, Belgium, Japan, and Mexico.

Bruno Kreisky and Swedish-born Vera Alice Führt, to whom he was married on April 23, 1942, still converse in Swedish. Both their children, Peter Staffan and Suzanne Christine, were born in Stockholm. Mrs. Kreisky is a graduate of Stockholm University where she studied modern languages. Her blue-eyed, blond husband stands about five feet eight inches tall and weighs about 176 pounds. Although political activities engage much of his time, Kreisky occasionally reads poetry and history.

As a spokesman for a small nation which lies between the Western and Eastern power blocs, Kreisky has scrupulously avoided a policy of commitment, but as a representative of a country that desires good relations with its neighbors, he has stressed the need for active cooperation with adjacent countries. As he has explained in his article, "Austria Draws the Balance" (*Foreign Affairs,* January 1959): "For Austrians, the first concern is for peaceful solutions, even if they seem makeshift and even if they prove temporary. It is not only the grand design that matters; the little steps on the path of progress count also."

References

Who's Who in Austria, 1957-58
World Biography (1954)

KROEBER, A(LFRED) L(OUIS) June 11, 1876-Oct. 5, 1960 Anthropologist; university professor; taught for forty-five years at the University of California at Berkeley (1901-46); author of *Anthropology* (1923, 1948), an authoritative textbook, and many books on linguistics, psychology, physical anthropology, and the philosophy of history. See *Current Biography* (October) 1958.

Obituary

N Y Times p41 O 6 '60

KURCHATOV, IGOR V(ASIL'EVICH) 1903-Feb. 7, 1960 Soviet physicist; instrumental in developing the atomic bomb for the Soviet Union; directed the Institute of Atomic Energy of the Soviet Academy of Sciences and belonged to its Presidium. See *Current Biography* (November) 1957.

Obituary

N Y Times p1+ F 8 '60

LA GORCE, JOHN OLIVER Sept. 22, 1879-Dec. 23, 1959 Editor; associated with the National Geographic Society since 1905; president of the society and editor of the *National Geographic Magazine* (1954-57). See *Current Biography* (November) 1954.

Obituary

N Y Times p19 D 24 '59

LANDRUM, PHIL(LIP) M(ITCHELL) Sept. 10, 1907- United States Representative from Georgia; lawyer

Address: b. House Office Bldg., Washington 25, D.C.; h. Jasper, Ga.; The Congressional, Washington 3, D.C.

Before his election to the United States Congress in 1952 to represent Georgia's Ninth District, Phil M. Landrum's interests and experience had been largely in the fields of education, law, and farming. He made his most significant contribution in the House of Representatives, however, in labor legislation, and he is nationally known as co-author with Republican Robert P. Griffin of Michigan of the Landrum-Griffin labor reform bill which became an amendment to the Taft-Hartley Law in the summer of 1959. Landrum is currently the second Democrat in rank on the House Education and Labor Committee and the chairman of its subcommittee on labor statistics.

A native of the chiefly agricultural area that he has represented in Congress for the past seven years, Phillip Mitchell Landrum was born on September 10, 1907 in the Stephens County village of Martin in northeast Georgia. His parents were Phillip Davis and Blanche (Mitchell) Landrum. In 1932 he became athletic director and coach for the high school at Bowman, Georgia and three years later moved to a similar post at Nelson, where in 1937 he was appointed superintendent of public schools.

Continuing his own education, Landrum took courses at Mercer University in Macon, Georgia and Louisiana State University in Baton Rouge and was awarded the B.A. degree from Piedmont College in Demorest, Georgia in 1939. During part of his four years as superintendent of schools in Nelson, he also attended night and summer classes at the Atlanta Law School. He received his LL.B. degree and his admission to the Georgia bar in 1941.

Nelson, like Landrum's present home of Jasper, is in Pickens County, one of the eighteen counties making up Georgia's Ninth Congressional District. As early as 1942 Landrum tried to become the representative of this district at Washington, but was defeated for the Democratic nomination in the summer of that year. Later in 1942 he joined the United States Army Air Forces and served for the duration of World War II.

In 1946 Landrum was appointed assistant attorney of Georgia and for two years, beginning in 1947, he was executive secretary to Governor M. E. Thompson. He then settled down in Jasper to become, as he has said, "a country lawyer who does a little farming on the side." Apart from farming, including poultry raising and processing, the economy of northeast Georgia depends upon a few textile mills. Landrum became interested in labor because some sections of that area attempted to develop industries that would absorb surplus agricultural labor.

Although relations between labor and management were never particularly a problem in Georgia's Ninth District, its veteran Congressman, John S. Wood, was "a strong anti-labor man," according to Peter Edson (New York *World-Telegram and Sun,* August 22, 1959). Wood decided not to seek re-election in 1952, and in the state primary that year six candidates, including Landrum, battled for the Democratic nomination to succeed him. Landrum won the nomination and in November was unopposed for election.

Upon taking his seat in January 1953 in the Eighty-third Congress, Landrum was assigned to the House of Representatives Education and Labor Committee. In July of the following year he became a member of a subcommittee set up to study the government's role in education, especially that of the Education Office. As a freshman legislator, he opposed an increase in funds for public power (April 1953) and favored private development of power resources at Niagara Falls (July 1953). Other important measures to which he objected included the Hawaii statehood bill (March 1953) and the St. Lawrence Seaway authorization (May 1954). Throughout his years in Congress he voted almost always against foreign aid and mutual security appropriations.

In the Education and Labor Committee hearings in the summer of 1955 on raising the minimum wage from 75 cents to $1 an hour, Landrum was the only Democratic member to support President Eisenhower in opposition to the increase, although later in July he voted for the $1-an-hour bill. During 1956 Landrum headed a special three-member subcommittee of the Education and Labor Committee named to

PHIL M. LANDRUM

investigate the administration of labor union trust funds, including those of the American Federation of Musicians.

Representative Landrum was among the Southern Congressmen who pledged in March 1956 to use "all lawful means" to reverse the Supreme Court's desegregation ruling. In July of that year he voted against the Powell amendment to the school construction aid bill, against the bill as a whole, and against the civil rights bill. The following year he helped kill the school construction bill by voting to strike the enacting clause (July).

Also during 1957 he approved the President's Mideast Doctrine (January), but opposed permitting Britain to defer seven debt interest payments (April). As he had done in the past, he voted in 1958 in favor of farm price supports (March). He opposed granting statehood to Alaska in 1958 (May) and to Hawaii in 1959 (March). Among his other 1959 votes were a "nay" on United States participation in the Inter-American Development Bank (July) and a "nay" on extending the life of the Civil Rights Commission (September).

The Education and Labor Committee had meanwhile, in May 1958, set up a special subcommittee to study a Senate-approved measure for reporting financial operations of employee welfare and pension funds. Landrum was appointed to this subcommittee and at the same time, as chairman of the regular labor-management subcommittee, prepared to hold hearings on broad legislation to curb abuses in unions. The committee, however, reported out no major labor legislation in 1958. The next year, in July, it endorsed a moderate measure sponsored by Carl Elliott of Alabama that in most respects resembled the Kennedy-Ervin bill passed by the Senate during the previous April.

Landrum's opinion that the Elliott bill was "too weak" was shared by the ranking Repub-

LANDRUM, PHIL M.—_Continued_

lican on his subcommittee, Representative Robert P. Griffin of Michigan, who began working out substitute provisions on his own. Realizing the importance of bipartisan backing, they collaborated on the measure known as the Landrum-Griffin bill, which on July 24 was introduced to the House with the support of most Republicans and Southern Democrats.

Labor forces charged that it was sponsored by the National Association of Manufacturers and the United States Chamber of Commerce, but on August 6 President Eisenhower made a special radio-television address describing the Elliott measure as "not effective" and the Landrum-Griffin bill as "a good start toward a real labor reform law." On August 13 the House approved substituting the Landrum-Griffin bill for the Elliott bill, which in turn had been presented as an amendment to the Taft-Hartley Law. A compromise version was passed in September by both the Senate (95-2) and the House (352-52) and signed by the President.

The amended measure, in part, provided for financial reports by unions to the Secretary of Labor, with stiff penalties for willful violations; assured secret balloting in union elections; extended to state courts jurisdiction over cases not handled by the National Labor Relations Board; tightened bans on secondary boycotts; and forbade picketing by a union at any plant legally represented by another union. In an address on December 3, 1959 Landrum urged further amendment of the Taft-Hartley Law to cope with such "national emergencies" as renewal of the steel strike and a threatened railroad strike, and declared the Landrum-Griffin amendment "only the beginning of real reform."

"He . . . mixes his Southern vowels with a slight Scottish burr and will continue wearing his Southern colonel broad-brimmed hats," a Washington _Post_ reporter wrote of Landrum soon after his arrival in Washington in 1953. Landrum is six feet tall and weighs 200 pounds. Drew Pearson once called him a "hot-headed Georgian"; Robert P. Griffin has described him as "a very competent lawyer who is about as non-partisan as anyone I've ever been associated with" (New York _Herald Tribune_, August 14, 1959). He belongs to the Georgia Bar Association, the American Legion, and Veterans of Foreign Wars; he is a Baptist, a Mason, and an Elk. Phil M. Landrum and Laura Brown of Dewey Rose, Georgia were married on July 30, 1933 and have a son, Phillip Mitchell, and a daughter, Susan.

References

N Y Herald Tribune p1 Ag 14 '59 por
N Y World-Telegram p3 Ag 22 '59 por
Washington (D.C.) Post p27 Ja 20 '53 por
Congressional Directory (1960)
Who's Who in America, 1958-59

LANGER, WILLIAM Sept. 30, 1886-Nov. 8, 1959 United States Senator from North Dakota since 1941; Governor of North Dakota (1933-34; 1937-39); Republican; lawyer. See _Current Biography_ (February) 1952.

Obituary

N Y Times p1+ N 9 '59

LAUREL, JOSÉ P(ACIANO) Mar. 9, 1891-Nov. 6, 1959 Philippine political leader; President of the Japanese-sponsored Philippine Republic (1943-45); Senator (1952-57); Associate Justice of the Supreme Court (1936-42); lawyer; faculty member of universities. See _Current Biography_ (June) 1953.

Obituary

N Y Times p29 N 6 '59

LEAKE, CHAUNCEY D(EPEW) Sept. 5, 1896- Scientist; educator; organization official

Address: b. Ohio State University, Columbus, 10, Ohio; h. 2873 Charing Rd., Columbus, 21, Ohio

A Renaissance man in modern dress, Dr. Chauncey D. Leake is a pharmacologist, physiologist, chemist, editor, administrator, and philosopher and historian of science. He is even a poet of sorts. The president, for 1960, of the American Association for the Advancement of Science, he succeeds Paul Ernest Klopsteg as chief executive of the foremost scientific organization in the United States. In addition, he remains assistant dean, professor of pharmacology, and lecturer in the history and philosophy of medicine at the College of Medicine of Ohio State University.

Chauncey Depew Leake was born in Elizabeth, New Jersey, on September 5, 1896, the first child of Frank Walter and Helen Caroline (Luttgen) Leake. His father, a coal shipper, came from a family of English potters; his mother's family were German cutlers. Following his graduation from high school in Roselle, New Jersey, at the age of sixteen Leake entered Princeton University.

It was at Princeton, where he took a dual major in biology and philosophy, that Leake's broad interests first manifested themselves. Moreover, at Princeton he achieved an important personal triumph: because he had stuttered as a child, he took up public speaking in an effort to overcome this defect. Not only did he cure his stammer, but he became so successful an orator that he was admitted to the American Whig Society, the nation's oldest debating club. He still wears the gold medal of the society on his watch chain.

Following graduation from Princeton, which awarded him the degree of Bachelor of Letters in 1917, Leake entered the United States Army. Assigned to the Chemical Warfare Service, he fulfilled the major part of his military duty with a unit stationed at the University of Wisconsin. Upon his discharge from the Army in 1919, he returned to the

University of Wisconsin to complete his studies, receiving an M.Sc. in physiology in 1920 and a Ph.D. in physiology and pharmacology in 1923. During his graduate work, he also held the position of instructor in physiology.

Leake remained at the University of Wisconsin for five years after he received his doctoral degree. He was assistant professor of pharmacology from 1920 to 1925 and associate professor of pharmacology from 1925 to 1928. While at the University of Wisconsin he discovered divinyl ether, an anesthetic still generally used for brief surgical operations. For this discovery he received an honor award from the International Anaesthesia Research Society in 1928.

In 1928 Leake was given the rank of full professor and called upon to reorganize the pharmacology department of the University of California Medical School in San Francisco. There he instituted a seminar program in pharmacology which he conducted at a redwood forest retreat in the Santa Cruz mountains; together with his students he developed Vioform and carbarsone, two drugs important in the treatment of amoebic dysentery. He also conducted research programs in the chemotherapy of leprosy.

At the University of California Leake's interests ranged far beyond his field of specialization, and his influence was felt far beyond the campus. A vigorous promoter of art, he was largely responsible for the fact that most of the available wall space on campus was eventually covered by original paintings. When students petitioned for a course in sex education, he agreed to teach it, "on the condition that the students would receive no credit and the teacher no salary . . . [and that] the course be called 'human relations' since sex is only a small part of the whole picture." Twenty-six hundred students appeared for the first lecture. Away from the campus, Leake worked at the Family Relations Center in San Francisco from 1935 to 1940 and, for some time, headed the organization. He also took an active interest in city planning and in public housing.

In more scholarly endeavors, Leake founded the University of California Publications in Pharmacology in 1943, helped to organize the California Academy of Science, and served as librarian of the University of California medical center. He also served as chairman of the board of St. Luke's Hospital in San Francisco from 1937 to 1939.

In 1942 Leake went to Galveston, Texas as executive director of the University of Texas Medical Branch. There, in addition to building up the school's physical plant, he introduced "a reorganized curriculum and a revitalized faculty, adventurous paramedical courses, and a healthy basic research program" (*Science*, February 20, 1959). He took an especially active role in expanding the school's psychiatric training program, explaining his preoccupation with mental health by saying: "I'm interested in people, and in broad social problems generally. It all starts with the individual."

CHAUNCEY D. LEAKE

At Galveston, Leake founded and edited the Texas Reports on Biology and Medicine, and contributed to the development of the M.D. Anderson Hospital and the Baylor Medical School in Houston, and of the Southwestern Medical School in Dallas. He was at least as well known for promoting such cultural enterprises as civic music programs and art exhibits and for his crusades for civic improvement as he was for his administration of the medical school. Wanting to devote more time to teaching and research, Leake left the University of Texas in 1955 to assume his present position at Ohio State University.

Leake's election as president of the American Association for the Advancement of Science climaxes many years of leadership in that organization and in many other scientific societies. In 1940 and again in 1954 he served as vice-president of the A.A.A.S. and chairman of the section on the history of medicine and the philosophy of science. He represented the A.A.A.S. at the first World Conference on Medical Education, held in London in 1953, and has served on its board of directors since 1955.

Founded in 1848 as a general scientific society, the A.A.A.S. today has 58,000 members representing all branches of the social, biological, and physical sciences and 286 affiliated scientific societies. It publishes the weekly journal *Science* and technical symposia in a variety of fields, sends traveling libraries of scientific books to elementary and high schools, and works for the improvement of teaching in science and mathematics. During 1959 the A.A.A.S., together with other interested organizations, conducted a large invitational conference on basic research in the United States, and co-sponsored the first International Oceanographic Congress.

A prolific author, Leake has written on pharmacology, physiology, medical history, and the relationship between science and ethics.

(Continued next page)

LEAKE, CHAUNCEY D.—*Continued*

His tercentenary translation, with annotations, of William Harvey's *Exercitatio anatomica de motu cordis et sanguinis in animalibus (Anatomical Studies on the Motion of the Heart and Blood)*, published by Charles C. Thomas in 1928, has gone through four editions and become a classic. Leake also translated and edited Percival's *Medical Ethics* (Williams and Wilkins, 1928), and edited a facsimile edition of William Clowes' *Profitable and Necessarie Booke of Observations* (Scholars, 1945) and Ashbel Smith's *Yellow Fever in Galveston, Republic of Texas, 1839* (University of Texas, 1950). His scholarship in the field of ancient Egyptian medicine is reflected in *Old Egyptian Medical Papyri* (University of Kansas, 1952). He has been invited to do further research into the subject by the Institute for Advanced Study at Princeton, New Jersey.

In his specialized fields of pharmacology and physiology, Leake has written *Prolegomenon to Current Pharmacology* (University of California, 1938), *Some Founders of Physiology* (American Physiological Society, 1956), and, most recently, a comprehensive review of the stimulating drugs, *Amphetamines: Their Actions and Uses* (Charles C. Thomas, 1958). With Patrick Romanell he also wrote *Can We Agree? A Scientist and a Philosopher Argue About Ethics* (University of Texas, 1950), in which he attempted to give a purely scientific formulation to the foundation of ethics.

In addition to books, Leake has written more than 300 articles for such publications as *Science*, *Scientific Monthly*, the *Saturday Review*, and *This Week* and for many scholarly periodicals. He is editor of the *American Lecture Series in Pharmacology*, associate editor of *Geriatrics*, and a member of the board of trustees of *Biological Abstracts*. Since 1940 he has written an informal mimeographed monthly, *Calling Attention To*, containing comment on new books and articles, which he sends to 1,600 friends throughout the world.

Leake has served as consultant for the United States Public Health Service, the California and Texas state health agencies, the National Library of Medicine, the National Research Council, the Veterans Administration, the Research and Development Board, and the United States Air Force.

Scientific societies in which he has held office include the American Society for Pharmacology and Experimental Therapeutics (president, 1958-59) and the American Federated Societies for Experimental Biology (chairman, 1959). He was also president of the History of Science Society in 1937, vice-president and chairman of the pharmacology section of the American Medical Association in 1937, and vice-president of the Society for Experimental Biology and Medicine in 1948. He is a member of the American Physiological Society, the Texas Academy of Science, and the Philosophical Society of Texas, and an honorary Fellow of the American College of Dentists.

A lifetime member of San Francisco's Bohemian Club, Leake takes charge of the lighting of the club's outdoor dramatic productions in the redwood groves every summer. He also belongs to the Chit-Chat Club in San Francisco, the Cosmos Club in Washington, and the Kit-Kat Club in Columbus, Ohio.

His many interests have not interfered with Leake's liking for poetry, although his choice of subjects may be somewhat unpoetic. In *Letheon: The Cadenced Story of Anesthesia* (University of Texas, 1947) he undertook to put into free verse the history of anesthetics, and in a poem he read before a meeting of the world's leading authorities on viruses he discussed the intellectual crisis brought about by the current state of our knowledge in physics and biology.

Leake was married to Elizabeth Wilson, a microbiologist, in 1921. They have two sons, Chauncey, a lawyer, and Wilson, an anesthesiologist. Tall and sturdy, Leake has a thatch of white hair, blue eyes, and what one reporter called a "Santa Claus laugh." His hobbies include gardening, hiking, and the collecting of books about the history of science and of medicine. In 1959 he was awarded an honorary L.H.D. degree by Kenyon College. He has always taken a decided stand against governmental interference with the freedom of scientific investigation.

References

Sat R 41:38+ Ja 4 '58 por
Science 129:468+ F 20 '59 por

American Men of Science vol 2 (1955)
Who's Who in America, 1958-59

LEECH, MARGARET (KERNOCHAN)
Nov. 7, 1893- Writer; historian
Address: b. Harper & Brothers, 49 E. 33d St., New York 16; h. 120 East End Ave., New York 28

NOTE: This biography supersedes the article which appeared in *Current Biography* in 1942.

A scholar's respect for assiduous research, an artist's eye for telling detail, and a novelist's power to bring characters to life have assured Margaret Leech a place in the front ranks of contemporary American historians. Her two historical books—*Reveille in Washington* (1941), a comprehensive view of the nation's capital during the Civil War, and *In the Days of McKinley* (1959), a study of President William McKinley and his times—each won her a Pulitzer Prize for History. Dramatic as well as documentary, zestful as well as informative, her writing is like a tapestry that weaves together innumerable and colorful pieces. It illuminates the pattern of an era.

Margaret Kernochan Leech, the daughter of William Kernochan and Rebecca (Taggert) Leech, was born in Newburgh, New York on November 7, 1893. Early in the nineteenth century her great-grandfather had moved from County Antrim in northern Ireland to the United States and had settled in Newburgh.

In an interview with Lewis Nichols for the New York *Times Book Review* (November 1, 1959) she recalled that when President McKinley was shot in 1901, she was almost eight years old and she wrote a short poem about the assassination. It ran: "I am oh so sorry that our President is dead,/ And everybody's sorry, so my father said;/ And the horrid man who killed him is a-sitting in his cell/ And I'm glad that Emma Goldman doesn't board at this hotel."

After completing her preparatory education at private schools in Newburgh and Poughkeepsie, New York, Margaret Leech entered Vassar College in Poughkeepsie and in 1915 received her B.A. degree. In the fall of that year she went to New York City to work for the Condé Nast publishing company, writing trouble-shooter letters to subscribers who complained about not receiving their copies of magazines. Among her other early jobs was one in an advertising agency. Her publicity work in various World War I fund-raising organizations led to her joining the staff of Anne Morgan's American Committee for Devastated France. While serving the committee in Europe, she contributed articles to American periodicals.

During the 1920's, after she returned to the United States, Miss Leech was chiefly occupied with writing novels. For the setting of her first, *The Back of the Book* (Boni & Liveright, 1924), a story about a refined young office girl in New York, she could draw upon her own direct observations and experiences. *Tin Wedding* (Boni & Liveright, 1926) concerned the thoughts and feelings of a woman on her tenth wedding anniversary. With *The Feathered Nest* (Liveright, 1928), a study of possessive mother love, she added what has been called another "panel in a screen of American family life." Giving generally favorable notices to all three novels, critics called attention to qualities that Miss Leech developed fully in her later writings: skillful and psychologically sound characterization, perceptive selection of significant detail, and grace and clarity of style.

In 1927 Miss Leech had turned temporarily from fiction to write in collaboration with Heywood Broun the biography *Anthony Comstock: Roundsman of the Lord* (Boni), in which she and Broun wrote and signed separate chapters. Their portrait of the reformer and vice crusader, who lived from 1844 to 1915, was based on research rather than rumor and was praised as much for being factual and fair as for being lively and witty. The book was the first choice of the Literary Guild.

Miss Leech was married to Ralph Pulitzer on August 1, 1928. As an author in her own right and as the wife of the publisher of the New York *World* (his father, Joseph Pulitzer, had founded the Pulitzer Prizes), she belonged to a distinguished literary circle that included publishers, playwrights, actors, journalists, and other writers. Collaborating with Beatrice Kaufman, she wrote her only play, *Divided by Three,* in which Judith Anderson starred in the fall of 1934. The production was disappointing.

G. D. Hackett

MARGARET LEECH

"We had every advantage there was, except talent," Miss Leech told Lewis Nichols some twenty-five years later when discussing her efforts as a playwright. She has said on more than one occasion that she likes brief, compact literary forms, such as plays and short stories, but feels that she is not inventive enough to write fiction.

The sprawling, factual type of book turned out to be Margaret Leech's particular vehicle to fame. In 1935 she began a five-year investigation into life in Washington during the Civil War, carrying on research in the New York Public Library and in the Library of Congress. By alternating research with periods of writing, she was able to see from her own re-creation that she had sometimes failed to take sufficient notes from a certain source. Some of her thousands of notes, on the other hand, turned out to be irrelevant. She studied letters, memoirs, photographs, and whatever pertinent government documents were made available to her. Most of the details that brighten her book throughout, however, came from old newspaper files. These she considered the best sources she could find, even though, as she has pointed out, some historians hold news accounts to be inadequate.

Reveille in Washington, 1860-1865 was first serialized in the *Atlantic Monthly* and in the summer of 1941 was published in book form by Harper & Brothers. Its appearance coincided with America's awakening to another national crisis—World War II. After being widely circulated as a Book-of-the-Month Club selection and establishing itself as a best seller, it was awarded the Pulitzer Prize for History in 1942.

Humorous and tragic episodes, scandals, anecdotes, portraits of personalities of the times, and descriptions of streets and buildings

LEECH, MARGARET—*Continued*

all contributed to the excitement and authenticity of Miss Leech's panorama. "Despite its color and dramatic vigor," MacKinlay Kantor commented, "few other histories of any nation or period bear more hammer-marks of an implacable concern for the grim and bitter truth" (New York *Herald Tribune Books,* August 31, 1941).

Miss Leech's next book, *In the Days of McKinley* (Harper) was published in November 1959. Asked about the long interval between her two histories, she replied that she had spent twelve years on the McKinley book, working slowly and "most ostentatiously." She chose the subject because no good biography of McKinley had yet been written.

The 704-page *In the Days of McKinley* combines a life of the President with a picture of the period from 1861 to 1901. John Morton Blum called it a "first-rate study of a second-rate President" (New York *Times Book Review,* November 1, 1959). Again Miss Leech's scholarly thoroughness yielded a graphic and discerning portrait of an epoch. Besides uncovering an abundance of little-known information, she brought a fresh and independent point of view, both sympathetic and critical, to her subject. In his review for the New York *Herald Tribune* (November 1, 1959), William Miller wrote that "Miss Leech's engaging volume is not the last word on McKinleyism; but on McKinley himself it provides illuminating and pleasurable reading."

Like Miss Leech's earlier history, *In the Days of McKinley* was a Book-of-the-Month Club selection and won for her a Pulitzer Prize (1960) as the preceding year's outstanding work in history. It was also awarded a Bancroft Prize by Columbia University (1960), which annually grants stipends of $3,000 for distinguished studies in American history or international relations.

Margaret Leech has been a widow since the death of Ralph Pulitzer on June 14, 1939. She is the mother of Susan (Pulitzer) Freedberg; another daughter, Margaretta Pulitzer, died in infancy. Interviewers have found Miss Leech direct, brisk, and pleasant in answering their questions. She is tall and has blue eyes and gray hair. Among her enjoyments are travel, the theater, and good conversation. Her enthusiastic persistence in research and writing she explained in part to Lewis Nichols: "There's a challenge in taking something obscure and trying to find out what you can."

References

N Y Times p34 My 3 '60 por
N Y Times Bk R p8 N 1 '59
National Cyclopaedia of American Biography current vol F (1942)
Twentieth Century Authors (First Supplement, 1955)
Van Gelder, Robert Writers and Writing (1946)
Who's Who in America, 1960-61
Who's Who of American Women, 1958-59

LEFFINGWELL, R(USSELL) C(ORNELL) Sept. 10, 1878-Oct. 2, 1960 Former United States Assistant Secretary of the Treasury (1917-20); board chairman of J. P. Morgan & Company (1948-50); lawyer. See *Current Biography* (March) 1950.

Obituary

N Y Times p31 O 3 '60

LEMASS, SEÁN F(RANCIS) July 15, 1899- Prime Minister of Ireland

Address: b. Government Bldgs., Upper Merrion St., Dublin, Ireland; h. Hillside Dr., Rathfarnham, Dublin, Ireland

By the unanimous nomination of Ireland's governing party, Fianna Fáil, and the approval of the Dáil Eireann (the lower house of Parliament), Seán F. Lemass was chosen in June 1959 as Prime Minister of the Republic of Ireland. He succeeded Éamon De Valéra, who had been elected earlier in the month to the now ceremonial office of President. Like De Valéra, Lemass had been a leader in the Irish struggle for independence from Great Britain and one of the founders in 1926 of the Fianna Fáil party. During his many years in the positions of Minister for Industry and Commerce and Deputy Prime Minister, Lemass' principal concern was the economic growth of Ireland. As Prime Minister he continues to promote an industrial development program in an effort to decrease unemployment and discourage emigration.

Seán Francis Lemass was born in Dublin, Ireland on July 15, 1899. He was educated in the Christian Brothers' schools in Dublin and was still in school when he became interested in the nationalist movement for Irish independence. During the unsuccessful Easter Week Rebellion of 1916, led by the Irish Revolutionary Brotherhood, sixteen-year-old Seán Lemass fought in the streets of Dublin and then with other rebels held out in the city's General Post Office for several days against British forces before being captured. In suppressing the revolt, the British executed many of the insurrectionists; but Lemass, who was considered too young for the firing squad or other punishment, was released from prison and sent back to school.

Unrest and violence continued, however, with Irish forces fighting British troops in guerilla fashion, attacking barracks and convoys. Lemass, who served in the Irish Republican Army, was taken prisoner during an outbreak of hostilities and interned until a truce was declared in July 1921. An Anglo-Irish treaty negotiated later in the year established the Irish Free State and gave it dominion status within the British Commonwealth. Irish negotiators for the treaty were representatives of Éamon De Valéra, head of Sinn Fein, the nationalist party, and President of the Republic of Ireland.

Although the Irish Parliament ratified the treaty in January 1922, De Valéra repudiated it —chiefly because it provided for a separate government in the six counties of Northern Ireland and because it required members of Parliament to take an oath of loyalty to the

Irish Press

SEÁN F. LEMASS

British crown. Civil war then broke out between the pro-treaty forces and the Republicans. Lemass fought again in the Irish Republican Army, and during the first week of the conflict, in July 1922, he was captured in an attack on the Four Courts garrison in Dublin. He soon escaped, however, and was appointed to the headquarters staff of the Irish Republican Army. In December 1922 he was again captured and interned.

The civil war ended in the spring of 1923 with the defeat of the Republicans, who continued to boycott the Free State Parliament. Soon, however, certain Republican leaders, including De Valéra and Lemass, decided that they would try to achieve their goals by working through the government. They withdrew from the Sinn Fein and in 1926 formed a new organization, Fianna Fáil (Soldiers of Destiny). The following year members of De Valéra's party entered the Dáil Eireann. Lemass had become Deputy for Dublin South in the 1924 by-election and has served continuously since then. (In the redistribution of seats in the Dáil in 1948 his district became Dublin South-Central.)

From 1927 to 1932 Lemass was director of elections for Fianna Fáil and honorary secretary of the party organization. During that period the party grew so strong that in the 1932 elections the Republicans gained enough seats to secure, with the support of the Labor party, a majority in the Dáil. De Valéra became President of the Executive Council and formed his first cabinet, naming Lemass as Minister for Industry and Commerce.

The Fianna Fáil party continued in power without interruption for the next sixteen years, and Lemass held a portfolio in all of De Valéra's cabinets. In 1939 he left the Ministry for Industry and Commerce to become Minister for Supplies, and in this position until 1945 he kept Ireland's supply lines open during World War II. Meanwhile, in 1941, he had again been appointed Minister for Industry and Commerce, and after the war he took over the additional duties of Deputy Prime Minister (Tánaiste). He filled both offices until Fianna Fáil lost its majority in the Dáil in the 1948 election.

The Republicans had gradually eliminated most of the differences between the Irish Free State and Great Britain, including the oath of allegiance. A new constitution drawn up in 1937 created a sovereign, independent, democratic state and restored the name Ireland (Eire). In April 1949 Ireland withdrew from the British Commonwealth and became officially the Republic of Ireland.

During the period from 1948 to 1951, when John A. Costello headed a coalition cabinet in which Lemass did not serve, Lemass was managing director of the *Irish Press,* the Fianna Fáil newspaper established in 1931. In the election of June 1951 Fianna Fáil again won control of the Dáil. De Valéra returned as Prime Minister and again named Lemass Deputy Prime Minister and Minister for Industry and Commerce. He lost these positions in 1954, when Ireland had another coalition government, but regained them in 1957. After De Valéra's election to the Presidency and resignation as Prime Minister in June 1959, Fianna Fáil chose Lemass to succeed him as head of the government (Taoiseach). On June 23 the Dáil ratified the nomination by a vote of 75 to 51.

Throughout his career in government, Lemass has worked especially for the economic goals of Fianna Fáil, which advocates government investments to encourage developments in agriculture, manufacturing, and transportation. In 1953 he made a tour of the United States and Canada, inviting foreign capital investment, and some years later he suggested that United States industrialists might consider the advisability of servicing European markets from plants located in Ireland. To help solve the unemployment problem his Ministry for Industry and Commerce promoted tourism as well as manufacturing and export trade. In 1957 Lemass said that the next five years would prove whether Ireland could survive as an independent economic unit.

In reviewing Ireland's economic gains for 1959, Hugh G. Smith reported in the New York *Times* (January 12, 1960), "Since Prime Minister Seán Lemass assumed office there is a new spirit of realism and enterprise abroad that is being felt in every state-sponsored activity. He is behind the decision of Irish Air Lines to enter the jet field of trans-Atlantic traffic." There was a notable decline in unemployment and emigration and a rise in industrial exports during the year.

A major objective of Fianna Fáil that has not been achieved is the reunification by peaceful means of the Republic of Ireland with the six counties of Northern Ireland. A few weeks after becoming Prime Minister, Lemass proposed that the partition be ended by establishing a federation in an all-Irish state, with the Northern Irish Parliament retaining the same powers that the British Parliament now delegates to it. Later in July 1959 he urged im-

LEMASS, SEÁN F.—*Continued*

mediate co-operation on economic matters between the two divisions of the island.

Lemass was married to Kathleen Hughes in 1924. They have one son, Noel, and three daughters: Maureen (Mrs. Charles Haughey), Margaret (Mrs. John O'Brien), and Sheila (Mrs. John O'Connor). He is a Roman Catholic. He was awarded the Grand Cross of the Order of Gregory the Great in 1948. In 1953 Iona College in New Rochelle, New York awarded him an honorary LL.D. degree, and in 1954 the National University of Ireland awarded him an honorary D. Econ. Sc. degree. Jack White pictured Lemass in the *Manchester Guardian* (June 9, 1959) as "a cool, shrewd, realistic thinker, who sees politics in terms of bread and butter rather than pipe-bands and bunting," and added that "a modern generation will recognize him, by contrast with many of his colleagues, as a modern man."

References

Christian Sci Mon p7 Je 24 '59
N Y Post Mag p7 S 13 '59
U S News 47:24 Jl 6 '59
International Who's Who, 1959
International Year Book and Statesmen's Who's Who, 1959
Who's Who, 1959
World Biography (1954)

LEONARD, BILL Apr. 9, 1916- Radio-television news correspondent and producer

Address: b. Columbia Broadcasting System, 485 Madison Ave., New York 22; 15 W. 81st St., New York 4

The potential that Bill Leonard foresees in the new but already influential field of television journalism is so vast that he regards its present degree of development as only the "covered wagon stage." As sportscaster, political reporter, commentator, interviewer, staff correspondent, and producer for the Columbia Broadcasting System, he has gained considerable respect for radio and television as responsible media of reporting. Known for many years principally for his news and feature stories about New York City, mainly presented on local radio and television stations, he has recently extended his coverage to all news-making areas of the world on nationally broadcast documentary TV programs, particularly the *CBS Reports* series.

A native New Yorker, William Augustus Leonard 2d was born on Manhattan's West Side on April 9, 1916. His father, James Garfield Moses, was a lawyer; his mother was Ruth (Leonard) Moses, now Mrs. Richard C. Harrison. He has a brother, James G. Leonard, an investment banker with Lehman Brothers in New York City, and a sister, Elizabeth M. Leonard, who is personal secretary to former New York Governor and United States Senator Herbert H. Lehman.

Bill Leonard's boyhood home town was Westport, Connecticut and he attended preparatory school in the same state, the Avon School

at Avon, where he was captain of the baseball, football, and track teams. After graduation in 1933 he entered Dartmouth College in Hanover, New Hampshire and majored in sociology. He served as president of the Dartmouth Amateur Radio Club, and acted with The Players. In his senior year he was managing editor of the *Daily Dartmouth,* and held the title of class orator. He received the B.A. degree in 1937.

"At about the age of twelve," Bill Leonard has said, "I was bitten by the radio bug, contracted by listening to distant stations late at night on the broadcast band. At sixteen [I was] bitten again, this time by the newspaper germ, caught by exposure to Budd Schulberg, then editor of the *Dartmouth.* By graduation, unable to shake either illness, I continued to live with them." His first job after leaving Dartmouth was as a newspaper reporter for the Bridgeport (Connecticut) *Post-Telegram.* In 1940 he went to New York City to work in the radio and research departments of the Newell Emmett advertising agency.

Entering the Navy as an ensign in 1941, Leonard took courses during the following year in advanced communication at the United States Naval Academy in Annapolis, Maryland. He spent the remaining years of World War II mostly in the Mediterranean theater of operations, serving on destroyers, destroyer escorts, and command ships. As officer in charge of guided missile countermeasures in the Mediterranean, he was involved in the first push button war in history. He was awarded the Presidential Unit Citation and the Secretary of the Navy Commendation and was discharged with the rank of lieutenant commander in 1945.

A few months later Leonard joined the Columbia Broadcasting System and by early 1946 he had created the radio program *This is New York.* Although originally designed as an early morning program in which he reported headline news stories of the night, the show proved so successful that it was soon broadcast at a more popular hour. Leonard expanded his program to include interviews, public service items, and reviews of motion pictures, books, and plays so that gradually he covered almost all aspects of life in New York City.

In addition to *This is New York,* which he broadcast until 1957, Leonard was heard for some years on radio as moderator of the discussion program *Let's Find Out,* beginning in 1955, and as star of the *Bill Leonard Show,* from 1958 to 1959. He made his debut on television in early 1947 with a series of "remote" telecasts based on *This is New York* and in 1954 first appeared on *Eye on New York,* a Sunday morning local program. Five evenings a week from 1952 to 1956 he was also seen on CBS-TV's *Six O'Clock Report,* on which he presented a brief feature story about New York.

Eye on New York, in part a public service discussion program, usually covers the top news story of the week through interviews with guests as well as special film. Leonard, who helps to write and produce the show, also serves as commentator and interviewer. Among the subjects that he has handled are wire-tapping scandals, problems of treating narcotic addicts, and slum clearance projects. In October 1956 his program took viewers on a tour of the State Training School at Wassaic, New York, an institution for the mentally retarded. The film, "The Wassaic Story," brought Leonard the Albert Lasker Award for Medical Journalism.

Another much-praised film on which Leonard worked, as narrator, was the CBS-TV documentary "Harlem—A Self Portrait," shown in August 1959. Since becoming staff correspondent for CBS News in February 1960, he has spent much of his time reporting and producing assignments for the *CBS Reports* series. The program's hour-long documentaries, presented monthly, have treated among other subjects the population explosion, organized crime, the new African republics, and Trujillo of the Dominican Republic.

Skill in interviewing has been a particular asset to Leonard as a radio-television reporter. "Compared with many of the network news bigwigs, Mr. Leonard is a breath of journalistic fresh air," Jack Gould of the New York *Times* (May 21, 1956) wrote in a review of *Eye on New York*. "He knows the art of interviewing and follows through on an unexpected answer; he keeps his own face off the screen as much as possible and allows the person being interviewed to have the stage; he doesn't always talk as if his words were being recorded for posterity. Mr. Leonard, in a phrase, is a civilized reporter who has not let television go to his head."

Since his college days Leonard has been an enthusiastic amateur radio operator and since 1950 he has broadcast the weekly "Amateur Radio Notebook" on the Voice of America. Through his station, W2SKE, he competes in the international Distance Radio Operators contests and has held the world's record for single-operator contacts, having once talked to about 800 stations in ninety-six hours. He is president of Hanover Electronics, a supply company for amateur radio.

From 1948 to 1951 Leonard was radio co-ordinator for the New York City Civil Defense Director. He is the author, with Andrew Hepburn, of *New York City Guide* (1951) and has written articles for *Sports Illustrated, Today's Health,* and other magazines.

By his marriage to Adele Wilde on April 25, 1942 Bill Leonard is the father of six sons—David M., William A. 3d, Andrew H., Nicolas D., James, and Oliver. Leonard was divorced in 1956 and on May 11, 1957 was married to Mrs. Norma (Kaphan) Wallace, the former wife of TV reporter-interviewer Mike Wallace. Leonard's clubs are the Regency, Dutch Treat, and Riverdale Yacht, all in New York City, and the Coral Beach in Bermuda. He is a Democrat and an Episcopalian.

At one time a strenuous athlete, Leonard boxed a round each with Joe Louis and Ezzard Charles to get background material for their fight on September 27, 1950. He is five feet nine inches tall, weighs 180 pounds, and has brown eyes. His hair began turning gray when he was twenty-five. He calls himself a

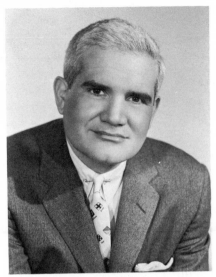

BILL LEONARD

confirmed hobbyist, plays contract bridge like a top amateur (according to his friend Charles Goren), and enjoys cooking and eating Chinese food.

References

N Y Herald Tribune II p1 My 11 '57
N Y Times II p13 S 11 '55 por
N Y World-Telegram Mag p6 My 21 '55 por
Who's Who in America, 1960-61

LOLLOBRIGIDA, GINA (lō-lō-brē′jĭ-dä⁾ July 4, 1928(?)- Actress

Address: b. c/o Metro-Goldwyn-Mayer, 1540 Broadway, New York 36

Three traits that have made Gina Lollobrigida the most glamorous and highly paid Italian star on the international film scene are her Mediterranean beauty, her driving ambition, and her business sense. Although a *Time* (August 16, 1954) writer characterized her as a "dark little nymph who seems to wake the satyr in men," and Philippe Halsman rated her figure as finer than that of any actress he had ever photographed, some of her motion-picture associates have sometimes referred to her in less flattering terms.

Although she did not make her film debut until the post-World War II period, Miss Lollobrigida bears a strong resemblance to the temperamental stars of the 1920's. She keeps scrapbooks of her clippings, maintains an extensive wardrobe, and, sensitive to adverse criticism, has been involved in as many as ten lawsuits at one time. American audiences have seen her in many films, including *Fanfan the Tulip* and *Love, Bread, and Dreams* and more recently in *Solomon and Sheba* and *Never So Few.*

(Continued next page)

Metro-Goldwyn-Mayer

GINA LOLLOBRIGIDA

Gina Lollobrigida was born on July 4, 1928 (some sources give 1927) in Subiaco, Italy, the second of four daughters of Giovanni and Giuseppina Lollobrigida. Her father was a moderately successful furniture manufacturer, and young Gina received private lessons in singing, dancing, drawing, and languages. After Allied air attacks had destroyed the family home and factory, the Lollobrigidas fled to Rome, where Gina contributed to the reduced family finances by singing, sketching portraits of American G.I.'s, and posing for *fumetti*, the Italian comic strips which use photographs rather than cartoon figures.

After the liberation Gina resumed singing lessons and, having won a scholarship to Rome's Academy of Fine Arts, she studied sculpture and painting there for three years. One day in 1947 the Italian film director Mario Costa spotted Gina on the street and promptly offered her a job in the movies.

Beginning her acting career as an extra for $3.30 a day, she soon became a stand-in for a star. She explains that this arrangement ended when the star became jealous of Gina's good looks. Her first major role was that of a beauty contestant in *Miss Italy* (1949). The part was appropriate, for two years earlier she had won the title of "Miss Rome" and had been a runner-up in a "Miss Italy" contest.

In 1949, reportedly as a result of seeing her in a bikini, RKO's Howard Hughes brought Miss Lollobrigida to Hollywood for a screen test. Gina's account of the next six weeks mentions forced English lessons, rehearsals, and attendance at "orrible RKO peectures" (*Time*). She won her freedom by signing a contract which she says she did not understand at the time and which gave Hughes an option on her services. Although he never exercised this option, Hughes prevented Miss Lollobrigida from making any pictures in the United States until 1959.

Miss Lollobrigida was introduced to the American public via the art movie theaters. Her earliest films exhibited in the United States were *The White Line* (1949) and *The Young Caruso* (1950), but it was in the French farce, *Fanfan the Tulip* (1951), released in America in 1953, that she first drew widespread attention. Typical of the reviews of Miss Lollobrigida's performance in this film was the one written by Bosley Crowther who called her "most fetching as a recruiting sergeant's daughter with ample charms" (*New York Times*, May 5, 1953).

Following *Fanfan,* she co-starred with Vittorio de Sica in one of the six playlets making up *Times Gone By* (1951). She then acted in *Beauties of the Night* (1952), *The Unfaithful,* (1952), and *The Wayward Wife* (1952). In *Beat the Devil* (1953) Miss Lollobrigida appeared for the first time with an American cast, including Humphrey Bogart and Jennifer Jones. She then made *Crossed Swords* (1953) and *Card of Fate* (1953), after which she again performed with de Sica in the highly successful *Bread, Love, and Dreams* (1954). Reviewers commented favorably on her acting, as well as her other attributes. The New York *Herald Tribune* critic wrote (September 1954): "Miss Lollobrigida is charming as a half-innocent peasant lass owning nothing but a torn frock and a winning smile." She also starred in the film's sequel, *Bread, Love, and Jealousy* (1954).

In the Fox movie *The World's Most Beautiful Woman* (released in America as *Beautiful But Dangerous,* 1955), her first picture for a major American studio, she played the Italian soprano Lina Cavalieri, who was more acclaimed for her beauty than for her voice. The more acerbic critics felt that the same might be said of Miss Lollobrigida, who did her own singing in this film.

Miss Lollobrigida next starred in the Hecht-Hill-Lancaster production of *Trapeze* (1955) which, released amidst much ballyhoo, opened to lukewarm reviews. After appearing in *The Hunchback of Notre Dame* (1956), *Anne of Brooklyn* (1957), and *The Law* (1958), Miss Lollobrigida starred in the United Artists 1959 release, *Solomon and Sheba.* In that year she arrived in Hollywood to make *Never So Few* (MGM, 1960), co-starring with Frank Sinatra, and later made another MGM film, *Go Naked in the World* (1960).

Other films in which Miss Lollobrigida has appeared include *Opera Fans* (1947), *Love of a Clown* (1948), *Tocsin* (1948), *Anselmo is in a Hurry* (1950), *A Dog's Life* (1950), *Achtung Banditi* (1951), *The City Defends Itself* (1951), and *Girl of Rome* (1954). Miss Lollobrigida's phenomenal output is made possible by her willingness and ability to work hard. She makes movies twelve months out of twelve, memorizes entire scripts in advance, and responds immediately to directors' advice. She also devotes meticulous care to her costumes (which she sometimes designs herself) and make-up, as well as other details of her screen image. "I am an expert on Gina," she once said, and, according to Louis Berg (*This Week,* October 7, 1956), she "is prepared to fight to the death to have her own way in everything she does."

One item for which she fights is money. When Harold Hecht once asked her in reference to future films what she would like to make, she promptly replied, "I'd like to make a million dollars American." After receiving $48,000 to make *Bread, Love, and Dreams,* she demanded—and got—$96,000 for its sequel, *Bread, Love, and Jealousy.* When she insisted on half the profits as her share for making a third film, *Bread, Love, and Nostalgia,* however, the producers balked and hired Sophia Loren instead. Gina Lollobrigida is also known for her litigiousness.

Miss Lollobrigida received the Grolla d'Oro (the Italian equivalent of the Oscar) for her acting in *The Wayward Wife* and the highest award of the Italian Journalists Guild for her performance in *Bread, Love, and Dreams.* The French film industry honored her with its Victoire award as the best foreign actress in 1953, 1954, and 1955. She won the International Cinema Clubs' "David" for *The World's Most Beautiful Woman,* and *Anne of Brooklyn,* which she and her husband produced with Vittorio de Sica, received that organization's prize as the best film of 1958.

Belgian and German polls voted her the most popular star in 1957, 1958, and 1959, and she regularly heads exhibitor and audience polls in France and Italy. In addition to making films, she has entertained at benefit galas and on television shows. She can sing in French, English, and Italian in a pleasant, though not exceptional, soprano voice.

The star was married to Drago Milko Skofic, a Yugoslavian-born physician, in 1950. Her husband is her manager and runs the three corporations they have set up to handle her career and investments. The Skofics have one son, Andrea Milko (some sources cite Milko Spyros), born on July 28, 1957. When leisure permits, Gina and her husband enjoy playing tennis and swimming. She has maintained her interest in painting and sculpture and, since the birth of her son, has developed a talent for photography.

Early in 1960 the family moved to Canada to establish a national status and, hopefully, citizenship for Dr. Skofic and his son. Gina denies (Toronto *Globe and Mail,* June 9, 1960) that tax difficulties with the Italian government, which alleged that Miss Lollobrigida reported less than half her 1956-57 income, are responsible for the move.

Miss Lollobrigida is five feet six inches tall, weighs about 120 pounds, and has black hair and brown eyes. Her measurements vary around thirty-six, twenty-two, thirty-five. Like many another film beauty, she wants to be known as an accomplished actress.

References

This Week p10 O 7 '56 por
Time 64:54+ Ag 16 '54 por
Who's Who in Italy, 1957-58

LONDON, JULIE Sept. 26, 1926- Singer; actress
Address: b. c/o William Morris Agency, 151 El Camino, Beverly Hills, Calif.

One of the busiest young actresses and singers in the entertainment industry today is Julie London who, although she had had a brief career as a motion-picture starlet in the 1940's, was a relatively unknown performer when she suddenly became successful with her best-selling record, "Cry Me a River," and her memorable performance in the movie *The Great Man.* The year was 1956, when *Theme* magazine voted her the "most exciting new vocalist" of the year. Since then, she has continued to make hit recordings, has appeared in leading roles in many motion pictures, and has carved new careers for herself in television and in the supper club circuit.

Julie London was born in Santa Rosa, California on September 26, 1926 to Jack and Josephine (Taylor) Peck, song-and-dance entertainers in vaudeville and radio, who between engagements ran a photography studio. Julie made her radio debut at the age of three, when she sang "Falling in Love Again" into a microphone. When Julie was a child, the family moved to San Bernardino, California, where the Pecks sang on a local radio station. Julie attended Arrowview Junior High School in San Bernardino; there she developed a lifelong aversion to formal education. In 1941, when her parents moved to Los Angeles, she left school to go to work as an elevator operator in a department store on Hollywood Boulevard. She was only fifteen years of age at the time. (Miss London has told reporters that she had to falsify her age to get the job.)

While she was running the department store elevator, a chance meeting took place that changed her way of life. Sue Carol, the actors' agent and wife of Alan Ladd, was so struck by the beauty of the girl that she suggested that Julie come to her office to talk about a possible career in motion pictures. Not knowing who Sue Carol was, Julie was about to dismiss the proposal, when an actor employed part-time at the store told her that Sue Carol was an important actors' agent. A successful screen test followed.

During the next four years, Miss London appeared in bit parts in several movies, including *The Girl and the Gorilla,* an item still telecast on post-midnight shows, in which she played a girl terrorized by a gorilla. (Miss London says she is now terrorized by the thought that some television viewers may recognize her in that exhibit.) But all of the roles were so minor that if Miss London was mentioned at all by the movie reviewers, she was mentioned only in passing. Between movie assignments, she went back to her $19-a-week job in the department store. Although she was in the movies, she obviously was no star.

In 1947 Miss London was married to Jack Webb, who was then an obscure radio artist. At the time of the marriage, she was more important in the entertainment world than Webb, especially after her film appearance in

Universal Pictures

JULIE LONDON

The Red House (United Artists, 1947) with Edward G. Robinson, but after Webb struck a rich lode with the *Dragnet* television series in 1950, she retired from show business. The Webbs had two daughters, Stacy and Lisa. In November 1953 they were divorced, and Webb settled a large amount of money on his wife and children.

After a period of inactivity and what she has called a failure of self-confidence, Miss London resumed her career, aided in large measure by Bobby Troup, a song writer and jazz musician, who is now her husband. Miss London met Troup in 1954 at the Celebrity Room in Los Angeles, where he was appearing with a jazz combination. He first heard her sing at a private party and was impressed by what he heard. He later told Pete Martin of the *Saturday Evening Post* (August 17, 1957): "For about a year and a half I tried everything I could to get her to sing when somebody was around to hear it who could do her some good, but when I put a mike in front of her, she'd freeze and wouldn't."

She finally agreed to sing in John Walsh's 881 Club in Los Angeles, and the supper club became the scene of her first success. Walsh had booked her for a three-week engagement, but she stayed on for ten. In short order, she became a recording and motion-picture star. In 1956 she cut her first album for Liberty Records under the title *Julie is Her Name*. The album contained her most popular song, "Cry Me a River," which, when later released as a single, remained on the best-seller lists for months.

Miss London has built her success on a voice that has been characterized by jazz connoisseurs as husky, breathy, haunting, sultry, intimate, sullen, sad, and as "a voice for a smoke-filled room." She has specialized in blues and torch songs, and would like to think that she has waged a successful campaign against rock 'n' roll by bringing the blues classics up to date.

Pete Martin quotes her as saying: "Someone said I have just a little old thimblefull of a voice, which is another way of saying it's very small. I'm a girl who needs amplification. You can put that down to my style. Somebody else said I have a well-smoked voice. By that maybe he meant that I smoke too many cigarettes. As for what you call 'breathy,' I've never learned how to breathe properly. I always run out of breath during a song; then I gasp in the wrong places. . . . I have to stay real close to the mike—almost in it, in fact. And if the mike's close it accentuates everything, including that breathy quality. . . . If I have to, I can belt songs out, but I don't like them that way. That's not the natural me."

In 1956 José Ferrer offered Julie London a role in a motion picture that established her as an accomplished actress. The film was *The Great Man*, based on Al Morgan's novel of the same title; in it Miss London played an alcoholic singer with a blurred vision of reality. A *Variety* critic who reviewed the movie in the issue of November 28, 1956 wrote: "Another big surprise is Julie London, who digs into a dramatic role and socks it across with all the aplomb of an actress with many years of seasoning."

On the basis of her performance in this picture, acting offers began to pour in. Her pictures in recent years have included: *The Crime Against Joe* (United Artists, 1956); *Drango* (United Artists, 1957); *Man of the West* (United Artists, 1958); *Voice in the Mirror* (Universal, 1958); *Saddle the Wind* (MGM, 1958); *Night of the Quarter Moon* (MGM, 1959); *The Wonderful Country* (United Artists, 1959); and *The Third Voice* (Twentieth Century-Fox, 1960). In *Drango* she played a secret drinker, in *Man of the West* a worldly dance hall singer who fails to get her man, and in *Voice in the Mirror* the suffering wife of an alcoholic.

Concurrently with her movie and singing career, Miss London began to appear on television as a guest singer. She has sung on many television shows, including *The Bob Hope Show, The Steve Allen Show, The Dinah Shore Show,* and *The Perry Como Show.* She used to have her songs recorded before the telecast, only pretending to sing them during the performance, but she now performs them "live."

In 1957 Miss London was interviewed by Edward R. Murrow when she opened her home in North Hollywood, California to the cameras of the *Person to Person* television show. Richard E. Shepard in the New York *Times* of September 14, 1957 reported that "Julie London broke up the show. . . . The singer's two children proved the rule that the unexpected makes for best television as they hid their heads and refused to perform for Mr. Murrow."

Over the years, Miss London has continued to record songs for Liberty Records. In addition to *Julie is Her Name*, her albums include:

Lonely Girl; About the Blues; Make Love to Me; Julie; London By Night; Calendar Girl; Swing Me an Old Song; and *Your Number, Please.* She has also recorded many best-selling single recordings.

In May 1959 Miss London informed Marie Torre, the television columnist for the New York *Herald Tribune,* that she had made a pilot film of a projected television series entitled *Maggie Malone.* In it Miss London played a woman who owns a night club in partnership with Steve Brody. She said that while it had a "gangster plot," it differed from the other gangster shows on television in that it had music. The pilot film was telecast in June and repeated in September on *The David Niven Show.*

On December 31, 1959 Julie London was married for the second time. Her groom was Bobby Troup, the man largely responsible for getting her to resume her career after her divorce from Jack Webb. Troup had previously been married to the dancer Cynthia Hare, by whom he had two children, Cynthia and Ronnie. Miss London, who has blue eyes and shoulder-length hair of golden-brown, stands five feet three inches in height and weighs 108 pounds. In addition to being an expert swimmer, she is a devoted football fan who has complete technical knowledge of the game. Disliking pretense and preferring informality, Miss London likes to dress in a sloppy sweater and blue jeans when not fulfilling engagements. She loves the desert, especially that surrounding Palm Springs.

References

Coronet 44:61+ Je '58
Look 22:85+ S 16 '58 por
N Y Post Mag p3 Jl 28 '57 por; p3 N 15 '59 por
Sat Eve Post 230:24+ Ag 17 '57 por
International Motion Picture Almanac (1960)

LONG, EARL K(EMP) Aug. 26, 1895-Sept. 5, 1960 Former Governor of Louisiana (1939-40, 1948-52, 1956-60) ; Democrat; younger brother of Huey P. Long. See *Current Biography* (December) 1950.

Obituary

N Y Times p1+ S 6 '60

LOOMIS, DANIEL P(ITTINGER) Apr. 6, 1905- Railroad executive; lawyer

Address: b. 915 Transportation Bldg., Washington 6, D.C.; h. 3252 S St., N.W., Washington 7, D.C.

Since the middle of the nineteenth century, railroads have been one of the chief means of transportation in the United States. In the middle of the twentieth century, they face gigantic problems induced by government regulation, labor union policies, and fierce competition from trucks, buses, and air lines. The man most directly concerned with grappling with these problems is Daniel P. Loomis, who, as president of the Association of American Railroads, oversees an organization that gathers together all of the nation's principal lines. He serves as chief spokesman for the management on matters of common concern in all aspects of railroading. A lawyer by training, Loomis began his career as a legal counsel for a single railroad company. Since 1942 he has been an executive for various railroad associations.

Daniel Pittinger Loomis was born in Burlington, Vermont on April 6, 1905 to Daniel A. and Mary D. (Pittinger) Loomis. He attended Union College in Schenectady, New York, receiving his B.A. degree in 1925. From there he went to the Harvard University Law School; he was graduated in 1928 with the LL.B. degree, and was admitted to the bar of New York the same year.

For the next eight years Loomis worked as an attorney for the Delaware & Hudson Railroad Corporation in Albany, New York. He was promoted in 1936 to assistant to the general counsel for the line and in 1939 to assistant general counsel. During these years he was concerned with labor relations. In 1939-40 he served as counsel for the carriers special committee of the Fair Labor Standards Act, from 1938 to 1940 as chairman of the Conference Trunk Line Counsel, and in 1941 as chief counsel for the Eastern Carriers Conference Committee.

Resigning from the Delaware & Hudson in 1942, Loomis accepted a position in Chicago as executive director and chairman of the executive committee of the Association of Western Railways, a group which handled labor problems for Western lines. He served as the organization's chairman from 1948 to 1957. (He was admitted to the Illinois bar in 1942.)

During his fifteen years with A.W.R., Loomis acted as the spokesman for the entire industry in many key labor-management arbitrations. He was chairman of the Western Carriers Conference Committee from 1942 to 1957 and was a member of the management-labor manpower advisory committee for the Office of Defense Mobilization from 1950 to 1953. In the early 1950's he came into the news as an outspoken defender of management during a series of railroad disputes that threatened to cripple Korean war production.

Loomis moved to Washington, D.C. to become president of the Association of American Railroads on August 1, 1957, succeeding William T. Faricy. Although the association, which includes the principal railroads of the United States, Canada, and Mexico, was formed in 1934, it grew out of earlier railroad associations dating as far back as 1867. Loomis presides over an organization that deals with matters of common concern to the whole field of railroading, such as operations, maintenance, engineering, research, finance, taxation, legal questions, and relations with the public.

As the chief spokesman for railroad management, Loomis must deal with economic pressures coming in from three sides: the stiff competition of other kinds of transportation, government regulations, and labor union policies. He

Chase, Ltd.

DANIEL P. LOOMIS

has directed his fight mainly against government regulation of fares, tax policies, and union featherbedding.

Shortly after taking over his position, early in 1958, Loomis outlined the changes in government regulation that railroads need if they are to remain solvent. He asked for legislation providing freedom in setting rates, the right to enter other forms of transportation, the repeal of excise taxes on freight and passenger business, changes in tax laws with respect to depreciation and tax deferral, closer regulation of truck transportation exempt from Interstate Commerce Commission authority, and the placing of authority for abandonment of unprofitable passenger services in the hands of the ICC.

The Eisenhower administration responded with a railroad-aid proposal that included a $700,000,000 loan. The proposal did not, however, consider excise tax repeal or special depreciation provisions for tax relief. Loomis termed the proposal "distinctly disappointing" because it offered temporary relief which would prove inadequate in the long run. Congress later passed the Transportation Act of 1958, which made, Loomis said, "positive contributions to sound national transportation policy and to the relief of the railroads from some of the competitive handicaps" (New York Herald Tribune, August 3, 1958).

Other problems remained. In September 1959 Loomis said that the railroad industry was still determined to fight "patchwork policies of oppressive taxation, discriminatory regulation and government favoritism toward other carriers" (New York Herald Tribune, September 23, 1959). Speaking to the American Association of Traffic Officers meeting later in 1959, he cited the case of Washington's Union Station which bore the highest tax assessment of any piece of property in the District of Columbia in 1958. "Yet right across

the river in Virginia," he said, "lies the Washington National Airport, also built at the cost of $32 million—but of taxpayers' money—which serves the competing airlines year after year without paying a cent in property taxes" (New York World-Telegram and Sun, October 6, 1959).

Loomis has been outspoken in his criticism of some labor union policies, especially featherbedding practices which he feels keep the railroads from competing with the other transportation media. During 1959 the association carried on an eight-month campaign against union "make-work" practices such as the rule that firemen who tend no fires must nevertheless accompany diesel locomotives, or the rule that a passenger train running between Chicago to Denver must change its crew eight times. Union leaders have denounced the charges as false and deny that the make-work practices exist.

As the end of the railroad unions' three-year contract approached in November 1959, Loomis underscored the need for new management and labor co-operation and denounced present practices. Speaking to the 1959 gathering of the American Short Line Railroad Association, he said: "We hope labor leaders will see the deadly boomerang they wield in their blind defense of inefficient work practices and their resistance to the drastic operating changes that must be made if the railroads are to stand up in the competitive battle for survival" (New York Herald Tribune, September 23, 1959).

In other transportation and labor relations activities, Loomis has served as chairman of the transportation committee of the Y.M.C.A., director of the Transportation Association of America, and American delegate to the Inland Transportation Committee of the International Labor Office in Geneva in 1947. He has lectured on railroad labor relations at the universities of Wyoming, Wisconsin, Minnesota, Chicago, and others. He was chairman of the 1955-56 section on labor relations law for the American Bar Association.

Middlebury College awarded Loomis an honorary LL.D. degree in 1958. He is a trustee of Union College and a member of the American and New York state bar associations, the American Academy of Political and Social Science, and the Industrial Relations Association. He is a Mason and a member of Phi Delta Theta.

Daniel Loomis was married to Marie Hegeman Bremner on December 31, 1931. They have one daughter, Mary Elizabeth, now Mrs. Gordon M. Simms. Golfing and fishing are his principal forms of recreation. His social clubs are the Chevy Chase Club, Burning Tree Country Club, Chicago Curling Club, Glen View Club, and the Lake Mansfield Trout Club in Stowe, Vermont. He also belongs to several business clubs. He is an Episcopalian and a Republican.

References

Who's Who in Commerce and Industry (1957)
Who's Who in America, 1958-59

LOPEZ, AL(FONSO RAMON) Aug. 20, 1908- Professional baseball manager

Address: b. Chicago White Sox, Comiskey Park, Chicago, Ill.

In the annual Associated Press poll, Al Lopez, the unassuming but brilliant manager of the Chicago White Sox, was named the American League Manager of the Year for 1959. He was honored for guiding the White Sox to their first pennant in forty years and for defeating the New York Yankees in the process.

The victory of the Chicago White Sox marked only the second time since 1949 that the New York Yankees had failed to win the flag of the American League. The other instance occurred in 1954 when the Cleveland Indians, with Lopez as their manager, outdistanced the New Yorkers with 111 winning games, an American League record for the most wins in a single season. In twelve years of managing (three with Indianapolis of the American Association, six with Cleveland, and three with Chicago), Lopez has guided teams that have never finished in less than second place.

Lopez' distinction as a manager comes as a sequel to his resplendent career as a major league catcher. In eighteen National League seasons and one American League season Lopez caught 1,918 games, a major league record. He also batted over .300 twice and was twice named to National League All-Star teams. He is the only living major league manager to have a baseball field bear his name—Al Lopez park in Tampa, Florida, where the White Sox hold spring training.

Alfonso Ramon Lopez was born August 20, 1908 in Ybor City, the Spanish-speaking section of Tampa, Florida, to which his parents had moved from Madrid, Spain to work in the cigar trade. As a child, Lopez learned to speak Spanish before English, a language the neighborhood children considered unmanly. He also quickly learned the disadvantages of the cigar trade. One of his earliest memories is of the odor of tobacco from the factory. He has said, "I vowed never to work in one." At sixteen he left school to play professional baseball with the Tampa Smokers. "They offered me $150 a month," he remembers. "I took it before they changed their mind" (New York *Times*, September 27, 1959). In the same year he was called upon to catch the formidable Walter Johnson in an exhibition game. At its conclusion, the soft-spoken Johnson, perhaps the finest pitcher of all time, told Lopez: "Nice game, kid. You're going to make a great catcher some day."

In 1925 Lopez was playing with Tampa in the Florida State League. In 1927 he was advanced to Jacksonville, then in the Southeastern League. At the end of the season, Jacksonville, having purchased Lopez for $1,000, sold him to the Brooklyn Dodgers for $10,000. He played three games with Brooklyn in 1928 but he failed to manage a base hit. The following year he was with Atlanta in the Southern Association. He played 143 games and hit .327. When Brooklyn recalled Lopez in 1930, he was in the major leagues to stay.

AL LOPEZ

He remained with Brooklyn six years, enjoying two of his finest seasons during that period. His average in 1930 was .309; in 1933 it was .301. In 1934 he was named to the National League All-Star team. He repeated as an All-Star member in 1941, while playing with the Pittsburgh Pirates. In between, he spent a little over four seasons with the Boston Bees of the National League.

Lopez was traded to Pittsburgh in the middle of the 1940 season. Yankee manager Casey Stengel was then guiding the Boston Bees, whose financial affairs were hovering on the verge of bankruptcy. One day Stengel took Lopez aside for a confidential talk. "We can't meet the payroll unless we sell somebody pretty soon," he said. "You and Eddie Miller are the only ones we can get money for. So we'll sell Miller." Lopez carried the word to shortstop Miller, who refused to believe him. They finally bet a $100 suit of clothes on which one would be traded. Lopez lost the wager.

Lopez was a bulwark of the Pittsburgh Pirates until 1946 when, through no fault of his own, an incident occurred that embarrassed the management. The executives of the Pirates had been considering firing Frankie Frisch as manager and a Pittsburgh newspaper conducted a fan opinion poll, asking its readers to suggest his successor. The overwhelming majority named Lopez. In the next year he was traded to Cleveland.

He played the 1947 season with Cleveland and then, in 1948, began his managerial career with Indianapolis. It was an auspicious beginning. Lopez piloted the club to the American Association pennant and then to its finishes in second place in 1949 and 1950.

On November 10, 1950 Lopez was back with the Cleveland Indians. The Indians discharged their popular player-manager, Lou Boudreau, and hired Lopez at $35,000 a year. Lopez spent six seasons with Cleveland, and in that time the

LOPEZ, AL—Continued

Indians never won fewer than 88 out of 154 games. They also captured one pennant. That victory, in 1954, was somewhat spoiled when the New York Giants beat the Indians four games to none in the World Series.

Lopez resigned from the Cleveland Indians on September 29, 1956. A month later he was hired to manage the Chicago White Sox at a salary of $40,000 a year. Arthur Daley, writing in the New York *Times* (September 24, 1959), said: "Lopez is a matchless handler of men, the most important qualification a manager needs. But he has everything else, including a magnetic personality. One extra qualification is his adaptability. When he managed Cleveland he had slow-footed power hitters. So he let them slug away, always playing for the big inning. With the White Sox he had speed and no power. So he had them running and inside baseball was his strength. And he did just as well with the rapier as with the bludgeon."

As a matter of fact, Lopez did better with the rapier. With Cleveland it took him four years to catch the New York Yankees; with Chicago it took him only three. In the 1957 and 1958 seasons the Chicago White Sox finished in second place, and Lopez' work in 1957 earned him the award as American League Manager of the Year.

Toward the end of the 1958 season Lopez announced that he would return as manager of the Chicago White Sox in 1959. There had been talk that he would retire because of his continuing frustration over the apparently invincible New York Yankees. Lopez said: "I wouldn't have taken the job if I didn't feel the club had a chance to win the pennant. . . .I'm not in this thing for the money. Fortunately, I'm pretty well fixed. But I love baseball and I think we have a good chance of winning the pennant" (*Christian Science Monitor*, September 15, 1958).

This was a familiar Lopez battle cry and the majority of experts proceeded to choose the New York Yankees in preseason polls. But the Yankees never got started and by the beginning of August it was apparent the league championship would be resolved between Cleveland and Chicago. In late August the White Sox swept a four-game series with the Indians and were never headed. They clinched the pennant in Cleveland September 22 with a 4-2 victory.

The White Sox subsequently met the Los Angeles Dodgers in the World Series and were beaten four games to two. Lopez accepted the defeat with his usual graciousness. "They played good ball, real good ball," he said, "and (Walter) Alston did an extra-fine job of managing."

In the middle of the 1959 season Lopez was mentioned as a possible successor to Stengel as manager of the New York Yankees; instead, he signed to manage the White Sox in 1960 at approximately $60,000. "This club," he said after the 1959 World Series, "with only a little help is good enough to win the pennant again."

Alfonso Ramon Lopez was married to the former Evelyn M. Kearney on October 7, 1939. They have a son, Alfonso Ramon, Jr. Away from the baseball field Lopez likes to fish and hunt, but he is even happier on the golf course. He shoots between 78 and 83. In the baseball world Lopez is known as "a nice guy," but Bill Veeck, president of the Chicago White Sox, admits that Lopez is "a man of very strong convictions. The fact that he doesn't shout doesn't mean he's weak."

References

Life 44:76+ My 5 '58 por
N Y Times Mag p17 S 27 '59 pors
N Y Herald Tribune II p1 O 26 '57
Christian Sci Mon p10 S 15 '58

LOPEZ, VINCENT Dec. 30, 1895- Band leader; pianist

Address: Hotel Taft, New York 19

To millions of radio listeners in the United States, the phrase "Hello, everybody — Lopez speaking" has served for nearly forty years to introduce the rhythms of Vincent Lopez. Since 1941 the indestructible Lopez has made his professional headquarters in the Grill Room of the Hotel Taft in New York City, where, as pianist and band leader, he has played the longest continuous engagement of any personality active in show business today. In addition to being a band leader, pianist, song writer, and music publisher, Lopez is a philatelist and numerologist. His autobiography, *Lopez Speaking,* was published in 1960.

Of Portuguese descent, Vincent Lopez was born in Brooklyn, New York on December 30, 1895. His father, Antonio, was a former jeweler and naval bandmaster turned music teacher; his mother, Virginia, Baroness Gonsalves, was from an aristocratic family. He has one sister, Marie. Brought up in conformity with the Old World ideas of his father, Vincent was, in his own words, a "child without a childhood." He was kept at piano practice three hours a day during the school year and six hours daily during vacations. Antonio Lopez was preparing his son for the Roman Catholic priesthood, however, rather than for the piano. At the age of twelve, before he could be "contaminated" by the outside world, Vincent was sent to St. Mary's Passionist Monastery in Dunkirk, New York.

Even at the monastery, it was music that most moved Lopez. To this day he remembers the Gregorian chant he heard there as "man's closest approach to the infinite," and it was in playing the piano for his fellow students that he found his greatest happiness. Three years at St. Mary's convinced both Confrater Anthony (the religious name he had taken) and his teachers that the church was not his true vocation. He left with the blessings of his spiritual Fathers, but his own father never understood or forgave this step.

Disappointed in his efforts to make his son a priest, Vincent's father next determined that business was his proper field and enrolled him in Kissick's Business College in Brooklyn. Vincent dutifully attended his classes and, upon graduation nine months later, took a job his father had found him as secretary to the president of a milk company. The piano remained his first love, however, and after a full day at his secretarial duties he pounded the keyboard from 9 p.m. to 1 a.m. at Clayton's, a Brooklyn saloon. It was there that a rival pianist named Jimmy Durante dubbed the seventeen-year-old Vincent "the pianner kid."

Inevitably, Lopez' lack of sleep led to the loss of his job at the milk company (and at Clayton's, too, the same day) and launched him on a full-time career as an unemployed musician. There followed a series of engagements in the rough-and-tumble world of Brooklyn beer halls, where Vincent, who was fired from one job because he drank nothing stronger than celery tonic, was thrown into contact with "hopheads, prostitutes, grifters [and] petty criminals." He finally landed a job at the Pekin restaurant in Times Square, where he was pressed into service one day as a substitute for band leader Ed Fischelli. When Fischelli left, shortly thereafter, Lopez found himself "the youngest orchestra leader in . . . Big Time."

Kept out of the United States Army by gout, Lopez remained at the Pekin during World War I, and, in those years, was one of the first band leaders to shift to the Dixieland style. Then came Prohibition, which forced both liquor and Lopez out of the Pekin. After an engagement at Perry's at Coney Island, Lopez toured in *Rings of Smoke,* a highly successful vaudeville dance revue. Next came another stage venture, Sigmund Romberg's *Lovebirds,* but that closed after a short run. Then, following an engagement at Ross Fenton's Farms in Asbury Park, Lopez landed his first job as hotel band leader—at the Grill of the Hotel Pennsylvania (now the Statler Hilton) in New York City.

While appearing at the Hotel Pennsylvania, Lopez and his band traveled to the WJZ studio in Newark, New Jersey on November 27, 1921, to broadcast "live" dance music for the first time over the air waves. Suffering mike fright, all Lopez could manage to say was "Hello, everybody—Lopez speaking." A month later he was broadcasting regularly direct from the Hotel Pennsylvania—radio's first "remote" pickup.

Established as a radio star, Lopez was snapping at the heels of Paul Whiteman for the title of King of Jazz. To defeat the lion in his own lair, Lopez returned to vaudeville, and opened at the Palace on August 7, 1922. On this program he introduced to show business the use of scenic effects for band presentations. Both his sets and his band were sensations, and what had been a tentative one-week engagement stretched to eleven weeks.

Competition with Whiteman continued. One result was that when Whiteman gave a concert at Aeolian Hall, Lopez countered, on November 23, 1924, with a concert at the Metropolitan Opera House. That winter, capitalizing on the artistic success of his Met program, Lopez took his band on a jazz concert tour. One date he played was President Coolidge's inaugural ball,

James J. Kriegsmann

VINCENT LOPEZ

where the taciturn President, a Lopez fan, told him: "I still listen to you on radio . . . but I notice you're talking too much in between the songs."

The following summer Lopez took his band to England to introduce Londoners to American jazz. Commenting on Lopez' Hippodrome appearance, a critic for the *Manchester Guardian* wrote: "There are some among us who cherish the hope that when the children of jazz grow out of the nursery stage they will scream a little less lustily. However, the audience loved every minute."

Night clubs flourished during the 1920's, and on October 15, 1925 Lopez opened his own establishment, the Casa Lopez. Although it was described by one critic as "a mélange of Spanish gardens and everything else," it was generally considered elegant. But the Casa Lopez was burned down in a blaze estimated to have caused $200,000 worth of damage, and on October 13, 1927 Lopez opened a second Casa Lopez, which the band leader himself has called "a cheap imitation of the first." It failed in a few months.

The next home base for the Lopez band was the St. Regis Roof, which Lopez opened in June 1928. In his review, society columnist Cholly Knickerbocker had predicted that Lopez would "be a favorite at the Roof for the entire summer." As a matter of fact, Lopez stayed at the St. Regis for seven years and, in 1930, signed a ten-year, million-dollar contract, the first ever signed by a band leader.

In 1934, with the Depression in full force, financial troubles forced the St. Regis to let Lopez go. There followed seven years of cross-country wanderings during which Lopez played everything from Florida dog tracks to Buffalo gambling dens. It was not until 1941 that he settled down in the Grill Room of the Hotel

LOPEZ, VINCENT—*Continued*

Taft. His original three-month engagement there has been extended so long that it has been said that he "goes with the lease."

A perpetual pioneer, Lopez arrived early on the television screen. After he appeared on the Ed Sullivan show in 1949, he was given his own fifteen-minute daily program which ran for two and one-half years on the Dumont network. In 1950 he again made broadcasting history when *Dinner Date With Lopez*, which was telecast from the Taft Grill, became the first regularly-scheduled "remote" TV show.

Because he has an eye for talent that matches his ear for music, Lopez has been the boss, at one time or another, of Xavier Cugat, Artie Shaw, Glen Miller, Tony Pastor, Rudy Vallee, Red Nichols and both the Dorsey brothers. Betty Hutton was one of his major discoveries and her sister Marion, another. But his talent for scouting has misfired occasionally: the young Ted Lewis was unable to land a job with Lopez and he turned down Jimmy Durante because of his looks.

Despite his professional success, Lopez felt "a vague discontent with the loose ends of life" until he found a faith through numerology. He recorded in detail the story of his spiritual journey, as well as of the vicissitudes of his career, in *Lopez Speaking; My Life and How I Changed It* (Citadel, 1960), which a *Variety* reviewer called "a warm and human document."

Numerology has given Lopez a secondary career. His extensive output in the field includes a column for the San Francisco *Chronicle*, numerous magazine articles (*American Astrology* pays him $1 per word), a book of predictions, *What's Ahead?* (David McKay, 1944), and a musical horoscope. He features his forecasts (for which he claims eighty-five per cent accuracy) on his own shows and in guest appearances and attributes to numerology his success in renaming Betty Darling (Hutton), Sonny Schuyler (Skylar), and Edna Mae (Deanna) Durbin.

Somewhat short and stocky, Lopez has blue-green eyes and black hair. He was married on March 5, 1921 to May Kenny, who died on July 5, 1938. The Lopezes had one daughter, Kay. On August 8, 1951 Lopez was married to the former Bettye Long. As hobbies Lopez collects air mail stamps and matchbook covers. During his musical career he has rewritten *The Star Spangled Banner* to make it more singable, given a series of jazz appreciation lectures at New York University, and experimented with the effects of "swing therapy" on mental patients. Now that his autobiography has been published, he is reported to be writing a novel about the prohibition era, tentatively entitled *The Days of Instant Scotch.*

Lopez attributes his durable popularity to a willingness to move with the times. "What happened years ago, weeks ago, even a day ago," he says, "isn't important. It's what is happening today, what will happen tomorrow. The past is good for only one thing—guidance, the benefit of experience." Whatever the secret of his success, his summer engagement at the 1960 Aquarama in New York proved him still very much in the swim, with every likelihood that his theme song, "Nola," which, according to his estimate, he has played more than 350,000 times, will be heard for many years to come.

Reference

Lopez, Vincent Lopez Speaking (1960)

LÓPEZ (PUMAREJO), ALFONSO Jan. 31, 1886-Nov. 20, 1959 Colombian Ambassador to Great Britain (since 1958); President of Colombia (1934-38; 1942-45). See *Current Biography* (September) 1942.

Obituary

N Y Times p23 N 21 '59

LÜBKE, HEINRICH (lüp'kĕ) Oct. 14, 1894- President of the Federal Republic of Germany

Address: Hammerschmidt Palace, Bonn, Germany

When he was elected President of the Federal Republic of Germany in July 1959, Dr. Heinrich Lübke said: "The main goal of all Germans is a Germany reunified in justice and freedom and serving the peace of the world." Dr. Lübke took office in September 1959, succeeding Theodor Heuss. In West Germany the President is chief of state, while the Chancellor is the head of the government—a position now occupied by Konrad Adenauer.

Dr. Lübke served in the Bundestag as a Christian Democrat; from 1953 to 1959 he was Minister of Food, Agriculture, and Forestry in the Adenauer government, where he was known as a sound administrator and a proponent of the "Green Plan" to put West German agriculture on a rational basis. Before World War II he had been prominent in the affairs of agricultural organizations. Because of his opposition to the Nazis, he was arrested and put in prison for twenty months.

Heinrich Lübke, the son of Friedrich-Wilhelm and Karoline (Becker) Lübke, was born in Enkhausen (near Arnsberg), Germany on October 14, 1894. His father was a small farmer and artisan. After his graduation from the Gymnasium, Lübke studied geodesy, architecture, engineering, political economy, agriculture, and community development at the universities of Bonn, Berlin, and Münster. He received his degree as an engineer. During World War I he served as a lieutenant in the German Army and won two Iron Cross medals.

After World War I, Lübke became active in agricultural organizations. Having come to the conclusion that a large number of independent farmers' organizations was detrimental to agricultural planning, Lübke brought these smaller organizations into the Deutsche Bauernschaft (Combined German Farmers Federation). He served with the federation as its director from 1926 to 1933; during this period he also founded and directed Bauernland, a land-settlement organization.

Lübke's interest in politics had grown, and he became a member of the German (Catholic) Center party. He was elected as their representative to the Prussian Landtag (legislative assembly) in 1931. When the National Socialists came to power in 1933, Lübke was dismissed from all his positions; he was imprisoned for a total of twenty months during the Nazi regime. Between 1935 and 1944 he worked on and off as a building worker for a Berlin construction firm.

When the Hitler era came to an end, Lübke helped to organize the Christian Democratic party (CDU) in Westphalia. He was elected as the CDU member of the North Rhine-Westphalia Landtag in October 1946 and served until 1953. Appointed Minister of Food and Agriculture for North Rhine-Westphalia in January 1947, he faced the huge task of reconstruction when food was scarce and farm lands lay devastated. Lübke encouraged the introduction of modern machine farming techniques to replace older methods, some of which had been in use since the Middle Ages. Before mechanization could take place, some farms had to be consolidated. Until 1952, Lübke remained the Minister of Food and Agriculture in North Rhine-Westphalia.

Meanwhile, in 1949, Lübke had been elected as CDU representative to the first Bundestag, the lower house of the federal German parliament. He was re-elected in 1953 and in 1957. Chancellor Adenauer named Lübke to his cabinet in October 1953 as Minister of Food, Agriculture, and Forestry. He served in this position until 1959.

During his six years in this office, Lübke was continually concerned with reconciling the interests of the farmers, who wanted high prices for their goods, and the demands of the consumers, who sought low-priced, but high-quality foods. His ability to achieve a fair balance is indicated by the fact that both sides came to respect his objectivity, firmness, and administrative ability.

Perhaps Lübke's greatest achievement lay in his success in modernizing German agriculture. His Green Plan for aiding agriculture was supported by all parties. Unfavorable conditions for farmers were driving the population away from the countryside, and mechanization was not making up for this heavy loss each year. Lübke proposed that the central government spend a fairly large sum of money every year in the form of tax relief, indirect subsidies, and improvements in public facilities in farm areas. This plan, which was passed by the German legislature, would enable the small farmers in particular to share in the German postwar economic boom.

Another problem facing his department was that of liberalizing federal agricultural policies to meet the West German obligations to the European common market, composed of West Germany, France, Italy, the Netherlands, Belgium, and Luxembourg. In 1956 Lübke came to the United States for a three-week tour, during

HEINRICH LÜBKE

which he visited American agricultural experimental stations, and studied methods of research in soil fertility.

Chancellor Adenauer announced in April 1959 that he would run for the presidency of West Germany; in the following month he changed his mind and announced that he would remain in his present position. This set off a domestic crisis and precipitated a quarrel between Adenauer and Ludwig Erhard, the leading contender for the chancellorship. Adenauer then proposed Lübke as the CDU's candidate for President, and in June 1959 the CDU chose Lübke to run. On July 1, 1959 the Federal Assembly, meeting in Berlin, elected Lübke as the second President of the Federal Republic of Germany, to succeed Theodor Heuss. Lübke won the election on the second ballot, defeating Carlo Schmid of the Social Democratic party and Max Becker of the Free Democratic party.

Lübke took office on September 15, 1959. In West Germany the President is the head of state and serves for a term of five years. He is limited constitutionally to two consecutive terms. The President must stand above party politics. Among his principal duties are representing the nation in international law; signing treaties for his nation; accrediting and receiving ambassadors; and appointing the Federal Chancellor (after he has been elected by an absolute majority of the Bundestag), federal ministers (at the Chancellor's suggestion), federal judges, officials, and officers of the armed forces.

Lübke was married to Wilhelmine Keuthen in 1929. He is five feet six inches tall and has white hair. He is a Roman Catholic. For recreation he enjoys reading, playing the piano, and taking walks. He has been awarded an honorary doctoral degree from the University of Bonn and a medal from the Federal Republic of Germany; he has been elected as a senator in

LÜBKE, HEINRICH—*Continued*

the Max Planck Institute. He is known for his stern sense of duty, irreproachable character, and high quality of work.

References

> Christian Sci Mon p4 Je 16 '59
> N Y Times p2 Jl 2 '59
> International Who's Who, 1959
> Wer ist Wer? (1958)
> Who's Who in Germany (1956)

LUCCOCK, HALFORD E(DWARD), REV. DR. (lŭk'ŏk) Mar. 11, 1885- Theologian; author

Address: b. The Christian Century, 407 S. Dearborn St., Chicago 5, Ill.; h. 176 Carmalt Rd., Hamden, Conn.

> *Bulletin*: The Reverend Dr. Halford E. Luccock died on November 5, 1960.

A militant clergyman, the Reverend Dr. Halford E. Luccock has conducted a campaign in his writings and sermons against social and economic inequities, nationalism, and the causes of war, urging his readers to recognize the "corporate responsibility for human welfare." Dr. Luccock, a Methodist Episcopal minister, has been called the "most quoted preacher among preachers in the United States." In his column for the undenominational *Christian Century*, written under the pseudonym of Simeon Stylites, Dr. Luccock since 1948 has treated religious and moral issues with many a metaphor and pertinent quotation. His slogan as a columnist is: "I believe in comforting the afflicted and afflicting the comfortable."

For twenty-five years Dr. Luccock was a professor of homiletics at Yale University Divinity School and in 1953 he became professor emeritus of homiletics. He has written twenty-five books in which he has demonstrated his scholarship in several fields.

Halford E. Luccock was born in Pittsburgh, Pennsylvania on March 11, 1885 to Naphtali Luccock and Etta F. (Anderson) Luccock. His father was a bishop in the Methodist church. Halford studied at Northwestern University, earning his B.A. degree in 1906. He then enrolled at Union Theological Seminary in New York City, where he was awarded the B.D. degree in 1909. In the same year he received an M.A. degree from Columbia University.

Ordained in the Methodist Episcopal ministry in 1910, Dr. Luccock served successively as pastor of a church in Windsor, Connecticut (1910-12); an instructor at Hartford Theological Seminary in Connecticut (1912-14); pastor of St. Andrew's Church in New Haven, Connecticut (1914-16); registrar and instructor in the New Testament at Drew Theological Seminary in Madison, New Jersey (1916-18); editorial secretary of the Methodist Board of Foreign Missions (1918-24); and contributing editor of the *Christian Advocate,* a Methodist weekly (1924-28). He was also a member of the Conference of the Methodist Board of Foreign Missions from 1924 to 1936.

From the *Christian Advocate* Dr. Luccock went to Yale University Divinity School in 1928 as professor of homiletics. He remained in this post until 1953 when he became professor emeritus of homiletics. During the twenty-five years he taught at Yale, his sharp insights and sprightly presentation endeared him to many classes of divinity students.

At the time of his retirement from Yale, Dr. Luccock delivered a series of lectures in which he took to task what he called "comfortable" preaching. He criticized the "Rocking Horse Sermon . . . which moves but does not go on, always charging but never advancing," "the Mockingbird Sermon . . . all the notes of someone else, either stolen or just imitated," the "Confectioner's Sermon, like a wedding cake, a great, airy structure with candy chateaux . . . and hearts of purest whipped cream." He also warned prospective preachers against packaging the Christian message as a "sort of glorified aspirin tablet." "We have a moral obligation to be interesting," he concluded, "for our gospel is loaded with life-and-death interest for people. . . . The aim of preaching is not the elucidation of a subject, but the transformation of a person."

While teaching at Yale Dr. Luccock served from time to time as guest preacher at various churches. At the Christ Methodist Church in New York City on September 26, 1943, he cautioned the United States government against supporting Pietro Badoglio or the House of Savoy as successors to Mussolini in Italy. He warned that the use of American power to restore the "reactionary rule of near-fascism" would indicate that the United States had lapsed back into its old isolationism; it might also be viewed as a symptom of the "newer brand of isolationism which incorporates in it an American imperialism" (*New York Times,* September 27, 1943).

Beginning with the issue of December 9, 1948, Dr. Luccock's weekly column, written in the form of letters to the editor, has brightened the pages of the *Christian Century.* The pieces have attracted much notice for their witticisms and puns. Dr. Luccock signs the articles "Simeon Stylites" in honor of the Syrian ascetic who became the first of the column saints.

Under the Simeon Stylites by-line, on March 2, 1960 he rose to the defense of the bear in the old song "The Bear Went over the Mountain." He concluded that people often see only their own side of a controversial question, and that a trip over the mountain to see the other side "is necessary for the acquiring of real and complete sympathy; there is no other way to see how life looks to the other person and how his burdens cut cruelly."

A prolific author, Dr. Luccock has been writing books on religion, literature, and contemporary problems for some forty-five years. Some of these reveal his unusual ability to express the quintessence of Christianity in provocative and relevant terms. One of his first books, *Fares Please! And Other Essays on Practical Themes* (Abingdon Press, 1916). posed moral issues and conveyed common-sense advice largely by means of anecdotes and quotations.

With Paul Hutchinson, Dr. Luccock wrote *The Story of Methodism* (Methodist Book Concern, 1926), a one-volume history of the sect beginning with John Wesley. When the book was reissued by Abingdon-Cokesbury Press in 1949, it was praised by reviewers as a spirited and accurate narrative that found room for the pageantry and adventure of the growth of Methodism.

In *Preaching Values in New Translations of the New Testament* (Abingdon Press, 1928), Dr. Luccock excerpted the translations of Drs. James Moffatt, Edgar J. Goodspeed, and Richard F. Weymouth and explained the meaning of the texts. Religious leaders disagreed over the merits of the book. Dr. Harry Emerson Fosdick (*Christian Century*, April 12, 1928) commented: "Dr. Luccock has done a provocative and stimulating piece of work. The use of the volume will not prove, I think, a crutch to lean on, but is much more likely to be tonic and invigorating." But Dr. John Haynes Holmes (New York *Herald Tribune Books*, August 5, 1928), wrote: "The fact that his outlines are almost irresistible from the standpoint of illumination, wisdom, courage and ripe discernment makes his offense only the more serious. With however innocent a motive, Dr. Luccock has undertaken to do other men's thinking for them."

Turning from the New Testament to the Old Testament, Dr. Luccock wrote *Preaching Values in the Old Testament in the Modern Translations* (Abingdon Press, 1933). Written in an original and arresting manner, the book is a collection of short homilies based on James Moffatt's translations. Avoiding the weighty moralizing and hair-splitting criticism of Biblical scholarship, Luccock recast the eternal truths of ancient Hebrew philosophy into modern language for application to present-day issues.

In the following year Willett, Clark & Company published Dr. Luccock's *Contemporary American Literature and Religion* (1934), a discussion of American literature since World War I. With Frances Brentano and others Luccock edited *The Questing Spirit; Religion in the Literature of Our Time* (Coward-McCann, 1947), an anthology of the prose and poetry of twentieth century writers, including Jews, Protestants, Catholics, and agnostics. Liberal religion set the tone of the book.

Another book of Dr. Luccock's literary criticism, *American Mirror; Social, Ethical and Religious Aspects of American Literature, 1930-1940,* appeared under the Macmillan Company imprint in 1940. Although Dr. Luccock called the 1930's an "era of cruising in a world of low visibility," he nevertheless predicted that contemporary literature would relate itself to public affairs after a long period of social apathy. Oxford University Press has published two collections of Dr. Luccock's pieces in *Christian Century;* they are *Like*

REV. DR. HALFORD E. LUCCOCK

a Mighty Army; Selected Letters of Simeon Stylites (1954) and *Living Without Gloves; More Letters of Simeon Stylites* (1957).

In *Preaching Values in the Epistles of Paul; Volume I, Romans and the First Corinthians* (Harper, 1959), Dr. Luccock used the Revised Standard Version and the J. B. Phillips translations of the New Testament. Using a text from I Corinthians 11:22 ("Do you humiliate those who have nothing?"), Luccock applied this to the problem of segregation in some churches. "When we have a greater fear of getting into a scrape over nonsegregation," he wrote, "than of denying our Lord, we do not get into scrapes. But we do get into a mausoleum for the spiritually dead. In seeking to avoid humiliation to any children of God by exclusive fences . . . we must go from the word of God to its resultant acts of brotherhood . . . across all barriers of border and breed and birth."

Inspired by Romans 12:9 ("Hate what is evil"), Dr. Luccock remarked in *Preaching Values in the Epistles of Paul,* "We explain it and account for it, but many of us do not hate evil any more. . . . It is easy to denounce juvenile delinquency. It is not so easy to see and hate the indifference of citizens and cities which refuse to pay for facilities for recreation of young people."

Halford E. Luccock and Mary Louise Whitehead were married on June 17, 1914. They have two children, Mary Etta and Robert Edward, a minister and author. Luccock has been awarded the honorary D.D. degree by Syracuse, Wesleyan, and Vermont universities; the D.Litt. degree from Allegheny College; and the D.S.T. degree from Northwestern University.

References

Who's Who in America, 1952-53
Who's Who in Methodism (1952)

LUMUMBA, PATRICE (EMERGY) (lŏŏ-mŏŏm-bá) July 2, 1925- Former Premier of the Republic of the Congo

Amid joyous shouts of "Independence!" from many of its 14,000,000 inhabitants, the Republic of the Congo was created June 30, 1960. The first Premier of this new African state, formerly known as the Belgian Congo, was a thirty-five-year-old firebrand named Patrice Lumumba, once a discredited postal clerk who rose to power as a leader of the political party Mouvement National Congolaise.

Adored by his enthusiastically loyal followers, distrusted and feared by his enemies among both native leaders and former colonists,

United Nations

PATRICE LUMUMBA

Lumumba won election as Premier only nine days before the declaration of independence, and not until he had defeated his strongest rival, Joseph Kasavubu, in a bitter power struggle. Lumumba faced many problems as head of the new republic, which is the richest of the new African nations, but is beset by a faltering economy, lack of qualified administrators and technicians, dangerous tribal animosities, and secessionist movements.

Unable to control the army, to prevent civil disorder, or to maintain national unity, Lumumba was deposed September 1960 and attempts were made to assassinate him. His regime was succeeded by several short-lived governments.

Patrice Emergy Lumumba was born on July 2, 1925 in Katako Kombe, a town in Congo's Kawai Province. Son of a tribesman of Batetelas, he attended Belgian mission schools in the Congo and completed his high school studies. Lumumba, a brilliant but erratic student, was dismissed from one school because of fights with teachers (New York *Herald Tribune*, August 25, 1960).

Having been trained in a school for postal employees, Lumumba began working at the Stanleyville post office at the age of nineteen. He continued his education by studying law and literature through correspondence courses. Eleven years after joining the postal service, he was convicted of embezzling $2,500 from the post office by fraudulent conversion and was sentenced to serve a term in Stanleyville Prison (New York *Times,* May 18, 1960). Lumumba later told followers that he stole the money to further his nationalist activities. Upon his release from prison, Lumumba was a salesman for the Bracongo beer company, of which he became commercial director in August 1958. He left the firm, in whose employ he is said to have amassed a sizeable fortune, in 1959.

During the three years preceding Congolese independence, Lumumba was active in various nationalist groups. In 1957 he was a member of the African section of the Liberal Club, served as president of the temporary committee of the Mouvement National Congolaise (M.N.C.) in 1958, and helped to organize a congress of native political parties in Luluabourg in April 1959. He was a Congolese delegate to the All Africa People's Conference in Accra, Ghana in December 1958, where he was elected a permanent member of the co-ordination committee. He has also aided the nationalist movement through his activities on various newspapers; he was a correspondent of the *Croix du Congo, Voix du Congolais,* and *Le Stanleyvillois* and is now director of *Indépendance.*

The political fortunes of Lumumba were most directly connected with the development of the M.N.C. When it was formed by prominent businessmen and community leaders in 1958, Lumumba typed out a roster of officers, with himself listed as president, and released it to the press (New York *Herald Tribune,* June 25, 1960). Other members were shocked, but decided to let the published list stand. Ten months later, moderate leaders of M.N.C., contemptuous of his fiery speeches and extreme nationalism, voted to expel Lumumba. Thereupon the party split into two factions, with Lumumba's wing becoming increasingly powerful.

In November 1959 Lumumba was jailed for having addressed a rally the previous month which led to rioting, in which twenty natives were killed by Belgian troops. In his speech, he had promised that the M.N.C. would initiate a "positive plan for the immediate liberation of the Congo." Calling for civil disobedience and nonviolence, Lumumba said that the enemy was "the government in Brussels, not the Europeans in the Congo."

A conference of Belgian and Congolese leaders to determine the political fate of the Belgian Congo was held in Brussels in January 1960. The principal leader of the native independence movement at that time was Joseph Kasavubu, president of the Association of the Lower Congo (Abako). Upon the insistence of delegates of the M.N.C., Lumumba was released from prison to attend the round-table discussions, at which plans were made for the election of government officials in May 1960 and the liberation of the Congo on June 30, 1960.

In the race for leadership of the forthcoming state, two men ran neck and neck: Lumumba and Kasavubu. Results of the May elections seemingly established Lumumba as the dominant figure in Congo politics; his party controlled thirty-six seats out of 137 in the new National Assembly. Unable to arrange the coalition necessary for a majority, Lumumba was by-passed by the Belgian authorities in favor of Kasavubu, who was asked to form the new government. Lumumba, however, refused to concede defeat and managed to gain support of eighty-four members of the National Assembly. On June 21, 1960 he recaptured the reins of leadership and successfully formed a government. In a conciliatory gesture, Kasavubu was named President, a largely ceremonial post.

With Patrice Lumumba at its helm, the new Republic of the Congo was launched on the last day of June 1960. During the Independence Day ceremony, in which King Baudouin I of Belgium participated, Lumumba astonished guests from many nations by attacking Belgian rule of the Congo, which dated back to 1885. He shouted: "Slavery was imposed on us by force. . . . We have known ironies and insults. We remember the blows that we had to submit to morning, noon and night because we were Negroes!" Later, however, Lumumba attempted to placate Belgian authorities by praising them for their decision to free the Congo.

As head of the new nation, Lumumba faced grave problems: dissension among savage tribes, an extremely low literacy rate, a severe lack of trained native leaders, and a standstill of the entire economy and governmental machinery resulting from the exodus of Belgians, who were fearful of native attacks. Almost immediately after the independence proclamation, civil order came to an end when tribal rivalries flared. There were widespread mutinies of the Force Publique, the Congolese army, against Belgian officers, and the Belgian government rushed units to the Congo. Lumumba's troubles were multiplied with the secession on July 11 of the province of Katanga, which provided two-thirds of the Congo's revenues, and its request that Belgian troops remain in Katanga. In August part of the Kasai Province also seceded.

To meet the rapidly deteriorating situation Lumumba set out on two courses. First, he announced a state of emergency which soon became rule by martial law, and he took steps to quiet opposition. Secondly, he looked for help outside of his country and on July 10 appealed to the United Nations for aid in reorganizing the armed forces.

The U.N. Security Council responded to the pleas of the infant nation on July 14 by calling upon the Belgians "to withdraw their troops from the territory of the Republic of Congo" and by authorizing its Secretary-General Dag Hammarskjöld to give the Congo military assistance. Within several weeks there were over 16,000 U.N. troops in the Congo.

On July 22 Lumumba flew to New York to seek economic and political support from the U.N., the United States, and Canada. Later the United States gave the Congo a $5,000,000 credit through the U.N. as part of the American contribution to the rehabilitation of the new republic. The money does not have to be repaid.

After he returned home, Lumumba began making personal attacks on Hammarskjöld and on August 19 formally demanded the withdrawal of all white U.N. troops (later he said this did not apply to military staff members or technical personnel), requested U.N. planes to transport soldiers to quell dissension in the interior, and asked for the establishment of an African-Asian committee to advise Hammarskjöld. On August 22 the Security Council gave Hammarskjöld a "vote of confidence" to pursue his policy of military, technical, and economic assistance and of noninterference in the dispute between the Republic of the Congo and Katanga. The Secretary-General did, however, appoint an advisory committee with a majority of members from the African-Asian bloc.

The political views of Lumumba emerged from the many speeches and public statements he made after his accession to power. Concerning the world rivalry between East and West, he said, "for us there is only one group. We are not Communists, Catholics, Socialists. We are African nationalists." The Congo Republic will choose its friends "according to the principle of positive neutrality."

Answering expressions of fear on the part of United States officials about the status of American investments in the Congo, he declared that they would not be expropriated. He assailed the Belgians for having "systematically neglected political education" in the Congo, which lagged behind the hospitals, universities, and schools they established.

Patrice Lumumba is married to a woman who was also born in a jungle town. They have four children, three boys and a girl; according to Lumumba, the children will attend European schools. He is a slender man, over six feet tall, and wears a goatee. He has been said to look like "a dark, bespectacled Davy Crockett under his chieftain's headdress—a feathered sheepskin cap" and has a reputation for having a quick wit, social poise, calm confidence, unlimited energy, and insatiable ambition. After becoming Premier, he was decorated with the Belgian Order of the Crown.

References

N Y Herald Tribune p4 Je 25 '60
N Y Times p4 My 18 '60
Washington (D.C.) Post p10A Jl 18 '60

LYDENBERG, HARRY MILLER Nov. 18, 1874-Apr. 16, 1960 Librarian; associated for forty-five years with the New York Public Library in several capacities, including director (1934-41); director-librarian of the Biblioteca Benjamin Franklin in Mexico City (1941-43); active in library associations. See *Current Biography* (September) 1941.

Obituary

N Y Times p92 Ap 17 '60

MCINTIRE, ROSS T. Aug. 11, 1889-Dec. 8, 1959 Surgeon general and chief of the bureau of medicine and surgery, United States Navy (1938-46); personal physician to President Roosevelt (1935-45). See *Current Biography* (October) 1945.

Obituary

N Y Times p45 D 9 '59

MCKNEALLY, MARTIN B(OSWELL)
Dec. 31, 1914- Organization official; lawyer
Address: h. 329 1st St., Newburgh, N.Y.

Numbering some 2,700,000 members in nearly 17,000 posts, the American Legion is the largest veterans organization in the United States. Its national commander for 1959-60 is Martin B. McKneally, a lawyer from Newburgh, New York and a former New York state commander, who was the unanimous choice of the 3,062 delegates who attended the forty-first convention of the American Legion in August 1959. He succeeds Preston J. Moore.

According to the New York *Times* (August 28, 1959), McKneally has for his main object an attack on communism on a more "intellectual" plane, proving in every instance that com-

Chase, Ltd.

MARTIN B. MCKNEALLY

munism is wrong and that the American way is right. In December 1959 he revoked the license of the American Legion's fun-making affiliate, the 40 and 8, for retaining a clause in its constitution barring nonwhites from its membership.

The grandson of English and Irish immigrants, Martin Boswell McKneally was born on December 31, 1914 in Newburgh, New York. His mother is the former Ellen Leahy; his father, George F. McKneally, developed a prosperous business as a building contractor.

Martin McKneally has a brother, George F., Jr., who now heads the business, and three married sisters.

Scouting and other forms of outdoor activity were Martin McKneally's favorite recreations when he attended the Broadway public grammar school at Newburgh and the Newburgh Free Academy. He developed an early interest in American history, and his proficiency in public speaking, debating, and dramatics at the Newburgh Free Academy helped to form his ambition to become a lawyer. As an undergraduate at the College of the Holy Cross in Worcester, Massachusetts, where he took his B.A. degree, McKneally continued debating and dramatic activities and belonged to the History Club. He received the LL.B. degree in 1940 at the Fordham University School of Law in New York.

Inducted into the Army on March 17, 1941, he was serving with the field artillery when a call went out from the Adjutant General's Office for officer candidates with legal training. McKneally, who was sent to the Officers Candidates School, was commissioned a second lieutenant in September 1942. He was assigned first as an instructor in military law and Army administration at the Officers Candidates School at Grinnell College in Iowa, and later as an assistant professor of military science and tactics at the University of Minnesota in Minneapolis. Transferred to the Tenth Army in Hawaii in December 1943, he was subsequently ordered to join the staff of Lieutenant General Robert C. Richardson, Jr., commander, central Pacific area. He remained in that assignment until his release from the service, in the rank of major, in January 1946.

Returning to civilian life, McKneally opened his own law office in Newburgh and at the same time joined a New York City law firm, from which he later withdrew. In 1950, when he was still practising in New York City, he headed a committee sponsoring Peter W. Hoguet as a coalition candidate in opposition to United States Representative Vito Marcantonio. It was James G. Donovan, however, who won the Republican-Democratic-Liberal nomination and later defeated Marcantonio.

In Newburgh McKneally attracted the attention of Justice Samuel W. Eager of the Ninth Judicial District of the New York Supreme Court. He was appointed the justice's confidential secretary and continued in that post until after he was elected national commander of the Legion.

In June 1959 Governor Nelson Rockefeller named McKneally to the New York State Defense Council, which had just been reactivated after having been dormant for several years. Under the provisions of the Defense Emergency Act, the council is the principal policy-making body for civil defense; in the event of war, it has broad powers to supersede local governments and to replace the state Legislature if it is unable to function. Later in the same summer McKneally was designated as New York state chairman for the March of Dimes. He has also served on the New York Governor's Committee on Youth and Delinquency and was president of the Newburgh Board of Education in 1955-56.

Martin B. McKneally, who has been described as "single-mindedly dedicated to the defense of fundamental 'Americanism,'" looks upon the late Senator Joseph R. McCarthy as the "symbol" of his mission (New York *Times*, August 28, 1959). He has worked toward his goal of forwarding Americanism through the American Legion since 1946, when he joined the Judson P. Galloway Post 152.

In his local post McKneally served as chairman of the Americanism committee and as judge advocate. Later, while holding the office of chairman of the New York state Americanism committee, he warned in January 1954 of two anti-Semitic publications being sent to Legion posts from Union, New Jersey and urged that they be destroyed. In the following year he was made commander of the Newburgh post, parliamentarian at the Legion's national convention in Miami, Florida, and member of the national Americanism committee.

Elected New York state commander for 1956-57, McKneally assailed in August 1956 a ruling by Dr. James E. Allen, Jr., of the State Board of Education that teachers could not be dismissed for refusing to identify others as Communist party members. McKneally called the ruling "shocking" and "another glaring example of the incredible failure on the part of some public officials to understand the nature of Communism."

While serving as state commander, McKneally began his bid for the position of national commander, according to a biographical sketch in the New York *Times* (August 28, 1959). "He logged more than 150,000 miles by air, in a campaign that, it has been estimated, cost between $35,000 and $40,000. The committee that raised the money was headed by Morton Downey, the singer, and Roy Cohn, a close associate of Senator McCarthy."

Like many other Legionnaires, reported Scripps-Howard correspondent Jim G. Lucas, "McKneally takes a dim view of the United Nations Educational, Scientific, and Cultural Organization, federal aid to education, cultural exchanges with Russia, left-wingers in general and Russians in particular. He wants to keep the nation strong militarily, but he is not sold on the United Nations" (New York *World-Telegram and Sun*, August 28, 1959).

At the forty-first national convention of the American Legion in late August 1959, McKneally supported a number of resolutions opposing the impending United States tour of Soviet Premier Nikita S. Khrushchev. "I think," McKneally declared, "that great harm could come from the visit because the captive nations . . . could conclude that we are building a sympathy for Khrushchev" (New York *Herald Tribune*, August 25, 1959). The delegates eventually voted to urge Americans to "accept the Soviet Premier's visit with the dignity common to free men."

The majority attending the convention, however, went on record against further exchange visits by top leaders, summit conferences, cultural exchanges, and trade agreements with the Soviet Union. They also defeated a proposal

for a $100-a-month pension for all World War I veterans regardless of need. Unsympathetic to this proposal, McKneally expressed his disapproval of "wild-eyed . . . pension schemes" and of fiscal irresponsibility in general (Jim G. Lucas).

The only candidate nominated to succeed Preston J. Moore, McKneally was unanimously elected 1959-60 national commander on August 27, 1959. The office entails a $18,000 salary and a $65,000 expense account. Founded in March 1919, the American Legion has now almost 3,000,000 members. It maintains its national headquarters at 700 North Pennsylvania Street, Indianapolis 6, Indiana.

The day before McKneally was elected national commander, convention delegates rejected a resolution declaring "in violation of the Legion constitution" a clause in the constitution of the 40 and 8 (its "fun and frolic" affiliate) which bars Negroes and Orientals from membership. Immediately afterward, however, the delegates adopted another resolution "to secure the sympathetic support of the 40 and 8 to a re-examination . . . of its eligibility clause for membership." On October 9 the national executive committee empowered McKneally to prohibit "the use by the 40 and 8 of the names 'The American Legion' and 'American Legion'" if it did not revise its constitution. After several weeks of fruitless conferences, in early December McKneally notified the president of the 40 and 8 that the license of the organization was revoked. Delegates to the national convention of October 1960 voted to sustain McKneally's action, but indicated that the 40 and 8 could return to the fold of the Legion if it dropped its membership restrictions.

The national commander supported the Hamilton County (Ohio) council of the American Legion in December 1959 when it censured United States Senator Stephen M. Young of Ohio for his plans to address the Emergency Civil Liberties Committee. Later that month Young addressed the group, which is not on the Attorney General's list of Communist-front organizations. McKneally pointed out that the House Un-American Activities Committee in 1957 accused the Emergency Civil Liberties Committee of undermining the government's anti-Communist programs (New York *Herald Tribune*, December 12, 1959).

Martin B. McKneally is a bachelor who lives with his widowed mother. Husky and well built, he has graying dark hair, "heavily angular brows, a strikingly moulded face, judicious thoughtful appearance, erect and soldierly posture." He stands five feet seven inches and weighs about 182 pounds. In religion he is a Roman Catholic; in politics, a Republican. He belongs to the Elks and to the American Bar Association. He sometimes plays the piano and would like to take up golf and skiing when he has more spare time.

References

Am Legion Mag 67:17 N '59 pors
N Y Herald Tribune p6 Ag 28 '59 por
N Y World-Telegram p31 Ag 28 '59 por
U S News 47:22 S 7 '59

MAHER, ALY 1883-Aug. 24, 1960 Former Premier of Egypt (1936, 1939-40, 1952); held various cabinet posts; served in the Egyptian Senate (1930-32; 1939-46). See *Current Biography* (March) 1952.

Obituary

N Y Times p29 Ag 25 '60

MALINOVSKY, RODION Y(AKOVLE-VICH) (mä"lē-nôf-skē' rôd-yôn') Nov. 23, 1898- Minister of Defense of the U.S.S.R.; Soviet Army officer

Address: U.S.S.R. Ministry of Defense, Moscow, U.S.S.R.

NOTE: This biography supersedes the article which appeared in *Current Biography* in 1944.

The attention of the world was again focused suddenly on Marshal Rodion Y. Malinovsky in May 1960, when he appeared at the abortive Paris Summit Conference as the constant companion of U.S.S.R. Premier Nikita S. Khrushchev. After becoming Soviet Defense Minister in October 1957, Malinovsky had remained a background figure. His renewed emergence into the limelight at Paris was interpreted both as a reminder of the force at Khrushchev's command and as a symbol of one of the forces pressing upon Khrushchev.

Rodion Yakovlevich Malinovsky was born November 23, 1898, in Odessa, a seaport on the Black Sea coast of the Ukraine. Reportedly the son of a worker or a peasant, he became a farm laborer at the age of twelve, and later a shop messenger. During World War I he fought in the Imperial Russian Army as a machine gunner. According to one report, he was wounded and decorated.

In 1917 he was sent to France with a Russian Army division, making the slow journey to the Western Front via Siberia, Singapore, the Indian Ocean, and the Mediterranean. In France he served side by side with British and American troops, and in later years spoke highly of them. When the news of the Russian revolution reached his division, many of the men refused to fight, demanding to return to Russia. "Our camp was surrounded by Allied troops," Malinovsky said. "The French tried to pacify us with artillery fire."

Malinovsky was elected chairman of a regimental committee of the soldiers. Later he was arrested by the French and sent with other dissident Russian troops to North Africa. After World War I had ended, he made his way back to Russia by way of Vladivostok and Siberia. In Russia he joined the Red Army as a machine gun instructor, and fought in the civil war that convulsed Russia until 1920. During that war he rose to command posts, and when it was over he remained in the Red Army. In 1926 he joined the Communist party. The Army sent him to the Advanced Training School for Officers, and in 1930 he was graduated from the M. V. Frunze Military Academy.

When Hitler attacked Russia in 1941, Malinovsky was a major general in command of an army corps in Bessarabia. After a two-month retreat before the German onslaught Malinovsky's men were surrounded at Nikolayev, but they managed to break out of the encirclement and rejoin the Russian forces without losing their equipment.

As an army commander, in 1942, Malinovsky took part in the defeat of the Germans at Stalingrad. In 1943 he was promoted in rapid succession from lieutenant general to colonel general to general, and placed in command of the south Russian front where he led a series of operations for the liberation of the Donets River Basin and the southern Ukraine.

In April 1944 the army under his command liberated his birthplace, Odessa. In August, when he had been promoted to marshal, he led his men in a new drive that resulted in the occupation of Bucharest, Rumania—the first enemy capital to be captured by the Soviet Army. In that city, on September 12, 1944, he signed an armistice agreement with Rumania on behalf of the Soviet and Allied commands. His troops entered Belgrade, Yugoslavia in October 1944, and in January 1945 they battled from house to house in Budapest, Hungary. Three months later they marched into Vienna, and when the Germans capitulated in May, they were driving toward Prague in Czechoslovakia.

At the end of the war in Europe Marshal Malinovsky was transferred to the Far East where he took command of the Transbaikal Army for its drive against the Japanese in Manchuria in August 1945. By the spring of 1946 his troops withdrew to Soviet territory, with the Chinese Communist troops moving in behind them to take over. Malinovsky then became the Soviet commander in the Far East, with headquarters at Vladivostok. He had an estimated 450,000 men under his command, out of the total Soviet Army strength of 3,000,000. In 1946 he was elected a deputy to the Supreme Soviet of the U.S.S.R., and has been re-elected every four years since then.

The outbreak of the Korean War in 1950 greatly enhanced the importance of his command, and on November 7, 1951, during the Korean armistice negotiations, he was chosen to deliver the traditional address from Lenin's tomb at Red Square in Moscow on the anniversary of the Russian revolution. At the Nineteenth Congress of the Communist party of the Soviet Union in February 1952, he was named an alternate member of the party's Central Committee.

In February 1956, at the Twentieth Congress of the Soviet Communist party, Malinovsky was named a full member of the Central Committee. At the same time he was shifted from his Far Eastern command to the post of commander in chief of Army ground forces. This post carried with it the rank of Deputy Minister of Defense.

On October 26, 1957 Malinovsky was appointed Minister of Defense of the U.S.S.R., replacing Marshal Georgi K. Zhukov. A few days later the Central Committee of the party removed Zhukov from his party posts and accused him of glorifying himself and his accomplishments, while curtailing Communist party control over the armed forces.

Under Malinovsky's direction there was wholesale replacement of the personnel in the political administration of the Army, but no purge of military commanders. The political training of officers was made more rigorous, and enrollments in the Communist party increased. (These innovations were formalized in a new code of military discipline issued in 1960.) But at the same time Malinovsky stressed the importance of unified command, and warned against weakening the authority of military commanders.

Malinovsky also presided over the continuing reduction of the armed forces. These had reached a postwar peak strength of 5,763,000 in 1955. Through the end of 1957, when Malinovsky took over, they had been reduced by 1,840,000 men. Since then cuts of 1,500,000 men have been ordered, with the intent of bringing Soviet strength by the autumn of 1961 down to 2,423,000 men—approximately that of the United States.

This reduction was part of a basic shift in Soviet military emphasis from that of a mass land army, which had outnumbered strategic air and naval forces, to reliance on missiles. Malinovsky outlined this new policy before the Twenty-first Congress of the Communist party in February 1959.

"The imperialists . . . threaten us with the power of their air force and navy," he said. "To this we can reply that these are now relatively obsolete means of warfare, that there is a newer and more dreadful weapon—the intercontinental ballistic missile. There is no antiaircraft device that can stop it, and it is capable of. . . delivering a hydrogen charge of colossal power to any point on earth. I emphasize the word point—it is a very accurate weapon."

As Defense Minister, Malinovsky accompanied Premier Khrushchev on a number of trips abroad—to East Germany in July 1958; to Peking, China, in August of that year; and to Albania and Hungary in May 1959. He also visited Austria in June 1959 as the guest of that country's Defense Minister.

On April 9, 1960, although the world did not know it at the time, a United States reconnaissance plane flew over the Soviet Union from Afghanistan. "Our military, to put it mildly, let a chance slip by," Premier Khrushchev said later. "And we, as one says, took them to task for it." A few days later, without any public announcement, a change was made in top military staff.

On May 1, 1960 another United States reconnaissance plane crossed over the same border and was shot down near Sverdlovsk. As Malinovsky prepared to review the annual May Day parade in Red Square, Khrushchev congratulated him on the feat. Malinovsky, however, said nothing of the incident and talked instead about the determination of the Soviet Union to settle questions which were to be considered at the approaching Summit Conference.

Wide World

MARSHAL RODION Y. MALINOVSKY

Three days later, on May 4, the Central Committee of the Communist party met in Moscow, and on May 5 the Supreme Soviet convened. Toward the end of a long speech on economic matters Premier Khrushchev, "on instructions from the Soviet Government," revealed the plane incident. At the concluding session of the Supreme Soviet on May 7, Khrushchev said the incident should not become an excuse to increase military appropriations or halt the reduction of the Army. But he revealed that the rocket forces had been organized as a separate branch of the armed services. A government decree of the same day appointed 298 new generals and admirals.

Two days later, on May 9, Malinovsky told a Moscow meeting commemorating the defeat of Germany: "Today's equipment is so improved that it unerringly shows us from what airfields violators take off, and we have a right to take any measures in such an event against the bases and airfields and can demolish these bases so that nothing is left of them." Several days later it was announced that Malinovsky and Foreign Minister Andrei A. Gromyko would accompany Premier Khrushchev to Paris for the Summit talks.

After the Paris meeting had collapsed, Malinovsky accompanied Khrushchev to meetings in Berlin, and then returned to Moscow. There, on May 30, he told a meeting in the Kremlin that he had ordered the commander of the Soviet rocket forces "to strike at any base from which a plane might fly to violate the territory of the Soviet Union or the socialist countries."

Physically, Malinovsky is a great bear of a man, who stands five feet seven inches tall, and weighs nearly 300 pounds. He has short-cropped gray hair and a bulldog face. One

MALINOVSKY, RODION Y.—*Continued*

American correspondent has called him a "cheerful extrovert, unassuming, a man of sheer physical power." An American diplomat has described him as "a slow, unreasoning, Communist party member."

Within the Soviet Union he is known as the champion of the enlisted man and the enemy of those who do everything by rote. "The first thing a commander should know is what the soldier is thinking and how he is reacting," he has said. "You must be creative and avoid standard patterns if you are to solve practical problems correctly and intelligently," he has told his young officers, "for standard patterns are the worst enemy, both in training and in battle."

Malinovsky was married in 1925 and has two sons, who, he has said, are more interested in photography than military affairs. He has been awarded five Orders of Lenin; the Order of Victory; the Order of Suvorov, first class; two Gold Star Medals; the title Hero of the Soviet Union; and many other decorations.

References

N Y Times O 27 '57 por; My 16 '60 por
Biographic Directory of the U.S.S.R. (1958)
Gunther, John Inside Russia Today (1957)
Hearst, William R., Jr., Considine, Robert, and Conniff, Frank Ask Me Anything (1960)
International Who's Who, 1959
World Biography (1954)

MALLORY, L(ESTER) D(EWITT) Apr. 21, 1904- United States government official; agricultural economist

Address: b. Department of State, Washington, 25, D.C.; h. 1618 44th St., N.W., Washington 7, D.C.

During his good-will visit to South America in early 1960, President Eisenhower clarified United States foreign policy in this area and reaffirmed his government's aim "to help in any way it soundly can" in solving Latin-American economic problems. The task of translating this goal into a program is the responsibility of L. D. Mallory, Deputy Assistant Secretary of State for Inter-American Affairs.

With an unusual combination of training and experience as an agricultural economist and a career diplomat, Mallory served in the Department of Agriculture's foreign service before it became part of the Department of State in 1939. Since that time his overseas assignments have included posts in Mexico City, Paris, Havana, and Buenos Aires. Later, as United States Ambassador to Jordan from 1953 to 1957, he represented his government during the Jordanian crisis of 1957. Before assuming his present duties in 1960, he was Ambassador to Guatemala for over a year and a half.

In appraising the course which his professional life has taken, Mallory wrote: "The point of interest I find in the career that has developed is the considerable role of coincidence. A number of changes in direction happened which at the time appeared radical, but each had a natural reason and a worthwhile turn."

Lester DeWitt Mallory was born to Enrique and May (DeWitt) Mallory at Houlton, Maine on April 21, 1904. He grew up in Oregon and in the Canadian province of British Columbia, where his brother Donald is now a rancher. In 1922 Lester was graduated from Oak Bay High School in Victoria, British Columbia.

Although he had first intended to study medicine, Mallory majored in horticulture at the University of British Columbia in Vancouver, where he was a member of the football, rowing, and debating teams. He won an important scholarship in his junior year and received the B.S. degree in 1927. Remaining at the university as an assistant for the next two years, he studied the economics of fruit growing and conducted a survey on fruit trees. At the end of this period he had completed the requirements for an M.Sc. degree.

"Plans for academic life in pomology," Mallory stated, "were diverted into economics when studies of the fruit industry turned to business aspects." He made an analysis of the California grape industry while at the University of California in Berkeley as a research assistant from 1929 to 1931. Continuing to work in the field of agrarian economics, he wrote his doctoral dissertation on the French wheat stabilization scheme and received the Ph.D. degree from the University of California in 1935.

Because academic openings were scarce during the Depression, Mallory joined the United States Agriculture Department's foreign service in 1931. Assigned to the post of assistant agricultural commissioner at Marseilles, France, Mallory was chiefly concerned with meeting competition and increasing demand for American farm products in the Mediterranean area. In 1933 he became an assistant agricultural economist with the Agricultural Adjustment Administration and in the following year assumed the duties of assistant agricultural attaché at the Embassy in Paris. There he was a delegate to the Annual Show of Breeding Animals of the Equine Race in 1938 and later went to Rome as an expert with the International Commission for Horticultural Statistics. Advanced to agricultural attaché at Paris in 1939, he received the French decoration Mérité Agricole.

When the Department of Agriculture's foreign service was transferred to the Department of State in 1939, Mallory was "involuntarily incorporated" into the latter. Mallory had written that "Work in the economics of competition and demand for American farm products was an odd introduction to diplomacy. However, the years abroad stood well, and subsequent assignment to countries with agricultural dominance made early experience and background useful." Sent to the American Embassy in Mexico City as agricultural attaché in 1939, Mallory was also adviser to the United States delegation to the Inter-American Agricultural Conference, held in Mexico City in 1942, and a member of the Mexican-United States Agricultural Commission (1943-44).

In the next few years Mallory served successively as agricultural attaché in Paris (1944-45), agricultural liaison officer at the Department in Washington, D.C. (1945-47), counselor at the Embassy in Havana, Cuba (1947-49), and counselor at the Embassy in Buenos Aires, Argentina (1949-53). In August 1950 he attained the personal rank of Minister.

Appointed by President Eisenhower in July 1953, Mallory succeeded Joseph C. Green as Ambassador Extraordinary and Plenipotentiary to the Hashemite Kingdom of Jordan. In July 1955 he was advanced to the grade of Career Minister. During the time that Mallory served in Jordan, world attention was focused on that Middle Eastern country because of its unstable condition, its strategic importance, and the decay of British power in the area. Yielding to extreme nationalists in his country, in March 1957 King Hussein I of Jordan formally abrogated the Anglo-Jordanian defense and aid treaty of 1948, thereby sacrificing an annual subsidy of $30,000,000.

In early 1957 Hussein began to indicate an interest in replacing British help with assistance provided by the Eisenhower Middle East Doctrine. After his pro-Nasser Premier Suleiman Nabulsi denounced the doctrine, Hussein dismissed him on April 10. This led to a crisis which threatened to topple the throne. Meanwhile, it was reported that Egyptian and Syrian troops might intervene, and it was made clear by Israel that any interference by foreign troops would be viewed with concern.

Following a conference between Hussein and Ambassador Mallory, the United States attempted to strengthen the King's position by moving units of the Sixth Fleet from the western to the eastern Mediterranean. On April 24 the White House called the "independence and integrity" of Jordan "vital to the national interests of the United States." In the following weeks the Eisenhower administration announced that it would grant the Jordanian government $30,000,000, which, Mallory explained, would "assist in the economic development and political stability in Jordan." In March 1956 Mallory had also created much good will in Jordan by the gift of a 4,000-volume library.

Mallory's next diplomatic mission was to Central America, where he succeeded Edward J. Sparks as Ambassador to Guatemala in February 1958. Within two years, on October 28, 1959, Mallory resigned the Guatemalan post to accept an appointment as Deputy Assistant Secretary of State for Inter-American Affairs beginning in early 1960. In this capacity he shares with the Assistant Secretary of State for Inter-American Affairs, R. R. Rubottom, Jr., the responsibility for the operations of the bureau of Inter-American affairs, with its six subdivisional offices.

Dept. of State—Whit Keith, Jr.

L. D. MALLORY

One of these, the office of Inter-American regional political affairs, co-ordinates United States policies in regard to the Inter-American system and with respect to United Nations affairs affecting Latin America. Another subdivision, the office of Inter-American regional economic affairs, co-operates with the International Cooperation Administration and co-ordinates United States policies in Latin America concerning technical and financial assistance.

Lester DeWitt Mallory and Eleanor Mercedes Struck y Bulnes were married on February 21, 1946. They are the parents of a son, Lester DeWitt, Jr. The blue-eyed, white-haired diplomat stands at five feet eleven inches and weighs about 180 pounds. His favorite recreations are hunting, fishing, and woodworking.

In summing up his unusual career, he wrote: "One thing easily leads into another and understandings gained in one sphere help in another. I grew up with some appreciation of the American Indian. This feeling for another mode of thought helped much in adjusting to facets of Latin America and subsequently going back to one of the mainsprings of Spanish origins and motivations among the Arabs. . . . I have been grateful for the background I did have and the coincidences as they developed. I have a mild curiosity as to just what the next aberration may hold—hopefully among a rustic, primitive society with deep archeological roots to be explored."

References

American Men in Government (1949)
American Men of Science (1949)
Department of State Biographic Register, 1959
International Who's Who, 1959
Who's Who in America, 1960-61
Who's Who in Egypt and the Near East, 1957-58

MARCUS, JACOB R(ADER) Mar. 5, 1896-
College professor

Address: b. Hebrew Union College, Clifton
Ave., Cincinnati 20, Ohio; h. 401 McAlpin
Ave., Cincinnati 20, Ohio

In Jacob R. Marcus, the founder and director of American Jewish Archives in Cincinnati, devotion to Judaism and love of America combined to make him a pioneer in the challenging new field of American Jewish history. He is also Adolph S. Ochs Professor of American Jewish History at Hebrew Union College-Jewish Institute of Religion in Cincinnati and former president of the Central Conference of American Rabbis. The president of Hebrew Union College, Nelson Glueck, has described Jacob Marcus as the man who "more than anyone else, has established the study of American

JACOB R. MARCUS

Jewish history on a scientific basis and has caused the principal resources for that study to be assembled in one place."

The second of four children of Aaron and Jennie (Rader) Marcus, Jacob Rader Marcus was born in Connellsville, Pennsylvania, on March 5, 1896. His father was a Lithuanian immigrant who had peddled notions, tinware, and clothing before settling down as a merchant, first in Homestead, Pennsylvania and later in Pittsburgh, Pennsylvania and Wheeling, West Virginia. Raised in these states, Jacob Marcus sold newspapers and helped in his father's various stores (and somehow found time to read numerous historical novels), while simultaneously attending public school and cheder (Jewish religious school).

At the age of fifteen, Marcus went to Cincinnati to begin rabbinical training at Hebrew Union College. Continuing his double-school program, he attended Woodward High School and later Hughes High School in the morning

and took classes at Hebrew Union College in the afternoon. He spent some of his free time swimming and hiking. Upon graduation from high school in 1913 he matriculated at the University of Cincinnati and, in 1914, also took courses in church history at Lane Theological Seminary, Cincinnati. He spent one of his summer vacations at the University of Chicago Divinity School waiting on tables and studying Egyptian history. At Hebrew Union College he served as editor of the student literary magazine.

On April 30, 1917, although exempt from the draft as a theological student, Marcus volunteered as a private in the United States Army. He fought for ten months in France with the AEF and was discharged in May 1919, with the rank of second lieutenant. He had received his A.B. degree in European history from the University of Cincinnati in 1917, just after joining the Army.

Ordained a rabbi in 1920, Marcus began his teaching career as instructor in Bible and rabbinics at Hebrew Union College. In 1921 he taught his first courses in Jewish history. The following year, because he felt the need for further background in the field, Marcus went to the University of Berlin in Germany to continue his studies. Since university authorities there would not accept a doctoral dissertation on a Jewish subject, Marcus wrote his thesis on mercantile relations between England and Germany.

After he had received his Ph.D. degree in 1925, Marcus did additional postgraduate work at École Rabbinique in Paris in 1925 and at the University of Jerusalem in 1926, returning to Hebrew Union College in 1926 as assistant professor of Jewish history. He became associate professor in 1929 and full professor in 1934. In 1946 he was named Adolph S. Ochs Professor of Jewish History and in 1959 he became Adolph S. Ochs Professor of American Jewish History when the name of his chair was changed.

Throughout his extensive writings Marcus has tried to be an objective scholar with "no special angles as a Jew writing history." His first major work, *Israel Jacobson* (published in the *Central Conference of American Rabbis Yearbook,* 1928), was a study of the founder of the German Reform movement. In Marcus' opinion, it is among his best books.

Six years later he published *The Rise and Destiny of the German Jew* (Union of American Hebrew Congregations, 1934), which George N. Shuster, writing in the New York *Times* (January 13, 1935), called a "scholarly, factual, but nevertheless impassioned book." He also praised its objectivity, but found it "not a very skillfully organized treatise." Though sound on facts, the volume was not so sound on prophecy, for in it Marcus had written of the Jews of Germany that "wholesale expulsion or massacre . . . seem rather remote."

His next major work was *The Jew in the Medieval World; a Source Book: 315-1791* (Union of American Hebrew Congregations, 1938), which W. E. Garrison (*Christian Century*) described as "neither a defense of the

Jew nor an attack upon his persecutors, but a superbly edited body of source materials for a history of the Jews within the limits assigned."

Although trained in European Jewish history, Marcus had been veering toward American Jewish history since almost the beginning of his career. Throughout the 1930's he placed more and more emphasis on American Jewry in his courses on general Jewish history, awarding prizes for themes and approving subjects for dissertations in that field. He traveled to libraries and historical societies in every state of the union to track down source materials in American Jewish history and, as early as 1934, became a member of the American Jewish Historical Society. In 1942, sensing the growing importance of American Jewish history, he taught the first required course in the subject ever given, and the following year he drew up *A Brief Bibliography of American Jewish History* (published in *Jewish Book Annual*, 1943-44).

In the early 1940's Marcus helped to start a collection of American Jewish historical materials at the Hebrew Union College Library, and in 1947 one of his great dreams materialized when the American Jewish Archives was established as a separate institution, with its own building and staff and with Marcus himself as director. In the period since its founding, the Archives has become a major research center for the study of American Jewish history. It houses huge collections of the minutes of Jewish congregations and various Jewish societies, letters and papers of prominent merchants and rabbis, and such fascinating side lights on history as the diary of a Jewish cavalry scout who fought the Sioux on the Western frontier.

The Archives publishes a semiannual journal, *American Jewish Archives,* which Marcus has edited since its inception in 1948. In 1956 it established the American Jewish Periodical Center, of which Marcus is director, to microfilm every Jewish periodical published in America from 1823 to 1925 and a sampling of those published at a later date. The growth of the archives, according to Nelson Glueck, is due primarily to Marcus: "The able leadership which he has supplied has turned the Archives from a bare idea into a living reality."

Marcus' first book in the field of American Jewish history was the two-volume study, *Early American Jewry* (Jewish Publication Society of America, volume 1, 1951; volume 2, 1953). This was followed by *Memoirs of American Jews, 1775-1865* (Jewish Publication Society of America, 1955), a three-volume collection of autobiographical materials. He has assisted in the research underlying virtually every volume on American Jewish history published since the establishment of the Archives. He prepared the handbook, *How to Write the History of an American Jewish Community* (American Jewish Archives, 1953), to encourage amateurs to enter his field. He has toured the Caribbean area and South America in search of source materials and, in the summer of 1952, led an expedition of scholars to retrace the route of the first Jewish settlers of the United States.

Dr. Marcus has also written *A Brief Introduction to the Bibliography of Modern Jewish History* (Hebrew Union College, 1935), *An Index to Jewish Festschriften* (with A. T. Bilgray, Hebrew Union College, 1937), *Communal Sick-Care in the German Ghetto* (Hebrew Union College, 1947), and *American Jewry: Documents; Eighteenth Century* (Hebrew Union College, 1958). He contributed the article on Jews to the *Encyclopædia Britannica* and has written numerous articles for Jewish and scholarly periodicals. His complete bibliography numbers well over 150 items.

In 1949 Marcus was elected president of the Central Conference of American Rabbis, the Reform rabbinical association, of which he is also chairman of the committee on contemporaneous history and literature. He is honorary president of the American Jewish Historical Society, vice-president of the Jewish Publication Society, and a member of the executive committee of the American Academy for Jewish Research. He serves on the board of trustees of the training bureau for Jewish Communal Service and was appointed in 1951 to the special committee on reassessment of the National Community Relations Advisory Council. He belongs to the Jewish Academy of Arts and B'nai B'rith.

Dr. Marcus was awarded an honorary LL.D. degree by the University of Cincinnati in 1950 and by Dropsie College in 1955, when he also received the Frank L. Weil Award of the National Jewish Welfare Board for his contribution to American Jewish culture. In 1955 Phi Epsilon Pi gave him its national service award, previously won by Bernard M. Baruch and Albert Einstein. In 1959 *Essays in American Jewish History,* a jubilee volume marking the tenth anniversary of the founding of the Archives (but appearing a year later) was published in his honor.

Marcus was married to Antoinette Brody, a musician, in Paris on December 31, 1925. (His doctoral dissertation, published that year, was dedicated to "Pretty Nettie Brody.") Their only child, Merle Judith, was born in 1929. Mrs. Marcus died in 1953. The gray-haired, brown-eyed scholar is five feet eleven inches tall and weighs 175 pounds. He is an independent in politics.

Summarizing his principles as an historian, Dr. Marcus said in 1957: "One must fanatically detest falsehood; one must search his soul every time he writes a sentence. The fact scrubbed clean is more eternal than perfumed and rouged words. The historian's desk is an altar on which he must sacrifice his most cherished prejudices. One must be dedicated to the truth."

References

Essays in American Jewish History (1959)
Who's Who in America, 1960-61
Who's Who in World Jewry (1955)

MARPLES, (ALFRED) ERNEST Dec. 9, 1907- British Minister of Transport
Address: b. House of Commons, Westminster, London S.W. 1, England; h. 33 Eccleston St., London S.W. 1, England

The most publicized member of British Prime Minister Macmillan's cabinet, Ernest Marples, Minister of Transport, represents the breakthrough of the self-made businessman into the highest circles of the traditionally aristocratic Conservative party. Delaying his entry into politics until he had made a fortune in apartment building, he was one of the few Conservatives to win a Commons seat in the elections of 1945, and has represented the Wallasey Division of Cheshire in Parliament since that date. He held various noncabinet posts, including that of Postmaster General, before his appointment as Minister of Transport in October 1959.

The only child of working-class parents, Alfred Ernest Marples was born on December 9, 1907. His father, the late Alfred Ernest Marples, Sr., was an engineer-foreman in the turbine shop of the British Westinghouse plant in Trafford Park, Manchester, and a trade union leader. His mother, the late Mary Marples, used to put bands around bowler hats in a factory in the Manchester suburb of Stockport. Ernest Marples was brought up in the poverty-stricken back streets of Manchester, moving with his family from the Hazelgrove section of the city to the sections of Levenshulme and Stretford successively.

Marples was educated at Victoria Park Council School, Manchester. One of his teachers, John Corlett, later Labour member of Parliament, urged him to obtain a scholarship to what is now Stretford Grammar School. It was in behalf of Corlett that Marples in 1923,

British Inf. Services
ERNEST MARPLES

at the age of fifteen, made his first experiment in politics, campaigning on the Labour side with great energy.

During a summer vacation Marples took his first job, with a firm of ship brokers in the Manchester Guardian Building on Cross Street in Manchester. As a young man he also sold cigarettes at football games. He quit school to take a full-time job with a firm of accountants, where he audited the books of bankrupt firms. The experience, Marples says, "taught me how not to run a business."

In 1928 he qualified as a chartered accountant and that same year, at the age of twenty-one, went to London to seek his fortune. He soon abandoned accounting and, with money saved from his first London job and twenty borrowed pounds, began converting Victorian houses into flats. He became so successful in the real estate and building business that he could have retired after ten years. His firm, before and after the war, built new apartments, docks, wharves, and power stations (including the Poplar power station and the Skelton Grange station at Leeds).

Just before the outbreak of World War II, in 1939, Marples joined the famous London Scottish regiment of the Territorial Army as a private. Within the year he became a sergeant major. In January 1941 he received the commission of second lieutenant in the Royal Artillery, was shortly thereafter made a captain, and served with the Royal Artillery until he was injured and invalided out of the Army in 1944.

Marples, who had sworn not to enter politics until he was financially independent ("so I should not be tempted to take a post or make a speech because my job depended on it"), ran for Parliament in 1945 and was one of the few Conservative candidates to emerge victorious in the Labour landslide of that year. In Commons, where he assumed the Wallasey seat, building and housing were among his main interests, and he became secretary of the Conservative Housing Committee.

For the big debate on housing in Parliament in the fall of 1950, Winston Churchill called on Marples to represent the Conservatives against the formidable Aneurin Bevan. Marples' success on that occasion brought him political standing overnight. When the Conservatives came back to power in 1951, with Churchill as Prime Minister and Macmillan as Housing Minister, Marples was selected to assist the latter in fulfilling the heroic Conservative campaign pledge to build 300,000 houses within one year.

Marples held the office of Parliamentary Secretary to the Ministry of Housing and Local Government from 1951 until 1954, when he became Joint Parliamentary Secretary to the Ministry of Pensions and National Insurance. He resigned from the latter post in December 1955, eight months after Churchill had retired and had been succeeded by Sir Anthony Eden, who apparently disapproved of him.

After a year on the back benches under Eden, Marples was called up front again when his old chief, Macmillan, became Prime Minister. Named Privy Councillor and successor to Dr. Charles Hill as Postmaster General in January 1957, he attacked Britain's telephone, telegraph, and mail problems with his usual decisiveness and *élan*. With news photographers following, he walked the rounds with letter carriers, helped sort letters, traveled on all-night mail trains, worked a switchboard. Criticized by many as a publicity seeker, he was credited by others with rooting out and solving long-festering telephone and postal problems "almost singlehanded" and with being "the best Postmaster General in years" (London *Observer*, January 3, 1960).

When Marples moved into the cabinet on October 14, 1959, replacing Harold Watkinson as Minister of Transport, he was described by Don Cook in the New York *Herald Tribune* (November 12, 1959) as the "new Beau Geste" of "Britain's 'most fired upon' government department." Knowing little about transport, he read every book about modern traffic published in English, inspected bridges and motorways in Germany, examined the control of traffic flow in Paris, and in January 1960 spent thirteen days in the United States, collecting ideas on traffic.

As Minister of Transport, Marples has approached his problems with the boldness, exuberance, and flair for publicity which observers had come to expect of him. His daring introduction of a "no parking" solution for London's "traffic thrombosis" in early December of 1959 shocked British motorists, but thousands of holiday shoppers and other pedestrians warmly praised the result, and the temporary program for the easing of Christmas traffic was retained when the holidays were over. Marples was on his way in a sweeping program to prevent the automobile from driving "the amenities into oblivion" in Britain.

Although Marples sees many innovations necessary, such as the marking of traffic lanes, more-legible road signs, one-way streets, gearing of traffic lights to rush-hour traffic, and abolition of right-hand turns, he knows that the over-all remedy for British traffic problems is an efficient method of enforcement. In the debate in Commons in December 1959, he said he needed supreme control of traffic in the central area of London for two years. Commons supported him with a 301 to 232 vote, and by late December he was taking measures to gain more direct control over traffic police and to build vast garages under Hyde Park, increase traffic fines, and rebuild roads. The Butler-Marples traffic bill, slated for Parliamentary vote in 1960, provided for traffic wardens and rigid ticket fines.

Other plans included improving the state-owned railway system, by electrifying some routes and dieselizing others. Also concerned with British shipping, in early 1960 Marples began discussing with United States shipping officials the problems created for Britain by some of the maritime policies of the United States, chiefly the Cargo Preference Act, which requires that 50 per cent of all cargoes sponsored by the United States government and destined for foreign ports be carried in American ships.

In *The Road to Prosperity* (Staples Press, 1947), Marples argues that the co-partnership of capital and labor is the industrial policy most consonant with the progressive Conservative preference for diffused power and individual initiative. The book was prompted by his desire to dispel the temptation of Conservatives to turn Socialist after their overwhelming defeat in the elections of 1945.

Marples resigned as chairman of Marples, Ridgway and Partners, the civil engineering firm which he founded, when he became a junior minister in 1951. In January 1960 he announced that he was selling his shares in the firm to avoid conflict of interest.

Of average size and compact build, with neat wavy hair, Marples is a high-powered and athletic type, fitting squash and tennis into a schedule that is an efficiency expert's dream. He is an excellent skier and mountain climber, has wrestled judo style and played football (as wing-half for Dulwich Hamlet, one of Britain's leading amateur teams). As indoor hobbies he enjoys cooking and gadgetry. He is quick-witted and has a talent for comedy. His heroes are said to be Marcus Aurelius and Lord Nelson; and his favorite authors, Gibbon, Wordsworth, and Lamb.

On July 7, 1956 Marples, who himself had been married previously, was married to Mrs. Ruth Dobson. He and his wife have twin green, eight-speed bicycles, and they often cycle on the Continent together during holidays, especially in France, where he hunts out the casks of wine he later bottles himself in his cellar. He reportedly has drawers filled with maps showing in detail almost every spot of earth where grapes are grown and pressed.

References

London Observer p9 Ja 3 '60 por
N Y Times p2 Ja 1 '60 por
Time 58:31 O 22 '51 por; 75:23 Ja 4 '60 por
International Who's Who, 1959
International Year Book and Statesmen's Who's Who, 1959
Who's Who, 1959

MARQUAND, J(OHN) P(HILLIPS) Nov. 10, 1893-July 16, 1960 American novelist of manners; *The Late George Apley,* a satirical study of a Boston Brahmin, won the Pulitzer Prize in 1938; other novels include *Wickford Point* (1939); *Point of No Return* (1949); *Melville Goodwin, U.S.A.* (1951); and *Sincerely, Willis Wayde* (1955). See *Current Biography* (April) 1942.

Obituary

N Y Times p1+ Jl 17 '60

MARSH, ERNEST STERLING Jan. 10, 1903- Railroad executive

Address: b. Atchison, Topeka and Santa Fe Railway System, 80 E. Jackson Blvd., Chicago 4, Ill.; h. 233 E. Walton Pl., Chicago, Ill.

An opponent of government subsidies for any form of transportation, including railroads, Ernest Sterling Marsh has been president of the Atchison, Topeka and Santa Fe Railway since 1957 and chairman of its executive committee since May 1959. As president, he heads the longest railroad in the nation, with over 13,000 miles of track and with the fourth highest operating revenue.

In the service of Santa Fe for over four decades, Marsh specialized in the financial affairs of the carrier. He became executive assistant to Fred G. Gurley, his predecessor

Santa Fe Railway
ERNEST STERLING MARSH

as president, in 1945 and vice-president for finance in 1948. "Modernization and improvement on the Santa Fe is the keynote in our dedication to service to the customer," Marsh has said. "And the people of the Santa Fe continue to be the important element in performing that service."

A native of Lynchburg, Virginia, Ernest Sterling Marsh was born to John Sterling and Hattie (Leftwich) Marsh on January 10, 1903. When he was a fifteen-year-old student at Clovis (New Mexico) High School, he became a file clerk in April 1918 in the Atchison, Topeka and Santa Fe Railway division offices in Clovis. He had taken the job on a temporary basis in order to save enough money to complete his education. Instead of returning to school, however, March remained with Santa Fe, having decided that he had the abilities required for a career in railroading. By

August 1918 he had been promoted to assistant timekeeper and two years later to chief timekeeper.

When his job was abolished during the depression Marsh was confronted with the alternative of taking another position in the operating department or entering the financial branch of the company; he chose the latter. He then served in a succession of accounting positions: assistant divisional accountant at Clovis (1926-32), department head in the division accounts bureau in Amarillo, Texas (1932-37) and auditor of disbursements in Topeka, Kansas (1940-42).

Transferred to Chicago in 1942, Marsh was appointed chief clerk in the office of Edward J. Engel, president of Santa Fe. His ability was soon recognized. He was advanced in 1944 to assistant to Engel and in the following year to executive assistant to Fred G. Gurley, who had meanwhile succeeded Engel.

Chartered in 1859 to link Topeka, Kansas with the Missouri River and subsequently with Santa Fe in New Mexico, the Atchison, Topeka and Santa Fe Railway became in the course of the next eighty years the operator, through ownership or lease, of a huge system. It extended eastward to Chicago, westward to Los Angeles and San Francisco, northward to Denver and southward to El Paso, Laredo, and Galveston in Texas.

In the decade that followed World War II Gurley expended some $532,000,000 for capital improvements. At the same time the road continued to pay dividends. In 1954, through a gross of $532,000,000 and net of $66,000,000, it was able to pay off the last of its equipment debts. This was made possible to a considerable degree by Ernest Sterling Marsh, who had been elected vice-president for finance in 1948.

After having been president for fourteen years, on May 1, 1957 Fred G. Gurley became chairman of the board. Marsh succeeded him as president. Gurley continued to head the system with the new title of chief executive officer, but Marsh took over the responsibility of operating it.

During the first year that Marsh was president, freight tonnage had fallen off. In explaining the decline, Marsh stated at the end of 1957 that live-stock loadings had been reduced because herds had been depleted in drought areas, and that grain yields were low because heavy rains had fallen during an unfavorable time in the growing period. He also claimed that, considering the prevailing inflation, the rate structure is unrealistic.

The company has also been losing ground in passenger service. Marsh has, however, expressed "great confidence in the future of rail passenger business—especially coach business. . . . The airlines have speed in their favor. . . . However, there are many people, too, who are interested in enjoying a comfortable trip and seeing the townspeople and scenery along the way."

Although the Santa Fe's operating revenues for 1957 were higher than for 1956, the railway's net income fell from $70,213,171 to $61,941,791. In January 1958 revenues were

7.4 per cent lower and earnings off by as much as 57.6 per cent. Other Western railroads were experiencing similar reverses, although in somewhat less degree. Passenger service was being curtailed or abandoned almost everywhere, especially on feeder lines.

To explore the financial difficulties of the nation's railroad industry, the United States Senate Interstate and Foreign Commerce surface transportation subcommittee, headed by George A. Smathers, conducted a series of hearings from January to April 1958. Testifying before this subcommittee, Marsh attacked the principle of subsidies, particularly to the airlines. "I don't believe," he said, "in subsidies for anyone. Transportation is a business in this country, and I don't think the general taxpayer should be required to pay a part of the cost of any transportation business." If the airlines had to earn operating costs and profits from their passengers, he feels, a fare differential favoring the railroads would come into existence.

As a result of the surface transportation subcommittee's investigation, the Transportation Act of 1958 was enacted. It provided relief to railroads by making it easier for them to acquire loans, increase their rates, and abandon certain lines. Another law, the Excise Tax Technical Changes Act of 1958, repealed the 3 per cent tax on freight shipment.

On May 1, 1958 chairman Gurley yielded the post of chief executive officer to Marsh. When Gurley retired as chairman of the board early in 1959, the board of directors of the Santa Fe elected Marsh to succeed him as chairman of the executive committee. They also voted to leave the post of chairman of the board vacant. Improvements introduced under Marsh's leadership in 1958 included the reduction of transit time for Santa Fe freight trains between Chicago and San Francisco Bay, the opening of an electronic-freight-classification yard in Chicago, the acceleration of freight shipments from the southwest to Chicago, and the ordering of 600 piggyback freight cars. In July 1959 the company reported a 17 per cent gain in operating revenue for the first half of 1959 and a 43 per cent increase in the income.

A director of the Santa Fe and its affiliates since April 1956, Ernest Sterling Marsh is also a director of the Harris Trust & Savings Bank in Chicago, Association of American Railroads, and Illinois Chamber of Commerce. He is on the executive committee of the Association of Western Railways, and a member of the National Industrial Conference Board, Traffic Club of New York, Newcomen Society, Illinois Society of Sons of the American Revolution, and Defense Orientation Conference Association. He is a Republican and a Methodist.

Mrs. Marsh is the former Agnes LaLonde. Married since January 14, 1922, the Marshes have three daughters, Neva Jo, Peggy Anne (Mrs. Thomas E. Lambert), and Colleen (Mrs. John T. McCarthy); two sons, Jack and Larry; and several grandchildren. Robert E. Bedingfield (New York *Times*, March 29, 1959) has described Marsh as "a big man" with a "ruddy complexion and a rather heavy step," somewhat "intense and yet soft-spoken, choosing his words with obvious care and deliberation." In 1953, when he took courses in the advanced management program at the Harvard Graduate School of Business Administration, he was selected by the other students as chairman of the group. In past years, when his responsibilities were not so great, Marsh was a bowler who scored 300, a billiard player, and a golfer; he also enjoyed collecting toy trains. More recently, however, he has given up all hobbies because of the demands of his work, except that he finds time occasionally to attend the theater.

References

> Chicago American p21 F 9 '59 por
> Christian Sci Mon p15 N 5 '57 por
> N Y Times p61 My 1 '57 por
>
> Business Executives of America (1950)
> Poor's Register of Directors and Executives, 1959
> Who's Who in America, 1958-59
>   America (1959)
> Who's Who in Railroading in North

MARSH, JOHN, REV. DR. Nov. 5, 1904-
Educator; theologian; clergyman
Address: Principal's Lodgings, Mansfield College, Oxford University, Oxford, England

Principal since 1953 of Mansfield College, the Congregationalist college at Oxford University, the Reverend Dr. John Marsh has distinguished himself internationally and interdenominationally by his work with the World Council of Churches and by his writing and editing of books about the Bible, worship, and church order.

John Marsh was born in Brighton, Sussex, England on November 5, 1904, to George Maurice and Florence Elizabeth Ann Marsh. His father was a postman and his mother managed a shop. An older brother, George, died in infancy. A sister, Eva, now resides in Canada. Reared in East Grinstead, Sussex, Marsh received his secondary education at Skinners' Company School, Tunbridge Wells, Kent.

Although he began his career as a pharmacist, Marsh's choice of studies after secondary school early indicated the direction his career would take. He studied philosophy at Edinburgh University in Scotland, taking his degree with first class honors in 1928. At Edinburgh he also won several scholarships and prizes, including the John Baxter Scholarship and the Class Medal in philosophy, psychology, and moral philosophy. He was an assistant to Professor A. G. Taylor at the university from 1926 to 1928. To the M.A. degree he earned at Edinburgh, the university added an honorary doctorate in divinity in 1955.

Marsh continued his studies at Oxford University, as a member of Mansfield College, then a nonresidential foundation independent of university jurisdiction, and also as a member of St. Catherine's Society. (Membership in the latter society permits students who are not members

Stone Studio

REV. DR. JOHN MARSH

of a university college to be admitted to the university.) At Oxford he won the Mill Hill Prize (1928) and the Procter Scholarship (1931), among others, and earned the M.A. and Ph.D. degrees, the latter in 1946. He also studied at Yorkshire United College in Bradford, England.

The Reverend John Marsh embarked upon his life's work as a Biblical lecturer and Sunday-school teacher at Westhill Training College, Birmingham in 1932. Two years later he left Westhill to become pastor of the Congregational Church in Otley, Yorkshire.

Back at Oxford in 1938, he became chaplain of Mansfield College, where he took part in one of the most valuable contributions of Oxford University to British education—tutoring. As a tutor he recommended to his charges courses of reading and lectures to attend and conferred with them weekly. In 1944 he became a lecturer at Mansfield College and in 1947 a professor. He went to the University of Nottingham in 1949 to become its first professor of Christian theology.

Marsh again returned to Oxford in 1953, this time as principal of Mansfield College. Mansfield was founded by the Congregationalists in the 1880's to take the place of Spring Hill College, Birmingham. When Marsh was a student there the college was a nonresidential hall for postgraduate students of theology only. In 1946 it became residential and began admitting undergraduates pursuing subjects other than philosophy and theology. Graduate students must still be in the latter fields, since the college is primarily for the training of "dissident" ministers, chiefly Congregational. In 1955 the college was given the status of "permanent private hall" by the university.

His job at Mansfield College has not prevented Marsh from keeping in active contact with schools and institutions other than Oxford.

In 1953 he became governor of William Temple College, an adult education school in Rugby, England, and he is still vice-president of the Friends of William Temple College. He has been a visiting lecturer at such institutions as Union Theological Seminary, New York City (1956).

Since the founding of the World Council of Churches Marsh has been deeply engaged in its activities. He was a delegate to the council's first assembly, held in Amsterdam, the Netherlands from August 22 to September 4, 1948. He took part in a World Council symposium on Biblical authority for the churches' social and political message today, published by Westminster Press as *Biblical Authority for Today* (1951) and edited by Alan Richardson and W. Schweitzer. His essay "Congregational Worship" appeared in *Ways of Worship* (Harper, 1951), the report of a World Council faith and order commission edited by Pehr Edwall and others.

The World Council of Churches called a World Conference on Faith and Order in Lund, Sweden in 1952, with the purpose of attempting to overcome the differences in doctrine and church order among the churches. The conference appointed a continuation committee, with John Marsh as secretary of the latter's theological commission on intercommunion. Marsh, with Donald Macpherson Baillie, edited the commission's report, *Intercommunion* (Harper, 1952).

In 1953 Marsh became a member of the working committee of the World Council's faith and order department. He was a delegate to the World Council's second assembly in Evanston, Illinois, in 1954, and wrote *The Significance of Evanston* (Independent Press, 1954), a small paper-bound book. In 1955 he became a member of the World Council's European commission on Christ and the church.

Marsh's literary output has not been confined to the books he has written for the World Council. In July 1942 he took part in a conference of Congregational ministers, including the Reverend Dr. Hubert Cunliffe-Jones, at Wadham College, Oxford; he later edited the proceedings in a volume called *Congregationalism To-day* (Independent Press, 1943). One of the contributions was his own "Obedience to the Gospel in Terms of Churchmanship and Church Order."

With William John F. Huxtable and others, he compiled *A Book of Public Worship* (Oxford University Press, 1948) for the use of Congregationalists. From the German he has translated Ethelbert Stauffer's *New Testament Theology* (Macmillan, 1955) and he has written an introduction and commentary to *Amos and Micah* (1959) for the Torch Bible Commentaries series of the Student Christian Movement Press. Among his other books are *The Living God* (1943), published by the Independent Press in its Forward Books series; *The Fulness of Time* (Harper, 1952), a Christian interpretation of history; and *A Year with the Bible* (Harper, 1957).

Interested in broadcasting, Marsh became chairman of section two of the British Council of Churches' commission on broadcasting in

1949; a member of the central religious advisory committee to the BBC in 1955; and a member of the religious advisory panel to the Independent Television Authority, also in 1955.

John Marsh was married to Gladys Walker, a teacher, on September 3, 1934. They have three children, John, George, and Mary. The theologian is five feet ten and one-half inches tall, weighs 180 pounds, and has blue eyes and brown hair. He has been described as pleasant in manner, confident but not overly aggressive, with a lively sense of humor. He likes to read or go to the theater when he is in a sedentary mood. Fishing, walking, rowing, and the coaching of rowing take up his time when he feels more athletically inclined.

References

Congregational Year Book (1955)
Who's Who, 1959

Angus McBean

LOIS MARSHALL

MARSHALL, LOIS 1924- Singer

Address: b. c/o Columbia Artists Management, Inc., 113 W. 57th St., New York 19

After overcoming serious physical handicaps caused by a childhood attack of polio, the Canadian soprano Lois Marshall has gone on to win distinction for her solo recitals and operatic and oratorio performances. Miss Marshall, whose voice ranges from mezzo-soprano to coloratura, is a favorite in her native country and has met great success in the United States and Europe. Among her admirers have been such celebrated conductors as Sir Thomas Beecham and the late Arturo Toscanini.

Born in Toronto, Ontario in 1924, Lois Marshall was one of the seven children of David and Florence Marshall. Her father, of Irish-Scottish descent, was a sales clerk in a Toronto store. At the age of two and a half, Lois Marshall suffered an attack of paralytic polio which made it impossible for her to attend school until she was eight. During these years of convalescence, she found satisfaction in listening to the operatic and symphonic recordings collected by a musically inclined older brother.

Lois Marshall's earliest educational training outside her home took place at the Wellesley School in Toronto. At the age of fourteen, she was admitted to Toronto's Royal Conservatory of Music because her vocal abilities were already evident. There she received voice instruction from Weldon Kilburn, who is still her accompanist and coach, and also studied the interpretation of lieder with Emmy Heim, a Viennese *emigrée*. She gave her first public recital when she was fifteen.

During World War II Miss Marshall not only sang at military camps but also held a position in a church and appeared in oratorio performances. In 1947 she was engaged by Sir Ernest MacMillan to sing the soprano solo parts of Bach's *St. Matthew Passion* and Handel's *Messiah* with the Toronto Mendelssohn Choir and the Toronto Symphony Orchestra, an orchestra with which she has continued to make frequent appearances. Other Canadian engagements of this period included performances with orchestras in Winnipeg, Vancouver, Victoria, and Kitchener.

In 1950 Miss Marshall won the Eaton Graduate Award of $1,000 and the Singing Stars of Tomorrow Grand Prize. In that year, at her Toronto debut recital and during the concert tour of Canada that followed, critics commented on her engaging stage presence and impeccable technique. As a Canadian representative for the Sesquicentennial Celebration, she sang with the National Symphony Orchestra in Washington, D.C.

A winner of the Naumburg Musical Foundation Award in 1952, Miss Marshall made her New York bow at Town Hall on December 2, 1952 under the auspices of the foundation. She presented a diversified program including Schubert's difficult *Dem Unendlichen* and Samuel Barber's *Three Songs to Poems of James Joyce.* Impressed by her musicianship and technical control, critic Peggy Glanville-Hicks wrote that Lois Marshall is "a new young singer who has to be heard to be believed" (New York *Herald Tribune,* December 3, 1952).

Arturo Toscanini was the conductor when Lois Marshall sang the solo soprano music of Beethoven's *Missa Solemnis* with the NBC Symphony Orchestra and the Robert Shaw Chorale at Carnegie Hall in the spring of 1953. The noted conductor is reported to have murmured *"Brava"* and later *"Bravissima"* during Miss Marshall's tryout for this assignment, and his enthusiasm was later echoed in the reviews of the concert. Performing with Jerome Hines, Eugene Conley, and Nan Merriman, Miss Marshall, with the highest range, could be heard above the massed ensemble. "Her florid passages had a liquid sound and her phrasing a natural warmth that her colleagues, for all their greater experience, never quite matched,"

MARSHALL, LOIS—*Continued*

wrote a *Time* critic (April 6, 1953). Later, Miss Marshall was among the singers who recorded the *Missa Solemnis* with Toscanini for RCA Victor.

During the 1953-54 season Miss Marshall made a concert tour of the United States. She included in her itinerary New York appearances as soloist both in a concert of Canadian music conducted by Leopold Stokowski at Carnegie Hall on October 16, 1953 and in performances of the *St. Matthew Passion* and *Messiah*, again with Sir Ernest MacMillan and the Toronto Symphony Orchestra.

In the 1955-56 season an important event took place in her career. She made her first appearance in England at the Royal Festival Hall in London with the Royal Philharmonic Orchestra under Sir Thomas Beecham in May 1956. Her artistry (especially her interpretation of Mozart's *Exsultate Jubilate*) aroused a jubilant reaction from the audience and warm responses from the critics. Under Sir Thomas' direction she recorded Mozart's opera *Die Entführung aus dem Serail* and Handel's oratorio *Solomon* for Angel Records. Before the London concert Miss Marshall was almost unknown in Europe; after it, requests for appearances flooded in from all over Great Britain and the Continent.

Remaining in England, she sang at the Harrogate Festival with the Hallé Orchestra under Sir John Barbirolli, at the National Eisteddfod of Wales, and on BBC radio and television broadcasts. She sang in Hamburg, Germany in June 1956, when her immaculate phrasing evoked superlatives from the critics.

Dividing her time between the New World and the Old, Lois Marshall presented concerts in the United States, Canada, England, and on the Continent during the 1956-57 season. In August 1957 she participated in the Edinburgh International Festival. In October 1958 Miss Marshall sang in the U.S.S.R. to reportedly wild public acclaim.

Although Lois Marshall has a great love for the operatic repertoire and has made known this feeling by recording her performances in several operas and by including operatic arias on her solo programs, the lasting effects of her bout with polio make it difficult for her to move about the stage with the ease necessary for most operatic roles. It was not until January 29, 1959 that she made her debut in a fully staged grand opera. On this occasion she sang the role of the tubercular Mimi in Puccini's *La Bohème* with the Boston Opera Company.

Lois Marshall, who is not married, continues to make her home in Toronto. As a token of the city's pride in a celebrated native daughter, Miss Marshall received on January 4, 1957 a sterling silver plate inscribed: "Presented by the City of Toronto to Lois Marshall, distinguished Toronto-born soprano, in recognition of her brilliant success in the musical centres of the world."

Brown-eyed and brown-haired Lois Marshall weighs about 135 pounds and is five feet two inches tall. Her tastes in clothing and coiffure are simple and restrained. She told Robert Sabin of *Musical America* (March 1957) of her fondness for food. "Before every concert," she said, "I must eat a steak for strength, and after it, a ham sandwich for the letdown."

Her enjoyment of music extends beyond the classical repertory; she also likes poetry and drama. Two of her favorite performers are Danny Kaye and Harry Belafonte. She is easily moved by music or literature. "I'm awfully emotional," she told interviewer Frank Rasky (*Saturday Night,* March 16, 1957). "Tears have been a bugbear all my life. I've never broken down in public. But when I'm learning a piece of music that's poignant and heartfelt, I'm so deeply affected that I feel I must escape it to weep." In a conversation with another reporter, Florence Schill (Toronto *Globe and Mail,* January 1, 1957), the soprano said that she has no favorite roles or compositions. "Whatever I am doing at the moment is the most important thing in the world to me."

The antithesis of the stereotyped, flamboyant prima donna, Lois Marshall respects the musical tradition to which she contributes. Robert Sabin wrote in *Musical America* (March 1957) that "to her, music is obviously not so much a key to power and fame or an outlet for self-assertion as it is a way of life, an inward experience that gives meaning to the whole world around her. She has enjoyed brilliant success, but she speaks of it only in terms of what it has meant to her musically."

References

Mus Am 77:9 Mr '57 por
Canadian Who's Who, 1955-57

MARTÍNEZ TRUEBA, ANDRÉS 1884-

Dec. 19, 1959 President of Uruguay (1951); chairman of the National Council (1952-55); banker. See *Current Biography* (November) 1954.

Obituary

N Y Times p60 D 20 '59

MASTROIANNI, UMBERTO (mäs″-trō-yän′nē) Sept. 21, 1910- Italian sculptor

Address: Strada Cavoretto 26, Turin, Italy

The angular bronze forms of the celebrated Italian sculptor, Umberto Mastroianni, although initially known only in Italy, have within the past decade attracted attention on four continents. Mastroianni's work has been recognized and shown throughout Europe since 1951, when his first one-man show outside of Italy was held at the Galerie de France in Paris. In 1958 he received the international grand prize for sculpture at the twenty-ninth Venice Biennale, an achievement which soon won him the notice of the American art world. He participated in the Carnegie International Exhibition of Contemporary Painting and Sculpture in Pittsburgh in the winter of 1958-59 and gave one-man shows in New York at the Juster Art Gallery in 1959 and the Kleemann Galleries in 1960.

Umberto Mastroianni, the son of Vincenzo Mastroianni, a civil servant, and Luisa (Conte) Mastroianni, was born on September 21, 1910 not far from Rome in the village of Fontana Liri, where he and his five brothers and four sisters were raised. His family originally came from nearby Arpino, an ancient Roman town which is the center of a flourishing pottery industry that produces ceramic sculpture of a popular type. His uncle Domenico, a sculptor who was born in Arpino, encouraged Umberto to follow his artistic inclinations.

At Fontana Liri, Umberto learned to work with clay and later went on painting expeditions in the Liri valley with his uncle and his cousin Alberto. He soon turned instinctively to sculpture. Mastroianni's impulses in this direction were, he says, "born on the banks of the Liri River where one still finds a sandstone that would inspire any sensitive man to sculpture."

Mastroianni attended a technical school in Fontana Liri and at the age of fourteen moved to Rome. There, he modeled clay in his uncle's studio on the Via Margutta during the day and studied at the Accademia di San Marcello al Corso in the evening. In 1926 he moved to Turin, where he still resides. During the next ten years he was confronted with serious economic and artistic problems. Rebelling against the prevailing taste for neoclassic sculpture with its academic formulae, Mastroianni struggled to find a new sculptural expression for ideas and feelings which originate in fantasy and instinct. Working in both marble and bronze, he slowly developed his distinctive style.

During the early 1930's Mastroianni began to exhibit his work. In 1933 he participated in a show at Florence and the following year displayed his sculpture at Naples and at the Cassa di Risparmio competition in Turin, where he won a prize. In 1935, Mastroianni first took part in the Rome Quadriennale and the same year contributed some pieces to an exposition of modern Italian sculpture which was shown in Berlin, Vienna, and Budapest. His work was included in the Venice Biennale as early as 1936. That year he also won a prize in Turin at an exhibition sponsored by the Sindicale Nazionale di Belle Arti.

Although his work occasionally won prizes in group shows, he received no major recognition and no commissions. He had, however, encouragement from the art critics Filippo de Pisis and Emilio Zanzi. In a review of the 1936 Venice Biennale, Zanzi wrote in the Turin newspaper Gazzetta del Popolo on June 2, 1936: "Mastroianni is one of the best of to-day's young Italian sculptors. And as portraitist no one surpasses him. In his work there is no trace of mannerism, but instead the search for psychological expression in the flow of line and the balance of masses."

Mastroianni studied at the Academy of Fine Arts in Milan during 1939. The year before, the Galleria Genova (Genoa) presented his first one-man show. His work continued to be exhibited regularly at important Italian expositions like the Rome Quadriennale and the Venice Biennale, and in 1940 a retrospective

UMBERTO MASTROIANNI

one-man show of his sculpture was arranged at the twenty-second Biennale. The same year he won a prize at the Premio del Turismo exhibition in Turin.

During the latter part of World War II he fought as a partisan against the Italian Fascists. In 1946 his design for a proposed memorial to the partisans in Turin won first prize in a national contest, and later that year he created the Monument to the Partisan. From 1945 to 1947 he contributed articles on art to newspapers and magazines. He organized, with his friend Luigi Spazzapan, several exhibitions of contemporary art, and they held a joint showing of their own work in 1948 at the Galleria La Bussola (Turin). The following year Mastroianni received the Saint Vincent prize at the National Exhibition of Contemporary Art, held in Saint Vincent.

In 1950 the world outside Italy began to open to Mastroianni. He participated in the international exhibition at the Royal Scottish Academy in Edinburgh and in the first international open-air sculpture exhibition at Antwerp. That same year he met Gildo Caputo of the Galerie de France in Paris, who arranged a one-man show of Mastroianni's work at this gallery in 1951. It was well received by the critics. Frank Elgar wrote (Carrefour, November 25, 1951): "Freedom of the imagination, a sense of the concrete, the joy of creation, an exceptional and native talent as sculptor such as we rarely find today, permit Mastroianni to articulate with a persevering passion the planes, the dense masses, the ample, alternating rhythms."

Examples of Mastroianni's sculpture were included in an exhibition of prize-winning work of the 1951 Rome Quadriennale, which toured the French provinces in 1953. That year he was also represented in showings in Tokyo and Antwerp and the following year in a touring

MASTROIANNI, UMBERTO—*Continued*

display of contemporary Italian art which was seen in Sweden, Norway, Denmark, and Finland. One-man shows of Mastroianni's work were presented at the Galerie de France in 1956 and in Brussels, Rotterdam, and São Paulo (Brazil) in 1957. Residents of Bonn, Berlin, and Darmstadt first saw Mastroianni's work that year.

Mastroianni was appointed professor of sculpture at the Academy of Fine Arts in Bologna in 1957. Already an internationally renowned sculptor, Mastroianni first received the attention of the American art world after he had been awarded the coveted international grand prize for sculpture at the 1958 Venice Biennale. His work was first seen in the United States at the Carnegie International Exhibition in Pittsburgh, held in 1958-59. Later, shows exclusively devoted to his work were organized in New York at the Juster Art Gallery in 1959 and the Kleemann Galleries in 1960.

His portrait heads and abstract sculptures are usually done in bronze treated to look like stone. Characteristically, they are heavy compact chunks of material whose surfaces fling out forcefully in angular or curved shapes. "Here is an audacious, exhilarating display of talent," wrote Dorothy Adlow (*Christian Science Monitor*, January 30, 1960) of Mastroianni's show at the Kleemann Galleries. "Clear to see is an artistic affiliation with cubists, with abstractionists. . . . In each item is a figuration of planes—oblique, pointing, thrusting forth from a core of design. Contours are heaving and jagged. Surfaces are rough, raked, scored, undercut, or deeply bored with holes. His objective is not an embodiment of physical form, but a concentration of force."

Photographs of many of Mastroianni's creations are reproduced in G. C. Argan's *Umberto Mastroianni* (1958). In addition to his sculptures in the round, he has done paintings and bas-reliefs. His work is represented in many private and public collections in Italy and other countries, including museums in Antwerp, Berlin, Brussels, Rome, Rotterdam, and Elath (Israel). From time to time he has executed commissions: a statue for the entrance hall of the central station of Rotterdam and several cemetery monuments in Turin and other Italian cities. He is a member of the Italian committee for plastic arts which co-operates with the United Nations Educational, Scientific, and Cultural Organization.

Umberto Mastroianni was married on December 21, 1936 to Dina Cibrario, who died in 1956. He has one son, Gabriele. The sculptor stands five feet nine and one-half inches tall, weighs 183 pounds, and has black hair and black eyes. He is a Roman Catholic and describes his political convictions as "liberal and progressive," but disclaims ties with any particular party. Fencing is his favorite sport, and he likes to drive sports cars.

In an article for *L'Espresso* (February 14, 1960), the art historian Lionello Venturi wrote of the sculptor: "Mastroianni has learned to infuse his sense of humanity into a style whose dynamism recalls Boccioni. His recent works are new objects which do not know whether they are sculpture or painting. They have all the splendor, the vibrations, the direct spiritual expression of painting, while of sculpture they have the certainty, the strength, the weight that comes from the solidity of the material. The originality, the novelty, the character borne by the creations of Mastroianni are evident and enchant the art lover."

References

Argan, G. C. Umberto Mastroianni (1958)
Bénézit, E. ed. Dictionnaire Peintres, Sculpteurs, Dessinateurs et Graveurs (1948-55)
Chi è? (1957)
Who's Who in Italy, 1957-58

MATTINGLY, GARRETT May 6, 1900-
Historian; university professor
Address: h. 308 W. 104th St., New York 25

Garrett Mattingly, who won a 1960 Pulitzer special citation for his best-selling history, *The Armada,* is a leading authority on early modern European diplomatic history. For the past twelve years he has been a professor of history at Columbia University, and he has been appointed George Eastman Visiting Professor at Oxford University for the academic year 1962-63. The scholarship and artistry of the books and articles that have won him the praise of his colleagues and critics have also helped him to obtain three Guggenheim Foundation Fellowships and a Fulbright research grant.

Garrett Mattingly was born in Washington, D.C. on May 6, 1900 to Leonard Howard and Ida Roselle (Garrett) Mattingly. He attended elementary schools in Washington until his family moved to Kalamazoo, Michigan in 1913, when he entered Kalamazoo Central High School. In 1916 his parents moved again, this time to nearby Allegan, Michigan. They considered sending Garrett to a private school to give him better preparation for college, but, strongly resisting the projected move, he completed his high school work at Kalamazoo Central. He recently explained: "I held out strongly for staying on at Kalamazoo Central High, living with friends and going home to Allegan weekends. I have never been sorry. I don't think any private school in the country could have given me a better education . . . or that I would have had more fun anywhere than I did in that warm and lively community." He was graduated from the school in 1918.

In June of that year Mattingly joined the United States Army and served until 1919 with the 43d Infantry Division. After his discharge, he entered Harvard University. When asked by a panel of Harvard professors what he wanted to study, he answered without hesitation "history." But then, Mattingly recalls, he was asked to name the century in which he was particularly interested. "I hadn't really thought about it" he says, "so I replied with the first one that came to mind—the sixteenth."

Mattingly received his B.A. (1923), M.A. (1926), and Ph.D. (1935) degrees from Harvard University. While still an undergraduate, he won a Sheldon Traveling Fellowship and studied in Europe from 1922 to 1924. As a young man, he tried his hand at writing a novel and poetry and did some reporting for French and Italian newspapers. He began his teaching career in 1926 at Northwestern University in Evanston, Illinois. Two years later, he joined the faculty of Long Island University in Brooklyn, New York, where he remained until 1942.

In 1936 Mattingly received his first Guggenheim Foundation Fellowship. It was granted to him so that he could engage in research on the life and times of Catharine of Aragon, first wife of Henry the Eighth, with special reference to her influence on English foreign policy and the development of English humanism. His studies of diplomatic history of the sixteenth century—particularly Anglo-Spanish relations during that period—resulted in the publication of *Catharine of Aragon* by Little, Brown and Company in 1941. The book was a Literary Guild selection in 1942. Thirteen years later the Houghton Mifflin Company published *Renaissance Diplomacy,* Mattingly's analysis of the origin and evolution of modern diplomacy.

During World War II Mattingly served with the United States Navy from 1942 to 1945. In July 1946 he joined the faculty of Cooper Union (a college in New York City that provides free education in engineering and art) as professor of history and chairman of the division of social philosophy. In the latter capacity, Mattingly was responsible for scheduling and moderating a series of lectures and discussions on topics of interest to the students and the public. Mattingly received a Guggenheim Foundation Fellowship in 1946. He left Cooper Union in June 1948 to join the faculty of Columbia University as a professor of history.

Mattingly's book, *The Armada,* was published in 1959 by the Houghton Mifflin Company. Favorably reviewed by critics and historical scholars, it was a Book Society choice in England, and a selection of the History Book Club and the Book-of-the-Month Club in the United States. The book describes the creation of the "invincible" Spanish Armada, its sailing, and its eventual defeat in 1588 against a political and diplomatic background. In the course of his research, Mattingly consulted original Spanish, English, French, and Dutch sources.

English historian A. L. Rowse, reviewing *The Armada* for the New York *Times* (October 18, 1959), wrote: "This will be the classic account of that famous year . . . 1588. It is quite simply, a historical masterpiece. . . . 'The Armada' is a work of art as well as of scholarship. . . . It is so skillfully constructed, it reads like a novel—but an accomplished novel, by one of the best writers."

Mattingly has explained that the idea for writing the book came to him during the Battle of Britain in 1940. "It seemed to me then for the many years I worked on it that the sixteenth century was very similar to the twentieth. I can't think of any two periods in history

Werner J. Kuhn

GARRETT MATTINGLY

where changes have been so rapid. In the sixteenth century . . . the Protestant Reformation was in full force and I'm sure that Queen Elizabeth and the Protestants appeared as dangerous to Philip II and the Catholics as the Communists do to us today. . . . They discovered, as we must, that two different systems can live in the world quite peacefully; indeed, they can grow together."

In January 1960 Columbia University named Mattingly the first incumbent of a new professorship in European history. The new chair was established to honor the late William R. Shepherd, a member of the university's department of history from 1896 to his death in 1934. Also in 1960 Mattingly was awarded his third Guggenheim grant for studies leading towards a narrative and interpretative history of the Italian Renaissance.

Mattingly is the author of articles and reviews in such publications as the *Journal of Modern History, Foreign Policy Bulletin, Saturday Review,* and the *Publications of the Modern Language Association.* He also edited *Hero and Leander* by Christopher Marlowe (Maddox and Gray, 1927) and *A Further Supplement to the Calendar of State Papers, Spanish, 1513-1543,* for the British Publications Record Office. His sixty-page appraisal of the American novelist, historian, and literary critic, *Bernard De Voto,* was published by Little, Brown and Company in 1938.

Garrett Mattingly was married to Gertrude McCollum, a former teacher, on June 22, 1928. He is a Democrat, an Episcopalian, and a member of the American Historical Society and Phi Beta Kappa. Mattingly has been described (New York *Post,* February 1, 1960) as looking somewhat like Edward G. Robinson in the role of board chairman and sounding somewhat like Lionel Barrymore. *The Armada* fulfilled Mat-

MATTINGLY, GARRETT—*Continued*

tingly's long-standing desire "to write about fighting." He has two books in progress (one on the Italian Renaissance and a second on the growth of European civilization), and he plans to write an historical novel some day. "But it would have to be after I retire," he says. "Right now I'm not sure my professional standing would permit it. My colleagues probably wouldn't approve."

References

N Y Post F 1 '60 por
Who's Who in America, 1960-61

MAUDLING, REGINALD   Mar. 7, 1917-
President of the British Board of Trade

Address: b. Board of Trade, Horse Guards Ave., London S.W. 1, England; h. Bedwell Lodge, Essendon, Hertfordshire, England

In appointing in October 1959 Right Honourable Reginald Maudling to the British cabinet post of President of the Board of Trade, the government of Harold Macmillan indicated the immense importance that it attaches to bettering its relations with countries on the Continent, especially in matters of trade. For two years Maudling had been chief British negotiator in the attempts to keep the six-nation European Common Market from spelling economic disaster to the rest of Europe.

Active in the Conservative party since 1945, Maudling was the party's drafter of policy on economic affairs after World War II. He has been Member of Parliament for the Barnet Division of Hertfordshire since 1950 and has held a number of ministerial appointments, including Paymaster-General, an assignment that he retains along with heading the Board of Trade.

Reginald Maudling was born in London on March 7, 1917, into a background which he himself has described as "North London suburban professional middle class." His father was a consulting actuary. Maudling attended Merchant Taylors' School and Merton College, Oxford University. At Oxford he is reported to have displayed his typical nonchalance, spending much time drinking beer, dining with friends, and playing golf. He missed a "blue" in golf, according to a friend, only because he could not be bothered with practice. He is said to have found undergraduate politics a bore and adult politics somewhat repulsive. He took first class honors in *Literae Humaniores* (Greats) and did particularly well in philosophy and logic. The latter studies helped shape his skepticism into a disciplined empirical outlook.

After an unsuccessful attempt to become an Oxford don through an All Souls College Fellowship, Maudling decided on law and was called to the Middle Temple Bar in 1940. World War II cut off his career as a barrister at its start. He served in the Royal Air Force as a staff officer and in the Air Ministry as private secretary to the Minister for Air, Sir Archibald Sinclair, who was leader of the Liberal party at the time. Sinclair's character and

intellect evoked deep admiration in Maudling and changed his view that politics encourages the second-rate.

Entering politics in 1945, Maudling unsuccessfully contested the Heston and Isleworth seat as Conservative candidate in the general election of that year. The election proved a disaster for Tories generally, and Richard Austen Butler gathered around him in the Conservative research department a team of talented young men to rethink Tory philosophy. Maudling was among the first of these "backroom boys." He specialized in economics and finance, became head of the party's economic secretariat, and personal adviser on economic matters to Winston Churchill, then leader of the opposition.

In 1950 Maudling won the Barnet seat in Parliament with a majority of 10,500 votes (which he increased to 13,000 the following year). His maiden speech in the House of Commons was on inflation and its cure.

His first ministerial assignment came in April 1952, when he was named Parliamentary Secretary to the Minister of Civil Aviation. Seven months later he moved to the Treasury. As Economic Secretary to the latter he was right-hand man to Chancellor of the Exchequer Butler and concerned with the supervision exercised by the Treasury of all economic policy at home and with all matters affecting the United Kingdom's external economic relations. Maudling came prominently to public notice while with the Treasury by offering, during an appearance on television, to answer any question about Conservative party policy telephoned in. Some 20,000 calls immediately came in to London from all over England, jamming the telephone system.

When he was appointed in April 1955 as Minister of Supply (succeeding Selwyn Lloyd), Maudling also became a Privy Councillor. During his first months as Minister of Supply he tackled head on a problem plaguing the British aircraft industry: too many prototypes and too little mass production. He threw the balance from design to production by remanding a number of prototypes already on order (including the Vickers V-1000, then Britain's hope in the jet airliner field) and decreeing that designs disapproved by the Ministry must be abandoned by manufacturers.

On January 16, 1957 Prime Minister Macmillan appointed Maudling Paymaster-General. The title is nonfunctional (the departmental duties being carried out by the Assistant Paymaster-General, a civil servant) and permitted Maudling to act as a sort of minister without portfolio. He represented the Minister of Power in Commons, reporting on questions of fuel and power. In Commons he also answered for the government on questions on scientific research that fell within the responsibility of the Lord President of the Council.

Late in 1957 Maudling, with over-all responsibility for economic relations with Europe, became chief negotiator in European free trade area talks. After Chancellor of the Exchequer Peter Thorneycroft resigned in January 1958, Maudling added to his other duties that of assisting the new Chancellor, Derick Heathcoat

Amory, over the whole range of economic matters. While Paymaster-General, Maudling was raised to full cabinet rank. A writer in the London *Observer* (February 23, 1958) noted that Maudling, with the vast range of his various responsibilities at the time, gave the impression of being a "kind of junior Prime Minister."

As chairman of the ministerial committee of the Organization for European Economic Cooperation, Maudling worked for the creation of a free trade area among the seventeen nations of the organization to overlap and mitigate the international economic effects of the impending six-nation Common Market (which would cut down tariff walls between France, West Germany, Italy, Belgium, the Netherlands, and Luxembourg). Talks began in October 1957 and reached a standstill in February 1958. Although they were subsequently resumed, in late 1958 Reginald Maudling conceded defeat: the Common Market began operating on January 1, 1959 without the larger free trade area attached. Maudling thereafter tried to help to form a Free Trade Association among the nations left outside the Common Market. He attended a meeting for the drafting of plans for such an association in Stockholm in July 1959. A convention establishing the European Free Trade Association was initialled in November 1959 by Foreign Ministers of seven nations, including Great Britain.

On October 14, 1959 Maudling was appointed President of the Board of Trade. This senior cabinet position makes him responsible for United Kingdom commerce, overseas trade, and industry (except that which falls specifically within the jurisdiction of other ministries). His chief assignment is still to head off a trade war with Continental Europe, an assignment Joseph C. Harsch has described as "the most difficult and urgent business of the day for London" (*Christian Science Monitor,* October 16, 1959). Maudling's problem is to make concessions which will broaden British trade with France and West Germany without damaging the newly and hard won solvency of the pound sterling.

In politics and world affairs Maudling is mainly concerned with practical solution of problems. Talk of Conservative party "principles" or "mission" reportedly does not interest him. He is liberal on issues like divorce and education. Conservative in other ways, he opposes repeal of capital punishment and was not among the Tories who had private misgivings over government policy during the Suez crises.

Not talkative by nature, when called upon to speak he is fluent, simple, concrete, and persuasive, even on the most complicated matters. He frequently makes long, detailed speeches from a few scribbled headings and has a talent for rational, calm discussion.

Tall and heavily built, Maudling has a fleshy, solemn face which breaks easily into a broad, boyish smile. His walk, like his voice and his whole demeanor, is leisurely and has been described variously as "shambling" and "lumbering." Although he has on occasion been razor-tongued in Commons debates, he is generally

British Inf. Services

REGINALD MAUDLING

reported to be remarkably consistent in his good temper and never intentionally rude. He calls himself a "born optimist." He makes friends easily and has a large circle of them.

Maudling was married to Beryl Laverick in 1939. Mrs. Maudling is interested in local government work and is a former member of the Hertfordshire County Council. They have three sons and a daughter. Maudling spends most of his spare time with his family. He frequently relaxes at golf or shooting, but enjoys doing, he says, "whatever the others want to do."

References

London Sunday Times p3 S 29 '57 por
International Who's Who, 1959
International Year Book and Statesmen's
Who's Who, 1959
Who's Who, 1959

MAY, CATHERINE (DEAN) May 18, 1914-   United States Representative from Washington

Address: b. House Office Bldg., Washington 25, D.C.; h. 201 N. 24th Ave., Yakima, Wash.

A former writer, commentator, and producer of radio programs, Catherine May is the first woman ever elected to the United States House of Representatives from the state of Washington. Mrs. May, who is a Republican, was elected by the Fourth District of her state in November 1958 and was seated in the Eighty-sixth Congress in January 1959. Before coming to the nation's capital, Mrs. May had served three terms in the House of Representatives of the state of Washington at Olympia. She is now a member of the Agriculture Committee of the United States House of Representatives.

(Continued next page)

CATHERINE MAY

Catherine Dean Barnes was born in Yakima, Washington on May 18, 1914 to Charles H. Barnes, a real estate broker, and Pauline (Van Loon) Barnes. Since the death of her husband, Mrs. Barnes has continued to manage the real estate brokerage office in Yakima. Catherine attended grade school and high school in Yakima, and then enrolled at Yakima Valley Junior College, where she was graduated with sociology as her major subject. During her three years as an undergraduate at the University of Washington in Seattle, where she received her B.A. degree in 1936, she majored in English and speech, and also took a summer course in speech at the University of Southern California. She wrote for the University of Washington *Daily News* and belonged to the speech correction clinic. She also acted at the Penthouse and Studio theaters and became a college fashion counselor for a department store during her summer vacations.

From 1936 to 1940 Catherine Barnes taught English at the high school in Chehalis, Washington. While teaching, she did graduate work at the University of Washington, which granted her a degree in education in 1937. In 1940 she left teaching to become women's editor and news broadcaster for radio station KMO at Tacoma. The following year she became a writer and special events broadcaster for KOMO-KRJ at Seattle. She then headed the radio department of the Strang and Prosser Advertising Agency and the radio and motion-picture department of the Federal Insurance Company, both in Seattle. It was at a USO in Seattle that Catherine Barnes first met James O. May, whose wife she became on January 18, 1943.

While waiting for her husband to be discharged from the United States Army, Mrs. May worked for two years at radio station WEAF in New York City as a writer and assistant to the commentator Adelaide Hawley. When he returned to civilian life, James O. May established a real estate and insurance business in Yakima, while his wife added to her domestic responsibilities those of women's editor for the local radio station KIT.

The Mays believe that a woman can combine marriage and a career, if the marriage is a genuine partnership. "But," Mrs. May has said, "I feel strongly that any woman who pursues a career outside the home without her husband's blessing is in for trouble. I would not have gone into politics if my husband had not wanted me to" (*Christian Science Monitor*, December 30, 1958).

The young couple became interested in politics through Charles H. Barnes, Mrs. May's father. "I hope you don't make the mistake I did," he once told them. "I never got out and fought for the things I believe in." The Mays joined the Young Republican Club and became zealous precinct workers.

In connection with her radio work, Mrs. May often addressed civic groups. In 1952, at her husband's insistence, she became a candidate for Representative of the Fourteenth (Yakima) District in the Washington state Legislature. "I was his campaign contribution," she likes to explain. "We couldn't give the party much money, so Jim donated me as a candidate." She became the second woman in the history of Yakima County to be elected to the Olympia legislature.

Re-elected in 1954 and 1956, Mrs. May was a member of the Education Committee throughout her three terms. She took a special interest in retarded children and in the problem of juvenile delinquency. She also served as vice-chairman of the Governor's State Wide Committee on Educational Television and was a member of the Governor's Safety Council. Serving on the Appropriations Committee, she discovered that the management of government finances was "very unbusinesslike in many cases" and that "we need more sense in the way we appropriate money."

In 1958 Mrs. May became a "reluctant candidate" (by her own description) for United States Representative from the Fourth Washington District. Observers regarded her as the "underdog" in her contest with Frank Le Roux, a Democrat who had narrowly missed unseating the Republican incumbent, Hal Holmes, in 1956. "In my campaign," Mrs May has said, "our team had neither power politics nor money on our side. We made a good, old-fashioned direct-contact type of campaign, working the district precinct by precinct." Although she campaigned with handbills, while her opponent covered the landscape with billboards, she won over Le Roux by 66,544 votes to 56,308 at the election on November 4. She became the first woman ever to represent the state of Washington in the federal legislature.

When she visited the White House about a month after her election victory, Mrs. May received the congratulations of President Dwight D. Eisenhower. She assured him that she would use her incumbency to fight runaway prices and promised to support his anti-inflationary programs.

Representing twelve counties that are mostly agricultural in the south-central and southeastern area of her state, Mrs. May is interested in education, agriculture, reclamation, the development of hydroelectric power, and atomic energy. She was seated in the Eighty-sixth Congress on January 7, 1959 and assigned to the House Agriculture Committee. She also belongs to the subcommittees on forests, on livestock and feed grains, on domestic marketing, on family farms, and on research and extension.

In March 1959 Mrs. May sponsored legislation promoting the consumption of turkeys and turkey products; in April she supported the bill giving the rural electrification administrator final authority to approve or disapprove loans, although she later voted against overriding the President's veto. In May she opposed the bill authorizing self-financing of the Tennessee Valley Authority through $750,000,000 in revenue bonds; in July she supported the President by voting against a motion to "disapprove" his Reorganization Plan No. 1, which transferred authority over the national forest from the Secretary of the Interior to the Secretary of Agriculture. The bill was passed. Although she represents an important wheat district, Mrs. May also supported the President by voting in June against the House wheat bill (later vetoed) which would have raised price supports to 90 per cent of parity.

In February 1959, Mrs. May voted against a veterans' housing bill increasing by $300,000 the amount which could be drawn from the United States Treasury for housing loans. In March she opposed passage of a federal airport construction bill with higher appropriations than the President favored. Mrs. May also supported the President on increasing the United States subscription to the International Monetary Fund and World Bank (March) and on the Mutual Security Act of 1959 (June). Early in March 1959 she introduced a bill to strengthen and improve state and local programs to combat juvenile delinquency.

Representative May received the Togetherness Award of *McCall's* magazine in March 1959 and the Theta Sigma Phi Matrix Table Award in April. She belongs to Alpha Chi Omega sorority, the American Association of University Women, and the National Congress of Parents and Teachers. She is a past president of the Yakima Women's Republican Club, a board member of the Young Republican Club, and a member of the Washington State Board of Republican Women's Clubs. She is also affiliated with the Washington Association for Retarded Children, the United Good Neighbors, the American National Red Cross, the Yakima Valley Art Association, and the Yakima Little Theater. She is an honorary member of the Altrusa and Zonta clubs.

George Dixon of the Washington *Post and Times Herald* has described Catherine May as "a comfortable-looking matron . . . with a pleasant face and homey smile," who "looks, acts and talks like one of the neighbor women

—in the finest sense of the term" (December 15, 1958). She is blue-eyed and brown-haired, five feet three inches in height, and around 165 pounds in weight. To her relatives and friends she is known as "Billie." She belongs to St. Michael's Episcopal Church at Yakima, where she has been a Sunday School teacher. James and Catherine May have one son, James Collins, and one daughter, Melinda Ellen. Mrs. May's favorite recreations are fishing, gardening, writing, and swimming.

References

Christian Sci Mon p2 D 30 '58 por
Ladies Home J 73:70+ Ap '56
Nat Bsns Woman 38:12 F '59 por
Washington (D.C.) Post p19A D 15 '58; p2 D 21 '58
Congressional Directory (1959)
Who's Who of American Women, 1958-59

MEADOWS, A(LGUR) H(URTLE) Apr. 24, 1899- Business executive
Address: b. Meadows Bldg., Dallas 6, Tex.; h. 6601 Turtle Creek, Dallas 5, Tex.

Skill in corporate finance has placed A. H. Meadows among Texas' most successful oilmen. He has been chairman since 1950 of the General American Oil Company of Texas, which he helped found in 1936. Within twenty years after its establishment, it had grown into the thirtieth largest oil company in the United States; in fiscal 1959 it produced 8,231,449 net barrels of crude oil. Meadows had begun his career in the oil industry as an accountant with the Standard Oil Company of Louisiana in 1921 and later, in partnership with Ralph G. Trippett, organized a loan-agency business which evolved into an oil company.

Algur Hurtle Meadows, the third of seven children of Dr. John Morgan and Sally Marie Elora (Dailey) Meadows, was born on April 24, 1899 in Vidalia, Georgia. He had one brother and five sisters. His father was a physician in general practice. As a high school pupil, at Vidalia Collegiate Institute, he shared in all sports activities and held a part-time job.

In 1915 Meadows was graduated from high school and entered the Georgia and Alabama Business College in Macon, Georgia. He later attended Mercer University, also in Macon, taking liberal arts courses and becoming a member of Sigma Nu fraternity and the ROTC. At the end of the year he left Mercer to go to work at a Ford agency in Metter, Georgia.

As a prelude to a projected trip around the world, Meadows and a friend traveled about the South during the next few years, moving from one job to another. They set out for Florida in 1919 to work as house-to-house agents for a photographer. In Jacksonville, Meadows was employed for a few months at a branch of Armour & Company and then went on to Louisiana, where the Standard Oil Company in Shreveport hired him as a clerk.

(Continued next page)

Gittings

A. H. MEADOWS

In his work in accounting for the Standard Oil Company from 1921 to 1929 Meadows began to show his exceptional aptitude for corporate finance. After attending a class in commercial law offered by the Chamber of Commerce, he took courses at night and weekends at the Centenary College of Louisiana Law School in Shreveport. He was graduated in 1926 and admitted to the Louisiana state bar in the same year.

While studying law Meadows met Ralph G. Trippett, with whom he planned the loan company from which the General American Oil Company of Texas eventually developed. The General Finance Company, founded in the fall of 1928, was one of the first to be set up under Louisiana's new Uniform Small Loan Law. The success of the company, of which Meadows was vice-president, led to the establishment of several other loan companies in Louisiana and Texas. Meadows and Trippett merged their companies in 1930 into the General American Finance System, Inc. This organization withstood the Depression even though at its height about $1,000,000—half of the capital on loan—was uncollectible.

Since the General American Finance System conducted much of its business with the oil industry, Meadows saw that the organization would benefit by association with a petroleum expert. In 1935 he and Trippett joined an oil operator, J. W. Gilliland, to form the Gilliland Producing and Refining Corporation. After the General American Finance System acquired the assets of this company, the General American Oil Company of Texas was formed, on July 1, 1936, to acquire the assets of the Finance System.

The headquarters of the General American Oil Company were originally in Shreveport, but in 1937 were moved to Dallas, which had become the center of the oil industry after the opening up of the East Texas Oil Field in 1930. When the company was formed, Trippett was made president, while Meadows filled the positions of vice-president, secretary, and assistant treasurer. Two years later the company paid off its obligation to Trippett; Gilliland, who became president at that time, withdrew from the company in 1941, leaving Meadows as president and major stockholder. He was elected chairman of the board in 1950.

Among the important changes that Meadows has seen his company undergo was the growth in the number of net wells from 194, in the East Texas Oil Field, in June 1937 to 2,990, in some fifteen states and Canada, by June 1959. At the end of its first fiscal year General American Oil had a book equity of about $4,000,000; in 1959 its common stockholders equity was over $78,000,000.

Much of General American Oil's rapid expansion of operations, beginning in late 1937, became possible because of a method that Meadows originated for acquiring oil-producing properties. The company paid for its new properties with a comparatively small amount of cash down; it made the rest of the payment in oil and also paid the interest on the reserve payment in oil.

According to John William Rogers' account in *The Story of General American Oil Company of Texas,* "Since Mr. Meadows devised interest-bearing oil payments, the Company has acquired deals involving more than $100,000,000 worth of properties, 75 to 80 per cent of which have been payable in interest-bearing oil payments. The purchase price in each case was the same as the price in cash would have been, because of the interest clause." Meadows' innovation of interest-bearing oil payments has since spread throughout the oil industry, and he has discussed the subject in talks before financial and security analysts' societies in New York, Boston, Philadelphia, San Francisco, Los Angeles, and other cities.

General American Oil Company's international investments are somewhat recent. Canadian operations were begun in the 1953 fiscal year and are maintained through the wholly owned General American Oils, Ltd., and the partly owned Fargo Oils, of both of which Meadows is president. In 1952 the company formed an American syndicate to drill for oil in Spain in association with the Spanish government's National Institute of Industry, and in the future it may explore a part of the Spanish Sahara. General American Oil also owns shares in International Egyptian Oil Company, Inc.

The Meadows Building, General American Oil Company's $4,000,000 headquarters built in suburban Dallas in 1955, reflects Meadows interest in architecture and landscaping. A patron of the arts and a collector, he is a sponsor of the Dallas Museum for Contemporary Arts. Music is another of his interests, and he belongs to the Terpsichorean Club. He is a commissioner of the City of University Park in Dallas County and is active in a number of community organizations such as the local Red Cross.

A year or so after he had decided to settle down in Shreveport, on December 11, 1922 Meadows was married to Virginia Stuart Garrison of that city. They have a son, Robert Al Meadows. With his white hair and blue eyes, Meadows is a striking man who stands five feet ten inches tall and weighs 185 pounds. He is a Protestant, a thirty-second degree Mason (Shriner and Knight Templar), and a member of many professional and social organizations, including several clubs where he can enjoy his favorite outdoor recreation—golf.

References

Elliott, Osborn Men at the Top (1959)
Who's Who in America, 1958-59

MELLETT, LOWELL Feb. 22, 1884-Apr. 6, 1960 Former United States government official; newspaperman; administrative assistant to President Franklin D. Roosevelt (1940-44). See *Current Biography* (May) 1942.

Obituary

N Y Times p35 Ap 7 '60

MENDENHALL, THOMAS CORWIN (2D) June 14, 1910- College president

Address: Smith College, Northampton, Mass.

The sixth president of Smith College, Thomas Corwin Mendenhall, once remarked that American education should emphasize the training of the mind above everything else. This is a principle to which he had adhered for twenty-three years as a teacher, historian, and administrator at Yale University. Taking office on July 1, 1959, three and a half months before his inauguration, he succeeded Dr. Benjamin F. Wright as president of the largest independent women's college in the United States. Dr. Mendenhall was formerly an associate professor of history at Yale, specializing in English and maritime history, and was for ten years the master of Berkeley, one of the university's ten residential colleges. He also directed the office of teacher training, a program enabling undergraduates of Yale, Smith, and Vassar to enroll in a two-year course in the Yale Graduate School to prepare them for teaching in high schools. He believes that the small residential school such as Smith can offer its students academic and social opportunities that large universities cannot give.

Born on June 14, 1910 in Chicago, Illinois, Thomas Corwin Mendenhall 2d is the son of Charles Elwood and Dorothy Mabel (Reed) Mendenhall. His father was for many years the chairman of the physics department at the University of Wisconsin and his grandfather, for whom he was named, was a physicist of more than national reputation. Dorothy Mendenhall, who graduated from Smith College in 1895 and received an honorary degree from the college in 1930 for her achievements in medicine, was a well-known pediatrician.

Tom Mendenhall, as he is called by friends and colleagues, grew up in Madison, Wisconsin with his brother, John Talcott, a Harvard Med-

THOMAS CORWIN MENDENHALL

ical School graduate who is now a surgeon in Wisconsin. Tom attended public schools in Madison, the Phillips Academy at Andover, Massachusetts, and secondary schools in Switzerland and France before entering Yale University in 1928. As a child he had a fondness for boating and sailing which continued as a lifelong enthusiasm for everything to do with rowing and crew.

At Yale, where he elected history as his major subject, Mendenhall wrote for the student magazine, the *Yale Record*, ran cross-country and track, and joined Delta Kappa Epsilon, a social fraternity. He was graduated *cum laude* with a B.A. degree in 1932 and elected to Phi Beta Kappa. Following a year's graduate study at Yale, he went as a Rhodes Scholar to Balliol College, Oxford and took B.A. (1935) and B.Litt. (1936) degrees there. He made many close friends in England and scored the triumph of being the first American ever to captain an Oxford college rowing crew. In 1938, after two more years of graduate study at Yale, he received a Ph.D. degree in history.

Mendenhall began teaching maritime and English history as an instructor at Yale in 1937. Because he tried always to bring history to life and to stir the imagination of his students, his assured and authoritative lectures became popular. Mendenhall was promoted to assistant professor in 1942 and to associate professor in 1946. For fifteen years, he headed the large freshman course in history and for several years taught summer session classes. In 1943 he was named assistant to the provost, a position he held until 1949.

At the end of World War II, Mendenhall and several colleagues in the history department developed the "problem method" of teaching history. Under this system, students supplement conventional lecture hours by examining source materials on specific historical problems and then meet in small discussion groups to recon-

MENDENHALL, THOMAS CORWIN—
Continued

struct in detail the facts about and reasons behind past events. Together with Basil D. Henning, Archibald S. Foord, and later Archibald W. Allen, he published five volumes of "historical problems"—source materials for the use of students in understanding the nature and methods of historical research. They were: *The Quest for a Principle of Authority in Europe, 1715 to the Present* (Holt, 1948); *Ideas and Institutions in European History, 800-1715* (Holt, 1948); *The Dynamic Force of Liberty in Modern Europe: Six Problems in Historical Interpretation* (Holt, 1952); *Foundations of the Modern State: Four Problems in Historical Interpretation* (Holt, 1952); and *Problems in Western Civilization* (Holt, 1956).

At Yale, Mendenhall took an active interest in curriculum planning. In 1940 he represented Yale College at a meeting for secondary school teachers which promoted integration of school and college work in history. For seventeen years, five of them as chairman, he served on Yale's committee on the course of study and helped establish the directed studies program at the end of World War II. In 1953 he was a member of an eight-man committee, headed by Yale president A. Whitney Griswold, which proposed major revisions of the first two years of the undergraduate curriculum. The proposals gained nationwide notice among college educators. In 1958 Mendenhall was named director of the office of teacher training, heading the joint program inaugurated by Yale, Smith, and Vassar colleges in March 1958. Undergraduates of the three schools enroll in Yale's graduate school for a two-year training course designed to fit them for teaching positions.

During World War II Mendenhall played a major role in Yale's activities supporting the defense. From 1944 to 1946 he co-directed the foreign area studies program begun in 1942, which tried to make military personnel going to Europe, Asia, Africa, and the Pacific familiar with the language, customs, and government of foreign countries. In 1942 he was acting chairman of the faculty committee on war literature and served as secretary of a committee on student preparation for war service. He directed the civil officers' training school during the war, and in 1946 and 1947 headed the summer session program for veterans resuming their studies.

Although his teaching responsibilities and associated duties had occupied a great deal of his time, Mendenhall's desire to engage in historical research remained unabated. In a "quiet period," in 1949, he returned to Balliol College, Oxford, this time with his family, where he embarked upon a year's research in English economic history. It resulted in the publication of his book, *The Shrewsbury Drapers and the Welsh Wool Trade in the Sixteenth and Seventeenth Centuries* (Oxford, 1953). Unable to refrain from teaching, he also did some tutoring while at Oxford.

Although Mendenhall is primarily a classroom teacher and not a prolific scholar, he has written several articles on historical and educational topics for such periodicals as *Social Education,* the *University Quarterly, School and Society, American Historical Review,* and the *Yale Alumni Magazine.* He is currently editing the letters of J. F. Schlezer, a seventeenth-century diplomat. In 1956 Mendenhall became a research Fellow of the Huntington Library at San Marino, California.

As master of Berkeley college from 1950 to 1959, Mendenhall earned the devotion and respect of his students, who responded to his "warmth, curiosity, and desire to help." A portrait in the *Smith Alumnae Quarterly* (winter, 1959) notes that he and his wife "gave a fine demonstration of what can be done to create a stimulating group life there." As a Fellow of Yale, he had been instrumental in organizing the Berkeley Players, a dramatic group, and had later established a Berkeley tool workshop for students. He took an active interest in Berkeley's sports teams and was the only faculty member ever to have rowed on a college crew when the Berkeley team was short one man.

Mendenhall feels that the residential college, with its fellowship and close conjunction of students and faculty, preserves the character of a university as a community of scholars. "The thing that interests me at Smith," President Mendenhall once declared, "is that the college has turned more and more to the honors program, not trying to do everything, but seeking to give the most to the best."

In 1938 Thomas Corwin Mendenhall was married to Cornelia Baker of Ohio. They have three daughters: Bethany Reed, Mary Thomas, and Cornelia Morgan. Mendenhall is six feet two inches in height and weighs about 200 pounds. A *Time* profile (November 24, 1958) reported that Mendenhall was known at Yale for his "imaginatively disreputable wardrobe of checks and tweeds" and for his rather disorderly office in which the books, stacked into cliffs, were always threatening to tumble down on the heads of visitors. (Mendenhall once fished an examination paper requested by a student from under his office rug.) His favorite sport is rowing. He often watched the Yale crew practising and used to write articles on crew meets for the *Yale Alumni Magazine,* on whose board of editors he served for many years. He "perfected a crushing game of croquet" at Berkeley, and liked to watch Berkeley's champion football team play.

Before moving to Berkeley college, the Mendenhall family lived in Bethany, Connecticut, where they owned a small house surrounded by thirty-five acres of wooded countryside. They continued to vote in Bethany and attended town meetings there, even after they had moved to the Yale residential college. Mendenhall was for four years a chairman of Bethany's local school board and a "valued member of the volunteer fire department." The loss for Yale and the gain for Smith, when Mendenhall moved to the women's college was voiced by one of his Yale colleagues: "It is hard for me to think of the Yale I know, like and honor without Tom

Mendenhall," he said. "If a real crisis arose here, he is the only person I should turn to for counsel and help."

References

N Y Herald Tribune p2 N 12 '58
N Y Times p39 N 12 '58
Smith Alumnae Q 50:68+ F '59 por;
  51:10+ N '59
Yale Alumni Mag 4:3 D '40; 9:5 Ja '46;
  14:16+ Ja '51 por
Directory of American Scholars (1957)
Who's Who in America, 1960-61

MÉRIDA, CARLOS (mä'rē-*th*ä) Dec. 2, 1891- Artist
Address: Avenida Alvaro Obregón, 159-D, Mexico, D.F.

A leading abstract painter of Mexico, where he has lived for about three decades, Guatemalan-born Carlos Mérida has been hailed in recent years as the "father" of the colorful mosaic murals that adorn the walls of many important buildings in Mexico, Guatemala, and Brazil. He was earlier responsible to a large extent for the revival of the art forms of his Guatemalan ancestors, and much of his painting can be identified by his preference for Mayan motifs and symbols. His work is included in important private collections and museums in the Western Hemisphere. His several publications, which have widened the influence of his painting and teaching, include *Modern Mexican Artists* (1937) and *Trajes Regionales Mexicanos* (1945).

Carlos Mérida was born on December 2, 1891 in Guatemala, in the highlands at Quezaltenango, to Serapio Santiago and Lupe (Ortega) Mérida. His father was a lawyer. "I am a mixture of Maya-Quiché Indian and Spanish," Mérida wrote in his article, "Self-Portrait," in *Américas* (June 1950). "I began to paint late, after I realized I could never be a pianist. [A childhood illness had left him partially deaf.] I studied music—piano, composition, and theory. I still have the love for the art of sound that enlivened my childhood impressions." (Mérida often speaks of his paintings in musical terms.)

At the age of eighteen, after graduating from secondary school in Guatemala City, Mérida went to Paris for four years of study and painting. He became well acquainted with Picasso and Modigliani, who lived in the same studio building as he did, and he visited with the Dutch painter Kees van Dongen and the Spanish painter Anglada Camarasa, as well as Modigliani. Travels in France, Spain, Belgium, and the Netherlands were also part of his first trip abroad.

On his return to Guatemala in 1914, Mérida felt a new appreciation of his country—the landscape, customs of the Indians, and ancient art at Quiriqua. He started a pro-Indian movement in art, basing modern painting and sculpture on pre-Hispanic themes. He was aided in this project by the sculptor Yela Gunther. Failing to arouse much interest in

CARLOS MÉRIDA

Guatemala, in 1919 Mérida went to Mexico, where the people were more receptive to his folk themes. His first paintings exhibited at the National Academy of Fine Arts in Mexico City in 1920 were "strongly geometric"; the colors were those used in textiles woven by Guatemalan Indians.

When Diego Rivera began his frescoes in the National Preparatory School in Mexico City in 1922, he hired Mérida, Xavier Guerrero, and Jean Charlot to help him. Mérida's technical soundness was an asset to Rivera. Later Mérida, alone, painted a mural at the children's library in the Ministry of Education. His interest in nonobjective art and abstract surrealism increased, and he soon drifted away from Rivera and the Revolutionary Syndicate of Technical Workers, Painters, and Sculptors, and returned to easel painting.

Mérida's work was exhibited in New York in 1926. Discussing his paintings in *Arts and Decoration* (February 1927), Carleton Beals praised his "subtle combination of super-simplicity, restrained handling, and sudden dramatic bits of flamboyant decorative beauty . . . the color clashes reach a synthesized climax and give a unique focus to the paintings. A baffling contradiction of super-sophistication and absolutely barbarous naïveté!"

After Mérida's second visit to Paris, from 1926 to 1929, his painting went through what he has called "a profound transformation." In the 1930's he began his work in personal, plastic painting, inspired particularly by the sculptured forms in the ruins of his Guatemalan birthplace. His guiding principle became: reduce everything to essentials. He explained in his *Américas* article that to obtain lyric reality one must bore deep, "absorb the essence. Abstract painting provides the best route of approach. I love it more than anything else, for it permits free expansion, free

MÉRIDA, CARLOS—*Continued*

expression. It is the most real of all painting, for it is based on reality. The reality may be the local color, the environment, traditional forms, space, light, music."

From 1930 to 1933 Mérida was professor of painting at the Central Academy of Plastic Arts in Mexico City. His love for the dance led him in 1931 to accept the directorship of the Mexican Ministry of Education's School of Dance. There he carried on interesting experiments with Indian dances and produced, between 1932 and 1934, a portfolio of documentary colored lithographs depicting costumes worn in native dances. A second portfolio, published in Mexico in 1940 under the title *Carnival in Mexico*, represents exotic dress worn at regional *fiestas*. *Mexican Costume*, for which Mérida prepared the text and twenty-five color plates, was published by the Pocahontas Press, Chicago, in 1941.

Three Mérida paintings of the 1940's with characteristic themes derived from ancient Indian art forms are *The Three Messengers, Time Has Stratified Eternity,* and *The Sleeping Dragon.* Teaching, as well as painting, occupied Mérida during some years of the 1940's. From 1941 to 1943 he was artist in residence and instructor at North Texas State College in Denton. In 1949-50 he was director of the Mexican Art Workshop in Taxco, Mexico. Beginning in 1950 he served for a time as cultural attaché at the Guatemalan legation in Rome, Italy, where an exhibition of his work was held in early 1951.

Long concerned with what he calls "the integration of the arts," Mérida works with architects and sculptors to make painting and sculpture a part of architecture. He experiments with industrial plastics in his polychromed bas-reliefs and works with stone cutters and with mosaic craftsmen. Recent notable examples are in the Reaseguros Alianza and Crédito Bursatil buildings in Mexico City and the social security building in Guatemala City.

"The little dancing abstracts of Mérida," noted Bernard S. Myers (*Mexican Painting in Our Time,* Oxford University Press, 1956), "done in silicon on square concrete plaques on the façade of the Benito Juárez Housing Project, and his staircase mural in the same building (1949) represent another attempt to fit modern design to the needs of Mexican mural decoration."

Mérida believes that easel painting is an art for minorities, while mural painting, when related to architecture, is an art for majorities, for all eyes to see. He has occasionally designed sets and costumes for the theater and for several ballets, among them some in which his daughter danced. His commercial activities have included furniture units, book illustrations, magazine advertisements, and Christmas wrappings.

In his *Mexican Journal* (Devin-Adair, 1958) Selden Rodman observed that Mérida is "more subtle and sophisticated in his art than any Mexican save Tamayo." Also like Tamayo, Rodman added, Mérida suffers "from the in-difference of the Mexican public. His paintings and mosaics command high prices (almost in Tamayo's bracket), but in São Paulo or Caracas, not here."

Carlos Mérida and Dalila Gálvez were married on December 18, 1919. They have two children, Alma and Ana. The painter is tall and slender, weighing 130 pounds; he has brown eyes and silvery gray hair. His hobby is collecting jazz records. Of a restless, wandering nature, he enjoys traveling and says that he feels at home anywhere. His church affiliation is Catholic. He has no political affiliation and does not like propaganda in paintings. "Painting is not a narrative art," he explains. "It is a plastic medium and, as such, the emotion which is produced must come from the painting itself."

References

Américas 2:24+ Je '50 por
Mexico This Month p21 My '59 por
Time 46:79 O 15 '45

Stewart, Virginia 45 Contemporary Mexican Artists (1951)
Who's Who in Latin America pt 1 (1946)

MESSERSMITH, GEORGE S(TRAUSSER) Oct. 3, 1883-Jan. 29, 1960 Career diplomat; former Assistant Secretary of State (1937-40); Ambassador to Cuba (1940-41); Ambassador to Mexico (1941-42); Ambassador to Argentina (1946). See *Current Biography* (October) 1942.

Obituary

N Y Times p21 Ja 30 '60

METZMAN, G(USTAV) June 23, 1886-Apr. 11, 1960 Business executive; president of the New York Central Railroad (1944-52); director of several companies. See *Current Biography* (July) 1946.

Obituary

N Y Times p33 Ap 12 '60

MEYER, ALBERT (GREGORY), CARDINAL (mī′ĕr) Mar. 9, 1903- Roman Catholic prelate

Address: b. 719 N. Wabash Ave., Chicago, Ill.; h. 1515 N. State St., Chicago, Ill.

Elevated by Pope John XXIII to the Sacred College of Cardinals in November 1959, Albert Gregory Meyer received the red hat, symbol of his rank, at the consistory in Vatican City the following month. About a year earlier, in September 1958, when Meyer had been named to replace the late Samuel Cardinal Stritch as Archbishop of Chicago, many Roman ecclesiastics were surprised, because they had never heard of him. The reason was his life-long fidelity to the ideal of self-effacing scholarship and prayer, to which he used to exhort his students at St. Francis Seminary in Milwaukee and to which he adhered even through twelve years of public life as Bishop of Superior, Wisconsin and Archbishop of Milwaukee.

Time (October 6, 1958), when reporting his appointment to the vital Chicago see, commented that the "scholarly, quiet man . . . has rarely committed himself on social issues." Before his first year as Archbishop of Chicago had gone by, however, *America* (May 23, 1959) could hail his forthright stand on race relations as "shining proof that the mantle of leadership . . . has indeed fallen on resolute shoulders."

Albert Gregory Meyer was born in Milwaukee on March 9, 1903, the third child of Peter James Meyer, a small but prosperous grocer of German descent, and Mathilda (Thelen) Meyer. The Meyers had two other boys, both of whom became executives in industry, and two girls, both of whom became nuns.

One of Albert Meyer's sisters recalls that when he was five he used to play at being a priest, using an old table as an altar. Almost from the time he entered grade school he told his family he would grow up to be a priest. At fourteen he entered St. Francis Seminary in Milwaukee. He continued his studies in philosophy and theology at the North American College in Rome and was ordained there on July 11, 1926, one year ahead of the rest of his class. After ordination he continued studying in Rome at the Universitá de Propaganda Fide, where he received the degree of Doctor of Sacred Theology in 1927, and at the Pontificio Istituto Biblico, where he received the Licentiate of Sacred Scripture in 1930. From Rome the young priest went to St. Joseph's Church, Waukesha, Wisconsin, a town a few miles west of Milwaukee, where he served as a curate for one year.

Cardinal Meyer has strong views on education, the central one being that teachers should goad the wills of students as well as train their minds and not leave "to the home and the Church the right and duty of striving to make men good." Applying this philosophy to seminary teaching, he once said that the teacher of Sacred Scripture "must . . . inflame the heart while enlightening the mind, as our Lord did on the way to Emmaus."

Meyer's opportunity to implement this philosophy came in 1931, when he was assigned to teach Biblical archaeology and dogmatic theology at St. Francis, the seminary where he himself had begun his studies for the priesthood. After six years as a professor he replaced the Most Reverend Francis J. Haas as rector of the seminary when the latter became Bishop of Grand Rapids. "Live among these books . . . meditate upon them . . . know nothing else . . . seek nothing else." It was this admonition of St. Jerome, so much heeded in the rector's own life of scholarship and so influential in his life as a whole, which he held before students during his direction of the seminary. As rector he exhibited that conservative nature he would later reveal as a prelate, becoming, in his own words,

Wide World

ALBERT CARDINAL MEYER

"sensitive, in a negative way" to suggestions of additions to the seminary curriculum. While rector, in 1938, he was made a monsignor, with the title of Domestic Prelate to Pope Pius XI.

The prelate entered the ranks of the episcopacy in February 1946, when he was assigned to fill the pastoral chair left vacant in Superior, Wisconsin by the transfer of Bishop William O'Connor to the diocese of Madison. He became known in Superior as "a man who conducts his office with the primary purpose of getting things done."

After Archbishop Moses E. Kiley of Milwaukee died, Pope Pius XII transferred Meyer to his home diocese. He received the crosier, symbol of his office, in St. John's Cathedral. Milwaukee in late 1953. During his tenure in Milwaukee, the Pope sent him the pallium, a vestment worn by the Pope and sometimes sent by him to ecclesiastics as a token of the fulness of their ecclesiastical office. The National Catholic Educational Association elected him in April 1956 to succeed the Most Reverend Joseph E. Ritter, Archbishop of St. Louis, as its president general.

"He has not dealt with every administration detail personally," a New York *Times* (September 25, 1958) writer observed of the prelate's work in Milwaukee, "but when a crisis has arisen and a decision needed to be made, the Archbishop has made it and remained calm and good-tempered." During his pastorate the population of the Milwaukee archdiocese grew by almost 100,000, fourteen new parishes were established, six missions were elevated to parishes, fifty-six new schools were built, thirty-three churches, fourteen convents, seven hospitals, and three seminary buildings. Besides being an able administrator, he was, according to one of his associates in Milwaukee, "a most fatherly Bishop to all his people and his priests."

Archbishop Meyer was in Baltimore officiating at a consecration in September 1958, when

MEYER, ALBERT, CARDINAL—*Cont.*

he received a special delivery letter from Apostolic Delegate Amleto Giovanni Cicognani informing him that he was to take over the vacant see of Chicago. The appointment was one of the last official acts of Pope Pius XII. Two days after the appointment, when the news was made public, the newly designated pastor of Chicago recalled, for the benefit of the press, the appointment of his predecessor. "I remember when Cardinal Stritch was appointed to go to Chicago. He told me that the problems are the same wherever you go. A bishop's duties are to teach and to rule and to help the people strive for sanctity."

When the Archbishop handed the Chicago archdiocesan consultors the papal bulls confirming his designation on November 15, 1959, he became the fifth prelate to head what is now the largest archdiocese in the United States. His pastoral domain encompasses 2,027,243 Catholics, including 2,722 priests, 8,601 nuns, 405 brothers; 428 parishes, 400 elementary schools, eighty-six high schools, and seven colleges and universities. Three auxiliaries (two bishops and one other archbishop) aid him in the care of his fold.

On November 16, 1959 Pope John XXIII appointed eight new Cardinals, raising the membership in the Sacred College of Cardinals to seventy-nine, the largest in history. Meyer was one of two Americans named; the other was Archbishop Aloisius Joseph Muench of Fargo, North Dakota. The public consistory for the consecration of the Cardinals-elect was held on December 14, 1959.

"Religion cannot be separated from life," Meyer once said. "The Christian gospel applies to politics, business, social and domestic life." Despite his quiet, conservative bent, he has evidenced this belief in his Chicago pastorate by the interest and encouragement he has given Catholic social action groups such as the Young Christian Students and by his uncompromising stand against racial inequality in housing. "We are no longer permitted to adopt a detached attitude of wait and see," he stated before the President's Commission on Civil Rights when it visited Chicago in May 1958. "Gradualism would be merely a cloak for inaction if we do not turn our immediate attention to the legitimate claims of middle class Negroes who wish to leave the ghetto."

Albert Cardinal Meyer is a slender man, more than six feet tall, whose appearance has been described as "ascetic" and "contemplative." He occasionally relaxes from the tensions of his office by lighting a pipe, watching a baseball game on television, or going fishing. "Fishing is the apostolic recreation," he once told a friend, and observers say that the determination which characterizes his Church work carries over into his fishing trips. The number of these trips—to Wisconsin's North country in the summers—have necessarily diminished as the weight of his office has grown, but when he was younger, his colleagues say, he held the muskallonge-catching championship among them. The favorite recreation of Meyer, however, will always be among books, especially those on Church history.

References

Cath World 163:84 Ap '46
N Y Herald Tribune p23 S 25 '58 por
N Y Times p26+ S 25 '58 por
Newsday p50 S 25 '58
Newsweek 52:84 O 6 '58 por
Time 72:70 O 6 '58 por
Catholic Directory, 1959
American Catholic Who's Who, 1958 and 1959
Who's Who in America, 1958-59
World Biography (1954)

MONTAND, YVES (môn-tän') Oct. 13, 1921- French singer; actor
Address: b. c/o Jacques Canetti, 53 ave. Franklin Roosevelt, Paris 8, France; h. 15 Place Dauphine, Paris 1, France

Yves Montand first came to Broadway in the fall of 1959 equipped with a few scraps of English and the reputation of being the most popular singer of *chansons populaires* in France since World War II. His one-man show of twenty French *chansons*—songs which portray the lives of ordinary people—won the unqualified approval of the critics. Montand is also known to American audiences for his dramatic film roles in *Le Salaire de la Peur (The Wages of Fear)* and *Les Sorcières de Salem (The Witches of Salem)*, Jean-Paul Sartre's adaptation of Arthur Miller's *The Crucible*.

Born Yves (or Yvo or Ivo) Livi at Monsummano, Tuscany in Italy on October 13, 1921, Yves Montand is the third child of Luigi and Louise (Montand) Livi, an Italian peasant couple. He was two years old when his father, a broommaker, became so alarmed over the rise of Italian Fascism that he moved his entire family to Marseilles in southern France. Yves grew up in the tough slums of the Mediterranean port city and willingly left school at the age of eleven to go to work as a delivery boy.

While still in school Yves had picked up the trick of entertaining his classmates with imitations of Mickey Mouse, Flip the Frog, Fred Astaire, and the cowboys he saw in imported American westerns. Entertainment, however, became purely incidental as he earned a living at a succession of short-lived jobs—waiter, apprentice bartender, welder, factory worker, longshoreman, and hairdresser.

When Montand was seventeen, he mustered up enough courage to appear at a rough-and-tumble amateur show, held every Saturday night in the open air of a public square near his home. He escaped without catcalls or flying missiles and was sufficiently emboldened to begin singing in suburban cafés of Marseilles. Encouraged by his favorable reception, Montand obtained his first professional booking at a small music hall in Marseilles, where his performance included two songs of Charles Trenet, one of Maurice Chevalier, another of Fernandel, and an imitation of Donald Duck.

Thereafter he appeared in small music halls and suburban cinemas in provincial cities like Marseilles, Lyons, Toulouse, and Carcassonne, singing contemporary French songs and his own versions of pseudo-American western songs like "Les Plains du Far West." His entertainment pay, supplemented by his income from occasional dock-hand chores, financed intensive singing and dancing lessons during this six-year apprenticeship period. At this time, Montand also took part in the French Resistance movement fighting against the Nazi occupation of France.

The Allied armies were approaching France from the west when Yves Montand arrived in Paris in June 1944. He quickly obtained a booking at the ABC Theater and went on the bill as the final act, following the headliner. Although this spot is regarded by entertainers as anticlimactic (audiences usually leave after they have heard the main performer), Montand scored a success in it.

To increase his income and his Parisian following, Montand took on late-evening engagements in small cabarets. At the Moulin-Rouge he met Edith Piaf, an established *chanteuse,* and became her protégé. She persuaded Montand to drop the synthetic American western songs he had featured in his act, and he went further, playing down his imitative numbers and developing a distinct style of his own. Montand's new program was fairly well received at Lyons and Versailles shortly after the liberation of Paris, but two months later he played the same act at the Théâtre de l'Etoile in Paris with resounding success. Montand presented his first one-man show at the Théâtre de l'Etoile in 1951 and later returned to the same theater for long runs in the 1953-54 and 1958-59 seasons.

Montand's style, since perfected in more than 200 recorded songs and in personal appearances on five continents, derives from the tradition of the French *chanson populaire.* Maurice Chevalier, Charles Trenet, and Edith Piaf had worked this vein with conspicuous success. Since *chansons* are specifically composed for certain performers, Montand's songs are all written especially for him. They feature lyrics with which audiences can identify themselves, because they deal with the everyday experiences of ordinary people. As Montand recently explained, "I try to sing of the small joys, the small sorrows, the small annoyances that are the same all over, like *l'amour.*"

Chansons populaires sometimes find their way into a singer's repertoire and then go into general circulation for many years. Montand introduced "Les Feuilles Mortes" ("Autumn Leaves") fourteen years ago, for example, and "Luna Park" has been identified with him for more than a decade. These and other songs from Montand's repertoire have appeared on records such as *One Man Show: Yves Montand* (Columbia), *Yves Montand* (Capitol), and on several discs with an Odéon label: *10 Chansons Pour L'Ete, Recital Yves Montand,* and *Succès du Recital 1958.* A recent recording is a Monitor disc, *Chansons Populaires de France.*

Montand made his American debut at the Henry Miller Theatre on September 22, 1959 with a one-man show of twenty French *chan-*

YVES MONTAND

sons. Received vociferously by both the public and the critics, Montand extended his original engagement from three to six weeks. "Montand is widely regarded as France's best and he was very good," New York *Times* reviewer Kenneth Campbell wrote (September 23, 1959). "He showed a remarkable range of emotion . . . and didn't try for effect; he just sang in a direct, straightforward manner." A New York *World-Telegram and Sun* reviewer noted that Montand "is an excellent mime; he can tell tales with his face and in a rubbery, rhythmic way he is a superb dancer" (September 23, 1959).

Through Edith Piaf, Montand had obtained his first motion-picture engagement, a minor part in *Étoile Sans Lumière (Star Without Light),* in 1945. The following year he starred in *Les Portes de la Nuit (The Doors of Night),* after Jean Gabir, who had been expected to play the leading role, withdrew from the enterprise. Other French movies in which he has appeared are *L'Idole* (1949), *Paris est Toujours Paris* (1950), *Paris Chante Toujours* (1951), and *Premier May* (shown in America in 1958). His performance as a hard-grained and ruthless truck driver in *Le Salaire de La Peur (The Wages of Fear),* a film produced in France in 1952 and seen here three years later, won warm reviews from American critics.

In 1949 Montand met Simone Signoret, already a leading French actress, and they were married on June 15, 1950, following her divorce from French film director, Yves Allegret. The Montands appeared together in *Les Sorcières de Salem (The Witches of Salem),* a stage version of Arthur Miller's *The Crucible,* for a one-year run in Paris in 1954 and shortly thereafter in a movie version (American release, 1958). Jean-Paul Sartre wrote both the stage and screen adaptations. "Perhaps the outstanding performance is that of Yves Montand

MONTAND, YVES—*Continued*

as the weak Puritan husband who succumbs to the lusts of the flesh and then struggles through a tormenting succession of vacillations until he goes to a heroic death," Bosley Crowther of the New York *Times* wrote (December 9, 1958). A New York *World-Telegram and Sun* writer on the same day called the Montands' performance "immensely moving."

Other recent motion pictures in which Montand has played leading roles are *Les Héros Sont Fatigués (Heroes and Sinners),* released in America in 1959, and *La Loi,* which was seen here as *Where the Hot Wind Blows.* Montand also starred with Marilyn Monroe in *Let's Make Love,* a Twentieth Century-Fox film released in the summer of 1960. The Montands say they are willing to make American films, if they are offered suitable roles and if they are able to obtain permission from the United States Department of State to make extended stays in this country. The State Department, which denied them visas for several years because of their association with leftist causes, had granted them a temporary six-month waiver for their 1959-60 visit.

The Montands appeared in April 1960 at the nationally televised presentation of the 1959 awards of the Academy of Motion Picture Arts and Sciences in Hollywood. Simone Signoret received the award as best actress for her performance in the motion picture, *Room at the Top,* and Montand did a ten-minute singing stint as a guest star on the Academy Awards telecast. Montand also was seen on *The Dinah Shore Chevy Show* and, with his wife, on *Person to Person.*

Montand first entertained in Canada in December 1959. His previous visits to London, Egypt, Yugoslavia, Germany, Switzerland, Russia, Poland, Romania, Bulgaria, Hungary, Czechoslovakia, Israel, Japan, and South America have proved that his appeal is universal. Montand is a large-nosed, large-mouthed man with a tall, wiry build and a slightly weatherbeaten face; his best feature is his warm, spontaneous smile. His regular stage costume consists of a dark-brown shirt, open at the collar, and matching brown slacks.

On the stage, Montand appears casual and relaxed, but there is nothing happy-go-lucky about the preparations for his appearances. He runs the entire show, rehearsing rigorously, planning every detail of the staging and lighting, and fussing endlessly to make every cue and prop exactly right. He chooses his material with the utmost care, then goes through it until every last detail has been permanently fixed in his mind.

When the Montands are not on tour or working in Paris, they spend their time at their large house in Normandy. Even at home, they show little inclination to take it easy. They run a small stock farm, and Montand, trying out new song routines, rehearses inside the house or, on pleasant days, hauls a microphone and its wires out on the lawn to continue his singing there. They watch important films at their home motion-picture theater, or spend hours

talking with their friends and fellow artists. He drives a $25,000 Bentley.

References

N Y Herald Tribune p1+ S 20 '59
N Y Post Mag p4 S 20 '59 por
New Yorker 35:33 S 26 '59
Reporter 21:35 O 29 '59
Dictionnaire Biographique Français Contemporain (1954)
Who's Who in France, 1959-60

MOORE, ARCHIE   Dec. 13, 1916(?)-

Boxer; actor

Address: h. San Diego, Calif.

Since 1952 the venerable boxer Archie Moore has reigned as the light-heavyweight champion of the world. During his long pugilistic career that began in 1936 he has knocked out 128 opponents, more than any other boxer in the history of the prize ring. Today, Moore is a success in the unrelated arts of professional boxing, motion pictures, and—to a lesser extent—literature. Moore became a film actor in 1959, when he played the role of Jim, the Negro slave, in Metro-Goldwyn-Mayer's film version of Mark Twain's *The Adventures of Huckleberry Finn.* In 1960 the McGraw-Hill Book Company, Inc., published Moore's candid, philosophic, and sometimes bitter autobiography, *The Archie Moore Story.* Although the book may not win any literary awards, it is warmed throughout by the personality of the man whose life it records.

One prize so far has eluded Moore's grasp. He has twice fought for and failed to win the heavyweight championship of the world. In 1955 he was knocked out in the ninth round of a fight with Rocky Marciano, but not before Moore had knocked down the champion. In 1956, after Marciano retired, Moore fought Floyd Patterson for the crown, and Patterson won by a knockout in the fifth round.

Archibald Lee Moore was born (according to his own account) on December 13, 1916 in Benoit, Mississippi, the son of Thomas Wright, a farm laborer, and Lorena Wright. He was christened Archibald Lee Wright. His mother gives his birthdate as December 13, 1913. Moore finds speculations about his age amusing, and wins a great deal of publicity from the controversy surrounding his birthdate.

His early years were darkened by emotional insecurity. While he was still a baby, his parents separated, and Archie and his older sister were given to the care of an uncle and aunt, Cleveland and Willie Pearl Moore, of St. Louis. He dropped the name of Wright and adopted the surname of his uncle and aunt because, as he has said, "It was less questions to be called Moore." Growing up in St. Louis, Moore attended the Dumas School, the Jefferson School, and Lincoln High School. Eventually he came into conflict with the law when he began to run around with a street gang. He bought his first pair of boxing gloves with the proceeds from a couple of oil lamps he had stolen from home.

"It was inevitable that I would be caught," Moore has written in his autobiography. "I think I knew this even before I started, but somehow the urge to have a few cents in my pocket made me overlook this eventuality. So I was caught. I was caught three times. The third time I had stolen money from a streetcar. . . . I was sentenced to three years in reform school and eventually served twenty-two months."

At the age of seventeen, Moore was released from what is now known as the Missouri Training School at Booneville, Missouri. He joined the newly formed Camp 3760 of the Civilian Conservation Corps at Poplar Bluff, Missouri. Aware that there was more money for Negroes in boxing than in baseball, Moore took up amateur boxing. In 1936 he engaged in his first professional bout, starting as a middleweight, when he knocked out Kneibert Davidson in two rounds. He won his first thirteen fights by knockouts; then he lost three bouts in succession. He won his seventeenth fight by a decision and reeled off fourteen consecutive knockouts before he lost on June 24, 1938 to Johnny Romero. Three months later he knocked out Romero in a return bout. Moore's early record in the ring followed a pattern: he would win a number of fights, lose one or two, then start winning again.

In 1940 Moore toured Australia, where he won seven out of seven fights. There he discovered a way of losing weight, which for years he kept secret, insisting that he had picked it up from an aborigine. When *The Archie Moore Story* was published in 1960, the curious were finally initiated into the mysteries of the secret diet. To their disappointment, they learned that the key to the secret diet was the chewing of meat to extract all of its juices without swallowing the bulk, and the drinking of sauerkraut juice.

From Australia, Moore returned to the United States, ranking fourth among the middleweights of the world. Early in 1941 he suffered from a perforated ulcer and underwent surgery. During the operation he lapsed into a coma and remained unconscious for five days. In addition to the ulcer, he endured both peritonitis and pneumonia, and when he was discharged from the hospital he looked years older, and weighed a little over 100 pounds.

In 1942 Moore returned to the ring. By 1946 he was the leading contender for the light-heavyweight championship, and he remained so throughout the reigns of three champions: Freddie Mills of England and Gus Lesnevich and Joey Maxim of the United States. When Maxim won the title, Moore began to conduct a campaign to obtain a fight with the champion.

"I took matters into my own hands," Moore has written. "I began a letter writing campaign to sports writers all over the country. I pleaded, I cursed, I demanded a shot at Maxim's crown." His persistence was rewarded on December 17, 1952, when he fought Maxim, and by winning a unanimous decision, became the world's light-heavyweight champion. Moore and Maxim met again on June 24, 1953, and

ARCHIE MOORE

Moore won by a decision. Their third and final bout took place on January 27, 1954. Moore was again the victor by a decision. Later Maxim went on to defeat Floyd Patterson before Patterson won the heavyweight title. Then he faded from sight.

Challenged next by Harold Johnson, Moore retained his championship by winning by a knockout in the fourteenth round. Wanting, at that point, a fight with heavyweight champion Rocky Marciano, Moore paved the way in a fight with Bobo Olson, who was then middleweight champion. On June 22, 1955, at the Polo Grounds in New York, Moore knocked out Olson in the third round. Moore met Marciano on September 21, 1955, at the Yankee Stadium in New York. In the second round Moore dropped Marciano for a count of two, but Marciano weathered the storm and knocked out Moore in the ninth round. Moore has said: "I think a knockout is the only way to end a championship fight and I went out the way a good fighter should, taking the full count." He made one more attempt to win the heavyweight crown when he fought Floyd Patterson on November 30, 1956, in Chicago. Since Marciano had retired, Moore and Patterson were considered the two outstanding contenders. Patterson won by a knockout in the fifth round.

Thwarted in his ambitions for the heavyweight title, Moore concentrated on guarding his light-heavyweight title, and he has unquestionably succeeded. On September 30, 1957 he knocked out Tony Anthony in seven rounds. He next defended his title on December 10, 1958, against the Canadian Yvon Durelle in Montreal. The contest developed into one of the more exciting fights of the decade. Durelle knocked down Moore three times in the first round, and again knocked him down in the fifth round. But Moore survived the ordeal and won by a knockout in the eleventh round. With his

MOORE, ARCHIE—*Continued*

usual panache, Moore says of the fight: "It was my finest hour."

On the basis of his title defense, Moore was named Fighter of the Year and awarded the Edward J. Neil trophy for 1958 by the Boxing Writers Association. The knockout was the 127th registered by Moore in his career. It broke the record for the most knockouts by one fighter, a mark formerly held by William L. (Young) Stribling. When Moore fought Durelle a second time on August 12, 1959, he won by a knockout in three rounds.

In 1959 Archie Moore began his acting career when he played the role of Jim, the Negro slave, in the Metro-Goldwyn-Mayer production of *The Adventures of Huckleberry Finn*. The movie itself received uncharitable notices from some critics. A *Time* magazine reviewer, for example, remarked that "while the story goes down the river, the picture heads up the creek" (June 13, 1960). Moore fared much better with the critics. Richard L. Coe wrote in the Washington *Post and Times Herald*: "There is a most winning performance, one of great dignity, from Archie Moore as the slave" (June 22, 1960). Moore has said that he would like to try his hand at roles in re-makes of such films as *The Green Pastures, The Champ*, or *Carmen Jones*.

Archie Moore was married on August 20, 1955 to Joan Hardy, a former New York model and sister-in-law of Sidney Poitier, the actor. Moore's four previous marriages ended in divorce. The Moores have two daughters, Joan and Rena, and make their home in San Diego, California. Moore is a heavy-set man with a furrowed face that usually wears a wide grin. He is five feet eleven inches tall, weighs between 175 and 212 pounds, although his title imposes a weight limit of 175 pounds, and measures 19, 12, and 48 in the biceps, forearms, and chest, respectively. He looks flabby in the prize ring, even when he is in prime condition.

To get into that condition, Moore runs, skips rope, and relies on his once secret method of losing weight. He neither smokes nor drinks. To relax, he plays the cornet, listens to jazz on his tape recorder, does some target shooting, develops photographs in his darkroom, and writes letters to correspondents all over the world. He makes his family the center of his existence. He sometimes drops into a language of his own coinage, in which such words as "summate," "relaxism," and "escapology" occur again and again. One of the most generous persons in the world of sports, he gives his money away to so many causes that his wife once reproached him for draining the family's financial resources. "I'm not giving anything away," he told her. "I'm just sharing." He is also one of the most philosophic members of the boxing fraternity. "My career is like a river," he has said. "I would like to have it end by fulfillment, by flowing into the mighty ocean. I don't want it to dry up before it reaches there."

Reference

Moore, Archie   The Archie Moore Story (1960)

MOORE, ELISABETH LUCE   Apr. 4, 1903-   Social worker; organization official

Address: b. Institute of International Education, 1 E. 67th St., New York 21; h. 1000 Park Ave., New York 28

Since the launching of the first Sputnik, the increasing recognition that many world leaders have given to the importance of education and of cultural exchange among individuals of one nation and another, has heightened the value of the purpose of the Institute of International Education. In November 1959 Mrs. Elisabeth Luce Moore, succeeding Columbia University President Dr. Grayson Kirk, became the first woman to serve as chairman of the IIE, which was founded in 1919 by the Carnegie Endowment for International Peace "to promote international exchange of ideas in all aspects of education." She met the qualifications for her position through many years of work in cultural, civic, religious, and social service agencies, especially in the YWCA and in several organizations devoted to strengthening the ties between the United States and Asia.

Much of the interest that Elisabeth Luce Moore takes in international and educational causes may be traced to influences in early life. She was born in Shantung Province, China on April 4, 1903, one of four children of the Reverend Dr. Henry Winters and Elizabeth Middleton (Root) Luce. Her father, who had gone to China under the Presbyterian Board of Foreign Missions, was associated for some years with Shantung Christian University and was instrumental in developing the United Board of China Christian Colleges. Her mother was related to the noted statesman Elihu Root, who had a share in establishing the Institute of International Education.

The other three children in the Luce family were Henry R., who became the editor and publisher of *Life, Time*, and *Fortune* magazines; Emmavail (now Mrs. Leslie Severinghaus); and Sheldon. With her brothers and sister, Elisabeth Luce was tutored at home by a German governess. Their parents supplemented their education with lessons in history, English literature and composition, and comparative religion.

Once when Dr. Luce was on a leave of absence, Elisabeth, then about ten years old, studied for a time at a school in the Harz mountains in Germany. Returning to Asia for a few more years, she attended the Shanghai American School and other schools. She completed her preparatory training at Abbott Academy in Andover, Massachusetts and then entered Wellesley College in Wellesley, Massachusetts, where she chose philosophy as her major subject and in 1924 received her B.A. degree.

For about a year following her graduation she was employed in editorial work for Charles E. Merrill Publications and beginning in 1926 wrote book reviews for *Time*. She was married on September 17, 1926 to Maurice Thompson Moore, a New York attorney, and for some years after her marriage continued to write for her brother's periodicals. Her article on the Rothschild family appeared in the first issue of *Fortune*, January 1930.

Active also in volunteer social work, Mrs Moore served as chairman of the library exhibitions of the New York Junior League from 1931 to 1935. Over a period of many years she has contributed greatly to the undertakings of the Young Women's Christian Association of the United States. She became a member of its national board and chairman of the board's foreign division in 1944. In the latter position she has traveled in many countries of Asia, Africa, South America, and Europe to help carry out YWCA programs directed toward developing women's capabilities and sense of responsibility as citizens.

Another office that Mrs. Moore held in the YWCA was chairman of the round-the-world reconstruction fund, which in 1947 raised over $2,000,000 to finance the organization's projects in countries devastated by the war. She was also chairman of publicity for the YWCA centennial fund campaign. As a delegate of the American YWCA, she attended the World YWCA Council meeting in Lebanon in 1951, in England in 1955, and in Mexico in 1959.

During World War II, in 1942, Mrs. Moore had also become chairman of the National United Service Organizations (USO) Council and remained in that post until 1946, playing a considerable part in the development of services for men and women in the armed forces of the United States. After the war the Secretary of Defense appointed her a member of the Advisory Committee on Women in the Services (DACOWITS).

The United States government again called on Mrs. Moore, in 1949, to serve as a member of the advisory committee of the Economic Cooperation Administration (ECA), which administered the Marshall Plan. In 1951 she was an American delegate to the International Conference of Women, the first to be held in postwar Germany.

On November 9, 1959 Mrs. Moore was elected chairman of the board of trustees of the Institute of International Education, after having served as vice-chairman since 1950. The United States' largest private multinational organization for international exchange, the IIE develops and carries out programs annually involving some 5,000 persons. Each year it sends about 1,500 American students to foreign countries and arranges for thousands of students from more than eighty countries to study in the United States. It administers the program for the exchange of scholars under the Fulbright Act of 1946 and scholarships for the Ford, Rockefeller, and Carnegie foundations and other private organizations, as well as for governments of some foreign countries. IIE's president is Kenneth Holland (see *C.B.*, March 1952).

Throughout her career in public service Mrs. Moore has shown special concern for promoting good will and understanding between Asian countries and the Western world. She was vice-president of United Services to China in 1948, has been a trustee of the China Institute of America since 1945 and vice-president since 1949, vice-chairman of Aid to Refugee Chinese Intellectuals since 1952, a member of the board

Bradford Bachrach

ELISABETH LUCE MOORE

of directors and trustee of the Asia Foundation since 1954, and trustee of the United Board of Christian Higher Education in Asia since 1953. As early as 1938 she had become chairman of the Wellesley-Yenching section of the United Board of China Christian Colleges.

A member of the board of trustees of Wellesley College, Mrs. Moore has also recently helped direct the drive in New York for the college's $15,000,000 faculty salary advancement fund. She has received honorary degrees from Trinity University and Adelphi College and in 1955 was awarded the gold medal of the National Institute of Social Sciences for "unique and unselfish service" and for contributions "to greater understanding and good will among nations." Hobart and William Smith colleges gave her the Elizabeth Blackwell Medal in 1959 for distinguished services. Mrs. Moore is a Presbyterian. In recent years she has taken an active part in politics on behalf of the Republican party. During 1958 she was co-chairman of Nelson A. Rockefeller's campaign for Governor of New York State.

Elisabeth Luce Moore and Maurice T. Moore have two sons, Maurice Thompson and Michael. In an article in the *Ladies' Home Journal* (October 1956), "When I Entertain," Mrs. Moore is described as "a sparkling, delightfully energetic person" who combines her work in civic and cultural causes with " a busy life as one of New York's most charming and capable hostesses." She recently said in an interview for the *Christian Science Monitor* (March 21, 1960) that her interest in international relations was part of her "natural way of looking at things." After she had lived for some years in the United States, she explained, she "became dismayed because so many Americans were so preoccupied with their own problems at home that they didn't realize how great an impact world affairs were to have on their

MOORE, ELISABETH LUCE—*Continued*

personal lives—or appreciate the importance of the part each individual can play in international affairs."

References

Christian Sci Mon p4 Mr 21 '60

Who's Who in America, 1960-61
Who's Who of American Women, 1958-59

MOORE, MRS. MAURICE T(HOMPSON) *See* Moore, Elisabeth Luce

MUENCH, ALOISIUS (JOSEPH), CARDINAL (mĭnch) Feb. 18, 1889- Roman Catholic prelate

Address: The Roman Curia, Vatican City

In a brilliantly colorful ceremony in St. Peter's Basilica, Vatican City on December 17, 1959, Pope John XXIII conferred the rank of Cardinal of the Roman Catholic Church on Archbishop Aloisius Joseph Muench of Fargo, North Dakota, and Papal Nuncio to West Germany since 1951. Installed with six other Roman prelates (the eighth, Paolo Cardinal Marella, received his red hat in Paris) on the fourth and final day of ceremonies, Cardinal Muench received the additional honor of being appointed to the Roman Curia, the central administrative agency of the Catholic Church. Although the second American Cardinal summoned to the Curia, he will be the first to sit with this administrative body. Samuel Cardinal Stritch of Chicago had been called but his death in May 1958 prevented him from ever serving. Cardinal Muench was appointed to the Vatican diplomatic corps in 1946, the first United States citizen to be an accredited diplomatic representative of the Vatican. During his thirteen years in West Germany he became dean of the diplomatic corps in Bonn.

Born in Milwaukee, Wisconsin on February 18, 1889, Aloisius Joseph Muench was the oldest of eight children of German emigrant parents, Joseph and Teresa (Kraus) Muench. Like many other American boys, he sold newspapers during his school days. Called to the priesthood, he entered the Seminary of St. Francis de Sales, Milwaukee in 1904. He was ordained on June 8, 1913. Then twenty-four years old, Father Muench was appointed curate in St. Michael's Church, Milwaukee, where he served until 1917. He was then assigned as curate at St. Paul's Chapel, University of Wisconsin, and chaplain of St. Mary's Hospital, both located in Madison.

While serving as both curate and chaplain, Father Muench enrolled in the university's graduate school to study economics. Two years later the university awarded him his master's degree. Sent to Europe that year, 1919, he entered the University of Fribourg, Switzerland. For the next two years he studied for

his doctorate in social science and in 1921 was awarded his degree *summa cum laude*. Remaining abroad for another year, he took graduate courses at the universities of Oxford, Cambridge, and Louvain and at the Sorbonne. Before returning to the United States, he traveled through many European countries still showing the devastating effects of World War I, particularly Germany, where he spent much time.

Upon his return to America, Father Muench was appointed professor of dogmatic theology, social sciences, homiletics, and catechetics at the Seminary of St. Francis de Sales in Milwaukee. He was subsequently named dean of the theology department and was appointed rector of the seminary in 1929.

In teaching and directing young men studying for the priesthood, Father Muench exhibited more than an academic knowledge of economics and allied social problems. His interest in Catholic Social Action dated back to his own seminarian days when he had been named a delegate to the Chicago convention of the National Catholic Central Verein (union), held in 1911, two years before he was ordained. He had impressed the leaders with his knowledge and his readiness to participate in their program. In the following years he attended the CCV's social study courses and after his return from abroad in 1922 became one of its most respected lecturers. He was known for his firm adherence to the elucidation of principles.

Such elucidation was evident in his writings, too. In an article "The State and the Worker," published in *America* (May 2, 1931), Father Muench re-emphasized the principles of social justice set down by Pope Leo XIII in his celebrated encyclical, *Rerum Novarum,* published forty years earlier. Stressing the state's obligation in justice to protect its great element of economic prosperity—the working class—Father Muench advocated a sound program of social legislation based on Christian principles. When employers failed to provide minimum wage laws, humane working conditions, security of employment, social insurance, Father Muench believed, the state should live up to its high duty by providing such legislation for the welfare of its labor force. For, wrote Father Muench, "by insisting on social justice for labor the State in the end serves the best interests of all."

On September 21, 1934 Father Muench was named domestic prelate to Pope Pius XI and given the rank of monsignor. Eleven months later he was elevated to bishop. Concluding his duties as seminary rector, he was elected to the See of Fargo, North Dakota. He was consecrated in Milwaukee on October 15, 1935, by Archbishop Amleto Giovanni Cicognani, Apostolic Delegate to the United States. Through all his promotions he maintained an active membership and leadership in the Catholic Central Verein. Before being elected bishop he had been named chairman of its social action committee and also chairman of its resolutions committee. Known for his intense interest in rural life, Bishop Muench was in 1939 named president of the National Catholic Rural Life Conference and was co-author of the *Rural Life Manifesto* published that same year.

During the Allied occupation of Germany, in June 1946, Bishop Muench was named official American representative to act as liaison officer between the Church in Germany and military government authorities in the American occupation zone. The following month Pope Pius XII appointed him apostolic visitor to Germany, a strictly ecclesiastical post. Muench, who has said that he went in "on the backs of the occupation armies," was named head of the Papal Relief Commission that same month. Reviewing his work, *The Bulletin,* weekly publication of the Bonn government, noted in its February 24, 1959 issue: "Thus the man who today is the dean of the Diplomatic Corps in Bonn did not come to Germany as a career diplomat but for work of a pastoral and religious nature. During the 2 years following his arrival 10,000 CARE parcels were brought in on his initiative alone; this was a great deal more important at the time than diplomatic routine."

In 1949 Bishop Muench was named regent of the papal nunciature in Germany and the following year he was given the personal title of Archbishop. At the time that diplomatic relations were restored with Germany in 1951, he was named Papal Nuncio with both diplomatic and ecclesiastical responsibilities. He was the first diplomat to present his credentials to President Theodor Heuss at Villa Hammerschmidt. During his thirteen years in the diplomatic service of the Holy See, he remained Bishop of Fargo. He made frequent trips home to his North Dakota diocese, never interrupted his series of Lenten pastorals which he started in 1936, wrote monthly articles for his diocesan newspaper that explained his work in Germany, and treated events current in his own diocese.

After receiving his *galero,* the red hat symbolizing his office, on December 17, 1959 Cardinal Muench took possession of his titular church in Rome, the Church of San Bernardo alle Terme, a Roman ruin converted to Christian use. The assignment preserves the tradition that the first Cardinals of the Church were Roman pastors who served as consultants to the Holy Father, also Bishop of Rome. On the same day he received his assignment of new duties in the College of Cardinals. They include membership in the Sacred Congregation for Extraordinary Ecclesiastical Affairs, connected with the Vatican Secretariat; the Congregation of Rites, which handles liturgical matters as well as causes of beatification and canonization; and the Congregation of Religious, which handles all matters pertaining to religious orders and congregations.

In addition to lecturing and writing on socioeconomic subjects, Cardinal Muench is the co-author of *The Church, Fascism and Peace* published by Our Sunday Visitor in 1944. Now honorary chairman of the social action committee of the Catholic Central Verein, he is also a member of the pontifical commission for sacred sciences of Catholic University of America, the Bishops' Peace Commission, asso-

Wide World
ALOISIUS CARDINAL MUENCH

ciate member of the administrative board of National Catholic Welfare Conference, charter member of Pax Romana for promotion of peace among university students, charter member of the Catholic Conference on Industrial Problems, and an assistant on the postwar reorganization of the International Association of Labor Legislation, Basle, Switzerland.

A stocky man, who only in recent years gave up his lifelong hobbies of hunting and fishing, Cardinal Muench is seventy-one years old, but after his first audience with Pope John XXIII in February 1959, the Holy Father remarked, "The Nuncio of Germany looks like a young man of 50" (*Social Justice Review,* May 1959). With his easy-going, informal American manner and Midwestern humor, he is said to be far removed from the prototype of Vatican diplomats.

References

Advocate p5 N 19 '59
N Y Herald Tribune p29 N 15 '59; p14 Je 28 '60 por
N Y Times p23 N 17 '59
Time 74:44 N 30 '59 por
American Catholic Who's Who, 1960 and 1961
Dictionary of the American Hierarchy, 1940
Who's Who in America, 1958-59

MUIR, JAMES 1892(?)-Apr. 10, 1960
Banker; president (since 1949) and chairman (since 1954) of the Royal Bank of Canada. See *Current Biography* (May) 1950.

Obituary

N Y Times p31 Ap 11 '60

MULLIGAN, GERRY Apr. 6, 1927- Musician; composer; arranger
Address: b. 745 5th Ave., New York 22

As arranger, baritone saxophonist, and composer, Gerry Mulligan has taken a leading role in making "modern" or "cool" jazz accepted on the world musical scene. He has done much to expand the audience for jazz in the last ten years, even in such unlikely places as the Orient and in countries behind the Iron Curtain. In helping to make jazz respectable, he has won over some admirers of classical music. Mulligan, who represents the mainstream of jazz, merges traditionalism with modernism. The jazz buff who listens closely to Mulligan's music can hear the sure and solid beat of New Orleans pulsing under the jazz sounds of the future. More adaptable than some of his colleagues, Mulligan can fit into any style of jazz.

Mulligan mainly earned his reputation by working with the small jazz ensemble (quartet or sextet), but he recently took steps to broaden his activities. He formed a jazz ensemble of thirteen men, making up what in jazz circles is called a "big band." For it he plans an ambitious program of tours and appearances at jazz clubs and festivals. In 1960 Mulligan also began to act in Hollywood films.

Gerald Joseph Mulligan was born on April 6, 1927, in Queens Village, Long Island, the youngest of the four sons of George Vincent Raphael and Louise Frederika (Shannon) Mulligan. His father, a management engineer, was required by his work to move about the United States, and Gerry spent his childhood in Marion, Ohio; Franklinville, New Jersey; Lockport, New York; Chicago, Illinois; Kalamazoo and Detroit, Michigan; and Reading and Philadelphia, Pennsylvania.

From an early age, Gerry Mulligan evinced strong musical instincts. Starting with the piano and progressing to the ocarina, and later

GERRY MULLIGAN

to more complex wind instruments such as clarinets and saxophones of various pitches, Mulligan showed promise both as a performer and composer. He composed a song called "You and Me and Love," later copyrighted, at the age of seven.

Despite his precocity, Mulligan insists that his early formal music instruction contributed little to his development as a musician and that he has learned principally on his own. However, Mulligan does acknowledge one teacher, Sammy Correnti, with whom he began to study in Reading in 1943. In Reading high school Mulligan was already playing in school ensembles and in small outside groups of his own. He kept up these extracurricular music activities when he entered the West Philadelphia Catholic High School for Boys in 1944.

In Philadelphia, Mulligan began his professional career when he made two arrangements for the band conducted by Johnny Warrington over radio station WCAU. He was paid $35 apiece. In the summer of 1944 he was engaged by Alex Bartha's band as a tenor saxophonist for an Atlantic City engagement. Planning to tour with the group (the tour never materialized), Mulligan left school. He soon found a job as an arranger with Tommy Tucker's orchestra.

On tour with the Tucker band, Mulligan was for the first time exposed to some of the more original trends in modern jazz when he listened to Chicago performances of the Billy Eckstine ensemble. After thirteen weeks with Tucker, he returned to Philadelphia as an arranger for Elliot Lawrence's new WCAU band. He remained in the position for about a year. Through the late alto saxophonist Charlie Parker he won an opportunity to perform as a tenor saxophonist with Dizzy Gillespie's quintet in Philadelphia.

In January 1946, after moving to New York City, Mulligan was hired as an arranger for Gene Krupa's band, with which he also toured as a performer on tenor and alto saxophones. After a year with Krupa, Mulligan found himself without a job, and he was forced to sell all his instruments except a baritone saxophone. He thus acquired a mastery over the instrument with which he is now most closely identified as a performer.

Returning to New York in 1947, Mulligan joined forces with another arranger, Gil Evans, to develop a new conception of jazz. Later known as "cool jazz," it embodied subtler effects and a wider range of instrumentation than those usually found in jazz ensembles of the period. As performed by a group headed by Miles Davis, first at New York's Royal Roost night club and later for Capitol records, these arrangements by Evans, Mulligan, and John Lewis have had an enormous influence in jazz circles.

From 1948 to 1950 Mulligan worked as baritone saxophonist and arranger for Benny Goodman, Elliot Lawrence, Claude Thornhill, Kai Winding, Charlie Parker, and Miles Davis. In 1951 he did arrangements for Stan Kenton's band. But Mulligan's career did not gain full momentum until 1952, when Richard Bock, a producer at the Haig, a Los Angeles night club, hired Mulligan for his Monday night jazz productions.

By this time Mulligan had decided that he could dispense with the piano in jazz ensembles. He formed a group that comprised himself on baritone saxophone, Chet Baker on trumpet, Bob Whitlock on bass, and Chico Hamilton on drums. Bock recorded Mulligan's group for his Pacific Jazz record company, first on a single disc and later on a ten-inch long-playing record that sold 30,000 copies and brought Mulligan into national prominence.

Since late in 1953 Mulligan has organized several jazz quartets and sextets. His combinations have played in night clubs, concerts, and at jazz festivals, in the United States and abroad. Mulligan first performed outside the United States at the Salle Pleyel in Paris in June 1954, where his group won an enthusiastic reception. His ensembles have recorded for several companies, including Pacific Jazz, Columbia, Mercury, and Verve. Mulligan has been reluctant to sign long-term contracts with any one company because he wants to be free to record when, where, and what he likes.

A spokesman for jazz as a serious form of art, Mulligan resents playing at night clubs where the audience is not likely to be attentive. He also objects to festival programs and concerts that present many groups in sequence, because he feels that no one ensemble has time to reach its best level of performance in the short time allotted. Moreover, he selects the halls in which he performs on the basis of their acoustical values.

Despite his stern code, Mulligan is happiest when playing before live audiences. "During a period when the mode in jazz has often been an introverted 'coolness' or a rather arch propriety," John S. Wilson wrote in the New York Times (April 12, 1959), "Mr. Mulligan has been one of the few jazz musicians generally accepted as à la mode who has given outward evidence of thoroughly enjoying his contacts with audiences, a pleasure that is reflected in the wit and spirit of his playing."

His bit parts in such films as *The Subterraneans, The Rat Race,* and *The Bells Are Ringing* have not swerved Mulligan's principal interest from the world of jazz. His recently formed big band has attracted much favorable comment. A *Variety* critic reported that it is "a quiet, relaxed band which features much muted brass. Modern in sound, it still retains a melodic, swinging style characteristic of Mulligan's small groups" (April 13, 1960).

Mulligan entertains some strong opinions on at least one nonmusical subject: narcotics addiction. An admitted addict for a period beginning in the late 1940's, he has been arraigned several times and in 1953 spent three and one-half months in a California prison as a result of the habit. Although he is now cured, he still protests the legal approach to the problem in the United States and feels that help, not punishment, is in order for drug addicts.

In February 1953 Gerry Mulligan was married to Jeffie Lee Boyd. The marriage was annulled in the same year, and in May 1953 he was married to Arlyne Brown, by whom he had one son, Reed Brown Mulligan. The marriage ended in divorce in March 1959. Although he was born a Roman Catholic and at an early age was attracted to the priesthood as a vocation, Mulligan now considers himself an agnostic.

Gerry Mulligan, who is six feet one inch tall, is thin and angular in build. His closely cropped, reddish-gold hair accentuates his youthful appearance. He dresses carefully in the idiom of the Ivy League, eschewing the extremely casual clothes sometimes affected by jazzmen. Mulligan belongs to the American Society of Composers, Authors, and Publishers and to the American Federation of Musicians.

References

New Yorker 35:51+ Mr 21 '59; 35:39+ Mr 28 '59

Who's Who in America, 1960-61

MUNIZ, JOÃO CARLOS Mar. 31, 1893-June 18, 1960 Former Brazilian Ambassador to the United States (1953-56) and to Argentina (1956-58); Representative to the United Nations (1946-53). See *Current Biography* (September) 1952.

Obituary

N Y Times p31 Je 20 '60

MURPHY, GARDNER July 8, 1895- Psychologist; writer
Address: b. Menninger Foundation, Topeka, Kan.; h. 3007 E. 21st St., Topeka, Kan.

Although Gardner Murphy has never been a popularizer of psychology, he is one of the best-known psychologists in the United States. Since 1952 he has directed the research work of the Menninger Foundation in Topeka, Kansas, an organization that has pioneered in the improvement of mental health. Earlier, he had been on the faculty of Columbia University, from 1921 to 1940, and City College of the City of New York, from 1940 to 1952. During the past twenty-five years several of his many scholarly books have been used as textbooks, on personality or social psychology. Because of his integrative, reflective, and speculative way of handling the enormous amount of research material at his command, he has attracted readers who are interested in both man's capacity to overcome present world crises and his developing potentialities to solve future problems.

Gardner Murphy, the son of Edgar Gardner and Maud (King) Murphy, was born in Chillicothe, Ohio on July 8, 1895. For his college preparatory training he studied at Hotchkiss School in Lakeville, Connecticut from 1910 to 1912, and then attended Yale University, where he took his B.A. degree in 1916. He received his M.A. degree the following year from Harvard University.

Military service in World War I forced Murphy to postpone further graduate study. Entering the United States Army in 1917, he fought with the American Expeditionary Forces until July 1919. He began his almost twenty-year association with Columbia Univer-

GARDNER MURPHY

sity in 1921 as a lecturer in psychology. He also resumed his graduate work and was awarded the Ph.D. degree from Columbia in 1923. His dissertation, *Types of Word-Association in Dementia Praecox, Manic-depressives, and Normal Persons,* was published in the *American Journal of Psychiatry* (April, 1923) and reprinted in 1923 in book form. For three years beginning in 1922 Murphy was also the Hodgson Fellow in Psychology at Harvard University.

From 1925 to 1929 Murphy was an instructor in psychology at Columbia and from 1929 to 1940 held the position of assistant professor of psychology. During these years, while directing the research of candidates for M.A. and Ph.D. degrees, he published a number of books which made him known to students of psychology and laid the foundation for his scholarly reputation, especially in personality and social psychology.

In 1929 he edited *An Outline of Abnormal Psychology* (Modern Library) and wrote *An Historical Introduction to Modern Psychology* (Harcourt). With his wife, Lois B. Murphy, he collaborated in 1931 on *Experimental Social Psychology* (Harper), which was published in a revised edition in 1937. He was co-author, with Friedrich Jensen, in 1932 of *Approaches to Personality* (Coward-McCann); and his *General Psychology* (Harper) appeared in 1933, with a simplified form, *A Briefer General Psychology,* in 1935.

Under the auspices of Columbia University's council for research in the social sciences, in 1938 Murphy prepared with Rensis Likert *Public Opinion and the Individual* (Harper). This psychological study was an examination of the opinion of students on public questions, with a retest on attitudes after five years.

Moving to City College of the City of New York in 1940 as professor of psychology, Murphy became chairman of the department of psychology and collaborated with honors stu-

dents on a series of studies that showed the role of emotion and feeling in perception, memory, and other processes. Among his books during his tenure at City College was *Human Nature and Enduring Peace,* which he edited in 1945 in association with Gordon W. Allport and other specialists. The volume, a third annual yearbook of the Society for the Psychological Study of Social Issues, is a symposium of some fifty-three scientifically trained men, mostly professional psychologists, who applied their knowledge in an effort to answer problems regarding war and peace and other urgent questions in public affairs.

Gardner Murphy's principal systematic work, *Personality: A Biosocial Approach to Origins and Structure* (Harper), published in 1947, is a comprehensive survey of "the little" that is known about personality (present data and systematic theories) and an effort to show the probable relation of this material to the tremendous area of knowledge yet to be comprehended. "The psychology of personality is spreading in all directions," Murphy stated in his Foreword, "and no one can make it stand still to be assessed. One thing that might practically be done is to formulate problems in terms of types of significant and manageable research tasks that lie just beyond present thresholds. . . . No two of us will agree as to what is closest to the threshold, or of course upon the fertility of the soil just beyond."

Book reviewers in general recognized Murphy's grasp of the problems of complexity, variety, and confusion that surround his subject in *Personality.* H. A. Murray commented in *Survey Graphic* (March 1948) that "the more confident books on personality when placed around it, look like little peaks of arrogant sectarianism." While one critic, however, praised the clear presentation and avoidance of unnecessary technicalities, another critic found the style difficult and the organization involved.

In 1950 Gardner Murphy and his wife went to India at the invitation of the government of India as consultants of the United Nations Educational, Scientific and Cultural Organization to the Ministry of Education at New Delhi. An account of their mission, *In the Minds of Men* (Basic Books, 1953), was related to a series of studies conducted by social scientists in a project on the investigation and control of social tensions in India, especially those regarding the Moslem-Hindu conflict. "Without sacrificing scholarly objectivity," Joseph Bram noted in *Library Journal* (June 15, 1953), "they brought to their tasks a wealth of compassion and reformist zeal."

Since September 1952 Murphy has been director of research at the Menninger Foundation, where he shares administrative supervision of the department with Robert S. Wallerstein. The Menninger Foundation, a nonprofit center for psychiatric education, research, treatment, and prevention of mental illness, was established by Dr. Charles Frederick Menninger in 1919. From the beginning it was an unusual clinic which pioneered in techniques of developing case histories based upon physical and neurological examinations and laboratory tests and of maintaining careful recordings of findings and treatments in regard to each patient.

As director of research at Menninger, Murphy has assisted in the development of three major projects: the psychotherapy research project, the perception project, and the infancy project. Working with John F. Santos as co-director, he has concentrated particularly on studies in perceptual learning, a project supported by grants from the United States Public Health Service.

The primary interest of the perceptual learning project is "to investigate the process by which people come to organize, interpret and understand the environment in which they live and to which they respond." Murphy and his colleagues are using clinical, experimental, and exploratory methods which have opened up new avenues of research. The Menninger Foundation report of progress for 1958-59 noted that the researchers have shifted their emphasis "from sheer demonstrations that feeling and emotions *can* influence what we perceive, remember, and imagine to more systematic investigations of factors which might be responsible for changes in our perception of the world." *Development of the Perceptual World* (Basic Books, 1960), written by Gardner Murphy and Charles M. Solley, grew out of the project.

A belief in man's capacity for change, for self-fulfillment through self-discovery and self-understanding, accounts for the optimistic outlook of Murphy's *Human Potentialities* (Basic Books, 1958), in which he draws upon his great reservoir of research information and philosophical knowledge to support his views on human development. Although the Virginia Kirkus bulletin (September 1, 1958) suggested that "its jargonized and muddled manner make this a work of dubious validity," many reviewers agreed with George Adelman (*Library Journal,* October 1, 1958), who recommended the book as "an inspiring, beautifully written credo."

In "A Cosmic Christmas Carol" (*Saturday Review,* December 13, 1958), an article adapted from *Human Potentialities,* Murphy pointed out that in the process of discovering more about how he is made, man is changing himself. "The potentialities of this process," Murphy wrote, "are radically new kinds of human nature. What is needed now is a readiness for bold, even extravagant, informed and serious guessing as to potentialities utterly different from those that can be extrapolated from man's present and past behavior."

Murphy was chairman in 1938 of the Society for Psychological Study of Social Issues, president in 1941-42 of the Eastern Psychological Association, and president in 1943-44 of the American Psychological Association. He has also been president of the Society for Psychical Research in London and is a member of the American Association for the Advancement of Science. In 1932 he was awarded the Butler Medal of Columbia University.

On many of his psychological studies, Gardner Murphy's collaborator has been his wife, Lois Barclay Murphy, to whom he was married on November 27, 1926. She is now principal

investigator of the "coping" project in the research division of the Menninger Foundation. The Murphys have two children, Alpen Gardner and Agatha Margaret. In a biographical note on Murphy in the *Saturday Review* (December 13, 1958), Roberta Silman wrote that "his interest in the highly controversial field of extra-sensory perception is an example of his unwillingness to deny anything that may be called a human experience. . . . Shy at first meeting, Dr. Murphy is, to those who know him better, a warm, quietly humorous man. When relaxed he will sing folk songs or talk about folk music, which he knows and loves."

References

American Men of Science vol lII (1956)
National Cyclopædia of American Biography current vol H (1947-52)
Twentieth Century Authors (First Supplement, 1955)
Who's Who in America, 1958-59
World Biography (1954)

MYERS, C(HAUNCIE) KILMER, REV. DR. Feb. 14, 1916-   Clergyman

Address: b. 550 W. 155th St., New York 32; h. 540 W. 155th St., New York 32

When teen-age gang violence flared on New York's Lower East Side during the summer of 1959, after three years of truce, no one was more distressed than the Reverend Dr. C. Kilmer Myers, then vicar of the Lower East Side Mission of Protestant Episcopal Trinity Parish and "chief keeper-of-the-peace on the Lower East Side." His distress did not mean, however, a turning from the policy of assistance and friendship which had won him the trust of gang members and raised many an angry, suspicious youth above the ways of violence. While police began a "get tough" policy and many voices rose in favor of stronger punitive measures, Father Myers continued as a leader of those urging patient and understanding rehabilitation. About a year later, in October 1960, Father Myers was transferred from the vicarage of the Lower East Side Mission to the vicarage of the Chapel of the Intercession, also in New York's Trinity Parish.

Chauncie Kilmer Myers was born in Schuylerville, New York on February 14, 1916 to Harry Edward Myers, a postal employee, and Addie Beatrice (Greene) Myers. He has one sister, Marjorie. Next door to the Myers' residence was the parish rectory, where lived Rev. Charles Kinney, who became a close friend of young Myers and a great influence on his life. "Kim", as he is called by his friends, took part in track, wrestling, and dramatics while studying at Schuylerville High School.

Upon graduation in 1934, he entered Rutgers University, New Brunswick, New Jersey, where he majored in sociology and was president of the campus Philosophy Club and of the Christian Association. He obtained his B.A. degree in 1937. Entering Yale University's Berkeley Divinity School, he studied theology and earned his S.T.B. degree in 1940. He was made a

REV. DR. C. KILMER MYERS

deacon of the Episcopal Church in May 1940 and ordained a priest in December of that same year.

Father Myers remained in New Haven after ordination, doing graduate study at Yale University and teaching church history at Berkeley Divinity School. In 1943 he moved to Buffalo to assume the rectorship of St. Mark's Church there. From 1943 to 1946 he was a chaplain in the United States Naval Reserve, entering as lieutenant (j.g.) and leaving as lieutenant (s.g.). In 1946 he became an instructor at General Theological Seminary of the Protestant Episcopal Church in New York City. After his assignment in 1949 to Grace Church in Jersey City, New Jersey, he remained on the staff of General Theological as lecturer in pastoral theology and liturgics until 1953.

As a member of the Associate Mission, Grace Church, Father Myers learned how to grapple with interracial and other problems of an urban slum parish. When he went to the Lower East Side in 1952 as vicar of Trinity Parish's two chapels, St. Christopher's and St. Augustine's, on Henry Street, he took with him three basic principles developed at the "open rectory" of Grace Church.

The first principle was hospitality. "The Church has to become a center for the parishioners. Our center was the kitchen table of the rectory," Father Myers says. For months after his arrival at Henry Street, the hospitality was unaccepted. Gradually, however, "the visitors at the kitchen table became the core of a Christian community."

The second principle was identification. "For a minister to identify himself," Father Myers says in an article in the journal *Christianity and Crisis* (March 17, 1958), "he must look down the dismal streets of his parish and be able to say in truth: 'This is my home; here is where I belong. These are my people.' He cannot play at being a 'slum priest.'" The vicar must, however, combine with his identi-

fication with his parishioners a philosophical approach, without which he would be "completely overwhelmed by the tragedy and grief of these people." He must also keep a constant awareness of his position as pastor of a flock. The priest, he believes, "must not condone lawlessness or be a party to it *ever*. He will be tempted to do so in his efforts to win the acceptance of the souls that confront him. But if he destroys the father-image the youth hold of him, he takes a long step toward destroying them."

The third principle he brought to the Lower East Side vicarage was teamwork, which makes it possible for priests to come and go without jeopardizing clerical leadership. The team at St. Christopher's and St. Augustine's is made up of several social workers, secretaries, vergers, other priests, and Sisters of St. Margaret, whose Episcopal convent is nearby on Oliver Street.

The work of this team has created what James E. McCarthy, executive director of the Big Brother Movement, calls "an integrated haven of warmth and acceptance" for hundreds of bored, frustrated youngsters (and many adults as well) from overcrowded tenements and streets tense with ethnic change. The progress achieved by the Lower East Side Mission can be measured in terms of chapel statistics: 500 communicants, 800 children in Sunday school, and 1,000 youngsters of all ages in the youth program. Another indication of the headway made is the relaxed participation of gang members in the dances which the Mission sponsors. These have assumed the same place in the social life of some teen-agers once held by those unchaperoned, dimly lit affairs in neighborhood apartments where liquor used to be sold to the children. To Father Myers the greatest sign of progress is the increase in conversation. "The deepest need of our youth," he says, "is to talk in depth—with adults."

One of the means Father Myers uses to encourage conversation is a boat he keeps moored at New Rochelle, New York. In the summer of 1957, as an experiment, he spent a week afloat on Long Island Sound with two teen-agers and one other adult from his parish. In this "last frontier" away from the city slums, he found that walls of silence and suspicion tended to break down. About 350 parish adults and youths used the boat in the summer months of 1959.

When gang war broke out on the Lower East Side in the middle of August 1956, Father Myers and his associates persuaded the leaders of the gangs involved to get together and talk over their differences. The result was a truce which New York Police Commissioner Stephen P. Kennedy called an "appeasement," but which, under the supervision of Father Myers and the Lower Eastside Neighborhoods Association, kept peace on Lower East Side streets for three years.

When a rash of violence occurred again in the late summer of 1959, Father Myers turned his parish's usually festive St. Augustine's Day celebration into a procession of mourning for the two children who had been killed as a result of the gang skirmish. He refused, however, to back down to those calling for punitive measures. He continued to insist that the desperate needs of youth were not being met by adequate services because "it is easier to punish" (*Life,* September 7, 1959).

Father Myers records his experiences with a gang which he calls "the Knights" in *Light the Dark Streets* (Seabury, 1957). The late Meyer Berger, writing of the book in the New York *Times Book Review* (October 20, 1957), said: "The vicar's great compassion for the lost and bewildered souls he tries to bring out of darkness flows to the reader out of black printer's ink." Father Myers has also written *Behold the Church* (Seabury, 1958).

The vicar of the Lower East Side Mission and his associates worked with many agencies. He was a member of the board of the Lower Eastside Neighborhoods Association (LENA) and chairman of its youth committee. As president of the board of the George W. Henry Foundation, he heads a program for assisting sex deviates in trouble with the law. He is also a board member of the Manhattan Society for Mental Health and of the Mobilization for Youth, Inc., which provides services to youth as a study-action project.

Father Myers is six feet tall, weighs 170 pounds, and has brown hair and gray eyes. Politically, he is a Democrat. He has been often eulogized in print ("brave shepherd," "pioneer in clerical urbanity") and rewarded for his contributions to the community (the Berkeley School of Divinity gave him an honorary S.T.D. degree in 1958), but his greatest honor is paid him on Henry Street. Rev. Dr. John Heuss, rector of Trinity Church, describes this honor: "It is an experience, never to be forgotten, to walk down Henry Street with Father Myers. He is known, loved and trusted by all kinds of people. He is the friend of those who are least understood, and he is the person many turn to when violence and fear engulf the community."

On September 20, 1958 Father Myers was married to Katie Lee Stuart. He has a ward, Albert James Williams, and he has adopted a Korean boy, Jonathan Ki. At the Lower East Side Mission his apartment was turned over almost nightly to teen-agers wanting respite from their own crowded, dismal flats. "Many of these kids have problems of love, acceptance and identity," the vicar pointed out. "A night stick will only aggravate the situation." In assessing Father Myers' work, Alfred A. Gross (*Christian Century*, December 11, 1957) concluded: "Kim Myers has set himself a heroic task . . . to deal daringly with the problems of human weakness, human deprivation, human rejection."

References

Life 43:89+ Ag 26 '57 pors; 47:36+
S 7 '59 pors
Look 23:102+ O 13 '59 pors

NEILL, STEPHEN CHARLES, BISHOP
Dec. 31, 1900- Churchman; author
Address: c/o Midland Bank, Cambridge, England

All his life, Bishop Stephen Charles Neill, the general editor of World Christian Books

BISHOP STEPHEN CHARLES NEILL

and former associate general secretary of the World Council of Churches, has worked throughout the world to promote the cause of Christian unity. A productive scholar, able church administrator, and dynamic evangelist, he served for twenty years as a missionary to India and has led many missions to student groups at Oxford, Cambridge, and other universities.

An Irish Anglican whose family had long been devoted to India and to missionary work, Stephen Charles Neill was born after the turn of the nineteenth century, on December 31, 1900. His maternal grandfather, James Monro, had sailed for India in 1858 as a member of the civil service. His parents, the Reverend Charles and Margaret (Monro) Neill, were married in India, served there as medical missionaries, and now lie buried there. Stephen Charles Neill was educated at Dean Close School and at Trinity College, Cambridge. After his graduation in 1922, Trinity College elected him a Prize Fellow of the College (1924-28) and awarded him an M.A. degree in 1926.

In 1924 Neill went to India as a missionary in the diocese of Tinnevelly and Travancore. He spent most of his time there in small, remote villages, as evangelist, pastor, and theological teacher. So fluent did he become in Tamil, the Dravidian language of the region and a language in which he has preached more often than in English, that he still dreams in that tongue from time to time.

From 1930 to 1938 Neill served as warden (an officer having the duties of a dean) of Bishop's Theological College, Tirumaraiyur, Nazareth, in south India. In 1938 he was elected Bishop of Tinnevelly by an electorate which was 96 per cent Indian. He thus became the spiritual leader of a diocese composed of 130,000 Christians scattered among 1,453 villages over an area of 5,381 square miles.

(Continued next page)

NEILL, STEPHEN CHARLES, BISHOP
—Continued

As Bishop of Tinnevelly, Neill was responsible for developing the Tinnevelly Theological Series, a publishing project designed to aid the village workers of his diocese. In five years twenty-two books were published, of which seven were written in Tamil by the Bishop himself. From 1939 to 1944 he also served on the committee for the revision of the Tamil Bible; the new version was published in 1957.

Neill first participated directly in the cause of Christian church unity in India, where, for ten years, he was a leading figure on the joint committee on church union in south India. After twenty-eight years of negotiation, the efforts of this committee resulted in 1947 in the establishment of the Church of South India, a merger significant in that it was the first to bridge the gaps between the three major forms of church polity: episcopal (government of the church by a body of bishops), presbyterian (government of the church by presbyters, or elders), and congregational (government of the church by the assembled brotherhood of each local church).

In addition to his other activities, Bishop Neill wrote, while in India, two works dealing with the church: *Out of Bondage; Christ and the Indian Villager* (Society for the Propagation of the Gospel in Foreign Parts, 1930) and *Builders of the Indian Church* (Society for the Propagation of the Gospel in Foreign Parts, 1934); as well as *Foundation Beliefs* (Lutterworth Press, 1942) and *Wrath and the Peace of God* (Lutterworth Press, 1944).

Having shepherded his diocese through all the strains and difficulties of war, Neill was forced to return to England in 1944 because of ill health. Although he claims, since that time, to have felt like an airman no longer allowed to fly, he has, figuratively if not always literally, flown all over the world, visiting five continents and numerous countries as missionary, lecturer, and leader in ecumenical affairs.

Upon his return to England, Neill became chaplain of Trinity College, Cambridge and lecturer in theology. He was University Lecturer in Divinity (1945-47), Hulsean Lecturer (1946-47), and Birkbeck Lecturer (1949-50). In 1950 he was Godfrey Day Lecturer in Missions at Trinity College, Dublin and from 1947 to 1950 he served as Assistant Bishop to the Archbishop of Canterbury.

When he led the evangelistic mission to Oxford University in 1947, Neill's direct and unrhetorical approach proved so effective that it was said: "No one thought any mission could ever be as good as Temple's, but this one was." (Frederick Temple, 1821-1902, was an English divine, at one time headmaster of Rugby and later Archbishop of Canterbury, who was renowned for his deeply impressive school sermons.) When rumors of Neill's success spread to Canada, he was asked to head the mission to Toronto University in 1949 and, in 1950, he took part in university evangelistic missions at Harvard, Yale, Princeton, and the University of California at Berkeley.

Soon after his return from India, Neill resumed his active participation in the movement for Christian unity. He joined the World Council of Churches in 1947 as co-director of the study department. He was a key figure at the Amsterdam Assembly of 1948, at which the World Council was formally constituted and, from 1948 to 1951, served as associate general secretary of that organization.

Described by Neill as "a new stage in the evolution of the Christian society," the World Council of Churches is composed of 173 churches in more than fifty countries. It is not a central ecclesiastical authority, but an instrument of fellowship and co-operation between these churches, which differ from each other in doctrine, creed, ministry, and tradition. The four major groups which are still outside the fold of the World Council are the Southern Baptists and the Missouri Synod (Lutheran) in the United States, the Russian Orthodox Church in Russia, and the Roman Catholic Church.

In the late 1940's, the cause of church unity took Bishop Neill to the Orient where he helped to plan the 1949 East Asia Conference and worked to develop the ecumenical idea in the younger churches. He has reported on his visit to eleven countries in *The Cross Over Asia* (Canterbury Press, 1948). Continuing his world-wide travels, Neill toured East and West Africa in 1950 for the International Missionary Council and the World Council of Churches, to investigate theological training for the ministry in Tanganyika, Kenya, Uganda, Nigeria, the Gold Coast, and Sierra Leone.

When ill health again interfered, Neill resigned his formal responsibilities with the World Council of Churches, but continued, as editor, author, and lecturer, to serve the ecumenical cause. In *Towards Church Union, 1937-1952* (Allenson, 1952), published for the faith and order commission of the World Council, he surveyed thirty-nine examples of union achieved between independent churches and of negotiations for union then in progress.

In *The Christian Society* (Harper, 1953) Bishop Neill examined, in the words of his preface, "the Christian people as a society of men and women, existing in time and space, acting and reacting continually with its environment." Virginia Kirkus (April 15, 1953) praised this study as "a book which churchmen and theologians active in the ecumenical movement will hail with delight, but which should also have a wide reading among the more thoughtful pastors and laymen."

At the same time that he was writing his own books, Neill for many years helped to edit *The History of the Ecumenical Movement, 1517-1948* (Westminster Press, 1954), which Nash K. Burger, writing in the New York *Times* (August 15, 1954), called a "comprehensive volume [covering] the growth of the churches toward unity and cooperation, topically, geographically and chronologically." Commenting on the editing, the London *Times Literary Supplement* (April 30, 1954) said that it must have been "an immensely difficult task, and it has been admirably carried through for, contrary to what one might perhaps expect, the work never ceases to be easily readable."

In 1953 Neill accepted the position of general editor of World Christian Books, a project sponsored by the International Missionary Society. As a contributor to this series, he has already written two volumes, *The Christian Character* (Association Press, 1955) and *The Christians' God* (Association Press, 1955), and translated another, *Mark's Witness to Jesus Christ,* by Eduard Lohse (Association Press, 1955).

The late 1950's saw Bishop Neill once again on his world-wide travels, delivering the Cody Memorial lectures in Toronto in 1956, serving as Visiting Professor of Missions at the University of Hamburg, 1956-57, delivering the Carnahan lectures in Buenos Aires in 1958, and acting as Duff Lecturer in Missions in Edinburgh and Glasgow, 1958-59. He returned to Africa in 1957 to attend the International Missionary Council Assembly in Ghana and, in 1958 and in 1960, he again traveled to the United States.

Among Bishop Neill's other works are *Christ: His Church and His World* (Eyre, 1948), *Fulfill Thy Ministry* (Harper, 1952), *Christian Partnership* (Allenson, 1952), *Under Three Flags* (Friendship Press, 1954), and *Christian Holiness* (Harper, 1960). Neill has also contributed to *Chambers' Encyclopedia, Die Religion in Geschichte und Gegenwart, Evangelische Kirchenlexikon,* and *Weltkirchenlexikon,* and has written articles for *Fortnightly* and the *Christian Century.*

Bishop Neill received an honorary doctorate in divinity from Trinity College, Toronto in 1950 and from Culver-Stockton College, Canton, Missouri in 1953. He was given an honorary doctorate in theology by the University of Hamburg in 1957. He is unmarried and is described as a versatile conversationalist with a ready sense of humor.

Reference

Who's Who, 1959

NELSON, GAYLORD (ANTON) June 4, 1916- Governor of Wisconsin

Address: b. State Capitol, Madison 2, Wis.; h. 101 Cambridge Rd., Madison, Wis.

Strengthening the political trend which in November 1958 marked the resurgence of the Democratic party in several states, Gaylord Nelson became the first Democrat to win the Governorship in Wisconsin since the landslide that made Franklin D. Roosevelt the President of the United States in 1932. Despite his ten years in the state Senate, Nelson was a political unknown compared with his Republican opponent, Governor Vernon W. Thomson, whom he succeeded in January 1959 for a two-year term. Since his discharge from the Army after World War II, Nelson had practised law in Madison, Wisconsin.

A traditional family interest in politics probably directed Gaylord Anton Nelson toward a career in government. His great-grandfather had helped to organize the Republican party, and his father was a devoted supporter of Robert M. La Follette's Progressive party. Gaylord Nelson, who is of Norwegian and Irish ancestry, was born in Clear Lake, Wisconsin

GAYLORD NELSON

on June 4, 1916 to Anton and Mary (Brandt) Nelson. He has two sisters and a brother.

Clear Lake is a small village of some 600 inhabitants in Polk County, where his father practised medicine as a country doctor. Gaylord Nelson grew up there and was graduated from Clear Lake High School in 1934. He then attended San José State College in San José, California, the home of one of his sisters, and he played the trumpet in the college dance band. During the summers he went back to Wisconsin to work as a timekeeper and foreman at a pea-canning plant. In college he chose economics as his major subject and philosophy and anthropology as his minor subjects. After his graduation in 1939, he entered the University of Wisconsin Law School and received his LL.B. degree in 1942.

Called into military service during World War II, Nelson fought for forty-six months in the Army, including the Okinawa campaign, and achieved the rank of captain in the Quartermaster Corps. By 1946 he was back in Wisconsin, campaigning for a seat in the state Assembly from Polk County. He ran on the Republican ticket, as did many other Progressive followers of the younger Robert M. La Follette, and was defeated.

Later in 1946 Nelson moved to Madison, where he established a practice in law that continued until 1959. Having changed his political affiliation, he was elected as a Democratic candidate to the state Senate from Dane County in 1948 and re-elected in 1952 and 1956. In a race for a seat in the United States House of Representatives from the Second Wisconsin Congressional District he was defeated in 1954 by Glenn R. Davis.

During most of his years in the Wisconsin Legislature, Nelson was the Democratic leader in the state Senate. He served for four years on the joint committee on finance, for four years on the Senate committee on education and

NELSON, GAYLORD—*Continued*

public welfare, and for two years on the Senate committee on conservation. He was also a member of interim committees on taxation and universities policies. Among the measures for which he worked especially hard were an increase in educational aid, establishment of a state-wide scholarship program, and a reduction in costs for parents' supporting mentally retarded children in state institutions. He was regarded as the Senate's "intellectual" leader of the Democrats.

On November 4, 1958, running for the Governorship in his first state-wide contest for office, Nelson drew 53.6 per cent of the votes. His victory over incumbent Governor Vernon W. Thomson, together with the election of Democrat William Proxmire to the United States Senate, broke the hold of the Republicans upon Wisconsin. Nelson's support came not only from labor, but also from voters in normally Republican rural areas who were apparently dissatisfied with the federal government's farm program. In the state Legislature, although the Republicans held their control over the Senate, the Democrats succeeded in gaining a majority in the Assembly.

Gaylord Nelson was inaugurated on January 5, 1959 as the first Democratic Governor of Wisconsin in a quarter of a century. Reporting on the new administration three months after Nelson's inauguration, Godfrey Sperling, Jr., of the *Christian Science Monitor* noted that Nelson had been "moving with prudent slowness, feeling his way along." With the help of experts in budget, taxation, and public administration, he worked toward more efficient governmental organization. He planned a department for economic development, for example, that would combine the responsibilities for industrial, agricultural, and community expansion previously handled by separate agencies. In the area of conservation, one of Nelson's particular interests, he wanted to fill membership on the conservation committee with professional specialists rather than political appointees.

Wisconsin has traditionally been the scene of an early primary election that tests the strength of Democratic Presidential aspirants. Looking ahead to the primary of April 5, 1960, Governor Nelson showed concern in June 1959 over the possibly "bloody fight" that might break out between Senators John F. Kennedy of Massachusetts and Hubert H. Humphrey of Minnesota because of the religious issue. To avoid a rift in the Democratic party within his state, he offered to support Senator Proxmire as a favorite son candidate. He later said, however, that he would not argue against other candidates' entering the primary, but during the following months he maintained a position of neutrality in the Kennedy-Humphrey contest.

Said to be "no joiner," Nelson belongs to only a few organizations, among them the American Legion, Veterans of Foreign Wars, and the Eagles. He served as first chairman of the Madison Council on Human Rights. He is an excellent debater and keeps well informed through regular reading of a large number and variety of newspapers and magazines. His tastes in literature range widely; he has a special preference for the writings of Shaw and Ambrose Bierce. He also enjoys outdoor activities, but apparently is not enthusiastic about games or sports as an end in themselves. One of his hobbies is cooking, and Chinese dishes are his favorites.

While in the Army during the war, Nelson met Carrie Lee Dotson, a Virginia-born nurse who served in the Army Nurse Corps in the Okinawa campaign. They were married after the war, on November 15, 1947, and have a son, Gaylord, Jr., and a daughter, Cynthia. Nelson's seven-year-old son also has his nickname of "Happy," which the Governor acquired in childhood when a Swedish hired girl in the Nelson home remarked that "gay lard" meant "happy grease." Nelson is five feet ten inches tall and weighs 190 pounds. Newspaper interviewers have described him as not a bold, sensational political figure, but a hard-working man of direct and unpretentious manner.

References

> Christian Sci Mon p8 N 26 '58; p3 Ap 3 '59 por
> Let's See p8+ F 6-19 '59 pors
> New Repub 139:9+ N 3 '58

NEUBERGER, RICHARD L(EWIS) Dec. 26, 1912-Mar. 9, 1960 Journalist; author; Democratic member of the Oregon Legislative Assembly (1948-54); United States Senator from Oregon (since 1955). See *Current Biography* (February) 1955.

Obituary

> N Y Times p1+ Mr 10 '60

NICHOLS, DUDLEY Apr. 6, 1895-Jan. 4, 1960 Screenwriter; motion-picture producer; author of the screen play for *The Informer, The Plough and the Stars, Pinky,* and other important films. See *Current Biography* (September) 1941.

Obituary

> N Y Times p35 Ja 6 '60

NIEMEYER (SOARES FILHO), OSCAR (nē'mī-ĕr) Dec. 15, 1907- Architect

Address: h. Estrada dos Canoas 2350, Gavea, Rio de Janeiro, Brazil; b. Edificio Banco Boavista, Rio de Janeiro, Brazil; Novacap Urbanizing Co. of the New Capital of Brazil, Brasília, Brazil

The boldness and originality of the Brazilian architect Oscar Niemeyer have been given free play in his designs for the federal buildings of Brasília, the new capital of Brazil. While striving to preserve the native and spontaneous qualities of Brazil's traditional architecture, he has won international renown for his startling and iconoclastic designs for schools, hotels, office buildings, churches, and homes, in Brazil, Japan, Cuba, Venezuela, and West Berlin. Niemeyer's work, integrating architecture, sculpture, painting, and landscaping, may often be recognized by his use of poured concrete to attain free-flowing and undulating form.

Niemeyer was one of the architects who collaborated on the United Nations buildings in New York City. His design for the Museum of Modern Art in Caracas, Venezuela, is considered one of the most original in the world, and his Ministry of Education and Health building in Rio de Janeiro, on which he worked with architects Lúcio Costa and Le Corbusier in 1936, is regarded as one of the most beautiful.

Oscar Niemeyer Soares Filho was born on December 15, 1907 into a middle-class family of six children in Rio de Janeiro, Brazil. His father, Oscar Niemeyer Soares, was a businessman; and his mother, the former Delfina Ribeiro de Almeida, died when he was a baby. In his youth Niemeyer gave most of his time to sports and other forms of entertainment, to the neglect of his education. His interest in drawing, however, eventually led him to study architecture at the School of Fine Arts of the University of Brazil in Rio de Janeiro.

Shortly before graduating with an architectural degree in 1935, he went to work in the office of Lúcio Costa, who is recognized as the leader of the contemporary Brazilian architectural movement. It is a common saying in Brazil that "Oscar Niemeyer is the creator, but Lúcio Costa is his master." Niemeyer himself regards Costa as the great figure of Brazilian architecture. The friendship and mutual respect of the two architects has continued for more than a quarter-century. With Costa he worked on designs for Brazil's Ministry of Education and Health building in 1936. Le Corbusier, the noted Swiss architect, was the consultant. Niemeyer proved an eager student of Le Corbusier and their skyscraper, faced with blue, louver-like sun breakers (called *brise soleil* or *quebra sol*) to temper the glare of the sun in Rio de Janeiro, became an architectural milestone.

Niemeyer's first major project on his own was commissioned in 1941 by Juscelino Kubitschek, at that time mayor of Belo Horizonte in Brazil. In designing Pampulha, a new suburb of Belo Horizonte, Niemeyer adapted some of Le Corbusier's ideas, making provision for Brazil's climate and terrain, and combined them with his own quality of lightness and preference for free-flowing form. A restaurant, a yacht club and casino, and the Church of St. Francis were among the buildings. Suggesting a hangar in design, the church was so untraditional that the archbishop of the area rejected it as "unfit for religious purposes." Although it had been completed in 1943, it was not consecrated until April 1959.

Since the completion of Pampulha, Niemeyer has designed hundreds of buildings, ranging in size from the small Dom Bosco roadside shrine in Brasília to the vast, curved apartment hotel, Quitandinha, at Petrópolis, housing 5,700 families. It is thirty-three stories high and more than a quarter of a mile long and has been called a "one-building town." In the early 1950's Kubitschek commissioned Niemeyer to plan additional buildings in Belo Horizonte. One of them, an auditorium for a secondary school, has a sloping floor and vaulted ceiling; functional in its unusual shape, it is among Niemeyer's most striking designs in poured concrete.

John and Bini Moss

OSCAR NIEMEYER

Outside Brazil, Niemeyer worked with Costa on the designs for the Brazilian Pavilion at the New York World's Fair in 1939. He represented Brazil in 1947 on the United Nations Board of Design Consultants, and, according to José Guilherme Mendes (*Américas,* September 1959), his plan for the U.N. group of buildings in New York was the one finally selected as the basis for the work of the collaborating architects. He also designed an apartment building for Hansa, a sector of West Berlin which had been bombed out during World War II. For the Museum of Modern Art (not yet built) in Caracas, Venezuela, he designed an inverted pyramid-shaped building, whose extensive, luminous roof allows the interior to be flooded with controllable light.

In December 1953 the second biennial International Exhibition of Modern Art in São Paulo, Brazil, was held in two of several large concrete buildings designed by Niemeyer. "A concrete marquee or portico," noted Aline B. Louchheim (New York *Times,* December 8, 1953), "shaped like an assymetrical starfish, makes a gigantic covered walk joining the five most important structures." Some were supported on V-shaped stilts (variously called butterfly stilts or kite-shaped stilts) which lift the building off the ground and which are an identifying feature of Niemeyer's work.

When Juscelino Kubitschek became President of Brazil in 1956, he told Niemeyer that he intended to keep his election campaign promise to move the federal capital to the interior of Brazil (590 miles from Rio de Janeiro), and he asked Niemeyer to design the new city. Later, speaking at the celebration of Niemeyer's fiftieth birthday in December 1957, Kubitschek paid tribute to the architect. "To undertake the most audacious work of urban planning and architecture in our history, the construction of Brasília," he said, "I did not hesitate for one moment to entrust him with the plans for pub-

NIEMEYER, OSCAR—Continued

lic buildings and with the supervision of the architectural part of the new Capital."

Niemeyer had agreed to design the governmental buildings, but proposed a national competition for a master plan for Brasília. His old friend and mentor, Lúcio Costa, won the competition. The pilot plan, resembling a cross (or, as some observers say, an airplane), calls for a "monumental axis," five miles long and 820 feet long, crossed at right angles by a curved six-lane "residential axis," seven and a half miles long and giving access to a series of residential blocks enclosed within belts of trees. The monumental axis leads to the Palace of Three Powers, where the legislative and judicial buildings and the Presidential Executive Palace are grouped in a triangular-shaped plaza.

For the President's residence (the Alvorada Palace, sometimes called the Palace of Aurora), Niemeyer designed a two-story structure resting on twenty-two arched concrete pillars, each faced with 250 carved sections of marble. Adjacent to the palace is the President's private chapel, to which Niemeyer gave the shape of a snail. His model of a glass-walled, crown-shaped cathedral, still under construction, has caused much controversy. The building of Brasília began in 1957, and an estimated 40,000 persons worked to have the capital ready for the government's move from Rio de Janeiro in the spring of 1960.

In his own home, which has a curved concrete roof and glass walls, Niemeyer has embodied many of his ideas about plasticity, "conquest of space," and response to terrain. He has been accused of being too facile and of delighting in the unusual for its own sake. Critics in general, however, share Le Corbusier's admiration for Niemeyer: "He knows how to give full freedom to all the discoveries of modern architecture." His work was represented in a major exhibition of Latin American Architecture since 1945 at the Museum of Modern Art in New York City in November 1955.

Oscar Niemeyer and Anita Niemeyer were married while he was still a student of architecture at the University of Brazil. They have a daughter, Ana Maria, who has studied interior decorating with her father and is one of the leaders in her profession. She is in charge of furnishing the Presidential Alvorada Palace at Brasília. Niemeyer is also a grandfather.

"A small, gentle-voiced man, with brown eyes and a large forehead, Niemeyer has a strong face that slopes like a Modigliani sculpture" (*Vogue*, March 15, 1958). Mendes pictured him in *Américas* as "unpretentious, almost timid in manner . . . a complex man of many whims and deeply rooted personal tastes." His fear of air travel is well known. He calls himself a Communist, but is not active in the party.

References

Time 72:48 Jl 28 '58 por

Papadaki, Stamo Oscar Niemeyer (1960)
Who's Who in Latin America pt 6 (1948)
World Biography (1948)

NILSSON, (MÄRTA) BIRGIT May 17, 1918- Singer

Address: b. c/o National Concert & Artists Corp., 711 Fifth Ave., New York 19

When Birgit Nilsson, the Swedish dramatic soprano, helped to spearhead the current Wagner renaissance at the Metropolitan Opera House with her debut on December 18, 1959 in *Tristan und Isolde,* critics inevitably compared her to Kirsten Flagstad. But Nilsson's career had been notably different from that of her great Norwegian predecessor. When Flagstad, who had been singing in opera for about twenty years, first astonished New York as Sieglinde in *Die Walküre* in February 1935, she was virtually unknown outside Scandinavia. Birgit Nilsson, who had been singing in opera for only about twelve years at the time of her Metropolitan debut, had already dazzled audiences in most of the world's great opera houses.

The daughter of Nils Svensson and Justina Pålsson, Märta Birgit Nilsson was born on May 17, 1918 at West Karup, Sweden, a small town near the coast about sixty miles north of Malmö. "I sang before I could walk," she told New York reporters soon after her debut. "I spoke very early and I sang very early. . . . I sang even in my dreams." When she was five, she sang at a Christmas concert at school, accompanying herself on the organ while her mother lay on the floor to work the pedals Birgit could not reach.

In spite of the child's obvious vocal talent her father adamantly opposed Birgit's taking up a musical career. "He needed a son to take over the farm," Miss Nilsson told Fern Marja of the New York *Post* (December 27, 1959). "It is a very old farm. I am the seventh generation. And, because I was the only child, I had to do everything. . . . My parents were not poor, but they did not want to spoil me." So Birgit worked away at her farm chores, but at every opportunity she sang—for her neighbors, for her schoolmates, for the church congregation. At school she learned to read music at sight and discovered that she had absolute pitch.

When Birgit was fifteen, she went to Båstad, several miles away from West Karup, to audition for the choirmaster there. Predicting that she would become a great singer, he urged her to go to Stockholm for intensive study. Fortified with financial help from a legacy her mother had inherited, she set out for Stockholm, but not without bitter opposition from her father, who wept on her departure. Her mother, however, who was an excellent amateur singer, felt that the girl should at least try a vocal career.

In Stockholm Miss Nilsson was one of two candidates chosen from forty-eight applicants to study at the Royal Academy of Music, a training ground for world-famous opera singers since the days of Jenny Lind. There she received the Christine Nilsson Scholarship, named in honor of the great nineteenth century soprano. After the first year, her funds ran out, and Miss Nilsson was forced to support herself. "I sang at weddings and funerals," Miss Nilsson informed an interviewer from *Newsday* (January 5, 1960). "I sang at weddings and funerals, in choirs, and played small roles in films. I had scholarships too. When I went home in the summer to work on the farm... sometimes I would be down to my last pennies. . . . But I was proud. I never would ask them for money."

In 1946 Birgit Nilsson took advantage of an unexpected chance to sing the role of Agathe in *Der Freischütz* at Stockholm's Royal Opera House. She learned the role in three days, and so impressed officials that they awarded her a contract. In 1947 she made her formal debut at the Royal Opera House as Lady Macbeth in Verdi's *Macbeth,* singing under the baton of Fritz Busch, whose son, Hans Busch, had chosen her for the production. A correspondent for *Musical America* in the audience was enough impressed to write (November 15, 1947): "She showed herself a distinguished artist from the start. . . . Her beautiful soprano, if not yet technically finished, is voluminous and rich enough to carry over the heaviest choral and orchestral masses." Miss Nilsson has remained on the roster of the Royal Opera House ever since, and in 1954 she received the title of *Hovsångerska,* or Court Singer.

Outside Sweden, Birgit Nilsson received her first major engagement at the Glyndebourne Festival near London, England on June 20, 1951 as Elettra in *Idomeneo.* Early in 1954 she made her debut at the Vienna State Opera, and has since appeared there from time to time in many roles. At the 1954 Bayreuth Festival she sang Elsa, and returned as Isolde in 1957 and 1959. She scored one of her greatest successes at the Teatro alla Scala in Milan on the opening night of the 1958-1959 season as Princess Turandot. Her Isolde later in the season was hailed as one of the finest ever heard at La Scala. Miss Nilsson has also sung in the opera houses of Naples, Venice, Rome, Florence, Munich, Zurich, Lisbon, and Barcelona and in major cities of Belgium and France.

In the Western Hemisphere, Miss Nilsson was first heard in 1955 at the Teatro Colón, Buenos Aires, as Isolde. In 1956 she appeared there again, as the Marschallin in *Der Rosenkavalier* and as Donna Anna in *Don Giovanni.* She made her debut in North America on August 9, 1956 in the Hollywood Bowl with the Los Angeles Philharmonic Orchestra, singing excerpts from *Tristan und Isolde* and *Die Götterdämmerung.* The first operatic role she undertook in the United States was that of Brünnhilde in *Die Walküre* with the San Francisco Opera Company on October 5, 1956. On that occasion Marjory Fisher of *Musical America* (November 1, 1956) found the debut "somewhat a disappointment," but Howard Taubman of the New York *Times* (October 7, 1956) called Miss Nilsson "the real thing. . . . She makes it easy to grasp why she is Wotan's favorite among the Valkyries." A few weeks later, Miss Nilsson made her debut with the Chicago Lyric Opera in the same role.

Covent Garden audiences first heard Miss Nilsson in the fall of 1957, when she sang Brünnhilde in a complete cycle of *Der Ring des Nibelungen.* "Thrilling . . . potentially as

BIRGIT NILSSON

great as any since Frida Leider," was the verdict of William Mann in *Opera* magazine (November 1957). He went on to say that he considered her "already unrivalled by the resident Queens of Wagnerland."

In the 1958 and 1959 seasons of the Chicago Lyric Opera, Birgit Nilsson sang four different roles for the first time with that company. Her performances as Princess Turandot, Isolde, Amelia in *Un Ballo in Maschera* and Senta in *Der Fliegende Holländer* were praised as unexceptionable by both the local and out-of-town critics.

When Birgit Nilsson made her New York debut as Isolde in a new Metropolitan Opera House production of *Tristan und Isolde* on December 18, 1959, she received the most thunderous applause accorded any Metropolitan artist since the debut of Ljuba Welitch in *Salome* on February 4, 1949. At the end of the four-hour production, members of the audience gave Miss Nilsson an ovation that lasted fifteen minutes and deluged her with roses. Whatever reservations the critics may have entertained about the flagging forces of Karl Liebl as Tristan, the *tempi* of Karl Boehm, and the surrealistic sets of Teo Otto, they all agreed that in Birgit Nilsson, Rudolph Bing had found a Wagnerian soprano of the first magnitude.

Still fresh after her taxing role, Miss Nilsson announced that she could "sing Turandot right now," and thanked in English, Swedish, and German the members of the cast who congratulated her. She shrugged her shoulders noncommittally when reporters asked if she considered her Metropolitan debut her best performance as Isolde, but her husband, when asked the same question, replied: "Ja, ja, ja."

Critics saw no reason to recant during the succeeding months of the season, when Miss Nilsson reappeared as Isolde and added to her New York repertoire the roles of Brünnhilde in *Die Walküre* and Leonore in *Fidelio.* On December 28, 1959 she sang her Isolde to the

NILSSON, BIRGIT—*Continued*

accompanying raptures of three Tristans (one for each act) when tenors Karl Liebl, Ramon Vinay, and Albert da Costa pleaded inability to sing the entire opera because of illnesses. Comparing her first New York Leonore with the interpretations of Kirsten Flagstad and Lotte Lehmann, Howard Taubman of the New York *Times* (February 14, 1960) found that while Nilsson's had more temperament than Flagstad's, it lacked only Lehmann's ardor to make it "incomparable."

In addition to the roles already mentioned, Miss Nilsson includes in her repertoire Salome, Aïda, Tosca, Venus, and Elisabeth in *Tannhäuser,* Sieglinde in *Die Walküre,* Lisa in Tchaikovsky's *Pique Dame,* and the title role in Rolf Liebermann's *Penelope.* Although she usually likes best the role she is singing at the moment, she considers Princess Turandot and Isolde her most enduring favorites.

Birgit Nilsson has rarely sung anything but dramatic soprano parts. Her voice is of such soaring power that it can knife through the massed forces of the Wagnerian orchestra, yet remain limpid and steady in the pianissimo passages. Some critics, while praising her security throughout the entire dramatic soprano range, have noted that she tends to "sharp" her notes on occasion, and a few have deplored the lack of tone color or "whitishness" in her voice. Recordings by Birgit Nilsson for the Angel label include a complete recording of Puccini's opera, *La Fanciulla del West* (*The Girl of the Golden West*), and recitals consisting of substantial excerpts and arias from the German and Italian repertoire.

Birgit Nilsson was married to Bertil Niklasson, a Swedish restaurateur with interests in the frozen food industry, on September 10, 1949. The Niklassons maintain homes in Zurich and Stockholm. Offstage, Miss Nilsson exhibits none of the emotional display associated with divas. Dark-haired and dark-eyed, she has a figure that for a Wagnerian soprano is athletic and slim, and a stamina for which she can probably thank her Swedish farming ancestry. By now she is weary of being compared with Flagstad, whose voice, she believes, differs from her own. "Hers is darker and larger than mine," she told Fern Marja. "I am a little higher, I think. And I sing Verdi and Mozart. . . . I prefer to be a not-so-good Nilsson than a second Flagstad."

References

N Y Times p32 D 21 '59 por
N Y Herald Tribune p2 D 20 '59 por
N Y Post Mag D 27 '59 por
Newsday p35 Ja 5 '60 por
Opera 8:617+ O '57
Vem är Det, 1959

OBERLIN, RUSSELL (KEYS) Oct. 11, 1928- Singer

Address: h. 40 W. 11th St., New York 11

Considered by many critics the outstanding countertenor before the public today, Russell Oberlin has done much to restore to popularity this unusual vocal range and the music originally written for it. But the praise he has received is not solely due to the rare quality of his voice. A reviewer for the New York *Herald Tribune* (December 26, 1959) has written: "If there is a singer working in any medium—now before the public—who has Mr. Oberlin's uncanny sense of phrasal delivery, all-'round musicality, and sensitivity to the shape of a vocal line this reviewer has not heard him."

The countertenor voice is a very rare and exceptionally high-pitched male voice between the tenor and soprano ranges. Oberlin, whose voice spans well over two octaves from the lyric tenor into the alto range, stresses that he does not resort to vocal artifice in order to produce his high, floating tones. "Occasionally, in print," he says, "I have been described as a falsetto singer. This is *not* true. I have a naturally high tenor voice which enables me to sing the countertenor repertoire without resorting to the falsetto voice."

Russell Keys Oberlin, the son of Mary Ethel (Keys) and John Russell Oberlin, was born on October 11, 1928 in Akron, Ohio, where he was reared and where he attended the John R. Buchtel High School. His one sister, Jean Ann, presently lives in California. Oberlin is a descendant of Jean Frédéric Oberlin, an eighteenth-century clergyman and educator for whom Oberlin College (Ohio) was named.

Oberlin's musical career began as a soprano in Akron, where he performed in boy choirs long before he could read the words in the score. When he was about fourteen, Oberlin's voice changed to a baritone tenor and then rose until, two years later, he was a light tenor. He became a tenor soloist for a Cleveland church and began studying voice.

Upon graduating from high school in 1946, Russell Oberlin enrolled in New York's Juilliard School of Music, where he majored in voice. While there, he held tuition scholarships and also undertook professional singing engagements. At this time, however, he did not sing any music composed before the time of Bach nor any music above the normal tenor range. He was graduated from Juilliard in 1951 with a diploma in voice.

Oberlin had been a leading soloist with New York's Pro Musica Antiqua from its inception in 1953 until 1959. The Pro Musica, a group of singers and instrumentalists under the direction of Noah Greenberg, is dedicated to the performance of forgotten music of the Middle Ages and the Renaissance. One of Oberlin's first assignments with this group was to participate in a recording of sixteenth-century Italian madrigals for Esoteric Records. Having previously confined his singing to tenor roles, Oberlin now experimented with the alto parts and was so successful that he became "typed" as a countertenor. His many outside commitments forced Oberlin to resign as a regular member of the group in 1959, but he continues to make guest appearances with it.

Russell Oberlin has appeared with many of America's most important musical organizations, principally in performances of operas and oratorios of such composers as Bach, Handel, and Monteverdi. Among the groups to employ

Oberlin's talents are the New York Philharmonic-Symphony Orchestra, the Chicago Symphony Orchestra, the American Opera Society, the Washington Opera and Choral Societies, and New York's Little Orchestra Society. He has sung several of Handel's works, including the *Messiah, Julius Caesar, Israel in Egypt, Judas Maccabeus, Acis and Galatea,* and the *Passion According to St. John.* Other Oberlin performances include Monteverdi's *Orfeo* and Bach's Magnificat, the *Passion According to St. Matthew,* and the *Passion According to St. John.*

Reviewing Oberlin's appearance with the New York Philharmonic under Leonard Bernstein in Handel's *Messiah,* Paul Henry Lang commented in the New York *Herald Tribune* that "among the soloists Russell Oberlin, countertenor, demonstrated absolute mastery of the style as well as impeccable taste and musicianship" (December 28, 1956).

Russell Oberlin's work with the Pro Musica and with the larger American musical groups has not prevented him from appearing with smaller organizations, among them the Clarion Concert groups, the Cantata Singers, Collegium Musicum, American Concert Choir, Caramoor Summer Festival, and Collegiate Chorale. He has also sung frequently in American universities, museums, and churches.

When Oberlin performed in Bach's Cantata No. 54 with the Collegium Musicum under Fritz Rikko in an outdoor concert in New York's Washington Square Park, Eric Salzman in the New York *Times* praised the presentation and noted that "part of the effect was due to the fine countertenor of Russell Oberlin. Although a couple of things got away from him in the final aria . . . most of the time he was right on the button musically as well as technically" (August 18, 1959).

Russell Oberlin has also enjoyed success as a singer and actor in the legitimate theater. In the 1955 Broadway production of Lillian Hellman's adaptation of Jean Anouilh's *The Lark,* which starred Julie Harris, Oberlin was heard in incidental songs especially composed for him by Leonard Bernstein. Two other noted contemporary American composers, Virgil Thomson and Marc Blitzstein, have provided Oberlin with musical material for his appearances with the American Shakespeare Festival Theatre in Stratford, Connecticut. In the summer of 1959 he was featured in the Cambridge (Massachusetts) Drama Festival production of Shakespeare's *Twelfth Night.*

Since 1957 Russell Oberlin has been a featured soloist in the New York Pro Musica's production of the medieval drama *The Play of Daniel,* given in New York during the Christmas season. He also appears in the Decca recording of this production, and he was a member of the company when the United States State Department sponsored a European tour of the production in the summer of 1960.

Television and radio have provided Russell Oberlin with numerous engagements. He offered musical illustrations for Leonard Bernstein's lecture on Bach on the television series, *Omnibus,* and was featured in Bernstein's per-

CAI

RUSSELL OBERLIN

formance of Bach's Magnificat on the *Ford Startime* show in 1959. With the NBC Opera he appeared in a presentation of Mozart's *The Magic Flute,* and has also been seen on the series *Camera Three.* During two recent visits to England he was heard as soloist on the British Broadcasting Corporation.

In addition to his many recordings with the Pro Musica Antiqua for Decca and Columbia, Russell Oberlin has also made solo recordings of Purcell songs (Counterpoint) and recorded Dowland lute songs, English medieval melodies, and troubadour and trouvère ballads for Expériences Anonymes. His Decca disc of Handel opera and oratorio arias has given listeners a rare opportunity to hear the selections performed in the countertenor range for which they were originally written. With the New York Philharmonic, Oberlin can be heard on Columbia records as soloist in Handel's *Messiah* and Bach's Magnificat.

A bachelor, Russell Oberlin makes his home in New York's Greenwich Village. He is five feet eleven inches tall and weighs 170 pounds. His hair is red and his eyes, blue. An Episcopalian, Oberlin attends the Church of the Ascension in New York. The scholarly attention which he lavishes upon music may be discerned by the fact that a few years ago he was chosen to co-edit a set of songs by Purcell for the Associated Music Publishers.

Reference

House & Gard 111:30 My '57

O'CONOR, HERBERT R(OMULUS)
Nov. 17, 1896-Mar. 4, 1960 Democratic Governor of Maryland (1939-47); United States Senator from Maryland (1947-53). See *Current Biography* (February) 1950.

Obituary

N Y Times p19 Mr 5 '60

ODETTA Dec. 31, 1930- Folk singer
Address: b. Universal Music Associates, 141 Jackson Blvd., Chicago, Ill.; h. 5021 S. Dorchester, Chicago, Ill.

One of the more exciting singers to emerge during the current renascence of interest in American folk music is Odetta, who belongs to the great tradition of Leadbelly, Bessie Smith, and Mahalia Jackson. Combining flexible vocalism with sincerity and emotional depth, Odetta brings to her heritage of Negro folk music a sophistication and finish all her own. She specializes in work and prison songs, accompanying her dusky contralto on the guitar, but finds herself equally at home with blues, lullabies, ballads, and spirituals.

During the past decade, Odetta has moved from West Coast night clubs that feature folk music to national prominence on the concert stage, recordings, and television. For her achievements in television she won a Sylvania Award in 1959. She added acting to her list of accomplishments in 1960, when she signed for the role of Nancy in a screen version of William Faulkner's *Sanctuary*.

Odetta was born Odetta Holmes on December 31, 1930 in Birmingham, Alabama to Reuben Holmes, a worker in a steel mill, and Flora (Sanders) Holmes, who was employed as a domestic. Her father died shortly after she was born, and her mother was married to Zadock Felious, a janitor, who gave his surname to the child. When Odetta was six years of age, the family, including her stepbrother and stepsister, moved to Los Angeles.

The piano in her grandmother's house first awakened Odetta's interest in music. In junior high school she joined the glee club and took vocal lessons for a time. But when she realized that her voice instructor entertained visions of turning her into a second Marian Anderson,

running against the grain of her already strong sense of individuality, Odetta dropped her lessons.

Upon graduating from Belmont High School in Los Angeles in 1947, Odetta received the high school achievement award presented by the Bank of America. She then found work as a housekeeper during the day and began studying music at night at Los Angeles City College, in preparation for a career in the classical field. To folk music she had never given a thought. By her own admission, at that point in her life she felt condescending towards any kind of music other than art songs and lieder.

Odetta's first professional appearance as a singer and her breakaway from classical music came in 1949 when she joined the chorus of the West Coast production of *Finian's Rainbow*. While on tour in San Francisco, Odetta was introduced to folk music through friends. "I knew I was home," she says today. Since that time she has concentrated on folk music, finding in it the expressive freedom she sought.

The discovery of folk music as her natural heritage set Odetta to teaching herself to play the guitar, and her guitar accompaniment has become an integral part of each of her musical numbers, different in style with each song. Odetta prefers finding her own way, in music or anything else, and may spend many months over each of her interpretations before she feels satisfied that she has made it truly her own.

San Francisco's headquarters for beatniks and folk singers, the hungry i, soon recruited Odetta from among its unpaid entertainers in the audience. She sang one song and was hired instantly, but when the featured singer on the bill objected, the offer was withdrawn. The experience led Odetta to a year's engagement at the Tin Angel in San Francisco, and her reputation spread as an interpreter of work songs, blues, ballads, and spirituals. When she was invited to perform for a month at the Blue Angel in New York City, she won new audiences and the admiration of other folk singers, including Pete Seeger and Harry Belafonte.

After her success in New York, Odetta returned to California for work in the film *Cinerama Holiday,* in which she sang a rousing version of the sea chantey "Santy Anna." She then enjoyed a run of two years at the Turnabout Theatre in Los Angeles before she returned to the Eastern half of the United States. Her first engagement after her return was at the Gate of Horn, a Chicago night club featuring folk singing.

Tradition Records released her first record album, *Odetta Sings Ballads and Blues,* in 1956. The collection rounded up such traditional favorites as "Joshua," "Deep Blue Sea," and "I'm On My Way," among others, and introduced Odetta as the latest inheritor of the Bessie Smith and Leadbelly tradition. Reviews of her first album made special mention of her "striking contralto voice" and "electrifying sincerity." This was followed in the next year by a second record for Tradition, *Odetta at the Gate of Horn.* On this disc she applied her developing musical powers to songs as varied as "He Got the Whole World in His Hands," "Take

Vanguard Records

ODETTA

This Hammer," and "Greensleeves." After this album was released, her reputation as one of the country's leading folk singers widened, leading to successful concert engagements in the United States and Canada, including Chicago, Boston, Toronto, and Vancouver.

In April 1959 Odetta made her Town Hall debut in New York City in a concert that brought acclaim from the critics. John S. Wilson of the New York *Times* (April 25, 1959) called her "a highly cultivated singer . . . bringing to everything she sings the strong imprint of her warm, positive, and enormously skillful musical personality." Jay S. Harrison of the New York *Herald Tribune* (April 25, 1959) said that Odetta "gave us the picture of a strong and indomitable people . . . in organ sounds and cathedral colors."

Not without reason, Odetta has sometimes been called a protegée of Harry Belafonte. It was he who wrote the introductory notes for her Vanguard album *My Eyes Have Seen,* lauding her dramatic insight into Negro folk music and her artistry. Included in the album are Odetta's popular interpretation of "I've Been Driving on Bald Mountain" and her much-praised version of "Water Boy." In reviewing the album for the New York *Times* (March 6, 1960), Robert Shelton called Odetta "the most glorious new voice in American folk music" and deplored the fact that she "has a voice so large and a physical presence so commanding, recordings have yet to do her complete justice."

For her appearance on the much-discussed, hour-long television special *Tonight With Belafonte* on December 10, 1959 Odetta won a Sylvania Award. More kind words from the New York critics followed for her subtle showmanship, sensitive interpretations, and warm and flexible voice after her Carnegie Hall recital of May 8, 1960.

Ballads for Americans, with music by Earl Robinson and lyrics by John Latouche, was a natural choice for Odetta's next record album for Vanguard. Introduced by Paul Robeson in the late 1930's, the composition became a landmark in the breaking down of the hard-and-fast demarcation between "popular" and "art" music. It draws upon the reservoir of American folk music and expands to symphonic breadth. Backed by the DeCormier Chorale and the Symphony of the Air, Odetta did a "tremendous job" as narrator, according to Robert Gustafson of the *Christian Science Monitor* (April 19, 1960).

On May 29, 1960 Odetta appeared with William Warfield, Eddie Hodges, Bill Hayes, Bud Collyer, and Rosalind Elias on the WNBC-TV half-hour special *Parable in the Park* on behalf of the fund appeal of the Protestant Council of New York. She was one of the featured singers at the Newport Folk Festival, held at Newport, Rhode Island on June 25 and 26. Her performance there the year before had been a highlight of the gathering. On July 9, 1960 she was signed for the screen version of William Faulkner's *Sanctuary* in the role of the servant Nancy, who goes berserk and murders a child.

Odetta Felious was married in Chicago on May 1, 1959 to Dan Gordon. They make their home in Chicago. A robust young woman of commanding physical presence, Odetta has sometimes impressed reviewers at her concerts as having the bearing of a princess six feet tall. Actually, she is five feet eight and one-half inches in height. Although her speaking voice is subdued and delicate, her singing voice is described variously as basso, baritone, or contralto, depending upon what vocal forces she chooses to unleash at the moment. Since she works constantly to increase her already huge repertory of songs, she spares little time for hobbies or favorite recreations. She is a member of the Congregational Church and has been active in fund-raising activities for the Protestant church. She belongs to the American Federation of Musicians, American Guild of Variety Artists, and the American Federation of Television and Radio Artists.

OLIVETTI, ADRIANO Apr. 11, 1901-Feb. 28, 1960 Italian industrialist; president of Ing. C. Olivetti & Company since 1938; founder (1948) of Comunità town-planning movement; member of Chamber of Deputies since 1958. See *Current Biography* (January) 1959.

Obituary

N Y Times p27 F 29 '60

O'NEILL, FRANCIS A(LOYSIUS), JR.
Apr. 3, 1908- United States government official; lawyer

Address: b. National Mediation Board, 1230 16th St., N.W., Washington 25, D.C.; h. 2151 California St., N.W., Washington 8, D.C.; 314 E. 41st St., New York 17

A chief mediator of the federal government, Francis A. O'Neill, Jr., works to keep peace in a vital area of American industry by helping to settle disputes between railroad and airline companies on one hand and their employees on the other. In length of service he is the senior member of the three-man National Mediation Board, having continuously won reappointment since President Truman made him a Republican member in 1947. From time to time he has served a year's term as chairman of the board and was chairman during 1960 when the NMB mediated the Long Island Rail Road strike and the Pennsylvania Railroad strike. O'Neill is a lawyer and former chief trial examiner for the New York State Labor Relations Board.

Francis Aloysius O'Neill, Jr., is the only son of a New York attorney, Francis Aloysius O'Neill, and Elizabeth (Evans) O'Neill. He had one sister, now deceased. Born in New York City on April 3, 1908, he attended St. Stephen's elementary school and was graduated from St. Francis Xavier High School in 1926. Within three years he completed his undergraduate course at Fordham University in New York, where he majored in psychology. Receiving his B.A. degree in 1929, he entered Fordham University Law School, which awarded him the LL.B. degree in 1932. The following year he was admitted to the New York state bar and for the next six years practised

FRANCIS A. O'NEILL, JR.

law with his father, a former United States commissioner who had been mainly concerned with prohibition violations.

In March 1939, during the gubernatorial tenure of Herbert H. Lehman, O'Neill was appointed an attorney for the New York State Labor Relations Board, which is authorized to decide the appropriate unit for collective bargaining and to conduct hearings and take action in cases of alleged unfair practices. He was promoted to trial examiner of the board in 1941, but soon left his position for World War II service in the United States Naval Reserve. Entering as a lieutenant (j.g.) in January 1943, he fought for a time as a gunnery officer on board merchant ships, and after a period of duty in 1944-45 as a labor relations officer in Cincinnati, Ohio, he was discharged on December 25, 1945 in the rank of lieutenant.

Having returned to the New York State Labor Relations Board in 1946, O'Neill was serving as its chief trial examiner when President Truman appointed him on March 7, 1947 as Republican member of the National Mediation Board for a three-year term ending in 1950. (No more than two members of the three-man board may belong to the same political party.) Late in April 1948 he was one of two mediation board members whom the President ordered to confer with union leaders in Chicago and try to find means of averting a threatened nationwide railroad strike.

During the first half of 1950, after O'Neill had been reappointed to the National Mediation Board for a second three-year term and while he was serving as chairman, the board played an important part in several notable settlements. In March it worked out an agreement that ended an eleven-day strike of 4,600 American Airlines ground employees, and in April it helped to negotiate a new contract between Pan American World Airways and the CIO Transport Workers Union in which a job-security clause had been the major obstacle.

Other negotiations that O'Neill conducted led to an agreement in May 1950 ending a six-day strike by members of the Brotherhood of Locomotive Firemen and Enginemen against the New York Central, Pennsylvania, Santa Fé, and Southern rail systems. This agreement had hardly been reached, however, before O'Neill and his fellow board members were called upon to negotiate first a postponement and later the settlement of a strike that began late in June against five Western and Midwestern railroads by the AFL Switchmen's Union of North America, which demanded forty-eight hours' pay for forty hours' work.

The board also mediated in September an International Brotherhood of Teamsters strike against the Railway Express Agency over wage increases and other demands. O'Neill and board member Leverett Edwards participated in December 1950 in the meeting between President Truman's assistant, John R. Steelman, and railway union leaders that brought to an end a Brotherhood of Railway Trainmen's strike after the President had called the strike a danger to national security and had demanded an immediate return to work. The memorandum of agreement provided for wage increases for yardmen and service workers and a three-year no-strike moratorium on wage and rules demands by the unions.

Again the chairman of the National Mediation Board in 1952, O'Neill with Leverett Edwards was intermediary in a dispute between the New York Central System and three unions that was settled in September without a strike. In November of 1952 O'Neill, who is also a member of the Railroad and Airline Wage Board, helped in settling a strike called by the Flight Engineers International Association, AFL, against United Air Lines as the result of a pay dispute.

Reappointed in 1953, O'Neill was instrumental during the year in averting a railroad shop-workers' strike and a conductors' strike. At the end of May 1955 he was complimented by President Eisenhower for his skillful work in mediating the fifty-eight-day Louisville & Nashville Railroad strike. In the following September a threatened strike by Long Island Rail Road trainmen was averted after what a New York *Herald Tribune* editorial (September 24, 1955) described as a "final marathon conference called by Mr. O'Neill that lasted no less than twenty-nine continuous hours." The editorial went on, "The work of the National Mediation Board deserves far more public recognition than it gets. . . . No less than 90 per cent of railroad disputes are settled by mediation."

Among the disputes that O'Neill helped settle during his next term on the board were a wage disagreement between the Brotherhood of Locomotive Firemen and Engineers and the nation's 140 major railroads (September-November 1956), a strike of mechanics against Capital Airlines (October-November 1958), and a walkout by flight engineers of Eastern Airlines (November-December 1958). Eisenhower once again reappointed him to the mediation board, in January 1959, for his fifth consecutive term.

During the summer of 1960 O'Neill, who had been again designated chairman of the NMB, worked strenuously but without success to avert a strike on July 10 by 1,350 members of the Brotherhood of Railroad Trainmen, who halted operation of the Long Island Rail Road. Some 200,000 daily passengers on the country's busiest commuter railroad were left without usual means of transportation until the strike was settled on August 3 with the help of federal mediators. Almost immediately the NMB had to turn its attention to the Pennsylvania Railroad strike, which began on September 1. When employees returned to work twelve days later, O'Neill was praised in newspaper editorials for his indefatigable efforts in getting both sides to agree through bargaining.

Francis A. O'Neill, Jr., is a Roman Catholic and has been honored with the Berlin Award of Holy Cross College. He is a member of the New York County Lawyers Association, the National Academy of Arbitrators, the Fordham Alumni Association, and the Knights of Columbus. The husky, brown-eyed, gray-haired mediator is six feet one-half inch tall and weighs 197 pounds. He finds outdoor relaxation on the golf course or in his flower garden at his "little place" in Manasquan, New Jersey. Cooking is another of his hobbies. Mrs. O'Neill is the former Lillian C. Gerner, to whom he was married on September 16, 1939.

"I have never found a textbook that would cover the problems involved in any major labor dispute," O'Neill has remarked. "I try to follow a philosophy which is based on the recognition that I am dealing entirely with human beings and not with commodities in commerce" (New York *Times*, September 2, 1960). He says that since his appointment to the NMB in 1947 he has never had four weekdays off "back-to-back," but new challenges that each case presents keep him devoted to his work.

References

N Y Times p12 S 2 '60 por
Who's Who in America, 1960-61

ORR, LOUIS M(CDONALD) Sept. 27, 1899- Physician; organization official

Address: b. 1300 Kuhl Ave., Orlando, Fla.; h. 750 Gatlin Ave., Orlando, Fla.

Installed in June 1959 for a one-year term as the 113th president of the American Medical Association, Dr. Louis M. Orr of Orlando, Florida is nationally known as an urologist who is also interested in nuclear medicine and cancer treatment and research. He is an outspoken opponent of both socialized medicine and mandatory retirement ages for the elderly. "Because a person reaches the age of 65 or 62 or 60 with his capabilities . . . still alive and strong," he contends, "such a person should not be fenced apart from everyone else by artificial barriers." Dr. Orr has criticized the Forand bill to provide wide medical benefits for the aged as tending to "make senior citizens semi-dependent

Alan Anderson, Orlando, Fla.

DR. LOUIS M. ORR

wards of the Federal government and be a foot in the door" for socialization.

Louis McDonald Orr can offer no explanation for becoming a doctor; as far as he knows there were no medical men among his ancestors. He was born in a covered wagon at Cumming, Georgia on September 27, 1899 while his parents, Louis M. and Etta (Wise) Orr, were making a trip. He spent his early childhood in Greensboro, Georgia, where his father was in the lumber business, and in Dothan, Alabama. When his family moved back to Georgia, Louis attended Glynn Academy in Brunswick, before becoming an undergraduate at Emory University in Georgia in 1917. Drafted by the Army in 1918, Orr was assigned first to the infantry unit attached to the college and later to Officers' Training School in Louisville, Kentucky. After the armistice he resumed his studies, receiving the B.S. degree in 1922 from Emory and the M.D. degree in 1924 from its Medical School.

During one summer he worked at Peter Bent Brigham Hospital in Boston as a voluntary assistant to Dr. Merrill C. Sosman, head of the X-ray department. In his final year as a medical student he won the appointment as surgical house officer at Peter Bent Brigham, where he served until the end of 1925. From Peter Bent Brigham he went to Lakeside Hospital in Cleveland as resident in general surgery and urology, but soon returned to Boston for further special training in urology as an associate of Dr. Arthur L. Chute.

Although he was strongly urged by Dr. Harvey Cushing of Harvard to remain in university medicine, Orr decided to practise privately, at least for a while. His brother, Clifton, was a businessman in Orlando, Florida, and he liked this central Florida city with its picturesque lakes. In February 1927 he opened an office in Orlando and there he has continued to prac-

ORR, LOUIS M.—Continued

tise (except for interruption by World War II service) until the present time. He was appointed chief of the urology department of the Orange Memorial Hospital in Orlando in 1927, and he now serves the institution as a consultant in urology as well as director of postgraduate education. At the hospital the nation's fourth blood bank was opened in 1938, made possible by financial gifts of Dr. Orr and his wife. Later, he established the Louis M. Orr Foundation for Cancer Research which furnished all the equipment for an isotope program at the Orange Memorial Hospital.

Among the fifty or more contributions Dr. Orr has made to scientific literature, several were published in Southern medical journals during his first years at Orlando. These articles treat such subjects as intravenous urography, resection of the prostate, and kidney removal.

Commissioned a major in the Army Medical Corps, Dr. Orr began four years of World War II military service on July 11, 1942. Sent to England, he served as executive officer and later commanding officer of the Fifteenth Hospital Center. During his military service he was a member of the Allied Nations Friendship Committee, which was organized to cope with the problems of men detached from their units. Orr was discharged in 1946 with the rank of colonel. He received the Bronze Star, a special tribute from the British-American Liaison Board, and a service rating of "superior—outstanding and exceptional performance."

Long a member of medical societies, Dr. Orr was a founder of the American Board of Urology, and he was one of the first Orlando doctors to be named a Fellow of the American College of Surgeons, in 1933. He also belongs to the American Urological Association (president of the southeastern section, 1943), American of Genito-Urinary Surgeons, International Society of Urology, Southern Medical Association, Southeastern Surgical Congress, Society of Nuclear Medicine, and, of course, the American Medical Association.

Named president-elect of the 170,000-member American Medical Association at the annual convention in San Francisco in June 1958, Dr. Orr had previously served the association as vice-speaker of the house of delegates, a member of the council on medical service, ex officio member of the council on constitution and bylaws, and chairman of the federal medical services committee. An opponent of socialized medicine, he referred to the Veterans Administration as a "Trojan horse" (*Arizona Medicine,* January 1958). In an address at Salt Lake City during his year as A.M.A. president-elect he warned that "any governmental medical program . . . would be compulsory, financially back breaking, subject to political whim and pressure and hopelessly snarled by red tape."

After succeeding Dr. Gunnar Gundersen as A.M.A. president in June 1959, Dr. Orr said that voluntary health insurance programs must be broadened and improved to provide greater medical benefits at reasonable costs. To reduce the costs of hospital administration and relieve the shortage of doctors and nurses, Dr. Orr has recommended that revolutionary plastic hospitals equipped with electronic devices be built. Such hospitals would reduce staffs to one-third their present size.

Dr. Orr serves on the consulting staff of the medical division of the Oak Ridge Institute of Nuclear Studies in Tennessee. A director of the United States committee of the World Medical Association, he attended general assemblies of that body at Istanbul, Turkey in 1957 and in Montreal in 1959.

In 1935 Dr. Orr became president of the Central Florida Civic Music Association, which has sponsored the concert appearances of famous musical artists in central Florida; in 1952 he was made honorary president for life. For fourteen years, beginning in 1937, he served as a trustee of Rollins College, Winter Park, Florida. In February 1946 he received the highest honor given by the college—the Algernon Sydney Sullivan Award. He has been a member of the Florida Medical Committee for Better Government.

Dr. Orr has been as successful in his hobbies as he has been in his profession. When he was a teen-ager he was so good a golfer that he considered becoming a professional player, and he has since taken part in many amateur championship contests. An expert rifleman, he has managed big game hunts in Wyoming. He has won prizes at flower shows with camellias from his garden, and he has successfully adapted tulips to the Florida climate. He is a skilled amateur photographer and likes to fish and to travel.

Louis McDonald Orr and Dorothy Brown were married on December 16, 1927; their children are Louis McDonald, Jr., and Doris Brown Orr. Dr. Orr has served on the chapter of the Episcopal Cathedral Church of St. Luke in Orlando. He has been described as a "perfectionist, short-tempered on occasion but possessor of a dynamic personality."

References

J Am Med Assn 167:1249+ Jl 5 '58 por
Miami (Fla.) Herald p1C Je 10 '59
American Medical Directory, 1958
Directory of Medical Specialists (1957)

ORVILLE, HOWARD T(HOMAS) June 16, 1901-May 24, 1960 Meteorologist; United States Navy officer (ret.); chairman of the United States Advisory Committee on Weather Control (1953-57). See *Current Biography* (May) 1956.

Obituary

N Y Times p33 My 26 '60

OTTLEY, ROI (VINCENT) Aug. 2, 1906-Oct. 1, 1960 Journalist and author of nonfiction books about the American Negro; reporter on Negro affairs for the Chicago *Tribune* since 1953. See *Current Biography* (October) 1943.

Obituary

N Y Times p84 O 2 '60

PAEPCKE, WALTER P(AUL) (pĕp'kĕ)
June 29, 1896- Corporation executive

Address: b. Container Corporation of America, 38 S. Dearborn St., Chicago 3, Ill.; h. Drake Hotel, 140 E. Walton Pl., Chicago 11, Ill.

> *Bulletin*: Walter P. Paepcke
> died on April 13, 1960.

In a period when the design of packaging for consumers' products has become increasingly important, the Container Corporation of America has taken the lead in the manufacture of paperboard cartons and other paper products. Its forty-three plants manufacture containers for commodities ranging from frozen food to ammunition. Its board chairman and chief executive officer, Walter P. Paepcke, is known not only as a successful businessman, but also as the founder of the Aspen Institute for Humanistic Studies in Colorado. Paepcke organized the Aspen experiment to stimulate the interest of businessmen in the liberal arts; it established the pattern for similar institutes that have sprung up across the United States.

Born in Chicago on June 29, 1896, Walter Paul Paepcke was the only boy in a family of four children. His parents were Paula (Wagner) and Hermann Paepcke, a German immigrant who became president and principal owner of the Chicago Mill & Lumber Company. Walter Paepcke was educated at the University School for Boys and the Chicago Boys' Latin School and studied music at home. At Yale University, where he majored in economics and history, he was elected to Phi Beta Kappa and was awarded the B.A. degree in 1917.

After his graduation from Yale, Paepcke entered the family business as an assistant treasurer. For two years he spent his evenings studying at the Kent College of Law in Chicago. By 1921 he had become president of the Chicago Mill & Lumber Company. Except for nine months of service in the United States Navy during World War I, when he earned the rank of ensign, Paepcke has continuously been in business.

In 1926 Paepcke predicted that paper cartons would replace wooden boxes and crates for many uses. By floating $6,000,000 in securities, he raised enough capital to buy two more companies. When he decided to call his new concern the Container Corporation of America, his attorney told him that this was a "big name for such a small company." Paepcke replied: "We'll take the name and grow into it." His promise was fulfilled: within a year sales topped $11,500,000; by the end of World War II assets were $43,000,000; and in recent years the company grossed about $275,000,000 annually. Paepcke served as president of the Container Corporation until 1946, when he became chairman of the board.

Explaining the problems of a newcomer in a highly competitive field, Paepcke once said: "Lower prices are the weapons a new business uses when starting. Your competitor meets you. Prices level off. Then you go in for better quality, better paper, stronger boxes. Soon you discover everybody else is doing the same thing. So you get your engineers and production people to help you give better service—say, 48-hour delivery instead of a week" (*Pathfinder*, June 14, 1950).

Shelburne Studios

WALTER P. PAEPCKE

Since the end of World War II the Container Corporation of America has invested some $160,000,000 in expansion projects. During World War II it developed solid fiber boards which were used in the military packaging of such items as dried eggs, field rations, and ammunition for small arms.

Fashioning many of its products from waste paper, the Container Corporation of America has attained leadership in manufacturing paperboard, corrugated, and solid-fiber shipping cases, folding cartons, and other paper products. It also makes fiber cans for frozen foods and automotive parts. It was the first to manufacture multi-can and mixed-commodity containers, and cartons with four-color screen printing.

Since 1955 the company has invested about $11,000,000 in West German and Latin American subsidiaries. Paepcke believes that the foreign income of the Container Corporation of America will soon account for 25 per cent of the company's sales.

In designing their colorful and functional packages, the executives and staff of the Container Corporation of America have been much influenced by modern art. "We believe in elegance," Paepcke has said. "That doesn't mean expensive. It just means the best possible taste." The company has reproduced abstract paintings in their series of advertisements on the United Nations during World War II and in their series on the Great Ideas of Western Man, containing quotations from famous statesmen, philosophers, and writers.

Paepcke and his wife first became interested in Aspen when they saw the deserted silver-mining city on the juncture of Roaring Fork River and Castle Creek during a Colorado vacation in 1945. Since that time Paepcke has poured about $800,000 of his own capital

PAEPCKE, WALTER P.—*Continued*

into projects in Aspen and its vicinity. Impressed by its mountain scenery and natural charms, he envisaged Aspen as a perfect location for a ski resort. With the aid of friends Paepcke built a 14,000 ski lift, one of the largest in the world, and other athletic facilities. He renovated the historic Hotel Jerome, restoring its former Victorian grandeur. He still serves as a director of the Aspen Skiing Corporation and as president of the Aspen Company.

His next objective was to turn Aspen into a musical center. In 1949 he inaugurated the annual Aspen Music Festival, which in its first summer celebrated the bicentennial of the birth of Goethe and featured Dr. Albert Schweitzer. The Aspen Music Festival and its summer music school attract to its roster of performers and teachers such composers, conductors, and pianists as Darius Milhaud, William Steinberg, and Madame Rosina Lhevinne.

Perhaps Paepcke's most abiding interest in Aspen has been the Institute for Humanistic Studies, which he established in 1950 to restore the mental and physical vitality of businessmen. Since then about 170 companies have sent some 400 executives to the two-week summer session, which includes calisthenics, hot and cold baths, massages, sports, concerts, and attendance at seminars.

Designed to promote the application of philosophical thinking to political and economic problems, the seminars feature group discussions of the works of Western thinkers and state documents of the past and present. The discussions try to promote an understanding of democracy and capitalism, on the assumption that these are the central ideologies of American society.

"A treasurer who goes to Aspen," Paepcke has said, "will not learn one single thing about being a treasurer . . . but two weeks in Aspen will equip that treasurer . . . to function better as a human being . . . and consequently as a businessman. Aspen turns executives away from the urgent to the important." Paepcke continues to serve as chairman of the board of the Aspen institute. Since he introduced the Aspen seminars many educational institutions and corporations have offered special seminars and courses in the liberal arts for businessmen.

In addition to his duties with the Container Corporation of America and the Aspen Institute for Humanistic Studies, Paepcke is a director for the U.S. Gypsum Company, the K.W. Battery Company, Inc., Encyclopaedia Britannica, Inc., and Encyclopaedia Britannica Films, Inc. He is also a director of the Fund for the Advancement of Education of the Ford Foundation, chairman of the board of Passavant Memorial Hospital in Chicago, Chicago Orchestral Association, and the Art Institute of Chicago. Paepcke is a member of the Newcomen Society, Alpha Delta Phi, and social clubs in Chicago, New York, and Denver. He served on the paperboard code authority of the National Recovery Administration and on the advisory committee of the Joint Army and Navy Munitions Board during World War II.

Among the awards Paepcke has received are an honor award from the Artists Club of Chicago in 1953; the 1953-54 honor citation from the Chicago chapter, American Institute of Architects; Industrial Advertising Man-of-the-Year award in 1955; and the Daniels and Fisher Creativity Award in 1957. The honorary LL.D. was conferred on him by the University of Denver (1950) and Occidental College and the L.H.D. degree by Wesleyan University (1954), Trinity College (1954), Oberlin College (1958), and Colorado College (1959).

On April 16, 1922 Walter P. Paepcke was married to Elizabeth Hilken Nitze, an artist and daughter of Professor William A. Nitze of the University of Chicago. The couple had four children: Walter Paul (deceased), Mrs. Anina Hilken Woods, Mrs. Paula Alexandra Zurcher, and Mrs. Alice Antonia DuBrul. Paepcke, a blue-eyed and athletic blond, weighs 175 pounds and stands five feet eleven inches. In religion he is a Presbyterian; in politics, an independent. His favorite sports are tennis, swimming, riding, and squash rackets. In less active moments he enjoys chess, bridge, and conversation.

References

    Forbes 82:11+ O 1 '58 pors
    Newsweek 49:94 Je 10 '57 por; 54:79+
      Jl 20 '59 por
    Business Executives of America (1950)
    National Cyclopædia of American Biography current vol G (1943-46)
    Who's Who in America, 1958-59
    World Biography (1954)

PALMER, ARNOLD Sept. 10, 1929-
Golfer

Address: b. Latrobe Country Club, Latrobe, Pa.; h. Latrobe, Pa.

During the year 1960 the iron-fisted, steel-nerved golfer Arnold Palmer captured the coveted Masters title, won the National Open and other competitions, and amassed more than $70,000 in winner's stakes, earnings which made him the best-paid player of the year. In the six years since he gave up his amateur standing, he has placed first in some twenty tourneys, more than any other full-time regular on the tournament circuit of the Professional Golfers' Association (PGA). Palmer, who was also Master champion in 1958, has been hailed as the finest player in a group of young professionals challenging veterans like Sam Snead and Ben Hogan for top honors, and in the 1960 PGA poll was elected professional golfer of the year.

Arnold Palmer, the oldest of four children, was born in Youngstown, Pennsylvania on September 10, 1929 and was reared in Latrobe, Pennsylvania, an industrial community thirty miles east of Pittsburgh. His German-Irish ancestors had settled in the region in the early 1800's as farmers. Palmer's parents have always lived "within a brassie shot" of the Latrobe Country Club, where his father, Milfred

Jerome ("Deacon") Palmer, has worked in various capacities for thirty-nine years and has served since 1933 as greenskeeper and teaching professional. Palmer has one brother, Milfred, Jr. ("Jerry"), and two sisters, Sandy and Mrs. Ronald Tilley.

When he was three years old Arnold got his first golf club—an old iron with a sawed-off shaft. His father, who taught Arnold almost everything he knows about golf, first showed him the proper overlapping grip and always impressed on him the importance of keeping a firm hold on the club. At every opportunity, particularly on Mondays when the Latrobe Country Club was closed to members, the boy would rush off to practise his golf. He played with the club caddies and with his mother, who, he said, was "quite good for a woman and a real stickler for keeping a scorecard" (*Saturday Evening Post*, June 18, 1960). By the time he was nine years old he had shot nine holes at forty-five.

Arnold attended Latrobe High School, where he was first player on the golf team for four years. During this time he lost only one match and won the Western Pennsylvania Junior three times and the Western Pennsylvania Amateur five times. In high school he learned an invaluable lesson for any professional golfer: how to control his temper. Infuriated by flubbing a shot in a junior match, he sent his club sailing over a poplar grove. After the match he found his father in a grim mood. "Pap told me that this was a gentleman's game," Palmer explains, "and he was ashamed of me. If he saw or heard of me throwing a club again, he was through with me as a golfer. That did it."

When Palmer, then a high school senior, was competing in the Hearst national junior tournament in Los Angeles, he met Bud Worsham, brother of the golfer Lew Worsham. Bud said that Palmer could get a golf scholarship at Wake Forest College, North Carolina. "I leaped at the idea," Palmer remembers. "Pap . . . had a tough enough time trying to keep me in golf balls, much less financing a college education for me."

Bud Worsham and Palmer were roommates at Wake Forest College, which Palmer entered in September 1947. Although he majored in business administration, the main thing on his mind was golf. He won a host of amateur tournaments, including the Southern Intercollegiate, and was twice a medalist, although not the winner, in the National Intercollegiate. In Palmer's senior year, Worsham was killed in an automobile accident. "I became restless," Palmer has explained, "and quit school to join the Coast Guard." He spent a few months of his three-year service period in New Jersey and Connecticut, serving the remainder of the time in Cleveland, Ohio.

In January 1954 Palmer returned to Wake Forest for a semester but he did not take his degree. He then became a salesman for W. C. Wehnes and Company, a Cleveland painting supplies company. The job involved morning work only, and Palmer played golf in the afternoons. He frequently felt frustrated, however, because he was unable to leave for extensive

Wide World

ARNOLD PALMER

periods to play in tournaments. Palmer did play in the 1954 National Amateur championship competition of the United States Golf Association. He defeated a former British Amateur champion, Robert Sweeny, on the thirty-sixth hole of their match contest for the National Amateur title.

"Ever since I was able to walk I have been swinging a golf club, and ever since I was big enough to dream I have wanted to be the best golfer that ever lived," Palmer has said (*Saturday Evening Post,* June 18, 1960). "At one time I was certain that someday I would duplicate Bob Jones's 'grand slam' of 1930—that is, sweep the United States Amateur and Open championships and the British Amateur and Open in a single year. Then I found out—to my disillusionment—that to devote the necessary time to golf, yet still remain an amateur, I would need either tremendous wealth or a high-paying job with no responsibility."

Since neither prospect was forthcoming, on November 17, 1954 Palmer signed a contract with the Wilson Sporting Goods Company and turned professional. During the next six months Palmer sustained himself and his wife, to whom he was married in December of 1954, by winning $750 in a special professional-amateur competition in Miami, Florida and collecting $1,300 for a second-place tie in another non-PGA event in Panama. It was not until August 1955 that he won his first major professional tourney by capturing the Canadian Open golf title with a four-round total score of 265, at that time the second lowest total in the forty-six-year history of the tournament. The win was worth $2,400 to Palmer.

In 1956 Palmer won three contests. The most important of these was his victory over Ted Kroll in the Insurance City Open in Wethersfield, Connecticut. He captured four tournaments in 1957, including the Azalea

PALMER, ARNOLD—Continued

Open, held in Wilmington, North Carolina; the Rubber City Open in Akron, Ohio; and the San Diego (California) Open. Palmer was the fifth leading money winner that year, with $27,802.80.

Palmer won three championships in 1958, and all were important. In late March he captured the St. Petersburg (Florida) Open. Two weeks later he took the Masters title at Augusta, Georgia. Playing consistent golf during the four days of competition, Palmer had finished with a seventy-two-hole total of 284, one stroke better than Doug Ford, the defending champion, and Fred Hawkins, both of whom scored 285. In June 1958 Palmer picked up $9,000 for finishing first in the Pepsi golf tournament at East Norwich, Long Island. His total winnings for the year were $42,607.50.

In 1959 Palmer's playing declined. He won no major titles, although he managed to win three tournaments, including the Thunderbird Invitation at Palm Springs, California in January. His over-all winnings for the year fell to $32,462.14.

After winning the Palm Springs (California) Desert tournament in February 1960, Palmer had three consecutive victories: the Texas Open, the Baton Rouge (Louisiana) Open, and the Pensacola (Florida) Open competitions. He again wore the green jacket which denotes a Masters champion after achieving a dramatic victory over Ken Venturi, who has been called Palmer's keenest rival for top place among golf's "young guard." Trailing Venturi by two strokes with two holes to play in the final round, Palmer knocked in two amazing birdie putts on the seventeenth and eighteenth greens for a four-round total of 282, one stroke better than Venturi's final score. Palmer also captured the National Open championship, which was played in June 1960 at the Cherry Hills Country Club in Denver, Colorado. After trailing seven strokes behind the lead throughout the tournament, Palmer surged ahead in the final round, winning the competition with a four-round total of 280. The same month at Portmarnock, Ireland, Palmer, again showing a last-minute spurt of energy, was instrumental in winning the Canada Cup for the United States.

Although coldly precise in his study of the game, he is not imperturbable during a round. He can drive the ball far from the tee and is especially accurate with long iron shots, his No. 1 iron being one of his pet clubs. Among his fellow professionals, Palmer is respected for the skill with which he is able to "scramble" or "finesse," that is, to find ingenious ways out of trouble. He can, for instance, play an intentional hook, find swinging room in a thicket, and blast a ball out of water.

A *Time* (May 2, 1960) writer describes Palmer as "a splendidly built athlete . . . with strength in all the right places: massive shoulders and arms, a waist hardly big enough to hold his trousers up, thick wrists, and leather-hard, outsized hands that can crumple a beer can as though it were tissue paper." He is five feet eleven inches tall and weighs 177 pounds. Off the course, Palmer's two main hobbies are bridge and flying. The Latrobe Airport is only about a mile from his home, and he has logged almost 100 hours of solo flying. "I'm looking forward to the day I buy my own plane and can sky-hop between tournaments," he says.

Arnold Palmer was married to Winnie Walzer on December 20, 1954. He had met her while he was playing in an amateur tourney in Shawnee on Delaware, Pennsylvania and had proposed three days later. The Palmers have two daughters, Peggy and Amy. They live in a white ranch house near the Latrobe club.

Palmer plans to play another ten years on tour and then take a job at a country club as a teaching professional. Although his first ambition was to duplicate the feats of Bobby Jones in amateur golf, Palmer's present goal is to cement his place in golfing history by achieving a professional grand slam, i.e., following up his Masters and National Open triumphs with victories in the British Open and the PGA tournament. No golfer has ever won all four contests in one year, and in 1960 Palmer was defeated in the British Open contest and lost in the PGA tourney. "In all the time golf has been played," a *Herald Tribune* (April 12, 1960) writer said of Palmer, "it is unlikely we ever have had a champion more bold who yet could calculate the chances so accurately and was so little afraid of taking them."

References

Sat Eve Post 232:24+ Je 18 '60 pors
Time 75:54+ My 2 '60 pors

PARKINSON, C(YRIL) NORTHCOTE

July 30, 1909- Author; historian
Address: h. "Les Câches House," St. Martin's, Guernsey, Channel Islands, Great Britain

About three years ago, administrators were chuckling at a joke on themselves. The source of their somewhat uneasy amusement was *Parkinson's Law* (1957), a collection of essays that satirized managerial bureaucracy in business and government. When the title essay was first published anonymously in the London *Economist* (November 19, 1955), many readers thought that Professor C. Northcote Parkinson, discoverer of the law, was the fanciful creation of jesting editors. As Parkinson has pointed out, "Rumors of [my] nonexistence . . . proved to be unfounded or at least grossly exaggerated." By the time he made his first visit to the United States in June 1958, his book had become a best seller, and he had come to be regarded as an authority on organizational efficiency.

A noted British historian, Parkinson served as Raffles Professor of History at the University of Malaya in Singapore from 1950 to 1958. He has written or edited some fifteen books on naval and Malayan history. *The Evolution of Political Thought* (1958) traces the development of political systems in the Western world and the Orient. *The Law and the Profits,* written in a vein similar to that of *Parkinson's Law,* was published in 1960.

Cyril Northcote Parkinson, the younger son of William Edward and Rose Emily Mary

(Curnow) Parkinson, was born at Barnard Castle in the county of Durham, England on July 30, 1909. He and his brother, who is now the Reverend Ronald Curnow Parkinson, were reared in York. Cyril attended St. Olive's School and then received his secondary education at St. Peter's School, from which he was graduated in 1929. During his school years he devoted most of his leisure to painting and journalism, and after his graduation he decided to follow his father's example and pursue a career as an artist. His lifelong interest in maritime and naval history stems from this period in his life, when he, like his father, painted ships and seascapes. Parkinson maintains that the sense of humor which produced his *Law* "seems to have been innate." In his youth he was much influenced by G. K. Chesterton, whom he believes to have been one of the great men of his time.

Law was the second vocation that Parkinson considered, but at Emmanuel College, Cambridge University he majored in history. He was granted a Drapers Company scholarship and a history exhibition, and was graduated with honors in 1932, receiving B.A. and M.A. degrees. After three years of postgraduate study he was awarded the Ph.D. degree in 1935 by Kings College, University of London, which also gave him the Julian Corbett Prize. His dissertation was entitled "Trade and War in the Eastern Seas, 1793-1813." A part of this document was later expanded and published as *Trade in the Eastern Seas* by the Cambridge University Press in 1937. Another book by Parkinson, *War in the Eastern Seas,* was published by Allen and Unwin in 1954.

Like Charles L. Dodgson, the mathematician who created *Alice in Wonderland,* Parkinson devoted most of his adult life to a vocation unrelated to the achievement for which he became widely known. Beginning as a Fellow at Emmanuel College, Cambridge in 1935, he taught history in a series of academic posts for seventeen years. From 1937 to 1938 he served as senior history master at Blundell's School, Tiverton; he was a master at the Royal Naval College in Dartmouth from 1939 to 1940. After serving in the British Army during World War II, Parkinson became a lecturer in naval and maritime history at the University of Liverpool in 1946. He left Liverpool in 1950 and moved to Malaya, where he was Raffles Professor of History at the University of Malaya until 1958.

His scholarly publications include *Edward Pellew, Viscount Exmouth* (Methuen, 1934); *Always a Fusilier* (Low, 1949); *The Rise of the Port of Liverpool* (University Press of Liverpool, 1952); *Portsmouth Point, the Navy in Fiction, 1793-1815* (University Press of Liverpool, 1948); and *The Trade Winds* (Allen and Unwin, 1948), which he edited. In Singapore, Parkinson found the historian's Utopia: a history of Malaya had never been written. He soon corrected this deficiency by writing *A Short History of Malaya* (Moore, 1954; 1956); *Templar in Malaya* (Moore, 1954); *Marxism for Malayans* (Moore, 1956); and, with his wife, *Heroes of Malaya* (Moore, 1956). He also began to edit twelve projected volumes of original research in Malayan history, of which

C. NORTHCOTE PARKINSON

the first, *The History of Malaya, 1867-1877,* was published by the University of Malaya Press in 1960.

During World War II Parkinson served for five years with the British Army. Entering the Army in 1941 as a lieutenant, he was an instructor at 166 Officer Cadet Training Unit for a year. In 1942-43 he was assigned to the Royal Air Force and, having been commissioned a major in 1943, was transferred the following year as a general staff officer to the War Office, where he served until he was demobilized in 1946.

It was largely in the Army that Parkinson gained the firsthand experience that enabled him to formulate his first law: work expands to fill the time available for its completion. Administrators make work for each other, he says in *Parkinson's Law* (Houghton Mifflin, 1957; J. Murray, 1958). Since executives are anxious to multiply subordinates rather than rivals, they gradually erect a pyramid of command in which "the executive's importance is enhanced by the number of his subordinates." The managerial ranks swell inevitably, he says, "irrespective of the amount of work (if any) to be done." This increase he estimates to be between 5.7 and 6:56 per cent annually.

Parkinson exposes the ludicrousness of much bureaucratic behavior with poker-faced sobriety. Among his targets are the committee, which grows organically, "flourishes and blossoms, sunlit on top and shady beneath until it dies, scattering the seed from which other committees will spring"; the executive meeting (the less a new item will cost, the more impassioned the discussion); organization offices (the more lavish the office, the more desiccated the firm); and cocktail parties (VIP's circulate on schedule from left to right).

Some 100,000 copies of the book were sold in the United States. It was translated into many languages, including Italian, German,

PARKINSON, C. NORTHCOTE—*Cont.*

Swedish, and Icelandic. In an article in the New York *Times Magazine* (July 10, 1960) Parkinson ascribes its universal appeal to the fact that "it has double impact. It is read initially as a joke . . . but the sequel to laughter is the shock of realization that the absurdity is based on fact, that the statistics are accurate, that the wildest statement is literally true."

The newly popular author left his post at the University of Malaya and visited the United States for the first time in June 1958. That summer he taught British history at Harvard University summer school and in the fall lectured from coast to coast on *Parkinson's Law*. After spending several months in Britain, he returned to America in August 1959. During the first half of the academic year 1959-60, he was George A. Miller Visiting Professor of History at the University of Illinois, and during the spring semester he taught history at the University of California in Berkeley.

Although *Parkinson's Law* primarily criticized government inefficiency, response from the business community convinced him that he had found a universal pattern of administrative behavior. "I also learned that the business man, unlike the civil servant, wants to do something about it," he has explained, and this realization led, in turn, to his writing *The Law and the Profits* (Houghton Mifflin, 1960).

In this book, which a *Time* (February 29, 1960) reviewer has called "twice as long and half as funny [as *Parkinson's Law*]," the author expounds his second law: expenditure rises to meet income. The administrative ranks of government can expand indefinitely, he asserts (New York *Times Magazine*, July 10, 1960), because "the multiplication of public administrators is unchecked by any thought of the total expenditure. . . . Politicians and economists see no reason at all to call a halt in the raising of taxes." Parkinson warns that excessive taxation may sap the vitality of a nation. He advocates a balanced budget with expenditures limited to available revenue.

"Professor Parkinson's book is brilliantly written," Nate White commented in the *Christian Science Monitor* (February 25, 1960). "He pierces government waste in Britain and the United States with startling clarity. The reader should be on guard, of course. Professor Parkinson's economic views put him in the extreme right. He might be classified as an 'economic cave man,' since he apparently thinks that great nations can run themselves without people and with greatly reduced revenue. Having put Professor Parkinson in the proper economic corner, one can proceed to enjoy his jibes. He has a point on government waste, and he makes it well."

Parkinson received critical acclaim for *The Evolution of Political Thought* (Houghton Mifflin; University of London, 1958), in which he describes a tendency for political regimes to follow a cycle from monarchy through aristocracy, democracy, chaos, dictatorship, and back to monarchy again. He has contributed articles to the New York *Times Magazine*, *Fortnightly*, the *Encyclopaedia Britannica*, *Punch*, and the Manchester *Guardian*. He was chairman of two government commissions of the Colony of Singapore, is a Fellow of the Royal Historical Society, and a member of the French Académie de Marine, the Society for Nautical Research in Britain, and the United States Naval Institute. His religious affiliation is with the Church of England. He is a Liberal in politics and belongs to the National Liberal Club in London.

By his marriage in 1943 to Ethelwyn Edith Graves, Cyril Northcote Parkinson has two children, Alison Barbara and Christopher Francis Graves. After his divorce in 1951 he was married to Elizabeth Ann Fry, a former subeditor of *Women's Illustrated*, on September 23, 1952. They have two children, Charles Nigel Kennedy and Antonia Patricia Jane. The stocky, genial Englishman has brown eyes and graying brown hair. He stands five feet nine inches tall and weighs 190 pounds. His favorite pastimes are painting, sailing, badminton, and travel. Expressing some surprise at the celebrity he has achieved, the humorist credits it to sheer persistence. "While always confident that I should succeed in some capacity," he says, "it has taken me thirty years to produce anything that could possibly be accepted as proof."

References

N Y Herald Tribune Bk R p2 Jl 6 '58
N Y Times Bk R p8 Jl 13 '58
International Who's Who, 1959
Who's Who, 1960

PASSMAN, OTTO E(RNEST) June 27, 1900- United States Representative from Louisiana; businessman

Address: b. House Office Bldg., Washington 25, D.C.; 118 Walnut St., Monroe, La.; h. The Congressional, Washington 3, D.C.; Loop Rd., Monroe, La.

Chairman of the House Appropriations' foreign operations subcommittee since 1955, Congressman Otto E. Passman of Louisiana has been "wielding a countryman's axe" on foreign assistance outlays, and his subcommittee has cut sums ranging from $627,000,000 to $1.4 billions from annual mutual security bills. Feeling that he has been "placed in the wrong light," Passman has explained that it is not his mission to cripple the foreign assistance program, but to end "this crazy system of spending more money every year than we take in" (New York *Times*, June 14, 1960).

Known as a fast-talking and articulate spokesman for whittled-down government spending, Passman opposes civil rights measures and advocates high price supports for farmers and curbs on labor unions. A well-to-do manufacturer and distributor of restaurant equipment, he has represented his state's Fifth District since 1947.

Self-described as "just a country boy," Otto Ernest Passman, of Irish-French-Dutch extraction, was born on a farm near Franklinton, Louisiana on June 27, 1900. His parents, Ed and Pheriby (Carrier) Passman, were sharecroppers, and Otto left Pine Ridge grade school at thirteen to earn his own living. In the course of the next sixteen years he worked at a variety of jobs in Louisiana, Arkansas, and elsewhere. Continuing his education in the evenings, Passman attended Baton Rouge (Louisiana) High School and Commercial Business College in Bogalusa, Louisiana and was graduated from both schools.

Moving to the industrial city of Monroe, Louisiana in 1929, he established the Passman Wholesale Equipment Company, manufacturers and distributors of commercial refrigerators and hotel and restaurant accessories, and became the owner of the Delta Furniture Company at Monroe, the Commercial Equipment Company of Fort Smith, Arkansas, and an investment company. Since his election to Congress in 1946, he spends most of his time in Washington, but he receives daily, weekly, and monthly statements of the sales and profits of these flourishing businesses. He estimates his current net financial worth at $750,000.

After the United States entered World War II, Passman joined the Navy as a lieutenant on October 11, 1942. He served as matériel and procurement officer until his discharge on September 5, 1944 with the rank of lieutenant commander. During the war Passman decided to enter politics, and in 1946 he filed for the Democratic nomination for United States Representative from the Fifth Louisiana District. Having defeated the incumbent Congressman, Charles E. MacKenzie, at the primary, Passman was elected to the Eightieth Congress on November 5, 1946. His subsequent biennial renominations and re-elections have usually been unopposed.

Louisiana's Fifth District is largely rural, Monroe being the only community with a population of over 15,000. As a freshman legislator, Passman voted (May 1947) for restoration of cuts made in that year's agricultural bill. Later he favored the coalition farm bill (July 1949), $2 billion for farm-price supports (May 1950), and preventing reductions in agricultural-price props and acreage allotments below 1957 levels (March 1958). He opposed flexible (versus rigid) farm-price supports (July 1954).

Sent to Congress from an industrial city as well as agricultural areas, Passman in 1947 approved the banning of portal-to-portal pay suits (February) and overriding the veto of the Taft-Hartley bill (June). Twelve years later (August 1959) he voted for additional restrictions on union practices embodied in the Landrum-Griffin amendment to the 1959 labor bill. On the other hand, he favored raising the minimum wage to $1 an hour (July 1955).

On civil rights and desegregation issues, Passman has an unvarying record dating from his opposition, in July 1947, to that year's anti-poll tax bill. In July 1956 he voted against the Powell amendment to the school-construction bill, as well as the bill itself. He called "yea" on the jury trial amendment to the civil rights bill and "nay" on the bill in its final form (June 1957). He endorsed a measure introduced by Representative Howard W. Smith of Virginia to define and limit the cir-

Wide World

OTTO E. PASSMAN

cumstances in which federal laws could supersede state laws on the same subject.

In his speeches on the floor of the House he has demonstrated a flair for reciting budget figures by memory and an ability to run through many arguments in a few minutes of fiery oratory. In December 1950 he showed alarm at government expenditures that amounted to "$9,500,000 an hour and $226,000,000 a day." "At that rate," he declared, "America easily could spend itself out of existence. . . . In my opinion the present preparedness program should be placed on a pay-as-you-go basis, but if the demands continue for the expansion of domestic and welfare programs it will be impossible for the government ever to operate on such a basis."

To counteract a growing federal debt, Passman has consistently worked for the reduction of foreign aid and foreign operations. He cast votes for limiting assistance abroad to $200,000,000 (May 1947) and cutting $350,000,000 from economic help to Europe (August 1951). Negative votes were recorded for Passman on the Voice of America bill (June 1947), military assistance abroad (September 1949), and Korea-Formosa economic aid (February 1950).

His program to withhold help from other countries was given freer rein in 1955 when he became chairman of the foreign operations subcommittee of the House Appropriations Committee. Later that year the subcommittee slashed $627,000,000, including $420,000,000 which had been earmarked for military purposes, from mutual security appropriation bill. After the Senate Appropriations Committee restored $566,600,000 of the cuts, Passman charged that the Senate body had acted on "misinformation" supplied by high-ranking officials in the Eisenhower administration (New York *Times*, July 21, 1955).

(Continued next page)

PASSMAN, OTTO E.—*Continued*

In the following year, after Passman's unit and both House and Senate approved a $4 billion ceiling on foreign aid, President Eisenhower asserted that Congress would make "a grave mistake" if it failed to raise the appropriation to agree with his original request. Passman answered Eisenhower and his supporters by warning that "the best way to destroy friends [overseas] . . . is to start supporting them with gifts and favors" (New York *Herald Tribune,* July 10, 1956). The bill as enacted in July assigned $3.7 billion for operations abroad, some $1 billion lower than the sum originally recommended by the administration.

In 1957 the Passman subcommittee voted a cut in foreign aid funds of $809,650,000, of which $500,900,000 was placed back into the bill by the Senate. In May 1958 Passman suspended that year's mutual security hearings, scoring "propaganda agents" of the executive branch of government for subjecting the subcommittee to "pressures of unprecedented proportions" (New York *Times,* May 23, 1958).

A special target of the Passman group in 1959 was the Development Loan Fund, an executive agency making long-term, low-interest loans in underdeveloped countries. In July 1959 the subcommittee released testimony about waste in the foreign aid program. Passman, who had undertaken fact-finding trips in European and Middle and Far Eastern countries in the fall of 1959 and returned to the Far East in early 1960, reported "plenty of indications of unsound management," but no evidence of wrongdoing (New York *Times,* November 22, 1959). After the President requested a $4.2 billion appropriation for overseas operations for fiscal 1960, the House, influenced by recommendations of the Passman subcommittee, passed a $3.7 billion foreign aid bill. It was later signed by Eisenhower.

In characterizing Passman (who believes he has saved taxpayers over $4 billion since he became head of the foreign operations subcommittee), a New York *Times* (June 14, 1960) writer noted: "The effectiveness of this energetic, intensely serious Democrat lies mainly in the faculty of articulating among conservative House members a widespread distrust of the whole concept of foreign aid. The pattern has been for the Appropriations Committee and the House to accept cuts imposed by his subcommittee and for the Senate to repair part of the damage. The final Senate-House compromise is always far below the Administration's original request."

Interested in the charitable, civic, and veterans' affairs of his region, Passman has been active in the Salvation Army, Society for Crippled Children, Mississippi Valley Flood Control Association, American Veterans of World War II, and American Legion. He was grand master of the Masons of Louisiana and board chairman of the Masonic Temple Commercial Building in New Orleans, and he is a Shriner, Knight Templar, honorary thirty-third degree Mason, and member of the Red Cross of Constantine.

Otto E. Passman is married to the former Willie Bateman of Franklinton. A dapper, gray-haired man, he maintains a schedule that allows him little relaxation and recreation, despite his heart attack early in 1958. When Congress is in session, he works from twelve to fourteen hours each day at his office or nearby hotel. Every morning he performs calisthenics to keep his six-foot frame trim at 175 pounds. He once said his hobbies are good food and decent clothes, and he has a wardrobe that includes ninety-six shirts and forty-eight suits. In his home town he is a member of the First Baptist Church.

References

Biographical Directory of the American Congress, 1774-1949 (1950)
Congressional Directory (1960)
Who's Who in America, 1960-61
Who's Who in the South and Southwest (1959)

PASTERNAK, BORIS (LEONIDOVICH)

Feb. 10, 1890-May 30, 1960 Russian author; awarded Nobel Prize for Literature in 1958 which he declined under political pressure; wrote poetry, short stories, an autobiography, and the novel, *Doctor Zhivago* (Pantheon Books, 1958). See *Current Biography* (February) 1959.

Obituary

N Y Times p1+ My 31 '60

PATTERSON, FLOYD Jan. 4, 1935- boxer

Address: Rockville Centre, Long Island

When Floyd Patterson knocked out Ingemar Johansson at 1 minute 51 seconds of the fifth round in their fight at the Polo Grounds in New York City the night of June 20, 1960, he accomplished what no boxer before him had been able to achieve: he regained the world's heavyweight boxing championship. In winning the fight, Patterson reversed the result of the match in which he lost the championship to Johansson on June 26, 1959 at Yankee Stadium in New York. On that night, the heavyweight from Göteborg, Sweden, knocked Patterson to the canvas seven times before the referee stopped the one-sided contest.

Defeating Johansson was to Patterson "easily the most gratifying moment of my life." He has had a number of such moments. In 1951, at the age of sixteen, he won the Golden Gloves open middleweight title. In 1952 he scored five straight knockouts at Helsinki, Finland, while on his way to capturing the Olympic middleweight crown. In 1956 he knocked out light heavyweight champion Archie Moore to become the youngest heavyweight champion in history. (Joe Louis at twenty-three was the youngest previous champion.) For his boxing achievements, Patterson was named "Fighter of the Year" by the New York Boxing Writers Association, and was given the *Ring* magazine championship belt.

Floyd Patterson was born on January 4, 1935, in a cabin in Waco, North Carolina, the son of Thomas, a manual laborer, and Annabelle Patterson, a domestic, and factory worker. He was a small boy when the Patterson family, searching for a better way of life, moved to the slum-ridden Bedford-Stuyvesant section of Brooklyn, New York. Floyd was one of eleven children. Life in the cramped apartment and on the violence-filled streets the boy found unbearable. Shy from his earliest days, he had nowhere to retreat but within himself. Floyd's mother had a photograph taken when he was two years old, showing Floyd, his older brothers, Billy and Frank, both boxers, and an uncle, Charley Johnson, also a boxer. The picture was taken at the Bronx Zoo and for many years it hung over Floyd's bed. Time and again he told his mother, "I don't like that boy," pointing to himself. One day, when Floyd was about nine, his mother found that he had scratched three large "X's" over his face with a sharp instrument, in an apparent attempt to eliminate the one person he couldn't live with—himself (New York *Post,* September 10, 1957).

At the age of eleven, Patterson was sent to Wiltwyck School near Esopus, New York. In Brooklyn he had been looked upon as a budding delinquent and a chronic truant from school. He was unable to read. He refused to talk, and when spoken to, he could not bring himself to look another person in the face. One person whom Patterson credits with helping him to emerge into the world of reality was the late Vivian Costen, a teacher at Wiltwyck. "She was like a mother to me," Patterson explains. "She gave me individual instruction and I began to catch on. I was learning to read. I even liked school." Miss Costen and Walter Johnson, then the athletic director, encouraged Floyd to take up boxing while at Wiltwyck. His interest in the sport continued to grow after he returned to Brooklyn in 1947. By the time Patterson was nearing the age of fifteen he was working out with his brothers at the Gramercy Gym on New York's Lower East Side. The gym was owned and operated by Constantine (Cus) D'Amato, who was later to become Patterson's manager. Patterson continued his education at P.S. 614, one of New York's five schools for maladjusted children, and at Alexander Hamilton Vocational High School before he had to leave and take a job to support his family.

Floyd was scarcely fifteen when he entered the New York Golden Gloves 147-pound sub-novice competition, and lost a disputed decision in his second bout. He continued to train, however, and the following year he won the Golden Gloves open middleweight title. He won nine amateur crowns in all in 1952, climaxed by his winning of the Olympic middleweight championship.

Patterson made his professional boxing debut on September 12, 1952, knocking out Eddie Goodbold in five rounds in New York. Fighting then as a "heavy middleweight," he kept his weight between 160 and 170 pounds. Patterson won two fights in October and another in December, all by knockouts. In 1953 he fought

Wide World

FLOYD PATTERSON

five times, winning three by knockouts and two by decisions. In 1954 he participated in ten bouts, registering three knockouts and winning six decisions. He lost that year to former light heavyweight champion Joey Maxim in a highly disputed decision in New York. In 1955, as a full-fledged light heavyweight himself, Patterson knocked out all nine of his opponents. While Patterson's star was rising, Rocky Marciano was holding forth as one of boxing's finest heavyweight champions. When Marciano retired, undefeated, in April 1956, the stage was set for Patterson to meet Moore, as the two men adjudged by boxing officials to be the most worthy contenders for the crown.

Patterson and Archie Moore, the light heavyweight champion, clashed on November 30, 1956 at Chicago Stadium. The younger fighter took command at the outset and kept pressing Moore through the first four rounds. "The end came with dramatic suddenness," Joseph C. Nichols reported in the New York *Times* (December 1, 1956), "Patterson setting his man up with a left hook that was truly artistic in its delivery. The punch was landed midway in the [fifth] round. It dropped Moore flat on the canvas. It appeared to fans that Archie was certain to remain down for the full count. But he stirred at six and succeeded in dragging himself to his feet at nine. He was up, but he had nothing left. Patterson sprang at him—this time with no finesse, but with both hands swinging. The flurry had force. Again Moore went down." When the referee stopped the fight at 2 minutes 27 seconds, Patterson, at twenty-one, reigned as the youngest heavyweight champion in the history of boxing.

At that moment Patterson was the most sought after man in his profession. What followed took on an almost tragic aspect. The shy and inexperienced Patterson placed his trust in D'Amato, who had embarked on a

PATTERSON, FLOYD—*Continued*

campaign against the powerful International Boxing Club, which at that time almost controlled the sport. "The campaign, which had some merit at the beginning, became a vendetta so extreme that, to punish fighters who worked for the IBC, D'Amato matched Patterson against incompetents. . . . The result was a bad press, a sharp decline of general interest in heavyweight boxing. . ." (*Newsweek*, July 4, 1960).

Patterson's first title defense was against light-hitting Tommy (Hurricane) Jackson on July 29, 1957 at the Polo Grounds, when the champion pounded Jackson into a helpless hulk. The referee stopped the fight at 1 minute 52 seconds of the tenth round. On August 22, 1957 Patterson fought former Olympic heavyweight champion Pete Rademacher in Seattle. Rademacher, engaging in his first professional fight, was knocked out at 2 minutes 57 seconds of the sixth round, but not before he had knocked down the champion in the second round. On August 18, 1958 Patterson met Roy Harris, of Cut 'n' Shoot, Texas, at Los Angeles. Patterson scored a technical knockout at the end of the twelfth round, but Harris was able to knock him down in the second round. Not until May 1, 1959 did Patterson again defend his title, when his opponent was Brian London of England. The match was considered a warm-up for the fight with Johansson. London proved an inept adversary and was knocked out at 51 seconds of the eleventh round.

There is little doubt that Patterson, with good reason, underestimated Johansson when he trained for their first fight. Johansson's training methods were unorthodox, and although he often referred to his powerful right hand, he rarely used it in training. On June 26, 1959 the two men met at Yankee Stadium. The first two rounds were almost devoid of action, with Patterson jabbing now and then, and Johansson pawing with his left hand. Johansson moved from his corner at the start of the third round and threw eleven left jabs without a return. He then hooked a slow left to Patterson's head, and landed a powerful right to Patterson's nose. The champion dropped to the canvas, and arose at the count of nine, helpless. Johansson knocked him down six more times before the referee stopped the bout at 2 minutes 3 seconds.

Before the second contest it was Johansson, not Patterson, who was the favorite. Ridiculed since the conclusion of the first fight as a mediocre boxer, Patterson entered the ring on the evening of June 20, 1960, fully determined to reverse the loss to Johansson. He took charge from the beginning, managed to escape damage from a right-hand punch by Johansson in the second round, and used two devastating left-hand punches to defeat Johansson at 1 minute 51 seconds of the fifth round.

Fully vindicated, Patterson said after the fight: "It was worth losing the title for this. This is easily the most gratifying moment of my life. I never for a moment thought of losing, but to win this way, it's just perfect.

I can't tell you how happy I am. I'm champ again. A real champ this time."

Floyd Patterson lives in Rockville Centre, Long Island with his wife Sandra, to whom he was married on July 12, 1957, his daughters Seneca (who was born on the night Patterson defeated Archie Moore) and Trina, and his son, born in July 1960. His parents and brothers and sisters live in a house in Mount Vernon, New York that Patterson bought for them. His first marriage to Gloria Wanamaker, in November 1953, ended in divorce on June 14, 1956. He has two children by his first wife. In 1955 Patterson was converted to Roman Catholicism.

Retiring by nature, Patterson avoids most public appearances except those for children's charities, but he sheds his shyness and sensitivity once he enters the ring. Unlike Johansson, he takes a Spartan view of training, and has been known to sleep twelve hours a night at camp. Weighing between 180 and 185 pounds and standing six feet in height, Patterson has a panther-like physique, and a long and usually impassive face. For recreation, he listens to records, watches westerns on television, and indulges in an occasional game of pool or blackjack. "I have never been more than seventy per cent of myself," Patterson once said. "My ambition is to be a hundred per cent."

References

N Y Post p48 S 10 '57
N Y Times p24 D 1 '56; p37 Je 21 '60
New Yorker 35:96+ My 23 '59
Newsweek 56:80+ Jl 4 '60 por
Sat Eve Post 230:25+ Jl 27 '57 por; 231:20+ F 28 '59

PATTERSON, JOHN (MALCOLM) Sept. 27, 1921- Governor of Alabama; lawyer

Address: b. State Capitol, Montgomery, Ala.; h. 1142 S. Perry St., Montgomery, Ala.

In November 1958 Alabama voters chose John Patterson, the youngest Governor ever elected in the state, to direct a four-year administration during a troubled period in the history of Alabama. The state had become a focal point in the Deep South for tense racial conflict and the testing of states' rights. Suddenly and dramatically in 1954 Patterson had emerged as a dominant political figure. He won election to the state attorney generalship soon after his father, who was also his law partner, had been murdered in an heroic effort to free vice-ridden Phenix City of its rackets. Both as attorney general and as Governor, he has been a spokesman for Alabama segregationists.

The oldest of four sons of Albert Love and Agnes Louise (Benson) Patterson, John Malcolm Patterson was born on September 27, 1921 in Goldville, Tallapoosa County, Alabama. His brothers are Maurice, Samuel, and Jack Patterson; his sister is deceased. Both his parents were schoolteachers, but his father studied law, took his degree in 1927, and became a practicing attorney.

In 1933 the family settled in Phenix City, where John Patterson attended Central High

School. Earlier he had studied in grammar schools in Rockford, Opelika, and Alexander City and in the Alexander City High School. Graduating from high school in 1939, he entered the Army as a private the following year, and during World War II he fought in North Africa, Sicily, Italy, southern France, and Germany. He served in the 5th field artillery battalion of the First Infantry Division and the 17th field artillery battalion.

After his discharge from the Army at the end of the war with the rank of major, Patterson studied law at the University of Alabama in Tuscaloosa, where he was a member of the social fraternity Alpha Tau Omega, the legal fraternity Phi Alpha Delta, and the Farrah Order of Jurisprudence and Phi Eta Sigma honorary societies. During 1948-49 he belonged to the board of *Alabama Law Review,* for which he has also written articles. In 1949 he was awarded his LL.B. degree, was admitted to the Alabama bar, and began law practice with his father in Phenix City.

Two years later, in 1951, during the Korean conflict Patterson was recalled into the Army. He served in the 42d field artillery battalion, Fourth Infantry Division, and in the judge advocate general's section of that division. In the latter assignment he participated in the prosecution and defense of criminal cases for the United States Army in Germany. He was discharged from active duty in December 1953 and now holds a Reserve commission as a major in the field artillery.

Patterson resumed law practice as his father's partner in Phenix City, which at that time had the reputation of being "the wickedest city in America." A center of vice and gambling, it was run by racketeers who controlled a corrupt political machine. In an article for the *Saturday Evening Post* (November 27, 1954), Patterson described "normal channels of life" in the city: "As a boy, I would spend my leisure time playing the slot machines with no sense of wrongdoing. . . . As I grew older, I bought 'wildcat' whiskey within a few hundred yards of the high school."

An opponent of Phenix City underworld leaders, his father, Albert Patterson, campaigned for the office of state attorney general in 1954 with the promise of driving the gangsters out of the city. He won the Democratic nomination, but shortly afterward, in June, he was assassinated. Until that time, John Patterson had shown little interest in politics or a career in public life. Now determined to take his father's place as a fighter against crime, he was an active campaigner in a sensational, nationally publicized clean-up drive in Phenix City in 1954 and 1955.

Also in place of his father, he was elected attorney general of Alabama and took office on January 17, 1955. During his four years as attorney general he concentrated on working against organized crime and for enforcement of the state's insurance laws and competitive bidding laws. He became noted, as well, for his efforts to maintain segregation in Alabama and for his legal attacks on the operations of the National Association for the Advancement of Colored People in the state. He also took legal

JOHN PATTERSON

action against Negro boycotting of stores in Tuskegee and buses in Montgomery.

Patterson's record of firmness in upholding the traditional racial policies of his state aided him in his campaign for Governor' in 1958. During the campaign two Alabama newspapers linked him with leaders of the Ku Klux Klan. Since an attorney general had never before in Alabama moved directly to the Governor's office, professional politicians doubted that he could gain the Democratic nomination, and his campaign slogan was "Nobody but the people for Patterson." In the run-off primary in June he won 315,353 votes to the 250,451 cast for his opponent, Circuit Judge George C. Wallace.

Not unexpectedly, as the Democratic candidate in a Deep South state, Patterson was victorious over Republican W. L. Longshore in every Alabama county in the election of November 4. He was inaugurated as his state's forty-ninth Governor on January 19, 1959 and immediately afterward presented a program of economy and efficiency in government. Called into special session, the Legislature unanimously approved his request for the issuance of $60,000,000 in revenue bonds for a four-year highway construction project.

A controversial issue of special gravity that Governor Patterson has had to meet concerns the efforts of the United States Civil Rights Commission to investigate complaints of discrimination in Negro voting registration in Alabama. He has led state officials in defying the authority of the commission on the grounds that its investigation is an unwarranted invasion of states' rights by the federal government.

In the matter of racial integration, whether in public schools or at lunch counters, he has warned that a departure from the traditional way of segregated living would lead to violence and bloodshed. He has charged repeatedly that Negro passive resistance tactics are actually designed to cause riots. In March 1960 the Gov-

PATTERSON, JOHN—*Continued*

ernor, as chairman of the Board of Education, ordered the expulsion of a number of students from Alabama State College for Negroes, who had protested against lunch-counter segregation. He maintained that his action was necessary to forestall further tension.

On March 29, 1960 the New York *Times* published an advertisement soliciting funds for the Committee to Defend Martin Luther King and The Struggle for Freedom in the South. The advertisement included the charge that state authorities had padlocked the dining room on the Alabama State College campus in order to "starve into submission" students who took part in protests and demonstrations against segregation. Governor Patterson charged the *Times* with publishing "false and defamatory matter," and the newspaper retracted two paragraphs of the advertisement. On May 30, however, Patterson filed a $1,000,000 libel suit against the *Times* and five Negro leaders, saying that the newspaper had not published a "full and fair retraction."

At the annual Southern Governors Conference, held in Asheville, North Carolina in October 1959, Patterson argued that Southern delegates should remain loyal to the party during the 1960 Democratic National Convention and should resist any encouragement by "radical elements" to have Southerners bolt the Democratic party. As he had done on earlier occasions, he expressed a preference for Senator John F. Kennedy for the Presidential nomination.

In 1956 the United States Junior Chamber of Commerce chose Patterson as one of the Ten Outstanding Young Men in America, and the Alabama Junior Chamber of Commerce named him among the Four Outstanding Young Men in his state. He is a member of the American and Alabama bar associations, the National Association of Securities Commissioners, the National Association of Attorney Generals, the Veterans of Foreign Wars, and the American Legion. He belongs also to the Dixie Lions Club and the Woodmen of the World. He is a Methodist.

While a law student at the University of Alabama, John Patterson was married to Mary Jo McGowin on October 19, 1947. Their children are Albert Love Patterson 3d and Barbara Louise Patterson. Governor Patterson has green eyes and black hair, weighs 185 pounds, and is five feet ten inches tall. He enjoys watching his university's football games and for more active recreation turns to hunting, fishing, and tennis.

References

Sat Eve Post 227:20+ N 27 '54 por
Who's Who in America, 1960-61

PAVELIĆ, ANTE May 19, 1889-Dec. 28, 1959 Fascist President of Croatia during World War II; was sought by Yugoslav government as a war criminal from 1945. See *Current Biography* (August) 1942.

Obituary

N Y Times p21 D 30 '59

PERKINS, ANTHONY Apr. 4, 1932-
Actor
Address: b. Music Corporation of America, 598 Madison Ave., New York 22

A new star who is still in his twenties, Anthony Perkins has enjoyed notable success on the Broadway stage, in Hollywood films, and on television. A teen-age idol, the tall, lanky actor has also made a favorable impression on more mature critics for his portrayals of moody, introspective young men troubled by the problems of approaching manhood. He has been honored with the Antoinette Perry Award as best actor of the 1957-58 Broadway season (for *Look Homeward, Angel*) and with an Academy of Motion Picture Arts and Sciences nomination as best supporting actor of 1956 (for *Friendly Persuasion*). Acting to Perkins is "the instantaneous accumulation of past experience. It's pouring boiling water on the instant coffee of what you've already experienced."

Born in New York City on April 4, 1932, Anthony Perkins is the only child of Osgood and Janet (Rane) Perkins. His father, who died at the age of forty-five in 1937, was a noted movie and stage actor. His mother, who has never remarried, managed the Boston Stage Door Canteen during World War II.

Anthony Perkins was raised in New York City and in Brookline, Massachusetts. He attended Browne & Nichols School in Cambridge, Massachusetts, later enrolled in Rollins College in Winter Park, Florida, and finally transferred to Columbia University. Perkins left Columbia shortly before his scheduled graduation in 1954 in order to replace John Kerr as the gentle, sensitive adolescent, Tom Lee, in the hit Broadway play *Tea and Sympathy*. He stayed with the drama for the remainder of its Broadway run, a total of fifty-four weeks.

Despite his youth, Anthony Perkins had had considerable theatrical experience before joining *Tea and Sympathy*. He always wanted to be an actor, and since his first professional engagement in Brattleboro, Vermont in 1946, he had worked regularly in summer stock and had appeared in dramatic roles on television. He had also played a featured part in a Hollywood film, *The Actress* (MGM, 1953). It was his Broadway stint in *Tea and Sympathy,* however, which alerted movie makers to his capabilities, and he returned to Hollywood to appear in *Friendly Persuasion* (Allied Artists, 1956). The film was a critical success, and Perkins' interpretation of Josh Birdwell, a young Indiana Quaker torn between religious belief and the need to defend the family homestead during Morgan's Raids, attracted special praise. It also resulted in a nomination from the Academy of Motion Picture Arts and Sciences as best supporting actor of 1956.

In the following year Paramount released three films starring Anthony Perkins. In *Fear Strikes Out,* based on the true story of Jim Piersall, Perkins, a natural athlete, was cast as the Red Sox outfielder who had a serious mental breakdown and fought his way back to sanity. In the psychological western *The Lonely Man,* he played Riley Wade, who hates his father, believing he was responsible for his mother's death. And in *The Tin Star,* as Ben Owens he enacted the inexperienced young sheriff who finally learns of the weighty responsibilities accompanying his badge.

Long an admirer of Thomas Wolfe, Anthony Perkins was delighted to appear in the central role of Ketti Frings's Broadway adaptation of Wolfe's autobiographical *Look Homeward, Angel.* The reviewers, in turn, were delighted with the play and with Perkins' courageous and poignant acting.

Look Homeward, Angel, which came to New York on November 28, 1957, won both the Pulitzer Prize as best American play of 1957 and the New York Drama Critics Circle Award as the best Broadway drama of the 1957-58 season. For his characterization of Eugene Gant, the gawky, sensitive youth who dreams of the greater world beyond his home town, Perkins took the Antoinette Perry Award as best dramatic actor of that season.

Critical reaction was divided on Perkins' work in the motion picture *Desire Under the Elms* (Paramount, 1958). While some reviewers found much to admire in his characterization of Eben Cabot, the scheming son, in this film version of Eugene O'Neill's smoldering drama, William K. Zinsser reported that "Perkins is insipid to the point of being neuter" (New York *Herald Tribune,* March 13, 1958). But he was uniformly well received for his work in the film adaptation of another Broadway play, Thornton Wilder's farcical *The Matchmaker* (Paramount, 1958). Another Perkins' movie released in 1958 was *This Angry Age* (Columbia).

Early in 1959 MGM displayed its film version of the classic W. H. Hudson novel of life in the jungles of South America, *Green Mansions.* Neither the film nor its stars, Audrey Hepburn and Anthony Perkins, enjoyed much success. Perkins fared better with *On the Beach* (United Artists, 1959), the adaptation of Nevil Shute's book, in which he played an Australian naval lieutenant in a world destroyed by nuclear explosions.

Again taking advantage of his natural athletic abilities, he was the college basketball star faced with academic and romantic problems in *Tall Story* (Warner, 1960). His versatility was apparent when he acted the part of the young motel keeper and amateur taxidermist who surrounds himself with stuffed owls and ravens in Alfred Hitchcock's macabre thriller *Psycho* (Paramount, 1960).

Although he had made several popular records for Epic Records and RCA Victor, including one notable hit entitled "Moonlight Swim," Anthony Perkins had never sung on the stage before assuming the leading role in *Greenwillow,* Frank Loesser's musical version of B. J. Chute's novel. "In one way, it was a sense of failure that made me want to sing on Broadway," Perkins explained to Varney Lefferts. "I made some records a few years ago of very low, soft singing that I was ultimately, if not immediately, dissatisfied with" (New York *Times,* February 28, 1960).

ANTHONY PERKINS

When *Greenwillow* opened on Broadway on March 8, 1960, Perkins sang and acted the part of the small town youth Gideon Briggs, who feels that he can never marry because he has inherited his father's wanderlust. Most reviewers shared Brooks Atkinson's opinion that "in addition to being an impressive actor, Mr. Perkins turns out to be first-rate in his singing" (New York *Times,* March 9, 1960). But some of the critics had serious misgivings about other aspects of this musical fantasy, and it closed on May 28 after ninety-five performances.

Aside from his motion pictures, stage plays, and popular records, Anthony Perkins has made numerous television appearances. Early in his career he acted in dramas on *Studio One, Kraft Theatre,* and *Goodyear Playhouse.* Since achieving celebrity, he has been a guest on such variety programs as the *Steve Allen Show.*

Having received no formal stage training, Perkins believes he learned to act in summer stock and in Broadway plays. "You do not learn about acting from being in movies," he told Robert Johnson (*Saturday Evening Post,* January 9, 1960). "Movies are made so mechanically. You do the best you can as fast as you can. It's the rehearsal that you are shooting." When making a film, he is interested in many of its phases: the titles, the music, and the actors who take the bit parts.

Anthony Perkins is six feet two and one-half inches tall and weighs 160 pounds. His hair and eyes are dark brown. In private life he wears steel-rimmed spectacles to counteract his nearsightedness. He prefers casual clothes and, in general, a casual way of life. When in New York, he still lives in the small midtown apartment he occupied when he was a student at Columbia, the walls of which are decorated with his own paintings. He also maintains a home on the West Coast. In addition to his

PERKINS, ANTHONY—*Continued*

art work, Perkins enjoys riding, tennis, swimming, attending movies, playing the guitar and piano, and reading such authors as Thomas Wolfe, Charles Dickens, and F. Scott Fitzgerald. At present he is undergoing psychoanalysis.

Perkins' informal off-screen behavior has given rise to much publicity typing him as a Hollywood eccentric in the tradition of Marlon Brando and James Dean. But he insists that he does not consciously foster this impression and that he has made many concessions to his fame. "I'd even walk barefoot—I used to," he said in an interview (*Look,* June 24, 1958). "The trouble with being someone like me is that everything I do seems suspect. Actually, everybody is nonconformist in some way or other, but nobody admits it."

His slightly gawky appearance, shy mannerisms, and bashful grin give to all Anthony Perkins' characterizations a sense of troubled, brooding adolescence. A *Newsweek* (March 3, 1958) writer has analyzed his appeal in these terms: "Notable among his precocious gifts is an ability to play young men at the brink of maturity without delivering either of dramaturgy's current stereotypes—the comical puppy or the darkling member of the 'beat generation.' Perkins' young men actually possess dignity and a certain elevation of spirit."

References

N Y Post Mag p10 Ja 19 '58 por
N Y Times II p5+ D 8 '57 por
New Yorker 33:20+ D 28 '57
International Motion Picture Almanac, 1960
Who's Who in America, 1960-61

PERKINS, GEORGE W(ALBRIDGE) May 2, 1895-Jan. 10, 1960 Assistant Secretary of State for European Affairs (1949-53); represented the United States on the council of NATO (1955-57); former official of Merck & Company, Inc., chemical and drug firm. See *Current Biography* (April) 1950.

Obituary

N Y Times p47 Ja 12 '60

PERLMAN, PHILIP B(ENJAMIN) Mar. 5, 1890-July 31, 1960 Solicitor General of the United States from 1947 to 1952; won forty-nine of sixty-one cases he argued before the United States Supreme Court; opposed racial discrimination. See *Current Biography* (July) 1952.

Obituary

N Y Times p23 Ag 1 '60

PHILLIPS, PAULINE ESTHER FRIEDMAN *See* Van Buren, Abigail

PIECK, WILHELM Jan. 3, 1876-Sept. 7, 1960 President of East German Democratic Republic since 1949; Social Democratic member of the Reichstag (1906); Communist member of the Reichstag (1928-33); a founder of the Spartacists (1915). See *Current Biography* (December) 1949.

Obituary

N Y Times p35 S 8 '60

POLLITT, HARRY Nov. 22, 1890-June 27, 1960 General secretary (1929-39, 1941-56) and chairman (since 1956) of the British Communist party; unsuccessful candidate for the House of Commons on eight occasions. See *Current Biography* (May) 1948.

Obituary

N Y Times p31 Je 28 '60

POST, EMILY (PRICE) Oct. 3, 1873-Sept. 25, 1960 Arbiter of etiquette; wrote novels, books on manners and interior decoration, and a syndicated column; was a radio commentator. See *Current Biography* (March) 1941.

Obituary

N Y Times p1+ S 27 '60

POWELL, LAWRENCE CLARK Sept. 3, 1906- Librarian; writer

Address: b. 405 Hilgard Ave., Los Angeles 24, Calif.; h. 31820 Broad Beach Rd., Malibu, Calif.

Crusader, bookish humanist, sentimentalist, visionary enthusiast, great professional leader, America's most provocative bookman—such are the epithets used by his associates to describe Lawrence Clark Powell, who is university librarian, director of the William Andrews Clark Memorial Library, and lecturer in English at the University of California at Los Angeles. Powell believes that books are basic to the good life and that librarianship is a dedicated calling similar to the ministry. His conviction has made him a controversial figure in his profession, but at the same time a man who commands the respect of librarians and bookmen on both sides of the Atlantic.

Born of Quaker parents on September 3, 1906 in Washington, D.C., Lawrence Clark Powell is the son of G. Harold and Gertrude Eliza (Clark) Powell. His father was a scientist with the Bureau of Plant Industry of the United States Department of Agriculture, who specialized in co-operative agricultural marketing. Both parents collected and read books, encouraging their son to lead a bookman's life and influencing his career as librarian and writer. Powell once wrote: "Encouragement to lead a bookman's life came from my mother from my earliest years, when she started me on *Grimms' Fairy Tales,* the *Home Book of Verse,* and scores of other good books, and my ultimate career as librarian and writer confirmed her faith in me which was unfailing from childhood."

In 1911 the Powell family settled in South Pasadena, California. Larry attended the South Pasadena High School, from which he was graduated in 1924. During his junior year he worked at the Link-Belt Pacific Company in San Francisco as a dictaphone stenographer. In the fall of 1924 he entered Occidental College in Los Angeles, where he majored in English and was "yell leader, actor, sports editor, jazz pianist, saxophonist, and fraternity president." He interrupted his undergraduate courses in 1925 to join the *President Harrison*'s jazz orchestra for Dollar Steamship Lines on a round-the-world cruise. When he returned to the United States he resumed his college studies and obtained his B.A. degree from Occidental College in 1929. He had earned part of his college expenses by leading his own dance orchestra.

After his graduation Lawrence Clark Powell taught English at Occidental College for a short time. He then worked as a shipping clerk in Vroman's Bookstore in Pasadena for a year. In 1931 he went to France to study for his doctorate at the University of Dijon. Majoring in English and American literature, he wrote a dissertation entitled "An Introduction to Robinson Jeffers," for which he was awarded a Ph.D. degree in 1932.

When Powell came back to the United States, he entered an apprenticeship in the antiquarian book business by working in rare book stores in Los Angeles. He also acquired some first-hand experience of publishing by working with Western Publishers from 1934 to 1936. He soon became acquainted with local writers, book dealers, book collectors, printers, and librarians. Among the latter were Althea Warren and Albert Read of the Los Angeles Public Library. Miss Warren, who was director of the library, and Read, who was a member of the order department, both stimulated Powell's already active interest in books and recruited him for the library profession. Before beginning his new career, however, he served for a short time as an editorial assistant at the University of California press. He then enrolled at the School of Librarianship at the University of California in Berkeley; in 1937 he was graduated with a Bachelor of Science degree.

Equipped with his professional degree, Powell joined the staff of the Los Angeles Public Library, working as an assistant in the order department and the branch libraries. From this beginning he went on to become junior assistant in the acquisitions department of the University of California library at Los Angeles in 1938. Within six years he became the university librarian and the director of the William Andrews Clark Memorial Library, which houses the rare book collections on the university campus.

Books have always been Powell's ruling interest. From the time when, as a boy, he had gratified his book hunger with volumes from the South Pasadena Public Library, he has had a "passion for books." He has said: "Three loves I have: collecting books, keeping books (which includes reading them), and giving books away." He frequently visits bookshops

LAWRENCE CLARK POWELL

from Los Angeles to London, ferreting out old and rare treasures for both the libraries of the University of California at Los Angeles and for his own private book shelves. But Powell does more than merely accumulate; he says that he takes home an armful of books every night and "goes through" perhaps several hundred books a month, skimming some, choosing others on which he will spend years.

Under his directorship, the libraries of the University of California at Los Angeles have tripled in size. The William Andrews Clark Memorial Library, specializing in books on English civilization of the seventeenth and early eighteenth centuries, grew from 16,000 volumes in 1934 to more than 60,000 volumes in 1950.

Powell's desire to build up his own personal library is as insatiable as his interest in adding to the collections in the university libraries. His private library encompasses a wide range of specializations, including novels with settings in or around Los Angeles, Chinese poetry translated into English, books about the sinking of the Titanic, books about fountains, and the works of authors from Shakespeare to D. H. Lawrence. He used to own one of the best John Steinbeck collections in the United States until he gave it to Harvard University.

Nevertheless, Powell somehow finds the time to be productive as a writer. Betty Rosenberg's *Check-list of the Published Writings, 1931-1958, of Lawrence Clark Powell, University Librarian* numbers over 300 items: books, magazine articles, literary criticism, essays, biographies and memorials, forewords and introductions to books, and bibliographies of printers and writers. The subjects range over history and travel, especially of the American Southwest, the book trade, libraries and librarianship, rare books, the University of California, and book collecting.

(Continued next page)

POWELL, LAWRENCE CLARK—*Cont.*

Many of Powell's writings are autobiographical; all of them set forth his evangelistic belief in books and reading. *Islands of Books* (Anderson & Ritchie, 1951) and *Books: West Southwest* (Ward Ritchie, 1957) bring together his enthusiastic papers about writers and readers. In *Alchemy of Books* (Anderson & Ritchie, 1954) he reports on his experiences as a Guggenheim Fellow in Great Britain during 1950-51. *A Passion for Books* (World, 1959) and *Books in My Baggage* (World, 1960) are further installments in the continuing story of his adventures as a reader and book collector.

In 1953 Powell was the Randolph G. Adams Memorial Lecturer at the University of Michigan; in 1954 he was the University of Tennessee library lecturer and a visiting professor of library science at Columbia University; and in 1957 he delivered the annual lecture at the meeting of the Library Association of Great Britain at Harrogate. Its title was "Books Will Be Read."

His belief in librarianship as a profession is as impassioned as his belief that books and reading are basic. The two, in fact, are closely associated in the mind of Lawrence Clark Powell. In *A Passion for Books* he maintained that the "two chief attributes of a good librarian are that he be a reader of books and a servant of those in need of help." He is impatient with the current stress on the new technological developments in libraries and has often criticized the courses taught in the library schools for being more concerned with "mechanical housekeeping techniques" than with a knowledge and understanding of books.

For more than a decade Powell had worked for the establishment of a library school on the campus of the University of California at Los Angeles. He envisioned such a school as having for its objective "the training of librarians who are concerned with the contents of books and the needs of their patrons; aware of their responsibilities as guardians of man's right to read all books; and equipped with the professional skills necessary to fulfill their responsibility." In the fall of 1960 the University of California at Los Angeles will open its new School of Library Service, with Lawrence Clark Powell as its first dean. In early 1960 he announced that he would relinquish the university librarianship in June 1961, but continue as head of the Clark library.

Lawrence Clark Powell was married to Fay Ellen Shoemaker on March 26, 1934. They have two sons, Norman Jerrold and Wilkie Haines. Slight in build, Powell is five feet six inches tall and has brown hair and brown eyes. In religion he is a Quaker, in politics he is a Democrat, but during the 1960 Presidential campaign was on the Scholars for Nixon Committee. Beachcombing, gardening, and music, in addition to reading and book collecting, are his favorite recreations. In 1955 Occidental College granted Powell an honorary Doctor of Letters degree, and in 1960 the American Textbook Publishers Institute gave him the Clarence Day Award. He belongs to numerous professional and bibliographical associations, including the American Library Association, the Association of Research Libraries, the California Library Association (president, 1950), and the Bibliographical Society of America (president, 1954-56). His social fraternity is Phi Gamma Delta and his clubs are the Grolier Club (New York), Caxton Club (Chicago), Roxburghe Club (San Francisco), Rounce and Coffin Club (Los Angeles), and Zamorano Club (Los Angeles).

References

ALA Bul 48 :553+ N '54 por
Bul Bibliography 20 :225+ Ja-Ap '53 por
Powell, Gertrude C. The Quiet Side of Europe (1959)
Who's Who in America, 1960-61
Who's Who in Library Service (1955)

POWER, DONALD C(LINTON) Dec. 25, 1899- Utilities executive; lawyer

Address: b. General Telephone & Electronics Corp., 730 3d Ave., New York 17; Power, Griffith & Jones, 50 W. Broad St., Columbus 15, Ohio; h. Manhattan House, 200 E. 66th St., New York 21; 2036 Berkshire Rd., Columbus 21 Ohio; "Don Power Farm," R.R.1, Galloway, Ohio

The chairman of the board and chief executive officer of the General Telephone & Electronics Corporation, Donald C. Power, is responsible for the largest independent (non-Bell) telephone system in the United States. As president of the General Telephone Corporation from 1951 to 1959, he had brought about tremendous growth in the firm and negotiated its merger with other units, the latest of which was with Sylvania Electric Products, Inc., in 1959. At that time Power assumed his present position with the new firm. For over thirty years he has been associated in Columbus, Ohio with the law firm now known as Power, Griffith & Jones (formerly, Postlewaite & Bricker).

Donald Clinton Power, the only child of George and Dorothy (Brooks) Power, was born on Christmas Day, 1899, in Paine Station, Ohio. His father was a geologist, and as a youth Donald Power intended to make geology his career. He attended Newark High School in Newark, Ohio and played on the baseball team. After graduation he studied at Denison University in Granville, Ohio from 1918 to 1920. Then, having changed his mind about becoming a geologist, he transferred to the Ohio State University College of Commerce in Columbus, from which he received the B.S. degree in business administration in 1922. He spent the summer in a training program of the National Cash Register Company in Dayton, Ohio, but returned to Ohio State University as an instructor in economic geography.

While teaching, Power studied law and economics, and was awarded the LL.B. degree in 1926 and the M.A. degree in public-utility economics in 1927 by the university. He continued to teach on a part-time basis, rising to the rank of associate professor in 1934, and also entered law practice in Columbus with the firm of Postlewaite & Bricker in 1927.

In 1930 he argued successfully an important case before the Ohio Supreme Court for the Ohio Associated Telephone Company, a part of Associated Telephone Utilities (A.T.U.). He was then offered the responsibility of handling all of A.T.U.'s legal work in Ohio. From 1933 to 1936 he served as assistant attorney general and counsel for the Public Utilities Commission of Ohio under John Bricker, who was a partner in his law firm. He was chairman of the Ohio Republican campaign committee in 1938, 1940, and 1942, and when Bricker became Governor of Ohio in 1939, Power served for four years as his executive assistant.

Returning to the law firm in 1943, Power was retained to handle the rate cases for the entire system of the General Telephone Corporation, the successor of Associated Telephone Utilities. In arguing for rate increases based on fair value, he became an expert in wage problems and operating expenses of the telephone firm; he also handled rate negotiations for many other independent companies.

Power was first asked to accept the presidency of the General Telephone Corporation in 1949; he finally accepted in June 1951. The corporation was at that time a holding company for about fifteen operating subsidiaries in the United States and had an annual revenue of about $80,000,000. In the eight years of Power's incumbency, the firm has climbed to a position high up among the United States' fifty largest corporations.

General Telephone's gross revenue rose to over $1 billion in 1959-60. The number of telephones in its system has increased by 169 per cent; its total sales has increased by 660 per cent; and its net income has increased 1,128 per cent. It is the nation's largest independent (non-Bell) telephone system. Part of its phenomenal growth is due to its policy of merging with other companies.

The two major moves in its series of acquisitions since 1951 were the mergers with Theodore Gary & Company in 1955 and with Sylvania Electric Products, Inc., in 1959. In the 1955 union, General Telephone gained skilled talent; control over the Automatic Electric Company, the largest telephone equipment-maker outside of the Western Electric Company; international interests in Canada, the Dominican Republic, and the Philippines; and increased domestic operations in seventeen states in America.

The 1959 merger again joined complementary characteristics, skills, and facilities. According to *Fortune* (September 1959), the union with Sylvania Electric Products, Inc., achieved for the firm a balanced operation that combined the stability of a utility with the growth potential of a wide-ranging industrial. It also gained the electronics capabilities needed for the telephones of the future and for complex communications systems. The new name of the firm is the General Telephone & Electronics Corporation; Donald Mitchell is president, and Power is chairman of the board and chief executive officer.

Fabian Bachrach

DONALD C. POWER

As a result of the merger, General Telephone & Electronics Corporation was prepared in the spring of 1959 to manufacture and sell about a thousand different products for the home, for industry, and for national defense, including photoflash bulbs, television sets, and giant digital computers. Power hoped to increase military electronics production and sales, making the corporation a leading contender for defense contracts.

Power's *Law of Contracts Condensed* was published by Hedrick in Columbus, Ohio in 1933; he has also written a number of articles about public utilities. He is a director of twenty-four companies in the United States, the Dominican Republic, the Philippines, and Canada, including the Irving Trust Company, Curtiss-Wright Corporation, Canada Dry Corporation, Copper Range Company, and the British Columbia Telephone Company.

A member of the American Bar Association, Power served as vice-chairman and chairman of its section on public utility law. He also belongs to the Ohio and Columbus bar associations. From 1942 to 1946 he was vice-chairman of the Ohio Administrative Law Commission. He is a trustee of the Committee for Economic Development and a board member of the National Industrial Conference Board and of the Armed Forces Communications and Electronics Association. He served as a captain, major, and lieutenant colonel in the Ohio National Guard, 37th Division.

The utilities executive received Ohio State University's Distinguished Service Award in 1954, the Significant Sig award of Sigma Chi fraternity in 1955, *Forbes* magazine award as one of today's fifty foremost business leaders in 1957, Governor's Award of the state of Ohio in 1959, and election as business executive of the year by the Congress of National Sales Executives—International—in 1959. He was

POWER, DONALD C.—*Continued*

awarded an honorary LL.D. degree by Upsala College in 1958 and an honorary Doctor of Business Administration degree from Rio Grande College in Ohio in 1959. He is a trustee of the latter college as well as of Ohio State University and the University of Tampa in Florida.

Donald C. Power was married to Catherine Hamilton on June 6, 1927. Their daughters are Jane (Mrs. Peter S. Mykrantz) and Charlotte Harriet. Power has brown eyes and brown hair, is five feet ten inches tall, and weighs 189 pounds. He is a Presbyterian and a thirty-second degree Mason (Knights Templar and Shriner). Horseback riding, swimming, and fishing are his favorite forms of exercise; he also enjoys watching college and professional football and basketball games. He and his family frequently leave New York City to spend the weekend on their 215-acre farm near Columbus, and he belongs to several social clubs in Ohio as well as in New York.

References

> Fortune 60:114+ S '59
> N Y Times III p3 Ag 12 '56
> N Y World-Telegram p47 S 15 '59
> Newsweek 43:67 My 31 '54
>
> Who's Who in America, 1958-59
> Who's Who in Commerce and Industry (1959)
> Who's Who in the Midwest (1949)

PRENTIS, HENNING WEBB, JR. July 11, 1884-Oct. 29, 1959 Business executive; president (1934-50) and chairman (since 1950) of the Armstrong Cork Company; president of the National Association of Manufacturers (1940). See *Current Biography* (September) 1940.

Obituary

N Y Times p33 O 29 '59

PROUTY, WINSTON L(EWIS) Sept. 1, 1906- United States Senator from Vermont

Address: b. Senate Office Bldg., Washington 25, D.C.; h. Newport, Vt.; 2500 Q St., Washington 7, D.C.

One of the co-sponsors in April 1960 of a private health insurance plan for the aged which would be financed jointly by subscribers and the state and federal governments, Winston L. Prouty, Republican Senator from Vermont, has generally gone along with his party's conservative policies during his ten years in Congress. Elected in November 1958 to the seat previously occupied by Ralph E. Flanders, Prouty had been Vermont's only member in the House of Representatives from 1950 to 1959. Although Prouty favors limited foreign and domestic expenditure by the federal government, he was a co-sponsor of the 1959 health-for-peace bill which would have appropriated $50,000,000 annually for the establishment of an international medical research program. Prouty

has repeatedly urged that the United States and Canadian governments construct an inland waterway from New York City to the St. Lawrence Seaway via Lake Champlain.

Born September 1, 1906, Winston Lewis Prouty is a native of Newport, in northern Vermont. He received his elementary education in Newport public schools and his secondary schooling at the Bordentown Military Institute in New Jersey. Prouty also attended Lafayette College in Easton, Pennsylvania before joining his family business at Newport, the Prouty & Miller Lumber Company, of which he is now a partner. He is also a director of the National Bank of Newport and of Associated Industries of Vermont.

Becoming interested in politics in 1938, Prouty began the first of three one-year terms as Mayor of Newport that year. He was elected, as a Republican, to the 1941, 1945, and 1947 sessions of the Vermont House of Representatives and served as Speaker of the House in 1947. The following year Prouty sought the Republican nomination for Lieutenant Governor, but lost at the primary to an old guard conservative, Harold J. Arthur, who later became Governor.

Named chairman of the Vermont State Water Conservation Board in 1948, Prouty resigned that position in May 1950, after incumbent Congressman Charles A. Plumley decided not to run again. Prouty competed against four other candidates for the Republican nomination for Representative-at-Large, one of whom was Governor Arthur. At the September primary Prouty defeated Arthur by a five-to-four margin and in November won an easy victory over his Democratic opponent in a state which has been loyal to the Republican tradition for over a century. At three subsequent biennial primaries Prouty drew only token opposition for the Republican nomination.

Seated in the Eighty-second Congress in January 1951, Prouty was appointed to the Veterans Affairs Committee, on which he served through 1956. Following a visit to Camp Pickett, Virginia, the training site of the Army's New England 43d Division, Prouty assailed a magazine article that described the unit's morale as low and its food, quarters, and training as bad. He said the unit which had been labeled a "cry-baby division" by some Pentagon officials, was now a division "of which the Army and the nation may well be proud" (New York *Times*, June 16, 1951). In 1952 Prouty was one of nineteen petitioners urging General Dwight D. Eisenhower to campaign for the Presidency.

Prouty was assigned to the House Foreign Affairs Committee in January 1953; in the spring of that year he was one of five Congressmen who made a two-week tour of France and Italy. When they returned, members of the group charged France and Italy with conducting "a faulty arms program" and asserted that the North Atlantic Treaty Organization would "bog down except for United States leadership" (New York *Times*, May 17, 1953).

In 1954 Prouty and Representative Lawrence H. Smith of Wisconsin visited nine countries in the Middle East. After they came back, they submitted a report recommending that the United States consider cutting off financial aid to nations who refused to comply with the decisions of the United Nations. They also recommended that the United States press for an end to the Arab blockade and boycott of Israel and the boycott of United States companies doing business with Israel. They suggested that the Arab refugees settle in Arab countries and that Israel compensate them for their loss of homes and land. In January 1957 Prouty voted in favor of authorizing the President to undertake a program of military and economic co-operation with Middle Eastern nations in order to counteract Communism.

Prouty's voting record during his eight years in the House of Representatives usually followed right-wing Republican policy. He favored limits on federal expenditures for public power developments (April 1953) and public housing (March 1952) and opposed extending unemployment benefits (July 1954) and veterans benefits (June 1956). He also approved of cutting the number of federal employees by 10 per cent (April 1952), reducing TVA appropriations (March 1952), setting a ceiling on military spending (April 1952), and ending consumer price and rent controls (June 1952). Prouty voted against the majority of Republicans, however, when he favored maintenance of high-level price supports for farmers (June 1952).

Prouty's efforts toward the creation of a big-ship canal to link the Hudson River with Lake Champlain and the St. Lawrence River began in February 1952 when he introduced a bill to provide federal grants to Canada for deepening the Canadian side of the waterway. Two years later he proposed a definite plan for a ship canal forty-one feet deep and 300 feet wide to extend from the Hudson River at Albany to deep water in Lake Champlain. In 1957 (despite little encouragement from the Canadian government), he co-operated with Senator George D. Aiken of Vermont in sponsoring bills that authorized Army engineers to survey the American part of the proposed inland water route. In June 1959 Prouty went to Canada for the dedication of the St. Lawrence Seaway and the Canada-United States Interparliamentary Group Conference.

Long before Senator Ralph E. Flanders made public his decision not to seek re-election, Representative Prouty and former Vermont Governor Lee Emerson had both announced their candidacies for the Republican nomination for Flanders' seat in the United States Senate. Prouty won the nomination by a two-to-one margin, but in the election campaign he faced Frederick J. Fayette, the Burlington lawyer, whom Democrats regarded as a strong candidate for the Senate. There was some dissatisfaction with the state's Republican leadership, and the 1958 contest turned out to be a close one. In a traditionally Republican state, Prouty carried the election with only 64,900 votes to 59,536 votes for Fayette.

A member of the Senate's District of Columbia, Labor and Public Welfare, and Public Works committees in the Eighty-sixth Con-

Wide World

WINSTON L. PROUTY

gress, the junior Senator from Vermont also serves on the Senate's Select Committee on Small Business and on the Special Committee on Unemployment Problems. In July 1959 he was named by Secretary of State Christian A. Herter to the United States Commission for the United Nations Educational, Scientific, and Cultural Organization. This 100-man commission includes three other members of Congress and representatives of the executive department and private organizations.

Prouty was one of the sponsors of the health-for-peace bill in May 1959. Throughout the first session of the Eighty-sixth Congress he supported President Eisenhower's mutual security, foreign aid, and military spending programs. He supported Senator Clinton P. Anderson's motion to amend the filibuster rule of the Senate (January 1959) and was one of the Senate minority favoring confirmation of Lewis L. Strauss as Secretary of Commerce (June 1959).

As for housing legislation, Prouty agreed with the President that certain 1959 bills proposed excessive spending. The President had criticized provisions for two $50,000,000-direct-loan programs for construction of college classrooms and homes for the elderly and for the erection of 37,000 new public housing units. Prouty co-sponsored in February 1959 a bill authorizing a five-year program of indirect assistance to local school districts and higher educational institutions for construction of school facilities. In April Prouty voted for labor reform amendments which would protect union members against unfair actions by their unions and which would ban secondary boycotts. The same month he submitted measures that sought to amend the Kennedy-Ervin labor bill by strengthening controls against financial and election misconduct among union officials.

(Continued next page)

PROUTY, WINSTON L.—*Continued*

A New York *Times* writer characterized Senator Prouty as "serious and intense," but with a "better sense of humor than appears on the surface" (November 6, 1958). Prouty attends the Congregational Christian Church. His favorite relaxation is playing the organ. Mrs. Prouty is the former Frances C. Hearle.

References

Congressional Directory (1960)
International Who's Who, 1959
Vermont Legislative Directory, 1959
Who's Who in America, 1958-59
Who's Who in the East (1959)

PUTT, DONALD L(EANDER) May 14, 1905- Research corporation executive; former Air Force officer

Address: b. United Research Corporation of Menlo Park, P.O. Box 365, Menlo Park, Calif.; h. Atherton, Calif.

During thirty years of active service in the United States Air Force, Lieutenant General Donald L. Putt was chiefly occupied in technical development and intelligence. In recent years he became an acknowledged expert in missile and satellite planning. Shortly after he retired from the Air Force in the summer of 1958, he accepted the position of president of the United Research Corporation of Menlo Park, California, which had been newly organized by the United Aircraft Corporation to carry out research in solid and liquid propellants, rockets, and advanced propulsion systems. For four years before his military retirement, he had served at Air Force headquarters as Deputy Chief of Staff for Development and as military director of the Chief of Staff's scientific advisory board. In November 1959 he was

Don Shapero
DONALD L. PUTT

elected president for 1960 of the Institute of the Aeronautical Sciences.

Donald Leander Putt, the son of Harry Edwin and Lucy Hollis (Preslar) Putt, was born in Sugarcreek, Ohio on May 14, 1905. Trained as an engineer, he was graduated from the Carnegie Institute of Technology in Pittsburgh, Pennsylvania in 1928 with a B.S. degree in electrical engineering. He had early decided upon military aviation as a career and in May 1928 was commissioned a second lieutenant in the United States Army Signal Corps Reserve. (The Army's aeronautical service was then under Signal Corps command.) A month later he was appointed a flying cadet.

After he had completed flight training at Brooks and Kelly fields in Texas, on June 28, 1929 he was commissioned a second lieutenant in the Air Reserve; three months later he received his regular commission. His first assignment after flight training was to the 17th Pursuit Squadron at Selfridge Field, Michigan. In September 1930 he entered the Air Corps Technical School at Chanute Field, Illinois, and upon graduating from the armament course there in April 1931 he returned to Selfridge Field to join the 36th Pursuit Squadron.

From February 1933 until August 1936 Putt served as a test pilot at Wright Field, Ohio. He then studied for a year at the Air Corps Engineering School before being sent to the California Institute of Technology in Pasadena, from which he received the M.Sc. degree in aeronautical engineering in June 1938. Reassigned to Wright Field, he held among other positions that of chief of the experimental bombardment aircraft branch during the development of the World War II bombers B-24, B-29, and B-36. During the last months of the war, from October 1944 to August 1945, he was assigned to the United States Army Air Forces in Europe as chief of technical services.

When Putt returned to Wright Field after the war, he served for over a year as assistant chief of staff for intelligence, Air Materiel Command Headquarters. He was named deputy chief of the engineering division in December 1946 and in this office, having advanced through the ranks over the years, was promoted to brigadier general (temporary). The Air Force was set up as a separate service in July 1947, and in September 1948 Putt was appointed director of research and development in the office of the Deputy Chief of Staff for Materiel at Air Force Headquarters in Washington, D.C.

One of Putt's responsibilities in this headquarters post was to supervise the experimental test flights for three new jet-propelled "penetration fighters" capable of operating far behind enemy lines. He was made Assistant Deputy Chief of Staff for Development in April 1951 and later in the same year served for three months as acting Deputy Chief of Staff.

On June 30, 1953 Putt assumed command of the Air Research and Development Command in Baltimore, after having served as vice-commander for eighteen months. During part of that period, from February to June 1952, he was also commanding general of the air development center at Wright-Patterson Air Force

Base in Ohio. His promotion to lieutenant general was confirmed by the United States Senate in July 1953. The following April he returned to Air Force Headquarters in the dual capacity of Deputy Chief of Staff for Development and military director of the scientific advisory board to the Air Force Chief of Staff.

Very much concerned with the air and missile races between the United States and the Soviet Union, Putt believed, as he told the Washington Aero Club in March 1956, that for psychological and propaganda reasons it was tremendously important that Americans forge ahead of the Russians in development of an intercontinental ballistic missile. When questioned by a special Senate air power subcommittee later in the year, he outlined what appeared to be major deficiencies in a series of research and development programs, including radar, aircraft engines, earth satellites, rockets, and various new weapons. He predicted Soviet superiority in both quality and quantity if existing budget limitations on research and development continued indefinitely.

On a visit to the Soviet Union with the Air Force Chief of Staff, General Nathan Twining, in June 1956, Putt found the Russians somewhat behind in electronics development but advanced in metallurgy and engine work. After his return home, he concurred in Twining's impression that the Soviet Union was closing the "quality gap" with the United States. He also asserted that the Air Force would have been further ahead in development of a supersonic bomber if it had not been for lack of research funds.

An interservice dispute involving Putt occurred in February 1958 when he criticized as premature a directive to the Air Force by Defense Secretary Neil H. McElroy to drop work on the weapons phase of its Wizard project and leave experimentation on an anti-ICBM missile to the Army. A week later he called on Congress to back an Air Force space-exploration program calling for a rocket shot at the moon in 1958 and the early launching of a manned satellite.

The White House announced in March 1958 the imminent retirement of Putt from the Air Force active list, after thirty years of service, and the appointment of Major General Roscoe C. Wilson as the new Deputy Chief of Staff. After Putt's retirement became effective, at the end of June, he was briefly occupied as special assistant to Dr. Theodore von Kármán, director of the summer study group jointly sponsored by the National Academy of Sciences and the Air Research and Development Command.

In October 1958 Putt was appointed assistant director of research for the United Aircraft Corporation of East Hartford, Connecticut. At the same time he became president of the United Research Corporation of Menlo Park, California, a newly formed subsidiary for research. As its initial undertaking United Research Corporation sponsored research in advanced high-energy propellants for missiles and space craft to be conducted in co-operation with the independent, nonprofit Stanford Research Institute of Menlo Park, an affiliate of Stanford University. Putt moved to California

to direct the program, while retaining his association with the Air Force as chairman of its scientific advisory board.

Elected president of the Institute of the Aeronautical Sciences for 1960, Putt heads a professional association of some 20,000 American scientists and engineers in the "aerospace" field. He is also on the board of trustees of the Systems Development Corporation and the Space Education Foundation, for nine years was a member of the National Advisory Committee for Aeronautics, and is an honorary Fellow of the Canadian Aeronautical Institute.

Among Putt's decorations are the Distinguished Service Medal, the Legion of Merit with oak leaf cluster, the Bronze Star with oak leaf cluster, and the French Croix de Guerre with palm. He was awarded an honorary D.Eng. degree by Brooklyn Polytechnic Institute in June 1954. He belongs to the Scabbard and Blade and to several Greek-letter societies. On December 27, 1933 he was married to Margaret Wile Yent; they have a son, William Donald, an officer in the Air Force.

References

Aviation W 58:64 Ap 27 '53 por
Gen Army 2:17+ Je '54 por
U S News 44:19 Mr 7 '58

American Men in Government (1949)
American Men of Science vol I (1955)
Who's Who in America, 1958-59
Who's Who in United States Aviation (1954)
Who's Who in World Aviation (1955)

QUASIMODO, SALVATORE (kwä-sī′ mō″dō) Aug. 20, 1901- Poet; translator; critic; professor

Address: b. Conservatorio di Musica Giuseppe Verdi, 12 Via del Conservatorio, Milan, Italy; h. 15 Via de Cristoforis, Milan, Italy

Many eyebrows were raised when the 1959 Nobel Prize for Literature went to Salvatore Quasimodo, Milan poet, critic, translator, and professor of literature, "for his lyrical poetry, which with classical fire expresses the tragic experience of life in our time." Little known throughout the world, because his work was little translated, he was a "dark horse" even in his native Italy, where the excellence of his poetry was generally recognized, but where his political nonconformity had isolated him from his contemporaries. During the totalitarian blackout of the Mussolini regime he concealed his heresies within the obscurities of his "hermetic" poetry, but he now often makes public his views on the social role of the poet. Although his poetry has changed, it has not become political. "But he has dared," wrote Sidney Alexander from Florence, "to a degree unusual in this tradition-ridden society, to employ his limpid, sensitive, classical idiom to confront 'social' themes" (*Reporter*, December 10, 1959).

Salvatore Quasimodo was born to Gaetano and Clotilde (Ragusa) Quasimodo at Modica, in the province of Syracuse, Sicily, on August

Wide World

SALVATORE QUASIMODO

20, 1901. The family was of Sicilian-Greek descent. He has a sister and a brother. Salvatore lived as a boy in Messina, where his father was a railroad official. His mother persuaded him to enroll in the local technical institute rather than in the Gymnasium where he might have pursued an academic course, because the Gymnasium was farther away and because, both parents felt, the academic education would not be as practical as the technical training.

From Messina's technical institute Quasimodo went to Rome, where he took polytechnical courses for two years. Lacking the financial means for the further study necessary for a degree in engineering, he had to content himself with a degree in surveying. In Rome a Sicilian priest, Monsignor Rampolla, encouraged him to indulge his interest in the humanities. He began studying Greek and Latin on his own. He had already begun to write poetry.

Unsure of himself as a writer, he began to support himself at the kind of job for which his formal education had prepared him. In 1920 he became a technical designer in a construction firm and four years later moved to a hardware store. In 1926 he became an official in the state civil engineering corps, a post which he kept for several years and which took him to Reggio di Calabria, Sondrio, and other places in Italy. He might not have stayed at this work as long as he did if his hostility toward the fascists had not closed to him the possibility of entering the more congenial field of writing through journalism.

Quasimodo was meanwhile writing poetry. In 1930 he went to Florence with three of his poems, to show them to the editors of *Solaria*. The poems were immediately published in the review. His work as a civil engineer took him north; he settled in Milan, where he became one of the "young emigrants"—the writers and artists who flocked to Milan in the 1930's, most of them from southern Italy.

By 1938 he had produced five slim books of poetry: *Acque e terre,* published in Florence by Edizioni di Solaria in 1930; *Oboe sommerso,* published at Genoa in 1932; *Odore di eucalyptus e altri versi,* published in Florence in 1933; *Erato e Apollion,* published by Vera in Milan in 1936; and *Poesie,* published in Milan in 1938. The five books established Quasimodo as a leading practitioner of the "hermetic" school of poetry. The "hermetic" poets, who traced their origins to French symbolism on one hand and the oppressive political climate of Italy under Mussolini on the other, tried to achieve a purity of utterance by using phrases of extreme simplicity. Critics soon recognized the "verbal and rhythmic sensitivity, at times exquisite," in the youthful poems of Quasimodo.

The early poems were only preludes. Even admirers like Sergio J. Pacifici at times found them "almost purposely involute, bordering on the dangerously experimental" (*Saturday Review,* November 7, 1959). "In his first books his genius is indeed at work but not in its full range," C. M. Bowra has pointed out. "He is intimate, discerning, sensitive, but he has not yet found the extraordinary power which is all the more impressive for being held in strict control and is now his most characteristic gift" (New York *Times Book Review,* November 15, 1959).

Residence in faraway Milan had moved Quasimodo to sing of his native Sicily, "distant in the south,/warm with tears and mourning." Two other influences further matured Quasimodo as a poet. One was his translating, which strengthened his mastery of words and rhythms, burnished his technique, and broadened his sensibility. "The poetic education and in no small part the achievement of Quasimodo has lain in his own translations of classical Greek lyrics," said Cecil Sprigge in the Manchester *Guardian* (October 23, 1959). His translation of various Greek lyrics, *Lirici greci,* was published by Edizioni di Corrente in 1940 and reissued by Mondadori in 1945. His translation of much of Virgil's *Georgics* was published during World War II under the title *Il fiore delle georgiche* (Gentile, 1944). Other translations he has made from the Greek include Homer's *Odyssey: Dall'Odissea* (Rosa e Ballo, 1945); Aeschylus' *Choephori: Le coefore* (Bompiani, 1946); the *Gospel according to St. John: Il Vangelo secondo S. Giovanni* (Gentile, 1946); and Sophocles' *Electra: Elettra* (Mondadori, 1954). From Latin he has translated the *Canti* of Catullus (Mondadori, 1955). From Spanish he has translated the *Poesie* of the Chilean poet Pablo Neruda (Einaudi, 1952).

Quasimodo's several translations from English include the poetry of Ezra Pound, E. E. Cummings, and Conrad Aiken, and, notably, the plays of Shakespeare. Cecil Sprigge attributed "some portion of his renown to his deft and sensitive translation of Shakespeare's 'Romeo and Juliet,' which shortly after the war had memorable performances in the ancient Roman theatre of Verona" (Manchester *Guardian.* October 23, 1959). He has also translated *Macbeth* (Einaudi, 1952), *Richard III: Riccardo III* (Mondadori, 1952), and *The Tempest: La tempesta* (Einaudi, 1956). "The translations, especially from Greek and Latin, are fresh limpid re-creations, not transcriptions, and, in the judgment of many, represent Quasimodo's highest achievement," commented Sidney Alexander in the *Reporter* (December 10, 1959). Giovanni Grazzini, literary critic of *La nazione,* the Florence daily newspaper, believes that Quasimodo's "superlative translations" assure him of "lasting fame."

The other great influence that matured Quasimodo as a poet was World War II. "The agony of his beautiful country, the degradation of humanity, the horror of bloodshed struck him in the center of his being and made a great poet of him," says C. M. Bowra. Four of the five books for which Quasimodo received the Nobel Prize for Literature on December 10, 1959 were postwar: *Giorno dopo giorno* (Mondadori, 1947), *La vita non è sogno* (Mondadori, 1949), *Il falso e vero verde* (Schwarz, 1954), and *La terra impareggiabile* (Mondadori, 1958). The fifth book, *Ed è subito sera* (Mondadori, 1942) includes prewar work. Not all critics regard this earlier work as inferior to his postwar efforts. Sidney Alexander reports that some Italian critics are worrying about "whether Quasimodo's more recent work has not lost force and beauty precisely to the degree that he has committed himself to a too narrowly conceived 'engagement.' "

Quasimodo's "engagement" springs from a passionate concern with the fate of his country and, beyond it, with the fate of mankind. It is first of all a poetical engagement, the nature of which he clarified in the "Discourse on Poetry" accompanying *Il falso e vero verde.* He views poetry as committed to an involvement, not with the provincial, with the past or with itself, but with contemporary man. He considers it capable of recreating man by its own power of creation. "He has sought, with words, and with all the intellectual resources at his disposal, to illuminate for himself and for us the meaning of life and man's condition in the universe," Sergio J. Pacifici observes (*Saturday Review,* November 7, 1959). "Discreetly, but convincingly, he has taught us to be braver and stronger, and to 'ask neither grace nor confusion.' "

His engagement sometimes takes the form of direct action. During World War II he joined with several other writers to participate in the struggle which ended in the liberation. At one point in Bergamo he was imprisoned for his activities. When the war was over, he joined the Communist party, but left after three months because he refused to write political poems. In late 1958 he went to Moscow to attend a writers' conference, suffered two heart attacks while there, was hospitalized, and did not return to Italy until May 31, 1959. After he returned he wrote articles which aroused much controversy.

The only poem by Quasimodo that has been widely accused of political bias is "To The New Moon." Appearing in the Communist organ *L'Unità* shortly after the Soviet Union launched Sputnik I in October 1957, the poem compared the man-made star to "those which moved/since the creation of the world." Italian Catholics were outraged. To religious and political charges hurled against him, Quasimodo replied: "The sputnik is just the source of new poetic factors. . . . I am not an atheist. I do believe in God, even if I do not observe any religious rule or proceeding."

Few of Quasimodo's poems are available in English translation. Allen Mandelbaum translated eleven of them, including "Lament for the South" and "To Pilgrim Me," in *Poetry* (July 1950). "And Suddenly It's Evening" and "Ancient Winter" appear in *1001 Poems of Mankind,* compiled by Henry W. Wells (Tupper & Love, 1953). "Ancient Winter," translated by G. R. Kay, also appears in the *Penguin Book of Italian Verse.* "The High Sailboat" appears in *A Little Treasury of World Poetry,* edited by Hubert Creekmore (Scribner, 1952). "Insomnia," translated by Sonia Raiziss and Alfredo De Palchi, was published in the *Atlantic Monthly* (December 1958). Other of his poems appear in translation in *The Promised Land and Other Poems,* an anthology edited by Sergio J. Pacifici (Vanni, 1957). Farrar, Straus & Cudahy published *The Selected Writings of Salvatore Quasimodo* (1960), the first major collection of his work to appear in the United States.

Since 1941 Quasimodo has been professor of Italian literature at the Giuseppe Verdi Conservatory of Music in Milan. He is also a drama critic for *Tempo,* the Milan magazine of which he was an assistant editor from 1938 to 1940.

Salvatore Quasimodo is a dark, balding man of average build. He is quiet in manner and reported to be shy to the point of diffidence. He is separated from his wife and has a grown son, Sandro, and a daughter, Orietta.

References

Christian Sci Mon p2 O 22 '59 por
Life 47:94 N 9 '59 pors
N Y Herald Tribune p7 O 23 '59
N Y Times p3 O 23 '59; p47 My 14 '60 por
N Y World-Telegram p1+ O 22 '59 por
Pub W 176:28+ N 2 '59
Chi è? (1957)
Panorama Biografico degli Italiani d'Oggi (1956)
Who's Who in Italy, 1957-58

QUESADA, E(LWOOD) R(ICHARD) (kā-sä′dä) Apr. 13, 1904- United States government official; former Air Force officer

Address: b. Federal Aviation Agency, Washington 25, D.C.

NOTE: This biography supersedes the article which appeared in *Current Biography* in 1950.

The Federal Aviation Agency, which began to function in January 1959, incorporates under independent authority the Civil Aeronautics Administration, the Airways Modernization Board, and the safety rule-making section of the Civil Aeronautics Board. Its first administrator is E. R. Quesada, retired lieutenant gen-

E. R. QUESADA

eral of the Air Force, who at the time of his appointment by President Eisenhower in September 1958, was serving as the President's Special Assistant for Aviation Facilities Planning and as chairman of the Airways Modernization Board. From 1949 until he resigned from the Air Force in 1951 Quesada had commanded Joint Task Force Three, which carried out a series of tests that included the detonation of the world's first thermonuclear device. From 1951 until 1958 he was engaged in private industry, and in late 1960 he headed a group that won certification from the American League to operate a baseball franchise in Washington, D.C.

Of Spanish and Irish extraction, Elwood Richard Quesada is the son of Lope Lopez and Helen A. (McNamara) Quesada. He has a brother, Graham, and a sister, now Mrs. Walter B. Kennedy. He was born on April 13, 1904 in Washington, D.C. and attended Washington public grade and high schools. He later studied at Wyoming Seminary in Kingston, Pennsylvania, the University of Maryland, and Georgetown University. In 1924 he joined the Regular Army as a private, became a flying cadet, and later was commissioned a second lieutenant in the Air Reserve. After about sixteen months of inactive status, he was commissioned on January 23, 1927 as a Regular Army officer in the Air Corps.

As pilot for General James Albert Fechet, then Chief of the Air Corps, Quesada took an active part in the rescue of the crew of the German aircraft *Bremen*, which crashed in Labrador in 1928 after making the first East-West transatlantic flight. In January 1929 he was relief pilot under Major (later General) Carl Spaatz of the monoplane *Question Mark*, which remained aloft over San Diego, California for six and a quarter days, establishing a world's record for endurance and proving the efficacy of air refueling. For this feat he and

the other crew members were awarded the Distinguished Flying Cross. When the Army flew the air mail for a period in 1933-34, he was chief pilot of the New York-Cleveland route. On May 7, 1934 he made a coast-to-coast flight in forty-nine minutes under the existing record.

Quesada attained the rank of brigadier general (temporary) on December 11, 1942, a year after the United States had entered World War II. Early in 1943 he was named Commanding General of the Twelfth Fighter Command and Deputy Commander of the Northwest African Coastal Air Force. Popular with his men (by whom he was nicknamed "Pete"), he was frequently referred to as "the pilots' general."

During the war Quesada took part in more than ninety combat missions, many of them in the North African and Italian campaigns. Transferred to England as Commanding General of the Ninth Fighter Command in October 1943, he directed the United States air effort before and during the invasion of Normandy. Then in the Allied sweep across Europe he co-operated with the army on a tactical operation.

As soon as the fighting ended in Europe, Quesada returned to Washington as Assistant Chief of Air Staff for Intelligence. In March 1946 he was appointed head of the newly formed Tactical Air Command and in October 1947 was promoted to lieutenant general. By the National Defense Act of 1947 the Air Force became a separate service, and in November 1948 the Tactical Air Command was merged in a new Air Defense Command. At that time Quesada was made special assistant to the Air Force Chief of Staff, General Hoyt S. Vandenberg.

The Joint Chiefs of Staff named Quesada in August 1949 to head a special planning project which three months later was disclosed to be the creation of Joint Task Force Three, representing the Army, Navy, Air Force, and Atomic Energy Commission. At Eniwetok Atoll, Joint Task Force Three carried out under Quesada's command a series of tests, called Operation Greenhouse, which included the detonation of the first hydrogen bomb.

In July 1951 Lieutenant General Quesada, then forty-seven years old, revealed that he had renewed an application to retire from military services that he had first submitted two years earlier. Placed on the retirement list, he went in mid-October to the California Institute of Technology as a temporary consultant on atomic and radar problems. In December 1951 he was elected a director and vice-president of Olin Industries, Inc., in East Alton, Illinois, to work on the expansion contemplated by the company in the field of cellulose and minerals.

From 1953 to 1955 Quesada was vice-president of the Lockheed Aircraft Corporation in California where he worked on problems of developing electronic guidance for long-range rocket missiles. In July 1956 he was elected chairman of the board and chief executive officer of Topp Industries, Inc., a Los Angeles electronics research development and manufacturing concern. Other business positions that he has held are directorships in Olin-

Mathieson Chemical Corporation and United Service Life Insurance Company.

In aviation, Quesada was active in the Flight Safety Foundation, Inc., of which he became a director in January 1953. President Eisenhower appointed him on June 14, 1957 as his Special Assistant for Aviation Facilities Planning, succeeding Edward P. Curtis. Two months later he was confirmed by the Senate as chairman of the Airways Modernization Board. On September 30, 1958 the President nominated him to be administrator of the Federal Aviation Agency, effective in November. (The Senate confirmed this interim appointment on March 11, 1959.)

The act of Congress which created the Federal Aviation Agency in August 1958 stipulated that its administrator must be a civilian. To accept the appointment Quesada formally resigned his commission as a lieutenant general on the Air Force retired list. In September 1959, however, Congress passed a special bill to restore Quesada to his military status when he leaves the FAA and to permit him to collect his retirement pay.

Objectives of the FAA are to regulate air commerce; control navigable air space and regulate civil and military flight operation; develop and operate a common system of air traffic control and navigation for civilian and military aircraft; develop a plan for functioning in the event of war; and prescribe minimum standards for design, materials and workmanship in construction of aircraft and other aviation elements.

In safety-promoting actions the agency has warned air-line pilots not to leave their cockpits while in flight and has ordered that all pilots over sixty years of age be grounded. Together with the Weather Bureau it has started development of a new forecasting system utilizing electronic computers and automatic observation stations. In June 1959 it proposed that all airliners be equipped with weather radar.

During the summer of 1959 Quesada submitted plans to the President to build up an efficient new cargo aircraft fleet by transferring to private carriers the bulk of the routine "pipeline" traffic of the Air Force's Military Air Transport Service and by encouraging private loans made for cargo aircraft purchases. MATS strongly opposed the proposal. In October Quesada announced that his agency was preparing to assume operation of about 2,095 military air traffic control facilities under what was given the code name of Project Friendship.

E. R. Quesada was married on October 12, 1946 to Mrs. Kate Davis Pulitzer Putnam, granddaughter of Joseph Pulitzer of the New York *World* and widow of Captain Ware Putnam. He has two stepdaughters, Kate Davis and Hope Ware Putnam, and two sons, Thomas Ricardo and Peter Wickham Quesada. Sturdily built, Quesada is five feet eight inches in height and about 180 pounds in weight; he has wavy brown hair and brown eyes. He plays golf and tennis. His political affiliation is with the Republican party. Among his many foreign awards are the British Order of the Bath, Commander of the British Empire, French Legion of Honor, and Belgium Order of the Couronne with Aviation Palm.

References

Gen Army 2:23+ Mr '54 por
N Y Herald Tribune p7 O 1 '58 por
N Y Times p1+ O 1 '58 por; p20 O 4 '58
Time 74:66 Jl 6 '59 por
U S News 45:21 O 10 '58 por
Who's Who in America, 1958-59
World Biography (1954)

QUOIREZ, FRANÇOISE *See* Sagan, Françoise

RAHMAN, SIR ABDUL, PARAMOUNT RULER OF MALAYA Aug. 24, 1895-Apr. 1, 1960 First king of new Federation of Malaya; elected for a five-year term as ruler in 1957; served as ruler of Malayan state of Negri Sembilan (1933-57). See *Current Biography* (December) 1957.

Obituary

N Y Times p33 Ap 1 '60

RAMSEY, ARTHUR MICHAEL, ARCHBISHOP OF YORK Nov. 14, 1904- English primate

Address: Bishopthorpe, York, Yorkshire, England

If the Church of England has been afflicted of late with "caretaker" bishops, as some Anglicans maintain, the Most Reverend and Right Honorable Dr. Arthur Michael Ramsey is not one of them. The strong sentiments, pro and con, which greeted his meteoric rise to the primatial See of York in 1956 bore witness to the forcefulness of the Archbishop. A forthright High-Churchman, prolific in writing and eloquent in speech, he appeared to some liberals in the church as a threat to the cause of Christian reunion. While his Anglo-Catholicism did not bear the fruit feared by these critics, neither did his antifundamentalism abate. Four days after his election to York he published an attack on American evangelist Billy Graham which received world-wide attention. Ramsey, who succeeded the late Cyril Forster Garbett as Archbishop of York and Primate of England, ranks second to the Archbishop of Canterbury.

Arthur Michael Ramsey was born on November 14, 1904, into a family with traditions of the Christian ministry on both sides. His paternal grandfather was a Congregationalist minister and his maternal grandfather, an Anglican clergyman. His father, Arthur Stanley Ramsey, a mathematics don at Cambridge and a Congregationalist, was confirmed in the Church of England by his son before his death in 1955. His mother was Agnes (Wilson) Ramsey.

(Continued next page)

British Inf. Services

ARTHUR MICHAEL RAMSEY
ARCHBISHOP OF YORK

During the years that Ramsey attended the public school of Repton, Dr. Geoffrey Fisher, the present Archbishop of Canterbury, was headmaster. He continued his studies at Magdalene College, Cambridge University. His father was president of the college at the time. Arthur took second class in classical tripos in 1925. He was a member of the University Union, the famous Cambridge debating society, and its president in 1926. He won his B.A. degree and took first class in theological tripos in 1927. He also studied at Cuddesdon Theological College near Oxford. In 1930 he received his Cambridge M.A. degree and in 1950, his B.D. degree.

Ramsey was ordained a deacon in the Church of England in 1928 and a priest in 1929. His first ministerial assignment was to the Church of St. Nicholas in Liverpool, where he served as a curate from 1928 to 1930. In 1930 he became subwarden at Lincoln Theological College, a position which he held until 1936. While subwarden at Lincoln College he also served as examining chaplain to the Bishop of Chester, from 1932 to 1939. He later performed the same duty—examining candidates for the ministry—for the Bishop of Durham from 1940 to 1950 and the Bishop of Lincoln in 1951-52. During his tenure as subwarden at Lincoln College he was also select preacher to Cambridge University (1934). He was again select preacher there in 1940 and 1948 and was select preacher to Oxford in 1945-46.

From 1936 to 1938 Ramsey was lecturer—an ancient title still used for certain parochial posts in the Church of England—of Boston Parish Church in Lincolnshire. From Boston he was transferred to Cambridge, where he was vicar of St. Benedict's Church. In 1940 he went to Durham and stayed there for ten years as canon of the Cathedral and Van Mildert Professor of Divinity in the University of

Durham. From 1950 to 1952 he was at Cambridge as a Fellow of Magdalene College and Regius Professor of Divinity in the university. During part of this time he was also canon of Caistor and prebendary in Lincoln Cathedral (1951-52).

Having become well-liked at Durham during his ten years there as canon and professor, he was nominated for election to the See of Durham in 1952 and was consecrated Lord Bishop of Durham on September 29 of that year. It is an historic privilege of the bishops of Durham to attend the Queen during her coronation. The "nice old bishop" who stood by the side of the Queen throughout the coronation service in Westminster Abbey on June 2, 1953, and who was thus seen by millions of television and movie viewers throughout the world, was Dr. Ramsey.

Some ecumenical liberals fear Dr. Ramsey because he hindered some of their efforts at church reunion during the Assembly of the World Council of Churches in Evanston, Illinois in 1954. His contribution to the Church of England's York Convocation the following year, however, gave a quite different impression. Dr. Cyril Forster Garbett, then Archbishop of York, was ill, and Dr. Ramsey presided over the convocation, held in July 1955. in his place.

Although Anglo-Catholic in his own thinking, Dr. Ramsey played a notable part in steering through the convocation a measure that many Anglo-Catholics considered a heresy: the resolution to admit the United Church of South India to closer communion with the Church of England. The decision allowed for a period of thirty years, during which, it was hoped, the Church of South India would achieve a complete acceptance of episcopacy. A colleague described Dr. Ramsey's contribution to the convocation as "immense" and his statesmanship in steering through the South India decision as "wise."

Archbishop Ramsey again displayed his conviction of the need for church unity after he ascended to the See of York. In July 1956 he headed an eight-member delegation to an Anglican-Orthodox theological conference in Moscow. "We are going to discuss the extent of unity in belief and practice between our two churches," he explained as he left for the conference.

Dr. Ramsey had succeeded to the episcopacy of York after the death of Archbishop Garbett on December 31, 1955. Queen Elizabeth announced her approval of his nomination in a statement issued from the Prime Minister's office on January 5, 1956. An Anglican correspondent observed in the Manchester *Guardian* (January 5, 1956), "The haste with which his appointment has been announced contrasts strongly with the long delays in other episcopal appointments." The same correspondent also said, "Among the more extreme Anglo-Catholic elements in the Church of England Dr. Ramsey's appointment will be welcome. Some others may tend to regard him as a party candidate."

On January 30 of the same year, in a ceremony 700 years old, he was elected by the dean and chapter of York. The Queen confirmed the election on March 16, and Ramsey was enthroned as Archbishop of York and Primate of England in York Minster on the afternoon of April 25, 1956. The episcopal seat held by Dr. Ramsey is second in importance only to Canterbury. It carries a salary of 5,000 pounds ($14,000) a year.

As Archbishop of York, Ramsey is a Lord Spiritual, entitled by his office to sit in the House of Lords. He took part in an epochal scene in Westminster on the night of July 10, 1956, when the House of Lords rejected by a vote of 238 to 95 a bill to abolish capital punishment in Britain, a bill which the House of Commons had already passed. Among the 95 votes against capital punishment were those of ten of the Lords Spiritual, including that of Archbishop Ramsey. (Only one Lord Spiritual, the Bishop of Rochester, voted to retain capital punishment.)

Dr. Ramsey is the author of several theological works: *The Gospel and the Catholic Church* (Longmans, 1936); *The Resurrection of Christ* (Presbyterian Board of Christian Education, 1946); *The Glory of God and the Transfiguration of Christ* (Longmans, 1949); *F. D. Maurice and the Conflicts of Modern Theology* (Cambridge, 1951), consisting of lectures he had delivered three years previously; and *Durham Essays and Addresses* (Society for Promoting Christian Knowledge, 1956). The Hale Memorial Lectures of 1959 delivered by Dr. Ramsey at the Seabury-Western Theological Seminary in Evanston, Illinois were published under the title *An Era in Anglican Theology; From Gore to Temple* (Scribner, 1960).

Dr. Ramsey gives vent to his Anglo-Catholic feeling occasionally, and with more sensational impact, in topical outbursts. In "The Menace of Fundamentalism," an article in the February 1956 issue of the Durham diocesan bulletin, he condemned fundamentalism as a whole as "heretical" and Billy Graham in particular as a teacher of the "grossest doctrines." "Where the message is addressed to less than the whole man as a being with a mind," he said, "dishonor is done to the image in which man was created" (*Newsweek*, February 20, 1956). Graham commented: "The present Archbishop of York has long been opposed to the message I preach. I have never answered his criticism nor do I intend to now" (New York *Times*, February 4, 1956).

An outspoken advocate of priest workers in England, Ramsey suggested in an article in the *York Quarterly* in early 1958 that the legislation forbidding clergymen to engage in "trade" should be ended, so that bishops might be able to ordain men at all levels of society. "We have yet to discover what possibilities there may be for priesthood in the context of different crafts and trades." In the same article he seconded the plea of Canon Stockwood of Great St. Mary's, Cambridge, for greater apostolic impact by laymen in industry and the professions and greater lay participation in the legislative bodies of the church.

Dr. Ramsey received an honorary doctorate in divinity from Durham University in 1951 and from Cambridge, Edinburgh, Leeds, and Hull universities in 1957. He has been an honorary Fellow at Magdalene College, Cambridge since 1952.

On April 8, 1942 Ramsey was married to Joan Alice Hamilton, daughter of Lieutenant-Colonel F. A. C. Hamilton and until that time secretary to the Bishop of Jarrow. They have no children.

Ramsey is a hulking, broad-shouldered man whose white hair and stooped posture make him look much older than he is. He likes to walk, and when he was Bishop of Durham he spent much spare time touring the districts around Auckland Castle. He is not the kind of prelate who gets lost in administration. "I love to know the parishes and what is going on in them," he has said.

References

> Manchester Guardian p1 Ja 5 '56 por
> Time 67:70 Ja 16 '56 por
> Author's & Writer's Who's Who (1948-49)
> Crockford's Clerical Directory, 1957-58
> International Who's Who, 1959
> Who's Who, 1959
> Who's Who in America, 1958-59

RANDALL, JOHN D(ANIEL) Nov. 30, 1899- Attorney; organization official
Address: b. American Bldg., Cedar Rapids, Ia.; h. 328 Forest Dr., S.E., Cedar Rapids, Ia.

During the year 1959-60, as the eighty-third president of the American Bar Association, John D. Randall heads one of the most influential professional groups in the United States. An organization largely of practising lawyers, the A.B.A. concerns itself with all important questions of jurisprudence and administration of justice. Among the issues of chief interest to the A.B.A. during Randall's term in office have been the problem of achieving world peace through law, the debate on the role of the United States in the World Court, and the controversy over Supreme Court rulings on civil rights and subversion. Randall, a practising attorney in Cedar Rapids, Iowa for thirty-seven years, has long been prominent in bar association activities.

John Daniel Randall was born in Lisbon, Iowa on November 30, 1899, the son of Mac J. and Katherine R. (Stahl) Randall. He was educated in local schools, attended Coe College in Cedar Rapids, and then transferred to the Law School of the University of Iowa, where he received his LL.B. degree in 1923.

Soon after graduation, Randall was admitted to the Iowa bar and began a private practice in Cedar Rapids. He has lived and practised law in that city ever since, specializing in insurance law—investigation and adjusting. His work has brought him into association with realtors, bankers, public accountants, insurance attorneys, adjusters, and underwriters.

Throughout almost all of his career Randall has been active in professional organizations. His role as a leader in bar association work began in 1946 when he was elected chairman of the unauthorized practice committee of the

JOHN D. RANDALL

Iowa Bar Association, a position that he held until 1952. In 1947-48 he was president of his local Linn County Bar Association.

Since 1948 he has held important positions in the American Bar Association. He served as Iowa delegate to the A.B.A. house of delegates, the association's policy-making body, from 1948 to 1954 and was chairman of the house of delegates, the second-highest post in the association, from 1954 to 1956. He was chairman of the rules and calendar committee from 1952 to 1954 and of the regional meetings committee in 1956. During three years, in 1952, 1956, and 1957, he served as co-chairman of a five-man committee representing the bar association on the Joint Committee on Professional Responsibility in co-operation with the Association of American Law Schools.

The A.B.A. house of delegates nominated Randall as president of the organization in February 1959, and the following August he was unanimously elected to office at the eighty-second national convention, in Miami Beach, Florida. He succeeded Ross L. Malone of Roswell, New Mexico for a one-year term during which he presided over 95,000 members in the fifty states and Puerto Rico. The association, founded in 1878, has its national headquarters at 1155 E. 60th Street, Chicago, Illinois.

At the 1959 convention one of the major topics of discussion was the possibility of applying the rule of law to achieve world peace. President Eisenhower wrote to the lawyers gathered at the session: "It is gratifying to note that one of the important matters which your convention will consider is the concept of world peace through law. Peace cannot prevail until men and nations recognize that their conduct must be governed by respect for and observance of the law."

As soon as he was elected president of A.B.A., Randall threw his full weight behind the committee formed to study the possibilities of peace through law. "We're going to make it the most terrific committee in the history of the A.B.A.," he said. In pledging to continue the bar association's drive for peace through law, Randall announced that the committee would be broadened to include lawyers with experience beyond the practice of law. The committee now includes two United States Senators, a federal judge, a law school chancellor, and three former bar association presidents.

In addition to the peace-through-law proposal, the association made some controversial recommendations on the Supreme Court and civil rights legislation during 1959. Through its house of delegates, in February it called upon Congress to modify the effect of recent decisions of the Supreme Court dealing with communism and internal security matters. It asked Congress to let states enact their own laws against sedition. It sought a strengthening of the Smith Act of 1940, which makes it a crime to conspire to teach and advocate the violent overthrow of the government. It asked that all federal employees be barred from refusing to answer questions about possible communist connections by any authorized agency of inquiry. Not all members of the association agreed with the recommendations, and some members resigned from the group.

In 1960 the American Bar Association pressed for Congressional action on an omnibus bill that would provide more judges for American courts. Randall told an American Bankers Association meeting in New York in February that forty-three new judgeships were necessary to ease a "staggering backlog of cases," including 64,000 civil cases and 7,500 criminal cases. "The right to be heard by the courts is a sham if parties to the action have to wait three, four and even five years to be heard," he said. "The denial of justice is the very antithesis of a system of justice," he pointed out, adding that delays were often the equivalent of the denial of justice.

Randall has in addition proposed that Congress consider legislation for the mandatory retirement of all judges who have passed their seventieth birthday. His association has also urged that the United States government take a more active role in the World Court and that the United States abandon its veto power on jurisdiction of the World Court.

As a representative of the American Bar Association, Randall has served as a member of numerous joint national conferences, including the National Conference of Lawyers and Life Underwriters, the National Conference of Lawyers and Adjusters, and the National Conference of Lawyers and Representatives of American Bankers Association Trust Division. He served as co-chairman of the National Conference of Lawyers and Realtors in 1945-46, and as co-chairman of the National Conference of Lawyers and Certified Public Accountants in 1950. From 1954 to 1956 he was a director of the American Bar Foundation.

Working for committees concerned with unauthorized legal practice led Randall to write a number of articles on that subject for professional journals. He is a member of the

American Law Institute, the American Judicature Society (of which he is the Iowa director), the International Association of Insurance Counsel, and the Association of Insurance Attorneys.

In 1955 Randall was appointed to the United States commission for celebration of the 200th anniversary of the birth of Chief Justice John Marshall. He has received several honorary awards, including an honorary LL.D. degree from his alma mater, Coe College; the Golden Key from Loyola University in Chicago; and the Order of the Coif from the University of Iowa.

John D. Randall and his wife, the former Margaret E. Graham, were married on June 20, 1952. They have a daughter, Margaret Sue (Mrs. William J. Jameson, Jr.) and a son, John Daniel, Jr. His son is also a lawyer, having been admitted to the Iowa bar in 1959. Randall is a Shriner and a member of the American Legion, the Selden Society, Sigma Phi Epsilon, and Phi Alpha Delta. His clubs are the Pickwick of Cedar Rapids and the Union League of Chicago. He is a Presbyterian and a Republican.

References

Martindale-Hubbell Law Directory, 1959
Who's Who in America, 1958-59
Who's Who in Commerce and Industry (1959)

REMINGTON, JOHN W(ARNER) Jan. 10, 1897- Banker; lawyer

Address: b. Lincoln Rochester Trust Co., Rochester 3, N.Y.; h. 76 Oliver St., Rochester 7, N.Y.

During a one-year term that began in November 1959 John W. Remington, as president of the American Bankers Association, heads an organization of more than 17,000 banks and branches devoted to promoting the usefulness of banks in the public interest. He succeeded Lee P. Miller. A lawyer by training, Remington practised law for several years in Rochester, New York before entering the banking business in 1930. Since 1954 he has been president of the Lincoln Rochester Trust Company, the largest bank in his city.

A native and lifelong resident of Rochester, John Warner Remington was born on January 10, 1897. He is the fifth of the seven children (five sons and two daughters) of Harvey Foote Remington, a prominent Rochester lawyer and judge, and Mary Agnes (Brodie) Remington. He attended Rochester public schools, then entered the University of Rochester, and in the summers following his freshman year worked as a conductor on the Rochester and Manitou Interurban Electric Railway, now defunct. In his spare time he played baseball. He received his B.A. degree in 1917.

When the United States declared war on Germany in April 1917, Remington enlisted in the Naval Reserve for World War I service, and in the rank of seaman he was assigned as a cook aboard a submarine chaser. After eight months of cooking for a crew of fourteen, he

JOHN W. REMINGTON

was sent to an officer training school. Commissioned an ensign, he returned to command the ship on which he had been the cook. Subsequently, he served as assistant navigation officer aboard the battleship USS *Vermont*.

After being discharged in 1919 as a lieutenant (j.g.), Remington entered the Harvard University Law School, where he received the LL.B. degree *cum laude* in 1921. Admitted to the New York bar in the same year, he began private practice of law in Rochester in association with his father and an elder brother. They were joined in 1923 by Kenneth B. Keating (who was later elected to the United States Senate), and the firm became Remington, Remington & Keating.

For fourteen months in 1924-25, on the recommendation of William J. Donovan, then United States Assistant Attorney General, Remington served as assistant United States attorney for the Western District of New York. From his offices in Rochester he was chiefly engaged in prosecuting narcotic and liquor violations. For the next five years he was again in private law practice.

Because of his experience in handling estates and corporation matters, Remington was chosen in 1930 by Raymond N. Ball, president of the Lincoln-Alliance Bank & Trust Company, as trust officer of his Rochester bank. Remington advanced to vice-president in 1935 and was holding that office when the bank merged with the Rochester Trust & Safe Deposit Company in 1944 to form the Lincoln Rochester Trust Company. He became executive vice-president and trust officer of the Lincoln Rochester Trust Company in 1950, and in 1954 he succeeded Ball as president of the bank, which at the end of 1958 had deposits of $357,104,231.54.

Rochester business and manufacturing enterprises of which Remington is a director include the Alling & Cory Company (paper products); Curtice Brothers Company (canned vegetables);

REMINGTON, JOHN W.—*Continued*

Haloid Xerox, Inc. (photocopying machines); the Stecher-Traung Lithograph Company; and Superba Cravats, Inc. He is president of the Rochester & Genessee Valley Railroad, which is leased to the Erie, and in September 1958 was elected a director of the Gannett Newspaper Foundation, which controls newspapers and television and radio stations in New York, New Jersey, Connecticut, Illinois, and California.

As a trust officer, Remington was early active in both the New York State Bankers Association and the American Bankers Association. He took the three-summer course of advanced study for bankers on the officer level which is offered by the A.B.A.'s Stonier Graduate School of Banking at Rutgers University, New Brunswick, New Jersey, and for graduation in 1937 wrote the thesis *Trust Business in the Future— Its Association with Banking,* published in book form by the A.B.A. research council.

Especially interested in the work of the A.B.A. trust division, Remington was a member or chairman of several of its committees, vice-president in 1948-49, and president in 1949-50. He was a member of the organization's economic policy commission from 1953 to 1958. At the A.B.A. convention in September 1958 he was elected vice-president, and Lee P. Miller of Louisville, Kentucky was elected president.

An important development at the 1958 convention was the association's decision to support the controversial Mason income tax reform measure which would increase income taxation for savings banks and savings and loan associations while reducing it for commercial banks. As a result of this endorsement, some 222 savings banks resigned from the association and another 142 did not renew membership. The issue was again discussed during the A.B.A. convention the following year.

Remington was elected the seventy-fourth president of the American Bankers Association without opposition on October 27, 1959. At the end of its fiscal year in August 1959 the association had a total membership of 17,690 banks and branches, including 146 in foreign countries. This membership is said to represent more than 98 per cent of the banks in the United States and over 99 per cent of the nation's banking resources. The A.B.A. operates through four major divisions (national bank, state bank, savings and mortgage, and trust), and as an educational section it maintains the American Institute of Banking, which had 86,800 enrollments in its 1958-59 classes.

When the United States Department of the Interior was preparing to end government trusteeship of the Klamath tribe of Indians, it called upon Remington as a consultant. He took part as a trust officer in negotiations which led to an agreement in 1957 whereby each member would receive $25,000 from the sale of tribal timber and land in Oregon and the state of Washington. In February 1959 President Eisenhower appointed Remington to the Annual Assay Commission. He is currently serving a second consecutive three-year term as director of the Buffalo branch of the Federal Reserve Bank in New York.

In Rochester, Remington is a trustee of the Chamber of Commerce and the Bureau of Municipal Research, Inc.; he is also a director of the local chapter of the American Red Cross, the Society for the Prevention of Cruelty to Children, and Genesee Valley Medical Care, Inc., a Blue Shield agency. He is a past president and a director of the Community Chest; in 1947-48 he served as president of the alumni association of the University of Rochester and in 1954-55 as president of his college fraternity, Alpha Delta Phi. He retains membership in the Rochester, New York state, and American bar associations. The Stonier Graduate School of Banking presented him with its Ayres Leadership Award in 1955.

Mrs. Remington is the former Margaret Alcock of Baltimore, Maryland. The Remingtons were married June 17, 1922 and have two daughters, Edith (Mrs. Richard R. Haig) and Martha (Mrs. John A. King); one son, John; and many grandchildren. The Rochester banker has been described in the house organ *Gannetteer* as "cooperative without being effusive . . . down to earth without being buddy-buddy." He keeps his early interest in baseball and is a long-time director of Rochester Community Baseball, Inc., though the outdoor sports in which he is now principally active are golf and water skiing. He belongs to the University and Genesee Valley Country clubs in Rochester and to the American Legion and Veterans of Foreign Wars.

References

Banking 52:46+ N '59 pors
N Y Times p51+ O 28 '59 por
Poor's Register of Directors and Executives (1959)
Who's Who in America, 1958-59
Who's Who in Commerce and Industry (1957)

RIGGIO, VINCENT Nov. 4, 1877-Sept. 6, 1960 Former president (1946-50) and board chairman (1950-51) of the American Tobacco Company. See *Current Biography* (July) 1949.

Obituary

N Y Times p41 S 7 '60

RIVERS, L(UCIUS) MENDEL Sept. 28, 1905- United States Representative from South Carolina

Address: b. House Office Bldg., Washington, D.C.; 13 Broad St., Charleston, S.C.; h. 3643 Trinity Dr., Alexandria, Va.; Wappoo Heights, Charleston, S.C.

As the Congressman from the First District of South Carolina, L. Mendel Rivers represents the conservative element in the Democratic party and the traditional viewpoint of Southern legislators. He has been a key figure in the South's fight against civil rights legislation. A high-ranking member of the House Armed Services Committee, he has been a proponent of a strong national defense. Rivers represents nine counties around Charleston, South Carolina, with a total 1950 population of 345,953 persons. A lawyer by profession, he has spent most of his adult life in elected positions in politics, including three years in the South Carolina legislature and twenty years in the United States House of Representatives.

Lucius Mendel Rivers was born on September 28, 1905 in Gumville, Berkeley County, South Carolina, the son of Lucius Hampton and Henrietta Marion (McKay) Rivers. He was educated in the public schools of Charleston County. At the age of twenty-one, Rivers enrolled in the College of Charleston, where he studied for three years. He then transferred to the Law School of the University of South Carolina, from which he received his law degree in 1931. He was admitted to the South Carolina bar in 1932 and admitted to practice in the United States Supreme Court in 1940.

Almost immediately after beginning his legal career in South Carolina, Rivers entered politics. He won his first election in November 1932 when he was chosen to serve in the South Carolina state legislature. He remained in the state legislature until 1936, acting as chairman of the Charleston County House delegation from 1934 to 1936. He was employed by the federal government from 1936 to 1940 as a special attorney with the United States Department of Justice. In 1940 he returned to political office when he was elected on November 5 to the Seventy-seventh Congress of the United States from the First District of South Carolina.

Rivers has been re-elected to each succeeding Congress and is now in his tenth consecutive term, having served longer as United States Representative than any other Congressman in the history of his district. As a Democrat, he has encountered practically no opposition for his seat in Congress. In the 1956 election, for instance, his district recorded 31,112 votes for him and only two votes against him.

In Congress Rivers has long served on the powerful House Committee on Armed Services, which handles all legislation dealing with common defense, including bills affecting the Department of Defense, military establishments, and the size, composition, and appropriations of the Army, Navy, and Air Force. He is the third-ranking Democratic member of the committee and serves as chairman of the permanent third subcommittee, which handles all reserve and National Guard matters.

In February 1960 Rivers became chairman of a special subcommittee on the national military airlift dealing with important cold-war policies on military air transportation. He is also a member of the Merchant Marine and Fisheries Committee, serving on the Coast Guard, coast and geodetic survey, navigation, and fisheries and wildlife conservation subcommittees. Chairman of a House Naval Affairs subcommittee, he headed a group of Congressmen who in 1946 toured naval installations in the Pacific to check progress on demobilization and the need for post-war American bases.

L. MENDEL RIVERS

As a Southern Congressman, Rivers has consistently voted against anti-poll tax (1945; 1947; 1949) and civil rights (1957; 1960) legislation. He supported state jurisdiction over tideland oil fields (1951; 1952; 1953) and voted for the Smith states' rights bill (1958). He once cried out in Congress that an anti-lynching bill would "lynch the Constitution" (New York *Times,* March 3, 1948). He figured prominently in the Southern secession from the Democratic party in the 1948 election. In 1952 and 1956 he demonstrated his conservative views by backing Republican candidate Dwight D. Eisenhower rather than his own party's candidate, Adlai E. Stevenson.

In 1960 Rivers accused both parties of using civil rights as a political weapon. Of pending civil rights legislation he said: "This has become a contest between the so-called Democrats of the North and the Republicans to see who can go to the conventions in July to win the political support of the NAACP" (*Congressional Quarterly,* March 18, 1960).

Rivers has consistently favored strong national defense measures. In 1946 and 1959 he voted to extend the existing draft programs; in 1952 he opposed shelving a universal military training bill. Although he was against draft exemption for teen-agers in 1946, he favored priority inductions (over eighteen year-olds) for older men and those in the 4-F classification (1951). In 1952 Rivers opposed a bill to place a $46 billion ceiling on military spending. Since 1957 he has supported liberal annual defense appropriations.

During the early years of his Congressional career, Rivers regularly supported foreign economic aid. He approved a $3.75 billion loan to Britain (1946), aid to Greece and Turkey (1947), Voice of America appropriations (1947), extension of the Marshall Plan (1949), and liberal foreign assistance bills (1951; 1953; 1954). In recent years, however, he

RIVERS, L. MENDEL—*Continued*

has voted against President Eisenhower's requests for mutual security legislation that would offer military aid to many foreign countries (1957; 1958; 1959; 1960).

With regard to domestic issues, Rivers usually supported liberal spending. In 1946 he favored a $400,000,000 housing subsidy. Although he voted to limit public housing development in 1951, 1953, and 1954, he supported the Housing Act of 1959 that provided increased indirect and direct aid to public housing projects. Rivers voted for social security increases in 1948 and 1958 and for a new minimum wage bill in 1949. He also supported federal employee salary increases in 1954 and 1960.

Rivers favored strike control legislation (1946), voted to use Taft-Hartley provisions to stop the steel strike of 1952, and supported the Landrum-Griffin Labor Bill (1959). In 1947 he joined the Republicans in voting for a two-term limit to the presidential term.

In 1948 Rivers made national headlines when he introduced legislation to repeal federal taxes on oleomargarine. Congressional opponents from dairy states fought bitterly to maintain the fifty-year-old levies to protect butter from what they called unfair competition. A coalition of legislators from urban areas and Southerners, whose states produce oils from which margarine is made, succeeded in passing the measure.

Rivers favored the establishment of a permanent Committee on Un-American Activities (1945). He supported subversive activities control measures in 1948 and 1950, and in 1954 cast his vote to make membership in the Communist party a crime. He opposed admission of large numbers of immigrants from European displaced persons camps (1948) and of 217,000 refugees from Communism (1953).

On many occasions, Rivers has been recognized for his achievements. In June 1959 The Citadel, a military college in South Carolina, awarded him an LL.D. degree, citing him "for distinguished service to the state and nation; for at all times exhibiting great initiative, courageous leadership, and unselfish devotion to duty." The Reserve Officers Association of the United States gave him its highest honor, the Minute Man Hall of Fame Award. The European department of that association cited him "for serving the national defense of the United States well, faithfully, and with great credit."

Lucius Mendel Rivers was married to Margaret Simons Middleton on September 1, 1938. They have two daughters, Margaret Middleton and Lois Marion, and one son, Lucius Mendel Rivers, Jr. The family lives in Alexandria, Virginia, but also maintains a home in Charleston.

The South Carolina Representative is known in Congress for his distinguished-looking mane of rather long silver-white hair; writers have often noted his handsome appearance. In addition to being an honorary member of the American Dental Association and the South Carolina Dental Association, he is a member of the Elks and Masons, a life member of the Exchange Club, and he attends the Grace Protestant Episcopal Church in Charleston.

References

Congressional Directory (1960)
Who's Who in America, 1960-61
Who's Who in the South and Southwest (1959)
Who's Who in United States Politics (1952)

RIVERS, THOMAS M(ILTON) Sept. 3, 1888- Physician

Address: b. c/o National Foundation, 800 2d Ave., New York 17; h. 163 Greenway S., Forest Hills 75, N.Y.

One of the foremost authorities on virus disease, Thomas M. Rivers has been vice-president in charge of medical affairs for the National Foundation (formerly the National Foundation for Infantile Paralysis) since 1957. He retired from the Rockefeller Institute for Medical Research as an emeritus member in 1955 after an association of thirty-three years, during which he headed its hospital (1937-53) and served as a director and vice-president.

Rivers has been associated with the foundation since 1938 when he was invited to head its virus research committee in an advisory capacity. In 1954 he was the chairman of the foundation's vaccine advisory committee which gave the final verdict on the safety of Jonas E. Salk's polio vaccine and he was acclaimed for his work in supervising the Salk vaccine field trials. Rivers joined the staff of the foundation in 1955 as an assistant to its president and in 1956 he served as its medical director.

Born in the rural community of Jonesboro, Georgia on September 3, 1888, Thomas Milton Rivers is one of the four children of Alonzo Burrell Rivers and his wife, the former Mary Martha Coleman. Two brothers are now deceased and a sister, Sarah Rivers Turner, still lives in her native town. The elder Rivers worked as a cotton buyer and warehouse man in Jonesboro, where Thomas was reared and educated. The young man attended Emory College in Oxford, Georgia (now Emory University in Atlanta), where he majored in biology and participated actively in athletics, particularly in tennis competitions.

After graduating from Emory in 1909 with a B.A. degree, Rivers entered the Johns Hopkins University Medical School. When he had completed two years of training, he took a leave of absence (1912-13) to work at the Santo Tomás Hospital in Panama. He was awarded the M.D. degree in 1915 and remained in Baltimore to complete his year of internship at the Johns Hopkins Hospital. The following year he accepted the post of assistant resident physician in pediatrics, and in 1917 he was named resident pediatrician at the hospital and instructor in that subject at Johns Hopkins University Medical School.

Rivers' pediatric work was interrupted in February 1918 when he was commissioned a first lieutenant in the United States Army

Medical Corps. He served on the permanent pneumonia board and sat on commissions studying respiratory diseases, the advance of pneumonia following an attack of measles, and empyema, a collection of pus in the pleural cavity of the lungs. When he received his honorable discharge in January 1919, Rivers returned to Johns Hopkins University where he served first as an instructor (1919-21) and then as an associate (1921-22) in the bacteriology department. From 1920 to 1922 he also worked as a pathologist at St. Joseph's Hospital in Baltimore.

During these early years Rivers devoted himself primarily to research on the respiratory diseases. He published several significant papers discussing his investigation of the influenza bacilli, including his discovery of Hemophilus parainfluenzae. In 1922 the Rockefeller Institute for Medical Research, one of the world's greatest medical centers, invited Rivers to become an associate on its staff. Three years later he was named an associate member and in 1927 he assumed full membership.

At the Rockefeller Institute, Rivers switched to the study of virus diseases. During the winter of 1929-30 he extended his investigations to make an exhaustive study of psittacosis, or parrot fever, which afflicted many persons in the Eastern United States at that time. Rivers proved that a virus caused the disease and found a reliable method of detecting its presence by tests on laboratory mice. In 1934 he announced that he had perfected a psittacosis vaccine for human and animal immunization.

Rivers also devoted particular attention to a study of sleeping sickness, a form of encephalitis. In 1934 he read a paper before the New York Academy of Medicine in which he traced the disease to two separate viruses, one of which causes the American form of the sickness, the other the type prevalent in Africa. Rivers also studied the viruses that cause measles, chicken pox, poliomyelitis, and lymphocytic choriomeningitis, and he discovered Virus III, an agent which is pathogenic for rabbits. The modern technique of producing tissue cultures of the virus germs is based upon Rivers' research.

In 1937 Rivers was appointed the director of the Rockefeller Institute's department of the hospital. With the outbreak of World War II Rivers' knowledge of virus diseases was considered important to the war effort; in February 1942 he was commissioned a reserve officer in the United States Navy Medical Corps. Although he was on a leave of absence from his post at the Rockefeller Institute, Rivers continued to work at the hospital, where he organized and directed a medical unit conducting virus research. During the last year of the war Rivers organized and became the commanding officer of Naval Medical Research Unit II, which was stationed in Guam and operated in the south and central Pacific. In 1945 he was promoted to the rank of commodore, and after his discharge in September 1946, the Navy awarded him the Legion of Merit.

The election of Dr. Rivers to the post of vice-president and director of the Rockefeller

DR. THOMAS M. RIVERS

Institute was announced in June 1953. He retired in October 1955 as an emeritus member to accept an assignment as assistant to the president of the National Foundation for Infantile Paralysis. When he took this position, Rivers had long been familiar with the battle against this crippling disease, having conducted research on the polio virus during the 1930's.

Rivers headed the committee on virus research and epidemiology of the National Foundation for Infantile Paralysis from 1938 to 1955, supervising hundreds of scientists working in laboratories and universities throughout the country with funds supplied by the March of Dimes. In this capacity he approved the grants to Dr. Jonas E. Salk for the development of his anti-polio vaccine. In 1954 Rivers served as chairman of the foundation's vaccine advisory committee, which had the responsibility of judging the safety of the Salk polio vaccine before launching a mass inoculation of school children.

When the vaccinations were completed in 1955, Rivers accepted the report of the results and congratulated the scientists on behalf of the polio foundation and the "yet unborn generations" whose usefulness would never be impaired. "I do not know," Rivers said, "whether we realize how very exacting was the assignment of evaluating the greatest field trial and one of the greatest endeavors in the history of preventive medicine."

In October 1956 Rivers became medical director of the National Foundation for Infantile Paralysis, and his appointment as vice-president for medical affairs of the National Foundation was made public in October 1957. The foundation no longer limits itself to study of the polio virus. Rivers now directs research on other virus afflictions, including the common cold and influenza. According to Rivers, the tiny organisms cause disease by invading a cell and controlling its functions. As the cell dies, it re-

RIVERS, THOMAS M.—*Continued*

leases hundreds of virus particles which infect more cells. The virus infection thus spreads in a geometric progression.

In his long career Rivers has published approximately 150 papers in foreign as well as American journals. He wrote a section for E. L. Opie's *Epidemic Respiratory Diseases* (C. V. Mosby Co., 1921) and was the editor of and a contributor to *Filterable Viruses* (Williams & Wilkins Co., 1928). *Viral and Rickettsial Infections of Man* was published under his editorial direction in 1948, 1952, and 1959 by the J. B. Lippincott Company.

Honorary degrees have been presented to Rivers by Emory University (1936), Rochester University (1938), and the University of Chicago (1941). In 1958 he was named to the polio Hall of Fame for his distinguished work with the foundation. He has served on the Armed Forces Epidemiological Board, the New York state advisory committee on polio, the New York City Board of Health (1939-57) and as member and chairman of the research council of the New York City Institute of Scientific Research. Rivers was president of the Third International Congress for Microbiology held in New York in 1939.

Professional memberships held by Rivers include the American Medical Association, the American Public Health Association, the American Pediatric Society, the American Society of Experimental Pathology, the American Epidemiological Society, and the Association of American Physicians. He also belongs to the American Association of Pathologists and Bacteriologists, the National Academy of Sciences, the Harvey Society, and the American Philosophical Society. He served as president of the American Society for Clinical Investigation (1932), the Society of American Immunologists (1934), the Society of American Bacteriologists (1936), and the Interurban Clinical Club (1942-43).

White-haired and distinguished in appearance, Thomas Milton Rivers stands five feet ten inches tall and weighs 175 pounds. He and his wife, the former Teresa Jacobina Riefle, to whom he was married on August 5, 1922, have no children.

References

N Y Herald Tribune p26 N 22 '42 por

American Men of Science vol II (1955)

Columbia Encyclopedia (1956)

Who's Who in America, 1960-61

World Biography (1954)

ROBERTS, (GRANVILLE) ORAL, REV.

Jan. 24, 1918- Evangelist; publisher

Address: b. Oral Roberts Evangelistic Association, 1720 S. Boulder Ave., Tulsa, Okla.; h. 2513 E. 38th St., Tulsa, Okla.

Through his Million Soul Crusades in the United States, Australia, South Africa, and other countries—as well as his far-reaching radio, television, and publishing activities—the Reverend Oral Roberts, a preacher of the Pentecostal Holiness Church, has become one of the best-known evangelists in the world. Because of what his critics calls his "high-pressure tactics" and because of the important place given to healing in his ministry, he is also one of America's most controversial revivalists. Often referred to as a faith healer, Roberts repudiates the designation. He declares that he himself has no power to heal and that he simply prays for the sick with faith that God will heal. He is the president of a well-organized enterprise, the Oral Roberts Evangelistic Association, Inc., which he founded in Tulsa, Oklahoma in 1948.

Granville Oral Roberts, the youngest of five children of Ellis Melvin and Claudius Priscilla (Irwin) Roberts, was born on January 24, 1918 in the backwoods about twelve miles from Ada, Oklahoma. On his mother's side he descends from Cherokee Indians. His father was a Pentecostal preacher who held revival meetings in towns along the pioneer trails of Oklahoma. One of Oral Roberts' sisters, Velma, died in childhood; he has another sister, now Mrs. Jewel Faust, and two brothers, Elmer and Vaden Roberts.

Childhood for Roberts was an ordeal of poverty and poor health. When he was twelve years old, the family moved to Ada, where he attended high school. A tall and gangling boy interested in sports, he played basketball for a time in school. Illness prevented him from finishing his high school education, but he was awarded a diploma in 1946. As he has related in his autobiography, *Life Story* (published by Oral Roberts in 1955), at sixteen he seemed to have reached the end of an unhappy life, afflicted by shyness, stuttering, and tuberculosis in both lungs.

Prayer with his father prepared him for what he regards as his salvation. This occurred when he was taken to see the Reverend George Moncey, an evangelist who had pitched his tent in Ada. Convinced that he was cured in answer to prayer, in 1935 Oral Roberts felt called to the ministry, particularly to tell the story of the healing power of Christ.

During the next twelve years he served in general evangelistic work and as pastor of churches in Enid and Shawnee, Oklahoma, in Toccoa, Georgia, and Fuquay Springs, North Carolina. His Pentecostal Holiness Church is a fundamentalist sect of some 2,000,000 members, concentrated mainly in Oklahoma, Georgia, and the Carolinas. In 1943, 1944, and 1945 he took courses at Oklahoma Baptist University in Shawnee; he has also attended Phillips University in Enid, which is under the control of the Disciples of Christ.

Several times during his life, according to Roberts, God has spoken audibly to him. One occasion was in 1947 when he felt that God's power to heal had been transmitted to him to take to others who had faith. In order to reach as many people as possible he decided to become a traveling evangelist and he began his mission in Tulsa. Reports of conversions and healings at his nine-week meeting there spread to other states. Roberts was soon conducting revivals in various parts of the country—generally under the sponsorship of local Pentecostal preachers, although Roberts calls his ministry nondenominational.

By 1955 Roberts required eight truck trailers to carry his $240,000 worth of campaign equipment on his crusades across the United States. His eight-pole canvas "cathedral tent," the largest in the world, seats 14,000 people. In 1948 he had established a nonprofit organization in Tulsa called Healing Waters, Inc., which became the Oral Roberts Evangelistic Association, Inc. Within eight years his enterprise had acquired a book value of $1,250,000 and during 1955 had received contributions totaling $3,000,000.

More than 450 people are now employed at the association's Abundant Life Building headquarters in Tulsa. Besides handling Roberts' campaigns and correspondence, the organization operates a large publishing and distributing program. Roberts' first publication was *Healing Waters,* which he began in 1947. It is now called *Abundant Life* and has a circulation of about 1,000,000. Other monthly publications of the organization are *Daily Blessing* and *Oral Roberts' True Stories,* a children's color cartoon book. It publishes at the rate of 25,000,000 or more pieces of literature annually and circulates tracts, pamphlets, and publications of various kinds in 115 languages. One of the projects in Roberts' "Outreach for the World" plan is the distribution of Hebrew-language Bibles in Israel.

Oral Roberts has written eight books, including *If You Need Healing, Do these Things* (1952); *God's Formula for Success and Prosperity* (1956, with G. H. Montgomery), and *Faith Against Life's Storms* (1957). These books were published either by Roberts or his organization. *Deliverance from Fear and from Sickness* (1954) was also published by Doubleday and Company, and his recent *God is a Good God* (1960) was published by Bobbs-Merrill Company.

Through his programs on hundreds of radio stations Roberts reaches about 95 per cent of the American audience, and since 1957 he has made short-wave broadcasts to Russia. His television programs, which he began in 1955, are seen on 150 or more stations in the United States, Canada, Mexico, Hawaii, and the Philippines. His organization spends over $1,000,000 a year for broadcasting time.

Roberts' use of the influential medium of television has increased the controversy centering around him. The programs consist of edited films of his crusades. Divided into two parts, they begin with a sermon in which Roberts seeks to strengthen faith in Christ as the Savior. In preparation for the second part, devoted to faith healing, he declares that he has no conflict with medical science. He often says, "God heals—I don't."

Many thousands of persons have maintained that through prayer Roberts has cured them of all types of physical ailments. His TV programs have been criticized for not showing the occasions when his ministrations have been unsuccessful. Some objection has also been made to his failure to keep medical files that would prove that organic changes had resulted from

REV. ORAL ROBERTS

purported healings. "Nobody knows," W. E. Mann wrote in *Christian Century* (September 5, 1956), "how many of the apparent cures are simply the result of mass suggestion and . . . psychological shock."

An intense and impassioned preacher, Brother Roberts undoubtedly owes to his oratorical skill much of his success in drawing huge audiences, usually well over 10,000. During his crusades he writes his sermons just before each meeting. "I become anointed with God's word," he has said (*Coronet,* October 1955), "and the spirit of the Lord builds up in me like a coiled spring. By the time I'm ready to go on, my mind is razor-sharp. I know exactly what I'm going to say and I'm feeling like a lion."

When Roberts hears himself criticized for commercialism or called a "supersalesman" of religion, he answers that he wants to apply every promotional device he knows to bring God to all people. W. E. Mann suggests that "perhaps Roberts' role is to mobilize faith in a loving and healing God among the unlearned masses." One of Roberts' weaknesses, Mann believes, is that he preaches a salvation that is "largely divorced from any social ethic and is thoroughly puritan in morality." But, he concludes, "anyway one looks at it, Oral Roberts is a figure to reckon with in America's religious life today" (*Christian Century,* September 5, 1956).

One of the six directors of the Oral Roberts Evangelistic Association is Roberts' wife, the former Evelyn Lutman, to whom he was married on December 25, 1938. She was a teacher before her marriage and has since been a partner in her husband's religious work. Their children are Rebecca Ann, Ronald David, Richard Lee, and Roberta Jean. The black-haired, blue-eyed evangelist stands six feet one inch tall and weighs 185 pounds. He is a Democrat and through his association participates in many

ROBERTS, ORAL, REV.—*Continued*

civic enterprises such as those sponsored by the Red Cross and YMCA.

In keeping with his Pentecostal background, he leads a somewhat austere private life, for the most part disapproving of the theater, dances, circuses, and the use of cosmetics and alcohol. Western stories are his favorite reading; he enjoys horseback riding and raises Aberdeen Angus cattle on his 240-acre Robin Hood farm south of Tulsa. He also plays golf and belongs to the Tulsa Country Club. He rejects the idea that religious people should be poor, and during his Australian crusade when newspapers disclosed that he was registered in a luxury hotel, he reportedly replied, "Christ has no objection to prosperity."

References

> Am Mag 161:21+ My '56 por
> Coronet 38:52+ O '55 por
> Life 30:73+ My 7 '51 por
> Time 66:41+ Jl 11 '55 por
> Roberts, Oral Life Story (1955)

ROBERTS, WALTER ORR Aug. 20, 1915-
Astronomer; physicist

Address: b. High Altitude Observatory, Boulder, Colo.; h. 1829 Bluebell Ave., Boulder, Colo.

The director of the National Center for Atmospheric Research since June 1960 has been Walter Orr Roberts. He is professor and chairman of the department of astro-geophysics at the University of Colorado and director of its High Altitude Observatory, acknowledged as one of the world's foremost institutions for solar observation. His assignment is to establish a research foundation that, by collaborating closely with university scientists, will stimulate them and help them to expand their efforts in the atmospheric sciences.

Dr. Roberts is an expert in the spectroscopic analysis of the corona and its prominences with the coronagraph, the huge "sun telescope" housed at the High Altitude Observatory in Boulder. He was one of the leaders of the American scientific effort during the International Geophysical Year, and he has written and lectured widely in the field of solar activity and its relationship to earthly weather phenomena.

Born in West Bridgewater, Massachusetts on August 20, 1915, Walter Orr Roberts is one of the three children of Ernest Marion Roberts and the former Alice Elliot Orr. His father was a farmer and a teacher. Roberts grew up on a farm near Brockton, Massachusetts and attended the local high school, from which he was graduated in 1934. He entered Amherst College, Massachusetts, joined the track team, and was undergraduate chairman of Fraternity Business Management. When he took his B.A. degree in 1938 he was awarded the Bancroft Prize in astronomy and the John Woodruff Simpson Fellowship for advanced study.

Roberts did graduate work at Harvard University and received his M.A. degree in 1940. In the same year he was appointed supervisor of the newly completed Harvard Observatory at Climax Station, Colorado, where astronomers had installed a coronagraph, one of three in the world. A boon to astronomical research, the instrument has a circular disc and produces artificial eclipses of the sun.

For his significant studies of the sun's activity, Walter Orr Roberts earned a Ph.D. degree from Harvard University in 1943. Three years later, when Climax Station was reorganized under the joint sponsorship of Harvard and the University of Colorado and renamed the High Altitude Observatory, Roberts was made its superintendent. During World War II he reported regularly from Colorado to Washington on solar disturbances that might interfere with short-wave radio communications. His vigilance helped the armed forces to make the most efficient use of their communication facilities. His military research provided the basis for his prediction that future world events (possibly even a war) might be gauged according to favorable sun-spot activity. He told the American Astronomical Society in 1946 that "the earth's gaseous envelope is responsible... for our weather vagaries and our ability to communicate over long distances by radio," and established a theoretical relationship between disturbances on the sun and the course of the earth's weather.

During the academic year 1947-48 Dr. Roberts was invited to teach at Harvard University and Radcliffe College. When he returned to Colorado in 1948 he established the research center and laboratory of the High Altitude Observatory. Three years later Dr. Roberts announced the construction of the "Big Eye," the world's largest coronagraph.

These exact instruments enabled Roberts and his staff to verify their hypotheses, and in 1953 they presented a radical concept of the corona to scientists of the American Astronomical Society. They explained the appearance of the corona and proposed "that it is spasmodically replenished by the infusion of gas from sunspot regions on the sun's surface." These observations of the sun and Dr. Roberts' theory that the corona affects the upper circulation of air and the wind flow were checked during the total eclipse that occurred in June 1955.

Working in conjunction with Dr. Robert J. Low, a staff astronomer, Dr. Roberts presented evidence in 1955 suggesting that sudden weather changes on earth were produced by "invisible but potent barrages of solar radiation that did not quite reach the earth." The variations produced in the upper atmosphere were held responsible for the big weather shifts on earth, though the scientists were not able to explain how these bursts influenced the lower atmosphere where the weather is produced.

The High Altitude Observatory ended its affiliation with Harvard University in 1955 and became a research institute of the University of Colorado. In 1956 Dr. Roberts announced the establishment of an institute for solar-terrestrial research to examine the relationship between the sun's states and the earth's weather. Roberts hoped that enough information would be collected to permit long-range weather forecasting for the use of the general public, business firms, farmers, and the airlines.

As chairman of the solar activities panel of the United States national committee for the International Geophysical Year, Dr. Roberts studied daily reports of the sun's activity. He offered an hypothesis establishing a link between solar flares, which are eruptions on the sun's surface, and magnetic storms in the earth's upper atmosphere. The effects of these storms on earthly weather phenomena include disturbances in the earth's magnetic field, the transmission of radio waves, and the appearance of the aurora borealis. Dr. Roberts made it clear that his evidence was inconclusive and that the manner in which these solar bursts affected weather conditions was unknown. Although many scientists support Dr. Roberts, his thesis was not sustained by observation during one period of heavy sunspot activity. In March 1958 Dr. Roberts' team reported an extraordinarily large number of flares, without the expected sudden radical changes in the weather.

When the United States government decided to create a research center to spur an investigation of the earth's weather, Dr. Walter Orr Roberts was selected as the director. The university corporation on atmospheric research, which is composed of fourteen member universities, was granted $50,000,000 to establish the center. Dr. Roberts' vision of the center "is that it will attract the most intelligent and best-trained people from virtually every branch of natural science . . . and that it remain primarily in an inspirational and coordinating role, sparking germinal research programs at the many institutions with which it is to work, and weaving the results into the grand pattern of furthering all human knowledge about the atmosphere."

Numerous articles by Dr. Roberts on the sun's activity and the solar-terrestrial relationship have appeared in domestic and foreign journals. He has also contributed chapters to *The Sun* (University of Chicago Press, 1953) and *Vistas in Astronautics* (Pergamon Press, 1958). Roberts is a member of the editorial boards of *Journal of Planetary and Space Physics* and the *Journal of Geophysical Research*.

Dr. Roberts is a Fellow of the American Association for the Advancement of Science and the Royal Astronomical Society. His memberships include the American Astronomical Society, International Astronomical Union, and the American Meteorological Society, of which he is a councilor. He is chairman of both the Colorado Weather Control Commission and the advisory panel for atmospheric sciences of the National Science Foundation. He is also a member of the advisory committee on grants of the Research Corporation and a trustee of the MITRE corporation. An honorary D.Sc. degree was conferred on Professor Roberts by Ripon College (1958) and by Amherst (1959) and he served as Sigma Xi lecturer-in-residence from 1951 to 1953.

WALTER ORR ROBERTS

Brown-haired, brown-eyed Walter Roberts is five feet eight inches tall and weighs 145 pounds. His medium build belies his vigor and exuberant energy, for the professor bicycles the half mile between office and home daily. He is an enthusiastic trout fisherman, tennis player, and skier. Dr. Roberts enjoys music, and he and his wife hold open house on Sundays for friends to listen to records.

Mrs. Roberts, the former Janet Smock, was a student at Wheaton College when she was introduced to the scientist by his mother. They were married on June 8, 1940 and are the parents of four children, ranging in age from nine to seventeen: David, Alan, Jennifer, and Jonathan. Roberts is an independent in politics and attends the Congregational Christian Church. Walter Roberts considers himself more the individualist than the organization man, preferring to keep close contact with his staff. He completes his administrative tasks during formal office hours and then usually remains late into the night to concentrate on "his more creative and contemplative work."

References

N Y Times p4 Je 27 '60 por

American Men of Science vol I (1955)
Who's Who in America, 1960-61

ROBERTSON, REUBEN B(UCK), JR.
June 27, 1908-Mar. 13, 1960 President of the Champion Paper and Fiber Company of Hamilton, Ohio (since 1950); United States Deputy Secretary of Defense (1955-57). See *Current Biography* (December) 1955.

Obituary
N Y Times p10 Mr 14 '60

ROCKEFELLER, JOHN D(AVISON), JR.

Jan. 29, 1874-May 11, 1960 Philanthropist; with his father made gifts of more than $1 billion; made possible Rockefeller Center and United Nations site in New York and restoration of Williamsburg, Virginia, among many other projects. See *Current Biography* (July) 1941.

Obituary

N Y Times p1+ My 12 '60

ROEBLING, MARY G(INDHART)

July 29, 1906- Banker

Address: b. 28 W. State St., Trenton, N.J.; h. 27 W. State St., Trenton, N.J.

Equally at ease in the worlds of high fashion and high finance, Mary G. Roebling has been president of the Trenton (New Jersey) Trust Company since 1937 and a governor of the American Stock Exchange since 1958. Mrs. Roebling is a glamorous widow who wears dresses by Dior and hats by Mr. John and would rather be late for a business conference than be caught wearing the wrong shade of lipstick. The only woman who heads a major American bank and the first woman to hold a policy-making position on any major stock exchange, Mrs. Roebling believes that any woman ". . . who wants to make her mark in business must make men forget she's a woman between nine and five, and must make them remember she's a woman for the balance of her waking hours."

Mary G. Roebling was born Mary Gindhart in West Collingswood, New Jersey, on July 29, 1906, the daughter of Isaac D. Gindhart, Jr., a telephone company official, and Mary W. (Simon) Gindhart, a music teacher. Raised in her native state, in modest though comfortable circumstances, she attended public elementary schools and Moorestown High School. After school the future "first lady of finance" sometimes picked strawberries at a penny a box, the entire proceeds of an afternoon's work, often as much as twenty-five cents, going toward the purchase of dill pickles. She also taught Methodist Sunday School.

While still in her teens, Mary Gindhart was married to Arthur Herbert, a great-nephew of the composer, Victor Herbert, but within three years she was left a widow with an infant daughter to support. Taking a job as secretary in a Philadelphia brokerage firm, she studied finance at night at the University of Pennsylvania with the object of working her way up to a position as customer's woman. She attained her ambition and stayed on the job until the day before her marriage to Siegfried Roebling, a great-grandson of the man who designed the Brooklyn Bridge and a successful banker and steel cable industrialist. Again her marriage was unhappily cut short and in 1936, soon after the birth of a son, she was left a widow for the second time in eight years.

Although this time it was not necessary to go back to work, Mary Roebling was not content to remain idle. Among the investments left to her by her husband was a controlling interest in the Trenton Trust Company. Determined to rescue the bank from its then shaky position, she became its president in 1937 and chairman of its board in 1941. Aware that her brief investment background had not sufficiently prepared her to assume these responsibilities, she took courses in banking and finance at New York University for six years and had herself privately tutored in law.

This solid background of financial training, combined with a highly feminine and personal touch, has produced an approach to banking which has not always been orthodox, but which has certainly been successful. In the years under her leadership the assets of Trenton Trust have climbed from $17,000,000 to more than $90,000,000 and by 1957 the number of depositors had increased by 300 per cent.

Although the eye she casts down a balance sheet may be as shrewd and appraising as any competitor's, Mrs. Roebling believes that banking can be glamorous and that money can be merchandised with as much skill as anything else. Applying these theories, she was the first banker to hold "financial teas" to introduce wealthy women to the advantage of trust funds, has turned board rooms over to women's clubs for their meetings, and has sponsored art shows and displays of customers' merchandise at her bank. Long before other banks featured giveaways and gimmicks, Trenton Trust, under her guidance, was employing professional window dressers, playing special music at Christmas, and distributing 50,000 pots of shamrock on St. Patrick's day. It was also one of the first banks to have a sidewalk deposit box.

Mary G., as she is sometimes called, finds the personal approach a professional asset. She is often described as a "politician-banker," probably because of her wide acquaintance with government figures, businessmen, and just plain people. She employs a full-time public relations man to handle her personal publicity and recently was named "the most publicized woman in the state" by the New Jersey Association of Newspaper Women.

In 1958 Mary Roebling received what she has called "possibly the most outstanding appointment I have had since becoming president of Trenton Trust" when she was elected the first woman governor of the American Stock Exchange. As one of the three public members, i.e., those not connected with the Wall Street community, of the thirty-one-man board of governors, her function is to report public reaction and thought to the board. In announcing Mrs. Roebling's appointment, Edward T. McCormick, president of the Exchange, said she had been selected "first, because of her stature and executive ability in the business field and secondly because she is a woman."

The second reason probably pleased Mrs. Roebling as much as the first, for she is an ardent feminist. She believes the world of banking and finance is wide open for women who can "think straight, reason correctly, and don't make clerical errors," and in accordance with these views, employs only women tellers at the main branch of Trenton Trust. So often has she advocated the nomination of a woman for Vice-President of the United States that admirers have proposed that she be named for the position. Mrs. Roebling is a Republican.

Although the Vice-Presidency of the United States has not yet come her way, Mrs. Roebling has held numerous offices in government, business, civic, and cultural organizations. In addition to her dual position at Trenton Trust, she is president and director of Wings, Inc., and of the Fleron Supply Company. She is also a director of Colonial Operating Company, Standard Fire Insurance Company, and of Walker-Gordon Laboratory Company.

Concerned with her community and her country, she is chairman of the Trenton Parking Authority and was formerly a member of the New Jersey State Unemployment Commission. She is also an emeritus member of the United States Defense Department's advisory committee on women in the services and vice-president and life member of the National Defense Transportation Association.

World-conscious as well, she is a member of the board of the International Rescue Committee and attended the White House Conference on the Refugee Problem. She was one of 100 American delegates to the Atlantic Congress of NATO, the purpose of which was to enlarge the activities and increase the understanding of the North Atlantic Treaty Organization. In 1956 she was the only woman delegate from the United States to the International Chamber of Commerce meeting in Tokyo and the following year, as a good will gesture, she entertained officially for the Japanese delegation to the United Nations. She is a trustee of the United States Council of the International Chamber of Commerce and, in April 1959, was chairman of women's activities for the Chamber's seventeenth congress held in Washington, D. C.

A founder and director of the American Women's Council, Mrs. Roebling is also a director of Girls' Clubs of America and of the Statue of Liberty Society and a trustee of Russell Sage College. Locally, she is a member of the board of governors of the Delaware Valley Council and belongs to the Trenton Chamber of Commerce. She is also a director of McKinley and Trenton General hospitals and the honorary chairman and founder of the women's committee of Donnelly Memorial Hospital.

Interested in music and in art, the indefatigable Mrs. Roebling is a member of the national council of the Metropolitan Opera Association and a trustee of the Columbus Boychoir and Westminster Choir schools. She is also president of the Greater Trenton Symphony Association and a member of the National Federation of Music Clubs and of the Philadelphia Museum of Art. A member of the national lay committee of Churches of Christ in the United States, she also belongs to the New Jersey Conference of Christians and Jews. She is also a member of the League of Women Voters and the ladies auxiliary of the American Legion.

Tracing her American ancestry back to the seventeenth century, Mrs. Roebling belongs to the Daughters of the American Revolution, the

Wide World

MARY G. ROEBLING

Daughters of Founders and Patriots, the Society of Mayflower Descendants, the Colonial Daughters of the Seventeenth Century, the Swedish Colonial Society, and the Genealogical Society of Pennsylvania. Professionally, she is a member of the American Institute of Banking and the American Bankers Association and belongs to numerous business and professional women's clubs. Her social clubs are the Zonta, Trenton Country, Lake Placid, Sea View Country, Huntington Valley Country, and Contemporary.

For her various achievements, Mary G. Roebling was honored by Ithaca College with an LL.D. and by Bryant College with an honorary D.Sc. in business administration. The city of Trenton declared a "Mary Roebling Day" in 1959 and she has had three flowers—a dahlia, a rose, and an orchid—named in her honor. She was interviewed by Edward R. Murrow on his *Person to Person* television show. Her jewel collection so impressed three viewers that they broke into her Trenton hotel suite and stole $375,000 worth of gems and furs. (They were apprehended the same day.)

In 1959 Mrs. Roebling built a luxurious home in the heart of downtown Trenton. Wedged between an optometrist's shop and a men's clothing store (and only seconds away from her office at Trenton Trust), it has been called "perhaps the only two-bedroom house in the country which cost upward of $500,000 to build." Furnished in an elaborate Louis XVI and Empire style, the house features a dining room that seats thirty-six, an oval bedroom, and a twenty-by-fifty-five-foot indoor swimming pool. It abounds with such special touches as twenty-three-carat gold sink fixtures, Picassos in the powder room, and Roman statuary around the pool. Mrs. Roebling also maintains an apartment in New York.

A tall (five feet seven inches) redhead with green eyes, Mary G. Roebling has been de-

ROEBLING, MARY G.—*Continued*

scribed as "sturdy, imposing, handsome." Named "best dressed banking woman" in 1958, she buys from Dior, Chanel, and Balenciaga when she goes abroad, but says her most successful fashions in recent years have been by American designers. In 1957 she was included among "America's Ten Richest Women" by the *Ladies' Home Journal,* which estimated her personal fortune somewhere between $125,000,000 and $200,000,000. Fittingly, she owns a silver Rolls Royce.

Mrs. Roebling's son Paul, who is a talented actor, partly designed and decorated her town house. Her daughter Elizabeth (Mrs. Andrew K. Dutch 3d) is the mother of four children. Mrs. Roebling's hobbies are playing golf and tennis and collecting old glass and silver, but she has said, "My job is my boss," and added: "I would honestly rather curl up with the *Wall Street Journal* or a good financial statement than any novel."

References

Christian Sci Mon p10 D 17 '59 por
Ladies Home J 174:60+ S '57 por
Nat Bsns Woman 38:7 O '59
Sat Eve Post 232:23+ My 21 '60 por
Business Executives of America (1950)
Who's Who in America, 1960-61

ROGERS, EDITH NOURSE Mar. 19, 1881-Sept. 10, 1960 United States Representative from Massachusetts since 1925; Republican; served in Congress longer than any other woman. See *Current Biography* (April) 1942.

Obituary

N Y Times p82 S 11 '60

ROGERS, PAUL Mar. 22, 1917- Actor

Address: b. c/o Music Corporation of America, 598 Madison Ave., New York 22

So skilled is his mastery of make-up, so complete his self-effacement in the roles he plays that a London critic once predicted of Paul Rogers that one evening he would walk on to the stage of the Old Vic looking like himself and not be recognized by anyone. Rogers is as convincing in his interpretation of the lecherous Pandarus in *Troilus and Cressida* as in his portrayal of the austere Lord Claverton in T. S. Eliot's *The Elder Statesman.* Groomed for stardom almost exclusively at the Old Vic, both in Bristol and in London, Rogers achieved top billing in England for his performances as Shylock, Cassius, Henry VIII, and Macbeth in the Shakespearean repertory. To these, he annexed brilliant portrayals of John of Gaunt, Mercutio, and Pandarus at New York's Winter Garden Theatre in the season of 1956-57.

Paul Rogers was born on March 22, 1917 in Plympton, Devon, England, the only child of Edwin Rogers, the headmaster of Newton Abbot Grammar School, and Dulcie Myrtle (Collier) Rogers. He was engaged by the West Regional Broadcasting Company to do his first

professional acting while still a student at the school which his father headed. At the age of nineteen he was graduated.

The year of his graduation Rogers was recommended to Michael Chekhov, former student of Stanislavski and nephew of Anton Chekhov; for three years he studied at the Chekhov Theatre Studio in Dartington, Devon. In 1938 he made his stage debut, at the Scala Theatre, as Charles Dickens in *Bird's Eye of Valour.* Shortly afterwards, Ben Iden Payne, then the director of the Stratford-on-Avon Shakespeare Memorial Theatre, hired Rogers as assistant stage manager and bit player. But Rogers did not long remain with Payne's group. He soon became a member of the Colchester Repertory Theatre, where he performed in *Othello, Payment Deferred, Eden End, Laburnum Grove, They Walk Alone, Outward Bound,* and *Billeted.*

His acting career was interrupted by military service during World War II. Beginning in 1940 as an ordinary signalman, Rogers was a crew member of destroyers in the North Sea and of small motor launches in the English Channel. When he was discharged in 1946 he had attained the rank of lieutenant in the Royal Naval Volunteer Reserve. Resuming his association with the Colchester Repertory Company, he was given the opportunity to play in *Romeo and Juliet, The Apple Cart, The Wind of Heaven, House of Regrets,* and other dramas. His next appearance was on the West End stage in London in *Tess of the D'Urbervilles* at the Piccadilly Theatre.

In September 1947, at the Theatre Royal in King Street, Bristol, Rogers began the association with the Old Vic that was to lead to stardom. For two years, as a member of the Bristol Old Vic Company, he played, among other roles, Roderigo in *Othello,* Polonius in *Hamlet,* Sir George Orreyed in *The Second Mrs. Tanqueray,* and Judge Brack in *Hedda Gabler.*

Rogers had the first important showcase for his talents when he was invited by Hugh Hunt to act with the Old Vic Company in London for the 1949-50 season. When he appeared as Don Adriano de Armado in *Love's Labour's Lost,* Lionel Hale wrote in *The Old Vic, 1949-50*: "The performance was as fine as anything in the season, and our hope for Mr. Paul Rogers will now run very high. He automatically suggests himself for many great Shakespearean parts."

In his first three years with the London Old Vic Company, Rogers was cast in a wide range of parts: Hardcastle in *She Stoops to Conquer,* First Player and Osric in *Hamlet,* Malvolio in *Twelfth Night,* Troubleall in *Bartholomew Fair,* the Greek tyrant Aegisthus in Sophocles' *Electra,* the old and deaf naval captain in Chekhov's *The Wedding,* and the French physician in *The Merry Wives of Windsor.* For his interpretation of old William Villon, the loyal and compassionate protector of François Villon, in James Forsyth's *The Other Heart* in 1952, Rogers received the Clarence Derwent Award for the best supporting actor.

When, in 1952, the second company of the Old Vic toured Rhodesia and the Union of South Africa, Rogers played Iago in *Othello,* endowing the schemer with great charm to make his malice and cunning more effective. In addition to playing Iago, he repeated the role of William Villon and played Bottom in *A Midsummer Night's Dream* and the Third Witch and Third Murderer in *Macbeth*.

With his first performance of Shylock in *The Merchant of Venice* in January 1953, Paul Rogers scored a triumph. Rejecting the interpretations that make Shylock a comic butt or a hounded victim, Rogers sees Shylock as a villain who is at the same time a human being. T. C. Worsley commented: "Rogers made a magnificent Jew throughout, dominating and in his pride of race, scornful, biting, on the attack."

Hard upon his Shylock, in the Old Vic *Julius Caesar* on February 24, 1953, Rogers gave a performance of Cassius that "thrust like a blade." He not only emphasized Cassius' irascibility, but his warmth and devotion to Brutus. He reached the peak of his 1952-53 season with his performance of the title role in *Henry VIII* on May 6, 1953. As the Tudor king who pines for an heir, Rogers won accolades from the critics, who saw in him a worthy successor to Sir Laurence Olivier and Sir John Gielgud.

A few months later Rogers was asked to play a very different role: that of Sir Claude Mulhammer in T. S. Eliot's *The Confidential Clerk*. The production was so successful at the Edinburgh Festival that it was moved to London on September 16, 1953 and ran there until April 1954.

Rogers returned to the Old Vic in the fall of 1954. After an introductory performance at the Edinburgh Festival the preceding August, Rogers repeated his portrayal of Macbeth on September 9 at the Old Vic theatre. "His Macbeth had vision and a kind of full-orchestra music, as well as subtlety of characterization and classical power," wrote Audrey Williamson (*Old Vic Drama, 1947-57*). He also added to his repertory Petruchio in *The Taming of the Shrew*, Touchstone in *As You Like It*, Sir John Falstaff in *Henry IV*, Parts I and II, and *The Merry Wives of Windsor*, and Leontes in *The Winter's Tale*.

On his first tour of the United States in 1956-57, Rogers was seen in four Shakespearean roles with the Old Vic company. As Macbeth, John of Gaunt in *Richard II*, Mercutio in *Romeo and Juliet*, and Pandarus in *Troilus and Cressida*, he again proved his ability to excite an audience. A typical critical reaction was that of Robert Coleman in the New York *Mirror*: "The performance of the evening was Paul Rogers' Mercutio. It was amazing to see an actor who had beautifully impersonated the aged John of Gaunt on the previous evening dominate the same stage as the dashing, youthful, vital victim of a feud."

In August of 1958 Rogers was chosen to play the leading role of Lord Claverton, in the world première of T. S. Eliot's *The Elder Statesman* at the Edinburgh Festival. This was one of his few appearances outside the Old Vic, for Rogers continues with the company, one of the few star actors made and developed almost

PAUL ROGERS

entirely within the framework of this British theatrical institution. His other than stage activities include radio and televison programs and work in such films as *Beau Brummel, The Beachcomber,* and *Svengali*.

Paul Rogers is a master of make-up who has appeared in many character disguises. He admits, wrote Anthony Merryn in the London *Stage,* that "he was born with a face too plain for a juvenile lead, a tragedian's nose and a Falstaffian laugh." He is five feet eleven inches in height, weighs about 168 pounds, and has brown hair and hazel eyes.

Married since July 7, 1955 to actress Rosalind Boxall, Paul Rogers is the father of a daughter, Lucy. In religion he is affiliated with the Church of England. He is a member of British Actors' Equity. His favorite recreations are swimming, walking, painting, and attending movies, and his favorite roles are Iago, Bottom, Shylock, and Don Adriano de Armado.

References

Who's Who in the Theatre (1957)
Williamson, A. Paul Rogers (1956)

ROMAN, NANCY G(RACE) May 16, 1925-
Astronomer

Address: b. National Aeronautics and Space Administration, 1520 H St., N.W., Washington 25, D.C.; h. 940 25th St., N.W., Washington 7, D.C.

Studying the Milky Way and the island universe by using satellites and other equipment of the space age is the special concern of Dr. Nancy G. Roman. Since February 1960 she has been chief of the astronomy and astrophysics satellite and sounding rocket program of the National Aeronautics and Space Administration. Dr. Roman is responsible for planning the co-ordination and supervision of vehicle launchings

NANCY G. ROMAN

After she received her B.A. degree in 1946, Miss Roman decided to make her career in astronomy. She was especially interested in the subject and realized that her ability lay in science. She enrolled in the University of Chicago for graduate work, and from 1946 to 1948 she was an assistant at the university's Yerkes Observatory in Williams Bay, Wisconsin. She wrote her thesis on Ursa Major, the most conspicuous of the northern constellations, which includes the Big Dipper. It was published in the *Astrophysical Journal* in September 1949. Miss Roman received her Ph.D. degree in 1949.

During the summer of 1949 Dr. Roman worked as a research associate with the Warner and Swasey Observatory of the Case Institute of Technology in Cleveland, Ohio, preparing a catalogue of high-luminosity objects and classifying objective prism spectra. In the fall she returned to the Yerkes Observatory, where she served first as a research associate and later as an instructor in stellar astronomy. There she taught a one-quarter course each year, conducted a home-study course in elementary astronomy, and supervised graduate students and visiting astronomers.

While at the observatory she carried out independent optical studies in stellar astronomy and galactic structure, with emphasis on radial velocity measurements, spectral classification, and photoelectric photometry. Her special fields of interest were clusters and stellar populations.

Deciding that a woman had greater opportunity in government service, she accepted a position with the radio astronomy branch of the United States Naval Research Laboratory in Washington, D.C. She held the title of physicist from 1955 to 1956 and then the title of astronomer from 1956 to 1958 as head of the microwave spectroscopy section.

Conducting research in galactic structure in both the radio and optical region, she concentrated on the spectra of radio stars, galactic distribution of radio emission, and radar measurement of the distance to the moon. She also was responsible for giving astronomical and radio astronomical information to other scientists in her branch. For her work she used a giant cast-aluminum mirror that had a fifty-foot span. In 1958-59 she was an astronomer (consultant) at the Naval Research Laboratory. In addition to continuing her other duties, she participated in the planning of branch programs and helped in branch projects like the lunar-dynamics problem.

"We are trying now to understand how stars are formed, how they age, their size, temperature, constitution," she told Harriet B. Blackburn (*Christian Science Monitor*, June 13, 1957) in explaining her work at the Naval Research Laboratory. "We know that thermonuclear reactions keep them too hot for living beings, but there is much more to know. Sometimes one works for weeks and months—even years—doing painstaking research without coming to any very important conclusions. Then, one day, all the computations made fit together, making a clear picture, and results are significant."

designed for astronomical observation. By obtaining unobstructed views of the heavens, scientists hope to gain information about the nature of the canals on Mars, the surface and atmosphere of planets, and the existence of solar systems other than ours.

Dr. Roman is an astronomer who received her doctorate from the University of Chicago in 1949. She remained with the university and its Yerkes Observatory, doing research and teaching, until 1955, when she joined the staff of the United States Naval Research Laboratory in Washington, D.C. She continued her research in optical and radio astronomy, particularly in spectral classifications and stellar motions, both there and at the National Aeronautics and Space Administration, with which she became affiliated in 1959. She has written many scientific articles and has attended such international astronomical conferences as the ones held in Soviet Armenia in 1956, in Sweden in 1957, and in Belgium in 1960.

Nancy Grace Roman, the only child of Irwin and Georgia Frances (Smith) Roman, was born in Nashville, Tennessee on May 16, 1925. Her father is a geophysicist who became associated with the United States Geological Survey in 1935. At the Western High School in Baltimore, Maryland, she took part in such extracurricular activities as sports and the Latin, French, and mathematics clubs.

Graduated from high school in 1943, she entered Swarthmore College, where she majored in astronomy and served as an assistant at the Sproul Observatory. Miss Roman was called a "wizard in math" by her contemporaries and was awarded the Joshua Lippincott Memorial Fellowship. The papers she wrote are still remembered as models of excellence by Dr. P. van de Kamp, head of Swarthmore's astronomy department. She also found time for such extracurricular activities as the outing club and the folk dance club.

In March 1959 Dr. Roman was named the head of the observational astronomy program of the office of space flight development of the newly organized National Aeronautics and Space Administration. There, she was responsible for the planning, co-ordinating, and instituting of a program of astronomical observations conducted in outer space by using rockets and satellites. This included plans for exploration of all the regions of the electromagnetic spectrum as well as projects on orbiting astronomical observation, orbiting radio astronomy, and gamma ray astronomy.

In February 1960 Dr. Roman was appointed the chief of astronomy and astrophysics in the office of satellites and sounding rockets of the National Aeronautics and Space Administration. Her duties with the agency include program planning for the co-ordination and supervision of rocket and satellite astronomy. She has announced that the NASA has decided to launch two satellite structures: the first is designed for solar research and will be sent aloft within a year. The second, which is larger and more complex, will be used for either solar or stellar experiments beginning probably in 1963.

Carrying payloads with astronomical telescopes, the satellites will be put into orbit about 500 miles into space, above the drag of the earth's atmosphere and below the Van Allen radiation belt. They will be used to increase man's knowledge about the surface and atmosphere of the planets, the nature of the canals on Mars, and many other questions concerning the various galaxies and the upper air. Astronomers hope that the program will culminate eventually in establishing an observatory on the moon.

Nancy G. Roman is a member of the American Astronomical Society, International Astronomical Union, Royal Astronomical Society, Astronomical Society of the Pacific, International Scientific Radio Union, Scientific Research Society of America, and American Association of University Women. Many of her papers have appeared in such scientific periodicals as the *Astrophysical Journal* and the *Astronomical Journal*. She is the editor of *Comparison of the Large-scale Structure of the Galactic System with that of other Stellar Systems* (Cambridge University Press, 1958), Symposium Number Five of the International Astronomical Union.

The astronomer has gray-green eyes and brown hair; she is five feet five inches tall and weighs 155 pounds. For recreation she enjoys swimming, photography, stamp collecting, cooking, and sewing. She weaves fabrics for her apartment on a hand loom. She belongs to a literary group and has taken advantage of early morning courses on television to acquire a working knowledge of shorthand and Russian.

References

Christian Sci Mon p4 Jl 18 '60
American Men of Science vol 1 (1955)

ROSENTHAL, A(BRAHAM) M(I-CHAEL) May 2, 1922- Journalist

Address: b. Palais des Nations, Geneva, Switzerland; h. Villa Les Pins, Coppet, Switzerland

When A. M. Rosenthal of the New York *Times* won the Pulitzer Prize in May 1960 for distinguished foreign correspondence, many newspaper readers felt that an appropriate citation for the award could be found in the condemnation written by the Polish Foreign Ministry spokesman who, six months earlier, had sought to justify a government decree ordering Rosenthal's expulsion from Warsaw. "You have written very deeply and in detail about the internal situation, party matters and leadership matters," the official had complained. "The Polish Government cannot tolerate such probing reporting." It was one of the highest unintentional professional compliments ever paid to a foreign correspondent.

Currently stationed in Geneva as chief of the local New York *Times* bureau, Abraham Michael Rosenthal was born on May 2, 1922, in Sault Ste. Marie, Ontario, the son of Harry and Sarah (Dickstein) Rosenthal. His father, who had immigrated to Canada in the early years of the century, was a farmer and, later, a fur trapper and trader in the Hudson Bay area. There were six children, five of them girls, of whom three died.

A. M. Rosenthal moved with his family from Canada to New York City as a boy. He attended elementary and high schools in the Bronx. (A member of the same January 1939 graduating class at DeWitt Clinton High School was playwright Paddy Chayefsky.) "Being a newspaper man was always the dream—but remotely, like being a fire engine chief or a pilot," Rosenthal has written. "But from the first day I joined the college newspaper—chiefly in a coffee-carrying capacity—there was no question but that this was to be for me."

At the City College of the City of New York, which he attended after illness had interrupted his education for two years, A. M. Rosenthal was editor in chief of *The Campus,* the undergraduate newspaper, and college correspondent for the New York *Times*. In February 1944, while still an undergraduate, he joined the city staff of the newspaper as a reporter. He completed his college courses at night—"very slowly, indeed," he admits, and received the degree of Bachelor of Science in social science in 1948. He became a United States citizen in 1951.

After two years of local reporting, he was assigned to the United Nations bureau of the New York *Times* in Lake Success, New York. He was a member of the New York *Times* staff that covered the General Assembly session in Paris in 1948. After eight years of covering UN proceedings, Rosenthal was assigned to New Delhi in 1954 as the New York *Times* correspondent in India and Pakistan. For four years Rosenthal covered those nations. His perceptive reporting earned him a citation from the Overseas Press Club. In 1958 the Taraknath Das Foundation, under the sponsorship of Columbia University, cited him for promoting

New York Times

A. M. ROSENTHAL

understanding between the United States and India.

In June 1958 Rosenthal was transferred by the New York *Times* to Warsaw, where he was assigned to cover Poland and other Eastern European countries. He summed up his first impressions of life behind the Iron Curtain in an article he wrote for the New York *Times Magazine* shortly after his arrival. "In Asia, the impressions that hit a newcomer hardest are the impressions of the way men live," he wrote. "In Eastern Europe, the sharpest impressions are of the way men think, and of the way foreigners react to the way men think. . . . The most difficult thing to become adjusted to in Poland, and perhaps the most important to try to understand, is the rationing of liberties. A complete absence of freedom is easy to grasp; so is the existence of real freedom. In Poland, there is neither and that makes for the nervous high plane on which so many Poles live, and for confusion in the mind of the foreigners."

So began the "probing reporting" that eventually resulted in Rosenthal's expulsion from Poland. He wrote about the effects of the Gomulka regime's relaxation of the Stalinist controls that had long choked Poland's political, economic, and cultural growth. When, some months after his arrival, the regime began to tighten the screws again, Rosenthal reported the new trend. Filing stories that the heavily censored Polish press dared not print, the New York *Times* correspondent disclosed the food shortage that required the Soviet Union to send meat to Poland. Rosenthal made known the Soviet Ambassador to Poland's denunciation of the Polish press for its admiration of Western literature, films, and art. He described in detail the chilly welcome given by the people of Warsaw to visiting Soviet Premier Nikita S. Khrushchev in July and the tumultuous greeting given to Vice-President Richard M. Nixon a week later.

The dispatch that triggered Rosenthal's expulsion was published by the New York *Times* on November 6, 1959. In it, he wrote that Polish Premier Wladyslaw Gomulka was becoming "moody and irascible." "M. Gomulka is more withdrawn these days and seems hotter-tempered than ever," Rosenthal reported. "He is said to have a feeling of having been let down —by intellectuals and economists he never had any sympathy for anyway, by workers he accuses of squeezing overtime out of a normal day's work, by suspicious peasants who turn their backs on the government's plans, orders and pleas."

It was this kind of human-interest reporting that had distinguished Rosenthal's dispatches from India during the four years leading up to his Warsaw assignment. But it brought an angry reaction from officials in Poland. Six days after the story was published, Gomulka ordered Rosenthal to leave the country within one week for "exposing too deeply the internal situation in Poland." Nobody made any specific accusations against Rosenthal. Asked whether Rosenthal's news stories from Warsaw were accurate, a Polish official replied that "the question of falseness or otherwise does not enter into the question."

The expulsion developed into an international incident. Jacob D. Beam, United States Ambassador to Warsaw, told the Polish Foreign Ministry that the United States regarded Rosenthal's expulsion as an action that would be "very harmful for United States-Polish relations." The protest was rejected, but the Polish action was further evidence, as a New York *Times* editorial put it, that "to Communists the primary function of a newspaper is that of a device for manipulating the minds and hearts of its readers in accordance with the needs of the current party line."

For his reporting from Poland, Rosenthal was awarded not only the Pulitzer Prize but also the annual award for foreign reporting of the Overseas Press Club, the Page One Award of the Newspaper Guild of New York, and the George Polk Memorial Award, sponsored by Long Island University, for "significant achievement in journalism."

To his New York *Times* assignment in Geneva, Rosenthal has brought the same reporting in depth and dedication to detail that characterized his work in India and Poland. Among the stories he has covered from Geneva have been the difficult negotiations between the United States and Soviet Russia in the fields of nuclear testing and disarmament. With Geneva as his home base, Rosenthal also covers fast-breaking news stories, summit conferences, and other events occurring in Western Europe.

Rosenthal is the author of a pamphlet *The United Nations: Its Record and Prospects* (Carnegie Endowment for International Peace, 1953) and of many articles for *Foreign Affairs* magazine, the *Saturday Evening Post*, and the New York *Times Magazine*. He is a member of the Overseas Press Club in New York City and the United Nations Correspondents' Association of Geneva.

On March 12, 1949 Abraham Michael Rosenthal was married to Ann Marie Burke, whom he met when they were both working for the New York *Times* in New York City. Miss Burke had been a secretary in the news department. The Rosenthals have three sons: Jonathan, Daniel, and Andrew. The time he spends with his small boys and his wide-ranging Geneva assignment afford him little leisure to enjoy what he describes as his favorite recreations: "sitting, reading, and book-collecting." "Off the job," says Rosenthal, "I have a wild talent for being sedentary."

RUBÍN DE LA BORBOLLA, DANIEL F(ERNANDO) May 20, 1907- Anthropologist

Address: b. c/o Museo Nacional de Artes e Industrias Populares, Avenida Juarez 44, México 1, D.F.; h. Galeana 115, Colonia San Angel Inn, Villa Obregón 20, México, D.F.

Tourists in Mexico City usually find their way to the National Museum of Popular Arts and Crafts, where the best available examples of Mexican handicrafts are exhibited and offered for sale. The director of the museum is Dr. Daniel F. Rubín de la Borbolla, a noted anthropologist and art historian, who administers the work of some 2,000,000 Mexicans making over 6,000 different kinds of products. The National Museum was founded in 1950 as a government institution to conserve, protect, and rehabilitate Mexico's peasant arts and crafts.

From 1940 to 1945 Dr. Rubín de la Borbolla was dean of the National School of Anthropology and History in Mexico City, an institution that he himself founded. He is chairman of the University Museum of the National Autonomous University of Mexico. Since 1951 he has been counselor for the rector and director general of the university.

Daniel F. Rubín de la Borbolla was born in Puebla in the state of Puebla, Mexico, on May 20, 1907 to Dr. Juan Rubín de la Borbolla, a physician, and the former Trinidad Cedillo. After his graduation from Evanston Township High School in Evanston, Illinois, Daniel attended the State College at Puebla. He then studied anthropology, law, and history at the University of Mexico in Mexico City, from which he was graduated in 1930.

In March 1931 the Secretary of Public Education appointed Dr. Rubín de la Borbolla as chief physical anthropologist on the staff of the National Museum of Anthropology. He held this post until December 1936, serving at the same time as professor of human biology at the National Preparatory School of the university. Whenever he could take time off from his teaching and administrative work, he went to Chicago, Illinois where he took courses toward his doctorate at Northwestern University. He received the Ph.D. degree in 1945.

As a professor on the faculty of philosophy and letters at the University of Mexico, Dr. Rubín de la Borbolla taught physical anthropology from 1931 to 1937. From 1932 to 1940 he explored Monte Albán, Oaxaca with Dr. Alfonso Caso. In the ruins of the Zapotec Indian

DANIEL F. RUBÍN DE LA BORBOLLA

civilization they discovered Tomb 7 which contained a great treasure of pre-Hispanic origin, consisting of exquisitely worked gold objects and jewels. Dr. Rubín de la Borbolla accompanied this treasure on board a special armored train from April to October 1933, when it was exhibited at the Chicago World's Fair and principal cities throughout the United States. It now reposes in the museum at Oaxaca. From time to time between 1933 and 1953 Dr. Rubín de la Borbolla did anthropological research at Tzintzuntzan, Michoacán, Chupicuaro, Guanajuato, and at Tlatilco, State of Mexico.

Established in 1950, the National Foundation for Popular Arts and Crafts has set up a museum and a shop. It now provides technical and economic assistance to the best craftsmen of each region, finds markets for their products in Mexico and abroad, furnishes materials and tools of high quality, educates craftsmen in the best examples of their ancient trades. The National Institute of Anthropology and History is responsible for the organization and functions of the foundation.

Housed in an old Spanish colonial church, the National Museum of Popular Arts and Crafts on Juarez Avenue, No. 44, in Mexico City, displays topical and changing exhibitions of folk art, and offers native handicrafts for sale. It has established the following museums as subsidiaries: the Regional Museum of Ceramics in Tlaquepaque, Jalisco; the Regional Museum of Popular Art in Uruapan, Michoacán, and the Museum of Lacquers in Chiapa de Corzo, Chiapas. There are workshops for rebozos (wool shawls) in Santa Maria del Rio and San Luis Potosi, and there is a workshop for ceramics in Tzintzuntzan, Michoacán. The museum has presented twenty-eight exhibitions of Mexican crafts in Cuba, Guatemala, the United States, and Europe.

By 1955 the museum had developed into a self-supporting enterprise, with a modest amount

RUBÍN DE LA BORBOLLA, DANIEL
F.—*Continued*

of profit to invest in materials, equipment, and craftsmen. The staff had successfully resisted the temptation to use synthetic materials which are frequently cheaper, but which inevitably debase the final product. It had educated its craftsmen in the differences between good and poor raw materials and in the solution of technical and economic problems.

The museum computes the price it charges for an article on the basis of the original cost of its materials and the amount that it costs a family to make the article if several members work on it, including living expenses. Field workers from the museum visit craftsmen in the villages to instruct them in the use of materials superior to the ones they have been using and in the application of more careful techniques.

"We may give technical advice," Dr. Rubín de la Borbolla has said, "but never aesthetic direction. We buy only what is good. Any true craftsman prefers to do his best, but if anyone likes to turn out shoddy work for other markets, he is naturally free to do so. The museum puts its stamp only on approved work, whether we sell it or not; we aim at no exclusiveness. And most merchants, once they understand that, are glad to get better work." Members of the museum staff keep in constant contact with more than 3,000 artisans who are considered the best in their respective fields.

"Mexican popular arts are made up of a complex of crafts," Dr. Rubín de la Borbolla has pointed out, "of native, European, and Asiatic origins, blended into an exciting and peculiar combination of styles. On the one hand, one finds objects of the purest Indian tradition, such as the *quichquemitl*—a handwoven and embroidered blouse—in use as far back as 1,000 B.C., and on the other hand, blown glass introduced by the Spanish in the sixteenth century. Mexico today is a place where many eras live simultaneously. . . . Its arts and crafts are unique expressions of powerful creative personalities."

Dr. Rubín de la Borbolla has written many articles for anthropological publications. He compiled *México Monumentos Historicos y Arqueologicos,* published in two volumes by the Instituto Pan Americano de Geographía e Historia, and has produced similar works on Guatemala and on Honduras. He belongs to the Mexican Anthropological Society, the Mexican Historical Society, the Mexican Folklore Society, the American Anthropological Society, the American Academy of Natural Sciences, the American Association of Physical Anthropologists, the American Museum Association, the Royal Anthropological Society, and other professional societies.

Daniel F. Rubín de la Borbolla and Sol Arguedas were married in October 1944. They have three children: Daniel Rubín de la Borbolla, Jr., Sol, and Maria de la Paz. Dr. Rubín de la Borbolla, who is tall and slender, has dark brown eyes and black hair. His favorite sports are tennis and swimming.

Reference

Who's Who in Latin America Part I Mexico (1947)

RUGAMBWA, LAURIAN, CARDINAL
July 12, 1912- Roman Catholic prelate

Address: Bishop's House, P.O. Box 33, Kamachumu, Tanganyika, British East Africa

The first Negro to enter the Roman Catholic College of Cardinals, Laurian Rugambwa of Tanganyika, received the red hat on March 31, 1960. "The color black was lacking and it also has arrived," Pope John XXIII said at the formal elevation three days earlier. Cardinal Rugambwa is bishop of Rutabo, the only Roman Catholic diocese in Africa whose bishop and staff are Africans.

Laurian Rugambwa was born three miles from his present ecclesiastical residence, at Bukongo, Kiyanja, on July 12, 1912. His father, who owned a small coffee farm, and his mother both came of royal tribal lineage. The name "Rugambwa" means of high renown. In accordance with tribal custom, it was given to Laurian by his grandfather.

On May 21, 1921 Laurian was baptized by the White Fathers of the Roman Catholic Church at the Kagonodo Mission in northwest Tanganyika along with his parents and brothers. While attending the mission school, Laurian became aware of all that the White Fathers were doing for his people. At the age of thirteen he decided to enter the junior seminary which the missionaries had built at Rubya. After completing his studies at the junior seminary, he went to the White Fathers' senior seminary at Katigondo in Uganda. He was ordained a priest on December 12, 1943.

For five years after his ordination he worked side by side with the White Fathers at the Rubya mission, running the school and riding a bicycle into the bush villages. "Riding a bicycle in the rain and sun, and always working is the way I lost my hair," he told journalist Sidney Fields of the New York *Mirror* (March 6, 1960). "No hair, but much joy."

Sent to Rome in 1948, Rugambwa spent three years studying canon law at the Pontifical Gregorian University. While in Rome he lived at the College of Saint Peter the Apostle. He received his doctorate in 1951; his doctoral thesis was on social and educational work in British East Africa.

Immediately upon his return from Rome in December 1951, Rugambwa received a telegram for the first time in his life. It informed him of his appointment as apostolic vicar in Lower Kogera, then a missionary territory in Tanganyika. He was also consecrated titular bishop of Febiana on February 10, 1952. Archbishop David Mathew, then apostolic delegate to British East and West Africa, officiated. He was assisted by Bishop Blomjous of Mwanza and Bishop Kiwanuka of Masaka. The latter was the first native bishop in Africa. (By 1959 there were twenty-seven native African bishops and 1,700 native priests.)

During 1952 the Roman Catholic Church changed its organization in Tanganyika from a missionary to a diocesan basis. When 4,000 square miles along the west side of Lake Victoria were formed into the diocese of Rutabo, Rugambwa became head of this jurisdiction.

The White Fathers relinquished to their protégé the seventeen primary schools they had established in the area. (Almost all teachers in the diocese, however, are trained in institutions founded and maintained by the White Fathers.) During Rugambwa's episcopate, the number of primary schools has been increased to more than thirty-five, and two junior high schools have been built. There are, in addition, four trade schools. "If we don't prepare Africans," he told Sidney Fields, "evil forces will do it for us." At the same time he has emphasized the willingness of Africans to help themselves. "Africans want to learn. Show them something and they know how to do it. They are so willing. I ask parents to help me build a school and they come bringing trees and stone."

The 60,000 faithful of the diocese are served through seven parishes and thirty small bush stations by thirty native priests, about the same number of native nuns, and a few native lay brothers. Only one priest in the diocese is non-African. The Roman Catholic Church had been trying to develop a diocese with African leaders for some seventy years.

Bishop Rugambwa was one of the seven prelates named to the cardinalate by Pope John XXIII on March 3, 1960. The Pope had already broken the precedent, followed for 375 years, of restricting the membership of the College of Cardinals to seventy. These and other new appointments made in March brought the number of cardinals to eighty-eight. Among the new appointees were Archbishop Peter Tatsuo Doi of Tokyo, the first Japanese to be so honored, and Archbishop Rufino J. Santos, who is the first Filipino cardinal.

Cardinal-designate Rugambwa, in Rome for the occasion, was formally notified of his elevation to the Sacred College after a consistory of cardinals on March 28, 1960. "African seminarians showed emotion," reported Arnaldo Cortesi in the New York *Times* (March 29, 1960), "when they saw white prelates and nuns, some much older than the new Cardinal, line up to kneel before him, kiss his ring and receive his blessing."

As Pope John embraced the Negro Cardinal at the presentation of the red hat on March 31, 1960, hundreds of onlookers broke into spontaneous applause in Saint Peter's Basilica. "The applause that greeted Cardinal Rugambwa," Barrett McGurn commented in the New York *Herald Tribune* (April 1, 1960), "underlined what Pope John himself has described as the widespread approval in non-Catholic as well as Catholic circles of the Church's unprecedented step in accepting a Negro into the Sacred College, which chooses the Popes."

An attorney for the National Association for the Advancement of Colored People, Arthur B. Spingarn, called the appointment "one of the most significant and encouraging indications of the growing prestige of Negro leadership today." Some saw behind Rugambwa's elevation the Vatican's awareness of the increasingly powerful drive of Islam south of the Sahara. Others saw the hope that the Negro Cardinal could become a force for peace in Africa.

British Inf. Services

LAURIAN CARDINAL RUGAMBWA

Rugambwa himself, in a press conference on March 22, 1960, expressed his intention to foster peace among whites and native Africans. He is, however, solidly on the side of Africans becoming masters of their own fate. He looks forward to the time when Tanganyika will change its status from a United Nations trust territory administered by Great Britain to an independent nation.

Shortly after the completion of the elevation ceremonies, the Cardinal, suffering aftereffects of malaria, was hospitalized in Rome. He recovered sufficiently to return to Tanganyika at the end of May. Cardinal Rugambwa is widely traveled. He spent three months in the United States in 1957, raising money for his diocese, and he has visited England twice in recent years. In 1959 he was one of the bishops who attended the conference of Roman Catholic clergy at Nijmegen in the Netherlands.

The Cardinal, whose cathedral church is a building of eucalyptus poles and handmade bricks, is deeply interested in the social problems of his people. The money he raised in the United States and elsewhere made possible the opening of a hospital, an orphanage, a technical school, and a school where girls might learn to care for children, among other projects. He also founded the Social Union of St. Augustine to train people for public life and has already had the satisfaction of seeing one of its members enter the Legislative Council of Tanganyika.

Laurian Cardinal Rugambwa is over six feet one inch tall, slim, erect, and athletic looking. He is an excellent tennis player. Although gentle, shy, and laconic, he is self-assured in manner and shrewd and hard driving as an administrator. His thoughtful face breaks easily into a smile. He speaks graciously and earnestly—most earnestly when the subject is

RUGAMBWA, LAURIAN, CARDINAL
—Continued

his people or their problems. He is said to be very approachable and much loved by his people.

Cardinal Rugambwa speaks Latin, German, French, and English in addition to Luganda and Swahili. Known for his prudence of judgment, he will not commit himself on a matter without thoughtful deliberation. A White Father who taught the Cardinal when the latter was a seminarian has said of him: "He's a remarkable person, very gifted, has tremendous charm and all kinds of interests."

References

N Y Times p3 Mr 4 '60 por
Newsday p28 Mr 29 '60 por
Catholic Directory of East and West
 Africa (1958)

RUGG, HAROLD (ORDWAY) Jan. 17, 1886-May 17, 1960 Educator; professor of education at Columbia University Teachers College (1920-51) and professor emeritus of education (since 1951); author of widely used social science textbooks for high school students. See *Current Biography* (May) 1941.

Obituary

N Y Times p41 My 18 '60

RUML, BEARDSLEY Nov. 5, 1894-Apr. 18, 1960 Financial expert; devised the pay-as-you-go plan for payment of federal income tax (1943); chairman of the Federal Reserve Bank of New York (1941-47) and of R.H. Macy & Company (1945-49). See *Current Biography* (May) 1943.

Obituary

N Y Times p1+ Ap 19 '60

RUTENBORN, GÜNTER, REV. Apr. 8, 1912- German clergyman; writer

Address: b. Jebensstrasse 3, Berlin-Charlottenburg, East Germany; c/o Kurt Hellmer, 52 Vanderbilt Ave., New York 17; h. Leiblstrasse 22, Potsdam, East Germany

From the unlikely quarter of the Soviet zone of eastern Germany a daring application of Christian teaching to the spiritual dilemma of twentieth-century man has reached the West in the writings of Günter Rutenborn, a pastor of the Evangelical Church. When his play *The Sign of Jonah,* written just after World War II, was produced in New York in May 1957, Brooks Atkinson of the New York *Times* noted that "in an hour's time it concentrates the passion of mankind" and praised Rutenborn as "a devout scholar" and "also a sophisticated theatre writer." Since 1956 he has served as pastor at the Holy Spirit Congregation in Potsdam, Germany (in the diocese of Bishop Otto Dibelius), where, he remarks, "there are shrinking congregations and increasing numbers of atheists."

Günter Rutenborn was born on April 8, 1912 in Dortmund, Germany to Otto Rutenborn, an engineer, and Sofie Rutenborn, whose maiden name was also Rutenborn. He has a sister who lives in Switzerland; his mother's home is still Dortmund, within what is now called West Germany. Reared also in Dortmund, he attended the city's Bismarck-Realgymnasium, where one of his special interests was Spanish, and was graduated in 1930.

Entering the University of Münster in Westphalia, Germany, Rutenborn studied theology, philosophy, and Oriental (Semitic and Indian) languages. In 1939 he was ordained to the Evangelical Lutheran Church, but, hindered by the Nazis from beginning his ministry, he was without a parish for more than a year as a result of the strife between the church and Hitler's regime. At one time he was fined 1,000 marks for speaking out against Hitler.

The flourishing of the Nazi movement in Germany was one of the reasons why Rutenborn chose to become a pastor. He believed that the people of Germany, receptive to both Nazism and, in part, to Communism, need the church, which in turn needs ministers. As a writer he has been guided by his conviction that German literature needs the Gospel. Referring to Goethe, Schiller, and Karl Marx, he has said, "German literature is literature of temptation to deny the Faith."

Because of a disability, Rutenborn was exempted from World War II military service, which he very likely would have resisted. "My war is the war of the Church," he has declared. During part of the war, from 1941 to 1943, he was pastor of several churches in Brandenburg, including Berlin. Exiled from Berlin in 1943, he was sent by his church to be a pastor in Senzke, a village of 500 inhabitants about thirty miles west of Berlin.

In eastern Germany, toward the end of World War II and later, he suffered much the same persecution under the Communists as he had under the Nazis. Reportedly, drunken Soviet soldiers once attempted to shoot him. As a pastor, he had become interested in the possibility of using the theater as a spiritual force and had written several plays for church audiences. After the war, in 1946, he wrote *Das Zeichen des Jona (The Sign of Jonah)* to be performed in church circles. "It was born," he recalls, "when there were bombed houses and piles of rubble everywhere" (*Life*, June 10, 1957).

For many Germans of the annihilated Third Reich, survivors of a regime that had brought about the devastation of cities and the extermination of millions of Jews, Rutenborn's inquiry into man's guilt had a compelling relevance. The play moved from church groups into the theaters of West Berlin's "Broadway." There and on the road in East Germany it was performed many hundreds of times. In 1949, the year in which Rutenborn founded the Christian stage of Berlin (Die Vaganten), it was awarded the Jochen Klepper plaque for the most successful performance of a Christian drama in Berlin. (Jochen Klepper was a young, gifted author who killed himself and his Jewish wife and stepdaughter in 1942.)

The Sign of Jonah, a one-act, nine-scene dramatic theodicy, or vindication of the ways of God to man, gives twentieth-century, or timeless, identities to Biblical characters (Jonah, for example, is a U-boat commander). Rutenborn brings mankind to a court trial and distributes among "innocent" bystanders and his audience—all sinners—the responsibility and guilt for human suffering, whether in Nineveh or Nazi Germany.

Pastor Rutenborn's Jonah play was published in Hamburg, Germany in 1950 (Wittig Verlag) and in New York in 1960 (Nelson). The American publication followed several productions of *The Sign of Jonah* in the United States, notably the presentation by the Union Theological Seminary in New York City in May 1957, which was directed by Professor Robert E. Seaver. Brooks Atkinson (New York *Times,* May 2, 1957) described it as "brilliantly composed . . . in a Pirandello style of speculation and inquiry." As Atkinson further observed, "Although he describes his craftsmanship as surrealism, he might just as well take credit for having written a poetic drama that is engaged in the proving of things unseen. He has written an indictment of the twentieth century. . . . Although 'The Sign of Jonah' is penetrating and bold, it is also personally modest. At the center of the horrors and meannesses it records, the core is sweet."

America (June 22, 1957) thought that next to *The Potting Shed* it was the most significant play produced in New York during the 1956-57 season. It was performed also at the general assembly of the Presbyterian Church in Omaha, Nebraska in May 1957 and at the Chicago Community Theatre in February 1958. In September and October 1960 the play was presented in New York at the off-Broadway Players Theatre.

Another of Rutenborn's works available in English translation is *The Word was God,* published in 1959 by Thomas Nelson & Sons (published in Munich in 1954 by C. Kaiser Verlag as *Biblische Fremdenführung*). It is a reading tour that Rutenborn as guide conducts through the books of the Bible.

Many of Rutenborn's plays remain unpublished. They include "Resurrection," about Dostoevski in Siberia; "Iphigenia in Aulis," about man's will to wage war, according to the classical myth; and "The Sword of Thoas," a tragedy written, he has explained, to refute "the humanistic falsifications in Goethe's *Iphigenia.*" He is also the author of "The Emperor Titus," the first of a cycle of plays about the Christian taming of state power, a theme close to his own experiences in Germany; and "The Case of Pilate," a mystery play that begins with the end of World War III.

He has written two comedies, "Happily Divorced" and "The Eternal Excellency," which he intends as "a bitter and hard laughing against dictators." According to *Life* (June 10, 1957), Rutenborn displays in his work, along with eloquence, "a pleasantly dry and sarcastic wit."

Wide World

REV. GÜNTER RUTENBORN

Life also believes that "he is likely to become Germany's most gifted living dramatist."

Residing and working in Potsdam since 1956, Günter Rutenborn occasionally visits West Berlin to see friends and discuss the production of his plays, but he otherwise seldom has the opportunity to leave the Soviet-controlled zone of East Germany. He has been married since April 30, 1943 to Angelika Wendland, who was a doctor's secretary, and had a son, Titus, who died in infancy. Pastor Rutenborn has blue eyes and once-blond hair that has now thinned and turned gray; he is tall and slender. He participates in no sports, but enjoys driving his car like a sportsman. Gardening and playing the piano are his recreations.

Rutenborn, who knows English, feels gratified by the reception of his writings outside the Soviet zone, since a Christian author is discouraged from producing or publishing his work under Communism. He regards the United States as a friend of freedom and as a deterrent to despair.

Reference

Life 42:121+ Je 10 '57 pors

SAGAN, FRANÇOISE June 21, 1935- Author

Address: b. c/o Éditions Julliard, 30 rue de l'Université, Paris 7e, France; c/o E. P. Dutton & Co., Inc., 300 4th Ave., New York 10

Whether or not France has another Colette in Françoise Sagan may be a subject of literary debate for some years to come. Her status, however, as one of the foremost controversial, and ambiguous, figures in contemporary literature was established six years ago. Ever since the Prix des Critiques was awarded to the teen-aged author of *Bonjour Tristesse* in

Rene Saint-Paul

FRANÇOISE SAGAN

1954, Françoise Sagan has been the focus of ballyhoo and fanfare and of legend and myth, and has drawn the attention of admirers like François Mauriac (though disapproving) and Janet Flanner. In her four brief novels, all with themes of troubled love, she is the spokesman for many of her restless contemporaries and a delineator of their lives of moral and philosophical vacuity. In France her books have been published by Julliard and in the United States, by E. P. Dutton & Company, Inc.

Readers who assume that Françoise Sagan's novels are autobiographical (some are written in the first person) search for details in her early life that might account for the amorality of her characters. The third child of Pierre Quoirez, a prosperous industrialist, and Marie (Laubard) Quoirez, she was born in Cajarc (Lot), France on June 21, 1935. Since Françoise Quoirez is younger by some ten years than both her sister, Suzanne, and her brother, Jacques, she became accustomed in childhood to older companions. She is said to have been timid as a child and to have been impressed by the comparative maturity and *savoir-faire* of her brother, who is possibly the prototype of some of her heroes.

Françoise Sagan's upbringing—in an apartment in Lyons, on a country estate in Vercors, and during part of World War II in Switzerland—was apparently sheltered and conventionally bourgeois. Her nickname was Kiki. She attended private schools, including the Couvent des Oiseaux and Couvent du Sacré-Coeur in Paris.

At the end of the war the Quoirez family moved to Paris, and there from the age of fifteen with numerous other teen-agers she spent her leisure hours in and around the cafés of the Latin Quarter, listened to jazz in cellars of Saint-Germain-des-Prés, and discussed existentialism at Les Deux Magots. These diversions,

in addition to writing poetry and short stories (as she had been doing since the age of thirteen) and reading the works of Marcel Proust and Stendhal, left her little time for formal education.

In her examinations at the end of her first year at the Sorbonne, she only half-failed, and after a summer of study she was able to resume classes. In her second-year examinations, however, in June 1953, she failed completely. Subsequent idleness and a desire to placate her family led her to begin work on a novel that she had been thinking about for a year or so. She wrote it during August, starting the story as a serial and reading installments to her friends.

The Paris publisher René Julliard accepted the manuscript within two weeks of receiving it. *Bonjour Tristesse* appeared in March 1954 under the pseudonym of Françoise Sagan. Recalling the Princesse de Sagan in Proust's *A la recherche du temps perdu*, Françoise Quoirez had appropriated this name because she liked its sound. The story is told from the point of view of an eighteen-year-old girl who is determined to prevent the marriage of her widowed father. The book received enthusiastic tribute in the French press and was awarded the Prix des Critiques. By the time it was published in the United States, in February 1955, more than 200,000 copies had been sold in France. Later translated into some twenty languages, it became a best seller in many countries.

The air of realism in *Bonjour Tristesse* and the young age of the heroine drew as much attention to the author as to the book itself. While some critics were impressed by the maturity and perceptiveness of Françoise Sagan, others felt that her literary talents made her age unimportant, and still others called the novel preposterous and deplored its seeming admiration of decadence.

The publication of *Un Certain Sourire (A Certain Smile)* in 1956 was almost as important a literary milestone as that of *Bonjour Tristesse,* because Mlle. Sagan was called upon to prove that she could duplicate the success of her first novel. Endorsement by some of France's most demanding critics, who compared her to Benjamin Constant and described her as "a Colette of the younger generation," guaranteed the novel's sales, which rose to 450,000 copies in France within a year and a half. Here Françoise Sagan treats a love affair between a twenty-year-old Sorbonne student and a married man twice her age.

Taking a phrase from Racine's *Bérénice,* Mlle. Sagan entitled her next novel *Dans un mois, dans un an* (In a Month, In a Year). The first printing sold out at once in Paris in September 1957, and the book appeared in the United States late the following month under the title of *Those Without Shadows.* In both countries it had mixed notices, with some reviewers praising it as her best work to date and others finding it inferior. The themes were the same as those of her previous books, as Nora Magid pointed out in the *Reporter* (November 14, 1957): "Aimless pleasures and half-hearted lusts, casual lies and knowing games.

the sea and whisky and reckless drives to lost weekends."

Before the appearance of this third novel, however, the name of Françoise Sagan made headlines for another reason. One day in April 1957, while she was living in a country house in Milly-la-Forêt rented from Christian Dior, she went for a ride in one of her four fast cars, an Aston-Martin, and almost lost her life in a smashup. A fractured skull, among other injuries, kept her in the hospital for two months. During the convalescence that followed she spent some time on the Riviera, and there in the summer of 1957 she occasionally visited the location of the filming of *Bonjour Tristesse,* of which Otto Preminger was producer-director. She is said to have been displeased with the movie, which generally fell short of expectation upon its release in the United States in early 1958.

Also while recuperating, Françoise Sagan had a visit from the young composer Michel Magne, with whom she worked out some ideas for a ballet. They were later joined by the painter Bernard Buffet and Roger Vadim (then married to Brigitte Bardot) in producing *Le Rendez-vous manqué* (The Broken Date), which deals with unhappy erotic relationships of modern youth. At its première in January 1958 in Monte Carlo, and later in Paris, it won thunderous applause, but elsewhere was less successful.

Like her first three books, *Aimez-vous Brahms . . .* (published in France in September 1959) is a story about love, this time involving a middle-aged businessman and his middle-aged mistress, with whom a much younger man also falls in love. (In 1960 a motion-picture adaptation of the book was produced by an American company.) Just about the time that the novel appeared in the United States in an English translation, Mlle. Sagan's first play, *Château en Suède* (Castle in Sweden), was produced in Paris. It opened in March 1960 to a warm reception from both the audience and critics.

Surveying her work as a whole, a number of serious literary commentators have come to interpret Françoise Sagan's success as evidence of her ability to understand and express the cynicism of French youth, particularly the philosophical, political, and religious disillusionment of many intellectuals. The world of her novels is one of boredom and fatigue, of aimlessness and frustration.

Completely appropriate to the tone of her subject matter, Françoise Sagan's manner of writing is restrained, economical, deceptively simple. Although she appears to compose in a haphazard way, snatching a few hours a day from swimming or dancing or horseback riding, few critics question her dedication to her craft or her technical skill. With a gift for maxims, she writes in the classical French tradition; and her style, which has received the compliments of imitation and parody, has been described as crystalline, lyrical, succinct, and acute. All her novels, really novelettes, run only to about 188 pages in the French editions and about 127 in the American.

"I have survived my own 'legend' (which frankly appalls me)," Françoise Sagan once told an interviewer. Personal reticence possibly accounts for why myths about her have been substituted for facts, and an effort to screen herself from overwhelming publicity may explain in part why she is always surrounded by gay young hangers-on. On March 13, 1958 she was married to Guy Schoëller, a publisher who is about twenty years older than she; the couple was divorced in the summer of 1960.

Françoise Sagan is of medium height and has a slim figure, gamin-cut dark hair, brown eyes, and a dimpled smile. Although she dresses for the occasion, photographs indicate a preference for casual clothes like blue jeans and shirts or sweaters. To interviewers she is well-mannered, forthright, and offhand. She likes animals (dogs, cats, horses, and birds), sports (swimming, tennis, and skiing), and jazz (including Louis Armstrong). She knows English, and among the American authors that she admires are William Faulkner and Truman Capote. Her favorite French writers are Proust, Gide, Sartre, Simone de Beauvoir, and several eighteenth-century authors. "I write as well as I possibly can," she told Carson Churchill of the Manchester *Guardian* (September 7, 1959). "It is not absolutely a joke to write—it is intimate, difficult, humbling, and even humiliating."

References

Atlan 205:87+ Mr '60
Cath World 185:258+ Jl '57 por
Cosmop 145:32+ Ag '58 pors
N Y Times Bk R p21 My 1 '55 por
N Y Times Mag p16+ O 27 '57 por
Sat R 43:19+ Mr 12 '60 por
International Who's Who, 1959
Who's Who in France, 1959-60

SAHL, MORT(ON LYON) May 11, 1927-
Comedian

Address: b. c/o Verve Records, Beverly Hills, Calif.

Because of his sardonic "little lectures" on the contemporary scene, Mort Sahl has become one of the highest-paid rebels without a cause in the entertainment business and the acknowledged leader of the new school of offbeat comedians. When Sahl appears at night clubs, wearing his uniform of slacks, sweater, and shirt open at the collar and carrying a rolled-up newspaper, he disparages everything with a nihilistic impartiality. Women and politicians, however, get the major share of his invective, which he delivers at breakneck speed and in a fractured syntax that, to be appreciated, should be heard rather than read.

To his annoyance, Sahl has often been called the first important political satirist to appear in American entertainment since the departure of Will Rogers. Sahl is more savage in his censure, more iconoclastic in his attitude than Rogers ever was. "I don't have the image of myself as a comedian," Sahl has said. "I never said I was one. I just sort of tell the truth and everybody breaks up along the way."

(Continued next page)

MORT SAHL   Wide World

Morton Lyon Sahl was born in Montreal, Canada on May 11, 1927. He has no brothers or sisters. His father, Harry Sahl, is an American who came from an immigrant family on New York's Lower East Side and who originally wanted to become a playwright. He was the proprietor of a tobacco shop in Montreal at the time of his son's birth, but later returned to the United States as a clerk with the United States Department of Justice. Harry Sahl's position for a while required considerable moving about the United States, but when Mort was seven, the family finally settled down in Los Angeles.

Early in life Mort Sahl displayed a talent for talking. (His mother has said that he began to talk at the age of seven months and at ten years of age spoke like a man of thirty.) Mort was so interested in radio broadcasting that he used to play with the discarded scripts from radio stations, but by the time he entered high school he had switched his interest to the military. As a leading light in the school's ROTC, he became, by his own admission, "something of a martinet." While still in high school, he lied about his age in order to enlist in the Army. He was ingloriously brought back by his mother after he had spent two weeks in service.

After his graduation from high school, Sahl enlisted again, this time in the Army Air Forces, and was assigned to the 93d Air Depot Group stationed at Elmendorf Field in Anchorage, Alaska. Although the highest rank he attained during his thirty-one months in service was private, he became a crew chief on a portable oxygen generator and also edited the post newspaper, *Poop from the Group.*

Sahl was discharged in 1947 and entered Compton Junior College in Compton, California under the GI Bill. After two years there, he moved on to the University of Southern California, where he received a B.S. degree in city management and engineering. His thesis was on the subject of city traffic flow. He aban-

doned his plans for graduate work in favor of three years of experimental theater and writing for little magazines in Los Angeles and San Francisco and their environs, supporting himself by odd jobs.

Late in 1953 Sahl obtained a job at a San Francisco rendezvous for the beatniks and college crowd—a night club called the hungry i ("i" for "intellectual"). Earning $75 a week, Sahl established the routine for which he has since become famous: a wide-ranging, often improvised commentary on life in the anxious age, delivered in a medley of academic and psychiatric jargon and the argot of the hipster.

Sahl's success at the hungry i eventually led to a crowded calendar of night club engagements. The spots where Sahl has scored notable successes include New York's Basin Street East and Copacabana, Chicago's Chez Paree and Mister Kelly's, Los Angeles' Crescendo, Miami Beach's Americana, and Las Vegas' Flamingo. His current night club salary is estimated at $7,500 per week, although, according to *Time* (August 15, 1960), "the hungry i still gets him for a sentimental $5,000."

Reviewing one of Sahl's appearances at the Copacabana, a *Variety* reporter (August 26, 1959) wrote: "Sticking to a tieless shirt and crew sweater, Sahl comes on like a beatnik, with this big difference: he's got something to say and a funny way of saying it. There is no subject that's safe from the Sahl scrutiny. President Eisenhower, Queen Elizabeth, veepee Nixon, Lewis Straus, Governor Rockefeller and he makes mince meat of them all. It's irreverent, but it's not irresponsible and the forty minutes he's on doesn't seem long enough to cover what's on everybody's mind."

But Mort Sahl does not appeal exclusively to audiences in the night club circuit. He has also performed successfully on radio and television. He has been heard regularly on the biweekly radio show *Nightline,* and he has appeared on the Steve Allen, Jack Paar, and Eddie Fisher shows. He has also been seen on special shows such as the 1958 presentation of the Academy of Motion Picture Arts and Sciences awards and a *Wide Wide World* production for NBC that analyzed American humor. Sahl's commentary on the 1960 Democratic convention was telecast locally over KHJ in Los Angeles.

He has not found it necessary to water down his material for his television appearances. He provides home viewers with the same mordant and irreverent remarks that he delivers to night club habitués. Because he would like to bring his ironic views of the passing scene to as large an audience as possible, he hopes some day to have his own regular show on television. In the meantime, the Sahl cultists who cannot get enough of him on television will have to solace themselves by listening to his monologues on the long-playing records that he has made for Verve.

On April 9, 1958 Mort Sahl opened on Broadway in a revue featuring Sahl. Entitled *The Next President,* it closed after only thirteen performances, but some reviewers attributed the failure not to Sahl but to the ineffective mode in which he was presented. "One act of Sahlism is stimulating," wrote Brooks Atkinson in the New York *Times* (April 10, 1958). "Although he does change his sweater for the second act, he changes nothing else except the subject, and by curtain time the brightness is wearing off. This is a problem in showmanship. For Mr. Sahl's conversation is fast, literate, witty and spontaneous."

The reviewer for *Time,* on the other hand, felt that much of the trouble with the show lay in Sahl himself. Admitting Sahl's refreshing brightness, he complained: "Beyond talking miles too long . . . his current great faults are too much smugness and too little showmanship. He could be more outrageous if he did not wait for laughs and even join in them. The danger with anybody as much commentator as jokester is that the mocking will become the messianic; already there is an atmosphere in the audience of followers rather than fans" (April 21, 1958).

Mort Sahl has appeared in two Hollywood war films, *In Love and War* (Twentieth Century-Fox, 1958) and the 1960 Columbia release *All the Young Men.* The character Sahl portrays in these films is essentially himself: his movie contract grants him the privilege of writing his own lines. Joseph Morgenstern in the New York *Herald Tribune* (August 27, 1960) reported that in *All the Young Men* "Mr. Sahl fires off some choice comments on warfare," but regretted that the film "must stand stock still" for Sahl's lines and that the comedian is "not in the picture, but grafted onto it."

Mort Sahl is five feet ten inches in height and weighs about 150 pounds. He has dark hair and a dark complexion, heavy-lidded eyes, and a frequent lupine grin. On June 25, 1955 he was married to Sue Babior; the marriage ended in divorce in 1957. Sahl seldom smokes or drinks, but he is addicted to coffee, which he drinks in large quantities in the West Coast coffee houses. He likes music, both jazz (especially Stan Kenton and Dave Brubeck) and classical, and often has a record blasting on one of his high-fidelity phonographs in the small hours of the morning. He likes to surround himself with electric razors, expensive watches, and the sleeker sports cars, perhaps because the mobility of his childhood imposed limits on the amount of material possessions that he could take along. His personal idols include Mark Twain, Herman Melville, Tom Paine, Albert Einstein, Edmund Wilson, and George Bernard Shaw. He resents being associated in the public mind with the so-called "sick" comedians. "My whole life is a movie," Mort Sahl has said. "It's just that there are no dissolves. I have to live every agonizing moment of it. My life needs editing."

References

Holiday 24:91+ S '59 por
New Yorker 33:43+ N 30 '57; 36:31+ Jl 30 '60
N Y Times Mag p32 F 8 '59 por

SALIT, NORMAN, RABBI June 8, 1896-July 21, 1960 Lawyer; author; president of the Synagogue Council of America (1953-55). See *Current Biography* (March) 1955.

Obituary

N Y Times p23 Jl 22 '60

SANTOS, RUFINO J(IAO), CARDINAL

Aug. 26, 1908- Roman Catholic prelate
Address: b. Archdiocese of Manila, 1000 General Solano St., Manila, Philippine Islands; h. Villa San Miguel, 50 Shaw Blvd., Mandaluyong, Rizal, Philippine Islands

Archbishop since 1953 of one of the largest sees of the Roman Catholic Church, Rufino J. Santos of Manila, Philippine Islands, was elevated to the rank of Cardinal by Pope John XXIII in March 1960. His elevation gave the only Christian country in the Orient its first representative in the College of Cardinals. For twenty-six years Cardinal Santos has served in various clerical capacities in Manila, where he solved many of the financial and organizational problems of the archdiocese. During World War II he was a prisoner of the Japanese occupiers.

Rufino Jiao Santos was born in barrio Santo Niño, Guaga, Pampanga, the Philippines, on August 26, 1908. He was the seventh of nine children of Gaudencio Santos and Rosalia (Jiao) Santos. His father was for a time overseer for some landowners in Pampanga, later moving his family to Manila, where he engaged successfully in a horse-drawn taxi business. When Rufino was seven his mother died and an aunt took over some of the maternal duties. Love and solicitude were also supplied by four unmarried sisters. His father died in 1957.

In July 1917, at the age of nine, Rufino entered the Manila Cathedral parochial school. His priestly vocation came to him in what he has described as a "flash" at the end of his fourth and last year at the school. Because of his photographic memory and dedication to scholarship, Rufino was one of the two boys who had particularly impressed Father José Tahon at the school. When the priest asked him about his plans for the immediate future, Rufino found himself saying: "I don't know, Father . . . because I want to be a priest."

At the age of twelve Rufino began his studies at San Carlos Seminary in Manila with the aid of a scholarship. After graduation, he left for Rome on September 27, 1927 to attend the Collegio Pio Latino Americano. He was salutatorian of his class when he received the D.S.T. degree from the Pontifical Gregorian University in July 1931.

Exempted from the canonical age requirement —he was only twenty-three—Santos was ordained a priest in the Basilica of Saint John Lateran in Rome on October 25, 1931. When he returned to the Philippines in February 1932, he was appointed assistant parish priest at Imus, Cavite. He was transferred to Marilao, Bulacan on September 24 of the same year. As parish priest at Marilao, he became known to the people as "Padre Pinong," a term of endearment.

Hearing much praise of the young priest, Archbishop Michael J. O'Doherty of Manila invited him to the episcopal palace for a weekend in 1932. The weekend stretched to fifteen years, during which time the aging Archbishop O'Doherty entrusted more and more of the

Wide World

RUFINO J. CARDINAL SANTOS

financial problems of the archdiocese to Father Santos. Appointed vice-chancellor of the archdiocese in August 1934, Father Santos also served as superintendent of religious instruction (1934-1938), member of the executive committee of the thirty-third International Eucharistic Congress (1936-1937), and secretary-treasurer of the archdiocese (1939). When Archbishop O'Doherty died in 1949, Segimund Pniower, an auditor for the archdiocesan administration, said of Santos: "He is now the only man—repeat, the only man—with a comprehensive knowledge of the financial problems of the archdiocese."

During the Japanese occupation of the Philippines Father Santos was imprisoned for one year. Roused from bed early in the morning of February 4, 1944, he was taken to Fort Santiago and was accused of listening to "enemy" shortwave broadcasts and aiding guerrillas and other underground workers. In spite of reported third-degree interrogations and physical torture, he refused to sign a document that would have been used against Irish-Amercan Archbishop O'Doherty. In August 1944, when his formal sentence began, he was transferred to a prison in Muntinglupa. With a rosary he had fashioned out of a handkerchief, he led other prisoners in the daily recitation of the rosary. His hair turned completely white during his incarceration and he almost died of dysentery. His seven-year sentence was cut short on February 5, 1945, with the entry of American-Filipino liberation forces.

Partly because of his experiences during World War II, Father Santos was named vicar-general by Archbishop O'Doherty in July 1945. As vicar-general, he was responsible for the chaplain service in the Philippine Army. He has been unhappy about the small number of chaplains, his ideal being one chaplain for every battalion or company.

After he was elected titular bishop of Barca on August 25, 1947, Santos experienced a spectacular rise in the hierarchy of the Church. On the same day he was named auxiliary bishop of Manila, and two months later he was consecrated bishop on October 24, 1947. Within two years, he assumed the duties of apostolic administrator of Lipa.

Recalled to Manila, Bishop Santos on December 2, 1950 became auxiliary to Archbishop O'Doherty's successor, the first Filipino Archbishop of Manila, the Most Reverend Gabriel M. Reyes. He was installed as military vicar for the Philippines on December 10, 1951; was appointed apostolic administrator of Manila on October 17, 1951; was appointed secretary general of the First Plenary Council of the Philippines in January 1953; and was elected administrative council president of the Catholic Welfare Organization in the same month.

On February 10, 1953, following the death of Archbishop Reyes, Santos became Archbishop of Manila. The archdiocese under his jurisdiction, comprising Manila and adjacent areas, has 3,800,000 communicants out of a total population of 4,000,000. In the 200 parishes of the archdiocese are eighty-five schools and other institutions. Many parishes, churches, and rectories have come into being during Archbishop Santos' administration. He has rebuilt the minor and major seminaries of San Carlos and the Cathedral of Manila, which had been severely damaged during World War II. (The new Cathedral was dedicated in 1958.) One of his first acts as Archbishop was the establishment of Catholic Charities in his archdiocese.

Archbishop Santos was appointed to the Sacred College of Cardinals on March 3, 1960. His appointment was approved at a secret consistory of Cardinals on March 28. This was the consistory that made history not so much by increasing the number of Cardinals to the all-time high of eighty-eight as by breaking the color line in the highest ranks of the Roman Catholic hierarchy. The break was represented not only by the appointment of Cardinal Santos but also by that of Laurian Cardinal Rugambwa, the first African to be so honored, and Peter Tatsuo Cardinal Doi, the first Japanese. Seven others were elevated, three of them *in pectore* (undisclosed for reasons of prudence). The process of elevation was completed on March 31, 1960, with the reception in Saint Peter's Basilica in Rome of the broad-brimmed hat, special badge of the rank of Cardinal, colored red to symbolize fearlessness in defense of the Roman Catholic faith "even to the shedding of blood."

His keen mind bent toward the practical, Rufino Cardinal Santos succeeded in extricating the Roman Catholic Archdiocese of Manila from financial and administrative problems during the 1930's. He is now the controlling stockholder of at least three Manila banks (Philippine Trust Company, Monte de Piedad & Savings Bank, and Bank of the Philippine Islands). He handles no money, however; that task is carried out by Father Benjamin Marino, his private secretary. Beyond such delegation, he is an executive who needs little secretarial help.

Rufino J. Cardinal Santos is five feet five inches tall and weighs 150 pounds. Besides Spanish and his native tongues of Pampango and Tagalog, he speaks Italian and English. He used to enjoy tennis when he was younger. Having lately turned to softball, he plays first base and hits well, but is a poor runner. There is a swimming pool at his residence, Villa San Miguel, but he seldom uses it. He mostly reads theological and philosophical works and *Filipinas,* the Manila archdiocesan paper that he founded, but he also scans the editorial pages of metropolitan newspapers. He occasionally indulges in a cowboy movie. He likes simple Filipino meals, but, because he is diabetic, they have to be well planned. His Eminence is a member of the Third Order of St. Francis and a Knight of Malta.

References

Manila Times special supplement Ap 8
'60 pors
N Y Herald Tribune p11 Mr 4 '60
N Y Times p3 Mr 4 '60 por
Time 75:48 Mr 14 '60 por
Asia Who's Who (1960)

Wide World

DALIP S. SAUND

SAUND, DALIP S(INGH) Sept. 20, 1899-
United States Representative from California; businessman

Address: b. House Office Bldg., Washington 25, D.C.; h. 3801 Connecticut Ave., N.W., Washington 8, D.C.; 392 S. Center St., Westmorland, Calif.

Fulfilling an aspiration to be "a living example of American democracy in practice," Indian-born United States Representative Dalip S. Saund has been proclaimed one of the most effective ambassadors of good will that America ever sent to India. He began his two-and-a-half-month mission to Asia in the fall of 1957, about a year after he had been elected to Congress as the first Democrat to represent California's traditionally Republican Twenty-ninth Congressional District. His victory over Jacqueline Cochran Odlum in the November 1956 election also made him the first Asian ever to serve in Congress. Saund is a prosperous dealer in fertilizer and a former Imperial Valley farmer who has lived in California since 1920.

A member of a well-to-do family of landowners and government contractors for canals and railroads, Dalip Singh Saund was born in the village of Chhajalwadi, northern India on September 20, 1899. His parents, Natha Singh and Jeoni (Kaur) Saund, were Sikhs—adherents of a Hindu sect that for centuries has opposed the caste system. Although both his father and mother were illiterate, they valued education and sent their children to schools in the Punjab town of Amritsar, near his native village. He graduated from the Sikh college there and then studied at the University of Punjab, which awarded him the B.A. degree with honors in 1919.

As a follower of Mahatma Gandhi's nationalist movement, Saund rejected opportunities for a career in India's British-controlled civil service. His interest in the ideals of Abraham Lincoln and Woodrow Wilson attracted him to the United States, and he decided to go to California to study the canning industry with a view to setting up his own business in India. In 1920 he enrolled in the University of California at Berkeley.

While studying food preservation, he worked during the summers in California canning factories. He also took courses in mathematics which led to the M.A. degree in 1922 and the Ph.D. degree in 1924, both from the University of California. His thesis was entitled "On Functions Associated with the Elliptic Cylinder in Harmonic Analysis."

From time to time Saund used to attend religious services at the Sikh temple in Stockton, California. There he met a number of Hindus who had become farmers in southern California's Imperial Valley, and in the fall of 1925 he began his own agricultural ventures in the valley. Before settling down to full-time farming, however, he felt impelled to write an answer to Katherine Mayo's best-selling book, *Mother India* (1927), which he thought presented an unfair picture of his native country. He started work on *My Mother India* in 1927 and had it published by Hetzel in 1930.

Like other farmers in the Imperial Valley, which has an unpredictable market, Saund experienced good and bad years. He grew a variety of crops from maize to watermelons and experimented in crops then new to the valley like sugar beets and Punjab flax. When the harvest or the market failed, he refused to file the customary bankruptcy proceedings —in India bankruptcy is shameful—and instead paid off his debts over several years.

Deeply interested in political and civic affairs, Saund became locally popular as a speaker always available for talks on India or on

SAUND, DALIP S.—*Continued*

Franklin D. Roosevelt before such groups as the Current Events Club in Westmorland and Democratic organizations in Imperial Valley towns. He was unable to run for public office because of citizenship restrictions against East Indians. He therefore helped to organize the India Association of America, of which he was president in 1942, and went to Washington, D.C. to urge the adoption of an amendment to the immigration law which would make Indians eligible to become citizens.

As soon as the bill was passed, in 1946, Saund applied for citizenship. He received his naturalization papers in 1949 and at once was made a member of the central committee of the Democratic party in Imperial County. The following year he became a candidate for the judgeship in Westmorland, a post somewhat similar to justice of the peace. Although he was successful in the 1950 election, he did not protest a petition that objected to his holding the position since he had not been a citizen for a full year.

Saund ran successfully again for the judgeship in the next election, and after taking office in 1953 as judge of justice court, Westmorland judicial district, Imperial County, he gave much of his attention to cleaning up prostitution, gambling, and narcotics in Westmorland. About this time he entered the chemical-fertilizer business and became the proprietor of D. S. Saund Fertilizers in Westmorland. He announced in late 1955 that he would campaign the following year for the seat in the House of Representatives of Republican John Phillips, who was not seeking re-election.

California's Twenty-ninth Congressional District, which covers Riverside and Imperial counties, is one of the largest districts in the country (11,460 square miles). Campaigning there against Republican Jacqueline Cochran Odlum, the well-known aviatrix, Saund argued that his victory would show the world that prejudice does not prevail in America and would help promote better understanding between Asian countries and the United States. In November 1956 he received 54,989 votes to Mrs. Odlum's 51,690 votes.

A few days after taking his seat in the Eighty-fifth Congress in January 1957, Representative Saund was appointed to the House Foreign Affairs Committee—an honor for a first-term Congressman. Assigned by the committee to survey the United States foreign aid program in Asia, he had the opportunity to carry out his campaign promise to go back to India and deny Communist propaganda about discrimination in the United States.

In the fall of 1957 Saund set out on his publicized tour of the Far East and the Middle East, a highlight of which was his invitation to address a joint session of India's houses of Parliament. The trip reinforced his belief that misunderstandings between Asians and Americans arose from the failure of the United States to make clear its motives and policies. He called for an expansion of the program for exchange of persons, especially in the fields of teaching and news reporting.

Among the foreign affairs bills that Saund supported in the House of Representatives were the President's Mideast Doctrine (January 1957), Mutual Security appropriations (July 1957, May 1958, and July 1959), postponement of interest payments on the British debt (April 1957), extension of the Reciprocal Trade Act (June 1958), an increase in United States subscriptions to the International Monetary Fund and World Bank (March 1959), and a provision for United States participation in the Inter-American Development Bank (July 1959).

On domestic issues Saund favored a bill for river-and-harbor flood control (March and June 1958), an increase in postal rates and salaries of postal employees (May 1958), an increase in Social Security benefits (July 1958), statehood for Hawaii (March 1959), an increase in grants for federal action against water pollution (June 1959), and an extension of the life of the Civil Rights Commission (September 1959).

Saund is a member of the American Mathematics Society and the Mathematics Association of America. He belongs also to Sigma Psi and the Toastmasters and the Lions clubs. In 1957 he won an Urban League award for bettering race relations and in 1958, a Lord & Taylor award for making "perhaps the most effective tour of India by an American on record."

On a visit to Los Angeles in the late 1920's Saund met Marian Z. Kosa, a University of California student who had been born in Massachusetts of Czech parents. They were married on July 21, 1928 and have a son, Dalip S., Jr. (a veteran of the Korean war), and two daughters, Julie G. (Mrs. Fred Fisher) and Eleanor B. (who is preparing to become a schoolteacher like her mother). Saund is a stocky man whose bushy black hair shows only slight signs of graying. He speaks with a slight British accent, in an even-tempered, engaging manner. Milton Mac-Kaye characterized him in a *Saturday Evening Post* article (August 2, 1958) as "an odd combination of meditative idealist and shrewd cross-roads politician."

References

Christian Sci Mon p6 N 21 '56 por
N Y Times p13 N 10 '56 por
Read Digest 73:175+ S '58 por
Sat Eve Post 231:25+ Ag 2 '58 pors
U S News 41:19 N 16 '56

Congressional Directory (1960)
Nine Who Chose America (1959)
Saund, Dalip S. Congressman from India (1960)
Who's Who in America, 1960-61

SCHOENBRUN, DAVID (FRANZ) (shōn' brŭn) Mar. 15, 1915- Journalist

Address: b. 33 Champs Élysées, Paris, 8e, France; h. 3 Avenue Bosquet, Paris 7e, France

One of the most informed and authoritative commentators on the people and politics of contemporary France is David Schoenbrun, who since 1947 has been the Paris correspondent for the Columbia Broadcasting System. Schoenbrun, who began his career as a high school teacher of French, often contributes to leading French and American newspapers and magazines. He is the author of *As France Goes* (Harper, 1957), an analysis of modern French civilization, in which he mediates between the French and the American people, trying, with his usual lucidity, to interpret each to the other.

David Franz Schoenbrun, the son of Max and Lucy (Cassirer) Schoenbrun, was born in New York City on March 15, 1915. He attended Townsend Harris Hall High School and City College of the City of New York, where he received a B.A. degree in 1934. Immediately after his graduation Schoenbrun, who was then nineteen, took a job as a French instructor at Townsend Harris and as a tutor in French at City College. The next year he taught French and Spanish at Far Rockaway and John Adams high schools in New York City.

In 1936 Schoenbrun left the teaching profession to become a labor relations adjustor and editor of a trade newspaper for the Dress Manufacturers Association. Four years later, he resigned so that he could devote his full time to free-lance writing. His articles on propaganda warfare for *Click* magazine, the Chicago *Sun,* and the New York liberal daily newspaper *PM* won him an appointment to the propaganda analysis division of the Office of War Information in 1942. He worked at the west European news desk.

Schoenbrun entered the United States Army in the spring of 1943 and was trained for military intelligence work. Two months after he was inducted, he was sent to Algiers and placed in charge of the Mediterranean theater news desk for the United Nations radio. He not only broadcast a weekly news commentary in this capacity in English and French, but directed the Allied Forces newsroom in Algiers.

In August 1944 Schoenbrun went to France as a Seventh Army combat correspondent and as a United States Army intelligence liaison officer with the French Army, covering the southern D-Day offensive. He reported from every battlefront throughout the French and German campaigns, and when the French Army broke through at Belfort Gap, he rode a tank through Alsace to become one of the first American soldiers to reach the Rhine.

After he was discharged from the United States Army in September 1945, Schoenbrun stayed in Paris to manage the bureau of the Overseas News Agency there. The following January he became a special correspondent for the Columbia Broadcasting System, continuing, at the same time, his duties for the news agency. In May 1947 he became a regular member of the CBS news staff.

As chief of the CBS Paris bureau, Schoenbrun covered the more than a score of cabinets that rose and fell during the French Fourth Republic. He witnessed the re-emergence of the present head of government, Charles de Gaulle. He was on the spot in Indochina when France was defeated there. He often travels to Tunisia, Morocco, and Algeria to observe and report on their relations with France.

David Seymour

DAVID SCHOENBRUN

The CBS newsman has left France to cover such events as the coronation of Great Britain's Queen Elizabeth II, the 1955 summit meeting, and the 1959 meeting of foreign ministers in Geneva. As a friend of Prince Rainier III of Monaco, he enjoyed a special advantage in covering the Prince's wedding to the American motion-picture actress Grace Kelly.

That Schoenbrun loves and understands France is obvious in his news commentaries on the politics and culture of his adopted home. In several articles he has analyzed the apparent contradictions in the manners, morals, and politics of the French, which, he feels, can be explained by the "cult of intelligence" which permeates every aspect of French civilization. He once maintained in an article called "Manners and Morals of the French" (*Harper's Magazine,* March 1957) that the cult is "the best and worst quality of the French. It has created the most civilized, literate society in the world. It is also a disease rotting that society. Intellectualism in France has reached the point of absurdity. . . . The Frenchman, the freest, most nonconformist thinker, becomes the slave of his own dogma."

Schoenbrun has often appeared on television to report on the crises that erupt in France and her dependencies. In 1957 he took part in a CBS production *Algeria Aflame,* in which he presented the French attitude toward the uprisings in Algeria. (Schoenbrun himself considers the Algerian situation a hopeless imbroglio.) In May 1958 he flew to New York to appear on a telecast *France at the Brink,* a special report on the French crisis over Algeria. During the program he termed Charles de Gaulle a "paternal autocrat" and a "mystic." When he took part in May 1959 in an evaluation by six CBS newsmen of the conference of foreign ministers in Geneva, a *Variety* reporter noted: "Schoenbrun and Schorr [the CBS Moscow corre-

SCHOENBRUN, DAVID—*Continued*

spondent] proved the most articulate and provocative of the lot with their probing remarks, frequently at variance with the views expressed by others at the powwow."

When David Schoenbrun's *As France Goes* was published by Harper & Brothers in 1957, it brought praise from most of the reviewers and won the 1958 Overseas Press Club award for the best book on foreign affairs. In the book Schoenbrun concluded that "the loss of the Empire may be the best thing that ever happened to France." He also predicted that if a republic of the world is ever established "it will have been a Frenchman who first proposed or drafted the World Constitution. There will probably be another Frenchman who will deliver the most brilliant analysis of its errors and vote against it."

Both the French and the Americans have recognized Schoenbrun's contributions to a better understanding of France and its people. In 1948 the French awarded him the Croix de Guerre and in 1952 they made him a Chevalier of the Legion of Honor. The Overseas Press Club cited him for distinguished reporting in 1951, 1953, and 1956. The TV program *Year of Crisis,* on which he was a panelist, won an "Emmy" award.

On September 23, 1938 David Schoenbrun was married to Dorothy Scher, the illustrator. They and their daughter Lucy live in an elegant apartment on the Left Bank of Paris. The "scholarly, war-toughened," and companionable reporter speaks French, Italian, Spanish, and German fluently. He has written articles for *Harper's Magazine,* the *Nation,* the *New Republic, Science Illustrated,* and other magazines. He belongs to the Association of Radio News Analysts, the Supreme Headquarters Allied Powers Europe Correspondents Association, the Overseas Press Club of America, and the American Press Club. He is a commander of the Confrérie du Tastevin de Bourgogne (the Brotherhood of Burgundy Winetasters).

Reference

Who's Who in America, 1958-59

SCHOMBURG, AUGUST July 3, 1908- United States Army Officer

Address: b. and h. United States Army Ordnance Missile Command, Redstone Arsenal, Huntsville, Ala.

When Major General August Schomburg became commanding general of the United States Army Ordnance Missile Command (AOMC) on February 1, 1960, he had completed nearly twenty years of service in the ordnance corps of the United States Army. A weapons expert and a mechanical engineer, he was deputy chief of ordnance in the Office of Chief of Ordnance in Washington, D.C. when he was named to succeed Major General John B. Medaris (see *C.B.,* February 1958) as head of the AOMC. Much of the Army's responsibility for space exploration programs has been transferred to the civilian National Aeronautics and Space Administration and to the United States Air Force. The AOMC retains jurisdiction, however, over the White Sands missile testing range in New Mexico and the Army Rocket and Guided Missile Agency in Huntsville, Alabama.

August Schomburg was born July 3, 1908 in Denver, Colorado, where his father, Sam Schomburg, was engaged in property management. His mother was Mary Harms before her marriage. He has one sister, Mrs. Ruth Bax. At West Denver High School, from which he was graduated in 1926, Schomburg was a member of the Junior Reserve Officers Training Corps, where he was appointed to the "top spot in the Colorado Junior ROTC," that of battalion commander.

After studying for a year at the Colorado School of Mines in Golden, he entered the United States Military Academy at West Point. There he received a B.S. degree in military science and a commission as a second lieutenant of infantry on June 11, 1931. Schomburg served as a platoon leader of a machine gun and howitzer platoon and as a company executive officer and regimental commander until May 1937. In August 1935 he had been promoted to the rank of first lieutenant.

For one year, beginning in June 1937, he studied at the Massachusetts Institute of Technology, from which he was graduated with an M.S. degree in mechanical engineering in 1938. After attending the Ordnance School at Aberdeen Proving Ground in Maryland until May 1939, he served for three years at the Proving Ground as an adjutant and post executive officer. During this time he was successively promoted to the ranks of captain (September 1940), major (February 1942), and lieutenant colonel (August 1942).

Schomburg next took command of the small arms section of the Ordnance Research and Development Center at Aberdeen. He also spent four months in Manitoba, Canada, as commanding officer of the Winter Proving Center there. Returning to Aberdeen in March 1943, he served for the next twelve months as executive officer and chief of the executive branch at the headquarters of the Ordnance Research and Development Command. His next assignment took him to Washington, D.C., where he was an organization and training staff officer with the general staff of the War Department. Promoted to the rank of colonel in August 1945, Schomburg served for three years (1946-49) as an assistant military attaché in Ottawa, Canada.

Appointed director of research, development, and engineering at the Watertown Arsenal near Boston, Massachusetts, Schomburg held this post from September 1949 to July 1952. The following month he entered the Industrial College of Armed Forces at Fort McNair in Washington, D.C., from which he was graduated in June 1953. Promoted to the rank of brigadier general in July, Schomburg was sent to Heidelberg, Germany, where he served as chief of the procurement branch, G-4, Logistics, for the United States Army in Europe until February 1956.

Schomburg attained his present rank of major general in May 1956, a month after he had been called to Washington, D.C. to succeed

Major General John B. Medaris as assistant chief of ordnance, research, and development in the Office of Chief of Ordnance. In May 1958 he was promoted to the position of deputy chief of ordnance in that office. In this capacity he supervised Army research on different kinds of new weapons and war equipment.

Speaking at an annual meeting of the American Ordnance Association in December 1958, Schomburg described the tentative development of a non-lethal gas, which could be used to diminish temporarily the enemy's will to fight. In September 1959 he announced that Army Ordnance was sponsoring experimentation on a Free Air Suspension System (FASS), a new propulsion system that would allow ground vehicles to fly over obstacles through the use of high-powered air pressure. At the same time Schomburg mentioned plans for the development of lighter rifles and of cartridges which would fire two or three bullets at one time.

Schomburg is familiar with research and development in missile and space activities. He played a leading role in expediting provision of satellite-launching vehicles to the National Aeronautics and Space Administration (NASA). He also took a major part in discussions which led to a cooperative agreement between the Army and NASA, under which the facilities of the Army Ballistic Missile Agency were made available to NASA and the Army's jet propulsion laboratory at the California Institute of Technology was transferred to NASA.

Schomburg was named to succeed Major General John B. Medaris as commanding general of the United States Army Ordnance Missile Command (AOMC) on October 27, 1959. From that date until his appointment became effective on February 1, 1960, he devoted a major portion of his time to working at the AOMC headquarters at Huntsville, Alabama. During Medaris' tenure the AOMC included the Army Ballistic Missile Agency, where rocket scientists led by Wernher von Braun had developed a short-range bombardment missile (the Redstone), intermediate-range Jupiter ballistic missiles, and the first earth and solar satellites. In October 1959, by an order of President Eisenhower which was approved by Congress, the Ballistic Missile Agency was transferred to the jurisdiction of the civilian National Aeronautics and Space Administration. It was also announced that the Air Force would eventually assume responsibility for space transportation programs.

Two subordinate installations of the AOMC have remained under Schomburg's command: the White Sands missile testing range in New Mexico; and the Army Rocket and Guided Missile Agency at Huntsville, which is primarily a maintenance and supply unit. Army Ordnance will continue development of limited-range missiles like the Lacrosse (for use as atomic artillery); SS-11 and Shillelagh (antitank missiles); Redeye, designed to meet low-level strafing attacks; and Mauler, a guided missile system. The day after he was named to his new post, Schomburg stated (*Christian Science Monitor*, October 28, 1959) that the transfer of the Ballistic Missile Agency would have

U. S. Army

MAJ. GEN. AUGUST SCHOMBURG

"no influence on military missiles" and that the mission of AOMC is unchanged.

August Schomburg and Fern Alice Wynne of New York City were married on June 12, 1931. They have two daughters, Alice Ruth (Mrs. R. M. D'Oliveira) and Augusta Ann (Mrs. Mead S. Gruver), and one son, August, who is a second lieutenant in the United States Army. Schomburg is six feet tall, weighs 165 pounds, and has blue eyes and black hair tinged with gray. He is a Roman Catholic and belongs to the Newcomen Society and the American Ordnance Association. His favorite pastime is collecting and repairing antique clocks, some of which are nearly 200 years old. The general has been decorated with the Legion of Merit (with oak leaf cluster) and the Commendation Ribbon (with oak leaf cluster).

References

Gen Army 2:20 Ag '54 por
Who's Who in America, 1960-61

SCHULZ, CHARLES M(ONROE) Nov. 26, 1922- Cartoonist

Address: b. c/o United Feature Syndicate, Inc., 220 E. 42d St., New York 17; h. 2162 Coffee Lane, Sebastopol, Calif.

When the United Feature Syndicate decided in 1950 to christen Charles M. Schulz's new cartoon idea *Peanuts,* the cartoonist entertained some misgivings. To him, the name sounded insignificant. Besides, he reasoned, new readers might become confused by the absence of any character named "Peanuts" from the strip. Time has proved Schulz right in his latter reservation; on the former, he could not have been more wrong. *Peanuts* soon became one of the most popular comic strips in the United States. It has earned for Schulz a "Reuben" award

CHARLES M. SCHULZ

from the National Cartoonists Society, the designation Humorist of the Year from Yale undergraduates, and the School Bell Award from the National Education Society. *Peanuts* now appears in more than 400 newspapers in the United States and in thirty-five newspapers in foreign countries.

Schulz's famous comic strip deals with very young children who think and talk like adults. *Peanuts* rewards its admirers with insights into the child mind without descending to the archness of cliché-ridden comic strips about children. Because of his cartooning, Schulz has been called "one of America's sharpest, if kindliest, social critics and analysts."

Charles Monroe Schulz, of Norwegian and German ancestry, was born in Minneapolis, Minnesota on November 26, 1922. He was the only child of a barber, Carl Schulz, and his wife Dena (Halverson) Schulz. Charles's mother died in 1943; his father still operates the Family Barber Shop in St. Paul as he has done for more than forty years. The boy's association with comic strips began early in life: when he was an infant, he was nicknamed "Sparky" after Sparkplug, the horse in the Barney Google cartoon. He still is known by the nickname. In later years he was called The Timid Soul, after H. T. Webster's famous Caspar Milquetoast in another comic strip.

According to Charles Schulz, he can trace none of his success as a cartoonist to his ancestors. "There were no artists in the family," he has said, "but there were a lot of funny people." From the age of six he wanted to become a cartoonist, when he could draw an easily recognizable Popeye in the first grade.

Otherwise, Schulz's achievements in primary and secondary school were somewhat less than breathtaking. Partly as a result of having skipped two and one-half grades early in elementary school, he soon found himself outclassed. As a consequence, he failed the eighth grade entirely. At St. Paul's Central High School later on, he flunked algebra, Latin, English, and physics.

His social life in high school was just as undistinguished. He was too shy to ask a girl for a date because he was afraid that he might be turned down. He lost even the consolation rounds when he played on the school golf team. He submitted some cartoons for the high school graduation yearbook, only to have them rejected. Like his own Charlie Brown, he was the "epitome of unachievement."

In the meanwhile, undiscouraged by his academic and social rebuffs, Schulz continued to draw. After his graduation from high school in 1940, he enrolled in a correspondence course given by Art Instruction, Inc., of Minneapolis. In 1943 he was drafted into the United States Army, and he was forced to give up his art studies for the duration.

As a soldier, Schulz served in France and Germany and, shortly before the end of the war, reached the front with the 20th Armored Division in Bavaria. He rose to the rank of staff sergeant in charge of a light machine gun squad. He recalls that he once refrained from throwing a grenade into an artillery emplacement because a little dog had wandered into it. "I guess I fought a pretty civilized war," he says.

After the war ended, Schulz returned to St. Paul, where for a while he joined the ranks of unemployed ex-GIs in the "52-20 Club," so called because its members received twenty dollars a week in benefits while hunting for jobs. He resumed his cartooning career when he obtained a job lettering the comic pages of a religious magazine that was published in St. Paul. Finally, to his surprise, he was summoned to Art Instruction, Inc., and on the basis of his prewar student drawings, was offered a position on its staff.

Schulz began to draw a weekly cartoon for a St. Paul newspaper, and in 1948 he sold his first cartoons to the *Saturday Evening Post.* His big opportunity came when the United Feature Syndicate bought his idea for a comic strip. It was then that *Peanuts* was born. (The name was bestowed by the United Feature Syndicate; Schulz had preferred to call it *Li'l Folks,* but that title had already been copyrighted by another cartoonist.)

The characters in the *Peanuts* cartoon include Charlie Brown, a juvenile version of Thurber's Walter Mitty, whose fantasies always come crashing to earth; Lucy, a little girl who constantly deflates Charlie's ego; Schroeder, an infant musical prodigy who plays a toy piano without any black keys; and Snoopy, a dog of many talents, not all of them canine. All of Schulz's little people talk and think like adults. Schulz says: "When I jam this adult approach and mature attitude into the characters of the little people . . . something has to give." The appeal of *Peanuts* has been attributed by a writer for *Time* (March 3, 1958) to "its sophisticated melding of wry wisdom and sly one-upmanship."

Peanuts was bought by eight daily newspapers in October 1950. By 1958 it was appearing in more than 400 newspapers, and Schulz was earning $90,000 a year. Carl Sandburg, the poet, and Harlow Curtice of General Motors are reported to be dedicated readers of *Peanuts*. Because of the strip, Schulz has acquired a reputation as an intellectual—a reputation that he protests is undeserved. The astuteness with which he has dealt with human foibles in *Peanuts* has given him a reputation as a semanticist, psychologist, and even as an existentialist. To Schulz, all this is a cause of wonder. After someone called him "the youngest existentialist," for example, he had to inquire what the term meant.

In 1955 Schulz was named Outstanding Cartoonist of the Year by the National Cartoonists Society. He was awarded its "Reuben" (the equivalent, among cartoonists, of an Oscar). In 1956 he won the Yale Humor Award as Outstanding Humorist of the Year. In 1960 he received the School Bell Award from the National Education Society.

Schulz has expanded *Peanuts* into a series of comic books for children and he has assembled several collections in book form for adults, the latest of which is entitled *Go Fly a Kite, Charlie Brown* (Holt, Rinehart, and Winston, 1960). The title alludes to a memorable episode in *Peanuts,* when Charlie Brown spent eight days holding on to the string of his kite that had been caught in a tree. It was the first time in the history of the seven lively arts that a cartoon character remained immobile for so long a period. Charlie Brown was finally forced to come indoors when it began to rain, but he won his victory over the kite when he learned that the kite, too, was getting wet.

As a clue to his own philosophy, Schulz points to Charlie Brown's encounter with the kite. Charlie's ordeal, according to Schulz, symbolized the little fellow with a problem who, because he is unable to do anything about it, has to wait until something happens. "You've just got to let things go along," he explains, "ride them out, and see how they turn out in the end. There's no use trying to solve all your problems in one day."

On April 18, 1949 Charles Monroe Schulz was married to Joyce Halverson, whom he met while he was working for Art Instruction, Inc., in Minneapolis; she was the sister of another member of the staff. They live with their five children—Meredith, Charles, Jr., Craig, Amy, and Jill—in Sebastopol, California. Schulz insists that his children seldom supply him with ideas for his cartoons.

Blue-eyed and blond-haired, Schulz stands five feet and eleven and one-half inches tall and weighs about 180 pounds. He grew up in the Lutheran Church, but now belongs to the Fundamentalist Church of God, where the members still observe the ancient custom of tithing. A deeply religious man, Schulz is active in the church both as Sunday-school teacher and as an administrative official. He does not smoke, drink, or swear. His entire vocabulary of expletives, he says, consists of "good grief" and "rats"—exclamations voiced by the children in his cartoons. His favorite recreations are golf (he shoots an excellent game), tennis, and bridge. But he spends most of his time in doing what he most enjoys: drawing a round circle, a dash, a loop, and two black spots. In various combinations, these elements go to make up the characters in *Peanuts*.

"If you read the Bible," Schulz has said, "you'll find an expression of how I feel in the Gospel of St. Luke. It's this verse: 'It were better for him that a millstone were hanged about his neck, and he cast into the sea than that he should offend one of these little ones.'"

References

Look 22:66+ Jl 22 '58 por
N Y World-Telegram Mag p5 My 5 '56 por
Sat Eve Post 229:34+ Ja 12 '57 por
Time 71:58 Mr 3 '58 por

SCHWARTZ, DELMORE Dec. 8, 1913-
Author; critic

Address: b. Doubleday & Co, Inc., 575 Madison Ave., New York 22; h. 725 Greenwich St., New York 14

When Delmore Schwartz was awarded the 1959 Bollingen Prize in Poetry in January 1960 for *Summer Knowledge,* he was tacitly recognized as one of America's foremost poets, joining such previous winners as Ezra Pound and Archibald MacLeish. At forty-six, he became the youngest winner of the award since it was established in 1948; yet Schwartz' work spans more than two decades of productive writing both in poetry and prose. In teaching (at Harvard University and elsewhere) and in editing (for the *Partisan Review* and *New Republic*) he also has a distinguished reputation.

Delmore Schwartz was born in Brooklyn, New York, on December 8, 1913, the son of Harry and Rose (Nathanson) Schwartz. He became a roving scholar after finishing high school, attending the University of Wisconsin in 1933, New York University from 1933 to 1935, and Harvard University from 1935 to 1937. He received his Bachelor of Arts degree in philosophy from NYU in 1935.

Apparently while still a student, Schwartz edited a "little magazine" called *Mosaic*. The young poet was published elsewhere at the same time, his first appearances in print being translations of the French symbolist poet Rimbaud and the philosophical writer Benda. In 1936, when Schwartz was twenty-two years old, *American Caravan* published his dramatic poem, "Choosing Company." Meanwhile, he was working on the manuscript of *In Dreams Begin Responsibilities* (the title is a paraphrased quotation from William Butler Yeats), a collection containing a story, a long poem, lyrics, and a play.

The publishing climate in 1936 was no more hospitable to new poets than it is today. In that year, however, James Laughlin launched his New Directions publishing house to specialize in hazardous ventures. Schwartz was one of Laughlin's first discoveries and was represented in his first *New Directions in Prose and Poetry* annual, published in 1937.

Two years later New Directions brought out *In Dreams Begin Responsibilities.* G. M.

Jane Lougee

DELMORE SCHWARTZ

O'Donnell, writing in *Poetry* magazine (May 1939), called it "one of those rare first books that oblige an immediate recognition of their genuineness as poetry. Indeed, no first book of this decade in American poetry has been more authoritative or more significant than this one."

New Directions published Schwartz' translation, with an introduction, of Rimbaud's *A Season in Hell* in 1940 and the following year reissued the work in its New Classics Series. Schwartz' essays in literary criticism reached a select audience through the pages of *Poetry,* the *Southern Review,* and the *Partisan Review.* These and other essays were collected in his unpublished "The Imitation of Life and Other Problems of Literary Criticism."

Schwartz' growing reputation was recognized by a Guggenheim Fellowship, which was awarded him in 1940, and in the same year by an appointment as Briggs-Copeland Instructor in English Composition at Harvard. While teaching at Harvard, Schwartz completed the manuscript of his verse play *Shenandoah,* which was published in a slim volume of twenty-eight pages by New Directions in 1941.

Shenandoah dealt with the naming rites of a Jewish child in the Bronx and contained both poetry and prose. The reviews were mixed. E. L. Milton wrote in New York *Herald Tribune Books* (November 23, 1941): "It has been obvious for some time that Mr. Schwartz writes too much and with too little self-criticism. He airs a not too well assimilated education, a knowledge of the work of many other poets and philosophers but no authentic view of his own." A different opinion was given by M. M. Colum in the New York *Times* (November 30, 1941): "The theme is a subtle one and is worked out with ironic humor and considerable profundity. Delmore Schwartz has been able to get dramatic tenseness and emotion into his

striking material, the significance of a name, of names."

In his long, introspective poem *Genesis, Book I* (New Directions, 1943), Schwartz depicted a sensitive young American of Russo-Jewish extraction growing up in New York. It was greeted as his most ambitious poetic work to date. In 1943, while maintaining his post at Harvard, Delmore Schwartz became editor of the *Partisan Review,* in whose pages he had often appeared as a contributor.

Schwartz had also written short stories for the "little magazines," and in 1948 New Directions published them under the title *The World is a Wedding.* "In so far as authenticity means truth, these short stories are the most authentic I have read in a long time," wrote critic John Hay in *Commonweal* (September 17, 1948). "They do not try to avoid the great pressures of the contemporary, but work within it and so mirror it faithfully. . . . *The World is a Wedding* is put together with impressive skill. It builds its patterns carefully and quietly. In a comparatively few pages some of the stories encompass generations of family tensions and frustrations without apparent strain. But the style, though quiet, has a kind of muted eloquence which testifies even more strongly to their author's talent."

Just a year after Schwartz had been advanced to assistant professor at Harvard, 1947, he left the university and also stepped down from the editorship of the *Partisan Review.* He remained with the magazine as associate editor, however, from 1947 to 1955 and appeared as a visiting lecturer at New York University, the Kenyon School of English, the Indiana School of Letters, Princeton University, and the University of Chicago. At the same time, he worked on a new volume of poetry and prose.

Vaudeville for a Princess and Other Poems (New Directions, 1950) was received more warmly for its prose passages than its verse. "The poetry of Mr. Schwartz suffers its most severe criticism at the hands of the author's own prose," wrote Rolfe Humphries in the *Nation* (November 25, 1950). Much the same view was held by Dudley Fitts in the *Saturday Review* (July 21, 1951): "From the beginning of his career . . . Delmore Schwartz has shown himself a master of a prose style of almost unbelievable subtlety and expressiveness. He carries it on in the *Vaudeville,* where it takes on a pseudo-ingenuous dead-pan, a parody of youthful seriousness, that the masterparodist, Joyce himself, might have envied."

For the next decade Schwartz was represented mainly by literary criticism and occasional poems and short stories in magazines and anthologies. He was associated with *Perspectives,* published by the Ford Foundation, in 1952 and 1953, and also served as literary consultant to New Directions. In 1955 he left his position as associate editor of the *Partisan Review* to become poetry editor of the *New Republic,* where he remained until 1957.

All the poems from Schwartz' first book, *In Dreams Begin Responsibilities,* as well as selections from his newer poetry, were reprinted in *Summer Knowledge: New and Selected Poems, 1938-1958* (Doubleday, 1959). On January 10, 1960 the Yale University Library named Schwartz the recipient of its 1959 Bollingen Prize in Poetry, carrying a stipend of $2,500. The award committee noted that the book included "poems in a great diversity of manners and meters, all marked by inventive workmanship, all spoken in a personal voice." For *Summer Knowledge,* Schwartz also won the Shelley Memorial Prize of $1,100 in 1960.

Delmore Schwartz has been twice married. His first wife was the former Gertrude Buckman. In 1949 he was married to Elizabeth Pollet. Schwartz lives in Greenwich Village, New York, where he is working on a book of stories, a novel, and a play. He has previously received awards from *Poetry* magazine in 1950 and 1959, from the National Institute of Arts and Letters in 1953, and was one of four *Kenyon Review* Fellows in 1957.

Conrad Aiken's *A Reviewer's ABC* (Meridian, 1958) contained a critical piece on Schwartz that Aiken wrote in 1940: "The two most completely satisfactory poets of the moment . . . are Mr. Dylan Thomas and Mr. Delmore Schwartz. . . . Mr. Schwartz, if a good deal drier [than Thomas], both linguistically and prosodically—at times almost imageless—is in his different way just as brilliant. His plain statements are not so plain, by any means, as they look—they are cunningly weighed and weighted, there are degrees in his dryness, and his psychological procedure is impeccable. He can even be lyrical, when he wants to. And surely his *Coriolanus and His Mother* is altogether the finest and profoundest long poem, narrative poem, which has come into English literature for a very long time."

References

Twentieth Century Authors (1942; First Supplement, 1955)
Who's Who in America (sup My '43)

SCHWARTZ, MAURICE June 18, 1890-May 10, 1960 Actor; director; producer; organized (1918) and acted with Yiddish Art Theatre (1919-1950, 1955); performed on Broadway stage, in American and Yiddish motion pictures, and in many parts of the world. See *Current Biography* (February) 1956.

Obituary

N Y Times p39 My 11 '60

SEABURY, DAVID Sept. 11, 1885-Apr. 1, 1960 Psychologist; author; educator; consulting psychologist for some forty years; founder of centralist school of psychology. See *Current Biography* (September) 1941.

Obituary

N Y Times p86 Ap 3 '60

SEARS, PAUL B(IGELOW) Dec. 17, 1891- Botanist; university professor; author
Address: b. Yale University, New Haven, Conn.; h. N. Forest Circle, New Haven, Conn.

As a botanist whose interests extend far beyond the plant kingdom, Dr. Paul B. Sears has not confined his activities to research and teaching nor his audience to students and scientists. Among Dr. Sears's chief concerns are man's stewardship of natural resources, the relationship of man to his environment, and the effect of present-day scientific research on the future of mankind. His research in plant ecology and plant history has caused considerable discussion among scientists, and his books, such as *Deserts on the March* (1935) and *Charles Darwin* (1950), have cast light on scientific problems for the general reader.

For ten years Dr. Sears served at Yale University as professor and head of the graduate program in the conservation of natural resources. In 1956 he was president of the American Association for the Advancement of Science. Dr. Edmund W. Sinnott, then chairman of Yale's division of sciences, wrote in 1955: "Paul Sears is a biological statesman, one of the group of men—all too few—who know the life sciences well but see them against the wider background of human affairs" (*Science,* February 18, 1955).

The son of Rufus Victor and Sallie Jane (Harris) Sears, Paul Bigelow Sears was born on December 17, 1891 in Bucyrus, Ohio. He attended Ohio Wesleyan University in Delaware, where he earned his B.S. degree in 1913 and won election to the Phi Beta Kappa and Sigma Xi honorary societies. Two years later he fulfilled the requirements for the M.A. degree at the University of Nebraska in Lincoln. In 1922 he earned his Ph.D. degree in botany at the University of Chicago. His doctoral dissertation, *Variations in Cytology and Gross Morphology of Taraxacum,* appeared in the *Botanical Gazette* (April and June 1922) and as a privately published book (1922).

His teaching career began in 1915 when he became an instructor in botany at Ohio State University in Columbus. Taking a leave of absence, he served in the United States Army in 1917-18. After returning to Ohio State for a year, Sears began in 1919 eight years' tenure at the University of Nebraska, first as an assistant professor and later as an associate professor. From Nebraska he went to the University of Oklahoma in Norman in 1927 in the capacity of full professor and chairman of the department of botany. For two years, 1936 to 1938, he was a research associate at Teachers College, Columbia University. He then joined the faculty of Oberlin College in 1938 as professor and chairman of the department of botany.

In 1950 he went to Yale University to assume the posts of professor and chairman of the new graduate program of research and instruction in the conservation of natural resources. For two years beginning in 1953 he was also chairman of the department of plant sciences. Having reached the mandatory

Yale News Bureau—
Alburtus

PAUL B. SEARS

retirement age of sixty-eight, Sears left Yale in June 1960.

One of Sears's continuing concerns is to define the obligations incumbent upon scientists. According to Dr. Sears, these include the conservation of human knowledge, the promotion of human well-being, an obligation to the universe, and the fulfillment of the duties of citizenship. A principal responsibility of the scientist is to provide politicians with facts, he said in August 1955, thus "reducing the area of uncertainty and dispute to a minimum." This gives scientists "a very definite relation to politics in the world today."

Closely related to Sears's convictions concerning the civic obligations of scientists is his belief in the importance of a long-range approach to scientific inquiry. Individual scientific projects, he believes, should not be solely prescribed by immediate and practical considerations; the broader social implications of scientific investigation should be carefully examined. Addressing the Ninth International Botanical Congress at McGill University in Montreal, Quebec in 1959, Dr. Sears declared that science, in order to progress, requires a considerable amount of idle speculation. "Today there seems to be no time for what I call fooling around," he said, "no time to permit great minds to contemplate this world and project their thought into realms from which vast ideas come." He reminded his listeners that leisurely contemplation had produced revolutionary discoveries in science by Charles Darwin, Sir Isaac Newton, and Louis Pasteur.

In the opinion of Dr. Sears, science must ultimately be guided by values and beliefs. "I'm personally much more concerned about the problem of control than the problem of speed [in making new discoveries]," Dr. Sears

said on the CBS-TV program *Great Challenge* in March 1958. "After all, science seems to me essentially a tool. But, like any tool, what happens depends on the user. So that checks back to our whole system of values and what we know and understand about ourselves."

In carrying out his own responsibilities as a scientist, Dr. Sears has written books in which he has popularized science for the general reader. Conservation and ecology have been the subjects of many of these works. One of his first books, *Deserts on the March* (University of Oklahoma Press, 1935), deals with the problems of soil erosion and land reclamation. Dr. Sears wrote the volume while he was at the University of Oklahoma, drawing on his observations of the havoc wreaked by drought and the improper use of land in the Dust Bowl during the 1930's.

A reviewer in the *Christian Science Monitor* (November 15, 1935) remarked: "Dr. Sears presents the situation, with its social-economic implications, and the way out, in nontechnical language, always simple, often dramatic, abounding in memorable and witty epigrams. He is not merely a prophet of doom, but he does sound a solemn warning against greed and expediency, and pleads for a long-time policy."

Perhaps Dr. Sears's most ambitious book is *Charles Darwin; The Naturalist as a Cultural Force* (Scribner, 1950). In it he presents Darwin's thoughts within the context of the history of scientific ideas, analyzes Darwin's role in interpreting the view that man is continuous with all organic nature, and assesses Darwin's influence on certain aspects of human life.

Other books by Sears include *This Is Our World* (University of Oklahoma Press, 1937); *Who Are These Americans?* (Macmillan, 1939); and *Life and Environment; The Interrelations of Living Things* (Teachers College, Columbia University, 1939), with I. James Quillan and Paul R. Hanna. In over fifty technical papers, Dr. Sears has written about fossil pollen; the techniques by which borings in peat bogs throw light upon vegetation of the past; postglacial changes in vegetation and climate in the Northern United States; the antiquity of maize; and Pleistocene climatic history. With the assistance of a $6,900 grant from the National Science Foundation he conducted a micro-paleo-botanical study of sediments.

The American Association for the Advancement of Science (A.A.A.S.) honored Dr. Sears by electing him its president for 1956. In his presidential address Dr. Sears discussed the burdens that a growing population and a rising standard of living impose on the food supply and on natural resources. "Our future security may depend less upon priority in exploring outer space," he said, "than upon our wisdom in managing the space in which we live." With "a population set to double in less than half a century, with a national space which, though vast, is finite both in area and quality, with each individual making growing demands . . . we have on our hands a problem without precedent in all geological history." The A.A.A.S. named him chairman of the board for 1957 and elected him a Fellow.

In addition to holding posts with the A.A.A.S., Dr. Sears served as general secretary of the Botanical Society of America (1924-28) and as president of the Nebraska Academy of Science, Ecological Society of America, and American Society of Naturalists. He is also a member of the American, Oklahoma, and Connecticut academies of arts and sciences and the Ohio Wildlife Council. His fraternities are Delta Tau Delta, Sigma Gamma Epsilon, and Phi Sigma (national president, 1928-29; national chancellor, 1929-33).

For the United States government, Dr. Sears served on the National Committee for the Development of Scientists and Engineers, which was formed in 1956. Two years later he was appointed to a six-year term as a member of the national science board of the National Science Foundation. Sears has worked as a consultant to the Virginia-Carolina Chemical Corporation and was elected a director of its board in 1956.

Paul B. Sears was married to the former Marjorie Lea McCutcheon on June 22, 1917. They have three children: Catherine Louise, Sallie Harris, and Paul McCutcheon, a writer of science books for children. Dr. Sears is an Episcopalian. He has received honorary D.Sc. degrees from Ohio Wesleyan University and Oberlin College, LL.D. degrees from the University of Arkansas, the University of Nebraska, and Wayne University, and a Litt.D. degree from Marietta College. His speeches are noted for their charm and eloquence. Edmund W. Sinnott wrote that Dr. Sears is "a man of thorough training, wide sympathies, and balanced judgment."

When Dr. Sears reviewed Joseph Wood Krutch's *Human Nature and the Human Condition* (1959), he allied himself with the humanist tradition. He wrote: "The humanist faith in the power of ideas is sustained by the rules of experience that have come from anthropology. We have already demonstrated our concern for the general welfare of contemporary mankind and our skill in using science as we please. If we extend our concern to our successors and our use of science to a thorough understanding of our own ecosystem, we have the basis for ideas that should go far toward insuring the future of the human adventure on this planet" (*Nation*, January 23, 1960).

References

N Y Times p27 Ja 16 '50 por; p59 Mr 27 '60 por

American Men of Science vol 2 (1955)
Who's Who in America, 1960-61

SEGRÈ, EMILIO (GINO) (sā-grā') Feb. 1, 1905- Physicist; university professor

Address: b. University of California, Berkeley 4, Calif.; h. 36 Crest Rd., Lafayette, Calif.

For the discovery of the antiproton, "a nuclear ghost which has haunted the world's physicists for a generation," Dr. Emilio Segrè has

EMILIO SEGRÈ

won a place among the Nobel Prize laureates of the world. He shared the 1959 physics award with his colleague at the University of California, Dr. Owen Chamberlain, for producing, and confirming in 1955 the existence of, the negatively charged proton that destroys itself as well as the matter it strikes. Their discovery of this atomic particle is regarded as the beginning of a new age in man's understanding of the universe.

The Italian-born physicist has made other significant contributions to nuclear physics. As a member of Dr. Enrico Fermi's team, he participated in research on the neutron which laid the foundation for the splitting of the atom. Dr. Segrè identified several new elements, developed a chemical method for dividing nuclear isomers, and was a co-discoverer of plutonium 239. In his efforts to learn more about the nature of the universe he has recently been involved in photographing the destruction of anti-matter. He does not rule out the possibility that somewhere in the universe exist galaxies of anti-matter that equal the galaxies of matter.

Born on February 1, 1905 in Tivoli, Italy, Emilio Segrè is one of the three sons of Giuseppe Segrè, an industrialist, and Amelia (Treves) Segrè. He attended schools in his native city and completed his secondary education at Liceo Mamiani in Rome in 1922. Segrè studied engineering at the University of Rome for five years before physics became his major interest. He came under the influence of Dr. Enrico Fermi, who became a Nobel laureate in 1938 and a leader in the United States atomic bomb project. The Ph.D. degree, which was the first to be conferred under Fermi's sponsorship, was awarded to Segrè in 1928 (one source gives the date as 1927).

After serving a one-year tour of duty in the Italian Army as a second lieutenant in the artillery, Segrè returned to the University of Rome as an instructor in physics. He was

SEGRÈ, EMILIO—*Continued*

named an assistant professor in 1930, the same year in which he received a Rockefeller Foundation Fellowship to study with Otto Stern and Pieter Zeeman. Two years later Segrè was promoted to an associate professorship.

During the early years of his career Segrè worked primarily in the field of atomic spectroscopy, molecular beams, and X rays. He obtained significant results in his investigations of the spectroscopy of forbidden lines and his studies of the Zeeman effect and the Stark effect. By 1934 he had switched his interest to nuclear physics and joined a group of scientists working with Professor Fermi on the production of artificial radioactivity by neutron absorption. As a member of the team, he participated in the discovery of slow neutrons and collaborated with Fermi and others on a series of papers which initiated the field of neutron physics and laid the groundwork for the development of atomic energy.

Dr. Segrè was appointed professor and chairman of the physics department at the University of Palermo in 1936. In the same year he visited the University of California, where he observed the working of the cyclotron and concluded that certain of its parts received a very strong bombardment of deuteron when it was in operation. Further examination of these parts in his Palermo laboratory, in collaboration with C. Perrier, led to the discovery of a new element, which Segrè named "technetium," from the Greek word *technetos*, meaning "artificial."

An opponent of Fascism, Dr. Segrè immigrated to the United States in 1938. He accepted an assignment as research associate in the radiation laboratory at Berkeley and lecturer in the physics department of the university. Within two years Segrè discovered another element, astatine, in collaboration with Dale R. Corson and K. R. MacKenzie. He followed these experiments with new researches in artificial radioactivity and nuclear isomerism, and with Dr. Glenn T. Seaborg, he developed a chemical method for separating nuclear isomers.

Dr. Segrè was a co-discoverer with Dr. Seaborg and others of plutonium 239, which they produced in the Berkeley cyclotron by fission of uranium. By means of tracer chemistry the scientists also established its fission properties. (Large-scale production of plutonium was started in 1944, and the element was used as one of the three atomic bombs of World War II.)

In 1941 Segrè and Seaborg announced that they had split atoms of uranium and thorium into equal parts. They succeeded in dividing uranium 235 into two atoms of palladium. The equal fission of uranium and thorium produced large quantities of energy, comparable to the results of unequal fission. Segrè's prewar studies of fission and atomic power proved invaluable to the United States war effort, and in 1943 he was invited to work at the Los Alamos Scientific Laboratory in New Mexico. As a group leader, Dr. Segrè conducted investigations in the field of spontaneous fission.

When Dr. Segrè returned to Berkeley in 1946, he was appointed a full professor in the physics department. Using the 184-inch synchro-cyclotron at Berkeley, Segrè conducted experiments on the scattering of neutrons and protons, including measurements of the effects of proton polarization. This research proved essential to an understanding of the forces between nuclear particles.

William L. Laurence (New York *Times,* January 30, 1955) reported that Segrè's experiments with high-energy polarized protons would "become a powerful new tool for probing the mysterious realms of the nuclei of atoms and the forces that hold the universe together." Segrè found that the proton, the positively charged constituent of every atomic nucleus, acted as a magnet with a north and south pole, and that its spinning was determined by the orientation of its poles.

Experiments showed that a beam of protons was simply a mixture of individual protons spinning in diverse directions. Polarized protons, on the other hand, moved in the same path since both the north and south poles were oriented in the same direction, being parallel to each other. Using the giant cyclotrons, which accelerated the speed of a beam of protons to several hundred million volts, Segrè obtained new information on the target nucleus as well as the polarized beam.

Professor Segrè pooled his efforts with Dr. Owen Chamberlain (see *C.B.,* March 1960), a colleague who was also working on proton polarization. Together they directed a classical series of experiments which resulted in the discovery of the antiproton, the negatively charged particle of the same mass as the proton. Although the idea of the antiproton had been suggested as early as 1928, physicists had not been able to prove its existence.

The Segrè-Chamberlain experiments revealed that antiprotons did not exist in nuclei, but were created only in high-energy nuclear collisions occurring in cosmic radiation or in the accelerated bombardments achieved in the Berkeley bevatron. The bevatron produced too few antiprotons, however, compared to the number of other particles, and it was Dr. Segrè who conceived the ingenious and subtle method of discovering and identifying the few antiprotons that entered his selective apparatus.

The award to Segrè and Chamberlain marked the sixteenth time the Nobel Prize in Physics was bestowed on Americans—"a record that speaks well for a climate of free scientific inquiry" (New York *Herald Tribune,* November 3, 1959). When Dr. Segrè received the news of his honor while teaching a class, he told his students that "looking for strange particles from here on is likely to be a kind of sport. There are other things . . . that are more important than the discovery of more particles."

Dr. Segrè has described his researches in scientific and professional journals in the United States and Europe and he has edited *Experimental Nuclear Physics* (Wiley, 1953). In this country and abroad he has lectured widely and is an honorary faculty member of San Marcos University in Lima, Peru. He has been elected to fellowships in the American Physical Society and the Società Italiana di Fisica and has been honored with membership in the scientific academies of the United States, Uruguay, Peru, and Germany.

Medals have been bestowed on him by the German Chemical Society and the Accademia Nazionale dei Lincei. He received an honorary degree from the University of Palermo and in 1959 he was named a commander of merit of the Republic of Italy. Segrè served as faculty research lecturer at Berkeley during 1959-60.

A cosmopolitan in manner, gray-haired, gray-eyed Emilio Segrè stands slightly over five feet six inches and weighs about 158 pounds. He was married to Elfriede Spiro, a former translator and interpreter, on February 2, 1936. They are the parents of a son, Claudio, and two daughters, Amelia and Fausta. Segrè has been a citizen of the United States since 1944. For relaxation he goes fishing, skiing, and mountain climbing.

References

N Y Times p1+ O 25 '59 por
Nature 184:1189 O 17 '59
American Men of Science vol 3 (1955)
Who Knows—and What (1954)
Who's Who in America, 1958-59

British Lion Films, Ltd., London

PETER SELLERS

SELLERS, PETER Sept. 8, 1925- Actor

Address: b. 37 Panton St., London S.W. 1, England; h. "The Manor House," Chipperfield, Hertfordshire, England

Hailed in England and the United States as a brilliant character actor and comedian, Peter Sellers is a radio, television, stage, and screen star whose talent for mimicry has earned him, among several other honors, the British Film Academy Award as the best actor of 1959. He first became widely known in the United States when he portrayed a woman and two men in *The Mouse that Roared* and a union czar in *I'm All Right, Jack*. Sellers views his mission in the world of entertainment as that of "ridiculing without being ridiculous; being serious without being solemn."

Peter Sellers was born on September 8, 1925 at Southsea, Hampshire, England to William Sellers, a pianist and musical director, and the former Agnes Marks, a character actress. The fact that his parents, a grandmother, and eight uncles were all in show business helped influence his choice of a theatrical career. Peter made his debut at the age of five, when he appeared with his parents in one of England's earliest revues, *Splash Me*, which was produced by his grandmother. Another job he held in his youth was that of "head sweeper outer" of theaters.

At St. Aloysius College in Highgate, Sellers was a poor student in every subject except drawing. Having decided to become a drummer, he studied the timpani and got a job with a dance band, with which he remained until he entered the Royal Air Force in 1943. While serving in India, Sellers entertained servicemen at camp shows with comedy skits and impersonations, and he later toured the Middle East

with the RAF Gang Show. At these performances he first displayed his formidable talent for mimicry.

Discharged with the rank of corporal in 1946, Sellers served for a short time as entertainment director at a holiday camp, and spent the next few years doing comic impersonations and playing the ukelele in such London vaudeville houses as the Windmill Theatre. He had in the meantime developed his talent for mimicry —especially vocal imitation—and he wanted to reach a wider audience. Making a telephone call to a program director of the British Broadcasting Corporation, Sellers successfully mimicked the voices of two stars of the BBC. Both voices recommended that the BBC hire a promising young comedian named Peter Sellers. Astonished at Sellers' brashness but much taken with the impersonations, the producer gave Sellers his first radio spot on *Show Time*.

In January 1952, with Spike Milligan and Harry Secombe, Sellers launched the *Goon Show*, a radio program that became a national hit and occasioned heated discussions between opposing camps on the merits of its nonsense. Clowning in dozens of voices, the three Goons, in eight years, managed to demolish many British pomposities. Sellers subsequently made television appearances on shows like *Gently Bentley*, Val Parnell's *Saturday Spectacular, Saturday Night at the Palladium,* and *Saturday Show-time.* When Milligan and he later produced their skits on *A Show Called Fred, Son of Fred,* and *Yes, It's the Cathode Ray Tube Show,* millions of devoted radio fans switched their attention to their TV sets. Tapes of the *Goon Show* have been broadcast in Canada and the United States.

While he was still appearing with the *Goon Show,* Sellers made his stage debut in the leading role of George Tabori's farce, *Brouhaha,* which opened in August 1958 at the Aldwych

SELLERS, PETER—*Continued*

Theatre in London. As a sultan who foments a minor disturbance in order to attract foreign intervention and capital into his impoverished Middle Eastern country, he received favorable notices from the critics.

Sellers had meanwhile appeared in small motion-picture roles, playing bit parts in *Penny Points to Paradise, Orders Are Orders,* and *Down Among the Z Men.* He got a bigger role when he was assigned the part of Harry, the youngest of a gang of rogues led by Alec Guinness, in *The Ladykillers* (United States, 1956). American audiences next saw him in 1957 in *John and Julie* and in *The Smallest Show on Earth,* in which he portrayed an alcoholic old film projectionist. The following year he was cast as a smirking villain in *Tom Thumb* (1958). His next role was a sizable one—that of a foxy Irish "bosun" in the farcical *Up the Creek,* released in the United States in 1958.

In *The Naked Truth,* released in the United States as *Your Past Is Showing* in 1958, he portrayed a television idol who bungles an attempt to murder a blackmailing publisher of a scandal sheet. "Major acting honors must go to Peter Sellers, top [United Kingdom] TV and radio comedian," a reviewer for *Variety* (December 11, 1957) wrote. "He shapes as a fine character comedian in a wide range of impersonations."

In 1959 *Carlton-Browne of the F.O.,* in which Terry-Thomas appeared with Peter Sellers, was released in Great Britain. (The film was released in the United States in 1960 as *Man in a Cocked Hat.*) The movie was the first that Sellers made for England's famous producer-director team, John and Roy Boulting, with whom he signed a five-year contract in 1959.

In *The Mouse that Roared* (1959), a screen version of Leonard Wibberly's best-selling novel, Peter Sellers made his first big impression on United States movie patrons. He played a prime minister, a duchess, and a constable in a small mythical European country that decides to ease its desperate financial situation by declaring war on the United States and allowing itself to be defeated and rehabilitated by the conqueror. Sellers was applauded for the finesse and "versatility in voice and subtle characterization" with which he created the three roles.

Reviewers and audiences were even more delighted with Sellers' performance in *The Battle of the Sexes,* based on James Thurber's short story *The Catbird Seat,* which was released in the United States in 1960. Sellers played an elderly chief accountant who plans to murder an American female efficiency expert determined to modernize the textile firm where he has worked for thirty-five years. "Sellers adds another to his gallery of shrewdly observed characters as the mild-mannered accountant," a reviewer for *Variety* (December 30, 1959) noted. "Softly throwing away his lines, gently blandishing his boss and the woman, Sellers gets his effects with the maximum of thought and the minimum of effort."

For his enactment of a self-important shop steward in *I'm All Right, Jack,* a satire on the skulduggery of management and labor, Sellers was honored with a British Film Academy Award as the best actor of 1959. He also received unanimous praise from American critics. "When . . . Sellers strides into the picture breathing fire and rattling off union specifications in an educated Cockney tone of voice, it is as if Mr. Chaplin's Great Dictator has come upon the scene," Bosley Crowther wrote in the New York *Times* (April 26, 1960). "He is all efficiency, righteous indignation, monstrous arrogance and blank ineptitude. . . . He is also side-splittingly funny, as funny as a true stuffed shirt can be."

Often dubbed by journalists as the man of total anonymity and a thousand voices, Sellers himself fosters this impression. "As far as I'm aware," he has said (New York *Times* Magazine, March 27, 1960), "I have no personality of my own whatsoever. That is, I have no personality to offer the public. I have nothing to project." He does, however, have an uncanny talent for animating the characters whom he plays. Master of some twenty British dialects alone, he has an unerring ear for accents of all kinds.

Sellers prepares a new role by first determining the correct voice for the character. He then fills out the rest of the part. Frequently compared to Sir Alec Guinness, he has pointed out a difference: "Alec likes to . . . work out just what he will do before he starts. I . . . have to 'get into the part'—feel it from inside." Sellers thinks of himself as a character actor rather than a comedian. A writer for the *Guardian* has perhaps described him most fittingly: "He is, to my mind, becoming funnier than ever—because and not in spite of the new humanity and pathos which he now achieves. From a music-hall jester he is becoming (if the term will not be misunderstood) a serious comedian."

Other films in which Sellers appeared in 1960 are *Two-Way Stretch; Never Let Go,* in which he plays a criminal; and an adaptation of George Bernard Shaw's *The Millionairess,* in which he portrays an East Indian doctor. An expert photographer, he produced an eleven-minute picture called *The Running, Jumping and Standing Still Film,* which won the Golden Gate Award at the San Francisco Film Festival as the best fiction short. The picture begins with a girl scrubbing a field with soap and water and exhibits other lunacies reminiscent of the *Goon Show.*

Peter Sellers was married to Anne Howe, an actress, on September 15, 1951. They have two children, Michael Peter Anthony and Sarah Jane. The brown-haired, brown-eyed actor stands five feet ten inches tall and weighs about 175 pounds. He usually wears black-rimmed spectacles. Sellers is Jewish and a Liberal in politics. He is vice-president of the London Judo Society and a member of the Marylebone Cricket Club. At his home he keeps equipment for other leisure-time activities: complex photographic paraphernalia, stereophonic records (mostly jazz), and a large set of trap drums. One of his ancient barns shelters some

500 feet of model railroad track. He belongs to the Royal Automobile Club and he is a compulsive car buyer. He has owned some fifty cars, including a Rolls Royce, but at present drives only three or four. In his best mahout manner, he also drives a giant mechanical elephant which he bought in 1958 for its publicity value and which appeals to his taste for gadgets.

References

Life 48:63 Je 20 '60
N Y Times Mag p64+ Mr 27 '60

SEWELL, (EMMA) WINIFRED Aug. 12, 1917- Librarian; organization official

Address: b. Squibb Institute for Medical Research, E.R. Squibb & Sons, 5 Georges Rd., New Brunswick, N.J.; h. 211 Cedar Ave., Highland Park, N.J.

A desire to follow a profession that would exploit her interests in both the sciences and the liberal arts led Winifred Sewell, the president of the Special Libraries Association for 1960-61, to choose a career in special library work. Since 1946 she has been senior librarian at the Squibb Institute for Medical Research and since 1949 she has also edited *Unlisted Drugs,* published by the pharmaceutical section of the science-technology division of the Special Libraries Association. Elected by some 5,000 members of the Special Libraries Association, Miss Sewell begins her term of office in June 1960, succeeding Burton W. Adkinson. She has been active in both the New Jersey and New York chapters of SLA, and has held numerous committee assignments. Before taking her position at Squibb, she was the librarian at Wellcome Research Laboratories, Tuckahoe, New York for four years. She often contributes to *Special Libraries* and other professional journals.

Born in Newport, Washington, on August 12, 1917, Emma Winifred Sewell is the daughter of Harold Arthur and Grace Winifred (Vickerman) Sewell. Her father is a civil engineer, and both of her brothers, James Arthur Sewell and George Vickerman Sewell, are engineers. She has two sisters, Martha Mae Oien, a former mathematics teacher, and Grace Elizabeth Kilsheimer, a biochemist.

While attending Newport High School, Winifred edited the school paper and belonged to the debating team. After she was graduated in 1934 she enrolled as a major in English at the State College of Washington, Pullman, Washington. While a student she worked as an assistant in the college library for "half to three-quarters time," and consequently had little time for extracurricular activities. She earned membership in Phi Beta Kappa and Phi Kappa Phi scholastic societies, and was graduated in 1938 with the B.A. degree.

"I had always been interested both in the sciences and liberal arts," Miss Sewell says, "and was delighted to find an occupation where I could carry on both interests." In 1940 she took her L.S. degree at Columbia University School of Library Service. "Linda Morley's course in special libraries at Columbia was

WINIFRED SEWELL

perhaps the greatest single determining factor in my becoming a special librarian," she recalls.

Continuing to earn her tuition by working in libraries, she was first a student assistant and later a junior assistant in the Columbia University library. After graduation she continued at Columbia, working in various departmental libraries and finally at the reference desk until 1942. She then became an assistant librarian in the pharmaceutical library of the Wellcome Research Laboratories in Tuckahoe, New York, and in 1943 was advanced to chief librarian, a post she held until 1946.

Beginning in 1946, she became senior librarian at the Squibb Institute for Medical Research, at that time located in Brooklyn and since 1954 at E.R. Squibb & Sons' Olin Mathieson division in New Brunswick, New Jersey. She heads one of the largest pharmaceutical libraries in the United States, with a staff of seventeen persons, eight of whom are chemists, and supervises an entire floor in one of the many Squibb buildings, where 40,000 volumes are kept. Dozens of chemists visit the library daily and telephone requests average about one hundred a week. Some questions come in by mail from all over the world, to which answers are obtained, typed, and sent back by air mail, and in some cases, by telegram. The librarians work closely with scientists in their search for technical information not usually available in public libraries.

"The librarian has no monopoly on classification," Miss Sewell wrote in *Special Libraries* (May-June 1957). "In its broadest sense it is almost synonomous with organization, and every time we put milk into the refrigerator and canned foods on a cupboard shelf, we are actually doing an act of classification." In her own particular domain, with a staff indexing references to some 400 scientific periodicals, she says that her problem of classifying is this: "We are asked for a form of classification which will cover all various types and quanti-

SEWELL, WINIFRED—*Continued*

ties of material which a man may collect in a limited, specialized field, and which will be so simple that it can be installed in no time and continued without any effort on the part of anybody."

Because she believes that it is imperative to maintain a close relationship with the needs of scientists and to obtain or improve the publications that serve them, Miss Sewell has taken courses in chemistry, physics, physiology, bacteriology, and other subjects at the various night schools of Hunter College, Columbia University, and the New School for Social Research. She also studied Russian to fill in the background for her present work.

The Special Libraries Association is an international organization of professional librarians who serve law firms, manufacturers, banks, corporations, newspapers, advertising agencies, and federal, state, and municipal government bureaus. It was organized in 1909 at Bretton Woods, New Hampshire and it retains its original purpose: "to promote the collection of specialized fields and to improve the usefulness of special libraries."

From 1944 to 1947 Miss Sewell was treasurer of the New York chapter of Special Libraries Association. Joining the New Jersey chapter when she moved to the Squibb's plant in New Brunswick, she devoted much of her off-duty hours to a vigorous campaign to "sell" industrial library careers to high school and college students, many of whom had not known of career opportunities in research departments of industries. Active in the SLA's pharmaceutical section of the science-technology division, she has edited its *Unlisted Drugs* since its beginning in 1949 and served as chairman of this section in 1952-53. *Unlisted Drugs,* which circulates to about 500 universities, hospitals, and drug stores, gives up-to-date facts about new drugs, including those of foreign countries, even before they are given brand names.

As a member of the Fédération International Pharmaceutique Commission on Pharmaceutical Abstracts, Miss Sewell attended meetings in Brussels, Belgium in 1958 and in Berne, Switzerland in 1959, the latter on a travel grant from the National Science Foundation. The objectives of the commission were to work out a "positive and realistic program for the publication of pharmaceutical abstracts." Miss Sewell worked with other pharmaceutical librarians to prepare a world list of pharmaceutical journals for the Berne meeting.

During the 1959 summer session at Columbia University, Miss Sewell taught a special course on pharmaceutical literature and librarianship. The course surveyed and evaluated library materials in the field of pharmacy and emphasized the methods of searching for answers to the types of questions that occur most frequently in pharmaceutical organizations.

Miss Sewell's articles have been published in the *Bulletin of the Medical Library Association* (October 1952; October 1959); *Special Libraries* (August 1944; February 1954; May-June 1957). She presented her paper "How *Unlisted Drugs* is Produced" at the SLA convention in June 1951 before the pharmaceutical section and a paper "A Key to Pharmaceutical and Medicinal Chemistry Literature" at the American Chemical Society convention in June 1956. She wrote a summary, "Cooperative Information Processing—Pharmaceuticals," published in Jesse H. Shera's book, *Documentation in Action* (Reinhold, 1956).

Gardening, traveling, hiking, bicycling, playing bridge, bowling, watching baseball games, and attending the theater are among Winifred Sewell's many interests. From her travels she has acquired maps with which she has decorated a wall of her home (a converted carriage house). Miss Sewell has ash-blonde hair ("going gray") and green eyes, stands five feet ten inches in height and weighs 160 pounds. In politics and in religion she is independent and unaffiliated.

Among the professional organizations to which she belongs are the American Library Association, the Special Libraries Association, the Medical Library Association, the division of chemical literature of the American Chemical Society, and the American Documentation Institute.

"We do, and should, recognize information as our 'end product,'" Miss Sewell has told fellow librarians, "the one toward which all other functions are keyed. The better our own relationships with all non-librarians and specialized fields of knowledge, the greater can be our own progress" (*Special Libraries,* September 1959). Discussing the problems of finding technical information, she wrote in *Special Libraries* (May-June 1957): "When there is no single perfect source in a field, a combination may be used even in searching for a specific item." She recommends "thorough and imaginative methods . . . not to limit checking to one or two abstracts or index services, but to study all constantly."

References

> Special Lib 50:287+ S '59 por
> Who's Who in Library Service (1955)
> Who's Who of American Women, 1958-59

SHIELD, LANSING P(ETER) Apr. 8, 1896-Jan. 6, 1960

Associated with the food chain store Grand Union Company since 1924, as president since 1947; introduced new methods in supermarket merchandising. See *Current Biography* (June) 1951.

Obituary

> N Y Times p29 Ja 7 '60

SHOLOKHOV, MIKHAIL A(LEKSANDROVICH) (shô′lŭ-ĸôf) May 24, 1905-
Russian writer

Address: Veshenskaya, Rostov Region, U.S.S.R.

> NOTE: This biography supersedes the article which appeared in *Current Biography* in 1942.

One of the visitors who accompanied Soviet Premier Nikita S. Khrushchev to the United States in September 1959 was Mikhail A.

Sholokhov, the leading novelist in the Soviet Union. Sholokhov told those Americans who interviewed him that he would not write anything about the United States because his observations could only be superficial. Never superficial in his writing, Sholokhov has started work on three gigantic novels in thirty-six years, but finished only one of them. They chronicle the three great epochs of Soviet history: the revolution, the collectivization of agriculture, and the war with Hitler, as seen through the eyes of the inhabitants of a single Russian village, Veshenskaya.

Mikhail Aleksandrovich Sholokhov was born on May 24, 1905, on a farm near that village, not far from the River Don in what is now the Rostov Region in the southern part of the Russian Republic. His mother was a Ukrainian, the widow of a Don Cossack—an hereditary class freed from feudal restrictions, but obligated to military service on the borders of the Russian Empire. His father had come from the Ryazan Region, southeast of Moscow, and was at various times a farmer, cattle buyer, clerk, and manager of a mill. When Sholokhov was seven his parents were formally married.

Sholokhov studied at the gymnasium, or public school, in Voronezh. It is said that his mother first learned to read and write so she could correspond with him while he was away at school. In his letters to her he began to experiment with the descriptive powers which he later developed so highly.

His schooling was interrupted by the civil war that swept through the Don basin in 1918. Two years later, when the war itself was over but terrorist bands still roamed the countryside, he joined a Red Army supply detachment, serving as a machine gunner. "We hunted down the bandits," he wrote, ". . . and the bandits hunted us. All went as could be expected. I was in many a tight spot, but nowadays this is all forgotten."

At the end of 1922 Sholokhov went to Moscow. There his first work, an essay, was published by a Communist youth newspaper in 1923. His first short story appeared the next year in another newspaper. But in the middle of 1924 Sholokhov returned to Veshenskaya; he was there in 1926 when his first collection of short sketches, *Don Stories,* was published in Moscow.

At home in Veshenskaya, Sholokhov also began to work on the first of his three great novels—*The Quiet Don,* a massive, four-volume account of revolution and civil war in a Cossack village. The first volume was serialized, beginning in January 1928, in the magazine *Oktiabr* (October). The second followed later that same year, and the third, begun in 1929, was not completed until 1932.

The Soviet critics appeared to be somewhat baffled by the first volume, which dealt with life before the revolution and seemed to have little political pertinence. The second, however, provoked sharp criticism, and Sholokhov was described as a man for whom the Whites were enemies but still heroes. Stalin himself objected, in a letter in 1929, to the characterization of two Communist party figures.

In the face of delays, Sholokhov turned to the second of his three great epics—*Virgin Soil*

Wide World

MIKHAIL A. SHOLOKHOV

Upturned, the story of the collectivization of agriculture. He completed its first volume in 1931, but again encountered political difficulties. One Soviet report says the Central Committee of the Communist party had to intervene in his behalf before it was published serially, starting in 1932, in the magazine *Novyi Mir* (New World).

It was in 1932, also, that Sholokhov joined the Communist party. He became a member of the party's regional committee, was elected to the Supreme Soviet in 1937 and thereafter, and in 1939 was named a member of the Academy of Sciences of the U.S.S.R. These were not just honorary posts—they entailed many political and cultural responsibilities both in his home region and in Moscow.

The fourth and final volume of *The Quiet Don* began to appear serially in *Novyi Mir* in 1937 and was finally completed in 1940. Meanwhile, the fame of Sholokhov had begun to spread throughout the world. Best-selling translations of the first two volumes appeared in Germany, France, Denmark, Sweden, Norway, Holland, and finally—in 1934—in England and the United States under the title *And Quiet Flows the Don.*

Using the pseudonym Stephen Garry, Harry C. Stevens translated the novel into English in London. It was published in England by G. P. Putnam's Sons and in the United States by Alfred A. Knopf. In the following year, 1935, a translation of the first volume of *Virgin Soil Upturned* appeared. In England that title was used, but in America it was called *Seeds of Tomorrow.* In the United States the final two volumes of *The Quiet Don* were published under the title *The Don Flows Home to the Sea.* Although Sholokhov's books were well received by the critics in the United States, they did not become best sellers. The combined sales, according to Knopf, are just

SHOLOKHOV, MIKHAIL A.—*Continued*

over 43,000 copies—compared with more than 22,000,000 copies sold in the Soviet Union.

John Chamberlain, reviewing *And Quiet Flows the Don* for the New York *Times* in 1934, said: "There is no propaganda in this book; merely drama." The following year, however, he wrote about *Seeds of Tomorrow*: "It is considerably more of a tract." Alexander Nazaroff, reviewing *The Don Flows Home to the Sea* for the New York *Times Book Review* in 1941, noted: "There is not a trace of the deadening 'Marxist approach' in his pages."

Professor Ernest J. Simmons of Columbia University has warned, however, that "readers of the English translation of *The Silent Don* may miss the degree of Communist tendentiousness and also obtain a somewhat distorted notion of Sholokhov's objectivity" because some of the most heavily political sections were removed to reduce the size of the English volume (*Russian Fiction and Soviet Ideology;* Columbia University Press, 1958).

During World War II Sholokhov went to the front to gather material for the numerous sketches, publicity articles, and stories he wrote to support the war effort. While he was there, in 1942, his mother was killed in a German bombing raid on Veshenskaya. Once again Sholokhov conceived an epic of the Soviet people—to be called *They Fought for Their Country.*

Pravda published the first fragmentary chapters of this work between May 1943 and February 1944. Other chapters appeared in 1949 and 1954. In 1958 the first volume of the projected trilogy was published. Consisting of tales of the days of disaster and retreat before the Germans in 1942, it was hailed by the *Izvestia* critic as "a significant work of Socialist realism that promises to become a genuine epic of the people."

After the war Sholokhov wrote many propaganda articles and made extensive revisions of his first two novels. When their new editions appeared in 1952 and 1953, both Soviet and foreign critics noted that Sholokhov had more clearly drawn the line between Communist good and evil. It was the imprecision of this line which had brought him his greatest criticism within the Soviet Union, and praise outside of it.

Sholokhov's fiftieth birthday in 1955 was made a national celebration. Newspapers printed articles about him, an entire issue of *Literaturnaya gazeta* was devoted to him, he won the Order of Lenin, and the serial publication of the second volume of *Virgin Soil Upturned* began simultaneously in *Pravda, Ogonyok,* and *Oktiabr.*

The conclusion of this novel was not published for some time. Harrison E. Salisbury of the New York *Times* contended that this was because the leaders of the Communist party were not pleased with the ending Sholokhov had written. Sholokhov, when he was in the United States, labeled this charge a "mad fantasy." When the last chapter finally appeared in *Pravda* in February 1960, he denied that he had revised the ending.

Before his United States trip, in the spring of 1959, Sholokhov visited Rome, Paris, Stockholm, and London. In England he made arrangements for the translation of the second volume of *Virgin Soil Upturned* and the first volume of *They Fought for Their Country.* *They Fought for Their Country* was serialized in *Soviet Literature* in 1959.

Few who write in English know the work of Sholokhov as intimately as his translator, Harry C. Stevens. "Even his simpler narratives have a literary quality that one can only describe as a richly colorful and human realism," Stevens has written. "He is a very slow worker, very thorough, and revises again and again. And until he is satisfied nobody in Russia or outside can get him to hand over his typescript. His own attitude to himself is that he is a teller of tales: he is not interested in propagating a philosophy: the philosophy in his books springs naturally from the characters, and not vice versa."

In 1941 Sholokhov won the Stalin Prize for *The Quiet Don,* and he has been awarded the Order of Lenin three times. He belongs to the Committee for Defense of Peace and in February 1956 was invited to address the Twentieth Congress of the Communist party.

Sholokhov is gray-headed and stocky, with a wisp of a white mustache and a gentle manner. He has what has been described as a "pleasant, good-humored, though thoughtful, face." He still lives in his native village, with his Cossack wife, Maria Petrovna Sholokhova, and their four children.

References

N Y Times p4 S 1 '59 por
Biographical Directory of the USSR (1958)
International Who's Who, 1959
Twentieth Century Authors (1942, First Supplement, (1955)
Who's Who, 1959
World Biography (1948)

SHOUP, DAVID M(ONROE) (sho͞op) Dec. 30, 1904- United States Marine Corps officer

Address: b. Headquarters, United States Marine Corps, Washington 25, D.C.; h. Commandant's House, Marine Barracks, Washington, D.C.

A hero of World War II and an experienced military administrator, General David M. Shoup took over the duties of the Commandant of the United States Marine Corps on January 1, 1960. In this post he succeeds General Randolph McC. Pate for a four-year term as the head of the nation's approximately 175,000 "leathernecks." General Shoup served in Iceland and the Pacific during World War II and won the Congressional Medal of Honor for "conspicuous gallantry and intrepidity" at Tarawa.

After six marine trainees died during a night march at Parris Island, South Carolina in April 1956, Shoup was appointed inspector general of recruit training. Four months later he became inspector general of the Marine Corps. Called a "marine's marine," he has the reputation of being a "sundowner" or rigid disciplinarian, who believes that the "defense forces of our country should be kept strong." He is the twenty-second Commandant in the history of the United States Marine Corps and serves on the Joint Chiefs of Staff.

Appropriately enough for a future military officer, David Monroe Shoup was born in Battle Ground, Indiana on December 30, 1904, one of the four children of John Lemar Shoup, a farmer, and Mary (Layton) Shoup. When David was fourteen the family moved to Covington, Indiana, and there he took part in basketball and track activities at Covington High School. Graduated in 1921, he won a Rector Scholarship at DePauw University, Greencastle, Indiana, majored in mathematics and education, and earned the B.A. degree with high distinction in 1926. In his spare time he had been on the rifle, football, and wrestling teams, and as a track star he established the present Indiana-Kentucky marathon record.

While at the university Shoup was also a member of the Reserve Officers' Training Corps; he later served for one month as a second lieutenant in the Army Infantry Reserve before entering the Marine Corps. Commissioned a marine second lieutenant on June 26, 1926, Shoup was ordered to Basic School, Navy Yard, Philadelphia. His studies, which had been twice interrupted by duty elsewhere in the United States and then by expeditionary duty in Tientsin, China, were completed in 1928.

In November 1934 Shoup returned to China, after various assignments, including two years of duty aboard the USS *Maryland*. He remained in China until early 1936, attached to the 4th Marines at Shanghai and later to the American Legation in Peiping. He was next stationed at the Marine Corps Schools at Quantico, Virginia, where he took the junior course and for two additional years served as an instructor. Shoup, who was transferred to the 6th Marine Regiment in May 1940, embarked for Iceland a year later with that unit.

When the United States entered World War II, Shoup was still in Iceland and was later awarded the Letter of Commendation with Commendation Ribbon for his services during the first three months of war. Joining the 2d Marine Division, he served as G-3 operations and training officer, while the division was in New Zealand preparing for combat. He was an observer of operations in New Georgia in the Solomon Islands in July 1943 when he suffered the wounds for which he later won the Purple Heart.

In command of the marines in the attack on Betio Island, Tarawa on November 20-22, 1943, Shoup earned the highest military honor for his valor. He was the twenty-fifth marine to win the Congressional Medal of Honor during the war. The citation read: "Although severely shocked by an exploding shell soon after landing at the pier, and suffering from a serious painful leg wound which had become infected, Colonel Shoup fearlessly exposed himself to the terrific relentless artillery machine gun and rifle fire from hostile shore emplacements and, rallying his hesitant troops by his own inspiring heroism, gallantly led them across the fringing reefs to charge the

U. S. Marine Corps
GEN. DAVID M. SHOUP

heavily fortified island and reinforced our hard-pressed, thinly-held lines."

His heroism on this occasion brought him not only the Medal of Honor presented by Secretary of the Navy James V. Forrestal on January 22, 1945, but also the British Distinguished Service Order, a gold star in lieu of a second Purple Heart, and the Legion of Merit with Combat V for his contribution in planning the assault on Tarawa.

As chief of staff for the 2d Marine Division from January to October 1944, Colonel Shoup served through the battles of Saipan and Tinian in the Mariana Islands and was awarded a second Legion of Merit with Combat V. In 1947, after nearly three years as a logistics officer at Marine Headquarters in Washington, Shoup was again ordered overseas to become commanding officer, Service Command, Fleet Marine Force, Pacific. He later was chief of staff of the 1st Marine Division and commandant of the Basic School at Quantico before assuming the duties of fiscal director of the Marine Corps in July 1953. He was elevated to the rank of brigadier general (permanent) in September 1953.

As an outcome of the drowning of six marines on a disciplinary night march at the Parris Island, South Carolina boot camp, Shoup was named on May 2, 1956 to the newly created post of inspector general of recruit training. In his first statement to the press after his appointment, he reported that a thorough re-evaluation had affirmed the soundness of marine training, "which has served us so well for so many years." He considered it essential that recruits be indoctrinated in unhesitating obedience to noncommissioned officers, but promised that mass punishment in any form would not be tolerated (New York *Times*, June 10, 1956).

(Continued next page)

SHOUP, DAVID M.—*Continued*

General Shoup next became inspector general of the Marine Corps, a post that he held from September 1956 to May 1957. Transferred to Okinawa in the Ryukyu Islands, he first was commanding general, 1st Marine Expeditionary Forces and then served as commandant of the 3d Marine Division. He was advanced to major general (permanent) in February 1958 and was sent back to Parris Island in May 1959 as commanding general of the recruit depot.

Major General Shoup stood tenth on the list of Marine Corps officers when President Eisenhower nominated him as Commandant of the Marine Corps on August 12, 1959, succeeding General Randolph, McC. Pate, who was scheduled to retire at the end of 1959. He was advanced over nine senior officers, including three lieutenant generals. In keeping with an administration policy of limiting the appointments of military leaders who serve on the Joint Chiefs of Staff, President Eisenhower had nominated Shoup for a term of two years. After it had been pointed out in the Senate Armed Services Committee that a term of four years is established by law, the administration yielded. On September 14 Shoup was confirmed by the Senate as Commandant for the four years beginning on January 1, 1960. When he assumed office, he received the rank of full general (permanent).

The honorary LL.D. degree was awarded to the general by his alma mater, DePauw University, on June 7, 1959. Shoup, who has been president of the Medal of Honor Society, is a life member of the American Legion and a member of the Veterans of Foreign Wars. His fraternity is Delta Upsilon. A number of his articles have appeared in the *Marine Corps Gazette*, but he is anxious to correct the mistaken belief entertained by some people that he wrote the book *Tarawa; The Story of a Battle* (Duell, 1944). The author is Robert Lee Sherrod, a correspondent who witnessed the battle.

Mrs. Shoup is the former Zola De Haven, who was a schoolteacher before her marriage on September 15, 1931. The Shoups have one daughter, Carolyn E., the wife of a marine officer, Joel S. Watkins, and one son, Robert. David M. Shoup stands at five feet eight and three quarters inches, weighs 175 pounds, has brown hair and brown eyes, and has been described as "stocky, taciturn and sharpwitted."

Once asked if he was a martinet, he replied: "I can be tough when it is required and compassionate when that is required." The Commandant lists billiards, golf, chess, checkers, bridge, poker, and pistol shooting as favorite recreations. He is a Methodist and attends church "wherever there is one." When he was nominated as Commandant, David M. Shoup gave vent to his feelings in this couplet: "One can attain a considerable height in this life, if he has an angel for a mother and an angel for a wife" (Washington *Post and Times Herald*, August 13, 1959).

References

N Y Herald Tribune p4 Ag 13 '59 por; p14 Ag 16 '59 por
N Y Times p15 My 3 '56; p21 Ag 13 '59 por
N Y World-Telegram p7 Ag 15 '59 por
Sherrod, R. L. Tarawa; The Story of a Battle (1944)
Who's Who in America, 1958-59

SHRIDHARANI, KRISHNALAL (JETHALAL) Sept. 16, 1911-July 23, 1960 Indian journalist and author; resided in United States from 1934 to 1946; in *My India, My America* (1941) and other books, interpreted his native land to the American public. See *Current Biography* (January) 1942.

Obituary

N Y Times p64 Jl 24 '60

SHUSTER, GEORGE N(AUMAN) (shoo'-ster) Aug. 27, 1894- Author; educator

Address: 279 Stamford Ave., Stamford, Conn.

NOTE: This biography supersedes the article which appeared in *Current Biography* in 1941.

Giving as the reason for his resignation his desire to attend more fully to his many off-campus responsibilities, George N. Shuster relinquished his position as president of Hunter College on August 31, 1960. He had held the post for two decades. Active for forty years in the academic world, Shuster had also distinguished himself in political and social action. He has served for the past two years as the United States representative on the executive committee of UNESCO, a body that he helped to create when he was a delegate to the Conference on International Education which in 1945 adopted UNESCO's constitution. Shuster has written many books on twentieth-century Germany, English literature, and education, and several works of fiction. An interpreter of Roman Catholicism to the modern world, he was for twelve years an editor of *Commonweal*, the Catholic weekly, to which he still contributes.

Born in Lancaster, Wisconsin on August 27, 1894 to Anthony Shuster, a building contractor, and Elizabeth (Nauman) Shuster, George Nauman Shuster is descended from German Catholic and German Lutheran families. At the age of thirteen, when his mother was taken seriously ill, George was sent to a Capuchin boarding school, St. Lawrence's College in Fond du Lac, Wisconsin, which, he says, "was a German Gymnasium transplanted to the New World." There he studied ancient and modern languages diligently, and became so proficient in German that he discovered he could write with more facility in German than in English. At the University of Notre Dame, where he later studied, Shuster was, he says, "a budding gawky oaf . . . who mooned over Sherwood Anderson, sighed over early Yeats, and sat up nights with *Jean-*

Christophe." He took his B.A. degree from this university in 1915.

At that time Shuster planned to enter the United States Military Academy at West Point but when World War I began he turned instead to journalism. For one year he worked in Chicago as a reporter. In 1917 he started his eighteen months of military service and participated, as a sergeant in the intelligence section of the United States Army, in nearly all of the major battles in which the Army engaged. He also served as an interpreter in the Army of Occupation. After the war he attended the University of Poitiers in France, which gave him a *certificat d'aptitude* in 1919. Shuster had seen much of post-war Germany and a good deal of "what went on round about the Peace Conference." It is to this period in his life that he attributes the beginning of his interest in modern Europe.

Returning to America, Shuster accepted a position teaching English at Notre Dame University. He and the President of the University, the Rev. Father James Burns, soon became fast friends and Shuster stayed at Notre Dame for four years. He took his M.A. degree in French literature in 1920 and served as head of the English department from 1920 until 1924. Having moved to New York City, Shuster taught English at Brooklyn Polytechnic Institute from 1924 to 1925. At this time he came into contact "quite accidentally" with the newly formed *Commonweal* group, which wished to publish a weekly magazine similar to the *Nation* and *New Republic,* but dedicated to Catholic religious principles. He served as an associate editor of *Commonweal* from 1925 to 1929 and as its managing editor from 1929 to 1937. From 1925 to 1926 Shuster studied at Columbia University. From 1925 to 1935 he taught English as a professor at St. Joseph's College for Women. He edited *Newman—Prose and Poetry* (Allyn and Bacon, 1925); the Malta Books (Holt, 1930); and the Century Catholic College Texts in English from 1932 to 1950.

Apparently his editorial and teaching work did not occupy Shuster sufficiently, for he was also a productive writer. To *The Catholic Spirit in Modern English Literature* (Macmillan) which he had written in 1922, Shuster added *English Literature* (Allyn and Bacon, 1926); a volume of short stories, *The Hill of Happiness* (Appleton, 1926); *The Catholic Spirit in America* (Dial, 1927); and *The Catholic Church and Current Literature* (Macmillan, 1930).

After 1929 Shuster became more and more concerned with contemporary Germany and visited it for long periods. He studied at the Hochschule für Politik in Berlin in 1930 and received fellowships from the Vereinigung Carl Schurz (1929-30), the Oberlaender Trust (1932), and the Carl Schurz Memorial Foundation (1933-34). In such books as *The Germans* (Dial, 1932), *Strong Man Rules* (Appleton-Century, 1934), and *Like a Mighty Army* (Appleton-Century, 1935) Shuster described the decline of the Christian churches in Germany as a new religion—the cult of Hitler—gripped its people. He also decried the Nazi party's program for a "final solution" to the Jewish question. Years later, in February 1960, Shuster

GEORGE N. SHUSTER

commended Chancellor Konrad Adenauer for trying to stamp out anti-Semitism in West Germany. He warned, however, that intensified teaching of Nazi crimes in West German schools might do more harm than good by "advertising" past misdeeds.

Shuster has translated from the German *Jesse and Maria* by Enrica Handel-Mazzetti (Holt, 1931), *Job the Man Speaks with God* by Peter Lippert (Longmans, 1936), and *The Vatican as a World Power* by Josef Bernhart (Longmans, 1939). In 1937 he became a Fellow of the Social Science Research Council at Columbia University and, having received a Carnegie Corporation grant to study the Weimar Republic and the Center party, he resigned his post on the *Commonweal* and spent the greater part of the next two years in Germany.

In 1940 Shuster edited and wrote the notes for the Reynal and Hitchcock edition of Adolf Hitler's *Mein Kampf.* His *Germany: A Short History,* written with Arnold Bergstraesser, was published in 1945 by W. W. Norton and Company. He served with Enemy Alien Board # 2 in New York City from 1942 to 1945 and was the chairman of the War Department's Historical Commission to Germany in 1945. Shuster was a Ford Foundation consultant in Germany during January and February 1956. He is now the president of the American Council on Germany, Inc.

When Shuster returned from Germany in 1939, he was invited by the Board of Higher Education of the City of New York to become academic dean and acting president of Hunter College. On September 1, 1940, soon after he received his Ph.D. from Columbia University, Shuster became president of the city college, where he served until August 31, 1960. Under his leadership Hunter instituted fifth-year and master's degree programs, extended teacher and adult education courses, and developed the

SHUSTER, GEORGE N.—*Continued*

Bronx campus which became a full four-year co-educational college in 1951. Shuster taught at least one course every semester, sometimes meeting his classes in comparative literature on Hunter's Park Avenue campus and sometimes driving to the Bronx campus to teach his special course in the dynamics of German politics. Meanwhile he continued to write. *Brother Flo* (Macmillan), a light, imaginative biography of a porter in a Catholic college, was published in 1938. His historical novel set during the Civil War period, *Look Away!* (Macmillan), and *Pope Pius XI and American Public Opinion* (Funk), written with Robert J. Cuddihy, appeared in 1939. The following year his *The English Ode from Milton to Keats* was published by the Columbia University Press and in 1942 he edited *The World's Great Catholic Literature* for Macmillan.

Long interested in promoting international amity, Shuster accompanied the American delegation to the London Conference on International Education which in 1945 adopted the constitution of UNESCO. He is a member of the United States national commission for UNESCO, of which he was chairman from 1953 to 1954. At a conference in São Paolo, Brazil during the summer of 1954, Shuster represented the UNESCO affairs division of the State Department. He participated as an American delegate in the 1956 Paris UNESCO Conference and has been a United States representative on the executive committee of UNESCO since May 1958.

Shuster's speculations on education, religion, and European affairs were set down in several books: *Cultural Cooperation and the Peace* (Bruce Publishing Co., 1952); *Religion Behind the Iron Curtain* (Macmillan, 1954); *In Silence I Speak* (Farrar, Straus & Cudahy, 1956), an account of the imprisonment of Cardinal Mindszenty and of the "new order of tyranny and poverty" in Hungary; and *Education and Moral Wisdom* (Harper, 1960).

Shuster was a member of the general advisory committee of the State Department's division of cultural relations from 1944 to 1945. He served on the University of Chicago's Commission on the Freedom of the Press from 1944 to 1947 and has been chairman of the Committee on Discrimination in the Nation's Capital since 1947. From 1948 to 1951 he headed the board of trustees of the International Institute for Education and from July 1950 to December 1951 was on leave from Hunter College to act as Land Commissioner for Bavaria. In March 1960 when the National Council on Naturalization and Citizenship joined with the American Immigration Conference, Shuster was elected president of the merged group. He has been on the board of directors of the National Educational Television and Radio Center since June 1960.

The Butler medal of Columbia University, given for service to education, was awarded Shuster in 1954. He holds the Great Gold Medal of Honor from the Austrian Republic (1957) and the Mariazell Award (1958). In 1955, as a result of his efforts to improve German-French relations, Shuster became a Chevalier in the French Legion of Honor, and three years later he received the Knight Commander's Cross of Order of Merit from Germany. In 1960 he was awarded the highest honor which Notre Dame University can confer on an outstanding American Roman Catholic layman: the Laetere Medal.

Shuster has received honorary LL.D. degrees from Columbia University (1954), from the College of St. Thomas in St. Paul, Minnesota (1950), and from Manhattan College (1958). In addition, he holds honorary degrees from the New York College of Music (Mus.D., 1954); the Jewish Theological Seminary (D.L. 1956); Loyola University (Litt.D., 1957); Dropsie College (L.H.D., 1957); University of Freiburg (Ph.D. honoris causa, 1957); Seton Hill College (Litt.D., 1958), and the Free University of Berlin (E.d.U., 1958). In 1960 he was awarded the degree of doctor of humane letters by Hunter College. This was only the third honorary degree to be given by the city college in its entire history.

George Nauman Shuster was married to Doris Parks Cunningham on June 25, 1924 in Notre Dame, Indiana. They have one son, Robert George. Shuster is a member of the Century Club and an independent politically. While at Hunter, he rarely failed to take part in faculty plays, but he has not found much time in recent years to indulge in his longstanding hobbies: gardening, fishing, and mountain climbing. In his letter of resignation the former president of Hunter College illuminated the forces which had motivated him throughout his long and busy career and indicated his future "retirement" plans: "All my life I have been tormented by twin demons. In the first place, I cannot stop writing. This is a disease as chronic and ravaging as malaria. Then, too, I feel a deep desire to concern myself with what strength will remain, with the basic institutions and ideas which are shaping the future destiny of mankind."

References

American Catholic Who's Who, 1960-61
Catholic Authors, 1930-47
National Cyclopaedia of American Biography current vol H (1947)
Romig, Walter Book of Catholic Authors (1948)
Twentieth Century Authors (1942; First supplement, 1955)
Who Knows and What (1954)
Who's Who in America, 1950-51; 1960-61
Who's Who in the East (1959)
World Biography (1954)

SHUTE, NEVIL Jan. 17, 1899-Jan. 12, 1960

Author; airplane engineer; wrote more than twenty novels, including *On the Beach* (1957), which was made into a motion picture. See *Current Biography* (July) 1942.

Obituary

N Y Times p47 Ja 13 '60

SIGNORET, SIMONE (sĕ-nyō-rā' sĕ-môn') Mar. 25, 1921- French actress
Address: h. 15 Place Dauphine, Paris 1ᵉʳ, France

To most American movie-goers, French star Simone Signoret seemed to achieve success all of a sudden when the Academy of Motion Picture Arts and Sciences chose her in 1960 as the most outstanding actress of the preceding year. She was very well known in France, however, for her work in some thirty films, and in England had been honored three times by the British Film Academy. Although at least two of her pictures, *Diabolique* and *Les Sorcières de Salem (The Witches of Salem)*, had prospered at the box office in the United States, she did not reach a nationwide audience here until given the opportunity to overcome the language barrier in her first English-speaking picture, *Room at the Top* (1959).

In this British production the part of the aging mistress that brought her the Oscar was a departure from the *femme fatale* role, usually a prostitute, in which Miss Signoret had been frequently type-cast (*Les Sorcières de Salem* provided a notable exception). Simone Signoret is herself a departure from the traditional concept of a movie queen: an unpretentious, mature, intelligent woman whose face has been described as both the saddest and most exciting on the screen today. She is the wife of the French actor and singer Yves Montand (see *C.B.*, July 1960).

Born Simone-Henriette-Charlotte Kaminker in Wiesbaden, Germany on March 25, 1921, Simone Signoret is the only daughter of André and Georgette (Signoret) Kaminker. She has two brothers, younger than she. Her father was a French army officer and a linguist who served as a chief interpreter in the League of Nations and later in the United Nations. Simone grew up in Paris in an intellectual atmosphere, acquiring from her mother some of her social conscience and tendency to become involved in causes.

At school in Paris she studied English among other subjects and when she was fifteen spent several months in England. After the Nazi invasion of France in 1940, her father left the family to join Charles de Gaulle's supporters in London. The German occupation of Paris was all the more difficult for young Simone Signoret because her father was part Jewish. She had earned a teaching degree, however, and was able to make a living by tutoring in English and Latin. She also worked as a typist for the paper *Le Nouveau Temps*.

During the tragic years of the German occupation, when French people were drawn closely together by common suffering, Simone Signoret formed a number of lasting ties with artists, writers, and actors whom she met at the Café de Flore in Saint-Germain-des-Prés. These friends encouraged her in her ambition to become an actress. She left her job on the newspaper, which had grown pro-German, and took whatever bit assignments she could get on the stage or in motion pictures.

By the end of the war she had become well established as a film extra. Then in 1946 Ray-

SIMONE SIGNORET

mond Rouleau gave her a role in one of his pictures, and soon afterward she was featured in Marc Allegret's *Des Démons de l'Aube*. Her first significant recognition as an actress came in 1947 when she won the Prix Suzanne Bianchetti for her performance in Jacques Feyder's *Macadam* (1946).

Also in 1947 Miss Signoret married Yves Allegret, a motion-picture director who had guided her in some of her early film work. About two years later while on vacation at Saint Paul de Vence on the Riviera, she met actor-singer Yves Montand, and they were married on June 15, 1950, soon after her divorce from Allegret.

From the beginning of her acting career many of Simone Signoret's successful roles were those of a prostitute, as in *Dédée d'Anvers*. She also took the part of a streetwalker in *La Ronde* (1950), a witty and sophisticated satire on sex adapted from *Reigen*, one of Arthur Schnitzler's plays about old Vienna. The picture received considerable publicity in the United States when it was banned in New York state in 1951 as immoral. When the Supreme Court ruled against the censorship in 1954, New York critics agreed with the court's action; to Bosley Crowther of the New York *Times*, *La Ronde* seemed innocuous.

The Prix féminin du Cinéma in 1952 and Grand Prix d'Interprétation féminine de l'Académie du Cinéma in 1953 assured Miss Signoret's stature as a dramatic actress. In 1953, also, she won the British Film Academy Award for her performance as the queen of the apaches in *Casque d'Or* (1951). Among her other notable films were *Thérèse Raquin* (1953) and *La mort en ce jardin*.

Henri-Georges Clouzot's mystery thriller *Diabolique* became one of the most financially successful and widely reviewed foreign films shown in the United States during 1955-56.

SIGNORET, SIMONE—Continued

Starring in the role of the cool-headed, fiendish mistress of a schoolmaster, whom she helps murder, Simone Signoret performed with assurance and subtlety, fully sensitive to both character and melodrama.

In striking contrast, she portrayed the outwardly austere Puritan wife, Elizabeth Proctor, in *Les Sorcières de Salem (The Witches of Salem)*, which was directed by Raymond Rouleau and adapted by Jean-Paul Sartre from Arthur Miller's *The Crucible*. Simone Signoret and her husband, Yves Montand, appeared together in the long-run production of the play on the Paris stage in 1954 before co-starring in the film version. Again Miss Signoret won the British Film Academy Award as the best foreign actress.

When released in the United States in late 1958, *The Witches of Salem* had a somewhat mixed reception, possibly in part because of political feelings arising from a parallel with McCarthyism. Most reviewers, however, agreed that the Montands had brilliantly expressed the terror and heartbreak of witch-hunt victims. A Canadian critic pointed out in the Toronto *Globe and Mail* (August 4, 1960) that Miss Signoret's "work has inward stillness and a capacity for stirring the emotions in the subtlest, but deepest, ways."

Room at the Top, the British screen version of John Braine's novel, a Romulus production filmed in 1958, gave Miss Signoret her most sympathetic role so far—an unhappily married older woman seeking love in an adulterous affair with an ambitious and egotistical young Yorkshireman, played by Laurence Harvey. A candid and tragic story of the social struggle of an "angry young man," the picture was internationally praised for its explicit dialogue, adult treatment of moral confusion, and satirical comment on class distinction.

The warmth and understanding of Simone Signoret's touching characterization compelled reviewers in general to describe her acting as superb. "Her performance," Paul V. Beckley noted in the New York *Herald Tribune* (March 31, 1959), "is always exact and achieves an unaffected naturalism while holding throughout to a clear sense of style." She won the 1959 best actress award of the British Film Academy and the Cannes Film Festival, as well as the Prize of the German Film Critics as the best foreign actress. In April 1960 the Academy of Motion Picture Arts and Sciences awarded her its Oscar as the outstanding actress. She is the first actress to receive the top award for work in a British film.

At the time of the Academy Award presentations, Simone Signoret was in Hollywood with her husband, and during April the Montands were interviewed on the television program *Person to Person*. Miss Signoret had earlier, in December 1959, appeared on TV in a very lively discussion with Agnes De Mille and Hedda Hopper on *Small World*. She made her TV acting debut on the *General Electric Theater* in a play called "Don't You Remember?" which some reviewers thought was a waste of her talent. The film was telecast in May 1960, but before that she had left the United States to go to Rome and play the part of an ex-prostitute in Zebra Films *Adua e le compagne* (Adua and Her Colleagues). The film was shown at the Venice Film Festival in 1960.

During her stay in the United States reporters and interviewers often asked Miss Signoret about her political beliefs because for two or three years the State Department had denied the Montands a visa under a law barring visitors for political reasons. In 1959, however, they had been granted a waiver which permitted them to come to the United States for six months. She has repeatedly denied that she was ever a Communist and has explained that in France and the United States the word "Left" has different meanings. In September 1960 she was one of a group of French intellectuals and artists who signed a manifesto upholding the right of a Frenchman to refuse to fight against the Moslem rebels if his conscience opposed it. Her fellow signers included Jean-Paul Sartre, Simone de Beauvoir, Françoise Sagan, and other internationally known French figures.

Along with her sophistication Simone Signoret has a quality of unpretentiousness and a tenderness that for her admirers surpass the conventional beauty of most movie stars. She is a little taller than five feet and has blue eyes. "Her robust charm," according to *Time* (April 4, 1960), "the shaggy, Chablis-tinted hair over soft, wide-set eyes, and the generous mouth that twists with Gallic wit as the words come tumbling out, all add up to a sultry but utterly unphony femininity."

At home in France when not working, the Montands enjoy living at their country home in Normandy with teen-aged Catherine, Simone Signoret's daughter by her marriage to Allegret. While she does not shun publicity, the actress declines to use the press to boost her professional standing and believes that quality of performance rather than the promotion of publicity men determines Academy Award winners.

References

Look 24:66+ Ag 30 '60 pors
N Y Herald Tribune II pl Mr 31 '59
Time 75:44+ Ap 4 '60 por
Dictionnaire Biographique Français Contemporain (1954)
International Who's Who, 1959
Who's Who in France, 1959-60

SIMIONATO, GIULIETTA May 12, 1916-
Opera singer

Address: b c/o Columbia Artists Management, Inc., 113 W. 57th St., New York 19; h. 29/C Via di Villa Grazioli, Rome, Italy

Some thirty years ago in a convent on the island of Sardinia an Italian girl in her early teens sang "for the Madonna." The girl was Giulietta Simionato, one of the world's foremost mezzo-sopranos, who commands a vocal range from a bottom G to a top B-flat in a repertory of more than fifty operatic roles. At the opening of the seventy-fifth season of the

Metropolitan Opera Company on October 26, 1959, her performance as the vengeful gypsy, Azucena, in Verdi's *Il Trovatore* won acclaim from both the critics and the audience. Later in the season she justified their high pitch of enthusiasm with her interpretations of Santuzza in Mascagni's *Cavalleria Rusticana* and of Amneris in Verdi's *Aïda*.

Giulietta Simionato was born in Forlì, a town of about 25,000 inhabitants near Bologna in Italy on May 12, 1916 to Felice and Giovanna (Truddaiu) Simionato, neither one of whom was musical. Her father, a Venetian who was one of twenty-four brothers, was director of the local prison. Her mother was a native of Sardinia, and when Giulietta was one month old she was taken to that island, where she remained until she was fifteen years of age. Her family then moved to Rovigo, near Padua in Italy, where the dark and vibrant quality of her mezzo-soprano voice was soon recognized.

At the convent in Sardinia, Giulietta had received her early vocal training from the nuns; she had even considered taking holy orders herself. Her childhood among the taciturn and reserved Sardinians may account for the timidity that kept her in the background during her early years at the Teatro alla Scala in Milan. It may also help explain her religious devotion and her loyalty to her friends.

When Giulietta began her vocal lessons, her mother, always opposed to secular singing, stopped them on the grounds that Giulietta should devote her talents to "singing for the Madonna." But after her mother's death, when Giulietta was fifteen, Ettore Lucatello, a music teacher in Rovigo, suggested to Signor Felice Simionato that Giulietta take up a professional vocal career.

While still a student under Maestro Guido Palumbo at Padua, Giulietta Simionato made her debut at Montagnana near Padua, as Lola in *Cavalleria Rusticana*. When she was eighteen she sang Maddelena in *Rigoletto* at Padua. Two years later her father died. Miss Simionato has said "Whatever I have accomplished, I have done it myself, for I was all alone and had to sing in order to live."

In a contest at Florence in 1933 Miss Simionato won the prize for *bel canto* singing, triumphing over 385 competitors. In 1938 she sang in Ildebrando Pizzetti's *L'Orseolo* at the Comunale in Florence. Two years later she made her bow at the Teatro alla Scala in Milan as Beppe in Mascagni's *L'Amico Fritz*. Paid a monthly salary, she sang *comprimario* (second lead) roles at La Scala for the following eight years.

The long apprenticeship at La Scala both rewarded and frustrated Miss Simionato. As a member of the company, she gained a wealth of stage experience, but because of her timidity few people paid any attention to her. At the end of the eight years she told the director of La Scala: "If I am going to be a *comprimario* all my life, tell me, and I will give up singing today." When he gave her an equivocal answer, she walked out of the opera house, determined to find a true measure of her vocal abilities.

Winning engagements at the opera houses of large cities and provincial towns, she sang

GIULIETTA SIMIONATO

Hansel, Cherubino, Dorabella, Carmen, Azucena, and many other roles. By 1947 rumors of her successes had drifted back to La Scala. In what she remembers as the greatest triumph of her career she returned to La Scala in the title role of *Mignon*. Since then she has been kept busy at La Scala in such operas as Rossini's *Il Barbiere di Siviglia, L'Italiana in Algeri,* and *La Cenerentola;* Donizetti's *Anna Bolena* and *La Favorita;* Scarlatti's *Mitridate Eupatore;* and Bellini's *I Capuleti ed i Montecchi.*

Word of the new operatic star reached managers abroad, and soon Giulietta Simionato was fulfilling engagements in the opera houses of Paris, London, Vienna, Rio de Janeiro, Mexico City, Madrid, Barcelona, Lisbon, Geneva, Salzburg, and other cities. In the United States she became famous through her long-playing recordings on the HMV, Cetra, London, and Decca labels. In 1954 the management of the Metropolitan Opera Company announced that Miss Simionato would appear in the title role of Gluck's *Orfeo,* but she was compelled to cancel her New York engagement because an attack of laryngitis had left her voiceless.

In 1954 Giulietta Simionato made her debut in the United States with the Chicago Lyric Opera when she sang Adalgisa to Maria Callas' Norma in Bellini's *Norma.* In 1955 she appeared with the San Francisco Opera for the first time. In October and November 1957 she sang in New York City, making her triumphant debut as Jane Seymour in two performances of a concert version of Donizetti's *Anna Bolena* with the American Opera Society. The following season she came back to sing Romeo in Bellini's *I Capuleti ed i Montecchi* under the same auspices. When, in November 1957, she appeared with the Dallas Civic Opera as Isabella in *L'Italiana in Algeri,* one critic for the Dallas *Times Herald* (November 23, 1957) compared her technical agility to that of a coloratura or the trumpet of Louis Armstrong.

(Continued next page)

SIMIONATO, GIULIETTA—*Continued*

When Miss Simionato made her debut at the Metropolitan Opera House on October 26, 1959 as Azucena in *Il Trovatore,* the New York critics showered her with superlatives. Newspaper columns resounded with such phrases as "a new artist of the first magnitude," "an extraordinary artist," and "a consummate artist of music drama." Five days later her Santuzza in *Cavalleria Rusticana* won further critical endorsement.

After the initial hubbub had subsided, the New York music critics set to work to analyze the mezzo-soprano voice of Giulietta Simionato. Winthrop Sargeant wrote in the *New Yorker* (November 7, 1959): "The designation [mezzo-soprano] is scarcely adequate, for she combines a rich contralto range with the agility and scope of a dramatic soprano." Irving Kolodin of the *Saturday Review* wrote: "The 'break' in her voice comes around A and B . . . but the compensation for this is a solid bottom down A and a top A (she can go to C) which many sopranos would envy" (November 7, 1959). Reviewers agreed that Rudolf Bing had added to his roster a true exponent of the art of *bel canto* singing.

Miss Simionato brings her formidable endowment of vocal agility and tonal coloring to a repertory of more than fifty roles. Her favorites are Octavian in *Der Rosenkavalier,* Leonora in *La Favorita,* Amneris in *Aïda,* Romeo in *I Capuletti,* and the title role in Giordano's *Fedora.* She has appeared in the United States and abroad with symphony orchestras and in solo recitals. She was a favorite of Arturo Toscanini, who chose her to sing for the festival commemorating Arrigo Boito in 1948 in Italy. She has also sung under the batons of such conductors as Dimitri Mitropoulos, Leopold Stokowski, Herbert von Karajan, Tullio Serafin, and Victor de Sabata.

Explaining her interpretation of operatic roles, Miss Simionato told an interviewer from *Musical America* (December 15, 1959): "I have only one method in interpreting a part. I put myself straight in the place of the person I must play. What would I do in a similar situation, I ask myself." She said that she makes her throat follow the commands of her brain and keeps her voice light or heavy as the composer demands. In her opinion, the true artist should be as tough as steel and never cancel an engagement. In twelve years of singing she has only canceled two.

The soaring sales of her long-playing records in the United States and abroad indicate that collectors disagree with her judgement that she does not sound well on records. For London, HMV, Cetra, and Decca she has recorded such complete operas as *Rigoletto, La Forza del Destino, La Favorita, Il Trovatore, Il Barbiere di Siviglia, La Gioconda,* and *La Cenerentola.* She is the leading mezzo-soprano for London Records.

Giulietta Simionato is five feet two inches tall and weighs about 120 pounds. She has titian-colored hair, lively brown eyes, and a pertly tilted nose. In spite of her diminutive stature, critics have commented on her queenly bearing on stage. She confesses to one superstition: she wears as a pendant on her bracelet an old Portuguese coin inscribed with seven (her lucky number) and a Latin motto reading "In this sign you will conquer." She says: "When I wear it, I know all will be well."

Fond of symphonic music, Miss Simionato attends concerts when her schedule permits. She despises "il jazz e il juke box." For relaxation she watches western movies, which she calls "bang bangs." For her wardrobe she prefers original creations by Givenchy and Lanvin and puts up a weak show of resistance when tempted by furs, hats, and antique jewels. When not on tour she retires to her villa in Rome, where she lives with her Afghan, Tommy, and her Yorkshire terrier; there she cooks such specialty dishes as *zucchini parmigiana.* Since she speaks no English, she has resorted to a macaronic mixture of Italian and French when interviewed by American newspaper reporters. She is hedged about by three self-imposed taboos: no smoking; no drinking; no *pasta.*

To Giulietta Simionato, her music is "passione, emozione e gioia." But she fears that the art in which she excels may be dying out because the young do not respond to the classical repertory and modern composers, she believes, write dissonant and unmelodic works that are not worth singing. "The dissonance," she says, "makes me very nervous."

References

High Fidelity 10:49+ F '60
Mus Am 79:9+ D 15 '59
N Y Herald Tribune p16 N 4 '60 por;
    IV p5 N 13 '60 por
N Y Times II p13 O 21 '59
N Y World-Telegram p23 O 21 '59
Time 74:43+ N 9 '59
Who's Who in Italy, 1957-58

SIMON, RICHARD L(EO) Mar. 6, 1899-July 29, 1960 Co-founder and partner (1924-57) of publishing firm, Simon & Schuster. See *Current Biography* (July) 1941.

Obituary

N Y Times p17 Jl 30 '60

SIMPSON, RICHARD M(URRAY) Aug. 30, 1900-Jan. 7, 1960 United States Representative from Pennsylvania (since 1937); champion of traditional Republican economic policy. See *Current Biography* (December) 1953.

Obituary

N Y Times p25 Ja 8 '60

SINATRA, FRANK Dec. 12, 1917(?). Singer; actor

Address: b. Sinatra Songs, Inc., 1619 Broadway, New York 19

NOTE: This biography supersedes the article which appeared in *Current Biography* in 1943.

Frank Sinatra, who first became popular in the early 1940's when his unusual style of singing love ballads made teen-aged girls squeal and swoon, is now regarded as one of the biggest show business attractions of the twentieth century. During his resplendent career—marked by a professional comeback after a popularity slump —Sinatra has developed into a baritone who charms lovers of popular music of all ages. He has also become a sensitive and versatile motion-picture actor, who won a 1953 Academy of Motion Picture Arts and Sciences Award as best supporting actor for his performance in *From Here to Eternity*. His annual income is estimated at $4,000,000; he can write his own contract at almost any night club; his Capitol albums are among the most popular records ever pressed; he appears frequently on television; and he stars in a number of motion pictures each year. In the world of entertainment, "The Voice" is coming through more loudly and clearly than ever before.

Francis Albert Sinatra was born in Hoboken, New Jersey on December 12, 1917 (some sources indicate 1915), the only child of Anthony Martin and Natalie (Garaventi) Sinatra. His father, who was for many years a member of the Hoboken Fire Department, and his mother, who often sang at social affairs, were both born in Italy.

Frank first became interested in music when his uncle gave him a ukulele, and on summer nights he would sit on a curbstone under a street light singing while he strummed on the ukulele. At Hoboken's Demarest High School he joined the school band and helped to organize the glee club. Later, he took courses at Drake Institute. In these years Sinatra developed another lasting interest, boxing; he grew up in a tough neighborhood and became a good boxer in order to protect himself. When he left school he went to work for the now-defunct *Jersey Observer* in his home town, first as a helper on a delivery truck and later as a copy boy.

Apparently, Sinatra's decision to become a singer was a spur-of-the-moment affair. One day in 1936 he and his fiancée, Nancy Barbato, went to a Jersey City vaudeville house to see Bing Crosby who was making a personal appearance there. Afterwards, Sinatra, who could not read music and who had never sung professionally before, suddenly announced that he, too, was "going to be a singer." He promptly quit his newspaper job and began singing with various local bands.

In 1937 Sinatra and three young instrumentalists from Hoboken performed on the *Major Bowes' Original Amateur Hour* as the Hoboken Four. They were awarded first prize and engaged for a tour with one of Bowes's traveling companies. After three months, a homesick Sinatra left the group and returned to Hoboken.

For the next year and a half, Sinatra sang at the Rustic Cabin, a North Jersey roadhouse, for $15 a week. When, in 1939, he got a $10 raise, he celebrated the occasion by marrying Miss Barbato. At this time Sinatra performed without compensation on many local radio shows, hoping to attract the attention of someone who could give him a good singing job.

Sinatra's efforts brought results: a trumpeter with Benny Goodman's band, Harry James, heard Sinatra sing on a broadcast from the

Metro-Goldwyn-Mayer

FRANK SINATRA

Rustic Cabin. James, who was organizing his own orchestra, offered Sinatra a one-year, $75-a-week contract in 1939. After several months with Harry James, Sinatra broke the contract to join Tommy Dorsey and his band.

For three and a half years Sinatra sang with Dorsey, eventually becoming as much a celebrity as the band leader. His discs of "I'll Never Smile Again," "Night and Day," and "This Love of Mine," made with the Dorsey group, smashed sales records. At this time Sinatra developed his distinctive singing style, characterized by pausing, phrasing, and glissandi. Sinatra had noticed that Dorsey's success had come from his unusual method of phrasing with his trombone. "I figured if he could do that phrasing with his horn, I could do it with my voice," Sinatra once explained. Tying phrases together with moans to heighten the song's emotional content and inhaling in the middle of a note so that his voice seemed to glide effortlessly from note to note without breathing became Sinatra trademarks.

By 1942 Sinatra had decided that he was ready to strike out on his own. He left Dorsey to become the first of many soloists who broke away from bands and made successful careers as individual singers. Obtaining a booking for a personal appearance at New York's Paramount Theatre, Sinatra crooned from the last day of 1942 until eight weeks later, a period longer than any other solo engagement at the Paramount up to that time. His growing popularity landed him a spot as soloist on the radio program *Your Hit Parade*, which he held from February 1943 to January 1945, and brought him to the attention of Hollywood producers.

It was during this period, 1942-43, that Sinatra became the idol of the bobby-soxers. This was in part a result of some high-powered press-agentry. E. J. Kahn in the *New Yorker* (November 9, 1946) magazine reported that Si-

SINATRA, FRANK—Continued

natra's publicists launched a drive to link the words "Sinatra" and "swoon." Such nicknames as "Swoonlight Sinatra" and "Mr. Swoon" were created. Ironically, the nickname that eventually caught on did not mention swoon in any way. To this day, Sinatra is "The Voice."

Throughout the United States girls and women formed Frank Swoonatra Fan Clubs. His performances, during which he stared intensely into the various eyes that were glued to him, were punctuated by shrieking and squealing and swooning and fainting. In the *New Yorker* (November 2, 1946) E. J. Kahn noted that it was during World War II that Sinatra became a teen-agers' hero, and that girls "turned to him as compensation for the absence of their young men."

The crooner's success outlasted the war years. In 1943 he made his debut as a film star in *Higher and Higher* (RKO) and went on to make other musical confections like *Anchors Aweigh* (MGM, 1945), *Till the Clouds Roll By* (MGM, 1947), *It Happened in Brooklyn* (MGM, 1947), *The Kissing Bandit* (MGM, 1949), and *On the Town* (MGM, 1949).

In addition to his professional activities, Sinatra at this time was working with youth groups to promote religious and racial harmony. He donated his services to the RKO short subject *The House I Live In* (1945), which had for its message the essential importance of tolerance in a democracy. This musical film won a special Academy Award.

In the late 1940's Sinatra's career suffered a setback. His record sales slumped, his throat began hemorrhaging, the adulation of his public declined, and his film studio, MGM, dropped him from its roster. During this period he became involved with Ava Gardner in a romance that the pair pursued in various parts of the world, usually followed by a contingent of unwelcome reporters. In 1951 Sinatra and his first wife were divorced and he was married to Miss Gardner. When Sinatra sought the dramatic role of Angelo Maggio in the screen version of James Jones's *From Here to Eternity*, he had to "undergo the humiliation of a screen test" and he had to accept a salary of only $8,000 instead of his customary $150,000.

His performance in *From Here to Eternity* (Columbia, 1953) was to prove a turning point. In this exposé of tarnished prewar Army brass and the injustices of barracks life Sinatra played a temperamental Italian-American GI who is confined to an Army stockade and killed by a sadistic sergeant. Many reviewers felt that Sinatra's acting was the biggest surprise of the film, and six years after the picture was made Alfred G. Aronowitz of the New York *Post* (October 27, 1959) wrote that as Maggio, "Sinatra, once strictly a song-and-dance man, had become an actor with a sensitivity that continues to overwhelm producers, directors, and critics." The film won seven Academy Awards, including one for Frank Sinatra as the best supporting actor of 1953.

In *The Man with the Golden Arm* (United Artists, 1956), an unrelenting examination of drug addiction, Sinatra portrayed a "junkie," Frankie Machine, struggling to "kick" the habit.

As an ex-soldier returning from World War II and floundering in his attempt to find a place in the civilian world, Sinatra played Dave Hirsh in *Some Came Running* (MGM, 1959). He appeared as a widowed hotel-owner in the comedy *A Hole in the Head* (United Artists, 1959).

Other motion pictures in which Sinatra starred are *Suddenly* (1954), *Young at Heart* (1955), *Not as a Stranger* (1955), *Guys and Dolls* (1955), *The Tender Trap* (1955), *Johnny Concho* (1956), *High Society* (1957), *The Joker Is Wild* (1957), *Pal Joey* (1957), *The Pride and the Passion* (1957), *Kings Go Forth* (1958), *Never So Few* (1960), and *Can-Can* (1960).

On television Sinatra captivated audiences of CBS's *The Frank Sinatra Show* from October 1950 to April 1952 and of ABC's *Frank Sinatra Show* from October 1957 to June 1958. He has also appeared as a guest star on various programs and on TV specials. He has interests in a Beverly Hills restaurant, the Sands Hotel in Las Vegas, Nevada, several music publishing companies, a talent agency, and Dorchester Company, a motion-picture producing concern. He has tried his hand at writing such songs as "This Love of Mine," "Peachtree Street," "Take My Love," and "Manhattan Skyline." With John Quinlan, from whom he has taken voice lessons, Sinatra wrote *Tips on Popular Singing* (Embassy Music Corporation, 1941).

Few people argue about Sinatra's prestige as a performer, but many disagree about Sinatra's personality. He appears to be a man riddled with contradictions. Outside his California home, which he protects with a ten-foot brick wall, there is a sign reading: "If you haven't been invited, you better have a damn good reason for ringing this bell!" He has carried on a feud with certain sections of the press, primarily over his desire for personal privacy. On the other hand, Sinatra's generosity with friends is legendary and he has aided the careers of many show business performers. He often surrounds himself with a retinue of business associates and stars known as "The Clan," who look to him as their leader.

Frank Sinatra and Nancy Barbato were married on February 4, 1939 and have three children, Nancy Sandra (who became the wife of the singer Tommy Sands), Franklin Wayne, and Christina. Although the couple was divorced in 1951, Sinatra remains devoted to his first wife and his children. On November 7, 1951 he was married to Ava Gardner; this marriage ended in divorce on July 5, 1957. Blue-eyed, brown-haired Sinatra is good-looking although emaciated, is five feet ten inches tall and weighs 140 pounds; his face is gaunt and bony. A Democrat, Sinatra favored a fourth term for President Franklin D. Roosevelt and campaigned for Democratic standard-bearers in recent Presidential elections.

References

Kahn, E. J. The Voice; The Story of an American Phenomenon (1947)

Who's Who in America, 1960-61

SIRIKIT KITIYAKARA, CONSORT OF RAMA IX, KING OF THAILAND Aug. 12, 1932-

Address: Grand Palace, Bangkok, Thailand

To demonstrate Thailand's friendship with the West, King Bhumibol Adulyadej (Rama IX) and Queen Sirikit Kitiyakara made a global good-will tour during 1960. In the course of it they also proved their own popularity with the people and press of the United States and a number of European countries. Sirikit is a strikingly beautiful queen—cosmopolitan, Western-educated, pleased with the growing emancipation of women in Thailand, and seriously occupied with social welfare work in her country. Since 1950 she has reigned with Bhumibol over the 22,000,000 people of the Southeast Asian constitutional monarchy, a country of colorful tradition and legend formerly called Siam. (See Rama IX, King of Thailand; *C.B.*, July 1950.)

Mom Rachawong Sirikit Kitiyakara was born on August 12, 1932, the daughter of Prince Chandaburi Suranath (Nakkhat Mongkol Kitiyakara), and his wife, Mom Luang Bua (Snidwongse) Kitiyakara. Prince Chandaburi is the third son of Prince Chandaburi Narunath and Princess Absarasman Kitiyakara. Princess Sirikit studied at the French Catholic St. Francis Xavier School in Bangkok. When her father was sent to Europe in the diplomatic service of Thailand, she accompanied him and continued her education in France and Denmark, where he was Minister, and in England, where he became Ambassador in September 1948. She learned to speak French and English fluently.

Later attending school in Lausanne, Switzerland, Princess Sirikit became acquainted with another student from Thailand, Bhumibol Adulyadej, a distant cousin whom she had met in Paris some years earlier. Bhumibol had succeeded to the throne of Thailand in June 1946 after the mysterious death of his older brother, King Ananda, who had been found shot to death in the royal palace. Postponing his coronation, Bhumibol had gone to Switzerland to study political science and law. He became engaged to Princess Sirikit in the summer of 1949, and after returning to Thailand, they were married on April 28, 1950, amid the ancient rites and splendor of the Buddhist faith, but in a ceremony relatively brief and simple for a Thai royal wedding.

The following month, on May 5, at the coronation of Bhumibol, who adopted the dynastic name of Rama IX, Sirikit was crowned Queen of Thailand. The royal couple then went back to Switzerland for about a year of further study, and their first child, Princess Ubol Ratana, was born to Queen Sirikit in Switzerland on April 5, 1951. Later in 1951 the King and Queen took up permanent residence in the palace at Bangkok, the birthplace of their other three children. Crown Prince Vajiralongkorn was born on July 28, 1952; Princess Sirindhorn, on April 2, 1955; and Princess Chulabhorn, on July 4, 1957.

Wide World

QUEEN SIRIKIT

In the ten years since King Bhumibol assumed the sovereign's responsibilities, his wife has helped considerably in carrying out royal duties. She frequently makes state visits with him; accompanies him to official functions, receptions, and ceremonies; and is said to be a thoughtful and conscientious hostess at the palace. From October 22 to December 7, 1956, when the King was entering the Buddhist priesthood and was residing at Bovornives Temple, Queen Sirikit acted as his regent. She performed her tasks so well that on the recommendation of the government she was given a title of very high distinction, Somdech Phraborom Rajininath.

Queen Sirikit became president of the Thai Red Cross on August 12, 1956, and when Prince Nagor Svarga, executive vice-president of the organization died in late 1959, she took over the additional duties of his office. Her own popularity and her active participation in fund-raising drives have aroused much public interest in Red Cross causes. She has also worked to encourage improvements in the country's educational system and public health programs. With King Bhumibol she campaigned for a vaccination program that saved the nation's poultry industry. She has traveled to remote parts of Thailand where members of the royal family have never before been seen, visiting leper colonies and village health centers. Like the King, she tries to keep in touch with the people and learn at firsthand about conditions in various parts of the country.

Since the end of World War II, Thailand, despite its proximity to Red China, has taken a pro-Western stand in the conflict between the Communist countries and the Free World. It is one of the three Asian members of the Southeast Asia Treaty Organization (SEATO), which has its headquarters in Bangkok. Bhumibol believes that one of the functions of a king is to try to bring peoples

SIRIKIT, QUEEN—*Continued*

of various countries closer together in order to improve relations throughout the world. In December 1959 he and the Queen made a state visit to Vietnam, and in early 1960 they visited Indonesia and Burma.

Their Majesties began their six-month tour of the West in June 1960 with a visit to the United States, which is of special interest to the King as the country of his birth (Bhumibol was born in 1927 in Cambridge, Massachusetts when his father was a medical student at Harvard University). During their four-day stay in Washington, where President Eisenhower and other high government officials met them at the airport, they were given "red-carpet" welcomes at numerous receptions. On their subsequent visits to thirteen European countries they were also received with much pomp and ceremony by heads of state, and at the Vatican in October, by Pope John XXIII. While the royal couple traveled in the United States, their children stayed in California, and in Europe the Prince and Princesses spent most of their time in Switzerland.

An admirer of Western fashions, to which she adds an Oriental touch, Queen Sirikit is reported to have dazzled spectators during the tour by her lavish wardrobe, mainly the creation of Paris designer Pierre Balmain, and by her jewelry, including pieces from the crown jewel collection. Several newspaper writers commented on her gay, informal manner and her poise and gracefulness. She smiles frequently, and her characteristic expressions of happiness and warm friendliness contrast noticeably with the King's air of gravity. "It is difficult to define the special quality of Queen Sirikit's beauty," a reporter for the Manchester *Guardian* (July 23, 1960) wrote during her visit to England. "There is a complete impression of loveliness, fragile as a painting on porcelain, delicate as lotus petals."

The Queen has said in press interviews that she makes a point of spending as much time as possible with her four children, who are being educated with about forty-five other pupils at a school built on the grounds of the palace at Bangkok. All the members of the royal family enjoy the beach near the summer palace at Hua Hin on the sea. Swimming, dancing and playing badminton are among Queen Sirikit's favorite recreations. A pianist who used to practise five hours a day, she shares her husband's well-known love of music, although, unlike the King, she prefers "sweet music" to jazz. Both the King and Queen tend to encourage the introduction of many Western customs into their country, while retaining what they regard as the best traditions of Thai culture.

References

Christian Sci Mon p5+ Je 12 '60 pors
N Y Times p28 Je 27 '60
N Y World-Telegram p10 Je 17 '60 por
Parade p14 Je 26 '60 pors
Washington (D.C.) Post pC21+ Je 30 '60 pors

Asia Who's Who (1960)

SISAVANG VONG, KING OF LAOS

July 14, 1885-Oct. 30, 1959 Ascended to the throne of Luangprabang in 1905; became King of all Laos in 1946; retired as head of government because of ill health in August 1959. See *Current Biography* (April) 1954.

Obituary

N Y Times p27 O 30 '59

SMITH, CARLETON SPRAGUE Aug. 8, 1905- Musicologist; educator; librarian

Address: b. Brazilian Institute, New York University, Washington Square, New York 3; h. "Waldingfield Farm," Washington, Conn.

An enthusiasm for music unifies the diversified career of Carleton Sprague Smith, whose contributions to education, library service, entertainment, and international relations have been equally distinguished. For twenty-eight years Smith was chief of the music division of the New York Public Library, a position he resigned in early 1959 to become the director of the Brazilian Institute of New York University. While Smith was directing a survey during 1960 in connection with the proposed national cultural center in Washington, D.C., he underscored the value of the performing arts as "our most effective" weapon in telling the story of America to the world. His remarks were characteristic of this internationally minded musicologist.

Carleton Sprague Smith, a native of New York City, was born to Clarence Bishop and Catherine (Cook) Smith on August 8, 1905 Educated at Harvard University, he received the B.A. degree in 1927, and during the following year while studying for the M.A. degree, conferred in 1928, he wrote musical criticism for the Boston *Transcript*. In 1928 he was a John Harvard Fellow and in 1929, a Woodbury Lowery Fellow. He went to Austria to complete his graduate study and was awarded the Ph.D. degree from the University of Vienna in 1930.

For the next twenty-eight years, from 1931 to 1959, Smith held the position of chief of the music division of the New York Public Library. His wide-ranging interests kept him also occupied in a variety of other appointments and activities. In the field of education he taught history at Columbia University from 1931 to 1933 and in 1939 became an instructor in music at New York University, where he later advanced to adjunct professor of music. Among the universities at which he has lectured are Leland Stanford in California in 1938, Indiana in Bloomfield in 1948, and Southern California at Los Angeles in the summers of 1950 and 1951.

Promotion of international exchange in music has long been one of Smith's major goals. In 1936 he was an official delegate at the International Music Education Conference in Prague, Czechoslovakia and attended the conference again in 1947. Particularly interested in music as a cultural link between the countries of North and South America, he became vice-chairman of the Committee on Inter-

American Relations in the Field of Music, formed by the Department of State in 1939. Under the auspices of the committee he made a good-will tour of South America from June to October 1940. One purpose of his trip was to investigate opportunities for musical research in archaeology, folklore, and musicology. In several of the fourteen countries that he visited he lectured on music in the United States, illustrating his talks with recordings of spirituals, ballads, and other folk songs.

At home, Smith also encouraged closer musical ties among the American republics as commentator during 1941-42 of "Music of the Americas," a *Columbia School of the Air* radio program presented over the Columbia Broadcasting System. He made another tour of South America in 1943 under the joint sponsorship of the Carnegie Foundation and the Office of the Coordinator of Inter-American Affairs, and in 1943 he lectured in Brazil at the invitation of Sociedade Felipe de Oliveira.

From 1944 to 1946 Smith served as the United States cultural attaché at São Paulo, Brazil. He also represented his government in a number of postwar assignments: as a delegate to the United Nations Educational Social and Cultural Organization conference in Paris in 1948 and as a member of the Mission for the American Council on Education in Germany in 1951-52.

Continuing his close association with the cultural life of Brazil, he attended the Luso-Brazilian Colloquia in Washington in 1950, in São Paulo in 1954, and in Lisbon, Portugal in 1957. He is the author of numerous articles on Brazil, including "Montparnasse of the Hemisphere" (*United Nations World,* October 1950) and "Song of Brazil" (*Américas,* October 1950), and edited a supplement on Brazil entitled "Perspective of Brazil" for the *Atlantic Monthly* in February 1956.

Since 1946 Dr. Smith had lectured on Latin American civilization at New York University's Institute of Public Affairs and Regional Studies. He was appointed director of NYU's Brazilian Institute on March 1, 1959, about a year after the official establishment of the institute. With Dean Thomas Clark Pollock of the Washington Square College of Arts and Sciences as director pro tempore, the institute became a working reality in July 1958.

A center for the encouragement of Brazilian studies on both undergraduate and graduate levels, the institute offers instruction in language, literature, fine arts, music, economics, politics, and history. It also provides courses for employees of United States companies with branches in Brazil, an exchange program for students and teachers, and special library and research facilities.

Shortly before becoming director of the institute, Smith had resigned as chief of the music division of the New York Public Library, in February 1959. He remains associated with the library, however, as music consultant to the chief of the reference department. One of the achievements of the music department during his tenure was the growth of the dance collection. In March 1956, when Genevieve Oswald, curator of the dance collection, won

N. Y. University—William R. Simmons

CARLETON SPRAGUE SMITH

the Capezio Dance Award, John Martin of the New York *Times* wrote that Smith was "a man with a broad background in the dance and a genuine enthusiasm for it, and it is in large part his sympathetic leadership that has made possible Miss Oswald's notable accomplishments with her department."

Besides assisting scholars in their musical researches at the library, Smith worked directly on several projects, including Hans Theodore David's edition of *Ten Sacred Songs for Soprano, Strings and Organ,* published by the New York Public Library in 1947, for which he adapted the English text. He also gave special encouragement to Sydney Beck's edition of Thomas Morley's *First Book of Consort Lessons,* a handsome volume on Elizabethan music that the C. F. Peters Corporation published in 1959.

Many of the organizations with which Smith is affiliated, like the International Music Fund and the Interamerican Music Center, are mainly concerned with cultural exchanges among countries. He has also taken part in the development of several projects to stimulate interest in the performing arts in the United States, including the Lincoln Center in New York City, for which he prepared a report on the library-museum.

As an investigator for the proposed national cultural center in Washington, he has called attention to shortcomings in the Congressional legislation that authorized the center on September 2, 1958. "This public law," Smith has said, "makes no mention of the national role the cultural center should play. It is a purely Washington operation. This naturally causes considerable resistance. Unless another law is passed that takes the nation into consideration the National Cultural Center will not come into being." Appealing for public support of the cultural center, Smith said in September

SMITH, CARLETON SPRAGUE—*Cont.*

1960 that the role of the performing arts is to place "our moral values under continual examination."

Smith is a director of the Aspen Institute for Humanistic Studies in Aspen, Colorado, where he lectured in the summer of 1950. He is a director of the Philharmonic Symphony Society of New York and a former director of the Metropolitan Opera Association. The many professional organizations to which he belongs include the Music Library Association (president from 1936 to 1938), the American Musicology Association (president in 1939-40), and the Academy of Political Science. He is also a member of the Council on Latin-American Studies and the Council on Foreign Relations. His clubs are the Century Association, Harvard (New York City), Grolier, and others.

As reported in *Américas* (October 1950), Smith's colleagues at the United States consulate in São Paulo described him "as gay, good looking, and charming, with tremendous energy." He was married to Elizabeth Cowles Sperry on June 30, 1934, and they have a daughter, Damaris Sayre Sprague. Smith plays the flute and has edited Prokofieff's Flute Sonata, Opus 94.

References

> Grove's Dictionary of Music and Musicians (1955)
> Thompson, O. ed. International Cyclopedia of Music and Musicians, 1956
> Who's Who in America, 1960-61
> Who's Who in New York, 1960

SNODGRASS, W(ILLIAM) D(EWITT)

Jan. 5, 1926- Poet; university professor

Address: b. c/o Wayne State University, Detroit 2, Mich.; h. 23805 Oxford, Dearborn, Mich.

For his first volume of poems, *Heart's Needle* (1959), W. D. Snodgrass was honored with the Pulitzer Prize for Poetry in 1960. Snodgrass is a confessional poet, who finds in his own experience universal meaning and moral implication. His poetry announces that "Snodgrass is walking through the universe" with dignity and with courage, in the face of domestic tragedy or human suffering in general. It is notable for its sincerity, delicacy, and restraint.

After having taught at Cornell University and the University of Rochester, Snodgrass is now an assistant professor of creative writing at Wayne State University in Detroit, Michigan. In addition to the Pulitzer Prize for Poetry, he has received a *Hudson Review* Fellowship and the Ingram-Merrill Foundation award.

William DeWitt Snodgrass, one of the four children of Bruce DeWitt Snodgrass, an accountant, and the former Jesse Helen Murchie, was born on January 5, 1926 in Wilkinsburg, Pennsylvania. The family later moved to Beaver Falls, Pennsylvania. William attended Beaver Falls High School, where he acted in school plays, belonged to the tennis team, and played the timpani in the orchestra. Graduated in 1943, he studied at local Geneva College until March 1944, when he joined the United States Navy as an apprentice seaman. At the end of three years of service he received his discharge with the rank of yeoman third class.

After returning to Geneva College, he became aware of its limitations in offering courses in poetry writing and he left for the State University of Iowa. A fellow student, Donald T. Torchiana (*Northwestern Tri-Quarterly*, spring 1960), remembers Snodgrass coming to Iowa City "resplendent in castoff Navy costume, great head of hair and flowing beard, and properly abstracted poet's eye." At Iowa State Snodgrass concentrated on Renaissance literature. There, according to Robert Lowell, Snodgrass "flowered in the most sterile of sterile places, a post war, cold war mid-western university's poetry workshop for graduate student poets." To supplement his GI Bill benefits, Snodgrass worked as a clerk in a hotel and as an aide at a Veterans Administration Hospital. He remained at Iowa State until 1955, and earned the B.A., M.A., and M.F.A. degrees in 1949, 1951, and 1953, respectively. He submitted original poems for both master's degrees.

From Iowa State Snodgrass went to Cornell University as an English instructor, but left within two years because he found the university dull. He then taught for one year at the University of Rochester. From June 1958 to June 1959, as the *Hudson Review* Fellow in Poetry, he had the opportunity to study, write, and give poetry readings of his work. Since September 1959 Snodgrass has been an assistant professor at Wayne State University in Detroit, where he teaches creative writing. During summer vacations he was the leader of poetry workshops at the Morehead Writers Conference in Kentucky in 1955 and at the Antioch Writers Conference in Yellow Springs, Ohio in 1958 and 1959.

While still a graduate student, Snodgrass began to write some of his important poems. His first poetic idol was William Empson, and later his work reflected his admiration of Marianne Moore, W. H. Auden, Kenneth Rexroth, and Donald Justice. Perhaps the most significant influence on his poetry was his experience at Iowa State: his imagery evokes such Iowa City scenes as rows of tin Quonset huts, snowdrifts at midnight, and the natural history museum in the old library. However, Snodgrass, who at first assimilated what he has called the "symbolist-metaphysical" tradition of the university, went on to develop a more flexible and laconic style of his own.

About 1954 the poems of Snodgrass began to appear in "little" magazines and literary quarterlies: *Western Review, Botteghe Oscure, Partisan Review, Paris Review, Transatlantic Review, Epoch, Fifties, Perspective*, and *Hudson Review*. Occasionally his work appeared in the *New Yorker*. His lyrics have been anthologized in the *Pocket Book of Modern Verse* (Pocket Books, 1954; Washington Square Press, 1960), edited by Oscar Williams; *New Poets of England and America* (Meridian Books, 1957), edited by Donald Hall and others; and *New*

World Writing (New American Library, 1957). In addition to writing his own poetry, Snodgrass has translated poems by Christian Morgenstern, Rainer Maria Rilke, and Arthur Rimbaud, and has written criticism on the works of D. H. Lawrence and Fyodor Dostoevsky.

The first volume of Snodgrass' poetry appeared in 1959 under the imprint of Alfred A. Knopf, Inc. Its title, *Heart's Needle,* derives from a phrase that occurs in an old Irish story: "An only daughter is the needle of the heart." The contents include nineteen short autobiographical poems about Navy service, revisiting his home town, sessions with his psychiatrist, personal integrity in the academic world, and his feeling of alienation in the wasteland of the 1950's.

The impressionistic title poem of *Heart's Needle* is a ten-part cycle that takes place from the winter of 1952 to the spring of 1955. Snodgrass experiences the agonies of a disintegrating first marriage and the dread of what his remarriage would do to his relationship with his daughter. About a trip to the zoo with his daughter in an effort to create common memories, he wrote in *Heart's Needle*: "If I love you, they said, I'd leave/ and find my own affairs./ Well, once again this April, we've come around to the bears;/ punished and cared for, behind bars,/ the coons on bread and water/ stretch thin black fingers after ours./ And you are still my daughter."

In his poetry, Snodgrass strives for personal honesty. In the *Partisan Review* (spring 1959) he wrote: "I believe the only reality which a man can ever surely know is that self he cannot help being, though he will only know that self through its interactions with the world around it. If he pretties it up, if he changes its meaning, if he gives it the voice of any borrowed authority, if in short he rejects this reality, his mind will be less than alive. So will his words."

To Snodgrass the happy family as an ideal for the individual parallels a peaceful world as an ideal for nations. He holds that man can best deal with the predicaments and uncertainties of life by evaluating them fearlessly and by doing what he can to resolve them. Lyrical in feeling and moral in import, his poems underscore his belief that individual responsibilty for every act is a cardinal principle.

A disciplined craftsman, Snodgrass employs imagery and description suggestively; he often reserves his expression of personal involvement for the end of the poem. When he views one of his poems as a failure he rewrites it in a longer version, developing ideas extensively that he first attempted to imply intensively. On occasion, however, the lyric seems to create itself. "Sometimes," he wrote, "a poem *does* surprise you by taking itself out of your well-meaning hands and deciding for itself what it will say. . . . You have approached something basic to that pattern of ideas and emotions and feelings which *is* your mind; you find something of what *your* meaning is" (*Partisan Review,* spring 1959).

Donald T. Torchiana has said that Snodgrass' "verses abound with the metaphoric crockery of mid-century life, realistic diction,

W. D. SNODGRASS

symbolic landscapes, double-dealing language, outrageous puns, partial rhymes, stretches of dead-pan prose, syllabic metres, and sudden line breaks, accent groupings, and a most polished surface. But he has not stopped there . . . these devices are not ends in themselves." Stanley Kunitz (*Harper's Magazine,* September 1960) credits Snodgrass with "the gift of transforming ordinary experience, including the domestic, into a decisive act of the imagination, remarkable for its pace and clarity and controlled emotion."

Some critics have pigeonholed Snodgrass as a bourgeois poet because he looks upon normal domestic relationships as both practical and desirable. The bourgeois group is distinguished from the "beat" artists who regard all aspects of middle-class conformity as blights upon the creative spirit. Conceding that schools of poetry do exist, Snodgrass asserts that "the members of either school in proportion as they represent that school, are bad poets. The bad poets of both schools are alike in being academic and doctrinaire imitators of what was once valid, personal invention. On the other hand, the good poets on both sides have more in common with each other, both in their private lives, personal beliefs, and even in the qualities of their writing, than they have in common with the lesser poets of their own 'school.'"

The Pulitzer Prize in Poetry for 1960 was given to W. D. Snodgrass for *Heart's Needle.* The award climaxed a series of other national honors he had won: the Ingram-Merrill Foundation award of $1,000, the Longview Literary Award, a grant of $1,500 from the National Institute of Arts and Letters, and a special citation and $250 stipend from the Poetry Society of America.

William DeWitt Snodgrass and his first wife, Lila, were married on June 6, 1946 and divorced on December 16, 1953. Their daughter is Cynthia Jean Snodgrass. On March 20, 1954 Snod-

SNODGRASS, W. D.—*Continued*

grass was married to Mrs. Janice Marie Fergu-son Wilson. They have two children: a son, Russell Bruce Snodgrass, and Mrs. Snodgrass' daughter by a former marriage, Kathy Ann Wilson. Snodgrass has brown eyes behind dark-rimmed glasses, brown, closely-cropped hair, and a bristly moustache. He is six feet tall and weighs about 185 pounds. In religion he is a Quaker. For relaxation he enjoys playing tennis, strumming on a guitar, and listening to music. In his poem "A Cardinal" Snodgrass wrote: "The world's not done to me;/ it is what I do;/ whom I speak shall be;/ I music out my name/ and what I tell is who/ in the world I am."

References

N Y Times p34 My 3 '60 por
Nation 189:257+ O 24 '59
Northwestern University Tri-Quarterly
2:18+ Spring '60 por

SPAIN, FRANCES LANDER Mar. 15, 1903- Librarian; organization official

Address: b. The New York Public Library, New York 18; h. 3840 Greystone Ave., Riverdale, New York 63

When Mrs. Frances Lander Spain was named president-elect of the American Library Association in June 1959, she promised that after she became president in 1960 she would work toward "introducing more books to more people" and "recruiting more promising young persons into the profession of librarianship." She was elected by the 23,000 members of the ALA, which was founded in 1876. Mrs. Spain, whose professional interests are library education and library work with children, has been co-ordinator of children's services at the New York Public Library since 1953. Her articles have appeared in numerous periodicals and books, and she edited "Books for Young People" in the *Saturday Review* from 1954 to 1959.

Frances Lander was born in Jacksonville, Florida on March 15, 1903, the daughter of Malcolm McPherson and Rosa Olivia (Dantzler) Lander. Her brother and sister died in infancy. Her grandfather, Samuel Lander, was the founder and president of Lander College in Greenwood, South Carolina (formerly the Williamston, South Carolina, Female Institute). Her father worked for the United States postal service and her mother became executive secretary of the YWCA in Jacksonville.

She attended the Duval High School in Jacksonville, and during her vacations she worked from 1919 to 1921 as an untrained assistant in the children's department of the Jacksonville Public Library. After her graduation from high school in 1921, she entered Winthrop College in Rock Hill, South Carolina. She was elected president of the student government association, and, after majoring in physical education, English, and history, she received her B.A. degree in 1925.

On October 10, 1925 Frances Lander was married to Donald Grant Spain. They had two children: Barbara Lander Spain (now Mrs. Porter Wiseman Dobbins, Jr.) and Donald Grant Spain, Jr. Mrs. Spain's son died in 1932, and her husband died in August 1934. She attended a summer session in 1935 at Florida State College for Women (now Florida State University) and then received a B.A. degree in library science in 1936 from the Library School of Emory University in Atlanta, Georgia.

Mrs. Spain became a librarian at the Winthrop Training School and head of the library science department at her alma mater, Winthrop College, in 1936. She remained in these positions until 1945, when she was made the librarian of the college. In the meantime, she had continued her formal education with the help of a General Education Board Fellowship (1939 to 1940) and tuition scholarships from the Graduate Library School of the University of Chicago in Illinois. She was awarded an M.A. degree in 1940 (her master's thesis was entitled "School Library Standards") and the Ph.D. degree in 1944. Her doctoral dissertation, "South Carolina Libraries: Their Origins and Early History, 1700-1830," was published in modified form as an article in the *Library Quarterly* in January 1947.

From 1949 to 1953 Mrs. Spain was the assistant director of the School of Library Science of the University of Southern California in Los Angeles. During 1951 and 1952 she was in Thailand, developing a program of library training in Chulalongkorn University in Bangkok under a Fulbright grant. Several of her articles explaining American university libraries and the role of libraries in a democratic society were published in Thai periodicals in 1951 and 1952 (in the *Magazine* of Chulalongkorn University and the Bangkok *Standard*). Her comments on libraries and teaching library science in Thailand appeared in several American publications, including the *Library Quarterly* (July 1952) and the *Wilson Library Bulletin* (December 1952).

In 1953 Mrs. Spain became co-ordinator of children's services at the New York Public Library, where she and her staff begin working with children from the age of two and up. She feels that, in spite of television, more children are reading more books than ever before; the library, according to the New York *Herald Tribune* (April 5, 1960), has a high percentage of attendance among young people under the age of nineteen, who still enjoy reading the classics of children's fiction, in spite of the demand for westerns and science books.

Mrs. Spain has been active in a number of organizations concerned with library work. She was a member of the library committee of the Southern Association of Colleges and Secondary Schools from 1940 to 1948. She served as chairman of the school library section of the South Carolina Library Association from 1941 to 1945, vice-president of the association in 1946, and president in 1947. From 1944 to 1945 she was chairman of the committee on certification requirements for school librarians of the South Carolina Department of Education, and in 1946 she was made a member of the conference on library statistics of the United States Office of Education.

From 1947 to 1948 Mrs. Spain served as a member of the executive board of the Southeastern Library Association, and as chairman of the intellectual freedom committee in 1951 and 1953 of the California Library Association. From 1956 to 1958 she was active in the scholarship and recruiting committee of the New York Library Association. She has also belonged to the School Library Association of California, Delta Kappa Gamma, and the Association of College and Reference Libraries.

In the American Library Association Mrs. Spain has been equally active. She was a member of the board of education for librarianship from 1950 to 1953, chairman of the Dutton-Macrae awards committee from 1952 to 1954. chairman of the Grolier Society awards committee from 1955 to 1956, second vice-president from 1955 to 1956, member of the council from 1957 to 1958, and secretary of the International Relations Round Table from 1958 to 1959.

At the seventy-eighth annual conference of the ALA, held in June 1959 in Washington, D.C., it was announced that Mrs. Spain had been elected vice-president and president-elect of the association. She was installed in these offices on June 26, 1959. She was inaugurated as president at the Montreal conference of the ALA when it held a joint meeting with the Canadian Library Association in June 1960. During 1959 and 1960 Mrs. Spain served as president of the library education division of the ALA.

Mrs. Spain has been a visiting lecturer at the School of Library Service at Columbia University in the summers of 1954, 1956, 1957, and 1960; at the Library School of Pratt Institute during the spring of 1956; at the Graduate School of Library Service of Rutgers University during the fall of 1958; and at the School of Library Science of Syracuse University during the summer of 1959.

From 1954 to 1959 Mrs. Spain was the editor of "Books for Young People," a monthly book list in the *Saturday Review.* Her articles, other than those previously mentioned, have appeared in such periodicals as *South Carolina Education, High School Journal, Library Trends,* and the *Annals of the American Academy of Political and Social Science.* She edited *Reading without Boundaries; Essays presented to Anne Carroll Moore on the Occasion of the Fiftieth Anniversary of Library Service to Children at the New York Public Library,* published by the library in 1956. Mrs. Spain contributed a chapter to a book by Ryan W. Carson and others entitled *Secondary Education in the South* (University of North Carolina Press, 1946), and to *The Library in General Education,* part two of *The Forty-second Yearbook of the National Society for the Study of Education* (1943). A lecture which she delivered at Simmons College in May 1955 was included in *Books and Publishing* (Simmons College, 1955).

Frances Lander Spain is a member of the American Association of University Women,

Clara E. Sipprell

FRANCES LANDER SPAIN

the Asia Society, and Beta Phi Mu. She is a Democrat and an Episcopalian. Mrs. Spain has hazel eyes and brown hair, stands five feet five inches tall, and weighs 135 pounds. For recreation she enjoys gardening, traveling, raising Siamese cats, and taking care of her four grandchildren.

References

ALA Bul 49:364+ Jl '55
Lib Q 17:60+ Ja '47; 22:305 Jl '52
N Y World-Telegram p9 Jl 11 '60
Washington (D.C.) Post pD3 Je 26 '59
Who's Who in America, 1960-61
Who's Who in Library Service (1955)

SPECTORSKY, A(UGUSTE) C(OMTE)
Aug. 13, 1910- Editor; author; publisher

Address: b. c/o Playboy Magazine, 232 E. Ohio St., Chicago 11, Ill.; h. 1347 N. State Parkway, Chicago, Ill.

The public knows A. C. Spectorsky best as the author of the much-discussed book, *The Exurbanites* (Lippincott, 1955), a witty commentary on the inhabitants of the counties that lie beyond Suburbia. An editor, anthologist, writer, and publisher, Spectorsky considers himself a "communicator," who has been involved in mass communication since 1929. As an anthologist, he has compiled works which, because of their de luxe format, have been regarded as models of book production. He has contributed articles and fiction to national magazines and has edited *Living for Young Homemakers, Charm, Park East,* and other publications.

Since 1956 Spectorsky has been associate publisher of *Playboy* magazine, which within a few years has climbed to an international

A. C. SPECTORSKY

circulation of nearly 1,000,000 male readers. Much in demand for his lectures on the craft of writing, he has made the keynote address for two consecutive years at Radcliffe College's annual course in publishing procedures.

Auguste Comte Spectorsky was born in Paris, France of American parents, Isaac and Frances (Herbert) Spectorsky, on August 13, 1910. His parents, who were multilingual, were primarily educators. His father founded the Educational Alliance of New York and was a dollar-a-year man in World War I. His mother was at one time an opera singer in Paris. Auguste spoke only French until he was four years old. When his parents moved to New York City, he attended the Ethical Culture School and the Columbia Grammar School. His special interests during his school days were music and sports.

After his graduation from the Ethical Culture School in 1929, Spectorsky went to work for Columbia Pictures in Hollywood, where he performed "various and menial" duties from 1929 to 1930. Returning to New York, he entered New York University, where he majored in physics. During college he worked as a camp counselor, teacher of horseback riding, and mathematics tutor. He earned the B.S. degree in 1934 and was elected to Phi Beta Kappa.

For a while after his college graduation, Spectorsky did graduate work in physics at Columbia; he then became a laboratory assistant with MP Concert Installations, in Fairfield, Connecticut. While working for this company, he made his first sale as a writer, to the New Yorker; "A sheer accident," Spectorsky says, "that filled me with a baseless courage for which I am grateful." He became an editorial associate on the New Yorker in 1938 and remained there until 1941.

"Spec," as his friends call him, continued writing, both fiction and nonfiction, for national magazines, including Cosmopolitan, This Week, Harper's Bazaar, Collier's, Reader's Digest, Good Housekeeping, and the New Yorker. He also wrote reviews for the New York Times Book Review section and the Chicago Sun. From 1941 to 1946 he was literary editor of the Chicago Sun.

As associate Eastern story editor of Twentieth-Century Fox Film Corporation, from 1946 to 1948, Spectorsky organized and administered writers' fellowships and purchased Letter to Three Wives, Gentlemen's Agreement, Lydia Bailey, and other books for filming. From 1948 to 1951 he was simultaneously advertising and promotion director of Charm magazine and managing editor of Living for Young Homemakers, both Street & Smith publications.

Invited to join the staff of the National Broadcasting Company in 1952, Spectorsky organized the NBC-TV Home show, a daily one-hour network production with a service magazine format. In 1954 he became senior editor for the television program. He also produced "remote origination" TV shows for the network.

From 1951 to 1954 Spectorsky was editor in chief of the now defunct Park East magazine; during his editorship the circulation of the publication rose from 5,000 to 70,000. After leaving Park East, he continued as a senior editor with NBC until May 1956, when he moved to Chicago to become associate publisher of Playboy magazine.

Launched in 1953 by twenty-seven-year-old Hugh Hefner, Playboy aimed at the young male market. Hefner, who had been associated with Esquire, felt that Esquire "had stopped being an entertainment magazine and had become a service magazine" (Fortune, May 1957). Since Spectorsky joined the staff, Playboy has become more staid than it used to be, and also more sophisticated; it features such well-known writers as John Steinbeck, Evelyn Waugh, and P. G. Wodehouse. Its circulation has rocketed to nearly 1,000,000, while that of Esquire has declined.

Asked about his magazine's resemblance to Esquire, Spectorsky replied: "Our readership is younger, richer, more urban, less married and (I would guess) happier and less neurotic . . . We are very young and vigorous, and by contrast Esquire is middle-aged."

During his various editorships Spectorsky continued his free-lance writing for national magazines and also wrote numerous books. He wrote the Midwest section of North, East, South, West (Howell, Soskin, 1945); a pamphlet, The Future For Books in America (Chicago Sun Publishing Company, 1945); Invitation to Skiing (Simon & Schuster, 1947); Man Into Beast (Doubleday, 1948); The Book of the Sea (Appleton, 1954); The Exurbanites (Lippincott, 1955); The Book of the Mountains (Appleton, 1955); The Book of the Sky (1956); The Book of the Earth (1957); The College Years (Hawthorn, 1958); and The

New Invitation to Skiing (Simon & Schuster, 1958).

Reviewers of *The Exurbanites* generally praised the book. *Commonweal's* critic (December 16, 1955) considered that Spectorsky, "as an ex-exurbanite deeply involved in symbol-manipulating, is . . . inclined to write not only knowledgeably but with sympathy for the predicament of the exurbanites." "Spectorsky has a gift for social insight and for illuminating an often hilarious anecdote," observed the San Francisco *Chronicle* (October 23, 1955). "Had his book been only witty and revealing, it would have been only absorbing. But because his observations are both daring and original, his book will be discussed and argued about not only in Exurbia but in all literate communities." The *New Yorker* (November 12, 1955) called it "an entertaining, if exceedingly parochial, field report by a disciple of the Russell Lynes school of social anthropology."

In the series of books about the mountains, the sea, the sky, and the earth, which Spectorsky edited for Appleton-Century-Crofts, *The Book of the Sea* received the widest acclaim. George H. Favre in the *Christian Science Monitor* called it a fascinating variety of selections (over eighty) from the history of man's first recorded ventures upon the sea's surface, to the latest phases of submarine exploration.

With ski instructor Fred Iselin, Spectorsky wrote *The New Invitation to Skiing* (Simon & Schuster, 1958), which uses stop-action photographs to illustrate its text. The book is designed for the beginning skiier.

In his preface to *The College Years* (Hawthorn, 1958), an anthology, Spectorsky wrote that he aimed, as editor, "to hold the literary mirror to college life in all its aspects. These are glimpses, some profound, some perhaps rosy with sentimental recall, others jaundiced and bitter, still others ebulliently young and carefree—but each and all contributing, it is hoped, to a view in the round of the university world."

Spectorsky was married to Joan Theodora Feigenspan, a book editor, in 1955. His two earlier marriages, to Lucille Hille and to Elizabeth Bullock, ended in divorce. By these marriages he has four children: Susan, Kathy, Lance, and Brooke. He is a member of the Society of Midland Authors; International P.E.N.; vice-president, the Shaw Society (Chicago); director, International Society for General Semantics; and member, the Authors' Guild and the Columbia Yacht Club (Chicago). He is over six feet in height, weighs 175 pounds, and has brown eyes and "charcoal gray" hair. His favorite sports are sailing, skiing, and riding. His hobbies are music, hi-fi, and travel.

References

Who's Who in America, 1958-59
Who's Who in Chicago and Illinois (1945)

SPITZER, LYMAN, JR. June 26, 1914-
Astrophysicist; university professor
Address: b. Princeton University Observatory, 14 Prospect Ave., Princeton, N.J.; h. 16 Prospect Ave., Princeton, N.J.

Project Matterhorn, a program for the development of techniques and instruments to control the hydrogen thermonuclear reaction, is headed by Dr. Lyman Spitzer, Jr., the Charles A. Young Professor of Astronomy at Princeton University. An authority on theoretical astrophysics, Spitzer also directs the Princeton University Observatory. He has supervised the expenditure of millions of dollars on research at his laboratories since 1951, when he first suggested that men could harness the energy released by the burning of hydrogen atoms at temperatures of about 10,000,000 degrees. Such energy would provide the world with sufficient power for over a billion years.

To accomplish his aim, Spitzer designed the "stellarator"—a man-made sun—recreating the processes in the solar interior. He has also conducted research on the origin of the stars and solar system, stellar atmospheres, and the broadening of spectral lines. Spitzer has also pioneered in the use of satellites for astronomical observation.

One of the four children of Lyman Spitzer and the former Blanche Carey Brumback, Lyman Spitzer, Jr., was born on June 26, 1914 in Toledo, Ohio. His father was a manufacturer of paper boxes and his two grandfathers, Adelbert S. Spitzer and Orville S. Brumback, were in banking and the law, respectively. He has a brother, who is a lawyer and manufacturer in Toledo, and two sisters.

Spitzer attended Scott High School in Toledo for two years before entering Phillips Academy in Andover, Massachusetts in 1929 to complete his secondary education. There he achieved an excellent scholastic record, served as editor in chief of the *Phillipian,* and participated in debating activities. At Yale University, Spitzer was also involved in extracurricular affairs as chairman of the *Yale Daily News* and as a member of Zeta Psi, Skull and Bones, and the Elizabethan Club. Majoring in physics, he was elected to Phi Beta Kappa and Sigma Xi for his high standing as a student.

After his graduation from Yale in 1935 with a B.A. degree, Spitzer received a Henry Fellowship to do research in physics and astronomy at St. John's College, Cambridge University, England. He returned to the United States in 1936 to continue his graduate work at Princeton University, which awarded him the M.A. degree in 1937. In the following year he earned a Ph.D. degree; his doctoral thesis was entitled *Spectra M Supergiant Stars* (1939.) Moving to Harvard University as a National Research Fellow, Spitzer engaged in postgraduate research on stellar atmospheres in 1938-39.

Dr. Spitzer returned to his alma mater in 1939 when he was appointed to the Yale faculty as an instructor in physics and astronomy. There his further studies on stellar atmospheres, particularly on the nebulae in the

Orren Jack Turner

LYMAN SPITZER, JR.

outer atmosphere, were highly praised. He demonstrated that these luminous masses are composed of stars and not of cosmic dust. He also discovered that the total amount of free atoms and dust in globular nebulae does not exceed 1-500 its total mass, but that in flattened systems that amount of dust is perhaps greater (New York *Times,* September 9, 1941).

After the coming of World War II Spitzer accepted an assignment in 1942 with the special studies group at Columbia University's division of war research doing antisubmarine warfare analysis. Two years later he was named director of the sonar analysis group to do underwater sound research for the bureau of ships of the United States Navy.

Returning to Yale and civilian research early in 1946, Dr. Spitzer became an associate professor of astronomy. His studies were devoted to investigation of the temperatures of interstellar particles and the formation of stars from the diffuse material in space. In an address before the American Astronomical Society, he explained that the "temperature of matter between the stars is very different for gases and for small solid grains, of the size of dust or smoke particles" (New York *Times,* September 12, 1946). The temperature of the solid grains would hover around the zero mark, while the gases would reach about 20,000 degrees Fahrenheit. If the gases were not ionized, their temperature would be reduced by the cooling effect of the grains. This indicated a significant factor in the continual formation of stars from diffuse matter spread out in space (New York *World-Telegram,* November 11, 1946).

Princeton University appointed Dr. Spitzer a full professor, chairman of the department of astronomy, and director of its observatory in 1947. Five years later he was honored

with the Charles A. Young Professorship of Astronomy. Spitzer, whose work at Princeton has covered all phases of astronautics, urged the launching of an earth satellite as early as 1947. He considers spaceship flight a certainty and has said that the conquest of atomic energy has made travel from an earthly satellite to other planetary satellites possible (New York *Times,* May 19, 1952).

In 1954 Dr. Spitzer reported that "a logical next step" in astronomy would be to establish a space observation point 500 miles above the earth's surface to record and photograph astronomical activities with exact precision (New York *Times,* June 17, 1954). This suggestion moved closer to reality in 1957 with Project Stratoscope, a photography program in which balloons carry cameras twenty miles into the sky. A satellite being constructed under Dr. Spitzer's direction at Princeton will hold a twenty-four-inch telescope which will study individual stars and will also contain a spectrograph permitting the analysis of elements in the stars and in interstellar space (New York *Times,* May 1, 1959).

Since 1953 Dr. Spitzer has been directing Project Matterhorn, a study sponsored by Princeton and the Atomic Energy Commission. Matterhorn is part of a larger AEC program, Project Sherwood, which co-ordinates research on thermonuclear power at several institutions. The research in progress under Spitzer's leadership grew out of a suggestion he made in 1951 that the fusion of heavy hydrogen atoms be harnessed for peaceful uses for the benefit of mankind. Thermonuclear burning takes place most readily with deuterium, a heavy isotope of hydrogen. The vast amounts of deuterium contained in ocean waters can provide more than the present rate of the world's energy consumption for over a billion years (*Life,* October 8, 1956).

To facilitate research related to taming the hydrogen bomb, a laboratory costing $450,000 was erected on the Princeton campus in 1956. A breakthrough in the work occurred with the invention of the stellarator. Built at an expenditure of several million dollars, the device consists of oblong, tubular vacuum chambers surrounded by coils. In it extensive amounts of magnetism and electricity are applied to deuterium which is converted into a mass of charged excited particles. When the excitation is prolonged the particles become fused. The occurrence of magnetic fields prevents the hot material from reaching the container's walls. The stellarator is only one of several methods being developed by American scientists to achieve controlled fusion of atoms.

Many articles by Dr. Spitzer have appeared in American and British scientific journals. He served as editor of the publication *Physics of Sound in the Sea,* prepared by the National Defense Research Committee (1946), and *Physics of Fully Ionized Gases* (Interscience, 1956).

Dr. Spitzer was elected to the National Academy of Sciences in 1952. He is a Fellow of the American Physical Society and a member of the American Academy of Arts and

Sciences, American Astronomical Society, Royal Astronomical Society (London), and the British Interplanetary Society. He served as trustee of the Woods Hole Oceanographic Institute, as a member of the Yale council, and as chairman of the Scientists Committee on Loyalty Problems. He sits with the advisory panel on astronomy of the National Science Committee and the Sherwood steering committee on controlled thermonuclear research of the Atomic Energy Commission. The Certificate of Merit was bestowed on Dr. Spitzer in 1948 in recognition of his achievements in wartime research.

Blue-eyed, brown-haired Lyman Spitzer, Jr., is six feet tall and weighs 165 pounds. He is a Republican, and his church affiliation is Congregational Christian. On June 29, 1940 he was married to Doreen Damaris Canaday, an archaeologist. The couple has four children: Nicholas C., Dionis C., Sarah Lutetia, and Lydia S. A ski enthusiast, Spitzer named his thermonuclear project in honor of a favorite skiing area in Colorado. He and his family also enjoy hiking.

References

N Y Herald Tribune p11 D 19 '57 por
American Men of Science vol I (1955)
International Who's Who, 1958
Who's Who in America, 1958-59
Who's Who in the East (1955)

SPRY, CONSTANCE Dec. 5, 1886-Jan. 3, 1960 British horticulturist; author of books on flower arrangement; was in charge of floral decoration at Westminister Abbey for coronation of Queen Elizabeth II (1953). See *Current Biography* (May) 1940.

Obituary

N Y Times p31 Ja 5 '60

STAFFORD, ROBERT T(HEODORE) Aug. 8, 1913- Governor of Vermont; lawyer *Address*: b. State House, Montpelier, Vt.; h. 64 Litchfield Ave., Rutland, Vt.

The first gubernatorial election in Vermont that required a re-count occurred in 1958 when Republican Robert T. Stafford was chosen chief executive by a plurality of only 719 votes in a state that had been steadfastly loyal to the G.O.P. At the same time it sent a Democrat, William H. Meyer, to the United States House of Representatives for the first time in over a century.

Robert Stafford, who has taken unequivocal positions on important issues, is an avowed opponent of capital punishment and recently welcomed a conference, held in Vermont in 1960, to plan further demonstrations against lunch-counter segregation in the South. As Governor, he has forthrightly confronted the problem of dangerous traffic conditions by proposing improvement and expansion of highways and urging rigorous regulation of careless and new drivers. Having announced that he would not seek a second two-year term, he stood for

ROBERT T. STAFFORD

election in November 1960 as Vermont's only United States Representative and defeated the incumbent, Meyer.

Robert Theodore Stafford was born in Rutland, Vermont on August 8, 1913 to the lawyer and banker Bert L. Stafford and the former Mabel R. Stratton. He has one brother, Thomas B. Stafford, and one sister, Mrs. Shirley S. Kelley. Robert attended Rutland public schools and was a member of the class of 1931 at Rutland High School, where his extracurricular activities included public speaking, participating in athletics, and writing for student publications.

Having received a special full-tuition scholarship from the state of Vermont, Stafford majored in political science at Middlebury College in Vermont. There he was active in campus affairs, playing tackle on the football team and serving as president of his fraternity. Awarded the B.S. degree in 1935, he continued his education as a graduate student at the University of Michigan in 1936 and later, in 1938, he received the LL.B. degree from Boston University School of Law.

In the same year Stafford was admitted to the Vermont bar and was made a partner in his father's law firm in Rutland. Not content with being a private practitioner, Stafford took on the additional responsibilities of city prosecutor in 1939. His career was interrupted in 1942 when he began four years of active World War II service as a lieutenant commander in the United States Navy. Later, from 1951 to 1953, he again served with the Navy during the Korean conflict and attained the rank of commander, a grade he now holds in the United States Naval Reserve.

Between his two military stints he had become senior partner of the Rutland law firm of Stafford & La Brake in 1946 and won election as Rutland County state's attorney in the

STAFFORD, ROBERT T.—Continued

same year. In 1953 he began his political career on a state level through appointment, by Governor Lee E. Emerson, as deputy attorney general, and in the following year successfully sought election as attorney general.

In this capacity the most controversial position that he took concerned state assistance to public schools. It resulted from the refusal of the Vermont Board of Education in December 1955 to give some $20,000 in state-aid-funds to various communities for tuition fees at private schools, including Roman Catholic institutions. Stafford stated in June 1956 that "there is neither legal nor constitutional authority for the payment of funds to non-public schools," and he defined public schools as "those receiving 51 per cent or more of their support from taxes or similar revenues from the general public" (New York *Times,* June 3, 1956).

When Stafford campaigned for the Republican nomination for lieutenant governor in 1956 his rival was Speaker John Hancock of the Vermont House of Representatives. Stafford defeated Hancock by a 2-to-1 vote and then, despite a strenuous Democratic bid to end "100 years of Republican control," was victorious in the November balloting.

Two years later, in the primary of September 9, 1958, Stafford was unopposed when he sought his party's designation for the governorship. At that time the Democrats chose Bernard J. Leddy as their nominee. The ensuing campaign centered around local issues. The Democrats again assailed the Republicans for their monopoly on state power. They also criticized the G.O.P. for its plank calling for a referendum on the "right to work" issue and for turning St. Lawrence power allocated to Vermont over to a private utility for transmission. The Republicans countered by citing their long experience in government and by proclaiming the necessity to shelter Vermont from outside influences.

A short time before the election the New York *Times* correspondent John H. Fenton wrote prophetically that Leddy "might make a good run on the strength of having some sort of platform for meeting state problems." Lieutenant Governor Stafford, Fenton added, had "not stated his position very vigorously" (October 18, 1958).

Dissatisfaction with conservative Republican leadership in Vermont was apparent at the election of November 4, 1958. For the first time since the 1851-53 Congress, voters chose a Democrat, William H. Meyer, for Vermont's seat in the United States House of Representatives. The new Republican United States Senator, Winston L. Prouty, won by only 3,595 votes, the lowest number of ballots cast for a Vermont Senator since the Civil War period. The closest contest, however, was the one between Stafford and Leddy; Vermont's Secretary of State announced that according to unofficial returns Stafford had a lead of only 918 votes, the smallest margin for a governor in the history of the state.

Leddy immediately called for a re-count and based his request on a long-ignored section of the state constitution stipulating that votes for a governor shall be tallied by a committee of both chambers of the legislature. Stafford agreed that this was "the only legal way to do it." Convened for its forty-fifth biennial session on January 7, 1960, the General Assembly named a fifty-six-member joint committee to re-count the ballots. By January 12 it had declared Stafford the winner with 62,222 votes to 61,503 for Leddy, or a majority of 719 for the new Governor. Leddy agreed that the re-count was made "fairly and impartially."

Immediately upon succeeding Governor Joseph B. Johnson on January 15, 1959, Governor Stafford urged that the state constitution be amended to provide for a prompt re-count in the event of any challenged elections in the future. He also proposed extending the governor's term to four years, holding annual instead of biennial sessions of the legislature, raising maximum old-age payments to $75 a month, creating a state scholarship board, and requiring prospective drivers to take a driving course and accident-prone drivers to be re-examined.

In his fiscal message of late January 1959, the Governor presented a $52,905,000 budget for the biennium of 1959-60. He also proposed a 20 per cent tax on tobacco products other than cigarettes and a 5 per cent tax on meals and rooms in public-lodging places, in an effort to overcome a state deficit of $4,000,000.

In support of the Governor's recommendations, the Republican-controlled legislature approved a general appropriation of $53,700,000 and a highway appropriation of $32,500,000. It passed a $3,000,000-highway-bond issue, authorized the use of $2,000,000 in bond funds for school construction, increased the cigarette tax, levied a 20 per cent tax on other tobacco products, and imposed a 3 per cent tax on rooms and meals in hotels, motels, and tourist houses.

Governor Stafford's position on some issues of national interest was made clear in April 1960 when he welcomed at Goddard College in Plainfield, Vermont a Protest and Action Conference on Equality to plan further demonstrations against lunch-counter segregation in the South, and when he revealed in a New York *Herald Tribune* poll that he was opposed to capital punishment. About a year after becoming Vermont's chief executive, Stafford concluded that he had "accomplished all he had set out to do as governor" and that he would not seek a second term.

Robert T. Stafford and Helen Content Kelley, who were fellow students at Middlebury College, were married on October 15, 1938. They are the parents of four daughters, Madelyn, Susan, Barbara, and Diane. The brown-haired, brown-eyed politician, who stands six feet two inches and weighs about 210 pounds, still finds time to continue his interest in athletics by skiing, boating, and playing tennis.

Stafford is a member of the Rutland County and Vermont bar associations, the American Legion, and Veterans of Foreign Wars and is a Lion, Eagle, Elk, and Mason. His church is the Congregational Christian. Boston University conferred an honorary LL.D. degree on

Governor Stafford in June 1959. In December 1959 he was honored with the Distinguished Service Membership Award from the National Republican Club and was called "one of the new leaders" of the Republican party in the East by William Mertens, the club's president.

References

Sports Illus 11:103 D 21 '59 pors
International Who's Who, 1959
Who's Who in America, 1960-61
Who's Who in the East (1959)

STEINMAN, D(AVID) B(ARNARD)
June 11, 1886-Aug. 21, 1960 Engineer; designer of over 400 bridges, including the Henry Hudson Bridge in New York and Mackinac Straits Bridge in Michigan; author of standard textbooks for engineers, books for juvenile readers, and collections of poems. See *Current Biography* (December) 1957.

Obituary

N Y Times p29 Ag 23 '60

STEPINAC, ALOJZIJE, CARDINAL
May 8, 1898-Feb. 10, 1960 Roman Catholic prelate of Yugoslavia; imprisoned by Yugoslav Communist government from 1946 to 1951 after his conviction on charges of collaboration with the Nazis in Croatia during World War II; Archbishop of Zagreb since 1937; elevated to Cardinal in January 1953. See *Current Biography* (February) 1953.

Obituary

N Y Times p1+ F 11 '60

STEWART, JAMES (MAITLAND) May 20, 1908- Actor
Address: P.O. Box 550, Beverly Hills, Calif.

NOTE: This biography supersedes the article which appeared in *Current Biography* in 1941.

During the quarter century that has elapsed between *Murder Man* (1935) and *The Mountain Road* (1960), James Stewart has starred in an average of two films a year and has sustained the appeal that has made him one of Hollywood's highest-paid actors. His hesitant drawl and awkward manner that reminded his fans of the boy next door became familiar to millions of prewar movie-goers. He did not reach top popularity at the box office, however, until 1950, when he freed himself from the stereotype and established a new screen image: a tougher man who is no longer boyish. He is, however, still the slow and courageous winner over odds.

Stewart received the New York Film Critics Award for the best male performance of 1939 for his role in *Mr. Smith Goes to Washington;* the Academy of Motion Picture Arts and Sciences award for the best performance in 1940 for *The Philadelphia Story;* and best starring actor awards in 1959 from the Venice Film

Columbia Pictures Corp.

JAMES STEWART

Festival, New York Film Critics, and annual *Film Daily* poll of writers for *Anatomy of a Murder.* He has been a winner in the *Motion Picture Herald-Fame* Poll almost every year since 1950.

James Maitland Stewart was born on May 20, 1908, in Indiana, Pennsylvania, where the prosperous Stewart family has run a hardware store since the middle of the nineteenth century. His devout Presbyterian parents, Alexander Maitland and Elizabeth Ruth (Jackson) Stewart, raised their children strictly with Scottish ideals of frugality, responsibility, prudence, and simplicity. A spindling boy who wore glasses, Jim liked to put on plays that he wrote himself and to play the accordion when not performing chores.

At Mercersburg Academy in Pennsylvania, Jim was interested in football, track, dramatics, the orchestra, and the glee club. He also served as art editor of the yearbook. During summer vacations he earned money by hauling bricks for a construction company and laying concrete with a highway-building concern.

Upon graduation from Mercersburg in 1928, Stewart, in keeping with family tradition, entered Princeton University. Invited to become a full member of the Princeton Triangle Club in his freshman year, he appeared in the club's annual musicals. Billy Grady, Sr., then a talent scout (later to become casting director) for Metro-Goldwyn-Mayer, who watched "a dozen guys dressed up as girls" in the 1932 show, told Pete Martin (*Saturday Evening Post,* September 15, 1951) that Stewart had impressed him as "the only one who didn't ham it up."

Graduated with a B.S. degree in architecture in 1932, Stewart left Princeton more interested in the theater than in architecture. He gravitated to Falmouth, Massachusetts to act with a summer theater group known as the University Players and to play the ac-

STEWART, JAMES—*Continued*

cordion at a tea room. When *Goodbye Again* had its pre-Broadway tryout in Falmouth, he won a very minor role (that of the chauffeur), but he managed to put so much humor into his two lines and three minutes on stage that he impressed summer audiences and visiting New York critics.

Making his Broadway bow in October 1932, Stewart played the supporting role of Constable Gano in the unsuccessful play *Carry Nation*. He again delivered the chauffeur's two lines in *Goodbye Again,* when it arrived in New York on December 28 of the same year. His first substantial role on Broadway was that of Sergeant O'Hara, the idealistic soldier-guinea pig in *Yellow Jack,* a dramatization of Walter Reed's fight against yellow fever. The play opened on March 6, 1934, but it failed to win a sustaining audience. Robert Garland (New York *World-Telegram,* March 7, 1934) described Stewart's performance as "simple, sensitive and true. . . . *Yellow Jack* might have been a more impressive spectacle had the other characters taken their cue from Mr. Stewart." There was again praise for his playing of Teddy Parish, a boy embittered by his mother's infidelity, in *Divided by Three* (1934). He also appeared on the New York stage in *Spring in Autumn* (1933), *All Good Americans* (1933), *Page Miss Glory* (1934), and *A Journey by Night* (1935).

Stewart entered motion pictures in a two-reel comedy made by Warner Brothers in Long Island City, New York. Later, Billy Grady, the Metro-Goldwyn-Mayer talent scout, persuaded MGM to give him a part in *Murder Man.* Stewart arrived in Hollywood by train in the summer of 1935 and established bachelor quarters with Henry Fonda, with whom he had roomed in New York. His performance as Shorty, a police reporter in *Murder Man* (1935), was not impressive. "I was all hands and feet and didn't know what to do with either," Stewart said later.

During his first five years in Hollywood Stewart made twenty-four movies, including *Next Time We Love* (1936); *Seventh Heaven* (1937); the Academy Award-winning *You Can't Take It with You* (1938); *Vivacious Lady* (1938); *The Shopworn Angel* (1938); *Destry Rides Again* (1939); and *No Time for Comedy* (1940). For his role as the idealistic young filibustering Senator in Frank Capra's *Mr. Smith Goes to Washington* he received the New York Film Critics Award as the best male performer in 1939. The Academy of Motion Picture Arts and Sciences gave him its best-actor award in 1940 for his performance as the reporter in *The Philadelphia Story.*

Rejected by the Army as underweight during World War II, Stewart stuffed himself with fattening foods, passed the weight test by one ounce, and entered the Army in March 1941. Already experienced in flying, he was assigned to the Army Air Corps. He resented the coddling and publicity inflicted on him during his first days in service, and the one time he used his influence was to request that he be treated like everyone else.

Winning his wings in August 1942, he instructed bombardier cadets until November 1943, when he went to Europe as the commander of an Eighth Air Force bomber squadron. He flew twenty-five missions over enemy territory, some of them as commander of a bomber wing. He returned to the United States in September 1945 with the rank of colonel and was decorated with the Air Medal and the Distinguished Flying Cross with oak leaf cluster. Still active in the Air Force Reserve, Stewart attained the rank of brigadier general in July 1959.

After his return to Hollywood, Stewart insisted that his war experience be kept out of film publicity. (He seldom talks about it even with his wife and friends.) The first postwar movies he made carried on the stereotype that he had created before the Pearl Harbor attack—the role described by Pete Martin as "the decent, homey Mr. Smith."

In Frank Capra's *It's a Wonderful Life* (1947), he played a civic-minded man saved from suicide by his guardian angel. Louella Parsons quoted Henry Fonda's comment: "When Jim stops pretending to be young, he'll become a great artist" (*Cosmopolitan,* February 1954). Jesse Zunser (*Cue,* October 11, 1947) found *Magic Town* (1947) a "saccharine offering" and said of Stewart's playing: "Jimmy is still exuding boyish charm in lethal doses."

Since the late 1940's, the screen Stewart has kept both his drawling speech and manner (part of the real Stewart) and his plodding but triumphant virtue (which reflects the credo of the real Stewart), but he has displayed them in new settings where they have lost the juvenile bumbling and gained variety. *Call Northside 777* (1948), in which he played a hard-boiled reporter, began a trend away from the "Stewart norm." The trend was evident in Alfred Hitchcock's *Rope* (1948), in which Stewart played the young murderers' suspicious former headmaster, and in *Malaya* (1950), in which he portrayed a patriotic World War II smuggler of Far Eastern rubber.

When, in 1950, he played Elwood P. Dowd, the drunk with an invisible giant rabbit for his companion, in a screen version of *Harvey,* Stewart emphasized Dowd's pixilation more than his inebriation. Although many critics saw that Stewart was bending the dipsomaniac to the old Stewart formula, their reaction, in general, was favorable. (Stewart had made his one return to Broadway in this same role, replacing Frank Fay during the summer of 1947.)

Winchester '73 (1950) witnessed the genesis of Stewart the raw frontiersman, who fell in love with an Apache maid in *Broken Arrow* (1950), led pioneers to Oregon in *Bend of the River* (1952), hunted down an outlaw in *Naked Spur* (1953), rooted out a villain selling guns to Apaches in *The Man from Laramie* (1955), fought rawhide outlaws who robbed his herd in *The Far Country* (1955), and foiled railroad payroll robbers in *Night Passage* (1957). Although some reviewers found it difficult to get used to Stewart riding the range with a day's growth of beard, the adult westerns opened up for Stewart a new vein of critical praise.

The Stratton Story (1949) began another line of portrayal that formed a pattern: the historic and popular hero (or potential hero). While *Carbine Williams* (1952), a biography of Marsh Williams, the chain gang prisoner who invented the 30 M-1 carbine rifle, was not received enthusiastically, *The Glenn Miller Story* was a great critical and popular success when released in 1954 and reissued in 1960.

As Charles A. Lindbergh, a role he had wanted for years, in *The Spirit of St. Louis* (1957), he drew critical attention to the ease with which he transformed himself into the young flyer, but the movie itself was a disappointment at the box office. He also played hero types in *Strategic Air Command* (1955) and *The F.B.I. Story* (1959). In half of these biographical and semidocumentary films, June Allyson played opposite Stewart. He likes to work regularly with the same actors and directors because of the time and trouble saved by customary co-operation and understanding.

Perhaps the most offbeat Stewart role was a minor part that he himself requested: the clown with the mysterious past who never takes the smiling paint off his sad face in *The Greatest Show on Earth* (1952). The starring roles in three suspense films made by Alfred Hitchcock during the 1950's are also among his credits: *Rear Window* (1954), *The Man Who Knew Too Much* (1956), and *Vertigo* (1958).

Other movies in which Stewart has appeared are *On Our Merry Way* (1948), *You Gotta Stay Happy* (1948), *The Jackpot* (1950), *No Highway in the Sky* (1951), *Thunder Bay* (1953), *Bell, Book and Candle* (1958), and *The Mountain Road* (1960). For his role as the defense lawyer in the trial of an Army officer in *Anatomy of a Murder* (1959) he won awards from the Venice Film Festival, the New York Film Critics, and the annual *Film Daily* poll of writers.

The end of the 1940's marked a turning point not only for James Stewart the actor but also for James Stewart the businessman. He worked out a payment plan (later used by other high-priced actors) whereby he would receive a percentage of net profits instead of a flat $250,000 salary. This participation arrangement made him one of Hollywood's highest-paid actors for several years. He has been called Hollywood's second-best businessman (after Bing Crosby): he has invested in various businesses and is a rancher.

James Stewart and Gloria Hatrick McLean were married on August 9, 1949. His father was quoted as saying, "He's too quiet. Gloria has brought him out a lot" (*Saturday Evening Post*, September 15, 1951). The Stewarts live in a large, vine-covered house in Beverly Hills. There are four children: two boys, Ronald and Michael, by Mrs. Stewart's previous marriage, and twin girls, Judy and Kelly, born on May 7, 1951. Stewart is a good companion to his children, but a strict disciplinarian. He is methodical to the point of being meticulous about his modest wardrobe, his tool room, his

photographic equipment, as well as the household in general.

Stewart and his wife do little entertaining, enjoy doing jigsaw puzzles, golfing, and fishing together, and picnicking with their children. Stewart holds a commercial pilot's license and owns a four-place Beechcraft Bonanza. After an interview in which Stewart talked about the Strategic Air Command, Richard Dyer Mac-Cann noted, "There is a sober enthusiasm . . . about his devotion to air power which makes you forget entirely that this is Jimmy Stewart, everybody's favorite home-town boy in the movies" (*Christian Science Monitor*, June 8, 1954).

Six feet three and one-half inches tall, James Stewart weighs 167 pounds and has graying brown hair and gray eyes. Louella Parsons has called him "the most nearly normal of all Hollywood stars" (*Cosmopolitan*, February 1954). He is a worrier, nervous when he's not working, nervous during previews of his films. A hard worker accustomed to accepting the discipline of his craft, he is willing to go over and over a scene until it is right.

The actor is an adviser to Princeton University's new Theatre in Residence, the first professional repertory company sponsored by an American university; a member of the executive board of the Los Angeles council, Boy Scouts of America; a member of the board of directors of the Air Force Association. He is a Presbyterian.

References

Adams, Jessie C. More than Money (1953)

International Motion Picture Almanac, 1959

Who's Who in America, 1960-61

Who's Who in the Theatre (1957)

STONE, WILLIAM S(EBASTIAN) Jan. 6, 1910- United States Air Force officer; educator

Address: United States Air Force Academy, Colorado Springs, Colo.

To his new post as superintendent of the United States Air Force Academy, Major General William S. Stone brings his experience as meteorologist, social scientist, administrator, educator, and airman. Succeeding General James E. Briggs, Stone became in August 1959 the third superintendent of the academy since its establishment in 1955. Before the Air Force Academy opened, Stone served on committees which planned its curriculum.

A West Point graduate, General Stone has served in the Air Force for almost twenty-five years. He has held such posts as director of AAF weather services in the Pacific theater of operations during World War II, associate professor in the department of social sciences of the United States Military Academy (1947-50), assistant deputy chief of staff for personnel of the Air Force (1956-57), and commander of the Atlantic section of the Military Air Transport Service (1957-59). For his outstanding service General Stone has been awarded

MAJ. GEN. WILLIAM S. STONE

the Air Medal, Bronze Star, and Legion of Merit with two oak leaf clusters.

William Sebastian Stone was born on January 6, 1910 in Cape Girardeau, Missouri to William M. Stone and his wife. After graduating from high school in St. Louis, he attended Hall War College in Columbia, Missouri and for a short time worked for the Shell Oil Company in St. Louis. Having decided upon a career in the nation's armed services, he obtained an appointment to the United States Military Academy in West Point, New York. At the time of his graduation on June 12, 1934, he was commissioned a second lieutenant in the field artillery.

Becoming a flight cadet, Lieutenant Stone attended primary and advanced flight schools and in October 1935 received a pilot's rating. Transferred to the Army Air Corps on June 29, 1936, he was assigned to the 32d Bomb Squadron at March Field, California. He did not remain in this position for long. His superiors recognized his talents, and the Army sent Stone to the California Institute of Technology in Pasadena, where he earned the M.Sc. degree in meteorology in 1938. He applied this newly gained knowledge as weather officer at Fort Lewis, Washington.

Changing his field of interest again, Stone became an instructor in economics, government, and history at West Point in 1940. After the United States entered World War II, he returned to meteorology in April 1942 as head of the Army Air Forces (AAF) weather project Caltech. He was next assigned as chief of the weather reports division at AAF headquarters in Washington, D.C. He received advanced leadership training at the Command and General Staff School at Fort Leavenworth, Kansas, completing his course of study in January 1943. After Fort Leavenworth Stone saw brief tours of duty as a weather officer in Washington, D.C. and in Asheville, North Carolina.

Promoted to the temporary rank of colonel, Stone served in the European, China-Burma-India, and Pacific theaters of operation. Returned to Asheville at the end of 1943, he was deputy commander of the AAF weather wing there. In the following May he was again in the Pacific as weather officer of the 21st Bomber Command, based in Hawaii. He became director of weather services for the AAF in the Pacific Ocean area in July 1944, and in July 1945 he went to Guam as head of weather services for the Strategic Air Forces, a post he held until the Japanese surrender. While in the Pacific he served as meteorologist for the long-range B-29 bomber raids on Japan for which he received the Legion of Merit. His other decorations were the Bronze Star and the Air Medal.

After World War II Stone assumed the duties of executive officer of the AAF's air weather service at Langley Field, Virginia and was chief of staff when that agency moved its headquarters to Washington, D.C. in July. In early 1947 he began three years' tenure as associate professor in the department of social sciences at West Point. He found time to do graduate work at Columbia University, and fulfilled the requirements for an M.A. degree in economics in 1950.

From West Point, Stone entered the National War College in Washington, D.C. to prepare for high-level policy, command, and staff functions and to study the power potential of government security agencies. Graduated in July 1951, Stone went to Air Force headquarters in Europe, at Wiesbaden, Germany. There, he was assistant chief of plans division, becoming chief of the division in April 1952. He attained the temporary rank of brigadier general in September.

Called to Washington in July 1953, Stone served as deputy director of personnel planning, became director in July 1955, and gained the permanent rank of major general in December 1955. He was advanced to the post of assistant deputy chief of staff for personnel in September 1956. For planning the use of personnel resources, Stone added an oak leaf cluster to his Legion of Merit.

General Stone's next duty was more directly operational. In June 1957 he took over the command of the Atlantic Section of the Military Air Transport Service (MATS). MATS was established under the Truman administration as a world-wide system for the transport of personnel and supplies for military and other authorized agencies. It is a crucial supply link in the defense system of the West. From MATS headquarters at McGuire Air Force Base in New Jersey, General Stone directed a fleet of over 300 four-engine transports and personnel of 35,000 stationed at seven bases from New Jersey to Scotland. The contribution that he made as head of MATS earned him a second Legion of Merit oak leaf cluster.

On August 17, 1959 Stone took office as superintendent of the United States Air Force Academy in Colorado Springs, Colorado. As early as 1950 Stone had been associated with the creation of an academy for the Air Force.

The organization of such a school had been advocated by many pioneer airmen, including General William (Billy) Mitchell, who had tried to persuade the government and private interests to establish one.

In 1949 Secretary of Defense James V. Forrestal appointed a board of civilian and military educators to study military education. In its report, the board concluded that the needs of the Air Force could not be met by expanding existing academies and recommended that an Air Force academy be established immediately.

In 1950 General Hubert R. Harmon, then special assistant to the chief of staff for Air Force academy matters, appointed General Stone to head a board charged with preparing a curriculum. Six years later Stone served on the curriculum review board, which examined the proposed curriculum and suggested several changes.

Congress authorized the establishment of an academy for the Air Force on April 1, 1954; on July 11, 1955 the academy was officially opened at its temporary quarters at Lowry Air Force Base, Denver, Colorado, with General Harmon as its first superintendent. Meanwhile, a 17,800-acre site at the foot of the Rocky Mountains near Colorado Springs was designated as the permanent home of the institution. Under the direction of the second superintendent, General James E. Briggs (see *C.B.,* June 1957), the academy moved from its makeshift quarters to its ultramodern buildings at Colorado Springs, which were constructed of aluminum, glass, and white marble at a cost of some $140,000,000.

As superintendent, General Stone administers a four-year curriculum of social sciences, humanities, pure and applied sciences, and military training. To meet the needs of the missile age the academy's department of astronautics offers courses in the fundamental physics of manned and unmanned flights into outerspace.

William S. Stone is married to the former Myra McCarthy and they have two children, Susan and William M. Stone. The general has been rated a command pilot and technical observer and has been described as a man who is a combination of military scientist and intellectual.

References

Gen Army 2:18 Ja '55 por
Time 74:58 Jl 6 '59

STOPH, WILLI July 8, 1914- East German Deputy Premier

Address: Berlin, East Germany

A Deputy Premier of East Germany since 1954, Willi Stoph was given special responsibility for carrying out and co-ordinating decisions of the Central Committee of the Socialist Unity party (SED) in 1960. As Minister of Defense from 1956 to 1960, he organized the 90,000-troop East German army. Of Stoph, whom Mayor Willy Brandt of West Berlin has called "a deadly, inhuman person," a ranking Western

Wide World

COL. GEN. WILLI STOPH

diplomat has said, "The Russians could not have picked a more dedicated, icy character if they had manufactured one."

Willi Stoph, the son of a manual laborer, was born on July 8, 1914 in Berlin (some sources give Magdeburg). After attending public elementary schools, Willi became an apprentice mason, advancing gradually to the positions of building foreman and construction engineer. At the age of fourteen he joined the Communist youth movement and three years later entered the Communist party of Germany (KPD) itself, in which he became noted for his organizational ability and efficiency. "He was a machine, even as a kid," a former comrade of Stoph once recalled.

During the prewar Nazi regime, Stoph worked at his building construction trade in Berlin. Meanwhile he organized, illegally, a courier system linking the German Communists with the Soviet Union. At the outbreak of World War II, Stoph was inducted into Hitler's *Wehrmacht*, where he served as a junior noncommissioned officer until his unit was captured by Soviet troops along the Eastern front. When the Red Army entered Germany in 1945 Stoph became an adviser in the military section of the Soviet military administration.

After the war Stoph devoted more and more time to building up the government machinery of the German Communist party (KPD) and its successor in the eastern zone, the Social Unity party (SED). The latter came into existence in April 1946 in the Soviet zone through the forced merger of the Social Democratic and Communist parties. Stoph became chief of the division of economics in the Executive Committee of the SED in 1947.

Since 1950 Stoph has been a member of the Volkskammer (People's Chamber) of the Ger-

STOPH, WILLI—*Continued*

man Democratic Republic (East Germany) and of the powerful Central Committee of the SED. Also in 1950 he was named head of the newly created economic section of the committee secretariat and in 1951 he was appointed chief of the Bureau for Economic Questions in Premier Otto Grotewohl's office. In these capacities, Stoph was responsible for reviving East Germany's light armament industry.

Beginning in 1948 Stoph started to build up the nucleus of an East German army. Ostensibly a conventional police force, the Barracks-Based People's Police (KVP) were organized into military units armed with Soviet weapons and dressed in uniforms resembling those of the Soviet army. Its sections were commanded in part by former Nazi officers, some of whom had studied after the war in Soviet military schools, and in part by veteran German Communists. Actual command, however, lay in the hands of Soviet army officers distributed throughout the KVP units. Within six years the KVP reportedly comprised about 100,000 men in land, naval, and air forces. "The People's Police will be brought into the hectic struggle for the preservation of the peace," Stoph wrote in the SED newspaper, *Neues Deutschland* (July 1, 1952). "They are ready to defend with all means our democratic German republic and its achievements as well as the cause of peace."

Stoph was named Minister of the Interior on May 9, 1952. After the workers' uprisings against the German Democratic Republic on June 17, 1953, he moved from the secretariat to the Politburo of the Central Committee of the party, and took control of the internal security apparatus. In addition to creating strong border and transport security forces, Stoph also directed the formation of militia units in factories and trade unions. On November 19, 1954 Stoph was named second Deputy Premier, ranking immediately below Walter Ulbricht, first Deputy Premier and head of the SED.

On June 30, 1955 Stoph unexpectedly resigned as Minister of the Interior. Two months later he was placed in charge of "questions of nuclear research and related industrial problems," and in January 1956 he was named East Germany's first Defense Minister and deputy commander under Marshal Ivan S. Konev, commander-in-chief of the armed forces of the Warsaw Pact nations. In February 1956 Stoph signed a resolution calling on the entire population of East Germany to learn how to shoot. Rifle practice, he contended, was designed to "raise the national defense capacity."

The East German Parliament on January 18, 1956 voted to set up a new People's Army. Stoph's police force (KVP), by exchanging their olive-green outfits for gray uniforms which (except for the helmets) closely resembled *Wehrmacht* issue, became the core of the People's Army. In contrast to the West German military organization which has issued American style uniforms and avoided references to Germany's military past, the East German army arouses the people's devotion to the Fatherland. "It would be very rash to

laugh at this . . . blend of Prusso-German patriotic traditions . . . with those of twentieth-century German communism," wrote Sebastian Haffner of the New York *Herald Tribune* (February 15, 1956). "It may appeal also, one day, to . . . West Germany's soldiers whose professional pride is inevitably bound up with the Prusso-German military tradition."

According to Stoph, the new military forces were needed to enable East Germany to fulfill her obligations as a nation participating in the Warsaw Pact. He indicated that the army would not be staffed by conscription and that it would be limited in numbers. In June 1956 the East German government reduced its army by approximately 30,000 men and announced plans to maintain the military corps at a level of approximately 90,000 men. Stoph holds the rank of colonel general in the People's Army.

Stoph was one of the seven deputy premiers who accompanied Premier Grotewohl on a mission to Moscow in July 1956. The German-Soviet talks resulted in a new economic agreement promising East Germany more Soviet aid and trade, and a cut in the annual bill to East Germany for the maintenance of the Red Army troops stationed there. Moscow leaders also agreed to give East Germany an atomic power station.

The statements that Stoph has made in recent years have done little to decrease the tensions of the cold war. In December 1956 he asserted that a "revival of militarism" in West Germany was "clearly directed" against the Soviet Union and its satellites. When the regime staged its National Army Day on March 1, 1957, Stoph made a threat that the Soviet army would crush any anti-Communist rebellion in East Germany. In April 1959 Stoph welcomed a military delegation from Communist China, saying that their visit symbolized the "close alliance in arms uniting us in the fight against imperialist warmongers."

In March 1957 Stoph was one of the two signers for the German Democratic Republic (East Germany) of treaties with the Soviet Union covering the temporary stationing of Soviet forces in East Germany. According to a United States Army estimate, these troops then numbered 400,000 men. Soon after Stoph had said that East Germany would build up its military air defenses, the East German Communist newspaper *Volksarmee* (April 20, 1957) said that the East German air force had received jet fighter planes from the Soviet Union. Western spokesmen said they did not believe these planes included anything more superior than an obsolescent MiG-15.

In February 1958 reports circulated in West Berlin of a conflict between Deputy Premier Walter Ulbricht and Defense Minister Stoph. The disagreement reportedly concerned Communist party work in the East Germany army. Ulbricht was said to have repeatedly charged Stoph with neglecting political education in the Army.

Willi Stoph, whose frame is slender but wiry, has gray-blue eyes and graying blond hair. He generally shuns publicity. He neither smokes, drinks, nor takes part in Berlin night life, and is slavishly devoted to his work. One of his former staff members is reported to have said that "efficiency is the only argument that convinces Stoph." His former wife, who lives in West Berlin, is supposed to have said of Stoph that "he lives for 'The Idea'—making Germany a Communist state. There is no warmth in him, no tenderness." They were divorced in 1945. In 1954 the German Democratic Republic gave Stoph the Gold Order of Merit for service to his country.

References

Army 7:39 Jl '57 pors
Christian Sci Mon p1 Ja 18 '56
This Week p15 My 8 '60 pors
International Who's Who, 1959
Wer ist Wer? (1958)
Wer ist Wer in der SBZ? (1958)

RUTH STRANG

STRANG, RUTH (MAY) Apr. 3, 1895-
Educator; writer
Address: b. University of Arizona, Tucson, Ariz.

For Ruth Strang, professor emeritus of education of Columbia University, becoming an authority on student personnel work has meant taking the world of ideas as her province. During almost forty years of teaching at Columbia's Teachers College she has earned international respect for her achievements in the fields of reading and communication, student counseling, development, and adjustment. In several hundred publications—books, pamphlets, and articles—she has not only reported her own research, but has covered the significant contributions of many other scholars in education. Since her retirement from Teachers College in 1960, she has been professor of education at the University of Arizona.

The daughter of a farmer, Ruth May Strang was born on April 3, 1895 in Chatham, New Jersey to Charles Garret and Anna (Bergen) Strang. There were also two boys in the family, Arthur (deceased) and Benjamin B. Strang. Growing up in the Greater New York City area, Ruth Strang attended Adelphi Academy in Brooklyn, played on the school's basketball team, and belonged to the German club and the walking club. For two years, from 1914 to 1916, after her graduation she studied household science at Pratt Institute in Brooklyn and during 1916 was employed as an assistant to an interior decorator.

Ruth Strang's career has been an unplanned one which grew as opportunities presented themselves. "I developed my interests and abilities," she has said, "and doors seemed to open." Having decided to be a teacher, she realized that she would need to be broadly educated in order to help children and young people make the most of their potentialities.

She began her work in education by teaching home economics from 1917 to 1920 in the New York City public schools. Resuming her own formal studies, she enrolled at Columbia University's Teachers College, where she be-

came a member of Sigma Xi, Kappa Delta Pi, and Pi Lambda Theta honor societies. She received the B.S. degree in home economics in 1922 and fulfilled requirements for the M.A. degree in 1924, at the same time working during 1923-24 as a research assistant in nutrition at Teachers College.

While studying for her Ph.D. degree, conferred in 1926, Miss Strang was an instructor in health education and supervisor of health education at Teachers College's Horace Mann School (1924-25) and research assistant in psychology at Teachers College (1925-26). When she had completed work for her doctorate, she accepted a research fellowship at Teachers College for 1926-27 in student personnel. She spent the summers of 1926, 1927, and 1928 at North Carolina College for Women in Greensboro as head of residence and instructor in psychology.

From 1929 to 1936 Dr. Strang held the title of assistant professor of education at Teachers College. She advanced to associate professor in 1936 and to full professor in 1940. Much of her work was in the department of guidance and student personnel administration. Through both her teaching and writing she has contributed greatly to knowledge and understanding in personnel work, a field in which very few studies had been published when she began her research in the mid-1920's.

Among her books on student personnel are *Educational Guidance: Its Principles and Practice* (Macmillan, 1947) and *The Role of the Teacher in Personnel Work* (Teachers College, 1953). In this subject alone her articles in professional journals, chapters in other books, and pamphlets number about a hundred. She was editor from 1935 to 1960 of the *Journal of the National Association of Women Deans and Counselors* (consulting editor since 1960)

STRANG, RUTH—*Continued*

and served from 1930 to 1939 as chairman of the research committee of the N.A.W.D.C. Other organizations in this field that she helped administer are the Alliance for Guidance of Rural Youth (vice-president) and American Child Guidance Foundation (member of the board of directors).

In the areas of mental hygiene, health education, and child psychology, as well as other aspects of general education such as testing, grading, and progress reporting, Miss Strang has also furthered the goals of various academic groups. Two of her most notable books, moreover, are in psychology: *An Introduction to Child Study* (Macmillan, 4th edition, revised, 1959) and *The Adolescent Views Himself; A Psychology of Adolescence* (McGraw-Hill, 1957).

Because of her concern for helping young people reach their full potential, Miss Strang became particularly interested in the problem of gifted children. She is treasurer and a director of the American Association for Gifted Children and author of *Helping Your Gifted Child* (Dutton, 1960). While most of her writing in this and other subjects is intended for professional people, she frequently addresses parents and pupils also. Her pamphlet *Guideposts for the Education of the Gifted* (Teachers College, 1958), for example, includes sections for administrators, teachers, parents, and children in which she points out how they can co-operate to overcome the social and psychological obstacles that sometimes hamper the development of brilliant students.

Since 1933 Ruth Strang has given special attention to the subject of improvement of reading, in large part as director of the high school and college reading center at Teachers College. She is a member of the board of directors of the International Council for the Improvement of Reading Instruction and was a consultant to Coronet Instructional Films on five 16mm. motion pictures on reading and communication. She regards reading as a continuing learning process that influences personality development, so that the teaching of reading is not simply concerned with remedial exercises but involves a vital causal relationship between a person's life and the books he reads. In collaboration with other authorities in the field of reading, she helped prepare certain volumes of *Teen-Age Tales* (Heath, 1954, 1955, and 1958) and *Gateways to Readable Books* (H. W. Wilson, 3d edition, revised, 1958).

As Amelia Melnik, also a specialist in reading, pointed out in "The Writings of Ruth Strang" (*Teachers College Record,* May 1960), Dr. Strang has carried on her research and has written her books and articles on her own initiative, on her own time, and at her own expense. The only special financial assistance that she has received was a small grant from the research committee of *Life* and *Time* magazines which she used in the preparation of *Explorations in Reading Patterns* (University of Chicago, 1942). Because she publishes

so prolifically, she gives the impression that she writes quickly and easily. "Instead," she has said, "I work hard and long on every book and article."

When Ruth Strang left Columbia University in June 1960 upon reaching the mandatory retirement age of sixty-five, she continued her work in teaching as professor of education at the University of California at Berkeley during the 1960 summer session. In the fall of 1960 she moved to the University of Arizona in Tucson as professor of education.

In 1960 also she became chairman of the board of directors of the National Society for the Study of Education, of which she had been a director since 1948; she has also been chairman of the society's yearbook committee. She was president in 1955 of the National Association for Remedial Teaching and belongs to the American Educational Research Association and the National Education Association. Several professional organizations have honored her with the title of Fellow, including the American Public Health Association, the American Association of Applied Psychology, and Her Majesty's Royal Society of Health (England).

Ruth Strang is a Republican and a Presbyterian. She has gray-green eyes and gray (formerly brown) hair, weighs 140 pounds, and is about five feet eight inches in height. Among her hobbies she includes interior decorating, once her chief professional interest, and children's stories. For more active recreation she turns to walking and swimming.

References

N Y Times p50 Je 19 '60 por
Teachers College Rec 61:464+ My '60
Leaders in Education (1948)
Who's Who in America, 1960-61
Who's Who in American Education, 1959-60
Who's Who of American Women, 1958-59

STRASBERG, LEE Nov. 17, 1901- Theatrical director; teacher
Address: b. Actors Studio, Inc., 432 W. 44th St., New York 36; h. 135 Central Park W., New York 23

"The Method" actor, caricatured on the one hand as a "mumbling back-scratcher," and hailed on the other as a "pioneer in a native American style of acting," learns his techniques at the Actors Studio in New York City which has been under the tutelage of Lee Strasberg, its artistic director since 1948. "The Temple," as the Studio is sometimes called, with Strasberg as its "high priest," has trained some distinguished devotees of the naturalistic style of acting, including Marlon Brando, Julie Harris, Paul Newman, Eli Wallach, Kim Stanley, Eva Marie Saint, and Geraldine Page.

Beginning his professional career as an actor and stage manager with the Theatre Guild, Strasberg later founded the Group Theatre, for which he directed *Johnny Johnson* and the

Pulitzer Prize-winning play *Men in White.* After he left the Group Theatre, he staged the Broadway dramas *Skipper Next to God* and *The Big Knife.* "Strasberg is a fine director," wrote Elia Kazan (New York *Herald Tribune,* February 27, 1955), "but first of all he is that extraordinary and unique phenomenon: a born teacher . . . our whole theater would have been less vital and less ambitious without the influence of this one man who has given so quietly and so unceasingly to so many people, because it is his nature to study and to think and to teach."

Lee Strasberg was born on November 17, 1901 in Budanov, then in Austria-Hungary and now in the U.S.S.R., to Baruch Meyer and Ida (Diner) Strasberg. Eight years later the family came to New York, where Baruch Strasberg went to work in the women's garment manufacturing district and Lee Strasberg attended Lower East Side public schools. Fascinated by the world of the theater before he was fifteen, he began acting in skits and plays at the Chrystie Street Settlement House and soon began directing some of its shows.

As soon as Strasberg obtained his first job—in a theatrical wig factory—he took dramatic lessons at the American Laboratory Theatre. Both of his instructors, Richard Boleslavski and Maria Ouspenskaya, had studied with Konstantin Stanislavski, a founder of the Moscow Art Theater. Stanislavski's style of acting, which became known as The Method, transferred the performer's attention from the external to the internal, from manners, customs, and facts to emotions, dispositions, and expressions.

Strasberg began his professional theatrical career when Philip Loeb of the Theatre Guild saw him in a settlement house production and invited him to join the Guild. He was assistant stage manager of the Guild's production of *The Guardsman* (1924), starring Lynn Fontanne and Alfred Lunt, and in 1925 acted in *Processional* and *Garrick Gaieties.* By 1926 he had the opportunity to be stage manager of a play—the second edition of *Garrick Gaieties.* Later he acted in *Red Rust* (1929) and *Green Grow the Lilacs* (1931).

During his association with the Theatre Guild, Strasberg met Harold Clurman (see *C.B.,* 1959) and Cheryl Crawford (see *C.B.,* 1945). Together they talked about the possibilities of a permanent theater where plays would be produced for their artistic rather than their commercial value. When the Theatre Guild presented the Jean Croué-Jacques Copeau adaptation of *The Brothers Karamazov* in January 1927, Clurman and Strasberg came to know Copeau and their hopes for an artistic theater were further stimulated by Copeau's ideas on acting and the stage.

Having decided to experiment with something new in acting, Strasberg, Clurman, and several actors, some employed and some unemployed, spent their spare time discussing, interpreting, and rehearsing Waldo Frank's play *New Year's Eve* for seventeen weeks in 1928. Next, they turned their attention to dealing with Padraic Colum's *Balloon.* In this way the laboratory workshop evolved.

Roy Schatt

LEE STRASBERG

At rehearsals Strasberg emphasized aspects of the Stanislavski "system": improvisation, requiring performers to act out extemporaneous situations emotionally analogous to the scenes in the play and what Strasberg called an "exercise in affective memory," or the memory of an emotion that an actor had felt. Recollecting such details would thus produce a "mood."

To carry out further Stanislavski's ideas on group acting, twenty-eight performers, with Strasberg, Clurman, and Cheryl Crawford as co-directors, rented a barn and several bungalows in Brookfield Center, Connecticut in the summer of 1931. This became the nucleus of the Group Theatre, an experimental, noncommercial company which exerted a notable influence on the American stage and screen.

The young people who established the new company were part of a generation, according to Strasberg, that came to the acting profession "on the wings of a dream." They dreamed of a theater that was "an art and worthy of the respect, dedication and devotion accorded to the other arts. The theatre . . . demanded the coherence expected of a trained ensemble, such as the great orchestras or ballet companies. The theatre was not a succession of separate productions, but each production was a link in the creative continuity that characterizes the activity of any artist" (New York *Times,* July 20, 1958).

The Group Theatre's first undertaking was Paul Green's *The House of Connelly,* directed by Strasberg and Miss Crawford. The play was later brought to Broadway in the fall of 1931 under the auspices of the Theatre Guild, and was highly praised. One reviewer wrote: "In this Group Theatre jaded Broadway seems finally to have young blood and new ideas for which many of us have been praying."

When Strasberg directed Sidney Kingsley's play *Men in White,* which opened in September

STRASBERG, LEE—*Continued*

1933, he and the Group Theatre scored a stunning success. Harold Clurman later wrote in *The Fervent Years; The Story of the Group Theatre and the Thirties* (1957) that the play was the group's most finished product and that "Strasberg had given it a dignity, a distinction all his own. For a fusion of all the elements of the theatre this was no doubt his masterpiece." *Men in White* won the Pulitzer Prize for drama in 1934.

In 1936 Strasberg staged *Johnny Johnson,* a comedy by Paul Green with a score by Kurt Weill. In 1937 Miss Crawford and Strasberg resigned from the Group because, he has explained, the members had "destroyed its leadership." The entire project disbanded in 1941.

With Cheryl Crawford and John Stillman, Jr., as producers, Lee Strasberg staged *All the Living* (1938), dealing with conditions in a mental institution. His next exhibit was Clifford Odets' *Clash by Night* (1941), in which a young wife becomes restive under the pettiness of her domestic life. In the early 1940's Strasberg went to Hollywood. There he underwent what he has called "an unfruitful but nonetheless educational experience" (New York *Times,* July 20, 1958).

Returning to Broadway in 1948, Strasberg directed *Skipper Next to God,* in which John Garfield played a captain with a shipload of Jewish refugees whom he cannot bring ashore. In 1949 Strasberg staged Odets' *The Big Knife,* again with Garfield in the leading role.

In 1947 the Actors Studio, Inc., was founded by Elia Kazan, Cheryl Crawford, and Robert Lewis, all of whom had been associated with the Group Theatre. Later that year Lee Strasberg was asked to join them. The Studio was founded with the conviction that it was an artistic necessity in the commercial theater. It is not a school, but a workshop where actors with stage experience can come to experiment, to grow, and to seek inspiration. The guiding spirit of the organization, Strasberg believes that "a career must develop in public, but one's talents grow only in silence." For Strasberg the Studio provides that silence. He has been its artistic director since 1948; Elia Kazan is now president, and Miss Crawford, vice-president.

Members do not pay tuition fees. The Studio receives contributions from benefactors in theatrical and other fields. Of some 1,000 actors who audition each year, less than twenty new members win admission; about 135 veteran performers are now acting members. Courses are also open to directors and playwrights. Affiliated with the Studio are many famous American stars, who return from time to time for new ideas and approaches. All in all, the Studio exerts an incalculable influence on American entertainment. Although Strasberg is guided by Stanislavski's system, no conceptions about the stage and performing are alien to him. His insight into the shortcomings of the actors and his uncanny ability to draw out their creativity spurs them to find the "truth" of the characters they are portraying. Strasberg has lectured on acting at many universities. He is a frequent contributor to the New York *Times* drama section, *Theatre Arts,* and the *Saturday Review.*

Lee Strasberg and Paula Miller, a former actress, were married on March 16, 1934. Their children are Susan and John; Susan starred in the Broadway production of *The Diary of Anne Frank.* Strasberg's first wife, Nora Z. Krecaun, died. He became an American citizen in 1936. He is small of stature and has thinning gray-black hair and intense black eyes behind thick glasses. In his soft and expressive voice he talks with effervescence, emotion, and brilliance. "The years have been kind to Lee Strasberg," wrote Sidney Skolsky (New York *Post Magazine,* August 22, 1958). "He has the appearance and mannerisms of a sage. His face projects kindness." One of Strasberg's hobbies is collecting rare books on the theater. He told Skolsky: "I have a rule. If a youngster tells me he wants to be an actor, I hear him out and see what can be done. But if he tells me he wants to be a star, I do everything I can to discourage him. You have to work hard to be an actor . . . it isn't an easy life. There are endless disappointments."

According to Strasberg, all the elements needed for a creative American theater are now present: talented and competent actors, directors who have developed a dynamic and romantic style, outstanding playwrights "who do not flee to Hollywood for refuge," a repertory of native classics, and receptive and enthusiastic audiences. "But while my hopes are optimistic," he concluded, "my practical vision is pessimistic. The conditions for great theatre today exist. But there exists equally too much of a tendency to confuse a theatre with the building which houses it, a dream against a ledger, great theatre with good manners" (New York *Times,* July 20, 1958).

References

Clurman, Harold The Fervent Years (1957)

Lewis, Robert Method—or Madness? (1958)

Who's Who in America, 1960-61

STROUSE, NORMAN H(ULBERT) Nov. 4, 1906- Advertising executive

Address: b. J. Walter Thompson Co., 420 Lexington Ave., New York 17; h. 2 Beekman Place, New York 22

The nation's oldest and one of its largest advertising agencies, J. Walter Thompson Company, for many years had led its competitors in billings, or the amount of advertising placed for its clients. Its president since June 1955 has been Norman H. Strouse, succeeding Stanley Resor who became chairman of the board after having served in the presidency for forty years. Strouse, who in clothes and temperament departs from the advertising executive stereotype, directs an agency with seventeen offices in the United States and thirty-two abroad. Its accounts cover such a broad field that, according to *Printers' Ink,* "it might be possible to get born, live a complete life, and die, using nothing but J. Walter Thompson advertised products and services."

Except for the time that he spent in military service during World War II, Strouse has been associated with J. Walter Thompson Company since 1929, when he joined the firm as an assistant space buyer. He is probably best known for waging the Ford Motor Company's advertising campaign to "put two cars in every garage"—one for the working husband, the other for the suburbanite wife. *Forbes* magazine on November 15, 1957 named Strouse to its list of America's Fifty Foremost Businessmen.

Norman Hulbert Strouse was born in Olympia, Washington on November 4, 1906 to John Quincy Strouse, a railroad clerk, and Harriet Elizabeth (Dyer) Strouse. He has a brother, J. Marvin Strouse, and a sister, Raibin A. Strouse. Strouse attended the local elementary schools and the local high school, where he played in both the school orchestra and band. His graduation from Olympia High School in 1923 marked the end of his formal education and the beginning of his lifelong process of self-education.

Shortly after his graduation from high school, Strouse was hired as secretary to the director of licenses of the state of Washington, a post in which he remained for one year. In 1925 he became secretary to the advertising director of the Seattle *Post-Intelligencer,* and in 1927 he was appointed as assistant to the national manager of the same newspaper. The four years that Strouse spent on the *Post-Intelligencer* introduced him to advertising and influenced him to choose it as his career.

His long association with the J. Walter Thompson agency began in 1929, when he became one of the assistant space buyers in its San Francisco office. In 1936 he was promoted to account representative in the San Francisco office, and in 1942 he was advanced to assistant Pacific Coast manager.

Military service during World War II provided an intermission in Strouse's advertising career. He entered the United States Army Air Forces as a private early in 1942 and was assigned to the Medical Administrative Officers Candidate School, from which he was graduated as a second lieutenant in 1943. From 1943 to 1945 he served as the executive officer of the information and education special staff section with General Douglas MacArthur's headquarters in the South Pacific. By the time Strouse was released from service in 1945 in the rank of major he had been awarded the Legion of Merit by the United States government and a special Medal of Merit by the Philippine government.

Returning to civilian status, Strouse rejoined J. Walter Thompson Company and was made account representative for the Ford Motor Company in Detroit, Michigan, the agency's most important client. He was assigned to the Ford account because of his solid background in advertising and because of his proved ability to get along with clients.

NORMAN H. STROUSE

When Strouse took over, Henry Ford 2d was in the midst of modernizing the obsolescent structure of the Ford Motor Company, recruiting young men for the firm and introducing new ideas to reverse its downward trend. Realizing that the public looked upon the Ford car as antiquated, Strouse tried to create a new image in the public mind: a car designed to meet the needs of fastidious suburbanites. He also inaugurated the campaign to put two Fords in every garage.

In 1947 Strouse was elected a vice-president of J. Walter Thompson Company. In 1948 he was named manager of the Detroit office, and in 1949 he became a director of the company. On June 28, 1955—twenty-six years after he joined the firm—Strouse was named president of J. Walter Thompson Company. Because of his success with the Ford account and his understanding of the company's operations and approach, he was handpicked by Stanley Resor to assume the responsibilities of the presidency over eighty-four other J. Walter Thompson vice-presidents. In June 1960 Strouse was also given the title of chief executive officer.

To make J. Walter Thompson Company secure in its position as the world's largest advertising agency was one of Strouse's first aims after becoming president. It also turned out to be one of his first accomplishments. In the years immediately following his appointment, the agency's billings increased by about $60,-000,000. Strouse not only helped to gain new business but also won back former major clients who had, for one reason or another, switched agencies. Among them was RCA. Until 1959 J. Walter Thompson had consistently held first place in agency billings.

Strouse holds firm and unorthodox views on how new accounts should be obtained. He believes that it is not the job of the agency to solicit business by presenting speculative ideas

STROUSE, NORMAN H.—*Continued*

or campaigns to possible clients. Senior staff members, alert to new developments in the advertising field, keep making new contacts. The agency maintains no "new business department" as such, and refuses to accept tobacco or alcoholic beverage accounts, with the exception of beer.

Looking into the economic future of the United States, Strouse sees the decade ahead as the "golden sixties," when consumers will grow in number, mobility, spending power, and in discrimination. Markets in the decade will be "more luxuriant," but it will take more imagination on the part of advertisers to sell products to consumers, according to Strouse.

Active in many civic, philanthropic, and social organizations, Strouse is on the board of directors and the executive committee of the New York chapter of the American Red Cross and was chairman of its public information committee during the 1956 and 1957 fund drives. He is also secretary-treasurer of the National Book Committee and will serve as chairman of its National Library Week for April 16-22, 1961. His club memberships include the Cloud Club, Pinnacle Club, the Grolier Club, and the Advertising Club in New York City, the Adcraft Club and the Athletic Club in Detroit, and the Advertising Club of San Francisco.

Norman Hulbert Strouse was married to Charlotte Auger on August 3, 1946. She has three children from an earlier marriage: W. Stanley Holt, Jr., Mrs. John Beresford, and Mrs. William H. Edwards. The couple live in a three-story penthouse apartment on Beekman Place overlooking the East River, which houses Strouse's collection of rare books, early manuscripts, autographs, and Wedgwood china.

Blue-eyed and brown-haired Norman H. Strouse is six feet tall and weighs about 205 pounds. He is a Republican. Although he never attended college, he has earned the reputation of being a scholarly man who, no matter what the pressures of business, relaxes with his planned reading program and his private printing presses. He has established his own private press, the Silverado, on which he has run off his own Christmas cards and essays by Thomas Fuller, Stevenson, and Santayana. When he plays golf, he shoots in the middle nineties.

A colleague at the J. Walter Thompson agency has described Strouse in the following terms: "I would sum up Norm Strouse as an all-around sound man. He's not a 'creative' man, but he has excellent advertising judgment. He's a very buttoned-up guy. I mean that he's thorough, touches all bases. And he's a worker, every night and weekend . . . a very disciplined man."

References

ALA Bul 54:862+ N '60 por
Ptr Ink 252:74+ Jl 15 '55 por; 262:42+ Ja 31 '58 por; 272:14 Jl 1 '60 por
Who's Who in America, 1960-61

STUMMVOLL, JOSEF (LEOPOLD) Aug. 19, 1902- Librarian

Address: b. Josefsplatz 1, Vienna 1, Austria; United Nations, New York 17; h. Flamminggasse 36, Baden, Austria

Tradition and progress find a meeting ground in Josef Stummvoll, general director since 1949 of the Austrian National Library, from which he is now on leave of absence as director of the library of the United Nations in New York City. He has improved the operation of the centuries-old Vienna library through the introduction of modern library techniques, without violating the library's baroque atmosphere.

Before working in his native Austria, Stummvoll had worked in Germany as research librarian and deputy director of the Berlin Patent Office library and as research librarian and director of the reading department at the Deutsche Bücherei in Leipzig. His services have frequently been enlisted in Turkey, Iran, and other countries. Stummvoll has written many articles on library science, documentation, research in scientific literature, and the history of science. He has edited among other works a volume on the Austrian National Library, *Die Österreichische National-bibliothek* (Bauer, 1948). He has been editor in chief of the Austrian bibliographic journal, *Biblos,* since its founding in 1952, and of *Biblos-Schriften,* and associate editor of *Libri,* international library review, since its founding in 1950.

Josef Leopold Stummvoll was born into an old family of Baden, a suburban health resort of Vienna on August 19, 1902. His father, who ran a small hotel, died in 1936. His mother, Maria (Gassler) Stummvoll, still lives in Baden. Josef has two sisters, Karoline Scheerer and Maria Hickel, both of whom live in Austria. A brother, Leopold, has been missing since early 1945, when he served on the eastern front.

Josef grew up in the tranquil atmosphere of Baden, augmented by the quiet joys of the Stummvoll family circle. In his first year at the local federal secondary school *(Bundesgymnasium),* he tutored fellow students in Latin and mathematics. After four years at the *Bundesgymnasium* (where the languages taught were Latin and Greek), he entered the Baden *Oberrealschule* (where the languages taught were French and English). He excelled in gymnastics and football. He was graduated from the *Oberrealschule* in July 1920, with the highest examination grade in the class of twenty-six students.

In the fall of 1920 Stummvoll entered the University of Technology, Vienna, where he studied physics and chemistry. He received his master's degree in science *(Diplom-Ingenieur)* in 1924 and his doctorate in science in 1951. While studying at the University of Technology, he also took courses at the University of Vienna.

In 1925 Stummvoll began working at the Deutsche Bücherei in Leipzig, where he remained, with interruptions, until 1939. His first two years at Leipzig constituted in-service training. He worked as a research librarian specializing in science during the days and took courses in the library school in the evenings.

His first interruption came in 1926, when he spent a few months in Kiel, Germany, as librarian at the library of the Institute of World Economics (Institute für Weltwirtschaft). In Kiel he studied in the philosophy faculty of the University of Kiel. Returning to Leipzig in the fall of 1926, he passed the examination for higher service in librarianship, and officially became research librarian and director of the reading department at the Deutsche Bücherei.

From 1928 to 1931, in addition to working at the Deutsche Bücherei, Stummvoll completed at the University of Leipzig his studies in journalism, philosophy, economics, and social science. Among his teachers were Hans Driesch, the parapsychologist, under whom he studied the philosophy of science, and Gerhard Kessler, the economist, one of the first professors expelled in Hitler's purge of the universities in 1933. Stummvoll passed the examination for his doctorate in 1932, and after the publication of his dissertation, *Tagespresse und Technik* (Risse, 1935), received his Ph.D. degree.

At the request of the Turkish government, Stummvoll took a leave of absence from the Deutsche Bücherei in 1933 to supervise the building and organization of the library of the College of Agriculture and Veterinary Medicine in Ankara, for which he had made the architectural plans. It was completed in 1933. He directed the library for four years, adding to the physical plant, increasing the number of volumes to 45,000, and seeing the average number of daily readers increase eightfold. Appointed expert for librarianship by the Turkish government, he lectured on library science at the college and elsewhere to students and librarians.

Returning to Leipzig in the fall of 1937, Stummvoll worked at the Deutsche Bücherei until 1939. On October 1, 1939 he became research librarian and deputy director of the library of the Patent Office in Berlin. He held this post for four years, lecturing on scientific, technical, and patent literature and documentation.

Drafted into military service in July 1943, Stummvoll was assigned to teach aerodynamics to German air force personnel. Later, because of his experience at the Patent Office, he was put in charge of German inventors attached to the air force. Taken prisoner by the Russians in May 1945, he was detained in a Russian prison camp until November. He arrived in his native Baden, at the home of his parents, at Christmas, 1945, where he was reunited with his wife and children, who had fled during the war, first to Baden, then—in April 1945—to Sweden.

In 1946, Joseph Bick, anticipating his retirement as director general of the Austrian National Library, asked Josef Stummvoll to come to Vienna. Stummvoll was appointed librarian (*Oberstaatsbibliothekar*) of the Austrian National Library in May 1946 and deputy general director in September 1946. Bick delegated to Stummvoll the reorganization of the library. Under Stummvoll's supervision, the time readers had to wait before obtaining seats or books was greatly reduced; a huge backlog of catalog

United Nations

JOSEF STUMMVOLL

cards was put in order; thousands of periodicals were bound; and daily statistics and annual reports were inaugurated. In September 1948 a complete inventory was taken for the first time in centuries and finished in six days. On March 31, 1949 Bick retired and Stummvoll took over his post.

The Austrian National Library, at one time the imperial library, was founded in 1526 but not completed until 1683. The library contains about 1,700,000 volumes, and its collections of incunabula, papyri, and manuscripts are excelled by few libraries in the world. The library collects all material published in Austria or concerning Austria or written by Austrians abroad, prints catalog cards, and makes interlibrary loans. It publishes the official Austrian bibliography *Österreichische Bibliographie,* a fortnightly list of new publications.

In April 1952 Stummvoll was appointed by UNESCO to the post of chief adviser for the development of Iranian libraries. For one year he gave courses in library science at the University of Teheran, organized the library of its medical faculty, and visited Iranian cities.

Stummvoll succeeded Dr. Rubens Borba de Moraes as United Nations librarian in January 1959. His term is due to expire in January 1961. At the U.N. library, he directs a staff of ninety librarians from twenty-four nations. In the fall of 1959 the United Nations received a Ford Foundation grant of $6.2 million for a new library building. The old one clashed with the design of the other U.N. buildings and proved inadequate for library use. The library and the offices of Stummvoll and his staff are being housed temporarily in the Secretariat building.

In addition to his editorial duties, Stummvoll has contributed many articles to American and foreign bibliographic and library periodicals. He is vice-president of the International Federation of Library Associations (FIAB) and

STUMMVOLL, JOSEF—*Continued*
Austrian delegate to its International Library Committee. He corresponds with scholars and authors all over the world.

On May 17, 1939 Josef Stummvoll was married to Luise Thorngren, a native of Sweden, whom he had known since they were teen-agers. The Stummvolls have three children: Asa Maria, Hans Krister, and Anna Louise. A music lover, Stummvoll was from 1956 to 1958 president of a fund-raising group for the Vienna Tonkünstler Orchestra. He plays the piano, but prefers to limit his audience to family and friends. He also likes to swim, hike, ski, and travel. Five feet seven inches in height, 165 pounds in weight, Stummvoll has gray hair and gray-brown eyes. He is a Roman Catholic. An energetic worker himself, he expects from his subordinates a strict adherence to duty, but has, nonetheless, a reputation as a good supervisor, who understands the personal problems of others.

References

Lib J 84:392 F 1 '59
International Who's Who, 1959
Who's Who in Austria, 1958-59

SULLAVAN, MARGARET May 16, 1911-Jan. 1, 1960 Stage and motion-picture actress; after successful appearances in such films as *Three Comrades*, achieved stardom in the theater with memorable performance in *Voice of the Turtle* in 1943. See *Current Biography* (July) 1944.

Obituary

N Y Times p1+ Ja 2 '60

SUSSKIND, DAVID (sŭs'kĭnd) Dec. 1920-Producer
Address: b. Talent Associates, Ltd., 234 W. 44th St., New York 36

Although he has admitted that he would like to become the Cecil B. De Mille of television, David Susskind, the producer, is a man of multiple talents who has not confined himself to the small screen. Talent Associates, Ltd., a firm which he owns in partnership with Al Levy, packages more live "specials" than the three major television networks combined. Yet Susskind has found the time to produce one motion picture and contract for four more, and to stage three plays for Broadway. He has crusaded for better drama on television, especially for live as against filmed television, and for more mature and intelligent programming in general.

David Susskind was born in December 1920 and was reared in Brookline, Massachusetts, on the outskirts of Boston. He has one brother, Murray, two years his junior, and a sister ten years younger. The elder Susskind was an insurance man who was affluent enough to afford a home on Brookline's Lancaster Terrace. David attended local public schools and was graduated from Brookline High School in 1938.

While in high school, Susskind had edited the student newspaper, played for the football team, and written a column for the weekly Brookline *Chronicle*. He decided to become a writer and to study at Harvard. His father, however, decided that agrarian liberalism in the La Follette tradition would be a broadening influence; accordingly, David entered the University of Wisconsin, which he attended for two years.

By 1940, Susskind had become a married man and a straight "A" student at the University of Wisconsin. That year he transferred to Harvard College, majoring in government, history, and economics. His wife transferred to Simmons College in Boston at the same time, and the couple settled down in a comfortable Cambridge apartment. Susskind had abandoned his writing goal: "At that time," he has recalled, "the only thing I wanted of life was a job at Harvard as a teacher." But World War II interfered with his plans. Following the United States' entry into the war, Susskind applied for a commission in the Navy. While waiting to be accepted, he was graduated *cum laude* from Harvard College in the class of 1942 with majors in history and government, and subsequently went to work as a junior economist with the War Labor Board in Washington, D.C.

The job lasted one month. Susskind received his commission as an ensign and was assigned as a government insurance officer in the Port of New York. Later he was transferred to sea duty as a communications officer aboard an attack transport in the Pacific, seeing service at Iwo Jima, Okinawa, and other invasion points. By the time he was discharged in 1946 he had acquired a new set of career goals.

"After the boredom of the Navy, teaching seemed too passive," he told Diane Leonetti of the New York *Post* (April 26, 1959). "I settled on show business as the most dynamic and interesting field I could get into, and went looking for a job in my Navy uniform." He was hired as a press agent by Warner Brothers studios, and in 1947 moved over to Universal Pictures in the same capacity.

Soon frustrated by the demands of successful press-agentry, Susskind decided to become a talent agent. He joined forces with Alfred Levy, whose own agency was breaking up because his partners wanted to move to the West Coast; Susskind came to New York to form Talent Associates, Ltd., with Levy. The "Ltd.," according to Susskind, was inspired by the company name on a pack of English cigarettes, and was added to give the agency a social tone. The new agency decided to package programs for the infant television industry and to represent its creative personnel rather than actors. Its first package sale was the *Philco Television Playhouse*, a one-hour drama series, and its first clients included some of the leading TV producers, directors, and writers.

Within a year, Susskind received an offer from Musical Corporation of America which he has labeled as "too good to turn down." He took a leave of absence from Talent Associates, Ltd., to join MCA's television program department, where he sold programs to sponsors and managed such entertainers as Dinah Shore and Jerry Lewis. He rejoined Talent Associates, Ltd., in 1953.

Almost immediately he was hired as producer of the *Philco Television Playhouse* in the temporary absence of Fred Coe, one of Susskind's clients. Before Coe returned to the staff, Susskind had produced five *Playhouse* dramas and developed an enthusiasm for the producer's craft. In quick succession he produced the *Justice* series, the *Kaiser Aluminum Hour,* and the *Armstrong Circle Theater.* He remained executive producer of the *Circle Theater* when it was extended to a one-hour biweekly series in 1955.

Susskind and Levy also formed Jonathan Productions, a motion-picture company. Its first effort was *Edge of the City,* starring Sidney Poitier and John Cassavetes, based on a Talent Associates, Ltd., television play and financed by Metro-Goldwyn-Mayer (which released it in January 1957). Adding a third dimension, Susskind then produced Robert Alan Aurthur's *A Very Special Baby* on Broadway; its première took place at the Playhouse on November 14, 1956.

Stage and screen interests did not slow down the video pace of Talent Associates. In 1957 and 1958 the firm continued to package the *Armstrong Circle Theater,* some plays for *Du Pont Show of the Month* (including Susskind's production of *The Bridge of San Luis Rey* on January 21, 1958), and in April 1958 took over the production of *Kraft Television Theater,* but later ended its association with that program.

Susskind returned to the theater in September 1958 as co-producer with the Playwrights Company of N. Richard Nash's *Handful of Fire.* It opened at the Martin Beck Theatre in New York on October 1, 1958 and closed on October 4. In October he also set in operation his own weekly discussion program entitled *Open End* (because no time limit was imposed), over WNTA-TV in New York City, and appeared before the camera himself as the host. He began work on *Revival,* the first of four motion pictures he had contracted to produce for Columbia studios. With Hardy Smith he produced *Rashomon,* Fay and Michael Kanin's adaptation of Ryunosuke Akutagawa's short stories, which opened at the Music Box in New York City on January 27, 1959 and ended its run on June 13, 1959.

By May 1959 Talent Associates, Ltd., had contracted for $9,000,000 in live shows, more than the combined efforts of the three major networks. Among them were nine "specials" for General Mills, four for Rexall, and eight for General Motors, in addition to the *Circle Theater* and Susskind's own *Open End.* In October 1960 he made headlines when he had Soviet Premier Nikita S. Khrushchev as his guest on *Open End.*

Bender, N.Y.

DAVID SUSSKIND

Susskind also added WNTA-TV's prestigious *The Play of the Week* to his roster when he agreed to produce four of its two-hour weekly dramas, beginning with Robinson Jeffers' adaptation of Euripides' *Medea,* starring Dame Judith Anderson (October 12-18, 1959). Before the fall television season was underway, he had added enough "specials" to his schedule to bring the total to forty-one and the budget to $15,000,000. He left *The Play of the Week* in April 1960, after having produced twenty-six plays on the series. George Foster Peabody Awards for 1959 were presented to *The Play of the Week* and to Susskind for his production of *The Moon and Sixpence* on NBC.

"Susskind's frenetic pursuit of both the television dollar and television quality has left many a competitor gasping in his wake," observed a *Time* critic (May 4, 1959). Susskind's comments about the medium have also startled his colleagues and critics (*Newsweek* termed him "television's most outspoken critic baiter"); often he is criticized for deploring mediocrity while offering nothing better, or for preferring to present established successes rather than untried original scripts.

David Susskind is married to the former Phyllis Briskin, whom he met while they were students at the University of Wisconsin. They have two daughters, Pamela and Diana, and one son, Andrew. Susskind is a personable but restless and hard-driving man who fortunately can draw upon an enormous fund of energy for his activities. He stands five feet nine inches in height. He dismisses the financial rewards of his career as unimportant, but maintains an apartment on Fifth Avenue and drives about in Carey Cadillacs. Working seventeen hours a day, he spares little time for what he considers the egocentric banalities of cocktail parties, but would stay up all night for the chance to talk with Harry S. Truman,

SUSSKIND, DAVID—*Continued*

Adlai Stevenson, or Justice Hugo Black. Politics is his hobby, and he calls himself a "consecrated Democrat." As for religion, he says: "I believe in God, but I'm not an orthodox practitioner. My children go to temple, so they'll know what they are."

Although he does not limit his productions to the television screen, Susskind realizes that it is through that medium that he must make his impact. "I want to have my own marquee value, like Sam Goldwyn and Cecil B. De Mille," he has said. "Then I wouldn't always have to bother about getting big stars for every show. If people accepted it as a Susskind production, that would be ideal."

References

N Y Post Mag p4+ Ap 26 '59 por
Time 73:54+ My 4 '59 por
Vogue 134:228 S 1 '59 por

SUTHERLAND, JOAN Nov. 7, 1926-
Singer

Address: b. c/o Messrs. Ingpen & Williams, 14 Henrietta Pl., London, W. 1, England

Some music critics regard the coloratura soprano Joan Sutherland of the Covent Garden Opera Company as a British challenge to the supremacy of Maria Callas and as a likely candidate to inherit the world fame of Nellie Melba. Like Melba, Miss Sutherland was born in Australia, and she too undertakes the most taxing lyric-coloratura roles in the Italian repertory, specializing in the heroines of operas by Bellini and Donizetti.

Miss Sutherland made her debut at Covent Garden in October 1952 in *The Magic Flute,* after having won several singing awards and scholarships in her native Australia. It was

British Inf. Services
JOAN SUTHERLAND

not, however, until she forsook the conventional repertory to concentrate on *bel canto* operas that she came into her own. After her triumphant performance as the mad heroine in *Lucia di Lammermoor* in January 1959 at Covent Garden, her reputation seemed assured. Since that time she has added further luster to it with her growing mastery of baroque music, especially the seldom-performed operas of Handel.

Joan Sutherland was born on November 7, 1926 in Sydney, Australia. McDonald Sutherland, her father, was a tailor; her mother was a nonprofessional mezzo-soprano who started Joan on her first vocal lessons. Joan attended St. Catherine's School and after graduation took a secretarial job, but she continued her vocal training and devoted all her spare time to singing. By 1947 she had made enough progress to appear in a concert performance of Purcell's *Dido and Aeneas*. Three years later, she won the Sun Aria competition and also the Mobil Quest award, which included a £1,000 prize for further training. She took part in many concerts and oratorio performances throughout Australia and sang the title role in Eugene Goosens 3d's opera *Judith* at the Sydney Conservatory of Music.

With the funds from the Mobil Quest award to subsidize her, Miss Sutherland went to London in 1951, where she studied under Clive Carey at the Royal College of Music. Although she aspired to Wagnerian roles, three auditions at the Covent Garden Opera Company led her later to admit: "My voice really isn't heavy enough for that, and I soon understood that I'd been forcing it along a road that was wrong for it."

The next five years Miss Sutherland spent in the hard work of learning new roles and in performing them at Covent Garden. In Verdi operas she sang the roles of Amelia in *Un Ballo in Maschera*, Gilda in *Rigoletto*, Desdemona in *Otello*, and Amneris and, finally, the title role in *Aïda*. She appeared on the Covent Garden stage as the Countess Almaviva in Mozart's *Le Nozze di Figaro* and as Pamina in *The Magic Flute*, and broadened her repertory with the roles of Olympia, Giulietta, and Antonia in Offenbach's *The Tales of Hoffman;* of Lady Penelope Rich in Britten's *Gloriana;* of Agathe in Weber's *Der Freischütz;* of Eva in Wagner's *Die Meistersinger von Nürnberg;* of Jenifer in the world première of Tippett's *The Midsummer Marriage;* and of Micaela in Bizet's *Carmen*.

Perhaps it was as Agathe in *Der Freischütz* in 1954 that Miss Sutherland realized her full vocal potential for the first time. In March 1957 she surprised many reviewers with the assurance and beauty of tone with which she sang the title role of *Alcina* for the Handel Opera Society. In the same year she sang arias from Donizetti's *Lucia di Lammermoor* at a celebration honoring the memory of another Australian soprano, Nellie Melba. On that occasion Harold Rosenthal, the editor of *Opera*, predicted that Miss Sutherland would one day sing Lucia at Covent Garden and that she would do so with tremendous success.

After Miss Sutherland's first appearance as Desdemona in December 1957, Rosenthal wrote in *Opera* (February 1958): "She sang with a purity and simplicity that was disarming, and moved and looked well." Her performance as the Israelite woman in Handel's *Samson* the following year moved William Mann of the London *Times* to observe in *Opera* (December 1958): "The finest singing of all came from Joan Sutherland in 'Let the Bright Seraphim'; it was worth waiting three hours to hear the liquid gold and springing mercury of her voice in this aria."

Taking the advice of her husband, Richard Bonynge, Miss Sutherland decided to concentrate on the coloratura roles of eighteenth- and nineteenth-century Italian operas. She soon mastered the difficulties of their florid passages and elaborate runs and trills. Sent by the Covent Garden Opera Company to Italy to study for the title role in *Lucia di Lammermoor,* she worked under the direction of the veteran conductor Tullio Serafin and the promising young producer Franco Zeffirelli. Both men developed faith in Miss Sutherland's ability, and, under their guidance, she turned the cardboard figure of Lucia, the young bride gone mad, into a creature of flesh and blood. As the coaching continued, she added to the tragic dimension of each scene, and revealed more and more dramatic and vocal riches in the part.

When *Lucia di Lammermoor* opened at Covent Garden on February 17, 1959, it was the triumph for Joan Sutherland that Harold Rosenthal had once predicted. It commanded so much approbation that, in response to public demand, the British Broadcasting Corporation broadcast a performance on February 26. Music critics praised the soprano's agility in difficult passages and the ease with which she managed the florid runs, trills, and ornaments. The acclaim led inevitably to press interviews, and offers flooded in from managers throughout Europe and North and South America.

An operation in the spring of 1959 and a subsequent slow recovery kept Miss Sutherland away from the opera house for several months. When she returned to Covent Garden, it was as the courtesan, Violetta, in *La Traviata.* She opened on January 8, 1960 with several handicaps: the production was not a new one, there was no coach like Serafin or Zeffirelli to guide her, and—to make matters worse—she suffered an attack of laryngitis. Although she sang superbly in many passages, she seemed nervous, uncertain, and ill at ease. Some British critics, including David Cairns, Andrew Porter, Noel Goodwin, and Desmond Shawe-Taylor felt that she lacked depth and genuine emotion as Violetta. Cairns observed in the London *Spectator* (January 15, 1960) that Sutherland was singing the role as if she were Lucia instead of Violetta and deplored the effects of publicity, which do not allow a young and gifted singer to consolidate her art and mature gradually.

In later performances Miss Sutherland disclosed a new and better Violetta. Few critics disagreed with Andrew Porter when he wrote in *Opera* (March 1960): "She is one of the few sopranos equipped to sing every part of the role. And now the delicate portamentos, the subtle and supple phrasing took on a new dramatic significance. There was a glitter, not merely vocal, which made one believe in a Violetta who had all Paris at her feet."

The famous Teatro Fenice in Venice provided the setting for Joan Sutherland's Italian debut on February 19, 1960, when she sang the title role in Handel's *Alcina*. By the end of the second act the volatile Italians were shouting "La stupenda!" and showering her with flowers. Italian music critics went so far as to compare Sutherland to their beloved Maria Callas.

In Palermo a month later, the usually hard-to-please Sicilians cast their reserve to the winds and applauded loudly as Sutherland sang Lucia, with Serafin and Zeffirelli again in attendance. She went on to Paris, where she repeated the triumph and received enthusiastic notices from the press. Génet, in describing Sutherland's Lucia for the *New Yorker* (May 21, 1960), noted: "It is an unbelievably great singing and acting performance. Her *bel canto* phrases are like crystal bubbles of sound; her pianissimi are technical marvels, as perfectly shaped as if they were miniature versions of full-throated song. Her trill is not an amplified vibrato but an alternation of two distinct notes, as if from two different woodwinds."

Critics in general agree that Joan Sutherland should rid herself of two faults: the somewhat frigid detachment of her acting and her need to develop a stronger and smoother legato. They feel that she could eliminate both of these weaknesses if she would submit to first-rate coaching and listen with undivided attention to the recordings of other *bel canto* artists, past and present.

When the twenty-sixth Glyndebourne Festival opened in Sussex, England in June 1960 with Bellini's *I Puritani,* Sutherland in singing the role of Elvira proved herself capable of more warmth than she had displayed before. Her vocal performance was further distinguished by a sense of style, accuracy, flexibility, and a remarkable control in the *fioritura* sections.

Joan Sutherland opened the 1960-61 season of the Covent Garden Opera Company, singing the title role in Bellini's *La Sonnambula.* American music lovers awaited her United States debut at the Dallas Civic Opera in November 1960. They also anticipated her appearance with the American Opera Society and a recital of Bach arias, both at Town Hall in New York City, and her Chicago concert, planned after the beginning of her United States tour in February 1961. They could also look forward to her scheduled appearance with the Metropolitan Opera during the season of 1961-62. The edge of their anticipation had been whetted by the samples of Sutherland's vocalism that had been released by London Records and its affiliate, l'Oiseau-Lyre, in the United States, including a recital of Donizetti arias and her performance as Galatea in Handel's *Acis and Galatea.*

(Continued next page)

SUTHERLAND, JOAN—Continued

In 1954 Joan Sutherland was married to Richard Bonynge, her friend from childhood, and they have one son. Bonynge, who is a pianist and authority on Italian opera, gave up his own concert career to promote that of his wife. The couple, who are experts on early nineteenth-century Italian opera, collect autographed opera scores, operatic lithographs, and books about noted singers of the era.

Joan Sutherland has been described by one observer as "a tall, old-fashioned type of woman with a strong chin who looks like a steel engraving portrait of Jane Eyre." Her dark hair, attractive face, and regal bearing are perfect attributes for her roles as Donizetti and Bellini heroines. Gracing the wall of her home in Kensington is a portrait of Elizabeth Billington, who brought *bel canto* opera to popularity in England in the early nineteenth century. She is an idol of Joan Sutherland, who hopes to perform the same mission for *bel canto* in the twentieth century. "I will be happy," she says, "if I can just sing in every opera Bellini ever wrote."

References

Time 75:48 Je 13 '60
Who's Who, 1960

SUZUKI, PAT 1930(?)- Singer

Address: b. c/o Vik Records, 155 E. 24th St., New York 10

When Pat Suzuki was signed to a leading role in the Rodgers and Hammerstein musical, *Flower Drum Song*, in 1958, the contract climaxed a year in which she made her American and Canadian television debuts and saw her first record album become a best seller. Since then the diminutive nisei with the long pony-tail has become a familiar figure on the TV screen and in newspaper feature columns. *Flower Drum Song* completed its Broadway run on May 7, 1960.

Chiyoko Suzuki was born in the California village of Cressey, the daughter of Chiyosaku Suzuki, probably in 1930, although some sources indicate that she is younger. She was by several years the junior of her two sisters and one brother. Her brother now manages the family farm; one sister, Mary, teaches school in Chicago, and the other, June, is married to the Presbyterian chaplain of Western Michigan University.

The elder Suzukis were first-generation Japanese-Americans who owned and worked a one-hundred-acre farm, on which they grew almonds, grapes, and peaches. The girl's given name (meaning "a thousand times good") was shortened to Chiby ("Squirt") by her family, and then to Pat by a local grocer who could not manage the Japanese name. She attended a two-room elementary school in Cressey, but remembers her childhood as a lonely one.

"I could hardly wait to grow up," she recalls (*Time*, December 22, 1958). "I didn't like being a kid, because I always had certain feelings I couldn't explain. The only things I could dream about in those days were the trucks going by on the highway all night long. I used to dream of all the places they had been that I would like to go some day."

One escape was singing. She learned from the family phonograph and sometimes sang at Sunday school (her parents were Methodists) and at county fairs, where her most popular number was "I Am an American." Following the attack on Pearl Harbor in December 1941, she learned that she was also Japanese. She and her family were moved to the Amache internment camp in Lamar, Colorado.

Pat continued her schooling at the relocation camp for the duration of World War II. After the war, her family worked for a year on a Colorado sugar-beet farm, renting their own land to accumulate capital so that they could begin farming again. In 1946 they returned to Cressey, where Pat finished high school. She enrolled at Mills College near San Francisco in 1948.

She transferred to Modesto Junior College and San Francisco City College before settling at San Jose State College for her final two years. She paid expenses by part-time jobs, including week-end singing engagements at a nearby night club where she developed a professional style. She also took formal classroom training in voice, although her major subjects were art and education.

After graduating from San Jose State in 1954 with a Bachelor of Science degree in education, Miss Suzuki went to New York City. She hoped to tour Europe before beginning her career as a teacher. She ran short of money in New York, however, and found a job as a walk-on in a road production of *Teahouse of the August Moon*, which took her back to the West Coast later that year.

In Seattle, Washington, she auditioned for Norm Bobrow, owner of the Colony Club, and was signed to a contract as a singer. Under Bobrow's guidance, her bouncy singing style soon won a local following. Her reputation grew when she was praised by Bing Crosby (who later wrote the jacket notes for her first album) and when she was called a "song belter of promise" by *Variety* in September 1955.

In 1957 Miss Suzuki signed a contract with Vik Records, and went to New York City for promotion appearances on the Lawrence Welk television program, and later on the Jack Paar and George Gobel shows. She was also signed for a series of television appearances over the Canadian Broadcasting Corporation's *Call for Music* show. A *Time* magazine reviewer wrote: "West Coast audiences and critics . . . like to argue whether she has the style of Billie Holiday, Jeri Southern, Judy Garland or Ethel Merman. The truth is that she sounds occasional echoes of all of them. But she also has a dead-sure sense of phrasing all her own and a warm-tinted, open voice which casts its own mellow glow over the familiar lyrics she handles" (July 22, 1957).

When Vik Records released a long-playing record album entitled *The Many Sides of Pat Suzuki* in 1958, the singer scored an immediate success. "New girl singers with big promotional build-ups turn up on records every month by the dozen," wrote Douglas Watt in the New York *Sunday News* (March 23, 1958), "but the first to live up to her advance ballyhoo in a long, long while is Pat Suzuki." A *Variety* reviewer (April 9, 1958) remarked, succinctly, that "the pre-sell hasn't oversold." Later her first single record for Vik, *Daddy,* became a best seller almost overnight.

In June 1958, after another appearance on the Jack Paar television show, Miss Suzuki was signed for a leading role in the Rodgers and Hammerstein musical, *Flower Drum Song.* She was cast as Linda Low, a Chinese-American dancer who has chosen American ways in preference to Chinese traditions. The show opened in Boston on October 27, 1958.

"The production is an achievement of pure delight," wrote a *Variety* reviewer (October 29, 1958), "coming up with [an] absorbing, exciting musical of conflict betwixt the old and new in San Francisco's Chinatown. The music is exuberant, although there are a few dull moments, but they are offset by a dozen rollicking songs . . . and an overall sense of audience acceptability."

Not all reviewers were equally enthusiastic, but when the show moved to New York's St. James Theatre in December it was clear that it was a popular success, with Miss Suzuki making a large contribution. Rodgers and Hammerstein "did not quite write *Flower Drum Song* for Pat," remarked a *Time* writer (December 22, 1958), "but at times it seemed close to becoming her show."

After *Flower Drum Song* opened, Miss Suzuki made several more television appearances, including an interview over Edward R. Murrow's *Person to Person* show. She performed on a *Voice of Firestone* program featuring the music of Richard Rodgers (May 4, 1959) and sang at the Newport, Rhode Island, Jazz Festival in July 1959.

Part of Miss Suzuki's appeal undoubtedly comes from the contrast between her vitality and her stature. She is four feet eleven inches tall and weighs 100 pounds; her dark hair is worn in an almost waist-length pony-tail which was five years in the growing and which was protected by a special clause in her *Flower Drum Song* contract. She can project her energy to an audience either in person or over television.

"If you meet Pat Suzuki, be prepared for anything," wrote Sally Hammond in the New York *Post* (May 19, 1958). "She's apt to skip onto the sidewalk and fling her arms toward the sun. Or she'll soberly confide her philosophy of singing. . . . Pat is the farthest cry from the stereotyped Japanese female—that 'submissive,' delicate, kimono-clad creature."

Knowing little about Japanese ceremony and tradition, Miss Suzuki lives in a modern apartment on Central Park West in New York City. A keen baseball enthusiast, Pat Suzuki is a New York Yankee fan. She was the pitcher for a softball team made up of girls from the cast of *Flower Drum Song,* and she pitched

PAT SUZUKI

several victories over rival teams from other Broadway shows. On March 28, 1960 she was married to Mark Shaw, a fashion photographer.

She carries this vitality into her singing, too. "I'm a little too young to be disillusioned about a great love," she has said (New York *Post*, May 19, 1958). "Even in my sad songs I can't leave it there. Just say I don't like despair in art. I think art should give people at least a little joy."

References

N Y Post Mag p1 My 19 '58 por
N Y Sunday News II p4 Je 21 '59 por
N Y World-Telegram Mag p1 My 24 '59 por
Time 70:45 Jl 22 '57; 72:44+ D 22 '58

SWANN, W(ILLIAM) F(RANCIS) G(RAY) Aug. 29, 1884- Physicist
Address: b. Bartol Research Foundation of the Franklin Institute, Whittier Pl., Swarthmore, Pa.; h. 609 Ogden Ave., Swarthmore, Pa.

NOTE: This biography supersedes the article which appeared in *Current Biography* in 1941.

In 1959 the distinguished theoretical and experimental physicist W. F. G. Swann resigned his post as director of the Bartol Research Foundation of the Franklin Institute in Swarthmore, Pennsylvania. He remains director emeritus of the foundation and special consultant to its staff members, and he will continue to do his own research there. The foundation, of which he had been director since 1927, is a nonprofit institution for fundamental research in physics. Since 1945 Swann has been the senior staff adviser to the Franklin Institute Laboratories for Research and Development in Philadelphia.

(Continued next page)

Eastman Kodak Co.

W. F. G. SWANN

W. F. G. Swann, who was born and educated in England, has held various research and teaching positions in his native country and in the United States. He has written about 250 articles and several books in his field. He is also known for his ability to explain difficult scientific problems to laymen. Swann is an accomplished cellist, has played in numerous orchestras in Great Britain and the United States, and has conducted orchestras in both countries.

William Francis Gray Swann, the only child of William Francis and Anne (Evans) Swann, was born at Ironbridge in Shropshire, England, on August 29, 1884. His father was an insurance executive. William was granted a scholarship to the York Place School in Brighton, England, from which he was graduated in 1900. He has said that he had a very bad memory when he was young, and that he disliked physics and mathematics in school.

He first thought of pursuing a career in music, then chose medicine because "it was said that one could make a living in that profession; and none of the other things in which I had so far acquired any interest seemed to afford the means of making a living." One day, while browsing in a bookshop, he came upon a very old volume—a treasury of algebra, trigonometry, conic sections, calculus, mechanics, dynamics, astronomy, and geodesy—which he bought for four cents. It turned out to be an excellent investment, for it was the reading of this book which prompted Swann to embark upon a scientific career.

Swann attended Brighton Technical College on a scholarship until 1903, when he matriculated at the Royal College of Science of London University, as a scholarship student. He was awarded the B.S. degree with first class honors in 1905, and the A.R.C.S. (Associate of the Royal College of Science) degree in 1906, tak-

ing first place. He also attended University College, King's College, and the City and Guilds of London Institute. He received his D.Sc. degree in 1910 from London University.

Meanwhile, Swann had worked as a junior demonstrator in physics at the Royal College of Science from 1905 to 1907. The success of one of his first experiments in the thermal properties of gases led to his appointment as an assistant lecturer and demonstrator in physics at the University of Sheffield in 1907. After six years there, he was invited to come to the United States; from 1913 to 1918 he served as the chief of the physical division of the department of terrestrial magnetism at the Carnegie Institution in Washington, D.C. A man of lively wit, Swann was once asked to deliver a series of lectures at the United States Bureau of Standards at eight o'clock in the morning. He protested these arrangements, saying that "an Englishman seldom stays up that late!"

During this period Swann did research in cosmic radiation and was responsible for the development and installation of atmospheric electric equipment on the institution's yacht, *Carnegie*. He contributed to *Ocean Magnetic Observations, 1905-1916, and Reports on Special Researches,* published in 1917 by the department of terrestrial magnetism of the Carnegie Institution. From 1917 to 1918 he also was a consultant to the United States Bureau of Standards. For the war effort, he devised a scheme for submarine detection and also investigated the cause of explosions in balloons.

Returning to teaching but continuing his research, Swann accepted a position as professor of physics at the University of Minnesota in 1918. He was also a member of the National Research Council from 1921 to 1923, and with three other persons on the council's committee on electrodynamics of moving media, he presented a report which was published by the council in 1922 under the title, *Electro-dynamics of Moving Media.* He became a professor at the University of Chicago in 1923, and in 1924 he became professor of physics at Yale University and director of its Sloane Laboratory.

For three years beginning in 1924, Swann served as chairman of the advisory research committee of the Bartol Research Foundation. Three years later he became director of the foundation, which had been established in 1925 by the Franklin Institute, through a bequest from Henry W. Bartol, a Philadelphia industrialist. Because the foundation is supported by private funds, scientists there have had the opportunity to do the kind of fundamental, theoretical research which Swann feels is the seed "to which all the trees and foliage of utilitarian effort owe their growth." The foundation was moved to its present site on the campus of Swarthmore College in 1928. Its program is concentrated in three principal areas: nuclear physics, cosmic radiation, and solid state and physical electronics.

During World War II, Swann, as director of the Bartol Research Foundation, supervised investigations that aided many different phases of the war effort. He also served, as a civilian, with the United States Office of Naval Research in 1944. Although he relinquished his position as director of the Bartol Foundation in 1959, he continues to serve as senior adviser to the Franklin Institute Laboratories for Research and Development, and he still conducts his own research at the Bartol Foundation.

Swann has made notable contributions to the field of physics in such areas as cosmic radiation, thermal measurements, relativity, electromagnetic theory, terrestrial magnetism, atomic structure, electroconductivity, atmospheric electricity, quantum theory, and electrodynamics. His scientific reports have appeared in professional journals like the *Physical Review, Science,* and the *Philosophical Transactions of the Royal Society.* He has also contributed to the *Encyclopaedia Brittanica* and to publications like the *Saturday Review.* He has been an associate editor of the *Physical Review* and of the *Journal of the Franklin Institute.*

With Ira M. Freeman he wrote *The Architecture of the Universe* (Macmillan, 1934) and *Physics* (Wiley, 1941), and he contributed to *The Story of Human Error* (Appleton-Century, 1936), edited by Joseph Jastrow. Swann and eight others presented papers in a general seminar conducted by the committee on training of the Brookings Institution in 1930 and 1931. These papers were published by the institution in 1931 under the title, *Essays on Research in the Social Sciences.*

Swann was awarded an honorary M.A. degree by Yale University in 1924, an honorary D.Sc. degree by Swarthmore College in 1929, and an honorary D.Litt. degree by Temple University in 1954. He received the Elliott Cresson Medal of the Franklin Institute in 1960. He is a Fellow of the Physical Society of London, the Imperial College of Science and Technology in London, and the American Physical Society, of which he was vice-president in 1929 and 1930 and president from 1931 to 1933

He was vice-president of the American Association for the Advancement of Science from 1923 to 1924, and is a member of the British Association for the Advancement of Science, the Optical Society of America, the Washington Academy of Sciences (vice-president, 1923-24), the American Geophysical Union (chairman, section D, 1923-24), the American Philosophical Society (secretary, 1940-46), the American Mathematical Society, and the Council of Learned Societies. His Greek letter societies are Gamma Alpha, Sigma Xi, and Sigma Pi Sigma. He belongs to the Cosmos, Yale, and Explorers clubs.

Since his youth Swann has had an abiding interest in music. As an accomplished violoncellist and orchestra conductor, he has attained a renown in musical circles that equals his fame as a physicist. Indeed, he prefers to regard these two spheres of achievement as independent areas, and many persons who delight in his musical performances are unaware of his status as a scientist. For many years Swann kept a 225-year-old Mateo Grofiller cello close by his desk at Bartol; at home he practised playing the instrument every morning before going to work. At informal chamber music sessions, Swann has played with distinguished artists like violinist Mischa Elman and pianist Agi Jambor.

In almost every place where Swann settled down to work as a physicist, he also found his way to the conductor's podium. He conducted the University of Sheffield Orchestra, the Bureau of Standards Orchestra in Washington, and he was an assistant conductor of the Main Line Orchestra in Philadelphia. In 1936 he founded the Swarthmore Symphony Orchestra, which he now conducts. Swann became an honorary Fellow of the Trinity College of Music in London in 1936, and he is a member and former chairman of the board of directors of the Philadelphia Academy of Music.

Dr. W. F. G. Swann was married to Sarah Frances Mabel Thompson, a violinist, on August 14, 1909; she died on May 25, 1954. They had three children: William Francis, Charles Paul, and Sylvia. On December 23, 1955 he was married to Helene Laura Diedrichs, a concert pianist. For recreation, in addition to his music, he formerly enjoyed playing golf and tennis. The scientist has white hair and brown eyes; he is almost six feet tall and weighs 145 pounds. Swann, who is an elector in the Hall of Fame at New York University, once listed the qualities which he thought essential to success: "Strong confidence in the present, and admission of necessity for improvement with equal confidence in the future"; hard work; ability to withstand discouragement; development of a hobby; and a good sense of humor.

References

Sci Illus 3:26+ D '48
American Men of Science vol 1 (1955)
International Who's Who, 1959
Who's Who, 1960
Who's Who in America, 1960-61
World Biography (1948)

SWART, CHARLES R(OBBERTS) Dec. 5, 1894- Governor-General of the Union of South Africa

Address: Government House, Cape Town, South Africa; Government House, Pretoria, South Africa

The ninth Governor-General of the Union of South Africa, His Excellency Charles R. Swart was sworn in on January 12, 1960 to represent Queen Elizabeth II in a country officially described as "a sovereign, independent state, freely associated with other sovereign states in the Commonwealth of Nations." Appointed by the Queen, acting on the advice of the Union's Prime Minister H. F. Verwoerd, he succeeded the late Ernest G. Jansen and is the fourth South African to occupy the office.

In representing the Crown, the Governor-General administers supreme executive authority in the Union, subject to advice by an Executive Council composed of heads of government departments. As the Minister of Justice under three Nationalist Prime Ministers from 1948 to 1959, Swart has been called the chief legislative architect of the National

CHARLES R. SWART

party's policy of complete racial segregation. A number of observers believe that if Verwoerd should succeed in his goal of making South Africa a republic, Swart might possibly become its first president. South Africa moved closer to this goal when on October 5, 1960 voters approved republicanism in an all-white referendum.

The Morgenzon farm where Charles Robberts Swart was born on December 5, 1894 was near the town of Winburg in what was then the Republic of the Orange Free State. Of South African Dutch descent, he was six years old when during the Boer War he was detained with his mother in a British concentration camp and, according to John Gunther, "has hated the British ever since" (*Inside Africa,* 1955).

Intellectually precocious, Swart completed high school at thirteen and received his bachelor's degree from Grey University College (now the University of the Orange Free State) in Bloemfontein at seventeen and his law degree at twenty. In 1914 he was briefly held in custody for taking part in a demonstration against South Africa's entry into World War I on the side of the British.

During 1914-15 Swart taught at the Ficksburg high school in his native province, and was subsequently appointed secretary of the Orange Free State examination board. Comparatively early in his variegated career, furthermore, he spent several months in the United States, acquired a special diploma from the Columbia University School of Journalism, and did reporting for New York and Washington newspapers. Before returning home, he visited Hollywood and played some bit parts in westerns. As a journalist in South Africa he contributed columns to *Die Burger* (the Capetown newspaper edited by Dr. Daniel

François Malan) and to papers in Bloemfontein and Johannesburg. Swart has also published two works of fiction, *Kinders van Suid-Afrika* (1933) and *Die Agterryer* (1939), both in Afrikaans (South African Dutch).

Swart's political career began when he became private secretary to General J. B. M. Hertzog, the Boer republican and champion of the "color bar" who founded the Nationalist party in 1913. Swart was the organization secretary for that party in the Orange Free State in 1919, the year in which the pro-Empire Jan Christiaan Smuts for the first time took office as Prime Minister of the Union of South Africa. Also in 1919 he became an advocate of the Supreme Court of South Africa and practised at the bar for the next four years. He served as legal assistant to the Bloemfontein city council and on the legal commission of the Dutch Reformed Church in the Orange Free State. He has been both a regularly appointed lecturer in law at the University of the Orange Free State and a visiting lecturer in agriculture legislation at Glen Agricultural College near Bloemfontein.

Deciding to devote more of his time to politics, Swart curtailed his law practice in 1923, ran for Parliament, and was elected to the Union House of Assembly as Nationalist member from Ladybrand in the Orange Free State. His prominence in the party increased as he became a member of its chief executive in 1928 and of its federal council in 1931.

Although Swart had lost his Assembly seat in 1938, he was chosen in 1940 to lead the Nationalist party in the Orange Free State. In 1941 he returned to Parliament as the member for Winburg, which he represented continuously from then until just before his appointment as Governor-General in late 1959. He served on numerous Parliamentary committees and was chief whip of the Nationalist party during some of the years in opposition, when Smuts was Prime Minister. At the general election of May 26, 1948 the Nationalists under Malan and the smaller allied Afrikaner party narrowly won over the United party of Smuts after a campaign waged largely on the issues of white supremacy and apartheid (strict racial segregation).

In Malan's "all-Afrikaner" cabinet, formed on June 4, 1948, Swart was appointed Minister of Justice. He also held the portfolio of Minister of Education, Arts and Science for a time and in 1950 became Chancellor of the University of the Orange Free State. As Minister of Justice he introduced a penal reform and rehabilitation system in the Department of Prisons and made radical changes in the police force structure. In May 1950 he introduced a bill for suppression of Communism which gave the Minister of Justice unusual powers to root out Communists from public jobs. He was also responsible for drawing up much of the repressive legislation of apartheid and pushing it through Parliament.

The aging Dr. Malan retired in November 1954 and was succeeded as Prime Minister by an even more extreme proponent of apartheid, Johannes Gerhardus Strijdom. Swart was named Deputy Prime Minister as well as Minister of Justice. Further apartheid legislation was quickly forthcoming, and in 1956 the Union Senate was enlarged to assure the adoption of a Constitutional amendment permitting the removal of thousands of "colored" (persons of mixed blood) from the common voting rolls. The right of the courts to test laws was also limited, and in December of that year 140 leaders of the African and Indian congresses and white sympathizers were charged with treason.

Just before Strijdom's death on August 23, 1958, Swart was named Acting Prime Minister. He was a candidate for the party leadership at the ensuing caucus, but lost to the former Minister of Native Affairs, Dr. H. F. Verwoerd, who was sworn in as Prime Minister on September 3. On the following October 20 Verwoerd reappointed Swart as Minister of Justice and leader of the House of Assembly, posts which he retained until his resignation from Parliament after the death of Governor-General Ernest G. Jansen in November 1959, when it became known that he would be recommended for appointment as Jansen's successor.

Appointment of Swart as Governor-General, announced on December 6, 1959, was strongly criticized in the British press, with the London *Daily Herald* calling him "the organizer of South Africa's color bar Police State" and the *New Statesman* stressing his unconcealed "detestation of the British connection and his determination to break it." He was, nevertheless, sworn into office on January 12, 1960, and three days later delivered to the Union Parliament the "speech from the throne" which outlined the Verwoerd government's legislative program including the placing of education under strong central control with Afrikaans as the language of instruction.

The apartheid policy, eight times previously condemned by the United Nations General Assembly as a violation of fundamental human rights, was denounced by the U.N. Security Council by a 9-0 vote on April 3, 1960 as a threat to international peace and security. During the mass revolt which had begun in South Africa on March 21 in protest against the law compelling native Africans to carry passes, the Governor-General was empowered to outlaw the Pan-Africanist, African National, and Indian congresses; and on April 7 he did so for a period of one year. The next day Prime Minister Verwoerd was seriously injured in an assassination attempt, amid new outbreaks of violence, large-scale arrests, and nationwide strikes.

South Africa's Governor-General Charles R. Swart is "an imposing" six feet seven inches tall and "looks gaunt and solemn," as a New York *Times* (January 16, 1960) sketch noted. However, "his friends say he has retained a sense of humor and can be genial and folksy." He has been married since 1924 to the former Nellie de Klerk and has one son and one daughter. He enjoys watching Rugby football and owns a fine private library.

References

Christian Sci Mon p4 D 7 '59
N Y Herald Tribune p5 Ag 27 '58 por; p17 D 7 '59 por
N Y Times p5 D 7 '59 por; p4 Ja 16 '60 por
Time 74:18 D 28 '59 por
U S News 15:20 S 5 '58 por
Author's and Writer's Who's Who (1948-49)
International Who's Who, 1959
International Year Book and Statesmen's Who's Who, 1959
South Africa Who's Who, 1956
Who's Who, 1960
Wie Ist Wie in Suid-Afrika (1958)

SWIRBUL, LEON A. Mar. 18, 1898-June 28, 1960 Aircraft company executive; a founder (1929), vice-president and general manager (1929-46), and president (since 1946) of the Grumman Aircraft Engineering Corporation. See *Current Biography* (April) 1953.

Obituary

N Y Times p33 Je 29 '60

TABER, LOUIS J(OHN) Sept. 19, 1878-Oct. 16, 1960 Former Master of the National Grange (1923-1941); helped the United States government to mobilize agriculture for World War II as a member of the Committee on Agricultural Production for Defense; board chairman of the Farmers and Traders Life Insurance Company since 1955. See *Current Biography* (June) 1942.

Obituary

N Y Times p29 O 17 '60

TANNER, VÄINÖ (ALFRED) Mar. 12, 1881- Finnish political leader
Address: b. Paasivuorenkatu 3, Helsinki, Finland; h. Hietalahdenkatu 18 C, Helsinki, Finland

No man is more responsible for Finnish resistance to Soviet expansionism than Väinö Tanner, who is the "grand old man" of Finland's Social Democratic party. He has been called the soul of Finnish socialism and "one of the last European survivors of the idealists who built parliamentary Socialism early this century."

During his long and varied political career, Tanner has experienced the honor of high office and the degradation of imprisonment. He served as Premier in 1926 and 1927, and among his cabinet posts was that of Foreign Minister during the Finnish-Russian War of 1939-40. Active in the Social Democratic party for over fifty years, Tanner was its chairman from 1919 to 1926 and has held this position again since 1957. He derives his political strength partly from his lifelong association with the Finnish

Wide World

VÄINÖ TANNER

co-operative movement, which has made him a leader of organized labor to an extent unmatched by any other Finnish politician.

Väinö Alfred Thomasson was born on March 12, 1881 in Helsinki, Finland, the son of Kustaa Alfred and Maria Sofia (Räsänen) Thomasson. The Swedish family name was changed to the Finnish Tanner in 1895. After completing his secondary education at the Helsingin Suomalainen Realilyseo, Tanner attended a business school in 1900-01. For the next four years he worked for co-operatives in Hamburg, Germany; Turku, Finland; and Viborg, Finland. During this period Tanner also studied law and took his degree at the University of Helsinki in 1911. He practised law from 1911 to 1915.

His leadership in the co-operative movement began in 1909, when he became chairman of the administrative board of the Co-operative Wholesale Society. Later, in 1917, he was made a director of the society. He has also held other posts such as member of the central board from 1910 to 1945 and chairman from 1927 to 1945 of the International Co-operative Alliance and head of the administrative board from 1916 to 1946 and again since 1950 of the Union of Co-operative Societies. Perhaps Väinö Tanner has been principally interested in the Elanto Co-operative Society. Under his guidance as managing director from 1915 to 1946 and board chairman since 1950, the organization has been considerably expanded.

Tanner has also contributed to the economic life of his country by his activities in the Bank of Finland. He was an auditor from 1908 to 1912 and from 1915 to 1916, deputy chairman from 1923 to 1924, chairman from 1933 to 1945, and a council member since 1919.

Running on the Social Democratic ticket, Tanner was first elected to Parliament in 1907. He was sent to the legislature by his constituents in 1913 and again in 1919. In 1919 he became Speaker of Parliament, serving until 1926 and from 1930 to 1945. When Finland was imperiled by the Russian Revolution of 1917, he was called upon to be chief of the Finance Department. After serving as Premier from 1926 to 1927, he was Minister of Finance from 1937 to 1939.

A member of the Finnish delegation to Moscow in the fall of 1939 to discuss Russian territorial demands on Finland, he is reported to have used few words other than *Nyet*. The Finnish delegation left Moscow on November 13. The Russians attacked Finland on November 30. Tanner was immediately named Foreign Minister.

As the undisputed leader of organized labor in Finland, he rallied even the extreme leftists among Finnish workers, on whom Russia had been counting for support, to the defense of their country against the invading Red Army. As the food situation in Finland deteriorated and as the Russians increased their bombing of Finnish cities, Tanner tried to reach a settlement with Russia, despite the opposition of the "win-or-die" faction. Under the Treaty of Moscow, signed on March 12, 1940, Finland ceded 13,558 square miles of territory to the Soviet Union. Shortly thereafter the Finnish cabinet was reorganized, and he was appointed Minister of Supply. By the end of the year, however, he had resigned.

"Whenever the Finns want to shorten sail and batten down the hatches to weather a gale, they always call Väinö A. Tanner into the Cabinet," wrote Lemuel F. Parton (New York *Sun,* September 16, 1941) of Tanner's re-entrance into the cabinet as Minister of Commerce and Industry in 1941. By 1942 he had again become head of the Finance Ministry.

Still fearful of further Soviet encroachment on Finnish territory, Finland fought on the Axis side during World War II. Although the country's leaders had considered making a separate peace with Russia in 1943, Finland's dependence on German economic aid and a reluctance to negotiate with a strong Russia led them to postpone the conclusion of a Finnish-Russian armistice until September 21, 1944.

After World War II, at Soviet insistence a Finnish court, under the supervision of an Allied Control Commission for Finland, sentenced Tanner to five and one-half years in prison for "war responsibility" early in 1946. Seven other Finnish wartime leaders were sentenced with him, for terms running from two to ten years. The Finnish government did not make the imprisonment uncomfortable for the sentenced leaders. Tanner received from his family all the paper, writing material, and extra food he needed, although he did have to cut down on smoking panatelas, from fifteen to five a day. He spent eight hours each day writing his memoirs and doing translations. "Thanks to my jailers, I have had the spare time I always wanted," he said on his release, "and I have used it to write . . . books about Finland and us Finns."

The memoirs, published between 1948 and 1957 and dealing with his youth and government service in peace and war, were popular in Finland for years. His account of the Finnish-Russian War of 1939-40, the first analysis of its political significance, was an immediate best seller. It has been translated into English as *The Winter War* (Stanford University Press, 1957). The book was roundly denounced by Communist critics in Finland as well as in East Germany and in Russia. Swedish reviewers also harshly criticized the book which partially attributed the severity of Russian demands to Sweden's refusal to co-operate sufficiently with Finland during the war. Other memoirs of Tanner relate the history of the co-operative movement, Finnish politics, and such critical periods as 1917-18 and 1943-44. He also translated several books into Finnish.

The jailing of Tanner was believed by many observers to have been devised by the Soviets chiefly to discredit him in the eyes of the working class. The actual effect was quite the reverse. He not only maintained a ruling hand in formulating Social Democratic policy from his cell, where he conferred with his party colleagues once a week, but emerged from prison in 1949 (pardoned by the late President Juho Kusti Paasikivi) a martyr and hero. Before the war he was more than once an unsuccessful Social Democratic candidate for President, seeking election in 1925, 1931, and 1937. "In any truly 'free' election since the war," a correspondent for the *Christian Science Monitor* (June 6, 1955) has quoted many Finns as saying, "Tanner would have been elected President by popular acclamation."

Immediately following his release from prison, however, Tanner shunned the political spotlight, lest he embarrass Paasikivi, who had advocated a policy of peaceful co-existence with Russia. He announced his intention of retiring to his farm near Helsinki to write books and cultivate his garden.

His retirement was temporary; in 1951 Tanner was again elected to Parliament, where he served until 1954, and was returned once more in 1958. In April 1957 the Social Democrats, who favored stringent action to counteract inflation, elected him as chairman of the party, Tanner, who had already announced that he was not a candidate for this post, had changed his mind in reaction to Soviet propaganda against his comeback. Early in 1960 Tanner stated that he wanted to step down from the chairmanship because of his age. He was persuaded to stay—reportedly for the sake of preserving a semblance of party unity.

The Social Democratic party, founded in 1899, has 100,000 members, most of them workers or small farmers. Its program is to work for socialism by constitutional means. Although it has often won the largest number of votes in postwar elections, the Social Democratic party has had to leave actual rule to the minority Agrarian party, because of the unacceptability of many Social Democratic leaders to the Soviet Union. There has been a movement within the party for teamwork with Agrarians and modifying of anti-Soviet policy. Tanner's re-election as party chairman on the night of April 17, 1960 represented a repudiation of the latter movement. Many Finns looked upon the re-election as a presage of a deepened impasse in Finland's politics.

Tanner was married to Linda Anttila on February 28, 1909. They have three sons, all of whom are civil engineers, and five daughters. Two of the daughters are civil engineers, one is a physician, another is a dentist, and another a veterinarian. Tanner is a burly man, weighing 154 pounds and standing five feet six and a half inches. He has white hair and gray eyes. The politician's smile has been described as ironic. He smokes cigars constantly, usually wears black boots, and takes streetcars home from official receptions. The University of Helsinki awarded him an honorary LL.D. degree.

References

N Y Times p11 Ap 18 '60 por
Kuka Kukin On (1954)
Vem Och Vad? (1948)
World Biography (1954)

TAWES, J(OHN) MILLARD Apr. 8, 1894- Governor of Maryland
Address: b. State House, Annapolis, Md.; h. Hall Highway, Crisfield, Md.

Having won the largest vote margin in Maryland's history, J. Millard Tawes became its fifty-ninth Governor on January 14, 1959. As successor to Theodore R. McKeldin in this post, he is the state's first Democratic chief executive since 1950. Tawes has had a long career in public office, having served as comptroller of the Maryland treasury for seventeen years and as state bank commissioner for three years. A conservative Democrat, he has defined his principal gubernatorial obligation as that of keeping Maryland "abreast of the times" while preserving the financial integrity of the state. During the first half of his four-year term, sound economic expansion has become an official governmental policy.

John Millard Tawes was born April 8, 1894 in Crisfield, Maryland to James and Alice (Byrd) Tawes. After attending the public schools of Somerset County and the Wilmington Conference Academy in Dover, Delaware, he continued his education at the Sadler's, Bryant and Stratton Business College, where he specialized in the study of banking and accountancy.

Tawes began his business career in the lumber and canning concerns founded and owned by his father. He continued to work with his father, and later with his brothers, as the family business enterprises were extended into shipbuilding, baking, and banking. From 1917 to 1919 he was secretary and treasurer of the Tawes Shipbuilding Company and from 1919 to 1945 vice-president and treasurer of the Tawes Baking Company. In addition to holding these positions, he was associated with the management of the Tawes-Gibson Lumber Company and the Tawes-Gibson Packing Company and is now a director of the Bank of Crisfield.

(Continued next page)

J. MILLARD TAWES

Entering politics in 1930, Tawes was elected clerk of court of Somerset County. He served two terms in that office, resigning in 1938 after having been elected comptroller of the treasury of Maryland in his first state-wide election campaign. In 1942 he ran without primary opposition for re-election and won a second four-year term at the general election.

In May 1947 Governor William Preston Lane, Jr., appointed Tawes state bank commissioner, a position he held until he was appointed in July 1950 to fill the unexpired term of the late James J. Lacy as state comptroller. He was re-elected comptroller without primary or Republican opposition in 1950 and again in 1954. Through his long years in Maryland public office Tawes was known as a political leader without enemies.

Making a bid for the governorship in 1946, Tawes lost out in a three-way Democratic primary race, to former Governor Lane. In 1954 Tawes stepped aside for his second cousin Harry C. ("Curly") Byrd who made an unsuccessful attempt to unseat the Republican Governor Theodore R. McKeldin.

Tawes became Maryland's first Democratic Governor in eight years when he defeated James P. S. Devereux by a record majority of 205,000 votes in the 1958 elections. He is also the first governor to be elected from the state's Eastern Shore since 1916. Democrats viewed the election as a critical test for the party. For almost a decade they had been in the uncomfortable position of having three times as many registered voters as the Republicans without being able to win state-wide elections. Both of Maryland's seats in the United States Senate have been held by the G.O.P. since 1952. Political observers have attributed Republican victories to continual squabbling within the Democratic organization and to the exceptional popularity of ex-Governor McKeldin.

On assuming office in 1959, Governor Tawes was granted broader executive power than had been conferred on any governor by the Maryland General Assembly in a decade. This occurred by means of the reorganization and expansion of four key agencies: the state roads commission, the racing commission, the planning commission, and the tidewater fisheries commission.

In addition to extending gubernatorial authority, the predominantly Democratic legislature during 1959 enacted a highway safety program to penalize habitual traffic violators and to institute voluntary chemical tests for suspected drunken drivers. It ratified the Potomac River compact to end the oyster war with Virginia and approved Maryland's participation in a metropolitan Washington transit authority. An editorial in the Washington Post and Times Herald (April 6, 1959) referred to the legislative session as "lackluster" and "rather routine" in view of the General Assembly's failure to pass important parts of Tawes's program, including a rise in teachers' salaries.

The General Assembly's biennial short session (thirty days as opposed to ninety days on alternate years) of 1960 enacted Governor Tawes's $477,000,000 budget with only minor cuts. It managed to avoid additional taxes for this fiscal period by balancing the operating expenses with surplus funds. A large part of the budget, $147,000,000, was earmarked for improving school facilities, and compensation for veteran teachers was increased. A $330,000,000 expenditure to complete a 400-mile network of arterial highways by 1965 was also approved.

Among the casualties of the session was the controversial Walsh commission plan for reapportionment of representation in the General Assembly. The plan sought to increase the voting strength of Maryland's "big four" suburban counties in the Washington-Baltimore area. The Eastern Shore's nine counties with a population of 248,000 can under the existing electoral scheme outvote the "big four" counties which together have 1,400,000 residents.

Another bill which failed to pass provided for outlawing segregation in hotels and restaurants. A measure approved by the legislature, which would have empowered the state government to regulate savings and loan associations, was vetoed by Governor Tawes. Maryland remains the only state in the Union without such controls.

At the prompting of Maryland's Economic Development Commission, Governor Tawes in May 1960 invited the chief executives of ten states to meet in Annapolis to seek a regional solution to a common problem, the chronically depressed Appalachian belt where 10,000,000 people live in economic privation. Tawes pointed out that "the Appalachian area is economically as well as topographically one entity and has become our nation's No. 1 economic problem."

In his first press conference after assuming the office of governor, Tawes indicated that he might be interested in standing for re-election. "If we do a good job and the people want Tawes for a second term, perhaps I'll run," he said.

John Millard Tawes was married to Helen Avalynne Gibson on December 25, 1915. They have two children, Philip, who lives in Crisfield, and Jimmie Lee (Mrs. William R. Wilson, Jr.) who lives in Limestone, Maine, and several grandchildren. The governor is a short, stocky man and has thinning gray hair. He rises early and is generally working at his desk by 8 A.M. A Methodist, Tawes is president of the board of trustees of Immanuel Methodist Church of Crisfield and was a delegate to the general conference of the Methodist Church in San Francisco in 1952.

Tawes holds honorary LL.D. degrees from Washington College and the University of Maryland. He is a member and former president of the National Association of State Auditors, Comptrollers and Treasurers, a member of the board of trustees of Wesley Junior College in Dover, Delaware and of Dickinson College in Carlisle, Pennsylvania, and is on the board of directors of the McCready Memorial Hospital in Crisfield. Tawes belongs to the Eastern Shore Society of Baltimore, the Chesapeake Bay Fishing Association, and the Hibernian Society. He is an Elk, a Mason, and a Knight of Pythias. His clubs are the Rotary in Crisfield and the Scimitar in Baltimore, and he is a member of the Crisfield fire department.

Reference

Who's Who in America, 1960-61

THACH, JOHN SMITH Apr. 19, 1905-
United States Navy officer

Address: Hdqrs., Commander, Antisubmarine Force in the Pacific, Pearl Harbor, Hawaii

For the past two years Vice-Admiral John Smith Thach has been responsible for perfecting United States Navy defenses against possible attack on the American continent by missile-launching submarines. Before he took command of the antisubmarine defense force in the Pacific in January 1960, he was commander of Task Force Alfa, a mobile submarine detection fleet in the Atlantic based on plans submitted by Thach in 1958. Noted for thirty years as an expert aviator and imaginative strategist, Thach, during World War II, evolved the aerial maneuver known as the "Thach Weave" that has since become a standard feature of plane warfare.

John Smith Thach, the third of four children of James Harmon Thach, an insurance executive, and Jo Bocage (Smith) Thach, a former teacher, was born on April 19, 1905 in Pine Bluff, Arkansas. When John was four years old, the family moved to Fordyce, a nearby town. The boy often accompanied his father on hunting trips, and at Fordyce High School, he was a better athlete than scholar. He was in his third year in high school when his brother James Harmon Thach, Jr., now a retired vice-admiral, was appointed to the United States Naval Academy at Annapolis, Maryland. The appointment turned John's mind toward the seas: "I had never even given them a thought before," he has said (*Time,* September 1, 1958). "I knew so little I was under the impression that if you took a handful of ocean water it would actually look blue."

At the Naval Academy, which he entered in 1923, Thach continued his participation in sports as a quarterback and a member of the wrestling team. It was there that he acquired the nickname of "Little Jimmy" or "Jimmy," as he is still known to navy colleagues today. Thach was graduated and given an ensign's commission in June 1927. He remained at the academy for a short course in aviation before joining the battleship *Mississippi.* Transferred to the USS *California* in June 1928, he served aboard the ship until March of the following year, when he went for flight training to the Naval Air Station at Pensacola, Florida. He became a naval aviator in January 1930.

For the next two years Thach flew with the famous Fighting Squadron One, known as the High Hat Squadron, which was commanded by Arthur W. Radford. One of the flying feats for which the squadron was noted was the formation in which nine planes, their wing tips tied together with manila rope, maneuvered in loops and snap rolls, and taxied into the field without breaking the lines. The High Hats performed all the stunt flying in the 1931 film *Hell Divers* that starred Clark Gable.

Fascinated with flying, Thach soon won recognition as one of the Navy's top aerial gunnery experts. For two years he was a test pilot of experimental aircraft at the Naval Air Base in Hampton Roads, Virginia. While on assignment (1934-36) with Patrol Squadron Nine, USS *Wright,* he flew the Navy's experimental seaplane XP2H-1, then the second largest in the world, on a nonstop twenty-five-hour test flight from Norfolk, Virginia to the Panama Canal. For the feat, he was commended by the Chief of Naval Operations.

After serving a year with Scouting Squadron Six-B and two years with Patrol Squadron Five-F, based at the Fleet Air Base in Coco Solo, Canal Zone, Thach became gunnery officer of Fighting Squadron Three. For his outstanding skill in aerial gunnery and for his achievements in training other pilots in plane warfare from 1939 to 1940, he received a Letter of Commendation. During this period Thach evolved new fighter plane tactics that substituted a two-plane weave pattern for the traditional, but less efficient, three-plane formation.

In command of Fighting Squadron Three when the Pearl Harbor attack occurred, Thach sailed into the Pacific aboard the USS *Saratoga* and, when that carrier was torpedoed, moved to the USS *Lexington.* On February 20, 1942 his squadron rose from the *Lexington* to meet enemy bombers that attacked the carrier in the Coral Sea. Using the "Thach Weave" for the first time, American planes shot down nineteen of twenty enemy fighters. For his part in this engagement, Thach received the Navy Cross. Some weeks later he led the Lexington air group in an attack on Japanese who were landing at Salamaua and Lae, New Guinea; in June 1942 he participated in the battle of Midway

VICE-ADM. JOHN SMITH THACH

Island. For exceptionally meritorious service during the first six months of the war, Thach received the Distinguished Service Medal in September 1942.

New aerial techniques developed by Thach proved so successful that he was recalled to Pearl Harbor to instruct Air Force and Navy pilots in their use. He also taught those tactics to new pilots at the Naval Operational Training Command in Jacksonville, Florida. In his next position as Air Operations Officer with the Fast Carrier Task Force, Thach designed a method of "blanket attack" to prevent enemy planes from leaving their airfields and bombing American troops invading the Phillipines. The method was used successfully in 1,000 air campaigns against Japanese airfields in that area. Thach also evolved Task force defense techniques against kamikaze attacks, with the result that, during the last two months of the war, not one carrier was exploded by the suicidal pilots of these diving planes. He was awarded the Legion of Merit and the Silver and Bronze Star medals for his participation in this phase of World War II.

Advanced to the rank of captain on March 20, 1945, Thach served for two years after the war as director of training on the staff of the Chief of Naval Air Training. After working for two years as special assistant to the Chief of Naval Air Training, he assumed command of the USS *Sicily* in June 1950. During the Korean War, the carrier provided air support of American ground forces in many crucial battles, including the Inchon landing. Captain Thach received a Gold Star in lieu of a second Legion of Merit for his part in this campaign.

Thach next served on the staff of the commander of Carrier Division Seventeen from August 1951 to January 1952; as naval aide to the Assistant Secretary of the Navy for Air;

as commander of the USS *Franklin D. Roosevelt* from March 1953 to April 1954; and as commander of Naval Air Bases, Sixth Naval District, with headquarters at Jacksonville, Florida. In August 1955 he was designated senior naval member of the weapons systems evaluations group in the Office of the Assistant Secretary of Defense, Research, and Development in Washington, D.C. He became a rear admiral in the United States Navy on November 1, 1955.

A new phase of Thach's career began in July 1957 when he took over command of Carrier Division Sixteen. As one of four Atlantic division commanders in the Navy's Hunter-Killer Force (HUKFOR), Thach applied his experience and ingenuity to the increasingly important problem of antisubmarine warfare. In response to a call from Chief of Naval Operations Arleigh Burke, he submitted a plan for a permanent floating task force that could experiment with new antisubmarine defense systems. His idea was adopted, and on March 24, 1958 Thach became commander of Task Group Alfa. The 5,000-man force, comprising the aircraft carrier *Valley Forge,* eight destroyers, two submarines, planes, a helicopter squadron, and magnetic and sonar detection equipment, first put out into the Atlantic Ocean in June 1958.

The major purpose of the exercises that Task Group Alfa has conducted in the Atlantic is to experiment with new devices and techniques for instant detection of unidentified submarines. The defense function of the mobile fleet has become crucial in an age of atomic-powered submarines that can launch nuclear warheads attached to guided or ballistic missiles. Thach has observed that every point on the American continent is within 1,500-mile missile range of such atomic underwater craft, which travel much faster and can stay submerged longer than ordinary submarines.

Although the fleet is equipped with such new weapons as atomic depth bombs, rocket-propelled torpedoes, and underwater missiles, it still lacks a detection device as infallible in water as radar is in air. "I am led to conclude that if the Russians had the potential of attack today with missile-firing subs, we'd be in trouble," Thach has said (*This Week,* November 9, 1958). "We could not stop enough of them."

In January 1960 Thach took command of the antisubmarine force in the Pacific. He sees his present task as one of forcing enemy submarines to lie offshore far enough to reduce their range and make it impossible for them to hit targets in the United States. Thach was promoted to the temporary rank of vice-admiral in January 1960.

While Thach was stationed in San Diego, California in the 1930's, he was married to Madalyn Jones. They have two sons, John Smith, Jr., an experimental psychologist, and William Leland. Thach is six feet tall and weighs about 160 pounds. Often referred to as "one of the Navy's most decorated pilots," he has been awarded, in addition to his other decorations, the Gold Star in lieu of the second Navy Cross; the Presidential Unit Citation; the Navy Unit Commendation; the American Defense Service Medal; the Asiatic-Pacific Campaign Medal; the Occupation Service Medal; the National Defense Service Medal; the Korean Service Medal; the United Nations Service Medal; and the Philippine Liberation Ribbon.

References

Time 71:21 Ap 7 '58 por; 72:9+ S 1 '58 pors

THALER, WILLIAM J(OHN) Dec. 4, 1925- Physicist

Address: b. Field Projects Branch, Office of Naval Research, Department of the Navy, Washington, D.C.; h. 1621 Tilton Dr., Silver Spring, Md.

Chief of the field projects branch of the Office of Naval Research, William J. Thaler has invented a monitoring system that can detect nuclear explosions and rocket launchings thousands of miles away. This recent major American scientific achievement has already proved its value in tracking Russian and American satellites. Its supporters believe that it can be used to extend the present warning time in case of an intercontinental ballistic missile attack, and to detect violations of a nuclear test ban if the United States and the Soviet Union reach an agreement.

Described as a "technological marvel," Tepee radar (for Thaler's Project) is still in its experimental stage. Dr. Thaler, who has dismissed the possibility of any insuperable technical obstacles, believes that a system capable of reliable detection over intercontinental ranges is feasible. His optimism is shared by naval officials who plan to set up the most powerful radio transmitter in the world to serve as a key component in the Tepee detection network. In the fall of 1960 Thaler accepted a professorship at Georgetown University in Washington, D.C., and announced his plans to leave the Office of Naval Research in about eighteen months.

Born on December 4, 1925 in Baltimore, Maryland, William John Thaler is one of the five sons of Thomas Joseph and the former Catherine L. (Russanowski) Thaler. His father was in the plumbing and heating supply business which his twin brother Joseph now heads. The oldest brother George is a professor of electrical enigneering; Thomas is a linguist, and Lawrence is a chemist.

Nothing in his early background indicated that Bill Thaler would become a scientific celebrity. He did not read avidly in the literature of science nor did he tinker in any homemade laboratory. Thaler attended St. James Parochial School and Loyola High School, where he majored in Greek and Latin and participated in debating, glee club, and the Gregorian choir. He was also a tennis star, who established his reputation at the age of thirteen, when he won the Middle-Atlantic Boys Tennis Championship. During his teens he won the Maryland State doubles championship five times.

WILLIAM J. THALER

After his graduation from high school in 1943, Thaler enlisted in the Air Force cadet program, but was not called up until July 1944. Meanwhile he enrolled at Loyola College in Baltimore as a science major and was able to complete his freshman year. During 1944-45 he studied at several colleges under the cadet program, but he returned to Loyola when he received his service discharge in November 1945. In his extracurricular activities he participated in tennis, basketball, and track and was a member of the mathematics and physics clubs. When he took his Bachelor of Science degree in 1947 Thaler was awarded two gold medals, in theology and psychology, respectively.

Continuing with his studies in physics, Thaler accepted a research assistantship at Catholic University (Washington, D.C.). "Physics appealed to me," the young scientist reports, "because it is an exact science based on mathematical theories and calculations. . . . Two plus two equals four . . . in the social sciences, two plus two might equal five because of emotional or a host of other factors that might enter into it" (New York *Times*, September 13, 1959). He received his master's degree in 1949 and the Ph.D. degree two years later. His doctoral dissertation was entitled *The Absorption and Dispersion of Sound in Oxygen as a Function of the Frequency-Pressure Ratio* and was published by the Catholic University of America Press in 1952.

Scientists at the Office of Naval Research (the Navy's organization for promoting basic research projects through the colleges and universities) recognized Thaler's "unusual amount of talent and creative ability . . . and imagination" while he was still doing graduate work in ultrasonics. In April 1951, with his doctoral requirements completed, Thaler accepted a job as physicist with the acoustics branch of the Office of Naval Research. A year later he was transferred to the field projects branch where

THALER, WILLIAM J.—*Continued*

he has concentrated on the planning and execution of tests of the effects of nuclear weapons. Thaler has participated in every firing of nuclear weapons, including the first hydrogen explosion.

Dr. Thaler was appointed chief of the field projects branch in 1955. He has described his bureau as a "kind of hush-hush, free-wheeling, idea group specializing to some extent in the bizarre" (New York *Times*, September 13, 1959). His successful handling of Project Argus, "one of the biggest and most ungainly scientific experiments ever performed," in the summer of 1958 catapulted him into a prominent position. Thaler supervised naval operations in this vast project in which three atomic bombs were detonated 300 miles over the South Atlantic. This created a shell of electrons that enveloped the earth for several days. The results yielded invaluable information on the earth's magnetic field and the radiation belt of the upper atmosphere.

The design for Project Tepee, the code name for Thaler's Project, originated in the summer of 1957, when the scientist first conceived the idea of detecting distant nuclear bomb tests and missile firings with radio signals. Dismissing his achievement with a casual "I don't know why someone didn't think of it before," Thaler utilized and combined basic information on ionized gases and reflected radio signals. Scientists had long known of the existence of backscatter, which results "when a low-frequency radio signal is bounced around the world. While most of the signal's energy propagates forward, a fraction is scattered back to the transmitter as it is deflected off the ionosphere and the earth. . . . From Thaler's own work in plasma physics [the study of the behavior of gases at temperatures of thousands of millions of degrees], he deduced that the hot gases of a rocket exhaust (and the bases of a nuclear fireball) are in reality tiny ionospheres, composed of the same electrically charged particles" (*Newsweek*, August 1, 1959).

The first test of Thaler's theory came in the late summer of 1957 when he used borrowed radio equipment to tune in on atomic firings in the Nevada desert. Although these results were inconclusive, Thaler, with the backing of scientists in government and industry, attempted to monitor the Cape Canaveral rocket launchings. He faced endless obstacles, for firing schedules were classified and Thaler received no information about them; furthermore, he had to readapt his monitoring equipment and obtain federal permission to use certain radio frequencies. But on November 8, 1957 Thaler was successful in detecting a Polaris missile test and in taking a photographic record of radio back-scattering from its exhaust.

This initial success brought Project Tepee an appropriation of $400,000 for research in 1958. With relatively simple and inexpensive equipment, placed within the continental boundaries of the United States, Thaler and his associates successfully detected high-altitude thermonuclear explosions in the South Pacific, the Argus Project in the South Atlantic, and Soviet missile and satellite firings. They claim that the monitoring system can pinpoint the location of missile-launching sites and judge the success or failure of a rocket. Enthusiasts believe that Tepee could be developed into a complete weapons system capable of doubling the present fifteen-minute warning in the event of a Russian missile attack. Unlike ordinary radar which cannot "see" below the curvature of the earth, the new system's radio frequency permits a view over the horizon and, under the right conditions, around the globe. Tepee stations, which are relatively low-powered and cheap, could be used to supplement radar stations which are already in existence and comprise the greater part of the United States defense network.

Authorities differ on the comparable advantages and disadvantages of Project Tepee and Project Midas, a rival missile detection system. They point out that although Tepee seems to be simpler and cheaper than Midas, it is more vulnerable to jamming and more open to the deceptions of decoys. Furthermore, Tepee seems unable to track a missile with the success of the Midas system.

Despite Thaler's youth and the brevity of his career, he has several significant articles to his credit published in the *Physical Review, Bulletin of the American Physical Society, American Journal of Physics* and the *Journal of Applied Physics*. He is chairman of the Navy's Special Weapons Effects Test Planning Group and his professional organizations are the American Physical Society, Acoustical Society of America and Sigma Xi. Thaler received a reward for co-ordinating Argus and the Navy gave him the Superior Accomplishment Award for Tepee's "entirely new theory of the greatest importance to national defense."

Black-haired and green-eyed, Bill Thaler is six feet tall and weighs 185 pounds. His religion is Roman Catholic, and he has no political affiliation. Thaler is married to the former Barbara Jane Jarnagin of San Francisco, who was a graduate student at Catholic University before her marriage to the scientist on June 16, 1951. The couple has three sons and a daughter, ranging in age from one to seven years. Thaler still plays a good game of tennis, drives a Volkswagen, watches television, and enjoys listening to recordings of folk singers.

Thaler's friends describe him "as the sort of fellow who does not care much about what other people think, so long as he is convinced he is right." He is dedicated to his work, although he could double his salary in private industry. "Making money is secondary," according to Thaler, ". . . [it] is not synonymous with success. I chose government because it seemed to me to offer the place for freedom of action in the scientific field" (New York *Times*, September 13, 1959).

References

N Y Herald Tribune p26 N 24 '60
N Y Times p4 Ag 8 '59 por
N Y Times Mag p34 S 13 '59 por
Sat Eve Post 233:38+ N 19 '60 por
Time 74:45 Ag 17 '59 por
U S News 47:23 Ag 24 '59

American Men of Science vol I (1955)

THOMAS, JOHN (CURTIS) Mar. 3, 1941- Track and field athlete

Address: b. Boston University, Boston, Mass.; h. 29 Field St., Cambridge 38, Mass.

At the age of seventeen, John Thomas, then a freshman at Boston University, electrified track and field enthusiasts when he established a new world record for the high jump by leaping 7 feet 1¼ inches at Madison Square Garden on February 21, 1959. On May 21, 1960 Thomas soared 7 feet 1¾ inches at Briggs Field in Cambridge, Massachusetts, capturing the world's outdoor high jump record. It marked the fifth successive outdoor meet in which Thomas had broken the 7-foot barrier in 1960 and the twenty-second time that he had cleared 7 feet, indoors and out. He returned to jumping in January 1960 after a severe injury to his left foot, with which he takes off, had interrupted his career for nine months.

Sports writers have predicted that Thomas will clear about 7 feet 4 inches in the future, but even if Thomas were to retire on the strength of his past record, he would leave an indelible mark on the track and field world as the first athlete to clear 7 feet with consistency. Meanwhile, he had placed himself on the road to Rome and the 1960 Summer Olympics. There, contrary to expectations, he came in third, after two Russians. He holds the Track Writers Association trophies as the outstanding athlete of the 1959 and 1960 indoor seasons.

John Curtis Thomas, the son of Curtis and Ida Kate (Shanks) Thomas, was born on March 3, 1941 in Boston, Massachusetts. His father is a bus driver for Boston's Metropolitan Transit Authority. John and his brother, Warren Melvin, and his sister, Rita Louise, were reared in the Boston suburb of Cambridge where John attended elementary schools and Rindge Technical High School.

From Tom Duffy, his coach at Rindge Tech, John learned most of what he knows about high jumping. Duffy, for instance, urged him to switch from an old-fashioned belly-roll jumping style to the straddle roll he uses today. The Cambridge coach imparted to John some of his own dedication to track and field, convincing him that he might become a really great jumper if he would work consistently toward this goal. When, in his junior year at Rindge in 1956, John thought of switching to tennis after he had had trouble in making a 6 feet 1 inch jump, Duffy persuaded him to stay in track. At Rindge Tech John belonged to the projection club, the safety patrol, the school newspaper, and the Boy Scouts. He was graduated in 1958.

It took him a year to acquire the straddle-roll technique; sometimes, almost in despair of learning the new style, he reverted to the belly roll. But, Duffy recalls, "he was always fighting to be the best." Before he was out of high school Thomas jumped 6 feet 8¼ inches and earned a trip to Japan with a touring AAU track and field group. There he took the Japanese high jump title with a leap of 6 feet 10⅝ inches. In the autumn of 1958, with the help of

Wide World

JOHN THOMAS

an athletic scholarship, Thomas entered Boston University, where he came under the guidance of field events coach Ed Flanagan.

The listed indoor high jump record at that time was 6 feet 10¾ inches. In his first competitive meet as a college student, Thomas topped the world's indoor record with a leap of 6 feet 11 inches at Dartmouth College on January 10, 1959. He repeated this feat a week later when he jumped 6 feet 11¾ inches at the Boston Knights of Columbus Games. On January 31 at the Millrose Games in New York, Thomas appeared to have cleared 7 feet—a previously unheard-of world indoor mark. The record was disallowed, however, because harried officials had not measured the height of the bar immediately after the jump.

Thomas jumped 6 feet 10¾ inches at the Boston Athletic Association Games on February 7, and the following week cleared 7 feet officially at the New York Athletic Club Games of February 14. Seven days later he successfully set the new world high jump mark at 7 feet 1¼ inches at the National AAU meet in New York. In a March 4 competition against Tufts College he won with a 6 feet 11¾ inch jump. He had also broken two Andover Cage records on February 18, 1959 when he leaped 6 feet 3¼ inches.

The Boston prodigy was stopped abruptly in his tracks when his left foot—from which he propels himself over the high jump bar—was severely injured in an elevator accident on March 24, 1959. The injury, which might have ended his career, was repaired through plastic surgery and skin grafting in three operations at the Massachusetts Memorial Hospital. When he left the hospital on May 17, Thomas took things easy for a while. Then he swam and sunned a bit at a New Hampshire Boy Scout camp and, back in Boston, resumed some tenta-

THOMAS, JOHN—*Continued*

tive running and weight lifting. On August 26, he jumped for the first time since the accident and then gradually regained his previous seven-foot level. Thomas, who had dropped out of school after the accident, entered his second freshman semester in September 1959.

Thomas jumped competitively for the first time since the accident at the Boston Knights of Columbus Games on January 16, 1960. He won the event with a leap of 7 feet ½ inch. From then on he slowly pushed his high jump up, seemingly without undue effort. On January 30, he added a quarter-inch to his world mark with a jump of 7 feet 1½ inches at the Millrose Games in New York. He tied this mark the following week at the Boston Athletic Association meet and cleared 7 feet at the Philadelphia *Inquirer* Relays on February 12.

Eight days later Thomas boosted the world record to 7 feet 2 inches at the National AAU championship competition in New York. He cleared 7 feet ½ inch at the I.C. 4-A meet on March 5, and he leaped 7 feet 2½ inches at the Chicago *Daily News* Relays on March 11. The next day, Thomas was so weary after this record-breaking jump that he was content to win the Greater Boston indoor intercollegiate high jump by taking off to a mere 6 feet 3¾ inches. He also broke the National Collegiate mark and tied the American outdoor mark by jumping 7 feet ½ inch in a dual meet between Boston University and Dartmouth College on April 23, 1960.

In the April 30 outdoor competition at the University of Pennsylvania Thomas chalked up a 7 feet 1½ inch score. On May 21, 1960 he soared to a world outdoor high jump record at Briggs Field, Cambridge, Massachusetts during the New England intercollegiate track and field championships when he leaped 7 feet 1¾ inches. The scene of this triumph is only a few blocks away from his home, and he had jumped there as a schoolboy only a few years before.

Later, he broke his own world outdoor record on two occasions. On June 24 he soared 7 feet 2 inches and on July 1, 7 feet 3¾ inches.

The key to Thomas' style is the powerful spring in his left heel. This he has developed through hours of lying on his back and hoisting 350-pound weights with his legs. He approaches the high jump bar from the left, using seven progressively longer strides. He springs off the left heel, kicks with his right foot, and rolls over the bar. Thomas appears remarkably unruffled in an event notorious for its psychological stress effects. At some level the bar becomes a frightening thing for most jumpers, but for Thomas the butterflies go away, he says, after the first jump.

A major factor responsible for Thomas' consistently excellent performance is his training program. He trains six days a week, working for an hour and three-quarters at a time. On some days he sprints and walks in addition to doing weight lifting and calisthenic exercises. Flanagan describes the training routine as body building, not to develop large muscles, but to build mobility, suppleness, speed and instant dynamic action.

"It would be an honor just to go," Thomas once said of the 1960 Summer Olympic Games in Rome. In the course of his short but spectacular career, he has won many other honors. Named as the outstanding performer of the 1959 and 1960 indoor seasons by the Track Writers Association, he has also received trophies as the outstanding performer in the 1959 and 1960 Millrose Games, the 1960 Boston Knights of Columbus Games, the 1960 Boston Athletic Association meet, the 1959 New York Athletic Club competition, the 1959 National Amateur Athletic Union games, the 1960 Chicago *Daily News* Relays, and the 1960 I. C. 4-A games.

Thomas was an honorary sheriff of Middlesex County, Massachusetts in 1959, and he is a chairman of the National Multiple Sclerosis Society's 1960 campaign. In addition, Thomas is a scout leader in the Boy Scouts of America and belongs to the National Association for the Advancement of Colored People. Thomas attends the Ebenezer Baptist Church. His hobbies are scouting, football, basketball, and dancing. He enjoys listening to progressive jazz records and occasionally plays card games like kitty whist and cribbage.

The sturdy Negro athlete is six feet five-and-a-half inches tall and weighs about 195 pounds. "He is an easy-moving fellow and carries himself with a shy sort of dignity," a *Sports Illustrated* (January 25, 1960) writer reported. "Although Thomas is exceptionally reserved with people he doesn't know, he is outgoing and mixes easily with his fellow students and people he knows well." Watching Thomas make higher and higher leaps, people frequently ask him how high he thinks he will go. To which he replies: "There is only one way for a high jumper to go—up."

References

Christian Sci Mon p15 Mr 6 '59 por
N Y Times p44 Ap 7 '59
N Y World-Telegram p30 F 25 '59
Sports Illus 12:14+ Ja 25 '60 por
Time 73:40 F 2 '59 por

THOMSON, ROY (HERBERT) June 5, 1894- Canadian and British newspaper publisher; television executive

Address: b. Kemsley House, Grays Inn Rd., London W.C. 1, England; 20 North Bridge, Edinburgh 1, Scotland; Thomson Bldg., 425 University Ave., Toronto, Ontario, Canada; h. 22 Braid Ave., Edinburgh, Scotland

Since becoming chairman and majority stockholder of Kemsley Newspapers Ltd. in August 1959, the Canadian-born financier-publisher Roy Thomson has controlled one of the largest newspaper enterprises in Great Britain. His publications in England and Wales include three London Sunday papers, eleven provincial dailies, and several weeklies. In Scotland, Thomson has owned the Edinburgh *Scotsman* since 1953, and since 1957 he has been the licensee for Scottish commercial television. In Canada, where he also prospered in radio and television undertakings, the Thomson Company Ltd. operates twenty-eight newspapers; in the United States it has six rural weeklies and one Florida daily.

Roy Herbert Thomson is of Scottish descent through his father, Herbert Thomson, who was a barber by trade; his mother, the former Alice Maud Coombs, was an Englishwoman from Somerset. One of two sons—his brother Carl Norman is deceased—Roy Thomson was born on June 5, 1894 in what has been described as a "seedy" midtown district of Toronto, Ontario. He attended the Church Street public elementary school and Jarvis Collegiate in Toronto.

At fourteen Roy Thomson started work as a clerk for $5 a week. He was later enrolled for a while in a Toronto business school and became successively a salesman, farmer, stenographer, and bookkeeper. By the time he was twenty, through investing his savings he had reportedly won and lost $20,000. Rejected for overseas service in World War I because of defective eyesight, he was assigned to the Canadian Militia, in which he held the rank of lieutenant.

For about twelve years after the war Thomson was engaged in a variety of occupations, including that of automobile-parts jobber. While selling radio sets during the depression in a somewhat remote part of Ontario, he realized that his sales would increase if reception were improved. He bought a transmitter, acquired a license to a broadcasting station, and was soon selling advertising time on the air as well as radio sets. His first radio station, the beginning of the chain to be known as the Northern Broadcasting Company, was CFCH in North Bay, Ontario in 1931. Two other Ontario stations followed closely: CKGB in Timmins in 1933 and CJKL in Kirkland Lake in 1934. Thomson acquired the Timmins weekly *Press* in 1934 and within three years had turned it into a daily.

Together with Ontario's Senator Rupert Davies, in 1942 Thomson formed the Brookland Company Ltd., operating radio stations CHEX and CKWS in Peterborough and Kingston, Ontario, respectively. Two years later he expanded his Ontario newspaper interests by acquiring the Galt *Reporter,* the Woodstock *Sentinel-Review,* the Welland *Tribune,* and the Sarnia *Observer.* Before the end of the 1940's he added several more papers in Ontario and two in Saskatchewan. In 1950 he bought a city of Quebec daily, the *Chronicle-Telegraph,* and the Port Arthur (Ontario) *News Chronicle.*

At present in Canada the Thomson Company operates nineteen papers in Ontario, two in Saskatchewan, one in Quebec, four in British Columbia, and two in Prince Edward Island. None can be regarded as large. The Sudbury (Ontario) *Daily Star* had the highest circulation—28,422 in 1959. In the main, the Thomson papers have been given uniform format, but editorial policy has been left largely to local discretion. "My papers are community papers," Thomson explains. "It would be foolish for me to try to tell an editor in . . . Moose Jaw what his community needs; he lives there, knows the people he serves and what they should have in the way of editorial interpretation" (quoted by

Bassano, London

ROY THOMSON

Gwyn Kinsey, *Saturday Night,* October 31, 1953). Thomson entered the Canadian commercial television field in 1951.

Thomson liked to pass the colder months of the year aboard his yacht off the coast of Florida, and in the spring of 1952, to give himself "something to do in the winter," he bought the St. Petersburg (Florida) *Independent.* To this evening and Sunday newspaper he shortly added six small rural Southern weeklies. In May 1953 he started the publication in London, England of the *Canada Review,* a weekly paper devoted to news of Canada.

A major development in Roy Thomson's career came in the late summer of 1953, when he acquired control of the long-established and dignified Edinburgh morning newspaper, the *Scotsman,* and its companion publications, the Edinburgh *Evening Dispatch* and the *Weekly Scotsman.* In gradually changing the conservative *Scotsman,* an influential voice of Scottish nationalism, Thomson put news on the front page instead of advertisements and increased the coverage of British Commonwealth affairs. The new editor, Alastair Dunnett, however, was given most of the responsibility for modernizing the paper, while Thomson concentrated on the business end. According to *Maclean's Magazine* (October 25, 1958), the circulation of the *Scotsman* "jumped ten thousand under Thomson's rule to a daily 65,000." Thomson also now controls four weekly papers in the north of Scotland as well as the Edinburgh *TV Guide.*

With the acquisition of the *Scotsman,* Roy Thomson made Edinburgh his new permanent home ("I look on myself as a Scot," he has said. "I am going to live in Scotland and I am going to die in Scotland"). At the same time he began to transfer the control of his Canadian properties to his son, Kenneth Thomson. The transfer was completed in 1956, when

THOMSON, ROY—*Continued*

Kenneth became president of the Thomson Company and Roy Thomson took the title of the chairman of the board.

Meanwhile, in 1955 Thomson tried, unsuccessfully, to purchase the Toronto *Globe and Mail.* "In 1956," the *Manchester Guardian* noted, "he secured the licence to supply independent television to Scotland. He held a controlling interest, but his board included Lord Balfour of Inchrye and Sir Edward Stevenson. The contract was, in a memorable phrase, 'a permit to print your own money.'" The 1958 profit of Scottish Television Ltd. amounted to £1,282,939 before taxation; during the first five months of 1959 the profit was £712,736.

Directors of the Kemsley newspaper group, one of the largest in England, announced in July 1959 that they had accepted Roy Thomson's offer to buy the newspaper chain for $31,500,000. Viscount Kemsley (see *C.B.,* January 1951) accepted $14,000,000 for his majority holding and recommended to other shareholders a merger with Thomson's Scottish Television. A month later the Kemsley shareholders ratified an unusual agreement whereby Lord Kemsley purchased all ordinary shares in Scottish Television and Thomson became chairman of Kemsley Newspapers Ltd. The transaction gave Thomson control of four Sunday newspapers, eleven morning and evening papers outside London, and eight provincial weeklies.

The most distinguished among the Kemsley newspapers is the *Sunday Times,* which has a circulation of 832,657; it is not connected with the daily *The Times* (of London). A second Kemsley Sunday paper in London is the illustrated *Graphic,* with a circulation of 913,648. A third Kemsley Sunday paper, the *Empire News & Sunday Chronicle,* was later sold by Thomson. Kemsley dailies include the Manchester *Evening Chronicle,* the Sheffield *Telegraph,* the Cardiff *Western Mail,* and the Aberdeen *Press and Journal.* In 1958 the Kemsley group made a profit before taxes of $4,317,000. The total circulation of Thomson's papers in England, Wales, and Scotland is about 4,500,000.

As described in the *Manchester Guardian,* Roy Thomson is "above all, a financier" who "runs his papers mainly to make money." He is "not a flamboyant person. His manner is quiet. He is a bulky man and generally peers through his heavy glasses. He is of surprisingly equable temperament . . . without arrogance. He will talk freely to anyone, regardless of rank." Thomson is five feet ten inches in height and about 196 pounds in weight, and he has blue eyes and gray hair. In 1916 he was married to Edna Annis Irvine; he has been a widower since 1951. He has one son, Kenneth Roy, and two married daughters, Mrs. Irma Jacqueline Brydson and Mrs. Phyllis Audrey Campbell.

Among Thomson's clubs are the Caledonian in London, the National in Toronto, and the Vancouver in Vancouver. He is a Presbyterian, a Mason, and an Elk. His newspapers tend to take an independent position politically, but Thomson himself is a Conservative and in 1953 ran unsuccessfully as a Progressive Conservative candidate for the Canadian House of Commons.

References

Christian Sci Mon p14 Jl 24 '59
Macleans Mag 67:9+ Ja 1 '54 pors;
  71:30+ O 25 '58 por
Manchester Guardian p4 Jl 18 '59
N Y Times p19 Jl 17 '59
Newsweek 39:90+ My 5 '52; 54:52 Jl
  27 '59 por
Sat Night 69:19+ O 31 '53 por
Time 74:48 Jl 27 '59 por
Toronto Globe and Mail p1 Jl 18 '59 por
Canadian Who's Who, 1955-57
International Television Almanac, 1959
Who's Who, 1959
Who's Who in America, 1958-59
World Biography (1954)

THOREK, MAX

Mar. 10, 1880-Jan. 25, 1960 Surgeon; founded the American Hospital in Chicago (1908) and the International College of Surgeons (1935). See *Current Biography* (January) 1951.

Obituary

N Y Times p33 Ja 27 '60

THURBER, JAMES (GROVER)

Dec. 8, 1894- American humorist; cartoonist
Address: b. c/o The New Yorker, 25 W. 43d St., New York 36; h. West Cornwall, Conn.

NOTE: This biography supersedes the article which appeared in *Current Biography* in 1940.

When Americans think of the humorist James Thurber, they think of his drawings of dogs, men, and women; the nonsense essays and stories, such as "The Secret Life of Walter Mitty" and "If Grant had been Drinking at Appomattox"; and his long association with the *New Yorker* magazine. By 1960 he had also written and illustrated about two dozen books, including his best-selling reminiscences about the *New Yorker* editor, *The Years with Ross* (Little, 1959), and he had been the inspiration or author of several successful plays, including *A Thurber Carnival,* which opened on Broadway in 1960, and of several movies like *The Battle of the Sexes,* which was first exhibited in 1960.

Thurber's approach to the foibles of human nature, dogs, and the continual warfare between the sexes is often lethal. An endless reviser, he has been known to rewrite a work as many as twenty-five times. His almost complete blindness now prevents him from decorating his writings with cartoon doodling, but he continues his steady production of books, essays, and stories.

James Grover Thurber, the son of Charles Leander (later changed to Lincoln) and Mary Agnes (Fisher) Thurber, was born in Columbus, Ohio on December 8, 1894. He had an older brother, William, and a younger one, Robert. His father was a politician who was appointed to various posts, but was never elected to office. When he was six years old one of his brothers shot James with an arrow, and as a result, he lost the sight in his left eye. He attended public schools in Columbus and then entered Ohio State University in 1913. He has recorded his memories of his family and early friends in *My Life and Hard Times* (Harper, 1933).

Toward the end of World War I Thurber began serving as a code clerk with the United States State Department in Washington, D.C., and then at the American Embassy in Paris. He returned to Columbus in 1920 and became a reporter for the city's *Dispatch* and Columbus correspondent for the *Christian Science Monitor*. During 1924 and 1925 he was a reporter for the Paris and Riviera editions of the Chicago *Tribune* and began writing humorous sketches for the New York *Sunday World*, *Harper's Magazine*, New York *Herald Tribune*, and Kansas City *Star*. He moved to New York as a member of the staff of the New York *Evening Post* in 1925.

His friend E. B. White took Thurber to Harold W. Ross, the editor of the *New Yorker* magazine, to see if Ross would hire him. Thurber left the interview as managing editor, a position which he soon found uncongenial. He then became one of the writers of the *New Yorker's* "Talk of the Town" and "Notes and Comments" sections. Subsequently, he resigned from the staff, but continued to be a regular contributor of humorous essays and sketches to the magazine. These pieces, with their seemingly casual gibes, often amused the very people whom Thurber was insulting. He reviewed his memories of the *New Yorker* editor and his other associates in *The Years with Ross* (Little, 1959).

Thurber began in the late 1920's to write a series of books, many of which included stories, essays, and illustrations which had first appeared in the *New Yorker*. His first books, which appeared under the Harper imprint were: *Is Sex Necessary? or, Why Do You Feel the Way You Do* (1929), with E. B. White; *The Owl in the Attic and Other Perplexities* (1931); *The Seal in the Bedroom and Other Predicaments* (1932); *The Middle-Aged Man on the Flying Trapeze* (1935); and *Let Your Mind Alone!* (1937).

With the advent of World War II appeared his *The Last Flower; A Parable in Pictures* (Harper, 1939), an antiwar fable even more frightening in the atomic age. There followed *Fables for our Time, and Famous Poems Illustrated* (Harper, 1940); *My World—and Welcome to It* (Harcourt, 1942); *Men, Women and Dogs* (Harcourt, 1943); and *The White Deer* (Harcourt, 1945). Harcourt had also published two books by Thurber for children: *Many Moons* (1943) and *The Great Quillow* (1944).

Continuing to be prolific, Thurber wrote *The Thurber Carnival* (Harper, 1945) and *The Beast in Me and Other Animals; A New Collection of Pieces and Drawings About Hu-*

JAMES THURBER

man Beings and Less Alarming Creatures (Harcourt, 1948). There then followed a number of books published by Simon and Schuster: *The Thirteen Clocks* (1950); *The Thurber Album* (1952); *Thurber Country* (1953); *Thurber's Dogs; A Collection of the Master's Dogs, Written and Drawn, Real and Imaginary, Living and Long Ago* (1955); *Further Fables for our Time* (1956); and *The Wonderful O* (1957). Harper published his *Alarms and Diversions* in 1957.

Thurber has also been active as a dramatist. With Elliott Nugent he wrote *The Male Animal* (published in 1940 by Random House). *The Male Animal* was presented on Broadway in 1940 and was revived in 1952. Three of Thurber's stories were adapted for the stage in 1955 by Paul Ellwood and St. John Terrell and were produced in New York under the title, *Three by Thurber*. In 1960 *A Thurber Carnival*, when it opened on Broadway, received enthusiastic reviews. Excerpts from it were recorded by Columbia Records in the same year. For about two months before *A Thurber Carnival* closed in New York on November 26, 1960, Thurber appeared as himself in the show.

Movies have been based upon Thurber stories. Among those released were *Rise and Shine*, *Unicorn in the Garden*, *The Male Animal*, *The Secret Life of Walter Mitty* (with Danny Kaye), and *The Battle of the Sexes* (with Peter Sellers). An operatic version of *The Thirteen Clocks* was shown on television in 1954, and a dance adaptation of *The Last Flower* was performed by a French ballet company in 1959.

The drawing of Thurber's somewhat fanciful dogs, with their innocent, wide-eyed stares, began about 1920, Thurber explained to a *Life* (March 14, 1960) writer, as "a form of nervous relaxation—I did them swiftly, almost absently, and threw them away. It was years before I

THURBER, JAMES—*Continued*

learned to my astonishment that they could be sold. Then I tried to draw slowly and carefully but my colleague E. B. White put a stop to that. 'If you ever became good,' he said, 'you'd be mediocre.' I went back to rapidity."

His drawings were first published in *Is Sex Necessary?* (Harper, 1929), and later in the *New Yorker* and in his books. Thurber has also illustrated *In a Word* (Knopf, 1939), by M. S. Ernst; *Men Can Take it* (Random House, 1939), by E. Hawes; and *How to Raise a Dog* (Simon and Schuster, 1953), by J. R. Kinney and A. Honeycutt. He drew a series of murals for Tim Costello's Third Avenue saloon in Manhattan and has had various one-man shows, including those at the Valentine Gallery in New York in 1933 and at the Storran Gallery, London in 1937. His articles and sketches have appeared in many magazines, in addition to the *New Yorker*.

The humorist received an honorary Litt. D. degree from Kenyon College in 1950, an honorary L.H.D. degree from Williams College in 1951, and an honorary Litt. D. degree from Yale University in 1953. He belongs to the Dramatists' Guild, Authors' League of America, Phi Kappa Psi, and Sigma Delta Chi.

James Thurber was married to Althea Adams on May 20, 1922. They have one daughter, Rosemary. They were later divorced, and he was married to Helen Wismer on June 25, 1935. Thurber has white hair, except for a black streak in front, weighs 154 pounds, and is six feet one and a half inches tall. He once said: "Everyone thinks I look like the man I draw—bald and 5 foot 1. Actually, I draw the *spirit* of the man I am—and I'm a pussycat" (*Life*, March 14, 1960).

Having developed a cataract in his good eye, Thurber underwent five unsuccessful cataract operations in 1940 and 1941. Thus the eyesight in his right eye gradually failed, and he can see only lights and shadows. He no longer draws or types, but he dictates his stories and articles. In preparation is a book called "The Nightinghoul," which Thurber says is "about the people of a typical town called Americanapolis and their reaction to a mechanical monster who pecks away at the cornices of their public buildings" (*Life*, March 14, 1960). The sure-fire best sellers he would like to write would carry such titles as "How to Make Love and Money," "How to Tell Your Blessings from Your Burdens," and "How to Pass the Joneses at a Dogtrot."

References

N Y Herald Tribune Bk R p4 O 8 '50; p2 N 3 '57

National Cyclopaedia of American Biography current vol G (1943-46)

Thurber, J. My Life and Hard Times (1933); The Thurber Album (1952); The Years with Ross (1959)

Twentieth Century Authors (1942, First Supplement, 1955)

Who's Who, 1960

Who's Who in America, 1960-61

TIBBETT, LAWRENCE Nov. 16, 1896-July 15, 1960 Baritone singer for the Metropolitan Opera (1923-1950); created leading roles in Deems Taylor's *The King's Henchman* and *Peter Ibbetson* and in Louis Gruenberg's *The Emperor Jones;* sang almost every principal baritone role in the Italian and French repertories. See *Current Biography* (February) 1945.

Obituary

N Y Times p1+ Jl 16 '60

TRIGÈRE, PAULINE (trē jàre') Nov. 4, 1912- Designer

Address: b. 550 7th Ave., New York 18; h. 525 Park Ave., New York 21

One of the "big name" designers in the elegant occupation of designing clothes for the carriage trade, Pauline Trigère has three times won the Coty American Fashion Critics' Award. In October 1959 she became a member of the Coty Fashion Hall of Fame. She also holds the Neiman-Marcus Award and has been cited as "the most original designer" by NBC-TV's *Today* show. With her brother, Robert, she founded Trigère, Inc., in New York in 1942, a business which in 1958 grossed over $2,000,000.

Although Pauline Trigère was born in Paris, she has made her career in the United States, where she has lived since 1937. Each year she designs four collections of some eighty outfits in each, priced from $130 to $1,500. Although some of her creations may strike the beholder as conservative, Miss Trigère has actually pioneered in many fashions, including reversible coats and wool evening dresses.

Among the fashions that Miss Trigère has introduced are mobile collars, black dresses with sheer tops, sleeveless coats, inverted trumpet silhouettes, cape-collared coats, spiral jackets, and tunics. She receives her inspiration wherever she happens to be: at home, at a concert, at the theater, or at the opera. She scrawls her programs full with notes and sketches. Whatever their source, all her creations are notable for their understatement and restraint.

Pauline Trigère was born in Paris, France on November 4, 1912 to Alexandre and Cécile (Coriene) Trigère. She lived with her family in the back of her father's tailoring business in Place Pigalle, then still an artists' quarter of the city. At the age of ten Pauline could operate the Singer sewing machine and help her mother with custom tailoring for women. At fourteen, the clothes she made for herself to wear were the envy of her friends.

For a time she studied at Collège Jules Ferry, and then at Collège Victor Hugo in Paris, where she received the B.A. degree. While in school she worked in the salon of Martial et Armand on the Place Vendôme. In a short time she had mastered the subtleties of bias cut and fabric, a skill that distinguishes her creations today.

Following a marriage in 1929, and separation, she moved with her mother, brother, and two sons to New York. She worked briefly for Ben

Gershel and then for Hattie Carnegie. In 1942, with her brother, she started her own dress design business in a loft and with only three sewing machines. Robert took his sister's collection of twelve outfits in a huge valise and traveled by cross-country bus to leading stores. The entire collection was sold to department store executives who immediately recognized her intimate knowledge of French high fashion and her talent for design. Buyers sought out Miss Trigère in her tiny loft, where she had hung her gowns on electric light fixtures for lack of better facilities. The creations waved in the breeze as the door opened and shut.

When, in 1949, Miss Trigère was named winner of the seventh annual Coty American Fashion Critics' Award, the highest honor in her profession, her citation read: "For her high and original talent in fashion design . . . and for her imaginative ideas which have set major trends." In 1950 she received the Neiman-Marcus Award and in 1951 a Return Award from the Fashion Critics.

In 1959 Miss Trigère was named a winner of the Fashion Critics Award for the third time, and thus became eligible for the Coty Fashion Hall of Fame. She is one of only four American designers to be so honored by the fashion critics. (The other three designers are the late Claire McCardell, Norman Norell, and James Galanos.) In the same year she also won the Cotton Award, the textile industry's annual salute to the designer who has made the best use of cotton during the year. Mayor Robert F. Wagner of New York City presented her with the award. "Cotton is a fabric to which you can talk," she says in her throaty voice with a marked French accent. "It is pliable. . . . When it comes to designing, the fabric is my master. I can't draw, I can't paint, I can't even sew, but put a piece of fabric in my hands and magic happens" (*Christian Science Monitor,* May 18, 1959).

Described by her friends as "vivacious, with an earthy sense of humor, unpretentious, generous, untrammeled," Pauline Trigère experiences, she says, "sheer joy from seeing something new coming out of a piece of material." Her production associate has said: "She will put a bolt of material on a model and cut, just getting the feel of the cloth. I have never in my thirty-five years' experience seen another designer do this."

Pauline Trigère, who became a United States citizen in 1944, once said: "Despite my love for France, I have found my niche here. The U.S. has been wonderfully kind to me." She lives with her mother and her two grown sons, Jean Pierre and Philippe. She is an active Democrat and often stages benefit fashion shows and serves on fund-raising committees for the Philharmonic Pension Fund, Visiting Nurses Service Association, the Federation of Jewish Philanthropies, the Damon Runyon Fund, and others.

Recently, Miss Trigère began studying yoga and also became an enthusiastic gardener. "Since

PAULINE TRIGÈRE

I have my garden and since I do Yoga," she said, "something has happened to me. I look better. I feel better. I can even stand on my head alone! That bathes the brain, like shaking a bottle" (New York *Post,* May 3, 1959). She gardens weekends at her Connecticut home, and once a week, even after a strenuous sixteen-hour working day, entertains informally at her New York apartment. In the kitchen the guests consume the specialties that Miss Trigère claims she can cook to perfection. They are also free to admire her arrangements of yellow flowers in an apartment keyed to colors of beige and gray and white and decorated with crystal and red glass accessories.

Pauline Trigère has blue eyes, ash-blonde hair, weighs 125 pounds, and is five feet four inches tall. Her hobbies are dancing, cooking, moving furniture around, gardening, reading, interior decorating, going to art galleries, the theater, and concerts.

Speaking on the television program *Night Beat* in April 1958, Miss Trigère said that she thought men's clothing is too conservative. She would like to see them wearing cardigans without collars and lapels. For the April 1959 issue of *Gentlemen's Quarterly* she designed fashions for men which, according to Eugenia Sheppard (New York *Herald Tribune,* April 27, 1959) the men promptly vetoed as "too faddish."

Surprisingly, if Miss Trigère had her way, American women would buy fewer and more lasting clothes. She recommends that women own two suits, one in black and one in gray, and that they express their love for novelty in a gay scarf, blouse, handbag, shoes, or gloves. Accessories, she believes, should be geared to one's own individuality. She advises women to read the fashion news, but with some caution. She says: "Just because a new hemline looks

TRIGÈRE, PAULINE—*Continued*

well on a model in a photograph there is no reason to think it will look well on you. The smart woman is her own boss in these matters."

References

McCalls 80:70 Jl '53 por
N Y Post Mag p5 Je 10 '56 pors; p2 My 3 '59 pors
Washington (D.C.) Post p5S Ja 15 '50
Who's Who in America, 1958-59
Who's Who of American Women (1958-59)

TRIMBLE, VANCE H(ENRY) July 6, 1913- Journalist

Address: b. c/o Scripps-Howard Newspaper Alliance, 1013 13th St., N.W., Washington, D.C.; h. 3510 Woodbine St., Chevy Chase 15, Md.

Washington news editor Vance H. Trimble of the Scripps-Howard Newspaper Alliance gained recognition as an ace reporter on national affairs in 1960 by winning journalism's "triple crown" for his series of articles exposing widespread payroll nepotism and secrecy in Congress. His honors were the Raymond Clapper Memorial Award for outstanding work by a Washington newsman, a Sigma Delta Chi award, and the Pulitzer Prize for distinguished reporting of national affairs.

With about ten years of experience as a reporter behind him, Vance Trimble had found his Washington desk job confining. An itch to investigate hints of irregularities in Congressional payrolls set him to work on his own time combing through files on Capitol Hill. His stories charging that at least one out of every five members of Congress had relatives

Wide World

VANCE H. TRIMBLE

on his staff brought about the Senate decision to publicize payroll information that had been kept secret since 1946.

The second of three sons, Vance Henry Trimble was born July 6, 1913 in Harrison, Arkansas to Guy L. Trimble and Josie (Crump) Trimble. He was reared in Arkansas and Oklahoma, where his father practised law. His older brother, Guy, Jr., an oil-well driller, lives in Wewoka, Oklahoma, and his younger brother, John C., is a real estate dealer in Houston, Texas.

While a freshman in high school at Okemah, Oklahoma, Trimble talked the editor of the *Daily Leader* into giving him small local reporting assignments, which he covered after school and on Saturdays. The editor for whom he worked recently described him as "a spindle-shanked newspaper boy who never wanted to quit work." The following year Trimble's family moved to Wewoka, a town in the next county. As a cub reporter for the Wewoka *Times-Democrat*, Vance worked before and after school, covering courthouse offices and serving as sports editor. He also found time to edit the high school paper. After he was graduated in 1931, he became a full-time *Times-Democrat* reporter for several months before moving on to a job as news editor of the Maud (Oklahoma) *Daily Enterprise*.

During the Depression, the possibility of earning even $2.50 a week more at a new job kept many journalists moving around the newspaper circuit. In 1932 Trimble became a desk man on the Seminole (Oklahoma) *Morning News*, but was fired two weeks later to make way for a former employee. Over the next few years he worked on several Oklahoma papers: the Seminole *Producer*, the Seminole *Reporter*, the Wewoka *Morning News*, the Shawnee *Morning News*, and the Muskogee *Times-Democrat and Phoenix*. He served as news editor on the Okmulgee *Times* for one year and as desk man and financial writer on the Tulsa *Tribune* for almost as long a period.

Trimble next went to Texas, where he became a reporter and desk man for the Beaumont *Enterprise* in 1937. After a few months he was hired by the Port Arthur *News* as a telegraph editor, and remained there until he joined the staff of the Scripps-Howard paper, Houston *Press*, as a copy editor, in 1939. Six months later Trimble was promoted to the post of city editor. When World War II began he was drafted into the United States Army signal corps as a private and sent to Camp Beale, California, where he edited the camp newspaper. After serving in the Army for twenty months, he was discharged in the rank of staff sergeant.

Returning to the Houston *Press*, Trimble became a special writer on many major beats. He also set up a promotion department and pioneered in radio and TV coverage of news from the *Press* city room. He served as managing editor of the *Press* from 1950 to 1955, during which time the newspaper attained its greatest expansion of circulation. In the summer of 1955 Trimble became news editor of the Washington, D.C. bureau of the Scripps-Howard Newspaper Alliance.

Trimble found his 3 to 11 P.M. desk job confining and chafed at being just another anonymous Washington newsman. He was anxious, also, to investigate hints of a new wave of nepotism in Congress. Beginnng in the fall of 1958, and working on his own time, he spent several hours a day searching through available Congressional payrolls, checking names and possible relationships. He also interviewed many of the people involved and photographed them.

The first detailed story establishing that one out of five members of Congress had relatives on his staff appeared in January 1959 just as the new Congress was meeting, but it brought no sharp public reaction. When new House payroll lists became available in February, Trimble's further investigations revealed that an Iowa Congressman paid his nineteen-year-old student son $11,870.30 a year as his public relations assistant; an Indiana Representative used the front porch of his home as an office and charged the government rent for it; and a New York Congressman used his office-help allowance to reward political cronies back home. These items awakened grass-roots interest, and at one time during the series of disclosures a picture of Trimble was put on the New House Office Building bulletin board with a sign reading: "Beware of this man—he's dangerous."

By March, the public had been made thoroughly aware of the Congressional payroll irregularities brought to light by Trimble's persistent research. His articles were inserted in the *Congressional Record* and debated on the floor. *Time* magazine (March 16, 1959) described the stories as "a solid series of solid beats."

Trimble filed suits on April 1, 1959 in the Washington, D.C. Federal District Court to compel the Senate and House to make public undisclosed payroll and expense records. According to Trimble, the suits were intended "to test whether Congress can maintain a veil of secrecy on records that should be open to the public." The Senate suit was later dismissed by United States District Judge Alexander Holtzoff, who maintained that a newsman had no legal right to insist on seeing Congressional records not open to the general public. Trimble's efforts were not wasted, however. On June 26, 1959 the Senate adopted a bill providing for the quarterly disclosure of the names and salaries of all Senate employees and an annual report of Senate expenditures. House legislation of April 1959, proposing publication of additional expense and pay information, was not passed.

Vance Trimble's initiative and hard work on this exposé series won for him the three top journalism prizes of the year, a feat rarely achieved in the profession. The Pulitzer Prize for distinguished reporting of national affairs, which carries an award of $1,000 in addition to a citation and a scroll, was awarded to him on May 2, 1960. He had previously been honored by receiving the $1,000 Raymond Clapper Memorial Award for "exceptionally meritorious" work by a Washington newsman, and the award of Sigma Delta Chi, a national journalistic fraternity, for making a "significant contribution to the public's right to know."

Trimble was married to his high school sweetheart, Elzene Miller, on January 9, 1932, when he was eighteen years old. They have one daughter, Carol Ann. The slender, strong-jawed newsman is a Democrat and belongs to the Southern Baptist Church. He is just under six feet tall, weighs 150 pounds, has blue eyes and graying hair, and favors bow ties. The hobby of photography ranks high on Trimble's list of interests. He is also an amateur architect and designed and supervised the building of two houses, including his own contemporary-style home in Chevy Chase, Maryland. He belongs to the National Press Club in Washington D.C.

References

Time 73:74+ Mr 16 '59 por
Who's Who in America, 1960-61

TSARAPKIN, SEMYON K(ONSTANTINOVICH) (tsä-rŏp′kĭn) 1906- Soviet diplomat

Address: Ministry of Foreign Affairs, Moscow, U.S.S.R.

Since October 31, 1958, when diplomats representing the United States, Great Britain, and the U.S.S.R. began to try to reach agreement on ending nuclear testing, the leader of the Soviet delegation has been Semyon K. Tsarapkin, one of the Soviet Union's most experienced diplomats. Officially ranked as an envoy extraordinary and plenipotentiary, Tsarapkin is in addition head of the international organizations department of the Soviet Ministry of Foreign Affairs and a member of its collegium, its top policy-making body. Tsarapkin has often represented the Soviet Union at United Nations meetings in New York City and was for some years Deputy Soviet Delegate to the United Nations, working under the late Andrei Y. Vishinsky. He was also the chief Soviet political officer in Korea in the years immediately following World War II.

A Ukrainian, Tsarapkin was born in 1906. He was at work in a smelting plant by the time he was seventeen, when government talent scouts spotted him, but he seems not to have been selected for advanced political training until he was in his twenties. He was educated in the Institute of Oriental Studies and Moscow, U.S.S.R.

Tsarapkin helped to negotiate the Soviet-Japanese nonaggression pact in 1941. From 1941 to 1944 he was chief of the second Far East department, U.S.S.R. Ministry of Foreign Affairs. He moved up from this post in 1944 to become head of the Foreign Ministry's American department. During World War II he was an official in the Soviet Embassy in Washington.

In 1944 Tsarapkin began a period of involvement with the United Nations that lasted ten years, starting as a delegate to the Dum-

United Nations

SEMYON K. TSARAPKIN

barton Oaks conference called to set up that organization. Then, in 1945, he was in San Francisco with the Russian delegation for the founding of the United Nations. He was seen at most U. N. conferences after that, usually well in the background, until 1946, when he was assigned to Korea to help set up Soviet and American spheres of authority. Later that year he was appointed minister-counselor in Washington, commuting between Washington and U.N. headquarters.

As a Soviet delegate to the U.N., Tsarapkin first came into prominence at the First Special Session of the General Assembly in the spring of 1947. Great Britain had just informed the U.N. that it was ending its mandate in Palestine. Tsarapkin took an active part in Palestine debates from the time of the partition report to the armistice arrangements Tsarapkin was also a member of the Second Special Session, as well as the first Soviet delegate to the Trusteeship Council, stepping in undramatically after the U.S.S.R. had boycotted that agency for a time. The same year, 1948, Tsarapkin became a member of the collegium—the policy-making body—of the Ministry of Foreign Affairs and was appointed chargé d'affaires at Washington.

Among other United Nations groups in which Tsarapkin represented the Soviet Union was the Atomic Energy Commission. As early as 1949, Tsarapkin contended that all atomic weapons should be prohibited and that the technical difficulties of establishing a control system were "imaginary and exaggerated." In substance, this is what he continued to maintain throughout the nuclear test talks in Geneva that began nine years later.

Also in 1949 Tsarapkin took over direction of the Soviet U.N. delegation in the absence of Deputy Foreign Minister Jacob A. Malik,

then permanent Russian delegate. As acting chief of mission, he was the first man appointed to the job of Soviet deputy delegate. That year he was promoted to the rank of Minister.

According to A. M. Rosenthal, "Mr. Tsarapkin seemed a forbidding, remote man at the U.N." (New York *Times*, May 24, 1959). A decade earlier, Rosenthal had reported that "at the council table or in the committee room Mr. Tsarapkin is sharp. He has a stand-offish reputation at the U.N. and is known as a stickler for details" (New York *Times*, July 24, 1949). But Mac R. Johnson of the New York *Herald Tribune* wrote on July 3, 1949 that Tsarapkin "is not addicted to the use of invective and refrains from being outright insulting."

The record shows that on July 12, 1948 Tsarapkin condemned Britain's governing of Tanganyika, and that Sir Alan Burns, the British delegate, responded with a defense that referred to Soviet occupation of the Baltic republics. Tsarapkin on July 13 charged that Sir Alan had loosed a "libelous attack on my country" and drawn from "the arsenal which was used by Goebbels."

In the Economic and Social Council, Tsarapkin on February 16, 1949 described an American Federation of Labor memorandum calling for an international investigation of slave labor practices as a "dirty pamphlet," whose authors were "either idiots or gangsters of the first grade." On November 21, 1951 Tsarapkin said that under "American bosses" Greece was living in a reign of terror, and warned a Chilean delegate not to "stick his nose into affairs of the Soviet Union."

Tsarapkin took part in some of the walkouts that characterized Communist delegations at the U.N. in 1950. On February 8, for instance, he participated in a walkout of Russian, Polish, and Czech delegates, the eleventh such boycott in twenty-five days. On March 27 he walked out of the Commission on Human Rights after its chairman, Mrs. Eleanor Roosevelt, gaveled him to silence for delivering what she called "propaganda speeches."

The next year found Tsarapkin demanding that the U.N. Security Council strike from its annual report any reference to meetings held from July 15 to July 31, 1950, when Moscow had boycotted it. He had recently condemned "private publishing monopolies" as the primary threat to the freedom of the press. He continued to sit in for the ailing Jacob A. Malik and in March 1953 was appointed Deputy Permanent Representative on the U.S.S.R. delegation to the U.N.

On June 25, 1954, while sitting in on the U.N. Security Council for Andrei Y. Vishinsky, then Deputy Foreign Minister and chief of the Soviet U.N. delegation, Tsarapkin was asked by Council President Henry Cabot Lodge, Jr., "For what purpose does the gentleman seek recognition?" Tsarapkin said, "I am not a gentleman, I am the representative of the Soviet Union." "The two are not necessarily mutually exclusive," said Lodge.

On September 15, 1954 Tsarapkin was replaced by Arkady A. Sobolev and returned to Moscow with his family. He was given a farewell party in his stateroom on the *Queen Elizabeth* by Vishinsky. Except for being identified as the head of the international organizations department, Ministry of Foreign Affairs, U.S.S.R., in 1955, Tsarapkin did not come into the news again until July 1958, when he was the only nontechnical delegate at a meeting of scientists from East and West, who gathered in Geneva, Switzerland to discuss standards for a nuclear test control system. When diplomatic test talks between the United States, Great Britain, and the Soviet Union got under way in Geneva on October 31, 1958, Tsarapkin was the chief Soviet delegate. Six months later, Tsarapkin said: "The gap between our positions is being narrowed day by day;" in July 1959, however, he said: "At the rate we are now going, the negotiations could drag on for three, four, or five years."

Although on January 27, 1960 Tsarapkin had said that his country would never accept any test ban of only large nuclear weapons, on March 19 he proposed just such a partial test ban and with controls, on the condition that the West agreed to a temporary ban without controls on tests of small nuclear weapons. Tsarapkin declared that a treaty could be worked out in a week if the West accepted the Russian formula.

Little is known about Tsarapkin's private and domestic life, except that he is married and has children. Since he has said that his wife enjoys baby sitting for their daughter in Moscow, it is apparent that he is a grandfather. Although his surname when translated into English means "one who claws," Tsarapkin can be affable, charming, and courteous on occasion. He speaks English fluently, but with a heavy accent. He likes civilized conversation at the dinner table, and relishes the novels of Charles Dickens and Stefan Zweig, but detests abstract art and contemporary music.

References

Biographic Directory of the USSR (1958)
International Year Book and Statesmen's Who's Who, 1959

TUTTLE, CHARLES E(GBERT) Apr. 5, 1915- Publisher; bookseller
Address: b. 15 Edogawa-cho, Bunkyo-ku, Tokyo, Japan; h. 740, 4-chome, Kita-Shinagawa, Shinagawa-ku, Tokyo, Japan

In his multifaceted activities as publisher, bookseller, literary agent, and encyclopaedia salesman, Charles E. Tuttle has more than earned the right to the motto of his publishing company: Books to span the East and West. Since he began publishing in Tokyo in the mid-1950's, Tuttle has ministered to the booming American curiosity in Japanese culture by producing a steady stream of books ranging in subject matter from Origami, the art of paper-

CHARLES E. TUTTLE

folding, to Karate, the art of mayhem. Like his motto, the dual location that appears in the imprint of his books: "Rutland, Vermont and Tokyo, Japan" symbolizes his successful mission to bridge the East and West. Edward H. Dodd, Jr., the chairman of the editorial board of Dodd, Mead & Company, has called Tuttle "the principal and perhaps the only literary agent in Japan, the man who arranges for most of the translations of our books."

Charles Egbert Tuttle was born on April 5, 1915 to Charles Egbert Tuttle and Sarah (Woolverton) Tuttle in Rutland, Vermont, the town in which his great grandfather had opened a bookstore in 1832. Tuttle has said: "The house I was born in was full of books and my father's antiquarian stock in trade consisted of more than a hundred thousand titles covering several hundred subjects. Given, in addition, a family tradition of printing and publishing, it was inevitable that my career would be in the world of books."

An only child, he was reared in Rutland, but, since his mother was a Canadian, he spent many summers in Woodstock and Campobello, New Brunswick. After attending Phillips Exeter Academy in Exeter, New Hampshire, from which he was graduated in 1933, he went to Harvard College, where he held various scholarships, worked in the Widener Library, and majored in American history and American literature.

Earning his B.A. degree *magna cum laude* in 1937, Tuttle then worked in the rare book division of the Columbia University libraries and took courses in the history of books and printing. In 1938 he returned to Rutland and joined his father's antiquarian book business, specializing in rare items of American literature, Vermontiana, the Negro in America, business history, genealogy, and the American Civil War. Significantly, the Tuttle catalogues were and

TUTTLE, CHARLES E.—*Continued*

still are called "Miscellanies." Neither father nor son took any special interest in Japan or the Orient at that time. Tuttle remained in Rutland with the family business until he entered the United States Army in May 1942 as a private in the chemical warfare service.

In October 1945, Tuttle went to Japan for the first time; serving as a captain on General MacArthur's military government staff, he classified Japanese art and cultural properties in the first foreign country that he had ever seen. Discharged in May 1946 with the rank of captain, he remained in Tokyo and discovered, while sending books to friends in the United States and to the store in Rutland, that the rage for things Japanese was already beginning. He began his publishing activity with *Baby-San* and *The World of Baby-San* by the Navy cartoonist Bill Hume and the writer John Annanino. These books of cartoons, which sold hundreds of thousands of copies in American Post Exchanges, featured the adventures of Baby-San, a typical Japanese girl friend of American soldiers and sailors.

Sensitive to the needs of American soldiers and civilians stationed in Japan, Tuttle published a map of Tokyo, a pamphlet on Japanese food, and similar materials. With the publication of Hugo Munsterberg's *The Landscape Painting of China and Japan*, issued in a de luxe edition in 1955, Tuttle made his entrance on the serious publishing scene.

Since Tuttle has his printing and binding done in Tokyo, where costs are low, he is often able to subsidize the publication of books that would not sell enough copies to cover costs if they were printed in the United States. This policy has sometimes resulted in the publication of "sleepers," or unexpected successes. One of the outstanding examples is *Flickering Flames*, an illustrated history of old lamps, lighting fixtures, candlesticks, and so forth, from earliest times up to the present. Its publication was sponsored by a private club in the United States that originally ordered a few hundred copies. Now in its third printing, *Flickering Flames* has sold over 4,000 copies.

The Charles E. Tuttle Company has extended its operations to include such activities as its sponsorship of a competition of contemporary Japanese wood blocks in 1959. The co-sponsor was James A. Michener, who wrote the text for *Japanese Prints, from the Early Masters to the Modern* (Tuttle, 1959).

The books on the Tuttle list have been praised not only because they are often the first or the only books on rather exotic subjects but also because they are so tastefully designed. Of Hokusai's *Sketch Books*, edited by James A. Michener (Tuttle, 1958), Edward Weeks wrote in the *Atlantic Monthly* (October 1958): "The format is beautifully in keeping, with quietly toned cover bound in raw silk, the running commentary of black and white sketches, and the soft-toned woodcuts on which to feast the eyes." Both critics and public, however, are aware that Tuttle's books are as useful as they are aesthetic.

The editorial offices of the Charles E. Tuttle Company are located on the second floor of a typical downtown Tokyo office building. The Oriental décor may be subdued, but the activity is not: proofreaders mumble their complaints about the abundant typographical errors on their galleys (Japanese printers are often totally unfamiliar with the English language) and telephones jangle constantly.

Meredith Weatherby, the editor of the Charles E. Tuttle Company, has been associated with it since it began to publish. Other chief members of staff are Bruce Rogers, the general manager, who was born in Anchorage, Alaska; Richard Brown, head of promotion, formerly of Massena, New York, and Toichito Katahira, who is in charge of translations.

By the end of 1959, Charles E. Tuttle had published over 350 titles and sold the rights to Japanese publishers for 1,400 American books. The wide range of titles that he has published since the middle 1950's reflects his own broad span of interests, including books on Origami, Japanese decorative design, architecture, Japanese gardens, cookbooks, Mah Jong, Buddhism, Paul Bunyan, New England covered bridges, and Chinese novels. Recently he has expanded his scope still further to include books on Persian and Indian art, classic Oriental literature (much of it previously unavailable in English), and translations into Japanese of Hemingway's *The Old Man and the Sea*, Nabokov's *Lolita*, and Pasternak's *Doctor Zhivago*. In 1959, under the terms of a special contract with John Wiley & Sons, Inc., the Charles E. Tuttle Company began to reproduce technical books for distribution in the Far East, offering works of top quality at prices within reach of the Oriental scholar and scientist.

Charles Tuttle also runs four retail bookstores in Tokyo, a rare book department, a literary agency for translations, a magazine subscription service, an encyclopaedia sales department, an import operation, a wholesale book and magazine distribution agency, and the American office in Rutland, Vermont. Every other year he renews contact with his native Vermont; he continually travels throughout the rest of the world, scouting for manuscripts, selling books, attending international book fairs, and exchanging information with fellow booksellers and publishers.

On February 16, 1952 Charles Egbert Tuttle was married to Reiko Chiba, a Japanese singer of classical music, whom he met while he was stationed with the United States Army of Occupation in Tokyo. Soft-spoken, with hazel eyes and brown hair, Tuttle is five feet eight inches in height and about 138 pounds in weight. He is known for his hospitality to visiting American soldiers, librarians, and bibliophiles, and has said: "It is vital that Americans get to know about this part of the world. I am sure this is happening and I hope we are helping." He is a member of the Harvard Club of Boston and the Harvard Club of New York; the Army and Navy Club in Washington, D.C.; and the American Club in Tokyo, where he ran often be found playing "liar's dice," a popular Oriental game. He is a Baptist and a Republican.

References

N Y Times Bk R p8 O 18 '59
Pub W 175:12+ Ap 27 '59

UREY, HAROLD C(LAYTON) (ū'rê)
Apr. 29, 1893- Scientist
Address: b. University of California, La Jolla, Calif.; h. 7890 Torrey Lane, La Jolla, Calif.

NOTE: This biography supersedes the article which appeared in *Current Biography* in 1941.

The American scientist Harold C. Urey is known throughout the world as an original worker in the field of physical chemistry and as a man who has not hesitated to reflect on the social and ethical implications of scientific advances. He received the Nobel Prize for Chemistry in 1934 for his discovery of deuterium or heavy hydrogen, and he later helped the United States to develop the atomic bomb during World War II. He is at present professor-at-large of chemistry at the University of California in La Jolla.

Urey has specialized in research on the structure of atoms and molecules, the thermodynamic properties of gases, and the separation of isotopes. He has worked on the production of heavy water and of U235 for the atomic bomb, and has investigated the chemical problems involved in the origin and evolution of the earth and the solar system.

Harold Clayton Urey, the son of Samuel Clayton and Cora Rebecca (Reinoehl) Urey, was born in Walkerton, Indiana on April 29, 1893. His ancestors had been pioneers in Indiana. His father, a schoolteacher and a minister of the Brethren Church, died when Harold was six years old. His mother subsequently married a clergyman. He has a brother, Clarence, a sister, Martha, and two half sisters, Florence and Ina. He attended country schools in De Kalb County in Indiana and high schools in Kendallville and Walkerton in that state. He was graduated from high school in 1911.

For the next three years Urey taught in country schools in Indiana and Montana. In 1914 he matriculated at Montana State University in Missoula, where his major was zoology and his minor, chemistry. He was awarded a B.S. degree in 1917. When the United States entered World War I, he went to Philadelphia to help manufacture war matériel as a research chemist at the Barrett Chemical Company from 1918 to 1919. He later said that this experience turned him away from industrial chemistry as a career and toward academic work.

From 1919 to 1921 he was an instructor in chemistry at Montana State University, and then he went to the University of California in Berkeley, where, studying under Professor Gilbert N. Lewis, he developed his interest in physical and mathematical chemistry. His major subject was chemistry and his minor, physics.

Wide World
HAROLD C. UREY

He received his Ph.D. degree in 1923. According to T. W. MacCallum and S. Taylor in *The Nobel Prize-Winners and the Nobel Foundation, 1901-1937* (1938), his thesis dealt with "the calculation of entropies of diatomic gases from molecular-spectra data and with the equilibrium distribution of hydrogen atoms among the steady states."

After receiving a grant as a fellow of the American Scandinavian Foundation, he attended the Institute for Theoretical Physics at the University of Copenhagen in Denmark from 1923 to 1924. There he studied under Niels Bohr, who was doing pioneering work in the theory of atomic structure. Urey returned to the United States in 1924 and for the next five years was an associate in chemistry at Johns Hopkins University in Baltimore, Maryland. From 1929 to 1934 he held the position of associate professor of chemistry at Columbia University in New York City and from 1933 to 1936 he was the Ernest Kempton Adams Fellow there. With Arthur Edward Ruark he wrote *Atoms, Molecules, and Quanta* (McGraw-Hill, 1930).

In December 1931 Urey announced that he, together with Drs. George M. Murphy and Ferdinand G. Brickwedde, had discovered the existence of heavy water, in which the molecules consist of an atom of oxygen and two atoms of heavy hydrogen or deuterium. The identification of deuterium has been called one of the foremost achievements of modern science and has had a significant effect on research in physics, chemistry, biology, and medicine. As the discoverer of this heavy hydrogen isotope, Urey was awarded the Nobel Prize for Chemistry in 1934. His Nobel Prize address, delivered on February 14, 1935, was entitled, "Some Thermodynamic Properties of Hydrogen and Deuterium."

(Continued next page)

UREY, HAROLD C.—*Continued*

Urey was appointed to the position of full professor of chemistry at Columbia University in 1934, and from 1939 to 1942 he was the executive officer of its chemistry department. He also served from 1933 to 1940 as editor of the *Journal of Chemical Physics.* He continued to study the problem of isotope separation at Columbia and his development of chemical exchange, distillation, and other methods of separation of isotopes enabled American firms to market as commercial commodities such materials as radioactive nitrogen. His work on the hydrogen isotope has dealt with its thermodynamic properties and those of its compounds, especially the vapour pressure of hydrogen and deuterium and the equilibrium constants of exchange reactions.

When World War II began, Urey, as one of the first Americans to realize that atomic weapons could be made, crucially influenced the early history of the American atomic projects. He was active in the development at Columbia University of the diffusion process for the separation of the uranium isotopes and during the war visited Great Britain in connection with this study. From 1940 to 1945 Urey served as the director of war research on the atomic bomb at Columbia University.

After the United States had used atomic bombs against Japan in World War II, Urey and many other scientists urged people everywhere to reconsider the ethical problems involved in the use of atomic weapons and the devastating results which could follow from their irresponsible use. He became in 1945 the distinguished service professor of chemistry at the Institute for Nuclear Studies at the University of Chicago, and from 1952 to 1958 he was the Martin A. Ryerson distinguished service professor of chemistry there. In 1958 he was named professor-at-large of chemistry at the University of California in La Jolla.

Since the war, in addition to his teaching, Urey has continued his research. He has done work on tritium in relation to the hydrogen bomb, and he has also done pioneering work in applying isotope research to problems of geology and paleontology. He discovered an oxygen thermometer which has been used by scientists to learn about ancient climatic temperatures through the study of fossils of several millions of years ago.

Over the years Urey has also studied the solar system. In 1951 he delivered the Silliman Memorial Lectures at Yale University, which, under the title, *The Planets: Their Origin and Development,* were published by the Yale University Press in 1952. He advanced a new theory about the formation of meteorites in an address he gave at Columbia University in April 1960. Since 1958 Urey has been a member of the space science board of the National Academy of Sciences, and in 1960 he prepared for the board two reports—one on the moon, the other on planets—in which he said that exploration of space might provide clues as to the origin of the solar system and as to whether life exists on distant planets.

Urey's articles have been published in the *Christian Century, United Nations World, Science, Scientific American, Bulletin of the Atomic Scientists, Saturday Review, Columbia University Quarterly,* and *Geochimica et Cosmochimica Acta.* He was the Montgomery lecturer at the University of Nebraska in 1952, the Hitchcock lecturer at the University of California in 1953, the George Eastman visiting professor at Oxford University from 1956 to 1957, and the Scott lecturer at Cambridge University in 1957. He was a co-editor of and contributor to *Production of Heavy Water* (McGraw-Hill, 1955).

Fifteen universities have conferred honorary degrees on Urey, including Princeton, Yale, Columbia and Oxford universities. He is a member of numerous scientific societies in the United States, Portugal, Belgium, Sweden, France, Norway, Ireland, India, Israel, and Great Britain. He belongs to the Sigma Xi, Epsilon Chi, Phi Lambda Upsilon, Gamma Alpha, and Phi Sigma fraternities.

Urey was awarded the Willard Gibbs Medal of the American Chemical Society in 1934. He also received the Davy medal of the Royal Society of London (1940), the Franklin medal of the Franklin Institute (1943), the Medal for Merit (1946), the Cordoza award (1954), the honor scroll award of the Chicago chapter of the American Institute of Chemists (1954), and the Joseph Priestley Award of Dickinson College (1955). He is vice-president and a member of the board of directors of the American Scandinavian Foundation.

Harold C. Urey was married to Frieda Daum in Lawrence, Kansas on June 12, 1926. She was a bacteriologist before her marriage. They have four children: Gertrude Elizabeth, Frieda Rebecca, Mary Alice, and John Clayton. Urey is a brown-eyed, gray-haired man who is five feet seven inches tall and weighs 175 pounds. His political affiliation is with the Democratic party, and he is a member of the science and technology panel of the Democratic National Committee's advisory council.

References

Nature 159:668 My 17 '47
Sci Illus 2:6 Ja '47

American Men of Science vol I (1955)
Farber, E. Nobel Prize Winners in Chemistry, 1901-50 (1953)
Fisher, D. F. American Portraits (1946)
International Who's Who, 1959
National Cyclopaedia of American Biography current vol E (1938)
Who's Who in America, 1960-61

VAN BUREN, ABIGAIL July 4, 1918-
Columnist

Address: b. c/o McNaught Syndicate, Inc., 60 E. 42d St., New York 17

A "jet-age sob sister who has brought a new and acid technique to the job of advising the lovelorn," Abigail Van Buren started her column, "Dear Abby," in the San Francisco *Chronicle* in 1956. Now syndicated in some

500 newspapers by the McNaught Syndicate, the column contains common-sense advice, free from mawkish sentiment, salted with wit and peppered with wisdom. It provokes some 3,000 letters a week, dealing mainly with marital instability and adolescent growing pains. Miss Van Buren hopes to give troubled people something to hold on to, if only an understanding friend.

Abigail Van Buren is the pseudonym of Mrs. Morton Phillips, who by raising her own two children, now teen-agers, has gained an insight into the problems of the "moot generation." Her chief competitor in her specialty is her identical twin, who writes under the pen name of Ann Landers. Miss Van Buren's books, *Dear Abby* (Prentice-Hall, 1958) and *Dear Teen-Ager* (Bernard Geis Associates, 1959) were best sellers.

Abby Van Buren was born Pauline Esther Friedman on Independence Day of 1918 in Sioux City, Iowa, to Abraham and Rebecca (Rushall) Friedman, who were both emigrants from Russia. Her father, an owner of movie theaters, was a benefactor of organizations ranging from the United Jewish Appeal to the Catholic Good Shepherd's Home. As a child, Pauline was first violinist in her school's orchestra and intended to become a musician. "Then I discovered fellers," she explains, "and that was the end of my musical career."

After graduating with honors in 1936 from Sioux City's Central High School, she majored in journalism and psychology at Morningside College, Sioux City, but did not complete her studies, although she earned "A" grades. Pauline ("Popo") and her twin, Esther Pauline ("Eppie"), together wrote gossip columns for their high school and college papers.

On July 2, 1939, two days before their twenty-first birthday, the twins were married in a double wedding ceremony. Esther was married to Jules Lederer, now president of Autopoint Company. Pauline was married to Morton Phillips, who has held such positions as vice-president of National Presto Industries, Inc., and president of M. Seller Company.

During the next seventeen years the Phillipses lived successively in Minneapolis, Minnesota; Eau Claire, Wisconsin; and San Francisco, California. Although Mrs. Phillips was busy bringing up her two children, Jeanne and Eddie, she found time to be active in philanthropic causes and in the Democratic party.

After her sister was hired to write the Ann Landers (see *C.B.*, November 1957) series in 1955, Mrs. Phillips began her own journalistic career. "She insists that her sister's coup had nothing at all to do with her own decision," reported *Life* (April 7, 1958). Blithely selecting the San Francisco *Chronicle*, which was publishing advice columns by Molly Mayfield, Mrs. Phillips arranged for an interview and submitted sample articles. The editors enjoyed her irreverent, engaging answers so much that they dropped Molly Mayfield and turned the job over to Mrs. Phillips.

Romaine-Skelton

ABIGAIL VAN BUREN

Under the by-line of Abigail Van Buren, a name of her own invention, she began her deftly written "Dear Abby" column in January 1956. Within a month Miss Van Buren signed a ten-year contract with the McNaught Syndicate; within a year the series appeared in over eighty newspapers, including the New York *Mirror*. At the present time it is published six days each week in some 500 papers throughout the world. Miss Van Buren's swift climb is most extraordinary, since her astringent comments seem to parody other lovelorn-ists. *Time* (January 21, 1957) called her replies "slicker, quicker and flipper than her twin sister's."

The two columns are as alike as Abigail Van Buren and Ann Landers. Sharing the same interests, both women believe the columns fulfill an important mission in their lives; maintain that religion and psychiatry provide the keys to the understanding of people and recommend that disturbed readers consult doctors, psychiatrists, and clergymen; feel that a shock and a laugh are better than a soft shoulder to cry on; promote stable marriages and believe that women who cannot make marriage work are ridiculous; deprecate premarital sexual relations and urge strict but understanding and loving parental guidance. Their rivalry has been a factor in their success. As soon as a newspaper contracts for one of the columns, its competitor in a given area buys the other twin's column to keep abreast of readers' tastes.

Examples of Abby's advice to adolescents are included in her book *Dear Teen-Ager,* excerpts of which were reprinted in *McCall's* (September 1959) and in *Reader's Digest* (December 1959). In answer to the query, "Should I go steady?" Abby replied: "Going steady means excluding everyone from your dates except your one-and-only. But how do you know 'the one' unless you have tried

VAN BUREN, ABIGAIL—*Continued*

going out with others—lots of others? Would you buy the first pair of shoes you tried on?" On another occasion Miss Van Buren cautioned a teen-age girl: "Keep away from tempting situations. Avoid overparking. Double date! Don't invite him over when nobody's home."

"My disagreements with parents are few," Abby wrote in an article for *Good Housekeeping* (May 1958), "but on one point I am ready to go to bat for the kids any time. That is when children confide in a parent only to have their confidence betrayed." Her own personal formula for happiness is "spare those around you as much unhappiness as you can; be kind; be forgiving."

Problem-ridden people who write to Miss Van Buren sometimes receive a personal reply. (She keeps a staff of four secretaries occupied.) No letters shock her. She respects persons willing to try to find a solution for their difficulties and often recommends that the troubled seek help from psychiatrists, clergymen, and social workers. Grateful correspondents send her all manner of gifts to express their gratitude, but she returns them. One man wrote to her: "Thanks, Abby, for giving me a kick in the pants when I needed it. It woke me up."

In her column Abby often answers letters with one terse and flippant sentence, and she is not averse to punning. "Putting a ring on her finger will help stop the circulation," she advised a young man, "but be sure she wants to stop circulating." To a cook, she wrote: "Quit snooping or the next thing you will cook will be your own goose."

Abigail Van Buren is five feet two inches tall, weighs 108 pounds, has black hair, greenish-blue eyes, and a heart-shaped face with dimples. Although her religion is Jewish, she took Roman Catholic instruction a few years ago in an effort better to understand other religions, and she warmly admires Bishop Fulton J. Sheen. She neither smokes nor drinks. Her hobbies are playing the piano, violin, and electric organ, and she likes to collect stamps with her children.

As clothes conscious as a movie star, the columnist favors Paris fashions, slacks, street frocks, and cocktail gowns in black, sport shirts, and Turkish slippers. She counts among her friends many celebrities from the entertainment world, and she took a small role in the motion picture *At War with the Army* (1951).

A subscriber to the belief that "husband and children come first," Miss Van Buren arises at cockcrow to help her husband and children off to work and school. The family live in a ten-room ranch house equipped with a swimming pool in the Hillsborough section of San Francisco. At an electric typewriter in her bedroom Miss Van Buren taps out her column and an endless stream of letters for four hours each day.

The heat of the battle between the twin sister-columnists has led Abby to advise: "Parents of identical twins should not dress them alike. Break up the vaudeville act. It may be good for the parents' ego but for the sisters it means double trouble."

References

Coronet 42 :52+ O '57 pors
McCalls 85 :54+ N '57 pors
Time 69 :70 Ja 21 '57 por

VAN DONGEN, KEES *See* Dongen, Kees van

VANIER, GEORGE PHILIAS (và-nyā')

Apr. 23, 1888- Governor-General of Canada; former army officer; former diplomat
Address: Rideau Hall, Ottawa, Ontario, Canada

The first French Canadian and Roman Catholic to become Governor-General of Canada, Major General George Philias Vanier was approved by Queen Elizabeth II on August 1, 1959 as the representative of the Crown in Canada and was inducted into office on September 15. A hero of the first World War and a diplomat who became Canada's first Ambassador to France, Major General Vanier succeeded the Honorable Vincent Massey, the first native Canadian to become Governor-General.

Like his sovereign in Great Britain, the Governor-General follows the advice of the Prime Minister; he signs, but cannot veto, legislation. His functions are thus largely ceremonial. "Yet in Canada, as in Great Britain," the New York *Times* (August 4, 1959) has commented editorially, "one must not be fooled into believing that the figure at the top is a piece of fiction and means nothing. The Governor-General is that touch of pageantry which makes Canadians and Britons kin. He has been called 'the symbol of a symbol.'"

The son of Philias and Margaret (Maloney) Vanier, George Philias Vanier was born on April 23, 1888 in Montreal. On his father's side he is descended from Norman-French settlers who were established in Canada by 1681. His mother was a native of Ireland. George, who was reared in the Roman Catholic faith, attended Loyola College and Laval University, both in Montreal. At the university he earned the B.A. degree in the humanities in 1906 and the LL.B. degree in 1911.

Called to the bar of Quebec, Vanier practised law with a Montreal law firm for several years, until the outbreak of World War I. "Today," he said in 1959, "I would have either been a lawyer, judge or dead—if the world war had not broken out" (Toronto *Globe and Mail*, August 3, 1959). A founding member of Quebec's Royal 22d (Vingt-Deux) Regiment, popularly known as the Van Doos, Vanier was ordered to the French front. There he led a group of men who devastated a machine gun post and was wounded. A short time later he directed the capture of a strategic village.

At Cherisy in 1918, as a major in command, he was again severely wounded, but rallying his battalion, he staged an important attack. As a result of the injuries he sustained, his right leg was amputated above the knee. His gallantry during the war won him the Military Cross with bar, the Distinguished Service Order, the 1915 Star, and the Chevalier's Rosette in the French Legion of Honor.

After briefly returning to the law, Vanier served in 1921-22 as aide-de-camp to Lord Byng, then Governor-General of Canada. Vanier missed army life, however, and applied to the Inspector General of Canadian Militia, Sir Arthur Currie, for permission to rejoin. "He looked at me, chuckled," Vanier remembers, "and asked how I expected to serve with only one leg and a tin one. . . . I made some jocular remark that the army could perhaps do with a few brains even if there was only one leg to go with them" (Toronto *Globe and Mail*, August 3, 1959).

The result was his appointment as second in command of his old regiment, two years at the Royal Staff College at Camberley in England, and advancement in 1925 to commander of the Van Doos. From 1925 to 1928 he also served as aide-de-camp to Lord Willingdon, who succeeded Lord Byng as Governor-General.

Promoted to the rank of lieutenant colonel in 1928, Vanier was transferred to Geneva, Switzerland, where in the next decade he served on such international bodies as the League of Nations permanent advisory commission for military, naval, and air questions. An advocate of disarmament, he was on the League's preparatory disarmament commission and attended the London Naval Conference in 1930.

Vanier was also a member of the Canadian delegation to the League's Assembly in September 1930 and technical adviser to the Canadian delegation to the Assembly in September 1936. Beginning in 1931 he was for eight years counselor and secretary of the Office of the High Commissioner for Canada in London. Other tasks he fulfilled were his assignments in 1936 as a member of the Commonwealth commissions for King Edward VIII's and King George VI's coronations.

The Canadian Minister to France from January 1939 until that country capitulated to the Germans in World War II, Colonel Vanier made a hazardous escape to England with the British Ambassador. "I have just come back from France," he declared shortly afterwards, "after having moved the Canadian legation twice in order to avoid capture by the German troops. . . . I have seen the misery of the refugees, broken by the horrors to which they have been subjected. Never before has an army had to contend with such heartbreaking conditions. A soldier may well become accustomed to seeing his comrade fall by his side, but never can he view without

William Notman & Son, Montreal

GEORGE PHILIAS VANIER

being profoundly disturbed, the assassination of women and children" (London *Times,* June 28, 1940).

From 1940 through 1942 Vanier was on the United States-Canada Joint Board of Defense and from 1941 to 1943 served, in the rank of brigadier, as commandant of Military District Number 5, with headquarters in Quebec. Confronted with the problem of French Canadians who opposed a "British war," Vanier toured Quebec to win support for the Allied cause.

After several European nations had been conquered by Germany, Vanier was transferred to England in 1943 to serve as Canadian Minister to Allied governments in exile in London and as representative to the French Committee of National Liberation. He hailed the scuttling of the French fleet at Toulon as the "glorious baptism of regenerated France" and declared that her people would now "hearken to the real voice of France, that great Frenchman, General Charles de Gaulle" (New York *Times,* December 1, 1942). Vanier formed a close friendship with de Gaulle in London and at Algiers. In 1944, twelve days after the liberation of Paris, Vanier was appointed the first Canadian Ambassador to France, the former legation having been raised to Embassy status.

Immediately after the war, as a Canadian delegate to the Paris Peace Conference of 1946, Vanier helped to draft treaties with Italy, Romania, Hungary, and Finland, and in February 1947 he was the signatory for Canada. In the following year he served as a Canadian delegate to the United Nations General Assembly at Paris.

After attaining the age of sixty-five, Vanier retired from the army with the rank of major general in 1953 and from the diplomatic service

VANIER, GEORGE PHILIAS—*Cont.*

in early 1954. In the succeeding years he displayed considerable talents as a financier in the posts of board director of the Bank of Montreal, the Crédit Foncier Franco-Canadien, and the Standard Life Assurance Company. He also was a member of the Canada Council and its investment committee; the council is a government body which distributes scholarships and grants to individuals studying and working in the arts.

Major General Vanier received the highest honor in his career when on August 1, 1959 Queen Elizabeth II gave formal approval to his appointment, recommended by Prime Minister John G. Diefenbaker, as Governor-General of Canada. Although everyone recognized the new Governor-General's high qualifications, some observers feared that his appointment marked the precedent of rotating office between Canadians of British and French extraction. Others questioned the propriety of having a Roman Catholic represent a monarch who heads the Anglican Church and whose titles include that of Defender of the Faith. It was pointed out, however, that the Queen may be the defender of faiths other than the Anglican, and Diefenbaker gave positive assurance on the rotation question. At the Governor-General's formal investiture in the Senate Chamber at Ottawa on September 15, the Prime Minister said: "The ceremony emphasizes the essential unity without regard to race or creed not only of the founding races but of all Canadians of every origin and religious faith" (Toronto *Globe and Mail,* September 16, 1959).

Governor-General Vanier holds honorary LL.D. degrees from the University of Ottawa (1945), Laval University (1946), the University of Lyons (1946), and the University of Montreal (1955). The United States award of Legion of Merit, degree of commander, was conferred on him in July 1946. He is a foreign associate of the French Academy of Moral and Political Sciences and a member of the Academy of Sciences, Belles-Lettres, and Arts of Rouen. His clubs are the University in Montreal and the Cercle de l'Union in Paris.

Tall, handsome, and courtly, with silver-white hair and mustache, Governor-General Vanier impressed the painter-photographer Roloff Beny more as a "humanist and man of letters" than as a soldier (*Maclean's Magazine,* September 26, 1959). He walks with a distinctive limp and the aid of a black walnut cane. Vanier is bilingual, speaking English and French with equal ease.

On September 29, 1921 George Philias Vanier was married to the "elegantly tall, easy and gay" Pauline Archer, daughter of the late Justice Charles Archer of Montreal. The couple's sons are George, a Trappist monk known as Father Benedict; Bernard, an artist; Jacques; and Michel. Their daughter, Thérèse, is a pediatrician. In his long career Governor-General Vanier has "developed a deep reverence for

the established order, and an air of conviction as impressive as his record of service to his country" (New York *Times,* August 3, 1959).

References

Christian Sci Mon p2 Ag 11 '59
N Y Herald Tribune p5 Jl 9 '59 por; p5 Ag 2 '59 por
N Y Times p1 Ag 2 '59 por
Washington (D.C.) Post p5A Ag 2 '59 por
Canadian Who's Who, 1955-57
Catholic Who's Who, 1952
International Who's Who, 1958
Who's Who, 1959

VERDON, GWEN Jan. 13, 1925- Dancer; actress

Address: b. Actors' Equity Association, 226 W. 47th St., New York 36

A Hollywood script writer assigned to do a success story in which a child barely able to walk finally becomes a Broadway musical comedy star could hardly do better than to write the true Gwen Verdon story. As a child, Miss Verdon wore corrective boots on her legs and for some twenty years practised her dancing in comparative obscurity. Unknown when she first appeared in *Can-Can* in 1953, she has since triumphed as the star of *Damn Yankees* (1955), *New Girl in Town* 1957), and *Redhead* (1959). Acclaimed as a dancer, singer, and actress, Miss Verdon has received four Antoinette F. Perry (Tony) awards for her Broadway musical appearances.

Gwen Verdon was born Gwyneth Evelyn Verdon on January 13, 1925 in Los Angeles, California. Her English-born parents, Joseph William Verdon, a former gardener, and Gertrude (Standring) Verdon, a vaudeville dancer, had emigrated via Canada to California, where her father became a stage electrician for Metro-Goldwyn-Mayer studios. Gwen attended public elementary schools and Hamilton High School in Los Angeles.

During childhood, Gwen wore corrective boots designed to support her legs, which had been badly bent since her infancy. Rejecting doctors' suggestions that the leg bones be broken and reset, Gwen's mother had her two-year-old daughter take dancing lessons. Two years later Gwen appeared with her mother in a dance recital in Los Angeles; at the age of six she was billed as the "world's fastest tapper" at the Million Dollar and Loew's State theaters in that city. As a teen-ager, she modeled for bathing suit pictures at Venice beach and danced in chorus lines in night clubs. She also appeared in the Los Angeles Civic Light Opera Company's first revival of *Showboat.* Gwen later studied ballet dancing with Ernest Belcher.

Miss Verdon interrupted her dancing career at the age of seventeen to marry a Hollywood writer, James Henaghan. When the marriage ended in divorce five years later, she returned to work, becoming an assistant to dance director Jack Cole. In this capacity she was employed for five years by motion-picture companies, principally by Twentieth-Century-Fox. Although she did manage to get small dance parts in several films like *Meet Me After the Show* (1951), *David and Bathsheba* (1952), *The Merry Widow* (1952), and *Mississippi Gambler* (1953), her performances were invariably cut, sometimes because she was too outstanding in her small role. The only released film in which she appeared briefly during that period was *The Farmer Takes a Wife* (1953), in which she danced with Betty Grable.

Instead of appearing in front of the cameras, Miss Verdon in those years worked behind them, teaching new dance routines or correct movements to Hollywood stars like Lana Turner, Betty Grable, Marilyn Monroe, and Jane Russell. She also danced with Cole in January 1948 in an abortive musical revue, *Bonanza Bound,* and she helped him to do the choreography for Heitor Villa-Lobos' *Magdalena,* which appeared on Broadway in November 1948. In January 1950 she was one of Cole's dancers in the short-lived Broadway musical, *Alive and Kicking.* "Her techniques, in the Cole tradition, are strong and precise," the editor of the *Dictionary of Modern Ballet* (1959) noted, "and she dances with tremendous verve and vitality."

Tired of winning no recognition, Miss Verdon in the spring of 1953 followed choreographer Michael Kidd's suggestion that she audition for the musical, *Can-Can,* then being rehearsed for Broadway. She was accepted, but soon proved so outstanding that she threatened to overshadow the show's French star, Lilo. As a result, the directors whittled down her part in out-of-town tryouts. Having so many times before been a victim of the censor's scissors, Miss Verdon, understandably discouraged, gave notice of her intention to leave the show. She was persuaded, however, to dance two numbers at the opening performance on May 7.

In this story of a strait-laced judge who drops his crusade against the can-can for the sake of an attractive blonde café owner, Gwen Verdon played a dancer who neglects her career to support the sculptor she loves. Her sensuous portrayal of Eve in Eden (before and after the apple) and her apache dance inspired first-night audiences to give her an ovation. Miss Verdon had returned to her dressing room after doing her specialty numbers, but was whisked back on stage in response to audience chants of "We want Verdon." Reviewers seconded this sentiment the next day—and Gwen Verdon emerged as a star. For her performance in *Can-Can* she won the Donaldson and the Antoinette F. Perry (Tony) awards.

In the 1955-56 season Gwen Verdon starred in *Damn Yankees,* a musical based on Douglass Wallop's novel, *The Year the Yankees Lost the Pennant.* She played Lola, the devil's disciple, who persuades a middle-aged baseball fan to trade his soul for a mighty batting

Wide World

GWEN VERDON

arm so that he can help the Washington Senators take the pennant away from the New York Yankees.

Every Broadway critic acclaimed her dancing and acting in this role. "Miss Verdon is just about as alluring a she-witch as was ever bred in the nether regions," L. Funke wrote in the New York *Times* (May 6, 1955). "Vivacious, as sleek as a car on the showroom floor, and as nice to look at, she gives brilliance and sparkle to the evening with her exuberant dancing, her wicked, glistening eyes and her sheer delight in the foolery." Miss Verdon won a Tony award for her acting in *Damn Yankees.* She also received a Lambs Gambol award for acting in 1956. *Damn Yankees* ran on Broadway for 1,022 performances. When Warner Brothers filmed *Damn Yankees* (1958), Miss Verdon played the role of Lola "with the same intensity and verve," according to Paul V. Beckley of the New York *Herald Tribune* (September 27, 1958). Remembering her past experiences, she stipulated, in signing the film contract, that no part of her performance could be cut without her permission.

In *New Girl in Town,* a musical based on Eugene O'Neill's *Anna Christie,* which opened on May 14, 1957, Gwen Verdon demonstrated that her success did not rest solely on her abilities as a comedy actress and dancer. Although most critics felt that O'Neill's bleak drama about an old Swedish tugboat captain and his unhappy ex-prostitute daughter, Anna, was intractable material for a musical book, they united in praising Miss Verdon. "The finest thing in *New Girl in Town* is Miss Verdon's reticent, moving performance as Anna," Brooks Atkinson of the New York *Times* (May 26, 1957) wrote. "There is nothing hackneyed or superficial about [her]

VERDON, GWEN—*Continued*

acting. It is an illuminating portrait of a wretched inarticulate creature." For her performance in this show Miss Verdon received her third Tony award.

Miss Verdon next appeared in *Redhead,* "a sort of pink-champagne-and-black-tights murder mystery in a London wax museum" (New York *Herald Tribune,* February 6, 1959), in which she played Essie Whimple, an English spinster who blossoms into a music-hall dancer. The critics, in welcoming Miss Verdon back, were unanimous in their acclaim. "The amount of physical activity in which this frail-seeming creature indulges is perfectly flabbergasting; spinning, prancing, leaping, curvetting, she is seldom out of sight and never out of breath. Yet beneath the athletic ebullience is something more rarified—an unfailing delicacy of spirit," Kenneth Tynan wrote in the *New Yorker* on February 21, 1959. The show ran for 453 performances and in the spring of 1960 toured Chicago, San Francisco, and Los Angeles. For her performance in *Redhead* Miss Vernon received a Tony award for the fourth time.

Television viewers have seen Gwen Verdon on the *Dinah Shore Chevy Show* (1958) and on *Person to Person* (1960). Before 1953 she had acted in a *Philco Playhouse* drama called *Native Dancer.* The RCA Victor recordings of *Redhead,* in which Miss Verdon and Richard Kiley sing their original stage parts, have proved popular.

Gwen Verdon was married to James Henaghan in 1942 and divorced from him in June 1947. They have a son, James O'Farrell, who is now studying acting. She was married to Bob Fosse in April 1960. Green-eyed Miss Verdon is five feet four and one half inches tall and weighs about 125 pounds. Unlike most performers, she worries about losing weight during a Broadway run, and she tries to maintain her weight by hearty eating. She has served as a member of the board of directors of the Karen Horney Clinic. Her hobby is making cabinets and refinishing old furniture; she also paints and works in sculpture.

"A slender and supple lady, with pointed features, an amiable grin, and a red top-knot," is Brooks Atkinson's description of Gwen Verdon (New York *Times,* February 6, 1959). "She does everything that anyone could expect of a musical performer. She can portray character like a fully licensed dramatic actress. She can sing in a russet-colored voice that is mighty pleasant to hear. . . . And Miss Verdon can dance with so much grace and gaiety that her other accomplishments seem to be frosting on the cake."

References

Am W p4 Je 28 '59 pors
Life 46:81 F 23 '59 pors
N Y Sunday News Mag p4 Ja 24 '60
N Y Times p12 F 7 '59 por
Dictionary of Modern Ballet (1959)
Who's Who in America, 1960-61
Who's Who of American Women, 1958-59

VILLA-LOBOS, HEITOR Mar. 5, 1884-Nov. 17, 1959 Brazilian composer and conductor; composed more than 1,400 musical works; directed the Conservatorio Nacional de Canto Orfeônico since 1942. See *Current Biography* (April) 1945.

Obituary

N Y Times p41 N 18 '59

WARREN, ALTHEA (HESTER) Dec. 18, 1886-Dec. 20, 1958 Librarian of the Los Angeles Public Library (1933-47); president of the American Library Association (1943-44). See *Current Biography* (February) 1942.

Obituary

Wilson Lib Bul 33:390 F '59

WARREN, FLETCHER Mar. 3, 1896-Former United States Ambassador to Turkey

Address: h. 5405 Stonewall St., Greenville, Tex.

In strategically important Turkey, probably America's strongest ally in the Middle East, United States Ambassador Fletcher Warren was responsible for maintaining a program of economic and military co-operation necessary to the collective security of the free world. Warren, who was appointed in early 1956 to succeed Avra M. Warren at Ankara, has been a Foreign Service career officer for almost forty years. An oil expert and specialist on Latin American affairs, he had served as Ambassador to Venezuela for five years before his transfer to Turkey. In September 1960 he resigned his ambassadorial post and later announced his plans to retire from the Foreign Service in early 1961.

The son of a Texas farmer, Fletcher Warren was born to Moses Abraham and Mary Elizabeth (Wilson) Warren on March 3, 1896 in Wolfe City, northeastern Texas. He was raised on the farm with his sister and two brothers and in his boyhood was kept busy doing chores around his home. He attended Wolfe City public schools, graduating in 1915 as valedictorian of his high school class.

While studying at the University of Texas in Austin, he helped pay his expenses by delivering newspapers, waiting on tables at a boarding house and at the university cafeteria, and working as a landscape gardener and later as a supervisor at the Texas School for the Deaf in Austin. His major subject was economics, and he also took as many courses as he could in government and foreign languages. In January 1918 he left college to become a private in the United States Army Quartermaster Corps, and for eighteen months during World War I he fought overseas.

After his discharge from the Army as a sergeant first class in October 1919, Warren returned to the University of Texas, which awarded him the B.A. degree in June 1921. His service as a soldier in France had made him interested in a career in foreign countries, and ten days after his graduation he passed the consular examination in Washington, D.C. for the Foreign Service.

Six months later Warren received his first assignment, as vice-consul in Havana, Cuba. He remained in that post for four years and then served the next four years as consul before being recalled to the State Department in Washington. In 1929 he returned to Latin America as a consul in Baranquilla, Colombia, leaving in 1931 to become consul in Budapest, Hungary. He was again sent to Latin America in 1934, this time as consul and second secretary in Managua, Nicaragua.

Warren returned to Europe in 1936, where he spent the next two years as consul and second secretary at Riga, Latvia. At this time World War II was brewing in Europe, and Latvia was involved in a last-ditch effort to preserve its integrity. In 1938 Latvian neutrality was declared, but two years later the country was incorporated into the Soviet Union.

From Riga, Warren was ordered to Kobe, Japan in 1938, but while he was on his way to his new assignment, the State Department had him stopped in Moscow and called him back to Washington. He served from 1938 to 1942 as executive assistant to George S. Messersmith, then Assistant Secretary of State, and beginning in November 1940 he had the additional responsibilities of chief of the division of foreign activity correlation. In 1944-45 he again was executive assistant to the Assistant Secretary of State, this time Adolf Augustus Berle, Jr. During the intervening period he had spent about a year and a half as counselor of the Embassy in Bogotá, Colombia. Under the leadership of President Alfonso López, Colombia had declared itself opposed to the Axis and was co-operating with the United States in its program of hemispheric defense.

Warren's first ambassadorial appointment, to Nicaragua in 1945, was one of several positions which brought him into intimate contact with vacillating governments, dictatorships, and *coups d'état* in Latin America. A United States Ambassador in Latin America found himself in the paradoxical and uncomfortable position of opposing dictatorships and rigged elections in theory, but in practice, because of United States nonintervention policy, being unable to answer the appeals of local democrats and liberals.

During Warren's stay in Nicaragua, President Anastasio Somoza ended martial law and called for democratic elections. In February 1947, shortly before the United States Ambassador left the country, elections were held. When Somoza's candidate won, his opponent appealed to Warren charging that the election returns were falsified.

In April 1947 Warren was sent as United States Ambassador to Paraguay, where he was again to witness a tumultous Latin American election. He arrived on the heels of a revolt which had attempted to oust the government of President Higinio Morínigo. This was followed by elections which brought in a government facing further political disturbance.

Warren put his experience in Latin America to good use when he returned to Washington in 1950 to head the State Department's newly

FLETCHER WARREN

created Office of South American Affairs. This office, which co-ordinated the work formerly dealt with by three separate departments, improved significantly the efficiency of the State Department's handling of relations with the ten South American republics.

After one year in Washington, Warren was named Ambassador to Venezuela. This country, rich in iron ore and oil essential to hemispheric defense, is regarded as one of the most important posts in Latin America. At the time of his appointment Warren hailed Venezuela for its adherence to free enterprise and "for fighting for the same ideals [as the United States] in today's clash of ideologies."

Close United States-Venezuelan relations stem in part from the fact that United States businessmen, 35,000 of whom reside in Venezuela, have invested substantial sums in the country's thriving economy. For this reason, among others, Warren feels that the United States position in Venezuela is crucial to its relations with all other Latin American countries. "If we can't get along with Venezuela, the other Latin American countries will feel we can't get along with anybody," he told George Dixon of the Washington *Post and Times Herald* (March 1, 1956).

While Warren was Ambassador in Caracas, the United States agreed in a 1952 trade negotiation to lower its duty on Venezuelan oil. In 1955 the United States signed with Venezuela an agreement concerning the peaceful development of atomic energy.

Assigned next to head the United States mission at Ankara, in March 1956 Warren went to the Middle East to apply his experience in oil-rich Venezuela to Turkey, where an oil boom was in progress. Turkey, which has been called "the eastern anchor of NATO and the western anchor of the Baghdad Pact" (*Business Week*,

WARREN, FLETCHER—*Continued*

April 13, 1957), is essential to United States defenses in the Middle East and gets a substantial amount of United States aid.

The economy of Turkey has been plagued by inflation due primarily to wasteful and extensive investments under an ill-planned development program. With help from the United States, the country is trying to stabilize its economy. One way to improve the situation, Warren has pointed out, is through better educational facilities. To this end the United States has in the past helped set up such institutions as Roberts College and the Istanbul Girls' College and is encouraging various co-operative cultural undertakings. "The investment of your time and money in this field," the Ambassador once told the Turks, "is an investment in the future and an expression of concern for your country." In May 1960 a military coup ousted the ten-year-old government of Prime Minister Adnan Menderes and set up a provisional government which announced its continued alignment with the West.

The University of the Andes in Mérida, Venezuela awarded Ambassador Warren an honorary LL.D. degree in March 1956. He belongs to Pi Sigma Alpha (an honorary political science society), the American Foreign Service Association, the American Legion, the Army and Navy Club in Washington, and the Country Club in Ankara. He is a Protestant and says that he has worshiped with members of a number of Protestant denominations as well as with Catholics, Jews, and Moslems. In Caracas he was a member of the Union Church.

On November 24, 1921 Fletcher Warren was married to Wilhelmina F. Kuenstler, a schoolteacher of Sweet Home, Texas. White-haired, brown-eyed Warren is six feet four inches tall and weighs 232 pounds. He lists as his favorite recreations walking, reading mystery stories, and studying peoples.

References

> Department of State Biographic Register, 1959
> International Year Book and Statesmen's Who's Who, 1959
> Who's Who in America, 1958-59
> World Biography (1954)

WARREN, LEONARD Apr. 21, 1911-Mar. 4, 1960 Leading dramatic baritone of the Metropolitan Opera Company for twenty years; among the twenty-six operatic roles in his repertoire his favorite was the title role in *Rigoletto*. See *Current Biography* (December) 1953.

Obituary

N Y Times p1+ Mr 5 '60

WARREN, WILLIAM C(LEMENTS) Feb. 3, 1909- Law school dean; lawyer

Address: b. Columbia University School of Law, New York 27; h. 325 Crest Rd, Ridgewood, N.J.

Since 1953, William C. Warren, a specialist in taxation and legal accounting, has served as the dean of the Columbia University School of Law. During his career he has been a corporation lawyer, a professor of law, a tax consultant to the Secretary of the Treasury, and a member of the United States tax mission to Japan. Warren has been an outspoken critic of what he believes to be the debasement of the Bachelor of Arts degree in recent years in the United States. He has edited several textbooks in his fields of specialization.

William Clements Warren was born in Paris, Texas, on February 3, 1909, the son of Archibold L. and Elma (Clements) Warren. His father was in the cotton business. The boy spent his early childhood in Paris, and when he was five years old the family moved to Wichita Falls, Texas, where William attended public schools and matriculated at Wichita Falls Junior College. He was a studious boy, who showed little interest in athletics or social activities.

William Warren attended the University of Texas in Austin at a time when his father lost all his money in the financial collapse of the Depression. To pay his own way in college, he joined a group that operated a tutoring school. He was also a university quiz master, worked in local bookstores, and washed dishes at his fraternity house. He majored in political science, minored in economics, and belonged to Delta Tau Delta and Pi Sigma Alpha. Elected to Phi Beta Kappa, Warren received a B.A. degree *summa cum laude* in 1931. After a year of graduate work, he received a M.A. degree.

Deciding to enter the legal profession, Warren matriculated at Harvard University Law School on a scholarship. He met some of his expenses by working during the summer vacations at bookstores on the campus of the University of Texas. At Harvard he engaged in extensive research in the fields of taxation and corporation law under the direction of Dean Erwin Griswold and Professor Barton Leach. In 1935 he received his LL.B. *cum laude*.

After his graduation from law school, Warren worked from 1935 to 1937 in the New York law firm of Davis, Polk, Wardwell, Gardiner & Reed. He was admitted to the Ohio bar in 1937. Having moved to Cleveland, he became a professor of law at Western Reserve University, teaching courses on taxation, international law, and corporate reorganization. Simultaneously he served as counsel with the Cleveland firm of Holiday, Grossman & McAfee. During the five years he spent with this firm he represented the Standard Oil Company of Ohio and other large corporations.

In 1942 Warren returned to New York and joined the firm of Milbank, Tweed & Hope, but left the position shortly afterward to do organizational work for the American Red Cross in Australia. At Melbourne he opened and operated the first military service club in the Pacific theater of operations. Returning to the United States after about nine months with the Red Cross, Warren was commissioned a captain in the United States Army.

His military assignments, mostly concerned with lend-lease affairs and matériel procurement and distribution, took him to England, Italy,

North Africa, Egypt, and France. While in England, Warren met Diana June Peel Willock, a popular British actress who belonged to Stars in Battle Dress, an affiliate of the Air Transport Service. Miss Willock's father was an air marshal in the Royal Air Force, and she is a direct descendant of the nineteenth-century British prime minister Robert Peel. When she met Warren, both were on leave on the Scilly Isles, off the southwest coast of England. They were married in London, January 13, 1945. Warren was discharged from the army in 1946, with the rank of lieutenant colonel.

Upon his return to civilian life Warren rejoined Milbank, Tweed, Hope, Hadley & McCloy, and in October 1946 was appointed to the faculty of the Columbia University School of Law. On September 1, 1947, John W. Snyder, Secretary of the Treasury, announced the appointment of three outstanding authorities to help prepare a new national tax program. Two of his appointees were Columbia professors, Warren and Dr. Carl Shoup, professor of economics and a well-known figure in federal tax research. The third was Harold V. Amberg, a Chicago banker and consultant for the Federal Reserve Board.

Until 1949, Warren served as tax consultant to the federal government. During the same period he helped Professors Adolf A. Berle and Roswell Magill to reorganize and modernize Columbia University's courses on corporations and taxation. In the summers of 1949 and 1950 he went to Japan to serve on a special tax mission that set up a comprehensive system of local and national tax revenues for the Japanese Diet. In 1952 he was admitted to the New York bar.

When Young Berryman Smith, dean of the Columbia University School of Law, resigned in November 1952, William C. Warren was made acting dean. He was officially named dean in March 1953. Less than a year after he was appointed, Dean Warren announced to the law school's alumni association that plans were being made for constructing a new building for the law school. The building would cost between six and seven million dollars. About $1,500,000 were then on hand.

When the Ford Foundation granted $1,500,000 for the new building in January 1955, Warren's drive was considerably aided. Ground for the new building was finally broken on November 7, 1958, one hundred years and six days after the law school was founded. All in all, $5,5000,000 had been raised for the new structure.

Since it was founded in 1858, the Columbia Law School had grown from a student body of thirty-five to one of 855, had produced two Supreme Court Chief Justices, and in 1929 had been the first law school in the country to admit women. In connection with the centenary celebration, Dean Warren said: "The role of law is going to become even more important as it seeks to keep up with the technological advances of the twentieth century. The opening-up of outer space, for example, presents tremendous legal problems."

WILLIAM C. WARREN

In the course of his career as professor and dean, Warren has come to the conclusion that the liberal arts graduates of today show "marked deficiencies" in their knowledge of political history and institutions, in economics, and in logic and philosophy. In his 1956 annual report to the president of Columbia University he wrote: "We are entitled to expect that the college graduate is able to read argumentative or expository prose swiftly, comprehendingly and retentively; that he is able to express himself in speech and writing grammatically, literately and precisely; that he has learned the basic lesson of using the dictionary. But we have found that few of our entering students, however carefully selected, possess these skills to the extent needed for the law study" (New York Times, February 6, 1956).

William C. Warren has written numerous articles that have appeared in legal periodicals. With Adolf A. Berle he edited Cases and Materials on the Law of Corporations (Foundation Press, 1948); with Stanley S. Surrey he edited a series of similar casebooks on federal income taxation and on federal estate and gift taxation.

Awarded the Legion of Merit and the Italian Order of the Crown for his service in World War II, William C. Warren also belongs to the societies the Order of the Coif and Phi Delta Phi. He is a member of the American Law Institute, the American Bar Association, and the American Society of International Law. He is a Democrat and a Presbyterian. He is five feet eleven inches tall, weighs 170 pounds, and has brown eyes and hair. The Warrens have three children, Robert Peel, Larissa Eve, and William Liversidge. For recreation the dean enjoys tennis, swimming, sailing, and golfing; Mrs. Warren writes fiction.

References

Who's Who in America, 1958-59
World Biography (1954)

WATKINSON, HAROLD (ARTHUR)

Jan. 25, 1910- British Minister of Defense
Address: b. House of Commons, London S.W.1, England; h. "Dibbles," West Clandon, Surrey, England

Through the redistribution of cabinet posts which followed the sweeping victory of British Prime Minister Harold Macmillan's incumbent Conservative government at the general election of October 1959, authority over Great Britain's armed services passed to the former Minister of Transport and Civil Aviation, Harold Watkinson, who became Minister of Defense. He succeeded Duncan Sandys, who was named to head a new Aviation Ministry. A member of Parliament since 1950, Watkinson has been identified with the progressive wing of the Conservative party. He was a director of a machine tool company before he took ministerial office.

British Inf. Services
HAROLD WATKINSON

The eldest son of Arthur Gill and Mary (Casey) Watkinson, Harold Arthur Watkinson was born January 25, 1910 at Walton on Thames, Surrey, England and was educated at Queen's College, Taunton, Somerset and at King's College, one of the schools of the University of London. He is by profession an engineer, and after six years (1929-35) in his family's business he was associated with various technical and engineering journals until the outbreak of war.

During World War II as a Royal Naval Volunteer Reserve officer, Watkinson served with convoys in the English Channel in 1940 and later in the Atlantic approaches. He took the gunnery staff course in 1943; was advanced to lieutenant commander in 1944; and in that rank in 1945 was placed in charge of training at the Eastney range and main naval antiaircraft gunnery school.

After his release from active duty in 1946, Watkinson made his home at West Clandon, near Guildford, Surrey, and resumed an industrial career which included experience in the timber, woodworking, building, and shipbuilding industries as well as general engineering. As director of a machine tool company, he served in 1948 as chairman of the Machine Tool Trades Association's production efficiency panel for southern England.

In the same year Watkinson became the first chairman of the Conservative Association for the new Dorking division of Surrey and then in 1949 was adopted as the prospective Conservative candidate for Woking, another new division. (Surrey borders London on the southwest, and because of postwar population shifts and growth, its representation in the House of Commons had been increased from seven to ten in a recent reapportionment of seats.) Although Woking's heavily industrial population indicates potential Labour strength, Watkinson topped the polls at the February 1950 balloting with 24,454 votes to 13,157 and 4,567 for his Labour and Liberal opponents, respectively.

In view of his appointment nine years later as Minister of Defense, it is significant that Watkinson's brief maiden speech in the Commons on March 16, 1950 warned that in future wars atomic attack would make convoying increasingly difficult. In another speech on July 26 he urged that "top priority in defense preparations . . . be given to overhaul and modernization of the convoy fleet in order to meet mass underwater attacks."

Watkinson was one of the six co-authors of the pamphlet *A New Approach,* released by the Conservative party several weeks before the October 25, 1951 election to show that "the solution to the problem of productivity lies by way of free and equal partnership between the State, the trade unions, and employers." The pamphlet also expressed the view that in the nationalized industries the government should pioneer improvements in labor relations and management practices to serve as an example to private enterprise.

At the October 1951 general election Watkinson was returned to Commons by his Woking constituency. Shortly after Winston Churchill took office as Prime Minister, Watkinson was appointed Parliamentary Private Secretary to John Maclay, the Minister of Transport and Civil Aviation in the new Conservative government. During the 1950-51 Parliament he had constantly advocated stronger ties with the United States, but in a letter published in *The Times* (London) on May 28, 1952 he warned that "what is a marginal and possibly desirable 'stake-out' in American economy would easily be a disaster for this country if we give too great a priority to dollar exports. . . . Britain should be the centre of a new sterling area which would include the Commonwealth and the countries of Western Europe, Scandinavia and the Middle East."

In his next position, as Parliamentary Secretary to the Ministry of Labour and National Service (1952-55), Watkinson had the opportunity to widen his knowledge of industrial conditions. He made tours of northern England and the industrial areas of Scotland to study problems of employment and production. He also served until 1955 as chairman of the National Advisory Committee on the Employment of Older Men and Women.

Anthony Eden became Prime Minister in April 1955 and the following December made a number of changes in his cabinet, including the appointment of Watkinson to succeed John Boyd-Carpenter as Minister of Transport and Civil Aviation. This was not then a post of cabinet rank, but it did carry membership in the Privy Council. During 1956 Watkinson had to face criticism for delays and revision of priorities in the government's highway-building program, a projected boost in railway rates and fares, and the possibility of restricting oil consumption during the Suez Canal crises.

When Harold Macmillan succeeded Eden as Prime Minister in January 1957, Transport and Civil Aviation Minister Watkinson advanced to full cabinet membership. He went to Ottawa in the summer of 1958 to confer with the Canadian Transport Minister; in July he paid a short visit to New York to discuss problems connected with the use of large jet aircraft in the North Atlantic service. He had already banned the Soviet TU-104 from London Airport as too noisy and indicated in New York that the same objection applied to the American Boeing-707.

Another problem confronting Watkinson in 1958 was Britain's lagging highway-construction program. To answer demands for better roads the government gave top priority to five new superhighway projects. Before these projects had advanced enough to silence complaints, the Prime Minister in December 1958 opened the new eight-mile Preston By-Pass in Lancashire, which had cost £4,000,000 and had taken two-and-a-half years to build. The surface collapsed within six weeks, and the road had to be closed.

The general election of October 1959 was a decisive triumph for the Conservatives. Some observers in London felt that Macmillan's subsequent cabinet reorganization reflected the increasing power of the progressive group within the party. In the redistribution of portfolios Harold Watkinson was appointed Defense Minister with control over the three armed services. The American magazine *Newsweek* noted that Watkinson was not only "a member of the progressive wing of the Tory party" but had already "proved his managerial skill." The *Guardian* conceded that he was "a conscientious and determined Minister who is likely to follow a firm course."

At the annual meeting of the ministerial council of the North Atlantic Treaty Organization at Paris in mid-December 1959, Watkinson joined United States Defense Secretary Thomas S. Gates, Jr., and West Germany's Defense Minister Franz Josef Strauss in strong support for military integration of NATO's command and forces.

Harold Arthur Watkinson and Vera Langmead, the youngest daughter of John Langmead of West Sussex, were married on November 18, 1939 and are the parents of two girls. The dapper, six-feet-tall statesman lists mountaineering, walking, and talking to people as his recreations. He has traveled widely, especially in the Scandinavian countries.

References

> N Y Times p2 F 17 '60 por
>
> Debrett's Peerage, Baronetage, Knightage and Companionage, 1959
> International Who's Who, 1959
> International Year Book and Statesmen's Who's Who, 1959
> Kelly's Handbook to the Titled, Landed and Official Classes, 1959
> Who's Who, 1959
> Who's Who in America, 1958-59

WELCH, JOSEPH N(YE) Oct. 22, 1890-Oct. 6, 1960 Boston lawyer; counsel for the United States Army in the Army-McCarthy hearings before the permanent subcommittee on investigations of the Senate Committee on Government Operations in 1954. See *Current Biography* (June) 1954.

Obituary

> N Y Times p1+ O 7 '60

WHEELOCK, WARREN Jan. 15, 1880-July 8, 1960 Sculptor and painter, especially of American historical figures. See *Current Biography* (March) 1940.

Obituary

> N Y Times p19 Jl 9 '60

WHITE, E(LWYN) B(ROOKS) July 11, 1899- Author; editor

Address: b. c/o The New Yorker, 25 W. 43d St., New York 36; h. North Brooklin, Me.

E. B. White's remarks on the vagaries, and sometimes the lunacy, of modern life and the wry humor with which he has invested them have refreshed and edified readers of the *New Yorker* since 1926. A consummate essayist, White regularly wrote the "Notes and Comments" editorials in the magazine's "Talk of the Town" section until 1938 and then, for the next five years, contributed a monthly column, "One Man's Meat," to *Harper's Magazine*.

Many of his articles from both periodicals have been published in book form. He has also written two children's books that have become classics, two volumes of poetry, and a tribute to New York City called *Here is New York*. White was awarded the gold medal for essays and criticism of the National Institute of Arts and Letters in May 1960. For the past twenty-two years he has lived on a Maine farm, which he manages with evident skill and relish and about which he often writes articles for the *New Yorker*.

"I was born of respectable people in Mount Vernon, New York [on July 11,] 1899," White has said. "There was an iron vase on the lawn

E. B. WHITE

and a copy of *Wet Days at Edgewood* on the library table. My parents came from Brooklyn: I presume they moved because Mount Vernon sounded tonier and would be better for the children." Elwyn Brooks White, the son of a piano manufacturer, Samuel Tilly White, and the former Jessie Hart, was raised in Mount Vernon with his two brothers and three sisters (one of whom is deceased). He attended local public schools and the Mount Vernon High School, from which he was graduated in 1917. White enrolled at Cornell University in Ithaca, New York, but left college in 1918 to serve in the United States Army as a private. Returning to Cornell, he majored in English and was editor in chief of the Cornell *Daily Sun*. He received his B.A. degree in 1921.

Soon after graduation White and a friend drove West in an old Model T. In Seattle White settled down for a year as a reporter for the Seattle *Times* and then, restless again, he signed as a messboy on a ship making a trading voyage to the Aleutian Islands and the Arctic. Returning to New York City, he worked for two years as a production assistant and copywriter in an advertising agency. "I also," White says, "spent several years in New York in comparative unemployment, ill at ease, lonely, and (as I recall it) poetically minded. Although I didn't write anything, this was the only genuinely creative period in my life, I think."

When the *New Yorker* was founded in 1925, White began to contribute sketches, poems, stories, and articles to the publication. Invited by Harold Ross, a founder and managing editor of the *New Yorker*, he joined the magazine's staff in 1926. During this period some of his pieces appeared in "The Conning Tower," a column conducted in the New York *World* by Franklin Pierce Adams (F.P.A.). Some years ago White recalled that the excitement con-

nected with borrowing and using his brother's Oliver typewriter had early implanted in him an ineradicable writing habit. "I liked to write," he recently explained, "and there seemed to be plenty to write about."

For twelve years White wrote the editorial essays for the *New Yorker's* "Notes and Comments." He also edited (but did not write) other parts of "Talk of the Town"; devised captions and taglines for the newsbreak fillers; and contributed sundry items of verse and prose. His work was often unsigned, but his unmistakable style soon attracted admirers, who combed through each issue for traces of White's hand.

In 1937 White moved to a farm in North Brooklin, Maine, from which he sent monthly pieces of informal comment to *Harper's Magazine*. The articles became a column, "One Man's Meat," which appeared in *Harper's* from 1938 to 1943. By 1945 White was again composing the *New Yorker's* "Notes and Comments" feature, this time on a free-lance basis. He still contributes to the magazine from time to time.

White's first two books were published in 1929 by Harper and Brothers: a volume of poems, *The Lady is Cold*, and *Is Sex Necessary?*, essays which led James Thurber satirizing pseudo-scientific sex literature. In 1931 and 1932 *Ho Hum* and *Another Ho Hum*, collections of amusing *New Yorker* newsbreak fillers with forewords by White, were published by Farrar & Rinehart, Inc. Shortly after White moved to Maine, his second book of verse, *The Fox of Peapack*, was published by Harper and Brothers (1938). The title poem concerned a fox in Peapack, New Jersey who, having taken a dislike to the local people, gathers up his belongings and sets out with his wife for other parts.

"White is a perceptive essayist," a *Time* writer once noted (July 4, 1960). "His topics range from the tremor of a leaf in the afternoon sun to the malaise of modern man." White's essays have been brought together, mostly from the *New Yorker* and *Harper's Magazine*, in several books published by Harper. *Every Day is Saturday* (1934) comments on the social activities, fads, politicking, and absurdities of the American people from 1928 to 1934; the thirty-seven essays in *Quo Vadimus* deal with topics like radio, non-stop aviation, and endorsement advertising.

After reading *One Man's Meat* (Harper, 1942; 1944), Lewis Gannett reported in the New York *Herald Tribune* on June 10, 1942: "White doesn't like oratory, loud speakers, cocksure theorists, or fraternities (he likes fraternity), and he is dubious about automobiles." The book won White the Limited Editions Club gold medal in 1945 as a work "most likely to attain the stature of a classic." John Chamberlain said of these essays (New York *Times*, June 30, 1942) that "they are full of quiet wisdom and odd humors, full of country sounds and the smell of Maine coast. Mr. White is a free man with a free mind . . . and he never hesitates to say a thing simply because it may be unfashionable."

In 1941 White and his wife, Katharine, co-edited *A Subtreasury of American Humor* (Coward-McCann), one of the few such collections to include humorous critical reviews and reportorial pieces. White's first book for children, *Stuart Little* (Harper, 1945), which describes the adventures of a boy who is only two inches high, was called "a genuine novelty in juvenile fiction" (New York *Sun,* October 17, 1945).

After World War II men turned toward the task of building a viable peace. According to White, a genuinely peaceful world can exist only if individual nations are prepared to give up full sovereignty and abide by the decisions of an international organization. In *The Wild Flag* (Houghton Mifflin, 1946), White pleads for justice based on world law as the only way to avoid wholesale extinction: "Government is the thing. Law is the thing. . . . Where do human rights arise anyway? . . . . They arise in responsible government. Where does security lie anyway? In brotherly love? Not at all, it lies in government. . . . Control lies in government because government is people."

Here is New York (Harper, 1949), a reprint of an article which first appeared in *Holiday* magazine, celebrates White's "long-standing love affair with New York." His second children's book, *Charlotte's Web* (Harper, 1952), is the fanciful story of Fern, a little girl who saves Wilbur, the runty pig, from being slaughtered and of Charlotte, the philosophical spider, who saves Wilbur's morale.

For *The Second Tree From The Corner* (Harper, 1954), White received the New York Newspaper Guild 1954 Page One Award. A collection of his best work over twenty years, the book demonstrated White's agility in many literary forms. "It is high time to declare roundly what a good many people have long suspected," Irwin Edman wrote in the New York *Times* (January 17, 1954). "E. B. White is the finest essayist in the United States. He says wise things gracefully; he is the master of an idiom at once exact and suggestive, distinguished yet familiar. His style is crisp and tender, and incomparably his own."

In 1959 White's revised edition of *The Elements of Style,* a small book on English composition written by his fondly-remembered Cornell professor, William Strunk, Jr., was published by the Macmillan Company. The book included an introduction and a new chapter on writing by White, and appeared for many weeks on the best seller lists.

Few Americans dissented when the gold medal for essays and criticism of the National Institute of Arts and Letters was awarded in May 1960 to E. B. White. The award, won previously by such writers as Edmund Wilson, Henry L. Mencken, and Van Wyck Brooks, was made not on the basis of a specific work, but for White's contribution to literature throughout his lifetime. White is a Fellow of the American Academy of Arts and Sciences. He has received honorary Litt. D. degrees from Dartmouth College (1948), the University of Maine (1948), Bowdoin College (1950), Hamilton College (1952), and Harvard University (1954). He holds an honorary L.H.D. degree from Colby College (1954).

Elwyn Brooks White was married to Katharine Sergeant Angell on November 13, 1929. They have one son, Joel McCoun. Mrs. White, an editor for the *New Yorker,* has two children by a previous marriage to Ernest Angell: Nancy (Mrs. Louis T. Stableford) and Roger. E. B. White is a slight man, with gray eyes and gray hair. Although he suffers from hay fever, he still prefers the existence of a farmer. "I like farm animals and usually keep a few around the place," he has said. "I enjoy tending them when they need something, and they almost always do."

Although E. B. White is a self-confessed "goodbye sayer"—both in and outside of books—he maintains that, notwithstanding "a few noisy and ill-timed farewells," he is "like a drunk at a wedding he is enjoying to the hilt and has no real intention of leaving."

References

International Who's Who, 1959
Twentieth Century Authors (1942; First Supplement 1955)
Who's Who in America, 1960-61

WHITE, ROBERT M(ITCHELL), 2D

Apr. 6, 1915- Editor
Address: b. New York Herald Tribune, 230 W. 41st St., New York 36; h. 1 Apawamis Ave., Rye, N.Y.

Although Robert M. White 2d, the editor and president of the New York *Herald Tribune* since August 1959 is a Democrat and his newspaper is Republican, he foresees no switch in party loyalties. He has taken in stride his move from the editorship of the Mexico (Missouri) *Ledger* (circulation of about 8,100) to that of the New York *Herald Tribune* (circulation of about 326,000).

The job of running the *Herald Tribune* was given to White by John Hay ("Jock") Whitney, United States Ambassador to the Court of St. James, who had been looking for a chief executive ever since he took financial control of the newspaper in 1958. White faces the difficult task of strengthening the position of the *Herald Tribune,* whose chief competitors are the stately New York *Times* and the mass-circulation tabloid the New York *Daily News.*

Robert Mitchell White was born on April 6, 1915 in Mexico, Missouri, a mule market and horse-breeding center, with a population of about 15,000 inhabitants. His parents are Leigh Mitchell White and Maude (See) White, and he has one married sister, Mrs. William Y. Burton of Portland, Oregon. As the child of a newspaper family, White has every right to say, "I grew up in the business." His grandfather, Colonel Robert M. White, bought the Mexico *Evening Ledger* (established in 1855) in 1876 when he was twenty-one and published and edited it up until the end of World War I.

(Continued next page)

Jean Raeburn, N.Y.

ROBERT M. WHITE 2D

After World War I his father, Leigh Mitchell White, took over as publisher and editor.

At the Missouri Military Academy in Mexico, Robert White won letters in football, basketball, and track, and joined the rifle shooting team. Graduated in 1933, he won an honor appointment to West Point, but left after six months when he failed in mathematics. He then attended Washington and Lee University in Lexington, Virginia, where he majored in history and played halfback on the varsity football team. In 1938 he received a B.A. degree. At Washington and Lee he was a member of Beta Theta Pi and Sigma Delta Chi and wrote for the college newspaper.

Long before he was graduated from college, White had been associated with newspapers in one way or another. Starting out as a newspaper carrier boy, he later served as school correspondent, sold advertisements, covered sports assignments, and, when he traveled to Africa, South America, and Europe in 1936 and 1938, se   back reports to the Mexico Ledger. In 1939 he joined the Kansas City bureau of the United Press.

From 1940 through 1945 White served with the United States Army, entering with the rank of second lieutenant in the field artillery and leaving with the rank of lieutenant colonel. He also served as a staff officer in military intelligence with both General Robert L. Eichelberger and General Douglas MacArthur. His last military assignment was in the White House as a public relations officer for the Department of War. For "meritorious service in the southwest Pacific area from 1942-1944" he was awarded the Bronze Star.

When White came back to Mexico, Missouri after the war, he shared with his father the duties of editor and publisher of the Mexico Ledger, and in 1947 he became vice-president,

secretary, and treasurer of Ledger Newspapers, Inc. His father continues to edit and publish the Ledger in Mexico, in an area which Time (July 20, 1959) called "Missouri's Little Dixie Region." In Mexico White's love of joining organizations made his name known in the newspaper world, and his contacts in journalism multiplied.

From 1956 to 1958 White was a special consultant to Marshall Field, Jr., the editor and publisher of the Chicago Sun-Times. Field is said to have given John Hay Whitney a "blue-chip recommendation" of White when Whitney was searching for a man to guide the New York Herald Tribune through the turbulent waters of metropolitan journalism. For all of its prestige, the Herald Tribune had had for years a troubled history. It was no secret in the trade that the newspaper was plagued by poor morale, circulation problems, lack of a definitive administrative policy, and a shortage of manpower that could compete with such a formidable rival as the New York Times. White confronts the problem of not only continuing the Herald Tribune in business but increasing its circulation in order to have it operate at a profit.

John Hay Whitney, who in 1958 bought control of the Herald Tribune from the Reid family, its owners since 1872, needed a man to set the newspaper on a new editorial course. That he finally found what he was looking for in a small town in Missouri occasioned some surprise among journalists. He had offered the job to several leading newspapermen, who had turned it down. He had rejected many candidates after "close examination" (Time, July 20, 1959). It is reported that Whitney, who was new to the newspaper field, had never heard of Robert White. When everyone he approached with his recruiting problem mentioned the name of the small-town journalist, he got in touch with White.

In June 1959 White flew to London to discuss the situation with John Hay Whitney. On July 13, 1959 Whitney announced that White had been appointed president, editor, chief executive officer, and member of the board of directors of the New York Herald Tribune. Whitney said: "I believe we have found a man with the dynamic ideas and sound newspaper background we were looking for. Bob White has been editor and publisher of one of the finest small daily newspapers in the nation. I know that he will bring new vigorous leadership to the Herald Tribune. The newspaper publishing field has recognized his ability and he has won national distinction for his publishing achievements. . . . Mr. White and I have only one target for the Herald Tribune—to make it a still greater newspaper, a still more vital and constructive force in the life of the city and the nation."

On the question of political allegiance Whitney commented: "It happens that Mr. White is a Democrat while I am a Republican. The paper will, of course, continue its policy of complete objectivity in its news columns and of independent Republicanism on its editorial page." White said: "I am more of a Southern

Democrat than anything else, so there are wide areas of philosophical agreement. If we still run into trouble there, well, I'm just going to have to live up to the editorial traditions of the paper" (*Newsweek,* August 17, 1959).

When he took charge of the New York *Herald Tribune* on August 3, 1959, White replaced Howard D. Brundage, who had served in the interim period as president. Before Brundage, the post of president and editor had been held by Ogden R. ("Brownie") Reid, who resigned in December 1958. Reid was subsequently appointed United States Ambassador to Israel. Whitney has said that he will take part in the management of the paper when he no longer is United States Ambassador to Great Britain.

White views his jump from a small-town newspaper to one of the nation's major dailies with a great deal of composure. "The difference between big papers and little papers is zeros—the zeros of the circulation figures," he has said. "No matter what the press run may be, the payoff is one guy and his wife. The paper either reaches them, or it doesn't" (*Newsweek,* August 17, 1959). In his first editorial for the *Herald Tribune* he wrote: "The most basic cause a newspaper can serve is telling you . . . the facts, the truth, the news."

The second editorial that White wrote for the *Herald Tribune* took the form of an open letter to Soviet Premier Nikita S. Khrushchev on September 15, 1959, the day that the Premier arrived in Washington, D.C. Published on the front page in both Russian and English, the editorial in November 1959 won an award from the Society of the Silurians, an organization of New York City journalists, for the best editorial to appear in a daily newspaper. In it White told the Premier: "For our greatest wealth, Mr. Khrushchev, is of the spirit. It lies in our people—a free people. A people who are volunteers, not conscripts, in citizenship, in labor, in their way of living."

White is a member of the American Society of Newspaper Editors, the National Press Club, and of the Missouri Press Association. He is chairman of the board and past president of the Inland Daily Press Association and a charter member and former member of the executive board of the National Conference of Editorial Writers. He is a director of the American Newspaper Publishers Association and the ANPA's Research Institute and serves on the executive council of Sigma Delta Chi, the professional journalistic fraternity and on the nominating committee of the Associated Press. He is a director of the New York Convention and Visitors Bureau, Christian College in Columbia, Missouri, and the Missouri Military Academy.

Before he came to the *Herald Tribune,* White won the Sigma Delta Chi Distinguished Service Award for Editorials (1952), and served on the Governor of Missouri's Committee for Education Beyond the High School (1958-59). In 1958 the past presidents of the Missouri Press Association named him "Missouri's Outstanding Young Newspaperman."

On August 19, 1948 Robert Mitchell White was married to Barbara Whitney Spurgeon, who comes from a family of manufacturers in Muncie, Indiana. They have three daughters: Barbara Whitney, Jane Randolph, and Laura Lea. Six feet one inch in height and 170 pounds in weight, White impressed a *New Yorker* interviewer as a "tall, rangy, blue-eyed, dark-haired, craggily handsome man of forty-four" (January 23, 1960). Sports cars (he owns a Jaguar), duck shooting, and quail hunting were his favorite recreations until he came to the concrete jungle of New York. He is a Methodist. "I have a deep and abiding respect for newspapers," White told the *New Yorker* interviewer. "I think they're the most important things on earth."

References

Christian Sci Mon p12 Jl 14 '59 por
N Y Herald Tribune p1+ Jl 14 '59 por
N Y Times p24 Jl 14 '59 por
N Y World-Telegram p36 Jl 14 '59 por
New Yorker 35:24+ Ja 23 '60
Newsweek 54:84 Ag 17 '59 por
Time 74:52 Jl 20 '59 por
Who's Who in America, 1958-59

WHITEHILL, WALTER MUIR Sept. 28, 1905- Librarian; historian
Address: b. Boston Athenæum, 10-1/2 Beacon St., Boston 8, Mass.; h. Old Berry House, North Andover, Mass.

The Director and Librarian of the venerable Boston Athenæum, Walter Muir Whitehill came into the library profession as an historian whose chief experience in libraries had consisted in using them for research on the history of medieval Spanish art and the maritime aspects of American history. Whitehill assumed his present post in 1946. On October 1, 1959 he took a year's leave of absence from the Boston Athenæum to direct a study of the research and publication problems of special libraries.

The only child of the Reverend Walter Muir Whitehill, an Episcopal clergyman, and Florence Marion (Williams) Whitehill, a painter, Walter Muir Whitehill was born in Cambridge, Massachusetts on September 28, 19 . His first experience with libraries came as a child, when, on returning home from visits to Dr. Geoffrey Brackett on Newbury Street, he would drop into the Boston Public Library and climb the Siena marble staircase to visit the lions that guard the landing. "Dr. Brackett assured me," he has recalled, "that if I pulled the lions' tails, they *might* roar, and I never failed to try."

The Boston Public Library played a more important part during his "two dreary years" at Boston Latin School. On his way to and from the "gloomy red brick monster" he would pass the library. "The Boston Latin School thirty-five years ago suited my temperament so poorly that I welcomed the daily opportunity to escape to the third floor of the Public Li-

WALTER MUIR WHITEHILL

brary, where I could wallow to my heart's content in architectural accounts of the palaces of Versailles."

Frank A. Bourne, an architect who had abandoned his practice to reorganize the Boston Public Library's fine arts department, gave the teen-ager an after-school job in the department. Whitehill's weekly wage ranged from a high of $2.50 to a low of 81 cents. "That period," he remarked later, "did give me the professional respectability of at least *beginning* in a library."

Whitehill finished high school at Wellesley High, graduating in 1922. He majored in English at Harvard University on a Matthews Scholarship and received his B.A. *cum laude* in 1926. From 1926 to 1928 he was a tutor in fine arts at Harvard, teaching art history. Working with Professor A. Kingsley Porter while an undergraduate, he had become interested in the middle ages. He pursued this interest through graduate work in the history of medieval art at Harvard (M.A. degree, 1929) and at the University of London (Ph.D. degree, 1934). His Ph.D. thesis was later published as *Spanish Romanesque Architecture of the Eleventh Century* (Oxford University Press, 1941).

Whitehill centered his interest in the history of medieval art on Spain, and he spent most of his time in Europe from 1930 to 1936 in that country. He was living and doing research there when the Spanish civil war broke out in 1936. Reluctantly, he dropped his research and went home to Massachusetts to wait for the war to end. While waiting, he worked as assistant director of the Peabody Museum in Salem. (The museum grew out of the East India Marine Society and has especially good collections on voyages of exploration.) Whitehill turned his interest to United States history, particularly its maritime aspects, while he was at Salem, and he never returned to Spain. His

new-found interest was signalized in such publications as his edition of the journal of Henry Edward Napier, lieutenant on H.M.S. *Nymphe: New England Blocaded in 1814* (Peabody Museum, 1939). Among later works which evidenced his continuing interest in maritime history was *Fleet Admiral King: A Naval Record* (Norton, 1952), written jointly with Ernest Joseph King. About the Peabody Museum of Salem he has written *The East India Marine Society and the Peabody Museum of Salem: A Sesquicentennial History* (Peabody Museum, 1949).

Whitehill served at the Peabody Museum of Salem from 1936 to 1942. In the latter year he went on active duty as a lieutenant in the United States Naval Reserve. He engaged in archival work on operational records of World War II in the Navy Department's Office of Naval Records and library until 1946, when he left active duty with the rank of commander, U.S.N.R. He is a member of the Secretary of the Navy's advisory committee on naval history.

In 1946 Whitehill attained his present post of Director and Librarian of the Boston Athenæum "without," as he has put it, "apprenticeship before the mast." "I became the head of a library as a result of having used many libraries in the course of my own historical investigations." The institution that he heads is a private library, the most prominent of those libraries set up in the late eighteenth and early nineteenth centuries by private societies for the use of their members. Founded in 1807, the Boston Athenæum progressively increased its general and special holdings and enriched the intellectual life of Boston throughout the nineteenth century. Its present role is that of a special library, open to members as well as to scholars who are not members. It has rich collections in New England history, American and British fine arts, belles-lettres, and literature. Among the special collections are early Boston newspapers, books owned by George Washington, King's Chapel Library (1698), first editions of American authors, prints of New England, broadsides, early United States documents, and Confederate imprints. At the Boston Athenæum, Whitehill directs a staff of over twenty persons. The library's volumes (including pamphlets and bound periodicals) number about 400,000. It circulates over 40,000 books a year.

Since October 1, 1959 Whitehill has been on leave of absence from the Boston Athenæum, directing a study of the research and publication problems of independent historical societies. Supported by a grant from the Council on Library Resources, Inc., the study is sponsored by the Massachusetts Historical Society (of which Whitehill is recording secretary), the Virginia Historical Society, the Historical Society of Pennsylvania, and the American Antiquarian Society (of whose council he is a member). The study has involved extensive travel on Whitehill's part. His leave of absence from the Boston Athenæum will end in October 1960.

Walter Muir Whitehill has been a member of the faculty of the Peabody Museum of Archaeology and Ethnology at Harvard University since 1951. He was Allston Burr senior tutor in Lowell House at Harvard from 1952 to 1956 and lecturer on history at Harvard during 1956 and 1957.

The published writings of Whitehill include *The Boston Public Library* (Harvard University Press, 1956), a centennial history written at the request of the trustees of the Boston Public Library; *A Brief Guide to the Institutions and Sites of Historic Interest in Boston* (Bostonian Society, 1957), prepared for the visit of military representatives of the North Atlantic Treaty Organization to the Bostonian Society on March 24, 1957; *Boston: A Topographical History* (Belknap Press of Harvard University Press, 1959), a series of eight lectures delivered at Lowell Institute, Boston, in the spring of 1958.

Among the works Whitehill has edited is *Letters to John Cotton of Plymouth* (American Antiquarian Society, 1949), from the seventeenth-century correspondence of Thomas Walley. He has contributed many articles to American, British, and Spanish scholarly journals. His "Bibliography of New England" has appeared annually in the March issues of *New England Quarterly* over the past several years. He is on the editorial boards of the latter publication and of *The American Neptune: A Quarterly Journal of Maritime History,* which he founded in 1941. He was on the editorial board of the *William and Mary Quarterly* until 1959. From 1954 to 1957 he was editor of the American Academy of Arts and Sciences; while serving in that capacity he changed the title of its official publication from the *Proceedings* of the Academy to its present title, *Daedalus.*

He is also editor of the Colonial Society of Massachusetts, librarian of the American Academy of Arts and Sciences, president of Boston's Old South Association, and director of the Thomas Jefferson Foundation. He served for nine years on the council of the Institute of Early American History and Culture, Williamsburg, Virginia, and as its chairman from 1954 to 1959.

Walter Muir Whitehill and Jane Revere Coolidge were married on June 5, 1930. Mrs. Whitehill, a graduate of Vassar and Radcliffe, edited the *Letters of Mrs. Gaskell and Charles Eliot Norton* (Oxford University Press, 1932). The Whitehills have two children: Jane Coolidge Whitehill (Mrs. William Rotch) and Diana Whitehill (Mrs. C. Christopher Laing). During most of the year the Whitehills live in the stately Old Berry House in North Andover, Massachusetts, where Whitehill likes to trim the hedges; for the last few summers they have retreated to a farm in Vermont.

David McCord, the humorist, has said of Whitehill that "he could pass in a crowd as the president of a college . . . a member of Parliament . . . a man who could speak up to Dr. Johnson and down to Mr. Boswell . . . an amused boulevardier in wax, an amiable walrus, or an ambassador between assignments." Whitehill is known for his engaging, witty, and meticulous speech. He smokes a huge pipe and carries a superannuated vellum valise with him wherever he goes. He is an Episcopalian and

a Republican. His recreations are gardening, collecting books and prints, printing, and cooking. Honorary degrees have been given to him by the University of New Brunswick (D. Litt., 1959) and Washington and Jefferson College (LL.D., 1959). He has been an honorary member of the Harvard Chapter of Phi Beta Kappa since 1951 and its president for 1959-60. His clubs are the Somerset, the Tavern Club, and the Club of Odd Volumes in Boston, and the Army and Navy Club in Washington, D.C. Of his work Whitehill has said: "It is extraordinarily pleasant to do what you most enjoy and have other people not only consider it work, but pay you for it."

References

> Directory of American Scholars (1957)
> International World Who's Who (1949)
> Who's Who in America, 1960-61
> Who's Who in the East (1955)

WIGGLESWORTH, RICHARD B(OW-DITCH) Apr. 25, 1891-Oct. 22, 1960 United States Ambassador to Canada since 1958; United States Representative from Massachusetts (1928-58); lawyer. See *Current Biography* (May) 1959.

Obituary

> N Y Times p88 O 23 '60

WIGNY, PIERRE (LOUIS JEAN JOSEPH) (wē-nyē') Apr. 18, 1905- Minister of Foreign Affairs of Belgium

Address: b. Ministry of Foreign Affairs, 8 rue de la Loi, Brussels, Belgium; h. 94 ave. Louise, Brussels, Belgium

During 1960 Pierre Wigny, the Minister of Foreign Affairs of Belgium, has been responsible for presenting and defending to the world his nation's position on the troubled events in the Republic of the Congo. The new state, which received its independence from Belgium on June 30, 1960, has been unable to maintain order among the Congolese. The necessity for United Nations help and the possibility of big power intervention called into question Belgian colonial policies in preparing the Belgian Congo for independence and caused Belgium to reconsider its relationship with its allies, its membership in the North Atlantic Treaty Organization, and its position within the European community.

Wigny, who has been Belgium's Minister of Foreign Affairs since 1958, had previously served as Belgian Minister of Colonies, from 1947 to 1950, when he outlined a ten-year program of development for the Belgian Congo. He has served in Belgium's Parliament and as a member of the Common Assembly of the European Coal and Steel Community and of the European Parliamentary Assembly. He was trained as a lawyer and has written numerous works on public law.

Pierre Louis Jean Joseph Wigny, was born in Liège, Belgium on April 18, 1905, the son of Henri Wigny, a lawyer, and his wife, whose

R. Kayaert, Brussels

PIERRE WIGNY

maiden name was Croisier. He was graduated from the University of Liège in international law and later received a J.S.D. degree from Harvard University in the United States. Beginning in 1930 he was employed at the Brussels branch of Guaranty Trust for five years. From 1935 to 1939 he was secretary-general of the Study Center for State Reform and during the Nazi occupation of Belgium in World War II was secretary of Pro Juventute. After the liberation of his country, he served in 1944-45 as the director of the Repatriation Commission. In 1946 he became president of the study center of the Social Christian party.

As the Minister of Colonies of the Belgian government from 1947 to 1950, Wigny drew up a detailed ten-year plan for the industrial and agricultural development of the Belgian Congo. The Belgian government would supervise the plan and supply about half of the $1 billion estimated cost; the other half would come from private investors in Belgium and abroad. The plan envisaged that projects in transportation, electrification, and agriculture operated by the Congo government would attract emigrants from Belgium, whose well-run, medium-sized farms would encourage the natives to come out of the bush, settle down as farmers, and imitate the colonists' farming methods.

The plan aimed also at the development of the rich mining resources in the Congo, although no mention was made of uranium, undoubtedly for security reasons; uranium mines in the Belgian Congo are a major source of supply for the United States. The establishment of light industries and projects for housing, education, and health were also outlined. Wigny proposed to eliminate the dual economy of the whites and the natives and urged a fight against racial discrimination: "This detestable policy attempts to save the situation of the white man by reserving for him a monopoly of certain professions and relegates the natives to inferior employment." During his three years in this office Wigny founded the Savings Bank of the Belgian Congo, the Institute for Scientific Research in Central Africa, and the Office of African Cities.

In 1949 Wigny became a deputy to Parliament from the district of Tournai-Ath as a member of the Social Christian party. This is a Catholic party whose members' views range from conservatism to leftism, although there is a strong central group. Its supporters are generally the nobility, Flemish peasants, industrialists, and labor groups; and it is stronger in Flanders than in French-speaking areas. The party has supported Belgium's membership in the North Atlantic Treaty Organization, Western European Union, the Common Market, and Euratom.

Chosen by the Parliament of Belgium, Wigny was a member from 1952 to 1958 of the Common Assembly of the European Coal and Steel Community (ECSC), composed of six nations: Belgium, the Netherlands, Luxembourg, France, West Germany, and Italy. From 1957 to 1958 he was president of the Christian Democratic group of the Common Assembly. In 1956 he headed the study group of the assembly for the establishment of Euratom and presented the "Preliminary Report on the European Problem of Energy," which compared Euratom plans with those being developed by the Organization for European Economic Cooperation. Euratom would provide for a common market for all materials used in nuclear processes and for the establishment of a supranational authority for the common development of research and industrial projects among the six nations.

The last session of the ECSC Common Assembly was held in February 1958, since parliamentary control over the community was henceforth to be exercised by the European Parliamentary Assembly of the communities of the six nations: ECSC, European Economic Community (Common Market), and the European Atomic Energy Community (Euratom)— the treaties establishing these latter communities went into force on January 1, 1958. Wigny became a member in 1958 of the new European Parliamentary Assembly and president of the Christian Democratic group there.

When Premier Gaston Eyskens formed his coalition cabinet of Social Christians and Liberals in November 1958, he appointed Wigny as Minister of Foreign Affairs. In this post he has been concerned with pointing out the responsibilities of the small powers in influencing the big powers and with asserting the right of the small powers to be heard. Other problems that confront him involve Belgium's relationship with the European communities and with NATO and events arising from the independence of the Belgian Congo in 1960.

In the fall of 1959 Wigny presented a plan to the Council of Ministers of the six-nation European communities for the acceleration of treaty provisions so that the Common Market would complete its economic merger by 1966. The harmonization of social, agricultural, fiscal, taxation, and other policies would also be accelerated, and a monetary union for accounting purposes would be established. Wigny also proposed the early adoption of provisions for a European assembly to be elected by universal suffrage and the merger of the three executives of ECSC, Euratom, and the Common Market. In 1960 the plan was being studied by the various nations concerned. In November 1960 the Benelux Economic Union of Belgium, the Netherlands, and Luxembourg came into being. Previously, the three nations had been joined in a customs union.

Because of the postwar pressures to grant colonies their freedom and demands from the Congolese, the Belgian government granted the Congo its independence on June 30, 1960. When the new Republic of the Congo was unable to maintain order, Belgium sent in its troops to protect Belgian and other nationals in the area. The United Nations acceded to the request to send its troops to the Congo to help keep order, and in the summer of 1960 the Belgian troops began to withdraw.

Wigny took part in the negotiations about the Congo situation and also, in speeches at home and at the U.N. Security Council and General Assembly meetings in New York, presented to his countrymen and the world the reasons for Belgian intervention and its position on the various issues there, including the secession of Katanga province from the Republic of the Congo. Belgium was particularly criticized for granting independence to a country whose Parliament contained only one university graduate and whose army had no African commissioned officers, although Belgium had made a beginning toward education and training a civil service.

Among Wigny's writings on law are *Essai sur le droit privé américain, Principes généraux du droit administratif,* and *Droit constitutionnel.* He is a member of the Royal Belgian Academy (1954), the Royal Colonial Academy (1957), and the Academy of Overseas Sciences of Paris (1958). He also belongs to the International Institute of Different Civilizations (secretary-general, 1951) and the Royal Society of Political Economy of Belgium (president, 1953).

He is a commander in the Order of Leopold (Belgium) and in the Legion of Honor (France), a grand officer in the Order of Merit (Italy), and a Chevalier in the Order of Orange-Nassau (the Netherlands). He received the Grand Cross of the Order of Saint Sylvester (Vatican), the Grand Cross of the Order of the Crown of Oak (Luxembourg), and the Grand Cross of the Royal Order of George I (Greece).

Pierre Wigny was married to Lily Borboux on July 30, 1929. They have four children: Jacqueline (Mrs. J. de Groete), Pierre, Henry, and Damien.

References

International Year Book and Statesmen's Who's Who, 1960
Who's Who in America, 1960-61
Who's Who in Belgium (1959)

WILLIAMS, ANDY Dec. 3, 1930- Singer
Address: b. c/o Connie De Nave, 1755 Broadway, New York 19

Known for his smooth delivery of love ballads and his relaxed and casual manner, Andy Williams has built up a nationwide following through his appearances on television and his best-selling recordings. A seasoned entertainer over radio and in the smarter supper clubs, Williams has been in show business for twenty years. Since he made his TV debut on Steve Allen's *Tonight* program in 1954, he has continued to enhance his reputation by a series of successful recordings, well-received summer-replacement shows on television, and video "specials." In November 1959 the Variety Club of Washington, D.C. bypassed celebrated television stars to honor the disarming Williams with its Personality of the Year award.

ANDY WILLIAMS

Andrew Williams was born on December 3, 1930 (some sources cite earlier dates) in Wall Lake, Iowa, a town with a population of under 1,000. His parents, Jay E. and Florence Bell (Finley) Williams, have three older sons, Richard, Robert, and Donald, and a daughter, Jane. Jay Williams, a railway mail clerk and amateur musician, trained his family into a choir to sing at the local Presbyterian Church. "We finally decided we were too good to stay home," Andy has recalled. The four Williams Brothers made their professional debut over radio station WHO in Des Moines, Iowa, when Andy was eight years old.

Until the early part of World War II, the Williams family moved with the engagements of their four singing sons. After Des Moines, they went to Chicago to appear on the *National Barn Dance* program over radio station WLS, then to Cincinnati's radio station WLW. Finally,

WILLIAMS, ANDY—Continued

in Los Angeles, the quartet was signed to a motion-picture contract with Metro-Goldwyn-Mayer Pictures.

The Williams Brothers were obliged to disband, however, when the two oldest brothers were called for military service. Andy, who had attended public schools along the family's route, settled down to finish his secondary education in Los Angeles, graduating in 1947. About this time the Williams Brothers reformed and teamed with comedienne Kay Thompson to create a night club act.

The team of Kay Thompson and the Williams Brothers made its debut in 1947. "They have since spent their time making money hand over fist," wrote a reviewer in *Harper's Magazine* a year later (July 1948). This critic described the brothers as follows: "Four young men, all of equal height and California complexion." Their singing, dancing, and buffoonery amused night club audiences in Europe and the United States for six years, until 1953. The brothers then dissolved their unit: Donald tried acting, Robert went into business, and Richard became a solo singer. "I was the youngest," Andy has said, "And I was in no hurry to do anything."

In 1954 Andy Williams recorded his first song and went to New York to market it. While there, he auditioned for a spot on the Steve Allen *Tonight* show and obtained a commitment for a two-week run. "After that no one said anything and I just reported each week and kept singing and they kept paying me," he has explained. He remained on the show for two and a half years, selecting his own songs and winning admirers with his warm voice and disarming smile. Besides singing, Williams noted, "I was called on to be anything from an Apache dancer to a gangster, from a precocious child to a Russian bartender. And it was great fun as well as a great professional experience."

Shortly after joining the *Tonight* program, Williams signed a contract with Cadence Records. Fans were soon buying discs of his mellow renditions of "Baby Doll," "Butterfly," "I Like Your Kind of Love," "Lips of Wine," "Are You Sincere?" and "Promise Me Love." His recordings of "Canadian Sunset," The Hawaiian Wedding Song," and "The Village of St. Bernadette" sold about 1,000,000 copies each. In 1956 Cadence released his first album, *Andy Williams Sings Steve Allen,* which was followed by *Andy Williams Sings Rodgers and Hammerstein* and *Two Time Winners.*

After leaving the Steve Allen program, Williams shared a minor summer-replacement series with June Valli on NBC-TV in 1957 and made several guest appearances on *The Dinah Shore Chevy Show.* Williams, who favorably impressed Miss Shore's sponsor, was chosen to replace another Chevrolet program, *The Pat Boone Chevy Showroom,* during the summer of 1958. He also impressed John Crosby, who admitted in the New York *Herald Tribune* on July 14, 1958 that he preferred Andy Williams to Pat Boone. "Not that I've got anything against Pat Boone," Crosby hastened to add. "Coming out against Pat Boone would be like

coming out against the American flag—but he is just so healthy and wholesome and normal that he puts me to sleep."

For thirteen weeks in 1958 *The Chevy Showroom with Andy Williams* serenaded summer audiences with such established favorites as "You Do Something to Me," "Swinging Down the Lane," and "Alexander's Ragtime Band." "This is perfect summer fare," said a New York *Herald Tribune* reviewer (July 4, 1958). "It is a lazy, good-natured show with an extremely pleasant host in Williams. He sings well in casual style and doesn't attempt to overpower you with personality."

Disappointed in his hope that the show would lead to a permanent commitment, Williams settled for guest appearances until the following summer, when he was signed to substitute for *The Gary Moore Show* on CBS-TV with a one-hour variety program, *The Andy Williams Show.* It was praised for its showmanship, simple but refreshing sets, and judicious selection of guest performers, including Carol Lawrence, the Mills Brothers, and Stan Freberg.

In the autumn of 1959 Williams began to concentrate on one-hour video "specials." The first was *Music from Shubert Alley* over NBC-TV on November 13, 1959. The hour's entertainment, with Williams as a vocalist and master of ceremonies, featured dances and songs from Broadway musicals of the last sixty years. In addition to entertaining on TV, Williams in 1959 returned to the night club circuit, appearing, among other places, at the Hotel Roosevelt in New Orleans. He also continued to record for Cadence, which in late 1959 released an album entitled *Lonely Street,* prompted by Williams' best-selling record with the same title. On November 21, 1959 he received the annual Personality of the Year award from the Variety Club of Washington, D.C.

Andy Williams lives in a small East Side apartment in New York, the walls of which are covered with original French impressionist and modern paintings he has collected in Europe and the United States. This is a recent hobby. "I filled my walls with all the prints I have always loved from da Vinci to van Gogh," Williams has said. "Then I made the mistake of buying one oil painting. From then on the prints went and the oils began!"

His other hobbies are travel, golf, tennis, spectator sports, and reading. He also enjoys playing with his Boxer, Barnaby. Williams is a rugged young man with a dimpled smile, thick brown hair, and blue eyes; he is five feet nine inches tall and weighs 150 pounds. He "looks and acts like just what he is, a country boy from the Midwest who has made good in the big city" (New York *World-Telegram and Sun,* August 14, 1959). In religion he is a Presbyterian. He is still unmarried.

With his relaxed singing style, Williams has benefited from a recent trend away from rock 'n' roll music. Behind the relaxation lies intensive work, however; he rehearses forty-eight hours for a single one-hour show.

After two decades as a showman, Williams plans no change in the whispered serenades or the easy-going style which have brought him success. "I've ignored rock 'n' roll because I think ballads are more welcome on TV," he has said (New York *Herald Tribune,* July 22, 1958), "but now and then I get on the fringe of rock 'n' roll for my recordings. . . .I wouldn't want to sing solely for teen-agers. Once they go to college, their musical taste changes, and then where would I be?" Kay Thompson, who teamed with the Williams Brothers thirteen years ago, said: "Stars like Andy, with a plain niceness about them, are the ones that last" (*Look,* September 1, 1959).

References

N Y Post Mag p3 N 1 '59 por
N Y Times II p3 Ag 24 '58 por
Wood, C. TV Personalities vol 3 (1957)

WILLIAMS, HARRISON A(RLINGTON), JR.

Dec. 10, 1919- United States Senator from New Jersey; lawyer

Address: b. Senate Office Bldg., Washington, 25, D.C.; 125 Broad St., Elizabeth, N.J.; h. 231 Elizabeth Ave., Westfield, N.J.

When Harrison A. Williams, Jr., was elected junior Senator from New Jersey in November 1958, he shattered state political precedents for the second time. The first New Jersey Democrat to hold a Senate seat since 1936, he also drew national attention in 1953 by becoming the first Democratic Representative (1953-57) of New Jersey's twenty-one-year-old Sixth District. Williams has supported the liberal wing of his party by advocating generous allotment of funds for foreign aid, housing and education, social security benefits, health and unemployment insurance, conservation, and urban renewal projects. He has favored civil rights legislation and opposed stringent labor control bills.

Harrison Arlington Williams, Jr., was born in Plainfield, New Jersey on December 10, 1919. His father, for whom he is named, is president of the Norwalk Vault Company in Plainfield. His mother was Isabel Lamson before her marriage. After attending elementary and secondary schools in Plainfield, Williams entered Oberlin College in Ohio, where he majored in economics and considered a possible career as a radio announcer. Having been graduated with a B.A. degree in 1941, Williams studied briefly at the Georgetown University School of Foreign Service in Washington, D.C. He earned his living by working as a copy boy on the Washington *Post.*

In the winter of 1941-42 Williams enlisted in the United States Navy. After one year as a seaman on a mine sweeper, he was transferred to the naval air division, where he soon received an officer's commission. Williams served as a pilot and flight instructor until December 1945 when he was discharged with the rank of lieutenant, junior grade.

Returning to civilian life, Williams was employed as a steelworker by the National Tube Company in Lorain, Ohio for several months. At that time he became a member of the United

Wide World

HARRISON A. WILLIAMS, JR.

Steel Workers of America, CIO. In the fall of 1946 he enrolled in the Law School of Columbia University, from which he received an LL.B. degree in 1948. The same year he was admitted to the New Hampshire bar, and practised law in Jaffrey, New Hampshire for one year.

He then returned to Plainfield, where he served for a time as "combination law clerk and baby-sitter" for the attorney, George F. Hetfield, whom he later opposed in the special Sixth District election of 1953. Admitted to the New Jersey bar in 1951, Williams joined the Newark law office of Cox & Walburg, and also became an instructor in business law at the Newark branch of Rutgers University. In 1951 he made an unsuccessful bid for a seat in the state assembly. The following year he failed to attain a seat on the Plainfield city council.

For twenty-one years after its formation in 1932 the staunchly Republican Sixth Congressional District of New Jersey refused to send a Democrat to the House of Representatives. When the popular liberal Republican incumbent, Clifford P. Case, resigned his seat in the House in August 1953, a special election to fill the vacancy was called for November. Chances of winning the contest were so poor that experienced Democrats were unwilling to run. When Williams agreed to become a candidate he was told by the Democratic National Committee that it was "against party policy to spend money in hopeless contests." Williams financed the campaign with $2,800 of his own and some borrowed money. He promised to follow Case's liberal policies, pledged support of President Eisenhower, and argued that he could do both better than his conservative Republican opponent, George F. Hetfield.

(Continued next page)

WILLIAMS, HARRISON A., JR.—*Cont.*

In the course of the campaign Williams first expressed publicly his views on various national issues for which he later voted as a Congressman. He favored strengthening of the Point Four program; strong military and civil defense measures; repeal of the Taft-Hartley labor law; and taxation based on ability to pay. Although he felt it was necessary to search out Communists in the government, this could be done "with less hysteria and with a traditional respect for the freedom of the individual by using some sort of court procedure." In November 1953 Williams prevailed over Hetfield by a narrow margin of 1,876 votes.

Williams' first major speech in the House of Representatives, made in June 1954, supported President Eisenshower's request for a three-year extension of the Reciprocal Trade Agreements Act. Shortly thereafter he introduced a bill, which he wrote with John F. Kennedy, to provide government assistance to businesses hurt by competition from low-priced imported goods. The legislation was offered as a substitute for high tariff protections.

During his first term in the House, Williams supported adequate mutual security appropriations and introduced an amendment which would have freed the employment of foreign aid workers from political patronage. As for domestic issues, Williams during 1954 favored flexible farm price supports, a comprehensive conservation program, government-supported slum clearance and urban renewal, extension of unemployment benefits, and authorization of the St. Lawrence Seaway construction.

Re-elected to a full two-year term in November 1954 by a plurality of over 20,000 votes, Williams was named to the Foreign Affairs Committee the following January. During the sessions of the Eighty-fourth Congress he supported a bill to provide $3.4 billion in foreign aid, but introduced an amendment which required termination of aid to Yugoslavia unless the country remained independent of Soviet control. In December 1955 Williams announced that he would submit a new immigration bill providing for a unified quota system, which would "rid us of the legalized snobbery of the national origins quota." The measure would also eliminate distinctions between native-born and naturalized citizens, in his opinion.

In 1956 Williams urged that the United States join the international Organization for Trade Cooperation. He continued to favor additional federal appropriations for highway and school construction, and he voted for the Powell amendment to the school aid bill, which made the provision that no federal funds be given to states which failed to comply with decisions of the United States Supreme Court. Williams supported higher veterans' pensions and postal workers' salaries, but opposed a raise in postal rates.

Williams was defeated by some 4,000 votes in his bid for re-election to the House in November 1956, when President Eisenhower carried the Sixth Congressional District. He resumed law practice in Elizabeth, New Jersey as a member of the firm of Pollis & Williams.

When Democratic Governor Robert B. Meyner sought a second term in 1957, Williams took over direction of the Meyner for Governor Clubs. "Williams spoke in behalf of . . . Meyner in nearly every county in the state," a New York *Times* (March 4, 1958) commentator noted, "and Mr. Meyner's 203,000-vote plurality made the Williams star glow."

Meyner designated Williams as the Democratic state organization candidate for United States Senator in March 1958. Having won at the April primaries over Mayor John J. Grogan and one other candidate, he defeated Robert W. Kean in the November elections for one of the two New Jersey Senate seats. In the Eighty-sixth Congress, Williams was named to the Banking and Currency, and the Labor and Public Welfare committees. He also served on the Select Committee on Small Business. Head of a Labor and Public Welfare special subcommittee on migratory labor, he conducted hearings throughout the nation's farm areas.

During 1959 Williams supported liberal mutual security and defense appropriations and favored United States aid to Soviet satellite countries. In a New York *Herald Tribune* (October 13, 1958) interview, however, he indicated that "we could be spending less money abroad if we did two things: [if we had] really competent people administering programs, and better definitions of what we are trying to do abroad." In 1958 Williams criticized the foreign policy of the Eisenhower administration as being one of stop-gap measures rather than long-term planned programs. He added that United States Mideast policy has been one of "massive appeasement of Nasser."

In 1960 Williams served as a co-sponsor of Senator Patrick V. McNamara's bill to provide health insurance for the aged. The bill was to include both hospital and other medical benefits and to extend coverage to those not eligible for social security.

Williams is an articulate and tireless political campaigner. He has often been up at dawn to greet workers as they arrived at the gates of industrial plants and he has frequently addressed women's and rotary clubs until after midnight. During his 1954 campaign he appeared on three fifteen-minute television programs, "all wonderfully simple, wonderfully inexpensive, and marvelously effective" (John Crosby, New York *Herald Tribune,* December 5, 1954). As a Congressman, Williams has maintained close contact with his constituents and has often polled voters on major issues. During 1955 he toured eighteen of his district's twenty-seven public, parochial, and private high schools, talking to the students and answering their questions. In the summer of 1954 he instituted a "congressional scholarship," offering to pay the expenses of a high school student who would "study government at its source," using Williams' Washington office as a classroom.

Harrison A. Williams, Jr. was married to Nancy McGlone on February 14, 1948. The couple, who live in a nine-room eighteenth-century house in Westfield, New Jersey, have four children, Peter, Wendy, Jonathan, and Nina, in addition to Nancy Nichols, Mrs. Williams' daughter by a previous marriage. The Senator, whose nickname is "Pete," is said to have "a clean-cut Ivy League appearance, an earnestness of manner and a resonant baritone voice befitting a radio announcer" (New York Times, March 4, 1958). He was awarded an honorary degree by Rutgers University in 1960. He is a member of the national advisory committee of the Unitarian Laymen's League, an Elk, and a member of the Ancient Order of Hibernians. He also belongs to the Reserve Officers' Association, the American Legion, and the Veterans of Foreign Wars.

References

N Y Herald Tribune p1 N 5 '53; p27 Mr 9 '58 por
N Y Times p25 Mr 4 '58
Congressional Directory (1960)
International Who's Who, 1959
Who's Who in America, 1960-61
Who's Who in the East (1959)

JOHN H. WILLIAMS

WILLIAMS, JOHN H(ARRY) July 7, 1908-   Physicist

Address: b. University of Minnesota, Minneapolis, Minn.

A former director of the Atomic Energy Commission's division of research, Dr. John H. Williams was the first staff official to rise within the ranks of the organization to a seat on its five-member board. He was appointed in July 1959 to fill the unexpired term of Dr. Willard F. Libby, who resigned. Williams began his scientific researches in X-ray natural line widths and spectroscopy. He changed to investigations in the nuclear physics field in the 1930's, concentrating on the study of light nuclei reactions and on the scatteration of light nuclei. At the University of Minnesota, where he has been on the faculty for some twenty-five years, he directed the proton-linear accelerator project supported by the AEC. In May 1960 he resigned as a commissioner of the AEC for reasons of health and returned to the university.

Born on July 7, 1908 in Asbestos Mines, Quebec, Canada, John Harry Williams is the son of Harry John and Josephine Lenore (Stockwell) Williams. His father, a mining engineer, moved the family to an apple farm in Kelowna, British Columbia when John was two years old. He attended high school in Kelowna; he now attributes much of his interest in science to one of his devoted teachers there. At the age of sixteen he matriculated at the University of British Columbia in Vancouver and earned the B.A. degree in physics in 1928.

Following his graduation Williams became a teaching Fellow at the University of California. He took his M.A. degree in 1930 and completed the requirements for a Ph.D. degree on a Whiting Fellowship in 1931. "X-rays were the big thing then," Williams recalls, "so I worked in . . . the basic physics of X-rays" (Minneapolis *Star*, April 17, 1958). From 1931 to 1933 he did postgraduate work in this field at the University of Chicago on a National Research Fellowship.

Dr. Williams' first teaching assignment was an instructorship on the physics faculty of the University of Minnesota. In 1934 he was named an assistant professor and three years later was promoted to associate. During World War II Williams took a leave of absence to serve in 1942 as an investigator for the Office of Scientific Research and Development.

The following year Williams became a member of the Manhattan Project as a group leader in the physics division of the Los Alamos Scientific Laboratory in New Mexico, where he supervised the making of the principal measurements for the A-bomb design. As assistant director of test operations, he participated in the firing of the world's first A-bomb in the New Mexico desert in 1945. He was also instrumental, in 1946, in selecting Bikini atoll as the site for the first atomic tests in the Pacific.

When Williams returned to the University of Minnesota in 1946, he was appointed to a full professorship. He resumed his research activities and teaching duties. Early in 1949 he was named by the AEC to supervise construction of a 50,000,000-volt, proton-linear accelerator at the university. Dubbed Linac by Williams and his staff, the atom-smashing device was completed in 1955 at a cost of $1,800,000. The instrument, which accelerates hydrogen positive ions (or hydrogen atoms stripped of electrons), forces the ions into the nuclei of other atoms. The results of this process provide data on the secret of the adhesion of the nucleus.

In the postwar decade Williams was a critic of growing anti-intellectualism, efforts to stifle free expression, and what he regarded as unnecessary security measures imposed on atomic projects. In 1954, when the AEC board sus-

WILLIAMS, JOHN H(ARRY)—*Continued*

pended its consultant J. Robert Oppenheimer, Williams's former superior at Los Alamos, for being an alleged security risk, Williams stated: "I worked under Oppenheimer three years and never questioned his ability to maintain proper security. The board's findings disappoint me greatly. It's a shame that a man to whom we owe so much must be treated so scurrilously" (Minneapolis *Tribune,* July 17, 1959).

A leave of absence from the University of Minnesota was granted to Williams in April 1958 when he was appointed director of the division of research of the AEC. When he accepted the new post, Williams said: "There's a job to be done and I hope the country will support basic research."

In his assignment Williams was responsible for supervising some 360 research projects in physics, chemistry, ceramics, and controlled thermonuclear reaction conducted in about 100 laboratories, colleges, and universities and supported by commission grants amounting to $25,000,000 annually. Williams and other scientists advised President Eisenhower to request in June 1959 a Congressional appropriation for the construction of a two-mile-long atom smasher at Stanford University. In 1960 Congress refused to grant an appropriation to build the atom smasher, but authorized $3,000,000 for additional design studies for the project.

A staff associate has said of Williams' achievement in dealing with Congress: "He has lent stability to the AEC's research program —by that I mean, without any reflection on his predecessors, that he is able to explain the program better to other people, including congressmen" (Milwaukee *Journal,* July 21, 1959).

The skill with which Dr. Williams handled the commission's basic research program was an important factor in his selection as a member of the Atomic Energy Commission in July 1959. The professor accepted the appointment at a sacrifice to his university career and his annual income, but his sense of responsibility as a scientist and a citizen dictated his decision to become a commissioner just as the year before it had prompted him to accept the post of research director.

"Every so often," Williams explained, "you have to put some chips back in the pot. I put some back in World War II, and for the last ten years I have been taking them out. Now I guess the time has come to put some more back in." The designation of Williams to the AEC as successor to Dr. Willard Libby for the unexpired term ending June 30, 1961 won Senate approval on August 12, 1959.

After Williams' appointment, the commission announced plans to erect a small nuclear power plant containing a pressurized-water reactor at Oak Ridge, Tennessee. The AEC also reported that it is conducting studies on the conversion of thorium into a material that can be used for atomic fission. As scientific member of the commission, Williams co-operated in developing methods of reducing radioactive fallout absorbed by foodstuffs. In September 1959 the AEC announced the development of new techniques in removing radioactive strontium 90 from milk.

In 1954 Dr. Williams founded the Midwestern Universities Research Association (MURA), whose members are some fifteen educational institutions; he served as its vice-president and president (1956-57). While in Minnesota he had served on the governor's committee on atomic development that urged the building of atomic power plants to aid industries in the state. He has been a consultant to the Los Alamos Scientific Laboratory since 1946 and a member of the policy advisory board of the Argonne National Laboratory. He sat with the board on neutron standards and measurements of the National Research Council (1946-48) and on the panel on ultra-high energy accelerators of the National Science Foundation. More recently, he was appointed to the special task force on materials of the Federal Council for Science and Technology. The task force is studying the development of new substances from which devices of the space age can be constructed.

Suave and urbane, Dr. John H. Williams is six feet two inches tall, weighs 190 pounds, and has steel-gray hair and gray-green eyes. His colleagues regard him as a "man's man, who tells witty anecdotes in uninhibited language, shoots a mean game of billiards . . . and goes on extended canoe trips in the wilds of Ontario" (Milwaukee *Journal,* July 21, 1959). Williams also enjoys poker and bridge, and he is a good golf player despite a chest cancer operation which cut into his shoulder muscles. He has been praised for his "quality of human warmth" and his "determination expressed in direct, blunt speech to subordinates or to members of Congressional committees" (New York *Times,* July 17, 1959).

John H. Williams was married to his college sweetheart, the former Vera Martin, in 1928. They have a son Lloyd, who is a practising architect, and two daughters, Ann and Susan. Dr. Williams became a citizen of the United States in 1942. He is a member of the American Physical Society, Phi Beta Kappa, and Sigma Xi. His alma mater, the University of British Columbia, awarded him an honorary D.Sc. degree in 1958.

References

Minneapolis Tribune p2+ Jl 17 '59 por
N Y Times Jl 17 '59 por
American Men of Science vol 1 (1955)
Who's Who in America, 1958-59

WINDUST, BRETAIGNE Jan. 20, 1906- Mar. 18, 1960 Stage director; actor; directed many Broadway hits, including *Life with Father* (1939), *Arsenic and Old Lace* (1941), and *The Hasty Heart* (1945) and several television productions. See *Current Biography* (March) 1943.

Obituary

N Y Times p21 Mr 19 '60

WITHEROW, W(ILLIAM) P(ORTER)
Apr. 15, 1888-Jan. 7, 1960 Industrialist; president of Blaw-Knox Company, Pennsylvania steel manufacturers (1937-52); president of the National Association of Manufacturers (1941-42). See *Current Biography* (April) 1942.

Obituary

N Y Times p25 Ja 8 '60

WITTE, EDWIN E(MIL) Jan. 4, 1887-May 20, 1960 Economist; helped to formulate federal Social Security Act of 1935; was professor (1933-57) and head of economics department (1936-41, 1946-53) at University of Wisconsin; held United States government posts; author. See *Current Biography* (July) 1946.

Obituary

N Y Times p86 My 22 '60

WOOLLEY, SIR (CHARLES) LEONARD Apr. 17, 1880-Feb. 20, 1960 Archaeologist; author; excavated cities in Syria, Turkey, and Mesopotamia; noted for his diggings at Ur of the Chaldees in Iraq. See *Current Biography* (December) 1954.

Obituary

N Y Times p92 F 21 '60

WORTHINGTON, LESLIE B(ERRY)
June 22, 1902- Corporation executive
Address: b. United States Steel Corporation, 71 Broadway, New York 6

A coal miner's son who reached the top echelon by working his way up through the ranks, Leslie B. Worthington is like a number of other United States Steel Corporation executives, notably Benjamin F. Fairless, formerly chairman and now a director, and R. Conrad Cooper, executive vice-president in charge of personnel services. Worthington's position as president of the corporation is one of the highest in American industry: he is the company's chief administrative officer, while Roger M. Blough, the chairman, is the chief executive officer. Before his election to succeed Walter F. Munford in November 1959, Worthington had been president of the corporation's Columbia-Geneva Steel Division in San Francisco.

During the fifty-nine years since its founding, the United States Steel Corporation has become a giant steel-making, mining, transportation, and construction complex employing more than 200,000 persons. Its estimated annual sales total $3,500,000,000, and in the first half of 1959 it set record earnings of more than $250,000,000.

Leslie Berry Worthington was born on June 22, 1902 in Duckmanton, England to John and Ethel (Berry) Worthington. The family, including another son, John Robert Worthington, immigrated to the United States in 1907 and settled in the small mining town of Witt, Illinois. There the father became one of some

Romaine Studio
LESLIE B. WORTHINGTON

3,000 coal miners. Leslie worked in the town's small general store after grammar school hours and during summer vacations to supplement the family's income. He was graduated in 1919 from the Witt High School in a class of two boys and three girls. He was known in school as "Whitey" Worthington, but his hair has since darkened.

Although Worthington had to work his way through the University of Illinois in Urbana, he had time for some extrascholastic activities and served as editor of the campus publication, the *Enterpriser*. He majored in business and was named a member of the Men's Honor Commission. In 1923, after receiving the B.S. degree, he began his career with United States Steel as a sales apprentice in the South Chicago Works of the Carnegie-Illinois Steel Corporation.

Ten years later Worthington became assistant manager of sales in the Chicago district of Carnegie-Illinois, and in 1936 he was appointed manager of the St. Paul, Minnesota district sales office. For five years, from 1936 to 1941, he worked at the Detroit sales office before being transferred to Pittsburgh, where he was in charge of sales of bar, strip, and semifinished materials for Carnegie-Illinois.

The next promotion for Worthington came in 1942 when he was elected vice-president of the United States Steel Supply Company in Chicago (now the steel supply division of United States Steel Corporation). He advanced to the company's presidency four years later and held that office for eleven years. In 1957 he became president of the corporation's big Columbia-Geneva Steel Division in San Francisco.

In May 1959 Clifford F. Hood retired as the sixth president of United States Steel and was succeeded by Walter F. Munford, who was recognized in big steel circles as an operations

WORTHINGTON, LESLIE B.—*Continued*

specialist. Beginning in mid-July the steel industry was shut down by a nationwide strike that continued until January 4, 1960. The mills, however, returned to operation in November after President Eisenhower invoked the Taft-Hartley law provision for an eighty-day cooling-off period. Negotiations continued into the new year without much progress until intervention by Vice-President Richard M. Nixon and Labor Secretary James P. Mitchell helped prevent resumption of the strike, which was scheduled for January 26.

In the midst of the labor unrest in the steel industry, meanwhile, United States Steel suffered the loss of its president, Munford, who died on September 28. As the board of directors of the corporation met in New York in October, speculation in the press as to the choice of a new president suggested that he would be an "inside man." Worthington was mentioned as a dark horse candidate.

The election of Worthington, however, occurred not at the regular board meeting, but at a special board meeting held on November 10, 1959 as the steelworkers were returning to work after the United States Supreme Court had upheld the Taft-Hartley law injunction. He also became chief administrative officer of United States Steel Corporation, a member of the board of directors, chairman of the executive committee, and chairman of the operations policy committee in Pittsburgh—all posts that Munford had previously held. The salary of the new president was not announced, but it was assumed to be at least $250,000.

In reporting Worthington's election to the presidency, commentators on business affairs called attention to his strong sales background and suggested that in selecting Worthington rather than an operations specialist, the company was returning to an earlier policy. Charles M. Schwab, who founded United States Steel in 1901, was an expert salesman, as were several of the corporation's subsequent presidents. Worthington's experience in sales distribution may help him to handle the emphasis expected to be placed upon marketing in the face of rising competition from both domestic and foreign steel producers.

When Worthington became president he was confronted immediately with many urgent questions arising from the longest strike in the industry's history. *Business Week* (November 14, 1959) pointed out that most of the issues concerned "people problems" and noted that Worthington's colleagues "say he combines an attractive personal warmth with firm, demanding leadership" and that he knows how to talk with warehousemen, machinists, automobile manufacturers, and other customers, as well as his own managers. Along with affability and a sense of humor, at work he also shows remarkable personal energy and a serious regard for punctuality.

Worthington is a member of the American Iron and Steel Institute and the American Steel Warehouse Association and is a director of the University of Illinois Foundation and the Stanford Research Institute. In both

Illinois and California he was a director of the chambers of commerce, and in San Francisco he was a director and member of the executive committee of the United Bay Area Crusade.

During his years as a sales apprentice in Chicago, Worthington met Dorothy Helen Rice, then a student at the University of Chicago. They were married on June 9, 1928 in Los Angeles. The Worthingtons have two married sons, John Rice, an attorney in Chicago, and Paul Leslie, a sales trainee in United States Steel's Pittsburgh office.

Trim in appearance, with gray eyes and brown hair, Worthington is five feet eight and a half inches tall and weighs about 165 pounds. He is a Republican and attends the Methodist-Episcopal Church. His chief hobby is golf, which he used to play at the Cypress Point Golf Club of Pebble Beach, California and the San Francisco Golf Club. He also likes various types of trapshooting. While in Chicago he took up curling, the old Scottish game and belonged to the Chicago Curling Club. He also is a member of the Duquesne Club of Pittsburgh.

References

Bsns W p156+ N 14 '59
N Y Times p49 N 11 '59 por
Newsweek 54:98+ N 23 '59
U S News 47:27 N 23 '59
Who's Who in America, 1958-59

YARBOROUGH, RALPH W(EBSTER)

June 8, 1903- United States Senator from Texas; lawyer

Address: b. Senate Office Bldg., Washington 25, D.C.; h. 2527 Jarratt Ave., Austin, Texas; Methodist Bldg., 100 Maryland Ave., N.E., Washington 2, D.C.

The junior Senator from Texas, Ralph W. Yarborough, is an Austin attorney and a leader of the liberal wing of the Democrats in his state. He was first elected to Congress in April 1957 to fill out the unexpired term of Price Daniel, who had become Governor of Texas the previous January. At the November 1958 election Yarborough was returned to the Senate for a full six-year term. As among his outstanding achievements during his first few years in Congress, he regards his co-authorship of the National Defense Education Act of 1958 and of measures for airport development and reduction of small business taxes, and his sponsorship of the Future Scientists of America program.

The seventh child in a family of three boys and eight girls, Ralph Webster Yarborough was born in Chandler, Texas on June 8, 1903 to Charles Richard and Nanny Jane (Spear) Yarborough. His father was a farmer and justice of the peace who wanted all his sons to be lawyers—they are. Yarboroughs have lived in Texas for a long time; Captain Harvey Yarborough, Ralph's grandfather, led the first company of infantry from Smith County, Texas to join Confederate armies.

Brought up in Chandler, Yarborough attended local public schools there through the junior year of high school. He then transferred to the Tyler High School in the adjacent county, where he played on the basketball team and completed his senior year of study. For one year after his graduation in 1919 he was a cadet at the United States Military Academy in West Point, New York.

Reductions in Army appropriations had made Yarborough believe that advancement in a military career would be too slow. For a few years he taught in small schools in Delta and Martin Springs, not far from Chandler, and took courses at the Sam Houston State Teachers College in Huntsville, Texas. Deciding to study in Europe, he worked his way to France on a freighter. When he failed to meet entrance requirements at the Sorbonne in Paris, he went to Germany, found employment at the American Chamber of Commerce in Berlin, and attended the Standahl Academy.

By the end of 1922 Yarborough had returned to the United States. He enrolled at the University of Texas in Austin and helped meet his expenses by taking a job at a boarding house. One summer he joined a threshing crew working through Oklahoma and Kansas, and other summers he helped build oil tanks at Borger, Texas during the oil boom. He also worked as a librarian and a quiz master. He received the LL.B. degree in 1927, graduating *cum laude*.

Admitted to the Texas bar in 1927, Yarborough began his career as an attorney with the El Paso law firm of Turney, Burgess, Culwell, Holliday & Pollard. Local conditions led to his taking a special interest in the law of land and water rights, and his testimony before a state legislative committee resulted in 1931 in his appointment as assistant attorney general representing the Permanent School Fund and the University of Texas Permanent Fund.

In the case of *Magnolia Petroleum Company v. Walker*, Yarborough saved for the Permanent School Fund the oil and gas bonus and royalty interest on 3,901,000 acres of land. He wrote the state's first underground water conservation law and also wrote an opinion asserting that Texas had the right to oil and gas rights in the offshore lands.

For about a year beginning in 1935 Yarborough practised law in Austin as a member of the firm of Brooks & Yarborough. During this period he also lectured on land law at the University of Texas Law School and served on the original board of directors of the Lower Colorado River Authority. From 1936 to 1941 he served as district judge of the fifty-third judicial district, Austin and for three of these years was presiding judge of the third administrative judicial district, embracing thirty-three counties in central Texas. In 1938 he was an unsuccessful candidate for Attorney General of Texas.

After leaving West Point in 1920, Yarborough had joined the 36th division, Texas National Guard for three years' service. When the United States entered World War II, he volunteered for active duty and after training at various Army camps was commissioned a captain and appointed to a position at the Pen-

Wide World

RALPH W. YARBOROUGH

tagon in Washington. "I requested combat duty and was assigned to the 97th Division." Yarborough has recalled. "I fought with Patton across Europe. After VJ Day, I was appointed military government officer for the central Honshu Province, and governed one-seventh of Japan's population and area." He was a lieutenant colonel when discharged in 1946 and is today a full colonel in the United States Army Reserve.

Yarborough resumed private law practice in Austin after the war. In 1952 he decided to run for the Democratic nomination for governor and made machine politics his campaign issue. At the July primary he lost to incumbent Governor Allan Shivers by 488,345 votes to 833,861. He went on to support the Stevenson-Sparkman Presidential ticket while Shivers was "swinging" the state to Eisenhower. In 1954 when he opposed Shivers for a third gubernatorial term, the latter's bolt to Eisenhower was made a principal issue. Running against "an almost unanimously hostile press and big oil money" (*Reporter*, August 17, 1954), he lost to Shivers in August by about 90,000 votes.

Making his third bid for the Democratic gubernatorial nomination in 1956, Yarborough lost at an August runoff primary to United States Senator Price Daniel by less than 4,000 votes. Daniel was elected governor in November, and on April 2, 1957 a special election was held for filling out his Senate term expiring in January 1959. The liberal Yarborough filed as a candidate and won by 364,605 votes to 290,803 for Representative Martin Dies, a Democrat, and 219,591 for Thad Hutcheson, a Republican. who split the conservative vote. Yarborough was sworn into the Eighty-fifth Congress on April 29.

During his first year in the Senate Yarborough served on the Government Operations Committee and its subcommittee on reorganiza-

YARBOROUGH, RALPH W.—*Continued*

tion, and on the Interstate and Foreign Commerce Committee and its subcommittee on surface transportation. In the 1958 session he was assigned to the Interstate and Foreign Commerce Committee, the Labor and Public Welfare Committee, and the Post Office and Civil Service Committee.

Again victorious when he ran for the Senate in November 1958, Yarborough was elected to a full term which expires in January 1965. In the Eighty-sixth Congress he added to his 1958 committee assignments membership on the Lincoln Sesquicentennial Commission. He was also chairman of the Interstate and Foreign Commerce Committee's three-man subcommittee to insure "freedom, fairness, and impartiality" in radio and TV handling of news.

Among the legislative proposals that Yarborough approved during 1957 were a single large federal dam at Hell's Canyon (June), a $32,220,000 multipurpose reclamation project at San Angelo in Texas (August), and the jury trial amendment to the Civil Rights Act of 1957 (August). During the summer he joined another Texan, Senator Lyndon B. Johnson, in support of the Eisenhower administration's policy of curbing "uncontrolled" oil imports. Yarborough supported in January 1959 the Lyndon Johnson motion to block consideration of new Senate rules and a curb on filibustering. He opposed confirmation of Scott McLeod as Ambassador to Ireland (May 1957) and Lewis L. Strauss as Secretary of Commerce (June 1959), and approved the nomination of Clare Boothe Luce as Ambassador to Brazil (April 1959).

A Yarborough motion to increase individual income tax exemptions to $800 was rejected in March 1958, and his amendment to increase Social Security benefits by 10 per cent was defeated the following August. In April 1959 his bill to extend college-education benefits and other privileges to those joining the armed services since January 1955 was opposed by the administration as too costly.

Senator Yarborough belongs to the American, Texas, and Travis County bar associations and to the American Judicature Society. Before World War II he was a member of the editorial board and a director of the *Texas Law Review*. In 1940 he served as director of the Texas State Bar and from 1947 to 1951 was on the Texas State Board of Law Examiners. He is a Shriner and a member of Phi Delta Phi, the Order of the Coif, the Acacians, and veterans' organizations.

On June 30, 1928 Ralph W. Yarborough was married to Opal Catherine Warren, who in childhood had lived next door to him in Chandler. She later became a home economics teacher in Pine Bluff, Arkansas. Their son, Richard W. Yarborough, practises law in Austin. The Senator is five feet ten inches in height, weighs 190 pounds, and has brown hair and brown eyes. He is a Baptist and used to teach a Sunday-school class in Austin. His favorite outdoor recreations are hunting and fishing. An-

other hobby is his library of Texan and Confederate imprints.

References

N Y Herald Tribune II p2 Ap 7 '57 por;
  p13 Jl 31 '58 por
N Y Times p23 Ap 4 '57 por
New Repub 138:8 Ap 22 '57 por
Newsday p48 Ap 14 '57 por
U S News 42:20+ Ap 12 '57
Washington (D.C.) Post p1F My 12 '57
Adams, Mark and Fath, Creekmore Yarborough: Portrait of a People's Senator (1957)
Congressional Directory (1959)
International Who's Who, 1958
Martindale-Hubbell Law Directory, 1958
Who's Who in America, 1958-59
World Biography (1954)

YOUNG, JOSEPH LOUIS Nov. 27, 1919-

Mosaic muralist

Address: b. Mosaic Workshop, 8426 Melrose Ave., Los Angeles 46, Calif.; h. 7917½ W. Norton Ave., Los Angeles 46, Calif.

The American artist Joseph Louis Young is a leading exponent of integrating the ancient art of mosaic with contemporary architecture and city planning. His murals and façades of colorful ceramic and glass tiles known as tesserae, that he designed for churches, synagogues, shopping centers, schools, parks, and office buildings, have won him recognition and election as a lifetime Fellow of the International Institute of Arts and Letters. His six-by-thirty-six-foot, six-ton glass mosaic mural, erected in the lobby of the Police Facilities Building in Los Angeles (1955), is the largest cantilever mosaic structure to be executed up to that time. It has been called a triumph of artistry and engineering.

Although his most important contribution has been mosaic murals, Young has created oils, *gouaches,* and monotypes which are included in private collections in various parts of the world. The art of mosaic has been known to mankind for some 5,000 years, and its utilitarian aspects were recognized from the beginning of its history. It was used by the ancient Egyptians and Greeks, and the Romans introduced floor mosaics throughout their empire.

The only son of Louis A. and Jennie (Eger) Young, Joseph Louis Young was born in Pittsburgh, Pennsylvania on November 27, 1919 and grew up in the adjacent community of Aliquippa. He is of Russian descent on his father's side and Romanian on his mother's. Much of his early interest in art resulted from his mother's activity as an artist. She was one of the first graduates of the Margaret Morrison School at the Carnegie Institute of Technology. At the age of eight he was taken to a Carnegie International Exhibition, where he was deeply moved by paintings of Georges Rouault and Pablo Picasso. Throughout his boyhood he continued to paint, often copying the works of the old masters that he found reproduced in the pages of library books.

For a career, however, Joseph had decided upon service in the United States Army. He transferred from Aliquippa High School to Randolph-Macon Academy in Front Royal, Virginia to prepare for the United States Military Academy, but his eyesight did not meet West Point's stringent requirements. His second choice was to follow his father's career as a business executive. After graduation from Randolph-Macon in 1937, he enrolled at Westminster College in New Wilmington, Pennsylvania to study business administration. During his freshman year he was encouraged by Professor H. J. Berman to change his major from business administration to English and journalism and to take art courses. Active in sports, he was on the college swimming team and was sports editor of the newspaper. He also was editor in chief of the yearbook, *The Argo*; was elected to Pi Delta Epsilon and Sphinx honorary fraternity; and was president of Kappa Phi Lambda.

After receiving the B.A. degree in 1941, Young became the director of the Stewart Howe Alumni Service in Pittsburgh. Frequent visits to the Carnegie Institute's museum led him to enroll in evening classes in art at the institute, and he soon decided to study art in New York City. There he worked as a copy boy with the United Press during the day and took classes with Moses Soyer in the evening. He rose rapidly on the staff of the United Press until his work was interrupted by World War II.

Inducted into the United States Army in 1943, Young was assigned to the Army Air Forces Special Services as a designer, writer, and orientation lecturer. Later, while directing the First Service Command's section of the national Army arts contest, he traveled throughout New England and saw for the first time the monumental frescoes of José Clemente Orozco at Dartmouth College in Hanover, New Hampshire, an encounter that stimulated his interest in the architectural uses of art. During his military service he painted murals for the Miami Beach quartermaster headquarters, made sets for the Basic Training Command, was an artist for the WAC recruiting art section, was an illustrator and cartoonist for various post newspapers, and a writer with a post historian's office.

After his discharge in 1946, he took courses at the School for Art Studies in New York, the Art Students League of New York, and the Cranbrook Academy of Art in Bloomfield Hills, Michigan. During the summer of 1946 he went to Mexico to examine the major frescoes in that country. When he returned in the fall, he embarked upon a five-year course of study at the school of the Boston Museum of Fine Arts, where two of his instructors were Karl Zerbe and David Aronson.

While studying at the school, Young painted a twenty-by-ten-foot war memorial fresco for its main hallway and taught painting from 1949-50. The school selected him for the first prize in oils in 1950 and conferred a graduating certificate with highest honors on him in 1951. He also received the Edwin Austin Abbey Fel-

JOSEPH LOUIS YOUNG

lowship of $1,500 (1949) and the Albert H. Whitin Fellowship of $1,500 (1951), the latter for the study of stained glass in Europe.

In Italy to study at the American Academy, Young took advantage of his opportunities to see the famous Byzantine mosaics, the Triumphal Arch and apse of St. Vitale in Ravenna, and other examples of mosaic architecture in Monreale and Venice. He later described his emotions during these visits as "the relief and exultation of finding what one knows exists."

In his essay, "The Walls of America, 1950," published in the architectural journal *Charette,* Young outlined the reasons why art within architecture would return to central importance. His thesis proved prophetic: art and architecture have since been unified in many instances, and mosaic, in particular, has become one of the principal architectural art forms.

Returning to the United States in 1952, Young and his wife, a concert pianist, both received residence fellowships from the Huntington Hartford Foundation in Pacific Palisades, California. His 1953 one-man exhibition of mosaics, oils, and prints at the Falk-Raboff Gallery in Los Angeles brought this comment from *Art News* (April 1953): "His show discloses a facile hand working in several idioms. Intense Expressionism, nonfigurative abstractions, and subtly-nuanced romantic drawings vie for attention. There's a promising future ahead for Young when he finds the metier most suited to his needs."

As a result of the success of his one-man show, Young won a commission to design and execute the mosaic mural for the main lobby of Los Angeles' Police Facilities Building. Devoting over two years of work to the prefabrication of this thirty-six-feet-wide by six-feet-high mural, he employed ambulatory perspective in the design of this panoramic history of

YOUNG, JOSEPH LOUIS—*Continued*

Los Angeles. Completed in 1955, it consists of 250,000 individually set tesserae in hundreds of colors.

Elaine K. Sewell in *American Artist* (September 1955) described the structure as "six tons of steel, copper, aluminum, and glass, fused into a monolithic mosaic panel of beauty and permanence that seems to float on air . . . it is a remarkable demonstration of what can be accomplished when logical architectural planning and imaginative art are integrated."

This commission led to others, notably mosaic murals for Temple Emanuel, Beverly Hills, California (1956); Southdale shopping center near Minneapolis, Minnesota (1957); Don Bosco High School, South San Gabriel, California (1957); Chapel of Our Lady of Lourdes in Los Angeles (1958); and for several private residences. One of his most challenging assignments was the 192-square-foot arch in bas-relief for Eden Memorial Park, San Fernando, California, completed in 1959. The mosaic arch, which depicts the twelve tribes of ancient Israel, is dedicated to the Jews who perished during World War II.

For his various projects Young cuts each tessera with a traditional mosaic hammer. He makes drawings, to scale, for his murals, from which he fashions a full-scale sketch on heavy cartoon paper. When he has determined the color design, Young cuts the cartoon paper into small sections. On these sections Young carefully glues each tile.

Young does much of his work as artist and teacher at his Mosaic Workshop in Los Angeles. He made his instruction on mosaics available to the public in his book *A Course in Making Mosaics; An Introduction to the Art and Craft* (Reinhold, 1957). As associate editor, he also writes for *Creative Crafts,* a southern California publication. He served in the dual role of artist-actor for the 16mm. sound-color documentary, *The World of Mosaic,* about the world-wide interest in mosaic and its cultural potential. The American Institute of Architects selected it for an award of merit, and the United States Information Service exhibited it abroad. He has lectured in Venice, Ravenna, Florence, and Rome at the invitation of the Italian Foreign Ministry of Trade, and he has delivered numerous lectures at American colleges and art schools.

Joseph Louis Young and Millicent Edith Goldstein, a concert pianist, were married on June 19, 1949. They have two daughters, Leslie Sybil and Cecily. He has gray eyes, brown hair, stands over five feet eleven inches tall, and weighs 160 pounds. Young is of the Jewish faith, and he is an independent in politics. His hobbies include color photography and documentary film making; his favorite sport is swimming. Young was elected a lifetime Fellow of the International Institute of Arts and Letters (1958) and awarded an honorary doctoral degree by Westminster College (1960).

As one of the very few American muralists who can execute their own designs in mosaic, Young is able to assure architects that their drafting board concepts will become a reality. He holds the conviction that the future of American art lies in developing architectural art forms which can function in everyday life.

References

Who's Who in American Art, 1956
Who's Who in Art, 1958
Who's Who in the West (1958)

YU HUNG-CHUN *See* Yui, O. K.

YUI, O. K. Jan. 4, 1898-June 1, 1960 Former Premier of Nationalist China on Formosa (1954-58); Chinese Finance Minister (1944-48); head of government banks. See *Current Biography* (May) 1955.

Obituary

N Y Times p33 Je 2 '60

YUST, WALTER May 16, 1894-Feb. 29, 1960 Former editor in chief of *Encyclopædia Britannica* and all associated publications (1938-60); reporter and editor of various publications (1917-30). See *Current Biography* (April) 1943.

Obituary

N Y Times p37 Mr 2 '60

ZHUKOV, GEORGY A(LEXANDRO-VICH) 1908- Soviet government official

Address: U.S.S.R. Council of Ministers' State Committee for Cultural Relations with Foreign Countries, Moscow, U.S.S.R.

When, early in 1957, the Soviet Union decided to pursue more aggressively the expansion of its cultural relations with other countries, the man chosen for the job was Georgy A. Zhukov, a newspaperman with many years of experience as a diplomatic correspondent in the capitals of the world. So well known was he abroad, in fact, that he was usually referred to as Yuri Zhukov, using the diminutive of his first name. He is not related to Georgy Konstantinovich Zhukov, the former Soviet Defense Minister, with whom he is frequently confused.

Georgy Alexandrovich Zhukov was born in 1908 in the Ukraine near what is now the city of Voroshilovgrad. According to one report, he began his working career in a railroad shop; according to another, he began it in an automobile factory. In any event, he soon switched to the profession of journalism, working at first for a number of small provincial newspapers. He was on the staff of several newspapers and magazines including the newspaper *Komsomolskaya Pravda,* the publication of the Communist youth organization, and the magazine *Novy Mir* (New World), an important and influential literary monthly.

In 1945 Zhukov joined the staff of *Pravda* and soon became a foreign correspondent, assigned to nearly every major international conference. From 1949 to 1952 he was based in Paris, from which he wrote about the Americans before whom "servile French cosmopolitans prostrate themselves." From Paris Zhukov was moved back to Moscow, first as a member of *Pravda's* editorial board, and then as assistant editor in chief—a post he held by the fall of 1953. He still made trips abroad to cover major diplomatic events, however.

He also began to take part in politics. In May 1955 he was elected to the Soviet Committee for the Defense of World Peace. In February 1956 the Twentieth Congress of the Communist party of the Soviet Union made him a member of the party's Central Inspection Commission. This powerful body checks on party finances, supervises the work of the party, and investigates all letters, petitions, and complaints sent to the Central Committee.

The editor in chief of *Pravda* since December 1952 had been Dmitri T. Shepilov, with whom Zhukov was supposed to be closely associated. When Shepilov became Foreign Minister in June 1956, Pavel A. Satyukov became the editor of *Pravda*. Zhukov, who had apparently been passed over for the editor's job, left the newspaper the next spring to become chairman of the newly created U.S.S.R. Council of Ministers' State Committee for Cultural Relations with Foreign Countries. Zhukov began his work by calling a conference with the foreign press corps in Moscow in May 1957. "Our desire is to liquidate once and for all the notorious iron curtain with the help of which some nations are trying to separate themselves from the Socialist countries," he declared.

Negotiations for a cultural, technical, and scientific exchange agreement with the United States were begun in Washington in October 1957, and successfully concluded on January 27, 1958. It was the first agreement reached between the two countries in almost three years. Under it, exchanges were to be increased fivefold, and would include television broadcasts, recordings, films, and plays as well as teachers, students, and artists. Three months later, in April, the presidium of the U.S.S.R. of the Supreme Soviet honored Zhukov on his fiftieth birthday by awarding him the Order of the Red Banner of Labor for "services to the Soviet State."

In November 1958 Zhukov came to the United States for a three-week visit in connection with the exchange program. While he was in America, his itinerary ranged from Cambridge, Massachusetts to Hollywood, California. It ended with a news conference in Washington, D.C., where the reporters asked Zhukov questions about Boris Pasternak's novel *Doctor Zhivago*. He said that he had not read it, but understood that the editorial board concerned had rejected the novel because it was "a slander on the Soviet people in general and on the revolution in particular."

As a result of the cultural exchange agreement, the United States sent an exhibition to Moscow in 1959 and the Soviet Union sent one to New York. Vice-President Richard M. Nixon went to Moscow to open the United States exhibit and then toured the Soviet Union

Wide World

GEORGY A. ZHUKOV

with Zhukov as his host. The New York *Times* correspondent who accompanied Nixon to the Soviet Union, Harrison E. Salisbury, wrote later in a book—*To Moscow—And Beyond* (Harper, 1960)—that no man had been more responsible than Zhukov for arranging the exchange of expositions between the United States and the Soviet Union; yet no man had done more to throw about the United States exhibition a blanket of unpleasantness.

"Why?" Salisbury asked. "There were two explanations. Either Zhukov was carrying on the classic Russian trick of trying to sabotage his own creation (having been put on the job for precisely that purpose) or he was attempting to appease the powerful faction . . . which makes no bones about its cold hatred for the new policy of objectivity."

In September 1959 Zhukov accompanied Premier Khrushchev to the United States. At a meeting with a group of Senators in Washington, D.C., Khrushchev said he had brought Zhukov in the hope of improving the cultural and scientific exchange program, and he charged the State Department with trying to reduce the number of exchanges. The next day, in New York, Khrushchev said: "The State Department has of late been somewhat afraid of this exchange of delegations."

Lincoln White, the press officer for the State Department, had at first said Khrushchev must be guilty of a "misunderstanding," and then said he must be "misinformed." The last statement he called "patently inaccurate and false." His remarks, White said, "were designed simply to put pressure on the Department of State to agree to anything and everything the Soviet representatives want without regard to United States reciprocal interests."

After he returned to the Soviet Union, Zhukov wrote an article saying the United States was trying to "foist an alien ideology" on other countries through the cultural exchange program. "We are for developing cultural exchanges, for having the people get to know each other better," he said. "But we are against cultural exchanges being exploited for subversion and interference in the affairs of other states."

Despite these harsh words, proposals for a two-year extension of the agreement had been exchanged, and the extension was successfully negotiated and signed in Moscow on November 21, 1959. The negotiator and signer of the first agreement had been the Soviet ambassador in Washington, Georgy N. Zaroubin. This time it was not done by the Foreign Ministry, but by Zhukov.

Zhukov was one of a group of twelve correspondents who contributed articles to a book, *Face to Face With America,* chronicling Khrushchev's trip to the United States. The group was awarded, in April of 1960, the Lenin Prize in journalism for the book, which was described as "an example of passionate and militant writing."

Late in April 1960 Zhukov made what was described as a "private" visit to Washington. While there he made inquiries about certain Voice of America broadcasts and speeches by Secretary of State Christian A. Herter and Undersecretary C. Douglas Dillon. He asked, particularly, if "the cold war has started up all over again."

"Judging from Mr. Zhukov's comments just before his departure from New York, the report he took back to Moscow was not very reassuring," Harrison E. Salisbury wrote in the New York *Times* (May 17, 1960) in an analysis of the factors leading to the breakup of the Summit Conference in Paris the next month.

Zhukov's Moscow offices are in a rambling old mansion at the head of Kalinin Street. He and his wife, Rose, live in an apartment some distance from the center of Moscow. Their seventeen-year-old son is a student, and their twenty-seven-year-old married daughter, the mother of a three-year-old, teaches history. Mrs. Zhukov, who speaks fluent French, formerly taught in the literature department at Moscow University. Now she is a member of the editorial board of the magazine *Soviet Woman.* She accompanied her husband on his trip to the United States in 1958.

Zhukov is about five feet ten inches tall and is sturdy and dark-haired. He speaks well in French. Journalists say he is overweight and appears to have heart trouble, and only with difficulty keeps up with Premier Khrushchev on their trips abroad. According to Harrison E. Salisbury, he is one of Premier Khrushchev's trusted confidants. Salisbury also says, in *To Moscow—And Beyond,* that "no Soviet bureaucrat has ridden to the top more rapidly than he. He has taken more and more of an empire under his control. He has practically put out of operation all other organizations for contacts with foreign countries. He has even taken bites out of the jurisdiction of the Foreign Office

and the Foreign Trade Ministry. He has become a Soviet bureaucrat par excellence, a past master at effrontery and bland rudeness."

References

N Y Herald Tribune p5 D 3 '58 por
U S News 47:28 N 16 '59
Salisbury, Harrison E. To Moscow—And Beyond (1960)

ZIMBALIST, EFREM, JR. (zĭm'bà-lĭst ĕf'rĕm) Nov. 30, 1923(?)- Actor; producer

Address: b. c/o American Broadcasting Company, 7 W. 66th St., New York 23

For an hour each week over ABC-TV, a sophisticated private detective named Stuart Bailey thrills millions of viewers of *77 Sunset Strip.* The part is portrayed by Efrem Zimbalist, Jr., a famous name in the theater to which television has given a new dimension. Although a veteran of seven plays and seven movies, as well as the co-producer of three Gian-Carlo Menotti operas, Zimbalist was almost unknown to the general public until he moved into the ranks of video sleuths in 1958.

Efrem Zimbalist, Jr., was born in New York City, the son of Efrem and Alma (Gluck) Zimbalist. Most accounts give his birthdate as November 30, 1923, although there is some suggestion that the year may have been earlier. His family name was derived from the profession of a Hungarian ancestor who played the gypsy *zymbal,* and certainly his has been a musical family. The elder Zimbalist is the famous Russian-born violinist and composer who in 1941 became the director of the Curtis Institute of Music in Philadelphia. Alma Gluck, who died in 1938, was equally famous as a concert soprano. Efrem has one sister, Mary Virginia (Mrs. Henry F. Bennett, Jr.), and a half-sister, the novelist Marcia Davenport.

The Zimbalist home in New York City was often visited by the great names of the musical world, including Sergei Rachmaninoff and Fritz Kreisler. Young Efrem studied piano and violin, although he never aspired to be a concert artist. He was graduated from the private Fay School in Southboro, Massachusetts and from St. Paul's preparatory school in Concord, New Hampshire.

Intending to study engineering, Zimbalist enrolled at Yale University, but was dismissed, as he has said, "for high jinks and low marks." Accordingly, he decided to become an actor, since the acting profession had long fascinated him. He returned to New York City to study drama at the Neighborhood Playhouse, where his fellow students included Gregory Peck and Eli Wallach.

World War II was already underway, however, and on April 2, 1941 Zimbalist enlisted in the United States Army. He gave his profession as actor and his age as twenty-two. While serving on active duty as a first lieutenant in the infantry, he met stage and motion-picture director Joshua Logan, who followed Zimbalist's subsequent stage career and eventually invited him to Hollywood.

Zimbalist returned to New York City after his discharge from the Army. His first stage appearance was in a minor role in *The Rugged Path*, starring Spencer Tracy, which opened on Broadway in November 1945. He then joined the cast of the American Repertory Theatre, performing at the International in New York. His first role was the Duke of Suffolk in Shakespeare's *Henry VIII*, which opened on November 6, 1946. "A spirited performance," wrote one critic of Zimbalist's part in the drama. Two days later he played the part of a butler in Barrie's *What Every Woman Knows* and on December 19, 1946 had the role of the *secutor* in Shaw's *Androcles and the Lion*.

After this demanding schedule, the American Repertory Theatre changed its program to one production at a time. Zimbalist gave a favorably received performance in a supporting role in *Yellow Jack,* a drama about yellow fever which was revived in February 1947. Following this, he temporarily abandoned acting to become a producer in collaboration with Chandler Cowles and Edith Lutyens.

In March 1947 the group purchased the rights to *The Medium* and *The Telephone,* two lyric dramas by Gian-Carlo Menotti. The double bill opened at the Ethel Barrymore Theatre on May 1, 1947, and was greeted as "disappointing" by many reviewers. It was scheduled to close in June, after running heavily into debt, but suddenly caught on with the public to become "the miracle on Forty-seventh Street," as a New York *Herald Tribune* writer phrased it. After a successful run in New York, the plays toured the United States and Europe during 1948 and 1949.

Meanwhile, Zimbalist had returned to the stage in the American Repertory Theatre's production of Ibsen's *Hedda Gabler*. He played the role of Eilert Lovborg in the play, which opened for a short engagement on February 24, 1948. Detouring briefly to Hollywood, he played a supporting role in the Twentieth Century-Fox production of *House of Strangers* (1949).

In 1950 Zimbalist went back to Broadway to produce (with Chandler Cowles) another Menotti lyric drama, *The Consul.* It opened at the Ethel Barrymore Theatre on March 16, 1950 for "an unquestioned and overwhelming success," according to Olin Downes in the New York *Times* (March 17, 1950). The Zimbalist-Cowles production later won a New York Drama Critics Award and the Pulitzer Prize in Music in 1950.

Zimbalist's wife Emily McNair Zimbalist, who had been suffering from a protracted illness, died in 1950. He abandoned his dual career after her death and until 1954 worked for his father at the Curtis Institute of Music in Philadelphia. Then, in the autumn of 1954, he began his comeback as an actor by starring in a daytime television series with Louise Albritton, *Concerning Miss Marlowe,* which was telecast over NBC-TV.

EFREM ZIMBALIST, JR.

Eventually he was signed to a motion-picture contract by Warner Brothers studio and in quick succession was cast in three films. He portrayed a Union officer in *Band of Angels* (1957), a Civil War film starring Clark Gable. He was described as "an interesting newcomer who shows promise" (*Variety*, October 30, 1957) when he appeared as the romantic lead in *Bombers B-52,* and earned stronger praise for his supporting role in *Violent Road* (1958). He has appeared in seven movies altogether, including *Home Before Dark* (1958), in which he co-starred with Jean Simmons and Dan Herlihy.

In 1958 Warner Brothers switched their "newcomer" to television films, casting him as private detective Stuart Bailey in the *77 Sunset Strip* series. The program made its debut over ABC-TV on October 10, 1958, with a special ninety-minute feature film. "As it turned out," wrote a New York *Times* reviewer (October 11, 1958), "the feature film, which forms the basis of the series, was a technically well-filmed, competent production well-acted. . . . It may not have transfixed viewers, but it was a somewhat better than routine handling of a very routine whodunit."

When *77 Sunset Strip* made its bow, ABC-TV held only 19.4 per cent of the viewing audience for that time period, according to the Nielsen ratings. Before mid-1959 the series had captured a 38 per cent segment of the audience, making it the leading program in its time period. The Trendex ratings in March 1959 ranked *77 Sunset Strip* as the eighth most popular program then being telecast.

Zimbalist's first marriage, to Emily McNair, ended with his wife's death in 1950. Their two children are Nancy and Efrem 3d. He was

ZIMBALIST, EFREM, JR.—*Continued*

married for the second time on February 2, 1956, to actress Stephanie Spaulding, and by this marriage has one daughter, Stephanie, Jr. The family lives on a small estate in Encino, California. Usually relaxed in both temperament and dress, Zimbalist is six feet tall and weighs 170 pounds; he has brown hair and brown eyes. He is an excellent swimmer and tennis player; sometimes he paints, plays the violin, or composes music. His eight-part choral setting of the 150th Psalm, *Laudate Dominum,* was performed by a chorus at Town Hall in New York City in 1955.

Despite his artistic accomplishments in music and on the stage, Zimbalist definitely aims for popular stardom in the movies. "I fought doing Stuart Bailey on the 'Strip' series," he has said (*Newsday,* March 31, 1959). "I now know I was wrong. The series did more for me than a half-dozen movies. I did seven pictures in all

for Warner Bros. and still had no real marquee value until this series came along."

References

N Y Post Mag p3 My 3 '59 por
N Y Sunday News Mag p4 My 24 '59 por
N Y Times II p13 Mr 15 '59 por
Newsday p1C Mr 31 '59 por
Newsweek 53:90 F 16 '59 por
Washington (D.C.) Post p3G Mr 22 '59

ZOLI, ADONE Dec. 16, 1887-Feb. 20, 1960 Former Premier of Italy (1957-58) and leading force in Christian Democratic Party; an inveterate anti-Fascist, he served as Minister of Justice (1951-53); Minister of Finance (1954-55); and Minister of the Budget (1956-57). See *Current Biography* (March) 1958.

Obituary

N Y Times p92 F 21 '60

BIOGRAPHICAL REFERENCES

Consulted by CURRENT BIOGRAPHY research staff.

American Architects Directory, 1956

American Bar, 1960

American Catholic Who's Who, 1960 and 1961

American Medical Directory, 1958

American Men in Government (1949)

American Men of Science vols 1-2 (1960) (vol 3, L-Z, in progress)

American Women, 1939-40

America's Young Men, 1938-39

ASCAP Biographical Dictionary of Composers, Authors, and Publishers (1952)

Asia Who's Who (1960)

Author's & Writer's Who's Who (1960)

Baker, T. ed. Biographical Dictionary of Musicians (1940)

Baseball Register, 1960

Bénézit, E. ed Dictionnaire des Peintres, Sculpteurs, Dessinateurs et Graveurs (1948-55)

Biographical Directory of the American Congress, 1774-1949 (1950)

Biographical Encyclopedia of Pakistan, 1955-56

Biographic Directory of the USSR (1958)

Burke's Landed Gentry (1952)

Burke's Peerage, Baronetage, and Knightage, 1959

Business Executives of America (1950)

Canadian Who's Who, 1955-57

Catholic Who's Who, 1952

Chemical Who's Who, 1956

Chi è? (1957)

China Yearbook, 1958-59

Chujoy, A. ed. Dance Encyclopedia (1949)

Congressional Directory (1960)

Congressional Quarterly Almanac, 1959

Davidson, G. Opera Biographies (1955)

Department of State Biographic Register, 1959

Dictionnaire Biographique des Artistes Contemporains, 1910-30

Dictionnaire Biographique Français Contemporain (1954)

Dictionnaire National des Contemporains (1936)

Directory of American Judges (1955)

Directory of American Scholars (1957)

Directory of Medical Specialists, 1959-60

Directory of Medical Women, 1949

Directory of the American Political Science Association, 1953

Ewen, D. ed. Composers of Today (1936); Living Musicians (1940; First Supplement, 1957); Men and Women Who Make Music (1949); European Composers Today (1954)

Grove's Dictionary of Music and Musicians (1955)

Hindustan Year-Book & Who's Who, 1954

Hoehn, M. A. ed Catholic Authors (1957)

Hvem er Hvem? 1955

Indian and Pakistan Year Book and Who's Who, 1948

International Motion Picture Almanac, 1960

International Television Almanac, 1960

International Who's Who, 1960

International Who's Who in World Medicine, 1947

International World Who's Who (1949)

International Year Book and Statesmen's Who's Who, 1960

Italian-American Who's Who (1946)

Japan Biographical Encyclopedia & Who's Who (1958)

Japan Who's Who, 1950-51

Junior Book of Authors (1956)

Kelly's Handbook to the Titled, Landed and Official Classes, 1957-58

Kraks Blaa Bog, 1954

Kürschners Deutscher Gelehrten-Kalender, 1954

Leaders in Education (1948)

Martindale-Hubbell Law Directory, 1960

Middle East, 1958

Nalanda Year-Book and Who's Who in India and Pakistan, 1958

National Cyclopaedia of American Biography current vols A-H (1926-52)

New Century Cyclopedia of Names (1954)

Österreicher der Gegenwart (1951)

Panorama Biografico degli Italiani d'Oggi (1956)

Quem é Alguém (1947)

Quien es Quien en la Argentina, 1958-59

Quien es Quien en Venezuela, Panama, Ecuador, Colombia, 1956

Radio and Television Who's Who (1956)

Religious Leaders of America, 1941-42

Slavonic Encyclopedia (1949)

Thompson, O. ed. International Cyclopedia of Music and Musicians, 1956

Turkin, H., and Thompson, S. C. Official Encyclopedia of Baseball (1959)

Twentieth Century Authors (1942; First Supplement, 1955)

Vem är Det, 1959

Vem och Vad, 1948

Warfel, H. R., American Novelists of Today (1951)

Webster's Biographical Dictionary (1957)

Wer ist Wer? (1958)
Who is Who in Music (1951)
Who Knows—and What (1954)
Who's Who, 1960
Who's Who in Advertising, 1957
Who's Who in America, 1958-59
Who's Who in American Art, 1959
Who's Who in American Education, 1959-60
Who's Who in Art, 1960
Who's Who in Australia, 1959
Who's Who in Austria, 1957-1958
Who's Who in Belgium, 1957-58
Who's Who in British Science, 1953
Who's Who in Canada, 1958-59
Who's Who in Chicago and Illinois (1950)
Who's Who in Colored America, 1950
Who's Who in Commerce and Industry (1959)
Who's Who in Engineering, 1959
Who's Who in France, 1959-60
Who's Who in France (Paris), 1953-54
Who's Who in Germany (1960)

Who's Who in Government (1932-33)
Who's Who in Insurance, 1960
Who's Who in Italy, 1957-58
Who's Who in Labor (1946)
Who's Who in Latin America Pts 1-7 (1946-51)
Who's Who in Library Service (1955)
Who's Who in Modern China (1953)
Who's Who in New England (1949)
Who's Who in New York, 1952
Who's Who in New Zealand, 1956
Who's Who in Philosophy (1952)
Who's Who in Railroading in North America (1959)
Who's Who in Switzerland: 1955
Who's Who in the East (1959)
Who's Who in the Midwest (1956)
Who's Who in the Nation's Capital, 1938-39
Who's Who in the South and Southwest (1959)
Who's Who in the Theatre (1957)
Who's Who in the United Nations (1951)
Who's Who in the West (1960)

Who's Who in U.A.R. and the Near East, 1959
Who's Who in United States Politics (1952)
Who's Who in World Aviation and Astronautics (1958)
Who's Who in World Jewry (1955)
Who's Who Israel, 1960
Who's Who of American Women, 1958-59
Who's Who of Southern Africa, 1959
Wie is Dat? (1956)
Winchester's Screen Encyclopedia (1948)
Women Lawyers in the United States (1957)
Women of Achievement (1940)
Wood, C. TV Personalities vols 1-3 (1955-57)
World Biography (1954)
World Diplomatic Directory, 1951

Yost, E. American Women of Science (1943)

PERIODICALS AND NEWSPAPERS CONSULTED

NOTE: Most of the publications below are listed in Wilson Company periodical indexes found in most libraries. For addresses, subscription price, etc., consult your librarian.

ALA Bul—American Library Association Bulletin
Am Artist—American Artist
Am Assn Univ Women J—Journal of the American Association of University Women
Am Bar Assn J—American Bar Association Journal
Am Hist R—American Historical Review
Am Mag—American Magazine (discontinued)
Am Mercury—American Mercury
Am Pol Sci R—American Political Science Review
Am Scholar—American Scholar
Am Sociol R—American Sociological Review
Am W—American Weekly
America—America
Américas—Américas (incorporating Bul Pan Am Union)
Ann Am Acad—Annals of the American Academy of Political and Social Science
Arch Forum—Architectural Forum, the Magazine of Building
Arch Rec—Architectural Record
Archaeology—Archaeology: A Magazine Dealing with the Antiquity of the World
Art N—Art News
Arts—Arts
Arts & Arch—Arts & Architecture
Atlan—Atlantic Monthly
Aviation W—Aviation Week and Space Technology

Barrons—Barron's
Bet Hom & Gard—Better Homes and Gardens
Book-of-the-Month Club N—Book-of-the-Month Club News
Books Abroad—Books Abroad
Bsns W—Business Week
Bul Atomic Sci—Bulletin of the Atomic Scientists

Can Hist R—Canadian Historical Review
Cath World—Catholic World
Chem & Eng N—Chemical and Engineering News
Christian Cent—Christian Century
Christian Sci Mon—Christian Science Monitor
Colliers—Collier's (discontinued)
Commonweal—Commonweal
Cong Digest—Congressional Digest
Cong Q—Congressional Quarterly Weekly Report
Coronet—Coronet
Cosmop—Cosmopolitan
Cue—Cue
Cur Hist—Current History

Dance Mag—Dance Magazine

Ed—Education
Ed & Pub—Editor & Publisher
Ed Res Reports—Editorial Research Reports
Etude—Etude (discontinued)

Facts on File—Facts on File
For Affairs—Foreign Affairs
For Policy Bul—Foreign Policy Bulletin
Forbes—Forbes
Fortune—Fortune

Gen Army—Generals of the Army and the Air Force and Admirals of the Navy (discontinued)
Good H—Good Housekeeping

Harper—Harper's Magazine
High Fidelity—High Fidelity; The Magazine for Music Listeners
Holiday—Holiday
House & Gard—House & Garden

Illus Lond N—Illustrated London News
Ind Woman—Independent Woman (continued as Nat Bsns Woman)

J Am Med Assn—Journal of the American Medical Association

Ladies Home J—Ladies' Home Journal
Lib J—Library Journal
Life—Life

Look—Look

McCalls—McCall's
Macleans Mag—Maclean's Magazine
Mag Wall St—Magazine of Wall Street and Business Analyst
Manchester Guardian—Manchester Guardian
Mlle—Mademoiselle
Mus Am—Musical America
Mus Courier—Musical Courier
Mus Mod Art—Museum of Modern Art Bulletin

NEA J—Journal of the National Education Association
N Y Herald Tribune—New York Herald Tribune
N Y Herald Tribune Bk R—New York Herald Tribune Book Review
N Y Post—New York Post
N Y Times—New York Times
N Y Times Bk R—New York Times Book Review
N Y Times Index—New York Times Index
N Y Times Mag—New York Times Magazine
N Y World-Telegram—New York World-Telegram and Sun
Nat Bsns Woman—National Business Woman
Nat Geog Mag—National Geographic Magazine
Nation—The Nation
Nations Bsns—Nation's Business
Nature—Nature
New Engl Q—New England Quarterly
New Repub—New Republic
New Statesm—New Statesman
New Yorker—New Yorker
Newsweek—Newsweek

Opera N—Opera News

Pol Sci Q—Political Science Quarterly
Pop Mech—Popular Mechanics Magazine
Pop Phot—Popular Photography
Pop Sci—Popular Science Monthly
Ptr Ink—Printers' Ink
Pub W—Publishers' Weekly

Read Digest—Reader's Digest
Reporter—The Reporter
Rotarian—Rotarian

Sat Eve Post—Saturday Evening Post
Sat Night—Saturday Night
Sat R—Saturday Review
Sch & Soc—School and Society
Sci Am—Scientific American
Sci Mo—Scientific Monthly (combined with Science)
Sci N L—Science News Letter
Science—Science (incorporating Sci Mo)
Spec—Spectator
Sports Illus—Sports Illustrated
Sr Schol—Senior Scholastic

Theatre Arts—Theatre Arts
This Week—This Week Magazine
Time—Time
Times Lit Sup—London Times Literary Supplement
Toronto Globe and Mail—Toronto Globe and Mail
Toronto Globe and Mail Globe Mag—Toronto Globe and Mail Globe Magazine
Travel—Travel

U N R—United Nations Review
U S Dept State Bul—United States Department of State Bulletin
U S News—United States News & World Report

Variety—Variety
Vital Speeches—Vital Speeches of the Day
Vogue—Vogue

Washington (D.C.) Post—Washington Post and Times Herald
Wilson Lib Bul—Wilson Library Bulletin
Womans Home C—Woman's Home Companion (discontinued)

Yale R—Yale Review

NECROLOGY

This is a list of biographees' obituaries that are in the Yearbook, including those of late 1959. Deaths that occurred in late 1960 are recorded in the early 1961 issues of CURRENT BIOGRAPHY.

Adams, Franklin P. (biog 1941)
Aly Khan, Prince (biog 1960)
Andrews, Roy Chapman (biog 1953)
Aranha, Oswaldo (biog 1942)

Bennett, Hugh H. (biog 1946)
Bevan, Aneurin (biog 1943)
Bjoerling, Jussi (biog 1947)
Brown, Charles H. (biog 1941)
Bryson, Lyman (biog 1951)
Bundesen, Herman Niels (biog 1948)
Burdick, Usher L. (biog 1952)

Carroll, John (biog 1955)
Castle, Lewis G. (biog 1958)
Clark, Bobby (biog 1949)
Claxton, Brooke (biog 1947)
Cochrane, Edward L. (biog 1951)
Cohen, Benjamin A. (biog 1948)
Cooke, Morris Llewellyn (biog 1950)
Crum, Bartley C. (biog 1947)

Defauw, Désiré (biog 1940)
Denny, George V., Jr. (biog 1950)

Fellows, Harold E. (biog 1952)
Flagg, James Montgomery (biog 1940)
Fletcher, Sir Angus (biog 1946)
Fowler, Gene (biog 1944)
French, Paul Comly (biog 1951)
Funk, Walther (biog 1940)

Gauss, Clarence E. (biog 1941)
Grace, Eugene Gifford (biog 1941)
Greenbie, Sydney (biog 1941)

Halifax, Edward Frederick Lindley Wood, 1st Earl of (biog 1940)
Hammerstein, Oscar, 2d (biog 1944)
Hansen, H. C. (biog 1956)
Haynes, George Edmund (biog 1946)
Hennings, Thomas C., Jr. (biog 1954)
Hennock, Frieda B. (biog 1948)
Hines, Frank T. (biog 1944)
Hudson, Manley O. (biog 1944)
Hurston, Zora Neale (biog 1942)

Ibáñez, Carlos (biog 1952)

Johnson, Arnold M. (biog 1955)
Jordan, Sara M. (biog 1954)

Kagawa, Toyohiko (biog 1941)
Kesselring, Albert (biog 1942)
Kilpatrick, John Reed (biog 1948)
Kirk, Norman T. (biog 1944)
Kluckhohn, Clyde (biog 1951)
Kroeber, A. L. (biog 1958)
Kurchatov, Igor V. (biog 1957)

La Gorce, John Oliver (biog 1954)
Langer, William (biog 1952)
Laurel, José P. (biog 1953)
Leffingwell, R. C. (biog 1950)
Long, Earl K. (biog 1950)
López, Alfonso (biog 1942)
Luccock, Halford E., Rev. Dr. (biog 1960)
Lydenberg, Harry Miller (biog 1941)

McIntire, Ross T. (biog 1945)
Maher, Aly (biog 1952)
Marquand, J. P. (biog 1942)
Martínez Trueba, Andrés (biog 1954)
Mellett, Lowell (biog 1942)
Messersmith, George S. (biog 1942)
Metzman, G. (biog 1946)
Muir, James (biog 1950)
Muniz, João Carlos (biog 1952)

Neuberger, Richard L. (biog 1955)
Nichols, Dudley (biog 1941)

O'Conor, Herbert R. (biog 1950)
Olivetti, Adriano (biog 1959)
Orville, Howard T. (biog 1956)
Ottley, Roi (biog 1943)

Paepcke, Walter P. (biog 1960)
Pasternak, Boris (biog 1959)
Pavelić, Ante (biog 1942)
Perkins, George W. (biog 1950)
Perlman, Philip B. (biog 1952)
Pieck, Wilhelm (biog 1949)
Pollitt, Harry (biog 1948)

Post, Emily (biog 1941)
Prentis, Henning Webb, Jr. (biog 1940)

Rahman, Sir Abdul, Paramount Ruler of Malaya (biog 1957)
Riggio, Vincent (biog 1949)
Robertson, Reuben B., Jr. (biog 1955)
Rockefeller, John D., Jr. (biog 1941)
Rogers, Edith Nourse (biog 1942)
Rugg, Harold (biog 1941)
Ruml, Beardsley (biog 1943)

Salit, Norman, Rabbi (biog 1955)
Schwartz, Maurice (biog 1956)
Seabury, David (biog 1941)
Shield, Lansing P. (biog 1951)
Shridharani, Krishnalal (biog 1942)
Shute, Nevil (biog 1942)
Simon, Richard L. (biog 1941)
Simpson, Richard M. (biog 1953)
Sisavang Vong, King of Laos (biog 1954)
Spry, Constance (biog 1940)
Steinman, D. B. (obit 1957)
Stepinac, Alojzije, Cardinal (biog 1953)
Sullavan, Margaret (biog 1944)
Swirbul, Leon A. (biog 1953)

Taber, Louis J. (biog 1942)
Thorek, Max (biog 1951)
Tibbett, Lawrence (biog 1945)

Villa-Lobos, Heitor (biog 1945)

Warren, Althea (biog 1942)
Warren, Leonard (biog 1953)
Welch, Joseph N. (biog 1954)
Wheelock, Warren (biog 1940)
Wigglesworth, Richard B. (biog 1959)
Windust, Bretaigne (biog 1943)
Witherow, W. P. (biog 1942)
Witte, Edwin E. (biog 1946)
Woolley, Sir Leonard (biog 1954)

Yui, O. K. (biog 1955)
Yust, Walter (biog 1943)

Zoli, Adone (biog 1958)

CLASSIFICATION BY PROFESSION—1960

Advertising

Bernays, Edward L.
Blackwell, Earl
Cornelius, John C.
Strouse, Norman H.

Archaeology

Rubín de la Borbolla, Daniel F.

Architecture

Breuer, Marcel
Candela, Félix
Fuller, R. Buckminster
Niemeyer, Oscar
Young, Joseph Louis

Art

Armstrong-Jones, Antony
Bonomi, Maria
Chagall, Marc
Dongen, Kees van
Duchamp, Marcel
Evergood, Philip
Ferber, Herbert
Halsman, Philippe
Mastroianni, Umberto
Mérida, Carlos
Rubín de la Borbolla, Daniel F.
Schulz, Charles M.
Young, Joseph Louis

Aviation

Grace, J. Peter
Putt, Donald L.
Quesada, E. R.
Stone, William S.

Business

Baker, Melvin H.
Bannow, Rudolph F.
Bernays, Edward L.
Blackwell, Earl
Buetow, Herbert P.
Burns, John L.
Candela, Félix
Canham, Erwin D.
Cornelius, John C.
Fong, Hiram L.
Galvin, Robert W.
Geis, Bernard
Grace, J. Peter
Halsman, Philippe
Hill, David G.
Jensen, Ben F.
Katz, Label A.

Kraus, Hans P.
Marsh, Ernest Sterling
Meadows, A. H.
Paepcke, Walter P.
Power, Donald C.
Prouty, Winston L.
Strouse, Norman H.
Thomson, Roy
Trigère, Pauline
Tuttle, Charles E.
Worthington, Leslie B.

Dance

Beriosova, Svetlana
Iglesias, Roberto
Kidd, Michael
Verdon, Gwen

Diplomacy

Belaúnde, Víctor Andrés
Bohlen, Charles E.
Dimechkie, Nadim
Green, Howard
Mallory, L. D.
Tanner, Väinö
Tsarapkin, Semyon K.
Vanier, George Philias
Warren, Fletcher
Wigny, Pierre

Education

Allport, Gordon W.
Burns, Eveline M.
Chamberlain, Owen
Coons, Albert H.
Dahanayake, W.
Eiseley, Loren
Eshelman, W. W.
Fischer, John H.
Flemming, Arthur S.
Hadas, Moses
Harkness, Georgia, Rev. Dr.
Hoyle, Fred
Ivey, John E., Jr.
Kistiakowsky, George B.
Leake, Chauncey D.
Luccock, Halford E., Rev. Dr.
Marcus, Jacob R.
Marsh, John, Rev. Dr.
Mattingly, Garrett
Mendenhall, Thomas Corwin, 2d
Moore, Elisabeth Luce
Murphy, Gardner
Paepcke, Walter P.
Parkinson, C. Northcote
Powell, Lawrence Clark
Roberts, Walter Orr
Sears, Paul B.
Segrè, Emilio
Shuster, George N.

Smith, Carleton Sprague
Snodgrass, W. D.
Spitzer, Lyman, Jr.
Stone, William S.
Strang, Ruth
Thaler, William J.
Urey, Harold C.
Warren, William C.
Williams, John H.

Fashion

Trigère, Pauline

Finance

Grace, J. Peter
Meadows, A. H.
Remington, John W.
Roebling, Mary G.
Tawes, J. Millard

Government—
Foreign

Barrette, Antonio
Belaúnde, Víctor Andrés
Betancourt, Rómulo
Chandy, Anna
Dahanayake, W.
Dimechkie, Nadim
Gaulle, Charles de
Green, Howard
Keita, Modibo
Kreisky, Bruno
Lemass, Seán F.
Lübke, Heinrich
Lumumba, Patrice
Malinovsky, Rodion Y.
Marples, Ernest
Maudling, Reginald
Stoph, Willi
Swart. Charles R.
Tanner, Väinö
Tsarapkin, Semyon K.
Vanier, George Philias
Watkinson, Harold
Wigny, Pierre
Zhukov, Georgy A.

Government—
United States

Berding, Andrew H.
Bohlen, Charles E.
Bolling, Richard
Brown, Edmund G.
Burgess, Robert W.
Byrd, Robert C.
Byrnes, John W.
Cannon, Howard W.
Combs, Bert T.
Ellington, Buford

Fascell, Dante B.
Flemming, Arthur S.
Fong, Hiram L.
Forand, Aime J.
Ford, Frederick W.
Griffin, Robert P.
Handley, Harold W.
Hartke, Vance
Hyde, H. van Zile
Inouye, Daniel K.
Jensen, Ben F.
Kintner, Earl W.
Kistiakowsky, George B.
Kowalski, Frank, Jr.
Landrum, Phil M.
Mallory, L. D.
May, Catherine
Nelson, Gaylord
O'Neill, Francis A., Jr.
Passman, Otto E.
Patterson, John
Prouty, Winston L.
Quesada, E. R.
Rivers, L. Mendel
Roman, Nancy G.
Saund, Dalip S.
Stafford, Robert T.
Tawes, J. Millard
Thaler, William J.
Warren, Fletcher
Williams, Harrison A., Jr.
Williams, John H.
Yarborough, Ralph W.

Industry

Baker, Melvin H.
Bannow, Rudolph F.
Buetow, Herbert P.
Burns, John L.
Cooper, R. Conrad
Elder, Albert L.
Galvin, Robert W.
Grace, J. Peter
Hill, David G.
Loomis, Daniel P.
Meadows, A. H.
Paepcke, Walter P.
Power, Donald C.
Putt, Donald L.
Quesada, E. R.
Worthington, Leslie B.

International Relations

Aly Khan, Prince
Belaúnde, Víctor Andrés
Bohlen, Charles E.
Dimechkie, Nadim
Green, Howard
Hyde, H. van Zile
Mallory, L. D.
Smith, Carleton Sprague
Stummvoll, Josef
Tsarapkin, Semyon K.
Warren, Fletcher
Wigny, Pierre

Journalism

Brinkley, David
Buchwald, Art
Canham, Erwin D.
Grosvenor, Melville Bell
Luccock, Halford E., Rev. Dr.
Rosenthal, A. M.
Schoenbrun, David
Schulz, Charles M.
Schwartz, Delmore
Spectorsky, A. C.
Thomson, Roy
Thurber, James
Trimble, Vance H.
Van Buren, Abigail
White, E. B.
White, Robert M., 2d

Labor

Cooper, R. Conrad
Cousins, Frank
Kennedy, Thomas
O'Neill, Francis A., Jr.

Law

Cannon, Howard W.
Chandy, Anna
Combs, Bert T.
Fascell, Dante B.
Fong, Hiram L.
Green, Howard
Griffin, Robert P.
Hartke, Vance
Inouye, Daniel K.
Katz, Label A.
Kintner, Earl W.
Landrum, Phil M.
Loomis, Daniel P.
McKneally, Martin B.
Nelson, Gaylord
O'Neill, Francis A., Jr.
Patterson, John
Power, Donald C.
Randall, John D.
Remington, John W.
Stafford, Robert T.
Warren, William C.
Yarborough, Ralph W.

Library Service

Powell, Lawrence Clark
Sewell, Winifred
Smith, Carleton Sprague
Spain, Frances Lander
Stummvoll, Josef
Whitehill, Walter Muir

Literature

Brooks, Van Wyck
Buchwald, Art
Eiseley, Loren

Frings, Ketti
Griffin, John Howard
Hart, Moss
Hellman, Lillian
Leech, Margaret
Quasimodo, Salvatore
Rutenborn, Günter, Rev.
Sagan Françoise
Schwartz, Delmore
Sholokhov, Mikhail A.
Shuster, George N.
Snodgrass, W. D.
Thurber, James
White, E. B.

Medicine

Alexander, Franz
Coons, Albert H.
Demikhov, Vladimir P.
Hyde, H. van Zile
Orr, Louis M.
Rivers, Thomas M.
Sewell, Winifred

Military

Beach, Edward
Davidson, John F.
Dennison, Robert Lee
Gaulle, Charles de
Kowalski, Frank, Jr.
Malinovsky, Rodion Y.
Putt, Donald L.
Quesada, E. R.
Schomburg, August
Shoup, David M.
Stewart, James
Stone, William S.
Stoph, Willi
Thach, John Smith
Thaler, William J.
Vanier, George Philias

Motion Pictures

Aherne, Brian
Bancroft, Anne
Bardot, Brigitte
Berg, Gertrude
Bergman, Ingmar
Bikel, Theodore
Buchholz, Horst
Burton, Richard
Cobb, Lee J.
Dillman, Bradford
Frings, Ketti
Griffith, Andy
Hayworth, Rita
Hellman, Lillian
Hitchcock, Alfred
Ives, Burl
Kidd, Michael
Lollobrigida, Gina
London, Julie
Montand, Yves
Moore, Archie
Mulligan, Gerry
Odetta

Perkins, Anthony
Rogers, Paul
Sahl, Mort
Sellers, Peter
Signoret, Simone
Sinatra, Frank
Stewart, James
Susskind, David
Zimbalist, Efrem, Jr.

Music

Bernstein, Leonard
Bikel, Theodore
Carter, Elliott
Chasins, Abram
Floyd, Carlisle
Gould, Glenn
Griffin, John Howard
Ives, Burl
London, Julie
Lopez, Vincent
Marshall, Lois
Montand, Yves
Mulligan, Gerry
Nilsson, Birgit
Oberlin, Russell
Odetta
Simionato, Giulietta
Sinatra, Frank
Smith, Carleton Sprague
Sutherland, Joan
Suzuki, Pat
Williams, Andy

Nonfiction

Alexander, Franz
Allport, Gordon W.
Beach, Edward
Bernays, Edward L.
Betancourt, Rómulo
Boyd, Louise A.
Buchwald, Art
Burns, Eveline M.
Canham, Erwin D.
Chasins, Abram
Cohen, Arthur A.
D'Arcy, Martin, Very Rev.
Dodge, John V.
Eiseley, Loren
Griffin, John Howard
Hadas, Moses
Halsman, Philippe
Harkness, Georgia, Rev. Dr.
Hunter, Dard
Leech, Margaret
Luccock, Halford E., Rev. Dr.
Marcus, Jacob R.
Marsh, John, Rev. Dr.
Mattingly, Garrett
Mendenhall, Thomas Corwin, 2d
Murphy, Gardner
Neill, Stephen Charles, Bishop
Parkinson, C. Northcote
Powell, Lawrence Clark
Ramsey, Arthur Michael, Arch-
    bishop of York
Schulz, Charles M.
Sears, Paul B.

Shuster, George N.
Spectorsky, A .C.
Strang, Ruth
Thurber, James
White, E. B.
Whitehill, Walter Muir

Organizations

Bannow, Rudolph F.
Canham, Erwin D.
Elder, Albert L.
Eshelman, W. W.
Grosvenor, Melville Bell
Katz, Label A.
Leake, Chauncey D.
Loomis, Daniel P.
McKneally, Martin B.
Orr, Louis M.
Randall, John D.
Remington, John W.
Sewell, Winifred
Spain, Frances Lander

Philosophy

D'Arcy, Martin, Very Rev.

Politics— Foreign

Barrette, Antonio
Betancourt, Rómulo
Cousins, Frank
Dahanayake, W.
Gaulle, Charles de
Green, Howard
Keita, Modibo
Kreisky, Bruno
Lemass, Seán F.
Lübke, Heinrich
Lumumba, Patrice
Malinovsky, Rodion Y.
Marples, Ernest
Maudling, Reginald
Stoph, Willi
Swart, Charles R.
Tanner, Väinö
Watkinson, Harold
Wigny, Pierre

Politics— United States

Bolling, Richard
Brown, Edmund G.
Byrd, Robert C.
Byrnes, John W.
Cannon, Howard W.
Combs, Bert T.
Ellington, Buford
Fascell, Dante B.
Flemming, Arthur S.
Fong, Hiram L.
Forand, Aime J.

Griffin, Robert P.
Handley, Harold W.
Hartke, Vance
Inouye, Daniel K.
Jensen, Ben F.
Kowalski, Frank, Jr.
Landrum, Phil M.
May, Catherine
Nelson, Gaylord
Passman, Otto E.
Patterson, John
Prouty, Winston L.
Rivers, L. Mendel
Saund, Dalip S.
Stafford, Robert T.
Tawes, J. Millard
Williams, Harrison A., Jr.
Yarborough, Ralph W.

Publishing

Blackwell, Earl
Cohen, Arthur A.
Dodge, John V.
Geis, Bernard
Roberts, Oral, Rev.
Spectorsky, A. C.
Thomson, Roy
Tuttle, Charles E.
White, Robert M., 2d

Radio

Berg, Gertrude
Brinkley, David
Chasins, Abram
Cullen, Bill
Ford, Frederick W.
Leonard, Bill
Lopez, Vincent
Sahl, Mort
Schoenbrun, David
Sellers, Peter
Thomson, Roy

Religion

Aga Khan IV, The
Cohen, Arthur A.
D'Arcy, Martin, Very Rev.
Doi, Peter Tatsuo, Cardinal
Harkness, Georgia, Rev. Dr.
Iakovos, Archbishop
Luccock, Halford E., Rev. Dr.
Marcus, Jacob R.
Marsh, John, Rev. Dr.
Meyer, Albert, Cardinal
Muench, Aloisius, Cardinal
Myers, C. Kilmer, Rev. Dr.
Neill, Stephen Charles, Bishop
Ramsey, Arthur Michael, Arch-
    bishop of York
Roberts, Oral, Rev.
Rugambwa, Laurian, Cardinal
Rutenborn, Günter, Rev.
Santos, Rufino J., Cardinal
Shuster, George N.

Science

Boyd, Louise A.
Chamberlain, Owen
Coons, Albert H.
Demikhov, Vladimir P.
Elder, Albert L.
Fuller, R. Buckminster
Grosvenor, Melville Bell
Hoyle, Fred
Hunter, Dard
Hyde, H. van Zile
Kistiakowsky, George B.
Leake, Chauncey D.
Rivers, Thomas M.
Roberts, Walter Orr
Roman, Nancy G.
Sears, Paul B.
Segrè, Emilio
Sewell, Winifred
Spitzer, Lyman, Jr.
Swann, W. F. G.
Thaler, William J.
Urey, Harold C.
Williams, John H.

Social Science

Alexander, Franz
Allport, Gordon W.
Boyd, Louise A.
Burgess, Robert W.
Burns, Eveline M.
Ivey, John E., Jr.
Leech, Margaret
Mattingly, Garrett
Mendenhall, Thomas Corwin, 2d
Murphy, Gardner
Parkinson, C. Northcote
Rubín de la Borbolla, Daniel F.
Strang, Ruth
Warren, William C.

Social Service

Burns, Eveline M.
Kirk, William T.

Moore, Elisabeth Luce
Myers, C. Kilmer, Rev. Dr.
Sirikit Kitiyakara, Consort of
    Rama IX, King of Thailand

Sports

Aly Khan, Prince
Chamberlain, Wilt
Conerly, Charles
Elliott, Herbert
Fox, Nellie
Lopez, Al
Moore, Archie
Palmer, Arnold
Patterson, Floyd
Thomas, John

Technology

Buetow, Herbert P.
Candela, Félix
Fuller, R. Buckminster
Galvin, Robert W.
Hunter, Dard
Putt, Donald L.
Thaler, William J.

Television

Bancroft, Anne
Berg, Gertrude
Bernstein, Leonard
Bikel, Theodore
Brinkley, David
Cobb, Lee J.
Cullen, Bill
Ford, Frederick W.
Griffith, Andy
Hitchcock, Alfred
Leonard, Bill
London, Julie
Lopez, Vincent
Odetta
Sahl, Mort

Schoenbrun, David
Sellers, Peter
Signoret, Simone
Sinatra, Frank
Susskind, David
Thomson, Roy
Williams, Andy
Zimbalist, Efrem, Jr.

Theater

Aherne, Brian
Bancroft, Anne
Berg, Gertrude
Bergman, Ingmar
Bernstein, Leonard
Bikel, Theodore
Buchholz, Horst
Burton, Richard
Cobb, Lee J.
Dillman, Bradford
Frings, Ketti
Griffith, Andy
Hart, Moss
Hellman, Lillian
Ives, Burl
Kidd, Michael
Montand, Yves
Perkins, Anthony
Rogers, Paul
Rutenborn, Günter, Rev.
Sahl, Mort
Signoret, Simone
Strasberg, Lee
Susskind, David
Suzuki, Pat
Thurber, James
Verdon, Gwen
Zimbalist, Efrem, Jr.

Other Classifications

Armstrong-Jones, Antony
Sirikit Kitiyakara, Consort of
    Rama IX, King of Thailand

CUMULATED INDEX—1951-1960

This is a ten-year cumulation of all names that have appeared in CURRENT BIOGRAPHY from 1951 through 1960. The dates after names indicate monthly issues and/or Yearbooks in which biographies and obituaries are contained.

For the index to 1940-1950 biographies, see CURRENT BIOGRAPHY 1950 Yearbook.

Blackall, Frederick S(teele), Jr. Jan 53

Blackwell, Betsy Talbot Jun 54

Blackwell, (Samuel) Earl, (Jr.) Nov 60

Blagonravov, A(natoli) A(rkadyevich) Feb 58

Blair, James T(homas), Jr. Apr 58

Blake, Eugene Carson, Rev. Dr. Sep 55

Blake, Francis G(ilman) biog Jan 43 obit Mar 52

Blakeslee, A(lbert) F(rancis) biog Oct 41 obit Jan 55

Blamey, Sir Thomas (Albert) biog Jun 42 obit Jul 51

Blanch, Arnold (Alder) Jan 54

Blanch, Mrs. Arnold (Alder) See Lee, D. (E.) Jan 54

Blancke, Harold Jun 57

Blanding, Don(ald Benson) biog Jan 57 obit Sep 57

Blandy, W(illiam) H(enry) P(urnell) biog Nov 42 obit Mar 54

Blank, Theodor Sep 52

Blankenhorn, Herbert (Adolphe Heinrich) Apr 56

Blanton, Smiley Jun 56

Blatnik, John A(nton) Feb 58

Blattenberger, Raymond Mar 58

Bliss, Henry E(velyn) biog Sep 53 obit Oct 55

Bliss, Raymond W(hitcomb) Jan 51

Blitch, Mrs. Brooks Erwin, Jr. See Blitch, Iris F. Apr 56

Blitch, Iris F(aircloth) Apr 56

Bloch, Ernest biog Sep 53 obit Oct 59

Bloch, Felix Sep 54

Block, Herbert (Lawrence) Jul 54

Blodgett, Katharine Burr May 52

Bloom, Claire May 56

Bloomgarden, Kermit Dec 58

Blough, Roger M(iles) Jul 55

Blücher, Franz biog Jan 56 obit Jun 59

Blume, Peter Mar 56

Blundell, Michael Mar 54

Blunt, Katharine biog Dec 46 obit Oct 54

Boatner, Haydon L(emaire) Jul 52

Bob and Ray See Elliott, Bob Oct 57

Bogart, Humphrey biog May 42 obit Mar 57

Boggs, Hale See Boggs, (Thomas) Hale Apr 58

Boggs, J(ames) Caleb Jul 56

Boggs, (Thomas) Hale Apr 58

Boheman, Erik (Carlson) Mar 51

Bohlen, Charles E(ustis) May 60

Bohrod, Aaron Feb 55

Boigny, Félix Houphouet- See Houphouet-Boigny, Félix Oct 58

Bok, William Curtis May 54

Boles, Ewing T(homas) Apr 53

Boles, Paul Darcy (WLB) Yrbk 56

Bolling, Richard (Walker) Mar 60

Bolt, Richard H(enry) Jun 54

Bolte, Charles L(awrence) Jan 54

Bolton, Frances P(ayne Bingham) Apr 54

Bolz, Lothar Sep 59

Bond, Horace Mann Mar 54

Bonner, Herbert C(ovington) Jul 56

Bonner, Paul Hyde (WLB) Yrbk 55

Bonomi, Ivanoe biog Aug 44 obit May 51

Bonomi, Maria (Anna Olga Luiza) Jul 60

Bonsal, Philip Wilson Jun 59

Bonsal, Stephen biog Aug 45 obit Jul 51

Boone, J(oel) T(hompson) Mar 51

Boone, Pat Jul 59

Booth, Shirley Apr 53

Borberg, William biog Nov 52 obit Sep 58

Borbolla, Daniel F. Rubín de la See Rubín de la Borbolla, Daniel F. Feb 60

Borden, Neil H(opper) May 54

Borgese, G(iuseppe) A(ntonio) biog Dec 47 obit Jan 53

Borgnine, Ernest Apr 56

Born, Max May 55

Borne, Mortimer Apr 54

Borst, Lyle B(enjamin) Jul 54

Bosustow, Stephen Jun 58

Bothe, Walther (Wilhelm Georg) biog May 55 obit Apr 57

Bourgès-Maunoury, Maurice (Jean-Marie) Jul 57

Bourguiba, Habib ben Ali Sep 55

Boutelle, Richard S(chley) Sep 51

Bovet, Daniele Jan 58

Bowater, Sir Eric (Vansittart) Sep 56

Bowditch, Richard L(yon) biog Jul 53 obit Nov 59

Bowen, Ira Sprague Jun 51

Bowers, Claude G(ernade) biog Sep 41 obit Mar 58

Bowers, Faubion Sep 59

Bowers, Mrs. Faubion See Rama Rau, Santha (WLB) Yrbk 59

Bowles, Chester (Bliss) Jan 57

Boyd, Alan T. Lennox- See Lennox-Boyd, Alan T. Jun 56

Boyd, Louise A(rner) Sep 60

Boyer, Harold Raymond Feb 52

Boyer, M(arion) W(illard) Jan 51

Brackett, Charles Feb 51

Brackman, Robert Jul 53

Bradbury, Ray (Douglas) Jun 53

Braddock, Bessie See Braddock, E. M. Jul 57

Braddock, E(lizabeth) M(argaret Bamber) Jul 57

Bradley, Preston, Rev. Dr. Mar 56

Bragdon, Helen D(alton) Feb 51

Brahdy, Mrs. Leopold See Rees, Mina S. Nov 57

Brailowsky, Alexander Jun 56

Brancusi, Constantin biog Sep 55 obit Jun 57

Brando, Marlon Apr 52

Brandt, Willy Jun 58

Braniff, T(homas) E(lmer) biog Apr 52 obit Mar 54

Bransome, Edwin D(agobert) Apr 52

Brattain, Walter H(ouser) Sep 57

Braun, (Joachim) Werner Jun 57

Braun, Wernher von See Von Braun, W. Jan 52

Breckinridge, Aida de Acosta Jun 54

Breech, Ernest R(obert) Sep 55

Brennan, William J(oseph), Jr. Jun 57

Brentano (di Tremezzo), Heinrich von Feb 55

Brenton, W(oodward) Harold Jan 53

Breslin, Howard (Mary) (WLB) Yrbk 58

Breuer, Marcel (Lajos) Jun 60

Brewer, Roy M(artin) Sep 53

Brice, Fanny biog Jun 46 obit Jul 51

Brick, John (WLB) Yrbk 53

Brickell, (Henry) Herschel biog Nov 45 obit Jul 52

Bricker, John W(illiam) Jul 56

Bridgman, P(ercy) W(illiams) Apr 55

Brier, Howard M(axwell) (WLB) Yrbk 51

Briggs, James E(lbert) Jun 57

Brigham, Clarence S(aunders) Jul 59

Brind, Sir (Eric James) Patrick Nov 52

Briney, Nancy (Wells) Jan 54

Briney, Mrs. Paul See Briney, N. (W.) Jan 54

Brinkley, David (McClure) Mar 60

Brinton, (Clarence) Crane Jun 59

Briscoe, Robert May 57

Britton, Edgar C(lay) Apr 52

Bro, Margueritte Harmon (WLB) Yrbk 52

Brod, Mrs. Albert Thomas See Hagy, Ruth Geri Oct 57

Brode, Wallace R(eed) Jun 58

Broglie, Louis (Victor Pierre Raymond), Prince de Sep 55

Bromfield, Louis biog Jul 44 obit May 56

Bronowski, J(acob) Sep 58

Brooke-Popham, Sir Robert (Moore) biog Oct 41 obit Jan 54

Brooks, C(harles) Wayland biog Sep 47 obit Mar 57

Brooks, D(avid) W(illiam) Jun 51

Brooks, James (D.) Feb 59

Brooks, Overton Jun 57

Brooks, Van Wyck Sep 60

Brophy, Thomas D'Arcy Sep 52

Brosio, Manlio (Giovanni) Sep 55

Brossard, Edgar B(ernard) Jul 54

Curry, Peggy Simson (WLB) Yrbk 58

Curry, Mrs. William Seeright See Curry, Peggy Simson (WLB) Yrbk 58

Curtice, Harlow H(erbert) Mar 53

Curtis, Carl T(homas) Sep 54

Curtis, Tony May 59

Cushing, Richard J(ames), Archbishop Jun 52

Cyrankiewicz, Józef Feb 57

Dahanayake, W(ijayananda) Apr 60

Dahlberg, Edwin T(heodore), Rev. Dr. May 58

Dalai Lama Jul 51

Dale, Chester Sep 58

Daley, Arthur (John) Sep 56

Daley, Richard J(oseph) Sep 55

Dali, Salvador Apr 51

Dallas, C(harles) Donald biog Apr 49 obit Jun 59

Dalrymple, Jean Sep 53

Daly, James (Firman) Oct 59

Damon, Ralph S(hepard) biog Jul 49 obit Mar 56

Damrosch, Walter (Johannes) biog Mar 44 obit Jan 51

Dangerfield, George (Bubb) Sep 53

Daniel, (Marion) Price Jan 56

Daniel, Robert Prentiss May 52

Daniel, W(ilbur) C(larence) Dan Jun 57

Daniel-Rops, Henry Mar 57

Daniels, Grace B(aird) Sep 59

D'Arcy, Martin (Cyril), Very Rev. Jan 60

Daringer, Helen Fern (WLB) Yrbk 51

Darré, R(ichard) Walther (Oskar) biog Nov 41 obit Jan 57 (died Sep 53)

Darrell, R(obert) D(onaldson) Sep 55

Darrow, Whitney, Jr. Dec 58

Da Silva, Vieira See Vieira da Silva Dec 58

Daud Khan, Sardar Mohammed Mar 57

Davenport, Russell W(heeler) biog Jan 44 obit Jun 54

Davidson, Garrison H(olt) Jun 57

Davidson, Irwin D(elmore) Jan 56

Davidson, Jo biog Apr 45 obit Feb 52

Davidson, John F(rederick) Nov 60

Davidson, William L(ee) Jul 52

Davies, Ernest (Albert John) May 51

Davies, Joseph E(dward) biog Apr 42 obit Jul 58

Davies, Ronald N(orwood) Sep 58

Davis, Benjamin O(liver), Jr. Sep 55

Davis, Bette Mar 53

Davis, Edward W(ilson) Sep 55

Davis, Elmer biog May 40 obit Sep 58

Davis, Mrs. Floyd (MacMillan) See Davis, G. R. Sep 53

Davis, Gladys Rockmore Sep 53

Davis, Harvey N(athaniel) biog Jul 47 obit Jan 53

Davis, James C(urran) Apr 57

Davis, Jess H(arrison) Jan 56

Davis, John W(illiam) biog Mar 53 obit May 55

Davis, Nathanael V(ining) Jan 59

Davis, Roy H(enry) biog Feb 55 obit Sep 56

Davis, Sammy, Jr. Sep 56

Davis, Tobé Coller Dec 59

Dawson, John A(lbert) Sep 52

Day, Doris Apr 54

Day, Edmund Ezra biog Sep 46 obit Apr 51

Day, Laraine Sep 53

Dayan, Moshe Mar 57

Deakin, Arthur biog Jan 48 obit Jun 55

Dean, Arthur H(obson) Mar 54

Dean, Dizzy Sep 51

Dean, Gordon (Evans) biog Sep 50 obit Nov 58

Dean, H(enry) Trendley Jun 57

Dean, Jay Hanna See Dean, D. Sep 51

Dean, Jerome Herman See Dean, D. Sep 51

Dean, William F(rishe) Sep 54

Deane, Martha See Young, M. Jun 52

Deasy, Mary (Margaret) (WLB) Yrbk 58

Déat, Marcel biog Jan 42 obit May 55

Debré, Michel (Jean Pierre) May 59

De Broglie, Louis, Prince See Broglie, Louis, Prince de Sep 55

DeButts, Harry A(shby) Apr 53

De Chirico, Giorgio See Chirico, Giorgio de Jan 56

DeCoursey, Elbert Sep 54

Defauw, Désiré biog Jan-Feb 40 obit Oct 60

De Galard Terraube, Geneviève See Galard Terraube, G. de Oct 54

De Gasperi, Alcide See Gasperi, A. de biog Dec 46 obit Oct 54

De Gaulle, Charles See Gaulle, Charles de Apr 60

De Givenchy, Hubert See Givenchy, H. (J. T.) de May 55

De Hevesy, George See Hevesy, George de Apr 59

Dehler, Thomas Jul 55

Dejong, Meindert (WLB) Yrbk 52

De Kauffmann, Henrik See Kauffmann, Henrik Apr 56

De Kiewiet, Cornelis W(illem) Jul 53

De Kleine, William biog Apr 41 obit Dec 57 Yrbk 58

De Kooning, Willem Jun 55

De La Colina, Rafael See Colina, R. de la Jan 51

De la Guardia, Ernesto, Jr. See Guardia, Ernesto de la, Jr. Jan 57

DeLany, Walter S(tanley) Dec 52

De Lima, Sigrid (WLB) Yrbk 58

Della Casa, Lisa Jul 56

Dello Joio, Norman Sep 57

Del Monaco, Mario See Monaco, Mario del Feb 57

De los Angeles, Victoria See Angeles, V. de los Feb 55

Demikhov, Vladimir P(etrovich) Jun 60

De Mille, Cecil B(lount) biog May 42 obit Mar 59

DeMott, Richard H(opper) Feb 51

De Moya, Manuel A. See Moya, Manuel A. de Nov 57

Dendramis, Vassili biog Jun 47 obit Jul 56

Denebrink, Francis C(ompton) Feb 56

Denham, R(obert) N(ewton) biog Oct 47 obit Sep 54

Deniel, Enrique, Cardinal Pla y See Pla y Deniel, E., Cardinal Feb 55

Dennis, Patrick See Tanner, Edward Everett, 3d May 59

Dennison, Robert Lee Apr 60

Denny, George V(ernon), Jr. biog Sep 50 obit Jan 60

De Onís, Harriet See Onís, Harriet de Apr 57

Der Harootian, Koren Jan 55

Derthick, L(awrence) G(ridley) Apr 57

Derwent, Clarence biog Nov 47 obit Nov 59

Desai, Morarji (Ranchhodji) Sep 58

De Sapio, Carmine G(erard) Sep 55

De Sica, Vittorio Jul 52

Dessès, Jean Jan 56

De Valera, Eamon Sep 51

Dever, Paul A(ndrew) biog May 49 obit Jul 58

Deviny, John J(oseph) biog Sep 48 obit Apr 55

De Voto, Bernard biog Sep 43 obit Jan 56

De Vries, Peter (WLB) Yrbk 59

Dewey, John biog Aug 44 obit Jul 52

De Wohl, Louis (WLB) Yrbk 55

Dexheimer, W(ilbur) A(pp) Feb 55

D'Harnoncourt, René Sep 52

Dhebar, U(chharangrai) N(avalshanker) Jun 55

Dial, Morse G(rant) Mar 56

493

El-Yafi, Abdullah See Yafi, Abdullah El- Jun 56

Emanuel, Victor May 51

Emerson, Faye Sep 51

Emerson, Lee E(arl) Oct 53

Emery, Anne (Eleanor McGuigan) (WLB) Yrbk 52

Emery, DeWitt (McKinley) biog Oct 46 obit Oct 55

Emmet, Evelyn (Violet Elizabeth) Mar 53

Emmet, Mrs. Thomas Addis See Emmet, E. (V. E.) Mar 53

Emmons, Glenn L(eonidas) Oct 54

Empie, Paul C(hauncey), Rev. Dr. Oct 58

Emrich, Duncan (Black Macdonald) Mar 55

Enckell, Carl J(ohan) A(lexis) biog Apr 50 obit Jun 59

Endeley, E(mmanuel) M(bela) L(ifaffe) Jul 59

Enders, John F(ranklin); Robbins, Frederick C(hapman); and Weller, Thomas H(uckle) Jun 55

Engle, Clair Mar 57

English, Mrs. William D. See Kelly, Judith biog Oct 41 obit Jul 57

Engstrom, E(lmer) W(illiam) Dec 51

Enters, Angna Jun 52

Epstein, Sir Jacob biog Jul 45 obit Nov 59

Erikson, Leonard F. Oct 53

Erkin, Feridun C(emal) Jan 52

Erskine, Sir George (Watkin Eben James) Jan 52

Ervin, Samuel J(ames), Jr. Jan 55

Eshelman, W(alter) W(itmer) May 60

Estenssoro, Víctor Paz See Paz Estenssoro, V. May 53

Ettinger, Richard P(rentice) Dec 51

Etzel, Franz See Armand, Louis Sep 57

Eustis, Helen (White) (WLB) Yrbk 55

Evans, Bergen (Baldwin) (WLB) Yrbk 55

Evans, Dale See Rogers, Dale Evans Sep 56

Evans, Dame Edith (Mary) Jun 56

Evans, Sir Edward R. G. R. See Mountevans, Edward R. G. R. Evans, 1st Baron biog May 41 obit Nov 57

Evans, Herbert M(cLean) Jul 59

Evans, Hugh Ivan, Rev. Dr. biog Nov 50 obit Jul 58

Evatt, Harriet (Torrey) (WLB) Yrbk 59

Evatt, Mrs. William S(teinwedell) See Evatt, Harriet (WLB) Yrbk 59

Evergood, Philip (Howard Francis Dixon) Oct 60

Ewing, (William) Maurice Jan 53

Exeter, David George Brownlow Cecil, 6th Marquis of—See Burghley, David George Brownlow Cecil, Lord Jan 56

Eyre, Mrs. Dean Atherton See Eyre, Katherine Wigmore (WLB) Yrbk 57

Eyre, Katherine Wigmore (WLB) Yrbk 57

Eytan, Walter Oct 58

Eyüboglu, Bedri Rahmi Sep 54

Fabian, Robert (Honey) Apr 54

Fabiani, Mrs. Alberto See Simonetta Dec 55

Fabray, Nanette Jan 56

Fadiman, Clifton (Paul) Oct 55

Fagg, Fred D(ow), Jr. Feb 56

Fairbanks, Douglas (Elton), Jr. Feb 56

Fairchild, David (Grandison) biog Jul 53 obit Oct 54

Fairchild, Henry Pratt biog Dec 42 obit Dec 56 Yrbk 57

Fairclough, Ellen (Louks Cook) Oct 57

Fairclough, Mrs. Gordon See Fairclough, Ellen Oct 57

Fairless, Benjamin F(ranklin) May 57

Falkenburg, Jinx See McCrary T. and J. (F.) Jul 53

Fanfani, Amintore Oct 58

Farmer, Guy (Otto) Feb 55

Farnsworth, Jerry Oct 54

Farnsworth, Mrs. Jerry See Sawyer, H. (A.) Oct 54

Farrar, John (Chipman) Jun 54

Farrar, Mrs. John (Chipman) See Farrar, Margaret Jul 55

Farrar, Margaret (Petherbridge) Jul 55

Farrington, Elizabeth Pruett See Farrington, (Mary) Elizabeth Pruett Jun 55

Farrington, Joseph R(ider) biog May 48 obit Sep 54

Farrington, Mrs. Joseph R(ider) See Farrington, (M.) E. P. Jun 55

Farrington, (Mary) Elizabeth Pruett Jun 55

Fascell, Dante B(runo) Apr 60

Fatemi, Hossein biog May 53 obit Jan 55

Fath, Jacques biog Apr 51 obit Jan 55

Faubus, Orval E(ugene) Oct 56

Faulkner, Nancy (WLB) Yrbk 56

Faulkner, William Jan 51

Faure, Edgar Feb 52

Faust, Clarence H(enry) Mar 52

Fawzi, Mahmoud Dec 51

Fechteler, William M(orrow) Sep 51

Feininger, Andreas (Bernhard Lyonel) Oct 57

Feininger, Lyonel (Charles Adrian) biog Jul 55 obit Mar 56

Feinsinger, Nathan P(aul) May 52

Feisal II, King of Iraq biog Jul 55 obit Oct 58

Feldmann, Markus biog Jun 56 obit Jan 59

Felix, Robert H(anna) Apr 57

Feller, Abraham H(oward) biog Nov 46 obit Jan 53

Fellini, Federico Jun 57

Fellows, Harold E(verett) biog Feb 52 obit May 60

Fels, William C(arl) Apr 59

Felt, Harry D(onald) Mar 59

Feltin, Maurice, Cardinal May 54

Felton, Ralph A(lmon) Sep 57

Ferber, Herbert Nov 60

Ferguson, Harry (George) Mar 56

Ferguson, Malcolm P(hilip) May 57

Fergusson, Erna (WLB) Yrbk 55

Fermi, Enrico biog Oct 45 obit Jan 55

Fermi, Mrs. Enrico See Fermi, Laura May 58

Fermi, Laura (Capon) May 58

Fermor, Patrick Leigh (WLB) Yrbk 55

Fernandel Oct 55

Ferren, John (Millard) Jul 58

Ferrer, José (Pepe) Figueres See Figueres Ferrer, J. (P.) Oct 53

Ferrier, Kathleen biog Oct 51 obit Dec 53

Feynman, R(ichard) P(hillips) Oct 55

Field, Betty Sep 59

Field, Henry Mar 55

Field, Marshall, 3d biog Mar 52 obit Jan 57

Fields, Dorothy Feb 58

Fields, Herbert biog Feb 58 obit Jun 58

Figueres Ferrer, José (Pepe) Oct 53

Figueroa, Ana Feb 52

Filho, Joao Café See Café Filho, J. (F.C.) Jan 55

Fine, John S(ydney) Sep 51

Finet, Paul Sep 51

Fingesten, Peter Oct 54

Finkelstein, Louis, Rabbi Mar 52

Finley, David E(dward) Feb 51

Finnegan, Joseph F(rancis) Apr 59

Finney, Gertrude E(lva Bridgeman) (WLB) Yrbk 57

Finney, Mrs. John Montfort See Finney, Gertrude E. (WLB) Yrbk 57

Finnie, Mrs. Haldeman See Holt, Isabella (WLB) Yrbk 56

Fischer, Carlos L. Feb 59

Fischer, John May 53

Fischer, John H(enry) Jul 60

Fisher, Eddie Oct 54

Hartford, (George) Huntington, 2d Jun 59

Hartke, (Rupert) Vance Mar 60

Hartman, Grace biog Nov 42 obit Oct 55

Hartman, Louis F(rancis), Rev. Jan 53

Hartnell, Norman (Bishop) May 53

Hartung, Hans (Heinrich Ernst) Jul 58

Harvey, E(dmund) Newton May 52

Haskell, William N(afew) biog Feb 47 obit Sep 52

Haskins, Caryl P(arker) Feb 58

Haslett, Dame Caroline biog Oct 50 obit Mar 57

Hass, Hans Feb 55

Hass, H(enry) B(ohn) Apr 56

al-Hassan, Prince of the Yemen Feb 57

Hatcher, Harlan (Henthorne) Oct 55

Hatfield, Mark O(dom) Nov 59

Hatoyama, Ichiro biog May 55 obit May 59

Hauge, Gabriel (Sylvest) Oct 53

Hauser, (Bengamin) Gayelord Jun 55

Havill, Edward (WLB) Yrbk 52

Hawkes, Anna L(orette) Rose Oct 56

Hawkins, Harry C(alvin) Apr 52

Hawkins, Jack Nov 59

Hawley, Cameron (WLB) Yrbk 57

Hayakawa, S(amuel) I(chiye) Nov 59

Haycraft, Howard Feb 54

Hayden, Carl T(rumbull) Jul 51

Hayden, Melissa May 55

Hayes, A(lbert) J. Oct 53

Hayes, Helen Oct 56

Hayes, Peter Lind Mar 59

Hayes, Samuel P(erkins) biog Sep 54 obit Sep 58

Hayes, Samuel P(erkins), Jr. Sep 54

Haynes, George Edmund biog Mar 46 obit Apr 60

Hays, Arthur Garfield biog Sep 42 obit Feb 55

Hays, (Lawrence) Brooks Jan 58

Hays, Will H(arrison) biog Jul 43 obit Apr 54

Hayward, Susan May 53

Haywood, Allan S(haw) biog May 52 obit Apr 53

Hayworth, Rita May 60

Head, Walter W(illiam) biog Apr 45 obit Jun 54

Heald, Henry Townley Feb 52

Hearst, William Randolph, Jr. Oct 55

Heathcoat-Amory, Derick See Amory, Derick Heathcoat Apr 58

Hébert, F(elix) Edward Nov 51

Heckart, Eileen Jun 58

Heckscher, August Oct 58

Hedden, Mrs. Walter Page See Hedden, Worth Tuttle (WLB) Yrbk 57

Hedden, Worth Tuttle (WLB) Yrbk 57

Hedin, Sven Anders biog May 40 obit Jan 53

Hedtoft, Hans (Christian) biog Mar 49 obit Mar 55

Heeney, A(rnold) D(anford) P(atrick) Jun 53

Hees, George (Harris) Oct 59

Heidenstam, Rolf (Magnus) von biog Oct 51 obit Oct 58

Heinlein, Robert A(nson) Mar 55

Heintzleman, B. Frank Jun 53

Heisenberg, Werner (Karl) Apr 57

Heiss, Carol E(lizabeth) Oct 59

Hektoen, Ludvig biog Dec 47 obit Sep 51

Helburn, Theresa biog Sep 44 obit Nov 59

Hellman, Lillian Jun 60

Henderson, E(lmer) L(ee) biog Jun 50 obit Oct 53

Hendl, Walter Jun 55

Hendrickson, Robert C. Nov 52

Henie, Sonja Jan 52

Hennings, Thomas C(arey), Jr. biog Oct 54 obit Nov 60

Hennock, Frieda B(arkin) biog Nov 48 obit Sep 60

Hepburn, Audrey Mar 54

Hepburn, Mitchell F(rederick) biog Dec 41 obit Feb 53

Hepworth, Barbara Feb 57

Herbert, Don(ald) (Jeffry) Feb 56

Herbert, Elizabeth Sweeney Feb 54

Herbert, Mrs. Leo J. See Herbert, E. S. Feb 54

Herblock See Block, H. (L.) Jul 54

Herod, William Rogers Mar 51

Herold, J(ean) Christopher (WLB) Yrbk 59

Herriot, Edouard biog Feb 46 obit Jun 57

Hershey, Lewis B(laine) Jun 51

Hersholt, Jean biog Dec 44 obit Sep 56

Herter, Christian A(rchibald) Mar 58

Herzog, Isaac Halevi, Rabbi biog Apr 59 obit Oct 59

Herzog, Maurice Jul 53

Hesburgh, Theodore M(artin), Rev. Jan 55

Hess, Dean E(lmer) Sep 57

Hess, Elmer Jan 56

Heston, Charlton May 57

Heusinger, Adolf (Ernst) Feb 56

Heuven Goedhart, G(errit) J(an) van biog Oct 52 obit Sep 56

Hevesy, George (Charles) de Apr 59

Heyman, Mrs. Marcus A. See Komarovsky, M. Oct 53

Hickman, Herman (Michael, Jr.) biog Nov 51 obit Jul 58

Hicks, Beatrice A(lice) Jan 57

Hicks, Henry D(avies) Oct 56

Higgins, Andrew J(ackson) biog May 43 obit Sep 52

Higgins, Daniel Paul biog Dec 50 obit Mar 54

Higgins, Marguerite Jun 51

Hightower, John M(armann) Nov 52

Higley, Harvey V(an Zandt) Oct 56

Hilaly, Ahmed Naguib biog Jul 52 obit Mar 59

Hildebrand, Joel H(enry) Feb 55

Hildred, Sir William P(ercival) Apr 56

Hill, David G(arrett) Apr 60

Hill, Edwin C(onger) biog Sep 40 obit Apr 57

Hill, Robert C(harles) Jan 59

Hill, William S(ilas) Mar 55

Hillary, Sir Edmund (Percival) See Hunt, Sir (H. C.) J.; Hillary, Sir E. (P.); and Tenzing Norkey Oct 54

Hilleboe, Herman E(rtresvaag) Jun 55

Hilliard, Jan (WLB) Yrbk 59

Hillings, Patrick J(ohn) Oct 57

Hillis, Margaret (Eleanor) Feb 56

Hilsberg, Alex(ander) Oct 53

Hilton, Frank C. Jul 52

Hilton, James biog Sep 42 obit Feb 55

Hines, Duncan biog May 46 obit May 59

Hines, Frank T(homas) biog Apr 44 obit May 60

Hinshaw, (John) Carl (Williams) biog Jul 51 obit Oct 56

Hinshelwood, Sir Cyril (Norman) Apr 57

Hinton, Sir Christopher Jun 57

Hitchcock, Alfred (Joseph) Jul 60

Hitchcock, Charles B(aker) Oct 54

Hitler, Adolf biog Mar 42 obit Jan 57 (died Apr 45)

Hoad, Lew(is A.) Sep 56

Hoare, Sir Samuel John Gurney, 2d Baronet See Templewood, Samuel John Gurney Hoare, 1st Viscount biog Oct 40 obit Jul 59

Hobbs, Leonard S(inclair) Oct 54

Hobby, Oveta Culp Feb 53

Hobby, Mrs. William (Pettus) See Hobby, O. C. Feb 53

Hodes, Henry I(rving) Feb 59

Hodges, Luther H(artwell) Jul 56

Hodgson, W(illiam) R(oy) biog May 46 obit Apr 58

Hoegh, Leo A(rthur) Jul 56

Hoey, Clyde R(oark) biog Oct 49 obit Jul 54

Hoffman, Joseph G(ilbert) May 58

Hofmann, Hans Oct 58

Hofstadter, Richard Oct 56

Hogan, Frank S(mithwick) Sep 53

Ironside, William Edmund Ironside, 1st Baron biog May 40 obit Nov 59

Irving, Frederick A(ugustus) Mar 51

Irwin, Helen G(ould) Oct 52

Irwin, Robert B(enjamin) biog Mar 48 obit Jan 52

Ishibashi, Tanzan Mar 57

Ishimoto, Tatsuo Apr 56

Iverson, Kenneth R(oss) Apr 51

Ives, Burl (Icle Ivanhoe) May 60

Ives, Charles E(dward) biog Jun 47 obit Jul 54

Ivey, John E(li), Jr. Jul 60

Jackson, C(harles) D(ouglas) Oct 51

Jackson, Henry M(artin) Oct 53

Jackson, Mahalia Oct 57

Jackson, Robert H(oughwout) biog Oct 50 obit Dec 54

Jackson, William H(arding) Mar 51

Jacobsson, Per Oct 58

Jacopi, Giulio Jan 59

Jagendorf, Moritz (Adolf) (WLB) Yrbk 52

Jamali, Moh(amme)d Fadhel Jan 54

James, Charles (Wilson Brega) Jul 56

James, F(rank) Cyril Oct 56

Jameson, William J(ames) Jul 54

Jansen, William Oct 51

Janssens, Jean Baptiste, Very Rev. See Janssens, John Baptist, Very Rev. Sep 59

Janssens, John Baptist, Very Rev. Sep 59

Jarman, Sanderford biog Sep 42 obit Dec 54 Yrbk 55

Jarring, Gunnar V(alfrid) Oct 57

Javits, Jacob K(oppel) Oct 58

Jaynes, Clare (pseud. of Mayer, Jane and Spiegel, Clara) (WLB) Yrbk 54

Jeanmaire, Renée Nov 52

Jeffers, William M(artin) biog Nov 42 obit Apr 53

Jenkins, Hayes Alan May 56

Jenkins, Ray H(oward) Jun 54

Jenkins, Sara (WLB) Yrbk 53

Jenner, William E(zra) Jun 51

Jennings, B(enjamin) Brewster May 51

Jensen, Ben(ton) F(ranklin) Feb 60

Jensen, Mrs. Clyde R(eynolds) See Bard, Mary (WLB) Yrbk 56

Jensen, Jack Eugene See Jensen, Jackie Jun 59

Jensen, Jackie Jun 59

Jensen, Mrs. Oliver See Stafford, J. (WLB) Yrbk 51

Jernegan, John D(urnford) Nov 59

Jiménez, Marcos Pérez See Pérez Jiménez, M. Nov 54

Jiménez (Mantacon), Juan Ramón biog Feb 57 obit Sep 58

Jimerson, Earl W. biog Sep 48 obit Dec 57 Yrbk 58

Jodoin, Claude Mar 56

Johansson, Ingemar Nov 59

John XXIII, Pope Feb 59

John, John P(ico) Oct 56

Johnson, Arnold M(ilton) biog Oct 55 obit May 60

Johnson, Charles Spurgeon biog Nov 46 obit Jan 57

Johnson, David M(offat) Jul 52

Johnson, Edward biog Mar 43 obit Jun 59

Johnson, Joseph B(laine) Jul 56

Johnson, Joseph T(ravis) Feb 52

Johnson, Lyndon B(aines) Jan 51

Johnson, Nelson T(rusler) biog Jan-Feb 40 obit Feb 55

Johnson, Osa biog Apr 40 obit Feb 53

Johnson, Philip C(ortelyou) Oct 57

Johnson, Roy W(illiam) May 58

Johnson, (Thomas) Walter Apr 57

Johnson, U(ral) Alexis Oct 55

Johnson, Walter See Johnson, (Thomas) Walter Apr 57

Johnson, Wendell (Andrew Leroy) Apr 59

Johnston, Alvanley biog Jun 46 obit Nov 51

Johnston, Clem(ent) D(ixon) May 55

Johnston, Eric A(llen) Oct 55

Johnston, Olin D(eWitt) Nov 51

Johnston, Wayne A(ndrew) May 51

Johnstone, Margaret Blair, Rev. Jan 55

Joliot-Curie, Frédéric biog Oct 46 obit Oct 58

Joliot-Curie, Irène biog Apr 40 obit May 56

Jones, Barry Mar 58

Jones, Sir Harold Spencer Mar 55

Jones, Jesse H(olman) biog Oct 40 obit Sep 56

Jones, Lewis Webster Oct 58

Jones, Robert Edmond biog Nov 46 obit Jan 55

Jones, Roger W(arren) Nov 59

Jones, Russell Oct 57

Jooste, G(erhardus) P(etrus) Apr 51

Jordan, B(enjamin) Everett Nov 59

Jordan, Mildred (WLB) Yrbk 51

Jordan, Sara M(urray) biog Mar 54 obit Jan 60

Jordan, W(ilbur) K(itchener) Mar 55

Josephs, Devereux C(olt) Jul 53

Jouhaux, Léon biog Jan 48 obit Jul 54

Jouvet, Louis biog Oct 49 obit Oct 51

Jowitt, William Allen Jowitt, 1st Earl biog Aug 41 obit Nov 57

Joy, C(harles) Turner biog Jun 51 obit Sep 56

Joyce, J(ames) Avery Mar 59

Juan Carlos, Count of Barcelona Oct 51

Juliana, Queen of the Netherlands Jan 55

Jung, Carl Gustav Oct 53

Kádár, János May 57

Kaempffert, Waldemar B(ernhard) biog Sep 43 obit Feb 57

Kaganovich, Lazar M(oiseyevich) Oct 55

Kagawa, Toyohiko biog Sep 41 obit Jun 60

Kahane, Melanie Jul 59

Kahmann, (Mable) Cheslev (WLB) Yrbk 52

Kaiser, Jakob Feb 56

Kai-shek, Chiang See Chiang Kai-shek May 53

Kalich, Mrs. Jacob See Picon, M. Jun 51

Kallen, Horace M(eyer) Oct 53

Kamau, Johnstone See Kenyatta, J. Oct 53

Kanin, Garson Oct 52

Kanter, Albert L(ewis) Jul 53

Kapell, William biog May 48 obit Jan 54

Kapitza, Peter L(eonidovich) Oct 55

Kaplan, Joseph Oct 56

Kappel, Frederick R(ussell) Mar 57

Karajan, Herbert von Oct 56

Karamanlis, Constantine E. May 56

Karami, Rashid Nov 59

Karfiol, Bernard biog Nov 47 obit Oct 52

Kármán, Theodore von See von Kármán, T. May 55

Karp, David (WLB) Yrbk 57

Karsh, Yousuf Dec 52

Kase, Toshikazu Apr 57

Kasner, Edward biog Nov 43 obit Mar 55

Kassem, Abdul Karim (el-) Nov 59

Katz, Label A. Apr 60

Katz-Suchy, Juliusz Jun 51

Kauffmann, Henrik (Louis Hans) Apr 56

Kaufman, Irving R(obert) Apr 53

Kaur, Rajkumari Amrit Oct 55

Kaye, Danny Nov 52

Kaye, Nora Jan 53

Kazantzakis, Nikos biog Jul 55 obit Jan 58

Kearns, Carroll D(udley) Sep 56

Kearns, Mrs. Carroll D(udley) See Kearns. Nora Lynch Sep 56

Kearns, Nora Lynch Sep 56

Kraus, Hans P(eter) Jul 60

Krautter, Elisa Bialk See Bialk, E. (WLB) Yrbk 54

Krebs, H(ans) A(dolf) Mar 54

Krebs, Richard Julius Herman See Valtin, J. biog Apr 41 obit Jan 51

Kreisky, Bruno Sep 60

Krekeler, Heinz L(udwig) Dec 51

Kress, Samuel H(enry) biog Oct 55 obit Nov 55

Krishna Menon, V(engalil) K(rishnan) Mar 53

Kristiansen, Mrs. Erling See Selinko, A. Jan 55

Kroeber, A(lfred) L(ouis) biog Oct 58 obit Dec 60

Krohg, Per (Lasson) Nov 54

Krupp (von Bohlen und Halbach), Alfred (Felix Alwyn) May 55

Krutch, Joseph Wood Nov 59

Kubelik, Rafael Feb 51

Kubitschek (de Oliveira), Juscelino Apr 56

Kubly, Herbert (Oswald) Feb 59

Kuchel, Thomas H(enry) Feb 54

Kuekes, Edward D(aniel) Mar 54

Kuiper, Gerard P(eter) Feb 59

Kumm, (Herman) Henry W(illiam) Jun 55

Kunitz, Stanley (Jasspon) Nov 59

Kuniyoshi, Yasuo biog Jun 41 obit Jun 53

Kurchatov, Igor V(asil'evich) biog Nov 57 obit Apr 60

Kurusu, Saburo biog Jan 42 obit May 54

Kusch, P(olykarp) Mar 56

Kuwatly, Shukri al May 56

Kuzmin, Iosif I(osifovich) Feb 59

Kuznetsov, Vassili V(asilyevich) Jan 56

La Cava, Gregory biog Dec 41 obit Apr 52

Lacoste, Robert Nov 57

Lacy, Dan (Mabry) Nov 54

La Farge, Oliver (Hazard Perry) Jan 53

La Follette, Robert M(arion, Jr.) biog May 44 obit Apr 53

Lagerkvist, Pär (Fabian) Jan 52

La Gorce, John Oliver biog Nov 54 obit Feb 60

La Guardia, Ernesto de, Jr. See Guardia, Ernesto de la, Jr. Jan 57

Lahey, Frank H(oward) biog Mar 41 obit Sep 53

Lahr, Bert Jan 52

Laine, Frankie Nov 56

Lall, Anand See Lall, Arthur S. Nov 56

Lall, Arthur S(amuel) Nov 56

Lamb, Willis E(ugene), Jr. Mar 56

Lambert, Janet (Snyder) (WLB) Yrbk 54

Lambert, W(illiam) V(incent) Nov 55

Lancaster, Burt(on Stephen) Jul 53

Land, Edwin H(erbert) Nov 53

Landers, Ann Nov 57

Landowska, Wanda biog Nov 45 obit Nov 59

Landrum, Phil(lip) M(itchell) May 60

Lane, Sir Allen (Lane Williams) May 54

Lane, Arthur Bliss biog Apr 48 obit Oct 56

Lane, Carl D(aniel) (WLB) Yrbk 51

Langer, William biog Feb 52 obit Jan 60

Langmuir, Irving biog Oct 50 obit Nov 57

Laniel, Joseph Feb 54

Lapp, Ralph E(ugene) Nov 55

La Roe, Wilbur, Jr. biog Mar 48 obit Jul 57

Larson, Arthur See Larson, (Lewis) Arthur Nov 56

Larson, Jess Jun 51

Larson, (Lewis) Arthur Nov 56

Lasker, Mrs. Albert D(avis) Oct 59

Lasker, Mary Woodard See Lasker, Mrs. Albert D. Oct 59

Laski, Marghanita (WLB) Yrbk 51

Lasky, Jesse L(ouis) biog Apr 47 obit Mar 58

Lassaw, Ibram Jan 57

Lasser, J(acob) K(ay) biog May 46 obit Jul 54

Latham, Dana Mar 59

Latham, Jean Lee (WLB) Yrbk 56

Latouche, John T(reville) biog Jan-Jun 40 obit Oct 56

Latourette, Kenneth S(cott) Nov 53

Lattre de Tassigny, Jean (Joseph Marie Gabriel) de biog Jan 45 obit Feb 52

Laurel, José P(aciano) biog Jun 53 obit Jan 60

Lauritzen, Jonreed (WLB) Yrbk 52

Lausche, Frank J(ohn) Nov 58

Lawrence, Mrs. Clarence A. See Lawrence, M. (WLB) Yrbk 53

Lawrence, David L(eo) Jun 59

Lawrence, Ernest O(rlando) biog Jan 52 obit Nov 58

Lawrence, Gertrude biog Aug 40 Sep 52 obit Oct 52

Lawrence, Mildred (WLB) Yrbk 53

Lawson, Edward B(urnett) Jan 56

Lawson, Robert biog Oct 41 obit Oct 57

Lawton, Frederick J(oseph) Mar 51

Layton, Mrs. Roy F(rancis) Jan 52

Leader, George M(ichael) Jan 56

Leahy, William D(aniel) biog Jan 41 obit Oct 59

Leake, Chauncey D(epew) Apr 60

Lean, David May 53

Leary, Herbert F(airfax) biog Aug 42 obit Feb 58

Leavey, Edmond H(arrison) May 51

Lebrun, (Fede)rico Sep 52

LeClercq, Tanaquil Jul 53

Lederberg, Joshua Mar 59

Lederer, Mrs. Esther Friedman See Landers, Ann Nov 57

Lee, Canada biog Dec 44 obit Jun 52

Lee, Clark (Gould) biog Dec 43 obit Apr 53

Lee, Doris (Emrick) Jan 54

Lee, John C(lifford) H(odges) biog Jul 44 obit Nov 58

Lee Kuan Yew Nov 59

Lee, Laurence F(rederick) Jun 52

Lee, Tsung-Dao Nov 58

Leech, Margaret (Kernochan) Nov 60

Leedom, Boyd (Stewart) Mar 56

Leffingwell, R(ussell) C(ornell) biog Mar 50 obit Dec 60

Le Gallienne, Eva Mar 55

Léger, Fernand biog Jan 43 obit Oct 55

Léger, Paul-Émile, Cardinal May 53

Lehman, Herbert H(enry) Jul 55

Leibowitz, Samuel S(imon) Jan 53

Leigh-Fermor, See Fermor, Patrick (WLB) Yrbk 55

Leighton, Margaret Mar 57

Leighton, Margaret (Carver) (WLB) Yrbk 52

Leiserson, William M(orris) biog Feb 42 obit Apr 57

Lelong, Lucien biog Nov 55 obit Sep 58

Lemass, Seán F(rancis) Mar 60

LeMay, Curtis E(merson) Nov 54

Lemkin, Raphael biog May 50 obit Nov 59

Lemnitzer, Lyman L. Nov 55

Lemonnier, André (Georges) Nov 52

Lennox-Boyd, Alan T(indal) Jun 56

Lentaigne, Walter D(avid) A(lexander) biog Jul 44 obit Oct 55

Lenya, Lotte Jun 59

Leonard, Bill Nov 60

Leonard, Lucille P(utnam) See Leonard, Mrs. N. P. Feb 53

Leonard, Mrs. Newton P(eckham) Feb 53

Leopold, Alice K(oller) Jan 55

Lequerica y Erquiza, José Félix de Jun 51

Lerner, Alan Jay and Loewe, Frederick Jul 58

Leser, Tina Jun 57

McClellan, Harold C(hadick) Oct 54

McClintock, Robert Mills Apr 55

McClinton, Mrs. Harold L. See McClinton, Katharine Morrison Mar 58

McClinton, Katharine Morrison Mar 58

McCloskey, Mark A(lexander) Nov 55

McCobb, Paul (Winthrop) Nov 58

McComas, O(liver) Parker biog Nov 55 obit Feb 58

McConachie, G(eorge) W(illiam) Grant Nov 58

McCone, John A(lex) Jan 59

McConnell, F(owler) B(eery) Jul 52

McConnell, Samuel K(erns), Jr. Nov 56

McCormack, Emmet J. Jul 53

McCormick, Anne O'Hare biog Mar 40 obit Jul 54

MacCormick, Austin H(arbutt) Jul 51

McCormick, Edward J(ames) Nov 53

McCormick, Edward T(heodore) May 51

McCormick, Lynde D(upuy) biog Feb 52 obit Oct 56

McCormick, Myron Jan 54

McCormick, Robert R(utherford) biog Aug 42 obit May 55

McCoy, Frank R(oss) biog Nov 45 obit Sep 54

McCrady, Edward Jan 57

McCrary, Jinx (Falkenburg) See McCrary, T. and J. (F.) Jul 53

McCrary, John Reagan, Jr. See McCrary, T. and J. (F.) Jul 53

McCrary, Tex and Jinx (Falkenburg) Jul 53

McDaniel, Glen May 52

McDaniel, Hattie biog Sep 40 obit Dec 52

McDermott, Michael J(ames) biog Feb 51 obit Oct 55

McDevitt, James L(awrence) Mar 59

MacDonald, Betty biog Feb 46 obit Apr 58

McDonald, David J(ohn) Jun 53

McDonald, Eugene F., Jr. biog Oct 49 obit Oct 58

Macdonald, John Ross See Millar, K. (WLB) Yrbk 53

MacDonald, Malcolm (John) Nov 54

Macdonald, Ross See Millar, K. (WLB) Yrbk 53

McDonnell, William A(rchie) Feb 59

McElroy, Neil H(osler) Apr 51

McFarland, Ernest W(illiam) Jan 51

McGinnis, Patrick B(enedict) Nov 55

McGranery, James P(atrick) May 52

McGraw, Curtis W(hittlesey) biog Jun 50 obit Nov 53

McGraw, Eloise Jarvis (WLB) Yrbk 55

MacGregor, Ellen (WLB) biog Yrbk 54 obit Yrbk 54

McGregor, G(ordon) R(oy) Mar 54

McGregor, J. Harry biog Oct 58 obit Dec 58

McHale, Kathryn biog Jan 47 obit Dec 56 Yrbk 57

Machold, Earle J(ohn) Nov 58

McIntire, Ross T. biog Oct 45 obit Feb 60

McIntyre, James Francis (Aloysius), Cardinal Feb 53

MacIver, Loren (Newman) Nov 53

Mack, Connie biog Jun 44 obit Apr 56

Mack, Lawrence L. Apr 57

Mack, Nila biog Dec 52 obit Mar 53

Mack, Ted Apr 51

McKay, David O(man) Jun 51

McKay, Douglas biog May 49 obit Oct 59

Mackay, John A(lexander) Feb 52

McKeldin, Theodore R(oosevelt) Oct 52

McKellar, K(enneth) D(ouglas) biog Jan 46 obit Jan 58

McKelway, B(enjamin) M(osby) Jan 58

McKenna, Siobhan Nov 56

Mackenzie, C(halmers) J(ack) Jun 52

MacKenzie, Gisele Nov 55

McKinney, Frank E(dward) Jan 52

McKinney, Robert (Moody) Jan 57

McKneally, Martin B(oswell) Mar 60

MacLaine, Shirley Dec 59

MacLean, Basil C(larendon) May 57

McLean, Robert Nov 51

MacLeish, Archibald Nov 59

Macleod, Iain (Norman) Apr 56

McLintock, (George) Gordon Nov 53

Macmahon, Arthur W(hittier) Apr 58

McMahon, (James O')Brien biog Dec 45 obit Sep 52

McMeekin, Clark See McMeekin, Isabel McLennan (WLB) Yrbk 57

McMeekin, Isabel McLennan and Clark, Dorothy Park (WLB) Yrbk 57

McMillan, Edwin M(attison) Feb 52

MacMillan, Sir Ernest (Campbell) Mar 55

Macmillan, Harold See Macmillan, (Maurice) Harold Jan 55

McMillan, John L(anneau) Nov 56

Macmillan, (Maurice) Harold Jan 55

McMinnies, Mary (Jackson) (WLB) Yrbk 59

McNair, Sir Arnold D(uncan) Feb 55

McNally, Andrew, 3d Nov 56

McNamara, Patrick V(incent) Nov 55

McNeil, Hector biog Dec 46 obit Dec 55

McNeil, Wilfred J(ames) Feb 58

McNellis, Maggi Jan 55

McNichols, Stephen L. R. Oct 58

McNutt, Paul V(ories) biog Jan-Feb 40 obit May 55

McSwigan, Marie (WLB) Yrbk 53

MacVeagh, Lincoln Jun 52

Macy, Edith Dewing See Macy, Mrs. E. W. Dec 52

Macy, Mrs. Edward W(arren) Dec 52

Macy, George biog Nov 54 obit Sep 56

Madden, Ray J(ohn) Apr 53

Maenner, T(heodore) H(enry) biog Nov 49 obit Mar 58

Magallanes, Nicholas May 55

Maggiolo, Walter A(ndrew) Jul 52

Maglie, Sal(vatore Anthony) Jun 53

Magloire, Paul E(ugène) Feb 52

Magnani, Anna Apr 56

Magsaysay, Ramón biog Dec 52 obit May 57

Mahady, Henry J(oseph) Jul 54

Mahan, John W(illiam) Jul 59

Mahendra, King of Nepal Jul 56

Maher, Aly biog Mar 52 obit Nov 60

Mahon, George (Herman) Mar 58

Maile, Boniface R. Feb 51

Main, Marjorie Oct 51

Makarios III, Archbishop May 56

Makins, Sir Roger (Mellor) Jan 53

Malamud, Bernard (WLB) Yrbk 58

Malan, Daniel François biog Apr 49 obit Apr 59

Malbin, Elaine Feb 59

Malcolm, George A(rthur) Nov 54

Malden, Karl Apr 57

Malenkov, Georgi M(aximilianovich) Jun 52

Malinovsky, Rodion Y(akovlevich) Nov 60

Mallakh, Kamal, El See El Mallakh, K. Oct 54

Mallory, C(assius) C(hester) biog Feb 56 obit Mar 59

Mallory, L(ester) D(eWitt) Sep 60

Malone, Ross(er) L(ynn, Jr.) Mar 59

Maloney, Walter E(dward) Oct 52

O'Meara, Walter (Andrew) (WLB) Yrbk 58

O'Neal, Edward A(sbury) biog Sep 46 obit May 58

O'Neil, Thomas F(rancis) Nov 55

O'Neill, C. William Jul 58

O'Neill, Francis A(loysius), Jr. Dec 60

O'Neill, J(ohn) E(dward) Jun 52

Onís, Harriet (Vivian Wishnieff) de Apr 57

Onsager, Lars Apr 58

Orlando, Vittorio Emanuele biog Feb 44 obit Jan 53

Orr, Louis M(cDonald) Apr 60

Orton, Helen Fuller biog Jan 41 obit Apr 55

Orville, Howard T(homas) biog May 56 obit Jul 60

Osborn, Robert C(hesley) Jun 59

Osborne, John (James) Jun 59

Ott, Mel(vin Thomas) biog Jul 41 obit Jan 59

Ottley, Roi (Vincent) biog Oct 43 obit Dec 60

Ötüken, Adnan Jun 54

Oursler, Fulton biog Oct 42 obit Jul 52

Overholser, Winfred Nov 53

Owen, Ruth Bryan See Rohde, R. B. O. biog Dec 44 obit Oct 54

Owens, James Cleveland See Owens, Jesse Nov 56

Owens, Jesse Nov 56

Paar, Jack (Harold) Apr 59

Paasikivi, Juho Kusti biog May 44 obit Feb 57

Pacelli, Eugenio See Pius XII, Pope biog Mar 50 obit Dec 58

Pacheco e Chaves, Joao Nov 54

Packard, Vance (Oakley) Apr 58

Packer, Fred L(ittle) biog Jul 52 obit Feb 57

Paddleford, Clementine (Haskin) Feb 58

Padover, Saul K(ussiel) Oct 52

Paepcke, Walter P(aul) biog Apr 60 obit Jun 60

Page, Geraldine Nov 53

Pagnol, Marcel (Paul) Mar 56

Paige, Janis Jan 59

Paige, Leroy (Robert) Sep 52

Paige, Satchel See Paige, L. (R.) Sep 52

Paley, William S(amuel) Dec 51

Palmer, Arnold Sep 60

Palmer, Hazel Jun 58

Palmer, Lilli May 51

Pant, Govind Ballabh Jan 59

Pantaleoni, Mrs. Guido See Pantaleoni, Helenka Nov 56

Pantaleoni, Helenka (Tradeusa Adamowski) Nov 56

Papagos, Alexander biog Nov 51 obit Dec 55

Parker, Buddy Dec 55

Parker, Cola G(odden) Sep 56

Parker, John J(ohnston) biog Dec 55 obit May 58

Parker, Raymond K(lein) See Parker, Buddy Dec 55

Parker, Roy H(artford) Oct 51

Parkes, Henry Bamford Mar 54

Parkinson, C(yril) Northcote Dec 60

Parkinson, Thomas I(gnatius) biog Apr 49 obit Sep 59

Parnis, Mollie May 56

Parrish, Wayne W(illiam) Nov 58

Parrish, Mrs. Wayne William See Knight, Frances G. Oct 55

Parsons, Harriet (Oettinger) Jan 53

Parsons, Rose Peabody See Parsons, Mrs. William Barclay Dec 59

Parsons, Mrs. William Barclay Dec 59

Partridge, Earle E(verard) Apr 55

Pascal, Gabriel biog Jan 42 obit Sep 54

Pasquel, Jorge biog Jul 46 obit May 55

Passman, Otto E(rnest) Oct 60

Pasternak, Boris (Leonidovich) biog Feb 59 obit Jul 60

Pastore, John O(rlando) Apr 53

Pasvolsky, Leo biog May 45 obit Jun 53

Pate, Maurice Jun 51

Pate, Randolph McC(all) Sep 58

Patel, Vallabhbhai (Jhaverbhai) biog Mar 48 obit Jan 51

Paton, Alan Jun 52

Patterson, Alicia Nov 55

Patterson, Floyd Oct 60

Patterson, John (Malcolm) Nov 60

Patterson, Robert P(orter) biog Oct 41 obit Mar 52

Patton, Frances Gray (WLB) Yrbk 55

Patton, Mrs. Lewis See Patton, Frances Gray (WLB) Yrbk 55

Paul, Elliot (Harold) biog Jan-Feb 40 obit Jun 58

Paulding, Mrs. C. Gouverneur See Peterson, V. Dec 53

Pauli, Wolfgang biog Jun 46 obit Mar 59

Pavelić, Ante biog Aug 42 obit Feb 60

Paxton, Robert Mar 59

Payne, Frederick G. Dec 52

Payne-Gaposchkin, Cecilia (Helena) Dec 57

Paz, Alberto Gainza See Gainza Paz, A. Apr 51

Paz, Hipólito Jesús Jan 52

Paz Estenssoro, Víctor May 53

Peale, Mundy I(ngalls) May 56

Peare, Catherine Owens (WLB) Yrbk 59

Pearkes, G(eorge) R(andolph) Nov 57

Pearson, Jay F(rederick) W(esley) Dec 53

Pella, Giuseppe Nov 53

Peltz, Mrs. John DeWitt See Peltz, M. E. (O.) Apr 54

Peltz, Mary Ellis (Opdycke) Apr 54

Penfield, Wilder Graves Nov 55

Peng Teh-huai Dec 51

Pennario, Leonard (Joseph) Oct 59

Penney, Sir William George Feb 53

Percy, Charles H(arting) Dec 59

Pereira, I(rene) Rice Nov 53

Pérez Jiménez, Marcos Nov 54

Perkins, Anthony Sep 60

Perkins, C(harles) H(arvie) Jun 55

Perkins, Dexter Jan 58

Perkins, George W(albridge) biog Apr 50 obit Mar 60

Perkins, R(ichard) Marlin Oct 51

Per Krohg See Krohg, P. (L.) Nov 54

Perlman, Alfred E(dward) Apr 55

Perlman, Philip B(enjamin) biog Jul 52 obit Oct 60

Perón, (Maria) Eva (Duarte) de biog Mar 49 obit Sep 52

Perrin, Francis (Henri) Jul 51

Persons, Wilton B(urton) May 53

Pervukhin, Mikhail G(eorgievich) Mar 56

Pétain, Henri Philippe biog Aug 40 obit Sep 51

Peters, Roberta Apr 54

Peterson, Roger Tory Apr 59

Peterson, Virgilia Dec 53

Petherbridge, Margaret See Farrar, Margaret Jul 55

Petiot, Henry Jules Charles See Daniel-Rops, Henry Mar 57

Petit, Roland Apr 52

Petitpierre, Max Dec 53

Petsche, Maurice biog Nov 49 obit Nov 51

Peurifoy, John E(mil) biog Jan 49 obit Oct 55

Pevsner, Antoine Mar 59

Pflimlin, Pierre (Eugène Jean) Nov 55

Pfost, Gracie (Bowers) May 55

Philbrick, Herbert A(rthur) Mar 53

Phillips, Lena Madesin biog Apr 46 obit Jul 55

Phillips, Pauline Esther Friedman See Van Buren, Abigail May 60

Phillips, Mrs. Robert J(ohn) Jan 59

Phillips, Ruth See Phillips, Mrs. Robert J. Jan 59

Phillips, Thomas Hal (WLB) Yrbk 56

Phillips, Wendell Nov 58

Pholien, Joseph Feb 51

Phoui Sananikone Sep 59

Piaget, Jean Dec 58

Pibul Songgram, Luang Sep 57

Pick, Lewis Andrew biog Jun 46 obit Feb 57

Pick, Vernon J. Nov 55

Rawlings, Marjorie Kinnan biog Jul 42 obit Feb 54

Razmara, Ali biog Oct 50 obit Mar 51

Reavey, Mrs. George See Pereira, I. R. Nov 53

Redfield, Robert biog Dec 53 obit Jan 59

Redpath, Anne Jan 57

Reed, Daniel A(lden) biog May 53 obit Apr 59

Reed, Ralph T(homas) Apr 51

Rees, Edward H(erbert) Jan 58

Rees, Mina S(piegel) Nov 57

Reese, Everett D. Mar 54

Reichstein, Tadeus Feb 51

Reid, Helen Rogers May 52

Reid, Mrs. Ogden Mills See Reid, H. R. May 52

Reid, Ogden R(ogers) Feb 56

Reid, Whitelaw Dec 54

Reinartz, F(rederick) Eppling, Rev. Dr. Jul 53

Reiner, Fritz Dec 53

Remington, John W(arner) Feb 60

Remorino, Jerónimo Sep 51

Renaud, Madeleine See Barrault, J. L. and Renaud, M. Mar 53

Renault, Mary Jan 59

Renner, Karl biog Sep 45 obit Jan 51

Renoir, Jean Dec 59

Reshevsky, Samuel Feb 55

Resnik, Regina Jan 56

Reuss, Henry S(choellkopf) Oct 59

Reuter, Ernst biog Oct 49 obit Dec 53

Reuther, Victor (George) Dec 53

Revelle, Roger (Randall) Mar 57

Revercomb, (William) Chapman Jun 58

Reynolds, Albert Pierce See Reynolds, A. Jun 52

Reynolds, Allie Jun 52

Reynolds, R(ichard) S(amuel), Sr. biog Feb 53 obit Oct 55

Rhoads, C(ornelius) P(ackard) biog Mar 53 obit Nov 59

Rhyne, Charles S(ylvanus) May 58

Ribicoff, Abraham A. Jun 55

Rice, Grantland biog Sep 41 obit Sep 54

Rich, Daniel Catton Dec 55

Richard, Maurice (Joseph Henri) Dec 58

Richards, Dickinson W(oodruff) Mar 57

Richards, James P(rioleau) Sep 51

Richards, John S(tewart) Jun 55

Richards, Robert E(ugene), Rev. Jun 57

Richards, Vincent biog Jul 47 obit Dec 59

Richards, Wayne E. Jul 54

Richardson, Seth (Whitley) biog Feb 48 obit May 53

Richter, Conrad (Michael) Jun 51

Rickenbacker, Eddie See Rickenbacker, E. V. Feb 52

Rickenbacker, Edward Vernon Feb 52

Rickover, Hyman G(eorge) May 53

Riddell, R(obert) Gerald biog Sep 50 obit Apr 51

Riddleberger, James W(illiams) May 57

Ridenour, Nina Apr 51

Riebel, John P(aul) Jan 57

Riesenberg, Felix, Jr. (WLB) Yrbk 57

Riesman, David, (Jr.) Jan 55

Riggio, Vincent biog Jul 49 obit Nov 60

Riiser-Larsen, Hjalmar Nov 51

Riley, Susan B. Feb 53

Riley, William E(dward) Nov 51

Rincón de Gautier, Felisa See Gautier, Felisa Rincón de Oct 56

Rinehart, Stanley M(arshall), Jr. Dec 54

Ripley, Elizabeth (Blake) (WLB) Yrbk 58

Ritchard, Cyril Jan 57

Ritchie, Jean Oct 59

Riter, Henry G., 3d biog Oct 55 obit Sep 58

Ritner, Ann (Gilliland) (WLB) Yrbk 53

Ritter, Thelma Dec 57

Rivera, Diego biog Jul 48 obit Feb 58

Rivers, L(ucius) Mendel Oct 60

Rivers, Thomas M(ilton) Jul 60

Rives, Hallie Erminie (WLB) biog Yrbk 56 obit Yrbk 56

Robards, Jason (Nelson), Jr. Oct 59

Robb, Inez (Callaway) Dec 58

Robbins, Frederick C. See Enders, J. F. Jun 55

Robbins, William J(acob) Feb 56

Robens, Alfred Jun 56

Roberts, C(harles) Wesley Apr 53

Roberts, Dennis J(oseph) Dec 56

Roberts, Dorothy James (WLB) Yrbk 56

Roberts, Goodridge See Roberts, (William) Goodridge May 55

Roberts, (Granville) Oral, Rev. Nov 60

Roberts, Owen J(osephus) biog Oct 41 obit Jul 55

Roberts, Robin (Evan) Dec 53

Roberts, Walter Orr Dec 60

Roberts, (William) Goodridge May 55

Robertson, Norman A(lexander) Dec 57

Robertson, Reuben B(uck), Jr. biog Dec 55 obit May 60

Robertson, R(obert) B(lackwood) May 57

Robertson, Walter S(pencer) Dec 53

Robinson, Boardman biog Dec 41 obit Oct 52

Robinson, Elmer E(dwin) Nov 55

Robinson, M(aurice) R(ichard) Dec 56

Robinson, Ray Mar 51

Robinson, Sugar Ray See Robinson, R. Mar 51

Robinson, William E(dward) Feb 58

Robitzek, Edward H(einrich) Dec 53

Robson, Flora Jan 51

Rockefeller, David Mar 59

Rockefeller, John D(avison), Jr. biog Jul 41 obit Jul 60

Rockefeller, John D(avison), 3d Jun 53

Rockefeller, Laurance S(pelman) Jun 59

Rockefeller, Nelson A(ldrich) Mar 51

Rockefeller, Winthrop Sep 59

Rodahl, Kaare Feb 56

Rodgers, Richard Apr 51

Rodino, Peter W(allace), Jr. Oct 54

Rodríguez, Jorge Alessandri See Alessandri, Jorge May 59

Rodzinski, Artur biog Aug 40 obit Feb 59

Roebling, Mary G(indhart) Oct 60

Rogers, Bruce biog Dec 46 obit Jul 57

Rogers, Dale Evans Sep 56

Rogers, Edith Nourse biog Apr 42 obit Nov 60

Rogers, Paul Mar 60

Rogers, Will, Jr. Dec 53

Rogers, William P(ierce) Feb 58

Rohde, Mrs. Borge See Rohde, R. B. O. biog Dec 44 obit Oct 54

Rohde, Ruth Bryan Owen biog Dec 44 obit Oct 54

Rojas Pinilla, Gustavo Jun 56

Roman, Nancy G(race) Dec 60

Romano, Umberto Mar 54

Romanoff, Alexis L(awrence) Dec 53

Rombauer, Irma (von) S(tarkloff) Dec 53

Romberg, Sigmund biog Mar 45 obit Dec 51

Romney, George Jun 58

Romulo, Carlos P(ena) Apr 57

Roncalli, Angelo Giuseppe See John XXIII, Pope Feb 59

Roney, Marianne See Cohen, Barbara and Roney, Marianne May 57

Roome, Mrs. Charles O. See Goertz, A. (WLB) Yrbk 53

Root, Oren Jul 52

Rootes, Sir William (Edward) Nov 51

Rooth, Ivar Dec 52

Schnurer, Carolyn (Goldsand) Mar 55

Schnurer, Mrs. Harold T(eller) See Schnurer, C. (G.) Mar 55

Schoenbrun, David (Franz) Jan 60

Schoeppel, Andrew F. Mar 52

Schomburg, August Nov 60

Schönberg, Arnold biog Apr 42 obit Sep 51

Schoonover, Lawrence (Lovell) (WLB) Yrbk 57

Schorr, Daniel (Louis) Sep 59

Schorr, Friedrich biog Jul 42 obit Jun 54

Schottland, Charles I(rwin) Dec 56

Schram, Emil May 53

Schreiber, J.-J. Servan- See Servan-Schreiber, J.-J. Jan 55

Schreiber, (Karl Rudolf) Walther biog Feb 54 obit Sep 58

Schriever, Bernard A(dolf) Oct 57

Schulberg, Budd (Wilson) May 51

Schulz, Charles M(onroe) Dec 60

Schumacher, Kurt biog Feb 48 obit Oct 52

Schwartz, Delmore Jun 60

Schwartz, Maurice biog Feb 56 obit Jul 60

Schwarzkopf, Elisabeth Dec 55

Schwebel, Stephen M(yron) Jul 52

Scoggin, Margaret C(lara) Jul 52

Scott, (Guthrie) Michael, Rev. Apr 53

Scott, W(illiam) Kerr biog Apr 56 obit Jul 58

Scribner, Fred C(lark), Jr. Dec 58

Seabury, David biog Sep 41 obit May 60

Sears, Paul B(igelow) Jul 60

Sears, Robert R(ichardson) Jul 52

Seaton, Fred(erick) A(ndrew) Nov 56

Sebald, William J(oseph) Oct 51

Sebrell, W(illiam) H(enry), Jr. May 51

Sedgman, Francis Arthur See Sedgman, F. Nov 51

Sedgman, Frank Nov 51

Seefried, Irmgard Feb 56

Segni, Antonio Dec 55

Segrè, Emilio (Gino) Apr 60

Segura, Francisco Sep 51

Seif al-Islam al-Hassan, Prince See al-Hassan, Prince of the Yemen Feb 57

Seif-ul-Islam Abdullah, Prince biog Dec 47 obit Sep 55

Seifert, Elizabeth (WLB) Yrbk 51

Seifert, Shirley (Louise) (WLB) Yrbk 51

Seitz, Frederick Apr 56

Seixas, E(lias) Victor, Jr. Jul 52

Selassie See Haile Selassie I, Emperor of Ethiopia Oct 54

Selinko, Annemarie Jan 55

Sellers, Peter Dec 60

Seltzer, Louis B(enson) Dec 56

Selye, Hans (Hugo Bruno) Jun 53

Semenov, Nikolai N(ikolaevich) Mar 57

Sen, B(inay) R(anjan) Dec 52

Senanayake, Don Stephen biog Apr 50 obit May 52

Senanayake, Dudley (Shelton) Dec 52

Serling, Rod Dec 59

Serov, Ivan A(leksandrovich) Dec 56

Serratosa Cibils, Joaquin Feb 54

Servan-Schreiber, J(ean)-J(acques) Jan 55

Seton, Anya (WLB) Yrbk 53

Settle, Mary Lee (WLB) Yrbk 59

Sewell, (Emma) Winifred Jun 60

Sforza, Carlo, Count biog Jun 42 obit Oct 52

Shabandar, Moussa (Mahmoud Al-) Feb 56

Shafer, Paul W(erntz) biog Jul 52 obit Oct 54

Shafik, Doria (Ahmad) May 55

Shahn, Ben(jamin) Dec 54

Shantz, Bobby See Shantz, R. C. Apr 53

Shantz, Robert Clayton Apr 53

Shapiro, Harry L(ionel) Dec 52

Shapley, Harlow Dec 52

Shaver, Dorothy biog Jan 46 obit Sep 59

Shaw, Ralph R(obert) Jun 56

Shay, Edith (WLB) Yrbk 52

Shay, Frank biog (WLB) Yrbk 52 obit Mar 54

Shea, Andrew B(ernard) Jan 57

Shearing, George (Albert) Apr 58

Sheen, Fulton J(ohn), Bishop Jan 51

Shehu, Mehmet Feb 58

Shellabarger, Samuel biog May 45 obit May 54

Shelly, Mary Jo(sephine) Oct 51

Shelly, Warner S(woyer) Feb 52

Shelton, James E(rrett) Feb 51

Shepherd, Lemuel C(ornick), Jr. Feb 52

Shepilov, Dmitri Trofimovitch Dec 55

Sherman, Forrest P(ercival) biog Mar 48 obit Sep 51

Sherman, Henry C(lapp) biog Jan 49 obit Dec 55

Sherwood, Robert E(mmet) biog Jan-Jun 40 obit Jan 56

Shidehara, Kijuro biog Apr 46 obit Apr 51

Shield, Lansing P(eter) biog Jun 51 obit Mar 60

Shields, James P. biog Mar 51 obit Sep 53

Shigemitsu, Mamoru biog Jun 43 obit Mar 57

Shimkin, Leon May 54

Shinn, Everett biog May 51 obit Jun 53

Shippen, Katherine B(inney) (WLB) Yrbk 54

Shivers, Allan Oct 51

Shockley, William Dec 53

Shoemaker, Samuel M(oor), Rev. Dr. Apr 55

Sholokhov, Mikhail A(leksandrovich) Feb 60

Shoriki, Matsutaro Feb 58

Short, Dewey Dec 51

Short, Hassard biog Nov 48 obit Dec 56

Short, Joseph (Hudson, Jr.) biog Feb 51 obit Nov 52

Shoup, David M(onroe) Jan 60

Shridharani, Krishnalal (Jethalal) biog Jan 42 obit Oct 60

Shull, Martha A(rvesta) Apr 57

Shulman, Harry biog Apr 52 obit May 55

Shulman, Irving (WLB) Yrbk 56

Shulman, Max Oct 59

Shuman, Charles B(aker) Feb 56

Shuster, George N(auman) Oct 60

Shute, Nevil biog Jul 42 obit Mar 60

Shvernik, Nikolai (Mikhailovich) Oct 51

Sidi Mohammed, Sultan of Morocco Oct 51

Siepi, Cesare Dec 55

Sigerist, Henry Ernest biog Sep 40 obit Jun 57

Signoret, Simone Dec 60

Sikorsky, Igor I(van) Dec 56

Siles Zuazo, Hernán Sep 58

Sillcox, Lewis K(etcham) Dec 54

Silva, Vieira da See Vieira da Silva Dec 58

Silva de Santolalla, Irene See Santolalla, Irene Silva de Dec 56

Silvers, Phil Dec 57

Simionato, Giulietta Apr 60

Simkhovitch, Mary (Melinda) K(ingsbury) biog Mar 43 obit Dec 51

Simmons, Jean Feb 52

Simms, John F. Sep 56

Simon, Edith (WLB) Yrbk 54

Simon, John Allsebrook Simon, 1st Viscount biog Jul 40 obit Mar 54

Simon, Richard L(eo) biog Jul 41 obit Oct 60

Simonetta Dec 55

Simons, David G(oodman) Dec 57

Simons, Hans Mar 57

Simpson, Harriette Louisa See Arnow, H. (L.) S. (WLB) Yrbk 54

Simpson, Howard E(dward) May 58

Simpson, Milward L(ee) Jan 57

Simpson, Richard M(urray) biog Dec 53 obit Mar 60

Sims, William L(ee), 2d Dec 56

Sinatra, Frank Oct 60

Stevens, George (Cooper) Apr 52

Stevens, Robert T(en Broeck) Jul 53

Stevens, Roger L(acey) Dec 55

Stevenson, Elizabeth (WLB) Yrbk 56

Stewart, James (Maitland) Dec 60

Stewart, Potter Dec 59

Stine, Charles Milton Altland biog Jan-Jun 40 obit Sep 54

Stirnweiss, George (Henry) biog Mar 46 obit Dec 58

Stoessel, Mrs. Henry Kurt See Chastain, Madye Lee (WLB) Yrbk 58

Stoica, Chivu Jan 59

Stokes, Richard R(apier) biog Sep 51 obit Oct 57

Stokes, Thomas L(unsford, Jr.) biog May 47 obit Sep 58

Stokowski, Leopold (Anton Stanislaw) Jul 53

Stolk, William C. Mar 53

Stolz, Mary Slattery (WLB) Yrbk 53

Stone, Abraham biog Mar 52 obit Oct 59

Stone, Edward D(urell) Jun 58

Stone, William S(ebastian) Jun 60

Stoph, Willi Oct 60

Storey, Robert G(erald) Nov 53

Stout, Ruth A(lbertine) Jan 59

Stout, William Bushnell biog Mar 41 obit May 56

Strachan, Paul A(mbrose) Jan 52

Stranahan, Frank (Richard) Sep 51

Strang, Ruth (May) Dec 60

Strasberg, Lee Oct 60

Strasberg, Susan (Elizabeth) May 58

Stratemeyer, George E(dward) Feb 51

Stratton, William G(rant) Apr 53

Straus, Jack I(sidor) Mar 52

Straus, Michael W(olf) Jun 52

Straus, Oskar biog Mar 44 obit Mar 54

Straus, Roger W(illiams) biog Jul 52 obit Oct 57

Strauss, Franz Josef Feb 57

Strauss, J(acobus) G(ideon) N(el) Jan 51

Stravinsky, Igor (Fëdorovich) Apr 53

Street, James (Howell) biog (WLB) Yrbk 46 obit Nov 54

Streibert, Theodore C(uyler) Feb 55

Streuli, Hans Apr 57

Strijdom, Johannes Gerhardus biog May 56 obit Nov 58

Stritch, Samuel (Alphonsus), Cardinal biog Apr 46 obit Sep 58

Stroéssner, Alfredo Dec 58

Strouse, Norman H(ulbert) May 60

Struble, Arthur D(ewey) Nov 51

Struther, Jan biog Jan 41 obit Oct 53

Stuhlinger, Ernst Nov 57

Stummvoll, Josef (Leopold) Jun 60

Stump, Felix B(udwell) Jan 53

Sturges, Preston biog Apr 41 obit Oct 59

Sturgis, Samuel D(avis), Jr. Jan 56

Sturzo, Luigi biog Feb 46 obit Nov 59

Subah, Abdullah al-Salim al, Sheikh See Abdullah al-Salim al Subah, Sir, Sheikh of Kuwait Jul 57

Sucksdorff, Arne (Edvard) Apr 56

Sugrue, Thomas (Joseph) biog Jun 48 obit Feb 53

Suhr, Otto (Ernst Heinrich Hermann) biog Apr 55 obit Nov 57

Suhrawardy, H(ussain) S(haheed) Apr 57

Sullavan, Margaret biog Jul 44 obit Feb 60

Sullivan, A(loysius) M(ichael) Dec 53

Sullivan, Brian Dec 57

Sullivan, Ed(ward Vincent) Sep 52

Sullivan, Francis L(oftus) biog Jun 55 obit Jan 57

Sullivan, Gael (E.) biog May 47 obit Jan 57

Sullivan, Henry J. Jun 58

Sullivan, Mrs. John B(erchmans) See Sullivan, L. (A.) K. Dec 54

Sullivan, Leonor (Alice) K(retzer) Dec 54

Sumac, Yma Dec 55

Summerfield, Arthur E(llsworth) Sep 52

Sumner, (Bertha) Cid Ricketts (WLB) Yrbk 54

Sumner, Mrs. G. Lynn See Picken, M. B. Dec 54

Sumner, James B(atcheller) biog Jan 47 obit Oct 55

Suslov, Mikhail A(ndreyevich) Feb 57

Susskind, David May 60

Sutherland, Graham (Vivian) Jan 55

Sutherland, Joan Dec 60

Sutton, George P(aul) Jul 58

Suyin, Han See Han Suyin (WLB) Yrbk 57

Suzuki, Daisetz T(eitaro) Oct 58

Suzuki, Pat Jan 60

Svanholm, Set (Karl Viktor) Dec 56

Sveda, Michael Dec 54

Swann, W(illiam) F(rancis) G(ray) Dec 60

Swart, Charles R(obberts) Jun 60

Sweeney, James Johnson Mar 55

Swigert, Ernest G(oodnough) Oct 57

Swing, Joseph M(ay) Apr 59

Swings, Paul See Swings, P. (F. F.) Dec 54

Swings, Pol(idore F. F.) Dec 54

Swirbul, Leon A. biog Apr 53 obit Sep 60

Swope, Gerard biog Sep 41 obit Feb 58

Swope, Herbert Bayard biog Nov 44 obit Sep 58

Syme, John P(rescott) Mar 57

Symes, James M(iller) Dec 55

Symington, (William) Stuart Jul 56

Synge, Richard L(aurence) M(illington) Nov 53

Szent-Györgyi, Albert (von Nagyrapolt) Jan 55

Szigeti, Joseph Mar 58

Szyk, Arthur biog Nov 46 obit Oct 51

Taber, Gladys (Leonae Bagg) (WLB) Yrbk 52

Taber, Louis J(ohn) biog Jun 42 obit Dec 60

Taffin de Givenchy, Hubert See Givenchy, H. (J. T.) de May 55

Taft, Robert A(lphonso) biog May 40 Apr 48 obit Oct 53

Talal, former King of Jordan Jan 52

Talbert, Billy Mar 57

Talbert, William F(ranklin) See Talbert, Billy Mar 57

Talbott, Harold E(lstner) biog Jul 53 obit May 57

Talbott, Philip M. Apr 58

Tallamy, Bertram D(alley) May 57

Tallant, Robert biog (WLB) Yrbk 53 obit Jun 57

Tallchief, Maria Nov 51

Tamayo, Rufino Mar 53

Tandy, Jessica Mar 56

Tani, Masayuki May 56

Tanner, Edward Everett, 3d May 59

Tanner, Väinö (Alfred) Sep 60

Tassigny, Jean (Joseph Marie Gabriel) de Lattre de See Lattre de Tassigny, J. (J. M. G.) de biog Jan 45 obit Feb 52

Tata, J(ehangir) R(atanji) D(adbhoy) Dec 58

Tatum, Edward L(awrie) Mar 59

Taubman, (Hyman) Howard Apr 59

Tawes, J(ohn) Millard Oct 60

Taylor, Elizabeth Jul 52

Taylor, Francis Henry biog Jan-Feb 40 obit Feb 58

Taylor, John W(ilkinson) Jan 54

Taylor, Myron C(harles) biog Jan-Feb 40 obit Jul 59

Taylor, Robert May 52

Taylor, Robert Lewis Dec 59

Taylor, Mrs. William Bolling See Young, M. Jun 52

Tchelitchew, Pavel biog Mar 43 obit Oct 57

Van Horne, Harriet Dec 54

Van Houtte, Jean See Houtte, J. van Mar 52

Vanier, George Philias Jan 60

Van Royen, Jan Herman See Royen, J. H. van Dec 53

Vansittart, Robert (Gilbert) Vansittart, 1st Baron biog Jul 41 obit Apr 57

Van Volkenburg, J(ack) L(amont) Jan 55

Vardaman, James K(imble), Jr. Apr 51

Vargas, Getúlio Dornelles biog May 51 obit Oct 54

Varnay, Astrid May 51

Vaughan, Sarah (Lois) Nov 57

Vaughan Williams, Ralph biog Dec 53 obit Nov 58

Velasco Ibarra, José María Nov 52

Velde, Harold H(immel) Mar 53

Velikovsky, Immanuel May 57

Ventris, Michael (George Francis) biog Jan 57 obit Jan 57

Vera-Ellen Feb 59

Verdon, Gwen Oct 60

Veronese, Vittorino Jun 59

Verwoerd, H(endrik) F(rensch) Mar 59

Victor, Sally (Josephs) Apr 54

Vidor, King (Wallis) Feb 57

Vieira da Silva, (Maria Helena) Dec 58

Vigneaud, Vincent du See du Vigneaud, Vincent Jan 56

Villa-Lobos, Heitor biog Apr 45 obit Jan 60

Villon, Jacques Jan 56

Vinson, Fred(erick) M(oore) biog Aug 43 obit Nov 53

Viscardi, Henry, Jr. Jan 54

Vishinskiï, Andrei (IAnuar'evïch) biog May 44 obit Jan 55

Vogel, Herbert D(avis) Dec 54

Vogt, William Mar 53

Von Braun, Wernher Jan 52

Von Brentano, Heinrich See Brentano (di Tremezzo), H. von Feb 55

Von Eckardt, Felix See Eckardt, Felix von Jan 56

Von Einem, Gottfried See Einem, G. von Jul 53

Von Heidenstam, Rolf See Heidenstam, Rolf von biog Oct 51 obit Oct 58

Von Karajan, Herbert See Karajan, Herbert von Oct 56

Von Kármán, Theodore May 55

Von KleinSmid, Rufus B. See Klein-Smid, Rufus B. von Jun 58

Von Kleist, Paul Ludwig See Kleist, P. L. (E.) von biog Jul 43 obit Jan 55

Von Mannerheim, Carl Gustaf Emil, Baron See Mannerheim, C. G. E., Baron von biog Apr 40 obit Feb 51

Von Neumann, John biog Jul 55 obit Apr 57

Von Rundstedt, Karl (Rudolf Gerd) See Rundstedt, K. (R. G.) von biog Nov 41 obit Apr 53

Von Szent-Györgyi, Albert See Szent-Györgyi, A. (von N.) Jan 55

Von Thadden-Trieglaff, Reinold See Thadden-Trieglaff, Reinold von Jul 59

Voorhees, Tracy S(tebbins) Feb 57

Voronoff, Serge biog Jan 41 obit Oct 51

Vukmanović-Tempo, Svetozar (N.) Dec 58

Vyshinsky, Andreï See Vishinskiï, Andreï (IAnuar'evïch) biog May 44 obit Jan 55

Wadsworth, James J(eremiah) Jun 56

Wadsworth, James W(olcott) biog Jul 43 obit Sep 52

Wagner, J(ohn) Addington May 56

Wagner, Robert F(erdinand) biog May 41 obit Jun 53

Wagner, Robert F(erdinand, Jr.) Feb 54

Wainwright, Jonathan M(ayhew) biog May 42 obit Nov 53

Wakehurst, John de Vere Loder, 2d Baron Dec 54

Wald, Jerome Irving See Wald, J. May 52

Wald, Jerry May 52

Walden, Amelia Elizabeth (WLB) Yrbk 56

Walker, E(dward) Ronald Dec 56

Walker, Eric A(rthur) Mar 59

Walker, Frank C(omerford) biog Oct 40 obit Nov 59

Walker, John May 57

Walker, Norma Ford Oct 57

Walker, Paul A(tlee) May 52

Walker, Ralph (Thomas) Dec 57

Walker, Walton H(arris) biog Sep 50 obit Jan 51

Walker, Waurine (Elizabeth) Feb 55

Wall, Art(hur Jonathan), Jr. Dec 59

Wallace, DeWitt and Lila (Bell) Acheson May 56

Wallace, Mrs. DeWitt See Wallace, DeWitt and Lila Acheson May 56

Wallace, Lila (Bell) Acheson See Wallace, DeWitt and Lila Acheson May 56

Wallace, Mike Jul 57

Wallach, Eli May 59

Wallenstein, Alfred (Franz) Apr 52

Waller, Fred(eric) biog Feb 53 obit Jul 54

Wallop, (John) Douglass (WLB) Yrbk 56

Walsh, Mrs. Richard J(ohn) See Buck, Pearl Jul 56

Walter, Francis E(ugene) Jun 52

Walton, Ernest Thomas Sinton Mar 52

Walworth, Arthur (Clarence, Jr.) Dec 59

Wambaugh, Sarah biog Apr 46 obit Jan 56

Wampler, (ElRey) Cloud Dec 52

Wan (Waithayakon), Prince Jun 54

Wang, Ping-nan Dec 58

Wangchuk, Jigme Dorji, Druk Gyalpo of Bhutan Oct 56

Warburton, Herbert B(irchby) Nov 51

Waring, Roane biog Dec 43 obit Dec 58

Warne, William E(lmo) Nov 52

Warner, Edward P(earson) biog Oct 49 obit Sep 58

Warner, Harry M(orris) biog Jan 45 obit Oct 58

Warner, W(illiam) Lloyd Dec 59

Warren, Althea (Hester) biog Feb 42 obit Feb 60

Warren, Avra M(ilvin) biog Feb 55 obit Mar 57

Warren, Earl Jan 54

Warren, Fletcher Jul 60

Warren, Leonard biog Dec 53 obit Apr 60

Warren, William C(lements) Jan 60

Washburn, Gordon Bailey Dec 55

Waterman, Alan T(ower) Jun 51

Waters, Ethel Mar 51

Watkins, Shirley (WLB) Yrbk 58

Watkinson, Harold (Arthur) Mar 60

Watson, Burl S(tevens) Apr 57

Watson, John B(roadus) biog Oct 42 obit Dec 58

Watson, Lucile Dec 53

Watson, Thomas J(ohn), Sr. biog Jul 50 obit Sep 56

Watson, Thomas J(ohn), Jr. Feb 56

Watt, Donald (Beates) Jan 58

Waugh, Samuel C(lark) Dec 55

Waverley, John Anderson, 1st Viscount biog Jul 41 obit Mar 58

Wayne, David Jun 56

Wayne, John Feb 51

Weafer, Elizabeth Jan 58

Weafer, Mrs. Eugene C(lyde) See Weafer, Elizabeth Jan 58

Weaver, Sylvester L(aflin), Jr. Jan 55

Weaver, Warren Apr 52

Webb, Aileen O(sborn) Dec 58

Webb, Jack (Randolph) May 55

Webb, Maurice biog May 50 obit Sep 56

Webb, Mrs. Vanderbilt See Webb, Aileen O. Dec 58

Webster, H(arold) T(ucker) biog Mar 45 obit Nov 52

Wouk, Herman (WLB) Yrbk 52

Wright, Anna (Maria Louisa Perrott) Rose (WLB) Yrbk 52

Wright, Benjamin F(letcher) Jul 55

Wright, Fielding L(ewis) biog Sep 48 obit Jul 56

Wright, Frank Lloyd biog Nov 52 obit Jun 59

Wright, Helen Mar 56

Wright, Jerauld Feb 55

Wright, Loyd (Earl) Jul 55

Wright, Martha Feb 55

Wriston, Henry M(erritt) May 52

Wrong, (Humphrey) Hume biog Oct 50 obit Mar 54

Wu, Chien Shiung Oct 59

Wu, W(uo) C(heng) Feb 53

Wyatt, Jane (Waddington) May 57

Wyeth, Andrew (Newell) Apr 55

Wyler, William Jan 51

Wyszynski, Stefan, Cardinal Jan 58

Yaffe, James (WLB) Yrbk 57

Yafi, Abdullah El- Jun 56

Yamut, Nuri May 52

Yang, Chen Ning Nov 58

Yang, You Chan Feb 53

Yarborough, Ralph W(ebster) Feb 60

Yates, Donald N(orton) May 58

Ydígoras Fuentes, Miguel Nov 58

Yeager, Charles E. May 54

Yeakley, Marjory Hall See Hall, Marjory (WLB) Yrbk 57

Yeakley, Mrs. Taylor B. See Hall, Marjory (WLB) Yrbk 57

Yeh, George K(ung-)C(hao) Mar 53

Yerushalmy, J(acob) Mar 58

York, Cyril Forster Garbett, Archbishop of—See Garbett, Cyril Forster, Archbishop of York biog Feb 51 obit Mar 56

York, Herbert F(rank) Dec 58

Yoshimura, Junzo May 56

Yost, Charles W(oodruff) Mar 59

Young, Alan Jun 53

Young, Joseph Louis Jul 60

Young, Marian Jun 52

Young, Milton R(uben) Dec 54

Young, Nancy Wilson Ross See Ross, N. W. (WLB) Yrbk 52

Young, Philip Dec 51

Young, Robert R(alph) biog Apr 47 obit Mar 58

Young, Stanley (Preston) (WLB) Yrbk 51

Young, Stephen M(arvin) Oct 59

Youskevitch, Igor Feb 56

Yu Hung-chun See Yui, O. K. biog May 55 obit Sep 60

Yui, O. K. biog May 55 obit Sep 60

Yust, Walter biog Apr 43 obit Apr 60

ZaBach, Florian Dec 55

Zablocki, Clement J(ohn) Jun 58

Zadkine, Ossip (Joselyn) Mar 57

Zaharias, Babe Didrikson biog Apr 47 obit Dec 56

Zahedi, Fazlollah Feb 54

Zahir, Mohammed Shah See Mohammed Zahir Shah Mar 56

Zaldívar, Fulgencio Batista y See Batista (y Zaldívar), F. Apr 52

Zanft, Mrs. Hattie Carnegie See Carnegie, Hattie biog Oct 42 obit May 56

Zanuck, Darryl F(rancis) Mar 54

Zápotocký, Antonín biog Jun 53 obit Jan 58

Zaroubin, Georgi N(ikolaevich) biog Apr 53 obit Jan 59

Zatopek, Emil Apr 53

Zeckendorf, William Mar 52

Zeineddine, Farid Feb 57

Zelomek, A. Wilbert Dec 56

Zerbe, Karl Feb 59

Zernike, Frits Feb 55

Zhukov, Georgi K(onstantinovich) Apr 55

Zhukov, Georgy A(lexandrovich) Oct 60

Ziff, William B(ernard) biog Oct 46 obit Feb 54

Zilboorg, Gregory biog Sep 41 obit Nov 59

Zim, Herbert S(pencer) Sep 56

Zimbalist, Efrem, Jr. Feb 60

Zimmerman, M(ax) M(andell) Jul 57

Zinn, Walter H(enry) Dec 55

Zinnemann, Fred Mar 53

Zirato, Bruno Dec 59

Zoli, Adone biog Mar 58 obit Apr 60

Zolotow, Maurice May 57

Zook, George F(rederick) biog Feb 46 obit Oct 51

Zorbaugh, Geraldine B(one) Dec 56

Zorin, Valerian A(lexandrovich) Mar 53

Zorlu, Fatin Rustu Dec 58

Zuazo, Hernán Siles See Siles Zuazo, Hernán Sep 58

Zubiría, Alberto F(ermín) Dec 56

Zuckert, Eugene M. Apr 52

Zulli, Floyd, Jr. Jan 58

Zwicky, Fritz Apr 53

(5772)